D1359499

Reader's Digest

THE STORY OF AMERICA

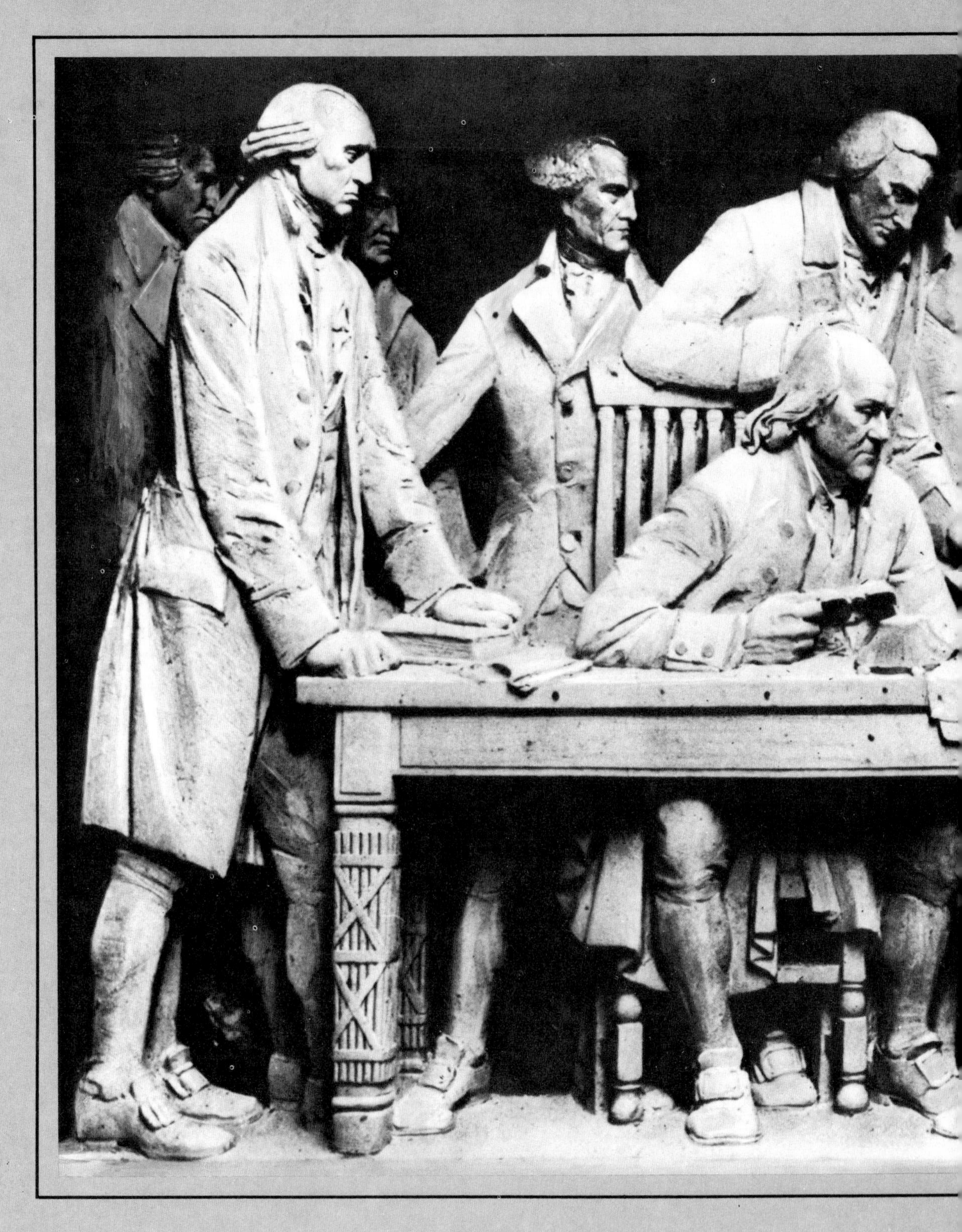

THE STORY

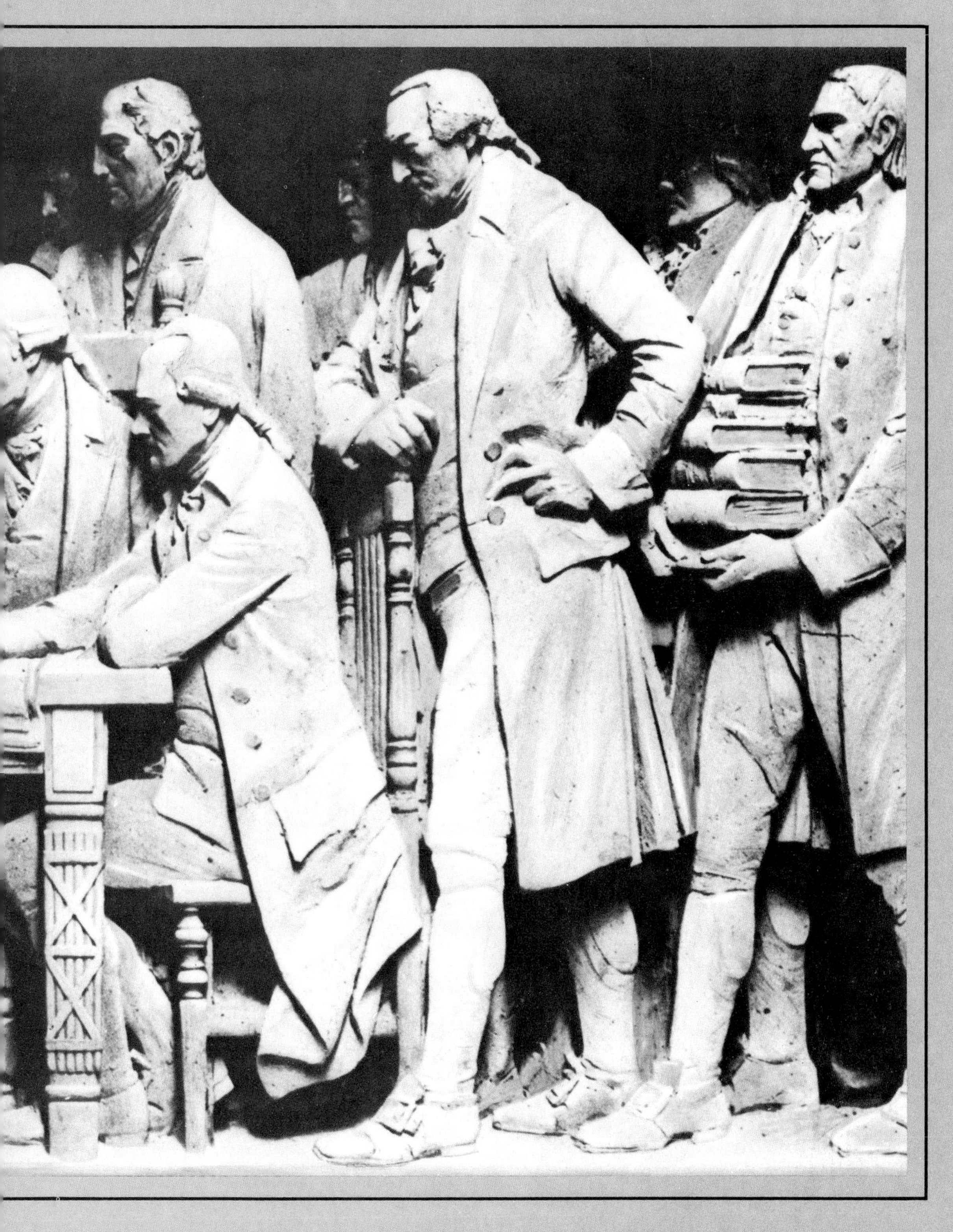

OF AMERICA

The Reader's Digest Association, Inc., *Pleasantville, New York*

The Story of America

Editor: Carroll C. Calkins
Art Director: Richard J. Berenson
Associate Editors: Priscilla B. Balaban, Mary Kelleher, Frank B. Latham
Assistant Editor: A. Denman Pierce-Grove
Editorial Assistant: Dolores H. Damm
Art Staff: Evelyn Bauer, Janet G. Iannacone, Barbara J. Schneit
Copy Editors: Rosemarie Conefrey, Robert V. Huber, Georgea A. Pace
Picture Editor: Robert J. Woodward
Picture Researcher: Richard J. Pasqual

The editors of Reader's Digest General Books wish to express their gratitude for the invaluable contributions of the following individuals:

General Consultant

Bernard A. Weisberger, Ph.D., *Visiting Professor of American History, Vassar College*

Special Consultants

Ralph K. Andrist
Author, The Long Death *and others*

James M. Banner, Jr., Ph.D.
Professor of American History
Harvard University

Annette Baxter, Ph.D.
Chairman, Department of History
Barnard College

Gert H. Brieger, M.D.
Associate Professor of History of Medicine
Duke University Medical Center

Stuart W. Bruchey, Ph.D.
Allan Nevins Professor of Economic History
Columbia University

Harold Claassen
Sports Editor (retired)
Associated Press

Robert Dahl, Ph.D.
Sterling Professor of Political Science
Yale University

Morris Fishbein, M.D., D.Sci.
Author; Founder, Morris Fishbein
Center for History of Medicine
University of Chicago

Eric Foner, Ph.D.
Professor of American History, The City
College of The City University of New York

William Goetzmann, Ph.D.
Director, American Studies Program
University of Texas at Austin

Jack P. Greene, Ph.D.
Professor of American History
The Johns Hopkins University

Norman E. Isaacs
Editor in Residence
Graduate School of Journalism
Columbia University

Richard Kostelanetz
Author, The End of Intelligent
Writing *and others*

Benjamin W. Labaree, Ph.D.
Ephraim Williams Professor of
American History Williams College

Richard M. Ludwig, Ph.D.
Professor of English, Princeton University

Martin E. Marty, Ph.D.
Associate Dean, The Divinity School
University of Chicago

Dan Morgenstern
Jazz historian and critic

Walter T. K. Nugent, Ph.D.
Professor of American History
Indiana University

William H. Pierson, Jr., Ph.D.
Massachusetts Professor of Art Emeritus
Williams College

Wayne D. Rasmussen, Ph.D.
Historian
U.S. Department of Agriculture

Marvin D. Schwartz
Consultant, Department of Public
Information, The Metropolitan
Museum of Art, New York

Robert Sherman
Program Director
Radio Station WQXR, New York

Douglas Sloan, Ph.D.
Associate Professor of History and Education
Teachers College, Columbia University

Russell F. Weigley, Ph.D.
Professor of History, Temple University

John Wilmerding, Ph.D.
Leon E. Williams Professor of Art
Dartmouth College

Library of Congress Catalog Card No. 75-3837

Printed in the United States of America

Where We Stand . . . in Terms of Time

The awesome panorama of people, places, objects, and events presented in this book took place in an incredibly short period of time. If we take as a beginning date the first meeting of the House of Burgesses in Jamestown, Virginia, in 1619, in 1976 we have a 357-year history of organized government in the United States. How remarkably short this time is, compared with the history of other countries, is illustrated here.

Each full layer on the base supporting the maps indicates a timespan of 100 years. Thus the United States is 3.57 units high, while Egypt, which has operated under various forms of organized government for 5,000 years, is 50 units high, and the other countries fall between the two.

1. United Arab Republic (Egypt)
2. Greece
3. People's Republic of China
4. France
5. Great Britain
6. Union of Soviet Socialist Republics (Russia)
7. Spain
8. United States of America

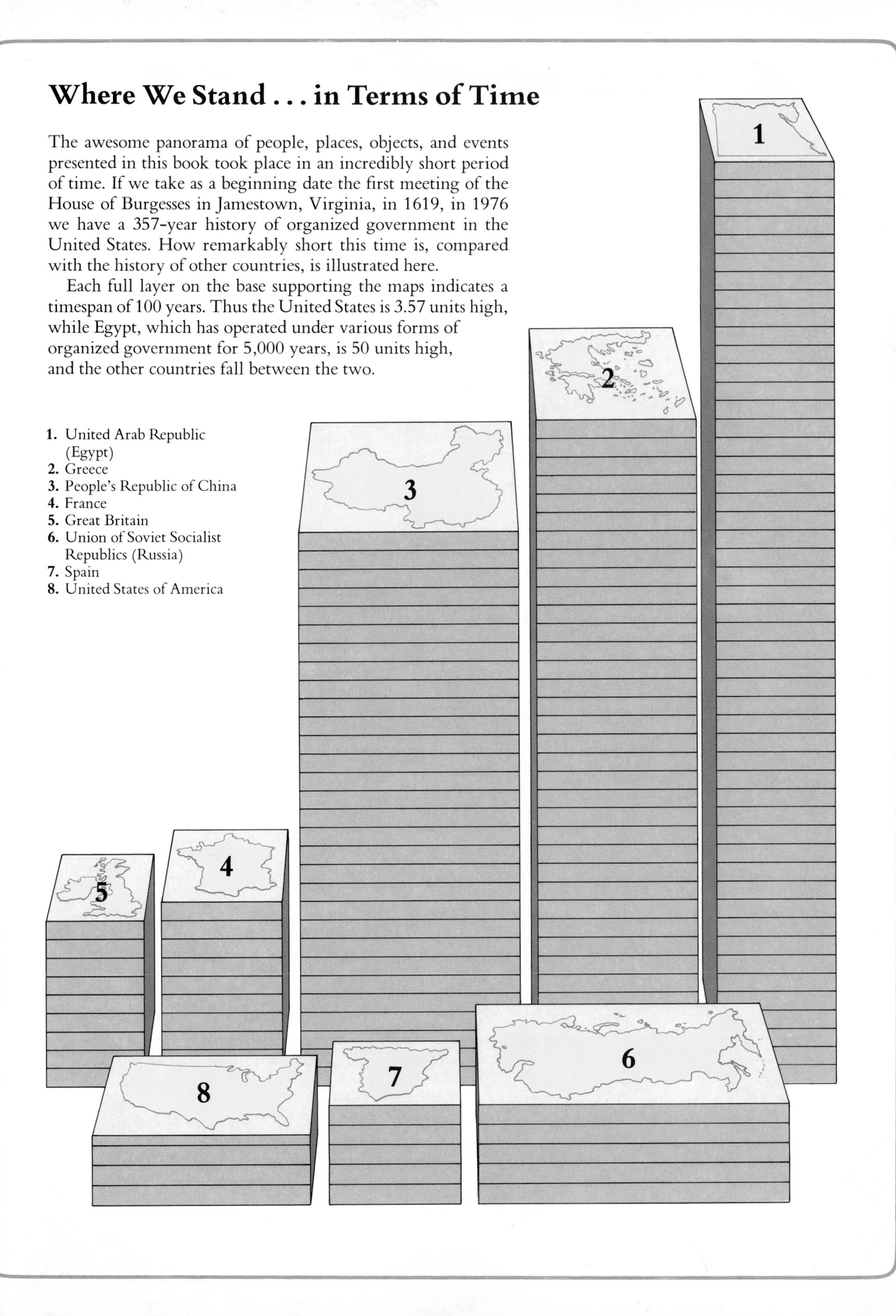

Contents

Why It Happened Here

Unprecedented in the history of the world is the explosion of social, political, and technical phenomena that occurred on this continent, particularly from the 1850's to the present. In that brief span mankind accelerated the rate of travel from the gallop of a horse to twice the speed of sound. Communication progressed from the pony express to the instantaneous. Comfort and convenience advanced from candlelight and an open flame to complete control of every nuance of light, heat, and humidity—and the list could go on and on.

There have been other changes, too. From the smoothbore musket of the 1700's, which could fire a single lead ball at a rate of three to five a minute, with reasonable accuracy for a distance of only 100 yards, we have progressed, if that is the word, to atomic weapons with the potential to destroy all mankind.

The damage and depredation that we are now wreaking on the topsoil, the rivers and seas, and the reserves of fossil fuel is another aspect of progress with consequences that are, as yet, incalculable.

While it is true that other countries helped to set the stage, the most dramatic breakthroughs in the last century or so happened here. How did this come to pass? Why here? What were the ingredients? There is no simple answer, but there have been some definable forces at work. While the harsh restrictive aspects of the Calvinist doctrine espoused by the Puritans of the Massachusetts Bay Colony in the mid-1600's no longer prevail, the Puritans' dedication to the practical virtues of hard work and self-reliance is still part of the American credo. The homely wisdom of Benjamin Franklin's Poor Richard, as presented in his popular Almanack of 1732–57, also helped sustain the belief that hard work would be rewarded. Horatio Alger, one of the bestselling authors of all time, pushed the concept to its furthest reaches. From the beginning this was a land where idleness was disdained; so what better setting for progress and development? This went hand in hand with the widespread belief of the rightness of our national goals and aspirations. The Puritans believed devoutly that this country, and they in particular, were the beneficiaries of God's special favor. They believed that theirs was a "Citty upon a Hill," a special protectorate of God. Puritan historian Edward Johnson wrote in the 1650's that the Lord had "sifted a whole Nation to plant his choice grain" in America's rich soil. Two centuries later this strain was still being played. Novelist Herman Melville believed that "we Americans are the peculiar chosen people, the Israel of our time; we bear the ark of liberties of the world." From the beginning the mighty engine that would subdue a wild continent was fueled by confidence, optimism, and faith.

In 1845 the fever of manifest destiny swept the Nation. In that year magazine editor John L. O'Sullivan wrote that no nation on earth should be allowed to interfere with America's "manifest destiny to overspread the continent allotted by providence for the free development of our yearly multiplying millions." It has been a recurring belief that as an agent of Providence whatever promotes America's fortunes is a blessing to the world at large. This is powerful medicine, and it helped produce some miraculous results.

It was easy to become a believer. One had only to look around for full evidence of the Lord's bounty. Here was some of the best agricultural soil on the face of the globe. Vast forests spread out for hundreds of miles, filled with deer, beaver, and wildfowl. The ocean and rivers teemed with fish. There were mountains of coal and iron ore, reservoirs of oil, and rich veins of gold and silver. This was truly a chosen land for a chosen people. And the people came: for the freedom and for the bounty of the land. The Indians showed the earliest settlers new crops and methods of planting. This amity did not prevail, but it was crucial at the time. With the successive waves of immigration, there was an ebb and flow of cooperation, as well as conflict. Some people came with fortunes to invest, others came in chains. They came from every land and brought their religion, language, dance, art, music, and cuisine. They worked, played, and learned together, and intermarried. This mix of people with varied points of view, skills, and interests produced miracles. Credit for our success belongs to all.

No single element determined why so much that is so felicitous happened here in such a short time. But a major aspect is our unique system of government, which strikes a workable balance between the rights of the governed and the rights of government itself. If we Americans hold fast to the concept that everyone has equal right to life, liberty, and the pursuit of happiness, as expressed by the Founding Fathers in the Declaration of Independence, and that the primary purpose of government is to maintain these rights, we will have done justice to that inspiring statue in New York Harbor that its sculptor, Frédéric Auguste Bartholdi, called "Liberty Enlightening the World."

In France *from 1685 until 1787 the Protestant Huguenots were killed or expelled. Thousands of them found refuge in America.*
In England *the cities were rife with the degradation engendered by poverty, crowding, squalor, disease, and enforced idleness.*
In Ireland, *as in most of Europe, the peasantry was hounded to harvest more for the landowners than the soil could possibly produce.*

Fear and frustration in Europe, hunger and illness, exploitation and persecution on all sides. Where could one turn?

America calls, with freedom to worship, to learn, to assemble, and to debate any issue; a new land where a family can find

a home, where there is work to do, where the people will be heard, and where they are free to come and go and seek a better life.'

Our natural bounty, from border to border and sea to sea, was incomparably varied and seemingly inexhaustible, but now we

begin to realize that unless we cherish this legacy and use it more wisely, it can be lost to future generations.

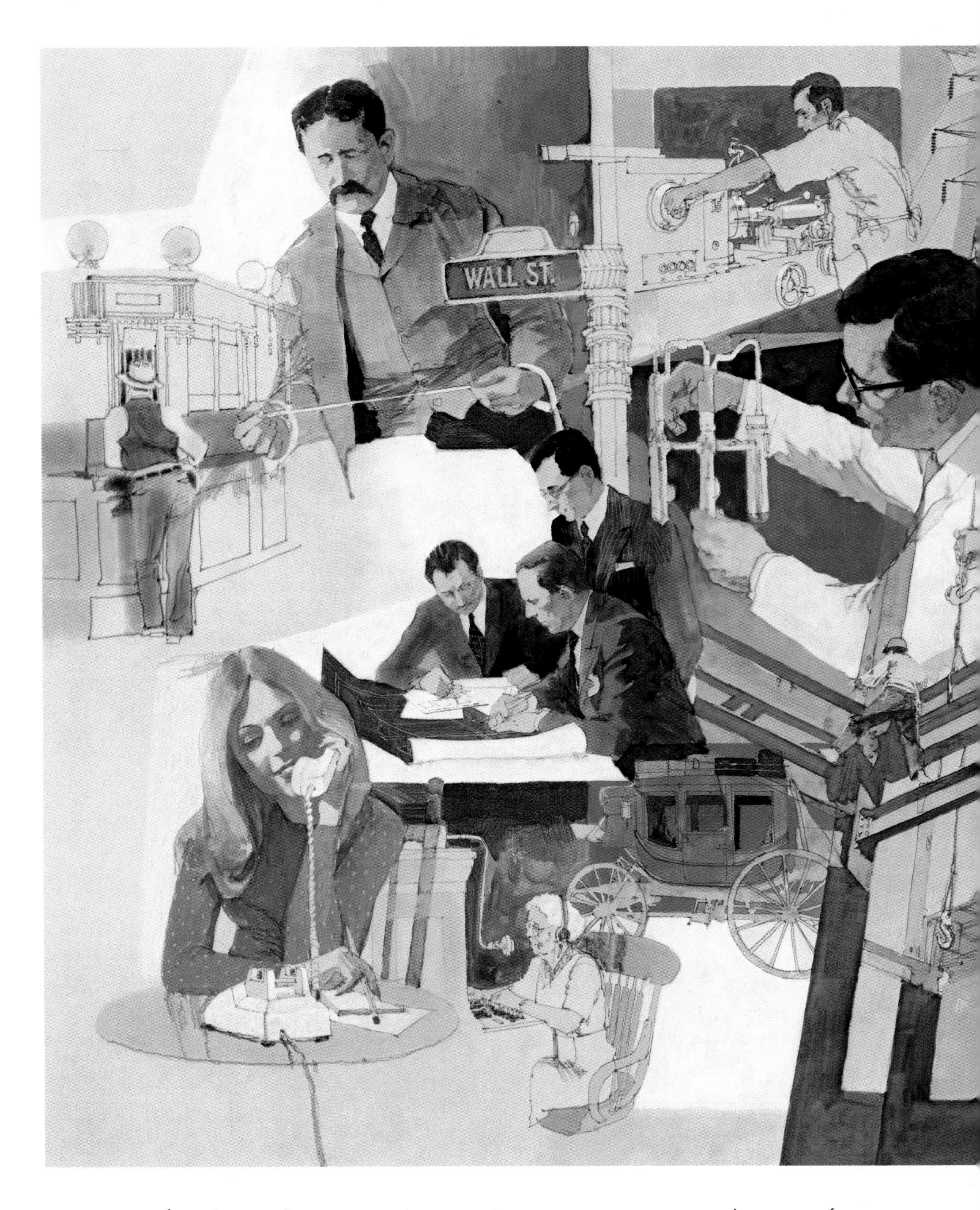

People working together with imagination, vitality, and persistence have produced triumphs of inventiveness and technology

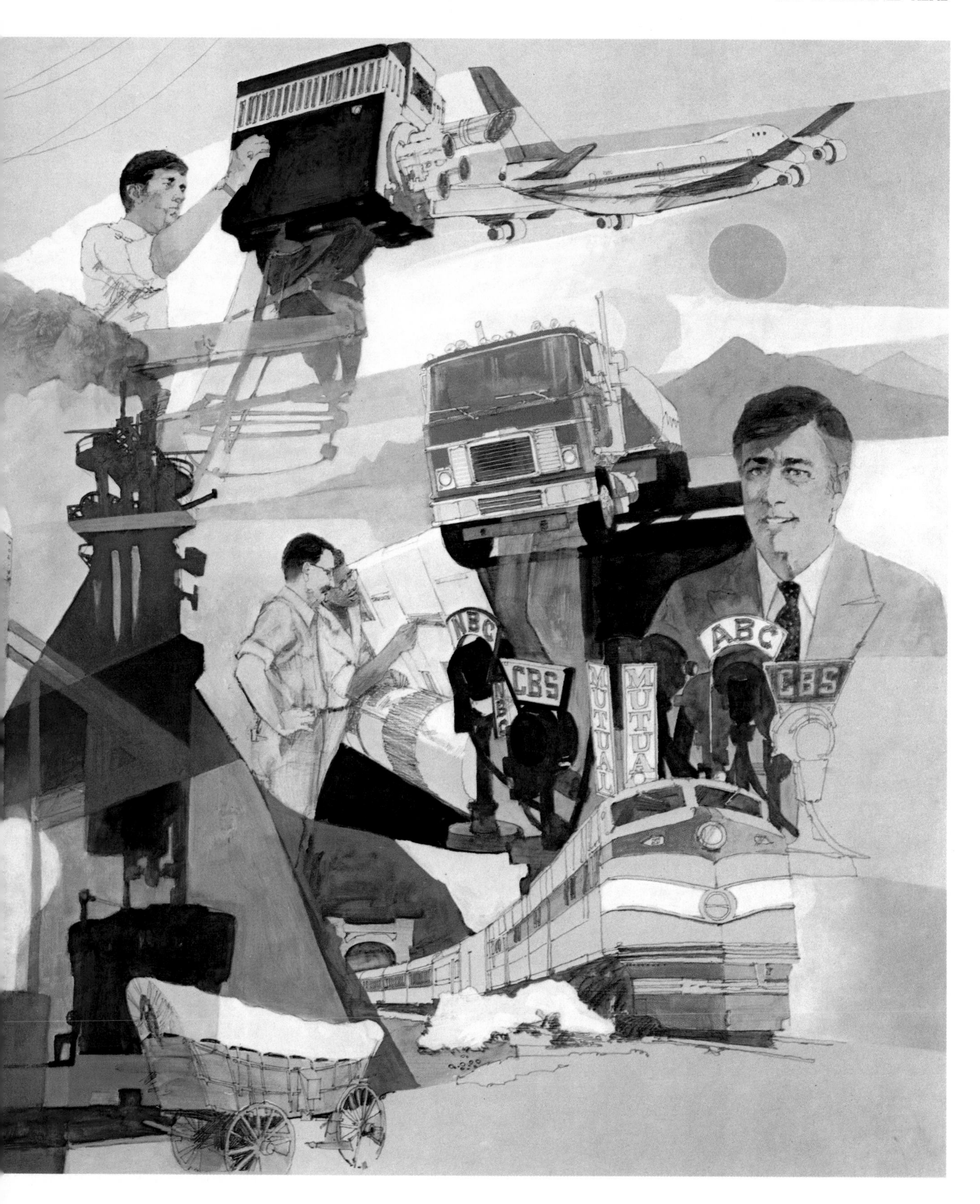

in commerce, industry, communications, and transportation beyond anything the world has ever seen or dreamed of.

CHAPTER ONE

Backgrounds and Beginnings

Although intrepid Norsemen skirted the New World's Northern shore about A.D. 1000, the news of their discovery remained veiled in the mist of Viking sagas fo centuries. The Americas were not visited again until 1492 when Christopher Columbus reached the Bahamas. North America was at first considered nothing but a vast, maddening obstacle between spice-hungry Europe and the riche of the Orient. For 150 years it remained largely unsettle by Europeans. During that time, however, Spanish adventurers roamed Florida, the gulf coast, and the Southwest in a vain search for treasure, French voyageurs brave the Canadian wilderness in pursuit of furs, and Dutch an

Eight decades before the Normans and Saxons clashed at the Battle of Hastings in 1066, the story goes, Norse seaman Bjarni Herjolfsson and his crew, lost in a thick fog while sailing between Scandinavian outposts in Iceland and Greenland, glimpsed an unknown land that was "level and covered with woods." They cruised along its coast for several days. The tale may not be true, but if it is, Bjarni Herjolfsson's men were the first Europeans to view the North American shore. It has been established that about a decade later Leif Ericsson, another Norseman, camped briefly on the Newfoundland coast, thus becoming the earliest known man from the Old World to set foot in the New. The Icelander Thorfinn Karlsefni may have followed in a year or two, but for four centuries thereafter the two vast, linked American Continents remained unknown.

The search for a sea route to Asia brought about the accidental rediscovery of the New World. In the mid-15th century the land passage that merchants had been using to bring the silks and spices of the Orient to Europe's Renaissance courts was blocked by hostile Turks. Enterprising mariners of many lands took to the sea to elude the blockade. Some favored sailing southward around the tip of Africa, but Christopher Columbus, a fearless Genoan financed by Spain, believed he could reach the Orient by voyaging westward across the uncharted Atlantic.

On October 12, 1492, after $6\frac{1}{2}$ weeks and several thousand miles of sailing, Columbus and his exhausted crew sighted a small island, in the archipelago now known as the Bahamas, and went ashore. Columbus named the island San Salvador and, convinced he had reached the Indies, dubbed the half-naked Arawaks he saw "Indians." Three later voyages did nothing to shake his belief; Columbus went to his grave in 1506 serenely confident that he had reached Asia.

Subsequent expeditions proved him wrong, and European countries continued to send mariners to probe the Eastern coasts of both continents in a frustrated search for a natural waterway to the Far East. The idea of colonizing the new lands began to grow. In 1565 Spain established St. Augustine, the first permanent settlement north of Mexico, and set up a chain of forts and missions in Florida and along the Southeastern coast to protect its claims to the land it called New Spain. In the Southwest the Spanish conquered the native Indians in 1598, called the region New Mexico, and 11 years later founded Santa Fe. Meanwhile the French were exploring the St. Lawrence River and the Great Lakes and laying claim to an area in the Northeast they called New France. After short-lived attempts to start colonies in Quebec, the Carolinas, and Florida, in 1605 France established a permanent settlement at Port Royal (later, under the British, Annapolis Royal) on Nova Scotia.

England Gains a Foothold

In 1584 Richard Hakluyt, a pious geographer who believed it a Christian duty to convert the Indians, penned his celebrated *Discourse on Western Planting.* Knowing that his fellow Elizabethans were less interested in souls than profits, he shrewdly marshaled all the material reasons he could think of for England to people the New World. English "Plantations," he argued, would provide bases from which to harass Spanish shipping. They would also offer new markets for English goods, timber for English ships, badly needed tax revenues for the royal purse, and worthwhile employment for "lustie youthes" idling at home. Hakluyt's logic and explorers' tall tales of gold and pearls for the gathering played their part in persuading daring Englishmen to emigrate. In 1585 Sir Walter Raleigh sent a group to establish a colony on Roanoke Island off what is now North Carolina, but it failed to survive.

Swedish traders established small outposts on the Northeast coast in present-day New York and Delaware.

The English, too, came looking for easy riches, but they proved more adaptable than their rivals and readier to see the possibilities of colonization. Between 1607, when the first ill-equipped settlers landed at Jamestown, and 1733, when a shipload of British debtors went ashore to found Georgia, Britain managed to establish a dozen bustling Colonies. Thirty years later, after France had met defeat in the French and Indian War and had ceded its Louisiana colony to Spain, Britain had all but eliminated its chief competitor from the North American Continent.

The British Colonies scattered along the Atlantic seaboard varied widely. Some were divided into hundreds of small farms, others had a few sprawling plantations intermingled with smaller holdings, but all drew sustenance from the production of agricultural raw materials for the mother country. The Colonies often quarreled among themselves, but loyalty to the King and faith in parliamentary self-government were common to all. As long as the distant rulers kept their hands off local matters, relations were generally friendly. It was only after 1763, when London sought closer control over their affairs without consulting them, that the colonists rebelled.

Explorers in a New Land *Sailors, Soldiers, Traders, and Priests Point the Way*

1000–1550. Norse sailor Leif Ericsson became the first known European to set foot on the New World—about A.D. 1000. No mariner matched his feat until Christopher Columbus reached the Bahamas in 1492, and John Cabot found the fish-rich Grand Bank in 1497 and began the futile search for a navigable Northwest Passage. During the next 53 years Spanish explorers probed the Southwest and as far east as Kansas seeking gold, and France staked its claim to the game-rich St. Lawrence Valley.

1551–1650. In this period Francis Drake claimed California for England; Juan de Oñate colonized New Mexico and blazed new trails east into Kansas and west to Lower California; and Samuel de Champlain founded Quebec in French Canada and pushed west to Lake Huron. Meanwhile Henry Hudson discovered the river that bears his name and Capt. John Smith charted New England's coast.

1651–1750. In the final 100 years of colonial exploration an Italian Jesuit, Eusebio Kino, founded the first missions in southern Arizona and northwest Mexico, but France scored the most spectacular successes. Fur trader Louis Jolliet and Jesuit priest Jacques Marquette paddled down the unmapped Mississippi to the Arkansas River to open up the fur trade in the Midwest. Robert Cavelier, Sieur de La Salle, descended to the mouth of the Mississippi and claimed all the land in the vast river system for France. Pierre Gaultier de Varennes, Sieur de La Vérendrye, and his sons, Louis and François, eventually extended the French fur empire all the way to the upper Missouri River.

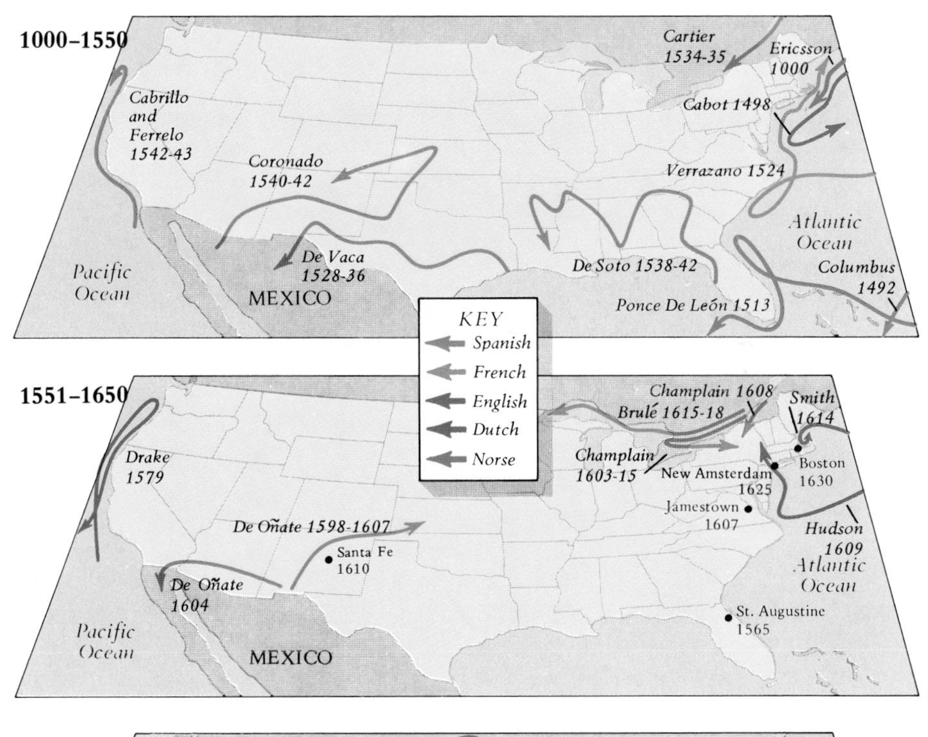

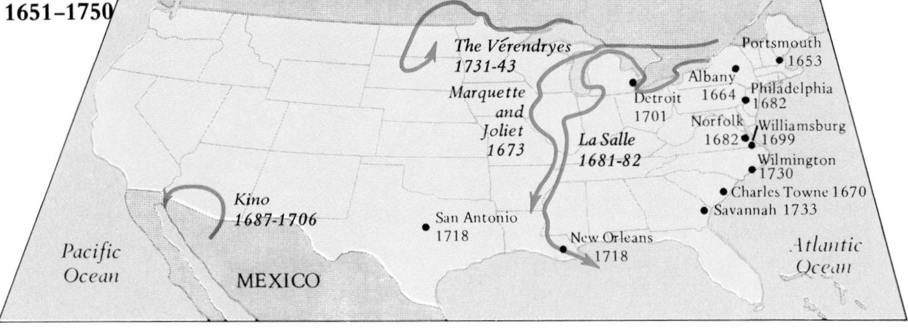

Europe's first glimpse *of the New World was through a series of bright watercolors painted at Roanoke in 1585 by John White, later the leader of the colony. The elaborately adorned Indian, above, was a member of a friendly Algonquian-speaking coastal tribe. At right is White's crude but handsome map of Virginia and the Southern coast. Some of the sea beasts shown on it are mythical; others are accurate renderings of the local fish. The coat of arms belonged to Sir Walter Raleigh, who was Roanoke's chief financial backer.*

Early Accounts of the New World
From French Writers and an English Artist

In 1564 a small French Huguenot (Protestant) colony called Fort Caroline was established on the shore of the St. Johns River in present-day northeast Florida. It did not survive for long; in 1565 armored troops from Catholic Spain marched in and killed every Frenchman they found. Among the few who escaped was Jacques Lemoyne de Morgues, an artist and writer. Some 20 years later he published the first eyewitness account of an American settlement. Here is his report of his first encounter with the Indians:

We found the seashore crowded with native men and women, who kept up large fires. At first we thought it necessary to be on guard against them, but very soon we realized that the last thing in their minds was to harm us . . . they gave numerous proofs of their friendly intentions. They were filled with admiration when they found out that our flesh was so much softer . . . than their own, and they praised our garments, which were so different from theirs. . . . They brought us grains of roasted maize, ground into flour, or whole ears of it, smoked lizards or other wild animals which they considered great delicacies, and various kinds of roots, some for food, others for medicine. And when they discovered that we were more interested in metals and minerals, they gave us some of those as well.

Nicolas le Challeux, another Fort Caroline colonist fortunate enough to have escaped the Spanish, also wrote a vivid memoir. He noted a common bond of faith between the colonists and the savage tribesmen:

As far as I could see, they are not without some idea of Divinity. I conjecture that under certain circumstances they might easily become civilized and made honest. They could also be converted to holiness and sound religion—if God in His mercy should so ordain it. For as soon as the bell rang for prayers at our fort, they would be there, stretching up their hands to Heaven as we did, even with reverence and attentive ear.

The Lost Colony of Roanoke

In July 1585, 108 Englishmen went ashore at Roanoke Island off the coast of what is now North Carolina. Backed by the adventurous Sir Walter Raleigh, they built a fort and houses, planted crops, and looked, in vain, for gold. Within a year hurricanes and hostile Indians forced them to go back to England. In 1587, undaunted by this failure, 118 colonists, led by John White, arrived on Roanoke. Among them were White's daughter and son-in-law, parents of Virginia Dare, the first English baby to be born in the New World. After several weeks White sailed back to England for more provisions. When he returned in 1591, he found Roanoke deserted; "CROATOAN" was carved on a tree. Roanoke's fate remains a mystery. Some believe the colonists were killed by Indians or Spanish troops from Florida, others that they went, peaceably or by force, to live with the Indians on nearby Croatoan Island.

The Roanoke failure brought a pause, but only a short one. In May 1607 three frail vessels landed some 100 eager adventurers near the mouth of the James River. There, in a malarial swamp, the newcomers built Jamestown, Britain's first permanent colony, and almost immediately began a fruitless search for treasure. They had been financed by a company of London merchants for whom they had contracted to toil for 7 years. Few of them were trained for survival in the wilderness, and half died during the first winter. Nevertheless the settlement managed to survive, due to the able leadership of Capt. John Smith and the aid of friendly Indians, who showed the men how to clear the forest and grow corn and sweet potatoes. The introduction of tobacco from the West Indies in 1612 made Jamestown a going concern. But since tobacco became popular only after the settlers' 7-year contracts had expired, not one shilling of profit ever reached their sponsors back in England.

A swashbuckling veteran *of several wars, Capt. John Smith pulled Jamestown through its hardest times, then returned to England to urge further colonization of America.*

The merchant company that backed the *Mayflower*'s voyage in 1620 fared no better. Many of these Plymouth colonists, who were led by the pious Pilgrim Separatists, also succumbed. The survivors earned their company no profits, but the Colony endured and eventually thrived. (In 1691 it joined the Massachusetts Bay Colony.) A decade after the *Mayflower,* John Winthrop led some 1,800 fellow Puritans to Massachusetts Bay, where they founded Boston and sought to establish a "City of God" in which they could practice their rigid faith. Restless colonists (some of whom were themselves dissenters from the Puritan code) spread inland to found more New England Colonies: Connecticut (organized 1639), Rhode Island (1644), and New Hampshire (1680). The craggy Maine coast was also settled early, but Maine was a part of Massachusetts until 1820.

Merchant companies having proved too risky, subsequent Colonies were founded by wealthy proprietors, court favorites who hoped to get rich by developing the far-off wilderness. In 1634 the Catholic Lord Calvert was awarded title to Maryland, which soon became a prosperous, tobacco-growing region. The vast area south of Virginia was first parcelled out by Charles II among eight courtiers in 1663. Named Carolina in honor of the King (the Latin form of his name is Carolus), it was split into North and South Carolina in 1691 but the two sections did not become separate Colonies until 1712. Twenty years later the King chartered the Colony of Georgia, which James Oglethorpe founded as a haven for debtors.

John Winthrop, *as Governor of Massachusetts Bay Colony for more than 10 years, believed in government by the elite among the Puritans, with the vote restricted to church members.*

By 1626 Dutch traders had settled along the Hudson River, establishing the colony of New Netherland; they swallowed up a tiny, short-lived Swedish outpost on Delaware Bay in 1655. Nine years later England occupied New Netherland, renamed it New York, and split off its southern portion into East and West Jersey (1676; united as New Jersey in 1702). In 1681 Quaker William Penn was named proprietor of Pennsylvania. The three Delaware counties, deeded to Penn by the Duke of York in 1682, were given the right of local self-government in 1701, but Pennsylvania retained ultimate authority over these "lower counties." In 1775 Delaware asserted its right to equality with the other Colonies and in 1776 declared its statehood.

The Making of a People

These entirely separate Colonies differed widely, and their differences generated almost constant sectional friction. There were bitter intercolonial squabbles over religion, trade, and boundaries. Southern planters denounced sharp-bargaining New England traders; many New Englanders deplored Southern slavery. (Many others, however, made money selling slaves to the South.) Within the Colonies, too, there were disagreements between factions, in some cases resulting in civil wars. Rough-hewn frontiersmen were pitted against the prosperous coastal dwellers who controlled colonial purse strings. "Fire and Water are not more heterogeneous than the different Colonies in North America," wrote one early visitor, and until 1754 even repeated threats of annihilation by France and its Indian allies failed to produce unity. Those Colonies that were not actually under fire customarily with-

The Pequot Indian War Denominator of Indian Conflicts

The pattern for scores of frontier conflicts was set by the Pequot Indian war of 1637. As Massachusetts Bay colonists worked their way into Connecticut and Rhode Island, they threatened to displace the Pequots, a proud people whose very name meant "destroyers," and who were themselves trespassers on the ancestral lands of the Narragansetts. Isolated incidents erupted into full-scale war when Pequot raiders, avenging an attack on one of their villages, killed some 30 frontiersmen. The New England Colonies promptly dispatched 250 armed militiamen and a band of perhaps 1,000 painted Narragansetts to do what one zealous clergyman called "the work of the Lord's revenge." They surprised and surrounded a palisaded Pequot village at the mouth of the Mystic River, set it ablaze, and shot or hacked to death all who tried to flee the flames. "It was a fearful sight," recalled one colonist, "to see them thus frying in the fyer, and the streams of blood quenching the same." The few who escaped were hunted down in a nearby swamp. Those not executed were handed over to the Narragansetts or sold into the West Indian slave trade. Their sachem's scalp was displayed at Hartford.

By the end of the following year the Pequots had ceased to be a people and the other New England tribes had seen what would happen to resisters. The Pequots were the first of countless tribes that were destroyed or placed on reservations during the next two and a half centuries of white expansion westward.

held men and arms from their less fortunate neighbors.

Yet, despite their differences, the colonists were slowly transformed into one quarrelsome but distinctive people. Several factors contributed to that process. Perhaps the most important was the fact that the colonists were overwhelmingly Protestant and English. They shared the English tongue, they believed in British customs and traditions of parliamentary self-government and trial by jury, and they were loyal to the British King. Their rich colonial culture—their books and buildings, fabrics and furnishings, portraits and poetry—was solidly based on British models. They saw themselves as transplanted Englishmen and called England "home," though after the first generation most had never been there. Major exceptions to this early homogeneity were the Dutch of New Netherland, Germans and Scotch-Irish on the backwoods frontier, and large numbers of African slaves.

Royal coats of arms *such as this one on the reconstructed Governor's Palace at Williamsburg, Virginia, symbolized nearly 170 years of colonial allegiance to the English Crown.*

The very act of leaving the settled life of the Old World for the uncertainties of the New bespoke a profound independence of mind and spirit. The vast majority of the colonists were farmers who owned and worked their land. A Frenchman, Michel Guillaume Jean de Crèvecoeur, expressed the feelings of most in his *Letters from an American Farmer:* "We are all animated with the spirit of an industry which is unfettered and unrestrained, because each person works for himself . . . without any part being claimed by a despotic prince, a rich abbot or a mighty lord." Such self-employment bred self-reliance and the determination to succeed.

Crown and Colony

Whatever their private wishes, the King and his ministers could maintain only minimal control over their far-off possessions, separated from them by some 3,000 miles of open sea. For the colonists, wrote historian Edmund S. Morgan, "the great thing about this empire, apart from the sheer pride of belonging to it, was that it let you alone." Some colonists lived a lifetime without ever encountering a royal official.

Each Colony had its own royal charter, which generally guaranteed the rights of Englishmen to all its citizens, but little further effort was made to standardize colonial law. By 1750 Pennsylvania (including the Delaware counties) and Maryland remained under proprietary rule, and Rhode Island and Connecticut were more or less self-governing. The rest of the Colonies were royal colonies, each with its own governor, royally appointed and usually British. The governors in turn nominated their own advisers, who were sometimes American. But beginning with the first meeting of the Virginia Legislature at Jamestown in 1619, every Colony had created its own popularly elected assembly. The Colonies were never true democracies in the modern sense; too many potential voters were disqualified because of color, poverty, or religious faith. They were, however, the closest thing to a democracy in the 18th-century world. The colonists had far more control of their own government than had their compatriots in Britain.

In theory the royal governors wielded great power: They directed defenses, called and dismissed the legislatures, and could veto virtually any assembly enactment. But they were dependent on the local legislatures for funds, and those bodies were able to exert a great deal of control over their actions. The attitude of many officials was expressed in 1736 by New York Gov. William Cosby, who said wearily after a jury had acquitted

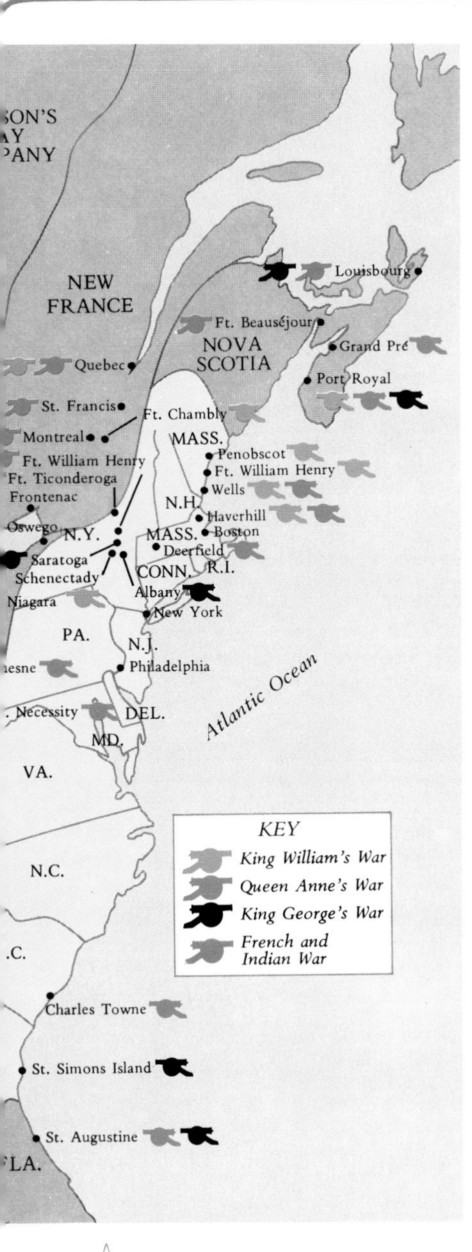

Struggle for a Continent

Four Little-Known, Easily Confused Conflicts

All of the international wars involving the Colonies between 1689 and 1763 were related to a century-long struggle for global supremacy between France and England.

King William's War (1689–97). In 1689, after England's William III entered the War of the League of Augsburg against France, French-led Indian attacks ravaged English settlements in New England and New York. New Englanders retaliated in 1690, seizing a key French base at Port Royal, Nova Scotia, then unsuccessfully besieging Quebec. The French retook Port Royal and English posts on Hudson Bay in 1691. Bloody but indecisive border skirmishes occurred for the next 6 years. The Treaty of Ryswick (1697) called on both sides to return to the prewar status quo.

Queen Anne's War (1702–13). The American phase of the War of the Spanish Succession, which pitted England against both Spain and France, was more decisive. Indians, under French and British command, pillaged forest settlements. Carolina volunteers razed Spanish St. Augustine in Florida and missions to the west, and British forces recaptured Port Royal. France lost the European war and, under the Treaty of Utrecht (1713), abandoned its claims to Nova Scotia, Newfoundland, and the Hudson Bay area, but kept Cape Breton Island, off the coast of Nova Scotia.

King George's War (1744–48). As fighting broke out again in 1744, the French, based at the supposedly impregnable fortress of Louisbourg on Cape Breton Island, attacked British posts in Newfoundland. Undaunted, 4,000 New England militia, commanded by William Pepperrell and aided by an English fleet under Sir Peter Warren, attacked Louisbourg and, after a 6-week siege, forced its surrender in June 1745. The same year French forces thrust into New York, burning Saratoga and harassing Albany. The 1748 Treaty of Aachen restored the status quo in North America.

The French and Indian War (1755–63). France and Britain almost immediately began preparing for renewed war. Both built new frontier fortresses and pushed into the Ohio Valley. On paper Britain had the edge—greater numbers, more resources, better strategic position. But France had powerful Indian allies. France struck first. In 1755 French and Indians destroyed a British force under Gen. Edward Braddock near Fort Duquesne in western Pennsylvania. They then laid waste to frontier towns. News of these forest battles sparked the worldwide Seven Years' War in 1756. In that year and the next French and Indian forces under the shrewd Marquis de Montcalm took British outposts in western New York, sealing off the invasion route to Canada. But the tide of battle turned in 1758. British and colonial troops seized Louisbourg and Forts Frontenac, Duquesne, and Ticonderoga, while Sir William Johnson's fierce Iroquois and a strong force of British regulars took Fort Niagara. French Canada was open to attack, and in late 1759 Quebec surrendered after a battle on the Plains of Abraham, in which both Montcalm and the British commander, Gen. James Wolfe, were mortally wounded. The following year English forces overran the final French stronghold at Montreal. The war in North America had ended. The Treaty of Paris (1763) ended more than a century and a half of French power in the New World.

MAKING DEMOCRACY WORK

The Albany Plan of Union

Anticipating a fourth wilderness war with France and her Indian allies, delegates from six Northern Colonies—New Hampshire, Massachusetts, Rhode Island, Pennsylvania, New York, and Connecticut—and Maryland met at Albany, New York, in June and July of 1754 to plan a united defense. To cement their faltering alliance with the mighty Iroquois Confederacy, they invited the chiefs of the Six Nations to the parley and, after much speechmaking on both sides, gave the Indians 30 wagonloads of trinkets and trade goods along with pledges of protection from further white encroachment into Iroquois territories.

But some delegates had a more ambitious program of unified action in mind. New Englanders, in particular, had learned in earlier wars the importance of working together against the enemy, and Pennsylvania delegate Benjamin Franklin had already used the pages of his newspaper, *The Pennsylvania Gazette,* to propose a plan of union. He called on the Colonies to come together voluntarily under one general government, with each Colony retaining its own identity and handling its internal affairs. A grand council would be elected by the colonial assemblies to work with a single president general, appointed by the Crown, to treat with the tribes regarding land purchases, to impose some taxes, to raise armies, and to build forts. Franklin's essay had been published alongside a celebrated cartoon (one of the first editorial cartoons to appear in the country) depicting a serpent cut in parts. The parts represented the Colonies; below the snake was the motto, "Join or Die."

The Albany Congress endorsed the plan, but the colonial assemblies, who disliked giving up any power to a central authority, refused to ratify it, and the Crown took no action. Nonetheless, the Albany Plan of Union had demonstrated a growing sentiment for united colonial action in a crisis and helped pave the way for the Continental Congress of 1774.

The bustling port of Philadelphia, *colonial America's largest and most prosperous city, as it looked in the early 1730's. Few signs of William Penn's "greene countrie towne" remained. Philadelphia was one of the largest cities in the British Empire; its merchants and bankers dominated much of the colonial economy; its intellectual and scientific community made it the most active cultural center in America.*

HUDSON'S BAY COMPANY
MASS.
NEW ENGLAND COLONIES
N.H.
Portsmouth
MASS.
Boston
Providence
Newport
R.I.
Hartford
CONN.
New Haven
QUEBEC
MIDDLE COLONIES
N.Y.
PA.
N.J.
New York
Perth Amboy
Philadelphia
Burlington
New Castle
MD.
Annapolis
DEL.
Proclamation Line of 1763
VA.
Williamsburg
INDIAN RESERVE
SOUTHERN COLONIES
N.C.
New Bern
Atlantic Ocean
S.C.
GA.
Charles Town
Savannah
EAST FLA.

The Face of America, 1763–74

All of these towns were at one time colonial capitals.

The Different Worlds of Colonial America

The Regional Variations, in General, Still Apply

New England Colonies. Massachusetts Puritans spread inland and along the coast to people this region's stony soil. Most became small farmers or artisans, dwelt in villages, and fiercely insisted on self-government. Others depended on the sea; they fished, built or manned ships, or traded with England and the West Indies. Busy ports, such as Boston and Newport, were havens for merchants who slyly evaded British attempts to tax and regulate their trade with French and Dutch colonies.

Middle Colonies. New York, New Jersey, and Delaware, first settled by Dutch and Swedish traders, and Pennsylvania, which under William Penn welcomed many nationalities, were the most cosmopolitan of the English Colonies. Most residents were prosperous farmers, but numbers of tradesmen, mechanics, and shippers clustered around Philadelphia and New York. More genial and tolerant than New England, more energetic than the South, the Middle Colonies best represented the creative ferment of classes and cultures that would characterize America after the Revolution.

Southern Colonies. Agriculture was the heart of Southern life, and the tidal rivers were its arteries. Along their banks flourished vast, self-sufficient plantations that shipped their crops to foreign markets from their own wharves. Because plantations were scattered and isolated, development of the South lagged behind that of the other Colonies; Charleston was its only real city until after the Revolution. Along the Appalachian frontier independent backwoodsmen cultivated small farms.

The gracious plantation home *of George Washington, Mount Vernon. Surrounded by lawns and shade trees, it overlooked the Potomac River and some 8,000 acres of forest and farmland. "No estate in . . . America," wrote its proud owner, "is more pleasantly situated than this."*

John Peter Zenger of charges of seditious libel, "I had more trouble to manage these people than I could have imagined." In most local affairs, the assemblies acted without hindrance from officials in London.

Only in matters of trade did England have a consistent imperial policy. The Colonies were expected to supply the mother country with an abundance of raw or semi-finished materials, including furs, fish, rice, tobacco, and timber. In exchange they received a host of manufactured goods from the homeland. Both sides profited handsomely. To ensure this steady flow of trade, Parliament passed a series of Navigation Acts starting in 1650 and continuing into the 1760's. These acts forbade foreign vessels to trade with the Colonies without a license, required that virtually all American goods be carried in British or colonial vessels and be sold only to British or British colonial buyers, and discouraged American manufacturing to protect British firms from competition. American trade with other nations or their colonies was officially forbidden. Since these statutes gave American shippers a virtual monopoly on trade with the British West Indies and generally served to formalize in law a system already eagerly pursued in practice, few colonists complained. They simply ignored the laws they did not like, such as a ban on the American manufacture of iron and prohibitive duties on molasses from the non-British West Indies (key to the profitable New England rum trade). At the same time, none of the acts was rigorously administered; royal officials grew rich from bribes and winked at widespread smuggling by the colonists.

Triumph and Trouble for the Crown

England's 1763 victory in the French and Indian War made George III the master of virtually all of North America east of the Mississippi. Yet within just two decades his American holdings would be nearly halved by revolt among his English-speaking subjects. The earnest young monarch, determined to "rule as well as reign," and his ministers unwittingly sparked the struggle by trying to tighten their grip on the Colonies.

Although their actions were denounced as despotic by revolutionists, they were motivated by ideological as well as purely pragmatic considerations. Outposts of the British Empire could be found halfway around the globe, and the Seven Years' War (of which the American conflict had been only a part) had doubled the national debt. If Britain's treasury was to be replenished and the Colonies well governed, new sources of revenue had to be found and the old system of colonial administration made more efficient. When Parliament tried to raise the money in England a series of riots quickly demonstrated that British taxpayers would not tolerate additional levies. Britain then looked to the Colonies for further income.

Toward that end Parliament moved to strengthen enforcement of the old Navigation Acts even before the end of the French and Indian War. Smugglers were tried without juries in vice-admiralty courts, the corrupt customs service was reformed, and writs of assistance were issued permitting officials without specific warrants to break into warehouses, ships' holds, and even private homes in search of contraband. New England merchants (many of whom were indeed smugglers) were outraged. Their fiery spokesman was James Otis, who resigned his post as the King's Advocate General in 1761 to denounce the writs before the Superior Court of Massachusetts. He declared them unconstitutional "instruments of tyranny" because they denied to British citizens abroad rights held sacred at home. Otis lost his case, but his ringing argument foreshadowed struggles to come.

A landmark of liberty, *Virginia's capitol, where the House of Burgesses met, has been reconstructed in the colonial Williamsburg restoration. Here George Mason, Thomas Jefferson, George Washington, and Patrick Henry debated how best to deal with Britain, and here, in 1765, resolutions were passed against the Stamp Act.*

London sought to appease the Indians and calm the frontier by barring white settlement west of the Appalachians after 1763. Veterans of the French and Indian War, many of whom had been promised free tracts of land in exchange for army service, were infuriated. So were a host of eager land speculators (including George Washington and Benjamin Franklin) who had hoped to make a profit by carving up tribal territories. But determined pioneers like Daniel Boone ignored the detested Proclamation Line of 1763; by 1782 some 30,000 had poured over the mountains into what is now Kentucky.

Relations between Crown and Colony were further impaired when Parliament dispatched a 10,000-man standing army to America to safeguard the frontiers against Indian attacks. Under the terms of the Quartering Act of 1765 the colonists were required to provide the troops with barracks and supplies. When soldiers took up stations in port cities, many Americans suspected that the troops had been sent to impose Parliament's will rather than to man the frontier.

Crucible of Conflict
Boston Before the Revolution

It was no accident that Boston became the flashpoint of the Revolution. Massachusetts had a long, proud heritage of self-government. And as New England's primary port, Boston depended for its livelihood on freedom of trade. No people were more determined than Bostonians to resist antismuggling measures imposed by Britain.

Boston had two leaders ideally suited to lead resistance: John Hancock and Samuel Adams. The elegant Hancock, one of America's wealthiest shipping magnates, provided the Patriot cause with money and a measure of respectability. Adams, a rumpled politician, contributed tactical brilliance, political ruthlessness, and a near-fanatic devotion to colonial rights. Backed by able allies, these two fanned the flames of discontent. They orchestrated mob demonstrations, urged harassment of occupation troops, persuaded the assembly to defy Parliament, and set up Patriot Committees of Correspondence to spread the spirit of resistance beyond the city.

The Boston Massacre, *according to John Adams, was triggered by a "motley rabble" of rock throwers. The squad of British soldiers fired under pressure, killing five persons and wounding others.*

Adams and Hancock played major roles in two of the most important incidents leading to the Revolution. In reality, the celebrated Boston Massacre, which took place on March 5, 1770, was hardly the heroic affair that the Patriots made it out to be. But this tragic brawl as reported by Samuel Adams came to be seen as another example of British tyranny against the Colonies. On the other hand, Adams' second cousin John Adams, despite his dislike of British policies in America, won acquittal for all but two of the nine soldiers involved in the incident.

The Boston Tea Party, too, involved Samuel Adams and Hancock. Gov. Thomas Hutchinson had stubbornly rejected the colonists' demands that three East India Company ships loaded with tea be allowed to return to England without paying hated duties. On the night of December 16, 1773, Adams and Hancock sent the Sons of Liberty, disguised as Indians, to the waterfront, where they boarded the ships and dumped their cargoes overboard. Britain retaliated by closing the port of Boston, an action that unified the colonists and hastened the outbreak of the Revolution.

Parliament passed a succession of bills aimed at raising revenues. The Sugar Act of 1764 put teeth into the 1733 Molasses Act and threatened to destroy the rum trade. Even more annoying was the Stamp Act of 1765. This required that virtually everything formally written or printed—from marriage licenses to playing cards—be inscribed on specially stamped paper dispensed by royal agents upon payment of a new tax or on paper brought to them and stamped for a fee.

No actions could have more enraged the colonists, who considered themselves patriotic Englishmen. Under the hard-won British parliamentary system, as outlined by 17th-century philosopher John Locke, property was inseparable from life and liberty; no man could be deprived of it except by his express consent or that of his elected representatives. Since the colonists had no voice in Parliament, Britain's recent acts deprived them of what the Massachusetts Assembly termed the "most essential Rights of Britons." However, the notion of total independence was still anathema to even the most radical Americans. But the Colonies were willing to defy the might of the world's greatest military power rather than meekly submit to "taxation without representation." A generation of extraordinary men, lawyers mostly but planters and pamphleteers as well, rallied to the colonial cause. Able men as different in their views as radicals Samuel Adams, James Otis, and Christopher Gadsden and conservatives John Dickinson and Joseph Galloway were united in their outrage against Britain's actions.

Beginning with the Virginia House of Burgesses—where the flamboyant oratory of young Patrick Henry carried the day—the colonial assemblies denounced the Stamp Act. In October 1765 delegates from nine Colonies met in New York to petition the King for relief. Almost against their will, the colonists were beginning to see themselves as Americans rather than Virginians or New Yorkers. An intercolonial boycott of British goods damaged the British economy. Meanwhile, urban mobs, led by the newly organized Sons of Liberty, set heaps of the hated stamps ablaze, looted the homes of customs officials, and forced stamp agents to resign their posts. Finally, on March 18, 1766, the Stamp Act was rescinded. The colonists were jubilant, celebrating, as John Adams recalled, with "such illuminations, bonfires, pyramids, obelisks, such grand exhibitions and such fireworks as were never before seen in America."

The Great Quarrel Intensifies

The celebration was short lived. On the very day it repealed the Stamp Act, Parliament also reasserted its unequivocal right to make laws binding on the Colonies "in all cases whatsoever." Its deeds soon matched its words. The 1767 Townshend Acts, named for Charles Townshend, Chancellor of the Exchequer, imposed stiff new duties on a host of popular British products (including glass, paper, lead, and tea) and established a new Board of Customs Commissioners whose income depended in part on how much revenue they could squeeze from American merchants.

The Colonies again resolved to resist. A new boycott of British imports saw wealthy colonists go without precious tea and fashionable lace. Homespun became a badge of honor. Workmen shunned British-made leather aprons. As a result of this resistance native industries thrived, and British exports fell 38 percent. Britain struggled to maintain order: Several colonial assemblies were suspended when they opposed the Townshend Acts, and British regiments were dispatched to recalcitrant Boston. Tense encounters between the troops and Bostonians became common. On March 5, 1770, the misnamed "Boston Massacre" occurred, and an accidental street skirmish became, in the hands of radical propagandist Samuel Adams, a symbol of British arrogance and brutality.

On that same day Parliament again temporarily backed down, repealing all the Townshend duties except the one on tea. For 2 years thereafter, relative peace was restored, marred only by angry confrontations between zealous (and often corrupt) customs men and dockside mobs. But in the spring of 1772 tension rose again. First a mob in Providence, Rhode Island, put a beached customs ship to the torch; then Gov. Thomas Hutchinson of Massachusetts announced that thenceforth he and the judges of the province were to be paid directly by the Crown; thus the people would no longer have any control over the activities of the officials. To alert other communities to British actions, Samuel Adams established a Committee of Correspondence. Soon a network of such revolutionary groups was spreading anti-British sentiment throughout the Colonies.

In the spring of 1773 Parliament awarded a monopoly on the sale of tea, still taxed under the Townshend Act, to the debt-ridden East India Company. Although it would have made East Indian tea cheaper than anything colonial merchants could offer, the issue of taxation overrode pocketbook logic. A supply of the tea, half a million pounds in all, was sent to the Colonies' four chief ports. In Philadelphia and New York tea merchants refused to accept the tea, and tea-laden ships simply turned around and sailed back to England. In Charleston the tea was unloaded and stored under bond rather than sold. But in Boston legalistic Governor Hutchinson insisted the

England's Point of View

The general British reaction to American unrest was anger and bewilderment. While Edmund Burke; William Pitt, the elder; Charles Fox; and John Wilkes sympathized with the colonials and their problems and foresaw the disaster that would befall the Empire if Parliament ignored them, most statesmen could not understand what the colonials were complaining about. Taxation without representation was nothing new. Large numbers of Englishmen at home were unrepresented in Parliament; yet they paid their taxes without rebelling. Anyway, the colonials had "virtual" representation, since all members of Parliament sought always to act in the best interests of the Empire. Then, too, the Americans seemed terribly ungrateful. English arms had rid Americans of the French menace at great cost in blood and treasure, and even then His Majesty's troops were protecting the colonial borders. Why shouldn't the recipients of all this royal beneficence pay their fair share of the cost?

Besides, the colonial agitators seemed a notably unsavory lot. They included urban rowdies (like the Boston toughs tormenting a hapless customs officer in the English cartoon below), smugglers, buckskin-clad frontiersmen, lawyers of dubious training, and Southern planters wishing only to be relieved of their debts to English merchants. All in all, royal officers assured the Commons, these were "raw, undisciplined, cowardly men. . . . The very sound of a cannon [will] carry them off. . . ." Few listened when Burke warned that force would win only temporary tranquillity and "a nation is not governed which is perpetually to be conquered." But events soon proved him right.

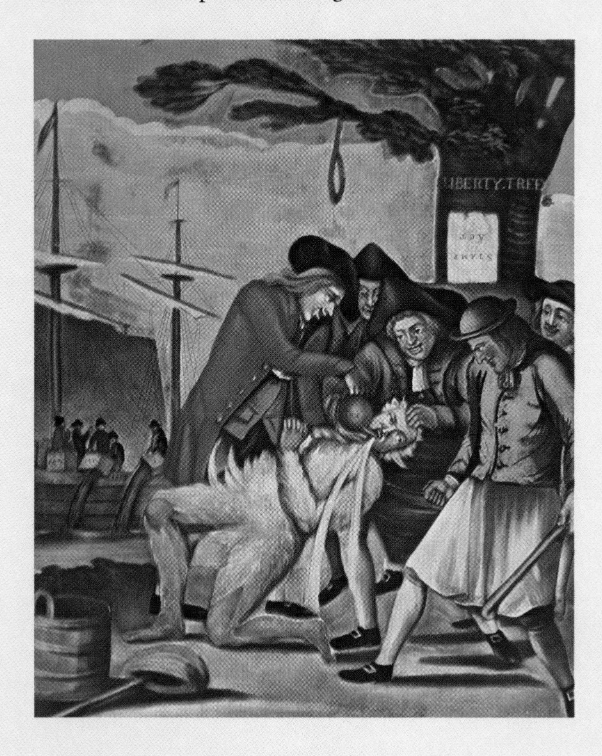

import duties be paid before the ships could leave the harbor. The loaded ships remained at anchor until Samuel Adams and some 50 painted Patriots boarded them and dumped 343 chests of the "accursed, dutied stuff" into the harbor.

This bold deed proved the final straw. The Crown came down hard on rebel Massachusetts. The port of Boston was closed, semimilitary government was imposed, an occupation army was brought in and housed in private homes, and civil liberties were curtailed. Simultaneously the Quebec Act extended the former French province of Quebec south to the Ohio River, dashing colonial hopes for westward expansion.

Patriot Samuel Adams, *as seen by John S. Copley. "He was born and tempered a wedge of steel," wrote his cousin John Adams, "to split the knot . . . that tied America to England."*

Intended to bring the Colonies finally to heel, these Intolerable Acts had precisely the opposite effect. At first only Parliament's power to tax had been questioned; now the angry colonists denied its right to intervene in any of their internal affairs. A complete break with England was still only the pipedream of such diehard radicals as Samuel Adams and South Carolina's Christopher Gadsden. Most colonists remained loyal to the throne and hoped for a new arrangement like the one later developed to keep such self-governing dominions as Canada within the Empire. But neither side was in the mood for compromise. In 1774 all the Colonies save Georgia sent delegates to the First Continental Congress and supported its call for a united stand against British demands.

To the King and his haughty Chief Minister, Lord North (who once declared, "I can never acquiesce in the absurd opinion that all men are equal"), these actions were evidence of treason pure and simple. The Prime Minister declared that "the New England governments are in a state of rebellion" and laid plans to crush them, assuring Parliament that "Four or five frigates will do the business without any military force." As the year ended, grimly earnest minutemen were drilling on frozen village greens. Supplies were on the way to beleaguered Boston from as far away as South Carolina. And open warfare was only months away.

MAKING DEMOCRACY WORK

The First Continental Congress

Parliament's passage of the Intolerable Acts, while aimed primarily at defiant Massachusetts, was looked upon by the other Colonies as a threat to their liberties. Accordingly they swiftly responded to a call from the Massachusetts House of Representatives for an intercolonial congress, which would take action necessary "for the recovery and establishment of just rights and liberties" of the Colonies. Only Georgia was not represented among the 55 delegates of the First Continental Congress that met in Carpenters Hall, Philadelphia, from September 5 to October 26, 1774.

The delegates were by no means united. Their first quarrel was over who should offer the opening prayer; they finally settled on the local Episcopal clergyman. After considerable wrangling, each Colony was granted one vote, regardless of size or population. At one point, a frustrated Patrick Henry appealed to his bickering colleagues to recognize that "the distinctions between Virginians, Pennsylvanians, New Yorkers and New Englanders are no more. I am not a Virginian, but an American!" No one yet dared openly to avow independence (not even such radicals as Samuel Adams), and many moderates feared that even a mildly worded protest to the King might bring disaster. There was considerable support for a conciliatory plan offered by Joseph Galloway of Pennsylvania. It would have created an American legislature, called a grand council, to oversee colonial affairs in association with a royally appointed president-general. The council was to be considered an overseas branch of Parliament, and agreement by both bodies would have been necessary to validate general colonial taxes.

Debate waxed hot over the Galloway Plan until Patriot Paul Revere galloped into Philadelphia and delivered to the Congress a copy of the newly adopted Suffolk Resolves. This set of resolutions, written by Dr. Joseph Warren and endorsed by delegates from besieged Boston and other towns in Suffolk County, enumerated colonial grievances and demanded that the British back down or suffer the consequences. They declared the Intolerable Acts unjust, illegal, and void; urged citizens to withhold taxes and to arm themselves in case British forces occupying Boston advanced into the countryside; and called for an intercolonial association to oversee a total boycott of British goods.

The Suffolk Resolves, which Galloway sourly called "a declaration of war against Great Britain," galvanized the Continental Congress. It adopted them on September 17 without change and then defeated Galloway's proposal by a single vote. Later a jubilant John Adams exulted in his diary: "One of the happiest days of my life. . . . This day convinced me that America will support . . . Massachusetts or perish with her." The Congress also approved a strongly worded Declaration of Rights and Grievances, but it still sought reconciliation with Britain and not American independence. It agreed, however, to reconvene on May 10, 1775, to consider stronger action if colonial grievances had not been redressed. An important step toward rebellion had been taken.

The Crucial Year: 1775 *A Time of Frustration and Foment*

After many years of Great Britain's confused and contradictory policies toward its American Colonies, by 1775 factions in both countries were preparing for war. Massachusetts in particular was the scene of martial activity. Had King George III shown any interest in the grievances of the colonists, war might have been avoided. It was not Britain's tyranny that led to bloodshed at Lexington, but its weakness and inconsistency. Once the battle was joined, a sense of unity and common purpose, which had been lacking among the colonists, began to build during 1775 until in time the Colonies were firmly resolved to be free of Britain.

Petition of the London Merchants for Reconciliation With America

As relations between Britain and the Colonies worsened, trade deteriorated also. The value of British exports to America, which amounted to nearly £5 million in 1772, dropped to around £2.5 million in 1774 and about one-tenth that sum in 1775. British merchants were being ruined. Fearing that war would prevent their collecting the large debts owed them by the colonial planters, they petitioned the King to come to terms with his American subjects.

Lord North

Lord North's Conciliation Plan

On February 20 Lord North, the British Prime Minister, presented to Parliament a number of propositions designed to conciliate the American Colonies. He asked Parliament to forgo taxation of the Colonies so long as the colonial assemblies themselves levied taxes to provide for their own civil administration and their own defense. Parliament approved Lord North's proposals, but the news of their passage did not reach the Colonies until April 24—5 days after the Battle of Lexington.

The Battle of Lexington

Edmund Burke Speaks Up for the Colonists

Many an Englishman thought the colonists had just cause for complaint. Edmund Burke, one of Britain's greatest statesmen, in an impassioned speech to Parliament declared: "An Englishman is the unfittest person on earth to argue another Englishman into slavery." Burke and many others believed the best way to keep the colonists' loyalty was to listen to them. Unfortunately the King and his ministers felt that the brash Americans deserved a lesson in manners rather than the opportunity for self-government. Supporters of this view took it as an insult that the Americans should presume to dictate to Britain.

Restraining Act

These differences among the English were exemplified by the members of Parliament, who approved Lord North's proposals yet within 6 weeks issued a restraining decree that effectively cut off the commerce of New England and five other Colonies with all countries outside the Empire.

Battle of Lexington and Concord

In April the Governor of Massachusetts, Maj. Gen. Thomas Gage, received orders from England to crack down on the dissidents in the Colony. Gage sent Lt. Col. Francis Smith at the head of some 800 men to destroy the munitions his spies told him were being assembled at Concord and to arrest rebel leaders John Hancock and Samuel Adams; who were in Lexington. On the evening of the 18th another rebel, Dr. Joseph Warren, guessing the unit's intentions, dispatched Paul Revere and William Dawes to spread the alarm and to warn Hancock and Adams. Early in the morning of April 19 the British advance guard arrived at Lexington green, where Capt. John Parker and 40 to 50 minutemen—so called because they were ready to march at a minute's notice—were assembled to meet them. The British leader, Maj. John Pitcairn, ordered the Patriots to disperse, and as Pitcairn, flourishing his sword, rode up to them, a pistol shot rang out—who fired it has never been ascertained. The British troops opened fire on the minutemen even as the colonists were retreating. By the time the shooting stopped, 8 minutemen were dead and 10 wounded. *(continued)*

The Crucial Year: 1775 *(continued)*

Reaching Concord, the British confiscated the few arms they found. Three British companies stationed at North Bridge were attacked by the colonists; three Redcoats were killed and eight wounded. As the British turned back toward Lexington, they were peppered with shot fired by minutemen from behind the rocks, trees, and shrubs that lined the road. More and more colonists joined the battle. By the time the British reached Boston, they could count some 270 dead, wounded, or missing. The colonists suffered around 95 casualties.

The Battle of Bunker Hill

Second Continental Congress Convenes

On May 10 the Second Continental Congress convened in Philadelphia to determine a course of action toward Britain. By June, 65 delegates had arrived, representing 12 Colonies (Georgia was not represented until September). The Congress was neither a unified nor a revolutionary body. Even after Lexington and Concord many delegates still hoped to remain Englishmen under a British sovereign if only Parliament would recognize the colonists' rights. This moderate faction was led by John Dickinson of Pennsylvania. The radicals predictably followed Samuel Adams.

Ethan Allen Captures Ticonderoga

Ethan Allen and the Green Mountain Boys Raid British Posts

With the encouragement of officials in Connecticut and Massachusetts, Ethan Allen led around 250 men in successful raids against British troops at Fort Ticonderoga (May 10) and Crown Point (May 12), both in New York. Benedict Arnold, then a colonel of the Massachusetts militia, accompanied the raiders. Because of his commission Arnold thought he should be sole commander of the expedition, but this was flatly rejected by the others. The Green Mountain Boys captured some 60 pieces of artillery, which were later used in the drive against the British in Boston. These daring movements assured control of Lake George and Lake Champlain and established an open route to Canada.

Address of the Continental Congress to the Inhabitants of Canada

One of the first acts of the Continental Congress was to appeal to the people of Canada to bring their country into an American union. This strategic move to protect the northern border was largely ignored by Canadians, but the Congress persisted in efforts either to win Canada's aid or to take over the country by force.

Battle of Bunker Hill

On the night of June 16 colonial militia led by Col. William Prescott, John Stark, and Israel Putnam took up positions on Breed's Hill, which was adjacent to Bunker Hill and overlooked Boston Harbor. If the Americans could mount cannon on Breed's Hill, they would command the harbor and British-occupied Boston. General Gage, strengthened by fresh troops and eager to avenge his losses at Concord, determined to take the hill. On June 17, 3,000 Redcoats, led by Gen. William Howe and Gen. Robert Pigot, marched up the hill in tight ranks. The Americans allowed the British to come within 40 paces and then opened fire. The British, with severe casualties, turned and fled. British officers rallied the soldiers, and again they advanced and again were routed. But when the British infantry charged for the third time, the colonists had run out of ammunition, and the Redcoats chased them away at bayonet point. In taking the hill, the British lost more than 1,000 men; the Americans lost around 440. Now misnamed the Battle of Bunker Hill, it was the bloodiest encounter of the war and proved to the colonists that the British were not invincible. Unfortunately, the glorification of the militia at Bunker Hill convinced many Americans that partly trained militia could be effective against the enemy—thus delaying far too long the enlistment and training of regular troops.

Washington Takes Command

George Washington Takes Command of the Continental Army

"Travel through whatever part of this country you will," wrote a colonist in July 1775, "you will see the inhabitants training, making firelocks, casting mortars, shells and shot, and making saltpetre." By then militia from the New England Colonies had been besieging Boston for more than 2 months. The Continental Congress had in June authorized the organization of the Continental Army and appointed George Washington as Commander in Chief. Washington refused any payment for his services, but asked that he be reimbursed for expenses. He arrived in Cambridge July 3 and took command of 17,000 mostly untrained militiamen whose enlistments would expire at year's end.

Declaration of the Causes and Necessity of Taking Up Arms

Three weeks after the Battle of Bunker Hill the Continental Congress proclaimed its policies toward Great Britain in a declaration defending the Colonies' right to liberty. Because the moderates objected to the strong language used in the first draft of the document, the Congress requested that Thomas Jefferson and John Dickinson, who were writing the final version, conclude on a conciliatory note. The final document, which has something of a split personality, indicates the range of American feelings about independence.

"We are reduced," the declaration states, "to the alternative of choosing an unconditional submission to the tyranny of irritated ministers, or resistance by force.—The latter is our choice.—We have counted the cost of this contest and find nothing so dreadful as voluntary slavery." This threatening tone softens: "Lest this declaration should disquiet the minds of our friends and fellow-subjects in any part of the empire, we assure them that we mean not to dissolve that union which has so long and so happily subsisted between us, and which we sincerely wish to see restored. . . . We have not raised armies with ambitious designs of separating from Great-Britain, and establishing independent states."

Olive Branch Petition

Not satisfied with the wording of the declaration of July 6, moderate leader John Dickinson received permission from the Congress to petition the King once more. In a humble and hopeful document, he put the blame for the colonial disorders on a corrupt ministry and begged George III, to whom the Colonies still owed allegiance, to keep Parliament from further abusing them. The petition was signed by John Hancock and most of the other delegates and conveyed to London, but the King, who felt that the Congress was sanctioning rebellious acts, refused to receive it.

Proclamation of Rebellion

On July 31 the Congress formally rejected Lord North's proposals of February 20, which granted only token control over the Colonies' civil affairs. Three weeks later the King issued a proclamation that labeled the Colonies unlawful and rebellious.

Invasion of Canada

In the fall of 1775 the Americans launched their first campaign. One force, led by Philip Schuyler who was later replaced by Richard Montgomery, attacked a key position of St. Johns, Quebec, on September 5. Another, led by Benedict Arnold, began a march into Canada about a week later. After suffering much hardship, Arnold's force arrived sick and starving at Point Lévis outside Quebec on November 9. When Montgomery arrived 3 weeks later, the Americans' total force amounted to little more than 900 men. For 3 weeks they laid siege to the English garrison at Quebec, and were themselves besieged by the Canadian winter and by smallpox. Finally perceiving that only a vigorous effort could keep the expedition from falling to pieces, Montgomery decided to launch a desperate assault against Quebec.

Prohibitory Act

In December Parliament resolved to bring the rebels to their knees. Provisions were made to send a force of 50,000 men to America; of these, 18,000 would be mercenaries from the German State of Hesse-Cassel. A law was enacted declaring that all colonies outside the protection of the Crown would have an embargo placed on their trade. It put a blockade on colonial ports and ordered the seizure of colonial ships on the high seas and the impressment of captured seamen. These measures outraged Americans and convinced even the moderates that all-out war was inevitable.

Battle of Quebec

In a blinding snowstorm on December 31 the combined forces of Montgomery and Arnold made their heroic attack against a strong British position at Quebec. The assault failed. Montgomery was killed, Arnold was wounded, and more than 400 men were lost. Arnold resumed the hopeless siege of the garrison, but when British reinforcements arrived in the spring, the Americans were forced to retreat in disorder. This had been the colonists' first costly failure. There were to be many more before Washington and Gen. Charles Cornwallis met at Yorktown 6 years later.

The Battle of Quebec

CHAPTER TWO

The War for Independence

The members of the Second Continental Congress belonged to the elite of colonial society. They were men of status and wealth, men who in normal circumstances might be expected to shrink from the very word "rebellion" and seek shelter under the comforting mantle of established authority. Yet in July 1776 these men—successful lawyers, merchants, ministers, plantation owners, and a sprinkling of artisans—signed their names to one of the most revolutionary documents of modern times in which they pledged to each other "our Lives, our Fortunes, and our sacred Honor" in the cause of American independence and the seemingly quixotic ideal that "all men are created equal."

They were no longer really colonials, but neither were they yet Americans. As the year 1776 opened, the farmers who had stood against the Redcoats at Lexington and Concord, the Vermonters who had swooped down on Fort Ticonderoga, the militiamen who had gone off on a doomed invasion of Canada were balanced precariously between their ancient loyalty to their sovereign, George III, and a forthright assertion of separatism. So, too, were the members of the Second Continental Congress sitting in Philadelphia. All through the stirring events of the preceding year the Congress had met, debated, and worried, but had failed to confront the supreme issue: independence. Instead its members had sought conciliation with King and Parliament; but their appeals for compromise had brought only proposals that they deemed inadequate and threats to crush what the monarch called a "desperate conspiracy." Late in 1775, when recruitment lagged, the King and his ministers engaged 30,000 German mercenaries—professional warriors whom Americans dubbed Hessians, although in fact they came from several German states.

"The Spirit of '76" *by Archibald M. Willard, first exhibited at the 1876 Centennial Exposition in Philadelphia, showed young and old marching to defend their country.*

No measure could have been better calculated to arouse resentment and to tip the balance toward war than this dispatch of German hirelings to suppress the liberties of those who thought of themselves as freeborn Englishmen. Early in 1776 colonial passions were further inflamed by a small pamphlet entitled *Common Sense,* the work of an unknown recent immigrant from England, Thomas Paine. Giving voice to the feelings of thousands, Paine wrote of the American struggle: "The sun never shined on a cause of greater worth. . . . Now is the seed-time of continental union. . . . O ye that love mankind! . . . stand forth! . . . and prepare. . . an asylum for mankind."

In a few weeks Paine's broadside found its way to village greens in New England, countinghouses in New York, and plantations in Virginia. Up and down the coast, men discussed his bold call for independence and increasingly found that his sentiments reflected their own. Suddenly the daring word "independence" was on everyone's lips, and a cause thought radical only a few months earlier had achieved an astounding degree of respectability. By late winter the tide of rebellion turned to full flood after the first great victory of Patriot arms. On March 4, 1776, with 50 or so cannon captured at Ticonderoga and hauled some 300 miles eastward through heavy snows and across hilly terrain, Gen. George Washington, commander of the Continental Army, fortified Dorchester Heights overlooking Boston. Sir William Howe, the Redcoats' commander inside the city, was faced with the choice of attempting a breakthrough in the teeth of Washington's artillery or evacuating his forces by sea. Discretion won over valor; the British abandoned Boston, and on March 17 Continental troops poured into the city without a fight.

In June the rebels scored another victory when a halfhearted British effort to land troops at Charleston, South Carolina, was repulsed. With Patriot arms triumphant North and South, the Continental Congress in early June

For 15 months Britain's North American Colonies had been in revolt. On July 4, 1776, representatives of those Colonies met in the Continental Congress to formalize that rebellion by adopting a Declaration of Independence. No man among those present could, on that day, foresee the outcome; yet each well knew that before peace was restored, he and his countrymen would have to endure a long period of privation and strife. For the next 5 years the sound of cannon and the flash of musketry were seldom stilled. American troops, most of them undermanned, ill-trained, and poorly equipped, harassed and stung British forces that were often overwhelmingly superior in numbers and weapons. Occasionally the Americans advanced, but more often they retreated; and often their cause seemed hopeless. Yet always a dedicated nucleus persevered until in 1778, after an American triumph at Saratoga, the powerful Kingdom of France came forward as an ally. Britain, having frittered away chances for compromise and having grossly underestimated the determination and courage of her erstwhile subjects, was confronted with a combination too powerful to conquer and was forced to yield. Thus was the United States of America born—not a nation at first, but a loosely knit confederation brought together by common dissatisfactions and shared aspirations.

Artist John Trumbull *has depicted the Declaration of Independence being presented by the drafting committee in Philadelphia's State House (now Independence Hall) on July 4, 1776. Left to right, standing at the table are John Adams, Roger Sherman, Robert Livingston, Thomas Jefferson (who wrote most of the text), and Benjamin Franklin. Facing them, also standing, is John Hancock, President of the Continental Congress. Around them Trumbull has shown the other members of the Congress, many of whom he knew personally. The declaration forced wavering colonists to take a stand and helped convince Britain and France that the Americans meant business. From that day to this, the declaration's sharp yet poetic language has served to rally oppressed humanity everywhere in battles against tyranny.*

The Declaration of Independence: America's Charter of Liberty

In CONGRESS, July 4, 1776.

A DECLARATION

By the REPRESENTATIVES of the UNITED STATES OF AMERICA, In GENERAL CONGRESS assembled.

WHEN in the Course of human Events, it becomes necessary for one People to dissolve the Political Bands which have connected them with another, and to assume among the Powers of the Earth, the separate and equal Station to which the Laws of Nature and of Nature's God entitle them, a decent Respect to the Opinions of Mankind requires that they should declare the causes which impel them to the Separation.

We hold these Truths to be self-evident, that all Men are created equal, that they are endowed by their Creator with certain unalienable Rights, that among these are Life, Liberty, and the Pursuit of Happiness——That to secure these Rights, Governments are instituted among Men, deriving their just Powers from the Consent of the Governed, that whenever any Form of Government becomes destructive of these Ends, it is the Right of the People to alter or to abolish it, and to institute new Government, laying its Foundation on such Principles, and organizing its Powers in such Form, as to them shall seem most likely to effect their Safety and Happiness. Prudence, indeed, will dictate that Governments long established should not be changed for light and transient Causes; and accordingly all Experience hath shewn, that Mankind are more disposed to suffer, while Evils are sufferable, than to right themselves by abolishing the Forms to which they are accustomed. But when a long Train of Abuses and Usurpations, pursuing invariably the same Object, evinces a Design to reduce them under absolute Despotism, it is their Right, it is their Duty, to throw off such Government, and to provide new Guards for their future Security. Such has been the patient Sufferance of these Colonies; and such is now the Necessity which constrains them to alter their former Systems of Government. The History of the present King of Great-Britain is a History of repeated Injuries and Usurpations, all having in direct Object the Establishment of an absolute Tyranny over these States. To prove this, let Facts be submitted to a candid World.

He has refused his Assent to Laws, the most wholesome and necessary for the public Good.

He has forbidden his Governors to pass Laws of immediate and pressing Importance, unless suspended in their Operation till his Assent should be obtained; and when so suspended, he has utterly neglected to attend to them.

He has refused to pass other Laws for the Accommodation of large Districts of People, unless those People would relinquish the Right of Representation in the Legislature, a Right inestimable to them, and formidable to Tyrants only.

He has called together Legislative Bodies at Places unusual, uncomfortable, and distant from the Depository of their public Records, for the sole Purpose of fatiguing them into Compliance with his Measures.

He has dissolved Representative Houses repeatedly, for opposing with manly Firmness his Invasions on the Rights of the People.

He has refused for a long Time, after such Dissolutions, to cause others to be elected; whereby the Legislative Powers, incapable of Annihilation, have returned to the People at large for their exercise; the State remaining in the mean time exposed to all the Dangers of Invasion from without, and Convulsions within.

He has endeavoured to prevent the Population of these States; for that Purpose obstructing the Laws for Naturalization of Foreigners; refusing to pass others to encourage their Migrations hither, and raising the Conditions of new Appropriations of Lands.

He has obstructed the Administration of Justice, by refusing his Assent to Laws for establishing Judiciary Powers.

He has made Judges dependent on his Will alone, for the Tenure of their Offices, and the Amount and Payment of their Salaries.

He has erected a Multitude of new Offices, and sent hither Swarms of Officers to harrass our People, and eat out their Substance.

He has kept among us, in Times of Peace, Standing Armies, without the consent of our Legislatures.

He has affected to render the Military independent of and superior to the Civil Power.

He has combined with others to subject us to a Jurisdiction foreign to our Constitution, and unacknowledged by our Laws; giving his Assent to their Acts of pretended Legislation:

For quartering large Bodies of Armed Troops among us:

For protecting them, by a mock Trial, from Punishment for any Murders which they should commit on the Inhabitants of these States:

For cutting off our Trade with all Parts of the World:

For imposing Taxes on us without our Consent:

For depriving us, in many Cases, of the Benefits of Trial by Jury:

For transporting us beyond Seas to be tried for pretended Offences:

For abolishing the free System of English Laws in a neighbouring Province, establishing therein an arbitrary Government, and enlarging its Boundaries, so as to render it at once an Example and fit Instrument for introducing the same absolute Rule into these Colonies:

For taking away our Charters, abolishing our most valuable Laws, and altering fundamentally the Forms of our Governments:

For suspending our own Legislatures, and declaring themselves invested with Power to legislate for us in all Cases whatsoever.

He has abdicated Government here, by declaring us out of his Protection and waging War against us.

He has plundered our Seas, ravaged our Coasts, burnt our Towns, and destroyed the Lives of our People.

He is, at this Time, transporting large Armies of foreign Mercenaries to compleat the Works of Death, Desolation, and Tyranny, already begun with circumstances of Cruelty and Perfidy, scarcely paralleled in the most barbarous Ages, and totally unworthy the Head of a civilized Nation.

He has constrained our fellow Citizens taken Captive on the high Seas to bear Arms against their Country, to become the Executioners of their Friends and Brethren, or to fall themselves by their Hands.

He has excited domestic Insurrections amongst us, and has endeavoured to bring on the Inhabitants of our Frontiers, the merciless Indian Savages, whose known Rule of Warfare, is an undistinguished Destruction, of all Ages, Sexes and Conditions.

In every stage of these Oppressions we have Petitioned for Redress in the most humble Terms: Our repeated Petitions have been answered only by repeated Injury. A Prince, whose Character is thus marked by every act which may define a Tyrant, is unfit to be the Ruler of a free People.

Nor have we been wanting in Attentions to our British Brethren. We have warned them from Time to Time of Attempts by their Legislature to extend an unwarrantable Jurisdiction over us. We have reminded them of the Circumstances of our Emigration and Settlement here. We have appealed to their native Justice and Magnanimity, and we have conjured them by the Ties of our common Kindred to disavow these Usurpations, which, would inevitably interrupt our Connections and Correspondence. They too have been deaf to the Voice of Justice and of Consanguinity. We must, therefore, acquiesce in the Necessity, which denounces our Separation, and hold them, as we hold the rest of Mankind, Enemies in War, in Peace, Friends.

We, therefore, the Representatives of the UNITED STATES OF AMERICA, in General Congress, Assembled, appealing to the Supreme Judge of the World for the Rectitude of our Intentions, do, in the Name, and by Authority of the good People of these Colonies, solemnly Publish and Declare, That these United Colonies are, and of Right ought to be, Free and Independent States; that they are absolved from all Allegiance to the British Crown, and that all political Connection between them and the State of Great-Britain, is and ought to be totally dissolved; and that as Free and Independent States, they have full Power to levy War, conclude Peace, contract Alliances, establish Commerce, and to do all other Acts and Things which Independent States may of right do. And for the support of this Declaration, with a firm Reliance on the Protection of divine Providence, we mutually pledge to each other our Lives, our Fortunes, and our sacred Honor.

Signed by Order *and in* Behalf *of the* Congress,

JOHN HANCOCK, President.

Attest.
CHARLES THOMSON, Secretary.

Philadelphia: Printed by John Dunlap.

agreed to debate Richard Henry Lee's resolution that "these united Colonies are, and of right ought to be, free and independent States." On June 11 a committee of five was chosen to give formal expression to Lee's initiative, and from this group Virginia's Thomas Jefferson was selected to draft a Declaration of Independence. Drawing on the philosophies of such European thinkers as John Locke, Jefferson asserted the natural rights of all mankind and held that the violation of those rights had driven the former Colonies to assume "among the Powers of the earth, the separate and equal station to which the Laws of Nature and of Nature's God entitle them. . . ."

On July 4, 1776, after having made several revisions in Jefferson's text, the Congress adopted the declaration. (One delegation, New York, abstained.) The United States of America was born, but its survival remained to be determined by the uncertain fortunes of war.

Captured Patriot spy *Nathan Hale is famous for the last words he spoke before the British executed him in 1776: "I only regret that I have but one life to lose for my country." The 21-year-old Connecticut ranger captain, caught spying behind British lines in New York City, freely admitted his guilt and was hanged without trial.*

Britain Strikes

Even as the signers of the great declaration were penning their names, the British were preparing a blow they felt confident would end the rebellion. After evacuating Boston General Howe regrouped and reinforced his army at Halifax in Nova Scotia and then moved south by sea to attack New York City. Having anticipated Howe's intent, General Washington rushed his small army from Boston to New York, where he was joined by militia units from Pennsylvania, Maryland, Delaware, New Jersey, and Virginia. He now had 19,000 men, the largest force of Americans he would ever command.

On July 2 a British fleet of more than 100 vessels entered New York Bay, and thousands of Howe's Redcoats landed on Staten Island. Howe remained there through July and into August, waiting for still more reinforcements of Hessians and of Redcoats from England. By mid-August Howe and his subordinate generals—Henry Clinton and Lord Cornwallis—boasted an army of some 32,000, plus scores of warships with which to bombard American positions. In an effort to contain this mighty array, Washington committed a tactical blunder that almost cost America the war: He split his forces between Brooklyn, on Long Island, and Manhattan Island.

On August 22 Howe finally moved his army across the Narrows to Long Island, and on August 27 he fell upon the American positions near Brooklyn Heights. Skillfully feigning a frontal attack and then outflanking the ineptly led Americans, Howe's soldiers drove them to the East River. But instead of pressing an all-out drive that might have destroyed Washington's army and ended the Revolution, Howe prepared for siege operations

The Penalties of Arrogance

To a degree impossible to exaggerate, the cause of American independence was aided by the clumsiness of Britain's wartime leadership, both civilian and military. Masters of a powerful empire, possessors of the world's greatest navy and a well-trained army of Redcoats and German mercenaries, beneficiaries of substantial support from Tories within the rebellious Colonies, the British managed to fritter away all their advantages.

On the throne was the unstable, stubborn, and badly advised King George III, who had suffered fits of mental instability as early as 1765. When delegates to the Second Continental Congress in mid-August of 1775 sent the King the Olive Branch Petition, seeking reconciliation, he refused to receive their emissary and, instead, proclaimed the Colonies in "open and avowed rebellion" on August 23, 1775.

The King's two chief advisers were his Prime Minister, Lord North, and his Colonial Secretary, Lord Germain. North was an indecisive politician who consistently underrated the strength of the rebellion and retained power by flattering his monarch; Germain, who has been blamed for most of Britain's strategic mistakes, had been dismissed from the Army for disobeying orders.

Britain's generals were as unequal as its political leaders to the task before them. The commander in chief in America, Sir William Howe, though a dutiful soldier, preferred high living to hard campaigning. After permitting Washington's battered army to escape time and again, Howe, in 1777, made the stunning error of moving on Philadelphia, the rebel capital, instead of driving north from New York City to link up with General Burgoyne's forces. The blunder cost Burgoyne his sword at Saratoga and Howe his command. Sir Henry Clinton, Howe's successor, was hampered by the meddlesome Lord Germain. Arrival of the French Fleet off the Virginia coast in 1781, which prevented Clinton from sending reinforcements to Yorktown, sealed the fate of General Cornwallis' army and virtually ended the war.

The Fight for Independence
An Overview of Battles, Year by Year

1776. The year opened with the American retreat from Canada after the failure of a costly invasion. This defeat was balanced by the British evacuation of Boston in March. But in September British troops under General William Howe struck again, invading New York from the sea and putting General Washington's Continental Army to rout. Only through luck and British ineptness was Washington able to keep his force intact for the long retreat through New Jersey into Pennsylvania. On December 26, in a surprise attack, Washington struck back, crossing the Delaware to destroy a Hessian force at Trenton.

1777. Before moving into winter quarters at Morristown, New Jersey, Washington inflicted another defeat on the British at Princeton. In late spring the British launched a two-pronged attack from Canada under Burgoyne and Lt. Col. Barry St. Leger. By August St. Leger had been checked, but Burgoyne continued southward under mounting American attack. Finally, at Saratoga in October, Burgoyne was forced to surrender by Americans under Gates and Benedict Arnold. Meanwhile, in September, General Howe captured the American capital, Philadelphia, and inflicted severe defeats on Washington's army nearby.

1778–1781. In June 1778, American arms were denied a major triumph at Monmouth probably because of Gen. Charles Lee's failure to obey orders. This was the last major battle in the Northeast. But far to the west, American frontiersmen under George Rogers Clark were conducting a successful drive to make the Illinois country U.S. territory. It was in the South, however, that the issue of U.S. independence was being decided. Beginning in 1779, the British under Clinton and Cornwallis won a series of victories but failed to destroy American forces under Generals Greene, Lafayette, Morgan, and Wayne. Victorious but bloodied at Guilford Courthouse in March 1781, Cornwallis took shelter at Yorktown, Virginia, only to be besieged by a strong Franco-American force on land and sea. Cornwallis' surrender on October 19 marked the end of the final large battle of the war.

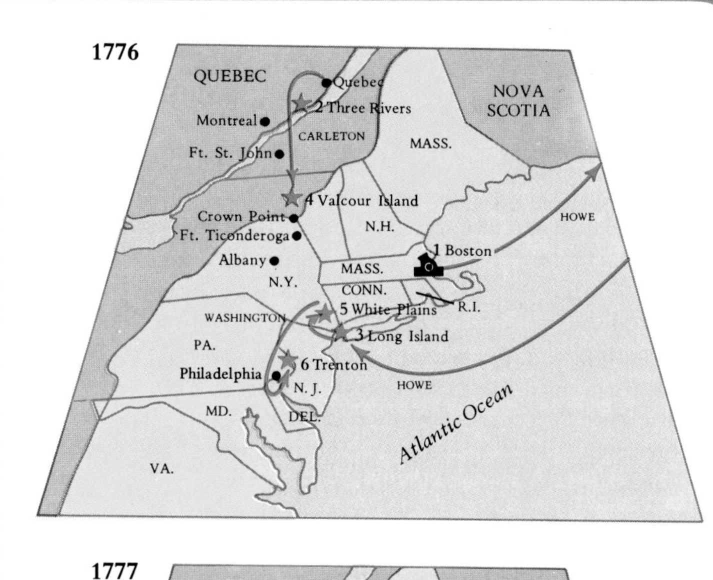

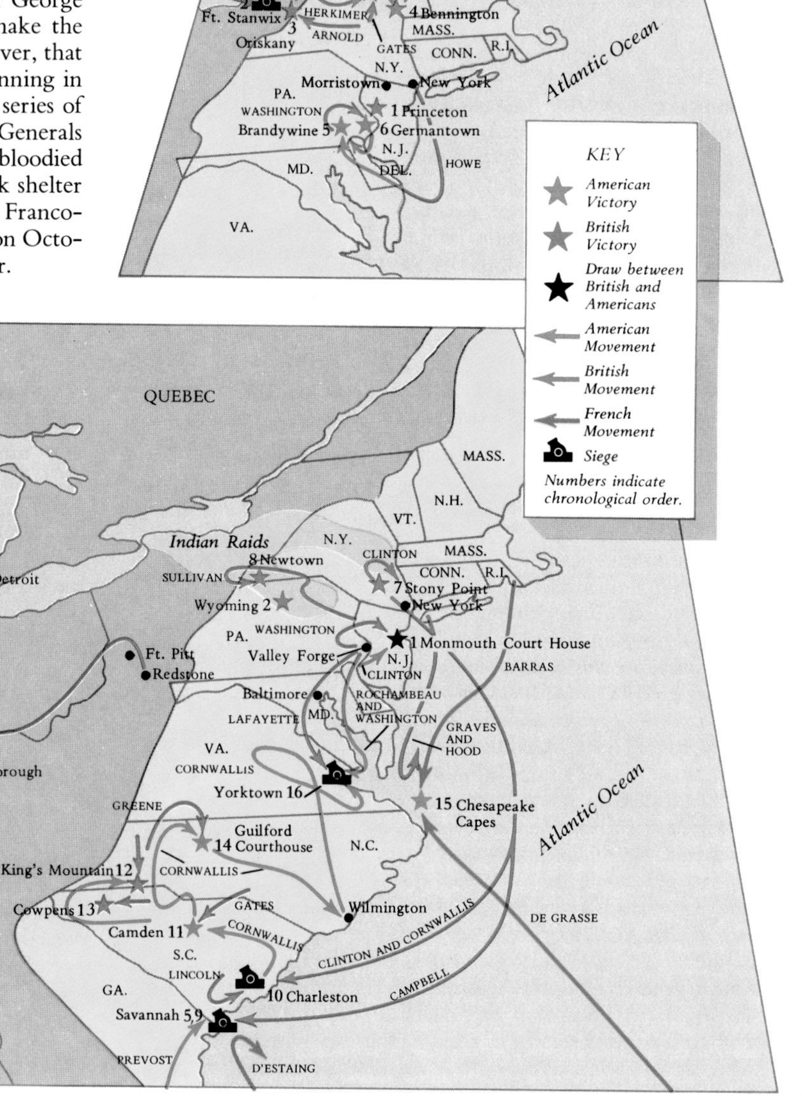

against the American fortifications on Brooklyn Heights. This delay permitted Washington to use Col. John Glover's experienced boatmen from Marblehead, Massachusetts, in a masterful evacuation of his army across the East River without the loss of a man.

The Fall of New York

Again Howe took his time about pressing offensive operations. On September 11 he met with American delegates on Staten Island, hoping to negotiate an agreement ending the bloodshed. When the talks failed Howe landed his troops at Kips Bay in Manhattan on September 15, accompanied by a cannonade from British warships cruising the East River. Initially the Americans fled; Washington, his temper flaring, rode among them and literally tried to whip them into line with a riding crop before withdrawing to his main defenses at Harlem Heights. For his part, Howe failed to take advantage of his foe's disarray, preferring to make a leisurely advance upon Harlem Heights in anticipation of an early rebel bid for peace. New York City, which then consisted only of the southern tip of Manhattan Island, was in his hands, but on September 21 a fire of mysterious origin leveled much of the town. Washington, evidently crediting a Patriot arsonist, remarked, "Providence, or some good honest fellow, has done more for us than we were disposed to do for ourselves."

In mid-September the Americans beat off a British attack on Harlem Heights. Washington, leaving behind a force to man Fort Washington on the northern tip of the island, retreated farther north to White Plains to avoid Howe's flanking maneuver. On October 28 a clash occurred at White Plains, and again the Redcoats carried the day. But Washington's men were permitted to retreat in good order while the British turned their attention southward, capturing Fort Washington on November 16 and forcing Fort Lee, across the Hudson River on the New Jersey shore, to yield 4 days later.

For America the cause looked bleak. In 3 months Washington had lost New York and Long Island, and his army of 19,000 had been reduced to fewer than 3,500 by casualties, desertions, and expired enlistments. Now, as winter was closing in, he and his battered force were in full flight across New Jersey and into Pennsylvania. In the Continental Congress, which was itself preparing to move to Baltimore in anticipation of a British occupation of Philadelphia, Washington's competence was under fire. The faint-hearted, certain of imminent British victory, laid plans to curry favor with the conquerors. Desertions mounted among the American forces retreating south through New Jersey. Of this moment of despair Thomas Paine wrote in *The American Crisis:* "These are the times that try men's souls. The summer soldier and the sunshine patriot will, in this crisis, shrink from the service of their country; but he that stands it *now* deserves the love and thanks of man and woman."

The outlook was grim for George Washington as he led the remnant of his army across the Delaware River to the temporary safety of Pennsylvania. To prevent the British from mounting a swift attack on his battered force, he ordered the transfer of all boats from the New Jersey to the Pennsylvania side of the Delaware River. Although its intent was defensive, this shifting of the boats enabled Washington to launch a surprise offensive of his own into New Jersey that winter. Meanwhile his men, many of them without shoes or coats, built rude shelters against the winter cold. Washington saw that a bold stroke was needed to raise morale and attract recruits. In the disposition of the enemy, spread thinly across New Jersey, he found his answer.

Garrisoned at Trenton, just across the Delaware from Pennsylvania, was a large Hessian force. In a snow and

Washington's crossing *of the Delaware late on Christmas night, 1776, is portrayed dramatically, if inaccurately, in this well-known painting executed in 1851 by German-born artist Emanuel Leutze. It would have been suicide for the American commander to stand up in a small, overloaded boat plying through dangerous ice floes, and the flag shown behind Washington was not designed until 1777. As a recording of history, the Leutze canvas was no masterpiece, but as a military maneuver, the crossing itself certainly was. In a raging sleet storm, Washington's ragtag troops negotiated the icy river and overwhelmed their surprised foes, chiefly mercenaries from Germany, at Trenton.*

Reviewing his tattered army, *Washington sits impassively astride a white horse as his weary men stumble through the snow into their bleak encampment at Valley Forge, Pennsylvania, where they spent the winter of 1777–78. Food was scarce and warm clothing, boots, and bandages virtually unavailable. Washington observed that "you might have tracked the army . . . to Valley Forge by the blood of their feet."*

The Ordeal of Valley Forge
Hardship Produces a New American Army

Some 20 miles from Philadelphia lies a plateau known as Valley Forge, where Washington's army made its winter quarters after defeats at Brandywine and Germantown. When the main column arrived on December 19, 1777, the men had only the meager provisions they carried. With their few tools they knocked together shelters of logs and clay. Their commander refused to quit his own leaky tent for more comfortable quarters until the men were provided for. Although the winter was fairly mild, shortages of food, clothing, blankets, and soap were chronic, sickness was rife, and approximately 2,500 out of 10,000 soldiers died in 6 months. The army not only endured but it became a toughened, unified fighting force, thanks largely to the efforts of its drillmaster, Baron von Steuben, and the men's faith in Washington.

Spring brought an unusually heavy run of shad up the Schuylkill River, which eased the food problem. With the warmer weather, too, came the enormously heartening news of the French alliance. By the end of June the Americans would be ready to strike Sir Henry Clinton's army at Monmouth in the last major battle of the Northern theater.

Drilling troops at *Valley Forge, Baron von Steuben, musket in hand, prepares awkward soldiers for action on the battlefield. His invaluable services won him the rank of major general, the position of inspector general, and fame as the first teacher of the American Army.*

sleet storm on Christmas night, when the Germans were groggy from their holiday celebrations, Washington gathered his men on the Delaware's west bank, loaded them into Durham boats (ordinarily used to carry freight), and ferried them to the New Jersey side. Again he called upon the skill of Colonel Glover's troop of Marblehead fishermen to handle this enormously critical task. Advancing in two columns from the north and south, Washington's men struck the sleeping Hessians on the morning of December 26. In a short, sharp encounter every man in the garrison was killed, wounded, or captured. Washington's casualties numbered six: two dead and four wounded—among the latter James Monroe.

The effect of this stunning victory was immediate. For the Americans the Patriot cause, which had seemed all but lost, gained new strength. For the British an enemy that had been dismissed as an undisciplined rabble was now regarded as worthy of respect. General Cornwallis rushed south from New York City toward Princeton with reinforcements. On January 2, 1777, his army reached Trenton, where he ill-advisedly decided to rest his men for a day. Washington slipped past Trenton in the night and surprised the Redcoat garrison at Princeton the following morning. Like Trenton, Princeton was a complete American victory, sweetened by Washington's capture of large quantities of desperately needed supplies. Now, with two quick triumphs to his credit, with Philadelphia no longer endangered, and with the British sufficiently alarmed to order most of their New Jersey garrisons evacuated, Washington moved north to winter quarters in Morristown, New Jersey. In just 2 weeks the American cause had been revitalized.

The War in the North

Midwinter in Northeastern America was no time for military combat in the style of the 18th century. Accordingly, while the British rested in their New York City snuggeries in January and February 1777, the Continental Army slowly regrouped and rallied new support in Morristown. By early spring Washington's force had grown to about 8,000 men, but the general feverishly sought more troops to use against the British when their offensive was resumed. It was not long in coming. Britain had a new plan to destroy the rebellion: From Montreal an 8,000-man army under Gen. John Burgoyne was to push south down the Hudson Valley; a second, smaller force, made up mostly of pro-British Americans (called Loyalists or Tories) and Indians, was to strike southeastward from Lake Ontario; a third army, commanded by Howe, would march north from New York City. The three forces would converge at Albany, after their combined offensives had chewed up all resistance along the way and had isolated New York and New England from the Central and Southern States.

The first part of the drive went off without a hitch as Burgoyne's force recaptured Fort Ticonderoga in early July before proceeding south. In late August, however, the second arm of the offensive met with disaster when the Loyalist-Indian army advancing from Lake Ontario clashed near Fort Stanwix with Patriot militia under Gen. Nicholas Herkimer. Severely mauled by Herkimer's men, the Indians later panicked on hearing rumors of a vast Patriot army about to descend on them. The Anglo-Tory-Indian forces then beat a hasty retreat westward and were lost to the British master plan. Yet, with the main force advancing south along the Hudson Valley, the strategy still seemed bound to succeed, particularly if General Howe did his part by moving north from New York City to link forces with Burgoyne.

But Howe had plans of his own, and they had nothing to do with Burgoyne. Instead of moving his army north, he had decided to capture the Patriot capital at Philadelphia. His attack on Philadelphia and the three-pronged drive on New England had both been approved by Lord George Germain, Secretary of State for the Colonies, in London. Perhaps Germain expected Howe to move so quickly that he could seize the capital and still have time to swing north to Burgoyne's aid. However, Howe decided against a frontal assault on Philadelphia via the Delaware River. Instead he determined to move on the capital from the south. He embarked 15,000 men on 260 ships and landed them on the northern edge of Chesapeake Bay, some 50 miles away, on August 25, 1777.

Washington and his Continentals, at first convinced that the British commander in chief's true intention was to move north to meet Burgoyne, were slow in recognizing the peril to Philadelphia. Once persuaded that the capital was in danger, the Americans moved the bulk of their army south of Philadelphia and guarded the fords of Brandywine Creek. With some 11,000 troops, including 3,000 militiamen, under his command, Washington dared the British to advance. This they did on September 10–11. A Hessian brigade feinted at the American center while the main body of Howe's army wheeled in a flanking attack to roll up the Patriots' right—a textbook maneuver that succeeded despite the fierce resistance of troops under Maj. Gen. Nathanael Greene. By nightfall of the 11th the road to Philadelphia lay open, and the victorious British marched along it, occupying the city on the heels of the fleeing Continental Congress.

Two Divided Homefronts

Neither Britain nor America went to war with anything like unanimity of opinion or purpose among their own peoples. In both countries fierce debate accompanied the drift toward war, with popular sentiment shifting as conditions changed and new developments arose. And throughout the conflict both countries had to deal with strong antiwar factions, as one man's patriotism was another man's treason.

The problem of divided loyalty was particularly acute in America, where perhaps as much as a third of the population, at the war's commencement, preferred royal rule to rebellion. Tory sentiment cut across sectional and class lines, and even divided families. Benjamin Franklin's illegitimate son, William, for example, was the Royal Governor of New Jersey. Patriot Gouverneur Morris' mother was a Loyalist, and his half-brother Staats Long Morris was a general in the British Army. Dozens of Tory regiments served under the British standard, and one Yankee loyal to the Crown remarked: "Nabour was against nabour, Father against the Son . . . and he who would not thrust his one blaid through his brothers heart was cald an Infimous fillon." In the end about 100,000 Tories fled America to sanctuary, mainly in Canada. One Canadian historian has said that the Loyalists, who were men of education and culture, "were the makers of Canada."

Britain, too, had its problems with disaffected subjects. Unable to recruit enough Englishmen to fight in America, King George III was forced to hire German mercenaries, while the Royal Navy's strength was maintained with help from impressment gangs, which kidnapped the unwary for sea duty. In Parliament an eloquent opposition, led by the great Edmund Burke and Charles James Fox, constantly assailed the war and its conduct. French intervention on the American side in 1778 greatly increased antiwar sentiment among the upper classes, who were pinched by the loss of American markets and feared the prospect of a resurgent France challenging British dominion throughout the world. The generous peace offered America in 1783 was more a reflection of Britain's desire to split America from France than a response to the actual military situation.

The War at Sea

American Seadogs Challenge British Supremacy

As the world's leading maritime power, Britain had little to fear from the infant American Navy established by the Continental Congress in 1775. Indeed, during the entire war only 13 frigates were completed for the Continental Navy's use, though some 40 merchantmen were converted into men-of-war. In addition, 11 of the individual States maintained their own small fleets for coastal defense, but these were generally ineffective.

When, on occasion, a State navy did sally forth on the offensive, the results were usually unimpressive. In July and August 1779, for example, a Massachusetts flotilla of 19 ships, backed by a strong militia force, sailed into Maine's Penobscot Bay in an effort to take that Tory stronghold. Thanks to inefficiency and command jealousies, the outgunned defenders were able to hold out until reinforcements arrived to shatter the Patriot attackers. Generally, however, British naval power in American waters faced few such challenges for most of the war. Royal Navy ships plied coastal waters at will, supplying His Majesty's troops, bringing in reinforcements, and transporting armies from one area to another.

In distant waters the American naval record was far better. Around 800 privateers, which ranged from the Caribbean to the English Channel, carried on a highly successful hit-and-run war, capturing some 600 British ships—including 16 men-of-war—and about $18 million in goods. The tiny Continental Navy followed suit, and such captains as John Paul Jones from Scotland, Joshua Barney, and Irish-born John Barry proved themselves adept at harrying British trade and heroic when challenged by British warships. Jones, the most famous of the Revolution's naval heroes, was only one of a number of captains. He later served in the Russian Navy and died in Paris at the age of 45.

In the end it was French naval power that proved decisive. The French outfought the British off Virginia in September 1781, thus completing the entrapment of Lord Cornwallis' army at Yorktown.

The "Bonhomme Richard" *(top), a leaky, converted merchant ship under Capt. John Paul Jones (above), engaged the frigate* Serapis *in a historic duel to death, September 23, 1779. Two heavy guns soon burst on the* Richard *and the English captain asked if Jones had surrendered. He bellowed his answer: "I've just begun to fight!" In the end the* Serapis *struck her colors; the battered* Richard *sank 2 days later.*

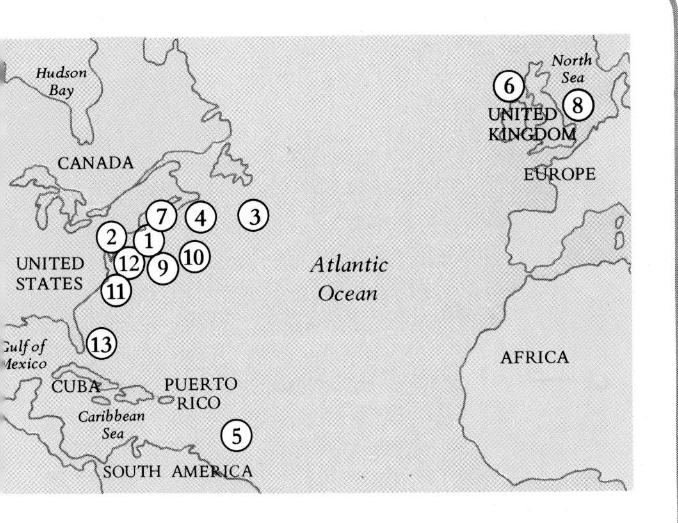

Major Naval Engagements of the Revolution

1. The first important capture by the Americans was made by Capt. John Manley's schooner *Lee*, which seized the British *Nancy* outside Boston harbor and provided Washington's army with arms and ammunition (c. August 27, 1775).
2. Commodore Esek Hopkins, first commander in chief of the Continental Navy, was humiliated when his fleet, which he led from aboard the *Alfred*, failed to capture the British frigate *Glasgow* (April 6, 1776). He was dismissed for incompetence.
3. The frigate *Hancock*, commanded by Manley, and the frigate *Boston*, commanded by Capt. Hector McNeill, captured the British frigate *Fox*, which was incorporated into the Continental Navy (June 7, 1777).
4. The *Hancock* and *Fox* were captured by three British warships while the *Boston* ran away. McNeill was dismissed from the Navy for failure to aid the *Hancock* (July 7, 1777).
5. The 32-gun *Randolph*, the first frigate built for the Continental Navy, was outfighting the 64-gun *Yarmouth* when a chance shot blew up the American vessel, killing her captain, Nicholas Biddle, and most of the crew (March 7, 1778).
6. After going ashore to destroy shipping and installations at Whitehaven, England—the only American landing on British home soil—Capt. John Paul Jones led his 18-gun sloop *Ranger* to victory over the British sloop *Drake* (May 1778).
7. The 32-gun American frigate *Raleigh*, commanded by Capt. John Barry, was overpowered and driven aground by the 50-gun *Experiment* and the 28-gun *Unicorn*, but Barry and most of his crew escaped (Sept. 27, 1778).
8. Jones' *Bonhomme Richard* defeated the *Serapis* in the greatest naval fight of the Revolution. The two ships exchanged cannon fire at pointblank range for 2 hours. (September 23, 1779).
9. The 30-gun frigate *Trumbull*, commanded by Capt. James Nicholson, fought a bloody draw with the 32-gun British privateer *Watt* (June 2, 1780).
10. Barry, commanding the 32-gun frigate *Alliance*, avenged the loss of his ship, the *Raleigh*, by capturing the *Atalanta* and the *Trepassy* (May 29, 1781).
11. Although most of his crew, largely British deserters, refused to fight, Nicholson resisted for more than an hour before the *Trumbull* was captured off Maryland by the 32-gun *Iris* (formerly the *Hancock*) and the *General Monk* (August 8, 1781).
12. Lt. Joshua Barney, commanding the 16-gun *Hyder Ally*, a converted merchantman of the Pennsylvania navy, outmaneuvered and subdued the 20-gun brig *General Monk* off Cape May, New Jersey (April 8, 1782).
13. In the last major naval action of the war, off Florida, Barry's *Alliance* severely mauled the frigate *Sybille* and escaped from two other British frigates (January 1783).

Despite 1,000 casualties at Brandywine, Washington again managed to keep his army from collapse. On October 4 he attacked the main British positions at Germantown on the outskirts of Philadelphia in a two-column pincers movement that unfortunately proved too complicated for the ill-trained Patriots. Insufficient ammunition and an impenetrable fog over the battlefield added to the confusion. Precious hours and supplies were wasted in fierce charges on a British strongpoint that might well have been bypassed. The two advancing American columns actually collided and in the chaos of battle opened fire on each other. When the smoke had cleared, the American troops were again in retreat, and the British occupation of Philadelphia was secure. But it was a costly triumph for His Majesty's forces; in taking the American capital instead of moving north to join forces with Burgoyne in New York State, Howe had contributed to the eventual doom of the British cause in America.

The Road to Saratoga

As Howe prepared his offensive on Philadelphia, Burgoyne was experiencing increasing difficulties along the route to Albany. Harried by New York and New England militia and running short of all the essentials of war, he dared not retreat into the wilds he had already traversed, yet each step he advanced increased his peril. In mid-August 1777 Burgoyne ordered an 800-man Hessian force to forage for supplies in and around Bennington, Vermont. There they collided with some 2,000 troops under John Stark; the exhausted Hessians were surrounded and cut to ribbons. A relief force was also heavily punished by the Americans.

Deprived of his Hessians and informed that help from Howe would be late in coming if it came at all, Burgoyne was faced with the prospect of dealing with a large and growing American army under Gen. Horatio Gates. Militiamen from Hudson Valley and New England towns were rallying to Gates' standard almost daily to be in on the kill. Stories that a woman living north of Saratoga, Jane McCrea, had been brutally murdered by Indians attached to Burgoyne's forces helped to inflame the Patriots, despite the fact that Jane was the fiancée of a Tory officer. Determined to uphold the proud traditions of British arms, Burgoyne decided on a daring attempt to break through American lines and on September 19 marched his men into the teeth of the Patriot positions at Freeman's Farm south of Saratoga.

At 1 p.m. Burgoyne's army, divided into three columns, emerged from the woodland into the open fields of Freeman's Farm, the blazing red of their uniforms bright in the sun. They were advancing cautiously in parade-ground formation when suddenly every tree surrounding the meadow seemed to spew forth bullets. Sharpshooting riflemen under Daniel Morgan mowed

Benedict Arnold and the British Spy

On September 23, 1780, a man in civilian dress (far right in the painting), who called himself John Anderson, was picked up by three Patriots in Westchester County, New York, while trying to make his way to the British lines. In his boots were found detailed plans of the key American defenses at West Point and, most damagingly, a pass signed by West Point's commander, Gen. Benedict Arnold.

"Anderson" proved to be Major John André, Sir Henry Clinton's adjutant general; his mission was to negotiate the betrayal of West Point, for which Arnold had demanded a lump-sum payment of £20,000.

During his trial André displayed a cheerful courage that earned him the admiration of many Americans, but he was nonetheless hanged as a spy. Arnold escaped and, as a British brigadier general, later led two savage raids against the Patriots, then lived out his days in London.

down the exposed Redcoats in the tall grass, and panic threatened the survivors. British officers averted a rout by riding among the troops, and the British beat an orderly retreat into the woods in the face of continuing American volleys. The Americans gave chase and in turn were routed by the bayonet-wielding Britons. All afternoon the carnage continued as first the British, then the Americans, advanced. At sunset the Americans retired when British reinforcements arrived, but Burgoyne had lost almost 600 men—losses he could not make good—while hundreds of militiamen were joining General Gates' army in and around the battlefield.

Burgoyne, looking for a way out of his predicament, decided on a probing attack on the American defenses at Bemis Heights, near the site of his recent defeat. On October 7, to the accompaniment of drum rolls, the British marched once more into the muzzles of Daniel Morgan's riflemen and Continentals, and once more were sent reeling. They rallied, but the Patriot firebrand Benedict Arnold suddenly led a charge that broke the British lines and forced their retreat. During this action Arnold took a bullet in the leg that ended his fighting days as an American officer. By the time he was able to take the field again 3 years later, it was as a British general; in the interim he had turned traitor and attempted to betray strategic West Point to the enemy.

Twice defeated by the Americans and weakened by 1,200 casualties, Burgoyne sought shelter in Saratoga. Now facing an American force more than three times the size of his own, he finally bowed to the inevitable, and on October 17 the British surrendered. To the astonishment of the world, seasoned British soldiers supported by highly trained German mercenaries had been defeated by a force of Continentals and green militiamen.

In London the news of Burgoyne's defeat was met with a dismay approaching hysteria, strengthening the hand of antiwar elements in Parliament. Lord North, the King's Prime Minister, dispatched a mission to Congress that offered repeal of all the laws to which the Colonies had objected. But the time for conciliation had passed. Flushed with the victory at Saratoga, the leaders of the Revolution would be satisfied with nothing less than British recognition of American independence.

Diplomatic Maneuvers

In France the American triumph was met with jubilation. As early as 1775 Congress had dispatched envoys to Paris seeking loans, munitions, and, if possible, a military alliance. From the first the French looked on the Revolution with cautious sympathy, seeing it as an opportunity to avenge their own recent defeats at the hands of Britain. Reluctant to commit the prestige of France to so risky a cause without strong indications of its success, the French at first proceeded warily, shipping arms to the rebels secretly through private intermediaries. The American mission in Paris was a focal point for recruiting foreign volunteers for Washington's army. Through this channel the gallant young Marquis de Lafayette, Tadeusz Kosciuszko and Count Casimir Pulaski from Poland, and Prussia's Baron Friedrich von Steuben found their way across the Atlantic. The best known and most beloved of this group was Lafayette, who became almost like a son to Washington. Kosciuszko, an engineer and artilleryman, built fortifications that played a major role in the victory at Saratoga. Pulaski, reaching the newly independent States in 1777, was appointed brigadier general and chief of cavalry later that year, and in 1778 organized Pulaski's Legion and led it south.

Perhaps the most valuable of all the foreign volunteers was Von Steuben, a born drill sergeant and martinet. Through the grim winter of 1777–78 at Valley Forge, Pennsylvania, the cocky, short-tempered Prussian spared neither himself nor Washington's troops in a largely successful effort to instill military discipline into the Continental Army. In one of his legendary rages he swore at the balky Americans in a torrent of broken English and French: "Sacré! Goddam de gaucheries of dese badauts! Je ne puis plus. I can curse dem no more." But curse them he did, and by the spring of 1778 his efforts had borne fruit in the creation of a military force that at least approximated the parade-ground dash of the British.

Far more important, however, than the recruitment of such idealists and adventurers was the diplomatic mission's ultimate success in gaining full and open support for the Patriot cause. Benjamin Franklin proved a happy choice as America's chief representative at the court of Louis XVI. Already world-renowned as a scientist, statesman, and journalist, Franklin brought tact and determination to his task. His charm and erudition made him socially popular as well. Still, all these qualities might have counted for little had not the French Foreign Minister, the Comte de Vergennes, perceived an alliance with the new, struggling Nation as the best means of furthering France's efforts to wrest world economic and political leadership from Britain.

After the British capitulation at Saratoga, events in Paris moved quickly as the French consulted with their Spanish allies on the wisdom of joining forces with the Americans. On February 6, 1778, a pact of Franco-American amity was signed and sealed in Paris, and 4 months later France declared war on England. By June 1780 Britain also found herself at war with Spain, although the Spanish still refused to recognize the American Colonies' right to independence.

If the French alliance ensured that eventually the Americans would triumph over their enemies, many months passed before promise became substance. Indeed, in the winter of 1778 victory appeared so far off as to be indiscernible even to the most optimistic eye. At his winter quarters in Valley Forge, Washington could do little but share the miseries of his troops, who lacked proper shelter, warm clothing, and nourishing food. For General Howe, wintering in occupied Philadelphia, it was quite another story. Wealthy Loyalists and onetime Patriots, now restored to their sovereign's favor, came to pay court to the King's general and to dine in sumptuous surroundings among elegantly uniformed officers. In May 1778, however, Howe relinquished command to his subordinate, Sir Henry Clinton, and sailed back to England to mend the damage to his reputation suffered by his failure to link forces with Burgoyne. Burgoyne also returned to England. Their roles in the war were ended.

A French Nobleman Serves a Noble Cause

Marie Joseph Paul Yves Roch Gilbert du Motier, Marquis de Lafayette, was the scion of an ancient French family who earned himself an honored place in American history. When the 19-year-old officer arrived in Philadelphia in July 1777, eager to offer his services to the Patriot cause, Congress at first looked coldly on this latest in a long line of European volunteers. Too many had demanded exalted rank and high pay as rewards for scant military experience. But Lafayette's offer to serve at his own expense won him a commission as a major general. On August 1 he joined Washington's staff and quickly earned the general's friendship. The marquis got his first taste of battle in September at Brandywine, where he was slightly wounded. By December he had his own command, a division of Virginia light infantry, and he cheerfully endured the winter of 1777–78 at Valley Forge, where his willingness to share the men's hardships earned him the title of "the soldier's friend."

In January 1779 Lafayette sailed for France to solicit military support for America, returning the next year with the heartening news that the Comte de Rochambeau would soon be bringing his expeditionary force to Washington's aid. Lafayette continued to badger his country for more help and acted as a valuable liaison between the Continentals and their French allies. In 1781 he displayed skill in the field as well, harrying Cornwallis' much larger army during its withdrawal to Yorktown and sending reports that brought Washington's Franco-American force south to trap Cornwallis. The Revolution won, Lafayette returned to France but later made two triumphant visits to America. In 1805 President Thomas Jefferson offered Lafayette the governorship of Louisiana, but the French hero refused it.

Missed Opportunity

As Howe set sail for his homeland, orders for General Clinton were crossing the Atlantic in the opposite direction. With France arrayed against her, Britain could no longer afford to concentrate all her efforts in the rebellious States. Clinton was ordered to dispatch 5,000 men to the West Indies and another force to Georgia and to stand on the defensive in the North. Acting on orders from London, Clinton prepared to abandon Philadelphia and move his army through New Jersey to reinforce the New York City garrison. Evacuation of Philadelphia began on the morning of June 18. The troops crossed the Delaware and were strung out in a vulnerable line of march along the New Jersey landscape.

If ever Washington had an opportunity to inflict a mortal blow, this was it. After much discussion and argument he appointed his second in command, Gen. Charles Lee, to lead the offensive. He could not have made a worse choice. Lee, a self-proclaimed military genius and a schemer who had long coveted Washington's position, was also a defeatist who thought the British Army invincible. His hesitation in committing his 5,000-man force to action and his blundering tactics turned what might have been a decisive American victory into a near rout.

On June 28 advance units of Lee's force encountered the British rear guard at Monmouth Court House, New Jersey. Lacking any battle plan, Lee gave no definite orders to his subordinates, and they launched uncoordinated attacks on the Redcoats. Upon hearing the rifle fire, Clinton sent several crack regiments toward the rear, and their appearance caused Lee to order a retreat that soon turned into a panic. At this moment General Washington appeared on horseback on the Englishtown road, his face set with determination. Lafayette, who witnessed the general's ride, remarked later that Washington's sudden appearance stopped the retreat, his dash toward the sound of battle rallying his troops and "restoring to our standard the fortunes of the fight. I thought then, as now, that never had I beheld so superb a man."

Unable to control his rage, Washington confronted Lee and rebuked him harshly. After dispatching Lee to the rear, Washington took personal command and managed to form a strong defensive line. For hours the combat continued in sweltering heat, and many on both sides died of sunstroke. By late afternoon the bloodletting had ended, and at midnight Clinton marched his men off to waiting ships at Sandy Hook and embarked for New York. Washington took his exhausted troops northward, crossed the Hudson River, and eventually installed his forces at White Plains. Both armies had suffered in the indecisive battle, but strategically the encounter was a grave disappointment for the Americans, who had missed the chance to cripple if not destroy Clinton's army. With the British now firmly ensconced in New York City, too strong to be dislodged but too weak to risk an offensive, the war in the North was stalemated, except for skirmishes and raids. The major theater of operations was shifting south to Virginia, the Carolinas, and Georgia.

Homefront Problems

Meanwhile in the midst of war, the 13 States were faced with the difficult task of creating a Union. While the Declaration of Independence laid the foundation of a new

Imperiously angry, *Washington (at center, brandishing sword) rides into a confused mass of retreating Americans at Monmouth Court House, New Jersey, on June 28, 1778. Gen. Charles Lee, the American field commander (at left, on white horse), had attacked the British troops without any plan of battle. After failing to direct his advancing troops, he had ordered a retreat that soon became disorderly. Denouncing Lee for his bungling tactics, Washington icily ordered him to the rear and personally rallied the Americans. They proved the value of Von Steuben's training at Valley Forge, beating off repeated attacks by Sir Henry Clinton's finest regiments. The battle raged all day and ended indecisively, although the Americans held the field.*

The Wilderness War
Sharpshooters Win the Day

In the summer of 1778 about 100 sharpshooting frontiersmen, led by Col. George Rogers Clark of Virginia, occupied Kaskaskia and Cahokia, on the Mississippi River, and Vincennes, 180 miles to the east. In the preceding months Clark had completed a daring campaign to destroy Britain's hold on the Illinois country. The tiny settlements, inhabited mostly by French fur traders and farmers, had surrendered readily to Clark's men.

In mid-December, however, the situation abruptly changed. Lt. Col. Henry Hamilton, the Lieutenant Governor of Canada, led a 500-man force of Indians, French militia, and British regulars from Detroit to Vincennes, where he overpowered a small American detachment. The French in Vincennes quickly switched allegiance to Britain. Deciding to wait for mild spring weather to launch an attack on Clark, Hamilton sent most of his French militia back to Detroit and let the Indians go. With his remaining force of 35 British regulars and 45 French militiamen, Hamilton rebuilt Vincennes' rundown fort, naming it Fort Sackville after the Colonial Secretary, George Sackville (later Lord Germain).

Knowing that Hamilton could reassemble an overwhelming force in the spring, Clark decided to beat him to the punch. On February 6, 1779, Clark left Kaskaskia with 170 men, nearly half of them French volunteers, and headed for Vincennes. The first 160 miles were relatively easy going, but the final 20 were a waterlogged ordeal of ice-cold rivers and flooded marshlands. Starvation threatened; the floods had driven off the usually abundant game. But the indomitable Clark pushed his exhausted men to Vincennes and then marched them back and forth across the rolling prairie to convince the French that he had a larger army than in fact he had. The attackers did outnumber Hamilton's men in the garrison, but they were protected by an 11-foot palisade of logs and four cannon.

During the night of February 23, Clark's men surrounded Fort Sackville. They had no artillery, but the Kentucky rifles carried by the frontiersmen were far more accurate than the British smoothbore muskets. At dawn on the 24th, Clark's sharpshooters started picking off British gunners each time they opened a port to fire a cannon. Later that day, Hamilton's French militia, already shaken by the sharpshooters and reluctant to die defending the fort, was demoralized by seeing the Americans capture and execute several Indian raiders who tried to enter the fort. Unable to count on his militia, Hamilton capitulated that evening, and America's claim to the Illinois country was established.

Slogging through floodwaters *knee deep to shoulder high, Col. George Rogers Clark leads his hardy Kentucky and Virginia frontiersmen and French volunteers on a 17-day march to a successful attack on Lt. Col. Henry Hamilton's British garrison at Vincennes.*

nation, the process of securing unity was to prove arduous in the extreme. The only central authority was the Continental Congress, and its hold over the States was vague and constantly under challenge. On July 12, 1776, the Congress had proposed the Articles of Confederation, a charter of union that left most powers in the hands of the States. Even this document, establishing a central control so weak as to be ineffectual, met with resistance from many State governments, and it was not until February 27, 1781, that the last of the 13 States signed the Articles, which Congress ratified 2 days later.

The Congress could only urge and cajole while attempting to deal with a multitude of problems, the most pressing of which was inflation. Despite large subsidies from France, bankruptcy was a constant threat. Early in the war the Congress had begun issuing paper dollars called Continentals. By 1780 millions of Continental dollars were in circulation, backed by little more than faith in the Patriot cause. But, where money was concerned, faith was in rather short supply, and by early 1780 a Continental was worth barely one-fortieth of its face value. State governments made the situation considerably worse by issuing their own currency—another $200 million in worthless paper money.

The financial picture improved somewhat in 1781 after banker Robert Morris became superintendent of finance and, with the aid of France, secured a large loan from Holland, but inflation continued to plague America throughout the war. Profiteers and speculators grew fat while the general populace, particularly the soldiers, suffered. Several times General Washington was faced with mutiny as his troops demanded pay. Gen. Robert Howe, ordered to put down a rebellion at Pompton, New Jersey, in January 1781, had the ringleaders executed, and a similar penalty for rebellion was also inflicted in Pennsylvania. But it was for the sharp businessmen who profited from their countrymen's plight that Washington reserved his most withering scorn. "I would to God," he once remarked, that speculators be "hung in gibbets upon a gallows five times as high as the one prepared by Haman. No punishment . . . is too great for the man who can build his greatness upon his country's ruin."

The War in the South

For America nationhood was proving hard to come by, yet Britain could not find effective means of heading it off. For 3 years His Majesty's forces had poured quantities of treasure and blood into their effort, and by the late spring of 1778 all they could show for their pains was the occupation of New York City and a few other centers. Desperate for a way to end the rebellion before the French could come to its aid in force, the British decided to launch an offensive in the South, where, according to their intelligence, Loyalist sentiment was strong and Patriot military power weak.

In the autumn of 1778 a large British force left New York by sea, and in December a combined land-sea assault was launched against Savannah, Georgia. The small and inexpertly led militia and Continental units in the area found themselves in the jaws of a British pincer, with Redcoat infantry advancing on their flanks and rear. Unable to cope with the attack, the Americans fled. Savannah fell on December 29, giving the British an important base in the Deep South. In an attempt to wipe out this foothold, a Franco-American force under French Admiral Comte d'Estaing and Gen. Benjamin Lincoln began siege operations against Savannah in September 1779. The siege guns made little headway against the British defenses, but when Count d'Estaing's naval captains began warning him of a possible attack by a British fleet, the French and American commanders decided to gamble on a general assault against the still powerful enemy defenses on October 9. As could have been expected, the well-entrenched British shot the French and American columns to tatters. Then Brigadier General Pulaski tried to save the day with a courageous cavalry charge, but his men were slaughtered and he was mortally wounded. Thus ended Count Pulaski's tragically short career in America.

Not long after fending off the attack on Savannah, the British mounted a major offensive in the South. In February 1780 Sir Henry Clinton—at the head of a large fleet and commanding a mixed force of Redcoats, Hessians, and Loyalists—set sail for Charleston, South Carolina, which 3 years earlier had successfully warded off a British invasion. Now, however, the situation was different. The British force was much larger and the city's defenses had deteriorated. General Lincoln made the fatal mistake of concentrating his entire 5,400-man army of Patriots within Charleston, allowing Clinton to land troops on his flanks and cut his supply lines and routes of escape. By the beginning of April Charleston was besieged, with British forces advancing on its defenses by land and a large British fleet standing offshore to prevent resupply or escape by sea. On May 12 the surrounded Lincoln laid down his arms, surrendering Charleston and his entrapped army to Clinton. About 4,000 militiamen and Continentals were thus wiped from the rolls of battle in a single stroke, and the Patriot cause lost tons of military supplies.

By mid-August the British were in control of all Georgia and South Carolina. With his campaign seemingly on the verge of complete success, Clinton returned to his New York headquarters, leaving behind a strong army under General Cornwallis to pacify the South. Cornwallis soundly thrashed an American force under General Gates at Camden, South Carolina, on August 16.

Patriot victory *at Yorktown, Virginia, in October 1781 was made inevitable by Cornwallis' poor judgment in placing his army with its back to the sea, in the expectation that British naval supremacy would extricate him if need be. Unfortunately for Cornwallis, the Patriots were now ready to undertake a joint land-sea operation with their French allies. In early September a French fleet under the Comte de Grasse blockaded Yorktown, holding firm when challenged by British ships, and late that month a combined Franco-American army under Washington's command took up siege positions on land. By October 9 the surrounded British were enduring daily, merciless poundings from siege guns, and on October 17 Cornwallis was forced to ask for terms. This painting shows the Redcoats marching out of Yorktown to lay down their arms on October 19.*

Despite ceaseless harassment by American guerrillas, led by Francis Marion and other partisan leaders, it appeared that there was no force capable of preventing British control of the entire South.

But in the autumn of 1780 the Americans struck back. Wilderness-hardened frontiersmen decimated a Tory force at King's Mountain in South Carolina on October 7, and a week later Washington sent General Greene south to succeed General Gates. Daringly splitting his small army of fewer than 2,500 men, Greene ordered Gen. Daniel Morgan's division to the west to collect supplies and raid British outposts. While Cornwallis concentrated on containing Greene, Morgan won a brilliant victory in South Carolina at Cowpens on January 17, 1781, killing, wounding, or capturing almost all of Banastre Tarleton's 1,000-man force. When Cornwallis went in pursuit of Morgan, Greene joined his colleague and led the British commander on an exhausting and frustrating chase through North Carolina and into Virginia. Once again Colonel Kosciuszko, who had contributed so much to the victory at Saratoga, served the Americans in good stead. Calling upon his engineering skill, the Polish nobleman contrived a fleet of amphibious baggage wagons to carry Greene's men and their supplies across flood-swollen streams.

After resting awhile in Virginia and recruiting reinforcements, Greene marched back into North Carolina and challenged Cornwallis at Guilford Courthouse on March 15. Cornwallis' superior artillery prevailed, but his losses were so heavy that he retreated to Wilmington, North Carolina. Failing to get aid from the now-discouraged Tories, Cornwallis marched into Virginia late in April and joined other British forces, including those of the traitor Benedict Arnold, to raid rebel supplies and obtain fresh troops. Greene meanwhile turned back into South Carolina and, with the cooperation of Francis Marion's guerrillas and the cavalry of "Light-Horse Harry" Lee, began mopping up British outposts, finally herding the remaining enemy forces into Charleston.

At first Cornwallis had things his own way in Virginia, raiding at will. As spring turned to summer, however, he met increased resistance from newly arrived troops commanded by Lafayette and Gen. "Mad Anthony" Wayne, an impetuous but canny leader. In late summer Cornwallis withdrew his 7,000-man army to Yorktown on the Virginia coast, expecting to make contact with a British fleet from New York. But Cornwallis had entered a trap of his own devising, his back to the sea and facing an ever-growing army under Lafayette and Wayne. When Lafayette sent news of the British commander's situation to Washington, whose main force was still garrisoned near New York, the American commander in chief saw an opportunity to strike a mortal blow at the enemy. Now he had not only his own Continentals but a seasoned 5,000-man French army under the Comte de Rochambeau. In addition a powerful French fleet with 3,000 troops aboard was heading north from the West Indies. Washington had mapped an assault on New York City, but, with Cornwallis bottled up at Yorktown, he changed his plans. The Franco-American army would march south to reinforce Lafayette, while the French fleet would engage and destroy British ships en route from New York to Yorktown and finally attack Cornwallis from the sea.

For once everything went exactly as planned. The French fleet under the Comte de Grasse appeared in Chesapeake Bay on August 26 and landed troops to reinforce Lafayette on September 2. Three days later the British fleet arrived to challenge De Grasse, but it was outgunned and outmaneuvered and took a fearful mauling before retiring to leave Cornwallis in the tightening trap. Unable to escape by land or sea, Cornwallis could only wait and hope some miracle would extricate him.

With the arrival of Washington at the head of a 20,000-man Franco-American army, Yorktown came under siege on October 9. For days on end, from land and sea, cannon poured destruction on the British defenses. Finally, on October 17, 1781, Cornwallis asked for terms. Two days later, as a Redcoat military band reportedly struck up the popular air "The World Turned Upside Down," the proud and once-powerful British units paraded between files of French and American soldiers to lay down their arms in surrender.

Peace at Last

The Battle of Yorktown did not conclude the war, but Cornwallis' surrender made its early end inevitable. Britain, faced with a powerful combination of enemies, was consumed with war weariness, and demands for peace grew daily louder and more insistent. In February

The formal signing *of the Peace of Paris on September 3, 1783, is shown in Benjamin West's painting, left unfinished because British representatives refused to pose. From left to right are American peace commissioners John Jay, John Adams, delegation chief Benjamin Franklin, commissioner Henry Laurens, a President of the Continental Congress, and William Temple Franklin, grandson of the elder Franklin and secretary to the commission. The Americans were under instruction to act only with the advice of France, but they tactfully avoided that, while at the same time obtaining British acknowledgment of American independence before serious talks began.*

1782 Lord North's ministry fell, to be replaced the next month by a peace cabinet. In Parliament that March a resolution was adopted denouncing "all those who should advise or . . . attempt the further prosecution of offensive war on the Continent of North America."

Still, many months of negotiation lay ahead before the independence of the United States was sealed by treaty. Despite indications that peace was at hand, Washington urged new exertions, commenting: "My only apprehension is lest the late important success . . . should produce such a relaxation in the prosecution of the war, as will prolong the calamities of it." But even Washington was convinced when the British evacuated Charleston and Savannah "in consequence of an unsuccessful war."

Now the scene of action shifted to Paris. When peace talks opened in the summer of 1782 the British Government at first hoped for a settlement that would give America something less than full independence. The first task of the U.S. delegation—headed by Benjamin Franklin, John Jay, and John Adams—was to dispel any British notion that increased autonomy might be an acceptable substitute for sovereignty. Finally, in September, Britain authorized its emissary to deal with the commissioners of the "13 United States," conceding that independence was an accomplished fact.

Before the United States could end hostilities or make a final settlement, England had to resolve her disputes with France and Spain. This was done on January 20, 1783, and on April 11 the U.S. Congress proclaimed the war was over. Finally, on September 3, in Paris, in the lodgings of the British emissary, British and American negotiators appended their signatures to the Peace of Paris.

On the whole, Britain showed generosity toward her former Colonies. Recognizing that the new United States, although no longer legally tied to the Crown, remained an Anglo-Saxon country in which bonds of sentiment and commerce might replace the broken governmental ties, Britain chose a course of enlightened self-interest. While denying U.S. claims to Canada and insisting that prewar debts to British merchants be acknowledged, Lord Shelburne's negotiators conceded the new Nation's title to a vast trans-Appalachian region in spite of French and Spanish attempts to prevent it, and confirmed the right of New England fishermen to ply their trade off Canada's coast. So generous were the British that one European diplomat remarked: "The English buy peace rather than make it."

Eight years had passed since the first shot was fired at Lexington green, and a conflict in which some 250,000 Americans had at one time or another taken up arms in freedom's cause had finally ended. Now that it was over, George Washington cast a prophetic eye to the future. "With our fate," he observed, "will the destiny of unborn millions be involved."

General Washington's Farewell to Arms

Emotions ran high at New York City's Fraunces Tavern on December 4, 1783, as Gen. George Washington met for the last time with a hastily assembled group of officers from the disbanding Continental Army. From June 1775 to this brisk winter day he had been their leader and had served among them and shared with them the bitter fruits of many defeats and, at last, the sweet taste of victory. Now it was time to say goodby, to turn his gaze homeward and his thoughts to the retirement from public life that he so much desired. Lifting a wineglass, he said: "With a heart full of love and gratitude, I now take my leave of you. I most devoutly wish that your later days may be as prosperous and happy as your former ones have been glorious and honorable." Then, after embracing each of the officers, he quickly departed.

The 2 years since the British surrender at Yorktown had not been easy. Pay and pensions, once freely promised the soldiers, had become a fading dream. In disgust some officers had issued the Newburgh Addresses (March 11 and 12, 1783), bluntly telling Congress that if their demands were not met they would refuse to disband when the war ended. Washington quashed this implied threat of a military takeover at a meeting on March 15 in which he persuaded the angry officers to be patient with Congress and trust it to meet their just demands. Then he wrote Congress, strongly urging the politicians to keep faith with the fighters: "If, retiring from the field, they [the officers] are to grow old in poverty . . . then shall I have learned what ingratitude is. . . ."

As he relinquished command, Washington pledged his Nation "my services to the utmost of my abilities. . . ." Though he sought only a quiet life, in the years ahead he was to redeem that pledge in full measure.

Evolution of the Flag *Not the Simple Story One Might Think*

Old Glory, that proud symbol of America, is the product of a rather haphazard series of events. From 1776 until 1912, when the flag was formalized, every flag maker was, in effect, a flag designer, and there were many versions of the Stars and Stripes. A precursor of today's flag was the Grand Union flag, which George Washington presented to the Continental Army on New Year's Day 1776. It incorporated the British Union flag because the colonists, although they had already fought at Lexington and Concord, had not yet decided to break away entirely from the mother country. No one knows who the designer was. On June 14, 1777, after independence, the Continental Congress decreed retention of the stripes but replacement of Britain's flag with a "new constellation" of stars symbolizing the united Colonies. The designer of the 1777 flag is also unknown. The only authority for the story that Betsy Ross made it was Betsy's grandson, who first told it in 1870. The new flag was flown mainly by ships, for identification; it was seldom used on land. But whether on land or sea, its stars—arranged in various ways—were as likely to be blue on white as white on blue and to have eight points as five. Often blue stripes were mingled with the red and white, and in some flags the stripes were vertical. Only the three colors were constant. In 1782 Congress proclaimed that the red stood for hardiness and courage, the white for purity and innocence, and the blue for justice, vigilance, and perseverance. In 1818 Congress eliminated some confusion by specifying 13 horizontal stripes, but it set no pattern for the stars. One popular motif was a single large star outlined by small stars, but the row arrangement became more common and in 1912 was made official.

Although Betsy Ross *was indeed a flag maker, for the Pennsylvania Navy, the meeting with George Washington depicted above by the artist John Ward Dunsmore is probably fiction.*

From the Cross of St. George to the Stars and Stripes

Cross of St. George, a Greek device, was brought to England by 13th-century Crusaders.

Cross of St. Andrew, of uncertain origin, has been Scotland's symbol since medieval times.

1606. British Union flag flew over the Colonies until the Revolution.

1705. On British Meteor flag, the Union was in the canton.

1776. Grand Union of the rebelling Colonies included the British Union.

After England and Scotland were united in 1603 through the accession to the English throne of James I, the Cross of St. George was superimposed on the Scottish Cross of St. Andrew to form the British Union. The Meteor flag, flown even today by British merchant ships (with Ireland's Cross of St. Patrick added to it), was equally familiar to the colonists, who striped its solid red field to form their Grand Union flag. In 1777 the newly independent Nation retained the stripes and added the stars. The 1777 design

Flags That Were Especially Designed for Rallying Around

Flags of the Revolution. State, regimental, and local militia units carried individual devices to identify themselves in battle and to show their pride and determination. Stars and stripes were popular, but so were the pine tree, taken from a coin, and the rattlesnake, personifying vigilance and retribution. Watchwords such as "Hope," "We Are One," "Don't Tread on Me," and "An Appeal to Heaven" also appeared. The American flag of 1777 was primarily a naval symbol, and John Paul Jones' sloop *Ranger* was the first to fly it in foreign waters and to receive the salute of a foreign navy—that of France—while on his way to raid enemy ships off the coast of Great Britain in the spring of 1778. "The flag and I are twins," he was quoted as saying proudly. But the ensign that he ran up on the British man-of-war *Serapis* after its defeat by his *Bonhomme Richard* was a different flag. This flag was documented by a painter in the Dutch port of Texel where Jones' fleet put in after the battle.

Rattlesnake Jack Used by Continental Navy

Pine Tree Flag Flown by New England Ships

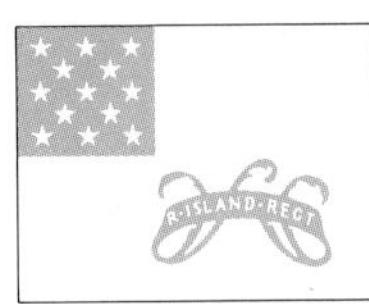

First Rhode Island Regiment Flag

Flag of the Green Mountain Boys

Flag That Flew at the Battle of Bennington, Vt.

Flag Raised on *Serapis* by John Paul Jones

John Trumbull used *an artist's license in painting the flag in "The Surrender of Cornwallis." Experts agree that this 14-striper, with 12 stars arranged in a square around a 13th, did not fly on that day in 1781 when active fighting in the Revolutionary War came to an end.*

'77. First use of Stars and Stripes -one of many versions.

1795. Second U.S. flag added stars and stripes for two new States.

1818. Third U.S. flag set the number of stripes at 13.

1960. Twenty-eighth, and current, U.S. flag has 50 stars.

shown above was only one of many. By 1795 two more stars and stripes had been added, representing the 14th and 15th States. This flag was the inspiration for "The Star-Spangled Banner" during the War of 1812. In 1818 Congress returned the number of stripes to 13, for the original Colonies. From then on only a new star was added for each new State—on the Fourth of July following the State's accession. The last such Independence Day celebration was in 1960, after Hawaii had become the 50th State.

Flags of the Confederacy. The first Confederate flag, the Stars and Bars, designed in 1861, so closely resembled the U.S. Stars and Stripes that it caused tragic confusion at Bull Run. A battle flag, the Southern Cross, was then designed. Its 13 stars represented the 11 Confederate States and the secessionist governments in Kentucky and Missouri. A second national flag displayed the Southern Cross on a white field. It looked like a flag of surrender, however, and a red stripe was added in 1865.

First Confederate National Flag

Confederate Battle Flag

Third Confederate National Flag

The Pledge to the Flag

I pledge allegiance to the flag of the
United States of America and to the Republic
for which it stands, one Nation under God,
indivisible, with liberty and justice for all.

Written by an editor of Youth's Companion, *the pledge was first recited by Boston schoolchildren in 1892. The original words "my flag" were changed in 1923 to "the flag of the United States of America"; "under God" was added in 1954.*

CHAPTER THREE

Creating a System of Government

When the Thirteen Colonies began their Revolution i 1775, their leaders had only the vaguest notion of wh kind of a united government would emerge once victor was won. Because of the history of uneasy relations wit England's monarch, most Americans believed that th broad form should be that of a republic. But they were war of granting great power to a central government, even on of their own making. The Revolution was waged and wo by a loose alliance of fiercely independent States under th leadership of the Continental Congress. The Articles Confederation, approved in 1781, soon proved inadequa once peace was restored.

MAKING DEMOCRACY WORK

The Articles of Confederation

Decades of struggle with the Crown had made Americans almost obsessively wary of centralized power. As they set about establishing the first independent republic since ancient Greece, they wanted to make sure that, having cast out a foreign tyranny, they were not merely exchanging it for a home-grown variety. It took 5 years of debate for all the States to approve the Articles of Confederation, America's short-lived first constitution, which went into effect on March 1, 1781.

The Articles established a Congress composed of delegates appointed by the State assemblies and authorized that Congress to make war, negotiate peace, conduct foreign relations, control the currency, borrow money, settle boundaries, and oversee relations with the Indian tribes. Except for the powers expressly delegated to this "firm league of friendship," each State was to "retain its sovereignty, freedom and independence, and every power, jurisdiction and right." Any proposed amendments of the Articles would require ratification by each of the 13 States.

It was a flawed document in many ways. Congress lacked the power to tax, to regulate commerce, or to enforce its own measures. There was no national judiciary, no chief executive, and only rudimentary executive departments. The States exploited Congress' weaknesses to the full, defying its decisions, trespassing on its prerogatives, and ignoring its requests for funds. Nonetheless the Articles of Confederation provided the fledgling Nation with vitally needed experience and precedents later used in establishing a viable national government. By 1787 the States themselves saw the need for greater Federal strength, and a few influential men already envisioned an entirely new constitution. It would not be long before their hopes would be fulfilled.

The American Revolution was a rare historical event. Unlike other successful uprisings it was not nationalistic. As historian Edmund S. Morgan has pointed out, "Our nation was the child, not the father, of our revolution." Thirteen quarrelsome Colonies were united by their common history, tongue, and customs; by their common sense of betrayal as British subjects; and by their common suspicion of remote and centralized power. But they took up arms as "Free and Independent States," with "full power . . . to do all . . . acts and things which independent states may of right do." The hard-fought 8-year conflict first brought them together as Americans, but once peace was won, the new States swiftly reverted to their old and independent ways.

Proposals for a formal constitution were heard, but they were without precedent. England had no such document; by custom and design her constitution was an unwritten, malleable instrument, based on precedent and practice. But in their conflicts with the King, the colonists had learned the importance of spelling out on paper the precise limits of governmental power.

Although the Continental Congress urged the drafting of a constitution for a confederacy of States as early as June 12, 1776 (3 weeks before independence was declared), the first order of business for the evolving country was the adoption of State constitutions. Aimed largely at righting old colonial wrongs, these documents were based on the principle first enunciated by Virginia that "all power is vested in, and consequently derived from, the people. . . . Magistrates are their trustees and servants and at all times amenable to them." By "the people" the drafters meant property-owning, white adult males, hardly a democratic definition in modern terms but at the time a radically broad electorate.

The State constitutions vested real power in the legislatures, which were believed most reflective of the peo-

With the Nation threatening to break apart even before emerged from infancy, the States sent 55 delegates to Philadelphia in 1787. There, for 4 hot months, they hammered out the U.S. Constitution, an extraordinary document by which America still abides almost two centuries later. Blueprinting a government based on the consent of the governed, it shrewdly balanced the rights of individuals and States with the interests of the Nation.

The new government was launched in 1789. Subsequent decades saw it survive a series of potentially disastrous storms. Thomas Jefferson's peaceful assumption of the Presidency in 1801 proved that the young Nation could withstand the buffeting of partisan politics. Three-quarters of a century of threats of secession by disgruntled States culminated in a Civil War to settle once and for all the question of the permanence of the Union. As the decades passed, the Central Government greatly expanded its scope to deal with a bewildering host of economic and social problems that dominated and tormented the 20th century. In this troubled era many nations turned to some form of authoritarianism for solutions, but the U.S. Government managed in the main to keep the democratic faith with the American people and fulfill the Constitution's pledge to "secure the blessings of liberty" for all citizens.

ple's will. Typically, these were divided into two chambers: a lower house, or assembly, elected by the people and an upper house elected by the assembly. In most instances the assembly was authorized to appoint the governor and judges, whose powers thus tended to be more limited than those of their prewar predecessors. Most State constitutions had bills of rights that guaranteed individual liberties against infringement; forbade standing armies and searches without warrants (two burning colonial grievances against Britain); and established trial by jury, habeas corpus (freedom from detention except by due process of law), and the right of petition. Feudal rights of inheritance and the bestowal of titles of nobility were outlawed.

Meanwhile the Continental Congress, driven from one temporary capital to another by the encroaching British and frequently without adequate funds from the tightfisted States, labored to support armies fighting in areas that were sometimes hundreds of miles apart. Preparing a national constitution had to wait. As a temporary device a committee of the Congress produced the Articles of Confederation, a tenuous alliance that scarcely nicked the sovereignty of the States. Even so, nearly 5 years of wrangling and delay preceded final ratification of this compact, in 1781, by the last of the 13 States.

The Articles created a new Congress, a weak body powerless to levy taxes or to make good on its decisions and mortally afraid of offending any State for fear it might secede. The Congress did manage, however, to establish departments of foreign affairs, finance, and the post office, which were embryonic precursors of today's huge Federal bureaucracies; and it provided for the future growth of the Nation by passing ordinances organizing new States in the Northwest Territory and allowing them to join the Union on an equal footing with the original 13 States. But the States freely trespassed on its powers. They individually borrowed money abroad, issued wildly inflated currencies, intrigued with foreign powers, maintained their own navies, warred with the western Indians—all actions only Congress was authorized to take. Sometimes they even neglected to send enough delegates to Philadelphia to form a congressional quorum. When debt-ridden Massachusetts farmers, led by Daniel Shays, rebelled against their aristocratic Boston creditors and officials in 1786, the national Government was powerless to stop the rebels; the rebellion was put down by the Massachusetts militia, supported by private funds.

The Founding Fathers Meet the Crisis

Clearly, the loose arrangement that had sufficed during the war could no longer meet the needs of a burgeoning, unruly Nation of almost 4 million. George Washington, in retirement at Mount Vernon, wondered whether the Revolution he had led had been worth all the blood and effort. "We are either a united people under one head, for Federal purposes," he wrote, "or we are thirteen independent sovereignties, eternally counteracting each other." Such able old comrades as Alexander Hamilton, John Adams, Gouverneur Morris, and John Jay agreed. The Central Government must be made far stronger, they argued, or the Union's components would inevitably fly apart and fall victim to native dictators or foreign predators. "Better . . . a supreme government now," wrote Morris, "than a despot 20 years hence." In 1786 five States agreed to dispatch delegates to Philadelphia the following May, there to "render the Constitution of the Federal Government adequate to the exigencies of the Union." The other States, with the exception of rebellious little Rhode Island, gradually fell in line, although the New Hampshire delegates arrived 2 months late.

Americans were by no means united in their desire for a stronger central government. Patrick Henry, Virginia's

Signing the Constitution *in Philadelphia's Independence Hall, September 17, 1787. Artist Howard Chandler Christy included a portrait of every signer. Among them: George Washington, standing on the platform; Benjamin Franklin, seated, with cane; Alexander Hamilton, whispering in Franklin's ear; and James Madison, seated at Franklin's left.*

The Constitutional Convention
Fifty-five Uncommon Men Set the Course

Thomas Jefferson hailed the 55 delegates to the Constitutional Convention as an assembly of demigods. Certainly they were an extraordinary group of citizen-statesmen. They were remarkably young (average age, 43) and generally prosperous—mostly lawyers, planters, or merchants seasoned in colonial and State politics. Many had fought in the Revolution; six had signed the Declaration of Independence. For 16 sweltering weeks (May 25–September 17, 1787) they debated the Nation's future behind closed doors, hammering out the government superstructure under which the United States has flourished ever since. Thirty-nine delegates signed the finished document, then hurried home to help win ratification by the necessary 9 of 13 State conventions.

The struggle took almost a year. Advocates insisted that the Constitution was essential to U.S. survival. Opponents retorted that the new Government's taxes would drain the States dry; that no national body could truly represent local interests; and that the document lacked a Bill of Rights to protect individual freedoms (a fault remedied in 1791). The national debate was brisk, and even some supporters had their doubts. "I consent to this Constitution," wrote Benjamin Franklin, "because I expect no better, and because I am not sure that it is not the best." New Hampshire became the ninth State to ratify, on June 21, 1788. A few weeks later Virginia and New York followed suit, assuring the new Government's success.

MAKING DEMOCRACY WORK

The Constitution

What emerged from the Philadelphia convention was a document—now the world's oldest written constitution—that kept the new Nation from splitting into as many as a dozen tiny ones; safeguarded its independence and republicanism against attack from both within and without; and struck a shrewd balance between State and Federal power. The ingenious system of checks and balances that it set up has protected the powers and prerogatives of the executive, legislative, and judicial branches of the Federal Government.

One secret of the Constitution's longevity lies in the flexible ambiguity its authors built into it. The framers wisely avoided the temptation to solve every foreseeable problem on paper; instead, they arranged that the Constitution should be adaptable to inevitable changes in circumstance without undue strain. Thus they made it possible—though not too easy—to amend the document, and created the U.S. Supreme Court to resolve disputes involving interpretations of the Constitution in relation to the laws of the land. The result was an instrument capable of surviving profound shocks—even civil war—without splintering. The Constitution may well be what John Adams called it in 1787: "The greatest single effort of national deliberation that the world has ever seen." It was, indeed, a work of collective genius that still commands our utmost respect.

Revolutionary firebrand, declared he "smelled a rat" and denounced the Philadelphia meeting; so did Samuel Adams of Massachusetts. And the State assemblies, still jealous of their powers, made sure their representatives understood that they were coming together only "for the sole and express purpose of revising the Articles of Confederation," and not to limit States rights.

Once a quorum had assembled, however, and the delegates had imposed strict secrecy on the deliberations—posting armed sentries at the doors and sealing the windows to thwart eavesdroppers—they took upon themselves the more momentous task of creating a new national government. The men who pointed them in that direction were both Virginians: James Madison and Gov. Edmund Randolph. For months Madison had steeped himself in volumes on history and government, seeking ways to balance the people's desire for personal liberty with the Nation's need for effective government. His plan, put forward by Randolph, called for a federal government divided into three coequal branches—executive, legislative, and judicial—each shrewdly calculated to serve as a check on the others. This scheme—which prevails to this day as a bulwark of democracy—was swiftly adopted, and its outline survived intact through 3½ months of hard, sometimes bitter debate over all-important details.

For all their differences, the delegates shared several basic beliefs. First all agreed that only a republic, deriving its authority from the people to whom it was ultimately responsible, would fulfill the promise of the Revolution. From this it followed that the people should have some voice in choosing those who made the laws. A measure of democracy was therefore inevitable, even though such conservative delegates as Massachusetts' Elbridge Gerry thought it "the worst of all political evils." With this much agreed, the spirit of creative compromise could dominate the convention.

The meeting almost broke down, however, over how the legislature should be apportioned. The large States supported Randolph's call for a two-chambered Congress—a House of Representatives and a Senate—in both of which each State would have members in proportion to population. The smaller States, led by New Jersey's William Paterson, feared they would be powerless under such an arrangement and instead demanded equal representation for each State, regardless of population. Neither side would budge until Roger Sherman and Oliver Ellsworth, both from Connecticut, offered an acceptable compromise: a House of Representatives apportioned according to population and elected by direct popular vote; a Senate made up of two members from each State, picked by the State legislatures.

Once this issue was resolved, the delegates concentrated on a host of important details, including the question of whether the executive should be a committee or a single man. Probably because most delegates expected Washington to be the Nation's first leader, they finally opted for the latter. Aware that further compromises might be needed to ensure ratification by the States, the framers gave their document flexibility. They specified that Congress could propose amendments to the Constitution by a two-thirds vote of both Houses; and the States, if two-thirds concurred, could call a convention to propose amendments; in either case, the amendments would become valid when ratified by three-fourths of the States. The first to ratify the new Constitution was Delaware; the last was recalcitrant Rhode Island, which waited until May 1790 to do so.

George Washington, *with "devout fervency," takes the oath as the first President of the United States on the balcony of New York City's Federal Hall on April 30, 1789. After more than 5 years of genteel retirement from public life at Mount Vernon, he confessed to a friend that he had embarked on the Presidency "with feelings not unlike those of a culprit going to the place of his execution." But he could not refuse. Wearing his dress sword and an American-made brown broadcloth suit (by way of encouragement to U.S. manufacturers), Washington was sworn in by New York State Chancellor Robert R. Livingston. "Integrity and firmness," he said in his inaugural address to a jubilant crowd, "is all I can promise."*

The Branches of Government
Controlled by Checks, Balances, and Wide Representation

Executive. The President heads this branch of government, assisted by the members of the Cabinet who administer 11 major Departments: State; Defense; Justice; Treasury; Commerce; Labor; Health, Education, and Welfare; Housing and Urban Development; Interior; Agriculture; and Transportation. Cabinet officers must be approved by the Senate. Though they rank as the President's chief advisers, in recent decades members of the White House staff have generally had more influence on him.

Judicial. The Supreme Court stands at the apex of the Nation's Federal judiciary system and hears cases on appeal from lower courts—the Federal District Courts and the U.S. Courts of Appeals. Though the primary function of the eight Associate Justices and the Chief Justice is to decide matters of law, rather than fact, the High Court's power to declare acts of Congress, State legislatures, and city councils unconstitutional can drastically alter the Nation's practices, as when it branded school segregation unconstitutional in 1954.

Legislative. Quartered in the Capitol Building, the two branches of Congress—the 435-member House of Representatives (blue, above) and the 100-member Senate—are responsible for enacting the Nation's laws. Though these days most major bills originate in the White House, all must be approved, disapproved, or amended by both Houses, and no measure becomes law until it has been passed by a majority in each House. The President may then sign or veto the bill, but a two-thirds vote in each House can override a veto.

The Birth of the Two-Party System

It was one thing to create a government on paper, quite another to make it work. To the eternal credit of George Washington and the Federalists who dominated his Cabinet, the fledgling Republic survived and flourished in the face of sectional claims and what Washington's successor, John Adams, called "the pernicious, baleful" doctrine of States rights. Under Treasury Secretary Alexander Hamilton, the prime Federalist theorist, a sound fiscal system was organized, and the Nation was set on the path toward commercial and industrial expansion through the imposition of Federal tariffs. When Pennsylvania farmers balked in 1794 at paying Hamilton's excise tax on whisky, Washington called out some 15,000 militiamen to enforce the Federal law. With this bold action the Federal Government proved it had the power to impose its will.

The Federalists were almost all propertied Northern merchants or their prosperous allies, with an instinctive distrust of those whom Harrison Gray Otis called "the mass of the people . . . turbulent and changing . . . [who] seldom determine or judge right." Without their sense of starchy self-esteem the Federalists might not have been able to cope with the many forces of disunion. But as the Federalist political party began to emerge under the leadership of Washington and Hamilton in the 1790's, they found that class pride served them poorly in the sweaty world of electoral politics.

The Founding Fathers had shared an aversion to what Washington called "the daemon of party spirit." Adams believed "faction" was "the greatest of political evils," and Thomas Jefferson once vowed that "If I could not go to Heaven but with a party, I would not go there at all." But Americans proved too fractious to feign a political unity they did not feel. Hamilton's economic nationalism and emphasis on the importance of "manufactures" alarmed hardscrabble farmers and prosperous planters alike and seemed to confirm the worst fears of those who had opposed ratification of the Constitution. The Government's determined neutrality during the French Revolution angered those who saw America's own struggle against monarchy mirrored in the blood-spattered Paris streets. And the "average man" grew increasingly resentful of rule by the rich and well born. In the late 1790's these disparate elements rallied to Jefferson and Madison to form the Democratic-

The Lawmaking Process. *The tortuous process through which a bill becomes law can generally begin in either House, with committee hearings. A bill on defense, say, might first be considered by the House Armed Services Committee and then, or simultaneously, by the Senate committee of the same name. These hearings may take months in each House, with scores of witnesses testifying and dozens of amendments offered. If the bill is reported out of committee, debate then takes place on the House and Senate floors, and new amendments may be offered before a vote is taken. Even if the measure passes both Houses, the two versions may differ substantially. A conference committee from both bodies then tries to write a compromise. Should this pass, the President may veto the bill, but his veto can be overridden by a two-thirds vote of both Houses. If the law is challenged, the Supreme Court may decide on its constitutionality.*

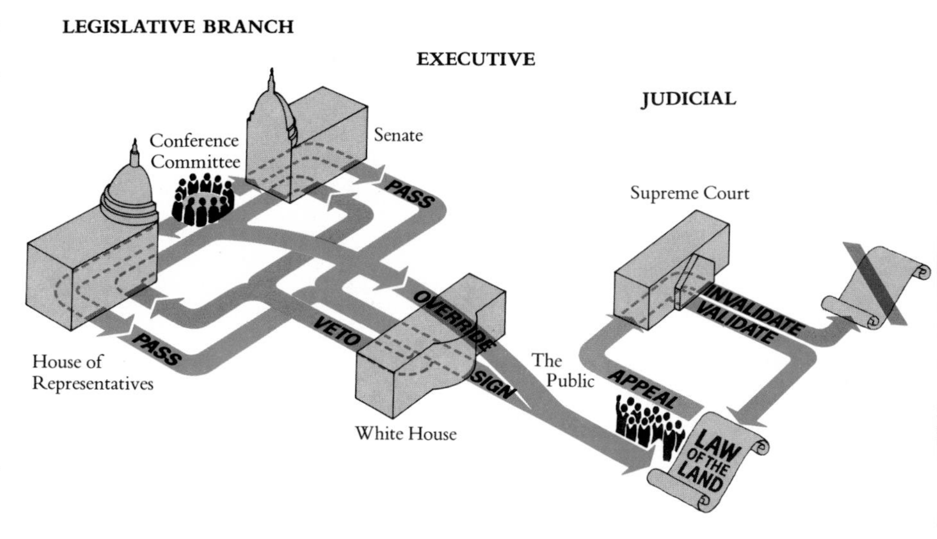

State, County, and City Administration

The States of the Union retain a significant measure of sovereignty. With a governor, a legislature, and a judicial system, each State parallels the governmental forms of the Federal system. All States have the right to levy taxes, and many services—such as education, health, welfare, and police—are supported either entirely or in large measure by State, rather than Federal, funds. The sovereignty of State governments has, however, been steadily eroded. Functions such as education, unemployment relief, public works, and the like—once considered entirely within State jurisdiction—are now matters of Federal concern as well.

County and city governments are solely the creations of the States, and the powers of such jurisdictions vary greatly from one State to the next. In Connecticut, for example, there are no county governments, while next door in New York, some counties, such as Nassau, have significant powers of taxation. So too with city governments, all of which derive their powers from the States. In some States the power of city governments to tax, to educate, and to operate broad-scale social services is great, while in other States the cities are virtually impotent in many areas. But, as befits our system, the balance can always be shifted.

Republican Party. Under its banner they championed a greater role for the States (thus winning support from the many opponents of centralization), increased popular democracy, and the virtues of rural life.

The two-party system had been born. Ever since, though party labels and political doctrines have changed to suit the times, three-quarters of the American electorate have identified with one or the other of two great national parties: Federalist and Democratic-Republican at first; then Democratic and Whig; and, since 1856, Democratic and Republican. America's vastness and the myriad interests of her different people have militated against ideologically oriented parties. Only rarely have U.S. parties offered voters clear-cut policy choices. Instead, each party seeks to make the broadest possible popular appeal.

The Federalist Party began its slide to extinction with the passage in 1798 of the Alien and Sedition Acts. These were ostensibly aimed at barring insubordinate immigrants; actually they were intended—and used—to muzzle the clamorous and shrewdly led opposition and to weaken Democratic-Republican support among immigrants. As it turned out, the acts served to make popular heroes of their political targets, and Jefferson was easily elected President in 1800. For some 15 years thereafter the embittered Federalists sought without success to regain national power. American politicians learned well the lesson of the party's demise. Never again would any significant political movement proclaim its distrust of the people or espouse government by aristocracy.

Peaceful Transfer of Power

The Federalists spared nothing, including personal slander, to prevent Jefferson's ascendancy to the Presidency. Among the semihysterical attacks against him by the press was that of the Hartford *Courant:* "There is scarcely a possibility that we shall escape a *Civil War.* . . . Murder, robbery, rape, adultery and incest will be openly taught and practiced." Instead a conciliatory Jefferson called for national unity, saying, "We are all Republicans, we are all Federalists." He won repeal of Federalist measures he deemed repressive but carefully left Hamilton's fiscal system intact and also did nothing to alter the existing balance between State and Federal power. Thus the Federal Government survived its first transfer of power from one party to another without trauma.

Party	1789	1792	1796	1800	1804	1808	1812	1816
Federalist Party	★ George Washington John Adams	★ George Washington John Adams	★ John Adams *(Presidential nominee)*	John Adams Charles C. Pinckney	Charles C. Pinckney Rufus King	Charles C. Pinckney Rufus King	DeWitt Clinton Jared Ingersoll	Rufus King *(No Vice-Pres. no*
Democratic-Republican Party			★ Thomas Jefferson *(Vice-Pres. nominee)*	★ Thomas Jefferson Aaron Burr	★ Thomas Jefferson George Clinton	★ James Madison George Clinton	★ James Madison Elbridge Gerry	★ James Monro Daniel D. Tomp

A Panorama of American Political Parties

The evolution of America's political parties is shown on these two pages. Although, traditionally, two major parties have dominated the political scene, minor (or third) parties have regularly put up Presidential candidates. They have rarely polled a combined percentage of more than 2 percent of the total popular vote, but several have had important impacts on U.S. history. One of these, the People's (Populist) Party of the 1890's, advocated far-reaching reforms that anticipated programs enacted under Presidents Theodore Roosevelt, Woodrow Wilson, and Franklin D. Roosevelt. This chart, which lists all Presidential and Vice Presidential candidates of the major parties and the most important minor parties, starts with the first national election in 1789 and goes across and down the page to the present day. Parties that have merged or split are so indicated.

Party	1852	1856	1860	1864	1868	1872	1876	1880
	John P. Hale George W. Julian	**Constitutional Union Party**	John Bell Edward Everett		**Prohibition Party**	James Black John Russell	Green C. Smith Gideon T. Stewart	Neal Dow Henry A. Thom
Republican Party		John C. Frémont William L. Dayton	★ Abraham Lincoln Hannibal Hamlin	★ Abraham Lincoln Andrew Johnson *called* **National Union Party** *in this election*	★ Ulysses S. Grant Schuyler Colfax	★ Ulysses S. Grant Henry Wilson	★ Rutherford B. Hayes William A. Wheeler	★ James A. Garfi Chester A. Art
	Winfield Scott William A. Graham	Millard Fillmore Andrew J. Donelson				**Liberal Republicans** *also nominate*		
	★ Franklin Pierce William R. King	★ James Buchanan John C. Breckinridge	Stephen A. Douglas Herschel V. Johnson	George B. McClellan George H. Pendleton	Horatio Seymour Francis P. Blair, Jr.	Horace Greeley Benjamin G. Brown	Samuel J. Tilden Thomas A. Hendricks	Winfield Scott Ha William H. Eng
		Northern Democrats	*No national nominees*		**Straight-Out Democrats**	Charles O'Conor Charles Q. Adams II		**Anti-Monop P**
		Independent (Southern) Democrats	John C. Breckinridge Joseph Lane				**Greenback Labor Party**	James B. Weav Benjamin J. Char
						Greenback Party	Peter Cooper Samuel F. Cary	
American (Know-Nothing) Party	*No national nominees*	Millard Fillmore Andrew J. Donelson						
							Socialist Labor Party	*No national nominees*

Party	1916	1920	1924	1928	1932	1936	1940	1944
	James F. Hanly Ira D. Landrith	Aaron S. Watkins David L. Colvin	Herman P. Faris Marie C. Brehm	William F. Varney James A. Edgerton	William D. Upshaw Frank S. Regan	David L. Colvin Claude A. Watson	Roger W. Babson Edgar V. Moorman	Claude A. Wats Andrew Johns
	Charles Evans Hughes Charles W. Fairbanks	★ Warren G. Harding Calvin Coolidge	★ Calvin Coolidge Charles G. Dawes	★ Herbert C. Hoover Charles Curtis	Herbert C. Hoover Charles Curtis	Alfred M. Landon Frank Knox	Wendell L. Willkie Charles L. McNary	Thomas E. Dev John W. Brick
								States Rights' Democrat (Dixiecrat) Par
	★ Woodrow Wilson Thomas R. Marshall	James M. Cox Franklin D. Roosevelt	John W. Davis Charles W. Bryan	Alfred E. Smith Joseph T. Robinson	★ Franklin D. Roosevelt John Nance Garner	★ Franklin D. Roosevelt John Nance Garner	★ Franklin D. Roosevelt Henry A. Wallace	★ Franklin D. Roos Harry S. Trum
	Farmer Labor Party	Parley P. Christensen Maximilian S. Hayes	*No national nominees*	Frank E. Webb Will Vereen	**Union Party**	William Lemke Thomas C. O'Brien		**Progressi Par**
		Progressive (La Follette) Party	Robert M. La Follette Burton K. Wheeler					
	Workers' (Communist) Party	*No national nominees*	William Z. Foster Benjamin Gitlow	William Z. Foster Benjamin Gitlow	**Communist Party** William Z. Foster James W. Ford	Earl Browder James W. Ford	Earl Browder James W. Ford	*No national nominees*
	Allen L. Benson George R. Kirkpatrick	Eugene V. Debs Seymour Stedman	Robert M. La Follette Burton K. Wheeler	Norman Thomas James H. Maurer	Norman Thomas James H. Maurer	Norman Thomas George Nelson	Norman Thomas Maynard C. Krueger	Norman Thom Darlington Hoc
	Arthur E. Reimer Caleb Harrison	William W. Cox August Gillhaus	Frank T. Johns Verne L. Reynolds	Verne L. Reynolds Jeremiah D. Crowley	Verne L. Reynolds John W. Aiken	John W. Aiken Emil F. Teichert	John W. Aiken Aaron M. Orange	Edward A. Teic Arla A. Albau

	1820	1824	1828	1832	1836	1840	1844	1848
Liberty Party / Free-Soil Party						James G. Birney Thomas Earle	James G. Birney Thomas Morris	Martin Van Buren Charles F. Adams
National Republican Party	*No national nominees*	★ John Quincy Adams Henry Clay Andrew Jackson William H. Crawford John C. Calhoun	John Quincy Adams Richard Rush	Henry Clay John Sergeant				
Whig Party	★ ames Monroe iel D. Tompkins				*No national nominees*	★ William H. Harrison John Tyler	Henry Clay Theodore Frelinghuysen	★ Zachary Taylor Millard Fillmore
Democratic Party			★ Andrew Jackson John C. Calhoun	★ Andrew Jackson Martin Van Buren	★ Martin Van Buren Richard M. Johnson	Martin Van Buren *(No Vice-Pres. nominee)*	★ James K. Polk George M. Dallas	Lewis Cass William O. Butler
Anti-Masonic Party			*No national nominees*	William Wirt Amos Ellmaker	William H. Harrison Francis Granger			

(Vice-Presidential nominee for all residential candidates)

EXPLANATORY KEY

- ★ Elected Candidates
- Roots of the Republican Party
- Republican Party
- Roots of the Democratic Party
- Democratic Party
- Prohibition Party
- Socialist Labor Party
- Socialist Party
- Communist Party
- Socialist Workers Party
- Short-lived Parties

	1884	1888	1892	1896	1900	1904	1908	1912
	ohn P. St. John William Daniel	Clinton B. Fisk John A. Brooks	John Bidwell James B. Cranfill	Joshua Levering Hale Johnson	John G. Woolley Henry B. Metcalf	Silas C. Swallow George W. Carroll	Eugene W. Chafin Aaron S. Watkins	Eugene W. Chafin Aaron S. Watkins
	ames G. Blaine ohn A. Logan	★ Benjamin Harrison Levi P. Morton	Benjamin Harrison Whitelaw Reid	★ William McKinley Garret A. Hobart	★ William McKinley Theodore Roosevelt	★ Theodore Roosevelt Charles W. Fairbanks	★ William H. Taft James S. Sherman	William H. Taft Nicholas M. Butler
National (Anti-Bryan) Democrats				John M. Palmer Simon B. Buckner				
Progressive (Bull Moose) Party								Theodore Roosevelt Hiram W. Johnson
	★ rover Cleveland mas A. Hendricks	Grover Cleveland Allen G. Thurman	★ Grover Cleveland Adlai E. Stevenson	William Jennings Bryan Anthony Sewall	William Jennings Bryan Adlai E. Stevenson	Alton B. Parker Henry G. Davis	William Jennings Bryan John W. Kern	★ Woodrow Wilson Thomas R. Marshall
People's (Populist) Party	njamin F. Butler bsolom M. West		James B. Weaver James G. Field	William Jennings Bryan Thomas E. Watson	Wharton Barker Ignatius Donnelly	Thomas E. Watson Thomas H. Tibbles	Thomas E. Watson Samuel W. Williams	
	njamin F. Butler bsolom M. West	*No national nominees*						
Union Labor Party		Alson J. Streeter Charles E. Cunningham						
Social Democratic Party					Eugene V. Debs Job Harriman			
Socialist Party						Eugene V. Debs Benjamin Hanford	Eugene V. Debs Benjamin Hanford	Eugene V. Debs Emil Seidel
	No national nominees	*No national nominees*	Simon Wing Charles H. Matchett	Charles H. Matchett Matthew Maguire	Joseph F. Mallony Valentine Remmell	Charles H. Corregan William Cox	August Gillhaus Donald L. Munro	Arthur E. Reimer August Gillhaus

	1948	1952	1956	1960	1964	1968	1972	1976
	laude A. Watson Dale H. Learn	Stuart Hamblen Enoch A. Holtwick	Enoch A. Holtwick Edward M. Cooper	Rutherford L. Decker Earle H. Munn	Earle H. Munn Mark Shaw	Earle H. Munn Rolland E. Fisher	Earle H. Munn Marshall D. Uncapher	
	homas E. Dewey Earl Warren	★ Dwight D. Eisenhower Richard M. Nixon	★ Dwight D. Eisenhower Richard M. Nixon	Richard M. Nixon Henry Cabot Lodge	Barry M. Goldwater William E. Miller	★ Richard M. Nixon Spiro T. Agnew	★ Richard M. Nixon Spiro T. Agnew	
National States' Rights Party / People's Party	trom Thurmond elding L. Wright	*No national nominees*	Thomas C. Andrews Thomas H. Werdel	Orval E. Faubus John G. Crommelin			Benjamin Spock Julius W. Hobson	
	★ arry S. Truman lben W. Barkley	Adlai E. Stevenson John J. Sparkman	Adlai E. Stevenson Estes Kefauver	★ John F. Kennedy Lyndon B. Johnson	★ Lyndon B. Johnson Hubert H. Humphrey	Hubert H. Humphrey Edmund S. Muskie	George S. McGovern Sargent Shriver	
American Independent Party	enry A. Wallace lenn H. Taylor	Vincent W. Hallinan Charlotta A. Bass				George C. Wallace Curtis E. LeMay	John G. Schmitz Thomas J. Watson, Jr.	
Socialist Workers' Party		Farrell Dobbs Myra T. Weiss	Farrell Dobbs Myra T. Weiss	Farrell Dobbs Myra T. Weiss	Clifton DeBerry Edward Shaw	Fred Halstead Paul Boutelle	Linda Jenness Andrew Pulley	
	enry A. Wallace lenn H. Taylor	*(Party deactivated by law)*	*(Party deactivated by law)*	*No national nominees*	*No national nominees*	*No national nominees*	Gus Hall Jarvis Tyner	
	orman Thomas ucker P. Smith	Darlington Hoopes Samuel H. Friedman	Darlington Hoopes Samuel H. Friedman	*No national nominees*	*No national nominees*	*No national nominees*	*No national nominees*	
	ward A. Teichert Stephen Emery	Eric Hass Stephen Emery	Eric Hass Georgia Cozzini	Eric Hass Georgia Cozzini	Eric Hass Henning A. Blomen	Henning A. Blomen George S. Taylor	Louis Fisher Genevieve Gunderson	

Concern With the Judiciary

Jefferson believed in a limited Presidency and devoted much of his time to behind-the-scenes management of legislation rather than open advocacy of his own aims. But when he saw a chance to double the Nation's size for just $15 million by the Louisiana Purchase, he did not hesitate to close the deal before consulting Congress.

But if Jefferson's relations with Congress were generally warm, those with the judiciary were tepid at best. He instinctively distrusted judges because they were appointed rather than elected, and when he found that outgoing President Adams had staffed 16 new circuit courts with loyal Federalists and had named John Marshall—a Federalist and a long-standing political foe—as Chief Justice of the United States, his suspicion turned to outrage. Fearing that his policies would be undermined, Jefferson tried but failed to purge the courts through impeachment of the judges by Congress.

America's greatest jurist, *John Marshall, as portrayed by Rembrandt Peale. John Adams, who named him Chief Justice, termed the appointment "the proudest act of my life."*

During Marshall's 34-year career as Chief Justice, he and his colleagues on the Supreme Court made some of the most momentous judicial decisions in U.S. history. First and most important, they established in 1803 the Court's power to invalidate Federal laws if it found them in violation of the Constitution. This power of judicial review made the judiciary truly coequal with the executive and legislative branches. Since then, as Chief Justice Charles Evans Hughes once pointed out, Americans have lived under the Constitution, but the judges have had the responsibility of interpreting it correctly. In addition, Marshall's Court held that the Court could review decisions made by State courts (1816), that the Constitution empowered Congress to "make all laws which shall be necessary and proper" for carrying out its powers (1819), and that Congress could regulate any aspect of interstate commerce without interference from the States (1824). Marshall's concepts of the function of the Court won power and public respect that has helped it to survive unpopular decisions and threats from Congress. Even President Franklin D. Roosevelt, fresh from an overwhelming election victory in 1936, was soundly beaten in the Senate when he sought to "pack" the Court by increasing the number from 9 to a maximum of 15 by adding one new justice for each one over 70 who would not retire.

Jefferson's immediate successors, James Madison and James Monroe, shared his political flexibility and his generally modest view of Presidential power. Monroe aroused so little hostility that when he sought a second term in 1820, he got every electoral vote but 1 of the 232 that were cast.

But Andrew Jackson, the first Chief Executive elected by nearly universal white male suffrage (1828), did much to originate the modern philosophy of an activist Presidency. Believing himself their "direct representative," he pledged to protect the American people and the Constitution "against the Senate or the House of Representatives, or both together." The President's duty was not merely to execute the laws, Jackson argued, it was to act

The People's President

Andrew Jackson's ascension to the Presidency in 1829 ended 40 years of rule by enlightened aristocrats—four gentlemen landowners from Virginia and two genteel Bostonians. The young Nation had sprawled westward to the Mississippi and Missouri Rivers, and pressure from its fast-growing, bustling middle class—entrepreneurs, mechanics, artisans, and farmers—had forced all but 5 of the 24 States to abandon the property requirements that had so effectively denied the vote to the common man.

A clamorous new breed of voters saw itself magnified to heroic proportions in rough-hewn "Old Hickory," the battle-scarred son of a Scotch-Irish pioneer who had made himself a successful attorney and planter, a hero of the Battle of New Orleans in 1815, and a popular Senator. Jackson was indeed self-made, but until he became President his political views were generally those of his conservative associates in Tennessee. His shrewd campaign adviser, Martin Van Buren (himself a future President), presented Jackson as the people's hero. Together the two men built a political organization that evolved into the modern Democratic Party and pioneered many of the campaign practices—from mass rallies to catchy songs and slogans—that have become a familiar part of Presidential politics.

As the first President elected by a broad popular vote, Jackson considered himself the "direct representative of the American people." He believed it his duty to dominate Congress and keep minority interests from blocking the working of the national will. He dismantled the second Bank of the United States in 1833–36 because he thought it rewarded a few capitalists at the expense of the less affluent; threatened military action rather than permit South Carolina to defy Federal tariff laws; and ignored the U.S. Supreme Court when its decisions went against his policies. "I have an opinion of my own on all subjects," he declared, "and when that opinion is formed, I persue it *publickly,* regardless of who goes with me." Jackson proved to be as good as his word.

vigorously to open the widest possible opportunities to all citizens. In his efforts to do this, Jackson zestfully clashed with Congress and the Courts and drummed up popular support for his policies through the newly created Democratic Party.

Though his outmaneuvered opponents vilified him as "King Andrew the First" and accused him of using the spoils system to fill Government jobs with his own partisans, "Old Hickory" remained the people's hero. By his actions he set a Presidential mark only his ablest successors could match. In the quarter century between his Administration and the Civil War, only James K. Polk showed equal aggressiveness and tenacity in the Presidency. Polk rode roughshod over his Whig opponents in Congress to fight and win the Mexican War (1846–48), which settled the boundaries of Texas and added Utah, New Mexico, and California to the United States.

Struggle Over States Rights

Despite the growing stability of the Central Government, problems of State and region dominated American public life from the Nation's birth until 1865. Though Southern slavery and States rights have become linked together in the American lexicon, States in every part of the country have at one time or another sought to evade Federal policies that they believed threatened their well-being. In this they mirrored the views of Virginia's John Randolph, who once quipped, "asking one of the States to surrender part of her sovereignty is like asking a lady to surrender part of her chastity." Although diehard New England Federalists were in most matters America's leading nationalists, they asserted the right to declare unconstitutional Jefferson's crippling embargo of 1807, which retaliated against British and French interference with American shipping. During the War of 1812, they talked of seceding from the Union. Twenty years later South Carolina declared Federal tariff acts null and void within the State. Such disputes, of course, had nothing to do with the thorny issue of slavery.

But slavery and States rights became inextricably connected as American political debate focused increasingly on Congress' power over slavery in new territories. Every milestone on the downhill road to the Civil War, from the Missouri Compromise of 1820 to the opening salvo at Fort Sumter, involved both issues. Since most Presidents shrank from taking stands on such divisive subjects, battle was generally joined in the halls of Congress, where legislative titans like Daniel Webster, John C. Calhoun, Stephen A. Douglas, and Henry Clay clashed and sought for compromises.

Further efforts to compromise the North-South clash over slavery were largely forgotten after Chief Justice Roger B. Taney delivered the majority opinion of the Supreme Court in the case of *Dred Scott* v. *Sandford.* Dred Scott, a Missouri slave, had sued for his freedom on the ground that residence with his master in the free territory of Wisconsin had made him a free man. In ruling against Scott, Taney declared that no slave or free Negro could be a citizen of the United States or of any State. Taney went on to say that Scott's living in Wisconsin did not make him a free man because the Missouri Compromise was unconstitutional. Slaves were property, and Congress could not keep them out of free U.S. territories. Taney and President James Buchanan both felt that a court decision denying Congress' power over slavery in the territories would settle this question for all time. But both men underestimated the bitterness and increasing

MAKING DEMOCRACY WORK

The Supremacy of Federal Law

As early as 1798 James Madison, Thomas Jefferson, and others of like mind argued that each State should have the right to reject any Federal law it believed unconstitutional. Their reasoning was simple: Since the States had drafted the Constitution to provide guidelines for the Federal Government, the States were the proper judges of whether Congress was overstepping its bounds. If a State decided that a statute violated the Constitution, it should be free to "nullify" the law so it would not apply to that State.

In 1828 Congress enacted the so-called Tariff of Abominations, leading to a nullification crisis. Designed to protect Northern industry from foreign competition, the act imposed crushing duties on imported goods. Fearing retaliation from foreign purchasers of cotton, rice, and tobacco, the South protested vigorously, holding with South Carolina's fiery John C. Calhoun, then Vice President, that a State had the right to declare an injurious Federal law "null and void." In 1832 a new tariff was enacted that was slightly less unpalatable to the South, but Calhoun's supporters in South Carolina's legislature passed an Ordinance of Nullification against both of these tariffs.

Nullification was a serious threat to Federal authority; if every State obeyed only those laws that pleased it, the Union was doomed. President Andrew Jackson surmounted this threat with a judicious blend of firmness and conciliation. He proclaimed nullification an "impractical absurdity" and warned that "disunion by armed force is treason." He urged Congress to modify the tariff, however, while at the same time obtaining passage of a bill empowering him to use the Army and Navy to enforce the laws. Jackson's willingness to intervene with arms, combined with passage of a milder tariff act, persuaded South Carolina to rescind its Ordinance of Nullification. Armed struggle was averted and the primacy of Federal law reasserted, not again to be seriously challenged until the secession movement in the South led to the Civil War.

Established Opinions
That Proved To Be Wrong

One virtue of the democratic process is the flexibility it affords, the ability to change with the times. Many positions that we now tend to regard as eternal verities were once hotly contested. Here are examples of opinions firmly held by leaders of the past—views that many of their contemporaries echoed but that few would care to espouse today.

He that willingly assents to [religious toleration], if he examines his heart . . . will tell him he is either an atheist, or . . . a captive to some lust. Polypiety is the greatest impiety in the world.
—Puritan pastor Nathaniel Ward, against freedom of worship, 1642.

. . . a democracy is among most civil nations, accounted the meanest and worst of all forms of government. . . .
—Massachusetts Governor John Winthrop, against increased democracy, 1644.

The people are turbulent and changing; they seldom judge or determine right.
—Alexander Hamilton, against votes for ordinary citizens, 1787.

What do we want with that vast and worthless area? . . . What could we do with the Western coast of three thousand miles, rockbound and cheerless and uninviting?
—Attributed to Senator Daniel Webster by foes of a transcontinental railroad, 1844.

Sensible and responsible women do not want to vote. The relative positions to be assumed by man and woman in the working out of our civilization were assigned long ago by a higher intelligence than ours.
—President Grover Cleveland, against women's suffrage, 1890's.

In a republic like ours, where all men are equal, this attempt to array the rich against the poor, or the poor against the rich is socialism, communism, devilism.
—Senator John Sherman, against the graduated income tax, 1894.

It is only to the man of morality that wealth comes. . . . Godliness is in league with riches.
—Episcopal Bishop William Lawrence, against social welfare legislation, 1901.

The rights and interests of the laboring man will be protected and cared for—not by the labor agitators, but by the Christian men to whom God in his infinite wisdom has given the control of the property interests of this country.
—Railroad magnate George F. Baer, opposing arbitration during the coal strike of 1902.

It is plain that you would have to go much further than most interpretations of the Constitution would allow, if you were to give the government . . . control over child labor throughout the country.
—President Woodrow Wilson, stating his views against a national ban on child labor, 1913.

Lincoln's Emancipation Proclamation *of 1863, freeing slaves in Confederate territory, is celebrated in this allegorical painting. But it was 5 years until the ratification of the 14th amendment erased Chief Justice Roger B. Taney's 1857 decision that no Negro could be a citizen.*

strength of the antislavery feeling in the Nation. Instead of settling the matter, Taney's decision so aroused the public that it seemed the question of slavery could only be settled by war.

When the election of Presidential candidate Abraham Lincoln caused seven Southern States to secede, President Buchanan declared their action illegal but argued lamely that the Federal Government had no power to use force against them. The secession led to the Civil War in April 1861, and President Lincoln did not hesitate to expand the limits of Presidential authority. In mobilizing the North to save the Union, he assumed emergency powers never imagined by the framers of the Constitution. He expanded the Armed Forces, blockaded the Southern coast, raised and spent vast sums of money, and even suspended the constitutionally guaranteed right of habeas corpus to combat sedition—all without waiting for congressional authorization. For these and other bold actions Lincoln was denounced as a dictator by the rebellious South and its Northern sympathizers. At the same time Radical Republicans in Congress pressed Lincoln to prosecute the war more vigorously. He patiently ignored his assailants and pursued an independent course. Had he done otherwise, many historians believe, the Union might never have been restored.

Although conflicts between State and Federal power still flare from time to time, the Civil War finally settled the question of a State's right to secede. As Woodrow Wilson once wrote, the Civil War "created in this country what had never existed before—a national consciousness. It was not the salvation of the Union; it was the rebirth of the Union."

Andrew Johnson, the martyred Lincoln's hapless successor, reaped the whirlwind of pent-up congressional anger when he tried to follow Lincoln's planned program of postwar moderation toward the defeated South. Congress sought first to reduce the President's powers, then to remove him from office through impeachment. Though it failed in that objective (by just one vote), Congress succeeded in intimidating Johnson's successors.

Distressing Decades

The $3\frac{1}{2}$ decades between the war's end and the turn of the 20th century saw a reunited America transformed from a rural, agricultural nation into an urbanized, industrial colossus. But in many ways this period was the least noteworthy in U.S. political history.

During Reconstruction the overwhelmingly Republican Congress took upon itself extraordinary powers. It dictated the terms under which the Confederate States could rejoin the Union; granted the vote and promised equal treatment under the law to the newly freed slaves; and supported governments run by Northern carpetbag Republicans, freedmen, and Southern white scalawags willing to risk their neighbors' wrath to profit from cooperation with Congress. Congressional motives were mixed—a complex blend of antirebel fervor, genuine concern for Negro welfare, and a pragmatic desire to ensure what hard-liner Thaddeus Stevens termed the "perpetual ascendancy" of the Republican Party throughout the South.

Instead, despite the generally progressive record of the Reconstruction regimes, Congress succeeded only in adding to the bitterness of the white South and ensuring almost a century of solid Southern support for the Democrats. And when disputed electoral votes from three Southern States hung in the balance after the election of 1876, Republican professionals had few qualms about deserting the blacks and ending Reconstruction in exchange for the White House. In a backroom deal that gave Rutherford B. Hayes a narrow margin of victory in the electoral college, the Republicans agreed to withdraw Federal troops and abandon the freedmen to the not-so-tender mercies of their former masters.

The crude cynicism of this arrangement set the tone of politics for the next 20 years. Weary of war and of efforts to solve the perplexing plight of the former slaves, and dazzled by the prospect of postwar profits, the Nation turned its attention to material advancement. During this Gilded Age vast financial baronies were carved from steel, oil, railroads, mining, and a host of other industries. The Nation grew and prospered as never before, but the fortunes of a few were often built on exploitation of the poor. Farmers were driven to desperation by exorbitant railroad charges, soaring tariffs, and high interest rates. Workers—including some 2 million children under 16—were often forbidden to organize unions and were forced to labor long hours for little pay under hazardous conditions. Immigrants choked the city slums. Southern blacks were denied full citizenship by white terror and Jim Crow laws. Women were denied the vote. Monopolistic trusts drove small businessmen into bankruptcy. While all the country wanted economic growth, many believed that the inequality, poverty, and degradation was too high a price to pay.

These problems, and others related to them, were central to domestic politics throughout the first half of the 20th century, just as States rights and sectionalism had dominated political debate 100 years earlier. But during the 1880's and 1890's the Government turned a mostly deaf ear to the beleaguered groups that sought its aid. While the unregulated Robber Barons bought and sold State legislatures and House and Senate seats, Democrats and Republicans alike sidestepped serious issues in a scramble for power and patronage. Government action with regard to business and industry was confined mostly to lavish subsidies and lofty protective tariffs.

MAKING DEMOCRACY WORK

The Pendleton Act

Andrew Jackson is often credited with having originated the Federal spoils system, which rewards a victorious candidate's political friends with Government jobs and punishes his foes with dismissal. Actually, the practice dates back to George Washington, who felt obliged to inquire into the loyalties of would-be officeholders when a Democratic-Republican revolt threatened his Federalist-dominated government. All of Washington's successors made room for their friends, but Jackson was the first to try to justify the high job turnover during his administration, although it was no greater than that of earlier Presidents. Jackson defended the spoils system, saying that it was a shield against turning the Government into a perpetual "engine for the support of the few at the expense of the many."

The lure of public employment did help to establish party loyalty, but the system eventually got out of hand. Loyalty rather than ability became the prime requisite for appointment; corruption spread into the Cabinet itself. Newly elected Presidents were plagued by swarms of office seekers. A weary Abraham Lincoln, badgered by job hunters as he grappled with the threat to the Union posed by the seceding Southern States, said: "I am like a man so busy in letting rooms in one end of his house, that he can't stop to put out the fire that is burning in the other."

Carl Schurz and other reformers condemned the spoils system, but powerful forces that lived by it routinely blocked corrective legislation. It took public outrage over the assassination of President James Garfield by a disappointed office seeker to force passage of the Pendleton Act in 1883. It created a Civil Service Commission authorized to hire thousands of Federal workers on the basis of open, competitive examinations. The act forbade the party in power to collect political contributions from Federal employees. Only 1 out of 10 Federal jobs was initially covered under the act. In the 1970's most Federal, State, and large-city employees worked under the system of merit with which the Pendleton Act replaced the spoils system.

Wielding his "big stick," *President Theodore Roosevelt is portrayed in this 1905 cartoon as the world's policeman. T.R.'s domestic activism did expand onto the global scene. An early champion of a U.S. overseas empire and a hero of the Spanish-American War, he dispatched the "Great White Fleet" to circle the globe in 1908–09 as a vivid demonstration of U.S. might; supplemented the Monroe Doctrine with a pledge to police the Western Hemisphere; orchestrated a Panamanian revolt that gave the United States the right to build and control the Panama Canal; and arranged talks that halted the Russo-Japanese War—a mediation effort that won him the 1906 Nobel Peace Prize.*

Government Grows To Meet New Challenges

Determined reformers—including middle-class progressives, rural grangers, and populists—had forced individual States to take some corrective actions by the late 1870's. But the problems facing them cut across State lines, and local government could offer little substantive relief. After the Supreme Court denied States the right to regulate interstate railroads, the reformers did manage to persuade Congress to create the Interstate Commerce Commission (1887), providing for Federal regulation of railroad rates, and to pass the Sherman Antitrust Act (1890), the first Federal law aimed at curbing monopoly. Dissent had grown so great by 1896 that William Jennings Bryan wrested the Democratic Presidential nomination from party regulars; but, despite a hard-fought campaign, he was outspent and outpolled by conservative Republican William McKinley. Patriotic fervor stirred by the Spanish-American War stalled reform for a time, but when McKinley was assassinated in 1901 and dynamic young Theodore Roosevelt succeeded to the Presidency, the Progressives at last had a vigorous ally in the White House.

Firmly convinced that the President was "the steward of the people" and that the Presidency was a "bully pulpit" from which to preach Progressive reform, T.R. sought to make the Government the arbiter of clashing economic forces, bigger than any, fair to all. "I did not usurp power," he recalled, "but I did greatly broaden the use of executive power." He did indeed. Armed with a gift for dramatizing complex issues, a shrewd sense of the possible, and the exuberant force of his magnetic personality, he won a reputation as a "trustbuster" by breaking up the gigantic Northern Securities Company. He also demanded, and got, a "square deal" for striking coal miners; rescued hundreds of thousands of wilderness acres from greedy lumber barons; and backed Federal meat inspection and a Pure Food and Drug Act, which empowered Washington for the first time to shield consumers from careless or crooked manufacturers.

Roosevelt's activism frightened businessmen accustomed to a free rein in their rush for profits and alarmed those who took literally Jefferson's celebrated dictum that held "that government [is] best which governs least." Roosevelt was roundly denounced as a Socialist and a revolutionary, although his actions—and those of his successors Woodrow Wilson and Franklin D. Roosevelt—were intended not to injure business or stifle competition but to save capitalism from its own excesses and to provide for every American what Daniel Webster once called "a clear and open field."

The Blue Eagle, *symbol of the National Recovery Administration (1933–35). The NRA helped reduce child labor and raise wages.*

The Constitution bids the Government "promote the general welfare." Since 1900 the Federal Government has adopted an increasingly broad definition of that charge. For better or worse the Nation has changed greatly since the framers met at Philadelphia, and the people have encouraged the Government to change with it.

Although Democrat Woodrow Wilson was a personal and political foe of Theodore Roosevelt, he was imbued with the same progressive, activist spirit. He won passage of more important legislation than any President since the Civil War. An eloquent, energetic leader who ruled his party in Congress with an iron hand, he established the Federal Reserve System, which gave the Government control over credit; stiffened antitrust laws; set up the Federal Trade Commission to bar unfair business practices; and provided farmers with low-interest loans.

New Deal and World Depression

Like the 1880's, the 1920's witnessed widespread prosperity and Government inaction. Calvin Coolidge's famous remark, "The business of America is business," could have served as the era's watchword. But two momentous events took place in the decade's first year: Women finally got the vote, and Prohibition became the law of the land after ratification of the 18th amendment. The national liquor ban, widely ignored, spawned bootlegging, corruption, and organized crime. Its repeal in 1933 was greeted with wide relief; the failure of the "noble experiment" had demonstrated conclusively that when the people flout any law, all law is denigrated.

It was the Great Depression that brought about the next and most profound expansion of Federal power. The economic crisis, which began with the Wall Street crash of 1929, was the worst and longest lived in U.S. history, and the cautious Republican Administration of Herbert Hoover seemed unable to cope with it. When Franklin D. Roosevelt entered the White House in 1933, the country was crying out for action, and it seemed to many Americans that the Government created by the Founding Fathers had proved unable to meet the demands of the modern world. Almost 15 million persons were out of work; 5,000 banks had failed; 32,000 firms had collapsed; and thousands of rural families had lost their mortgaged farms. Such extraordinary ills required extraordinary remedies. The self-confident new President pronounced himself prepared to recommend "the measures that a stricken Nation in a stricken world may require."

F.D.R. made good his pledge of action. The unprecedented flood of hastily created New Deal agencies provided jobs and relief for the jobless; bailed out failing businesses; pumped Federal funds into public works and conservation projects—all measures aimed at restoring the Nation's economic health. Meanwhile, the Government moved vigorously into areas of American life where it had only tentatively ventured before. It provided workers with social security; set minimum wages and maximum hours; guaranteed labor the right to organize and bargain collectively; insured bank deposits; regulated the stock exchange; fixed crop prices and production rates; and produced hydroelectric power for millions.

Some New Deal programs did not work. Others were outlawed by the Supreme Court, touching off a grave 1937 constitutional confrontation between the determined President and the stubborn Court. Twelve key New Deal statutes had been voided mainly on the grounds that they invaded the rights of the States by seeking to regulate local industries. After Roosevelt failed in his attempt to enlarge the Court, it reversed itself and handed down decisions giving Congress full power to legislate in such fields as labor relations, farm aid, abolition of child labor, and social security.

Though conservative critics denounced the New Deal as revolutionary, modern historians have shown that it was rooted in earlier actions taken by Theodore Roosevelt and Woodrow Wilson. Nor was the startling growth of the Federal bureaucracy anything new; the Govern-

MAKING DEMOCRACY WORK

The Ultimate Limitation of Presidential Power

The Founding Fathers, mindful that royal tyranny had helped spark the Revolution, well knew the risks they ran in creating a strong chief executive. Consequently, although the Presidency they fashioned was a powerful office, they hedged it about with effective institutional safeguards in the judicial and legislative branches. In addition they built into the Constitution the power of impeachment, which enables Congress to unseat any President or other Federal official it deems guilty of malfeasance in office. Because removal by this process is a drastic remedy, it was purposely made difficult. An official must first be impeached (formally indicted) by a majority of the House of Representatives on charges of "Treason, Bribery or other High Crimes and Misdemeanors." Actual removal requires a guilty verdict by two-thirds of the Senate.

Impeachment has only rarely been invoked, mostly against Federal judges, and only once against a President. In 1868 Andrew Johnson was impeached by the House but acquitted in the Senate. No other President was seriously threatened with impeachment until the Watergate scandal. After agents of Richard M. Nixon's reelection committee were arrested in June 1972, while trying to burglarize Democratic Party headquarters at Washington's Watergate complex, the attempted coverup was eventually revealed to have involved the President himself. In late July 1974 the House Judiciary Committee recommended three articles of impeachment, and on August 5 Nixon publicly released the transcripts of three tapes he was sending to Federal Judge John Sirica in response to a Supreme Court order. These tapes, implicating the President in a conspiracy to obstruct justice, cost him most of his dwindling support in the House and Senate. On August 9, 1974, in a letter to the Secretary of State Henry Kissinger, Nixon resigned—the first President to do so. A month later his successor, Gerald R. Ford, granted Nixon a full pardon, protecting him from prosecution for any Federal crimes he may have committed.

ment had mushroomed steadily since the 1880's. The Depression and New Deal only accelerated the process. F.D.R. himself had little patience with ideology. "This country needs bold, persistent experimentation," he once said. "It is common sense to take a method and try it. If it fails, admit it frankly and try another. But above all, try something." It was with that pragmatic, buoyant spirit that Roosevelt wore the mantle of his office.

The New Deal did not solve the unemployment problem; only the massive defense spending that began in 1939 accomplished that. But the New Deal did help restore America's faith in its own future and finally established the principle that the Federal Government has a responsibility for the national welfare and a duty to act vigorously to meet specific crises. Although Roosevelt and his works were bitterly attacked by his political opponents, most of the New Deal has since been endorsed by politicians of both major parties. Thanks to its innovations, the Government no longer need plead powerlessness in the face of national crisis. "Never again," declared GOP Presidential nominee Dwight Eisenhower in 1952, "shall we allow a depression in the United States."

Government Today

Since the 1940's the Central Government has grown steadily in size and power. New Deal programs intended

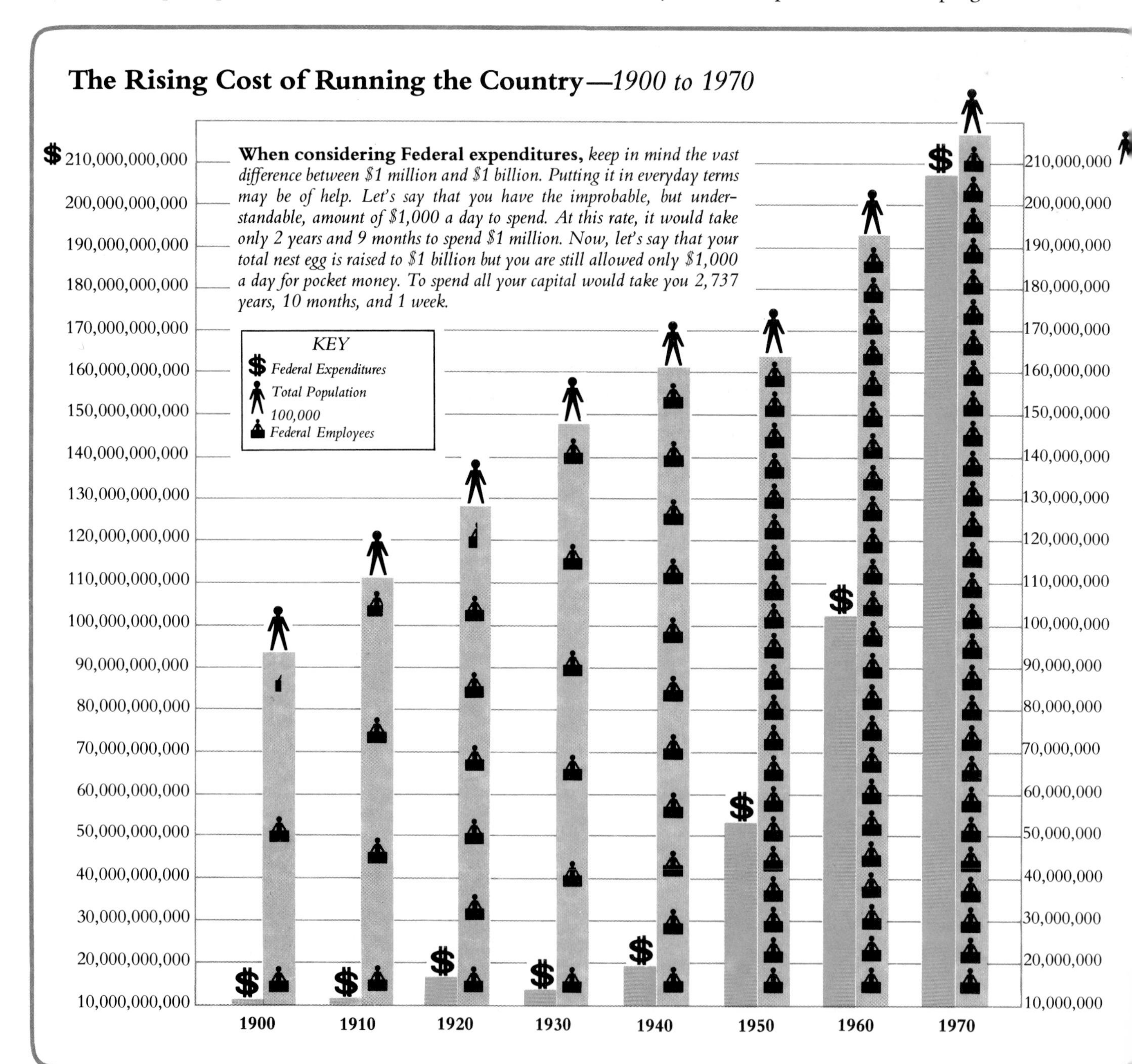

Proud symbol of self-government, *the white marble dome of the Capitol dominates the city of Washington, D.C. The building has grown with the country: Although George Washington laid the cornerstone in 1793, the dome was not finished until 1863, and many changes have since been made. Home to both House and Senate, the Capitol was once hailed by Nathaniel Hawthorne as "the center and heart of America."*

as stopgaps became permanent. The Military Establishment, reorganized as the Defense Department in 1949, grew to awesome size as a result of World War II and the cold war threat. A "fourth branch" of Government mushroomed, made up of the vast regulatory agencies; the Government became the Nation's largest civilian employer. Negro pressure for full equality during the 1960's produced congressional action that finally opened all kinds of public accommodations to everyone and virtually halted antiblack discrimination at the polls.

The flow of power toward Washington has continued unabated. Even Presidents Dwight D. Eisenhower and Richard M. Nixon, who sought to reverse the process and return power to local jurisdictions, met with little success. The vexing problems facing the American people during the final quarter of the 20th century—urban blight, industrial pollution, mass transportation, social health care, energy shortages, inflation, recession, explosive population increase—are primarily national in character and will require national action. Neither local nor State government has the authority, the resources, or the expertise to do much about them.

Americans still cherish the town-meeting, States-rights spirit inherited from their forefathers and prefer to retain local autonomy in such matters as education, policing, and, to the extent feasible, health and welfare. We tend to resist governmental arrogation of activities traditionally reserved to private enterprise. Other countries may nationalize public utilities and establish strong government control in areas considered vital to the public interest, but Americans are reluctant to adopt this course. Independent-minded and long convinced of the value of the capitalist system, we remain suspicious of a centralized bureaucracy. In our early history we learned that the more remote the seat of authority, the likelier it is to be both inefficient and tyrannical.

Nonetheless, centralization marches on, and many citizens feel increasingly isolated from the wielders of power; taxes increase to meet rising costs; bigness spawns waste; and those who have power seek even more. Yet our social and economic advances have eased life's burdens for many, helped establish history's highest national standard of living, and encouraged the "pursuit of happiness" promised by the Declaration of Independence.

On balance, the American Government has adjusted well to the complex modern world. A Constitution written by bewigged colonists for small seaboard communities has proved strong and flexible enough to serve the sprawling, fast-paced industrial giant that is America today. Ours is still a Government "by the people," and, in a world studded with tyrannies, that is a fact of which all Americans can be immensely proud.

Giants of the Senate *Declared Outstanding by Their Peers*

The 100 members of the United States Senate—2 from each State—wield great power. Until 1913, when ratification of the 17th amendment made them subject to popular vote, Senators were elected by the State legislatures. The Founding Fathers believed that the House of Representatives, directly elected by the people from the outset, would dominate the Congress. The Senate was expected to serve mainly as a brake on the supposedly capricious will of the people.

Over the years, however, the Senate has come to wield the greater power. There are several reasons for this. Representatives outnumber Senators by more than four to one; consequently, the individual member has less influence on House policies than on those of the Senate. Senators serve 6-year rather than 2-year terms and have more time to make their mark. The House carefully limits debates, but only a 60-vote motion for cloture can silence the Senate, so that a determined minority can sometimes thwart the will of the majority. Senators exert an important influence on foreign policy because of their power to ratify or reject treaties. They can also exert leverage on the executive branch by their right to confirm or reject Presidential appointments.

The Senate has produced many of our Nation's most able leaders. In 1957 a special committee chaired by Senator John F. Kennedy of Massachusetts was instructed to select five outstanding Senators who would exemplify the highest standards of that august body. The current members and living former members were ineligible and those selected were not necessarily to be considered the greatest of all time, a distinction that would be all but impossible to confer. Criteria for selection included long tenure, association with outstanding legislative measures, and choices that would represent the entire history of the Senate. Clay, Webster, and Calhoun, who formed the "great triumvirate" that dominated Capitol Hill in the decades before the Civil War, were the almost unanimous choices of the 150 scholars who served as advisers. La Follette and Taft, respectively, epitomize the modern progressive and conservative traditions.

The presiding officer *of the U.S. Senate, shown in session here, is the Vice President, or the President pro tempore, who sits on a dais facing the Senators—Democrats to his right, Republicans to his left. Also on the dais are the Sergeant at Arms, secretaries, and clerks. The galleries are open to visitors, except for the central section directly behind the dais, which is reserved for reporters.*

Henry Clay
Kentucky, 1806–07, 1810–11, 1831–42, 1849–52

In an era of strong partisan and sectional feeling, Clay was known as The Great Compromiser. He rejected extremism as "entirely too ultra," and in three crises during his political career his talent for accommodation helped forestall the Union's collapse. A Whig, he was Speaker of the House, Senator, and Secretary of State and thrice ran for President. Abraham Lincoln called him "my beau ideal of a statesman."

Daniel Webster
Massachusetts, 1827–41, 1845–50

The finest orator of his age, the majestic Webster represented New England Whigs for decades as Senator, Congressman, Cabinet officer, and Presidential candidate. The peroration of his reply to Southern Senator Robert Y. Hayne, a fiery States righter, gave nationalists a deathless watchword: "Liberty and Union, now and forever, one and inseparable." Webster's decision to back the Compromise of 1850 alienated abolitionists but helped delay the Civil War.

John C. Calhoun
South Carolina, 1833–44, 1845–50

Calhoun, a Democrat, began as a dedicated nationalist and ended up as the South's most eloquent and implacable champion. Senator, Congressman, Cabinet officer, and twice Vice President, he wrote the nullification doctrine and the theory of the concurrent majority, which arrogated to the South the power to veto acts of Congress. "He was wrong," wrote Arthur Schlesinger, Jr., "but he was a greater man and senator than many . . . who have been right."

Robert M. La Follette
Wisconsin, 1906–25

As Governor, Congressman, and Senator, "Fighting Bob" was an able progressive leader, spearheading Senate struggles for conservation, antitrust legislation, and banking reform. Never tempering his opinions to the political climate, he alienated most Americans by opposing war with Germany in 1917 and, later, U.S. entry into the League of Nations. In 1924 he was a strong Presidential candidate.

Robert A. Taft
Ohio, 1939–53

Integrity, not charm, won Taft the sobriquet of Mr. Republican. "It is not honest to be tactful," he once said, and he refused to compromise conservative principles for political gain. Taft won the respect of friend and foe alike for his often lonely battle against the New and Fair Deals. "He had," wrote William S. White, "a luminous candor of purpose . . . in a chamber not altogether devoted to candor."

Others of Similar Stature

These Senators were also deemed outstanding: **Alben W. Barkley** (*D-Ky., 1927–49, 1955–56*), able New Dealer and Vice President; **Thomas Hart Benton** (*D-Mo., 1821–51*), who sacrificed his Senate career by defending the Union: **William E. Borah** (*R-Idaho, 1907–40*), reformer, orator, and isolationist; **Stephen A. Douglas** (*D-Ill., 1847–61*), who espoused popular sovereignty as a slavery compromise; **Oliver Ellsworth** (*Federalist-Conn., 1789–96*), drafter of the 1789 law that organized the Federal judiciary; **Carter Glass** (*D-Va., 1920–46*), banking reformer; **Justin S. Morrill** (*R-Vt., 1867–98*), author of laws founding and expanding land-grant colleges; **George W. Norris** (*R-Independent-Nebr., 1913–43*), advocate of public electric power; **John Sherman** (*R-Ohio, 1861–77, 1881–97*), fiscal conservative, namesake of the Sherman Anti-Trust Act; **Charles Sumner** (*R-Mass., 1851–74*), crusading abolitionist and leader of Radical Republicans; **Lyman Trumbull** (*R-Ill., 1855–73*), ally of Abraham Lincoln and enemy of the spoils system; **Arthur H. Vandenberg** (*R-Mich., 1928–51*), creator of bipartisan foreign policy after World War II; **Robert F. Wagner** (*D-N.Y., 1927–49*), author of acts to clean up slums, protect labor's right to organize.

CHAPTER FOUR

The Advancing Frontier

If there is one quality that most Americans share, it a yearning that sets their eyes straining for a look beyon the horizon, their minds wondering what might be beyon their range of vision, and their feet on paths into the un known. The horizons keep expanding, but for 100 yea after the Declaration of Independence, the conquest of th continent provided ample outlet for the footloose, the ad venturous, and the homeseekers—the millions who brave the wilderness in a quest for independence and prosperit

It is doubtful whether any of the Founding Fathers en visioned an American dominion stretching beyond th Mississippi when they signed the Constitution in 178

Washington: Man of the West

George Washington was in his career a soldier, a statesman, a planter, and the first President of the country he helped to found, but he started out as a surveyor. The lands of what was then the West—the Virginia Piedmont, the Shenandoah Valley, and the Allegheny region—were just beginning to open to settlers in Washington's youth, and surveyors were badly needed to define boundaries. In 1748, when Washington was 16, he joined a surveying team and a year later was appointed official surveyor of Culpeper County, Virginia, a position that often took him into the back country. This limited experience may have prompted Gov. Robert Dinwiddie to appoint him, in 1753, to lead a small party to the forks of the Ohio and warn the French to stay off territory claimed by the Ohio Company of Virginia. Although the mission failed to dislodge the French, Washington gained invaluable knowledge of the wilderness, which he later put to good use, both as an officer in the French and Indian War and as a speculator who owned a considerable amount of Western acreage.

For the 1.2 million or so whites and Negroes who lived along the Atlantic seaboard in England's American Colonies, 1763 was a year of promise. After a century of intermittent warfare, France had at last yielded her claims to vast territories in North America. England had won a total victory, and thousands of Americans—as they were just beginning to be called—eagerly looked forward to reaping its fruits. Beyond the Appalachian mountain chain, running from inland Maine southward to the interior of Georgia, lay an immense wilderness, formerly claimed by France and inhabited only by Indians and a few fur traders. Here, many believed, an opulent future beckoned the colonists.

If the tales of the few intrepid souls who had pierced the Appalachian barrier were to be credited, the region beyond, which stretched westward to the Mississippi, was a potential El Dorado. The soil was rumored to be so rich that one had only to scatter seeds on the ground to assure an abundant harvest, and game was said to be so plentiful that a hungry man needed only to shake the nearest tree to bring down a shower of wild turkeys. In the settled regions of America, such stories sparked new ambitions in men who had once hoped for no more than a small dirt farm in New England or New York. Now they turned their eyes westward, where a veritable empire of land might be had for the clearing and claiming.

King George III had other plans for his new lands, however. He hoped to secure their valuable fur trade for his own profit and that of his court favorites. Success depended on cooperation from the Indians, and to appease them, the King, in October 1763, proclaimed the region west of the Appalachian crest (along which the King's Proclamation Line was established) closed to settlement. This unpopular action played no small role in arousing Americans against their monarch and creating the mood that ultimately touched off the Revolutionary War. It *'et a mere 16 years later that distant waterway was vaulted vith the purchase of the Louisiana territory. And before hat immense expanse had even begun to be digested, the ntire Southwest and California came under U.S. sover-ignty, while the Pacific Northwest was annexed in 1846.*

To exploit this wide realm, thousands of families pushed vestward across the prairies and plains and through the now-choked mountain passes. Many perished, but more urvived to clear the forests, plow the high grass of the prai-ies, and build cities. Only a few generations have passed ince the taming of the last frontier, but already the taking f the land has become legend—an American odyssey.

Columbia's spirit *inspired the westward-bound pioneers in this 1873 allegory depicting the taming of the vast continent.*

was clear that so long as George III ruled over America, the claims of squatters and speculators alike might at any time be disallowed. Thus the grievances of the East against the Crown found a ready echo among settlers who had already crossed the mountains, as well as among would-be pioneers and men of property who had invested heavily in lands west of the Appalachians.

Meanwhile, Americans streamed west as if there were no Proclamation Line. By the end of 1765 some 2,000 families, mostly squatters without legal title to their holdings, had settled along the forks of the Ohio River in western Pennsylvania near Fort Pitt (later to become the city of Pittsburgh). Five years later there were 10,000 families. Farther to the south, frontiersman Daniel Boone had hacked out the Wilderness Road through the Appalachians' Cumberland Gap to open a route into Kentucky and Tennessee. Boone's trail was primitive and would accommodate nothing larger than a pack animal, but it opened the way for an endless stream of pioneers. Even before the Revolution was underway, the Kentucky woods were filled with the sound of falling trees as settlers began clearing the forests.

By 1780 more than 55,000 Americans had crossed the mountains into Kentucky and Tennessee. Of the terrible hardships they endured in their trek to the "Promised Land," one observer wrote: "Women and Children in the Month of Decembr, Travelling a Wilderness through Ice and Snow, passing large rivers and Creeks without Shoe or Stocking, and barely as many raggs as covers their Nakedness. . . . Here is Hundreds Travelling hundreds of Miles, they know not what for Nor Whither, except its to Kentucky . . . the Land of Milk and Honey." The great westward migration was on, and it would not end until, more than 100 years later, the young Nation had stamped its imprint from the Atlantic to the Pacific, from the Great Lakes to the Rio Grande.

During the Revolutionary War the campaigns led by Gen. George Rogers Clark in the Illinois country northwest of the Ohio River lent a degree of reality to the American claims on the wilderness, but eventually it was Britain's sense of enlightened self-interest that gave the new United States a western border at the Mississippi. In the Peace of Paris (1783), the British, hoping to loosen the bonds between America and her French allies, yielded the region beyond the mountains to the victorious former Colonies—a step that was also intended to forestall a possible French occupation of that strategic area.

Independent America Moves West

Postwar economic conditions along the seacoast were bad, and the westward movement gained momentum. By 1800 Ohio, where scarcely a white man had lived 15 years before, had more than 45,000 people busily clearing farmland and building towns, and 5,600 pioneers had already pushed into the Indiana wilderness. Back east the question of how these territories were to be governed caused concern. Most of the lands west of the Appalachians had been claimed by several States. Eventually all yielded their titles to the Continental Congress, which in 1787 passed the Northwest Ordinance. This foresighted measure outlined the procedures under which new territories might advance to full statehood, a process that depended primarily on population growth and the establishment of representative government. Ever since, the rules laid down by the ordinance have provided the legal framework through which most new States have entered the Union.

The Northwest Ordinance, with its guarantee of gradual self-government for territories under the umbrella of Federal protection, further spurred westward immigration. For most settlers farmland was the goal. During the early 19th century an English visitor, Harriet Mar-

Life on the Frontier
The Family Was on Its Own

Although the settlement of the vast continent took some two centuries, certain aspects of life along the shifting frontier remained constant throughout the long process. For those who blazed the way into the forested Midwest, the windswept plains, and finally the Oregon wilderness, isolation and loneliness were constant facts of life. Homesteading families had to rely on their own resources for both the necessities and the simple pleasures of life. More often than not, medical care and defense against marauding Indians were family affairs. Only rarely was the isolation of the widely separated farms and cattle ranches broken by the visit of a distant neighbor or by a family outing to a revivalist camp meeting or a trip to market.

Still, hard though this life was, it offered compensations. Certainly the American dream of independence and self-sufficiency owes much to the experience of the frontier, where everything from building houses to making clothes was the responsibility of the homesteader and his family. And for the children of the pioneers, the wide-stretching forests and endless plains were both a playground and a school. Their chores completed, the young could roam at will in a boundless wilderness, learning nature's secrets, its benefits, and its dangers, and honing the skills they would some day need to push the frontier still farther.

Frontier dwellings *were built from materials close at hand. Log cabins were common in both the Eastern woodlands and Pacific Northwest, where trees were plentiful. On the plains, however, settlers built dugouts (as shown) or sod houses from the soil they plowed. These dirty, dark homes were replaced by dwellings of wood as soon as a farmer could afford lumber.*

tineau, commented on this land hunger. "The pride and delight of Americans," she wrote, "is in their quantity of land. I do not remember meeting with one to whom it had occurred that they had too much. . . . The possession of land is the aim of all action . . . and the cure for all social evils. . . . If a man is disappointed in politics or love, he goes and buys land. If he disgraces himself, he betakes himself to a lot in the West. . . . If a citizen's neighbors rise above him in the town, he betakes himself where he can be monarch of all he surveys."

Luckily the supply of land seemed inexhaustible. Beyond the Western border of the United States lay the vast region on the other side of the Mississippi River, with whatever riches it might hold. In 1800 France forced Spain to cede title to the area loosely called Louisiana, which stretched from the Gulf of Mexico northward approximately to the 49th parallel and westward to the Rockies. In 1803 Napoleon, fearful that Britain might try to wrest Louisiana from France, suddenly offered the entire region to the United States at the bargain price of $15 million. Although President Thomas Jefferson entertained doubts about his constitutional authority to purchase the 530 million acres of woodlands, prairies, plains, valleys, and mountains, the offer seemed too good to reject. On April 30, 1803, with the signing of the Louisiana Purchase treaty, the United States more than doubled its territory and gained control of an important means of transportation, the Mississippi River, as well as the established port of New Orleans. Even before the purchase was contemplated, Jefferson had ordered his young secretary, Meriwether Lewis, to plan an expedition through the Louisiana territory and into the Oregon country, a region whose ownership was disputed between the United States and Britain. It was not until after the Louisiana Purchase was sealed, however, that Lewis and his coleader, William Clark, began their historic 3-year exploration, which was to give Americans the first detailed knowledge of their new domain.

Thousands of Mexicans *storm the Alamo, a Franciscan mission founded in 1722 and later used as a fortress. Vastly outnumbered, the Texans within the fort were all killed in the siege.*

Slowly the map of a continent-spanning nation was forming. In 1810 and 1813 the United States took over sections of West Florida, a Spanish-held region east of New Orleans, and in 1819, by the Adams-Onís Treaty, it acquired the rest of Florida from Spain, after Gen. Andrew Jackson had deposed the Spanish governor.

In January 1821 Spain, hoping to encourage the development of sparsely settled Texas, took the unusual step of granting land there to speculator Moses Austin for the settlement of 300 American families. Austin died before he could carry out the plan, but his older son, Stephen F. Austin, led the first group of American families, who arrived early in 1822. Meanwhile, Mexico had revolted against Spain, securing her independence and taking Texas with her. After some delay the new government confirmed the deal with Austin and in the late 1820's made further grants to other American speculators. During this period Mexico held her Texas province on a fairly loose rein, but in 1834 the pompous Gen. Antonio López de Santa Anna established a dictatorship and resolved to tighten his hold on the Texans. Hoping to benefit from the change in government, the Texans had at first supported Santa Anna, but soon they were in full rebellion, led by Stephen Austin and Sam Houston, a former Governor of Tennessee. The war, which lasted a little more than a year, was marked by both savagery and heroism. Santa Anna, who styled himself the Napoleon of the West, marched in with an army of several thousand to quell the revolt. In February 1836 he laid siege to the Alamo, a fortified mission near San Antonio. Inside were fewer than 200 Americans led by Col. William B. Travis, mountain man James Bowie, and frontiersman-politician Davy Crockett. To Santa Anna's demand for immediate surrender, Travis replied: "I shall never surrender or retreat. . . . Victory or death!" Every defender died in the final Mexican bombardment and charge of March 6, 1836.

Neither the defense of the Alamo nor Santa Anna's determination to reduce the fortress seem to be important from a purely strategic point of view. But the 2-week siege gave the Texans time to rally an army under the Lone Star banner, and the final bloody assault seared the souls of all American settlers, strengthening their resolve to resist Mexico. "Remember the Alamo!" became the battle cry of the Texas army commanded by Sam Houston. On April 21, 1836, Houston and 800 men swept down on a larger Mexican force camped along the San Jacinto River. Taken by surprise, the Mexicans were routed, and Santa Anna was captured. With his army in full retreat, the imprisoned Mexican dictator was obliged to recognize Texas' independence. In 1845 Texas entered the Union; her admission led to the Mexican War of 1846–48. (For more about the Mexican War, see "Battles Fought in Foreign Lands," pages 442–459.)

The Expedition of Lewis and Clark
An Epic of Fortitude—and Good Fortune

In Meriwether Lewis and William Clark, President Thomas Jefferson had two men of exceptional intelligence, adaptability, and courage—qualities they needed to lead a party of 32 persons across the wilderness acquired by the Louisiana Purchase and through the Oregon Country. Accompanied by an additional group of soldiers and boatmen, the explorers and their men left their camp near St. Louis on May 14, 1804, aboard a 55-foot keelboat and two smaller vessels. By late autumn they had forced their way up the Missouri almost to the Little Missouri, where they went into winter quarters among the hospitable Mandan Indians.

While waiting for spring, the party was joined by the interpreter Toussaint Charbonneau, his Indian wife Sacagawea, and their infant son. Sacagawea proved invaluable when the expedition reached her Shoshone kinsmen's territory; there by chance she met her brother and his warriors, who provided horses and information about the trails to the west. Early in April 1805 Lewis and Clark resumed their travels, which were punctuated by parleys with tribal chiefs and delayed by difficult mountain portages around great waterfalls and rapids. Eventually they reached the westward-flowing Clearwater, Snake, and Columbia Rivers and, on November 7, 1805, came to the Oregon coast. At the mouth of the Columbia the explorers built a collection of rude cabins they called Fort Clatsop. There they spent a chilly, uncomfortable winter, but their sojourn buttressed the U.S. claim to the Oregon Country, finally purchased from England 40 years later.

When Lewis and Clark returned to St. Louis on September 23, 1806, they had completed a 7,689-mile journey, much of it through territory no white man had seen before. During their 28-month expedition they had made the first U.S. crossing from the Missouri River to the Pacific and had gathered extensive data on the Western Indians, the locations of the rich trapping grounds, and the region's flora, fauna, and climate.

Meriwether Lewis

William Clark

This elkhide-bound *notebook was one of many that Lewis and Clark filled with observations. The notes record a meeting with Indians who gave them skins and deer meat in exchange for a medal and some silk.*

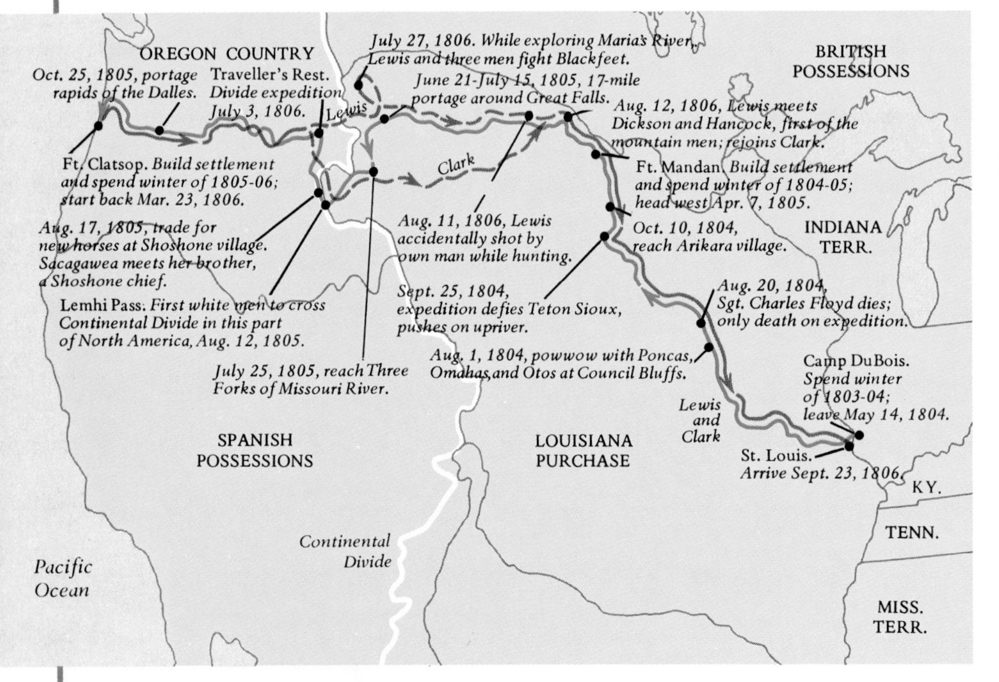

Flathead Indians arrive *to parley with Lewis and Clark in the shadow of a range of Rocky Mountains in Charles M. Russell's painting (right). President Jefferson had instructed the explorers to open friendly relations with the Indians of the Far West, and the two men proved themselves adept diplomats. The Flatheads proved most friendly, providing horses for a 9-day mountain portage. The weary expedition rested in this valley before going on to Lolo Pass.*

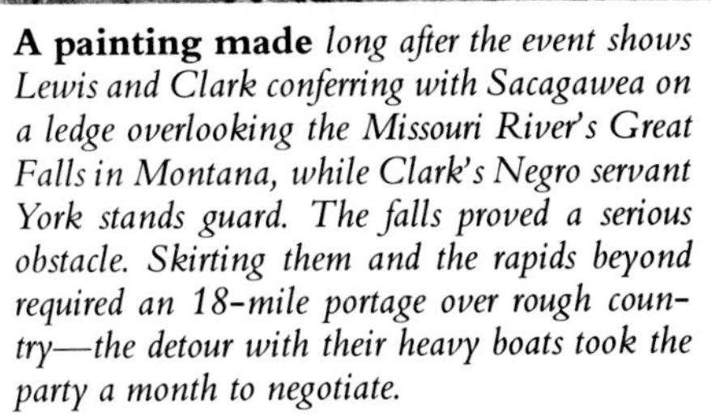

A painting made *long after the event shows Lewis and Clark conferring with Sacagawea on a ledge overlooking the Missouri River's Great Falls in Montana, while Clark's Negro servant York stands guard. The falls proved a serious obstacle. Skirting them and the rapids beyond required an 18-mile portage over rough country—the detour with their heavy boats took the party a month to negotiate.*

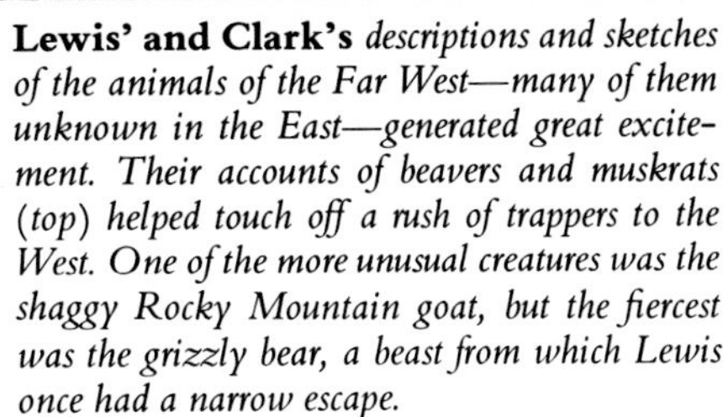

Lewis' and Clark's *descriptions and sketches of the animals of the Far West—many of them unknown in the East—generated great excitement. Their accounts of beavers and muskrats (top) helped touch off a rush of trappers to the West. One of the more unusual creatures was the shaggy Rocky Mountain goat, but the fiercest was the grizzly bear, a beast from which Lewis once had a narrow escape.*

Settling Down in the New Lands

Meanwhile, the old frontier east of the Mississippi was filling up with settlers, farms, and urban centers. For most of the pioneers life was a constant struggle against the Indians, the elements, and the land itself, which had to be laboriously cleared before it could be planted. Daniel Drake, a 19th-century frontier physician, recalled his childhood in Kentucky in terms that might well have been echoed by thousands. Describing his family's log cabin, Dr. Drake wrote that "in due . . . time [it] acquired a puncheon [split-log] floor below and a clapboard roof above, a small square window without glass and a chimney. . . . The rifle . . . lay on two pegs. . . . The axe and scythe were kept at night under the bed as weapons . . . in case Indians should make an attack."

Life was not always grim, but even the frontiersmen's pleasures—cornhuskings and quilting bees, wood-sawing contests, community barn raisings, and hunting—were mostly related to the pressing business of survival. Important in the settlers' lives, too, was religion, usually of the evangelical variety. Camp meetings provided solace and hope as well as a reason for widely scattered neighbors to congregate and enjoy each other's company.

MAKING DEMOCRACY WORK

The Preemption and Homestead Acts

As Americans moved westward the question of how the public domain was to be divided became increasingly acute. Speculators, who hoped to resell these lands at a great profit, sought legislation that would favor their interests by limiting sales to those who could afford to buy immense plots of wilderness land. Eastern commercial interests, fearing that cheap land would deprive them of their labor supply, generally stood with the speculators. But ordinary pioneers demanded cheap or even free land from their Government. At first the Government favored the speculators, but as popular pressure developed for inexpensive land, Congress began to yield. Actually, the Government had little choice, for by the 1830's thousands of pioneers had settled on unsurveyed land, improved it, and claimed it for their own. The Preemption Act of 1841 legitimized this situation by giving these squatters the right to buy 160 acres for $1.25 an acre.

This principle of cheap land, once established, was soon expanded. The Homestead Act of 1862 made much of the public domain virtually free. Under its terms, any adult male who would reside on and cultivate 160 acres for five years could achieve full title for a small fee. Both preemption and homesteading, though often abused for speculative purposes, helped make the family farm an American institution.

By the 1840's one source of worry along the old frontier had been eliminated. Through military actions and Government edicts, the Indians of the forests and swamps had been dispossessed. After signing numerous solemn treaties guaranteeing Indian rights, the Government, yielding to the land-hungry, had pushed the Indians into regions beyond the Mississippi.

Most whites believed the grasslands west of the great river were unsuitable for farming. This delusion stemmed from the reports of two Army officers. In 1805 Lt. Zebulon Pike led a group from St. Louis into Minnesota to explore the headwaters of the Mississippi. This successful trek won Pike command of a Southwest expedition that took him far into Spanish-held lands in 1806–07. In Colorado he discovered what is now Pikes Peak and then was captured by Spanish soldiers who took him to Chihuahua and later deported him to the United States. In an account of his journey, published in 1810, Pike described much of the region through which he had traveled as wasteland. This view was seconded by Maj. Stephen H. Long, who in 1820 followed the Platte River, traveled into Colorado where he discovered the peak that now bears his name, and returned through the present States of Kansas and Oklahoma. Long gave such a bleak report of this portion of the Great Plains that the entire plains area came to be called "The Great American Desert" and was avoided by early settlers.

The Mormon Exodus Into the Desert

Not all whites, however, were discouraged by such grim descriptions. Among those who saw in the vast and almost empty spaces a hope for salvation were the Mormons, members of a religious sect (officially named The Church of Jesus Christ of Latter-day Saints) founded by Joseph Smith in 1830. Their communal lifestyle and growing prosperity had aroused the jealousy and suspicion of their neighbors. The Mormon practice of polygamy had turned suspicion into hatred. Hounded from Ohio to Missouri and on into Illinois and Iowa, the Mormons, under the leadership of Brigham Young, Smith's successor, sought the isolation of the West where they might live in peace and build a "new Jerusalem."

In 1847 an advance guard of Mormons struck out westward over the prairie, crossed the High Plains, and struggled through the Rockies until, on July 24, they came to the dreary flats beside the Great Salt Lake in Utah. There, far from the nearest white settlement, Young established his theocracy. Within 3 years some 5,000 "Saints," as the Mormons called themselves, had migrated across the plains to devote their energies to making the desert bloom. Hardship and privation were the lot of these first pioneers in the Rocky Mountain region, but their faith kept their spirits high, and their zeal was crowned with success. One of Young's followers

Our Nation's Expansion
In Less Than 300 Years

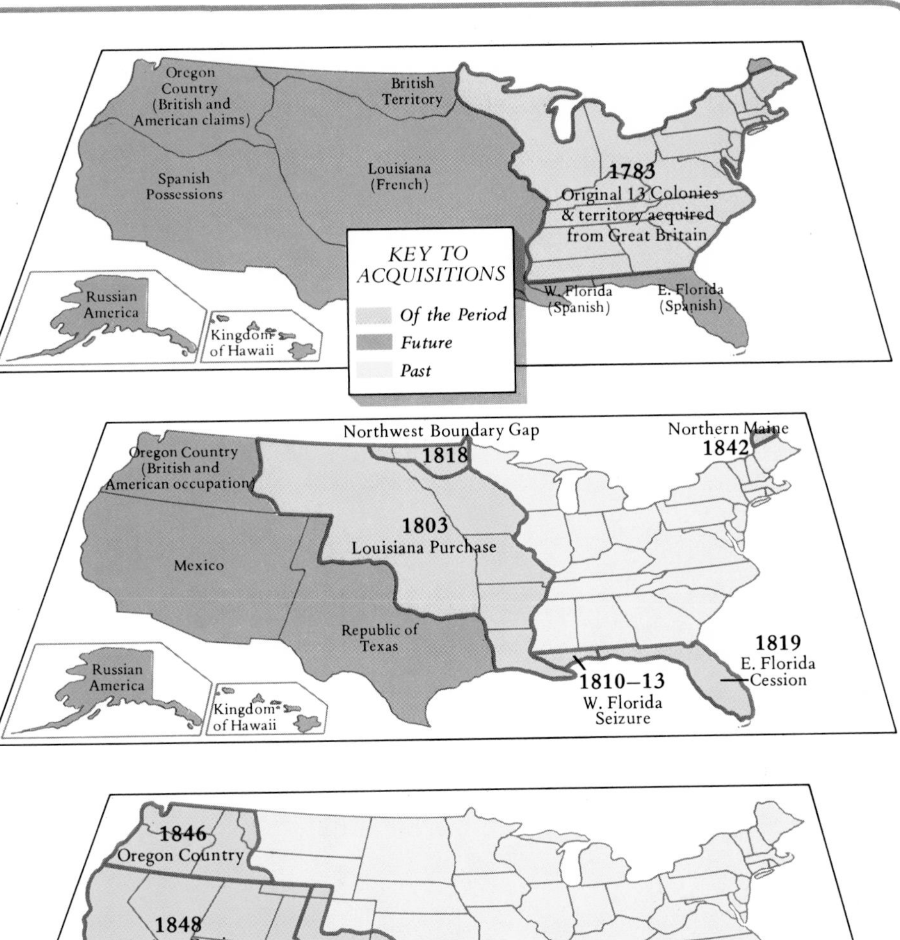

1607–1802. *For well over a century after the establishment of the first successful English colony, European settlement was limited to a narrow coastal strip. But by the time the Revolutionary War ended in 1783, American pioneers had already pushed beyond the Appalachians. Eager to conclude a peace treaty, Britain granted the United States sovereignty over the massive trans-Appalachian wilderness.*

1803–1844. *In one of history's greatest bargains, the United States, aided by French fears that her Louisiana territory might fall to British arms, was able to purchase the enormous region—stretching from Louisiana in the south to present-day Montana in the north and west—for $15 million. Seven years later the United States began chipping away at Spain's Florida colony, a process completed in 1819 with the Adams-Onís Treaty. Disputes with Britain over the Canadian border from eastern Maine to the Continental Divide were peacefully settled by treaties in 1818 and 1842.*

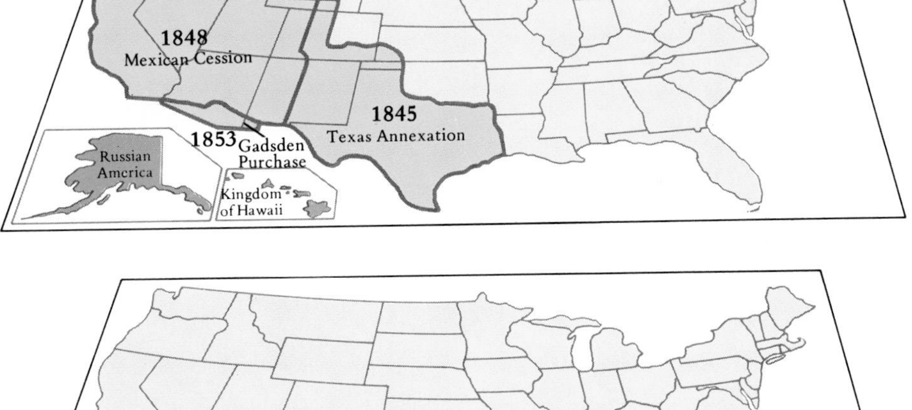

1845–1866. *After the annexation of Texas in 1845, a border dispute with Mexico led to war with that nation. After 2 years of fighting, the Treaty of Guadalupe Hidalgo, in which Mexico ceded California and vast stretches of the Southwest to the United States, was signed (1848). Meanwhile, the dispute with Britain over control of the Oregon Country was settled in 1846, with the United States gaining sovereignty of the region south of the 49th parallel. In 1853 U.S. negotiator James Gadsden arranged the purchase of a strip of land from Mexico to provide right-of-way for a railroad.*

1867–1898. *The Civil War had hardly ended before Secretary of State William Seward opened negotiations that led to the purchase of Alaska from the Russians. Though the vast region was bought for a mere $7.2 million, many Americans considered the purchase a total waste of money and the Secretary of State was roundly mocked for his largesse with public funds. Present-day U.S. borders were achieved with the annexation of Hawaii in 1898, an event that occurred 5 years after American settlers in those islands overthrew the ancient Hawaiian monarchy and established a republic.*

Dates of Statehood

Delaware	*Dec. 7, 1787*
Pennsylvania	*Dec. 12, 1787*
New Jersey	*Dec. 18, 1787*
Georgia	*Jan. 2, 1788*
Connecticut	*Jan. 9, 1788*
Massachusetts	*Feb. 6, 1788*
Maryland	*Apr. 28, 1788*
S. Carolina	*May 23, 1788*
New Hampshire	*June 21, 1788*
Virginia	*June 25, 1788*
New York	*July 26, 1788*
N. Carolina	*Nov. 21, 1789*
Rhode Island	*May 29, 1790*
Vermont	*Mar. 4, 1791*
Kentucky	*June 1, 1792*
Tennessee	*June 1, 1796*
Ohio	*Mar. 1, 1803*
Louisiana	*Apr. 30, 1812*
Indiana	*Dec. 11, 1816*
Mississippi	*Dec. 10, 1817*
Illinois	*Dec. 3, 1818*
Alabama	*Dec. 14, 1819*
Maine	*Mar. 15, 1820*
Missouri	*Aug. 10, 1821*
Arkansas	*June 15, 1836*
Michigan	*Jan. 26, 1837*
Florida	*Mar. 3, 1845*
Texas	*Dec. 29, 1845*
Iowa	*Dec. 28, 1846*
Wisconsin	*May 29, 1848*
California	*Sept. 9, 1850*
Minnesota	*May 11, 1858*
Oregon	*Feb. 14, 1859*
Kansas	*Jan. 29, 1861*
West Virginia	*June 20, 1863*
Nevada	*Oct. 31, 1864*
Nebraska	*Mar. 1, 1867*
Colorado	*Aug. 1, 1876*
North Dakota	*Nov. 2, 1889*
South Dakota	*Nov. 2, 1889*
Montana	*Nov. 8, 1889*
Washington	*Nov. 11, 1889*
Idaho	*July 3, 1890*
Wyoming	*July 10, 1890*
Utah	*Jan. 4, 1896*
Oklahoma	*Nov. 16, 1907*
New Mexico	*Jan. 6, 1912*
Arizona	*Feb. 14, 1912*
Alaska	*Jan. 3, 1959*
Hawaii	*Aug. 21, 1959*

Possessions and Other Holdings

Possession	Year
Navassa	*1865*
Midway Islands	*1867*
Guam	*1898*
Johnston and Sand Islands	*1898*
Puerto Rico (*Commonwealth status since 1952*)	*1898*
American Samoa	*1899*
Wake Island	*1899*
Canal Zone (*Leased from Panama "in perpetuity"*)	*1903*
Palmyra Island	*1912*
Virgin Islands of the U.S.	*1917*
Kingman Reef	*1922*
Baker Island	*1936*
Howland Island	*1936*
Jarvis Island	*1936*
Micronesia (*U.N. Trust Territory*)	*1947*

Fleeing persecution *in Illinois, Mormon refugees flock across the Mississippi River into Iowa during the winter of 1846. The next spring an advance guard of Mormons under the leadership of Brigham Young blazed the Mormon Trail westward beyond the Rockies into Utah. There, beside the Great Salt Lake, they established their Zion and, like the Israelites of old, they made the desert bloom. By 1850 Salt Lake City had a population of 5,000, and a decade later about 12,000 Mormons lived and prospered in the city and its environs.*

wrote: "When I commune with my own heart and ask myself whether I would choose to dwell here in this wild looking country amongst the Saints . . . or dwell amongst the gentiles with all their wealth . . . the soft whisper echoes loud . . . give me the quiet wilderness."

The isolation that the Mormons sought was illusory. The war between Mexico and the United States was being fought even as the first Mormons arrived at the site of their future capital, and in 1848 the Mormon state of Deseret—along with Colorado, New Mexico, Arizona, Nevada, and California—came under the Stars and Stripes. There followed a period of conflict between the Mormons and the U.S. Government, based on religious and political differences and misunderstandings. The difficulties were eventually ironed out, and the Mormon territory became the State of Utah in 1896.

Frémont the Pathfinder and the Route West

One of the men who helped bring California into the Union was John Charles Frémont, a young Army officer called the Pathfinder. Flamboyant adventurer, dedicated explorer, and ambitious officeseeker, Frémont had the good fortune to be wed to Jessie Benton, a daughter of Missouri's powerful Senator and longtime advocate of transcontinental expansion, Thomas Hart Benton. In 1842 Lieutenant Frémont was made the head of an expedition to explore the Far West and examine the Platte River-South Pass route to Oregon. With the famous Indian fighter and mountain man Kit Carson as its guide, Frémont's party moved up the Platte and the Sweetwater Valleys to South Pass, marched on to the Green River, and later explored the Wind River Range in Wyoming. Frémont's report, vivified by his wife's literary skills, brought him instant fame and created a surge of national interest in the unknown West. In May 1843 Frémont left on another journey in which he traversed an immense area of the Far West—including parts of Utah, Idaho, Oregon, and Nevada—and then moved into California, where he was impressed by both the potential of the country and the weakness of Mexican control.

A third expedition, begun in 1845, on the eve of the Mexican War, took Frémont into California again. There in June 1846 he participated in the Bear Flag Revolt by American settlers against Mexican authority, and in 1847 he led a battalion of settlers and his own men that helped wrest California from Mexico.

Frémont's well-publicized exploits made America more aware than ever of the "golden West," particularly the Oregon country. In his wake thousands began the long trip to the Pacific. The sudden influx of Americans fortified United States claims to the Oregon territory. In 1846 Britain, wishing no war over that distant piece of real estate, finally recognized American interests, and the border between America's Pacific Northwest and Canada was established at the 49th parallel, except for the extreme west where the borderline dipped south of Vancouver Island.

Two years later the Treaty of Guadalupe Hildalgo ended the Mexican War, and California and most of the Southwest became American in return for a token payment of $15 million. Only 85 years had passed since George III had established his Proclamation Line, only 72 since the Atlantic coast Colonies had declared their independence. Now the Nation encompassed a vast continental domain, though much of it remained to be settled and exploited.

John Charles Frémont, *famous as both a soldier and explorer, helped initiate the conquest of California by urging American settlers there to revolt against Mexican rule in 1846.*

California Strikes It Rich

On January 24, 1848, only 9 days before California was added to the American republic, gold was discovered at a sawmill at Coloma on the American River. The mill belonged to John Sutter, who ruled a huge domain from his stronghold of Fort Sutter (now within the city limits of Sacramento). By spring all California was in a frenzy. Entire towns lost all their able-bodied men. Hundreds of soldiers deserted their posts. In San Francisco Harbor ships were left to rot as seamen and captains alike hurried off to share in the bonanza.

When the news reached the East 6 months later, President James K. Polk thought it important enough to include in his message to Congress. Soon the Nation was infected with gold fever. Thousands laid down the tools of their trades to leave by land and by sea for California. Few struck it rich, but most stayed on to find jobs or to establish farms and businesses. California's population increased tenfold between 1848 and 1853.

COLEMAN'S CALIFORNIA LINE.
FOR
SAN FRANCISCO
CLIPPER OF SATURDAY, DECEMBER 25th
THE FIRST CLASS CLIPPER SHIP
DERBY
SAMUEL HUTCHINSON, Jr., Commander, is now rapidly loading at
PIER 15 EAST RIVER
WM. T. COLEMAN & CO.
88 WALL STREET, Tontine Building.
N.B. No SAL SODA taken by ships of this line.
Agents in San Francisco, Messrs. WM. T. COLEMAN & CO.
George F. Nesbitt & Co., Printers cor. of Pearl and Pine Streets, New-York.

Ships of every kind *and description ride at anchor in San Francisco Bay at the height of the Gold Rush. Of the tens of thousands who streamed into California in the late 1840's and early 1850's, many arrived on vessels such as these, a few of which were fast clipper ships that made the trip from the east coast around Cape Horn and up the Pacific coast in 100 days or less. Others were slower, older ships pressed into service to accommodate the thousands of gold-seekers willing to pay $300 and endure as much as 200 days of boredom—punctuated by bouts of seasickness—to reach California. Some California-bound prospectors chose a combination land-sea route, which included a trek through the jungles of the Isthmus of Panama. With optimum connections, this route could be negotiated in as little as 8 weeks, but for most of the travelers, even those lucky enough not to succumb to some tropical disease, there was a wait of many weeks for a ship out of Panama City to the golden promise of San Francisco.*

The Rush for Wealth in the Golden West

Immigrants From the World Over

The cry was "Gold!" and within a year of its discovery in 1848 at John Sutter's California sawmill on the south fork of the American River, the word spread near and far. From Oregon and New England, from Turkey and China, from France and Australia, men converged on California by the tens of thousands. At roaring gold camps, with names like Red Dog, Hangtown, and Rich Bar, they built huts and pitched tents and set about the business of panning the waters of the American or San Joaquin rivers or scratching in nearby hills in hopes that fortune would favor them.

Indeed, some were lucky, fabulously lucky. At Rich Bar on the Feather River, several prospectors averaged $2,000 per day for their labors while one group of four men working together actually cleared $50,000 between one dawn and dusk. There were stories, some of them true, of men literally picking handfuls of gold-rich pebbles off the ground. For most, however, even at the height of the Gold Rush, an average of $20 a day was considered an acceptable return, while for many, weeks of backbreaking labor yielded virtually nothing. Others made fortunes by supplying gold seekers with necessities.

By the late 1850's the California Gold Rush was over. Four decades later another major trek to new goldfields began. This time Eldorado was in Alaska, for rich strikes had been made near Nome and Fairbanks. Overnight, a region long scorned as a valueless icebox became the focus of feverish activity. Thousands of hardy prospectors, heedless of biting winds and subzero cold, made their desperate bids for wealth, as shown on the facing page.

The first tool *of the prospector's trade was simplicity itself: nothing more than a shallow-sided pan that the miner filled with gravel from a river bottom and carefully washed out with water. Heavy, gold-bearing particles, if any, settled to the pan's bottom. More efficient, if more complex, was the sluice, a long box with a ridged bottom. Miners shoveled gravel into the sluice, washed it with a continual flow of water, so the heavy gold-bearing pieces would collect behind the crosspieces at the bottom of the sluice. An improved technique was the use of water wheels to feed the sluices and speed up operations. This required the cooperation of several prospectors who generally worked for equal shares of whatever profits where realized. Eventually, as the relatively easy pickings were exhausted, large mining concerns entered the picture. They had both the capital and expertise to dig deep tunnels into the hills and exploit the veins of gold to the fullest.*

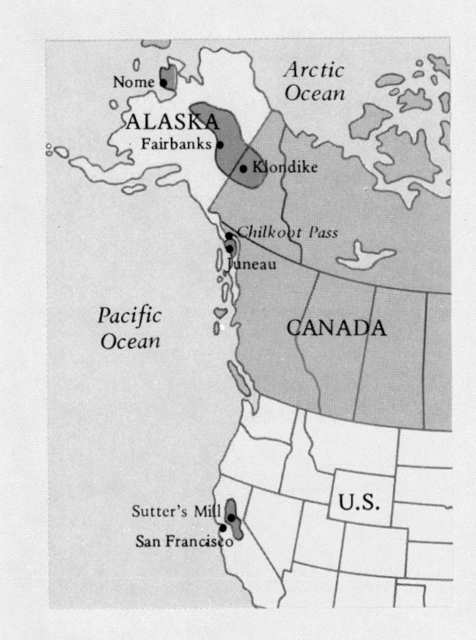

The Lure of Gold Leads to Statehood

Although a few thousand Americans had drifted into California by 1848, and many more had settled in the Oregon Country, the discovery of gold in California brought a population boom that in 1850 catapulted that territory to statehood, 9 years ahead of Oregon. Almost half a century later, the pattern was repeated far to the north. In 1897–98 prospectors had streamed into Canada's Yukon Territory, following the discovery of gold in Klondike Creek. Many who missed the Klondike rush headed west, into Alaska, where gold discoveries precipitated another rush. But it was another 60 years before Alaska became a State. Aided by a hospitable climate and transcontinental railroads, farming, commerce, and industry boomed in California. When Alaska's gold veins petered out, despite the area's rich resources of lumber and fish, economic growth was slow, hampered by a severe climate and the difficulties of transportation. World War II demonstrated Alaska's importance to national defense, and highway and air connections were vastly improved. Alaska's population more than doubled after the war (to 300,000 in the 1970's), and in 1959 Alaska became the 49th State. The discovery of huge petroleum reserves on the North Slope brought another boom to Alaska. An oil pipeline now goes to Valdez, one of the ports used by the Klondikers. The red areas on the map indicate the relative size and location of the gold-bearing areas that accelerated the movement into our Pacific frontier.

The Klondikers' goal *was the boomtown of Dawson in the Canadian Yukon Territory, which had a population of 25,000 by 1899. As this scene shows, the roistering town had a wide range of services, from saloons to dressmaking shops, general stores, hotels, and laundries.*

At least 100,000 people *dropped everything in their haste to join the Klondike rush in 1897–98. Thousands sailed up the Inside Passage to Dyea, where the fearsome Chilkoot Trail began. At the Scales (left) 1,200 steps cut in the ice and snow led over 3,500-foot Chilkoot Pass. Battered by incessant snow-laden winds, prospectors took at least 6 hours to climb 1,000 feet. An aerial tram, powered by electricity, carried equipment over the pass, but most of the prospectors could not afford this service. Chilkoot Indians, hired as porters, were said to have made more money than many Klondikers.*

Perils of the Westward Trek

Many of the tens of thousands who journeyed to the Pacific during the 1840's and 1850's took the Oregon Trail. In early spring wagon trains left Independence, Missouri, heading up the Platte Valley of Nebraska and crossing the Wyoming country to Fort Bridger. There the travelers veered northward to Fort Hall in Idaho, then west through the Blue Mountains, and north again to the Columbia River, which they followed to the coast. Travelers bound for California left the Oregon Trail at Fort Hall and headed southwest across Nevada and through the Sierra Nevadas into California before winter storms made the mountains impassable.

However they went, most pioneers could be certain of a full measure of hardship along the way—starvation, disease, thirst, and Indian harassment. None fared worse than the California-bound Donner and Reed families from Illinois. Instead of striking north from Fort Bridger to the turnoff at Fort Hall, 87 members of the Donner party elected to use the Hastings Cutoff, which took them southwestward across the savagely hot Great Salt Lake Desert before picking up the California Trail in Nevada. This shortened the route to California, but the desert heat took a heavy toll of the party's oxen and horses, and the wagon train fell behind schedule, reaching the awesome Sierra Nevadas when the passes were already blocked with snow. Low on food and weakened by hunger, the travelers built several cabins near Truckee (now Donner) Lake in the winter of 1846–47 and sent a small party out to seek aid. Although rescue parties from California were able to reach the group eventually, 39 had died of exposure or starvation, and several had survived only by eating the flesh of their dead comrades. But even such gruesome experiences could not dampen the pioneers' spirits for long. One Donner survivor, an adolescent girl, was soon writing a glowing account of the Far West to a friend back East, urging her to make the journey no matter what dangers she might encounter on the way.

"The Grand Canyon of the Yellowstone," *artist Thomas Moran's depiction of a natural wonder he said was "beyond the reach of human art," so impressed Congressmen that it helped persuade them to establish Yellowstone National Park in 1872. Moran, who journeyed to the Yellowstone Valley with an official survey team in 1871, made numerous sketches of the glories he observed. Together with equally dramatic photographs, taken by William H. Jackson, they provided eloquent testimony that such country was a national treasure, far too valuable for private exploitation or development. Yellowstone became the first reserve of its kind in the world and the model for our national park system.*

A Most Hospitable "Desert"

With the settlement of the west coast well under way by the end of the 1850's, Americans began to turn their eyes to the region between the Missouri River and the Rockies—the Great American Desert. Only the eastern fringe of this vast area—parts of Kansas and Nebraska—had been settled. After Kansas and Nebraska were made Territories in 1854, thousands of whites moved into Kansas alone. Among them were abolitionists and supporters of slavery. For several years before the Civil War began, these two groups fought for supremacy, giving the Nation a foretaste of the combat to come.

Large-scale exploitation of the Great Plains did not begin until the post-Civil War period when cheap, good land in the East and Far West became scarce. The Homestead Act, permitting settlers to claim 160 acres on payment of a small fee, spurred migration, especially after a burst of railroad building across the Plains in the 1860's and 1870's linked the West with Eastern markets. The Plains, far from being a desert, proved an ideal region for raising cattle. In time, too, as settlers developed the techniques of dry farming, they were able to raise bumper crops of grain on the less arid parts of the Great Plains. And for the expanding railroads, beef on the hoof and good grain harvests meant high profits.

To encourage settlement of the West, the railroads vigorously pushed the sale of the millions of acres of land the Government had granted them to make the building of the lines more attractive to investors. Agents were even sent to Europe to recruit settlers with tales of the wealth awaiting them in the American West. One clever promoter lured Germans to America by naming Bismarck, North Dakota, after the Chancellor of Germany.

Figures help to illuminate the story. Between 1870 and 1880, immigration from abroad was heavy. But, while States such as New York and Ohio were making relatively modest gains, South Dakota's population soared from 11,000 to 98,000, Nebraska's from 123,000 to 452,000, and Colorado's from 40,000 to 194,000. During this period of settlement and development of resources, the Federal Government sent such men as John Wesley Powell and Ferdinand V. Hayden on extensive geological surveys. Their reports focused national attention on the weather and the scenic wonders of the High Plains and mountain areas, and stimulated serious interest in the establishment of national parks.

As exploitation of the West continued, the Plains Indians were increasingly viewed as a threat to settlement, and the Government undertook by a variety of devices to remove them from desirable land. Armed expeditions brought tragic massacres, such as those at Sand Creek in 1864 and at Wounded Knee in 1890, as well as the engagement at the Little Bighorn, where Lt. Col. George Armstrong Custer and five companies of U.S. cavalry were wiped out in 1876. Fully as effective as military action in destroying the Plains Indians was the slaughter of the buffaloes on which they depended for meat and hides. For years the buffalo herds had been decreasing under the assault of so-called sportsmen and meat hunters for commercial butchering firms and for railroad construction crews; but the end came for the buffalo under the guns of the professional hide hunters during the 1870's and early 1880's. An estimated 15 million buffaloes were killed, and the great beasts came perilously close to extinction. Extinction, for all practical purposes, was also the fate of the Indians that followed the herds.

By the end of the 19th century the United States had secured its transcontinental realm. First had come the trailblazers who explored the land; then the soldiers who seized it from its former owners. Finally, millions of settlers poured in—from the Eastern reaches of the Nation and from Europe—to farm and mine the land, to put barbed wire around its grassy stretches, and to build small

MAKING DEMOCRACY WORK

Our National Parks

No nation had ever done anything like it. Indeed, the very idea of the Federal Government's setting aside a portion of the public domain for use as a national "pleasuring ground" instead of for private exploitation by farmers, ranchers, or miners had a faintly improper ring, particularly in the "robber baron" era of unbridled private enterprise following the Civil War. Nevertheless, depictions by artists and photographers and the reports of official survey teams all pointed to one inevitable conclusion: that the Yellowstone region of the Rocky Mountains was of such exceptional beauty, such awe-inspiring dimensions, that this sublime gift of nature must belong in perpetuity to the entire American people. Accordingly, Congress passed and President Grant signed legislation establishing Yellowstone National Park, which over the years has been extended to take in 2.2 million acres of breathtakingly beautiful country in Idaho, Montana, and—mainly—Wyoming.

Almost two decades passed before new national parks were created, and then, in 1890, Sequoia and Yosemite were both established in California. Subsequently, the pace quickened, particularly during Theodore Roosevelt's conservation-minded administration (1901–09), when eight new national parks were established. Today there are 38 national parks, most of them in the West, covering more than 14 million acres. Additional millions of acres have been set aside as national monuments, national recreation areas, national forests, and national seashores. Within these sanctuaries millions of vacationing Americans each year enjoy days or weeks of relaxation amid nature's most impressive splendors—preserved by man for posterity.

Closing in *on a herd of buffalo, Indians of the plains risk life and limb to secure the meat, hides, and tendons on which their very survival depends. The slaughter of the herds by whites destroyed the Indians' economy and helped force them onto reservations.*

A Disgraceful Record
Of Broken Treaties and Diminishing Indian Lands

Seizure of the land that supported the Indians' way of life started as soon as the first colonists stepped ashore. The incursions increased steadily and the red man's defenses were weakened by the superiority of the invaders' weapons, by broken treaties, and by the inroads of the white man's diseases. Inexorably, the Indians were pushed from their homes and hunting grounds into areas unwanted by the whites. Those diminishing areas are shown in green on the maps at right. In recent years there has been some effective effort to honor Indian claims to disputed lands. The Indian population, too, has made a comeback: from 248,253 in 1890 to 792,730 in 1970.

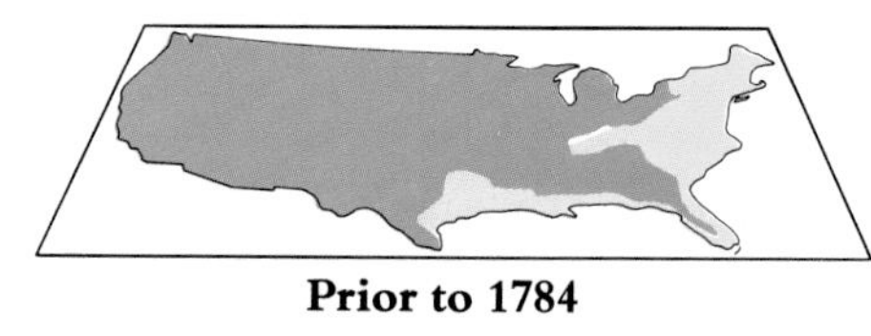

Prior to 1784

1784–1810

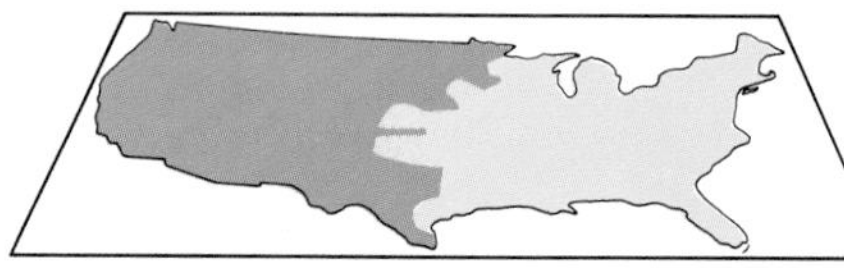

1811–1850

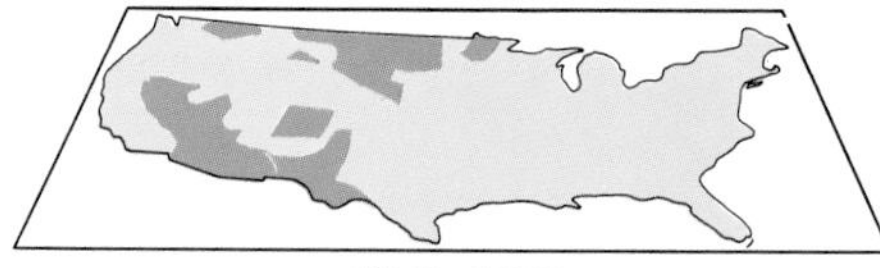

1851–1870

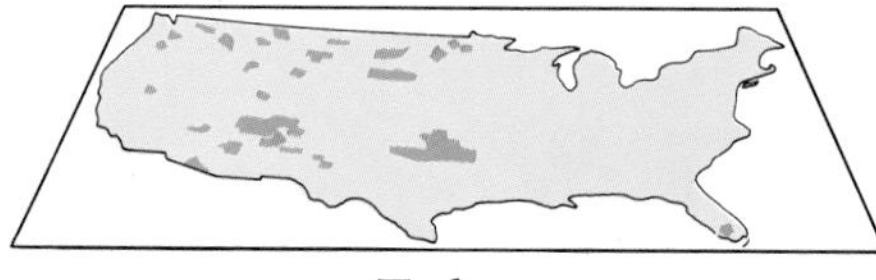

Today

On this treaty-ground *at Prairie du Chien, the United States sponsored a treaty among the warring Sioux and Chippewa tribes. This agreement, too, was doomed to fail.*

villages and great cities on its face. The frontier was a thing of the past, and with its disappearance an epoch of American history had come to an end.

The Ruthless Advance Across Indian Lands

For the Indians of the United States, the American Dream has been nothing less than a nightmare. From the landing of the first English settlers at the beginning of the 17th century, to the closing of the last frontier near the turn of the 20th century, the Indians have been the victims of almost unrelieved woe. Those tribes that escaped annihilation by the white man's bullets and diseases suffered instead something close to cultural genocide.

At the root of the centuries-long confrontation between red man and white was one inescapable fact: The Indians inhabited vast territories that the whites had to have in order to fulfill their "Manifest Destiny . . . as allotted by Providence" to develop the continent. It mattered little what precautions the Indians took to preserve their lands, what alliances they formed, what concessions they made, what solemn treaties they secured from the settlers; the story was always the same. Whenever the white moved west he displaced the Indian by force of arms, by destroying his hunting grounds, or by fraudulent treaties in which the uncomprehending red man often exchanged his patrimony for glittering trinkets.

Unlike the Indians under Spanish rule in South and Central America, the North American Indians did not provide the white man with cheap labor, and little effort was made to bring them into the white man's economic and social institutions. For as long as possible they held to their tribal ways in the face of a vacillating policy that, at one period, fed them in the winter and fought them bitterly in summer campaigns.

By the time of the American Revolution the destruction of the various tribal cultures of the east coast Indians was virtually complete. The process began with the Powhatans of Virginia. These, the first red men to rise in anger against incursions on their domains, killed some 600 settlers in two attacks, one in 1622 and another in 1644. The colonial militia in reprisal killed more than 7,000 of the 8,000 members of the tribe.

Massasoit, chief of the Wampanoags, kept his treaty of friendship with the Puritans of Massachusetts for 40 years, but his son Metacomet (also known by his Christian name, Philip, and dubbed King Philip by the whites) was determined to prevent further intrusion on Indian land. He forged an alliance with the powerful Narragansets of Rhode Island and led murderous attacks on New England villages in 1675–76. But the firepower of the settlers proved too great in the end, and the two tribes were destroyed. Most of the men, including Philip, were killed and the women and children sold into slavery.

Driven from their traditional territories, the remnants of the coastal tribes moved inland to the mountains and forests, there to make war on local tribes in a quest for new footholds. The settlers pursued them, felling trees, plowing the land, building villages, and pushing the Indians ever farther west. Time and again the Mississippi Valley tribes rose up, hoping to save some portion of their lands. Tecumseh, chief of the Shawnees, formed a far-reaching alliance with other Midwestern tribes early in the 19th century and waged fierce war on settlers. But all hope of maintaining a hold on areas east of the great river was dashed during the War of 1812, when American victories over the English and their Indian allies sealed the Eastern red man's doom.

In the decades after the War of 1812, the Federal Government adopted a policy of pushing the Indians to the grasslands west of the Missouri, where it was thought no white man would ever wish to settle. On their new holdings, solemnly granted by the Government for "as long as the grass shall grow," the displaced red men could either adopt the free-roaming existence of the local tribesmen, who followed the buffalo, or they could try to scratch out a livelihood by farming. But during the Civil War and in the years that followed, gold was discovered in the Black Hills of the Dakotas and silver in the Rockies, and the grasslands proved valuable for both stockraising and extensive cultivation.

Back east the voices of white defenders of Indian rights were drowned out by those demanding either the slaughter of the Indians or their removal to reservations. Among the minority who championed the Indian cause were abolitionists Wendell Phillips and the first Protestant Episcopal Bishop of Minnesota, Henry B. Whipple. During the Civil War, Bishop Whipple called on Americans to "rise up and with one voice to demand the reform of an atrocious Indian system which has always garnered . . . the same fruit of anguish and blood." On the other hand there was James M. Cavanaugh, Montana Territory's delegate to Congress, who stated: "I have never in my life seen a good Indian . . . except when I have seen a dead Indian." While many mourned the wanton slaughter of peaceful Indian women and children by Colorado militia at Sand Creek, Colorado, in 1864, others agreed with Gen. William T. Sherman, who held: "The more we can kill this year, the less will have to be killed in the next. . . . They all have to be killed or be maintained as a species of paupers."

General Sherman's view was heartily supported by the flamboyant Civil War hero Lieutenant Colonel Custer, who was eager to enhance his military reputation at the expense of the Indians. Custer minced no words:

The Trail of Tears

Some Indian tribes met the onrush of white civilization by adopting Christianity as well as the white man's dress and mannerisms, and turning to a wholly agricultural lifestyle. One such, the most renowned of the so-called Five Civilized Tribes, was the Cherokee Nation of western Georgia, which even had its own written constitution. But for the Cherokees, as for the other civilized tribes of the region, assimilation proved no protection against expulsion when white settlers began to clamor for their lands.

Although the Cherokee holdings were guaranteed by a 1791 treaty between the tribe and the Federal Government, the administration of President Andrew Jackson supported the efforts of the Georgia government to force the Indians off their land. Finally, in 1838, Jackson's successor, Martin Van Buren, dispatched Gen. Winfield Scott and 7,000 soldiers to Georgia with orders to expel the Cherokees and transport them to newly established Indian territory in distant Oklahoma. One soldier, sickened by his task, described an all too common scene that year: "I saw the helpless Cherokees arrested and dragged from their homes and driven by bayonet into stockades. In the chill . . . rain I saw them loaded like cattle or sheep into wagons and started toward the west."

The trek to Oklahoma, called by the Cherokees the Trail of Tears, took a tragic toll; many of them fell ill, and thousands died from exposure, disease, and starvation and were buried in unmarked graves.

"When the soil which he [the Indian] has claimed and hunted over . . . is demanded by [white civilization], there is no appeal; he must yield or it will roll mercilessly over him, destroying as it advances." Custer considered himself the archangel of this destruction, and on November 17, 1868, he led his 7th Cavalry in an attack on the Cheyenne camp of Chief Black Kettle along the Washita River in Indian Territory (later Oklahoma). More than 100 Cheyennes were killed (including Black Kettle and his wife and younger son), but the surprised Indians managed to kill or wound 35 of Custer's men.

With their backs to the wall, the Indians of the West set the plains and mountains afire in a decade-long struggle to retain something of their heritage. The superb horsemen of the Apache, Sioux, Arapaho, Cheyenne, and Crow Nations raided forts, settlements, wagon trains, farms, and ranches, spreading death and destruction. The Army responded with punitive campaigns, matching slaughter with slaughter. Finally, on June 25, 1876, the Indian wars of the West reached a climax when some 210 officers and troopers of the 7th Cavalry led by Custer himself were surrounded by Sioux and Cheyenne warriors near the Little Bighorn River in Montana and every Army man was killed. The battle, often called Custer's Last Stand, also proved to be the Indians' last major triumph. Enraged Americans became determined to "pacify" the Indians. Reinforcements were dispatched to the frontier to hunt down the last of the free-roaming tribes—an assignment that the Army carried out with cold efficiency, despite rearguard actions fought by some tribes and the brilliant retreat of the Nez Percés under the great Chief Joseph. For the Indians the days of pride and glory were ended forever when the 7th Cavalry killed or wounded some 200 Sioux men, women, and children while attempting to disarm their warriors at Wounded Knee Creek, South Dakota, in December 1890. The decades of frustration and repression on Government reservations for all the Indians had begun.

The Oklahoma Land Rush
First Come, First Served

Early in the 19th century the Federal Government selected the semiarid, windswept plains of Oklahoma country as a convenient dumping ground for the Indians of the East whose holdings were being transferred to white settlers. Later, the same territory was used to relocate numerous plains tribes displaced by pioneers. By the 1880's more than 30 tribes—among them the Cherokees, Creeks, Choctaws, Chickasaws, and Seminoles from the East, the Cheyennes, Arapahoes, Kiowas, and Comanches from the plains, and the Apaches from the Southwest—had received Government land grants in Oklahoma, which were to be theirs "forever."

But pressure from would-be settlers and from railroads that wanted to cash in on land sales along their rights-of-way forced the Federal Government to reconsider. By the early 1880's white adventurers—railroad hirelings called boomers—were regularly invading the Indians' territory to publicize its attractions for homesteaders. They helped generate a public outcry against leaving Oklahoma in the hands of "shiftless" Indians. In 1889 the Government began to yield to pressure and opened a portion of the territory to white settlement, precipitating the first great rush for farmland in Oklahoma.

By dawn of April 22, 1889, thousands of pioneers—some on foot, but most on horses and mules or in wagons and carriages—had lined up on the border of the Oklahoma lands; at noon the sound of a signal gun sent them racing into the flat, dry Indian territory. Would-be farmers carried sledges and stakes with which to mark off their homestead claims of 160 acres. Townsmen carried the tools of their trades so they could immediately set up shop to service the hordes of land seekers. Within several hours a deserted area near a rail depot had been converted into the town of Guthrie, where some 15,000 people milled about, clamoring to register land claims and secure the necessities of life from merchants selling their wares from tents.

The first Oklahoma *land rush opens amid swirling clouds of dust as would-be settlers, on horseback and in all manner of conveyances, engage in a frantic race to stake their claims.*

This first land rush was followed by several more, each one drastically reducing Indian holdings. The largest and wildest rush took place on September 16, 1893, when a part of Oklahoma called the Cherokee Outlet was opened for settlement. Finally, in 1906, the last portion of Oklahoma Territory was turned over to settlers. In 1907 Oklahoma entered the Union as the 46th State. Included within it was the land of the Five Civilized Tribes, who had hoped to have a state of their own.

Great Indian Leaders
Against Insurmountable Odds

Philip (*c. 1640–76*). Born Metacomet, King Philip was chief of New England's Wampanoag Indians, and in 1675–76 led a confederation of tribes in wide-ranging attacks through the white settlements. Although his swift raids on dozens of New England villages caused widespread death and destruction, he was unable to preserve Indian unity in the face of a white counter-offensive. After he was killed by an Indian scout serving with the colonists, his followers were dispersed or sold into slavery.

Pontiac (*c. 1720–69*). Chief of the Ottawas, Pontiac had been a strong supporter of France in the French and Indian War. Fearing that the English victory would bring a surge of white settlers in its wake, he led an alliance of 18 tribes against British forts and colonial settlements on the Western frontier in 1763. His short, but bloody uprising helped influence the British Government to establish the Proclamation Line of 1763, forbidding white settlement west of the Appalachians.

Black Hawk (*1767–1838*). Chief Black Hawk, disavowing a treaty by which the Sauk and Fox Indians had ceded their land in Illinois and Wisconsin, in 1832 led a small band of his people back across the Mississippi to plant crops on their old fields. Cries of settlers for protection brought troops who pursued the Indians—mostly women and children—through southern Wisconsin and defeated the remaining warriors at the Battle of Bad Axe. Before his death on an Iowa reservation, Black Hawk wrote his *Autobiography,* an eloquent but futile plea for the Indians' cause.

Tecumseh (*c. 1768–1813*) and **The Prophet** (*c. 1770–1834*). Tecumseh traveled from the Great Lakes to Florida in a valiant effort to unite the tribes in an Indian confederation to stand against the whites. Tecumseh's younger brother became a religious mystic, proclaimed himself a prophet and began a passionate crusade against all white ways. He was of great help to his brother, and the Shawnee capital on Tippecanoe Creek was named in his honor. But he was not a war leader, and while Tecumseh was away in 1811 he encouraged his braves to attack General William Henry Harrison. As the Prophet worked his "magic" at a distance, the Indians lost, and he was discredited.

Osceola (*c. 1803–38*). For 2 years (1835–37) Seminole leader Osceola waged a skillful guerrilla war against U.S. troops in Florida's dense and swampy Everglades. His purpose was to prevent the forced removal of his people from their hereditary lands to the distant West. Treacherously seized when he appeared for peace talks, Osceola died in prison in 1838, but a remnant of his followers survived and fought on until 1842. Many of the tribe live and work in Florida to this day.

Joseph, *chief of the Nez Percés*

Cochise (*c. 1812–74*). Chiricahua Apache Chief Cochise's friendly relations with the whites in Arizona ended in 1861 after he and other Apaches were seized during a flag of truce meeting with Army officers. Cochise escaped and led his warriors in merciless raids on settlements. The end of the Civil War freed troops for use against Cochise, and he was finally forced to surrender in 1872, agreeing to keep the peace when his friend the Army scout Thomas Jeffords was appointed Indian agent.

Geronimo (*c. 1829–1909*). In the Southwest, in the mid- and late-1800's, no one struck more terror into the hearts of Americans and Mexicans than Geronimo, a chief of the Chiricahua Apaches. A superb horseman and a skillful tactician, Geronimo led countless raids through New Mexico and Arizona and into Mexico. For 18 months, in 1885–86, he and his followers eluded the 5,000 U.S. soldiers sent to track him down. Captured at last, he lived out his final years as a farmer in Oklahoma, and, in 1905, rode in Theodore Roosevelt's inaugural parade.

Sitting Bull (*c. 1831–90*). When the Army set out to evict the northern Plains tribes from their western hunting lands, Sitting Bull, Sioux medicine man, joined with other Sioux and Cheyenne leaders to defend their rights. Their victory at the Little Bighorn in 1876 was followed by defeat; Sitting Bull withdrew with some followers into Canada until permitted to return in 1881. In 1885 he toured with Buffalo Bill's Wild West Show. Suspected of being a leader of the Ghost Dance cult that revived Indian hopes in 1890, he was killed when Indian police tried to arrest him.

Chief Joseph (*c. 1840–1904*). No one wanted peace more than Chief Joseph of the Nez Percés, a tribe living in Oregon. He had reluctantly agreed to Government demands that the Nez Percés cede their lands and move to a reservation. But when hotheaded braves killed 19 whites, he knew there would be Army reprisals. Joseph led his people in an epic retreat northward, fending off U.S. Army units in a number of battles before his 89 warriors and 329 woman and children were trapped only 30 miles from sanctuary in Canada. On October 5, 1877, Joseph surrendered and lived out his life on reservations.

Crazy Horse (*c. 1849–77*). As a chief of the Oglala Sioux, Crazy Horse was one of the Indian leaders most feared by white settlers, both for his military ability and for his skill at arousing resistance to white incursions. He was the master strategist of the Sioux-Cheyenne coalition that surrounded and wiped out one-third of Lt. Col. George Armstrong Custer's regiment at the Battle of the Little Bighorn in 1876. In May 1877, after a bitter winter campaign, Crazy Horse and his starving Oglalas were forced to surrender. Crazy Horse was killed a few months later, while still in captivity.

Geronimo, *Apache warrior chief*

The War of 1812 *An Inconclusive Conflict That Was Marked by Blunde*

On June 18, 1812, the United States formally declared war on Britain. The "War Hawks" of Congress, led by southerners Henry Clay (newly elected Speaker of the House) and his colleague John C. Calhoun, had barely got their way. President James Madison had at first favored peace. The powerful Federalists of New England wanted no war; they preferred to continue trading with the mother country. But 1812 was an election year, and Madison, throwing his weight toward the War Hawks, won reelection.

Little more than 30 years had passed since Cornwallis' surrender at Yorktown. Britain and France, at war since 1803, attempted to block U.S. and other merchant ships from each other's ports. The British Navy, harried by desertions, hunted down its sailors everywhere, even aboard American merchantmen on the high seas. As a result, "Freedom of the seas!" became the War Hawks' rallying cry.

The British had also been inciting Indian raids on the white settlers who were pouring into the Old Northwest. This led to the cry "Annex Canada!" Many Americans thought Canada would be easy prey, but the opening engagements of the war in the summer of 1812 brought swift disillusionment. Not only did U.S. forces prove too weak to invade Canada, but they yielded Detroit without firing a shot and lost control over Michigan Territory.

In the first year of the war little went right for the Americans on land, but their fighting ships won reassuring victories. The U.S.S. *Constitution* defeated and sank the British *Guerrière* off the coast of Nova Scotia in Au-

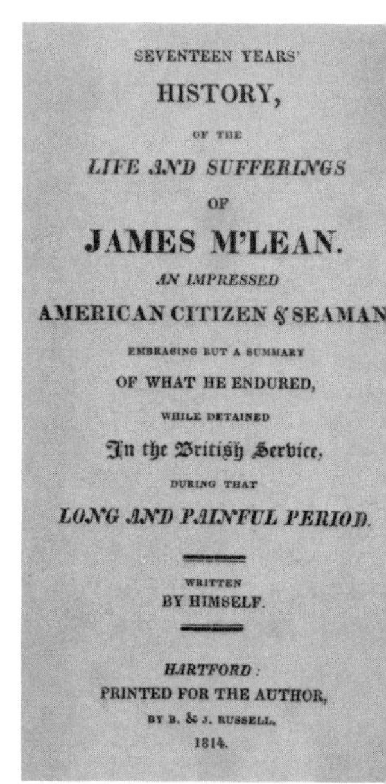

SEVENTEEN YEARS'

HISTORY,

OF THE

LIFE AND SUFFERINGS

OF

JAMES M'LEAN.

AN IMPRESSED

AMERICAN CITIZEN & SEAMAN

EMBRACING BUT A SUMMARY

OF WHAT HE ENDURED,

WHILE DETAINED

In the British Service,

DURING THAT

LONG AND PAINFUL PERIOD.

WRITTEN

BY HIMSELF.

HARTFORD:

PRINTED FOR THE AUTHOR,

BY B. & J. RUSSELL.

1814.

Of the many American grievances against Britain after the Revolution, none stirred more rancor than Britain's arrogant conduct on the high seas. At a time when Britain feared an invasion by Napoleon, its navy had been weakened by desertions from warships, which were notorious for cruel discipline, low pay, and wretched living conditions. British men-of-war regularly stopped American merchantmen to search them for deserters (right) and in the process forcibly impressed some 6,000 American seamen into British service. One particularly bitter incident involved a U.S. naval vessel, the *Chesapeake,* which in 1807 had four of her sailors removed by the British frigate *Leopard.* At the far right is the title page of an 1814 book describing the experiences of a victim of impressment.

Tecumseh, the magnetic Shawnee chief, had united Indian tribes in a pact to resist white settlement of the Old Northwest. Gen. William Henry Harrison, then Governor of Indiana Territory, led 970 well-trained men in a march against the Indians. Camped along Tippecanoe Creek, this force was attacked at dawn on November 7, 1811, by about 700 braves, led by Tecumseh's brother "the Prophet." Harrison broke the assault and counterattacked (right), then burned Prophetstown, the Indian capital. The campaign intensified anger against the British for inciting the Indians and increased talk of annexing Canada. Tecumseh died fighting for the British at the Battle of the Thames in 1813.

nd Heroism Brought a Surge of Self-respect and Unity

Both as Secretary *of State and as President, James Madison (left) had tried to settle America's quarrel with Great Britain by diplomatic means, but he was thwarted finally by two fledgling congressmen, War Hawks Henry Clay (center) and John C. Calhoun (right).*

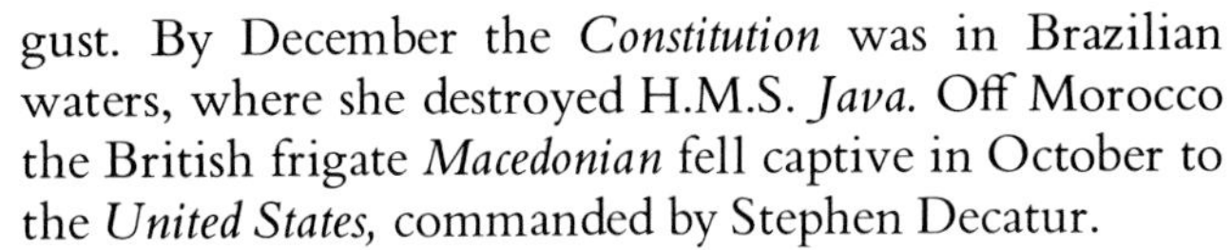

gust. By December the *Constitution* was in Brazilian waters, where she destroyed H.M.S. *Java.* Off Morocco the British frigate *Macedonian* fell captive in October to the *United States,* commanded by Stephen Decatur.

Many American ships were able to slip past the growing British blockade in 1813. A major loss, however, was the *Chesapeake,* captured off Boston in June. Capt. James Lawrence's impassioned cry as he lay dying on her deck became the Navy's motto: "Don't give up the ship!" But in September Capt. Oliver Hazard Perry gained a sweeping victory on Lake Erie, enabling Gen. William Henry Harrison to retake Detroit and mount a campaign in Upper Canada. The death of the Indian leader Tecumseh in battle a month later led to the collapse of Indian support for the British. *(continued)*

In August 1812 the 44-gun frigate U.S.S. *Constitution,* under Capt. Isaac Hull, slipped out of Boston Harbor. Off Nova Scotia on the 19th she encountered H.M.S. *Guerrière,* a 38-gun frigate whose crew included 10 impressed Americans. Hull brought his ship within 60 yards of his opponent and blasted her into submission (left). The *Guerrière* was so badly damaged that Hull ordered it destroyed rather than taken as a prize of war. This victory raised American morale, faltering after the surrender of Detroit 3 days earlier. On December 29 the *Constitution,* then under Commodore William Bainbridge, turned H.M.S. *Java* into a flaming ruin off Brazil, forcing her to strike her colors in surrender. In this action the *Constitution* weathered such heavy fire that it earned the name "Old Ironsides."

By early August 1813 Capt. Oliver Hazard Perry had nine vessels ready to challenge Britain's supremacy on Lake Erie. On September 10, off Put-in-Bay, his fleet clashed with six British ships in an action that could decide control of the Old Northwest. When his flagship, the *Lawrence,* was damaged, Perry was rowed to the *Niagara.* Followed by smaller ships, he passed through the enemy line with guns firing and forced the British vessels to surrender. Perry reported his victory with the words, "We have met the enemy and they are ours. . . ." American control of Lake Erie posed a new threat to the British. They evacuated Detroit and retreated into Canada, pursued by General Harrison.

The War of 1812 *(continued)*

A new American drive on eastern Canada in the fall of 1813 was ended by defeats on the Châteauguay River and at Chrysler's Farm on the St. Lawrence. In December the British took Fort Niagara and burned the town of Buffalo. The Niagara campaign of 1814 was a different story. After seizing Fort Erie, U.S. troops decisively defeated the British near Chippewa Creek on July 5. Three weeks later, in a bitterly fought battle at Lundy's Lane, the Americans severely damaged the British.

The abdication of Napoleon and his exile to the island of Elba in April 1814 enabled Britain to withdraw troops from Europe and send them to America. In August the British raided Washington, D.C., and put it to the torch. The next month they attacked Baltimore, but this time they were repulsed. The naval bombardment of Fort McHenry during that engagement inspired Francis Scott Key to write "The Star-Spangled Banner."

Meanwhile the Americans won a major victory on the Northern front. In September the British had launched an offensive down Lake Champlain, planning to wipe out a garrison at Plattsburg and invade the Hudson Valley. But a U.S. naval force won a hard-fought battle at Plattsburg Bay and so weakened the enemy supply lines that the invaders were obliged to withdraw to Canada.

Powerful peace movements were underway in both countries throughout the 2½ years of war. In England influential shipowners longed for a resumption of normal commerce. In the United States a group of New Englanders was agitating against the war and even threatening to secede. A convention of Federalist delegates from New England was held secretly in Hartford, Connecticut, in late December 1814 and early January 1815. The moderate majority prevailed; the resolutions that were

The British considered the burning of Washington, on August 24 and 25, 1814, justifiable retaliation for the Americans' burning of York (now Toronto), the capital of Upper Canada, the previous year. Public buildings put to the torch included the Capitol, the White House, the Treasury, and the War Office.

Supporting an invading force of 11,000 soldiers from Canada, British naval forces on Lake Champlain attacked the U.S. Fleet in Plattsburg Bay on September 11, 1814. Although his flagship, the *Saratoga,* was battered by the enemy, Capt. Thomas Macdonough won a stunning victory and forced the British to retreat.

Francis Scott Key, a lawyer from Washington, D.C., went aboard a British frigate in Chesapeake Bay with Col. John S. Skinner. Their mission was to negotiate the release of Dr. William Beanes, who was being held by the British. On September 13, 1814, when the British fleet sailed up Chesapeake Bay to bombard Fort McHenry, guarding Baltimore Harbor, Key, Skinner, and Dr. Beanes were transferred to a small cartel boat behind the fleet. On the 14th, "by the dawn's early light," Key saw the Stars and Stripes still flying over the fort. His poetic tribute to that flag was quickly printed on handbills and a week later appeared in the *Baltimore American.* Set to the English drinking tune "To Anacreon in Heav'n," the song soon became America's national anthem—although it was not until 1931 that it received official sanction.

drawn up did not contain a secession ultimatum. But before the resolutions could be acted upon, peace had come.

The Treaty of Ghent, which brought an end to the war, was signed on Christmas Eve 1814. So poor were communications that the war's greatest battle was fought in the South 15 days later. Seasoned British soldiers had been dispatched to New Orleans to open a new front. There they encountered powerful entrenchments set up south of the city by Gen. Andrew Jackson. The British frontal assault on the outnumbered defenders resulted in a disastrous loss for the British forces.

The Treaty of Ghent did not settle any of the major issues that had fomented the war. But America had seen its fighting men prove a match for Europe's finest campaigners and its ships achieve amazing triumphs against the world's greatest navy. The national anthem, the heroes and heroics, and the watchwords and slogans have become a vivid part of U.S. heritage.

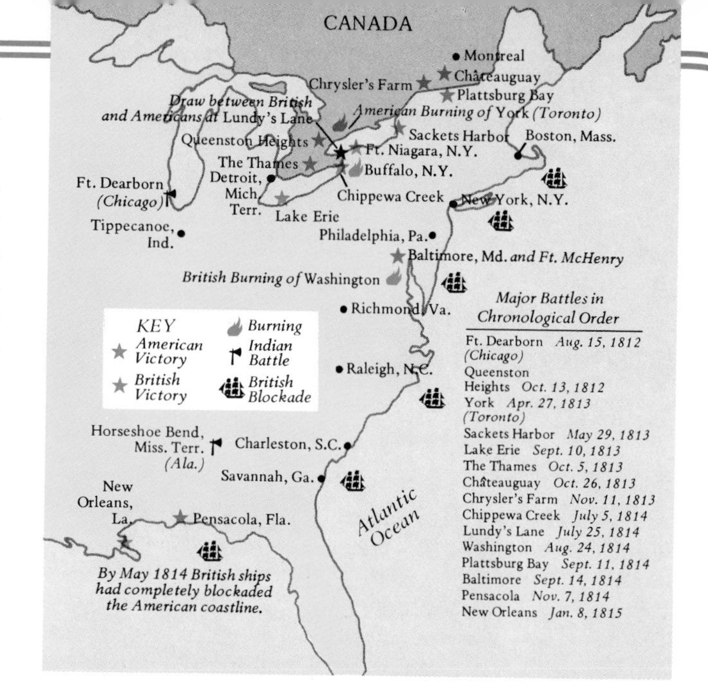

The war's greatest victory, the Battle of New Orleans, was won by U.S. forces under Gen. Andrew Jackson (right). "Old Hickory" had broken an uprising of Tecumseh-inspired Creek Indians at Horseshoe Bend in Alabama in March 1814. In November he took Pensacola in Spanish Florida, then proceeded to Louisiana to combat a British plan to take over the lower Mississippi Valley. Although the treaty signed in Ghent, Belgium, had ended the war in December 1814, it was weeks before U.S. and British commanders in America heard the news. On January 8, 1815, 5 miles below New Orleans, a British force of 5,300 under Gen. Sir Edward Pakenham attacked Jackson's troops. The Americans' defensive earthworks were impenetrable and the British, vulnerable. There were more than 2,000 British casualties; only 13 Americans were killed and 58 wounded. The Battle of New Orleans made Jackson's name familiar to the country and helped elect him President in 1828.

CHAPTER FIVE

Religion in a Free Country

From earliest times religion has offered strength and sola to Americans of many faiths. It has also been a factor i shaping the Nation's history. Centuries ago the glob rivalry between Catholicism and Protestantism helped spur exploration and colonization of the New World. Bri ain's chronic need for new settlers to people her empi encouraged her to allow her American Colonies a wi measure of religious freedom. That policy, in turn, estab lished America as a likely sanctuary for dissenters fro many lands. The Puritans of Massachusetts Bay soug to "shake the dust of Babylon" from their feet and crea a wholly righteous commonwealth in the wilderness; the

John Eliot, Apostle to the Indians

Almost alone among the Puritans, the Rev. John Eliot took seriously the Massachusetts charter's promise to "wynn the natives of the country to the knowledge and obedience of the onlie true God and Saviour of mankinde." Trained at Cambridge, Eliot emigrated from England in 1631, became minister to the Roxbury Puritans, then began preaching to the nearby Indians. He learned their tribal tongues as he wandered from village to village, sermonizing and offering food, clothing, and tools to any who agreed to embrace Christianity.

Eliot was an able, prolific writer, and his eloquent account of his activities, *The Day Breaking* (1647), caused a sensation among English churchmen. It led directly to the formation of the Society for the Propagation of the Gospel in New England, which provided financial and material support for his efforts. Eliot laboriously translated the entire Bible into an Algonquian dialect, a task that took years and included some interesting compromises. The word "heaven," for example, was rendered by an Algonquian word meaning "regions of the far west part of the skies," while "God the Father" became "God the Chief." His *Mamussee Wunneetupanatamwe Up-Biblum God,* or, literally, "The Whole Holy His-Bible God" (1661–63), was the first complete Bible ever printed in America and the first translation of the Bible into an Indian language.

By 1675 Eliot claimed 1,100 converts and had established 14 peaceful settlements of "praying Indians," who developed their own law codes and ran their own schools. But King Philip's War erupted in that year, and, although Christian Indian volunteers inflicted some 400 casualties on the marauding tribesmen, Eliot's frightened fellow colonists turned against the converts. Most of their towns were razed and many of the inhabitants banished to a barren offshore island, where starvation took a heavy toll. Despite these setbacks, Eliot remained devoted to his Indian charges until his death in 1690.

Religion played an important role in America long before the coming of the white man. Each of the many Indian tribes dwelling here had its own legends and rituals, uniquely suited to the life it led. Tribal faiths were dismissed as superstitious by early settlers, who lost little time in trying to uproot them. But ecology-minded modern observers have come to admire the Indian emphasis on living as a partner of nature rather than as its subjugator, and many tribal faiths have survived intact.

Missionary zeal helped spur Catholic Spain's expansion into the New World, and tonsured friars soon followed in the gory wake of the armored conquistadores in Florida and the Southwest. Catholic France, too, sought to combine soul saving with commerce in fish and furs. The early missionaries shared their countrymen's vicissitudes in an unknown and sometimes savage land; some acquired lasting fame as explorers and mapmakers for those who would follow.

Like the Spanish kings, the Protestant rulers of England and the Netherlands were persuaded to colonize America primarily by the promise of land and treasure. But the peopling of the Eastern seaboard was also motivated in part by a desire to build bulwarks against further gains by Catholic Spain and France. Originally Britain hoped all its overseas colonies would recognize the Anglican Church of England as the established (officially recognized and supported) faith. In the charter of Virginia (1606), James I decreed that the "true word and service of God" should be "preached, planted and used . . . according to the doctrine, rites and religion now professed and established within our realm of England." The first ship to anchor off Jamestown in 1607 carried an Anglican clergyman, and the colonists took time out from building their own shelters to fashion a crude church from freshly cut timber and tattered sails.

But London soon saw that if "the American Planta-

ailed in that lofty effort, but their pious example perma-nently marked the American psyche and helped foster the special sense of American mission that persists to this day. The great religious awakening of the 1740's helped unite the Colonies and expand education.

America became a safer haven for believers and nonbe-lievers alike when the Constitution and the Bill of Rights made freedom of conscience a matter of right rather than privilege for the first time in history. Succeeding decades saw old churches altered and many influential new ones born. And most of these churches involved themselves in causes ranging from temperance and foreign missions to Sabbath keeping and slavery. Overwhelmingly Protestant at first, America became increasingly pluralistic after the Civil War as successive waves of immigration brought more believers of the Roman Catholic, Jewish, and Eastern Orthodox persuasions. New religious concepts proliferated; by the mid-1970's there were more than 250 established cults, sects, and denominations.

While there have been unfortunate episodes of religious bigotry and violence, the history of religion in America has remained an inspiring story of a land in which men and women of widely differing beliefs met and made a nation while worshiping as they wished.

tions" were to prosper, other church groups would have to be made welcome: There were not enough willing Anglicans to go around. In later years all the Southern Colonies and (for a time) part of New York adopted Anglicanism as their official faith. But the church rarely played a central role in the South: The scattered planta-tions made organized parishes impractical, and the few clergymen dispatched from London were, by and large, indolent and ill-trained. One pious traveler from Puritan New England dismissed many of the southerners he met as "Nothingarians." Each Southern Colony saw the growth of large non-Anglican sects. Public worship by Roman Catholics, however, was generally forbidden.

Cecilius Calvert, Second Baron Baltimore, founded Maryland in 1634 to provide a haven for his Catholic coreligionists. But Protestants soon outnumbered Catho-lics, and to protect the latter, Lord Calvert caused the passage of the Toleration Act (1649), which prohibited the molesting of any professed Christian. It was the first legislative act concerning religious toleration passed in the Colonies. Anti-Catholic feeling and civil strife led to the repeal of the act a few years later, and in 1692 the Church of England was made the established church.

Profits, not piety, became the watchword of almost all the Colonies. "A free exercise of religion," declared the London Lords of Trade, "is essential to enriching and improving a trading nation: It should be ever held sacred in His Majesty's colonies." This "free exercise of reli-gion" was a revolutionary doctrine in the 17th century. As historian Perry Miller writes: "No nation of Europe had yet divided the state from the church; no government had yet imagined that religion could be left to individual conscience." This new freedom from religious constraint, tentatively sanctioned by England for purely pragmatic reasons, was later strengthened and embodied as a basic right in the first amendment to the U.S. Constitution.

The rich fruits of religious tolerance were most evident in the prosperous Middle Colonies. When England seized New Netherland and renamed it New York in 1664, British colonial officials were forbidden to interfere with the thriving Dutch Reform, Swedish Lutheran, French Protestant (Huguenot), Quaker, and Jewish congrega-tions they found there. The religious diversity of the re-gion increased in 1682 when Quaker proprietor William Penn launched a "Holy Experiment," throwing open the fertile Pennsylvania frontier to believers of every faith —Quakers, Scotch-Irish Presbyterians, and Mennonites and other pietists from Germany.

The Bible Commonwealth

In Puritan New England, however, church and state long remained inextricably linked. The Puritans left England because their opposition to the elaborate rituals and cen-tralized control of the Anglican Church had aroused official wrath. In the Massachusetts Bay Colony they strove to create a Bible commonwealth, a spotless "city set upon a hill" in which only the orthodox might live.

Safely ashore, the once-persecuted Puritans became persecutors in their own right. The very idea of religious toleration was anathema to them. Anyone willing to tol-erate another's faith, wrote pastor Nathaniel Ward, "ei-ther doubts his own, or is not sincere in it." The Puritans lived in fear that their Colony would be undermined from within, and they established a modified theocracy in which only propertied church members were allowed to vote. By 1640 some 3,000 Puritans controlled the des-tinies of 15,000 voteless fellow citizens.

Dissenters were harshly dealt with. Quakers were con-demned as a "cursed sect of hereticks." Quakers who dared enter Massachusetts were imprisoned, flogged, or otherwise abused; six were hanged. The New England Colonies banned Roman Catholic worship until 1783.

It would be hard to exaggerate the grim rigor of the Puritan code. Church attendance was compulsory for all, and no one was permitted to doze during the 3-hour sermons. Strict, paralyzing standards of decorum were set for almost every area of life. Householders were encouraged to spy on their neighbors and report breaches of discipline to church elders.

A body of stern blue laws banned both labor and frivolity on the Sabbath. These may have reached their zenith in 1656 when a Boston mariner spent 2 humiliating hours in the stocks for his "lewd and unseemly behavior" in daring "publiquely" to kiss his wife on Sunday when he arrived home after a 3-year absence at sea.

Anne Hutchinson

The Puritans came to Massachusetts Bay, in part, to be free to worship as they pleased; but they denied that right to others, believing that dissent would endanger their Colony's survival. The best known victim of Puritan intolerance was Anne Hutchinson, who came to Boston with her husband in 1634. Weekly theological discussions and intensive private study of Scripture convinced her that faith alone was enough to qualify anyone to communicate directly with God. There was no need, she declared, for submission to the clergy, prescribed prayer, church membership, or acceptance of many other tenets of the Puritan faith. Her revolutionary doctrine won a sizable following, and in 1637 she was brought to trial for "traducing the ministers." Found guilty by the General Court, she was sentenced to banishment and later excommunicated. She moved to Rhode Island and then to Dutch New Netherland, where, in 1643, she and 5 of her 14 children were killed by Indians.

Much of New England was settled by refugees from Massachusetts who had grown impatient with Puritan rigidity. Best known was Roger Williams, a stubborn clergyman who was banished to the wilderness in the winter of 1635 for having dared to challenge church power and to champion Indian rights. In the spring of the following year Williams founded Providence, the first settlement in Rhode Island ("Rogue's Island" to its detractors). Providence, together with other early settlements, formed a colony that was a sanctuary for all those "distressed in conscience." Williams welcomed both Quakers and Jews to Providence, and in 1639 he formed what some say was the first Baptist church in America. Throughout the colonial era Rhode Islanders' consistent advocacy of religious freedom reduced much of Puritan New England to frustrated rage.

Despite the rigidity of the code by which they tried to live, Puritans as a whole were not "puritanical." Modern scholars have shown that most were no more pious, no more reserved in human relations, nor less bawdy than their contemporaries. If Puritanism had its dark side, its followers also made lasting positive contributions to American life. Because they believed all men and women should be able to read and properly understand the Bible, they were among the earliest promoters of education in America. Their advocacy of learning helped to launch a native American literature, and their conviction that church members could run their own affairs helped to foster the American passion for self-government.

In the end the Puritans lost their battle to keep Massachusetts orthodoxy intact. Non-Puritans streaming into the flourishing Colony chafed under Puritan rule; cities and towns expanded, encouraging worldly ways. The Crown ended the last vestiges of theocratic rule by the Puritans in 1691, and the political power of the clergy was further weakened after the Salem witch trials that took place the following year had demonstrated the tragic events to which Puritan zealotry could lead.

The Great Awakening

The religious orthodoxy that helped hold some Colonies together during their embattled infant years began to wane by 1720. Prosperity, the growth of towns, increased contact with foreign lands, and the proliferation of churches encouraged by immigration all contributed to its decline.

The waning of religious fervor alarmed many clergymen, and from Georgia to New Hampshire fiery exhorters warned their flocks of dire consequences if they did not mend their ways. Though many local revivals erupted throughout the Colonies, four extraordinary preachers emerged as leaders of this Great Awakening of the 1730's and 1740's. The first was Massachusetts Congregationalist Jonathan Edwards, whose vivid preaching

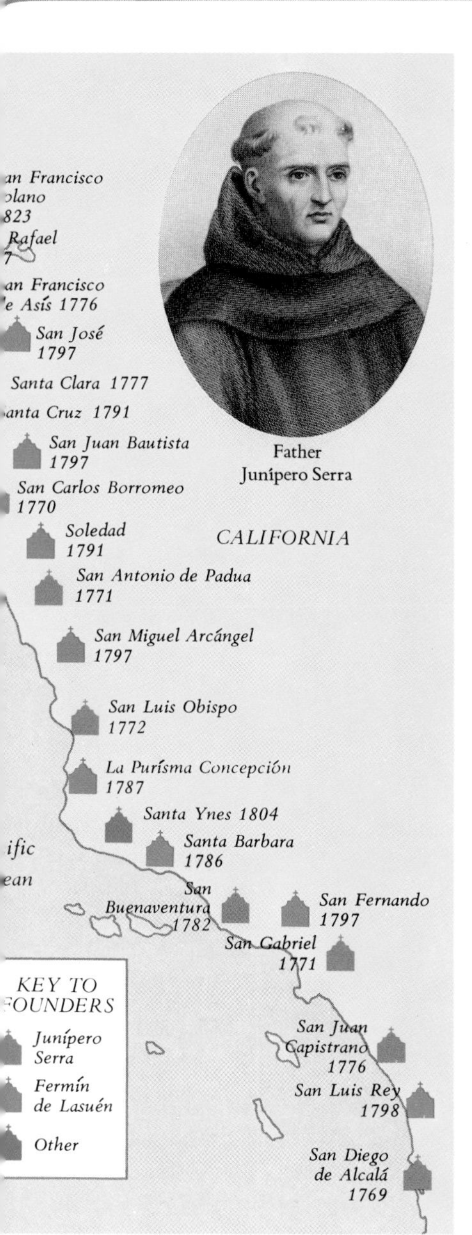

Father
Junípero Serra

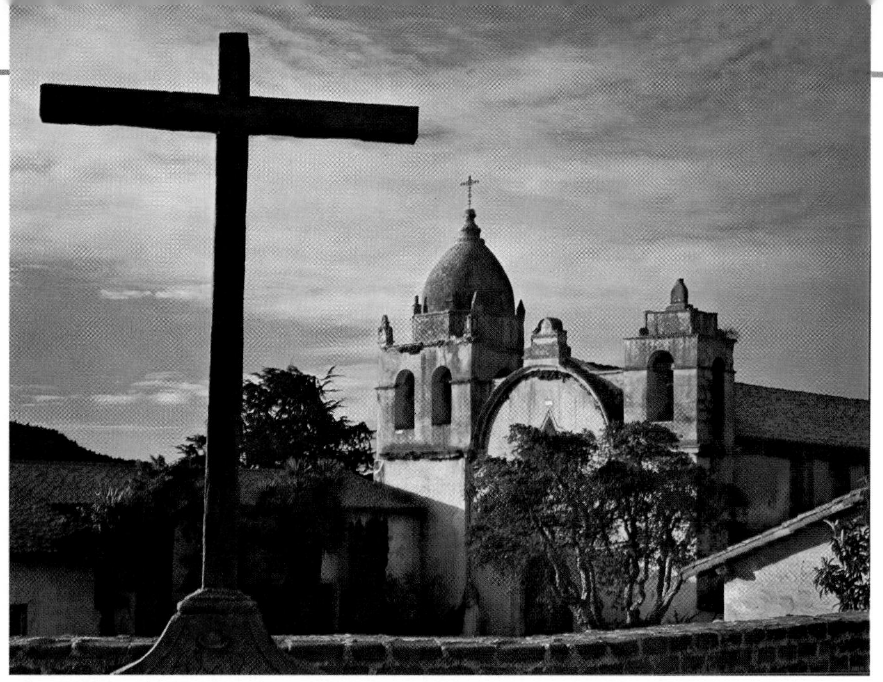

The Mission of San Carlos Borromeo *at Carmel was the headquarters of a peaceful conqueror. From this church, built in 1770, Father Serra supervised Upper California's missions.*

Christianity Came Early to California
Father Serra Started the Chain of Catholic Missions

In 1769 Spanish soldier Gaspar de Portolá led a dusty column northward out of Mexico to occupy Upper California. Perched on a plodding mule among Portolá's sweating men was Father Junípero Serra, a Franciscan monk who hoped to establish a chain of missions along the Pacific coast, continuing the work begun by Jesuit priests in Lower California and New Mexico. Despite official indifference and Indian hostility, the tireless friar managed to found nine thriving missions, stretching from San Diego to San Francisco, before his death in 1784. Nine more missions were established under Father Serra's successor, Fermín de Lasuén, and by 1823 there were 21 missions in all, with some 21,000 Indian converts. In 1821 Mexico won its independence from Spain and in 1833 began to bring mission property under secular control.

The missions did much for the Indians. While they were being imbued with Christianity, the once-nomadic tribesmen were taught farming, cattle and sheep raising, carpentry, spinning, weaving, and other useful crafts. Yet the story had its dark side. Ancient coastal cultures were destroyed. Mission Indians were forbidden to return to their ancestral hills. Backsliders were flogged. And mission schooling failed to equip the tribesmen to deal with the land-hungry whites that came with the Gold Rush of 1849. Thousands of mission Indians died from disease and violence.

persuaded hundreds to confess their sins, repent, and seek rebirth in worship. (In recent years Edwards has been hailed as America's first theologian and one of its best.) The Presbyterian William Tennent with his son Gilbert performed similar work among the faithful of Pennsylvania; their "log college" at Neshaminy trained scores of eager evangelists and served as a model for frontier seminaries of many churches.

The most celebrated orator of the Great Awakening was George Whitefield, an itinerant Anglican preacher who had worked with John Wesley in England but later broke with him to spread his own form of Calvinistic Methodism. He made seven trips to the Colonies, where he exhorted large crowds into a frenzy of repentance. So awesome were his skills that even that genial skeptic Benjamin Franklin was moved to empty his pockets into the collection plate at a Philadelphia revival.

The lasting effects of the Great Awakening are still debated by historians. It was one of the first movements to affect all the Colonies and therefore indirectly to help unite them; some scholars believe it was a more effective force for unity than the four colonial wars with France. It firmly established revivalism as a technique for strengthening the churches in America. It split several sects into two camps: those who followed the new evangelical path and those more sedate believers who distrusted public displays of emotion. It created a demand for trained ministers that resulted in the founding of a number of distinguished institutions of higher learning, including Princeton, Brown, Rutgers, and Dartmouth. The great evangelists paid little attention to doctrinal barriers separating Protestant groups and held forth in any church or meetinghouse that would have them, thus doing their bit to make Americans more tolerant of one

MAKING DEMOCRACY WORK

The Virginia Statute for Religious Liberty

At the outset of the Revolution, a majority of the 13 Colonies still had established tax-supported faiths. Three New England Colonies recognized the Congregational Church; five Southern Colonies and parts of New York were officially Anglican. During the war, church and state were separated in most Southern States, but the Anglican establishment maintained its strength in Virginia. With the aid of leading Patriots George Mason, James Madison, and Thomas Jefferson, the dissenters finally won a "declaration of the free exercise of religion" from the 1776 State constitutional convention. Three years later they managed to get all State aid to the Anglican Church cut off. But they were not satisfied, because prewar statutes that cast doubt on the legitimacy of non-Anglican weddings and granted special civic powers to Anglican vestrymen were still on the books.

In 1785 Jefferson's "Bill for Establishing Religious Freedom" finally was passed by the lower house of the State assembly. It declared "all men shall be free to profess, and by argument to maintain, their opinions in matters of religion" and guaranteed Virginians against being compelled to "support any religious worship, place or ministry whatsoever." The next year the senate accepted Jefferson's bill, including the historic principle of separation between church and state or, as some say, distinction between civil and religious realms. Five years later it influenced the writing and ratification of the first amendment to the U.S. Constitution.

another's beliefs. "God help us to forget party names," prayed Whitefield, "and to become Christians in deed and truth." Growing numbers of American Protestants came to share his generous view. But for all that, the Great Awakening only momentarily slowed the steady decline of churchly influence in the increasingly prosperous and self-confident Colonies.

Though the leaders of the American Revolution were not notably pious, religion gave momentum to the struggle in several ways. Fully 9 out of 10 Americans in 1775 were at least nominal Protestants, even if the vast majority were not enrolled church members. English statesman Edmund Burke attributed the colonists' "fierce spirit of liberty" both to their predominantly British heritage and to their support of those Protestant sects "most adverse to all implicit subjection of mind and opinion." Non-Anglican resentment at having to contribute to the established Anglican Church helped stir the Southern Colonies to action—especially after rumors swept the Colonies that England was about to dispatch bishops to America at the colonists' expense. The 1774 Quebec Act, which recognized the right of recently conquered French settlements to profess Catholicism, also angered many Protestants who feared "that hydra, popery," as much as they resented parliamentary tyranny.

All denominations were divided by the Revolution. Anglican clergymen were almost universally Loyalists, and many were driven into exile. Yet in the South, at least, most Anglican laymen solidly supported the Patriot cause. From England, John Wesley fulminated against the war, but most of his American followers favored rebellion. Quakers, Mennonites, and other pacifist sects angered Tories and Patriots alike by remaining above the battle. Churchmen of many denominations fought alongside their parishioners, echoing the brave sentiments of Anglican leader John Peter Muhlenberg, who stripped off his black robes in the pulpit to reveal a Continental officer's uniform in 1776. Paraphrasing the Book of Ecclesiastes, he said: "There is a time for all things, a time to preach and a time to fight, and now is a time to fight!"

Religion in the New Republic

At the end of the Revolution, American churches had reached their lowest ebb. Long-term ties with coreligionists in England were cut. Probably fewer than 7 percent of the people were enrolled as church members, although about twice that number attended services.

Historian Martin E. Marty has pointed out that "apathy, not antipathy" characterized the Founding Fathers' approach to religion in the new republic. While most Americans were more or less conventional in their beliefs, many of their most influential leaders were well-read products of the Enlightenment, champions of reason, science, "progress," and the natural rights of man. A few, including Franklin, Thomas Jefferson, and pamphleteer Thomas Paine, were deists—believers in a higher power to whom deference was due but who never intervened in the affairs of men. To such men doctrinal orthodoxy and sectarian squabbling were irrelevancies, unworthy of a free people and potentially disastrous for a fledgling republic made up of many faiths. Jefferson summarized their view. "It does me no injury," he wrote, "for my neighbor to say there are twenty gods or no God. It neither picks my pocket nor breaks my leg."

No clergyman attended the Constitutional Convention, and the Constitution itself contains not a single religious reference: The word "God" does not appear once. But even this was not enough for those who worried that the new government might still try to interfere with the religious beliefs of its citizens unless it was expressly forbidden to do so. Accordingly, the Bill of Rights, ratified in 1791, begins by declaring that the "Congress shall make no law respecting an establishment of religion, or prohibiting the free exercise thereof." For the first time in history a national government was forbidden to have anything to do with religion as such.

A backwoods preacher in full cry, *shown in this 1839 watercolor, whips a frontier camp meeting into a joyous frenzy. One convert from such a meeting recalled: "The noise was like the roar of Niagara. . . . Some of the people were singing, others praying, some crying for mercy in the most piteous accents. . . . I saw at least five hundred swept down in a moment as if a battery of a thousand guns had been opened upon them, and then immediately followed shrieks and shouts that rent the very heavens." In the excitement, some people spoke in unknown tongues.*

The Bill of Rights applied only to the Federal Government, but the States soon followed suit. Even before the Revolution, four Colonies had guaranteed religious liberty. During the struggle five States discontinued their support of official religions. Later Virginia, too, bowed to deists and dissenters and abandoned her official Anglican faith in 1786 after a bitter and protracted battle. Only in Congregational New England did established religion endure for a time. Massachusetts was the last holdout, finally abandoning official support for Congregationalism in 1833.

In a 1790 letter to the Jewish congregation of Newport, Rhode Island, President George Washington stated the Founding Fathers' basic attitude toward religious liberty. No longer, he wrote, was it "to be spoken of as if it was by the indulgence of one class of people that another enjoyed their natural rights. For . . . the United States, which gives to bigotry no sanction, to persecution no assistance, requires only that they who live under its protection should demean themselves as good citizens."

But if the new Constitution offered unprecedented freedom, the concomitant withdrawal of Government aid confronted the disestablished churches with awesome new challenges. Clearly, new techniques were required to meet them. First came a renewed emphasis on denominationalism. Protestants could no longer afford to quarrel over doctrine; they agreed to disagree on points of doctrine but to work together for the common cause whenever possible.

Meanwhile, the fulcrum of national power was steadily shifting westward as thousands of pioneers, most of them religiously unaffiliated, crossed the Alleghenies. If converts were to be attracted, dramatic new means were needed. Revivalism provided a partial answer. Beginning in Kentucky's Logan County in the 1790's, camp-meeting fever spread throughout the South and West, spurring a Second Awakening that helped double church attendance by 1835 and lasted until the Civil War. Presbyterian preacher James McGready was the movement's leather-lunged founder. He converted so many frontier sinners, he said, because "even the most prophane swearers and Sabbath-breakers [were] pricked to the heart." Soon camp meetings were a backwoods mainstay of social and religious life; some lasting several days with as many as 10 preachers sermonizing simultaneously amid hymn singing, ecstatic dancing, and speaking in tongues. In Kentucky alone 10,000 new Baptists were immersed in sanctifying waters in just 3 years; in the summer of 1811 there were some 400 Methodist camp meetings.

Faith Follows the Frontier

Although preachers of many denominations went west with the pioneers, it was the intrepid circuit riders of Methodism who proved most effective. A frontier saying had it that the first human sound to follow the *tunk* of the pioneer's ax in the wilderness was the "hello" of the Methodist preacher. Almost half of these wiry, Bible-toting men died before they reached the age of 30. Francis Asbury, the first American Methodist Episcopal bishop, set the rugged circuit-riding style, covering some 270,000 frontier miles between 1771 and 1816. The circuit riders preached from church pulpits, at camp meetings, on riverboat decks, and in bordello parlors—anywhere they could attract a crowd. Without them the West would have been far wilder than it was.

The rise of the cities, after 1820, offered another new frontier for preachers, and Presbyterian evangelist Charles G. Finney was the first to prove that revivalism could succeed among urban Americans. A skilled speaker and former lawyer who claimed to have a "retainer from the Lord Jesus Christ to plead His cause," he brought his message of "free and full salvation" to the fast-growing cities of upstate New York. His preaching lured so many eager listeners to one Rochester church that its brick walls bulged and partly collapsed; almost miraculously, no one was killed.

From earliest colonial times Americans had seen their triumph over the New World's "waste and howling wilderness" as sure evidence of God's special favor. The Lord had "sifted a whole nation," wrote Puritan historian Edward Johnson in 1670, to plant "His choice grain" in America's rich soil. The Puritans believed in this divine favor toward America with unique fervor, but almost all colonists shared the conviction to some degree. America's triumph in the Revolution, her survival as the sole successful democratic republic, her growing prosperity, and the success of the Second Awakening—all tended to rekindle belief in her special grace.

Bible in hand, *booted and spurred, with only an umbrella to ward off the elements, this Methodist circuit rider paused in his labors long enough for artist O. C. Seltzer to paint him.*

Clergy and laity alike shared novelist Herman Melville's view that "We Americans are the peculiar, chosen people—the Israel of our time; we bear the ark of liberties of the world." It became America's duty to set an example of Protestant piety for the rest of the world. A dizzying number of hard-working religious organizations formed to cleanse society of vice and indifference.

These organizations printed and distributed millions of Bibles and tracts; battled alcohol, tobacco, profanity, and Sabbath breaking; dispatched pastors to the frontier and missionaries to the "heathen" of the world; and crusaded against slavery and for peace, public health, prison reform, women's rights, and Sunday schools. Revivalism persuaded men and women to combat sin; reform movements focused their efforts on creating a righteous world. Until the advent of the New Deal in 1933, most American programs for human welfare remained in church hands, and throughout U.S. history churches and churchmen have often been at the forefront of movements for social and political reform.

Ferment and Friction

While all this activity often fostered Protestant unity, it sometimes spawned new schisms. Some congregations withdrew in horror from what one clergyman called the "artificial fireworks" of revivalism. Others objected to a blurring of doctrinal distinctions. "No such thing exists on the face of the Earth as Christianity in the abstract," warned old school Presbyterian Charles Hodge. "No one is a Christian in general." Many groups were permanently divided.

The late 18th and early 19th centuries saw the birth of the Unitarian and Universalist Churches, the phenomenal growth of the Disciples of Christ, also known as the Christian Church, and the arrival of the Rappites and other small perfectionist sects from abroad. The excitement engendered by revivalism is believed by most historians to have offered a favorable breeding ground for several native-born faiths, including Millerism, Spiritualism, and Mormonism. Most mid-19th-century Americans stopped short of church membership, but the vast majority regarded themselves as Protestants of some sort. Millions regularly read the prolific religious press, and most tried to follow churchly standards of conduct.

Just and Upright Men and Women
The Missionary Movement

The passion to win converts to the Christian God brought many devoted ministers and missionaries to colonial America. At first missionaries, like the Franciscan and Jesuit priests, worked among the Indians; they then followed the frontier westward to save souls among the settlers. Tireless missionaries such as Jason Lee and Marcus and Narcissa Whitman helped open the Pacific Northwest during the 1840's.

Roman Catholic missionaries from Europe had established Christianity in Central and South America, the Caribbean, and the Philippines, and introduced it into Asia, by the 16th century. The Protestant world missionary movement reached a peak in the 19th century, and inevitably missionaries from the United States were in the forefront of it. In 1806 five Williams College undergraduates felt a call to go to the aid of those millions of non-Christians who, they believed, lived trapped in the "moral darkness of Asia." The five students, who came to be known as The Brethren, were ordained as Congregational missionaries at Salem, Massachusetts, in 1812. Soon after, they set sail for India. The American Board of Commissioners for Foreign Missions was established to oversee their activities, and those of the Congregational, Presbyterian, and Reformed Church missionaries who followed in their wake. The Baptists later established a separate supervisory organization.

Soon a flood of pious, dedicated young men and women carried the Gospel, as well as literacy and health care, to Asia, Africa, South America, and the islands of the Pacific. Home mission societies backed their efforts and worked among immigrants and newly freed blacks following the Civil War. The American Bible Society, organized in 1816 to fill the demand for Bibles on the American frontier, soon began publishing translations.

Missionaries and their homefront supporters were a potent political force. Protestant mission efforts in the Pacific fanned enthusiasm for the annexation of Hawaii, and Protestant eagerness to overthrow the rule of Catholic Spain in Cuba was a factor in the Spanish-American War. The presence of Protestant and Catholic missionaries in China was related to the sending of U.S. troops to help quell the Boxer Rebellion of 1900.

Enthusiasm for missionary projects waned in the mainline churches in the 1900's, as the old mission fields were swept by the tides of nationalism. Even so, more North American missionaries were working abroad in the mid-1970's than ever before.

Under the watchful eye *of a benevolent angel, an American missionary preaches to a rapt outdoor audience of Asians, Africans, and South Sea Islanders. This allegorical engraving served as a frontispiece to an 1832 history of U.S. missions overseas. In recent years many missionaries have deemphasized evangelism in favor of greater stress on social work, engineering, public health expertise, and the application of other technical skills badly needed in underdeveloped parts of the world.*

The long, bitter struggle over slavery disrupted every area of American life, including religion. By 1845 the Nation's three largest Protestant denominations—the Baptists, Methodists, and Presbyterians—had all been split into Northern and Southern divisions. To some Northern churchmen, slavery was an unmitigated evil to be eradicated root and branch. Seminaries and religious colleges such as Oberlin produced scores of eager abolitionists. "The cause is worthy of Gabriel," thundered antislavery editor William Lloyd Garrison. "Yea, and the God of Hosts places Himself at its head."

In the South, however, slavery found ample support in the pulpit. Southern clergymen argued that slavery had scriptural sanction because the Bible did not forbid it, and the churches had no business meddling in political affairs anyway. "We defend the cause of God!" declared a Louisiana clergyman in 1861.

Once war began, each side claimed God's guidance. The words of Abraham Lincoln were almost lost in the clamor: "It is quite possible, that God's purpose is something different from the purpose of either party." The wounds of war healed slowly: Some denominations have never reunited their Northern and Southern branches.

During Reconstruction Northern churches shouldered the burden of educating 3.5 million unlettered freedmen. There were some 530 Congregationalist missionary-teachers at work in the former Confederacy by 1867, two-thirds of them women. Other denominations were almost equally active. The churches were largely responsible for establishing the first black schools—among them, Fisk, Atlanta, Talladega, Tougaloo, and Hampton Institute. At the same time thousands of freed blacks flocked into the Negro churches, which served as centers for social uplift and organized protest.

The Unique Role of the Black Church
From Its Beginnings a Focus of Strength and an Outlet for Self-Expression

Religion has had a special place in the history of black America. Colonial slaves were often baptized, but little effort was made at true conversion until the Great Awakening of the 1730's and 1740's, when Baptist and Methodist evangelists stormed through the Southern Colonies, exhorting slave and master alike. Most blacks still belong to one of these two denominations.

Separate black churches were forbidden on most plantations for fear they would foment rebellion. Slaves usually sat apart in their owners' churches, where, as one ex-slave recalled, they were told by the minister to do "whatsomever your master tells you to do." But plantation slaves often met to worship in secret, led by forceful, untutored slave preachers. Some of these gave hope to their listeners, assuring them that God would end slavery. Not all counseled patience, however. Nat Turner, who was preacher to his fellow slaves for several years, led an insurrection in 1831.

Northern blacks, excluded from most white churches, meanwhile, formed their own organizations, beginning in 1816 with the African Methodist Episcopal Church, whose first bishop was Richard Allen.

As the first American social body controlled by blacks, the church was usually the most important Negro institution in the community. Especially during the Jim Crow era in the South, it promoted education, offered aid to the poor, and provided hope for the future and sanctuary from white hostility. Bigotry and discriminatory laws barred blacks from Southern politics; at the same time, church elections offered them opportunities to hone electioneering skills and wield real, if limited, power.

Venerated by their flocks, black ministers were community leaders. They acted as spiritual shepherds, mediated disputes, and served as spokesmen in dealing with whites. Such modern black politicians and civil rights leaders as Adam Clayton Powell, Jr., Dr. Martin Luther King, Jr., Ralph Abernathy, and Andrew Young were solidly rooted in that tradition.

The massive 20th-century migration of the Negro poor from the rural South to Northern cities spawned new forms of black religion. By 1970 there were well over 35 all-black denominations, claiming nearly 10 million adherents, plus many smaller, less formally organized sects.

The black churches have reflected the needs of their people. In recent years black nationalism has permeated many Negro congregations and, in the Nation of Islam (the Black Muslims), has become a kind of religion in itself. In an America in which blacks are still all too often "last hired and first fired," religion remains a strong force for strength and unity.

A fervent Negro circuit preacher *exhorts an informal Tennessee congregation in about 1910. The watercolor was painted from a childhood memory by black artist Joe Delaney. Services often included spirituals and gospel melodies, whose sound inspired much modern popular music.*

American Catholics

Throughout the colonial period and for a while after the Revolution, America was essentially a Protestant nation. As late as 1790, when John Carroll, of Baltimore, was consecrated America's first Roman Catholic bishop, there were fewer than 40,000 U.S. Catholics, ministered to by a handful of mostly French priests. Only a few Catholics were nationally prominent, though Charles Carroll had signed the Declaration of Independence, and Daniel Carroll and Thomas Fitzsimons had helped frame the Constitution. The numbers of Catholics swelled as territory was acquired from predominantly Catholic Mexico and as wave upon wave of Catholic immigrants arrived—first from Germany and Ireland, then, after 1870, from Italy and Eastern Europe. There were well over 3 million Catholics in the United States by 1860; 60 years later there were more than 18 million, and Catholicism was the Nation's largest single denomination. This phenomenal growth took place despite Protestant opposition and internal division between the different ethnic groups.

As Catholic newcomers crowded the cities, urban culture and politics were permanently transformed. Displaced Protestants came to view Catholicism as an alien faith and its adherents as foreigners incapable of true American patriotism. Many believed that immigration itself was a Romish plot to subvert free institutions. Ethnic rather than religious friction dominated the nativist struggle, but Protestant-Catholic tension was an important constant.

Tactless remarks by a few embattled Catholic clergymen helped fan the flames. Some pronounced all Protestants infidels and hinted at the future conversion of the Protestant majority. Others attacked the public school system as godless and demanded public funds for parochial education. Protestant propagandists seized on these and similar remarks as further proof that Catholicism was indeed un-American.

Farsighted Catholic clergymen worked to calm nativist fears. Such men as James Cardinal Gibbons patiently explained that Catholics owed only their moral and religious allegiance to Rome; they could be just as patriotic as any other citizens. "American Catholics rejoice in our separation of church and state," Gibbons declared in 1887. "I can conceive of no circumstances . . . which would make a union desirable to either church or state." Despite the efforts of Gibbons and other eloquent advocates of amity on both sides, ill feeling did not entirely subside. Anti-Catholicism marred the 1928 Presidential bid of Catholic Democrat Alfred E. Smith, an outstanding Governor of New York. It was not until 1960, with the election of John F. Kennedy, the grandson of Irish immigrants, that the United States got its first Catholic President.

Meanwhile, the Roman Catholic Church hierarchy in America, mostly of Irish origin, was faced with a difficult job. It had to forge a single, cohesive institution out of disparate, often mutually antagonistic groups of newcomers who did not even share a common tongue. The clergy sought an answer in adapting to American ways as soon as possible. English was the teaching language used in parochial schools, even when the children were from homes where a different language was spoken. Seminaries sprang up to train a native-born priesthood. Catholic missionaries worked among the immigrants, both to fortify their faith and to teach the English language. The first American citizen to be canonized a saint, Mother Frances Xavier Cabrini, was especially effective in organizing charitable and religious work with the Italian poor of New York and other cities.

Americanization angered some Catholic traditionalists and saddened many immigrants who saw in the abandonment of European traditions the cutting of the last links with their homelands. Some Polish Catholics broke away in 1904 to form their own Polish National Catholic Church of America, entirely independent of Rome.

Other internal dissensions imperiled Catholic unity during the 19th century. One of the most serious was a dispute over the church's attitude toward temperance. In the lands from which most Catholics came, alcohol was simply a fact of life, neither good nor bad in itself. But in America (where alcoholism became common among discouraged immigrants) some Catholic clergymen, such as Archbishop John Ireland, joined forces with the Protestant-led temperance movement; others opposed temperance as an exclusively Protestant cause. The church's view of organized labor also created controversy. Most Catholic laymen were members of the working class, and many were early converts to unionism. But much of the hierarchy remained hostile toward the labor movement. An exception was Cardinal Gibbons, whose 1887 defense of the Knights of Labor to the church hierarchy both here and in Rome marked a milestone in U.S. labor history.

Finally, factions within the church clashed over parochial schools. Some argued that a national system of parochial schools was essential to perpetuate the faith and to shield children from the anti-Catholic propaganda that then riddled public school texts. Others countered that religious antipathy would never end as long as Protestant and Catholic children were educated apart. The church officially called upon Catholic parents to support a national system in 1884, and by 1970 there were more than 10,000 primary and secondary Catholic institutions, attended by about 13 percent of America's children. After decades of dispute a series of State and Federal court decisions ruled that direct public aid to these schools (and to those run by Protestants and Jews as well) is unconstitutional, but support for health care, transportation, and other noncurricular activities is permissible.

The same years that saw Catholicism become a major American power also witnessed the steady growth of the Eastern Orthodox Church, which since World War I has been divided into 18 national or jurisdictional groups with a total membership of more than 4 million. The Eastern churches remain the least Americanized of all large U.S. religious bodies. Although most of their members are now second- or third-generation Americans, the clergy that leads them remains largely foreign born and trained, and the churches have rarely altered or been altered by the mainstream of American history.

American Jews

Like Catholicism, American Judaism has overcome awesome challenges from within and without. Almost half the world's Jewry lives in the United States—some 6 million persons. While Jews have a long history in America, the vast majority spring from an immigrant wave that was at its height between 1880 and 1920.

Five members of Columbus' crews were Marranos, Spanish Jews forcibly converted to Catholicism during the Inquisition. There have been American Jewish congregations since 1654, when 23 refugees from Spain, Portugal, and a way-stop in Brazil stepped ashore at New Amsterdam. While colonial laws denied Jews certain political rights, they were almost universally permitted to worship as they pleased—an indulgence then rare in the Western World. There were just over 2,000 Jews in America in 1775, but no fewer than 20 served as officers in the Continental Army, and Jewish merchants helped provide vital financial backing for the Patriot cause.

Encouraged by the infant Republic's pledge of religious liberty, growing numbers of Jews, mostly from Germany, came to America before 1850. Many made their way west as itinerant peddlers and shop clerks, swiftly working themselves up to become successful merchants, wholesalers, and financiers. They developed their own tightly knit society dominated by cultured families of German origin, and many abandoned Orthodoxy for Reform Judaism under the leadership of Rabbi Isaac Mayer Wise. Reform Judaism offered easy accommodation with American life, including services in English, men and women worshiping together, and relaxed dietary laws. Conservative congregations, retaining many more of the fundamental traditions of Orthodoxy, offered a third choice. American Jewry is now divided more or less equally among the three branches.

Beginning in the 1870's large numbers of Eastern European Jews flocked to America in flight from brutal pogroms. Some 2,388,000 Jews arrived between 1881 and 1924 alone. Most were poor, Orthodox, and literate only in Yiddish. They became the targets of widespread anti-Semitism and were simultaneously disdained as foreigners and greenhorns by the descendants of earlier Jewish immigrants. In the Eastern cities communities of Yiddish-speaking Jews from Russia, Poland, Lithuania, Romania, and Austria-Hungary created their own literature and press and established synagogues, schools, and mutual-aid societies. In New York, where most of the newcomers settled on the teeming Lower East Side, many worked in the needle trades, and some became leaders of the labor movement.

Thanks largely to their love of learning and to their hard-won skill at surviving as an embattled minority, Jews have flourished in America despite having had to face many forms of bigotry. Their contributions to learning and literature, science and law, business and politics, and music and medicine have been far out of proportion to their numbers.

In the "Monkey Trial" *of 1925, Clarence Darrow (left) unsuccessfully defended John Scopes, accused of having taught evolution in defiance of a Tennessee law. William Jennings Bryan (right), for the prosecution, was ridiculed by many, including* Judge *magazine.*

Protestantism Reaches Its Peak

In the period after the Civil War, with the growth of science, culture, and philosophy in America, Protestantism faced many intellectual challenges. The teachings of Charles Darwin called the Biblical account of the creation into question. Some archeologists and scriptural historians challenged the Bible's strict historical accuracy. The new sciences of psychology and sociology seemed to encourage a view of religion as a social phenomenon rather than as divinely revealed truth. Finally, tardy inquiries into non-Western faiths convinced many students that Eastern religions had much to offer and that Christianity had no monopoly on the eternal verities.

Protestant churches did not retreat under this onslaught. Indeed, the years between 1890 and 1910 saw Protestantism reach new heights. Overseas missions mushroomed, and missionary concern for the souls of America's "little brown brothers" in the Philippines was among the influences that prompted a reluctant President William McKinley to pursue an empire-building course in the Pacific. New churches opened daily; attendance soared; celebrated ministers were hailed as heroes. Churchmen continued to lead the crusade against alcohol. State after State—and finally, in 1920, the Nation—went dry.

But many religious leaders reacted strongly against the new intellectual and social currents. Some reaffirmed their faith in the Bible's literal truth and denounced "godless science." In the South and Middle West these fundamentalists persuaded some State legislatures to forbid the teaching of any scientific theory that conflicted with their religious conviction. The struggle between fundamentalism and modernism threatened the unity of many denominations in the early 1900's and provided the country with vivid drama in the celebrated Scopes Trial of 1925.

Most clergymen, however, sought to reconcile science and religion. Many came to believe with historian John Fiske that "Evolution is God's way of doing things." Some preached the "Gospel of Wealth" advocated by multimillionaire Andrew Carnegie. Carnegie agreed with the Social Darwinists Herbert Spencer and William Graham Sumner that life was ruled by Darwin's principle, "the survival of the fittest." Men of ability and drive should accumulate wealth, Carnegie said, but they would die disgraced if they failed to use a large portion of it for the public good. Other millionaires, such as John D. Rockefeller and Henry Ford, agreed with this and indulged in massive philanthropy.

Stars of the Sawdust Trail. *Dwight L. Moody (top left), shown preaching in a giant Brooklyn tabernacle in 1875, was the leading revivalist in the late 1800's. He set the vigorous, pulpit-pounding style of modern evangelism. Among those who followed in the footsteps of Moody were ball-player-turned-preacher Billy Sunday (far left), very popular prior to World War I; Aimee Semple McPherson (above), leader in the 1920's and 1930's of her own Los Angeles-based International Church of the Four-Square Gospel; and Baptist Billy Graham (left), whose dynamic preaching made him one of the best known ministers in the world.*

The rise of the cities and the growth of industrialism afforded ample opportunities for religious work. Beginning in the 1870's spellbinding evangelist Dwight L. Moody stumped the cities, converting thousands. A former shoe salesman with a businessman's shrewd eye for organizational detail and a burning desire to preach the redeeming power of God's love, Moody pioneered the techniques of modern evangelism.

Moody's audiences were mostly middle class; more strenuous efforts were needed to reach the urban poor. The Young Men's Christian Association and the Salvation Army, both British in origin, worked in the slums; so did church-supported settlement houses and rescue missions. For some young clergymen, appalled at the inequities spawned by the industrial revolution, more drastic action was required. Their best known spokesman was Baptist Walter Rauschenbusch, who had battled big city poverty and vice firsthand as a minister in New York's notorious Hell's Kitchen. In radical opposition to Social Darwinism, he proposed a new Social Gospel. Modern capitalism rewarded selfishness, not goodness, he argued. Only by exchanging the hatred engendered by competition for the Christian love fostered by cooperation could the churches fulfill their proper role and the kingdom of God at last be attained. Partly in response to the Social Gospel, the Federal Council of Churches of Christ in America, forerunner of the National Council of the Churches of Christ in the U.S.A., was established in 1908 to strengthen the movement to ease social ills.

Rauschenbusch's dream of achieving the kingdom of God on Earth was dimmed by World War I and its isolationist aftermath. Clearly man was not progressing as the advocates of Christian Socialism had hoped. But the religious liberals' determination to improve man's lot survived in tempered form in the neoorthodoxy of theologian Reinhold Niebuhr and others. In *Moral Man and Immoral Society* (1932) and other influential works he argued that it was impossible for imperfect men ever to embody the will of a perfect God. He urged churchmen to work ceaselessly for social reform but with a realistic sense of their own limitations and an understanding of the human fallibility of all mass movements. Individual churchmen of all faiths continue to be active in social and political causes, as evidenced in the civil rights and anti-Vietnam War struggles of the 1960's.

Growth and Diversity

Since in matters of religion the United States has long been one of the most pluralistic of nations, it is not surprising that it has been a leader in the global ecumenical movement. The National Conference of Christians and Jews was established in 1928 to combat religious tension. Twenty years later American churchmen were instrumental in creating the World Council of Churches, dedicated to what one historian termed "the gathering tide of Christian reunion." The U.S. Catholic Church, initially cautious about interfaith cooperation, joined the surge toward ecumenism after Pope John XXIII convened the Second Vatican Council in 1962.

While church membership has generally risen for all faiths since the Revolution, the churches are no longer the linchpin of daily life for most Americans. This is largely due to the rise of science and secularism and the increasing complexity of modern life. Nonetheless, religion remains a vital part of the American scene. Some epochs have witnessed particularly rapid religious growth and ferment. The 1950's was such a period; for the first time a majority of the American people claimed membership in a church or synagogue.

The late 1960's and early 1970's seemed to signal still another. Traditional denominations suffered an internal turbulence that echoed the rapid change sweeping society. Clergy and laymen of every faith debated the proper attitudes toward peace and civil rights. Catholic priests and nuns challenged the doctrine of celibacy; women sought the Anglican priesthood; controversy over the ethics of abortion and birth control split congregations; the laity generally demanded a greater role in church affairs.

Meanwhile, other Americans followed unorthodox paths in search of truth, developing new faiths or adapting ancient cults to modern needs. Among the most striking phenomena were a new interest in astrology and the occult; enthusiasm for Eastern religions, particularly Zen Buddhism and offshoots of Hinduism that stressed yogic meditation; the infusion of Pentecostal practices, such as speaking in tongues, into once-staid denominations; and the "Jesus Movement," which attracted thousands of enthusiastic young devotees.

History suggests that some new religious enthusiasms will die away, others will merge with older denominations, still others may endure. But their extraordinary diversity bears vivid witness to the continuing richness of American religious life.

A Rich Heritage of Faiths

The Largest Religious Denominations in Ame

In no nation on Earth is religion more diverse than in the Unit States. The chart at right indicates the relative size of the 52 ma denominations whose membership exceeds 100,000. (Althou enrollments are measured differently, these are the best availa statistics.) The chart only hints at the rich and dynamic reali The *Yearbook of American and Canadian Churches* lists an astonis ing 223 sects, cults, and denominations—not counting groups li The First Church of Christ, Scientist, which provide no membe ship statistics, and other organizations whose adherents make in devotion what they may lack in numbers or prestige. To wh can we attribute this extraordinary richness? Some faiths—li Anglicanism and Catholicism—outwardly changed relatively l tle for many years. Others—like Quakerism and Congregatio alism—were greatly altered by life in the New World. Still oth arrived with the 19th-century immigrant tide or were "made America."

Fertile Ground for New Faiths

Most American faiths were brought here from Europe, but some were born and nurtured on U.S. soil. Five of the most important of these are outlined here.

Adventists. All five major U.S.-founded Adventist sects stem from the prophecies of William Miller, a Baptist evangelist who predicted that Christ's Second Coming, or Advent, would occur in 1843, then in 1844. Both deadlines passed, but enough followers remained to establish several Millerite, or Adventist, sects. All believe in a millennium set in the indefinite future.

The Church of Jesus Christ of the Latter-day Saints (Mormonism). Mormonism was officially founded at Fayette, New York, in 1830 by Joseph Smith. Moving westward, he established his church's headquarters in Kirtland, Ohio, in 1831. His tightly knit organization and novel doctrines (including advocacy of polygamy) alienated many nonbelievers, and Smith and his disciples were hounded from Ohio to Missouri to Illinois. Smith was killed at Nauvoo, Illinois, in 1844. In early April of 1847 Brigham Young led Smith's surviving followers to Utah, where they founded Salt Lake City.

Disciples of Christ. In backwoods Pennsylvania in the early 1800's, Thomas Campbell and his son Alexander, founders of the Disciples, held that the New Testament alone should guide Christians and that salvation was granted to all who believed in Christ. Today each local church elects its own officers and recognizes no outside ecclesiastical authority.

The First Church of Christ, Scientist. Christian Scientists follow the teachings of Mary Baker Eddy, who founded their church in 1879. She taught that God is the sole source or principle of being and that an understanding of His power heals both disease and sin, as in the early Christian Church.

Jehovah's Witnesses. Believing that "millions now living will never die," Witnesses look forward to an imminent Second Coming. They campaign aggressively to save the largest possible number of souls before the wicked are destroyed. Organized by Charles Taze Russell in Pittsburgh in 1872, they object to military service and much modern medicine on Scriptural grounds.

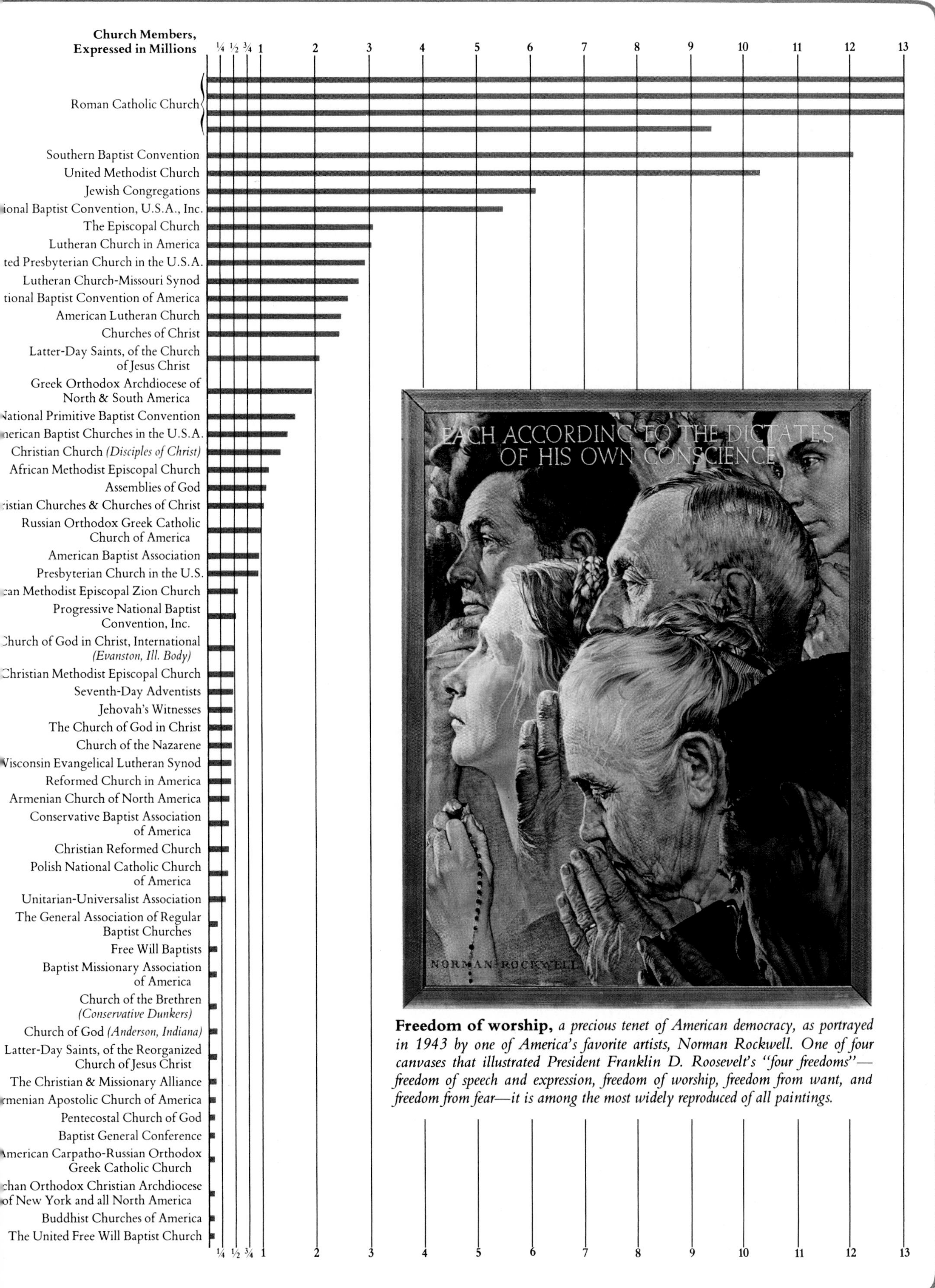

Freedom of worship, *a precious tenet of American democracy, as portrayed in 1943 by one of America's favorite artists, Norman Rockwell. One of four canvases that illustrated President Franklin D. Roosevelt's "four freedoms"—freedom of speech and expression, freedom of worship, freedom from want, and freedom from fear—it is among the most widely reproduced of all paintings.*

MAKING DEMOCRACY WORK

The Bill of Rights

FIRST AMENDMENT. Congress shall make no law respecting an establishment of religion, or prohibiting the free exercise thereof; or abridging the freedom of speech, or of the press; or the right of the people peaceably to assemble, and to petition the government for a redress of grievances.

SECOND AMENDMENT. A well regulated Militia, being necessary to the security of a free State, the right of the people to keep and bear Arms, shall not be infringed.

THIRD AMENDMENT. No soldier shall, in time of peace be quartered in any house, without the consent of the Owner, nor in time of war, but in a manner to be prescribed by law.

FOURTH AMENDMENT. The right of the people to be secure in their persons, houses, papers, and effects, against unreasonable searches and seizures, shall not be violated, and no Warrants shall issue, but upon probable cause, supported by Oath or affirmation, and particularly describing the place to be searched, and the persons or things to be seized.

FIFTH AMENDMENT. No person shall be held to answer for a capital, or otherwise infamous crime, unless on a presentment or indictment of a Grand Jury, except in cases arising in the land or naval forces, or in the Militia, when in actual service in time of War or public danger; nor shall any person be subject for the same offence to be twice put in jeopardy of life or limb; nor shall be compelled in any criminal case to be a witness against himself, nor be deprived of life, liberty, or property, without due process of law; nor shall private property be taken for public use, without just compensation.

SIXTH AMENDMENT. In all criminal prosecutions, the accused shall enjoy the right to a speedy and public trial, by an impartial jury of the State and district wherein the crime shall have been committed, which district shall have been previously ascertained by law, and to be informed of the nature and cause of the accusation; to be confronted with the witnesses against him; to have compulsory process for obtaining witnesses in his favor, and to have the Assistance of Counsel for his defence.

SEVENTH AMENDMENT. In Suits at common law, where the value in controversy shall exceed twenty dollars, the right of trial by jury shall be preserved, and no fact tried by a jury, shall be otherwise re-examined in any Court of the United States, than according to the rules of the common law.

EIGHTH AMENDMENT. Excessive bail shall not be required, nor excessive fines imposed, nor cruel and unusual punishments inflicted.

NINTH AMENDMENT. The enumeration in the Constitution, of certain rights, shall not be construed to deny or disparage others retained by the people.

TENTH AMENDMENT. The powers not delegated to the United States by the Constitution, nor prohibited by it to the States, are reserved to the States respectively, or to the people.

For all the genius of that remarkable document, the Constitution of the United States, it had a glaring defect, according to many critics. They deplored the absence of articles specifically prohibiting the Federal Government from invading an individual's rights of life, liberty, and property. But the consensus at the Constitutional Convention was that no Federal bill of rights was needed because the States guaranteed individual rights in their constitutions. However, Massachusetts, Maryland, and New York made their ratification of the Constitution contingent upon the adoption of a Federal bill of rights.

When the newly established Congress met in 1789, one of its first priorities was to amend the Constitution, provided for in Article V. James Madison proposed a series of amendments, and 12 of them were adopted by Congress. In 1791, 10 of the 12 amendments, as shown on the facing page, were ratified by the States.

The articles have stood the test of time, but the exact meaning of some is still debated. For example, should the second amendment's right "to keep and bear Arms" to maintain a "Militia" be interpreted as an all-inclusive right to keep firearms? Where do the modern forms of electronic eavesdropping stand in relation to the fourth amendment's stricture against "unreasonable searches and seizures"? In the light of the eighth amendment's statement on "cruel and unusual punishments" how should the death penalty be considered? Judicial interpretation will continue to shade their precise meaning, but the freedoms bestowed by these articles, as indicated in the breakdown below, are basic to our way of life.

At Home and in the Community

We are exempt from:	*We are entitled to:*
Unreasonable or unwarranted searches and seizures of persons, houses, papers, and effects	Worship as we please
The taking of property for public use without just compensation	Speak freely
The quartering of soldiers in our homes	Publish the truth
	Assemble peaceably
	Keep and bear arms

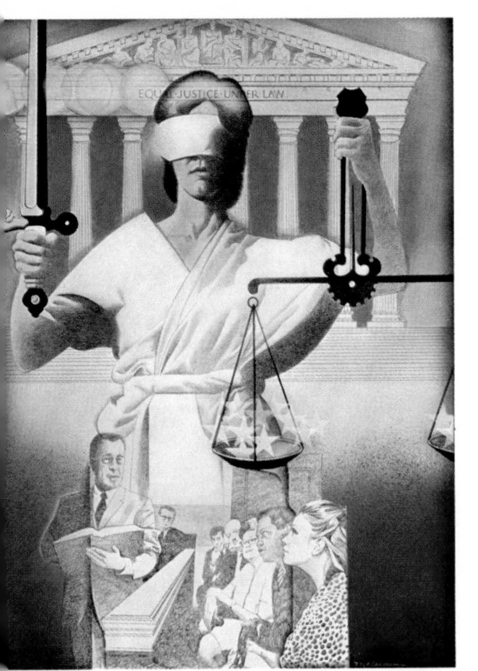

In a Court of Law

We are exempt from:	*We are entitled to:*
Being tried twice for the same offense	Petition for redress of grievances
Bearing witness against ourselves	Due process of law regarding life, liberty, and property
Excessive bail	Speedy public trial by impartial jury
Excessive fines	Be informed of the nature and cause of an accusation
Infliction of cruel and unusual punishments	Confront any witnesses against us
	Obtain witnesses in our favor
	Assistance of counsel for defense

CHAPTER SIX

Putting the Land To Work

The role of the American farmer in the making of Amer ica has often been taken for granted. Almost every Ameri can knows Daniel Chester French's statue "The Minu Man." That tall, forthright figure with musket in han has become a symbol of American independence; few re member that the minuteman is standing by a plow. Bu as the poet Ralph Waldo Emerson correctly pointed ou it was "embattled farmers" who faced the Redcoats a Concord and "fired the shot heard round the world."

Many of the Founding Fathers realized the importan of agriculture to the new Nation and urged America farmers to adopt more advanced scientific farming tech

Nothing about their new land impressed the early European settlers so much as its unbelievable lushness. "I thinke in all the world the like abundance is not to be found," wrote the captain of one of Sir Walter Raleigh's ships in 1584.

He had seen only the Eastern edge of one of the greatest of all forests, with trees 250 feet high and up to 13 feet in diameter. Little did he know that this magnificent woodland stretched 700 miles, from the sandy beaches of what Raleigh would christen Virginia to the Mississippi Valley. It was broken only by occasional meadows and small fields cleared by the Indians for their crops.

The greatest treasure was hidden beneath the tangle of plants on the forest floor. Here was the accumulated fertility of thousands of years of growth and decay. This was some of the richest soil man had ever known.

Many of the settlers were farmers, but at first the imported plantings and ways of cultivation failed in the New World. The newcomers did not know where to find the most fertile land nor how to prepare the soil nor how to sow their barley, wheat, and peas. Often the colonists arrived well after the spring planting season. William Bradford, the Governor of Plymouth Colony, where half of the original settlers died of disease or starvation, reported that the European crops "came not to good, eather by ye badness of ye seed, or lateness of ye season, or both or some other defecte." Fortunately for the survivors, friendly Indians taught them how to plant native crops, such as maize, beans, and squash, on hills around the stumps of felled trees, with a fish in each mound for fertilizer. Only after Indian tutoring, as Bradford said, did the colonists begin to enjoy "the sweetness of the land."

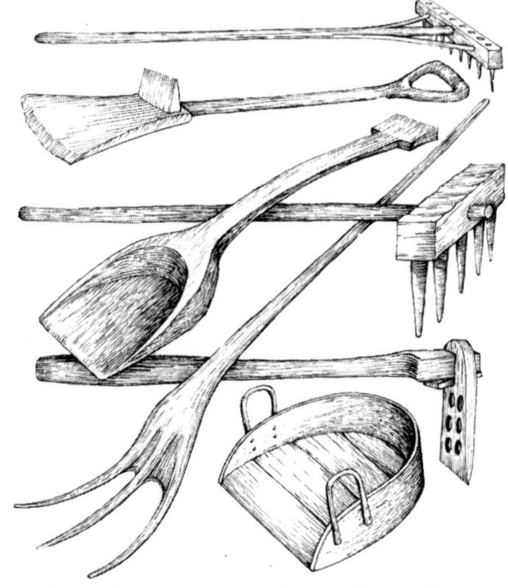

When the *American colonists began farming in the New World, plows and iron tools were scarce. Most of the work was done with primitive handmade wooden tools such as these.*

Old World ideas had to be discarded before colonial agriculture could thrive. The entire continent north of Mexico was claimed by the King of England, and he gave immense estates to his friends and to English land companies. The absentee landlords soon found, however, that few colonial farmers would work hard on someone else's land or even on communally owned property. Capt. John Smith of Virginia said, "When our people were fed from the common store, glad was he who could slip from his labor," but when farmers had their own land, "they will doe in a day" what had previously taken a week. Most of the proprietors turned to selling or granting the land, often for a small yearly fee, to those who lived on it.

As the settlers mastered farming techniques suitable to the New World, the Colonies progressed beyond their simple beginnings of wilderness outposts dependent on the mother country. The wooden handtools of agriculture had changed little from those used 3,000 years earlier in the Nile Valley. Clearing trees from a single acre might require months of dawn-to-dusk labor. A family could, however, raise just about everything it needed except salt, powder for the family musket, and iron for tools and hardware. Beside the farmhouse was an orchard with apple and peach trees grown from seed. In the garden European vegetables such as peas, turnips, cabbages, and lettuce grew alongside Indian plants—beans, pumpkins,

ques. Washington, Franklin, Jefferson, and Monroe be-
ıged to farm-improvement societies and experimented
th new kinds of tools and seeds. One agricultural inven-
n, Eli Whitney's cotton gin, changed the economic and
:ial structure of the South and contributed to the causes
the Civil War. During that war another farm tool,
yrus McCormick's reaper, helped preserve the Union.
ncoln's Secretary of War Edwin M. Stanton once re-
ırked, "Without McCormick's invention I fear the
orth could not win." Much later, during the two World
'ars, farmers' "battles of production" were of primary
portance in our ultimate military victories.*

U.S. farmers have shaped the Nation in more subtle ways. The American pioneer spirit springs from the farm families who crossed the frontier in covered wagons seeking new lands. The American fondness for wide-open spaces, many of our figures of speech—and doubtless some of our rambunctiousness—owe much to the Western cowboys who were employed by cattle farmers. Today farmers make up little more than 2 percent of the American population; but the amazing productivity of this small group supplies the raw materials for much of the industry in the United States and gives Americans the most varied diets for the least share of their incomes of any nation on Earth.

The Original American Farmers

Indians Helped the Colonists Get Started

Indians had been farming the land successfully for some 6,500 years by the time the first European colonists set foot in the New World. A thriving agriculture was the basis of the complex civilizations of the Incas in South America, the Aztecs and Mayas in Central America and Mexico, and the Pueblos and Mound Builders in North America.

The staple of these civilizations was maize, or corn, a native plant that had been domesticated from wild grasses. The first British colonists along the Atlantic coast found cornfields growing in neat rows near bark-covered houses, as in the Indian village seen at right. Other Indian crops were beans, pumpkins, tobacco, and sunflowers. The only domesticated animals were the dog, sometimes used as a beast of burden, and the turkey, an important source of meat and one of the first products of American agriculture introduced into Europe. Not all Indians were farmers; many were nomads who lived by hunting. Even the farming tribes supplemented their diets with fresh game and wild plants.

When early colonists faced starvation because they had neglected their planting or were faced with crop failures, the Indians taught the newcomers how to cultivate and use New World plants. Soon colonial gardens began to resemble those in Indian villages. Corn was planted in hills, often with fish or manure for fertilizer. After the corn sprouted, beans were planted in the hills so that the vines could use the stalks as poles. Hilling up the soil caused it to absorb more of the sun's heat and made the seeds germinate faster. Pumpkin and squash were sown between the rows. The squaws often scolded the colonists for neglecting the weeding. The Indians also taught the Europeans how to make maple syrup, dyes from plants, corncribs, and clamshell hoes. Small huts like the one in the midst of the "rype" corn at top were built in the cornfields. In them children with rattles earned their keep by serving as living scarecrows.

In 1585 artist *John White sketched this Indian village in what is now North Carolina. Well-tended fields of ripe, green, and newly planted corn grow beside the center street. White later became the leader of the colonists who settled on Roanoke Island.*

squash, and the mainstay, corn. As he cleared more land, the farmer found he could also grow old-country staple grains, such as wheat, rye, and oats. By the late 1600's New York and Pennsylvania were known as the bread Colonies. Cows, sheep, swine, and chickens, imported from England, were at first only half domesticated. In some Colonies, between the Tidewater and the Alleghenies, a range cattle industry developed. In other areas livestock was first herded and then kept behind split-rail fences or walls made from stones that had been cleared to make farmland and pastures. A good enclosure had to be "pig-tight, horse-high and bull-strong." Flax and wool provided cloth; honey and maple syrup, sweetening.

A Noxious but Profitable Weed

Corn had saved the first farmers from starvation; another New World plant —tobacco—became the Colonies' first big-money crop. In 1613 Virginian John Rolfe—who a year later married the Indian princess Pocahontas—grew a mild variety of tobacco from seed brought from the West Indies (the Indians had introduced the colonists to a harsher variety), and shipped a few barrels to England. In Europe love of Lady Nicotine, mostly in the form of snuff and pipe tobacco, "spread faster than any religion," as historian Samuel Eliot Morison has written. Virginia went tobacco-mad, growing the plants even in the main streets of Jamestown, until it seemed to one visitor that the Virginians were "rooting in the ground about tobacco like Swine."

Tobacco has been *a major U.S. export since John Rolfe sent the first shipment from Jamestown to England in 1613. Here an early British merchant advertises "best-Virginia."*

Tobacco was used as legal tender. Prices of goods, and even the salaries of the same ministers who agreed with James I that it was a "vile and stinking weed," were expressed in pounds of tobacco. Tobacco growing spread to Maryland and the Carolinas, and the crop became the most important export of colonial times. Within a few decades Virginia and Maryland were exporting 28 million pounds a year to Europe, and a planter could make his fortune in a single season. No effort was made to rest or feed the soil, and in 3 or 4 years it was exhausted. The grower then abandoned his ruined fields and cleared more forest. Virgin land was consumed at a great rate.

Tobacco required endless hours of painstaking labor, as it does to this day. It had to be seeded, transplanted to the field, suckered (pruned), cut, and cured; then the leaves had to be carefully stripped from the stalk and packed in hogsheads. English indentured servants—men and women who had agreed to work for a fixed period of years to pay their passage—did some of the work. But a new source of labor arrived in Jamestown in August 1619 when, John Rolfe reported, there "came a Dutch man of War that sold us 20 negars." The great profits that were soon to come were made from the toil of these unfortunates and the thousands who followed.

Another bonanza came to the Southern Colonies by accident, according to legend, when a storm forced a ship into Charleston harbor in 1694 with a hold full of seed rice from Madagascar. Rice, which requires flooded fields during planting, proved well suited to the low-lying coastal areas of South Carolina and Georgia. By 1765 the chief ports of these Colonies were shipping 65 million pounds of rice a year. Its cultivation required workers to put in 12-hour days under the blistering sun up to their knees in malarial swamps. More slaves were the answer. The unhealthy conditions took a great toll of lives. The workers contracted "all the plagues of Egypt," according to a planter's diary.

In the early 1740's Eliza Lucas of South Carolina demonstrated that indigo could also be grown profitably on plantations with slave labor. This blue dyestuff, so vital to the British wool industry that the Crown placed a bounty on its production, nicely complemented the rice harvest. Indigo could be grown on higher ground above the paddies and tended by the slaves when they were not busy with the rice. Lumber, resin, and tar from the great pine forests also helped to build Southern fortunes.

The rich planters, though a small minority, dominated the South culturally and politically. For them, life in the South was easy. English ships came right to the wharves of the riverside plantations, collected the crops, and delivered farm tools, furniture, servants, fine cloth, and all kinds of luxury items. There was little need to build factories or train craftsmen. Plantation blacksmiths and artisans, often slaves, fashioned the few additional products that were necessary, but almost nothing was made to be sold. Charleston, the colonial South's single big city, could not boast one outstanding craft or craftsman. As late as the mid-1700's, if a piece of fine silk was faded, it would probably be sent to England for redyeing. This comfortable, rural way of life would eventually set the South in conflict with the North and in little more than a hundred years would be destroyed.

In the North a more self-reliant, mercantile way of

Colonial Commodities
Sectional Differences Emerge

Almost from the first, long before anyone had dreamed of an independent United States, two nations were in genesis in colonial America. Climate and soil were perhaps the determining factors in creating these separate societies, but religion and class background were important as well. In the North, in New England and the Middle Atlantic Colonies, a generally chilly climate, rocky soil, and hilly terrain made subsistence farming the most practical form of agriculture. The family farm, producing vegetables, corn, wheat, and livestock for local consumption, was the usual agricultural institution, although in the Hudson Valley and in Pennsylvania large estates did flourish. Fishing for cod was a major New England enterprise and a source of trade with Europe. In general, small-scale enterprises dovetailed nicely with the egalitarian philosophies of the founders of many Northern Colonies.

The South presented a different picture. Here, in the rich, deep tideland plains, watered by broad rivers, plantation agriculture set the style of the largely rural South. There were, of course, many small subsistence farms, but in Virginia, tobacco supported large and increasingly elegant plantation manors, while farther to the south, rice and indigo were the crops of choice. The profitable cultivation of these crops required a large, cheap labor pool, which the aristocratic South found in slavery. By the mid-1700's Southern crops had overwhelmed their markets abroad, and prices plunged, while the prices of goods the southerners bought remained high. Many plantation owners became deeply indebted to agents in England and increasingly impatient with British control of the colonial economy.

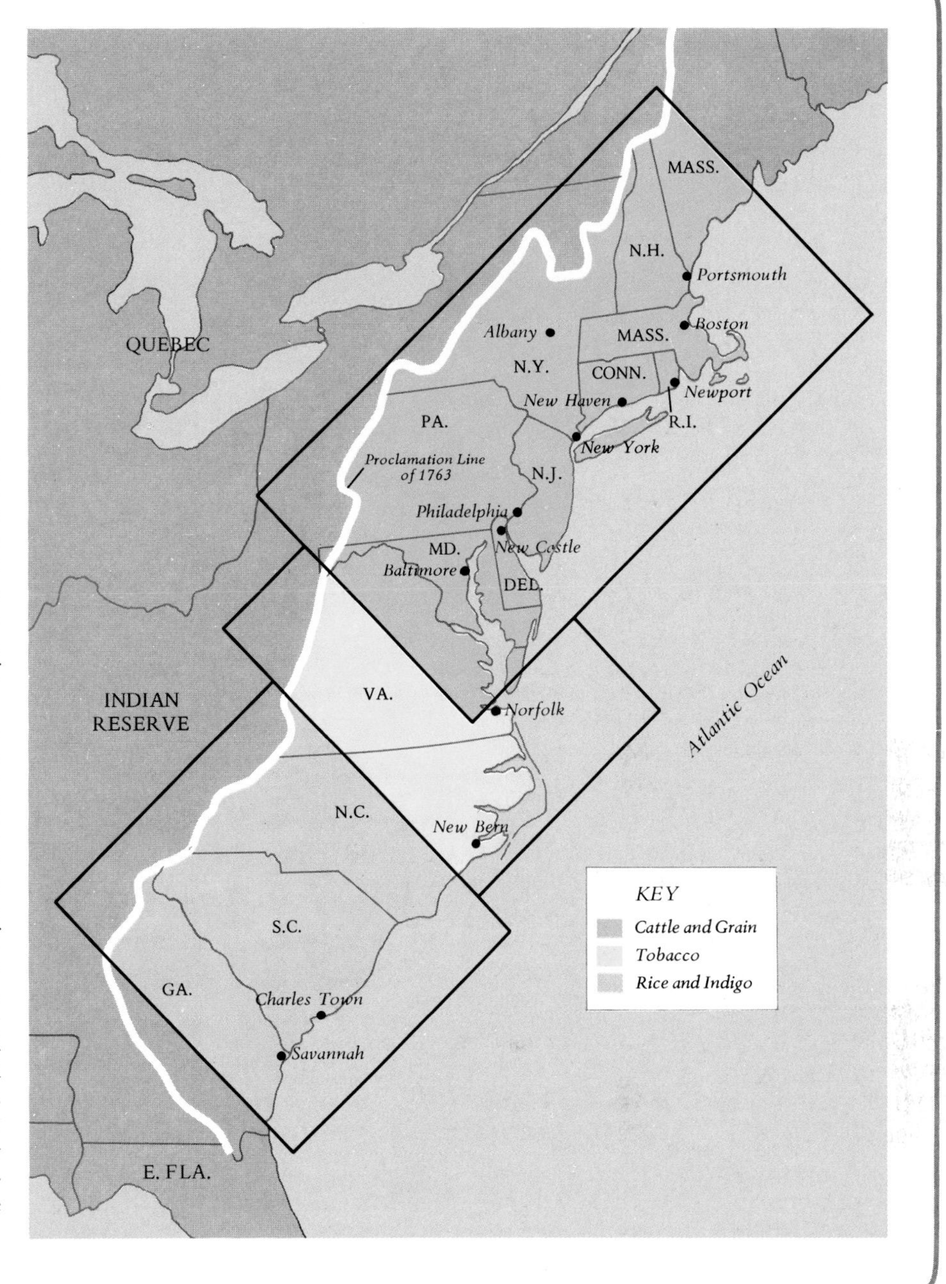

life developed. There few farmers had land holdings of more than several hundred acres. Corn, wheat, and barley surpluses were a drug on the foreign market. English merchant ships found less profit in Northern than in Southern waters. If a Massachusetts farmer wanted tools, furniture, or other household goods, he was likely to make them. During the long winters farm families turned out everything from leather breeches to wagons at their home spinning wheels, workbenches, and looms.

Yankee Traders Serve the South

Some things farmers could not make, and they had their surplus crops to dispose of. Boston, Salem, Newport, Portsmouth, Philadelphia, and other Northern ports began building merchant ships that roamed the seven seas to find sources and markets. Yankee skippers traded fish, lumber, and grain in the West Indies for sugar, which they then exchanged in England for manufactured goods. One infamous trade pattern involved West Indies molasses, received in exchange for Northern produce. It was brought back to New England and distilled into rum. Not all the rum was drunk in America although, as the scholar T. Harry Williams has noted, mighty efforts were made. The remainder was taken to Africa and used to buy slaves, who were carried to the West Indies and the Southern Colonies, completing the triangle.

Farm produce brought prosperity, but in New England the merchants called the tune. Northern farmers and Southern planters did have one attitude in common: They seemed to think that the natural resources were inexhaustible, and they squandered them recklessly.

While the statistics of the time show a trade balance

Farmer-Led Rebellions

Nearly all the soldiers who fought for America's independence were farmers, but, once the war was won, many turned against the new Government they had helped to bring into being.

New England's farmers suffered greatly in the postwar depression. Taxes on land and buildings were high and income from crops pitifully low. Many farms were confiscated and their dispossessed owners thrown into jail for inability to meet outstanding debts. In 1785, in Worcester County, Massachusetts, alone, 92 of these unfortunates were imprisoned.

Daniel Shays, a former captain in the Continental Army, organized and drilled a ragtag army of Massachusetts farmers, demanding tax relief, a moratorium on debt collection, and other fiscal reforms. During the late summer of 1786 armed bands of Shaysites broke up court sessions and prevented sheriffs' sales.

Wealthy merchants financed an army of state militiamen who battled Shays' troops in the winter of 1787, killing several and capturing others. The rebellion collapsed. Shays and about a dozen of his lieutenants were sentenced to death but later pardoned by Gov. John Hancock. Some of their demands for tax relief and debt postponement were met. But the most significant result was the impact on the majority of delegates at the Constitutional Convention in Philadelphia, who resolved to establish a federal government strong enough to meet such emergencies and to head off future unrest by improving the economy.

The new Government under the Constitution was soon challenged. In 1794 farmers of western Pennsylvania refused to pay an excise tax on whisky and assaulted Federal officers. This time the solution was not left to State authorities. President George Washington used his authority to call out 15,000 militiamen and ordered them to march into Pennsylvania. Unlike the Shaysites, who stood and fought, the Pennsylvanians saw the futility of resisting the overwhelming militia force. The rebellion quickly collapsed and the distillers meekly paid their taxes. The power of the Central Government had been asserted, although the Democratic-Republicans accused the Government of using excessive force.

that was favorable to the Southern Colonies throughout much of the colonial period, the data fail to reveal the hidden costs—most of which went into British pockets—for freight and insurance, commissions of the agents in London who handled Southern crops, and interest on debts and taxes. Although the value of colonial exports to Britain in the 1770's was seven times that of 1697, the trade deficit with Britain was almost £3 million in 1771. Indeed, Britain's insistence on the right to tax and regulate colonial commerce—and with it colonial agriculture—was to prove an important cause of the Revolution. In addition the British ban on settlement west of the Appalachians after 1763 aroused the antagonism of land-hungry settlers. When war broke out the farmers' attitude was summed up by one Reuben Stebbins, who heard the firing at the Battle of Bennington, Vermont, got out his horse and musket, and headed for the battle to see "who's goin' to own this farm."

The war had little effect on colonial agriculture. The Army called only a small portion of the able-bodied men. Most farmers continued as usual, particularly in New England, where few battles were fought after the first weeks of the war. In the Middle Colonies, where the bloodshed was heaviest, the influx of gold for Army payrolls and supplies raised the farm prices.

A Promising New Crop for the South

In the South, however, the planters suffered. The British raided Virginia and the Carolinas from 1778 to 1781 and confiscated slaves and crops. There the war had an important side effect: Loss of the British market all but ended the export of indigo and rice, and the planters hastened their experiments with a new crop, cotton.

In England gentlemen farmers with a scientific turn of mind, such as Jethro Tull (inventor of the grain drill) and Charles Townshend (nicknamed Turnip Townshend because he advocated the value of turnips in crop rotation), were starting another revolution—in agriculture. They developed improved crop varieties, better methods of cultivation, and selective stock breeding.

American farmers were slow to see the light of progress, but in 1785 the first society devoted entirely to the improvement of agriculture, the Philadelphia Society for Promoting Agriculture, held its initial meeting. Later the same year the Agricultural Society of South Carolina was formed. The Philadelphia group, which included George Washington and Benjamin Franklin, was the first to publish the results of experimental work. Members corresponded with English agricultural reformers and tried out new varieties of seeds, breeds of livestock, implements, and crop rotation. Societies such as these built the foundation for later agricultural development, which was nonetheless slow in coming in the new Nation.

The postwar recession was hard on many growers. Shays' Rebellion, in 1786–87, was a revolt of armed farmers against irksome Massachusetts economic policies. The Shaysites were defeated and dispersed. But many had feared the insurrection would lead to anarchy, and the rebellion impressed on the country the need for a strong central government to deal with internal strife and thus hastened adoption of the Federal Constitution.

A few years later, when farmers in western Pennsylvania rebelled against a whisky tax, President Washington quickly called up a militia force almost as large as the one he had commanded against the British. When the farmers saw these troops, most of them ran for home.

In the postwar South tobacco prices fell, rice production dropped, and indigo became less profitable. Southern planters still hoped for a miracle to make cotton more profitable. As early as 1786 Sea Island, or long-fiber, cotton was tried in America, but it was too susceptible to frosts, and although short-fiber, or upland, cotton flourished almost everywhere in the South, its green seeds were extremely hard to remove from the fibers.

Better Tools and Miraculous Machines

In the spring of 1793 a recent Yale graduate, Eli Whitney, visited Mrs. Nathanael Greene's plantation a few miles from Savannah. There, Whitney later recalled, he met "a number of very respectable gentlemen who all agreed that if a machine could be invented that would clean the cotton with expedition, it would be a great thing both to the country and to the inventor."

A week or so later Whitney "struck out a plan of a machine," which he called a gin (short for engine), to do the job. A revolving cylinder with wire teeth projecting through a grating pulled the fibers through and left the seeds behind. A revolving brush removed the lint from the teeth.

Although "absurdly simple," Whitney's gin transformed Southern agriculture and changed the course of a nation. Within a decade the cotton crop increased eightfold. Slavery, which had declined somewhat, now

The Impact of the Cotton Gin
The Invention That Divided North and South

When 27-year-old Eli Whitney invented his cotton gin in 1793, Southern agriculture was ailing. Prices of indigo, rice, and tobacco, the South's main cash crops, had dropped sharply after the Revolutionary War and the loss of the South's main market, England. As planters' profits declined, so did the advantage of keeping slaves. Northerners and southerners alike thought slavery would gradually die out.

Whitney's Yankee ingenuity changed that view. The new gin, powered by water, enabled a slave to clean the seeds from 50 times as much cotton as before, and soon horse- and mule-powered gins were available too. Production of cotton soared, and with it the need for slaves. By 1860 cotton made up 57 percent of all U.S. exports. The South had its cash crop. New England textile mill owners had a vital raw material, and Northern factory owners profited by selling manufactured goods to southerners.

Although the North welcomed the profits of the cotton-slave economy, it did not condone the "peculiar institution," and it steadily hardened its opposition to the South's demand that slavery be extended into Western territories. Other differences that divided North and South might have been resolved peacefully had not Whitney's gin made cotton king and slavery its handmaiden. Civil war was the resolution.

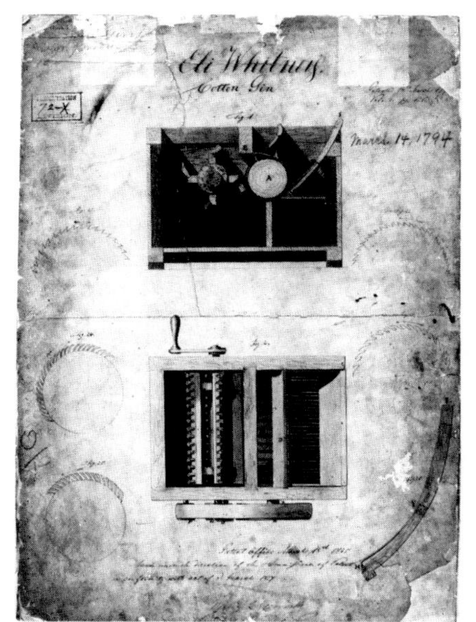

Whitney's cotton gin, *shown above in his patent drawing, was a model of simplicity. Slender wire fingers on a rotating wheel clawed at cotton held in a hopper and pulled the fibers through narrow slots at the bottom. The seeds, too large to pass through the slits, remained behind. Wire brushes on another wheel removed the fibers from the spikes. Earlier gins, like the one at right, were even simpler. Two rollers pulled the fibers one way and popped the seeds out in the opposite direction. Roller gins work for black-seed or Sea Island cotton, which is limited in output because it grows only in hot, moist coastal areas; more modern versions are still used for this type of cotton. Upland cotton grows almost anyplace that has 200 consecutive frost-free days and 24 inches of rain; but until Whitney's gin came along, upland cotton was unprofitable because its green seeds could be removed only by hand, at the rate of scarcely a pound a day per slave. Today's almost automatic cotton gin is based simply on improvements of Whitney's model.*

Thomas Jefferson *in the late 1700's invented this wooden forerunner of the modern moldboard plow. It broke the sod, he wrote, and had a "hind-end perpendicular to throw it over."*

seemed indispensable to southerners.

Thomas Jefferson, then Secretary of State, promised Whitney a patent (granted in 1794). Jefferson was working on an invention of his own, a plow with a moldboard to turn the sod into furrows. He calculated the design of least resistance by pulling various models through sand, much as aeronautical engineers develop aircraft designs in a wind tunnel. Jefferson's was the first major improvement in this basic implement since it was used by the Mesopotamians some 6,000 years earlier.

Another revolutionary invention was introduced on a hot July day in 1831. Polly Carson, a Virginia farm girl, was surprised to see two of her neighbor's slaves leading a strange parade down the lane past her house. The black men were doing their best to hold in check two frightened horses, hitched to a rattling, flapping contraption the like of which she had never before seen. A group of excited farmers walked alongside the odd machine.

Miss Polly was unimpressed. Curiosity did not arouse her enough to follow the parade to her neighbor John Steele's oatfield. Although she heard later that the "right smart curious" machine would not "ever come to much," Miss Polly had seen history going down her lane. The machine, a reaper, was the invention of another neighbor, 22-year-old Cyrus Hall McCormick. That afternoon it cut 6 acres of standing grain. As agricultural historian Grant Cannon wrote of the event: "From the time man first domesticated plants, no one had ever cut so much grain in such a short time."

Reaping and most other farmwork had always been done by manpower—or, in the case of most Indian tribes, womanpower. A muscular scytheman cut the grain and laid it in bunches; two or three banders tied the grain in sheaves; gatherers combined the sheaves into shocks; and gleaners collected what the others had missed. Two acres a day was a respectable speed for a cutter, even with frequent stops at a barrel of "ra-al Monongaly" (Monongahela), a potent Pennsylvania rye whisky used for "stimulation."

McCormick's invention gave the farmer an extra power source, the horse. With a team hitched to the reaper, two workers could cut 14 times as much wheat as they could with scythes. Dobbin was soon harnessed to many other newfangled rigs: mowers, binders, planters, cultivators, improved steel plows, and threshers, sometimes with the horse on a treadmill. Horses and mules, with their faster gaits, gradually replaced the oxen that had served so well since early colonial times—and which at the end of their 4-year working life often could be sold to the butcher for more than they had cost.

The decline of the ox, a romantic symbol of the pioneer farmer, marked the passing of a way of life. As he used more machinery, the farmer himself changed. He and his family no longer had to grow or manufacture all the necessities of life. He became a commercial specialist in one or several cash crops and used store-bought clothing, tools, and furniture.

Most of the leading industries in the booming new cities of the mid-1800's depended directly on agriculture. Of the 10 leading U.S. industries at the outbreak of the Civil War, 8 depended on agriculture for their raw materials. The flour and meal business, for example, which

The horse-drawn reaper *of young Cyrus Hall McCormick, first demonstrated in 1831, is celebrated in this commemorative print. It took two or three men a day to hand-scythe the quantity of grain that the Virginia Reaper could cut in a few hours. Although the machine revolutionized grain production, it contained nothing new. The vibrating horizontal knife, iron guides to hold the grain against the knife, a large reel to sweep the grain to the cutting edge, and a heavy wheel behind the horse to support and drive the reel and knife had all been tried before. However, McCormick was the first man to put them all together. The result, introduced into England in 1851, was a contraption that the* Times *of London called a "cross between a flying machine, a wheelbarrow and a chariot"—but it worked.*

Big-team hitches *of more than 30 horses were common in the West and Midwest during the late 1800's, when this photograph was taken in an Oregon wheatfield. The team is pulling a combine—a machine that cut the wheat and separated the grain from the straw and the kernels from the chaff in a single operation. Some combines weighed 15 tons and cut a swath more than 30 feet wide. These behemoths—along with mule team and horse-drawn gang plows, harrows, and planters—revolutionized agriculture by substituting animal muscle for manpower. The most popular draft horse was the high-spirited, hard-working Percheron, which usually stood more than 5 feet high at the shoulder and weighed over a ton. By 1930, when tractors began to be widely used, the time required to produce a bushel of wheat had been reduced from a total of 3 man-hours to just half an hour.*

grossed $250 million in 1859, relied on the grain crop.

Despite horse-drawn machinery, enlightened agricultural societies and journals, and men such as Edmund Ruffin—who proved on his Virginia plantation that the use of calcareous manure, crop rotation, and improved cultivation could double and triple crop yields—the farmers' main resource was still virgin land. The only substantial areas of new land lay to the west. In the late 1840's Mormons began growing corn by irrigation in Utah, and an epidemic of "Oregon fever" sent thousands of covered wagons on the long trails toward the Pacific. The object of the pioneers' quest was evident from the plows lashed to their wagons. As soon as they arrived and settled down, the migrants wanted even more land. Western settlers were only half joking when they said: "I don't want all the land. I only want what jines mine."

The Golden Age of Farming

By 1860 most of the Nation's corn, wheat, and wool were produced in Ohio and States farther west, while Texas was soon to become the realm of the cattle kings. Hungry markets brought closer by railroads, lands almost for the taking, and labor-saving machinery made this pre-Civil War period a golden age of farming. More than half the U.S. population were farmers, and about half of all Americans lived west of the Appalachians. Since the day when McCormick's reaper rattled past Miss Polly's place, wheat production had increased 75 percent; tobacco, 106 percent; and corn, half of it from the South, 40 percent. But cotton was king, accounting for nearly two-thirds of the Nation's total exports.

The Civil War was in many ways a conflict between wheat and cotton. The Southern States' faith in cotton encouraged them to secede. It was altogether appropriate that when the firing began on Fort Sumter in 1861, many of the Southern planters, Edmund Ruffin among them, were manning the batteries. Because the English and French needed Southern cotton, many southerners believed they would intervene and force the Union to recognize the Confederacy, and the war would be over.

But the emphasis on growing cotton impaired the South's war effort by increasing food shortages. By 1863 some Confederate soldiers were living on quarter rations of meat, and others were suffering from dysentery caused by unwholesome food. Even then many planters preferred to grow cotton rather than corn or wheat. The Confederacy limited planters to 3 or 4 acres of cotton for each field hand, but to little avail. As a writer in the Charleston *Mercury,* calling himself Clodhopper, said, even when planters observed the restriction, they saved their best land for cotton and babied it with "garden culture," meanwhile neglecting food crops.

Draft laws exempted every owner or overseer of 20 or more slaves from military service. This, plus the refusal of some planters to let their slaves be used for defense work and the fact that an exemption could be bought for $500, caused poorer southerners to call the conflict "a rich man's war, a poor man's fight."

The Balance Shifts to the North

While the Southern farmer watched his machinery wear out without hope of replacement, the North was putting new inventions to work. At the outbreak of the Civil War there were some 125,000 mowers and reapers in the

What Really Won the West
Three Innovations That Tamed the Land

In popular legend it was the blazing six-gun that won the West. But in fact, it was three less romantic innovations—the steel plow, barbed wire fencing, and the portable windmill—that made it possible for the pioneers to settle there. And the first farmers were a tough breed capable of making the best use of this readily available equipment; they often had to live off the wilderness for a year or so before they could get the land ready for crops or cattle.

The sea of grass covering the prairies grew from a dense network of roots that bound the soil like tangled twine. The typical plow of the early 1800's was not equal to this challenge because the heavy sod often broke the plow or stuck to the rough surface of the cast-iron blade. And even if it didn't break, the plow might require 10 or more oxen to pull it through the virgin soil.

It was not until the late 1830's, when John Deere developed plows of slick, smooth saw-blade steel, that the prairies could be farmed. With a Deere plow the heavy sod could be turned with one yoke of oxen or a span of horses. By 1857 Deere was selling 10,000 of his plows a year, mostly to prairie farmers. In 1868 James Oliver patented a process for hardening cast iron and used the material to make a chilled iron plow that was low in price and that sliced through prairie sod as smoothly as Deere's plow.

No sodbuster wanted to see a cattle herd driven through his fields once they had been plowed and planted, but often he was powerless to stop it. Then, in 1874, Joseph F. Glidden patented a practical type of barbed wire that was "lighter than air, stronger than whiskey and cheaper than dirt." The stinging wire could be ordered by mail and provided an efficient way to fence as large an area as the homesteader could afford. This enclosure of the land infuriated the cattlemen and led to some vicious battles on the range. By 1885 the Great Plains, which were crisscrossed by railroads and barbed wire, were too heavily stocked to support more cattle. Many big ranch companies were ruined by the terrible winter of 1886–87, which killed thousands of head of stock. The great cattle empires of the open range soon began to give way to grain fields and the fenced ranch, which produced a better breed of animal.

Meanwhile, windmills, turned by the almost ceaseless prairie wind, pumped water from deep wells into troughs and drinking pails, bringing life to thousands of acres of arid land. These sentinels, which came, disassembled, from the mail-order houses of the day, stood on nearly every farm or ranch in the Great Plains States until the 1930's, when they began to give way to electric power.

The windmill: *a miraculous mail-order waterhole.*

With the invention *of barbed wire it became possible for the first time to build an enforceable line around a piece of prairie property to keep the domesticated animals on the inside and wandering strays out. In 1890, $4 would buy 100 pounds of barbed wire similar to this sample of Joseph Glidden's invention. Today a collector would gladly pay $200 for an 18-inch length.*

This is the tool, *made by John Deere in 1837, that first broke the prairie sod.*

country; by 1864 the number in the North alone was 250,000. During the war years the North's production of wheat reached nearly 200 million bushels, more than the total national output in 1860. There were comparable increases in corn and other crops. The Northern farmer not only raised ample food to feed the Union but he produced significant amounts for export as well.

This surplus defeated the South's King Cotton diplomacy. Britain, faced with crop failures, desperately needed the food it bought from the North. The British were not prepared to risk a famine in order to recognize the South, and France followed Britain's lead. Neither country intervened on behalf of the Confederacy, and cotton rotted on the wharves of blockaded Southern ports. As a popular song put it: "Old King Cotton's dead and buried, brave young Corn is King." (Corn was the British name for wheat.)

When the southerners walked out of Congress after seceding from the Union, they took with them their opposition to measures that Northern farmers and westerners had been trying to push into law for as long as 40 years. Soon after the secession, in 1862, four laws were quickly enacted, which affect the country, and especially its agriculture, to this day.

The Homestead Act of 1862 gave settlers 160 acres of Federal land for a nominal filing fee if they would farm the land for 5 years. Some 15,000 homesteaders trekked westward on foot, on horseback, in covered wagons, by boat, and by train before the end of the war.

The Morrill Act of 1862 allowed every Union State 30,000 acres of public land for each Representative and Senator it was entitled to send to Congress. The land was to be sold and the proceeds used to aid in the establishment of agricultural and mechanical-arts colleges in every State. The act was the basis for the land-grant colleges and universities that are still the backbone of U.S. agricultural education. Establishment of the U.S. Department of Agriculture the same year ensured further Government aid to farmers.

The Pacific Railroad Act of 1862, and another act in 1864, provided Government land grants and loan bonds to build the West's transcontinental railroad. Although little work was done until after the war, these laws set the stage for the complete opening of the West. As historian Paul Gates has noted: "Without railroads . . . homestead would have been an empty promise."

Just about planting time in the spring of 1865, two military men faced each other across a bare parlor in the Virginia town of Appomattox Court House. As they arranged for the surrender of Confederate forces, the problems of the South's farmers intruded. Gen. Robert E. Lee, noble in defeat, hinted that it would mean a great deal to his men if they could keep their mounts. In the terms of surrender Gen. Ulysses S. Grant wrote: "Let all men who claim to own a horse or mule take the animals home with them to work their little farms."

All too often the farms turned out to be someone else's land on which the sharecropper scratched out a bare living. The freed slave usually found rural poverty instead of the 40 acres and a mule that had been promised him. In 1870 the South produced only about half its prewar quantities of cotton, livestock, sugar, rice, and tobacco; the figures on most of these products did not increase substantially until around the turn of the century.

Steam traction engines, *like this 1886 Case, proved far more efficient than draft animals for pulling large plows and combines, but smaller and more versatile gasoline tractors soon replaced these steam giants.*

MAKING DEMOCRACY WORK

The Hatch Act of 1887

Although their productivity increased spectacularly in the decades after the Civil War, farmers were bedeviled by serious problems. Much Eastern soil was worn out, Midwestern crop yields had to be increased to meet the competition from the growing numbers of farms farther west, and westerners needed assistance in finding new crops and techniques suited to their land.

Most farmers felt they had no place to turn for help. One writer charged that the new agricultural colleges established under the Morrill Act of 1862 were "asylums for classical idiots." Another critic wrote that most "educated" agriculturalists were not "competent to feed pigs." Although many agronomists were doing significant research, their findings were not reaching the ordinary farmer, often because the value of their work was not recognized by State and Federal bureaucrats. U.S. Department of Agriculture scientists were relegated to a cramped Washington basement, where fumes from their experiments often nearly suffocated them.

In 1887 Congress passed a bill sponsored by Representative William H. Hatch of Missouri, which gave Federal funds to each State to promote "scientific investigation" and to establish an agricultural experiment station. The act quickly resulted in a steady stream of improved techniques flowing from laboratory to farm that continues to benefit crops and livestock.

In the North and West the wartime prosperity continued. Cattle kingdoms sprang up in the Southwest, and that new breed, the cowboy, drove 1,000-head herds north to railheads at Abilene and Dodge City. On seemingly endless grainfields in Kansas and Nebraska farmers rode great combines that reaped and threshed in one operation. Driving huge teams—sometimes as many as 40 horses—they plowed, planted, and harvested ever-increasing crops of grain.

By 1900 almost every kind of farm machinery that could be powered by a horse had been invented. Because of this the human labor required to produce a bushel of grain had decreased from the 1830 time of 3 hours to 30 minutes. In 1920 there were 25 million farm horses and mules, and 76 million acres were required simply to fill their feedbags.

In the early 1900's, however, a gasoline-powered tractor began chugging across fields and gradually replaced the horse as a source of power in farming. Even the farmer's sleek carriage horse was not sâfe from the onslaught of internal combustion. By the 1920's Henry Ford's Model T had ended the remoteness of farm life. "Tennessee coupés"—pickup trucks—carried the farm family to town and crops to market or, with the back wheel jacked up and a homemade belt drive, did all kinds of chores from sawing wood to filling silos.

Luther Burbank *developed more than 800 new plant varieties, relying on his keen memory and powers of observation to detect changes in his breeding stock. One of his few failures was his proposal to apply sound plant-breeding principles to human procreation.*

George Washington Carver *was dedicated to his laboratory at Tuskegee Institute, where he developed hundreds of new uses for Southern crops other than cotton. Somehow he also found the time to help local dirt farmers and receive illustrious visitors from all over the world.*

Luther Burbank and George Washington Carver

Different Methods That Led to Great Successes

Although both Luther Burbank and George Washington Carver drastically changed the course of American agriculture (and were good friends), the methods of these two workers in the same field could hardly have been more dissimilar.

Burbank had little formal education beyond high school, but was inspired by Charles Darwin's *Variation of Animals and Plants Under Domestication* to pursue a career as a plant breeder. On his Massachusetts truck farm in 1872 he produced his first "plant creation"—a superior variety of potato still called the Burbank.

After moving to California a few years later, Burbank experimented with hundreds of thousands of plants and produced a steady stream of "creations" that earned him the sobriquet "The Plant Wizard." His most successful included new varieties of plums, prunes, berries, apples, peaches, citrus fruits, and ornamental plants, including the Shasta daisy. He produced a spineless cactus for cattle feed, but it failed to transform arid regions into productive cattle lands as he had hoped.

Burbank's pioneering opened the country's eyes to the productive possibilities of plant breeding when agricultural experimentation was in its infancy. However, the value of his contributions was diminished by his methods. He kept records only for his own use and thwarted attempts by scientists to study his work.

Carver, on the other hand, was a thorough and careful scientist. Working all the while, he attended high school in Kansas, Simpson College in Iowa, and Iowa State College, where he received a master's degree in 1896. That same year, when the eminent black educator Booker T. Washington offered him a lifetime of "hard, hard work," Carver accepted and joined the faculty of Tuskegee Institute in Alabama.

While Burbank concentrated on developing new plants, Carver sought new uses for existing plants. He produced some 60 synthetic products from the pecan and 100 from the sweet potato; he also found more than 300 uses for the peanut. He propagandized the planting of the soybean, a crop that now earns the country's farmers more than $3 billion annually. Although he hated to tear himself away from his laboratory, and often locked himself inside to begin his workday at 3 a.m., Carver found time to teach illiterate farmers how to increase crop yields and to publish nearly 50 scientific papers.

Born a slave, Carver managed to shake the tyranny of King Cotton by helping end the South's dependence on a single crop.

The Working Cowboy
A Most Improbable Hero

Unlike the glamorous figures of legend and fiction, real cowpokes of the 1870's and 1880's were usually hardy young men who labored long hours, often under wretched conditions, for little pay, in a bone-jarring, dangerous occupation.

One of the riskiest and most strenuous jobs began with the autumn or spring roundup, as depicted in the scene below by the "cowboy artist" Charles Marion Russell. The cowboys brought the longhorns in from their breeding grounds on the Texas range, counted them, and burned a mark on the calves born during the year. Examples of the brands appear on the map to the right, which also shows the four major trails over which the cattle were herded north from Texas to railhead towns such as Cheyenne, Abilene, and Kansas City. From there they were shipped to stockyards, such as the one above in East St. Louis.

Turn-of-the-century dime novels *(continued)*

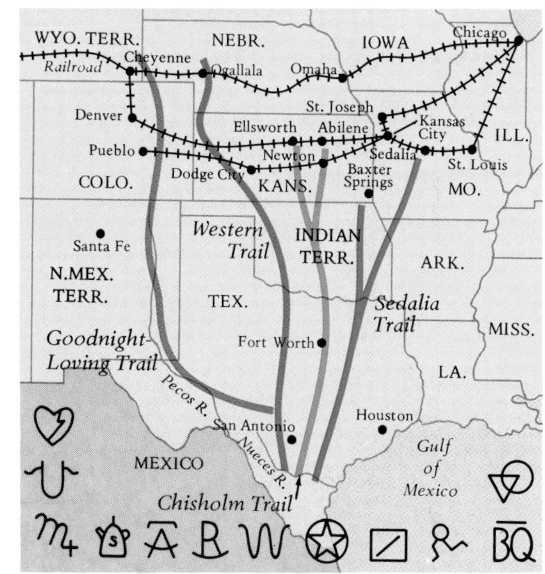

The Working Cowboy *(continued)*

and, later, Hollywood movies and television made the cowboy probably the most misrepresented and misunderstood worker of all time. Cowboys themselves fed the mythology. A mayor of Dodge City remarked that they "delight in appearing rougher than they are." Some cowboys were sturdy and dependable; others were cowardly, dishonest, and cruel to their animal wards. Their bosses often treated them with contempt. The $100 that a cowhand earned for driving 1,000 cattle for 3 months might be spent in one spree on the gambling, the rotgut whisky, and the "soiled doves" awaiting them in the cow towns at the end of the trail. Nonetheless, the cowboy's labors supplied the growing Nation with beef and helped settle one of America's last frontiers.

Hat, Boots, and Saddle Cost Twice as Much as the Horse

These are the prices *a top hand might pay for his outfit, although a youngster or someone past his prime would get by for half this total of about $135. Any cowboy who had the money would buy the best hat, boots, and saddle he could find. Most of the other prices are from Montgomery Ward catalogs of the 1880's.*

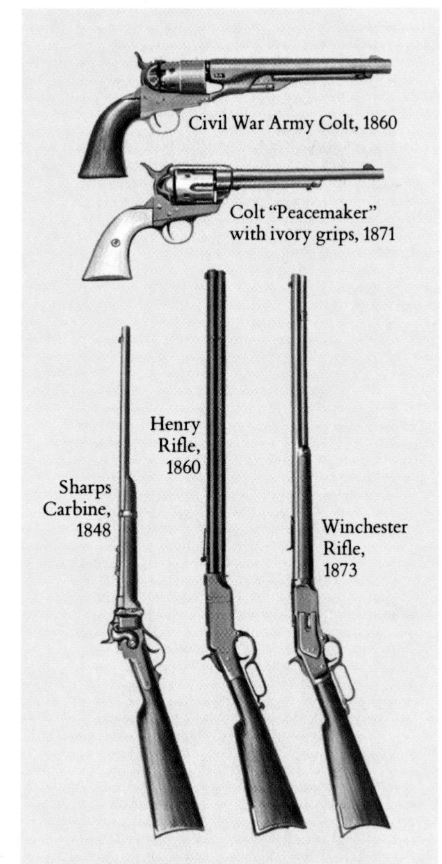

Two guns, *a pistol and a carbine or rifle, were the usual weapons. These models were most popular. The Sharps was a single shot.*

ıe herds the cowboys drove *to shipping ıters might number several thousand and ɛtch out almost as far as the eye could see. The ils were a gauntlet of hazards for man and ıst alike—Indians, rustlers, swirling rivers, ɔw, drought, stampedes. To the buckaroo, the ve was an endurance test that meant dusty eks in the saddle with very little sleep and ıcon and beans most every day."*

Stampedes, *the trail driver's most feared calamity, usually came at night and were often set off by a thunderstorm. In Charles Russell's "Stampede Lightning," a cowboy races the terrified cattle to reach the leaders and turn them so the herd will become a rotating wheel, which can be gradually slowed. Almost anything could start a stampede—a lighted match, a coyote's call, or jingling spurs. Once on their wild rampage, the animals might gallop 3 or 4 miles.*

The chuck wagon *was the center of the cowboy's life on the range. It contained nearly everything 10 or more hands might need during the semiannual roundups and cattle drives. The water barrel held only a 2-day supply, but the other provisions were good for up to 5 months. In the chuck box at the rear were the food and utensils the cook needed daily. Bulk food, guns, tobacco, bedrolls, and dozens of other items were stacked in the wagon bed. The handiest niches were reserved for the coffeepot and the bottle of "medicinal" whisky.*

"In Without Knocking," *another painting by Charles Russell, shows five cowboys indulging in one of their less endearing pastimes—"cleaning out a town." Such carousals, punctuated by blazing six-shooters, marked a last fling before months on the lonesome trail. The end of the drive was a likely occasion for another spree. Although escapades such as these were rare (most cow towns forbade gun toting), cautious gentlefolk kept off the streets when the cowboys hit town. The drovers swaggered along the board sidewalks, joking and shouting profane greetings to fellow roisterers. A merchant in Abilene, where Wild Bill Hickok was marshal in 1871, described his town as a "seething, roaring, flaming hell." In Dodge City, The Cowboy's Capital, 25 men were said to have been killed during the town's first year. Cattleman Joseph G. McCoy, writing in* Historic Sketches of the Cattle Trade *in 1874, said: "Few more wild, reckless scenes of abandoned debauchery can be seen on the civilized earth than a dancehall in full blast in one of these frontier towns."*

Overproduction and Government Control

Governmental prodding and high prices during World War I had encouraged farmers, in the words of historian Richard Hofstadter, to "feed the country and its allies and line their pockets in the process." Farm income went up by about a third during the war, but after the armistice the bubble burst. The increased use of expensive machinery, fertilizer, and hybrid seed—such as hybrid corn, introduced in 1926—raised operating expenses, while overproduction depressed prices. Although 13 million acres of farmland were withdrawn from production during the 1920's, output continued to rise. And as tractors replaced farm horses, the acres formerly used to feed the horses were switched to food crops, further aggravating the problem of overproduction. The Government was unwilling to impose production controls. "Every farmer is a captain of industry," President Warren G. Harding declared. Finally, in 1929, early in Herbert Hoover's Administration, the Federal Farm Board was created to stabilize farm prices. The next year brought the Government's first effort to raise prices by purchases of surplus wheat and cotton. But production increased, surpluses piled up, and farm prices continued to fall.

In 1933 Edward A. O'Neal, the usually conservative head of the Farm Bureau Federation, told a Senate committee: "Unless something is done for the American farmer we will have revolution in the countryside within less than 12 months." Two months later mobs of farmers in Le Mars, Iowa, blocked farm foreclosures and eviction sales, manhandled a local judge, and forced the Governor to call out the National Guard.

Drastic problems brought drastic solutions. In May 1933 one of the early initiatives of President Franklin D. Roosevelt's New Deal, the Agricultural Adjustment Act, became law. Under Agriculture Secretary Henry A. Wallace cotton farmers were paid to plow under a fourth of their crop, and 6 million young pigs were slaughtered. The irony of such destruction in a country where many were hungry and ill-clothed brought cries of protest, but the farmers were quieted. The plan fell short of expectations, but this was partly due to the farmers themselves. They took the Government checks that were paid for limiting the acreage under cultivation but farmed their remaining land more intensively to increase the yields.

New crop-quota systems took 30 million acres out of production in 1934 and 1935, and prices began to rise. Farm income more than doubled before the end of the 1930's, but it was the large-scale farmers who benefited most. Sharecroppers, farm tenants, and hired hands were not much better off than before. During a trip through the South in 1936, Secretary Wallace estimated that a third of all U.S. farmers lived under conditions "much worse than the peasantry of Europe." For many of these families, hopelessness and despair were compounded by the storms that whipped across the Dust Bowl in the Great Plains after the severe droughts of the mid-1930's. The Resettlement Administration, followed in 1937 by the Farm Security Administration, provided loans and other assistance; eventually 40,000 families were enabled to buy farms. However, the lot of many farmers did not improve much until World War II.

Agriculture Goes to War

When the bombs fell on Pearl Harbor in December 1941, the United States was possessed of a resource that would prove as decisive as any weapon or force of arms: the awesome capacity of the American farmer. For 10 years the farmer had tried to cut down on crops to adjust production to demand. Now he was told to pull out all stops: "Food will win the war and write the peace!"

Norris Dam *on the Clinch River, shown here before its completion in 1936, was the first major achievement of President Franklin D. Roosevelt's controversial Tennessee Valley Authority, one of his boldest New Deal measures, begun in 1933. Some 30 more dams followed, and the power from their hydroelectric plants enabled many farmers to electrify their properties much more cheaply than through private companies. People in seven Southern States also benefited from TVA programs to control floods, improve navigation, rehabilitate worn-out farms, and sell the fertilizer manufactured in TVA-owned factories at low prices.*

In April 1935 eroding winds *whipped over the desert-dry Great Plains and puffed up this cloud of dust near Liberal, Kansas. A conductor on the Santa Fe, explaining why trains were late, said: "Noon was like night. There was no sun and at times it was impossible to see a yard."*

The Dust Bowl

Years of Drought and Neglect Yield a Tragic Harvest

In the morning the dust hung like fog, and the sun was as red as ripe new blood. All day the dust sifted down from the sky, and the next day it sifted down. An even blanket covered the earth. It settled on the corn, piled up on the tops of the fenceposts, piled up on the wires; it settled on the roofs, blanketed the weeds and trees.

Thus did novelist John Steinbeck describe, in *The Grapes of Wrath,* the disaster that befell the farmers who lived in the Dust Bowl. High prices and unusually heavy rainfall during World War I had made it profitable to farm the arid Great Plains of the West. In some 100 counties in Arkansas, Kansas, Oklahoma, Colorado, New Mexico, Texas, and other States, virgin prairie sod was put under the plow.

When farm prices declined precipitously in the 1920's, farmers stopped cultivating huge areas of land and it lay idle, stripped of its protective cover of grass. With the onset of a severe drought in 1930, rainless days and a blazing Sun turned some 50 million acres into a virtual desert. Then, on May 11, 1934, a great duststorm howled across the parched plains, stripping them of precious topsoil. This "black blizzard" blotted out the Sun, reducing visibility to zero and interrupting rail schedules. Three hundred million tons of soil were scattered over the East. Dust from the plains settled on ships 300 miles out in the Atlantic.

In addition to blowing away valuable soil, the duststorms killed farm animals and damaged crops, machinery, and merchandise in stores. Some quarter of a million farmers were "dusted out" and took to the road on foot and in jalopies to seek work. Strapped to their backs and the sides of their battered cars was all they owned—water jugs, bedding, skillets, a baby's broken toy. Most of the Okies, Arkies, and other homeless and landless headed for California; but the men were often too defeated and dispirited to believe they would find work. In 1936 the Soil Conservation Act was passed; and contour plowing, strip planting, windbreaks, and other soil reclamation techniques gradually revived the land. Similar drought conditions have since occurred in the Dust Bowl, but with much less disastrous results.

Alexandre Hogue's *"Drought Stricken Area" shows the desolation of a 1930's Dust Bowl farm. Farmers watched helplessly as their soil blew away and cattle fell dead of suffocation.*

The Story of Corn

Corn, or maize, was first cultivated about 7,000 years ago by highland Indians near the present site of Mexico City. The ears were about the size of a pencil stub and contained some 50 kernels; the plant was the product of accidental crossbreeding of native grasses. By the time Columbus discovered America, corn was being grown from central South America to the region north of the Great Lakes. It saved many of the first New England and Virginia colonists from starvation. The multicolored ears that the Indians taught them to grow were similar to the corn we display at Thanksgiving.

In the 1870's Charles Darwin, the originator of the theory of evolution, described to American colleagues how he had obtained an almost explosive increase in the size and vigor of corn by crossing distantly related strains. In 1875 William Beal began similar experiments at Michigan Agricultural College. His work was continued in the early 1900's by three men who deserve to be called the fathers of hybrid corn—Edward M. East, George H. Shull, and Donald F. Jones. Jones encouraged farm editor and corn breeder Henry A. Wallace (later Secretary of Agriculture and Vice President under Franklin D. Roosevelt) to produce hybrid corn commercially. Wallace began doing this in 1926, and the new hybrids soon doubled and tripled corn yields across the country and around the world. Modern hybrid corn has ears more than a foot long, with some 1,000 plump kernels. The only important grain of American origin, its annual U.S. production surpasses that of all the Nation's other grains combined.

Production soared. Bumper crops kept the factories supplied with raw materials and fed the country, the American soldier, and his allies around the world. By 1945 farm yields and farm income had doubled—a fact all the more remarkable considering that during the war the number of farms, farmworkers, and acres under cultivation had decreased. As historian William Miller wrote: "The 'Battle of Production' was the first allied offensive victory of the war." This accomplishment, in which agriculture played the primary role, ". . . underlay all later successes and the ultimate allied triumph."

After the war production remained high, although demand slumped. This was partly because U.S.-donated seeds and livestock helped rebuild the agriculture of war-torn countries. At home Government farm subsidies increased along with the surpluses in Government warehouses. But World War II, unlike World War I, ended with the farmers wielding political power, which ensured reasonably high farm supports.

Just as the Civil War had hastened the use of horsepower and as World War I had accelerated the use of tractors, World War II triggered a new approach to farming: that of modern methods of management.

Methods and materials as sophisticated as the missiles and warheads being developed by the military became commonplace. The present state of the art of corn culture serves as a good example. The colonial farmer poked his seed corn into the ground with a stick, fertilized it with a fish, cultivated it with a clamshell hoe, and harvested it with his bare hands. The hybrid corn seed of today has been developed and selected by computer for high productivity and treated with a fungicide. It may be put in the ground by a 24-row planter, pulled by a 200-horsepower tractor. One man, in an air-conditioned cab with a two-way radio, can plant 200 acres a day. The planter simultaneously lays down a preemergence herbicide to prevent weeds from sprouting, pesticides to protect the seed from insects, and "pop-up" fertilizer to nourish the germinating corn. Other fertilizers, such as gaseous anhydrous ammonia as a source of nitrogen, have already been applied.

In the hundred or so days it takes to reach maturity, the corn is likely to have additional fertilizers, herbicides, and pesticides applied, perhaps from aircraft flying over it. When the corn is ready for harvest, a 7-ton, $30,000 corn combine moves over as many as eight rows at a pass, automatically removes the ear from the stalk, the husks from the ear, the kernels from the cob, and, at intervals, unloads the grain into one of the several trucks or wagons that shuttle back and forth between field and storage bin, all at a speed of about 8 miles an hour.

Computers Determine What Cows Eat

If the corn is to be fed to a dairy cow, chances are that it will be machine-mixed with other ingredients according to an analysis done by a computer somewhere in a land-grant university or a farmer-owned cooperative. The feed is mixed for each cow to ensure that the maximum amount of milk is produced for every unit of corn swallowed. The formula used for the feed depends on the current cost-profit analysis that is contained in the computer's memory banks.

Such technology costs money. In 1940 American farmers invested about $52 billion in land, livestock, buildings, and equipment. By 1973 the amount had climbed to $384 billion, even though farms had dropped in number from more than 6 million to fewer than 3 million. The amount of farm acreage under cultivation stayed about the same. It would take all the assets of all the corporations in the United States to surpass farm investments. Many people had to sell their small family farms because they could not find the necessary capital to run them. Nevertheless, about 95 percent of U.S. farms are still family owned, although nowadays they tend to be large and are often incorporated. Meanwhile, true corporation farms, supervised by boards of directors and professional managers, are increasing in number.

Food for Thought

The American farmer's success is one of the less publicized wonders of the 20th century. By the mid-1970's a single farmer could grow enough food to feed himself, 45 other Americans, and 8 foreigners. Agriculture is one of our biggest and most basic productive enterprises. It feeds the Nation and supplies raw materials to most industries. In a single year farmers in the United States grow crops valued at some $25 billion.

The ever-intensifying production has exacted its price. In an attempt to stabilize farm income, the U.S. Government has paid farmers billions of dollars in the past decade. Spokesmen for the consumers have charged farmers and the food-processing industry with sacrificing wholesomeness, nutrition, and taste in their efforts to mass-produce meat, poultry, fruit, vegetables, and grain products. Conservationists are concerned about the impact of farm chemicals on the environment.

Perhaps the future of farming can be read in the fields of some Louisiana rice farmers who are experimenting with a new crop: crawfish. Before the flooded fields are taken up with the growing of rice, a valuable crawdad crop can be harvested. Such unconventional intensive farming methods are necessary if the U.S. population—expected to total between 400 and 700 million by the year 2000—is to be fed. It is anticipated that by that time the number of American farms will be cut in half, to about 1.5 million, while the number of cultivated acres will remain about the same. Farm output, however, will probably double.

Much of the machinery *on U.S. farms is automated, like this irrigator watering Colorado corn. Timer-controlled and water-powered, the wheeled boom crawls in an arc over 160 acres.*

Some agriculturists envision a future where weather will be made to order, robots will operate the streamlined farm machinery, millions of identical cattle will be produced as clones from a single superior "parent," and crops will grow lush and green under a pollution-free sky as they orbit the Earth in space stations.

In more immediate terms, environmentalist Dr. Paul R. Ehrlich has pointed out that agriculture cannot hope to keep pace with an exploding population. The amazing productivity of American farmers and agricultural scientists has ensured that much of the world will have enough to eat for the next 20 or 30 years. Within that brief period man must come to grips with the population problem. Only if this is done, says Nobel Prize-winning wheat breeder Norman Borlaug, can the world's farmers provide "a decent standard of living for all mankind."

The Man Who Started a Green Revolution

A Plant Scientist Who Listens to the Wheat

Norman Borlaug, *the 1970 Nobel Peace Prize winner, can usually be found working in the high-yielding wheat he developed. The 15th American to win the prize, Borlaug said his was the first to go to a "dirty-handed" scientist.*

Norman E. Borlaug, the first agricultural scientist to receive the Nobel Peace Prize, embodies many of the qualities that have made American farmers the most efficient in the world. Born in 1914 to an immigrant family near Cresco, Iowa, in an area that is still known as Little Norway, Borlaug wanted to farm with better methods than his father had used. He worked his way through agricultural college and received his doctorate in plant pathology in 1940. Four years later he was chosen by the Rockefeller Foundation to be part of a team that the Mexican Government had requested to "bring the U.S. agricultural revolution to Mexico."

Borlaug set about improving the low-yielding wheat that Mexico had been growing for centuries. His methods were unorthodox, but he believed a fresh start was needed. "About every 25 years they ought to burn all the agricultural textbooks," he once remarked. By the 1960's Borlaug had developed new dwarf and semidwarf wheat that could hold heavier heads of grain on their short, sturdy stems than the older types. Mexico, long plagued with wheat shortages, became a wheat exporter. Other countries used the wheat to double yields, and Borlaug was dubbed "the father of the green revolution."

Professor Borlaug raised another "crop" in Mexico and on trips to the Middle East and Africa—a new species of plant scientist. Students abroad were amazed to see him working in the fields with his hands. "This wheat will talk to you," he told them, "but you can't hear it if you sit under a tree." He warned bureaucrats that "farmers will be after your scalps for failing to develop fertilizer factories or to provide credit."

When his wife rushed across a Mexican field in 1970 to tell Borlaug he had been awarded the Nobel Prize, the scientist, like a busy farmer getting in hay, postponed celebrating for a while, saying, "I still have a day's work to do here."

American Food and Drink

Known All (

Apple Pie. At its best, with a savory filling and crisp, light-brown crust, apple pie has long been a favorite on American tables. Apples and apple seed were among the precious supplies the early colonists brought to the New World. The first large apple orchards were planted near Boston by William Blaxton in the 1600's. When he moved to Rhode Island in 1635, he developed the tart Rhode Island Greening, still considered one of America's finest pie apples. As the fruit became abundant, many settlers ate apple pie at every meal. Garnished with a chunk of cheese, it was a favorite colonial breakfast dish. By the 18th century apple pie had become so popular that Yale College in New Haven served it every night at supper for more than 100 years. America's love affair with apple pie has remained constant. Today's housewives, pressed for time, can shortcut the traditional recipes by baking presliced canned apples in piecrust mixes or by buying the pastry readymade at bakeries and supermarkets. Many variations on the good old original are available, but the classic apple pie, irresistible when topped with a slice of rat-trap cheese or slathered with vanilla ice cream, is still America's favorite.

Carbonated Water. Carbonated, or soda, water was introduced in 1767 by an English chemist, Joseph Priestley, the discoverer of oxygen. In America Benjamin Silliman, Yale's first professor of chemistry, thought it had merit as a health drink and in 1807 began to bottle and sell it around New York City. In 1832 John Matthews developed the first equipment to make and dispense soda water (fountains, he called them), and a new industry was launched. In 1876 the three-stories-high Arctic Soda Water Dispenser was serving seven beverages and 16 different syrups at the Philadelphia Centennial Exposition. Soon the ice cream parlors and drugstores of America became favorite gathering places. Growing concern over the damage to health caused by excessive sugar intake and the use of artificial sweeteners have caused many doctors in recent years to recommend plain carbonated water as a safe noncaloric drink.

Coca-Cola. America's best known soft drink was first concocted by an Atlanta pharmacist in 1886. The syrup was cooked up by John S. Pemberton from extracts of coca leaves and the kola nut. He then organized the Pemberton Chemical Company, Inc., and Coca-Cola syrup mixed with plain water was sold in a local drugstore for 5 cents a glass. Sales were slow until in 1887 a prosperous Atlanta druggist, Asa G. Candler, bought the Coca-Cola formula—then as now a carefully guarded secret—and added carbonated water to the syrup instead of plain water. Advertisements stressing the words "delicious" and "refreshing" and carrying coupons for free Coca-Colas added to the increase in consumption. A system of independent local bottling companies was developed, and the flared bottle, familiar worldwide and said to resemble the hobble skirt, was designed in 1916. In 1919 Candler sold out for $25 million to a group headed by Ernest Woodruff. Under Woodruff's son, Robert W. Woodruff, who became president in 1923, Coca-Cola rapidly expanded its market. By the mid-1970's more than 150 million Cokes a day were being sold in countries all over the world, and applications had been made for bottling franchises on the Moon.

Doughnuts. It was the early Dutch settlers and the Pennsylvania Germans who introduced the yeasty, deep-fried doughnut to America. To the Dutch it was a festive food, eaten for breakfast on Shrove Tuesday, "dunked" into coffee or molasses as the last treat before the Lenten fast. Legend has it that the doughnut got its hole in 1847 when Hanson Gregory, a Maine lad later to become a sea captain, complained to his mother that her fried cakes were raw in the center and poked holes in the next batch before they were cooked. During World War I, when the Salvation Army served them to the troops, doughnuts really took off as popular fare. Since then, coffee and doughnuts have become a national institution. Chain stores sell them plain, sugared, frosted, honey-dipped, or jam-filled.

Graham Crackers. One of America's earliest health foods, graham crackers were originally unsalted, unleavened biscuits of whole grain flour promoted in the 1830's by Sylvester Graham. This New England preacher and self-styled expert on diet decried the consumption of meats and fats and urged the health-giving merits of bread made of coarse whole grain flour. He advocated a boycott of commercial bakers and bade women make whole wheat bread at home as a sacred obligation. When Graham made a public appearance in Boston, his disciples dumped slaked lime on an angry mob of bakers who stormed the gathering. As the Graham movement gained momentum, health food stores and Graham hotels in many parts of the country promoted Graham flour, bread, and crackers. Dr. Graham would be horrified by the honey, cinnamon, and chocolate-covered confections sold today under the misnomer of graham crackers.

Hamburgers. Modern hamburgers on a bun were first served at the St. Louis Fair in 1904, but Americans really began eating them in quantity in the 1920's, when the White Castle snackbar chain featured a small, square patty at a very low price. Chopped beef, tasty and easily prepared, quickly caught on as family fare, and today hamburger stands, drive-ins, and burger

chains offer Americans their favorite hot sandwich at every turn. The history of the hamburger dates back to medieval Europe. A Tartar dish of shredded raw beef seasoned with salt and onion juice was brought from Russia to Germany by early German sailors. The lightly broiled German chopped-beef cake, with pickles and pumpernickel on the side, was introduced to America in the early 1800's by German immigrants in the Midwest.

Hot Dogs. Tad Dorgan, a Hearst sports cartoonist, gave the frankfurter its nickname in 1906. Munching on a frank at a baseball game, he concluded that it resembled a dachshund's body and put that whimsy into a drawing, which he captioned "Hot dog!" Sausages go all the way back to ancient Babylon, but the hot dog was brought here shortly before the Civil War by a real Frankfurter—Charles Feltman, a native of Frankfurt, Germany, who opened a stand at New York's Coney Island and sold grilled sausages on warmed rolls—first for a dime apiece, later, a nickel. The frank appealed to busy Americans, who—as an early-19th-century comment put it—tend to live by the maxim of "Gobble, gulp and go." Nowadays Americans consume more than 12 billion frankfurters a year.

Ice Cream Cones. At the St. Louis Fair of 1904, a Syrian vendor named Hamwi was selling a wafflelike confection derived from an old Persian pastry. When an ice cream stand ran out of plates, he twisted his wafers into horn-shaped containers for his neighbor's scoopfuls of ice cream, and "The World's Fair Cornucopia" was born. Many variations have been played on the Hamwi theme—the spiral, the dripless, and the rocket cones among them—but nowadays we seem to have settled on the cup-shaped and the hard-sugar cones. It takes some 2 billion cones a year to accommodate the scores of ice cream flavors available. A Government antipollution expert described the ice cream cone as "the only ecologically sound package known."

Ice Cream Sodas. The ice cream soda was born in 1874 at a fair in Philadelphia. Robert M. Green, a concessionaire, ran short of the sweet cream he was putting into his flavored soda drinks, so he substituted vanilla ice cream. The mixture of syrup, carbonated water, and ice cream was an instant hit. Green's profits rose from $6 a day to more than $600 a day. As the ice cream soda grew in popularity, blue-nosed citizens began making it a target, and in some Midwest towns laws were passed prohibiting its sale on Sunday. In Illinois ingenious soda fountain owners got around the law by covering a scoop of ice cream with syrup, omitting the carbonated water. They called this a "Sunday soda"; later it was shortened to plain "Sunday," till someone with a taste for elegance rechristened it "sundae."

Jell-O. The largest selling prepared dessert in America was patented in 1845 by businessman Peter Cooper. Nothing much happened to his powdered, artificially flavored product until 1895, when Pearl B. Waite, a cough-medicine manufacturer from upstate New York, took over the patent and began producing a gelatin dessert commercially as Jell-O, a brand name coined by his wife. But Jell-O did not really catch on until Orator F. Woodward, who had bought the business in 1897, launched an advertising campaign proclaiming it America's most famous dessert. The magazine ads, featuring a pretty, yellow-haired "Jell-O girl," caught the public imagination. By 1906 annual sales had neared the million-dollar mark. Today, besides being American favorites, Jell-O's 15 flavors are sold all over the world.

Peanut Butter. Restaurants serve hot peanut-butter soup, airlines give passengers peanut-butter pie, Senator Barry Goldwater claims to have used peanut butter in a pinch as shaving cream. By running roasted peanuts through a kitchen grinder, a St. Louis doctor, whose name has been lost, developed peanut butter in 1890 as an easily digestible form of protein. Currently, more than 650 million pounds of shelled nuts are used each year to produce both smooth and crunchy kinds, so that Americans may delight in their peanut butter and jelly sandwiches.

Popcorn. Corn, the oldest American food, was grown in New Mexico more than 5,000 years ago and was introduced to the Pilgrims by the Indians at the first Thanksgiving feast, in Plymouth, Massachusetts, in 1630. To the settlers' amazement, heating one variety of corn on stones exploded the kernels to many times their size. Indians of many tribes used popcorn for adornment as well as food. As the world's first puffed breakfast cereal, it was served with cream and sugar to colonial children. With the coming of talking pictures and electric machines, the industry grew until nowadays more than 350 million pounds of popcorn are sold each year.

Potato Chips. George Crumb, an American Indian who was the chef at Moon's Lake House in Saratoga Springs, New York, in the mid-19th century, was irked when a finicky dinner guest kept sending back his French fried potatoes, complaining they were cut too thick. In exasperation, Crumb shaved the potatoes into tissue-thin slices and deep-fried them in oil. He had a dishful of crisp brown "Saratoga chips" presented to the guest, who was delighted with the new treat. Potato chips became the specialty of Moon's Lake House and, later, America's crunchiest between-meals snack.

CHAPTER SEVEN

Education for All

We Americans have long been inclined to look to forn education for solutions to many of our most serious pro lems. We have counted on education to serve a variety needs, from preserving a knowledge of the Scriptures in early New England Colonies to teaching a trade or profe sion that would lead to a better way of life and providi the social reforms of today and tomorrow.

We have fondly hoped that attendance at classes wou turn an immigrant into an American citizen, a slum ch into an acceptable member of an orderly society, and gi a black youngster equal opportunities. Good schools, have believed, would help rural and urban communiti

MAKING DEMOCRACY WORK

The Old Deluder Satan Law

The Massachusetts School Law of 1647, as it is officially called, required that towns with 50 or more families establish schools. Several secondary and some elementary schools were opened as a result of the edict, but many towns preferred to pay the fine imposed for ignoring the law. Although the law was not the beginning of publicly supported education, it was an important milestone. It provided a precedent that could be cited in later campaigns to make schools a matter for both public concern and governmental interest. The text follows:

It being one chiefe proiect of y^{e} ould deluder, Satan, to keepe men from the knowledge of y^{e} Scriptures, as in $form^{r}$ times by keeping y^{m} in an unknown tongue, so in these $latt^{r}$ times by perswading from y^{e} use of tongues, y^{t} so at least y^{e} true sence & meaning of y^{e} originall might be clouded by false glosses of saint seeming deceivers, y^{t} learning may not be buried in y^{e} grave of o^{r} $fath^{rs}$ in y^{e} church and commonwealth, the Lord assisting o^{r} $endeavo^{r}s$,—

It is therefore $ord^{r}ed$, y^{t} $ev^{r}y$ towneship in this iurisdiction, aft^{r} y^{e} Lord hath increased y^{m} number to 50 $household^{rs}$, shall then $forthw^{th}$ appoint one wth in their towne to teach all such children as shall resort to him to write & reade, whose wages shall be paid $eith^{r}$ by y^{e} parents or $mast^{rs}$ of such children, or by y^{e} inhabitants in $gen^{r}all$, by way of supply, as y^{e} maior part of those y^{t} ord^{r} y^{e} prudentials y^{e} towne shall appoint; provided, those y^{t} send their children be not oppressed by paying much more y^{m} they can have y^{m} taught for in oth^{r} townes; & it is $furth^{r}$ ordered, y^{t} where any towne shall increase to y^{e} $numb^{r}$ of 100 families or $househould^{rs}$, they shall set up a grammer schoole, y^{e} m^{r} thereof being able to instruct youth so farr as they shall be fitted for y^{e} university, provided, y^{t} if any towne neglect y^{e} performance hereof above one yeare, y^{t} every such towne shall pay 5 pounds to y^{e} next schoole till they shall performe this order.

In 1636, only 6 years after the Massachusetts Bay Colony was established, a college was founded. The proportion of university graduates among the first New England settlers was much higher than in the other Colonies. These men felt that institutions to train new leaders were essential. The fledgling college, opening 2 years later, was named for the Rev. John Harvard, who bequeathed to it his library and half his estate (about £780).

Candidates qualifying for admission were scarce. In the struggle for existence in the new land, many parents neglected their traditional role of educating their children. In 1642 a law was passed reminding Massachusetts citizens of their obligations to teach their children reading and catechism. In 1647 the Colony passed an act that became known as the Old Deluder Satan Law. This law, with its more positive requirements, is considered the foundation of publicly supported education in America.

The few schools resulting from the law offered a limited curriculum. Fluency in Latin was a requirement for admission to Harvard, so Latin grammar (secondary) schools concentrated on teaching that language and literature as well as Greek. In lower schools the emphasis was on religion. The Puritans insisted that a child be able to read the Bible. He learned to read first from a hornbook and then from the *New England Primer,* which was full of religious admonitions and reminders of mortality and the need for salvation. "Xerxes the great did die/And so must you and I," was the couplet illustrating the letter X in the rhyming alphabet. Reading, writing, and religion were the three R's. Arithmetic did not enter the curriculum in New England until the late 1600's.

In many villages the church was also the schoolhouse. Often teaching was only a sideline for the schoolmaster, whose main occupation might be the ministry, farming, medicine, or law. Many Harvard and Yale graduates taught for a while before entering the ministry. The *ould teach morals and ethics, and would give all children common background of basic knowledge. However, this ith in education has not always been justified.*

The history of the American way of education—how began, how it came to be counted on for such ambitious hievements, and what great progress has, in fact, been ade—is a continuing story of complacency, resistance to ange in the face of growing dissatisfaction, and occasional nstructive reform.

By the mid-19th century the concept of free elementary ooling was just gaining acceptance. As the years passed, e goal of universal education expanded to include high school and eventually college. As more and better schools became available, more students attended for a longer time. In 1870 only 2 percent of the 17-year-old population graduated from high school. By 1970 this had risen to 78 percent, of which 60 percent went on to college.

Our schools have grown and changed enormously over the years, and nearly every aspect of education has been a subject of heated controversy. Only one thing has remained constant: our faith in the power of education to improve us both as individuals and as members of society and thereby to create a better country and a better world. It is a faith sufficiently realized to have sustained itself.

teacher, although respected in the community, was poorly paid, and few remained schoolmasters for long without another job.

Children learned their catechism and ABC's very early in their own homes or at a dame school, where a woman kept toddlers busy with these fundamentals for 2 or 3 years for a small amount of money. For nearly 200 years most girls had no more formal education than the dame schools offered. The wife of one of the first Connecticut governors, said to have lost her wits from too much reading and thinking, was held up as a terrible warning to men willing to endanger the delicate minds of their wives and daughters with education. Gradually girls were reluctantly allowed to attend the lower schools. At first this was often limited to before and after regular hours or when the schools were empty because the boys were busy in the fields, and the teacher did not always appear. Even in Quaker Philadelphia, which had coeducational elementary schools, girls were not allowed to proceed to the secondary level.

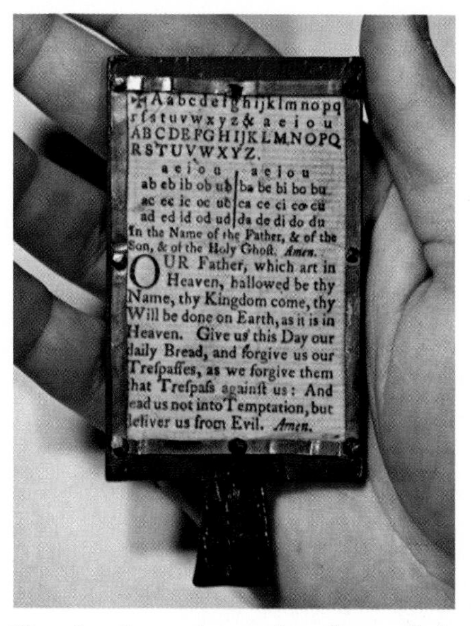

Hornbooks, *used to teach reading until the late 1700's, were made of a printed sheet of paper attached to a paddle-shaped board and protected by a transparent layer of horn.*

Educational financing varied from village to village. The settlers attempted to follow the English tradition of maintaining schools with donations and endowments of land. But donations were insufficient, and land was so plentiful that it afforded little income from rent because nearly every householder had property of his own. Other sources had to be found. Some towns reserved a certain percentage of ferry tolls. Others used the proceeds from marriage and liquor licenses. Parents were expected to provide firewood in addition to paying a small tuition fee. The shivering child, sitting farthest from the fireplace, was the one whose father had failed to supply his share of wood.

Public funding led to the schools being administered by the town selectmen, who controlled the money. Since these men were elected officials, the schools were more responsive to public opinion than were the English schools, most of which were controlled by wealthy trustees.

Along the Eastern seaboard the educational pattern varied according to local beliefs and local geography. Distances between the scattered plantations of the South made district schools impractical. The local minister often taught neighboring children, sometimes in an "old field school," which was built on land lying fallow after several years of use. By the 18th century affluent planters were importing tutors from Northern colleges and then exporting sons to England or the Continent to finish their education. Educated bond servants also served as tutors.

Privately operated schools for each sex began to appear in response to the needs of the growing middle class. These schools were usually run by one or two persons; when they moved, the school moved with them; when they retired, the school closed. For a fee freelance teachers offered evening courses for apprentices and workingmen. The newspapers were full of advertisements for pupils in mathematics, geography, history, navigation, foreign languages, and other subjects. These private lessons by individuals were not always well taught. However, the good ones provided some supplement to the narrow traditional patterns of elementary schools and apprenticeship for those of lesser means, and of Latin grammar school followed by college and possibly professional training for the wealthy.

Schools of higher learning were slow to develop in the Colonies. The second to appear was the College of William and Mary in 1693, and 8 years later the Collegiate School of Connecticut (now Yale University) opened its doors. In the mid-1700's, however, various religious denominations were active in founding what are now Princeton, Columbia, Brown, Rutgers, and Dartmouth. The College and Academy of Philadelphia (later the University of Pennsylvania), chartered in 1755, was the first officially nonsectarian institution of higher learning. It offered a wider range of studies than the other colleges, which were intended to train students for the ministry (although applicants for admission were not required to subscribe to the colleges' religious beliefs or to become ministers).

An Anglican mission group, the Society for the Propagation of the Gospel in Foreign Parts, set up charity schools in most of the American Colonies. The society also sent missions to Indians and to blacks and bought two slaves who were trained to teach other slaves. Slave-

"Licks and larnin'" *were not the schoolchild's only fare. Pupils played games such as Snap the Whip, as in the Winslow Homer painting above. In the Homer painting to the right, boys sit on one side, girls on the other (tots excepted). The teacher took them severally through the graded reader, according to age.*

The One-Room Schoolhouse
One of America's Most Enduring Institutions

The typical oldtime school was built of logs, with rough-hewn shingles for its roof. Its only interior ornament was the teachers' row of hickory sticks used for "humbling." In the earliest days one end of the room had a fireplace, replaced later by a stove, which ensured that in winter children would be perpetually either too hot or too cold. Sanitation was backward, and drinking was done from a common pail. Children came to school, often a distance of several miles, on foot or on horseback, though no State made attendance compulsory until Massachusetts led the way in 1852. Some teachers were itinerant, and few stayed long in one place. Often the teachers' knowledge extended little beyond the textbooks they taught from.

The earliest textbooks in wide demand were Noah Webster's speller, grammar, and reader. From the 1830's to the 1920's McGuffey's *Readers* were in almost universal use. They ranged from an elementary primer to anthologies of American and English literature. The first three *Readers*, which were for younger children, were simply but attractively illustrated. In the stories children were often rewarded materially for virtue, industry, and perseverance. Four of the *Readers* were compiled by William H. McGuffey, a frontier clergyman and college president, the fifth by his brother Alexander, a lawyer, and a sixth was later added by the publisher.

Whatever its imperfections, the country school taught a social philosophy well suited to a new and vigorous people of widely diversified origins, facing rapidly expanding problems and opportunities. Even after the bulk of the population had shifted from rural to urban areas, it continued to play a vital role in national life.

The schoolmaster *lays into Tom Sawyer in this Norman Rockwell illustration. Uncommon accessories were the map and globe.*

owners were assured that they could allow their slaves to become Christians and learn to read and write without being obligated to set them free. Most owners, while permitting conversion to Christianity, refused to allow their human chattels to become literate, and eventually the Southern Colonies enacted laws that forbade teaching slaves to read and write.

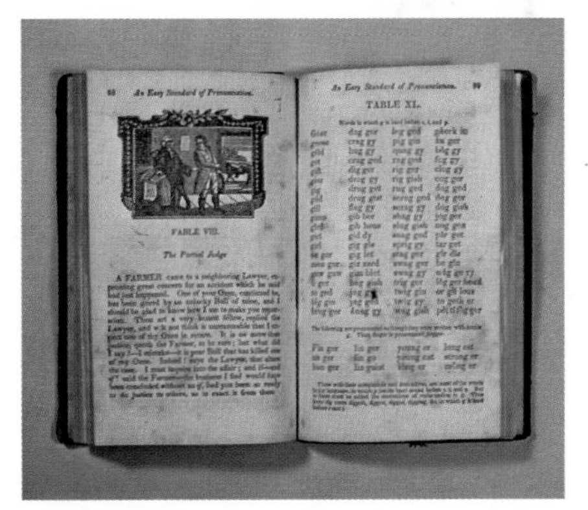

Noah Webster *wrote the first American spelling book in 1783. The great lexicographer's "blue-backed speller" sold more than 60 million copies in about 50 years.*

Independence and the democratic experiment in the government by the people made it even more important for Americans to be better educated. However, the right to vote was generally restricted to property owners, most of whom could normally afford to pay for their children's schooling. The Virginia Legislature, therefore, turned down Thomas Jefferson's farsighted plan for 3 years of free schooling for all boys and girls, with provisions for continued education for the best students. The legislators were equally unwilling to approve State-supported higher education for those who could pay. It took Jefferson 40 years to get the University of Virginia built, and he considered his role as father of the university his greatest accomplishment.

Despite the foot dragging, the trend to general education gradually gathered momentum. The Sunday school movement, which first gained prominence in England in the 1780's, was set up to teach reading, writing, and catechism to poor children on the week's one nonworking day. In America Sunday schools were a strong influence in the late 18th and early 19th centuries. When the churches took over this lay activity, however, more catechism, and less reading, was taught.

In the early 1800's charitable societies were formed in several cities to help provide schooling for the poor. One of the best known was the Free School Society in New York City (founded in 1805 and renamed the Public School Society of New York in 1826), which began classes for poor children who were not being taught by any of the religious denominations. Each member of the society, whose first president was DeWitt Clinton, mayor of New York, donated an annual sum and also solicited funds. In addition, the society received support from the State. (The city's public school department, created in 1842, later took over the schools begun by this farsighted group.) Also outstanding in the field of dedicated school reformers was the Society for the Promotion of Public Schools in Philadelphia.

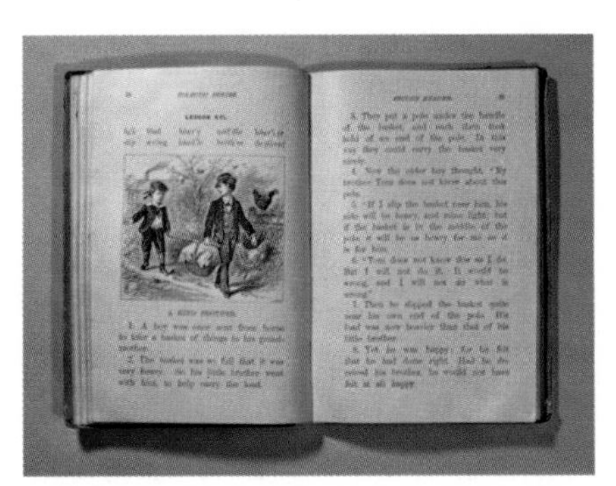

From 1836 to 1920, *122 million McGuffey* Readers *were published. They provided a common fund of knowledge and established standards of virtue for most Americans.*

As the property-owning qualifications for voting were slowly abolished, the dangers of ignorance and the problems of preparing children for citizenship won increasing recognition. Many poor parents refused to send their children to the "free schools," which bore the stigma of charity. The movement for free schools that would be open to all children, rich or poor, became particularly strong during the Jacksonian "era of the common man" in the 1830's, and a complicated State-by-State struggle developed, which was to continue for many years.

The Battle for Public Schools

New England had always taken pride in being the leader in education, but even there no consistent system was established for nearly 200 years after the Massachusetts School Law of 1647. In many districts school was in session for only 2 or 3 months each winter. In Massachusetts, for example, school buildings were seldom repaired, and nearly a third of the children had no educational facilities at all. Except in a few Catholic convents, no training was provided for the underpaid teachers who came and went each term. Most of them knew little about education in any real sense; they were mainly harsh disciplinarians who drilled lessons into their pupils' heads by rote.

Private academies and schools, some of which still exist, grew up all over the country, particularly in New England. These were larger, more permanent versions of the earlier privately owned schools, but included some elements of the Latin grammar schools. Parents paid to have their sons taught a combination of practical subjects in addition to the Latin and Greek traditionally considered necessary for cultured gentlemen.

In 1837 an influential group of men, many of whom had suffered at district schools, pushed a law through the Massachusetts Legislature creating a State board of education. Horace Mann was appointed its first secretary. Mann, who had attended school only a few weeks a year until he began preparing to enter Brown University, had strong ideas on what a common school system should be. During the 11 years he held office (1837–48) he greatly changed the Massachusetts schools. Through his efforts the school system was centralized, many high schools were established, teachers' salaries were raised, and the Nation's first State schools for teacher

Sequoya, Inventor of the Cherokee Alphabet

The Roman alphabet that we use took several thousand years to develop—from the picture writing of the ancient Egyptians through modifications by Phoenicians, Greeks, Etruscans, Romans, and others. Yet in just 12 years, one man invented an alphabet for his people. Sequoya, son of a Cherokee Indian woman and a white trader, was illiterate, but he wanted his people to have the white men's secret of the "talking leaves." He began by making a pictograph for each word in the Cherokee vocabulary. When his wife, angry at his neglect of the house and garden, burned his thousands of notations, Sequoya started again. This time, having concluded that picture writing was cumbersome, he made symbols for Cherokee sounds. Eventually he refined his system to 86 characters, which he presented to the council of chiefs in 1821. The response was phenomenal. Cherokees who had failed to master English lettering after months in a mission school learned to read and write their own language in a few days. Books and a newspaper were printed in the new alphabet. Sequoya was acclaimed a genius by his people, but today his name is remembered mainly because the giant redwoods of the Pacific coast (*Sequoia sempervirens*) were named for him.

education were opened. Mann went to Europe and Great Britain to study the school systems there and imported the teaching methods of Swiss educator Johann Heinrich Pestalozzi, who believed children should learn to think by examining objects closely and then discussing them, rather than by memorizing facts and dates.

At about the same time Henry Barnard, secretary of the new Connecticut Board of Education, was waging a similar battle. Although Barnard was voted out of office after 4 years, his efforts and those of Mann and others, such as John Pierce of Michigan, eventually led to a public system of common schools. For years this concept was the subject of wide controversy. Many people did not take readily to the idea of spending their own money to educate the children of others. Some rural areas, where children's help was needed on the farms, were opposed to financing such an unnecessary leisure-time luxury. Private schools and those run by religious denominations or by foreign-language groups felt threatened, although in some areas, notably the Midwest, Protestant groups gave their all-out support to public schools. State and local factions battled over control—State control meaning less discrepancy between richer and poorer districts, local control perhaps ensuring closer supervision.

The fight lasted for years and varied from State to State. Political offices were won and lost on the issue of free public schools. Legislation enacted one year was repealed another. Then, in the 1840's and 1850's, the problems presented by an increase of immigrants settled the question in favor of free public schools. The intensely nationalistic young republic was concerned about how to teach the new arrivals American ways and values and to incul-

MAKING DEMOCRACY WORK

The Morrill Act

In 1862, in the midst of the Civil War, President Lincoln signed the Morrill Act into law. The measure, named for Vermont Representative Justin S. Morrill, its sponsor in Congress, made the Federal Government an important force in higher education. Popularly known as the Land-Grant Act, it provided every State in the Union with 30,000 acres of public lands for each of its Senators and Representatives in Congress, and required that the land be sold to endow at least one college per State to teach subjects related to "agriculture and the mechanic arts."

The States used this money in several ways: To add agricultural and mechanical schools to established colleges, to further endow existing schools of science, or to open new colleges. Within a year after the enactment of this measure, nine States had established land-grant schools, democratizing higher education by offering students college training at low cost. Most students preferred the "mechanic arts" of engineering to agriculture, which was not considered a science until it was dignified by the work of experimental research stations established at the land-grant colleges in 1887 by the Hatch Act.

The second Morrill Act, passed in 1890, provided annual Federal funds for each land-grant institution and enabled Southern States to found similar colleges if they made equal facilities available for blacks and whites. By the early 1970's the 69 land-grant institutions, including such renowned schools as Purdue University and the University of Illinois, were educating one in five of all American college students.

cate loyalty to their adopted country. The answer was schools for the children—and through the children perhaps their elders could be reached.

Other 19th-Century Developments

By 1860 most States had free public elementary schools, but attendance was not compulsory. Even Massachusetts, which had enacted the first school laws, required attendance only 12 weeks a year, 6 of them consecutively. Colleges, mainly private and sectarian, had multiplied since a Supreme Court decision in 1819 that protected Dartmouth's charter as a private corporation. The few State universities were attended mostly by sons of the well-to-do. Free education was still largely limited to elementary schools. When some towns established free high schools without the benefit of special legislation, those opposed to carrying public education beyond the elementary level initiated legal action. But in 1874 a Michigan Supreme Court decision affirmed the Kalamazoo district's power to levy taxes in support of the local high school, giving legal blessing to public secondary education. High schools increased dramatically in number during the 1890's.

The cause of women's education was furthered by the growth of public schooling and the consequent need for trained teachers. A woman teacher received less than half a man's wage, and budget-conscious administrators soon recognized the wisdom of allowing women to be educated enough to teach so that they could fill the classroom vacancies.

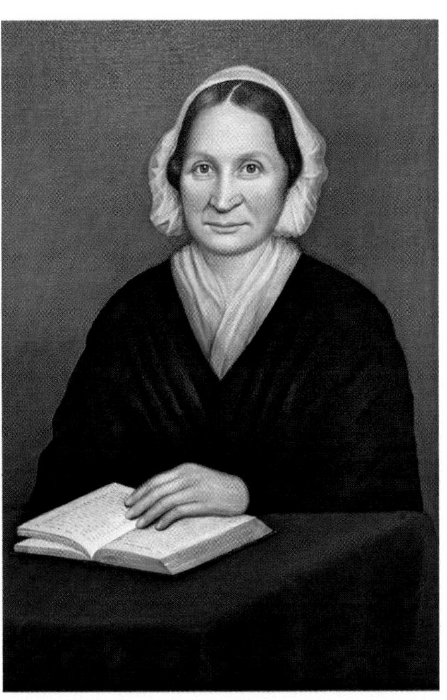

Mary Lyon *was one of the leaders in providing higher education for women. After raising the money to found Mount Holyoke Seminary, she served as its first president until her death.*

Private academies for girls still concentrated mainly on airs and graces, manners and morals. There were a few notable exceptions, such as Emma Willard's Female Seminary in Troy, New York (founded in 1821), Catharine Beecher's school for young ladies in Hartford, Connecticut (1824), and Mary Lyon's Mount Holyoke Seminary (later known as Mount Holyoke College) in South Hadley, Massachusetts (1837). These pioneers assuaged male fears that education for women threatened the sanctity of the home by emphasizing the domestic applications of the subjects they taught: Chemistry could be applied to cooking; mathematics would improve a woman's ability to keep her household accounts. Many graduates of the new seminaries also proved to be excellent teachers.

The first experiment in coeducation was at Oberlin Collegiate Institute (now Oberlin College), Ohio. Women were accepted at the secondary level from the start (1833). In 1837 women were admitted at the college level, and the first woman to earn a bachelor of arts degree received it from Oberlin in 1841.

Most women, no matter how eager, were too poorly prepared to undertake studies at the college level. Elmira (1855) and Vassar (1861) were the first all-women's schools to provide collegiate, as well as precollege, studies. Wellesley and Smith (founded in 1870 and 1871, respectively, and opening their doors in 1875) came next, followed by a number of others in the late 1880's and 1890's. The majority of State universities began admitting women not long after the Civil War, but the women were segregated and only gradually allowed to do collegiate work.

As early as 1826, Amherst College in Massachusetts and Bowdoin in Maine had graduated a black man. The first black woman to earn a B.A. received it at Oberlin in 1862. But pre-Civil War efforts to provide schools for Negroes in the North were sporadic. Before the Revolution Anthony Benezet ran an evening school for blacks in Philadelphia for 25 years and willed money to continue the work after his death. One of the best of the early schools for blacks was the New York African Free School, established by the Manumission Society in 1787. Boston opened a separate elementary school for children "of color" in 1820. Salem, Massachusetts, became the first town to allow children of both races to attend school together and even had a black teacher. In Connecticut, however, when Prudence Crandall, a young Quaker teacher, admitted a black girl to her school in 1831, parents withdrew their daughters. Miss Crandall then attempted to maintain her school for the black girls who soon flocked there from all over the Northeast. The school existed in a state of siege. Manure was thrown into the well, windows were broken, and food had to be smuggled in. Finally, in May 1833, Connecticut passed a series of "Black Laws," forbidding the establishment of schools for any person of color from outside the State without the consent of local authorities. The defiant Miss Crandall was arrested and convicted but was upheld by a higher court. She reopened her school in 1834, only to have it so badly damaged by a mob that she abandoned her efforts and moved west.

After the Civil War, through the Freedmen's Bureau and the efforts of many churches, thousands of Northern

Black Education
An Uphill Struggle To Learn

Negroes, except for a fortunate few, could not hope for any kind of formal education until the Reconstruction Era after the Civil War. New constitutions of the former Confederate States provided for public school systems, but white southerners soon passed segregation laws, which were upheld by Supreme Court decisions in 1883 and 1896. The gap between public expenditures on black and on white schools widened every year. "Separate and unequal" became tacit education doctrine in most sections of the country. Public money allotted to black schools was supplemented by philanthropic and charitable contributions, and black people dug into their own thinly lined pockets. Even so, few Negro schools met minimum white standards for buildings, equipment, and teachers' salaries. In the 1950's many towns began trying to provide equal facilities, but by 1954 the Supreme Court had decided that equality was not compatible with separation. The problem of giving all American children the same opportunities continued to preoccupy educators faced with stubbornly surviving difficulties.

This scene *was often repeated in the South after the Civil War. To learn to read and write, freed slaves of all ages flocked to the schools set up by missionary societies and the Freedmen's Bureau.*

The first Negro college *was founded in Pennsylvania in 1854, but black education did not gain momentum until after the Civil War. Howard University, Fisk University, and Hampton Institute opened between 1866 and 1868; other black institutions of higher learning were founded in the ensuing three decades. The distinguished scientist George Washington Carver is shown here in the chemistry laboratory of Tuskegee Institute. From modest beginnings in 1881, Tuskegee soon had an unusually large endowment, thanks largely to the fund-raising ability of its head, Booker T. Washington, who had more influence than any other black man of the early 1900's. The second Morrill Act, passed by Congress in 1890 and condemned by civil rights advocates because it affirmed the "separate but equal" doctrine, did help establish 17 Negro land-grant institutions. Most educated Negroes were products of all-black colleges, but this began changing after World War II. Since 1960 college enrollment of blacks has more than doubled, and the majority attend predominantly white colleges.*

men and women went south to teach the newly freed slaves. By 1872, when the bureau ceased its efforts, 21 percent of all Southern blacks could read; there were some 4,000 schools including more than a dozen black colleges; and a widespread public education system consisting of white schools as well as black had been initiated in the South. After 1872, however, black schools suffered from lack of funds and trained teachers for many years.

During the 1870's the growth of industry was beginning to change the balance of population from primarily rural to urban. The immigrants who streamed to America in the next decades tended to remain clustered in the cities. Many of these new arrivals were from southern and eastern Europe, and their cultural patterns differed from those who had preceded them. Societies were formed to help them adjust to the New World, and States began to enact compulsory education laws. By 1900 every State had laws requiring children between the ages of approximately 7 through 14 (the ages varied from State to State) to attend school, either public or private. The laws were enforced mainly in the cities, where it was important to keep children from roaming the streets in gangs or taking adults' jobs at lower wages.

Rural schoolhouses usually remained ungraded. In the cities, however, to ease the problem of discipline in schools that were bulging at the seams, children were locked by age into eight grades of elementary school and four grades of high school. The curriculum was widened to include domestic science and hygiene, and teachers found it necessary to tell children how to bathe and brush their teeth.

The schools, though a boon to many immigrant children, were repressive. The inadequate teaching staffs stressed efficiency and discipline. Rote recitation was still standard; bells ruled class life. The overcrowded buildings were poorly heated, inadequately lighted, and even unsanitary. Many late-19th-century politicians are remembered more for corruption than for public service: They soon recognized the opportunities presented by education funds. Administrative and even teaching appointments became political plums, and the price of new buildings skyrocketed to cover kickback costs.

One notable bright spot was the public school system in Quincy, Massachusetts, which Francis W. Parker began reforming in 1875. He discarded the speller, the reader, and the copybook, emphasizing understanding rather than memorizing, and informality rather than discipline. Because of his innovation in the field, Parker has been called the Father of Progressive Education.

The Progressive Movement

By the 1890's nearly every phase of American life was a target for mounting criticism. The traditional promise of the land of opportunity was not being fulfilled in the new industrial urban civilization. Something had to be done. The attempt to make good this promise was called progressivism, and education played a large part in it.

Social reformers, such as Jane Addams of Hull House in Chicago, became interested in education when they concluded that their settlement houses had to teach domestic science, hygiene, child care, and manual arts. They felt that the schools could help alleviate the suffering of the poor. Political reformers such as Theodore Roosevelt believed that freer and less repressive education would stimulate people to interest themselves and participate in government.

Business, management and labor, recognized that the apprentice system had so deteriorated that the schools had to help train young people to make a living. Agrarian reformers wanted children to become aware of the possibilities of rural life; to stay on the farm; and to have the technical knowledge to make the most of their opportunities there. These diverse interests shared the view that the schools were too narrow—that they should begin to include in their curricula more of what children used to learn at home or on the job.

Theories of psychology imported from Europe affected the new study of child development. Varying doctrines of educational reform arose, which could be grouped under the umbrella of progressive education. While Francis Parker has been called the father of the movement, Dr. John Dewey is considered its chief spokesman. Dewey's writing was sometimes opaque and ambiguous. As a result his intent was often distorted by people who did not understand his books but had no qualms about discussing and interpreting them.

Dewey's main thesis was that each school should be a community in itself; through membership and participation in this microcosm, a child would come to comprehend the larger society into which he would graduate. Learning should begin with a child's concrete experience and continually expand it. In 1896 Dewey and his wife opened a Laboratory School at the University of Chicago to carry out his theories. Other teachers believing in progressive principles also opened schools to test and develop their ideas. Before World War I progressive education was essentially experimental, and with the exception of a few public school systems, such as the one in Gary, Indiana, the experiments were carried out in private schools. Following the war, developments in progressive education took place mainly in the public schools.

Pedagogy was maturing into a science and a profession. The influential Teachers College of Columbia University was founded in 1888. During the 1890's the better normal schools, which trained elementary school teachers, changed from being secondary schools to colleges. Liberal arts colleges and universities added education departments and graduate schools of education. Stimulated by the Morrill Act of 1862, the State universities, once small and shaky, had become powerful institutions, particularly in the Midwest. At Harvard, President Charles William Eliot gradually abolished most required courses and widened and deepened the range of elective courses. Numerous other colleges followed suit.

With the new interest in manual training, methods were imported from Russia to teach such crafts as woodworking and metalworking. Secondary manual training schools opened to give students both mental and physical skills. Commercial high schools and courses to train clerks, bookkeepers, and typists gained favor. New approaches to nature study introduced in rural areas had such impact that even children in slum-area schools started to grow gardens in vacant lots. Efforts to teach mentally and physically handicapped children increased. After 1910, as the special difficulties of the adolescent were recognized, the grading pattern of the schools was changed to 6 elementary years, 3 (or 2) in junior high school, and 3 (or 4) in senior high school.

The first formally organized private kindergarten in the United States was opened in Boston in 1860 by Elizabeth Peabody. Public school systems began adding kindergartens in the 1870's, but they were not the gardens of well-nurtured growth that the name implies. On the contrary, highly structured routines kept restless little children immobile for long periods. The reaction against formalism in schools started with these young students.

One of the most notable theorists in early childhood development was an Italian doctor, Maria Montessori. According to Dr. Montessori, children must be afforded a free and favorable environment in order to grow intellectually; given the proper setting, they will spontaneously develop the ability to concentrate when they are ready and will learn eagerly when allowed to proceed at their own pace. Dr. Montessori found the methods she had devised in 1899 so effective in helping retarded children that, when given the opportunity, she applied the same techniques to normal children living in the slums of Rome. The progress of these children, ages 3 to 6, lent support to her theories, which spread through Europe.

The year 1912 saw the publication in the United States of *The Montessori Method,* which attracted wide attention and excited enthusiasm. Two years later William H. Kilpatrick, an influential professor at Teachers College, published a criticism, arguing that Dr. Montessori's emphasis on individuality precluded the social interaction stressed in American progressivist theories. He complained further that the teaching materials were not stimulating; that children learned to read, write, and figure too early; and that any good elements in the method were already contained in Dr. Dewey's theories, which went beyond those of Dr. Montessori. Dr. Kilpatrick's book had such impact that by 1918 the Montessori method was seldom mentioned in the United States, although it flourished elsewhere. (Fifty years later, however, the method was reimported to this country. In 1958 there was only 1 Montessori school; by 1972 there were more than 1,000.)

With America's entrance into World War I, interest in social and political progress waned. Separated from the larger movement, educational progressivism became more professional. The Progressive Education Association (PEA), founded in 1919 and open to all who were interested in exchanging ideas, was gradually taken over by theorists in pedagogy. Differences became sharper. Instead of moving forward together, educators sniped at one another in increasingly esoteric jargon. As a result the effectiveness of the movement dwindled over the ensuing years. (The PEA was disbanded in 1955.)

In the hands of less than dedicated teachers, schools that encouraged pupils to express themselves freely and often formlessly in the arts produced such chaos that progressive schools became a favorite subject for caricature. The lampoons ignored the real contributions that progressive education had made to the public schools. The progressive influence could be credited with many useful innovations: the junior high school, testing to establish levels

Maria Montessori *was the first woman doctor of medicine in Italy. Working with retarded children in a psychiatric clinic and later with normal children in the slums of Rome, she concluded that children enjoyed learning as long as the work contributed to their personal growth or helped someone around them. On the basis of these observations, she devised an educational approach that put teachers and children, usually of a 3-year age range, in a pleasant, noncompetitive environment containing a wide variety of special teaching materials. Under the Montessori method, materials for each subject are designed for a logical succession of uses. As shown here, the classrooms are open, and the children are free to move about at will, so long as they do not interfere with others. The teacher must be a careful observer and introduce new materials as the children are ready for them. If they are interested, they continue working on their own. An important goal of the system is to create motivation through successful work and mutual respect. Students are allowed to work together or alone on projects that interest them. The self-confidence, self-discipline, independence, and creativity that children seem to develop are considered as important as the specific skills they gain.*

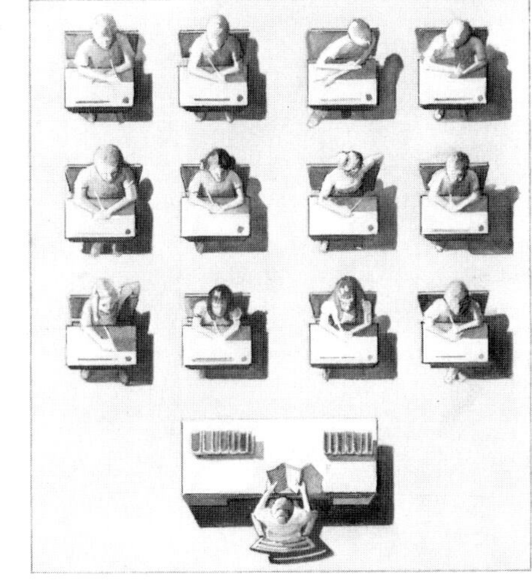

The Symmetrical School: *Its Effect on Education*

Few if any of us are unfamiliar with a school such as this, with its symmetrical facade, evenly spaced windows, central hallways, and identical rectangular classrooms with desks in perfect alignment, often bolted to the floor. Plain and purposeful, the building had no frills and was intended simply to provide space where teaching and learning could take place. The impression that it created was one of order and discipline. While this regimented arrangement may have suited the architect and school board, it was not designed to encourage individual motivation, cooperative effort, or easy exchanges between teachers and pupils, all of which most educators now consider best for everyone concerned.

Reaction against this traditional architecture has brought significant change in school design, which many educators consider to be a decided improvement over the old familiar form. And numerous communities are choosing more flexible plans, such as the one shown on page 139.

of competence, teacher-student "contracts" for work, expanded curricula, more and better gymnasiums and auditoriums, and increased extracurricular activities. More nursery schools and kindergartens were established, and more students remained through high school. The automatonlike recitations of the era of the McGuffey *Readers* were almost entirely discarded in favor of projects that combined work in several subjects.

During the 1920's rural one-room schoolhouses decreased in number as children from several districts were bused to one consolidated school. The expanded facilities of the larger school could offer much more than any single district school and they made possible the more efficient use of the always limited funds. Belated recognition of the virtues of the one-room schoolhouse—in effect, an open classroom—and the controversy over loss of control by local school boards have engendered criticism characterizing consolidation as a desire for efficiency that loses more than it gains.

High school attendance had been steadily growing, and the lack of available jobs during the Depression caused a great many students to remain in school. In 1900 there were 519,000 high school students; by 1935 there were more then 6 million. More than 1 million of these were aided by Federal funds through the New Deal Youth Administration. Although college enrollment increased slightly, most students were not continuing their education, and the majority of high schools had only a narrow college-preparatory curriculum.

Post-World War II

After the Second World War educational facilities and teacher shortages became major issues. In spite of the baby boom, taxpayers in local school districts, under the pressure of inflation, continually voted against increasing school expenditures.

Experience with some of the ideas of progressive education showed a need for further improvement and reform. Dewey's theory that the school should form a small community had been reversed, and the school went out into the larger community to study its needs. Testing, conceived as a helpful tool in properly placing and directing a child, came under attack as a form of typecasting that doomed him to a single self-fulfilling classification (intelligent, slow, one-sided, etc.). Too much reliance, it was found, had been placed on intelligence tests, which might be valid for a white middle-class suburban child but which tended to ignore other backgrounds.

Many critics charged the schools with closing doors rather than opening them. They felt that the public school, designed as a ladder of opportunity, had become a career selector. In junior high school, aptitude and achievement tests, combined with earlier intelligence tests, tended to set children on specific tracks from which escape was difficult. Many high schools offered commercial, vocational, and college-oriented courses under one roof, in an effort to afford students a common American background. However, a tendency to concentrate in one field meant that often the only experience students on different tracks shared in common was cheering for a high school team. Other high schools offered few alternatives to the college-oriented courses. Students with little chance of attending college found such studies boring and irrelevant, and they often dropped out of school.

The reward for finishing college was a good job and the chance to scale another ladder, that of the big corporation. Home and school pressure on students to be admitted to a "good" college intensified, putting a premium on learning how to excel at tests even in the early grades.

The colleges and universities had been changing slowly over the years, experimenting with honors programs and independent study. Some catered to special segments of the population, such as Catholics, Baptists, or upper-middle-class women. Several university projects, particularly those related to agriculture, had received Federal aid for decades. It was World War II, however, that brought a cascade of Federal money into the universities in the form of grants for research in the sciences and technology. At the close of the war, the GI bill of rights, providing veterans with money for tuition, books, and subsistence for up to 4 years of study, brought more funds and increased enrollments to institutions of higher education. Between 1945 and 1952 some 8 million men and women seized the opportunity. Personnel was added to handle the research and provide the additional teachers and administrators required by the increased enrollment, and some of the universities turned into large corporations. Graduate schools multiplied. Professors found opportunities to serve on committees, to act as consultants for the Government or foundations, to do research, to write books, and sometimes even to become

For nearly 40 years *children learned to read by chanting repetitive lines from books about Dick and Jane or imitators of this series. By 1970 such readers were fading from the classroom.*

The World's Great Books
For Discipline and Perspective

The concept of learning from great authors is as old as education itself. St. John's College at Annapolis, Maryland, bases its entire curriculum on detailed analysis of the works of more than 155 writers and composers. Listed below are most of the authors and a sampling of the books that are studied during the 4-year course.

Freshman Year

Homer ... *Iliad, Odyssey*
Aeschylus ... *Agamemnon, Prometheus Bound*
Sophocles ... *Oedipus Rex, Antigone*
Thucydides ... *Peloponnesian War*
Euripides ... *Hippolytus, Medea, Bacchae*
Herodotus ... *History*
Aristophanes ... *Clouds, Birds*
Plato ... *Republic, Symposium, Sophist, Phaedrus, Ion, Meno, Gorgias, Apology, Crito*
Aristotle ... *Poetics, Physics, Metaphysics, Ethics, On Generation and Corruption*
Euclid ... *Elements*
Lucretius ... *On the Nature of Things*
Plutarch ... *Pericles, Alcibiades*
Marcus Aurelius ... *Meditations*
Nicomachus ... *Arithmetic*
Antoine Lavoisier ... *Elements of Chemistry*
Essays by **Archimedes, Blaise Pascal, Gabriel Fahrenheit, Marcel Proust,** and others

Sophomore Year

The Bible
Apollonius ... *Conics*
Virgil ... *Aeneid*
Epictetus ... *Discourses, Manual*
Tacitus ... *Annals*
Ptolemy ... *Almagest*
Galen ... *On the Natural Faculties*
Plotinus ... *Fifth Ennead*
Diophantus ... *Arithmetic*
St. Augustine ... *Confessions, City of God*
St. Anselm ... *Proslogion*
Maimonides ... *Eight Chapters on Ethics*
St. Thomas Aquinas ... *Summa Theologica*
Dante Alighieri ... *Divine Comedy, Song of Roland*
Geoffrey Chaucer ... *Canterbury Tales*
Niccolò Machiavelli ... *The Prince, Discourses*
Nicolaus Copernicus ... *On the Revolution of the Spheres*
Martin Luther ... *The Freedom of a Christian*
François Rabelais ... *Gargantua and Pantagruel*
John Calvin ... *Institutes*
Michel de Montaigne ... *Essays*
Francois Viète ... *Introduction to the Analytical Art*
Francis Bacon ... *Novum Organum*
William Shakespeare ... *Richard II, Henry IV, Henry V, Hamlet, King Lear, The Tempest, As You Like It, Othello, Macbeth, Sonnets*
Johannes Kepler ... *Epitome IV*
John Donne ... *Poems*
William Harvey ... *Motion of the Heart and Blood*
René Descartes ... *Geometry*
Chevalier de Lamarck ... *Philosophical Zoology*
Charles Darwin ... *On the Origin of Species*
Gregor Mendel ... *Experiments in Plant Hybridization*
Poems by **Andrew Marvell** and other 17th-century poets
Essays by **Claude Bernard, August Weismann,** and others

Junior Year

Miguel de Cervantes ... *Don Quixote*
Galileo ... *Two New Sciences*
Thomas Hobbes ... *Leviathan*
John Milton ... *Paradise Lost, Samson Agonistes*
Francois de La Rochefoucauld ... *Maximes*
Jean de La Fontaine ... *Fables*
Blaise Pascal ... *Pensées*
Christian Huygens ... *Treatise on Light*
Baruch Spinoza ... *Theologico-Political Treatise*
John Locke ... *Second Treatise of Government*
Jean Baptiste Racine ... *Phèdre*
Isaac Newton ... *Principia*
Gottfried von Leibniz ... *Discourse on Metaphysics*
Jonathan Swift ... *Gulliver's Travels*
George Berkeley ... *Principles of Human Knowledge*
Henry Fielding ... *Tom Jones*
David Hume ... *Treatise of Human Nature*
Jean Jacques Rousseau ... *Social Contract*
Adam Smith ... *Wealth of Nations*
Immanuel Kant ... *Critique of Pure Reason*
Jane Austen ... *Pride and Prejudice*
Andrew Hamilton, John Jay, and **James Madison** ... *The Federalist*
Herman Melville ... *Billy Budd, Moby Dick*
Julius Dedekind ... *Essay on the Theory of Numbers*
Essays by **Ruggiero Boscovich, Thomas Young**

Senior Year

Molière ... *The Misanthrope, Tartuffe*
Johann von Goethe ... *Faust*
Georg Hegel ... *Logic, Philosophy of History*
Nikolai Lobachevski ... *Theory of Parallels*
Alexis de Tocqueville ... *Democracy in America*
Abraham Lincoln ... *Speeches*
Soren Kierkegaard ... *Philosophical Fragments*
Henry Thoreau ... *Walden*
Karl Marx ... *Communist Manifesto, Das Capital*
Fedor Dostoevski ... *Brothers Karamazov*
Leo Tolstoi ... *War and Peace*
Mark Twain ... *Huckleberry Finn*
William James ... *Psychology, Briefer Course*
Friedrich Nietzsche ... *Birth of Tragedy, Thus Spake Zarathustra, Beyond Good and Evil*
Sigmund Freud ... *General Introduction to Psychoanalysis, Beyond the Pleasure Principle*
Paul Valéry ... *Poems*
Carl Jung ... *Two Essays in Analytic Psychology*
Thomas Mann ... *Death in Venice*
Franz Kafka ... *The Trial*
Johann Heidegger ... *What is Philosophy?*
August Heisenberg ... *The Physical Principles of the Quantum Theory, Supreme Court Opinions*
Robert Millikan ... *The Electron*
Poems by **William Butler Yeats, T. S. Eliot, Wallace Stevens, Charles Baudelaire, Arthur Rimbaud,** and others
Essays by **Michael Faraday, H. A. Lorenz, J. J. Thomson, Alfred North Whitehead, Hermann Minkowski, Ernest Rutherford, Albert Einstein, Clinton Davisson, Niels Bohr, Erwin Schrödinger**

national figures. The country's hopes and expectations, which in the preceding decades had been focused on the high schools, were now directed toward higher education to provide answers to almost impossible questions and to be all things to all men.

Americans prefer not to choose between quantity and quality but to strive for both. As the idea became prevalent that everyone is entitled to more than a high school education, many communities opened 2-year colleges, some of which grew rapidly. Fairleigh Dickinson University in New Jersey, for example, which opened as a small community college in 1941, had 20,000 students on three campuses in the early 1970's.

Adult Education

Since the Nation's beginning Americans have been interested in self-improvement. Benjamin Franklin's Junto was a group of workingmen and apprentices who gathered to debate philosophical problems. The 18th and 19th centuries saw the opening of subscription libraries, reading rooms supported by mechanics institutes, and other establishments to encourage voluntary reading and stimulate individual study. The first town free library was opened in Peterboro, New Hampshire, in 1833. Other towns followed suit, although the idea did not really take hold until the 1870's.

During the first half of the 19th century lyceums multiplied rapidly. These local organizations, which sponsored debates and lectures on topics of current interest, were often large enough to attract such notable speakers as Ralph Waldo Emerson, Henry Ward Beecher, and Horace Mann. Later, chautauquas became increasingly popular. They originated in 1874 during a 2-week course to train Methodist Sunday school teachers in the rustic lakeside setting of Chautauqua, New York. So many enrolled that the next year the camp was opened to people of all denominations, and secular topics were introduced. Thereafter thousands gathered by Chautauqua Lake for 8 weeks every summer for lectures, classes, and musical performances. Correspondence courses were even developed for those who could not attend. Imitations sprang up all over the United States. Eventually several hundred towns had chautauqua-type assemblies, and traveling tent chautauquas became a national phenomenon. The movement declined during the Great Depression of the 1930's, and today only the original Chautauqua is still active, providing an annual summer program.

The chautauqua correspondence courses on literature gave diplomas that varied depending on the number of books read. Several publishing houses put out sets of the Western World's best literature. A popular series was the Harvard Five-Foot Shelf of Classics, published in 1909 and later accompanied by a series of lectures in book form to educate the serious student who had to abandon his

MAKING DEMOCRACY WORK

1954 Supreme Court Decision

In 1951 fourth-grader Linda Brown, of Topeka, Kansas, wanted to attend a public elementary school for white children near her home to avoid a long walk and a bus trip to the Negro school. When she was refused admission, her father sued the Topeka Board of Education. He lost, and the issue was appealed to the Supreme Court along with other cases showing a pattern of legal segregation. On May 17, 1954, the Court unanimously declared, "Separate educational facilities are inherently unequal" and unconstitutional.

The next year the Court ordered Southern States to desegregate their schools "with all deliberate speed." Many white southerners, regarding school segregation as the foundation of racial separation, resisted compliance with the decision. In Little Rock, Arkansas, desegregation had to be enforced by Federal troops.

Real progress toward desegregation began with the passage of the Civil Rights Act of 1964, which permitted Federal agencies to withhold Government funds from intransigent school districts. The effect of this act was reinforced by Supreme Court decisions that invalidated the closing of public schools to avoid integration and ordered school districts to end segregation "at once." Between 1968 and 1973 the number of black students in the South attending all-black schools was reduced from 77 percent to 21 percent.

However, if *de jure* (legal) segregation of schools was ended, *de facto* (actual) segregation resulting from residential patterns was not, particularly in the big cities in the North and West. Federal courts ruled that children be bused to schools out of their neighborhoods, in order to achieve racial balance—an ironic twist on Linda Brown's position. People of both races opposed long bus trips for their children. Picketing, school boycotts, and riots, which had erupted in the South during the late 1950's and early 1960's, were repeated in Northern cities in the late 1960's and early 1970's. In what many considered a backward step for integration, the Supreme Court barred busing across school district lines in 1974. More than 20 years after segregation was declared unconstitutional, the issue of integration in public schools was still far from being settled.

formal schooling. In the 1930's a few colleges experimented with 4-year college programs based on selections from the "great books" of Western civilization.

An explosive increase in adult education began in the late 1960's. With more leisure time available, many adults tend to return to school part time, either to earn an advanced degree or to take special courses. Community colleges, in particular, provide education for adults. From informal beginnings in the late 19th century, when a few professors occasionally traveled and gave lectures, university extension courses have developed into major departments. Some colleges have experimented with courses on television early in the morning or late at night and have even set up classes on commuter trains. Courses at YMCA's, libraries, and museums are widely attended, as are those offered by businesses for their employees.

Use of audiovisual *materials, such as the cassette recorder and slide projector shown here, is increasing in most schools. These electronic and mechanical aids, ranging from records to teaching machines and computers, can be used to facilitate individual study of any subject, freeing teachers to spend more time on nonroutine problems.*

Modern Education

American education, as always a subject of controversy, became the center of the furor that arose when the Russians surpassed the United States by launching *Sputnik* in October 1957. The blame for our lag in the space race was laid at the door of the educational system, and searching analyses were made of its faults. A spate of books on education were published. The U.S.S.R. was said to have better schools. Ivan could read, Johnny could not. Ivan had better teachers, better facilities, more knowledge of science. America did not emphasize science enough and did not train a sufficient number of technicians, mathematicians, scientists, or researchers. Marginal school activities, such as football and driver education, which helped to prepare Johnny for the good life, left him unprepared to enter any specialized field. The United States must train more technological experts.

The Smith-Hughes Act of 1917 had provided Federal money for vocational and agricultural training below the college level. Federal funds had been temporarily appropriated for educational agencies during the Depression. But most other efforts to aid elementary and secondary schools had been voted down, for fear that Federal funds would be followed by Federal control. Beginning with the National Defense Education Act in 1958, which specifically funded the sciences, mathematics, and foreign languages, Congress passed a torrent of legislation, showering Federal aid on every type of education from preschool to graduate level. Heated arguments continue to arise over whether such Federal aid should be extended to private and parochial schools.

The amounts of local money available for education have always caused discrepancies in the quality of school systems. The 1965 education bill was designed primarily to help children from impoverished homes. Students from middle-class homes start school with a cultural advantage over poor children, who fall further and further behind in achievement tests designed with their better-off classmates in mind. Recognition of this difficulty and of the importance of early experiences led to the Head Start Program for poorer preschool children.

New programs have been developed to reach those formerly left behind by the educational system. For the urban dropout there came street academies and schools without walls. Mobile classes, held in various locations around a city, as well as open classrooms, in which furniture is moved (or removed) to suit given projects or the wishes of a class, have helped to avoid the hemmed-in feeling of a big building full of rooms with straight rows of desks. Experiments have been carried out with year-round schools. Schools that teach manual skills have received new dignity. Attempts have been made to relate studies to the environment of the students—not a new idea, but one that had fallen by the wayside.

In the 1960's, too, many schools had more money available. On the whole teachers' salaries rose dramatically, making the profession more attractive. Many schools were able to establish new techniques and to set up valuable experimental programs, some federally funded, some funded by charitable foundations. In addition, many major corporations conducted or financed research in educational materials and methods.

Several systems of programed instruction have been

devised, tested, and modified in the schools. A wide variety of audiovisual aids, including television, is in use and constantly being improved. Children learn to read from an assortment of materials, which includes stories about more realistic characters than Dick and Jane. Conscientious revisions are being made to portray the female sex in a less limited and stereotyped way. Several paperback programs, such as Reading Is FUNdamental (RIF), offer stimulus to older children. Unfortunately, many schools—notably high schools in the larger cities—have been unable to make significant changes.

Although operating under the burden of soaring costs, the colleges and universities have devised new work-study plans and have opened up a whole new range of courses in such current concerns as environmental protection, urban planning, and black studies. Government projects and the well-funded programs for research had drawn many professors away from the classroom. Moreover, pressures on professors to do outside work—to "publish or perish"—had often led to the neglect of their teaching duties, and the students finally protested at the University of California at Berkeley in 1964. By the late 1960's many students had become disturbed about the social and political problems plaguing the Nation, and a series of student strikes spread across the country. The revolts, which frequently included the occupation of college buildings, resulted in a larger student voice in the administrations and curricula of a number of universities.

The educational and social upheavals of recent years have forced continuous scrutiny of the role of the schools. Arguments still rage about bureaucracy, centralization versus decentralization, the busing of children outside their neighborhoods, and the role of parents in the schools. There are disputes over textbooks, teaching methods, and finances. After more than a century of adding to the schools' educational burdens, Americans are increasingly aware that the school is only one of many educational forces in a child's life, and the resources of all of these, including the mass media, must be used in developing better education. There is now more emphasis on teaching students to think and prepare themselves to meet the unexpected in a rapidly changing world. Many problems still exist: Too little money, too few really good teachers, cultural differences, and the ever-expanding need for more years of education for more people. With the advances toward zero population growth, enrollment in elementary schools began declining in 1973. A few years ago, these schools were battling for more space. Now many must deal with the problems caused by over-expansion and at the same time they must cope with rising costs due to inflation. But despite the problems, we have learned that a good education is the best assurance of fulfillment for the individual and continued freedom and prosperity for the Nation.

The concept *of the open classroom, which provides freedom of movement and easy rearrangement of furniture, has been further developed in the design of open schools. These buildings provide more flexibility of use and are often less expensive to build than traditional schools. There are few partitioning walls, and the structural supports and heating and air-conditioning ducts are brightly painted to create interesting patterns of color and shape. The wide carpeted stairway shown here is used for seating or for temporary displays. Most teachers in such open schools as this one in Mt. Healthy, Indiana, are enthusiastic about the variety, flexibility, and efficient use of space. Advocates of these arrangements insist that the freedom of movement does not degenerate into confusion, nor is noise a problem. Other educators, however, question the effectiveness of the open-school approach. No matter which view prevails, these sophisticated new versions of the one-room schoolhouse are a far cry from the schools they are replacing.*

CHAPTER EIGHT

The Tragic Civil War

It has been called the irrepressible conflict, for so grave w the issues that gave birth to it, so intense the emotions evoked, that it seemed a war predestined by fate. For South the conflict was, and for many southerners rema to this day, the "War Between the States"—a phrase flecting the view that the Union had been a volunta association among sovereign powers, which could be fre terminated. For the North it was a civil war, a bloo drenched struggle foisted on the Nation by misguided a parochial countrymen, determined to sever the bonds o union that had been forged in revolution and sealed for time at the Constitutional Convention of 1787.

A Somber New President

A noticeably weary Abraham Lincoln sat for this portrait shortly after he arrived in Washington on February 23, 1861, for his first inaugural. Alexander Gardner, of Mathew Brady's studio, was the photographer. The President-elect had just completed a meandering, 2,000-mile trip from his home in Springfield, Illinois, touring five Northern States, attending receptions, shaking thousands of hands, and making more than 20 speeches in a futile attempt to calm a Nation hurtling toward the gravest crisis in its history. Lincoln's beard was a recent addition, presumably grown at the suggestion of an 11-year-old girl who had written him that his face was too thin and that a set of whiskers would make him look more dignified.

Despite the thin rays of sunshine that penetrated the somber sky, March 4, 1861, was a wintry day in Washington, D.C. The cold wind seemed to confirm the sense of foreboding felt by the city's 75,000 residents. The Capital of a young Nation that now stretched across the continent, Washington was also a sleepy Southern town where slaves were sold secretly at auction, belying the United States' proud and still revolutionary assertion that all humanity had a right to "Life, Liberty, and the pursuit of Happiness." Now, on Inauguration Day 1861, rooming houses and hotels were jammed with thousands of officeseekers from the new and victorious Republican Party. In these gathering places and in the sanctuaries of Government itself, the Capital was awash with rumors that Southern firebrands, whose States were on the verge of precipitating civil war, might kidnap or assassinate President-elect Abraham Lincoln before he could take office. Army sharpshooters were stationed along the route of the inaugural procession and in the windows of the still-unfinished Capitol, while the President-elect was provided with an escort of cavalry.

The rumor-fed fears did not materialize. The inauguration went through without a hitch, but the new President found little reason for comfort at the moment when he took the oath of office. The United States of America had reached a perilous juncture on that fateful day. Seven Southern States had already seceded, and at least four more slaveholding States were on the brink of secession, awaiting only an overt act by the Federal Government against their sister States before joining the newly formed Confederate States of America.

As far back as men then alive could remember, North and South had been moving toward this tragic confrontation. In the North, with its mixed agricultural-commercial-industrial economy and its fast-growing cities, most southerners saw an unbecoming bustle of

The philosophic question of Federal Union versus ates rights was complicated by the issue of slavery—its istence in the South and its possible spread to the new ritories under settlement. It was an issue that had be- viled the Union for decades, one that was cast into sharp ief by Abraham Lincoln in 1858. In his speech accept- the Republican nomination for U.S. Senator from Illi- is, he asserted: "'A house divided against itself cannot nd.' I believe this Government cannot endure perma- ntly half slave and half free." When Lincoln was elected the Presidency in 1860, the South saw its institutions avely threatened. Even before Lincoln arrived in Washington for his inauguration, seven Southern States had seceded and, meeting in convention early in February, had formed the Confederate States of America.

At its outset in April 1861 the war was viewed by most northerners as a struggle to save the Union, but in the end it became a crusade to free the slaves. In 4 years of bloody encounter the blue-clad Union armies and the gray-clad forces of the Confederacy ravaged the land, until at length a valiant but shattered South yielded to overwhelming force. At terrible cost the Union had been preserved and slavery eradicated. Perhaps now the noble principle that "all men are created equal" might become a reality.

John Brown *looms like a defiant Old Testament prophet in a mural painted by John Steuart Curry for the Kansas State Capitol. The fanatical abolitionist believed he had a divine mission to ensure Kansas' admission to the Union as a free State. Three days after militant advocates of slavery sacked Lawrence, Kansas, in May 1856, Brown led a reprisal assault against a proslavery settlement at Pottawatomie Creek during which five men were killed. Brown's larger purpose was to incite a widespread slave revolt, and this led him to attack the Federal arsenal at Harpers Ferry, Virginia, in October 1859. His death on the gallows that December made him a martyr for his cause.*

moneymaking. In the agricultural South, dependent on sales abroad—mostly to England—for its plantation-grown cash crop of cotton, northerners saw indolence and decay—a society propped up by the involuntary servitude of blacks, who enriched their white masters while virtually all hope of freedom was denied them.

Sectional divisions might have been compromised but for the crucial issue of slavery. Most white northerners did not consider blacks their equals nor advocate their immediate emancipation. But the northerners feared slavery's spread to the new Territories of the West and the consequent denial of land to free white men seeking to improve their condition. Southerners were equally fearful that the admission of the Western Territories into the Union as free States would in the end lead to the outlawing of slavery throughout the entire land.

For four decades Congress had vainly tried to reach a permanent compromise between advocates and opponents of the extension of slavery in the expanding country. In the 1850's the Territory of Kansas had been the chief battleground for the rival factions, as antislavery guerrilla bands and proslavery "border ruffians" struggled in bloody campaigns to control the Territorial government and thus determine whether Kansas would be admitted to the Union as a slave or free State. Then, at the end of the decade, in 1859, the fanatic abolitionist John Brown attempted at Harpers Ferry, Virginia (later West Virginia), what the South had always feared most: the fomenting of a slave rebellion. Although Brown found little support and his effort was quickly extinguished, the backing he had received in the North gave white southerners pause and sent a chill through their land.

The 1860 elections were held against this backdrop of violence. At the Democratic Party's national nominating convention, held in April in Charleston, South Carolina, the great split in the Democratic ranks became truly evident. The Northern wing of the party nominated Stephen A. Douglas of Illinois, the Southern wing nominated John C. Breckinridge of Kentucky, and a third-party candidate, John Bell, appeared. These divisions all but ensured a Republican victory. For their candidate the Republicans chose a dark horse, tall, raw-boned Abe Lincoln of Illinois, who hoped for the eventual peaceful emancipation of the black man in the South and stood firmly against the extension of slavery to the Territories.

Presidents Lincoln and Davis

In character, outlook, and temperament, no two men could have been more unlike than Jefferson Davis, the first and only President of the Confederate States of America, and Abraham Lincoln, 16th President of the United States, whose tenure was dedicated to the destruction of Davis' dream of a sovereign South. Davis' hair-trigger temper made him ill-equipped to deal with other ambitious and strong-minded Southern leaders. Lincoln, on the other hand, was generally a compromiser, anxious to balance conflicting points of view in the pursuit of his overriding goal of preserving the Union. Davis had the visage of a stern leader, upright, decisive, bold, and unyielding, while Lincoln cultivated a softer image. He conducted himself as a man of the people, folksy, sympathetic, and self-disparaging, turning his homely jokes against himself; but behind that seemingly gentle front lay a hard determination to crush secession at any cost.

For all their differences in style and substance, the two men had similar early backgrounds. Both were born in the first decade of the 19th century on the Kentucky frontier, and both were the sons of relatively unsuccessful farmers. Davis' family moved south to Mississippi where, with the help of his prosperous oldest brother, Davis became a successful planter. His feats during the Mexican War made him something of a celebrity, and, when he was 39, his State sent him to the U.S. Senate (1847–51). As Secretary of War for Franklin Pierce (1853–57) and during another term as U.S. Senator (1857–61), Davis became one of the staunchest proponents of Southern interests.

Lincoln's family moved west from Kentucky into Indiana and then into Illinois where young Abe worked at an assortment of jobs before acquiring enough learning to practice law in Springfield. As a country lawyer, an Illinois State legislator, and a one-term Congressman, he mingled with and came to understand a wide variety of people. Lincoln's experience enabled him to lead a Nation into war to preserve the Union. Later, when he judged the time ripe, he gave voice to the nobler aspiration of freedom for a race in bondage and used that crusade as a decisive weapon of war.

Southern States Secede

Lincoln was elected in November, though by a minority of his countrymen, and for the South the moment of decision had arrived. On December 20, 1860, South Carolina declared that it was independent and that the Union was dissolved. State conventions were called throughout the South, and by February 1, 1861, Mississippi, Florida, Alabama, Georgia, Louisiana, and Texas had followed suit. Then, on February 8, in Montgomery, Alabama, the seceded States formed the Confederate States of America and the next day elected Jefferson Davis of Mississippi as President. At his inauguration on February 18, Davis, a former U.S. Senator and Secretary of War, made a speech aimed largely at the North. In it he expressed the defiance of the new nation: "If a just perception of mutual interest shall permit us peacefully to pursue our separate political career, my most earnest desire will have been fulfilled. But if this be denied to us and the integrity of our territory . . . be assailed, it will but remain for us . . . to appeal to arms. . . ."

Secession presented the Union with so ominous a challenge that few men, in the winter of 1860–61, had the courage to respond. Serving out his last months in the White House, Democratic President James Buchanan of Pennsylvania was torn between his devotion to the Union and sympathy with the South. Buchanan had placed himself in an untenable position, declaring secession illegal but holding that the Federal Government had no power to prevent it. Now he could only hope to retire from office before events forced him to act.

As northerners debated what course to pursue, the Confederacy was busily asserting its sovereignty, seizing Federal property, and occupying Federal arsenals and forts. And throughout the Nation, Southern officers in the tiny 16,000-man U.S. Army were facing their own dilemmas: choosing between the flag they were sworn to protect and the seceded States that commanded their affection and loyalty. For most, ancestral ties to the South proved overwhelming, and they resigned their commissions, journeyed homeward, and prepared to serve the Confederacy. For none was this decision more difficult than for Col. Robert E. Lee of Virginia, who was widely regarded as the Union's most promising officer and who—in early spring, before Virginia seceded—had been offered the command of the Federal Army. Lee cared little about slavery and disapproved of secession; nevertheless, he finally decided that he could not "raise my hand against my relatives, my children, my home." Once having cast his lot with the South, he pursued a valiant struggle with a vigor that concealed his doubts, and he became the Confederacy's most celebrated hero.

Many northerners, too, were burdened with qualms, Abraham Lincoln among them. This was not apparent, however, in his inaugural speech, delivered beneath the

Opening shots *of the Civil War: Fort Sumter, in Charleston harbor, South Carolina, is fired on by Confederate batteries on April 12 and 13, 1861. The war had begun. South Carolina had seceded on December 20, 1860, but Sumter was one of two outposts in the newly formed Confederacy that remained in Union hands. Sumter's commander, Kentucky-born Maj. Robert Anderson, refused Gen. Pierre Beauregard's demand to evacuate the fort. The Confederate bombardment killed no one, but Anderson—short of supplies and menaced by raging fires—had to capitulate. (A Union gunner was accidentally killed in a powder explosion after the surrender.) Anderson and his men then departed by ship for New York.*

scaffolding of the unfinished Capitol dome. After giving assurances that he would not interfere with slavery where it already existed, the new President addressed himself to the secessionists; and here there was no hint of compromise. "In your hands, my dissatisfied fellow countrymen . . . is the momentous issue of civil war. . . . You can have no conflict without being yourselves the aggressors. You have no oath registered in heaven to destroy the Government, while I shall have the most solemn one to 'preserve, protect and defend' it."

Yet Lincoln's determination was tempered with extreme caution. By March 4, 1861, seizures of Federal property in the Confederacy had left only two forts under U.S. control: Fort Pickens off the Florida coast and the recently garrisoned Fort Sumter in the Charleston, South Carolina, harbor. To evacuate them would be an admission of Confederate sovereignty; to attempt their resupply would invite war. For a month Lincoln hesitated; then on April 6 he informed South Carolina officials that he intended to send supplies to Sumter. The Confederacy, wishing to show its independence and to force undecided States to join the Confederacy, decided to act. On April 11, with hundreds of South Carolina militiamen at his command, Confederate Gen. Pierre G. T. Beauregard demanded of Maj. Robert Anderson, commander of the small garrison, that he evacuate Sumter. Anderson refused, and at 4:30 a.m. on April 12, to the cheers of civilian onlookers, one of Beauregard's men fired the first shell of the Civil War toward the fort. Thirty-four hours later Major Anderson, having defended his command to the utmost and, miraculously, having suffered no fatalities in the battle, finally withdrew from the fort, marching his company out "with colors flying and drums beating," as the military code of honor required.

News of this assault on the Stars and Stripes stirred outrage in the North. Oliver Wendell Holmes wrathfully proclaimed: "The first gun that spat its iron insult at Fort Sumter smote every loyal American full in the face . . . for [over] those battered walls waved the precious symbol of all we most value . . . the banner under which we became a nation. . . ." But in the elated Confederacy, a Southern writer, George C. Eggleston, later recalled: "The unanimity of the people was simply marvelous. . . . Men got ready for war, and delicate women with equal spirit sent them off with smiling faces."

The Sides Are Established

To rouse men to battle was one thing; to organize, equip, train, and transport them, another. In urgent response to the attack on Sumter, President Lincoln on April 15 declared the States of the Confederacy to be in a condition of insurrection and called on the loyal States to provide 75,000 men for 3 months of Federal service so as to put the rebellion down. In most places the response was immediate. Men formed themselves into regiments, elected officers, and solemnly vowed to crush the rebellion before mid-July. But the States of the upper South—North Carolina, Tennessee, Arkansas, and, most significantly, Virginia—quit the Union rather than supply troops to fight fellow southerners, thus adding their resources to the Confederacy. In the restless Border States of Maryland, Kentucky, and Missouri many months were to pass before the Federal Government could fully assert its authority and ensure that they would not secede.

The resources of the North, with its population of 21 million, far outweighed those of the South, whose 9 million residents included some 3.5 million slaves. The North had about 1.2 million factory workers, compared with the South's 111,000. Railroad trackage stood at 21,700 miles in the North, only 9,000 miles in the South. And the North far outstripped the South in agricultural production. The South, however, had one major advantage: It was fighting on its own territory, which the North would have to invade and conquer.

The potential strength of Union land and naval forces was overwhelming; but for the time being, President Lincoln had only to glance out of a White House window to see, across the Potomac, the Confederate flag waving in the breeze. Washington, in fact, was virtually undefended until the fourth week of April, when Northern volunteers began to gather there. By early May 10,000 men had arrived, many in gaudy uniforms, armed with outdated weapons, and far from battle ready.

King Cotton Fails To Reign

The Confederacy entered the Civil War with an economy heavily dependent on cotton and, consequently, on the slaves who planted and picked it. Since the world's textile makers, particularly the great mills of Britain, presumably needed the cotton, the South was confident of European support. Southern leaders were certain that Britain and France, the two major world powers, would recognize the Confederacy and force the Union, despite its overwhelming superiority in men and supplies, to negotiate a peace. The French emperor was openly sympathetic to the Southern cause, as were the more influential elements of British society—especially the manufacturers, who saw an independent South as a vast potential market for British goods.

The Confederates, however, overestimated the importance of their cotton to the British textile industry and underestimated Britain's need for wheat from the North—as great as the demand for cotton and a strong reason for British neutrality. In the first months of the war, before the Union naval blockade became effective, the Confederacy made the mistake of withholding cotton that could have been traded for badly needed military supplies, hoping thereby to pressure the powers into recognition. But Britain had ample cotton reserves and was developing new sources in India and Egypt; and even after British textile workers lost their jobs because of dwindling supplies, they continued to back Lincoln and the Union. In the end French and British prudence overshadowed pro-Southern sentiment. The Confederacy's military position was never deemed strong enough to justify the risks of intervention, and Lincoln's preliminary Emancipation Proclamation of September 22, 1862, gave the North a strong moral advantage. Thereafter no nation was willing to give direct support to the slave-owning South.

The Confederacy was not sufficiently organized, however, to seize this initial advantage and march on Washington. In response to President Davis' appeal, 100,000 eager volunteers had rallied to the newly designed Stars and Bars, to be armed with weapons from captured Federal arsenals. The leadership included such superb West Point-trained officers as Lee, Beauregard, Joseph E. Johnston, and Thomas J. "Stonewall" Jackson. Davis could not ignore the North's great superiority in manpower and industrial might, but he cherished the hope that Britain, France, and other friendly European powers, which needed the raw cotton that was produced in the South to keep their mills in operation, would provide the major share of the South's supplies—a hope that was to prove ill-founded.

On May 23 Virginians voted overwhelmingly to ratify the month-old fact of their State's secession. In the face of the "Old Dominion's" rebuke, Lincoln moved quickly. On May 24 eight Union regiments crossed the Potomac, occupied Alexandria and Arlington Heights with no resistance, and established a symbolic force on Confederate territory. In the Virginia counties west of the Alleghenies the individualistic mountain folk, who had long nursed grievances against the dominant Tidewater counties, greeted secession with dismay. Gen. George B. McClellan, from his headquarters in Cincinnati, ordered his volunteers to invade and secure western Virginia. His successful campaign, which met with little military resistance and much civilian support, paved the way for the admission to the Union of the trans-Allegheny counties as the new State of West Virginia in 1863. These heady triumphs of June and early July were seen by some northerners as portents of an early Confederate collapse. But this illusion was soon dispelled in blood at a momentous battle the Union was to call First Bull Run; the Confederates, First Manassas.

Washington in early July 1861 was an armed camp. Some 30,000 soldiers—largely 3-month volunteers whose enlistments would soon be up—crowded the city, finding quarters in every place from a stable to the marbled sanctuary of the Capitol. Gen. Irvin McDowell was assigned the Herculean task of whipping this mass into a disciplined army. But he was given no time. About 25 miles from Washington, at Manassas, Virginia, near a stream called Bull Run, a Confederate army that now numbered some 25,000 men had been gathering under General Beauregard. Its presence so close to the Union Capital was viewed in the North as both an insult and a threat. Unionist newspaper editorials urged a forced march on the Southern troops, one glorious battle, and then an advance on Richmond, Virginia, which since late May had been the Confederate capital.

The President, too, was demanding battle before enlistments began to expire. To McDowell's pleas for time

The colorful ranks *of a Union Army Zouave regiment (above) parade up Washington's Pennsylvania Avenue away from the domeless Capitol shortly before their baptism of fire. Most were raw, undisciplined recruits, as their humiliating rout by equally green but better led Confederates demonstrated at First Bull Run on July 21, 1861. The period engraving at the right shows Gen. Irvin McDowell's Union force in full retreat from Bull Run. Joining their flight were frightened civilians who had come from Washington—like spectators flocking to a sporting event—to see an expected Union victory.*

to prepare the troops, Lincoln replied: "You are green, it is true; but they are green also. You are all green alike."

On July 16 McDowell yielded to the President's demands. Followed by a procession of carriages bearing Congressmen, their ladies, and newspaper reporters, all eager to witness the fall of the Confederacy, the general's hastily assembled troops marched out of the Capital for Manassas, where Beauregard and his forces—reinforced by an additional 9,000 troops under his superior, Gen. Joseph E. Johnston—lay in wait. The confident Beauregard had recently written: "If I could only get the enemy to attack me . . . I would stake my reputation on the handsomest victory that could be hoped for."

The South Shows Its Mettle

Beauregard's hopes and McDowell's fears were soon confirmed. Although the Union claimed a numerical superiority of some 5,000 men, they were attacking a well-entrenched enemy. Southern marksmanship and discipline first blunted the Union attack—which began before dawn on July 21—then pushed back the Union line, and finally, as the long summer day faded into dusk, turned a Union retreat into a rout. The disorganized troops streamed pell-mell back toward Washington, preceded by the panicky civilians, who soon infected the city with rumors that a Southern attack was certain.

This crucial battle, which resulted in Union casualties

of nearly 2,900 and Southern losses of about 1,900 (in killed, wounded, and missing), forced the North to acknowledge that it faced a determined and resourceful foe that could not be subdued by 90-day volunteers. In the aftermath of Bull Run, President Lincoln set his course for a long struggle. He ordered that 3-year recruitments be stepped up and the incipient blockade tightened, and he began a frustrating search for a Union general able to organize, train, and lead an army capable of defeating the Confederacy.

The South was jubilant, for in the blood-soaked fields of Manassas a new legend was born. It was there that Gen. Thomas J. Jackson earned his nickname, Stonewall, after rallying his troops by sitting stock-still upon his mount in the face of withering Union fire, and it was there that James Ewell Brown "Jeb" Stuart led his Virginia cavalry through the Union cannonade to military glory. The South had tasted the sweet fruit of victory, and the Northern cry of "On to Richmond!" was fading before the Confederate shout of "On to Washington!"

But the victorious army of Beauregard and Johnston was exhausted. In vain might Stonewall Jackson appeal for 5,000 "fresh men and I will be in Washington City tomorrow." The 5,000 were simply unavailable, and the hard-pressed Union thus gained a vital respite.

To reorganize the Union force, Lincoln called on General McClellan, conqueror of western Virginia, a vainglorious little man but a good administrator, capable of infusing his men with loyalty, discipline, and determination. Rushing to Washington in the wake of the debacle, McClellan quickly ringed the city with forts, which were manned by the 3-year volunteers who increasingly composed what had become known as the Army of the Potomac. By the year's end McClellan could boast a disciplined military force of 168,000 men, proud of their units and determined to win.

But the general thought his army too valuable to risk lightly. Certainly he would not repeat McDowell's error of marching into the teeth of the Confederate force still bivouacked at Manassas—an army only a fourth the size of his own but one that rumor and faulty intelligence had enlarged in McClellan's mind to immense proportions. So he sat, nurturing his force and holding interminable reviews, while General Johnston prepared his Virginia defenses. Meanwhile, armies of both the North and South gathered in the west, preparing for a battle to win control of the vital Mississippi River artery.

The "Trent" Affair

In this interim an incident occurred on the Atlantic Ocean that briefly sent Southern hopes soaring—the so-called *Trent* Affair. On November 8, 1861, a force from the Union man-of-war U.S.S. *San Jacinto* boarded the British mail steamer *Trent* and seized two Confederate

The Civil War at a Glance
Four Years of Anguish

These five stacked maps clarify the strategy of the opposing sides in the Civil War. To achieve its goal of conquering the South and restoring the Union, the North mounted offensives while Southern armies stayed on the defensive hoping to take so high a toll in lives that the North's will to fight would flicker out. Only twice did the South invade the North, at Antietam and at Gettysburg—with disastrous results.

By the end of 1863 the Union had achieved two goals—control of the Mississippi River, which split the South in two, and a strangling blockade of Southern ports—but no coordinated strategy to end the war was formulated until Grant took command in 1864. Coolly accepting heavy losses, Grant hammered Lee's army into submission in 1864–65 while Sherman slashed through Georgia and the Carolinas, destroying the South's last major source of arms and food.

KEY

Land gained by Union
Land controlle by Confederac
Land controlle by Union
Union Victory
Confederate Victory
Draw between Union and Confederacy
Union Movement
Confederate Movement
Union Blockade
Siege

Numbers indicate chronological order

Soldiers of Opposing Armies

The typical Union infantryman was dressed from kepi to boots (or hea shoes called gunboats) in a blue Government-issue uniform. His Co federate counterpart, for want of supplies from his Government, provi much of his own clothing—often from the Northern dead. The Sout official color was gray, but this soldier's jacket is yellowish brown—a obtained from a dye of copperas (made by soaking rusty iron in water) one made from butternut or walnut hulls. Most northerners carried Springfield rifled musket while southerners used either English-ma Enfields or Springfields that had been captured from Union troops.

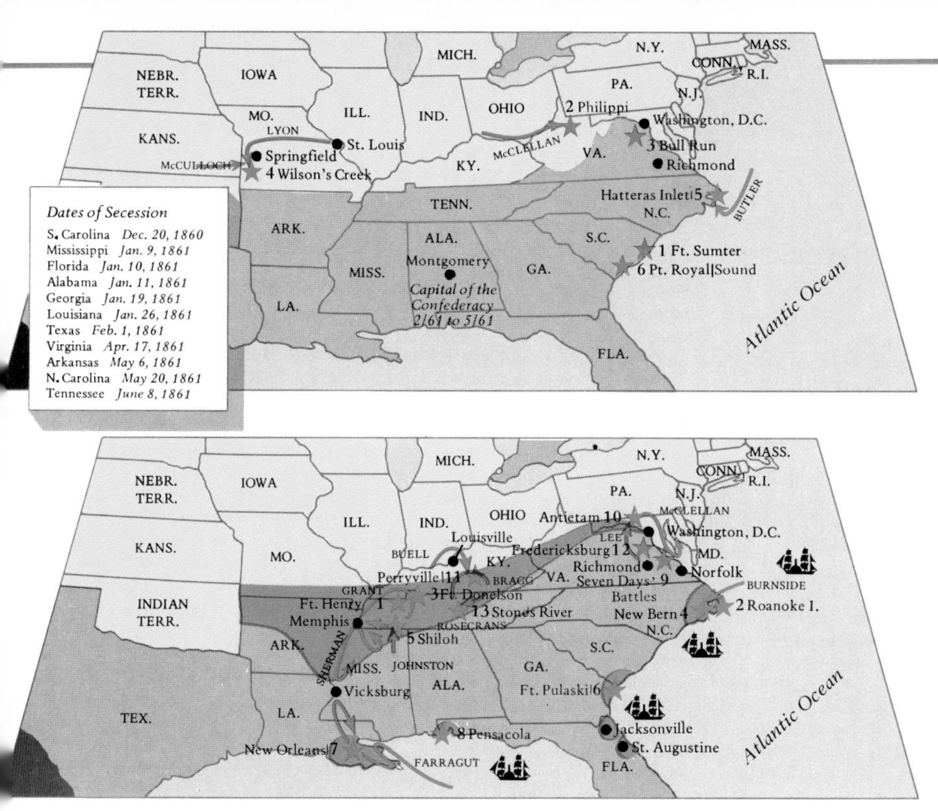

1861. *Combat began on April 12, when Confederate forces bombarded Union-held Fort Sumter in Charleston harbor, South Carolina, forcing its surrender. Union morale soared with McClellan's sweep through Virginia's western counties, which later became the State of West Virginia. The first major battle, at Bull Run on July 21, ended in a rout for the Union. This setback crushed Northern hopes for an easy victory. Lincoln then appointed McClellan commander of Union forces around Washington.*

1862. *Union troops under Grant cleared western Tennessee of Confederates in the battles of Forts Henry and Donelson in February and in the brutal engagement at Shiloh on April 6–7. On April 24 Union ships pierced New Orleans' defenses to force the surrender of the South's leading port. In the east, McClellan launched his Peninsular Campaign against Richmond in March but was thrown back with heavy losses in the Seven Days' Battles in June. Lee's army then invaded the North in September, only to be fought to a standstill at Antietam and forced to withdraw. McClellan's failure to pursue allowed Lee to regroup his forces.*

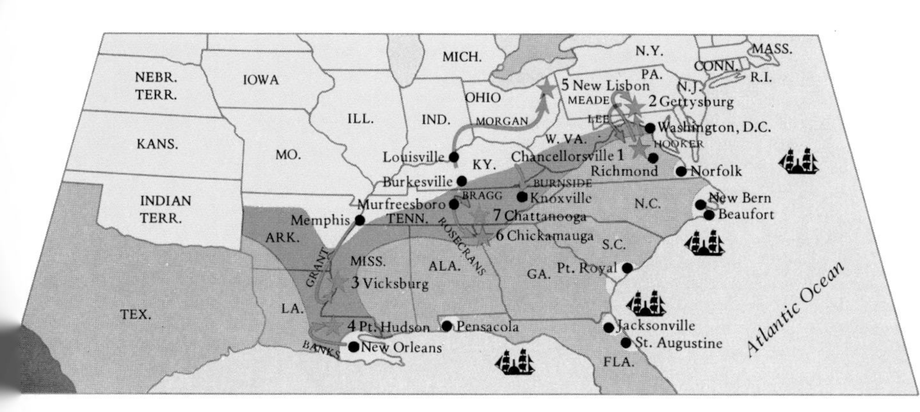

1863. *General Hooker's drive on Richmond was smashed by Lee at the Battle of Chancellorsville (May 1–4), encouraging the South to invade the Union once more. Lee moved north on June 3 and concentrated his forces near Gettysburg, Pennsylvania, on June 30. The Battle of Gettysburg (July 1–3) ended in Lee's withdrawal into Virginia. The South's bastion on the Mississippi, Vicksburg, fell to Grant on July 4, giving the Union control of all the Mississippi Valley and cutting the Confederacy in two. A series of bitterly fought encounters around Chattanooga (September–November) gave the Union a base for the invasion of Georgia.*

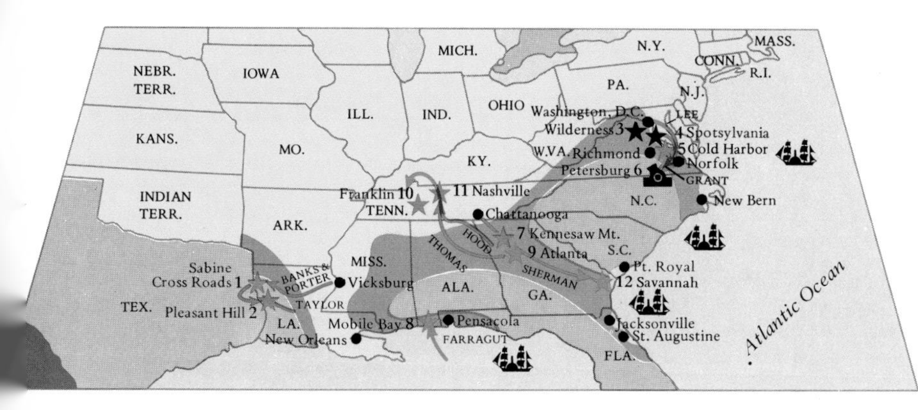

1864. *Grant, now commanding all Union armies, launched his Wilderness Campaign against Richmond on May 4. He was unable to crack Lee's defenses in a month of heavy fighting and suffered his worst repulse at Cold Harbor on June 3. Grant then outflanked Lee and struck at Petersburg, the vital Confederate rail-supply junction south of Richmond. Grant's bid for Petersburg failed when Union generals bungled the attack, and on June 18 Grant put the town under siege. Sherman's Union forces invaded Georgia in May, captured Atlanta on September 2, then swept to the sea, seizing Savannah on December 21 before swinging north.*

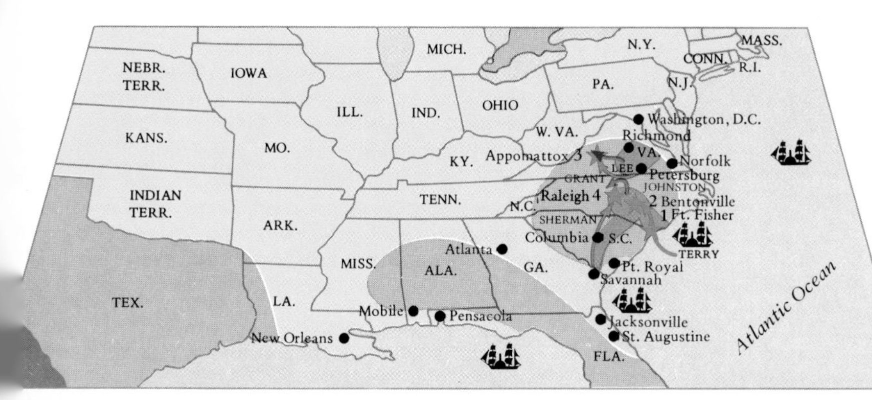

1865. *With Sherman slashing north through the Carolinas and Grant pounding at the gates of the enemy capital of Richmond, the Confederacy was doomed. Lee's dwindling army finally was forced to retreat from Petersburg on April 2, and Richmond fell the next day. Lee surrendered his army to Grant at Appomattox Court House on April 9. Johnston signed an armistice with Sherman on April 18, and the last Southern forces surrendered on June 2. The war was over. The Union had been restored.*

envoys, James M. Mason and John Slidell, who were bound for Europe to seek help for their cause. In London the incident was seen as a grave insult to the British flag; Her Majesty's Navy was mobilized and the Union was suddenly confronted with the unpleasant prospect of a foreign as well as a domestic war. At length the situation was saved by the diplomacy of Prince Consort Albert, husband of Queen Victoria, who redrafted a British protest note to U.S. Secretary of State William Seward in such a way as to allow the Union to return its two Confederate prisoners without a loss of dignity. Before the year was over the incident was closed; but throughout the war the South clung to the hope of foreign intervention. The shipyards of England and France continued to build Confederate vessels—blockade runners and cruisers—whose construction kept relations with Washington in a state of tension. But the settlement of the *Trent* Affair drastically lessened the chance of active intervention by European powers on behalf of the Confederacy.

When fighting resumed in February 1862, it was not in Virginia, but far to the west in Tennessee. The Union's western strategy was threefold: To occupy Tennessee and detach it from the rebellion; to seize control of the Mississippi Valley, denying the South access to the great river and cutting communications between the eastern and western Confederacy; and to seize the vital Southern port and commercial center of New Orleans.

The Emergence of General Grant

On February 6 Union volunteers and gunboats under a then little-known brigadier general, Ulysses S. Grant, captured Fort Henry in north-central Tennessee. Ten days later Grant took nearby Fort Donelson, capturing some 15,000 Southern soldiers and leaving Gen. Albert S. Johnston's Confederate Army of the West in deep trouble. To cut their losses and regroup, the Southern forces evacuated Nashville and moved south to Corinth, Mississippi, with Grant in pursuit.

The battle for New Orleans, *the South's greatest seaport, began with a savage bombardment of Forts Jackson and St. Philip, which guarded the approach to the city from the lower Mississippi. For 5 days Commander David Dixon Porter's 19 mortar boats lobbed shells into the forts with little effect. Finally Flag Officer David G. Farragut, as shown in this contemporary print, ran some 40 warships past the blazing guns of the forts on April 24, 1862; then shattered a small Confederate fleet and took the defenseless city the next day.*

On April 6 A. S. Johnston, having rallied his army, turned northward into Tennessee once more and fell upon an unsuspecting Grant at Shiloh Church, just above the State line. In the 2-day pitched battle that followed, the Confederates at first nearly routed Grant's army. But on the second day the Union received vital reinforcements from Gen. Don Carlos Buell, and the valiant southerners—whose commander had fallen in the fray—were pushed inexorably back. The price of the battle was 13,000 Union and 10,000 Confederate casualties. But the mangled Federal troops had secured all of western Tennessee, forcing their opponents into an almost permanently defensive position in the west.

On April 24, 1862, the Union objective of driving the Confederates from the Mississippi Valley came closer to realization as a fleet under Flag Officer David G. Farragut entered the Mississippi at its mouth and, with all guns firing, boldly ran by the Confederate forts protecting New Orleans. The next day the helpless city surrendered; it was promptly occupied by Federal troops and came under the harsh rule of Gen. Benjamin F. Butler.

After Shiloh and New Orleans, Union forces swooped down on one Confederate bastion after another along the Mississippi until the South's presence there was limited to its main stronghold at Vicksburg, Mississippi. To compound the disaster, the Southern ranks—initially filled in a burst of confidence with 12-month enlistees—had been depleted by heavy casualties; enlistments were sagging, and numerous soldiers, their terms up, prepared to return to civilian life.

Quick action was required, and on April 16, 1862, the Confederate Congress authorized the first conscription act in American history. All white Southern males between 18 and 35 were liable for service, though owners or overseers of 20 or more slaves and all those able to buy a substitute or contribute $500 to the Confederate war chest were exempted. Most southerners willingly obeyed the law at first, but the bitterness created by exemptions for the wealthy gave rise increasingly to the complaint, "Rich man's war, poor man's fight." The Governors of Georgia and North Carolina, alarmed at the act's threat to their cherished concept of States rights, clashed frequently with President Davis in their attempts to retain manpower within their States for local defense.

The South Gains Time

The troubled South could take some comfort from the Union's difficulties. Though Northern triumphs in the west had been greeted with jubilation, the President well knew that defeating the Southern armies in Virginia was far more crucial to the Union. McClellan, however, was not totally convinced that an all-out military victory was essential and still hesitated to commit his Army of the Potomac to battle. In vain did Lincoln plead with the general to mount an attack on the Southern forces. After long debate McClellan and Lincoln finally agreed on an advance on Richmond from the south. On March 17, 1862, supported by a strong Union fleet, McClellan began transporting his 112,000-man army to Fort Monroe, Virginia, on the tip of the Yorktown Peninsula. But then, instead of marching directly northward, McClellan decided to lay siege to and reduce every Confederate stronghold within range of his guns—thus beginning the long, frustrating Peninsular Campaign, which afforded Gen. Joseph Johnston's Army of Northern Virginia precious time to prepare its defenses.

By April 5 McClellan had advanced only as far as Yorktown, which he took after a month-long siege. His army then picked up speed, and on May 9 Norfolk fell, but thereafter his ponderous advance up the peninsula came under increasingly intense Confederate harassment. On May 31 General Johnston was severely wounded and was replaced by Gen. Robert E. Lee. On June 26 Lee launched the first of a series of engagements called the Seven Days' Battles, which pushed McClellan back from Richmond. His troops, evacuated from the peninsula August 14–16, were soon needed elsewhere.

On September 5 Lee's confident army crossed the Potomac into Maryland to open the first Confederate invasion of the North. Lee intended nothing less than the detachment of Maryland from the Union and the invasion of Pennsylvania. He hoped thereby to impress the horrors of war on the North and gain diplomatic recognition and military aid from the European powers. But on September 17 at Antietam Creek near Sharpsburg, Maryland, Lee met McClellan's reorganized and reequipped army in the bloodiest 1-day engagement of the entire war; after 12,000 Unionists and 13,000 Confederates had fallen, the southerners withdrew across the Potomac into Virginia.

Lincoln Proclaims Freedom

Although Antietam was by no means an unqualified Union victory—and McClellan's failure to pursue Lee led to his removal from command in November—it was the first heartening news the North had received in some time. Lincoln took the opportunity to announce his preliminary Emancipation Proclamation on September 22, 1862. In it he promised freedom to all slaves within those territories still in rebellion on January 1, 1863. His initiative was as yet unenforceable, but it set in motion an inevitable process. In a letter to abolitionist Horace Greeley, editor of the *New York Tribune,* on August 22, the President had stated: "If I could save the Union without freeing any slave, I would do it, and if I could save it by freeing all the slaves I would do it; and if I could save it by freeing some and leaving others alone, I would also do that." But by the fall of 1862 Lincoln decided that a decree granting freedom to Southern slaves would

Technology and Warfare
Destructive Weapons of an All-out Conflict

The Civil War was a surprisingly modern conflict in which railroads, the telegraph, observation balloons, torpedoes, ironclad warships, and crude submarines were used. Before the end of the first year, the relatively inefficient weapons of the past were being replaced. The war, in which more Americans died than in any other, proved the deadliness of muzzle-loading rifled muskets and artillery against attacking infantry. American companies had developed rapid-fire weapons prior to the war, but Army ordnance officers dismissed these guns as ammunition wasters. Ignoring these experts, Lincoln pressed for the adoption of breech-loading repeating rifles and carbines. The Union cavalry scored smashing victories in 1864–65 with 7-shot Spencer carbines, causing Confederates to complain that the damyankees loaded their guns on Monday and fired all week.

On guard at Washington, D.C., *Union troops man a 100-pound Parrott gun at Fort Totten, one of the National Capital's main defenses.*

The Dictator, *a 13-inch mortar capable of throwing a 200-pound explosive shell 3 miles, was used by Union troops at the siege of Petersburg in 1864. In the air, balloons, such as the one at left, guided by Prof. Thaddeus Lowe, gave valuable service as the eyes of the Union Army.*

The historic duel of the ironclads, *the Confederate* Merrimack *and the Union* Monitor, *foreshadowed the end of wooden warships. On March 8, 1862, the* Merrimack *had challenged the Union blockade of Hampton Roads, Virginia, by sinking one warship, capturing another, and running a third aground, but the next day she in turn was challenged by the little Union ironclad* Monitor, *the first ship with a revolving gun turret. The two vessels engaged in a slugging match, and after a 3-hour duel the leaking* Merrimack *withdrew, never to return.*

benefit the Union cause. It would give it new luster among influential antislavery northerners and would turn the struggle into a crusade in which any wavering European power would not dare intervene on the side of the slave master. The liberated slaves rallied to Union arms, and many revealed extraordinary courage in battle. Altogether, some 215,000 black troops served in the Army and Navy.

Lincoln's moral dilemmas might have seemed minor compared with the problems the South then faced. With Lee's retreat from Antietam and the tightening Northern blockade of Southern ports, all the materials of war were in short supply. In early 1862 the Confederacy's hopes had been briefly raised by the success of its ironclad warship *Virginia* (generally known by its earlier name, *Merrimack*), which on March 8 sank one Union warship, captured another, and drove a third one aground. But the next day the *Merrimack* was itself challenged by the ironclad *Monitor,* which ended its threat to the Union fleet. The battle of the ironclads not only marked a revolution in naval warfare but forcefully demonstrated the Union's ability to respond to any challenge the South might muster. And so the blockade went on. General Lee, attempting to rebuild and resupply his army in Virginia during the winter of 1862–63, described its sufferings: "In one regiment . . . there are only 50 men with serviceable shoes, and a brigade that recently went on picket was compelled to leave several hundred men in camp, who were . . . destitute of shoes and blankets. . . ."

The Draft and the Riots

On New Year's Day 1863 Lincoln issued his formal Emancipation Proclamation, and from then on Northern armies capturing new Confederate territory bore a message of liberation to the region's slaves. On March 3 the Union, which by then was experiencing extreme difficulty raising new regiments of volunteers, instituted conscription. The law required all men to register, but a man whose name was drawn could avoid that particular draft by paying $300 or could be permanently exempted by paying a substitute to serve in his place—provisions bitterly resented by the poor, who could ill afford to pay (at the time $300 was about two-thirds of the average workman's annual pay). A Norwegian immigrant described the feelings of many when he wrote: ". . . who is to go will be decided by drawing lots . . . we are in a mood of uncertainty and tension, almost like prisoners of war in this formerly so free country." On July 13 draft riots broke out in New York City, and mobs, mostly Irish immigrants, roamed the streets in a 4-day orgy of looting and burning. In their fury they focused on the city's Negroes as the cause of all their troubles, and before Federal troops could restore order, many black men had been beaten or lynched. Meanwhile, in April, a food riot among the poor of Richmond was quelled by President Davis, who addressed the rioters in firm tones and distributed to the crowd the money that he was carrying. Only then did he call on the militia to disperse them.

For all the war-weariness, frustration, and sorrow in both the North and South, each side remained determined to force its will on the other. Nowhere was this more evident than on the western front. In mid-May Grant began a siege of Vicksburg, which was the last important Southern stronghold on the Mississippi. One Southern soldier later recalled that "a cat could not have crept out of Vicksburg without being discovered." On July 4, with mass starvation threatening, the city surren-

MAKING DEMOCRACY WORK

The Emancipation Proclamation

"If my name ever goes down into history, it will be for this act, and my whole soul is in it." Thus did Abraham Lincoln appraise his preliminary Emancipation Proclamation, announced on September 22, 1862, and made official by Presidential signature on New Year's Day 1863. The document proclaimed:

> *. . . all persons held as slaves within any State or designated part of a State, the people whereof shall then be in rebellion against the United States, shall be then, thenceforward, and forever free; and the Executive Government of the United States . . . will recognize and maintain the freedom of such persons. . . .*

Eloquent though Lincoln's words were, they had no immediate power to end slavery in areas still under Confederate control. Border slave States loyal to the Union were not affected nor were sections of the Confederacy already restored to Federal jurisdiction; no longer enemy territory, the latter were not subject to the President's war powers, under which the proclamation was issued. Although the measure freed no slaves on January 1, 1863, it made inevitable the passage by Congress in 1865 of the 13th amendment, which finally ended slavery in the United States. And, for all its limitations, the proclamation dramatically shifted the moral basis of the conflict from a war fought to restore the Union to a battle for human freedom.

Reaction to the President's move ranged from Southern outrage—the Richmond *Examiner* called it "the most startling political crime . . . in American history"—to ridicule by extreme abolitionists, who acidly pointed out that emancipation applied only to areas where it could not be enforced. Many Union soldiers were indifferent, but most antislavery advocates exulted, and in London, U.S. historian Henry Adams wrote: "The Emancipation Proclamation has done more for us here than all our former victories and all our diplomacy. It is creating an almost convulsive reaction in our favor all over this country."

dered. In a master stroke, Grant paroled his 31,000 Confederate captives and sent them streaming homeward, under a pledge to take no further part in the war.

Terrible Days at Chickamauga

The scene then shifted to Chattanooga, the Confederacy's last bastion in eastern Tennessee. On September 4 Union Gen. William S. Rosecrans began a march on the city, which was garrisoned by a weaker force under Gen. Braxton Bragg. Rather than see his army decimated, Bragg evacuated it 25 miles south into Georgia, where reinforcements brought his strength up to 70,000; then he turned back into Tennessee and gave battle at Chickamauga Creek. In that 2-day bloodbath (September 19–20), Bragg sustained some 18,000 casualties but was in command of the field. The routed Union forces, whose losses amounted to more than 16,000, fled to the shelter of Chattanooga. The exhausted Bragg at first failed to pursue his foe, which brought an accusation of "criminal negligence" from an infuriated President Davis, but by September 23 he occupied Missionary Ridge and Lookout Mountain on the edge of Chattanooga, trapping the bumbling Rosecrans and his Army of the Cumberland.

Thus the entire Union position in the west was suddenly threatened. Grant, then commanding all Northern forces in the area, replaced Rosecrans with Gen. George H. Thomas and 8 days later forced open a supply line to the city's beleaguered defenders. On November 25 the heavily reinforced Federals stormed through a murderous hail of Confederate fire and won Missionary Ridge, Bragg's main line of defense.

With Chattanooga safely in Union hands, the war in the west was effectively over, and Gen. William T. Sherman began organizing the army that would cut a destructive swath through Georgia to the sea. In the east a train of events had occurred that would lead to the destruction of the Confederacy's war-making power. It began auspiciously for the South. At Chancellorsville, Virginia, on May 1–4, 1863, Lee won a smashing victory over the Army of the Potomac under its latest commander, Gen. Joseph Hooker, a triumph that set the scene for a final Southern invasion of the North. Despite President Davis' warning counsel—and the bitter blow dealt Lee at Chancellorsville by the death of Stonewall Jackson, his most talented subordinate—Lee determined once more to challenge the Union on its own ground and at the same time use the North's resources to provision his ragged army, which the weary land of Virginia could no longer afford to feed or clothe.

On June 3, 1863, Lee moved northward through the Shenandoah Valley, encountering little resistance. By the end of the month his troops had emerged near the little town of Gettysburg, Pennsylvania, where they collided with the Army of the Potomac, now under Gen. George G. Meade—who had replaced the inept "Fighting Joe" Hooker. For 3 days, July 1–3, the most decisive battle of the Civil War raged between about 90,000 northerners and some 75,000 southerners. On July 3 the Union line on Cemetery Ridge withstood a fierce Confederate charge, and the battle ended with a heartsick Lee counting about 20,000 casualties to Meade's 17,500. "It is all my fault," the Southern commander said. Once again, a Confederate invasion of the North had resulted in disaster. Lee and his forces withdrew once more into Virginia.

In the wake of Gettysburg the Confederacy entered its final agony. Sherman's 100,000 men in Chattanooga stood poised to strike through the heart of Georgia, where

Generals Lee and Grant

The Civil War's two top generals are often thought of as opposites: Robert E. Lee, the scholarly, gallant gentleman-soldier from Virginia, and Ulysses S. Grant, the unprepossessing, doggedly determined Ohioan. As the war began, the two men found themselves in very different positions. Grant had resigned his commission in 1854—possibly to avoid charges of drunkenness—and had spent the next 7 years eking out a living as a civilian. The war proved a chance to redeem his reputation. For Lee, civil strife was a national tragedy, and he was torn by conflicting loyalties. He disapproved of secession, but he could not turn against his beloved Virginia. Unlike as they were, however, the two men had certain features in common: Like most of the war's leading officers, both were West Pointers; both were descended from Patriot fighters in the Revolution; and both had served more than creditably in the Mexican War of 1846–48. Both, too, commanded the loyalty, in Lee's case, outright devotion, of their officers and men.

In one sense Grant and Lee had a similar task: to mold raw volunteers, and later resentful draftees, into disciplined soldiers. But whereas Grant had the overwhelming resources of the North on his side, Lee had to rely on Southern dash and the desperate courage of men defending their own soil; he had to make up in surprise and swiftness what he lacked in supplies and reserves. His tactics resulted in both brilliant victories and devastating defeats. Grant did not match Lee in daring, but he alone among the Union generals implemented President Lincoln's grand strategy of maintaining unrelenting pressure on the Confederate armies. Grant led the Union in its first major victories in early 1862 and masterminded the successful siege and capture of Vicksburg in 1863. As the war neared its end, Grant forced Lee into a series of punishing battles before finally hounding the remains of Lee's army into submission at Appomattox Court House on April 9, 1865. Here the man who had made his reputation as the war's most implacable commander displayed great tact and generosity. Lee, who shared with his opponent an awareness of the need for reconciliation between North and South, was much moved by Grant's magnanimity.

Fierce hand-to-hand combat *erupts as the spearhead of Pickett's Charge reaches Union lines on Cemetery Ridge south of Gettysburg. But the Southern flanks were under heavy fire and Union reinforcements poured in to stop the gallant assault. As the exhausted survivors among the 15,000-odd attackers straggled down the hill, Gen. Robert E. Lee hurried to rally his men to meet any Union counterattack.*

The Battle of Gettysburg
The Turning Point

In the spring of 1863 the tide of battle flowed favorably for Gen. Robert E. Lee's Army of Northern Virginia. In May, at Chancellorsville, Virginia, Lee's force inflicted a stunning defeat on the North's Army of the Potomac, and the next month, in a desperate gamble to destroy the Union's will to carry on the war, Lee invaded the North with 75,000 men. On July 1 these forces reached the town of Gettysburg, Pennsylvania, where a Union army of 90,000 under Maj. Gen. George Meade caught up with them to open the bloodiest and most decisive engagement of the war.

The battle began with a series of sharp, probing encounters that left Lee in control of Gettysburg while the Unionists took strong defensive positions on the hills south of the town. July 2 was a day of wrath. In an effort to outflank the center of the Union line on what was aptly named Cemetery Ridge, Lee sent one corps, under Lt. Gen. James Longstreet, against the south end, while a second corps, commanded by Lt. Gen. Richard Ewell, launched an attack on Culp's Hill to the north. Ewell's attack was late and ineffective, allowing Meade to shift troops that finally plugged gaps in the Union line and stalled Longstreet after desperate hand-to-hand fighting.

Thus frustrated, Lee ordered an all-out frontal assault against Cemetery Ridge on the next day, July 3. An intensive artillery bombardment of the ridge announced the Confederate intentions, and at 2 o'clock in the afternoon about 15,000 gray-clad men, commanded in part by Maj. Gen. George Pickett, moved into a clearing in front of the ridge and charged into the teeth of Union artillery and small-arms fire. Thousands fell; desperate remnants of the Confederate regiments dented the Union lines for a few bloody minutes, only to be overwhelmed by their stronger foe. The failure of what is called Pickett's Charge sealed the outcome of the battle. With casualties of approximately 20,000 irreplaceable men, Lee could only order a retreat into Virginia, there to organize a defensive stand against the inevitable Union onslaught.

MAKING DEMOCRACY WORK

The Gettysburg Address

On a mild November day in 1863, President Lincoln dedicated a cemetery at Gettysburg with this incomparable distillation of American ideals:

Four score and seven years ago our fathers brought forth on this continent, a new nation, conceived in Liberty, and dedicated to the proposition that all men are created equal.

Now we are engaged in a great civil war, testing whether that nation, or any nation so conceived and so dedicated, can long endure. We are met on a great battle-field of that war. We have come to dedicate a portion of that field, as a final resting place for those who here gave their lives that that nation might live. It is altogether fitting and proper that we should do this.

But, in a larger sense, we can not dedicate—we can not consecrate—we can not hallow—this ground. The brave men, living and dead, who struggled here, have consecrated it, far above our poor power to add or detract. The world will little note, nor long remember what we say here, but it can never forget what they did here. It is for us the living, rather, to be dedicated here to the unfinished work which they who fought here have thus far so nobly advanced. It is rather for us to be here dedicated to the great task remaining before us—that from these honored dead we take increased devotion to that cause for which they gave the last full measure of devotion—that we here highly resolve that these dead shall not have died in vain—that this nation, under God, shall have a new birth of freedom—and that government of the people, by the people, for the people, shall not perish from the earth.

Lying in ruins, *the Confederate capital at Richmond gives mute evidence to the ravages of war. It was evacuated on April 2, 1865, by the government of Jefferson Davis, which ordered the firing of bridges, warehouses, and shipping. Wind whipped the fires through the business district while mobs looted the city. The next day, Union troops entered Richmond and brought the flames under control.*

60,000 troops under General Johnston were making frantic preparations for defense. In the east the 115,000-man Army of the Potomac under General Grant, whom Lincoln had recently brought east and made commander of all Union armies, girded for the decisive campaign. Lee now had 60,000 effective fighting men but sorely lacked food, munitions, and medical supplies.

The Beginning of the End

For some months there was a lull in major combat as the two sides gathered strength for the ultimate confrontation. On May 4, 1864, Grant struck, moving his army across Virginia's Rapidan River to meet Lee in what became known as the Wilderness Campaign. On May 7–8 the two armies clashed head on at the crossroads town of Spotsylvania, and for the next 12 days Lee's men withstood a fierce artillery pounding and repeated Union attacks. The southerners inflicted some 20,000 casualties on the Federals before retiring to Cold Harbor, a scant 10 miles from Richmond. Grant then ordered a frontal assault on the deeply entrenched Confederate line, only to lose some 7,000 men in less than an hour. A Southern officer, surveying the battle site, remarked: "The dead covered more than 5 acres of ground as thickly as they could be laid."

Having failed to take Richmond by direct assault, Grant swung south toward Petersburg, hoping there to cut the main rail line to Richmond, destroying Lee's supply line and starving out the Confederate capital. On June 15 Grant's XVIII Corps reached Petersburg ahead of Lee's main force but bungled the opportunity to capture the vital rail junction when the corps commander halted to await reinforcements. By the time these arrived, Petersburg's garrison had itself been heavily reinforced; and after a series of assaults failed, Grant settled down to a 10-month siege. All told, the Wilderness Campaign cost Grant some 55,000 men, but they were quickly replaced by Union reserves. Lee had suffered lighter losses but had no such reserves on which to call.

Meanwhile, far to the west, Sherman had at last emerged from Chattanooga on May 6, 1864. By mid-July he was bogged down on the outskirts of Atlanta, his flanks and lines of communication under constant harassment. It was at this time that the Union's 1864 Presidential campaign was launched. For their candidate the Democrats picked the dismissed General McClellan. His running mate was Ohio Congressman George H. Pendleton. He was a close friend and associate of Clement Vallandigham, a fellow Ohioan whose loudly expressed Southern sympathies had once caused Lincoln to have him deported to the Confederacy. In the Democratic candidates and their peace platform the South saw its last, best hope for a favorable resolution of the war. Indeed, war-weariness pervaded the North, Grant's immense losses and Sherman's stalled offensive being partially responsible for the Democrats' peace campaign. Even Lincoln doubted his reelection, noting in late August that "it seems . . . probable that this Administration will not win. . . ."

The South sought to capitalize on Northern disaffection and to relieve the pressure on Lee's besieged army at Petersburg by launching a swift thrust through the Shenandoah Valley, using a small army under the command of Gen. Jubal A. Early. On July 6 Early, having bested several Union commanders, crossed the Potomac into Maryland and prepared to attack Washington. The panic-stricken Capital might have fallen, but Grant dispatched a corps to reinforce it. After a July 12 battle on the city's outskirts, Early was forced to withdraw; he was pursued into the valley and eventually overwhelmed by Gen. Philip Sheridan's Union army.

Lincoln Is Reelected

The Shenandoah gamble had failed, and on September 2 the western front broke as Sherman moved into Atlanta and began his march through Georgia to the sea. Sherman's victories and Early's defeat ensured Lincoln's return to office by an electoral vote of 212 to 21—a rousing affirmation of the Union's determination to see the war through to victory.

After taking Savannah on December 21, Sherman hacked a bloody trail northwestward through the Carolinas. Meanwhile, Grant was still stalled at Petersburg. Through the fall and winter of 1864–65, Grant continued pressing Lee's force, his artillery bombarding Southern positions in the town, his line moving ever westward in an effort to cut the rail link to Richmond and force Lee to thin out his own line in its defense. The despairing President Davis sought some means of holding on, and on March 13, 1865, the South tacitly abandoned slavery, for which it had so long struggled, by authorizing the enlistment of Negroes as combat soldiers.

But it was far too late. Twelve days later Lee launched a final doomed attack on Grant's lines, and on April 2 he was forced to abandon Petersburg. On April 9, at Appomattox Court House, the epic struggle ended as Lee yielded to the inevitable and surrendered his command to General Grant. For all intents and purposes, the Civil War was over. Its cost in lives—620,000—remains the highest toll in American history; its other costs, particularly in the South—wasted farms, burned-out cities, devastated communications—were incalculable. But the Union had been saved and slavery ended. Yet a true peace had still to be restored to all—to the emancipated slave and his former master, to the defeated Southern soldier and his victorious Northern counterpart. And it appeared that the structure of that peace lay solely in the hands of the Nation's President.

During the final months of the war, Lincoln was developing a plan for the reconstruction of the South and the readmission of the defeated States into the Union. In his second Inaugural Address, a month before Appomattox, the President fervently envisioned a peace of reconciliation while at the same time acknowledging that to expunge the sin of slavery, history might yet require that "every drop of blood drawn with the lash shall be paid by another drawn with the sword."

Whatever Lincoln's hopes for restoring the South to an honored position, they were shattered by an outrageous act. While attending a theatrical performance in Washington on the night of April 14—Good Friday—the President was struck down by an assassin's bullet, and he died the next morning. The Union, still in mourning for hundreds of thousands of its sons, had now to mourn

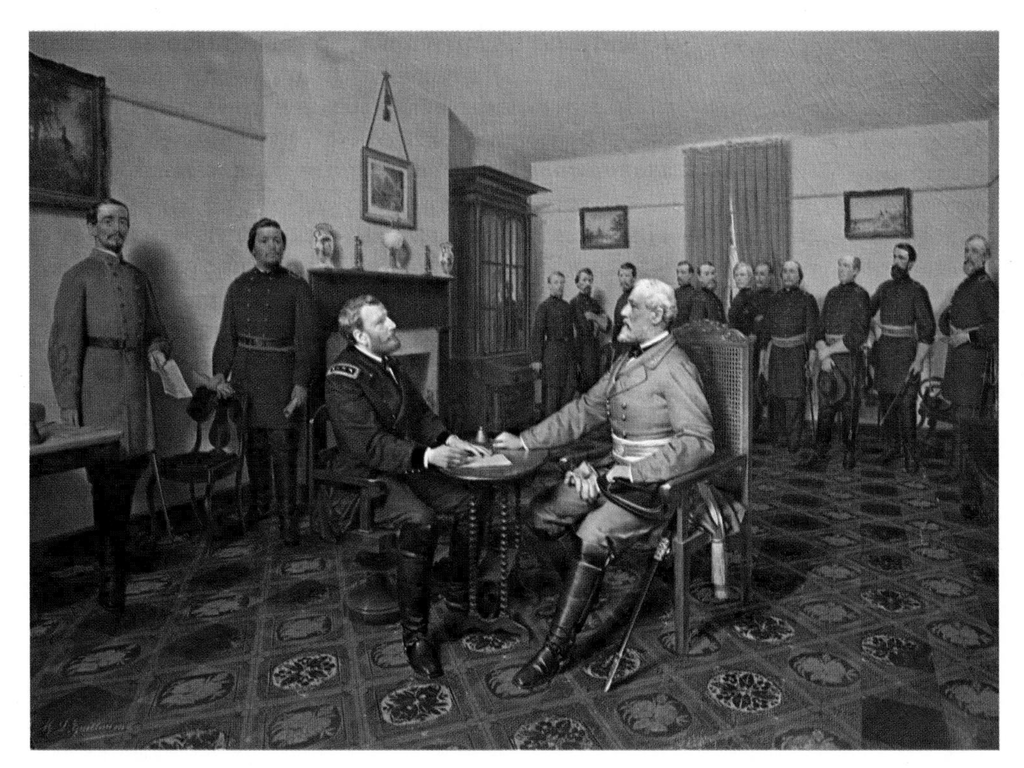

Lee's surrender *to Grant at Appomattox Court House on April 9, 1865, is depicted in this painting by French portraitist Louis M. D. Guillaume, who was present when the two generals signed the terms in the parlor of a local farmhouse. Behind Grant stood Col. Charles Marshall, Lee's aide, and Lt. Col. Ely Parker, a Seneca Indian on Grant's staff. Grant's terms ruled out the taking of prisoners or trials for treason. Officers were allowed to retain sidearms and baggage. Both officers and men could go home, taking their mounts with them, after signing a parole that they would no longer fight. Thereafter they were "not to be disturbed by United States authorities." After the papers were signed at 4 p.m., a "sad-faced and weary" Lee rejoined his beaten Army of Northern Virginia. Grant stopped his men from firing their artillery pieces in celebration; he preferred not to "exult" in the defeat of a courageous foe.*

Lincoln's Assassination

Ending the Nation's Hopes for Reconciliation

John Wilkes Booth, a lesser light in a famed theatrical family and an impassioned Confederate sympathizer, apparently believed that by killing Abraham Lincoln he would somehow be helping the fallen South. But his deranged act did just the opposite: The death of a great President evoked an enormous outpouring of grief and anger in the North and a demand for revenge against the South. With one squeeze of the trigger, Booth had killed the man who seemed to represent the best hope for a peaceful reconciliation between the former adversaries.

After Lincoln's death, Secretary of War Stanton fanned the flames of vengeance by making unsubstantiated charges that Jefferson Davis had been involved in the assassination conspiracy. Booth was trapped in a a barn and shot by his pursuers, and four of his alleged coconspirators (including his landlady, Mary Surratt, who had probably taken no part in the scheme) were sent to the gallows by a military tribunal on July 7, 1865. One of them, Lewis Paine, had seriously wounded Secretary of State William H. Seward in Seward's home. The Secretary later recovered.

A stricken President *recoils from Booth's fatal shot at Ford's Theater on April 14, 1865. Earlier that day Lincoln had told a friend that he had no desire to attend the evening's theater party but felt he must not "disappoint the people." The poster below was issued on April 20, 6 days before Booth was caught hiding in a barn in Virginia and shot.*

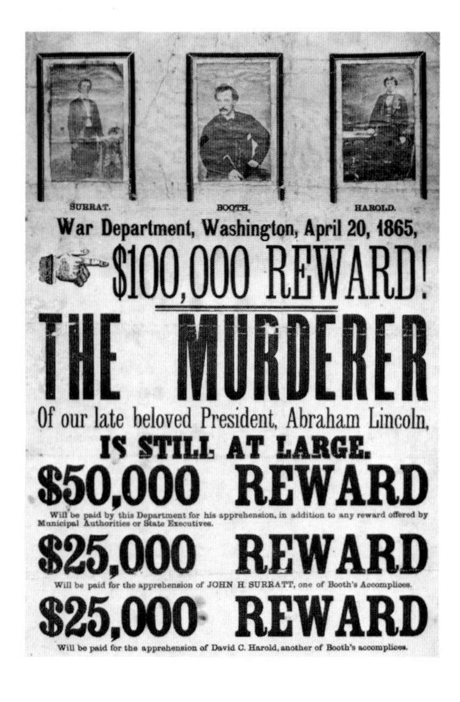

Lincoln's funeral cortege *winds through the hushed streets of New York City, where 100,000 mourners watched its passage. Many thousands more waited in the rain along the route of the President's funeral train as it made the slow, sad journey to Springfield, Illinois.*

its leader, victim of the deranged actor John Wilkes Booth, who had thought by his deed to avenge the South.

As the funeral train slowly made its way west, bearing the great President's body to its grave in Springfield, Illinois, a new mood developed in the North. Secretary of War Edwin Stanton, long an opponent of Lincoln's conciliatory peace proposals, stated publicly and without a shred of evidence that Lincoln had been the victim of an organized plot, supervised by the defeated leaders of the Confederacy, a charge that was echoed in Congress.

The new President, Andrew Johnson, was a former Democratic Senator from Tennessee who had remained steadfast in his loyalty to the Union throughout the Civil War. To the surprise of most Republicans in Congress, he granted readmission to the Union of the Southern States under terms so lenient as to leave the antebellum power structure virtually intact. Congress, however, was in a far different mood. Its leaders, known as Radical Republicans, insisted that black freedmen be raised to full citizenship and their rights as Americans be protected by the Federal Government. In the ensuing struggle between President and Congress, sectional strife again dominated the Nation's political life.

Adding fuel to the flames of sectional hatred was the now-open story of Southern mistreatment of Union prisoners. During the last years of the war the South had held some 125,000 Northern soldiers in makeshift camps that lacked even the most basic sanitary and medical facilities. The Confederacy, unable to feed and clothe its own troops, made little effort to supply these camps, and almost 10 percent of the prisoners died of starvation, exposure, and disease. At the worst prison, a 26-acre stockaded plot in the Georgia swamps near Andersonville, almost 13,000 of 32,000 Union soldiers died. Even before the war ended, the cry "Remember Andersonville!" increased hatred of the Confederacy in the North.

A Postwar Issue

In the aftermath of Lincoln's assassination, the suffering of Union prisoners became another argument to beat down pleas of compassion for the defeated Confederacy. Where prevailing opinion demanded revenge, it would have done little good to point out that even more southerners died in Northern camps, where there was less excuse for disease and starvation.

Over President Johnson's veto a civil rights act was passed in 1866 designed to cancel discriminatory laws in the South and to give the ballot to the Negro. And in 1867–68, Reconstruction Acts were passed to divide the South into military districts ruled by Army officers. Coalitions of blacks, sympathetic Southern whites, and Northern immigrants (called carpetbaggers) formed local and State governments. These regimes, while often fiscally irresponsible, brought to many Southern States their first real taste of democracy and instituted such reforms as the establishment of public school systems where none had existed before. White extremists began to retaliate, as night-riding vigilantes of the Ku Klux Klan and similar organizations spread terror among those blacks who tried to stand up for their hard-won rights. Gradually, as the North wearied of its duty to the liberated Negroes, the power of racist whites grew. During the late 1860's and early 1870's, as the States of the former Confederacy met Congress' conditions for readmission into the Union, new white regimes were established, and slowly the Negro was squeezed into a form of peonage that was little better than slavery. By 1877, when the Reconstruction period came to an end and the last Federal troops were withdrawn from the South, the groundwork had already been laid for the disenfranchisement of the Negro and the creation of a pattern of life built on race discrimination and segregation. These patterns were to survive into the mid-20th century, to inhibit not only the progress of the Negro but that of the white man as well. This, then, was the final tragedy of the Civil War from which the Nation is still emerging.

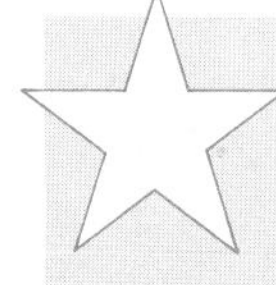

MAKING DEMOCRACY WORK

Three Constitutional Amendments

Perhaps no Government document or enactment since the Constitution itself has had so profound an effect on the shape of American society as the three constitutional amendments generated by the Civil War: the 13th, 14th, and 15th amendments. All three dealt with the status of the American Negro in the years just after the conflict. One, the 14th amendment, continues to exert a powerful influence on the laws and practices of the Union's 50 States to this day.

The 13th amendment, ratified by the States in 1865, put the decisive power of the Constitution behind the process of liberating the slaves. President Lincoln's wartime Emancipation Proclamation of January 1, 1863, had called only for the liberation of those slaves held in States still in rebellion. The 13th amendment completed Lincoln's initiative by emancipating all slaves within the United States and forbidding the institution of slavery for all time.

The 14th amendment, ratified in 1868, was far more complex. It stated that anyone born or naturalized in the United States was a citizen, and it sought to guarantee the rights of citizenship, including the vote, to the newly freed slaves with the following command:

No State shall make or enforce any law which shall abridge the privileges or immunities of citizens of the United States, nor shall any State deprive any person of life, liberty or property, without due process of law; nor deny to any person within its jurisdiction the equal protection of the laws.

Other sections of the amendment provided for the punishment of high Confederate officials and attempted to guarantee Negro voting rights by threatening to reduce congressional representation of any States that withheld such rights.

When it became clear that, despite the 14th amendment, Negroes were being barred from the polls, Congress enacted and the States ratified (1870) the 15th amendment, which specifically forbade States to deny the franchise "on account of race, color, or previous condition of servitude."

Most Southern States, however, managed to evade the 15th amendment by using such weapons as literacy tests and the poll tax to keep blacks from voting. The guarantees of full citizenship for Negroes contained in the 14th amendment were also vitiated by Supreme Court decisions that denied Congress the power to pass laws protecting the civil rights of blacks and upheld the passage by States of Jim Crow laws segregating blacks.

But in recent decades the amendment has become the basis of both the struggle for civil rights and the continuing battle to ensure the civil liberties of all Americans. The Supreme Court has reversed its earlier narrow interpretations of the 14th amendment. Using the "due process of law" clause as a wedge, the Court has broadened the scope of the U.S. Bill of Rights to include the rights of citizens vis-à-vis a State government as well as vis-à-vis the Federal Government. Thus, today, no State may abridge freedom of speech or deny a defendant the guarantee of a fair trial given in the fourth, fifth, and sixth amendments, any more than the Federal Government may. In its 1954 landmark decision in *Brown* v. *Board of Education of Topeka,* the High Court struck down school segregation as a denial to blacks of "the equal protection of the laws" guaranteed by the 14th amendment.

CHAPTER NINE

Trailblazers and Mountain Men

Even today, when superhighways and jet planes ha brought new perspective to distances, the traveler is bou to marvel at the expanse and variety of America. It is ha to imagine how formidable that vastness must have a peared in the early years when the few communities th had been established along the east coast and in the Nor and Southwest were no more than beachheads on the ma gins of limitless wilderness. And yet from almost the ve beginning a restless and hardy breed of men pushed in the forests, mountains, and deserts that stretched out in an unmapped continent. They were trappers, trade mountaineers, scouts, and—when required—warriors.

The Appalachian Mountains rise like a green wall between the east coast of America and forests, valleys, and vast plains to the west. Long before the hunger for land swept the English settlements along the Atlantic littoral, a few colonials were already probing the high wilderness—adventurers, traders, trappers, and fortune hunters, who left the relative security of the settlements almost as soon as there were settlements to leave.

The Virginia area produced many of the men who were soon to become legendary: self-reliant wayfarers clad in buckskin and carrying a rifle and a pack. In 1645 two posts were built west of the James River as fortifications against the Indians, who regularly raided on the fringes of Virginia settlements. It was at one of these posts, Fort Henry (where Petersburg, Virginia, now stands), that much of the trailblazing of the ensuing decades originated. This fort, in addition to being a stockade, was also a trading center, with warehouses stocked with goods for barter with the Indians. British guns, hatchets, kettles, blankets, and metal trinkets of all kinds, supplied from Fort Henry's warehouses, were carried by backpack through the dense Appalachian forests and exchanged for the most valuable currency the New World had to offer, the pelts of beavers, otters, and deer. Most of the expeditions originating from Fort Henry went unrecorded.

Among the few whose names survive was a German, John Lederer. Romantic tales of a rich new country and exotic Indians brought Lederer to America, where he entered the employ of William Berkeley, Governor of Virginia. Berkeley, still dreaming the old dream of a way to the Orient, sent Lederer westward to break a path through the mountains "to find out the East India Sea." Within a year and a half Lederer had captained three explorations; abandoned by his companions on his last one, in 1670, he went on alone with only an Indian guide. He was probably the first white man to reach the top of the Blue Ridge Mountains, and although he never succeeded in discovering a trail through the interminable westward ranges, he left in his journal a legacy of woodsmanship for those who were to follow. Take a small group of Indians with you on your expeditions, he said, to pacify the "nations in your way [who] are prone to jealousie and mischief towards Christians." Notch the trees along your path; a blazed trail means a way home again. As for trade goods, "gaudy toys and knacks of children" would do to relieve wilderness Indians of their furs, but Indians closer to the settlements wanted useful things—guns, hatchets, ammunition, and "sometimes brandy . . . or strong liquor."

A year after Lederer's final exploration Capt. Thomas Batts, heading an expedition out from Fort Henry, made the first recorded crossing of the Allegheny Mountains into the watershed of the Ohio River. Along the way he found several trees scored with English letters. Some anonymous trailblazer had been that way before him.

The French and English Traders

Traders and explorers were making good headway hacking out trails through the Southern mountains by the late 1600's. The wilder sections of the North yielded their secrets less readily. The Canadian-based French, with their Indian allies, effectively controlled large areas of the Great Lakes region and northern New England. Renegade voyageurs, hoping to get higher prices and to avoid the heavy taxes of their own country, often sneaked their furs south and traded them to the English settlers.

Best known of these French fur traders were Pierre Radisson and his brother-in-law, Médard Chouart, Sieur des Groseilliers. Since they had not bothered to obtain permission from the French authorities for a fur-trading sojourn in Indian country, one of their cargoes was confiscated. Soured by this treatment, they offered their

Although they were men of differing nationalities and *ces, they shared certain traits: Self-reliance, courage, love* *the unknown, a bent for solitude, and the ability to* *rvive under seemingly impossible conditions. Trailblazers* *l, they broke the way for the settlers who followed, though* *at was seldom their intent.*

When they mingled with others, it was with men of *eir own kind or with the Indians, from whom they* *arned much. Their relations with the Indians, however,* *ried with the individual: Some were adopted into Indian* *bes or lived with Indian women, some learned to hunt* *d fish and stalk their prey Indian fashion, and some died* *at the hands of hostile braves. If they had been asked why they chose so hard and dangerous a calling, few would have had a ready answer. Some were looking for wealth, which they seldom found. Others sought adventure and escape from the confines of farm and family.*

America owes much to these men, for they opened the land to the pioneers and settlers who made it great. Many of them ended their lives obscurely—killed in battles with Indians, drowned in the rapids of wild rivers, or lost in the savage bleakness of America's deserts. But a few of their names survive, affixed to mountain passes, peaks, streams, and trails from the Appalachians to the Pacific coast.

The Voyageurs
First of the Trailblazers

The lusty, energetic voyageurs, French-Canadian and often part Indian, were a breed apart. Even their name signified a special order of men: those who travel afar—usually by water. (The *coureurs de bois*—"woods runners"—were the French-Canadian equivalent of the American backwoodsman.) From the first days of French settlement, in the early 1600's, these intrepid explorers had paddled their way through the labyrinth of Canadian rivers and lakes and had captured the fur trade of the beaver-rich north country. They were distinguished by their gaudy dress (colored fringes, bright sashes, and beads), their passion for singing, and their short stature. Long legs were uncomfortable in canoes, and if a young Canadian "should stop growing at about 5 feet 4 inches, and be gifted with a good voice and lungs that never tire," wrote a 19th-century observer, he considered himself lucky.

Charles Deas *painted "The Voyageurs" in 1846. The short stature of the standing paddler was typical of the hardy boatmen. Deas had seen many of their kind during a long stay in the Midwest.*

Most of the voyageurs remain nameless, but one of the first, the adventuresome, ruthless Étienne Brulé, won a place in the histories of the time. In 1610 the French explorer Samuel de Champlain, determined to create a fur-trading empire in the virgin beaver country of Canada, sent the teen-aged Brulé as an advance agent among the Indians. Brulé, with a genuine fondness for Indian life and language, quickly succeeded in establishing friendly relations with the Hurons of the Great Lakes. Married into one of the tribes, dressed and painted like an Indian, Brulé paddled through the immense Great Lakes region as far as the westward tip of Lake Superior and explored the Susquehanna River south to Chesapeake Bay. A heavy drinker himself, he paid the Indians brandy for furs, and his tactics proved highly profitable; in 1626 alone Brulé and his colleagues brought in a fortune in beaver—some 22,000 pelts.

In 1629 Brulé turned traitor to France, selling his services to an English expedition that captured Quebec that year. In 1633 Brulé—who had gained a reputation for brutality and licentiousness—quarreled with some Hurons, who then murdered him and ate his remains. Brulé has been acclaimed as the first of the French explorers of the North American wilderness.

The voyageurs who came after Brulé likewise performed a great service in exploring and naming lakes and rivers and establishing settlements. As a group, these French-Canadians knew more about the Indians than any other white men until the days of Daniel Boone and the long hunters of the Allegheny frontier. Several French-Canadians served as boatmen, hunters, and interpreters for the Lewis and Clark Expedition to the Pacific in 1804–06. They helped to make the Hudson's Bay Company a commercial power in the Northwest, and they contributed, along with the mountain men, to the great trailblazing decades of the first half of the 19th century.

services to the English. While exploring the farthest reaches of Lake Superior in 1659–60, Radisson and Chouart had learned from the Indians of rich beaver country west of Hudson Bay. In 1665 the King's commissioners sent them to England, where they helped persuade Charles II to charter the Hudson's Bay Company (1670), the "Company of Gentlemen Adventurers" that eventually established a trading empire incorporating most of Canada and much of the Northwestern United States. Radisson later rejoined the French and plundered English trading posts, then returned to the English and lived out his final years on a pension from them. He was one of the few of his daring breed to reach the age of retirement.

North and South, other adventurers were finding new routes to the West in the century preceding the Revolution. Wherever they wandered on the mountainous frontier, the Indians took note, sometimes with surprise attacks, often with offers of furs and friendship. In 1692 Aernout Cornelissen Viele, a white man who had lived long among the Indians, left Albany, New York, to open the Southern fur country via a trail that would avoid the territory around the Great Lakes that was controlled by the French. Viele's path took him south through Pennsylvania to the Allegheny River, thence down to the Ohio River—a rich new country that would be the source of great wealth for coming generations of trappers.

There were many more adventurers of Viele's stamp in the South. Some, like Lt. Gov. Alexander Spotswood of Virginia, were aristocratic dreamers. His "Knights of the Golden Horseshoe" expedition of 1716 was a kind of wilderness joyride for himself and his gentlemen friends. Spotswood and the band of gallants failed to discover the "highway . . . between Virginia and the Great Lakes" that he sought, but they did reach the Shenandoah River beyond the Blue Ridge Mountains, and there buried a bottle containing a claim to the river on behalf of His Majesty George I.

Later, other men probed much deeper into the wilderness. In 1735 Polish trader Jan Sadowski crossed the Allegheny Mountains and set up a trading post at what is today Sandusky, Ohio. In 1750 Dr. Thomas Walker passed through the Cumberland Gap and blazed the first trail into Kentucky. The following year Christopher Gist traveled down the Ohio River to the Kentucky country. He was soon followed by the peddler and hunter John Finley, whose tales of the marvelous abundance of Kentucky game brought hunters over the mountains and through the gap, along the route that was to become famous as the Wilderness Road.

Daniel Boone and the Wilderness Road

One whose imagination was stirred by Finley's stories was 21-year-old Daniel Boone, who first met the Kentucky trader while serving in Gen. Edward Braddock's disastrous 1755 expedition against the French. Returning to North Carolina, where his family had settled after leaving their home near Reading, Pennsylvania, Boone worked on his father's farm and in 1756 married and settled down to raise a family of his own.

The relationship *between hunter and Indian—often hostile, but just as often sympathetic and cooperative—played a vital role in the opening of new territory. Alfred Jacob Miller sketched this scene in 1837, but it had often been enacted in earlier decades, from the Eastern forests to the Great Plains, as hunters blazed new trails westward. A group of trappers relax in camp, while their Indian companions wait stolidly on the fringes of the convivial circle. Fat buffalo ribs sizzle over the cooking fire. Trappers' tales flow, along with the drink in tin cups—in this instance, coffee, the great camping comforter that was always in short supply. One buckskin-clad hunter keeps his rifle close at hand, perhaps in deference to the trapper's rule that one never takes an Indian's friendliness for granted.*

"**Daniel Boone** *Escorting Settlers Through the Cumberland Gap" was painted by George Caleb Bingham in 1851, when Boone's opening of the Wilderness Road had already achieved legendary status. The dark mountains, blasted trees, and grimly determined settlers were part of the legend, although, in Boone's words, his group all "arrived safe without any other difficulties than such as are common to this passage."*

He never forgot Finley's tales of Kentucky, however, and in 1767 he explored westward as far as the Cumberland River area, returning home in the spring. Finley soon showed up with more stories of the West, and in 1769 Boone, his brother-in-law John Stuart, Finley, and three others traveled through the Cumberland Gap to the region of the Kentucky River. Joined later by his brother Squire, Boone spent months exploring the region, enthralled by a land where wild turkeys were so plentiful that flocks broke the branches on which they roosted, where creeks teemed with beavers and otters, where forests were alive with deer, and buffalo roamed the valleys.

During this period Col. Richard Henderson of the Transylvania Land Company began staking Boone to powder, shot, and other supplies in exchange for the information the woodsman gleaned in his long hunts in Kentucky. In 1775 Henderson's company purchased from the Cherokees almost 20 million acres of the land embraced by the Ohio, Kentucky, and Cumberland Rivers. The Indians sold the land, which had been chosen on Boone's advice, to the company in exchange for goods worth £10,000. Later that year Boone led the first group of land seekers to Henderson's holdings.

These men started building a fort on a site that became Boonesborough, but they were land speculators, not homemakers. None of them had brought his family, and all were interested only in staking out claims that could be sold at a profit to later settlers. In July 1775, when news of the fighting at Lexington and Concord reached Boonesborough, most of them fled back East. They doubted their ability to survive against the British and the always menacing Shawnees and Cherokees.

Early in September Boone returned to Boonesborough from a trip to his North Carolina home. During the journey he and a party of 20 men blazed and widened the Wilderness Road. More important, Boone was accompanied by his wife and daughters—the first white women to enter Kentucky. "With their coming," wrote Dale Van Every in *A Company of Heroes,* "what had been before a temporary camp of itinerant land seekers had made the vital transition to a permanent community of homemakers."

Of all Boone's triumphs, this moment, in which his wife shared, represented his greatest. Others had explored Kentucky long before him; the initiative in the establishment of Boonesborough had been taken by his employer,

Henderson. But Daniel Boone was Kentucky's first genuine settler, and his momentous trip over the Wilderness Road in the late summer of 1775 transformed the trail into a well-marked pathway for the pack trains of the thousands of homemakers who soon streamed into the newly opened lands. That same year James Harrod followed Boone's example and led settlers down the Ohio and up the Kentucky Rivers to establish Harrodsburg.

A New Breed of American

The Wilderness Road had been simply a narrow, hazardous trail over the Blue Ridge Mountains, through the Cumberland Gap, and down into the plains of Kentucky. The Indians knew the trail, and tribe had fought tribe fiercely for possession of "The Dark and Bloody Ground" that lay at the end of the trail. White hunters had also traveled it since the days of Thomas Walker. Among them were the long hunters, a group of restless woodsmen who trapped over the trail in the 1760's and earned their name by disappearing into the wilderness for months on end. In a sense, the making of the Wilderness Road embodies the accomplishments of all the men of the forest, who throughout their solitary lives blazed the small paths that became the arteries of civilization.

In important ways these men were alike. Many could not read; all hated the plow. And "As soon as the leaves were pretty well down," wrote Joseph Doddridge, a contemporary historian, ". . . they became uneasy at home. The house was too warm, the feather bed too soft. . . . I have often seen them get up early in the morning, walk hastily out . . . snuff the autumnal winds . . . then cast a quick and attentive look at the rifle."

When the hunter took to the trail, he wore a deerskin jacket, breeches, and moccasins, and carried the barest minimum for survival: A long rifle, a few tools to repair it, a flask of powder, lead for bullets, a knife, and an ax. Flint and steel for making a fire, a blanket, tobacco, and salt were in his leather pack. For the next week, or month, or even year, he would eat what he shot, and if he came home with his arms and legs intact and a few fur pelts to sell, he considered himself fortunate. That he found his way home at all was in itself extraordinary. Said Daniel Boone, speaking for all his kind: "I can't say as ever I was lost, but I was *bewildered* once for three days."

The Kentucky and the Hawken Rifles

Guns That Opened the Forests and Tamed the Mountains

The Kentucky rifle, carried by the hunters of the forests and plains east of the Mississippi, was the finest long-range weapon of the 18th century. This product of skilled Pennsylvania German gunsmiths—with its hair trigger, double sights, and barrel up to 48 inches long—was accurate at more than 200 yards when handled by an expert. But it took even the expert 30 seconds to load, prime, aim, and fire the Kentucky if he hoped to hit his target. First he had to measure loose gunpowder into the barrel and powder pan. Then he had to patch the bullet, a hand-molded lead ball, by covering it with a piece of greased linen or buckskin, and ram it down the barrel. The firing mechanism used a piece of flint, which, when the trigger was pulled, struck sparks to ignite the powder. Damp powder or a dull flint could cause the flintlock to misfire, an action described as a flash in the pan—bad business in a tight situation.

The mountain man of the Far West, who traveled long distances on horseback, needed a rifle that was easier to handle and fired a heavier ball at long range. The Kentucky rifle, which had gone west with the explorers and trappers of the early 1800's, was gradually modified by gunsmiths until it became the mountain rifle.

The most famous mountain rifle was made by Jacob and Samuel Hawken of St. Louis, Missouri. The Hawken had a shorter barrel with a larger bore, and the smashing power of its heavier ball could kill a buffalo or a grizzly bear at long range. But the Hawken still was a flintlock weapon that had to be loaded and primed with care. The Hawken brothers soon produced a percussion rifle ignited by a copper cap, which was more reliable than a flint in wet weather.

The mountain man also prized a good hunting and skinning knife. In the early days the best knives were British and were stamped "GR" (for George Rex) near the hilt, to assure Indians of their genuineness. But to the mountain man "GR" did not mean the British King but Green River, a stream in the fur country. So his shout, "Up to Green River!" meant to drive a knife into a foe all the way up to the "GR" mark. Later, American-made knives were stamped "Green River."

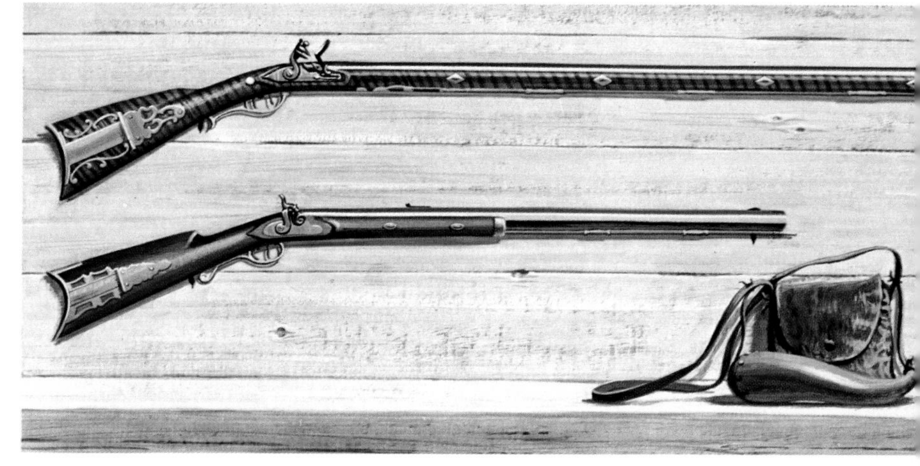

The Hawken percussion rifle *(bottom) was a more powerful gun than its forebear, the Kentucky rifle (top). Necessary accoutrements were the powder horn and bullet bag (right).*

The backwoodsman became for the world the embodiment of the free spirit of America. Lord Byron wrote in praise of Daniel Boone in his mock-epic poem "Don Juan." A biography of Boone was translated into French and German. Tall tales were told, and hard as they were to swallow, many were true. Escape from Indians, long hikes over rough country, battles with bears, incredible feats of marksmanship, all actually happened—if not to Boone, to others.

Such men as Boone's friend Simon Kenton were common on the frontier. Hardly more than a boy when he met Boone, Simon was already a daring scout and hunter. A story long told in Kentucky illustrates the matchless wilderness skill of these two. Once Kenton and Boone approached a river ford from opposite directions. Each knew that someone—perhaps an adversary—lurked on the far bank, and all day each maneuvered for position, using the available cover so adroitly that neither recognized his friend until near sundown.

Frederic Remington's *bronze captures the essential mountain man. The rider and his Indian pony seem a single creature, perpetually hazarding the steeply treacherous mountain trail.*

Boone appointed Kenton permanent scout for Boonesborough, where his superb talents for tracking, tricking, and fighting the elusive Indians proved vital. Kenton saved Boone's life three times during one fight and was himself captured by Indians and later escaped from them. In 1778 he served as a scout with George Rogers Clark's expedition in the Illinois country, rode with "Mad Anthony" Wayne to fight the Indians of the Old Northwest Territory in 1794, and at the age of 57 marched with a Kentucky brigade to the Battle of the Thames during the War of 1812.

All frontiersmen knew Indian ways and languages; some, captured on the trail, had lived in Indian camps. Boone was captured and adopted by the Shawnee war chief Blackfish, and became Sheltowee, or "Big Turtle." The adoption ceremony was long and painful. John Bakeless, in his book *Daniel Boone,* describes it: ". . . the hair of the head is plucked out . . . leaving a tuft on the crown for the scalp lock. . . . The candidate is then taken into the river in a state of nudity, and there thoroughly washed and rubbed, 'to take all his white blood out.' . . . His head and face are painted . . . and the ceremony is concluded with a grand feast and smoking." Boone lived among the Shawnees for 5 months, but he had no intention of making the adoption permanent. When he learned that the Shawnees planned to attack Boonesborough, he escaped from them in time to direct a successful defense of the settlement in September 1778.

Boone remained active in public and military affairs at Boonesborough and later at Boone's Station, holding several offices. Meanwhile, Virginia and North Carolina had disallowed Henderson's extensive land claims, and in 1785 Boone faced a series of legal challenges to his land titles. By 1798 he had lost all his holdings in the region he had done so much to settle and defend. Moving west to get "more elbow room," he settled around 1799 in what is now Missouri and obtained a large Spanish land grant. When this area was taken over by the United States as part of the Louisiana Purchase, Boone's land titles again were challenged. But Congress finally acted to restore a portion of his holdings. He lived in Missouri until his death in 1820.

Exploring an Unknown Land

For those living in thriving Boonesborough in the early 1800's, the American continent was made up of three unequal parts: The East, familiar, peopled, and relatively safe; the country to the west, where Daniel Boone had gone, stretching to the Mississippi River; and finally the vast, unknown region far to the west. In 1803 the United States bought 828,000 square miles of that land from the French. At the time the Louisiana Purchase seemed to many an act of mad extravagance. But President Thomas Jefferson knew better, and in order to find out more about this new territory, he asked Congress to authorize a series of expeditions, one of which was to become the most famous overland journey in U.S. history—the 1804–06 trip of Lewis and Clark. (For more about the Lewis and Clark Expedition, see pages 72–73.)

The newly opened region was immense, and no one can say how many men were already roving its plains and mountains while Lewis and Clark were on their journey westward. Nonetheless, if anyone deserves the title of "First of the Mountain Men," it must surely be the young Virginian John Colter. Colter had traveled all the way to the Pacific coast with the explorers; on the way back east, in August 1806, he began his own explorations. Not far from where the Yellowstone River empties into the Missouri, the Lewis and Clark group met two American trappers who, following the expedition's outward-bound trail, had already spent 2 years in the wilderness collecting beaver pelts and were prepared to stay longer. Colter, relieved of his duties with the expedition, joined the trappers and disappeared up the Yellowstone with his new companions.

Six months later, after having canoed down the Missouri River, Colter appeared in the camp of a trader from New Orleans, Manuel Lisa, at the mouth of the Platte River. Inspired by the Lewis and Clark reports of beavers in the north country, Lisa was determined to establish an organized trading system upriver on the Missouri. He needed a guide and hired Colter on the spot. Following Colter's lead, the Lisa party worked its way north into what is now Montana. Here, at the mouth of the Bighorn River, Lisa built Fort Raymond (named for his son) in 1808 and began his attempt to create a fur-trading alliance with the Crow Indians, an affable, easygoing people, and their sworn enemies, the Blackfeet.

John Colter Among the Indians

The Blackfeet were known as bad-hearted Indians, who took more trappers' scalps than any other tribe. Colter was sent out to find them and talk them into peaceful trading. Carrying only a 30-pound pack and a rifle, he walked west through the Valley of the Bighorn, picking up a party of Crow Indians who guided him across the Continental Divide at what is now Union Pass. On the other side of the mountains the Blackfeet attacked. With an arrow in his leg, abandoned by his Crow escort, Colter followed his nose back to Fort Manuel—as Fort Raymond was now called. His trip was extraordinary: He was the first white man ever to cross Union Pass, to see the Tetons, to stand at the headwaters of the Colorado and the Snake Rivers, and to see the boiling springs and geysers of what is today Yellowstone National Park.

Yet another historic first was in store for Colter: He became the first mountain man to fall captive to the Blackfeet and live to tell about it. It happened in the fall of 1808, when Lisa once again sent his best scout to try to make friends with the Blackfeet. While retracing his earlier route, Colter and one companion, John Potts, were attacked near the Three Forks of the Missouri River. Colter quickly surrendered, hoping to coax the Blackfeet into a good mood. But Potts panicked, shot one Indian, and was killed. This clash wrecked Colter's chances of a parley, and he was seized, stripped naked, and told to run for his life. He outran the entire Blackfoot band, racing 6 miles to the river, where he plunged under a mass of driftwood. Here he hid while the Indians thrashed the riverbank brush in a futile search for him. Then, still naked and with bleeding feet, Colter walked for 7 days and more than 200 miles back to Fort Manuel, with nothing to eat but berries and the roots he grubbed from the ground.

Colter's adventures were repeated, with variations, by the mountain men who followed him. Many survived incredible ordeals. One indestructible adventurer, Hugh Glass, left for dead after being mangled by a grizzly bear, is said to have crawled and stumbled 100 miles to safety. But others fell victim to the rigors of frontier life or to the enmity of the Blackfeet and other Indian tribes.

The Northwest Fur Trade

John Jacob Astor was no mountain man. He remained in the comfortable confines of his New York City office while building a fur-trading empire. This shrewd German-born businessman was already wealthy when he heard of the adventures of Lewis and Clark and decided to seize the Western fur trade for himself. He outfitted two expeditions to the Far West, one by sea around Cape Horn, the other overland from the Missouri River. The two groups were to meet at the mouth of the Columbia River in what is now Oregon, where they would build a trading post, entice the region's Indians to barter, and ship beaver and otter skins to a waiting market in China.

Despite great difficulties during the 6-month voyage, the ocean expedition reached the Columbia River and established Fort Astoria in April 1811. The land party

Old Bill Williams

He was Old Solitaire to the mountain men who knew him—a man who, even in that individualistic fraternity, was known for preferring his own company to that of all others. He became in his own lifetime an almost mythical figure, although he made no claims for himself, named no trails or peaks (there is one named for him—Bill Williams Mountain in Arizona), and left few written records. His legend comes to us through the writings and tale-spinnings of other mountain men.

William Sherley Williams began his career as a young, self-appointed backwoods preacher in his home State of Missouri. While doing missionary work among the Osage Indians, he married into the tribe and began the trapping, hunting, and trading that took him into the Western wilderness. He spent 40 years roaming that land, living alone much of the time. He suffered numerous bullet and arrow wounds in his brushes with Indians, but survived to establish his reputation as one of the best beaver trappers in the West. Occasionally he hired himself out as a guide to less seasoned travelers, especially in the Colorado–New Mexico region that had become his special province. A prodigious drinker and gambler, he could blow the profits of a whole season's trapping in a single afternoon. To the regret of California ranchers, he was an expert horsethief who could beat even the Indians at their specialty.

Williams' one recorded failure came when he attempted to guide the expedition of Capt. John C. Frémont over the southern Rockies in 1848. He had, however, warned the headstrong Frémont against challenging the snow-clogged Rockies in the winter. The expedition ended with 11 out of 33 men dead in the snows. Old Bill survived, but was killed shortly afterward by a band of Utes. When they realized who their victim was, they gave him a chief's funeral.

The Beaver
Trapping As a Fine Art

Early white hunters adopted the Indian technique of the winter hunt, invading the beavers' mud-and-stick winter lodges and netting and killing the animals when they tried to escape. The mountain man of the West absorbed Indian skills and insights, but he also had the white man's steel traps. He tramped along streams fringed by alders, cottonwoods, and willows, plying his trade—except during the heavy freezes and in the warm months from June to September when beavers shed their fur. Wading through water to obliterate his scent, the hunter sought fresh beaver traces and, where he found them, carefully baited and laid his underwater traps. The bait was castoreum, the musky sex-scent taken from the glands of trapped beavers. Setting six to eight traps along a promising stretch of stream in the evening twilight, the hunter returned in the dim light just before sunrise to claim his catch, which he skinned on the spot. He took only the pelt, the castoreum glands, and, usually, the tail. First charred to remove the horny skin and then boiled, the tail meat was considered a delicacy.

Moving upstream, so that any signs of hostile Indians in the area might drift downstream to alert him, the trapper sloshed away his solitary days, often tormented by the "trapper's complaint," rheumatism. Around mid-June he packed his furs off to the annual rendezvous. When the beaver holed up in his winter lodge, the trapper made his own shelter—a skin tepee or, occasionally, a log cabin. Here he made new clothes, repaired the old, and except for an occasional foray, waited out the winter for the spring thaw.

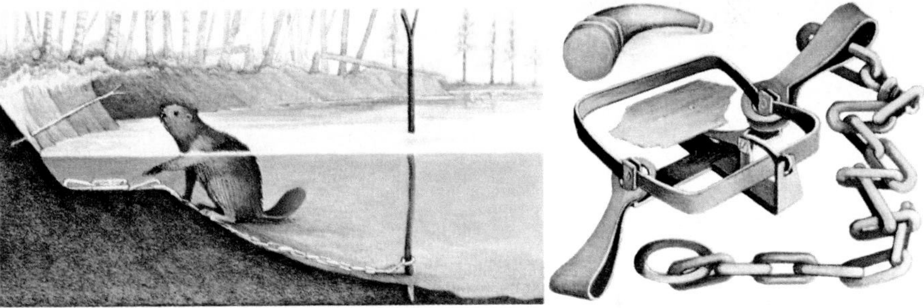

A trap chained *to the pole driven into deeper water is being set in the shallows in this 1837 Alfred Jacob Miller painting (top). A twig smeared with castoreum from the trapper's horn bottle will lure the beaver. When the animal is caught in the trap and dives to escape, the chain will slide down the pole and jam, holding the beaver under until it drowns.*

Raw material for the beaver hat: *In camp the pelts were rough-cured—scraped clean of all flesh and stretched on willow-frame hoops to dry. Marked with the trapper's symbol, they were pressed into packs by a makeshift chain-and-pole press or contraptions of logs and heavy stones. Each pack of about 60 pelts weighed 90 to 100 pounds. Carried two to a packhorse, or loaded into bullboats (shallow boats made of buffalo hides) or canoes, the packs were transported to the nearest trading post or to the annual rendezvous.*

This was the reason for it all

arrived half a year later, exhausted by terrible weeks of wandering in Idaho's mountains and wastelands and decimated by drownings in the white waters of the Snake River. Soon after, with the outbreak of the War of 1812 and the threat of a British naval attack on his new possession, Astor decided to withdraw for a time. In 1813 he sold out to a British firm, the North West Company, and for the next decade the Oregon territory remained a British enclave. But Astor was to return with his powerful American Fur Company. When he did, his rivals were no longer the British, but an American outfit, the legendary Rocky Mountain Fur Company.

Traders Change Their Tactics

The St. Louis *Missouri Gazette* of March 20, 1822, carried an advertisement calling for "100 young men to ascend the Missouri River to its source, there to be employed for one, two, or three years." The notice was placed by two enterprising businessmen who intended to revolutionize the fur trade: William H. Ashley, Lieutenant Governor of Missouri, and Andrew Henry, once second in command to Manuel Lisa. Many of the men who signed on for the Ashley Expeditions were to become great names in the roster of mountain men: Jedediah Smith, James Bridger, Thomas Fitzpatrick, and Jim Beckwourth. They not only changed the history of the fur trade but also inaugurated an era of exploration that opened the trails followed by thousands of emigrants to the new lands of the Far West.

Until the Ashley Expeditions, the mainstay of the fur trade had been the permanent fort, where the white trader would wait, often in vain, for the Indians of the surrounding country to bring in their skins. The system depended on the goodwill of the Indians, and when they proved, like the Blackfeet, implacably hostile, the trade was stopped dead. Ashley and Henry had a different design for the fledgling outfit. They would stop relying on the Indians and depend instead on trappers of their own. Their plan depended on the ability of their men. It proved enormously successful.

In the spring of 1822 Ashley and Henry, with their recruits divided into two groups, moved up the Missouri River in keelboats into the country that Manuel Lisa and John Colter had already made familiar. Familiar too was the reaction of the Indians in the area, the Crows proving as friendly to the travelers as always, the Blackfeet as hostile. That first year the Ashley Expeditions almost collapsed before a single beaver pelt had been shipped downriver. The Blackfeet attacked and robbed the first group, and Ashley's group was forced to fight its way out of an Arikara village in a wild melee that ended in the loss of men, horses, and supplies.

At the Green River *rendezvous of 1837 the Snake Indians set up an entire village and held the grand procession depicted here. At these riotous gatherings, the Indians generally set the holiday tone by thundering into the rendezvous site in full regalia, performing daring feats of horsemanship, and shooting off volleys of arrows and bullets. Afterward, the warriors, squaws, children, and dogs would wander over to the trappers' encampment, where the braves would barter their furs, scrounge whisky, and pick up needed trade goods—rifles, blankets, knives, beads, and bells. The painter of this picture, Alfred Jacob Miller, was entertained at the 1837 rendezvous with an Indian feast of dog and presented with a drawing of an Indian battle, sketched by the Snakes' Little Chief himself. Of the chief's drawing, Miller wrote: ". . . the enemy are diminutive creatures and he is spitting them like larks." In another part of the camp the white trappers were also whooping it up—trying to get enough celebration under their belts to hold them through another solitary year in the mountains.*

Convinced that the upper Missouri River region was effectively closed to them, Ashley and Company decided to find a more southerly route into the fur country. Over the next few years Ashley trappers followed new trails from the Missouri through the Rockies to the Green River Valley, and from there southwestward to the Pacific. Scouring a seemingly limitless land, they packed a wealth of beaver pelts back to civilization.

This treasure in skins was carried by horse, mule, or backpack, or, on the waterways, by boat to a rendezvous, another Ashley innovation. Every year in early summer Ashley's new and independent trappers went to some green and well-watered spot in the heart of the beaver territory, where they met packhorse caravans from St. Louis. The caravans brought wages, which the trappers usually squandered on a few days of wild drinking and gambling, and new supplies, including traps, knives, rifles, trade goods, tobacco, and whisky. When all the furs had been exchanged and all the whisky drunk, the trappers turned back into the wilderness for another year, and the fur-laden packhorses retraced the route east to St. Louis. Trappers and caravans would meet again at next summer's rendezvous.

For writer Washington Irving, who spent some time in the West gathering material for his chronicle *Astoria,* there was "no class of men on the face of the earth who lead a life of more continued exertion, peril and excitement . . . than the free trappers of the West." His descriptions of the trapper "buffeting his way across rapid streams, amidst floating blocks of ice . . . scaling or descending the most frightful precipices . . ." contributed to the popular image of the mountain man as an almost mythical superhuman. Yet many of the tales coming out of this era of American history are by no means exaggerated, and the stature of the great mountain men is truly heroic. If it is possible to choose among this remarkable group, the most phenomenal of them all may have been Jedediah Strong Smith, who traveled more than 16,000 miles, mostly through unmapped wilderness, during the 9 years he spent on the trail.

Jedediah Smith—One of the Best

Jed Smith was a New York State man who first appears in Western annals as a member of Ashley's 1822 expedition, when, at the age of 24, he barely escaped from the Arikaras. The bravery he showed during that bloody fight marked him as a leader, and Ashley chose him to command a group of hunters who were to explore the country west of the Black Hills. Smith was a tall, slender man who, unlike his companions, was deeply religious, modest, and a teetotaler. He carried a Bible in his pack and enjoyed singing Methodist hymns as he rode through the wilderness. But he was tough, resourceful, and incredibly durable. At one point on his first expedition he was attacked by a grizzly bear that laid open his scalp and left one ear hanging by a shred of skin. "You must try to stitch it some way or other," Smith said to his volunteer surgeon, Jim Clyman. "I put in my needle," Clyman wrote, "stitching it through and through . . . as nice as I could." Within 10 days of the incident Smith hit the trail and in due course the ear healed completely.

Smith and his men spent the winter of 1823–24 trying to find a breach in the Rockies that would lead into what the Indians assured them was good beaver country. Gale winds and man-high snow drifts frustrated their exploration for months. Finally in March 1824 they ascended the Sweetwater River and discovered a way through: a 20-mile-wide plateau that led them over the Continental Divide from the Wind River Mountains in what is now Wyoming. This was South Pass, one of the key openings through the Rockies and the future route for thousands of emigrant trains. The winter of 1824 also saw the discovery of the Great Salt Lake by another of Ashley's men, Jim Bridger, who paddled a bullboat down the Bear River into the lake. Finding the water salty, he reportedly concluded that he had reached the Pacific Ocean.

Smith and his party spent 1824–25 trapping along Idaho's Snake River and into Oregon—the first Americans to go that way since the Astorians had left more than a decade before. Since the region was being worked by the Hudson's Bay Company, Smith resolved to look for beaver where there would be no competition. Before he could seek new beaver lands, however, there was business to attend to. Ashley wanted to retire, and in July 1826 Smith, David Jackson, and William Sublette bought him out. The partners' plans called for Jackson and Sublette to work the beaver country around the Snake River to the north while Smith sought new trapping areas to the south. Smith was particularly interested in finding a much-talked-of river, called the Buenaventura, which was thought to flow west through the mountains to the Pacific. Such a discovery would open vast new trapping lands and would provide a convenient water route for bringing furs back east.

On August 16, 1826, Smith led 17 men southwestward from Bear Lake, on what is now the Utah-Idaho border, through a tumbled land of cliffs, mountain peaks, deserts, and blazing heat. Reaching the Colorado River, the party descended it to a village of the friendly Mojave Indians. The trappers had been savagely punished by this country and had lost more than half their horses. Still determined to find the Buenaventura, Smith got fresh horses from the Indians and pushed west across the scorching Mojave Desert. After climbing the taxing San Bernardino Mountains, he dragged his half-starved men into southern California.

Smith and his company were the first Americans to reach California by land from the east, and the startled Mexican officials were not glad to see them. Assuming these lean, heavily armed men to be spies, Gov. José Echeandia threatened to jail them. Eventually convinced that they were merely innocent trappers who had wandered too far west, Echeandia permitted them to leave on condition that they return the way they had come. Smith, however, had no intention of going east and swung his party north through the great central valley of California, once again in search of the mythical Buenaventura. To their east towered the seemingly endless Sierra Nevada, and it became evident that no river cut completely across this mountain barrier.

Reaching the American River, Smith attempted in early May 1827 to go up this stream and over the Sierra, but he was thwarted by 40-foot snowdrifts and dead-end canyons. He left his main party in California and with two men and nine pack animals on May 20 again assaulted the mountains. This time he and his companions got through—the first white men to cross the Sierra from west to east. Now they faced the bone-dry desolation of hundreds of miles of desert lands. For days they were without water. One by one, seven of their pack animals had to be slaughtered for food. Often the men buried themselves to their chins in the sand to preserve the moisture in their bodies. Amazingly, they conquered this forbidding land and became the first whites to cross the Great Salt Lake Desert. On July 3 the trio reached Bear Lake, site of that year's rendezvous, and were welcomed with a round fired from a cannon that had been brought up by caravan from St. Louis.

Within 10 days the tireless Smith set out again for California with 18 men. This time the Mojave Indians, angered by a clash with other trappers, took their revenge by ambushing and killing 10 of Smith's party. The survivors pushed on across the Mojave Desert and finally, in late September 1827, reached the men Smith had left behind 4 months earlier.

With the aid of friendly American and English ship captains in San Francisco, Smith scrounged supplies from Governor Echeandia, who was then in northern California, and headed northward to the Columbia River in Oregon. On the way Smith lost his furs and all but two of his men in an Indian ambush. Fortunately, John

Jim Beckwourth

The Life & Adventures of James P. Beckwourth must surely be among the most swaggering, extravagant, and gory life histories ever written. Told by the aging Beckwourth to a journalist who, while writing it, added a few embellishments of his own, the book was published in 1856 and became an instant classic. Its vivid portrayal of mountaineering life provided the style for all such stories, novels, and movies that came after it. Much of it may well be true. As was true of the many legends surrounding Daniel Boone, the adventures Beckwourth describes probably happened—if not to him, then to one of his colleagues. And however much Beckwourth may have exaggerated, his feats were still extraordinary.

Francis Parkman, the Western traveler and historian, knew Beckwourth and called him "a ruffian of the first stamp, bloody and treacherous. . . ." Mountain men themselves, hearing some incredible tale, would brand it "one of Jim's lies." He was notorious as a thief and a cheat, and his record as a horsethief rivals that of Old Bill Williams. Beckwourth was accused—falsely for once—of having sold smallpox-infected blankets to the Blackfoot Indians and of arranging the robbery—probably true—of fur-laden pack trains. This indestructible mulatto was adopted by the Crow Nation and made one of their chiefs. At least one authority vouches for his claim that, while leading the Crow in battle, he leapt into a Blackfoot fort, armed only with a battleax and scalping knife, and helped to take some 160 Blackfoot scalps in the ensuing carnage.

With all his faults, Beckwourth was one of the most trusted men of the Ashley fur expeditions. He later became an Army scout, an Indian trader in the Southwest, and a rancher in California. He eventually went back to Colorado and died among his people, the Crow Indians. For them, there was never any doubt about Jim Beckwourth's valor. They called him the Red Fish, the Bloody Arm, and the brave and wily Enemy of Horses.

The Major Trails of the Westward Movement
The Trailblazers Led the Way for the Covered Wagon and the Automobile

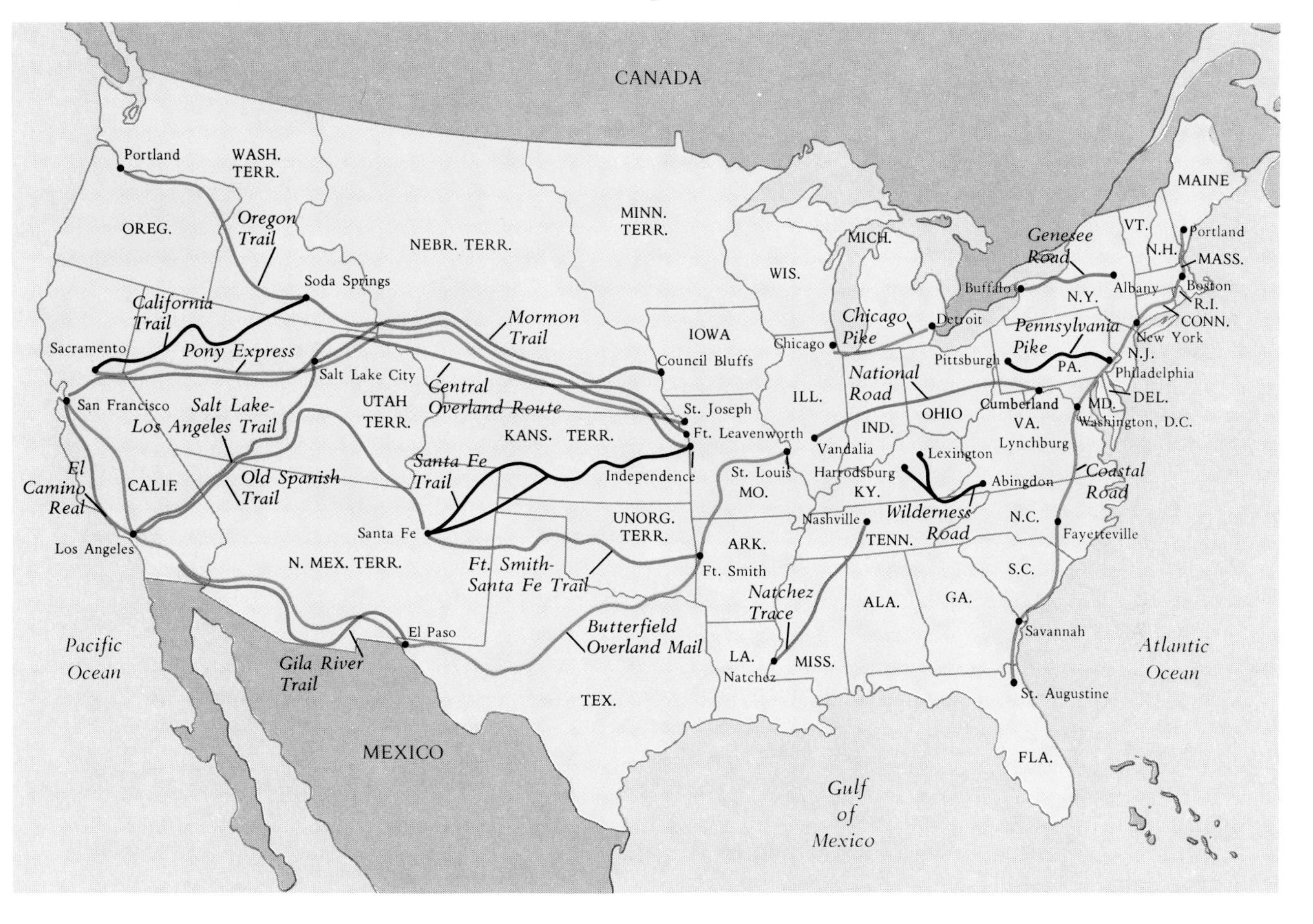

McLoughlin of the Hudson's Bay Company sheltered the survivors and helped them recover their furs. In March 1829 Smith and one companion headed east up the Columbia, joined David Jackson in northwestern Montana, and then journeyed south to meet William Sublette at Henry's Fork on the Snake River. At the 1830 rendezvous (to which Sublette transported goods by wagons rather than by pack animals, thus leading the first wagon train to cross the central plains), Smith and his partners sold out to Tom Fitzpatrick, Milton Sublette, Jim Bridger, Henry Fraeb, and Jean Gervais, who named their new firm the Rocky Mountain Fur Company.

Meanwhile, other trappers were marking new trails through the Southwest to the Pacific. James O. Pattie with his father, Sylvester, led a group along the Gila and Colorado Rivers and across the Colorado Desert to San Diego in 1827–28. In 1831 William Wolfskill pioneered the Spanish Trail across the Mojave to Los Angeles.

The Santa Fe Trail, leading from Missouri to the then Mexican city of Santa Fe, was opened as a wagon route in 1822 by the pioneer trader William Becknell. Despite savage Comanche attacks, the trail soon became a major trading route, thronged with wagon trains carrying Yankee merchandise to be sold at a great profit to the Mexicans. Jed Smith became a Santa Fe trader and in 1831, searching for water ahead of his southbound caravan, was ambushed and killed by Comanches near the Cimarron River. For a long time after his death, Smith was remembered only by other mountain men. It took years and the careful searching of old records and diaries to win him the recognition his achievements merited.

The Beginning of the End

The few short years between the first Ashley expedition in 1822 and the early 1830's saw the beaver trade reach its pinnacle and begin its decline. In some areas the beavers were almost trapped out. "We're goners, gone beavers," sang old-time mountain men, scouring the wild country for the ever scarcer pelts. But there were still rich pickings for those with skill and organization, and the Rocky Mountain Fur Company had what it took. The competition the Rocky Mountain men faced, however, was ruthless, powerful, and funded by the fortune of that wily old New York fur trader, John Jacob Astor.

At the end of the War of 1812 Astor had expanded the activities of his American Fur Company in the Great

The Buffalo
Source of Life for the Indian

Buffalo meat, if we can believe the gustatory tales told in its honor, was the epicure's delight, tender, rich, and gamy. But for the Indians of the Great Plains area the buffalo was the stuff of life itself: Food, shelter, weapons, and clothing all came from this prodigious animal.

Clumsy and phlegmatic, the buffalo lived and moved in massive herds, and it was in pursuit of the herds that the Indians lived and moved. The method of hunting was brutally simple: A part of the herd was surrounded, pursued as it stampeded, and shot at close range. To do this required fast, panic-proof horses and a lightning-fast ability to shoot hard and true. Arrows were the usual weapon—a brave could launch 8 to 10 arrows in the time it took to reload and fire a rifle and could shoot with such force that the arrow might pass completely through the buffalo.

The braves butchered their kill on the spot, taking the buffalo hump, hump ribs, and belly fat—favored delicacies—and whatever other portions could be packed back to camp, rolled in the animal's hide. The hide itself, properly cleaned and cured, had innumerable uses. It supplied bags, carriers, rawhide rope, the walls of tepees, bedclothes, moccasins, and the warmest of all coverings, the buffalo robe. Sewing thread came from the animal's sinews.

The meat that was not eaten immediately was preserved. Some of it was made into jerky—strips of meat dried in the wind and smoked over a slow fire for a full day. Pemmican, which was jerky pulverized and kept sealed with fat in a buffalo-skin bag, remained edible for years. Buffalo meat was also prized by the trappers, who often ate as much as 8 pounds of it a day—more when supplies were very plentiful—and carried pemmican and jerky with them on their hunts.

Neither trapper nor Indian visibly reduced the herds. When the railroad first rolled over the Great Plains in the late 1860's, buffalo could be seen packed for miles, to the horizon and beyond. But with the railroads came the professional meat hunters, who numbered their kill in the thousands. Buffalo hunting became fashionable for Eastern dudes and European royalty, who traveled west in comfortable caravans. Buffalo robes were suddenly the rage.

The buffalo were slaughtered by the millions until, by the end of the century, there were only a few small herds scattered here and there. And with the buffalo went the Plains Indians—destroyed, too, or driven into reservations where buffalo hump was a meal eaten only in dreams.

In the chase *to overtake the immensely powerful bull buffalo, portrayed in a painting by George Catlin, the Indian sometimes had to gallop his well-trained horse 5 miles across the plains.*

Buffalo shoots *sustained the men of John C. Frémont's expeditions. In this illustration from Frémont's memoirs, the horses are in among the stampeding buffalo to give the hunters a close shot. Although the mountain rifles used by hunters packed a wallop, the only sure way to down a buffalo with a single bullet was to hit him just behind the shoulder. Failing that, the hunter might need several bullets to stop the animal.*

Lakes area. By 1822 he had a branch office at St. Louis. Displaying his characteristic aggressiveness, Astor then bought up competing fur-trading companies and put the competent Kenneth McKenzie in charge of American's upriver operations. In 1829 McKenzie enlarged Fort Floyd, built the previous year, on the Missouri River at the mouth of the Yellowstone. Renamed Fort Union, it became the American Fur Company's most important upriver post. The Company (as American came to be known) had a stroke of good fortune in 1830 when Jacob Berger, a former Hudson's Bay Company trapper, encouraged the savage Blackfeet to stop fighting and start trading furs. The next year The Company began an all-out drive against the Rocky Mountain Fur Company, sending trapping brigades into the mountains and using bribes, theft, and force to break the opposition. Then, in 1832, The Company strengthened its supply and transportation setup with the steamboat *Yellowstone,* which plied the Missouri between St. Louis and Fort Union.

Astor's men also used whisky to influence independent trappers and Indians. The whisky was shipped upriver as raw alcohol, then "improved" with lacings of chewing tobacco, red pepper, molasses, and river water. More water was added as the buyers became drunk. The final product was mostly flavored water, but by that time no drinker was sober enough to notice.

In attempting to counter the ruthless methods of The Company, the Rocky Mountain men had one important advantage: experience. It amused such seasoned trappers as Jim Bridger to watch as The Company's novices dogged his men from creek to creek, awkwardly setting traps wherever his veterans did. However, the newcomers learned fast; the 1832 summer rendezvous at Pierre's Hole, a green valley lying on what is today the Utah-Idaho border, proved to be the largest and, for the Rocky Mountain Fur Company, the last successful one. Five Rocky Mountain brigades, carrying $85,000 worth of furs, met at the rendezvous; two Company outfits, with much slenderer packs, were also present. Independent trappers appeared from every cranny in the remotest mountains, along with bands of fur-laden Indians, all eager to sell their packs to the highest bidder or to the first outfit to get them drunk enough.

The Rocky Mountain supply train beat The Company caravan into camp. After 9 days of feverish trading, gambling, fighting, and drinking, the badly hung over trappers drifted out of Pierre's Hole and back to their fall hunting grounds, and the Rocky Mountain men counted up their richest profits. The Company's trappers were unable to meet expenses that year, but it kept up the struggle. It was bolstered by Astor's wealth, which enabled it to offer four times the actual value of the fur to eliminate competition, and by its system of steamboat transportation and forts in the upper Missouri country.

In 1834 the Rocky Mountain Fur Company was dissolved, and Bridger, Fitzpatrick, and Milton Sublette set up a new partnership. Facing increased competition from the Hudson's Bay Company, moving south from the Columbia, Bridger and his partners made a contract to supply furs to The Company and sold out to it soon after.

Bridger went on to become a famous guide and scout for the U.S. Army and in 1843 built Fort Bridger to supply emigrant wagon trains on the Oregon Trail. Irish-born Tom Fitzpatrick served as a wagon train guide, a guide for John C. Frémont's expeditions, and later as an Indian agent. Milton Sublette's life was shortened by an Indian wound; he died in a westward-bound caravan in 1836. Late in 1834 Astor, persuaded by reports on the scarcity of beaver and declining prices, sold his Western operations to subordinates.

The fabulous days were over. The kingdom of the mountain men was rapidly becoming domesticated, as wagon trains wore ruts in the trails the trappers had made. And of the thousands of settlers who pushed their way over the Oregon and California Trails, few ever heard or cared about the names of those extraordinary men who had opened the way for them.

The Legendary Kit Carson

Of all the mountain men, only Kit Carson (1809–68) won the praise of the Nation while he was still alive, and his fame was bestowed on him by that great publicist and official pathfinder, John C. Frémont. If Carson had not been Frémont's guide on three dramatically successful expeditions to the Rockies (1842–46), his name might have remained as obscure as those of his equally heroic colleagues in the fur trade.

A runaway saddler's apprentice at 16, Carson joined a trading expedition bound for Santa Fe in 1826. He learned trapping and Indian fighting in Arizona and southern California, then traveled through the Rockies as an independent trapper. By the time he met Frémont, Kit Carson was a master mountain man and a recognized and reliable leader.

Frémont's praise, lavished publicly on his guide after each of his expeditions, made Carson an instant hero. During the Mexican War Carson fought valiantly for the United States, and in 1847 the "clear, steady, blue-eyed" scout created his own headlines. With one companion, he rode horseback all the way across the continent to Washington, D.C., bringing news of the American seizure of California. In his later years he became a famous Indian fighter, a colonel who fought successful campaigns in the Southwest during the Civil War, and for more than 7 years, an Indian agent who won the trust of his charges. Carson was a modest man of few words, but he deeply impressed all who knew him. "His integrity is simply perfect," said Gen. William T. Sherman, who met him in 1866.

Heroes of Our Folklore *Some Real, All Larger Than Life*

Johnny Appleseed (*1774–1845*). This legendary free spirit walked barefoot through the Ohio Valley, wearing a tinpot hat and coffee-sack shirt and planting and distributing apple seeds and seedlings. He was John Chapman, a devoutly religious nurseryman, who exchanged the seeds for food and clothing. Any money he obtained usually went to buy and distribute Swedenborgian religious tracts. He left a living memorial of blossoming orchards dotting the land he loved.

Sam Bass (*1851–78*). A former lawman turned train robber, a good cowboy gone bad, Bass was glorified as the Robin Hood of Texas. Betrayed by a pal and shot by a Texas Ranger, he died on his 27th birthday.

Roy Bean (*c. 1825–1903*). Rough-talking and hard-drinking, "Fining Judge" Bean was said in his prime to be the only "law west of the Pecos." He dispensed a crude, arbitrary, and often ruthless brand of justice when he wasn't busy tending bar. His saloon, The Jersey Lily, was named after English actress Lillie Langtry.

Billy the Kid (*1859–81*). The short-tempered, cattle-rustling Kid (William H. Bonney, who was born in New York City and brought to the West as a child) boasted that he had shot 21 men, "not including Indians." When he was only 21, he was gunned down, after a daring jailbreak, by Sheriff Pat Garrett.

Daniel Boone (*1734–1820*). His courage as a hunter, sharpshooter, and Indian fighter made him a legendary figure in his own time—in Europe as well as America. In 1775 he blazed the Wilderness Road, which opened Kentucky to settlers, and won wide renown, but he lost most of his land holdings before he died.

Bowleg Bill. Seamen told of an 8-foot, 4-inch cowboy from Wyoming who was shanghaied aboard a whaleship. Bill never learned how to "sashay around them poles and wires," but he could ride a 2,000-pound tuna bronco-style.

Jim Bridger (*1804–81*). As a Rocky Mountain trapper and guide, he became one of the most celebrated of the mountain men and established a sound reputation as a teller of tall tales. He was hailed as the discoverer of the Great Salt Lake (1824), but his stories of the hot springs, geysers, and petrified rock that today make up Yellowstone Park were ridiculed as "Old Jim Bridger's lies."

John Brown (*1800–59*). Some considered this angry fanatic a madman, others, a divinely inspired martyr. Encouraged by other abolitionist sympathizers, he led bloody attacks on advocates of slavery. His 1859 raid on Harpers Ferry, Virginia (now West Virginia), with 21 followers, was intended to touch off a slave revolt. Captured by troops led by Col. Robert E. Lee, he was hanged as a traitor in December of 1859. After his death he became the subject of a famous song, and his name became a wartime Union rallying cry.

Buffalo Bill (*1846–1917*). A Pony Express rider, an Army scout, and Indian fighter before he was 20, William F. Cody killed 4,280 bison in less than 18 months to provide meat for crews constructing the Kansas Pacific Railroad. He was dubbed Buffalo Bill after winning a buffalo-killing contest with William Comstock near Fort McPherson, Kansas, in 1870. Cody went into show business at the age of 26. Shrewd publicity made him a star in his own Wild West Show.

Paul Bunyan. Woodsmen loved to swap yarns about a mighty lumberjack who combed his beard with a pine tree and bypassed 24 towns in a single stride. Babe, his big, blue ox, could haul a forest of logs in one load, and Paul could catch a blizzard in a box trap and nail it to a tree.

Calamity Jane (*c. 1852–1903*). Martha Jane Canary claimed to have been a Pony Express rider, a scout for General Custer, and the wife of Wild Bill Hickok. She got her nickname allegedly from her threat that calamity would be the lot of those who opposed her. Jane wore men's clothes, liked to drink with the boys, and was no beauty, but the dime novels transformed her into a "beautiful, buckskin-clad crusader for justice."

Davy Crockett (*1786–1836*). He was a backwoods hunter and a coonskin Congressman from Tennessee, who could "whip his weight in wildcats and shoot six cord of bear in one day." He was also known for his jokes, his political barbs, and his tall tales. After a spell as a poor farmer, he fought in the War of 1812, serving as a scout under Andrew Jackson in the campaign against the Creek Indians. Davy was elected to Congress for 3 terms, but was defeated in his bid for a fourth term in 1835. Davy died in Texas, helping defend the Alamo against Santa Anna.

Virginia Dare (*1587–?*). The first English baby born in America, she disappeared with her parents and all the other Roanoke Island settlers soon after the Virginia colony's founding. Later the Indians told of a milk-white doe, which, mortally wounded by a hunter's silver arrow, was heard to murmur, "Virginia Dare." On the dying doe's back sprouted the word "Croatoan." "Croatoan," the name of an island near Roanoke, was found carved on a Roanoke tree after the settlers' disappearance.

Mike Fink (*c. 1770–c. 1823*). "I'm a regular tornado, tough as hickory and long-winded as a nor'wester," said Pittsburgh Mike, one of nature's meanest bullies. Tales were told of how he shot the heel off a black man and set a flirtatious girl friend afire. A crack rifleman, an Indian scout, a fur trapper, and "King of the Mississippi keelboatmen," he was as unruly as the waters he rode. He died violently in Montana, after he had become a trapper, but exactly how no one knows. One story has it that he killed a companion in what had begun as a prankish exchange of gunfire; the victim's friend murdered Mike in revenge.

John Henry. The ballad says a ghost hammer still rings in the Big Bend railroad tunnel in West Virginia where this black steel-driving man won his race with the steam drill, "then laid down his hammer an' died." Based on a real rock-gang character, the John Henry saga traveled widely, and changed as it went. In the West he was

a railroad man; in the South, a champion cotton picker "with a cotton-hook for a right hand, a river song on his tongue."

Wild Bill Hickok (*1837–76*). As marshal of Abilene, Kansas, this gunfighter is said to have tamed the tough cow town, although detractors contend he was more gambler than lawman. By turns a stagecoach driver, a Union Scout in the Civil War, and an Indian fighter, he died playing poker in Deadwood, Dakota Territory, when Jack McCall shot him from behind.

Jesse James (*1847–82*). This notorious bank and train robber of the Midwest claimed that respectable enemies hounded him into a life of crime. After serving as a Confederate guerrilla in the Civil War, he became the leader of a murderous gang that operated in the Midwest for about 15 years. Jesse was killed by Bob Ford, a former member of the James gang, who shot him in the back for a reward.

Jonathan the Yankee. "Jonathan" was a term of contempt applied to Americans by British soldiers and Tories during the Revolution. But with his stage debut in 1787 as the comic Yankee in Royall Tyler's *The Contrast,* Jonathan began to evolve into a stage prototype. He ultimately became the personification of the shrewd Yankee farmer, bemused by urban airs and graces, often getting the better of his slick city cousins despite his seeming simple-mindedness. The hero of many plays, songs, illustrations, and anecdotes, he became a comic favorite all over the country.

Casey Jones (*1864–1900*). He died with one hand on the brake and the other on the throttle, giving his life to save his passengers. John Luther Jones, born near the Kentucky town of Cayce, which gave him his nickname, became the railroadman's symbol of courage and devotion to duty. A ballad celebrates his hard-driving ways with a steam engine.

Joe Magarac. A legendary giant of the Pennsylvania furnaces, Joe had a "steel body, steel hands, steel everything." The story goes that he melted himself down into ingots, so that his strength is now a part of every bar of steel.

Mose the Bowery B'hoy. New York City, too, had its comic hero—the brawling, dandified volunteer firefighter who made his bow in the theater in 1848. Traveling companies popularized Mose nationally for the next decade or so.

Annie Oakley (*1860–1926*). With her rifle, "Little Sure Shot" sliced playing cards edgewise at 30 paces, hit dimes in midair, and shattered cigarettes held in her husband's lips. She had married Frank E. Butler, a marksman in his own right, after defeating him in a shooting match. She became an international star, touring with Buffalo Bill's Wild West Show for years.

Sam Patch (*1807–29*). This Rhode Island daredevil dove into prominence from a 75-foot New Jersey cliff in 1827. Sometimes with a small bear in his arms, he jumped from ever-increasing heights until he plunged to his death over the Genesee Falls at Rochester, New York. "Here lies Sam Patch; such is Fame," said the epitaph on his gravestone.

Pecos Bill. Weaned on moonshine, teethed on a bowie knife, and raised by coyotes, Pecos Bill was the mythical supercowboy, tough but tenderhearted. He saddled and rode a wild mountain lion, whipping it along with a 10-foot rattlesnake. Barbed wire in his toddy was his undoing. When he died, his skeleton weighed 2 tons.

Pele. The Hawaiian volcano goddess, driven from her home by her sister, the goddess of the sea, took refuge in Hawaii's Kilauea crater. An earthquake signifies that Pele is stamping her feet in anger.

Rip Van Winkle. Writer Washington Irving's gentle idler, a simple Dutch farmer, one day went off into New York's Catskill Mountains with dog and gun. After meeting some tiny men who were bowling, and drinking their potent brew, he fell into a magical 20-year sleep. Irving based Rip, who appears in *The Sketch Book* (1819), on a German legend.

Sasquatch. In the Himalayas he is called the Yeti, or Abominable Snowman. In the Pacific Northwest he is Sasquatch, or Big Foot, a huge, hairy creature who walks like a man. Some who have found "footprints" and taken pictures say he exists, but adventurers are still searching for positive proof.

Stackalee. This legendary black rascal was a Mississippi River roustabout and ladies' man who, according to the song celebrating his fame, sold his soul to Satan for a "magical Stetson" that gave him supernatural powers. Stackalee's strength was such that he started the great San Francisco earthquake by tearing up a barroom in a brawl.

Superman. Faster than a speeding bullet, the "champion of the oppressed" flies through the air on his way to fight evil and injustice. Rocketed to Earth as a baby from the planet Krypton, he became Clark Kent, a mild-mannered reporter, who keeps his powers secret from his colleagues. Since 1938, when he first appeared in Action Comics as the brainchild of writer Jerry Siegel and artist Joe Shuster, Superman has delighted the Nation's children.

Uncle Sam. The story goes that Samuel "Uncle Sam" Wilson, of Troy, New York, an Army food inspector in the War of 1812, stamped "U.S." (for "United States") on barrels of salted meat. This prompted the sarcastic remark from opponents of the war that "these victuals are from Uncle Sam." The cognomen gradually attained respectability along with the whiskered cartoon character that went with it. James Montgomery Flagg, in a famous World War I recruiting poster, endowed his top-hatted Uncle Sam with strength and dignity, and Congress completed the ennobling process in 1961 by officially recognizing the old fellow as our national symbol.

CHAPTER TEN

A New Nation Goes to Sea

The Atlantic Ocean, which scoured the edge of the col nists' first narrow foothold on this continent, proved to both a challenge and an opportunity. With fish plenti and other food scarce, sturdy boats were built to gather t harvest from the sea. The industry and ingenuity that we to become hallmarks of this Nation produced remarkab seaworthy craft to meet the buffeting of the wind and wa along the rugged Northeast coast. The frigates and t privateers that challenged British shipping and men-c war during the War of 1812 evolved from vessels that h proved themselves on the fishing banks and the high se The men who had sailed as peaceful fishermen and trad

The farmers, tradesmen, craftsmen, and adventurers who journeyed to a new land seeking freedom and fortune did not in the main come here to be fishermen or sailors. After 40 days or more in small, crowded sailing craft pitching and rolling on heavy Atlantic seas, most of them might well have sworn never to step aboard another ship. But like it or not, many who came to the newly settled Colonies were heavily dependent on the ocean. Their villages faced the water along protected bays, inlets, and rivers, with dense and forbidding forests edging the small farms on the inland side. The water—for all its fearsome tides and currents, storms and fog—proved the best available means of transportation, as well as a welcome source of food.

The first settlers bartered with the Indians for canoes—birchbarks in the North, dugouts in the South—and ventured forth with hook and line to supplement their meager fare. The bountiful harvests to be had from the deep emphasized the need for larger and more seaworthy craft, and carpenters and coopers turned their hands to the task. Thus began a noteworthy chapter in the history of shipbuilding and seamanship.

It must be noted that the first ship built in America was constructed for a voyage away from the New World, not for commerce. The vessel was the 30-ton pinnace *Virginia of Sagadahoc,* launched in 1607 at the mouth of the Kennebec River in Maine by members of an unsuccessful settlement led by Sir George Popham. The *Virginia* took them back to England and survived to make other crossings, but it was the Yankee fishermen who set the style for the shipbuilding boom to come.

By the mid-1600's the immense schools of cod, haddock, and pollock off the New England coast were considered a major asset. British investors were willing to put up money for boats and equipment in exchange for a share of the profits. Favorable tax rules were enacted to encourage an industry destined to become the largest in early New England. A commission was established in Massachusetts to regulate the catch and protect the fish in the spawning season. The market for dried codfish became so important that a wooden image—"the sacred cod"—was hung in Massachusetts' State House, completed in 1798 in Boston, where it remains today.

Wind and Water Shaped the Boats

Along the Northeast coast the weather and water are remarkably varied. The winds are sometimes gusty, sometimes light, and they may help or hinder a loaded boat headed for port. Shallows and deeps, shifting shoals, rocky ledges, and vicious riptides bedevil the navigator. Small, seaworthy sloops and ketches were needed for New England. Farther south, the waters of Chesapeake and Delaware Bays are shallow and the winds light, so bugeyes, skipjacks, and log canoes were developed as specialized workboats for the fish and oyster trade.

Small boatyards were started, especially around Massachusetts Bay, where timber was abundant close to shore. In the pioneer tradition of doing whatever had to be done, the part-time shipwrights were also farmers, woodsmen, and fishermen. When the builders are the same men who take the boats to sea, they learn their trade thoroughly and practice it with care.

The first New England fishing boats were shallops—open-ended or partially decked, full fore and aft, and usually fitted with gaff-headed foresail and mainsail. It soon became apparent that larger and faster boats were required. The men fished on equal shares, so it was best to have boats of considerable capacity manageable by small crews. This also held true later, when each man was paid for what he caught "on his own hook."

Such everyday tasks as catching lobsters, harvesting oysters, and tending fish traps called for a stable "single-

on some critical victories at sea that gave needed resolve the fledgling Nation.

American clippers, the fastest commercial sailing ships er built, dominated the profitable tea trade in the mid-:00's, while Yankee whalers turned sleepy New England vns into thriving ports. But by the end of the century nerican interest turned from the sea to the land and the . Although prodigies of shipbuilding were performed ring World War II, and an American liner still holds transatlantic speed record, there is little indication that rchantmen flying the Stars and Stripes will recapture glory that once was theirs.

American Rigs

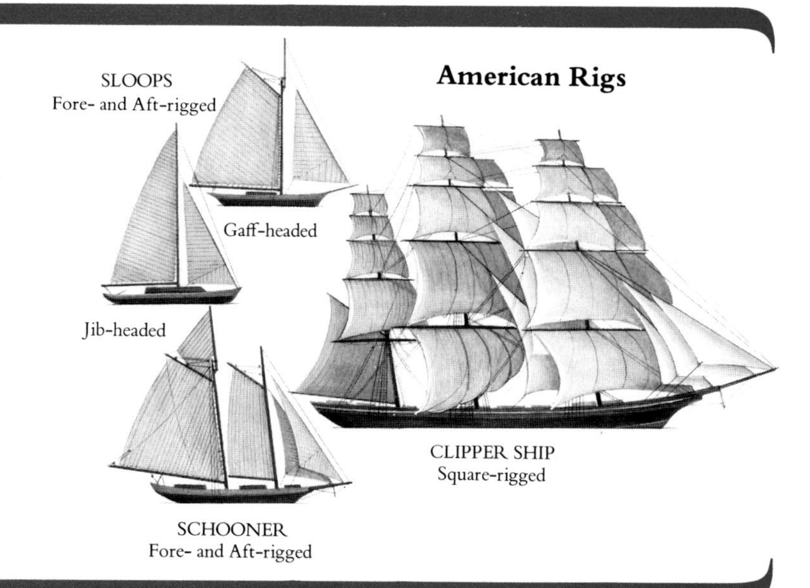

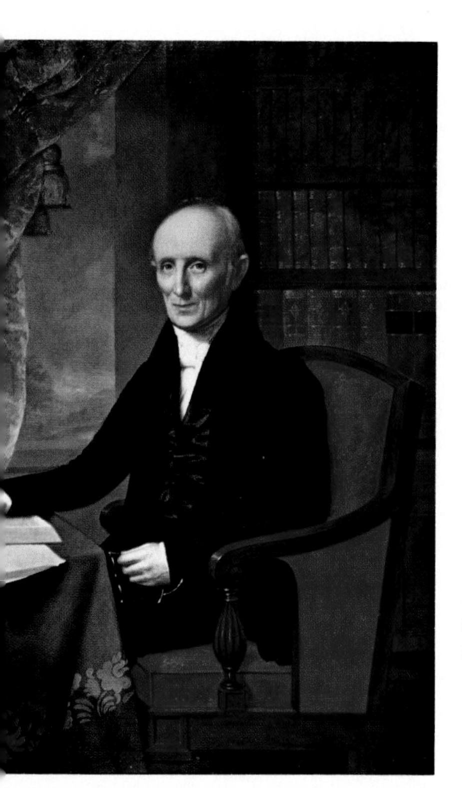

This portrait *by Charles Osgood seems to express Bowditch's precise manner and probing intelligence. His* Practical Navigator, *of which the cover and one of the maps is shown at right, was based on a consummate knowledge of the subject, continually checked and rechecked during his years at sea. He also sharpened his skills by teaching navigation to ambitious shipmates on their long voyages under sail. His book has been revised and reissued in more than 60 editions and in its latest form it still stands as a basic reference work on the critical and demanding subject of navigation.*

Nathaniel Bowditch

From Rags to Riches and Worldwide Renown

Nathaniel Bowditch left school at the age of 10 to work in his impoverished father's cooperage in Salem, Massachusetts. Later apprenticed to a ship's chandler, he developed a lifelong interest in the sea. With his quick, retentive mind, unquenchable thirst for knowledge, and disciplined study habits, he was able to teach himself algebra and Latin, and he later learned French, German, Spanish, and Italian.

In 1795, when he was 22, he went to sea as a supercargo (sales and purchasing agent). He worked his way up to a captaincy and after 8 years retired as a man of means. While at sea he applied his formidable knowledge of mathematics and astrology to navigation and found thousands of errors in the best available book on the subject, J. H. Moore's *The Practical Navigator.* He brought out a corrected edition in 1799 and in 1802 published his own book, *The New American Practical Navigator.*

His seafaring days over, he became president of the Essex Fire and Marine Insurance Company and applied his talent for mathematics to the establishment of actuarial tables. His interest in astronomy did not diminish, and at his own expense he published a translation and commentary of Pierre Simon de Laplace's 3,200-page *Mécanique Céleste,* a seminal work on the movements of heavenly bodies. The honors accorded Bowditch include a master of arts degree from Harvard, a fellowship in the American Academy of Arts and Sciences, and a fellowship in the Royal Society of London. When he died in 1838, ships of all countries flew their flags at half-mast in appreciation of his contributions to their safety on the high seas.

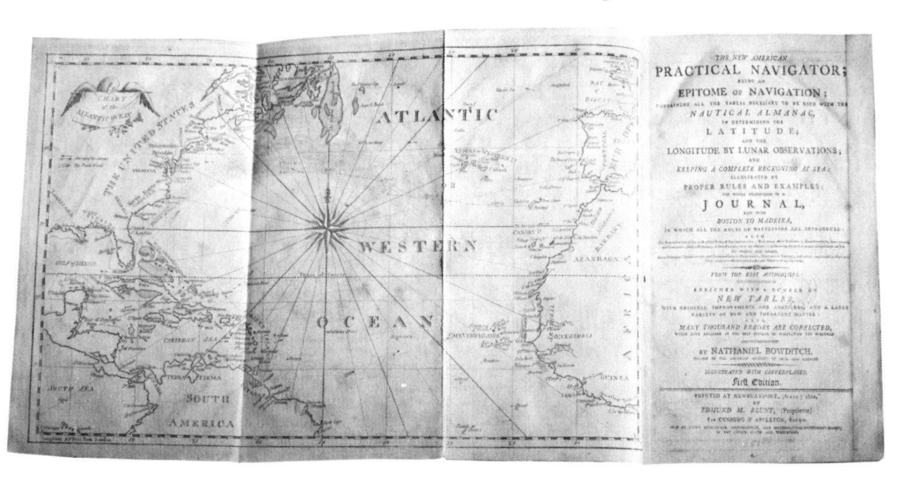

THE NEW AMERICAN
PRACTICAL NAVIGATOR;
BEING AN
EPITOME OF NAVIGATION;
CONTAINING ALL THE TABLES NECESSARY TO BE USED WITH THE
NAUTICAL ALMANAC,
IN DETERMINING THE
LATITUDE;
AND THE
LONGITUDE BY LUNAR OBSERVATIONS;
AND
KEEPING A COMPLETE RECKONING AT SEA:
ILLUSTRATED BY
PROPER RULES AND EXAMPLES:
JOURNAL,
BOSTON TO MADEIRA,
IN WHICH ALL THE RULES OF NAVIGATION ARE INTRODUCED:
FROM THE BEST AUTHORITIES.
ENRICHED WITH A NUMBER OF
NEW TABLES,
MANY THOUSAND ERRORS ARE CORRECTED,
BY NATHANIEL BOWDITCH.
ILLUSTRATED WITH COPPERPLATES.
First Edition.
PRINTED AT NEWBURYPORT,
BY
EDMUND M. BLUNT, (Proprietor)
FOR CUSHING & APPLETON, SALEM.

hander" that a man could safely sail by himself. The beamy catboats with a mast at the bow and a long boom; the handsome Friendship sloops, built in Friendship, Maine, and the salty double-enders used as pilot boats around Passamaquoddy Bay between Maine and New Brunswick, later evolved as good workboats; they are still built, with modern materials, as pleasure craft. The exceptionally seaworthy dory made in Amesbury, Massachusetts, set the standard for small, open workboats and is produced to this day for that purpose.

A small ketch or sloop with a crew of three or four could go out in some waters (such as Georges Bank, 50 miles off Cape Cod), catch a load of fish, and bring it safely back to port. But to work the Grand Banks off Newfoundland, perhaps the best fishing waters in the world, required bigger boats with larger crews.

Our First Major Contribution—The Schooner

Some historians say that in 1713 the schooner was created full-blown by a Capt. Andrew Robinson in Gloucester, Massachusetts. While Dutch paintings show that this rig was used in Holland at least 35 years earlier, there is no doubt that the schooner was perfected by American shipwrights and fishermen. The Dutch also developed efficient sloops that were so successfully adapted in Bermuda and Jamaica that the Bermuda sloops became famous in the late 1600's. Their hull shape, in particular, influenced the design of the American schooners.

The schooner was developed for the heavy weather encountered in fishing the Grand Banks, and it evolved to combine admirable qualities of speed, easy handling, seaworthiness, and generous cargo space. Some large schooners also had centerboards that could be raised for passage into shallow harbors.

The schooner, with its fore and aft rig, could sail closer to the wind than square-riggers of comparable size, and required about one-third as many men to handle the sails. A "topsail schooner" had a square-rigged topsail that could be hoisted for downwind use but did not need to be set unless it was convenient or advantageous to do so.

By 1776 some 500 schooners were fishing for cod off the Grand Banks. From fishing grounds nearer shore hundreds of smaller boats were bringing in mackerel and herring. The rugged life and constant vigil of tending sail in the shifting winds and navigating in the sudden fogs of these waters gave some of America's future Navy men and merchant seamen invaluable training.

Before the Revolution, Britain commissioned some of the fast and serviceable American schooners to be built as revenue cutters. During the Revolution, and again in the War of 1812, many of the fastest schooners were turned to privateering. To succeed at this risky business one needed a good ship, a fearless crew, and a Letter of Marque and Reprisal from the Government, which authorized privately owned vessels to capture any enemy ship. After a capture was declared legal in a prize court, the proceeds from the sale of ship and cargo were split by the privateer's owner, officers, and crew.

The ultimate two-masters were schooners and brigs made in Baltimore. Because they sailed at "a good clip," particularly upwind, they were called Baltimore Clippers. Effective as privateers in the War of 1812, these were the namesakes of the full-rigged clipper ships that were to become so famous.

While the schooners could not compete with the square-riggers for long hauls, where sustained speed was paramount and winds were fairly constant, they were ideal for maneuverability in varying winds. Their efficient performance in the fishing fleet set the standards for the new Nation's ships of war.

Although a frigate is a square-rigged fighting ship with a full gun deck, the hulls of those built for the Revolution and the War of 1812 were influenced by successful designs for the Grand Banks. With experience at sea, the frigates had been slowly improved, and reached their best fighting form in the 1750's. The *Randolph,* built in Philadelphia, is considered one of the finest frigates ever set afloat. In 1794 Congress authorized the construction of six frigates, which became the foundation of the American Navy. Among them, the U.S.S. *Constitution*—"Old Ironsides"—was unrivaled for firepower plus speed and maneuverability. (For more on American fighting ships, see pages 188–189.)

One sturdy ship, the 83-foot *Columbia* out of Boston, commanded by Capt. Robert Gray, earned an honored place in maritime lore. In 1789, after a winter of trading with Indians on the Northwest coast, Captain Gray set sail for Canton, China, with a load of sea otter skins and sandalwood picked up in Hawaii on the way. In China he traded his cargo for commodities and returned to Boston in 1790 with tea, silk, porcelain, and nankeen (a cotton cloth used for breeches), thus inaugurating the lucrative Northwest coast-Hawaii-China trade. On this venture the *Columbia* became the first American ship to sail around the world. On May 11, 1792, during the second trading voyage, Captain Gray sailed into the mouth of a great river and named it for his ship. His exploration of the Columbia River, some 12 years before the Louisiana Purchase and the Lewis and Clark Expedition, helped establish America's claim to the Oregon country.

The Black Ball Packets

Soon after the War of 1812, when world trade was expanding, a startling new concept in transatlantic travel was introduced. On October 27, 1817, five textile and cotton merchants, four of them Quakers, offered service between New York and Liverpool in packet boats that would "positively sail, full or not full." Sailing had been

Matthew F. Maury
Pathfinder of the Sea

Maury's curiosity about the sea was, seemingly, insatiable and he did more than any other man to investigate and document its tides, currents, winds, and topography. He was commissioned a Navy midshipman in 1825, and his scholarly bent was first demonstrated with publication in 1836 of an excellent treatise on navigation. Appalled by what he considered to be inefficient methods of naval administration and education, Maury urged formation of a naval academy such as Congress had established for the Army at West Point. His outspoken views did not endear the impetuous Maury to some of his starchy superiors who considered him to be an upstart. Lamed in a stagecoach accident in 1839, he was eventually given an innocuous assignment as head of the Navy's Depot of Charts and Instruments in 1842. Not content with a caretaker's job, Maury delved into the Navy's voluminous collection of charts and encouraged ships' captains to keep daily records of winds and currents and report to him. He coordinated these reports in his masterwork, *The Wind and Current Charts of the North Atlantic,* which saved weeks of sailing time on long runs. In 1855 he published *The Physical Geography of the Sea,* the first modern textbook on oceanography. His innovative work led to an international system of recording oceanographic data, which has been of immeasurable value in worldwide shipping.

The intricate detail *of Maury's charts is shown in this section of Newfoundland waters with "wind brushes" to indicate velocity and direction as recorded and reported by ships' captains over the years. In his patient compilation of reports of winds and currents, tides and temperatures around the world, Maury developed a total view of the major movements of wind and water that gave him a perspective far ahead of his time. He was a pioneer in the field of weather forecasting, and from 1868 until his death in 1873 he was professor of meteorology at the Virginia Military Institute.*

"positively" scheduled before this time, but the ships would usually not depart until they had a full cargo, and that could take weeks longer than anticipated.

These square-rigged ships had a black disk painted on the fore-topsail and on the company flag, and the company thus became known as the Black Ball Line. Service started from Liverpool, England, on January 4, 1818, and from New York City the next day. The packets soon were famous for keeping to their schedule. They averaged 24 days "downhill" from New York to Liverpool, with the prevailing winds, and 38 days westbound, or "uphill." By 1822 two competing lines and an augmented Black Ball service provided weekly sailings between New York and Liverpool and until 1838 carried most of the news, cabin passengers, and quality freight between America and Europe. Their often brutal "bucko mates" became infamous for their iron-fisted treatment of the "packet rats" who had to labor unremittingly to keep a sailing ship at maximum speed. Seamen did not relish working on the Black Ball Line and many were shanghaied and pressed into service. Nonetheless, no other country could match the performance of these American ships expertly handled by American captains.

When steamships became more common, after 1838, the packets switched to the immigrant business. Passengers who could afford first-class fares found luxurious accommodations, but the hapless souls who were crowded into steerage on these rough crossings never forgot the harrowing experience.

In 1819, slightly more than a year after the first packet boats sailed on schedule, a little-noticed but significant launching took place in Georgia. The *Savannah* was a strange-looking craft with stubby masts, full-rigged sails, paddle wheels, and an angled smokestack to carry off the smoke of a steam engine, the first ever used in an Atlantic crossing. Although the ship ran its engine less than 90 hours in a 29-day trip from Savannah to Liverpool, the voyage foreshadowed the development of steam and eventual decline of commercial sailing craft. However, there were still glorious pages in American maritime history to be written by the windjammers.

The Power and Beauty of the Clipper Ships

The most dramatic era of ships under sail began, in fact, when the 154-foot square-rigger *Rainbow* slid down the ways in New York in 1845. The designer, John Willis

Doing full justice *to her name, with most of her canvas set, the clipper ship* Flying Cloud *drives majestically over the waves in this painting by Frank Vining Smith. The builder was Donald McKay.*

What Made the Clippers Fly

No Other Ships Have Sailed So Far So Fast

More Sail. It was no secret that more sail on a ship of giv waterline length would drive her faster. But until the era of t clipper ships, no one had dared take that knowledge to su extremes. As it became evident that more speed would mean mc profits, taller ships were built. One of the tallest was the *Challer* with a sail plan specified by the record-setting Capt. Robert Waterman. The mainmast reached more than 200 feet above t water, and the canvas spread some 60 feet beyond the hull on ea side. It might have become the fastest ship of all, but Waterm never had a crew equal to the task. Later captains reduced t formidable expanse of canvas to more manageable size.

Sharper Hulls. There was more to a "sharp" ship than the na rower width and sharper bow shown in the overlay below. T underwater parts of the clipper ship's bow section also had a co cave shape, making the bow even sharper in effect. Anoth

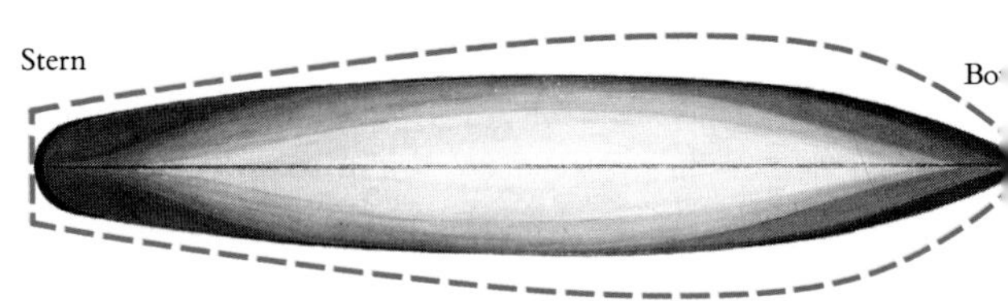

feature that improved the speed of these hulls was a relatively bottom or floor. This attribute was discovered by chance wh ships built for the cotton trade were made with flat floors, inste of the usual deep V-shaped profile, to float safely over shifti sandbanks in the delta country. This shape provided more car

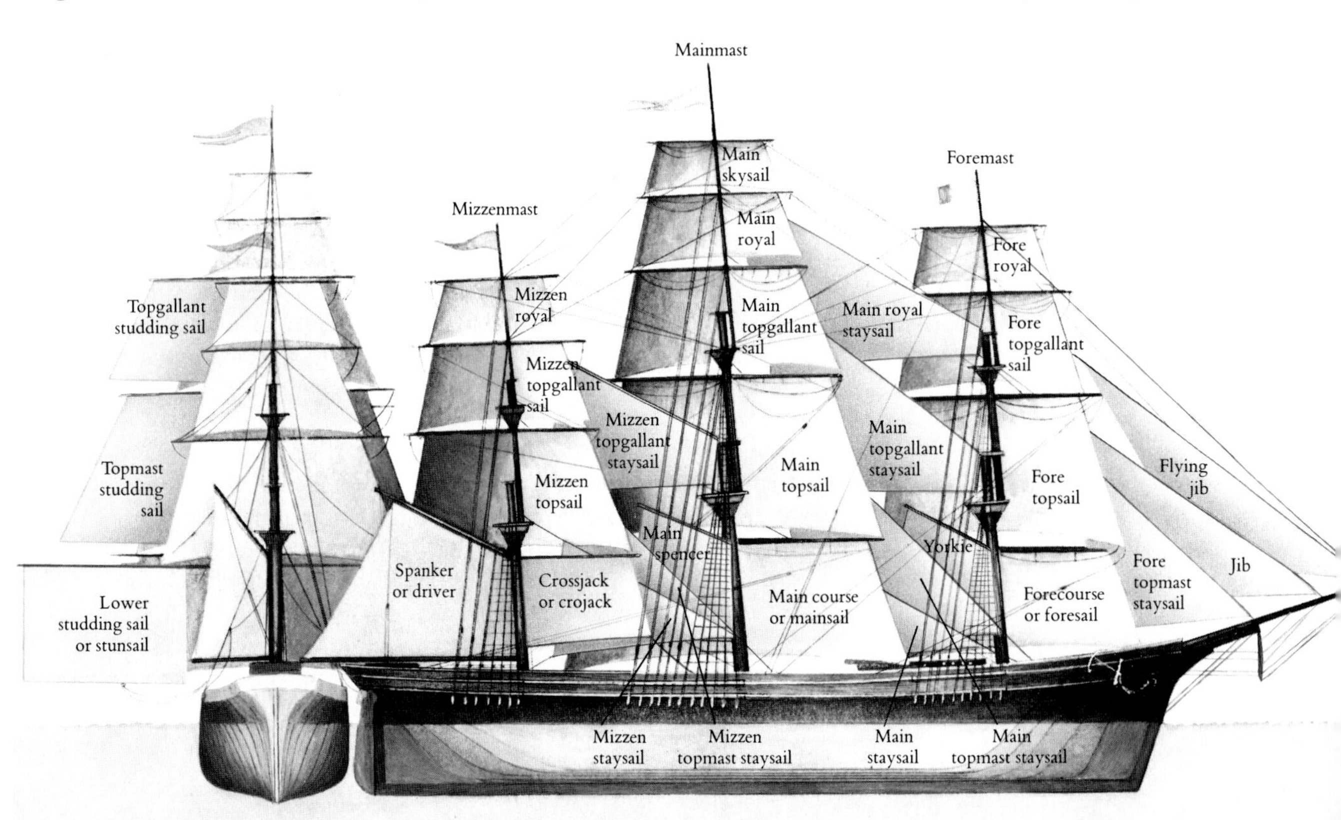

ıce and, to everyone's surprise, improved the sailing qualities. ıt even at best, the finer bow and stern and narrower beam luced the cargo capacity of the clippers as much as one-third ative to full-bodied hulls of the same length.

ırd-Driving Captains. No matter how superbly a ship was signed and rigged, it could not perform to its full potential less there was someone in command who knew how much ain the vessel could take and had the courage to hold as near ıt limit as possible. As one experienced skipper put it: "The pert sailor knows exactly how long his sails and spars will stand : strain. The lubber does not and therefore is apt to lose both." ıptains have been known to stand on the quarterdeck with ıded pistols, ready to shoot down any terror-stricken crewman ıo would try, if he had the chance, to cut the halyards and luce sail before the masts pulled out and took the ship and its ·w to the bottom of the sea. Many captains did overreach and owed rigging to break and sails to tear to shreds. American ppers were famous for getting the most out of their ships. Even the competitive tea trade, British ships would often slow down ıight. But once an American clipper was underway she would ve at maximum speed, unless becalmed, until the destination s reached.

Hard experience was the only teacher, and the more the bet- . Many captains started their careers as cabin boys at age 10 or , and many had earned a command while still in their teens or ly 20's. The demands were great, but so were the incentives. the great days of sail one good voyage could make the captain vealthy man for life.

Standing Records Under Sail

The sole purpose of the clipper ships, and the obsession of their owners and their captains, was speed—and more speed. For the owners speed meant premium rates for passengers and cargo, more frequent runs, and more profit. For the captains there were fat bonuses for fast trips, public acclaim, and the respect—not to mention envy—of competing captains. The most publicized records were from New York to San Francisco during the Gold Rush. With visions of wealth at the end of the voyage, passengers would pay as much as $1,000 for the fastest passage around the Horn to the Golden Gate. The magic number was "in two figures"—under 100 days. Lesser ships would take twice that long. The variety of records listed here indicates the dominance of the American clipper ships.

Ship	Route	Time or Speed	Date of Run
Sea Witch	*Hong Kong to New York,*	*74 days 14 hours*	1849
Oriental	*New York to Hong Kong,*	*80 days 10 hours*	1850
Swordfish	*San Francisco to Shanghai,*	*32 days 9 hours*	1853
Comet	*San Francisco to New York,*	*76 days 7 hours*	1853–54
Andrew Jackson	*New York to San Francisco,*	*89 days 4 hours*	1854
Champion of the Seas	*Logged 465 miles in 24 hours*		1854
James Baines	*Boston to Liverpool,*	*12 days 6 hours*	1854
Red Jacket	*New York to Liverpool,*	*12 days*	1854
Sovereign of the Seas	*Logged a speed of 22 knots*		1854
Mandarin	*New York to Melbourne,*	*69 days 14 hours*	1855–56
Sweepstakes	*New York to Bombay,*	*74 days*	1857

Griffiths, had tried models in a test tank and discovered that more than the usual speed could be expected with a hull of narrow beam, sharp bow, long waterline, and a flat floor or bottom. He also decided that such a hull could carry more canvas than any ship had ever handled. The evolution had been slow, but the characteristics of the American clipper ship were finally established.

Other designers were quick to appreciate *Rainbow*'s qualities, and the race to build bigger and faster clippers was on. Three of the most successful designers were William H. Webb, who built *Young America;* Samuel Hart Pook, whose masterpiece was *Red Jacket;* and Donald McKay, whose *Flying Cloud* and *Lightning* were among the greatest clippers ever built.

McKay was apprenticed at 16 to New York shipwright Isaac Webb, William Webb's father. McKay learned his craft well and was helped in his trade by his two marriages. His first wife, a shipbuilder's daughter familiar with the rudiments of marine architecture, taught him what she knew. His second wife was his secretary and business adviser and named his most famous clippers. McKay opened his own shipyard in Boston and in 1850 launched his first clipper, *Stag Hound,* which was then the largest merchant ship afloat. This was the beginning of a remarkable career. Of the 12 ships ever to make a speed of 18 knots or more under sail, 9 were designed by McKay. Of 14 ships to log more than 400 miles in 24 hours, 10 were by McKay, and his *Sovereign of the Seas* and *James Baines* both sailed at record speeds of more than 20 knots (23 miles an hour).

One of the great clipper ship captains was Nathaniel Brown Palmer, who at 14, during the War of 1812, shipped out on a blockade runner. In 1820, when he was only 21, Palmer commanded a 47-foot sloop, the *Hero,* on a sealing expedition to the Antarctic Ocean. On November 18, in his quest for seal, he sighted the Antarctic continent—probably the first person to do so. Palmer's Land, the southern part of the Antarctic Peninsula, and the nearby Palmer Archipelago are named for him. As a captain for the China traders, A. A. Low and Brothers, Palmer contributed to the design of some of their great clippers, including the *Oriental,* which made a record 81-day run from New York to Hong Kong in 1850.

The clippers sacrificed cargo space, comfort, and, in some cases, safety in the race for profit. They were queens of the seas when speed was important. They often carried tea, which soon lost its flavor in a ship's hold. Clippers were also used to rush cargo and passengers to the goldfields of California.

American sailing ships were technically the best afloat, but more important, they were manned by seamen who had in many instances grown up before the mast and were not held back by class distinctions. Any 12-year-old cabin boy could hope to become a captain some day. Some 35

At Salem, Massachusetts, *Crowninshield's Wharf, shown in this 1806 painting by George Ropes, vied with Derby's Wharf for the East India trade. The inset, not part of the painting, is the city seal and motto: "To the farthest port of the rich east."*

The China Trade
Cargoes of Luxuries

When the *Empress of China,* out of New York, dropped anchor at Canton's deep-water port in 1784, she unloaded a cargo of raw cotton for cloth, lead for bullets, furs to trim the imperial robes, and ginseng root for medicines and aphrodisiacs. These irresistibly desirable goods were exchanged for the tea, silk, and porcelain that would make fortunes for venturesome Yankee traders. The China trade ships were always racing against time, especially with tea, which was perishable and could command premium prices if they were first in port. In speed at sea the American clipper ships excelled, and the owners and the captains prospered greatly.

After 1842 China was forced to open several ports besides Canton to "foreign devils." As other nations developed spheres of influence in China, the United States insisted on an Open Door Policy, ensuring equal trading rights to all. In 1934 Japan, having meanwhile invaded Manchuria, nullified this policy.

Exotic treasures such as these *were the serendipitous by-products of the China trade: porcelain, Chinese silver cup, tea box and tea chests, ivory ball carved from one piece, and tea caddy.*

Off Whampoa Island, *about 12 miles down the Pearl River from Canton, proud clipper ships take on their exotic cargo for what their skippers hope will be a fast run homeward, free from the terrors of pirates and typhoons. When all went well, the profits on a single round trip could equal all of the original investment. This crisp and elegant painting, by an unknown Chinese artist, was made about 1855.*

crewmen on the 20 trips that Joseph Peabody's ship *George* made between Salem and Calcutta ultimately rose to become masters in their own right.

But the magnificent clippers, the most beautiful ships ever built, could not survive the competition of the noisy, dirty, awkward-looking new steam vessels that had the one insurmountable advantage sailors had always dreamed of: freedom from the vagaries of the wind. In 1853 more than 150 so-called clippers were launched. Two years later only 42 keels were laid, and shortly after the Civil War clippers were made no more.

The decline of the clippers did not mean the end of sail. There was still use for big windjammers to carry bulk cargo at relatively low cost. Best for this work were the stable, capacious, down easters, many of them Maine-built. They were called down easters because in sailing to Maine from Boston you generally went downwind and east, to take advantage of the prevailing southerly winds. Maine shipyards specialized in the practical but unglamorous down easters from 1865 to the 1890's. Long after steam had captured the prime cargo and passenger trades these sturdy vessels roamed the high seas, carrying such mundane cargo as grain, tobacco, naval stores, wool, and fish.

Sail was also economical for the coastal trade. The steady, maneuverable sloops, ketches, and schooners profitably plied the ports of the east, west and Gulf coasts, their holds loaded with cargoes of brick, stone, lumber cotton, tobacco, and coal.

Selling Ice, Tea, and Spice

Less commonplace was the cargo carried aboard Boston merchant Frederic Tudor's brig in 1806. Tudor cut large blocks of ice from New England ponds and rivers and shipped them to the Caribbean and the cotton ports of the South. By the 1830's he had developed a trade with the tea and spice port of Calcutta, and in the banner year 1856 he shipped 363 cargoes to 53 different ports. After trying many materials for insulation, Tudor finally settled on sawdust, a plentiful New England byproduct. A tireless and imaginative merchandiser, he convincingly argued that ice was a necessity for civilized living, and he built storage houses at a number of tropical ports for his "blocks of Yankee coldness." Demand was so great that by 1847 he had to go inland for his supply, and when author Henry David Thoreau saw ice being taken from his beloved Walden Pond, he wrote: "Thus it appears that the sweltering inhabitants of Charleston and New Orleans, of Madras and Bombay and Calcutta drink at my well."

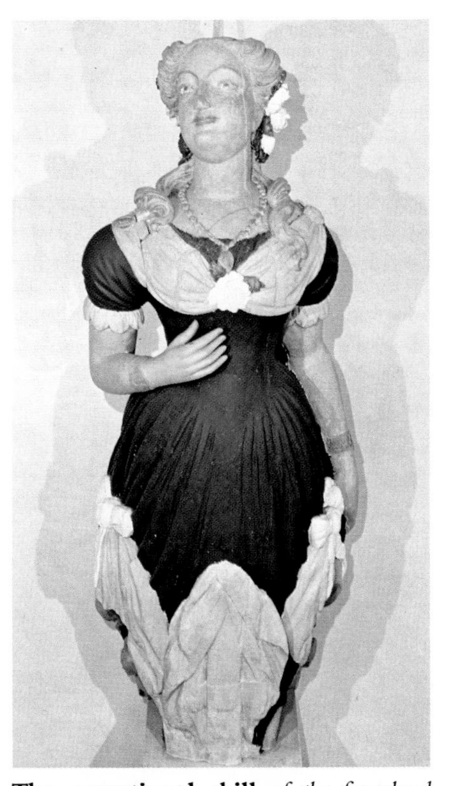

The exceptional skill *of the figurehead carver is evidenced in the fine detail of the hands, the stylish costume, and ornate jewelry of this flaxen-haired blue-eyed lady of the seas.*

The Giant Schooners

Owners were always on the lookout for ways to reduce the number of seamen required for the heavy work of handling sail. In the late 1860's, small, stationary, steam-driven donkey engines—so named for their strong pulling power—were put aboard the big schooners. Installation of a donkey for loading, unloading, and raising the sails permitted an increase in cargo space, masts, and canvas without the need for more hands. Soon there were three-masters, called terns, then schooners with four, five, and six masts. They were used largely in the coastal trade, especially for coal.

The largest of these leviathans was the 375-foot steel-hulled *Thomas W. Lawson,* launched at Quincy, Massachusetts, in 1903. The only seven-master ever built, it carried more than 44,000 square feet of sail. A crew working against the wind would find it almost impossible to put a ship of this size about. On its first transatlantic run in 1907 the *Lawson* was blown ashore near the Scilly Isles off southwest England and beaten apart on the rocks. Only 2 of the 19 crew members survived.

A Century of Whaling

From the early 1700's, when the whalers first put out from Nantucket and New Bedford, Massachusetts, until the 1860's, when kerosene was introduced, whale oil lamps gave the best light. At the peak of the whale oil industry in the mid-1800's the worldwide search for whales involved more than 700 American ships. Their home berths were all up and down the New England coast, on Long Island, and even in a few ports on the Hudson River. As the British statesman Edmund Burke once wrote of the American whalers, there was "no sea but what is vexed by their fisheries. No climate that is not witness to their toils."

Whaling ships were built for strength, stability, and carrying capacity, not for speed. They were usually square-rigged, like those shown in the painting on page 182, but at one time or another almost every kind of ship went out to seek the profitable oil. Between 1835 and

All aspects of whaling *are shown here: The kill (of a right whale); towing in a carcass with its identifying flag; peeling off the blanket piece from a whale alongside the ship; and rendering the oil in the smoking trypots. Here, too, is revealed the functional design of the sturdy, square, stable whaleship, as well as the sleek elegant lines of the lightweight whaleboats that were used for the chase and the kill.*

Big-Game Hunting on the Open Sea—*Danger, Dirty Work, and Stupefying Boredom*

The taking of the world's largest living creature was grueling work. Money was not the main attraction, but whaling did provide room and board of sorts. Only the whaler's captain and owners might be enriched; the crew had to settle mostly for the excitement and danger of the chase and catch.

When the quarry was sighted, the whaleboats were lowered, each under the command of a mate who manned the steering oar. Four crewmen, facing aft, plied pulling oars, while the boatsteerer, who was also the harpooner, took his place at the bow oar. If there was a good distance to go, the crew might rig a sail to draw near the prey and then take up their oars again. Under the exhortations of the mate, who was seldom subtle, they bent to the task of coming alongside the whale as it cruised on the surface. At pointblank range the harpooner would sink his sharp iron firmly into place and, if there was time, before backing frantically away, set another harpoon for good measure.

Fastened to the harpoon was one end of about 1,800 feet of tough manila line, which was artfully coiled in a wooden tub so it would play out as required to keep the whale hooked. Thus the battle was drawn, and the men were committed, as they put it, to "a dead whale or a stove boat."

The next move was up to the whale. It might sound (dive for the bottom) or flee on the surface in an attempt to escape. The aggressive sperm whale would sometimes turn and attack the boat. Even the more docile baleen whale could break a boat to splinters with its mighty tail as it dove.

If the beast chose to run, the men were in for a high-speed "Nantucket sleigh ride," until they could draw near enough for the kill. As the whale towed the boat, the harpooner went aft to take up his official duty as boatsteerer, and the mate replaced him in the bow, wielding the long, sharp killing lance as shown in the graphic illustration above. When the deed was done, there was hard, dirty work ahead and possibly weeks of boredom before another whale brought the crew closer to their dreams of a featherbed and hot food in Nantucket or New Bedford.

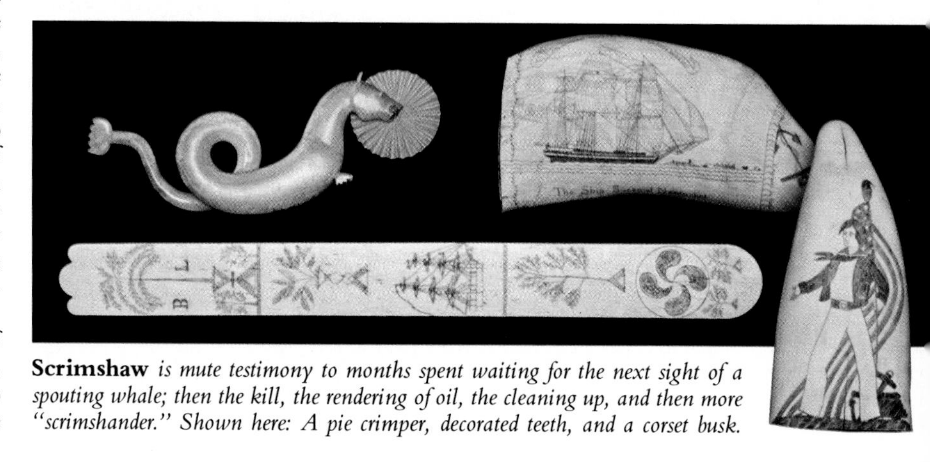

Scrimshaw *is mute testimony to months spent waiting for the next sight of a spouting whale; then the kill, the rendering of oil, the cleaning up, and then more "scrimshander." Shown here: A pie crimper, decorated teeth, and a corset busk.*

ketches From a Whaler's Journal

'he head was cut into sections *and brought aboard first. Here ɐe crew is shown bailing the pure oil—which was the most valuable—om the "case" in the sperm whale's head. The head also provided sper-aceti, a waxlike substance that made the finest candles. The teeth were ɪved to use for scrimshaw carving. Sperm oil has unexcelled rust-inhibit-ɐg characteristics. Some present problems with automatic transmissions ɐe attributed to the lack of a suitable substitute for whale oil now that haling has been sharply restricted.*

ɪreat chunks of blubber, *called horse pieces, were removed from the ntinuous blanket pieces, which were cut in a spiral, like peeling an apple. ackle in the rigging was used to lift the strip high enough to swing it oard, as can be seen in the lithograph at far left. The ship's officers ere not exempt from the hard labor of whaling. The captain and first ɪd second mates, ever mindful of the hungry sharks below, stood on a ippery, narrow platform rigged above the whale and used long cutting ades to strip away the blubber.*

/orking night and day *on 6-hour watches, the crew kept the trypots iling to render the oil from the blubber and drain it into the casks, which ɔuld be stored in the hold. Horse pieces were cut into long narrow sections ɪd sliced vertically to expose more surface. These "bible leaves" were opped into the pots as shown above. The fires were started with wood ɪd then fueled with the cracklings left after the oil was boiled out. The ɪale thus rendered itself up to the cause of better light and lubrication.*

1860 the industry's products averaged $8 million a year or more in value, sometimes exceeding all other fisheries.

In the tradition of New England fishermen, the crews worked on shares. The captain might get a "lay" of $\frac{1}{8}$ or $\frac{1}{10}$ of the ship's share; a forecastle hand as little as $\frac{1}{200}$. For the benefit of all, a ship stayed at sea until it had a full load—usually 3 to 5 years.

It is hard to imagine the conditions under which those years were spent. All possible space below deck was reserved for the cargo. The common sailors were crowded into the dark and fetid forecastle. The food was poor at best, and it got worse by the month. When no whales were in sight, the monotony was that of a prison ship. The men whiled away some of their time by singing chanteys, spinning tales, and roughhousing, but the most poignant evidence of the mind-numbing weeks of enforced idleness is the scrimshaw they created. These marvelous hand-wrought creations of ivory, bone, baleen, coconut shell, or tropical wood are a form of folk art unique to the American whalers.

When an idle ship was within hailing distance, the captain, with his wife (if she was aboard), and the ship's officers would exchange a neighborly visit, or "gam," and would often trade newspapers and books. For the other hands, the only escape from the ship's confines was a rare stop at an island for fresh water and supplies.

Only the sighting of a whale could end the daily boredom. When the lookout cried, "Thar she blo-o-ows!" the work that followed could be as exciting and demanding as any that man has ever done. The degree of danger depended on the quarry. There are basically two kinds of whales: those with jaws lined with flexible fibrous material, called baleen, and those with teeth. Among the baleen whales are relatively slow and unaggressive species that float after they are killed. The laconic New Englanders called these right whales because they were the right ones to go after. They produced a good percentage of oil, and the flexible baleen (also called whalebone) was valued for use in hoopskirts, corset stays, buggy whips, and umbrella ribs. Among the toothed species are the sperm whale, the most dangerous and valuable of all. They are fast swimmers and ferocious fighters, and sperm oil is a better lubricant and burns brighter than the oil of other whales. This whale also has a liquid in its head that hardens to a waxlike consistency as it cools. This is called spermaceti, and it made candles that were far superior to the common tallow tapers of the day. The whale's teeth and parts of its jawbone were saved for scrimshaw work. On rare occasions the intestines of a sperm whale would yield a hard yellow lump of ambergris, which was used in perfume making. In the 1800's a 100-pound piece of this rare stuff could bring as much as $7,000.

As soon as the lookout sighted the spout, the whalers knew what kind of battle to expect. The baleen whale has two blowholes, the sperm whale only one. The distinctive single spout of the sperm whale brought a mixture of hope for profit and well-founded fear. It was known that this monster might even attack a ship. In the Pacific Ocean, in 1820, an 85-foot sperm whale rammed the Nantucket whaler *Essex* on one side, came back and rammed again, staving it in beyond repair. The 20-man crew took to three whaleboats and headed southeast toward South America. After almost 3 months of rowing and sailing for more than 4,500 miles in the small open boats, five survivors were picked up about 300 miles off the coast of Chile.

The schooner "America" *humbled Britain's Royal Squadron in a race in 1851. Designer George Steers patterned the New York Yacht Club entry after his fast pilot boats.*

The era of American whaling ended in the 1860's, when the oil and baleen were replaced by more efficient materials. The United States, which built up the industry, now leads the world in the campaign to save the whale from extinction by hunters of other nations who still track it, using ships and weapons undreamed of by the hardy harpooners out of New Bedford and Nantucket.

Racing—For the Glory Alone

As constant as the tides is the urge to go faster on the sea and to win the grand prize, be it fame, fortune, or a silver cup. It is not surprising that a nation whose survival has so often depended on individual enterprise and spirited competition should produce men who excel at the exacting sport of yacht racing. The first significant triumph came in 1851, at the height of the era of the clipper ships, when the yacht *America* beat a flotilla of British yachts in a 60-mile race around the Isle of Wight and won a cup donated by the Royal Yacht Squadron of England. The win was decisive. Queen Victoria, watching from the Royal Yacht, was told that the American boat had just come into sight. "Oh indeed!" she said, "And which is second?" An officer replied, "I regret to report that there is no second."

In 1857 the Royal Yacht Squadron Cup was presented to the New York Yacht Club as a perpetual challenge trophy. Thereafter, in the 22 races held from 1870 to 1974, all challengers were defeated and the America's Cup—named after its first victor—remained in U.S. hands. In the matches' early days some regulations gave the advantage to the Americans, but in 1956 these rules were changed, and since then the race has been fair.

Among the many great yacht designers, perhaps the most influential was Nathanael G. Herreshoff, "The Wizard of Bristol," Rhode Island. His 37-foot sloop *Shadow,* launched in 1872, was unbeaten in its class for 16 years. He designed five America's Cup defenders between 1893 and 1920 and constantly advanced the standards for hull

Sailing Alone Around the World

A run of hard luck found Captain Joshua Slocum, age 51, ashore in Massachusetts with no prospect of another command. It seemed that his 24-year career as a master of sailing ships had come to an end. But the sea was a part of him and he decided to try what no other man had ever dared: to sail alone around the world. He found an old oysterboat on the Acushnet River near New Bedford and set about making her seaworthy. It cost him less than $600—but more than a year—to rebuild the *Spray* into a sturdy sloop 36 feet 9 inches long by 14 feet 2 inches wide.

After a test run he headed for Gibraltar on July 2, 1895, on the first leg of a voyage that secured him a lasting place in sea annals. In 33 days he made Gibraltar, where he was feted for his daring but warned to give up his plan to go through the Suez Canal into the pirate-infested Red Sea. To avoid this peril, Slocum set sail for South America and the Straits of Magellan. It took him 60 days and nights to make the 350-mile passage through the tempestuous Straits. In the comparative calm of the Pacific, he could lash the helm and count on *Spray* to make her way for days unattended. He headed west to Samoa and on to Australia, where he stayed for months. He crossed the Indian Ocean to South Africa, where he spent 3 months. Then, turning northwest across the Atlantic, he arrived at Newport, Rhode Island, on June 27, 1898. Two years later he published his book, *Sailing Alone Around the World.* On November 14, 1909, while he was cruising off Martha'a Vineyard, a sudden storm came up. The man and the sloop that had weathered the Straits of Magellan and sailed more than 46,000 miles of deep water were lost without a trace.

The two "Savannahs" *with sources of power that made seagoing history. The first had a wooden hull 100 feet in length. The second is made of steel and is 595 feet 6 inches overall.*

From Coal and Cordwood to Nuclear Power
Two Oceangoing Firsts for America

The *Savannah,* launched in 1819, was a strange-looking craft. Just over 100 feet long, she had stubby masts and an angled stack to direct the smoke and sparks of a steam engine away from the sails. The 72-horsepower engine was there to drive removable paddle wheels that would be installed and used when the wind failed. The engine was employed for less than 90 hours in a 29-day voyage from Savannah to Liverpool, but it was the first time steam was used on an Atlantic crossing. Although this country was the first to adapt steam power to ocean travel, it was more than 30 years before we did much more to take advantage of the steam engine's potential for driving ships.

In another bold experiment with a new source of power, a second *Savannah* was launched on July 21, 1959. Instead of the usual gigantic machinery in the engine room of a ship this size, there was a small nuclear reactor. This sleek passenger-cargo ship logged more than 450,000 miles and visited 46 countries. Although high costs in the operation of the *Savannah,* plus technical problems, have put her future in doubt, the success of nuclear submarines, carriers, cruisers, destroyers, and frigates has proved the value and efficiency of nuclear power.

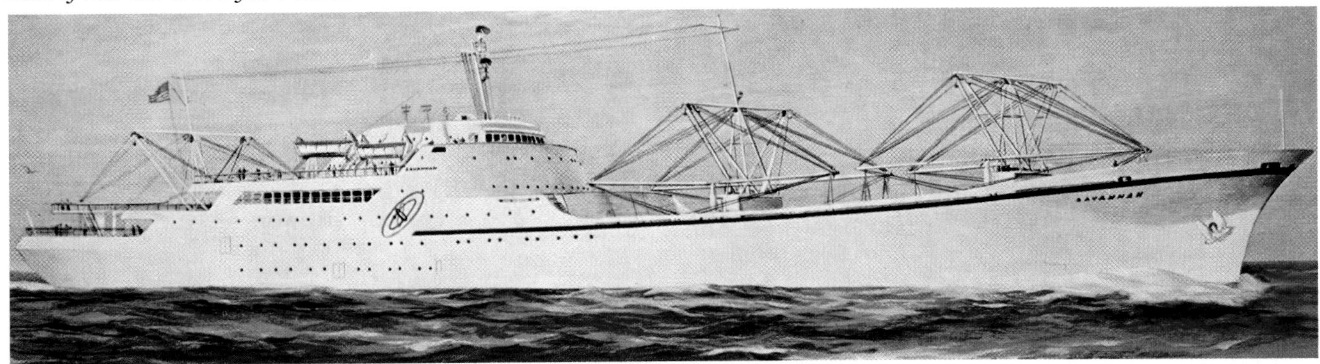

shape and sail plan. He also proposed the "universal rule"—a formula in which hull displacement, length, and sail area are all considered—to prevent one craft from having undue advantage over another.

Interest in ocean racing has continued to grow, as evidenced by the annual races from New England to Bermuda and from California to Hawaii and Ensenada, Mexico. These contests have been dominated by boats of American design, but only in this specialized field has U.S. leadership survived the inroads of time that have affected all other branches of American seamanship.

The Advent of Steam—And Our Decline

From the end of the Civil War until the outbreak of World War I we were winning yacht races, but American merchant ships had all but disappeared from the high seas.

Although this country was the first to put steam power to the test with the transatlantic crossing of the *Savannah* in 1819, more than 30 years passed before a regular American steamer schedule was established. In 1852, under the banner of the Collins Line, the wooden side-wheeler *Baltic* steamed from New York to England in less than 10 days to win the mythical transatlantic blue ribbon for the fastest crossing. Aided by Government funds, the line was off to a good start, but disaster struck in 1854 when the *Baltic*'s sister ship, the *Arctic,* was rammed in a fog and sank. Sixteen months later the *Pacific,* and all aboard, was lost in the North Atlantic without a trace. The subsidy was withdrawn and the Collins Line failed.

While the Collins Line was setting records on the Atlantic, the Pacific Mail Steamship Company was making a good start on the other side of the continent, also with subsidy aid. The company carried mail and passengers from New York to Panama, provided an overland link to the Pacific, and served all the major West Coast cities. By 1858 the line had 29 ships flying the American flag in the Pacific. In 1867 the largest wooden side-wheelers ever built began carrying its colors to Japan and China. Later, steel ships, also the largest of their kind until that time, were put on the run.

The transcontinental railroad, completed in 1869, offered overland service that eventually led to the demise of the Pacific Mail, although it remained the best known line on the Pacific until World War I. The opening of the Suez Canal, also in 1869, gave steam power the final advantage over sail. Until that shortcut was built, there were still some ocean runs that required sail because of the immense distances between coaling stations.

Boats for the Rivers, Lakes, and Coastal Trade

The oceangoing paddle-wheelers were made obsolete by the development of the screw propeller. Partly responsible for this breakthrough was John Ericsson, the Swedish-

American engineer who later designed the ironclad *Monitor,* which fought the historic standoff with the *Merrimack* in the Civil War. The propeller was developed in response to a British competition, in which Ericsson received part of the prize for his contribution to the solution. Working in this country with the Clyde Line in 1844, Ericsson first installed a propeller on the *John S. McKim.* The principle was sound, but it was many years before the efficiency of the screw propeller was fully recognized.

In 1842 more than 500 paddle-wheelers were plying the rivers of the West, but in the mid-1970's the famous *Delta Queen* was the only big stern-wheeler still in operation. (For more on the river boat, see pages 196–197 in "The American Knack of Getting There.")

One of the most successful steamboat routes was the water link between Boston and New York City via Fall River, Massachusetts. Started in 1847, the Fall River Line kept up its nightly schedules until the last trip of the *Commonwealth* in 1937. The 342-foot *Metropolis* made the 180-mile run on 60 tons of coal a night, averaging 20 knots—an amazing speed for the early 1850's. Among the most fondly remembered boats on this line was the *Priscilla,* "Queen of all steamboats" and the epitome of comfort and luxury in the early 1900's. The Fall River boats delivered finished cloth from the factories of New England to the garment center in New York and fresh seafood to Manhattan's Fulton Fish Market.

Two other famous steamers engaged in the coastal trade of that era were the Metropolitan Line's *Yale* and the *Harvard,* which also made overnight runs from Boston to New York. They were later chartered to a West coast line and kept a schedule from San Francisco to San Diego until World War I, when they were used to ferry troops across the English Channel. After the war both went back to the Pacific run until 1935, when the construction of improved highways finally ended coastal steamer travel. These ships survived as long as they did because they were stylish, comfortable, and steamed along at the respectable speed of 20 knots. Luxury and speed also accounted for the popularity of the big passenger boats that served the Great Lakes trade, but these, too, were at last outdated by rail and road travel.

Before World War I a few transports were built, and after the war they became the core of our merchant marine. One, the *President Harrison,* was converted to the passenger trade and became the first liner under the U.S. flag to keep a regular round-the-world schedule.

In 1936 Congress finally recognized the urgent need for Federal subsidy and passed the Merchant Marine Act to help shipbuilders and operators compete with the lower overheads of foreign competitors.

In World War II the British ordered that 60 Liberty Ships be built to a straightforward, well-tested English design; 30 were constructed on the east coast, the other 30 in west coast yards. This touched off the most productive era of American shipbuilding since the days of the whalers and clippers. As U.S. involvement in the war became imminent, we began to build for ourselves. More than 2,700 vessels—Liberty Ships and the larger Victory Ships—were turned out in a remarkable surge of production. Tankers and other merchantmen brought the total to more than 5,700 new ships in less than 4 years. By the end of World War II the U.S. had the world's

The S.S. "United States," *a magnificent passenger liner, was launched in 1952. She measured 990 feet from stem to stern, and 165,000-horsepower engines drove her at record-breaking speeds. But in an era of air travel at speeds faster than sound, an ocean crossing at 35 knots is hardly impressive nor, as was the case with the* United States, *which was retired in 1969, economically feasible.*

Exploring the Sea's Third Dimension

After Conquering Width and Breadth, Only the Depths Remain

The seas cover more than 70 percent of the world's surface, and only about 10 percent of the bottom of this underwater realm has been explored, mostly on the relatively shallow continental shelf. The vast deeps remain largely a mystery, although it is known that they are a potential treasure trove of oil and minerals.

The first step in plumbing the depths was taken near Bermuda in 1934 by William Beebe and Otis Barton. In Beebe's bathysphere (sphere of the deep) they descended to 3,028 feet, establishing a record that stood for 26 years. Then, in January 1960, a dive sponsored by the U.S. Navy set a record that may well stand forever. The dive was made in the *Trieste,* a bathyscaph (ship of the deep), designed by Swiss inventor Auguste Piccard. The two-man crew included Piccard's son Jacques and Navy Lt. Don Walsh. The site, 210 miles southwest of Guam, was the Mariana Trench, which at 35,800 feet is the deepest known place in all the oceans and more than a mile deeper than Mount Everest is high. It took 4 hours and 43 minutes for the *Trieste* to touch bottom. In the beam of their searchlight Piccard and Walsh saw a small flat fish swimming slowly by, proving for the first time that a living creature could withstand a pressure of 200,000 tons per square inch.

Undersea investigation continues, aided, in part, by the long-range capability of such nuclear-powered undersea craft as the *Nautilus.* The deepest secrets will ultimately be revealed and the sea may well become a major resource.

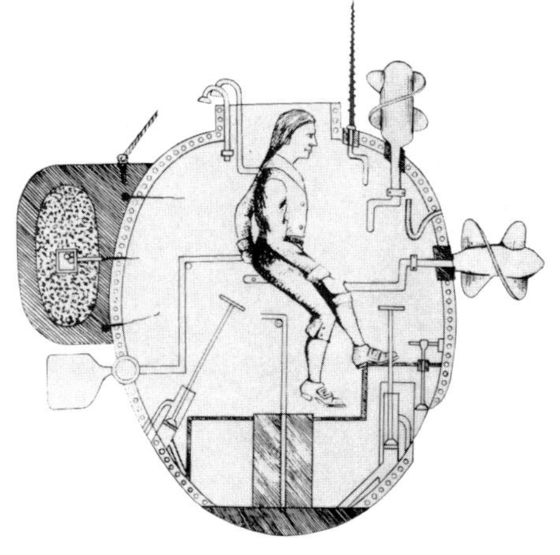

The first *American underwater craft was David Bushnell's* Turtle. *Of sound design, it failed only because the auger could not pierce the copper sheathing of the British warship* Eagle *in 1776 to attach a time bomb as planned.*

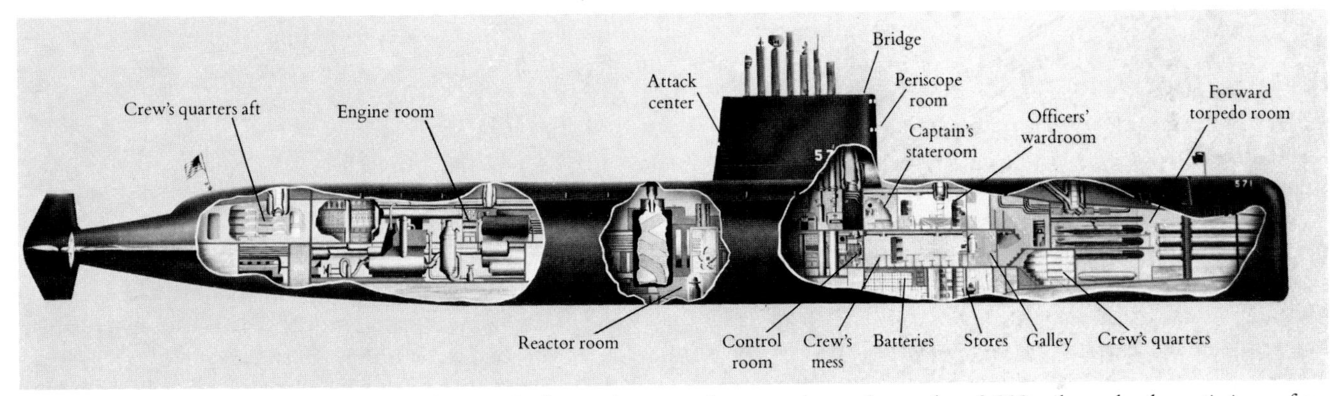

The "Nautilus," *launched in January 1954, was the first nuclear-powered vessel. In the shakedown cruise she ran 1,602 miles in 84 hours to break all records for speed and distance underwater. In 1957 the* Nautilus *ran submerged more than 2,000 miles under the arctic icecap from the Bering Strait to the Greenland Sea. Atomic energy is the perfect fuel for submarines because it requires no oxygen for combustion.*

largest merchant fleet, but the momentum was not sustained. From 1950 to 1965 many vessels were sold or taken out of service; by the 1970's our fleet had dropped to the seventh largest in the world in total tonnage.

Americans took the lead in promoting containerized shipping, starting in 1929 with the *Seatrain.* Freight cars could be rolled aboard a railed deck and rolled off onto railway tracks when the boat reached port. The further development of this concept resulted in standard-sized containers that fit interchangeably on ships, railway cars, trucks, and in some cases, airplanes.

A Last Proud Triumph

In 1952 Government subsidy plus outstanding American production skills culminated in the launching of an ocean liner with qualities unlikely to be surpassed. The S.S. *United States* was designed by William F. Gibbs and put together from component parts made by some 800 companies. She was smooth, fast, dependable, and comfortable, and, as the designer said, she was the prideful product of all American industry. On her maiden voyage in 1952 she logged an average speed of 35.59 knots (about 41 miles per hour). The crossing from Ambrose Light off New York to Bishop's Rock off Cornwall, England, was made in 3 days, 10 hours, 40 minutes. This run beat the record held by the *Queen Mary* by 10 hours, 2 minutes, and won again for America the transatlantic blue ribbon, which we had not held since the *Baltic*'s 1852 crossing.

Except for this triumph and the preeminence of our sporting boats, America has made few recent significant contributions to the history of nonmilitary ships and seamanship. The nuclear merchant ship *Savannah* failed to live up to expectations and her ultimate fate is in question. It is to be hoped that this ship will not be symbolic of our future maritime endeavors. If the American flag is to regain the prominence and prestige it once enjoyed on the high seas we must somehow rediscover that fortunate combination of talent, inspiration, and economic feasibility that created the great clipper ships, the whaling fleet, and the down easters.

Adapting to Warfare at Sea

Innovation and invention have been hallmarks of the American Navy since its birth in the Revolutionary War. Faced with the overwhelming power of the British fleet, the United States responded with a motley collection of converted merchantmen backed by a few frigates, and with the audacity of youth even raided the English in their home ports. In the following years what the American Navy lacked in size it often made up for in seamanship and the quality of its ships. The U.S.S. *Constitution,* for example, was perhaps as fine a frigate as ever plied the seas under sail. But if America often led in devising superior means of naval warfare—such as the ironclad, the submarine, and the aircraft carrier—other nations were frequently more foresighted in putting the innovations to use. In peacetime, Congress has hesitated to appropriate funds for major fleet improvements, and high Navy officers have occasionally resisted change. Thus the aircraft carrier and the submarine were important weapons in foreign arsenals before they gained acceptance in the United States. Yet in times of crisis the U.S. Navy has always overcome earlier neglect and made the changes necessary to emerge triumphant.

"Old Ironsides," 1797. With her bottom sheathed in copper furnished by Paul Revere and a hull of the strongest live oak, the frigate U.S.S. *Constitution* was a marvel of the shipwright's skill. In the War of 1812 she gave the infant United States several major victories including this triumph over the *Guerrière.* Because her hull proved to be almost impervious to cannonball, she was popularly dubbed "Old Ironsides."

The Battle of Ironclads, 1862. In an engagement that revolutionized naval warfare, the Union ironclad *Monitor,* looking like a cheesebox on a raft, according to one observer, exchanges fire with the ironsided Confederate *Merrimack.* Though no clear victor emerged from the battle, the encounter proved the superiority of iron-sheathed vessels. Soon navies around the world were scrapping their majestic wooden ships for ironclads.

A Workable Submarine, 1900. Though not the first undersea craft, John Holland's sub was the prototype for many navies. Measuring 53.3 feet, it employed a 45-horsepower internal combustion engine for surface operation and an electric motor for subsurface cruising. Its purchase by the U.S. Navy gave America a headstart in undersea warfare, but by World War I the Germans had the initiative.

The Seagoing Airstrip, 1911. The first landing aboard a ship, by stunt pilot Eugene Ely on the cruiser *Pennsylvania,* was described by the *Pennsylvania*'s captain as the "most important landing . . . since the dove flew back to the ark." Most Navy officers were less enthusiastic—the first carriers did not join the fleet until 1927—but in World War II sea-based airpower proved decisive.

Submarine Chaser, 1917. This speedy, 110-foot vessel was developed by the U.S. Navy to help Allied destroyers fight German U-boats during World War I. In World War II much more powerful destroyers—equipped with sonar for tracking down their prey and armed with depth charges, torpedoes, and guns—proved more than a match for enemy submarines and warships.

High-Speed Torpedo Boats, 1942. Hornets of the seaways, these World War II PT boats would dart among enemy ships to discharge their lethal stingers and speed off to safety. The designer of these boats was Andrew Higgins, who had long experience building speedy craft—some of which rumrunners used to good effect during the Prohibition era.

Nuclear Missile Submarines. Armed with atomic-tipped ballistic missiles that can be fired from beneath the sea's surface, each of the U.S. Navy's most modern undersea craft carries more potential destructive power than all of the bombs exploded in World War II. These nuclear-powered subs can cruise underwater for literally thousands of miles, an ability that would permit them to move secretly and silently to their action positions in case of war. The first atomic submarine, the U.S.S. *Nautilus,* was launched in 1954 after many years of debate about the feasibility of such craft. Shown here is the Ballistic Missile Submarine (SSBM) U.S.S. *John Marshall.* Craft of this type are now a first line of defense. They can cruise for months and launch missiles (far right) without surfacing.

Nuclear-Powered Frigate, 1961. The *Bainbridge* was the first nuclear-powered warship of her type. Her designation "frigate" harks back to the class of sailing ships such as the U.S.S. *Constitution* of War of 1812 fame. She is 550 feet long, and her turbines drive her at speeds in excess of 30 knots. The *Bainbridge,* really a superdestroyer, is larger than the light cruisers commissioned by the Navy during World War II. As an escort for other fleet units, this formidable vessel carries two twin Terrier surface-to-air guided missile launchers, four antiaircraft guns, and two triple torpedo launchers for antisubmarine warfare.

CHAPTER ELEVEN

The American Knack of Getting There

Americans are a restless people, always on the move a. eager to get where they are going as quickly and co veniently as possible. It was not until well after the Rev lution, however, with the need for opening up the lan to the West, that the Nation began to develop an integra system for transporting people and goods.

Interregional roads were the first components of such system. The concept of using Federal funds to build the was established in 1806 under President Jefferson, and t so-called National Road, which eventually linked Mar land with Illinois, was begun in 1811. This road help bring more business to Baltimore, to the detriment of Ne

Roads Before the Revolution

The old Boston Post Road was one of the earliest colonial routes. For decades it was nothing more than an ill-defined path that wandered vaguely through the empty countryside, vanishing wherever it met a stream or river. In 1704 Sarah Kemble Knight, an intrepid Boston schoolteacher, traveled the road on horseback, swimming her horse over water too deep to be forded, and ferrying across the river at Providence in a canoe. Traveling from dawn to dark, it took her 7 days to reach New York City, some 200 miles from Boston. A journey in winter would have been faster and easier; two-horse sleighs, called pungs (the one-horse variety was named a pod), glided smoothly over rocky New England trails that, in warmer seasons, were difficult for horses and almost impassable for carriages. But during the first half of the 18th century many country paths were widened, some were ribbed with logs to make "corduroy" roads; and regular ferry service was provided at major river crossings. Wagons, and soon stagecoaches, traveled the busiest routes—although no road was smooth enough to prevent the occasional overturn of some grand "Flying Machines," as the New York-Philadelphia stage was called. Despite the improvements, however, communication between New England and the Deep South took weeks rather than days.

"Man has always gone where he is able to go," said Michael Collins of the Apollo 11 team in explaining why he and his fellow astronauts dared to journey to the Moon. That ride in Apollo 11, which resulted in the first Moon landing in July 1969, took scarcely more courage than it had required some 350 years earlier to set out from England for North America. The voyage aboard crowded sailing ships—in conditions of almost unimaginable hardship and squalor—took from 6 to 8 weeks. And when immigrants arrived looking forward to the new opportunities and new freedom, they found danger and more hardship in a land devoid of any but the most elementary means of communication. The earliest newcomers and those who joined them in the next few decades clung to the coastal plain along the Atlantic.

For most of the first century of settlement, westward travel was limited to the winding Indian trails, which in a few places were widened to make primitive roads. Only the venturesome hunters and trappers pushed into the heavily forested mountains. On the water it was a different story; the rivers, inlets, and bays provided the easiest and safest means of transportation. Farmers floated their produce—wheat, corn, salted pork, logs, cotton, and tobacco—downriver to market on flatboats and rafts. Small sloops, ketches, bateaux, and log canoes carried people to church and on visits to neighbors or to market. Many New Englanders gave up cultivating their rocky lands and turned to the sea in sturdy fishing boats to harvest the haddock and cod. Merchants, traders, and passengers traveled between Boston, New York, Baltimore, and Charleston by boat. Although a water voyage usually involved many more miles than the same trip by land, most travelers preferred journeying by ship to risking the hazards of the road. Brigs, barks, schooners, and sloops, mostly built in New England, plied the lanes of commerce linking the New World with the Old.

rk City. The Empire State retaliated by building the ie Canal, connecting the Great Lakes with the Atlantic d establishing the Port of New York as a major trading iter. When the Erie was started in 1817, America had trained engineers, so the men who pushed the canal ough by 1825 had to teach themselves on the job. Ironi-'ly, several of them later helped build the transcontinental 'lroad, which in effect put the canals out of business. The 'lroad, finished in 1869, linked the two oceans and ified the continent.

Although Americans did not invent that mechanical irvel, the automobile, they made it their own by finding ways to improve it, mass-produce it, and sell it. Speed and movement soon became national obsessions.

The Wright brothers made their historic flight at Kitty Hawk, North Carolina, some 5 years before Henry Ford built his first Model T in 1908, but it took World Wars I and II to accelerate the evolution of the airplane. When all the technical challenges of travel on and around the Earth had been met, a new breed of traveler shot for the Moon, and made it. Next, spacecraft were sent to monitor the planets. But though time and distance have been conquered, solutions to the more difficult problems of safe, clean, comfortable travel still lie ahead.

Conestoga wagons and cattle drovers, *coaches and foot passengers all met at the roadside tavern. Here, the thirsty traveler could wash down the road dust and stay the night—sharing a dubiously clean bed with one or two others, or, if he were lucky, enjoying a "large and lofty apartment," and fine food and drink. Pictured is the Fairview Inn, or Three Mile House, a stopping place on the Frederick Road near Baltimore.*

The Slow Conversion to Wheels

Land travel increased slowly in the early 1700's. A horseback trip from New York to Boston took at least 7 days, and overnight accommodations ranged from the indifferent to the impossible. Most inns were little more than hovels—hot and dirty in the summer, cold and dirty in the winter. The food, often scarce, was usually coarse, greasy, and badly cooked.

As more Indian trails were widened into rough dirt or corduroy roads—the latter made of logs laid side by side—vehicles began to appear. The first conveyances for private travel were the chair, a graceful two-wheeled, two-passenger, one-horse cart, and the chaise, a more elegant two-wheeled carriage with a leather top and a body swung on leather braces to somewhat ease its bone-jarring ride. By the mid-1700's four- and six-horse carriages with coachmen or postilions and footmen were common among the prosperous Virginia planters.

Mail service was expanded from the Northern Colonies to Virginia in 1732, and when Benjamin Franklin became deputy postmaster general in 1753, he reestablished the weekly year-round service by post riders. By the time of the Revolutionary War, a network of dirt and corduroy roads had spread through the Northern Colonies, and north-south thoroughfares extended into Maryland, Virginia, the Carolinas, and Georgia.

The Prairie Schooner

This "Ship of the Plains" Took the Emigrants West

For the emigrants of the mid-19th century, the Great Plains were a challenge unlike anything they had known before. Family, food, and shelter had to be carried across many miles of open prairie. Unlike the previous denizens of the Plains—the Indians and mountain men who traveled light—these emigrants had literally to take their houses with them. And their houses were the wagons in which they moved, the far-famed prairie schooner.

A variant of the Conestoga wagon used for transport in the East, the prairie schooner was smaller, lighter, more maneuverable. Providing shelter and protection, its painted canvas covering was rain- and hail-proof. The wagon bed, about 10 feet by 4 feet, was large enough to hold a bit of furniture, perhaps even a feather bed; hanging off the edges of the wagon were a variety of essentials: A toolbox on the front, a feed trough at the back, a water bucket, a tar pot, which contained tar or tallow for greasing the axles, and an assortment of other needed bits and pieces. Three to six yoke of oxen or four to six mules pulled each wagon. Horses did not fare well on the Great Plains. The optimum loading weight was three-quarters of a ton; too heavy a load could mire a vehicle, and the trails were littered with stoves, trunks, and furniture jettisoned to lighten a load.

The safest way to make the hazardous journey was as part of a wagon train. A large company meant greater safety from Indian attack and more hands available in case of emergency. Aside from a guide, usually a mountain man, an experienced plainsman often was engaged as expedition "captain," and he ran his wagon train like a military company: Guards were appointed, hunting details sent out for game or to give advance warning of Indians. At night, or when the Indians attacked, the wagons were driven into a circle with the front wheel of one wagon locked into the back wheel of its neighbor to form a rigid defense barrier. The indispensable animals and the women and children took shelter inside and guards were posted.

Diseases, such as cholera, mountain fever, and dysentery, were perhaps the worst dangers. In 1850, the peak migration year, a cholera epidemic killed thousands until the emigrants reached the cold air of the Rocky Mountains. The Indians and the natural hazards of the Plains and mountains—drought, hunger, tornadoes, blizzards, floods, heat—also took their toll. In all it is estimated that for each of the 2,000 miles of Plains and mountains between the Missouri River and the coastal lands of the Pacific, some 17 people perished—in all, about 34,000 died on the trail to a better way of life.

With the development of roads, as bad as they were, came the growth of stagecoach and wagon transportation. The first regular stage line between New York and Philadelphia began operating on March 8, 1759. Passengers seated on hard benches in a springless wagon bounced over rutted roads for 18 to 19 hours a day. About 10 p.m. they put up at an inn or ordinary, slept fully clothed on cornhusk or straw mattresses, and arose at 3 a.m. the next morning, bleary-eyed and in winter half frozen, to resume the jolting journey. The 90-mile trip took 3 days. Small wonder that when the First Continental Congress convened in 1774 the delegates were for the most part acquainted with their colleagues and their problems and grievances only through correspondence.

The all-purpose vehicle for handling overland freight was the Conestoga wagon, which was developed by Germans in Pennsylvania's Conestoga Valley. Before the canals and railroads were built, the Conestogas in caravans of 10 to 12 did most of the heavy freight hauling.

On the eve of the Revolutionary War, the Transylvania Land Company hired Daniel Boone and his party to open the Wilderness Trail through the Cumberland Gap into Kentucky. It was, indeed, a trail suited only to hikers and horsemen. Not until 1796 was it widened to permit the passage of wagons. Farther north, on the Braddock and Forbes Roads, which had been hacked through the mountains during the French and Indian War, the heavy Conestogas carried freight and settlers into western Pennsylvania. A big boost to transportation came in 1795 with the completion of the famous Lancaster Pike from Philadelphia to Lancaster. This excellent 62-mile crushed-stone road was privately built and was the first profitable toll road in the Nation, with a tollgate (a long pike across the road) every 7 miles. Its success started a rush of turnpike building in the Northern and Eastern States, and by 1807 New York State alone had 900 miles of toll roads owned by 67 different companies.

As settlers continued to push west, Secretary of the Treasury Albert Gallatin persuaded President Thomas Jefferson and Congress to appropriate money for a public highway from the Atlantic seaboard to the Ohio Valley. Construction of the National (or Cumberland) Road, from the head of navigation on the Potomac River at Cumberland, Maryland, to Wheeling, Virginia (now West Virginia), on the Ohio River, began in 1811. (By 1840 it had reached Vandalia, Illinois.) Regular stagecoach travel was soon established. From dawn to dusk the road was crowded with droves of horses, cattle, sheep, and swine and with Conestoga wagons, mostly headed west and loaded with families and freight. When the wagons reached the Ohio River, many families built or bought boats or rafts on which they floated downstream to look for homes in Indiana and Illinois.

New Waterways Dug by Hand

The burgeoning traffic on the National Road brought prosperity to Baltimore, while New York City lost ground in trade and industry. But New York merchants, prodded by Mayor DeWitt Clinton, were mulling over a project that would in time make their city the leading commercial center in the country by tapping the rich trade of the new States in the Old Northwest Territory. Clinton's plan was to connect the Great Lakes and the Hudson River by a canal running 363 miles across the State from Buffalo on Lake Erie to Albany on the Hudson. As early as 1777 the far-sighted Gouverneur Morris, later to serve at the Constitutional Convention, had proposed a waterway from the Hudson to Lake Erie, which would be the longest canal in the world. The engineering problems involved in lifting barges nearly 600 feet above sea level by means of locks between the Hudson and Lake Erie seemed beyond the ability of the untrained engineers of the day. Far more modest canal projects had already failed. The $27\frac{1}{2}$-mile Middlesex Canal from Boston to the Merrimack River was the longest in the country up to then, and its operators were deeply in debt. The Patowmack Company, formed in 1785 with George Washington as president, had planned to dig a canal from the vicinity of what is now Washington, D.C., across the Appalachian barrier to the Ohio River, but ran out of money after completing a bypass around the worst rapids of the Potomac River. Against this background the Erie Canal proposal seemed ridiculously visionary. President Thomas Jefferson, still hopeful that the Potomac canal could be completed, brusquely dismissed New Yorkers seeking aid for the Erie: "It is a splendid project," he said, "and may be executed a century hence. It is little short of madness to think of it at this day!"

The Concord Coach and the Overland Express

Manufactured in the quiet New England town of Concord, New Hampshire, the world-renowned Concord Coach became a symbol of the Wild West in the period after the Civil War. Its tough, durable body, and a suspension system of leather straps (or thorough braces) that could handle the hard jolts from rutted roads, made the Concord the ideal coach for wild country. They were also visually splendid: ". . . the bodies red, and the running part yellow. Each door has a handsome picture, mostly landscapes, and no two . . . are alike," wrote a newspaperman in 1868, describing a railroad shipment of 30 coaches destined for Wells, Fargo and Company.

Wells, Fargo was founded in 1852 to provide mail and banking services for the gold camps of California, and by the 1870's it had won a monopoly of the express business west of the Mississippi. A Wells, Fargo Concord carried 9 to 14 people, plus baggage and mail, and a long trip in one was hardly luxurious. "Passengers becoming crazy with whiskey, mixed with want of sleep, are often obliged to be strapped to their seats; their meals, dispatched during their ten-minute halts, are simply abominable, the heats are excessive, the climate malarious; lamps may not be used at night for fear of . . . Indians; briefly there is no end to this Via Mala's miseries," wrote a disillusioned passenger. But the stagecoaches were the fastest means of travel in much of the Far West. Describing an 1865 trip, a journalist wrote: "One route of eight miles we traveled in 30 minutes! . . . We spent only 72 hours upon the 575 miles of desert road between Salt Lake and Virginia, Nevada. . . ."

Concords traveled rough country everywhere; they could even be seen jouncing on South African and Australian roads. But perhaps the most famous Concord was the incredibly durable Deadwood Stage, which traveled the long route from Cheyenne, Wyoming, to Deadwood, South Dakota, fighting off attacking Sioux and marauding highwaymen all the way, and creating a legend—even longer lived than the coach itself—of courageous drivers and the sharp-eyed men who "rode shotgun" beside them, ready to fend off all attackers.

Rivers and Canals: 1850
They United a Growing Nation

Less than 10 years after its completion, the Erie Canal had proven a glorious success. Cities within the canal's perimeter flourished beyond their founders' wildest dreams. New York City became the Nation's chief port, and shipping costs shrank to a fraction of precanal rates: On the Albany–Buffalo run, for instance, goods that had cost $100 per ton to ship via wagon were only $12 per ton on a canal barge. Investors now flocked to put their money into new canals: The Chesapeake and Ohio, paralleling the Potomac River; the Ohio and Erie, linking Lake Erie with the Ohio River; and almost 1,000 miles of canal in Pennsylvania alone. In the decade 1830–40 a total of 3,300 miles of new canal were built. The succeeding decade added another 3,600 miles. Ironically, despite the wealth these canals helped create, many investors were never repaid; States often repudiated their canal debts, particularly in the depression of 1837–43. With the rise of the railroads in the mid-19th century, the great canal building era ended.

Roadbuilding never rivaled canal construction during those early years. Aside from the short stretches of privately built turnpike (some 300 such roads had been built by 1810), there was only the great, federally financed National Road (begun in 1811), which by 1840 stretched west from Maryland to Illinois; a few more-or-less passable intercity roads; and a tangled remainder of wagon routes, dusty trails, and obscure pathways. By 1840 roadbuilding had virtually come to a halt—to be resumed only with the coming of the automobile, some 70 years later.

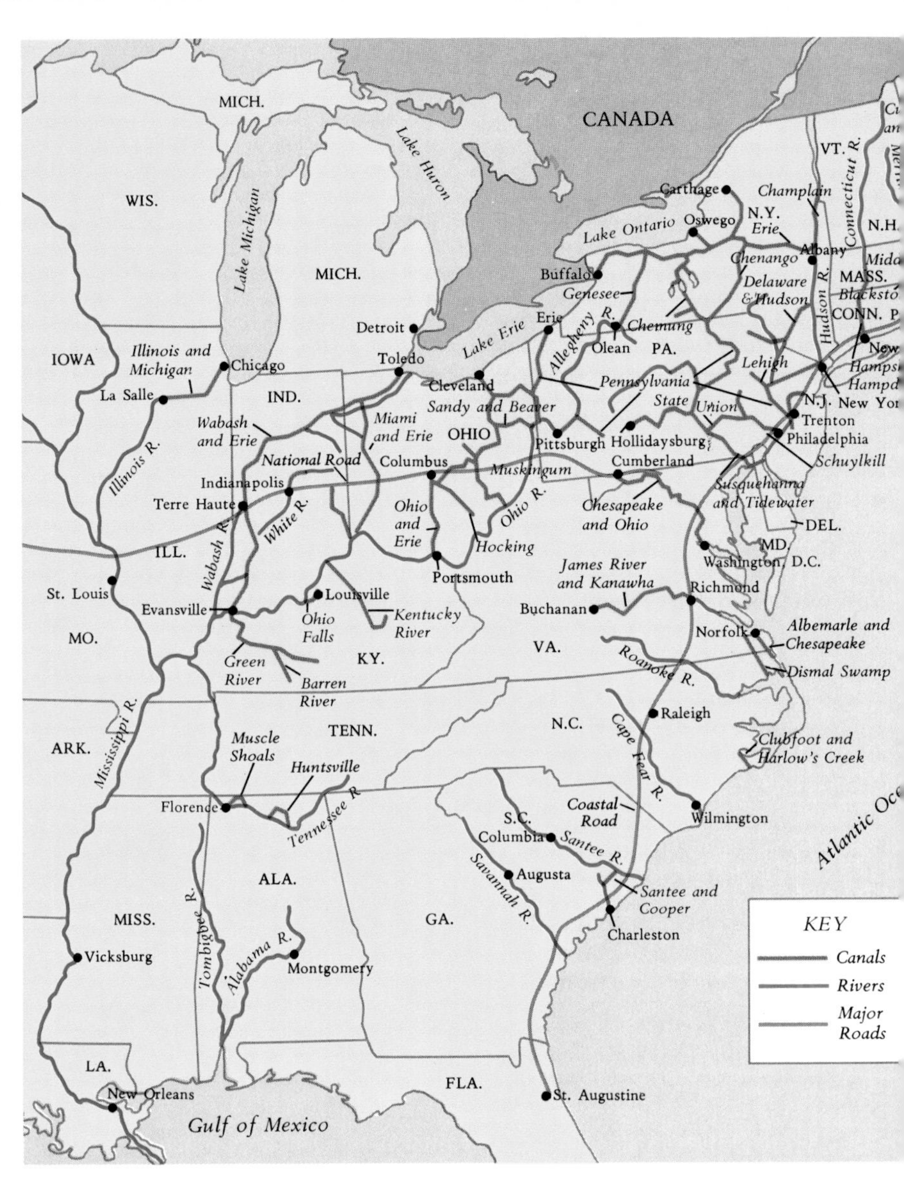

Madness or not, Clinton, who became a canal commissioner in 1810, mobilized support for the Erie among villagers along the proposed route of the canal and among New York merchants who were looking westward for new markets. In 1817 Clinton was elected Governor of New York on a build-the-canal platform, and work soon began at Rome, New York, on "Clinton's Ditch," as it was derisively called at the time.

The canal was 4 feet deep and 40 feet wide at the surface, sloping to a width of 28 feet at the bottom. A 10-foot towpath for the draft horses and mules that pulled the barges and boats flanked the canal for its full length of 363 miles. Eighty-three locks were required to raise and lower the boats a total distance of 688 feet. To build a canal of these dimensions was an astonishing achievement at the time even for experienced engineers.

As they stepped off the ships that brought them to America, Irish immigrants were recruited to work on the canal. They augmented the crews of lumberjacks who felled the trees, the pick-and-shovel men, and the cooks who prepared their food. Engineers improvised their machines on the job. One of the most ingenious consisted of a 30-foot axle with three huge wheels—a wheel 16 feet in diameter at either end and a 14-foot wheel in the center. This contraption straddled even the biggest tree stumps. A team of horses tugged a rope around the middle wheel, which turned the axle and wound up a chain fastened to the stump. In this manner 7 men and 2 horses could uproot 30 to 40 outsized stumps in a single day.

Nothing stopped the builders. They braved malaria in the swamplands. To cross deep valleys, they extended the canal overhead on great stone piers. No such elaborate aqueducts had been constructed since Roman times. At Lockport, Nathan S. Roberts, a self-taught engineer, devised a double set of five locks, cut through solid rock, to carry the canal up over cliffs and on to Buffalo.

To open the canal in 1825, a flotilla of five gloriously decorated boats left Buffalo with Governor Clinton and

Waiting their turn for the locks *(the small gateways at the center of the picture), boatmen and passengers relax in the canal at West Troy. The boats idling in the sunshine are typical of the craft that plied the canal: Long, flat barges that could haul quantities of lumber or grain; "lineboats," in which whole families, as well as their livestock, could live as they traveled; and the larger, more elegant "packet" boats, which carried passengers, fed them sumptuously, and bedded them down at night in narrow berths stacked three and four high inside the cabin. Packet boats used the best horses and made the best speed of any on the canal—sometimes 6 or 7 miles per hour. Canalboats coming from New York, where most of the passenger traffic originated, were towed by Hudson River steamers up to Albany. There, where the canal began, horses supplied the motive power, and the leisurely journey began.*

An emigrant barge *is working its way upstream on the Ohio River. Westward-moving families from the South often traveled by flatboat on the Ohio, which took them to the canals linking Cleveland and Toledo on Lake Erie with Cincinnati and points west.*

other dignitaries aboard. Nine days later they entered the Hudson River. In New York Harbor, crowded with ships of many nations, Governor Clinton dumped two kegfuls of Lake Erie into the Atlantic to symbolize the wedding of inland and ocean waters.

The Erie Canal was also a commercial triumph. Millions of tons of cargo and hundreds of thousands of emigrants moved inland, while grain and produce flowed back to the east coast. Passenger travel on the packet boats was faster and more comfortable than by road, although novelist Charles Dickens compared the four-tiered sleeping berths to library shelves. Travelers sunning themselves on the flat roof of the cabin had to watch out for the low bridges that crossed the canal at frequent intervals. Repeatedly the warning came from the steersman, "Low bridge! Everybody down!"

The success of the Erie launched a countrywide canal craze. The Pennsylvania system combined waterways, horse-drawn railways, and cable cars to cross the Alleghenies from Philadelphia to Pittsburgh. To make the steep half-mile ascent between Hollidaysburg and Johnstown, engineers built the Allegheny Portage Railroad. Cars rolling on iron-capped wooden rails were hauled up a series of five slopes by engine power. Rope was used on the winches until wire cable became available. Horses pulled the cars on the level sections between the slopes. The Portage Railroad was an engineering marvel that attracted tourists from all over the world.

Eleven more States soon joined the frenzy of construction that linked the Atlantic Ocean, the Great Lakes, the Mississippi River, and their tributary rivers into one great waterway. The canals brought expansion and undreamed-of prosperity to the Nation for many years. Not until the late 1860's did canal traffic start to dwindle in the face of the superior efficiency of the railroads.

Before the development of canal travel the rivers had teemed with boats, but sails, oars, poles, and towlines made only painfully slow progress upstream or into the wind. Dozens of inventors tried their hands at propelling a boat with steam. First to succeed commercially was Robert Fulton with his 133-foot *Clermont,* launched on the Hudson in 1807. Within 20 years steamers were plying all coastal waters and navigable rivers.

But it was on the Mississippi, queen of rivers, that steamboating reached its zenith. In 1811 Nicholas Roosevelt built the steamboat *New Orleans* in Pittsburgh and descended the Ohio and Mississippi Rivers from Pittsburgh to New Orleans in 14 days. A few years later Capt. Henry M. Shreve built the first shallow-hulled riverboat with boilers and engine on the main deck instead of below the waterline. "It could float on a heavy dew," one observer said. Ideal for the shallows and rapids of the Western rivers, Shreve's *Washington* became the prototype of nearly 1,000 side-wheelers and stern-wheelers on the Mississippi and its tributaries.

For a century the riverboats flourished, firing the imagination with their gilded salons, their decks packed to the funnels with cotton bales, their colorful and often unscrupulous gamblers, their occasional terrible wrecks, fires, and collisions, and their spectacular races—particularly the celebrated contest between the *Robert E. Lee* and the *Natchez* in 1870. Now they are all gone save for an occasional nostalgic survivor that gives tourists a brief opportunity to recapture the past.

Side-wheeler steamboats *round a bend on the Mississippi. Atop the decks is the pagodalike pilothouse where, alert against the ever-changing perils of the river, the pilot guided his flat-bottomed craft through the tangles of tree snags, whirlpools, rapids, sandbars, and shallows. Mark Twain, once a riverboat pilot himself, said that he had to "learn [the river] all over again in a different way every twenty four hours."*

The Iron Horse Comes To Stay

Canal and stagecoach operators spread dire tales about those newfangled railroads that were beginning to carry passengers and freight in England early in the 19th century. They spoke darkly of boiler explosions, derailments, and devastating fires set by sparks. But that hardly mattered to the Baltimore merchants who needed a way across the mountains to compete with the Erie Canal.

They got a charter for one of the first railroads, the Baltimore & Ohio, in 1827, and used horse-drawn cars on the tracks. In 1830 inventor Peter Cooper demonstrated the steam locomotive *Tom Thumb,* dubbed a "teakettle on a truck," on the B & O tracks. A few months earlier another steam engine, *The Best Friend of Charleston,* had made a pioneer run for the South Carolina Canal and Railroad Co. Extending its line south and west, the B & O reached Washington, D.C., in 1835; Cumberland, Maryland, in 1842; and the Ohio River in 1852. Other railroad companies quickly entered the field—the Pennsylvania Railroad linked Pittsburgh with the Atlantic coast, and the New York Central—formed by merging several small lines—operated between New York City and Buffalo. By 1857 passengers could travel by rail from the Atlantic coast to St. Louis, making only five changes on the way. In 1860 there were 30,000 miles of track and Chicago had become a leading rail center.

The Fabulous Steamboat Era
The Mississippi Was the Nation's Great Highway

At the height of the steamboat era, the tonnage on inland American waters was greater than that carried by the entire British merchant marine. An unending stream of shipping moved over the Missouri and Ohio Rivers and onto the Mississippi. The cities along the major routes were thriving centers of commerce. New Orleans, especially, grew so prosperous that by the 1840's it had become the second ranking port in the Nation. The traffic on the rivers varied, from magnificent side-wheeler passenger steamboats, to sturdy stern-wheelers (used mainly for pushing barges), to man-powered flatboats and keelboats that threaded through the shallower waters. Carrying an encyclopedic assortment of goods and human cargo, steamboats had, even before the Civil War, navigated more than 40 tributaries of the Mississippi, and made possible the opening up of a vast new area for settlement.

Steamboat gamblers *were a fixture on the river. Some made a good living from their skill alone, but many cheated. And major riverboat landings became famous for the large number of cardsharps they harbored. When Vicksburg, Mississippi, drummed its gamblers out of town in 1835, they all shipped downriver to the neighboring city of Natchez.*

The main cabin *of the steamboat* Grand Republic *was a study in ostentation: Acres of rich carpeting, carved paneling, and scrollwork surrounded a forest of cushioned chairs. The bill of fare was equally elaborate. Ten-course dinners were standard—and the diners were expected to consume them in toto. All cabin passengers sat together at mealtimes; otherwise the ladies kept to their own quarters. As an English lady traveler noted, although the men "do not scruple to chew tobacco and to spit . . . in the presence of women, they generally prefer drinking and gaming in their absence." Poker games and whittling passed the time—although whittling the woodwork was forbidden.*

With its cowcatcher *and its "balloon" smokestack, a midcentury steam engine chugs cross-country. Its coaches had adjustable seats and sleeping cars had berths. Until dining cars were added in the 1870's, hungry passengers had to rush the depot lunchroom for a quick snack.*

While the railroads were pushing to the Mississippi and Missouri Rivers, wagon trails were probing the wilderness area hundreds of miles to the west. Mountain men and Government explorers had marked the way for the Oregon Trail from Independence, Missouri, to Portland and Fort Vancouver, Oregon. In the 1840's this trail was deeply rutted by the prairie schooners—descendants of the heavy old Conestoga wagons. The prairie schooners, usually pulled by three to six yoke of oxen, were rolling homes for the pioneers; in case of Indian attacks they were arranged in a tight circle and served as a temporary fort. The trip west took from 4 to 6 months. Thousands of people died on the way—victims of Indians, disease, desert heat, and blizzards. After the discovery of gold in California in 1848, thousands of gold seekers took the California Trail turnoff from the Oregon Trail at Fort Hall in Idaho. They headed southwestward through Nevada and crossed the towering Sierra Nevada into California. Other trails that contributed to the romance and excitement of the era included the Mormon Trail from Nauvoo, Illinois, to the Great Salt Lake in Utah; the Santa Fe Trail from Independence to Santa Fe, New Mexico; and the Old Spanish Trail, established by Spanish monks, from Santa Fe to Los Angeles, California.

Development of the Locomotive *From Steam to Turbopower*

The powerful iron horse that thundered over the Great Plains could be traced back to tiny engines like the *DeWitt Clinton,* built in 1831 for the 17-mile Mohawk & Hudson Railroad. The passengers on this pioneer line sat in open cars resembling stagecoaches just behind the engine—bathed in black smoke and menaced by sparks from the smokestack. Although such engines performed yeoman service on short hauls, they were too heavy for the slender rails and too small to haul sizable loads. Later engines distributed the weight via several sets of wheels, with the front wheel-pairs mounted on swivels to ease the bulky machines around bends in the road. With the incorporation of the boiler into the body of the engine, the engine became more efficient and less dangerous in case of an explosion, and the steam locomotive began to assume a more modern shape. (The numbers under each

1831 *DeWitt Clinton* 0-4-0 steam

1836 *George Washington* 4-2-0 steam

1839 *Gowan & Marx* 4-4-0 steam

1867 *J. B. Turner* 4-4-0 steam

1889 No. 796 4-6-2 steam

1923 No. 3450 4-6-4 steam

As the mining camps in California increased in number, express companies—including Adams and Company and Wells, Fargo and Company—were organized to carry mail, gold dust, and other valuables. The stagecoach business also prospered with the inauguration between 1858 and 1861 of a semiweekly passenger and mail service from St. Louis to Portland by way of El Paso, Texas, and San Francisco. This 3,600-mile journey by Concord Coach took a month—more if there was an Indian attack or a herd of a million buffalo to avoid. For a brief 18-month period between April 1860 and October 1861, an undying legend of courage and endurance was created by the Pony Express riders. Racing through Nebraska, Wyoming, Utah, and Nevada, these horsemen carried letters written on lightweight paper (postage ranged from $2 to $10 an ounce) from one relay station to another. They covered the 1,966 miles from St. Joseph, Missouri, to Sacramento, California, in 11 days. The nature of the work is implied in the newspaper advertisements seeking riders who weighed less than 135 pounds, did not drink or carouse, and were "daring young men—preferably orphans." Completion of the overland telegraph in late 1861 put the Pony Express out of business.

Despite the progress made by the express and stage lines in providing passenger and mail service, farseeing men insisted that a transcontinental railroad was needed to provide quick and dependable transportation between the East and the Pacific coast. During the Civil War railroads proved invaluable to the Union cause. The North, with more than 3 miles of track for every mile in the South, had a great advantage in moving supplies and men toward the areas of attack. Gen. William T. Sherman contended that his decisive campaign against Atlanta, Georgia, would have been "impossible without the railroads." And it was during this conflict that the transcontinental railroad won the support of doubters who came to look

The transcontinental railroad *was completed on May 10, 1869. At Promontory, Utah, the Union Pacific's west-running tracks met the rails built eastward by the Central Pacific; and amidst cheers and acclamation, the two lines were joined by a golden spike.*

upon it as a military and political necessity—a link between the East and gold-rich California and the other States and Territories in the Far West. In 1862 Congress passed the Pacific Railroad Bill (amended in 1864), providing loans and land grants to the Government-created Union Pacific (UP) and the California-chartered Central Pacific (CP). The UP, building west out of Omaha, Nebraska, and the CP, building east out of Sacramento, laid 1,776 miles of rails without the aid of bulldozers, pneumatic drills, or computers. Grading crews using picks and shovels and plows and scrapers drawn by horses leveled the roadbed and dropped ties, 5 to the rail length. Then 10 "ironmen," 5 to each 700-pound rail (the CP rail weighed 500 pounds), pulled the iron from a wagon and dropped it onto the ties. Spikers and clampers quickly

engine define the engine type, indicating, reading front to back, the number of wheels in each wheel set.) Today, the more efficient electric, the diesel-electric, and the new, superfast turbine-powered trains have almost entirely replaced the steam engine. Only a few survive on tourist lines, in train museums, or as park exhibits for the nostalgic parents of children who have never heard the sweet, sad sound of a train whistle.

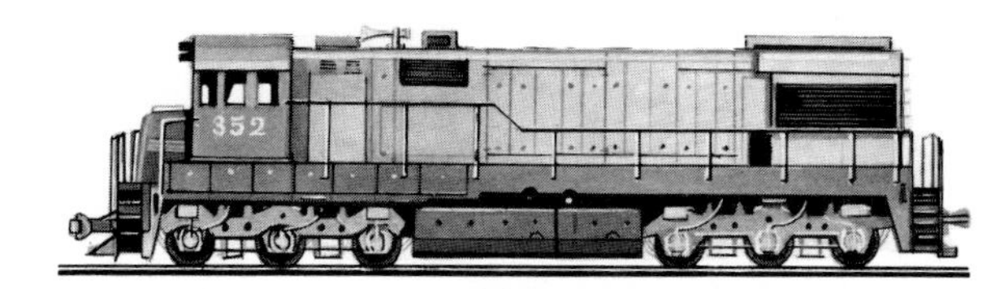

1966
U-28
2,800-hp diesel-electric

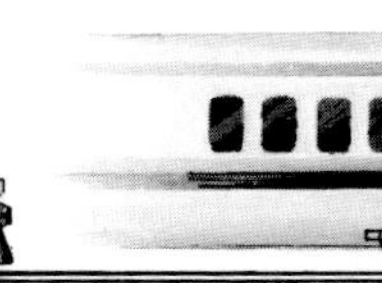

1949
F-7
1,500-hp diesel-electric

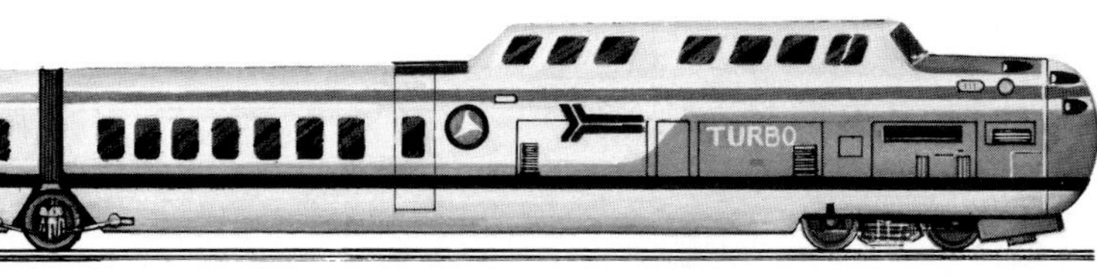

1969
Turbo Train
2,000-hp gas turbine

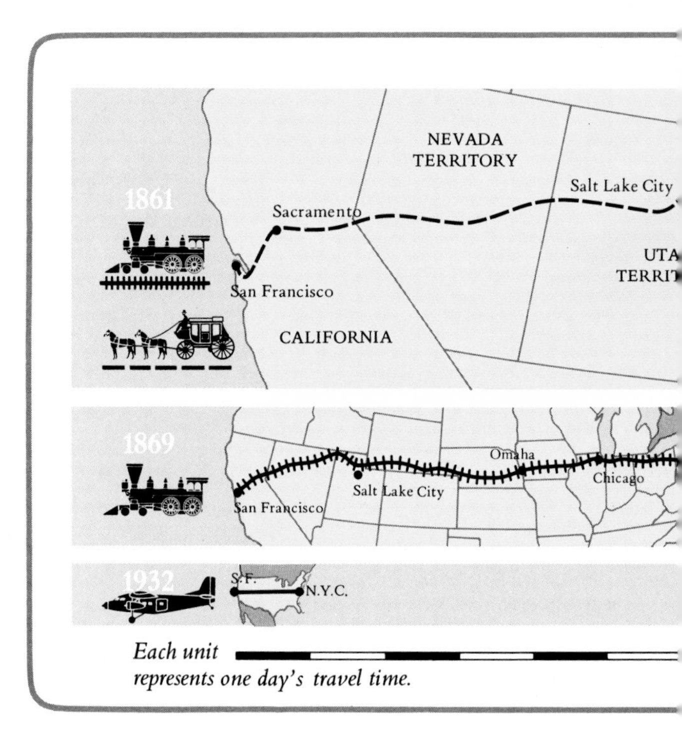

fastened it into place—taking only 30 seconds to fasten each pair of rails, 2 rail lengths to the minute. They struck 3 blows to each spike, and there were 10 spikes to the rail, and 400 rails—or 4,000 spikes and 12,000 blows—to the mile. Seldom was less than a mile of track laid in a day, and often 5 or more miles were laid. In the Sierra Nevada, the CP's patient, tireless Chinese laborers chipped their way through granite at the rate of 7 inches a day, then used gunpowder and later nitroglycerin to blast out 15 tunnels.

Since Government loans and land grants were based on the miles of track laid, the UP and CP engaged in a bitter race across deserts and through mountains. Finally, on May 10, 1869, the two roads met at an agreed point, and a golden spike was driven into a tie, signaling the completion of the transcontinental line. This road cut the travel time between the East and West to days instead of weeks. It linked the agriculture, commerce, and industry of the two coasts and opened the Great Plains of the West to settlement. It also set off the great boom in railroad building, which saw the construction of four more transcontinental lines in the next 25 years. This boom led to fierce financial struggles as rail tycoons Jay Gould, Cornelius Vanderbilt, Collis P. Huntington, Leland Stanford, Edward H. Harriman, J. P. Morgan, and James J. Hill fought to control huge railroad empires. When Harriman challenged Hill and Morgan for control of a rail line into Chicago, the resulting financial manipulations brought on a panic in the stock market in 1901.

Despite the financial turmoil churned up by the battling tycoons, railroads entered their grandest era. Such inventions as automatic couplers, telegraphic dispatch, and airbrakes enhanced the safety of rail travel, and comfort improved with every decade. At first cars were heated in winter by a stove in each coach. After 1890 steam heat from the locomotive circulated through the train. In the first sleeping cars, wooden bunks were triple-stacked. The passengers' coats were the only bed coverings. But in 1864 George Pullman built a remarkable new kind of car with sliding seats, better heating, and upper berths that folded into the ceiling in daytime. Called the *Pioneer* and decorated with carved woodwork, carpets, and mirrors, the car had a price tag of $20,000—four times the cost of any previous car—but thousands of Pullman's sleepers were ordered, and many generations of Americans delighted in the process of bedding down in an upper or lower berth or in a gadget-laden bedroom or roomette. They also enjoyed eating in the dining cars after Fred Harvey, a Kansas restaurant man, introduced the custom of serving meals on the Atchison, Topeka & Santa Fe Railroad.

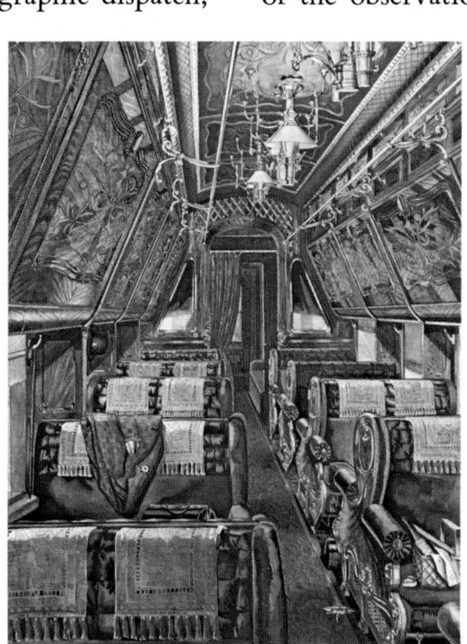
An early Pullman car *offered every comfort—plush upholstery, clean sheets, commodious washrooms. With the addition of dining cars, journeys by train became luxurious experiences.*

For the very rich, for opera and theater stars, and for Presidents, there were private railroad cars—elegant palaces on wheels—that were inlaid, filigreed, brocaded, tufted, gilded, and equipped with private kitchens and dining salons of unbelievable luxury. In Presidential elections the campaign train became an important tradition as millions of Americans flocked to the tracks in cities, towns, and whistle-stop hamlets to get a personal glimpse of a candidate speaking from the rear platform of the observation car. Harry S. Truman was the last president to campaign actively by rail. President Dwight D. Eisenhower, Truman's successor, rarely used the private Presidential car, the *Ferdinand Magellan,* and it was retired in 1959. The *Magellan,* an old Pullman private car, had been rebuilt for President Franklin D. Roosevelt during World War II with armor-plated sides and 3-inch-thick bulletproof windows.

Although railroad equipment was constantly being improved, for all their innovations—their clean, efficient diesel locomotives, their streamlined cars, and computerized scheduling—the railroads finally had to give way to the automobile, the truck, and the airplane. Track mileage dropped from a peak of some 254,000 in 1916 to 205,000 in 1970. At one time 65,000 steam locomotives thundered and screeched across America;

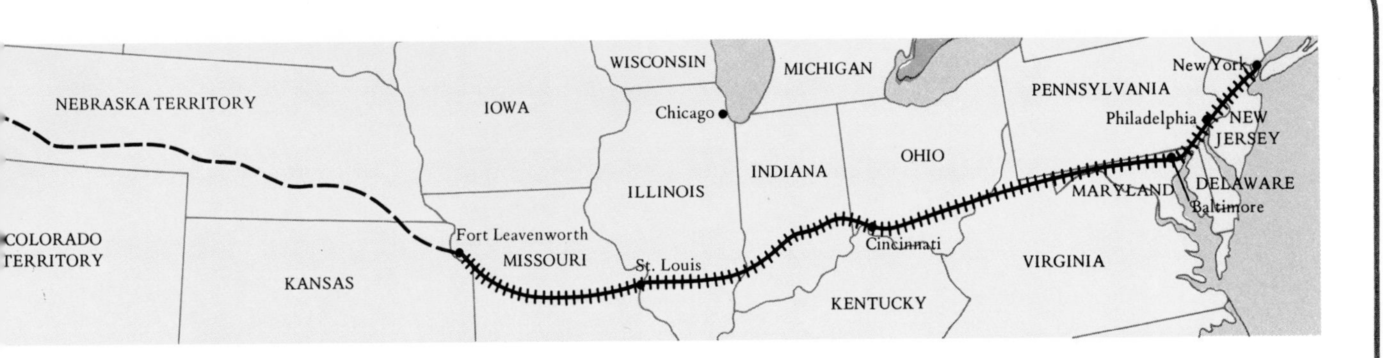

Making a Large Continent Seem Small— *Reducing the Time It Takes To Cross*

In 1861, when it was first possible to buy rail and stagecoach tickets and go straight through from coast to coast on public transportation, the continent could be crossed in 26 days—if there were no storms, floods, breakdowns, Indian attacks, or holdups. Before that time every traveler had been on his own, and the trip often took months. The next reduction in the size of the continent, in terms of travel time, was in 1869, with the completion of the transcontinental railroad. The fare was $190; several train changes were required. The first commercial air flights, made in the early 1930's, took 24 hours; today they take about 5 hours.

today there are only a few hundred such locomotives in existence, most of them exhibited in parks and museums like dinosaur bones. Monumental depots and terminals crumbled or were turned into schools or restaurants. In the early 1970's railroads carried less than 1 percent of the intercity passengers and less than 40 percent of the Nation's freight and miles of steel rails needed replacing. Compared to the heyday of the railroads, the decline in traffic and in earnings has been catastrophic.

It seems hard to believe that in 1934 the country was excited because a Union Pacific diesel train raced from Los Angeles to New York in 56 hours and 55 minutes, making all regular stops in its 3,258-mile trip. That was almost a mile a minute—hardly a stunning figure in the age of superjets. In the 1970's Amtrak, a Federal agency operating 1,500 passenger trains a week to more than 400 cities, tried to re-create the fun of rail travel and reestablish its reputation for efficient service to encourage people to travel by train again. Amtrak's glass-roofed observation cars were popular in the West, and its speedy Metroliner was well patronized on the heavily traveled New York to Washington corridor. Some families discovered the joy of loading their automobiles onto flatcars and relaxing on southbound trains en route to Florida.

As a result of the energy crisis, the Nation's ailing railroads took on a new importance. Many recalled the heyday of steam with wistful regret and cited the efficiency of some foreign railroads. Henry David Thoreau's

Urban Transit

In an effort to reverse the present, almost total reliance on automobiles, many municipalities are grappling with the need for improved mass transit—a need that is painfully evident in the car-clogged, pollution-blighted streets of America's cities. San Francisco's Bay Area Rapid Transit (BART) system may prove to be the prototype of future urban transportation. The 75-mile system links San Francisco, the city of Oakland across the bay, and the suburbs through high-speed, sway-free trains that travel at 80 miles an hour over a network of elevated and underground tracks. Each station was carefully designed to fit into the neighborhood around it. BART is completely computerized, down to its ticketing machines; the trains run without operators, guided by a computer control center that determines the position and speed of every train at every moment. Despite the comfort and service it offers, BART has been plagued with a high breakdown rate and runs a very limited schedule. Like other, less ambitious urban transit systems, BART has yet to prove itself as a replacement for the automobile.

poetic description once again stirred hearts: ". . . I hear the iron horse make the hills echo with his snort like thunder, shaking the earth with his feet, and breathing fire and smoke from his nostrils. . . ."

A Machine To Match Our Wanderlust

As the 19th century drew to a close, self-taught mechanics in bicycle repair shops, buggy works, and machinery barns around the country were busily experimenting with new ways to drive wheels by power. Trains and steamships took care of long journeys and cross-country freight, but people were beginning to think about improvement of individual, everyday travel.

In 1893 two brothers, Charles E. and J. Frank Duryea of Springfield, Massachusetts, fitted a single-cycle, four-horsepower gasoline motor to a secondhand buggy they had bought for $70. "It ran no faster than an old man could walk," Charles Duryea said later, "but it did run." They were the first of many Americans to make a successful car. In 1896 the Duryeas sold a dozen of their roofless motor buggies, with their wooden wheels, tufted seats for two, and brass kerosene headlamps. Although the brothers soon went their separate ways, they were both involved in the automobile business well into the 1900's.

The merry Oldsmobile, *circa 1902, mired in mud. The first car to be produced in quantity, it was easy to run and lightweight but sturdy enough to plow over most muddy roads.*

In 1897 a gearless, steam-driven car was built by the twin brothers Francis E. and Freelan O. Stanley in Newton, Massachusetts. Five years later they began to manufacture the car, which could achieve a speed of more than 25 miles per hour with no more sound than a sibilant hiss. In 1906 a racing model of a Stanley Steamer set a world speed record of more than 120 miles per hour. In 1903, 23 firms were making steamers, and the Stanleys continued turning out models until 1927.

The Oldsmobile of 1901 was a popular early combustion engine auto. It had a snappy curved dashboard and a steering device that looked like a tiller. During those first years of the 20th century fume-free electric runabouts were gliding noiselessly through city streets. Thomas Edison was convinced that the future of the automobile lay in the development of such electric cars, not in those using the smelly internal combustion engine. The 21st century may prove him right.

By 1906 the automobile was cutting loose from its horse-buggy parentage and developing a style of its own: Fenders, running boards, steering wheel, and paired lights front and back were added. If the automobile as we know it has a birthday, October 1908 will serve. That is when Henry Ford introduced his first Model T, a five-passenger, open touring car with a 20-horsepower four-cycle engine. The Model T cost $850 and its progeny came rolling out of Ford's factory so fast that by June 1909 some 100 cars a day were being made. More than 150,000 were manufactured in 1913, and three times that number were made in 1915. By 1924 the price was down to $260. When the Model T was finally discontinued 3 years later, more than 15 million had come off the assembly lines. America was on wheels. (For more information on early Fords, see pages 286–287.)

Although the earliest horseless carriages were often feared and hated, particularly by farmers, and even though livery stable owners fought them valiantly in an attempt to ward off the inevitable elimination of their jobs, Americans quickly fell in love with the automobile.

A car at the front door meant unprecedented mobility. A job no longer had to be around the corner; it could be many miles away. The ordinary working family could take a vacation in another State or visit relations 1,000 miles away. Young people could escape parental supervision. Women had new freedom. A farmer's wife put it succinctly when asked why her family owned a car but not a bathtub: "You can't go to town in a bathtub." It didn't matter that you got rained on or choked with dust in those early cars, or that you had to change tires frequently and crank the motor until your arm nearly fell off. All you had to do was put on your long canvas duster; tie on your hat or cap with a scarf and let the ends fly out behind you; don your goggles and long gauntlets; and you were ready to burn up the roads at a daring 30 miles per hour.

To catch up with Ford, other companies adopted mass production methods and raised wages to meet Ford's unprecedented $5 a day. Hundreds of automobile companies were formed, merged, and vanished. In 1927 Chevrolet sales overtook those of Ford, and ever since the two makes have competed for first place. Improvements in safety and performance came fast and with much fanfare. The electric self-starter, introduced in 1912, eliminated the need for brawny muscles to turn the starting crank, although for some years thereafter it was a luxury extra on most makes. The starter, more than anything else, put women behind the wheel. Competition among manufacturers brought a spate of improvements: Balloon tires, electric headlights, hydraulic brakes, automatic windshield wipers, shock absorbers, steel tops, built-in trunks, automatic transmission, power brakes and steering, automatic seat and window controls, exhaust emission controls,

From Imaginative Elegance for the Few to Monotony for Every Man
Putting a Nation on Wheels Was Not Without Its Cost

During the early years of mass automobile manufacture, Americans on the road were likely to pass—or to be passed by—cars of a rich and bewildering variety. In the 1920's, the golden years of the auto industry, the spare functionalism of the pioneer cars was replaced by a new elegance and craftsmanship. Custom coachwork and specially fitted interiors were the rule on luxury cars. Certain cars became symbols for envied lifestyles: the legendary Stutz Bearcat, with its long low lines and vivid colors, was the car driven by the moneyed, fast-living "Flaming Youth"; aristocratic, closed sedans belonged to solid wealthy types, who could pay as much as $20,000 for a rosewood-paneled limousine with gold door handles and cutglass flower holders by Tiffany. By the end of the decade such features as the enclosed car body and comfortable interior had been incorporated into low-priced cars, but charm and elegance were on the way out.

Father of the famous *Bearcat is this 1913 Stutz. Since it had neither top nor windshield, riding in it required a long duster, veils or goggles, a blanket, and perhaps a hot water bottle.*

The Duesenberg of 1929 *was typical of the classy, costly machines of the period. Duesenberg went on to build even more elegant models, priced at up to $20,000. His four-passenger touring car could reach the astonishing speed of 120 miles per hour.*

This New York City parking lot *represents look-alike cars in staggering numbers, and a major contemporary problem. In 1973 registered motor vehicles of all kinds totaled 125 million—more than one for every two Americans. The roads to carry them, the lots to park them in, the air to absorb their fumes, even the gasoline to power them are all in short supply. Prescription: more efficient modes of transport.*

America's Highways

Largest System in the World

In 1910 the price of a Ford flivver was $800; by 1916 anyone could buy a Tin Lizzie for $360—and a lot of people did. Rural roads swarmed with dust-shrouded cars, gouging road surfaces and miring hub-deep in mud in wet weather. The problems created by the ubiquitous car were nationwide in scope; and in 1921 Congress enacted the Federal Highway Act, the first national legislation for the development of interstate roads. By the 1940's the United States had the largest road network in the world. Yet its more than a million miles of roads were still inadequate for the ever-growing hordes of cars, trucks, and buses; and the traffic fatality rate was disastrous.

Postwar America laid down throughways and turnpikes at a feverish pace. But it was the passage of the 1956 Highway Act that finally took the Nation into the age of the automobile. The act called for a system of interstate highways, for which Washington would pay 90 percent of the cost, with funds from vehicle and gasoline taxes; 42,500 miles of limited-access, divided highway have been built, connecting 90 percent of America's cities and, with the addition of locally built superhighways, transforming the American way of life.

A mass movement from the cities into the now-accessible countryside took (by 1970) 37 percent of the American people into the suburbs. Trucks took more freight business from the ailing railroads. Highway motels supplanted city hotels. Drive-in chains fed the hurried motorist and his family. Everywhere, interminable lengths of concrete tied country with city, coast with coast. It is now possible to drive from Seattle to Boston—3,085 miles—without stopping for a single red light.

Los Angeles' freeway system—*more than 600 miles of superhighway—is vital to the city's life. With a population of 2.8 million, there are more than 3.7 million cars—and almost no other means of transportation. L.A.'s once unique inner-city railway system is defunct; buses are few and far between. L.A., however, boasts the largest concentration of trucks in the Western United States. The interstate system has created a smooth, efficient track for the fleet of semitrailer trucks (inset) that transport most of the Nation's goods from coast to coast.*

seatbelts, and stepped-up horsepower. Each added to the pleasure, safety, or ease of motoring—and, incidentally, to the cost of the cars, which became for most families the biggest single item in their budget.

Sales of closed cars exceeded those of open cars for the first time in 1925. But for those who still wanted the wind in their faces, first there was the rumble seat—which came into view when what is now the trunk on most models was popped open—and then the convertible, its collapsible top first operated by hand, later by vacuum, and finally by an electrical control.

While the main thrust of automobile production was toward assembly-line cars for mass markets, a few companies specialized in magnificent handmade vehicles of superb design. To this day fanciers of antique cars flock to exhibits and rallies to admire meticulously restored Stutz Bearcats and Duesenbergs, their leather shining, their metal bodies agleam. Enthusiasts also applaud parades of stately Packards, Marmons, Franklins, Pierce Arrows, and other now-discontinued makes of that golden era. In 1974 one Middle Eastern potentate offered to sell his 1932, 12-cylinder, bulletproof Packard, the only model of its kind in the world, for $100,000.

World War II halted U.S. passenger car production in 1942, but after the war the country went on a car-buying spree. Millions of families moved to the suburbs, where many of them found they needed two cars, and as the children of these suburbanites became old enough to drive and demanded automobiles of their own, families with three and four cars became commonplace. Passenger car production hit a peak of 9.3 million in 1965. By 1970 there were 90 million licensed American drivers, and 1 in every 7 persons in the entire labor force worked at some enterprise related to highway transport.

The automobile culture had its disturbing aspects. Deaths on the highways rose from 38,137 in 1960 to a shocking 56,600 in 1972. Downtown areas of cities fell into disrepair and decay as retail trade shifted to huge suburban shopping centers and malls. Thousands of acres of fields and woodland were leveled and paved with concrete to accommodate the automobile. Drive-in movies, roadside restaurants and food shops, and filling stations and used car lots—garish with neon signs and plastic pennants—turned highways into tawdry carnivals. Curtains of smog, blamed in large part on gasoline fumes, blanketed many urban areas.

The pollution problem inspired a multitude of save-the-environment movements, and the shortage and rising price of gasoline in the early 1970's reminded the country that natural resources were not inexhaustible. Smaller cars, car pools, lower speeds, rediscovery of the bicycle, and moves to revive mass transit signified that Americans were seeking more rational solutions to their transportation problems. But their love affair with the automobile seemed in no real danger of diminishing.

Transportation Takes to the Air

A notable feature of the American experience has been an impatience to travel farther and faster. The horse, the small boat, the steamship, the railroad engine, the automobile—each of these aids to mobility made its mark in turn on the Nation's history. Next came the airplane. It fell to the brothers Orville and Wilbur Wright, owners of a Dayton, Ohio, bicycle shop, to open up the skies as highways of human travel. On December 17, 1903, a cold and gusty day, their wood and canvas biplane, powered by a 12-horsepower engine, rose from its launching ramp and hovered in the air for 12 seconds. Later that day the plane remained airborne for 59 seconds and traveled a distance of 852 feet over the dunes of Kitty Hawk, North Carolina.

Now that flight in heavier-than-air vehicles was a proven fact, eager young mechanics and inventors went to work in their sheds and garages testing monoplanes against biplanes, developing aerial rudders, and devising ways to control climb, dive, and stability. Glenn H. Curtiss built the first successful seaplane; he designed the first lightweight plane engine made in this country, installed it in his airship, attached a pontoon to the plane, and took off and landed on the water in San Diego, California, in 1911. In World War I planes first served on scouting missions and later carried machine guns. The need for greater speed and maneuverability to evade machinegun fire in dogfights in the air stimulated many advances. When peace was restored, hundreds of pilots, who, despite the U.S. lack of military planes, had been trained in the wartime Army air service, continued to fly.

In 1918 the U.S. Post Office inaugurated the first airmail service between New York and Washington, D.C. When it proved a success, service was extended to other cities so quickly that by 1920 mail bags were being relayed by air from New York to San Francisco. Those hazardous runs recalled—in spirit and element of danger, at least—the pioneer overland ventures of a century earlier. Mail pilots in flimsy, open-cockpit planes flew in all weather, peering down through the murk for a reasonably level pasture that might serve in case of a forced landing. At night they navigated by the stars.

The barnstormer, too, played a role in American aviation. Daring, cocky, happy-go-lucky, he somehow scraped up $300 and bought himself a surplus trainer, which he put through hair-raising stunts at county fairs. He walked on the wings, changed planes in midair,

The Barnstormers

After World War I there was a brief era of aerial excitement, novelty, and danger known as barnstorming. There were few airports then, but planes could land in cow pastures and fields of stubble—and thus the name. On the day of the event the pilot might treat the townsfolk to a series of ear-shattering high-speed passes—at 80 miles per hour—just above their rooftops. Out at the field this wondrous machine, usually a biplane, could be viewed close up. It had gleaming, bright-colored fabric stretched over the wood skeleton, which showed every rib. Varnished-wood struts held the wings apart, and bright wire was pulled taut to hold it all together. The copper-tipped propeller of laminated wood and the exposed cylinders and exhaust of the engine had a beauty of their own.

At the appointed hour the pilot, wearing the obligatory leather helmet and goggles, a leather jacket, and white scarf of parachute silk, would take his craft aloft to demonstrate a breathtaking series of loops, barrel rolls, snap rolls, Immelmann turns, chandelles, stalls, and spins. Then it was back to Earth with the offer to take all comers for a spin, at $5 or so a head, or whatever the traffic would bear. From the open-front cockpit one experienced the noise and power of the engine, the rush of wind, and an amazingly unfamiliar perspective of familiar ground. There was Main Street, the church steeple, the schoolyard, and, if you were sharp-eyed, your own street and the house where you lived.

For larger audiences, such as at a county fair, an entire flying circus might appear. There would be aerial dogfights, wing walking, air-to-air transfers, and other hair-raising feats. This was risky business, and many pilots and stuntmen were killed.

The Civil Aeronautics Authority, established in 1938, soon set rules for regular inspection of planes, licensing of pilots, and other precautions that brought an end to barnstorming. But for many thousands of Americans, their first real experience of the miracle wrought by the Wright brothers was the plane that landed in a cow pasture on the edge of town.

Evolution of the Airplane

From Wire and Wood to Gleaming Metal Faster Than Sound

Flimsy as they were, the Wright brothers' planes embodied principles of aeronautical design that would remain basically unchanged for more than four decades. It was not until after the invention of the jet engine during World War II that a new species of plane was created, propellerless, capable of incredible speed and altitude, and able to carry hundreds of passengers and thousands of pounds of cargo. In the 1970's two supersonic jet airliners, the Anglo-French Concorde and the Russian Tupolev Tu-144 had begun flights, but the United States ended its development of the Boeing SST when questions were raised about sonic boom and damage to the upper atmosphere. Future air flight may rely on helicopters and more on short take-off and landing (STOL) aircraft.

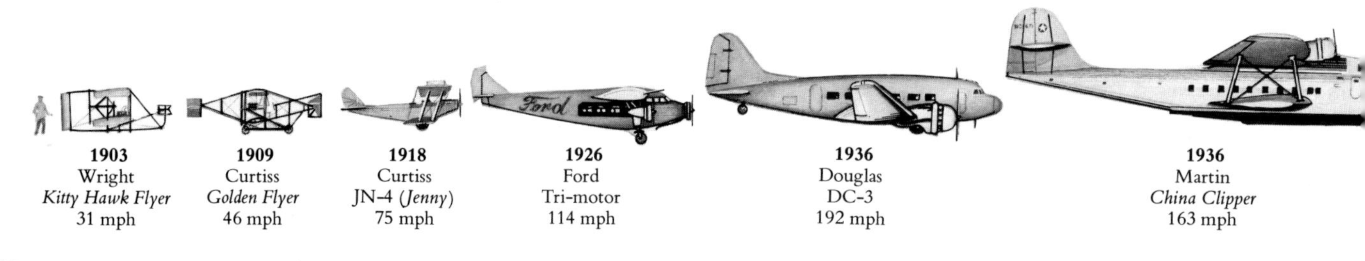

1903 Wright *Kitty Hawk Flyer* 31 mph

1909 Curtiss *Golden Flyer* 46 mph

1918 Curtiss JN-4 (*Jenny*) 75 mph

1926 Ford Tri-motor 114 mph

1936 Douglas DC-3 192 mph

1936 Martin *China Clipper* 163 mph

looped, and somersaulted. Between shows he took passengers up at $5 a head or, sometimes, a penny a pound.

A lanky youngster named Charles A. Lindbergh was both an airmail pilot and a barnstormer, and then he made a flight that brought the age of aviation to full flower. In 1927 Lindbergh flew nonstop in 33½ hours from Long Island to Paris aboard the *Spirit of St. Louis,* a single-engine, 223-horsepower plane.

The country and the world were enthralled and delighted. Flying to get places suddenly became the thing to do. Airlines were formed everywhere. The first scheduled flights had begun as early as 1914 over a 22-mile route between St. Petersburg and Tampa, Florida. (The fare was $5 per person—more for anyone weighing over 200 pounds.) In 1928, the year after Lindbergh's flight, 27 scheduled airlines carried some 53,000 passengers more than 10 million miles.

A flight on those early airlines was truly an adventure. Some planes were so small that a passenger could step into the cabin directly from the ground. Others were served by a small kitchen stepladder. Wicker chairs, for lightness, were standard cabin furnishing. Even after cabins were enclosed, pilots often wanted their cockpits open. In those days of seat-of-the-pants flying, when planes had no instrument gauges or navigational aids, a pilot judged speed by the sound of wind in the wires, kept his plane level by feel, and knew by the breeze on his cheeks if his plane was sideslipping.

But aviation was growing too fast to tolerate such primitive conditions. The Air Commerce Act, passed in 1926, set the first safety standards by licensing pilots, charting airways, and regulating the construction of aircraft and airfields. Cockpit instruments became increasingly sophisticated with Elmer Sperry's adaptation of the gyroscope to flight, and with improved altimeters, radio beams, variable pitch propellers, and wing flaps to facilitate landing. The first truly modern airliner was the Boeing 247, introduced in 1932. It carried a crew of 3 and 10 passengers and cruised at 180 miles per hour. A few years later the Stratoliner offered the first pressurized cabin, which enabled planes to cruise comfortably above most weather as high as 20,000 feet. A nontechnical improvement, but one that offered considerable comfort to air travelers, came in 1930, when Boeing Air Transport hired eight young nurses—stewardesses, they were soon to be called—to serve meals and to fluff cushions for passengers on its San Francisco–Chicago flights.

In World War II air power was an important key to victory. President Franklin D. Roosevelt's dramatic command to U.S. industry, after Pearl Harbor, to turn out 50,000 planes a year seemed almost beyond reach at the time; in 1944, however, 96,000 were produced. Under pressure to build planes that would fly higher and faster than the enemy's and carry bigger bomb and freight loads, the aviation industry made giant strides. The Germans were the first to put jet-propelled fighters in the air, but the United States was not far behind. At a secret base in California a strange, propellerless plane with two General Electric jet engines in a frame built by Bell Aircraft streaked into the air in September 1944. The jet age was born, and just in time: The piston plane had reached the limits of its size and speed.

After World War II travelers took to the air en masse. Early airports had been little more than mowed fields with wind socks, but by the early 1950's enormous complexes of terminals, hangars, shops, motels, and runways covering as much ground as a city were being built. The first commercial jet transport crossed the Atlantic from Great Britain in 1958, presaging the end of the mighty ocean liners that had long ruled the seas. American airlines converted almost entirely to jets in the 1960's and in the 1970's introduced the huge, double-aisled superjets that accommodated 400 passengers. Steak dinners and movies in the air became the norm of American long-distance travel. Traveling at speeds up to 600 miles an hour, a businessman could easily attend a conference 1,000 or more miles away and return home the same day. The first commercial faster-than-sound transports began

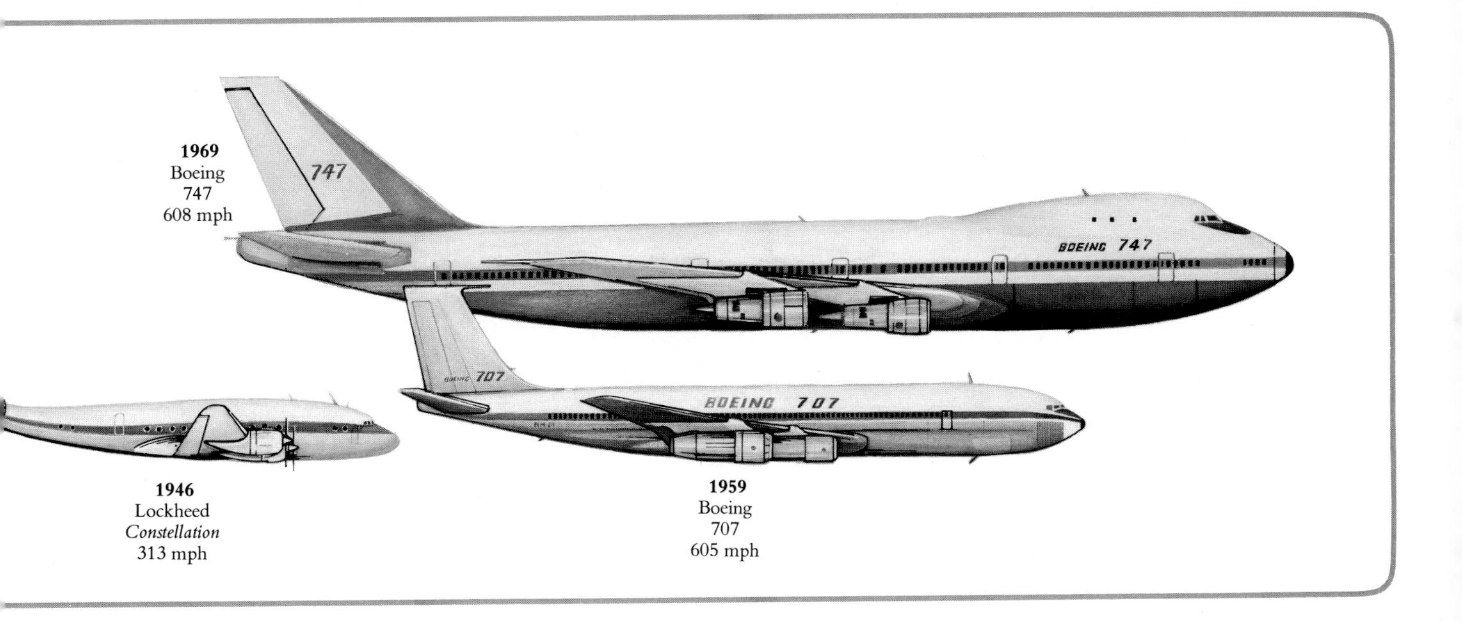

First Heroes of the Air

For an enthralled public, the men and women who flew their fragile craft incredible distances at unbelievable speeds were a breed set apart. Daring and sometimes reckless, always in danger of their lives and often losing them, they were the pioneers of the air who charted new pathways in the sky, often helped to improve the planes they flew, and changed flying from a daredevil stunt to a safe new mode of travel.

Floyd Bennett, as pilot, and Richard E. Byrd, as navigator, teamed up in May 1926 to make the world's first flight over the North Pole, an exploit that won both men Medals of Honor. Bennett was slated to serve with Byrd in the Antarctic when he undertook an air rescue mission to German transatlantic fliers downed in the Gulf of St. Lawrence. Taken ill with pneumonia, he died in Quebec on April 25, 1928, despite Charles A. Lindbergh's emergency flight from New York with serum.

Jacqueline Cochran learned how to fly to promote her cosmetics business. In the process she set a new world's speed record for women in 1937 and won the Bendix transcontinental race in 1938. She flew a bomber to England in 1941. In 1953 she became the first woman to exceed the speed of sound, in a Sabre jet F-86, and 11 years later she flew at more than twice the speed of sound. She was also the first woman to pilot a jet across the Atlantic.

Douglas "Wrong Way" Corrigan flew the Atlantic in 1938 without permission from air control. He claimed, tongue in cheek, that he had been aiming for California, but misread his compass. Hence his name and fame.

Howard Hughes, the millionaire tool manufacturer and moviemaker, used his fortune and his talents to develop new planes. Flying craft of his own design, he set a speed record of 352 miles per hour in 1935; in 1936 he flew across the continent in slightly less than 9½ hours—faster than any man had before; in 1938 he broke all records by flying around the world in 3 days, 19 hours. Hughes spent $25 million in the 1940's to develop a 200-ton plywood flying boat, which never became operational.

Lindbergh *stands beside the monoplane which was built for him especially for his flight across the Atlantic.*

Charles A. Lindbergh, doubtless the most famous of all air heroes, thrilled the world with his 1927 nonstop flight from New York to Paris. The French cheered him as though he were another Napoleon, and on his return to New York the "Lone Eagle" was given the greatest reception in America's history. Hundreds of thousands of people lined Broadway to welcome him. Lindbergh became the revered spokesman for the air industry and made flying seem respectable and safe. Thus in 1929 alone aviation manufacturers sold more than $70 million worth of planes and parts.

Wiley Post was the first to fly solo around the world. He and his Australian navigator, Harold Gatty, announced in 1931 that they would circle the globe in a mere 10 days. Flying the *Winnie Mae,* a small all-wood plane, they completed their 15,474-mile trip in 8½ days. Later, in 1933, Post scored a first by taking the *Winnie Mae* around the world alone—this time equipped with a newly developed automatic pilot, which lightened the burden of guiding the plane. Post's record-breaking time: 7 days, 18 hours, 49 minutes.

to cross the Atlantic from France in the mid-1970's, taking less than 3 hours for the trip.

Meanwhile the helicopter came of age. Pioneered before World War I in Russia and again in the United States a quarter of a century later by Igor Sikorsky with others, the vertical-lift craft with overhead rotors proved its worth in the Korean War as scout and ambulance. Today some 2,500 rotorcraft do yeoman service monitoring traffic, carrying the mail, rushing the sick and injured to hospitals, and taxiing passengers on short hauls.

By 1971 more than 131,000 American civilian aircraft of all types were flying 25 million hours a year and covering some 3 billion miles.

Robert Goddard *prepares to launch the first liquid-fuel rocket on March 16, 1926. The rocket flew 2½ seconds for a distance of 184 feet and was a portent of things to come.*

Space Flight Becomes a Reality

The dream of travel through the heavens is as old as mankind itself, and mythology and literature are full of fanciful flights to the Moon and beyond. In the 19th century the fictional descriptions of space travel became more realistic. Edgar Allan Poe's "Unparalleled Adventures of One Hans Pfaal," published in 1835, described in great detail a flight to the Moon in a balloon. The French novelist Jules Verne stirred the imagination of hundreds of thousands of readers with *From the Earth to the Moon.* His vividly imagined voyage approached the realm of scientific practicality when the Russian K. E. Tsiolkovsky formulated the basic laws of rocketry in the 1890's. In America Robert Hutchings Goddard, a young New England physics professor who became interested in rocketry as a way of achieving high altitudes, published a pamphlet in 1919 describing a prototypal meteorological rocket. He speculated that rocket propulsion ought to bring the Moon within reach and, although his theories were widely derided, he managed to interest a few wealthy patrons in his work. In 1926 he launched the first liquid-propellant rocket. Its 184-foot flight drew the mockery of the press ("Moon Rocket Misses Target by 238,799½ Miles"), but despite the discouragement of his supporters and the objections of neighbors disturbed by the noises of his launch pad, Goddard persisted. By 1940 he had built and sent aloft liquid-fuel rockets that in basic design were the models for those flown today.

Nazi Germany took rocketry more seriously. Late in World War II the Germans fired V-2 rockets into England from secret bases on the Continent. These terrifying weapons were the work of a research team headed by young Wernher von Braun, who came to America after the war to lead the U.S. rocket program. By 1956 Von Braun's team had perfected the Jupiter-C rocket, which flew an amazing 3,300 miles.

But it was the Russians who won the race into space. On October 4, 1957, using an ultrapowerful launching rocket, they sent out the first man-made satellite. Sputnik, a 184-pound metal sphere, circled the Earth about every 1½ hours at altitudes ranging from 140 to 550 miles. A month later, Sputnik II was launched—a 1,120-pound satellite carrying the first space passenger, a dog named Laika. America's answer to Sputnik was the Explorer 1 satellite, launched via a Jupiter-C rocket on January 31, 1958. It made known to the world a startling discovery: The Earth is surrounded by belts of high-energy radiation (named after James Van Allen, who identified them). Since that time satellites and space probes have added volumes of knowledge, from meteorological facts about the Earth and its atmosphere to discoveries about the nature of solar space. In the 1970's unmanned probes were penetrating our solar system, sending back a wealth of data and pictures of our planetary neighbors.

True to Jules Verne's fictional vision, man now lives in space and walks on the Moon. Since the first Apollo Moon landing on July 20, 1969, we have sent men to the Moon five times. And scientists, no longer earthbound, have lived and worked for weeks aboard American Skylabs orbiting high above the Earth.

It would seem that, compared to the awesome difficulties of space travel, the problems of getting quickly and comfortably from one place to another on the face of the Earth should be child's play. Yet, although we have traveled to the Moon, here on our own planet transportation advances have created their own problems: Congested highways, rundown mass surface transportation, overburdened airports, polluted air and water, distressing noise, and shortage of energy. As Americans stood on the brink of their third century in history, they were having to ask themselves many searching questions about their traveling habits. The answers, when they finally emerge, might well prove as revolutionary in their impact on transportation as the Model T automobile of an earlier era had been. In the main, however, most observers were confident that the same kind of energy and brilliance that had been applied to the space programs would ultimately solve the Nation's more mundane transportation problems, even though no ready solutions were currently in sight.

To the Moon
A Giant Leap Into Space

On July 16, 1969, the Apollo 11 spacecraft, powered by its giant Saturn V rocket, lifted off from Cape Kennedy on the first stage of an extraordinary journey. On July 20, at 10:56 p.m. eastern daylight time, astronaut Neil Armstrong became the first man to set foot on the Moon.

The technological accomplishment involved in sending men to the Moon—and bringing them safely back—is, in itself, awe inspiring. From 1961, when the first manned space flights were sent into Earth orbit, more than 20 American launchings had hurled men into space, for increasing orbital periods, and used an increasingly complex rocket and spacecraft technology. And since the epochal Apollo 11 flight, six subsequent Moon journeys (one unmanned) have sharpened space skills and returned to the Earth a treasure house of knowledge about the Moon.

The cost of this great space project has been immense. In 1974 alone the National Aeronautics and Space Administration, the agency responsible for the development of U.S. space programs, spent over $3 billion. And, although some of the benefits of space technology have already begun to appear here on Earth (especially in medicine, industry, and communications), it remains to be seen how Apollo and related programs involving an orbital space laboratory and unmanned space probes of the planets will influence terrestrial transportation. Will we eventually travel regularly to the Moon? Given the present speed of technological advance, we should know the answers soon.

The first lunar module *returns to the Apollo 11 spacecraft. Aboard are astronauts Neil A. Armstrong and Edwin E. Aldrin, leaving after more than 21½ hours spent on the Moon's surface. The lunar module will rendezvous with the orbiting command module, which will then return to the Earth. Earth can be seen here rising above the lunar horizon.*

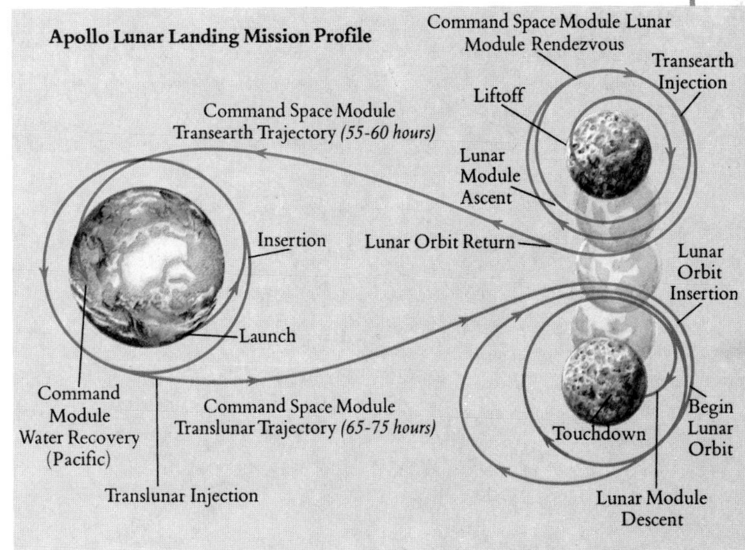

A schematic representation *of the flight of Apollo 11. The giant Saturn V launch rocket (shown at left) fired its three-stage engines in orbit around the Earth to send the lunar spacecraft—the top portion of the rocket—on course to the Moon. On the return trip, retro-rockets were fired to maneuver the spacecraft for a safe landing on Earth.*

CHAPTER TWELVE

Crafts and Craftsmen in a Growing Land

The work of a nation's craftsmen speaks eloquently a its people, their daily lives, interests, and tastes. C reflect a people's history, their esthetic sense, their skill, t ingenuity, and their pride in workmanship. The cra man's creations mirror not only his personal skill but the values of the persons for whom his works are inten

On the whole, the image reflected back to Ameri by our crafts has been an attractive one. Although we h produced our share of gimcracks, we have also been talen imaginative, and meticulous. We have combined bea utility, and durability in a wide range of objects made un differing circumstances for a variety of purposes.

Craftsmanship for Family, Friends, and Neighbors

The greatest treasure the early settlers brought to this country was an ingenuity which, born of necessity, made virtually everyone a jack-of-all-trades. Some of the settlers were skilled craftsmen, but there was more work than they could handle. The immediate need was for housing—followed by a demand for furnishings, for few people came to America with more than a minimum of household goods from their former homes.

In the early 17th century the genius of America's craftsmen—amateur and professional—showed itself in their ability to give distinction to even the simplest furnishings. Their primary concern was for utility, but their esthetic sense was strong. What their creations lacked in complex adornment, they made up for in their beauty of proportion. As the Colonies prospered and life became less arduous, everyday appurtenances became more elegant. By the beginning of the 18th century, carpenters (called joiners) had become competent cabinetmakers, and many pewterers found their products so much in demand that they no longer had to supplement their income by mending pots and pans. American artisans were becoming the equals of their European counterparts.

Handcrafted instruments, *fashioned in 18th-century style, are displayed in a music shop in Virginia's restored colonial capital at Williamsburg. Popular stringed instruments of the day included the violin, the viola da gamba, and a primitive type of banjo.*

Furniture for the Colonies

Space was at a premium in early colonial houses, and their furnishings were designed and built accordingly. Every article had to be functional; the more purposes it could serve, the better. The chest, an ideal multipurpose object, was used for storage, as a seat, and as a low table. The first chests were merely lidded boxes. If made by the man of the family, busy with many other chores, they were generally undecorated; if made by a carpenter, they might be embellished with carvings, such as the popular sunflower-and-tulip design of the Hartford chest. In time the drawer-chest combined drawers with the lidded box, and eventually drawers were added atop drawers. Thus the chest evolved into the chest of drawers.

Tables, too, were made so that they would conserve space. The trestle table—a long board resting on two or more footed supports held together by a horizontal bar —could be taken apart and stored against a wall. The gateleg table could be reduced to the width of a single board by dropping its leaves. Most ingenious was the chair-table, an armchair with a hinged tabletop serving as the back. The back stayed upright until a table was needed; then it was tilted down and rested on the arms.

A number of influences may be said to have shaped the s in America and to have given them vigor and vital- First, the rigors of the settlers' lives made virtues of the ssities of simplicity and sturdiness. Then the influences e many different European cultures represented here, with its own tradition, contributed diversity to our s and craftsmanship. Some of these European tech- es and tastes merged to produce a distinctively Ameri- style; others retained the character of the culture from ch they sprang. Another significant influence was the strial Revolution, which made machine work out of that had previously been done by hand. On the positive side this made more goods available to more people; the negative aspect of industrialization was that it encouraged the standardization of taste and of workmanship. Later, from England, came the Arts and Crafts movement, which grew up as a reaction against such standardization. The artistry and activity inspired by this movement helped to restore crafts and craftsmanship in the United States to their former high standards while retaining the benefits of mass production. And finally, there has been the influence of a new breed of craftsmen with intensely personal points of view and dedicated more than ever before to turning the products of their hands into useful works of art.

The rich glow of wood *adds warmth to this 17th-century New England room, now on display in the Winterthur Museum near Wilmington, Delaware. Part of a house built in Massachusetts about 1684, the room served as the core of family life and included all facilities for cooking, eating, and sleeping. The Jacobean court cupboard in the background, made of oak, was the household's most prized possession; pine was used for everyday furniture such as the stretcher-base table and bench. The plates, bowls, and spoons on the table are also of wood.*

This silver beaker and porringer *were made in the 1650's by John Hull and Robert Sanderson of Massachusetts. They minted the Pine Tree shillings, some of the first silver money in the Colonies. Beakers were used as communion vessels and as ordinary drinking cups.*

The 18th-century pewter *on the shelves of this walnut cupboard at Winterthur includes all the elements of a country family's finest table service. The charger, or platter, on the center of the top shelf, measuring 19 inches across, may be the largest of its type in America.*

For seating there were also stools, benches, and settles; the last named were long, high-backed benches with enclosed foundations that provided some storage space for household articles. Cane-seated chairs with wooden arms and backs were less commonly used. Two of the most popular pieces of seating furniture were the Carver and Brewster chairs, named after John Carver, the first Governor of Plymouth Colony, and William Brewster, a leading official of the Colony. Both types of chairs were made with lathe-turned posts connected by turned spindles. The back of the Carver chair had three vertical spindles set between the lower two of its three horizontal spindles; the more elaborate Brewster chair had more vertical spindles, with more turnings. These were fitted both over and under the seat as well as under the arms.

The tallest piece of furniture in the colonial home was the cupboard, which provided necessary storage room, since there were no closets in which to tuck away things not in daily use. The press cupboard had a shallow open space on top, while the lower sections contained either drawers or shelves with doors. The court cupboard had a larger open section, either at top or bottom, in which decorative items could be displayed.

No colonial family would consider being without its Bible, and the Bible was usually kept in a carved box that stood in a place of honor. The Bible box also contained the family's important papers. The top was hinged and frequently slanted, and the box often stood on long legs. The top could also be used as a desk.

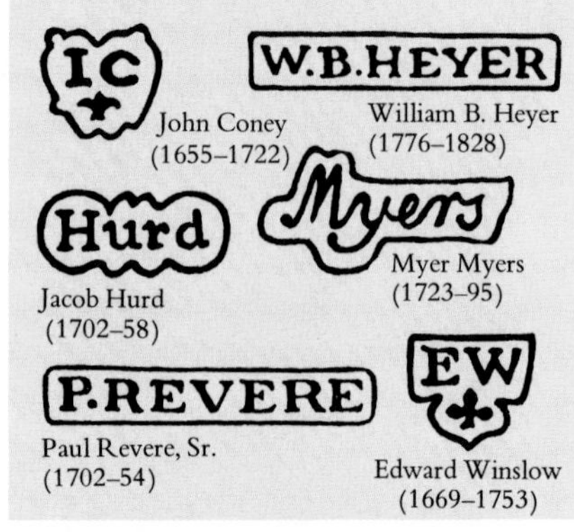

Early silver marks *were the stamp of the individual maker; the hallmark, used by English smiths to attest the metal's purity, did not appear in America until the early 19th century.*

Silver and Pewter

The colonial silversmith was not merely a skilled craftsman; he also served as an informal banker. Until the mid-18th century all the silver these artisans used was supplied by their clients, generally in the form of coins. Since silver objects were made to order and easily identifiable, they were safer from theft than coins; the silversmith's work also gave the metal added value.

The earliest silver pieces were simple, graceful, and restrained. Among the commonest silver objects were spoons, beakers, tankards, porringers, and the two-handled caudle cups used for "caudle"—a warm drink for the sick, made of spiced wine or ale. One of the earliest signed pieces of American-made silver is a caudle cup made in 1652 in the Boston workshop of John Hull and Robert Sanderson.

Although all but the poorest colonial families had some silver pieces, pewter was far more commonly used in everyday life. An alloy, the chief constituent of which is tin (usually combined with copper, lead, or antimony), pewter was worked in simple forms, and it was used for most of the same objects as silver. Because most pewterers followed more than one calling, we know of only a few 17th-century craftsmen in pewter. Among these are Joseph Copeland of Virginia and Richard Graves and Edmund Dolbeare of Massachusetts. Signed pewter work did not appear until the 18th century, when some of the most distinguished work was done by Johann C. Heyne of Pennsylvania and Peter Young of New York.

Accent on Style

In 1723 Apollos De Rivoire, an immigrant of French descent who had been apprenticed to the Boston silversmith John Coney, anglicized his name to Paul Revere and opened his own workshop. Twelve years later he fathered a son who bore his name and followed his profession. The two generations that separated John Coney and Paul Revere, Jr., saw dramatic changes in the silversmith's art. Coney and the senior Revere modeled their work on the Baroque and Rococo styling of their British counterparts. The younger Revere worked both in the Rococo and in an American adaptation of the more restrained Neoclassical (also known in the United States as the Federal) style, which flowered during the Revolutionary and post-Revolutionary periods.

The emergence of the Neoclassical style did not, however, mean the end of the elaborate. Philadelphia silversmiths remained partial to the Rococo, as is shown in the

Paul Revere, Silversmith

Skilled Craftsman and Legendary Patriot

A man whose abundant energies and talents flowed in many directions, Paul Revere was not only an accomplished silversmith and a celebrated Patriot but an expert engraver, a designer of ornamental false teeth "of real Use in Speaking and Eating," and a fabricator of church bells and cannons. Born in Boston in 1735, Revere learned his trade from his father, Apollos De Rivoire, who anglicized his name so that "the Bumpkins should pronounce it easier." Revere took over the family business at 19, after his father's death. His early work consisted largely of delicately chased tea and table services in the late Rococo style. In 1768 his deep commitment to the Patriot cause led him to design the most famous piece of early American silver ever made, the "Sons of Liberty" punchbowl. The piece was commissioned by the Sons of Liberty, of which Revere was a member, and inscribed with the names of the 92 members of the Massachusetts House of Representatives who "Voted NOT TO RESCIND" their complaints against Britain's hated Townshend Acts.

In 1774 Revere was made official courier for the Massachusetts Provincial Assembly, beginning the series of dispatch rides that culminated "on the 18th of April, '75," when he gave the alarm that the British were on the march—a feat immortalized in Longfellow's poem "Paul Revere's Ride." After the Revolution he devoted most of his time to his trade, specializing in elegant tea services in the Neoclassical manner, known in America as the Federal style. Revere Copper and Brass, Incorporated, traces its origins to Paul Revere, and the town of Revere, Massachusetts, is named for him.

This candid portrait *of Paul Revere, painted by John Singleton Copley around 1768, shows the silversmith in his working clothes, thoughtfully contemplating an unfinished teapot. Engraving tools lie on the table before him. Among his many other activities, Revere often designed and made the frames for Copley's portraits. The tea service at right, with its restrained lines and delicately engraved embellishments, is typical of his later style. The set includes a covered sugar bowl, a basket-shaped open sugar bowl, a creamer, and a teapot with its own silver tray. Shown above the teapot is the silver mark often used to identify Revere's work: the family name enclosed in a rectangle.*

REVERE

Paul Revere (1735–1818)

This pristine workroom *used by Shaker women of the Hancock Community near Pittsfield, Massachusetts, exemplifies the sect's orderliness and sense of form. The high-backed chairs were light enough to be hung on wall pegs when the floors were cleared for religious ceremonies, which included marching and dancing. Other pegs held spare clothing. The oval nesting boxes on the chests and open shelves were made of thin strips of maple, steamed and shaped around a mold.*

Shaker Craftsmanship
The Functional Designs of an Austere Sect

The Shaker, or "Shaking Quaker," sect, which originated in England and established its first American communal village in 1774 near Watervliet, New York, derived its nickname from the tendency of its adherents to go into trembling ecstasies during religious services. But the celibate society's way of life was as ascetic as its mode of worship was passionate. Shaker laws forbade any "fanciful styles" in building and dictated that "Whatever is fashioned . . . be plain and simple . . . unembellished by any superfluities, which add nothing to its goodness or durability." Guided by these precepts, American Shakers, whose farming communities flourished from the 1790's to about 1860, designed buildings and crafts whose spare, elegant functionalism would be called thoroughly modern today. Interiors were stripped down to essentials: Unadorned board floors and plaster walls, built-in shelves and cupboards, the plainest chairs and tables. But thanks to the skill of the Shaker carpenters and the precise, detailed planning of each village, the society's dwellings and their contents were impeccably finished to the last detail.

Shaker furniture and artifacts owed much to the country designs of early New England, but they achieved a rare purity of form. Although they occasionally used colored paints, the Shakers generally preferred light wood stains that revealed the natural beauty of the grain. The society's furniture and other crafts were much in demand in the outside world; by the 1880's, replicas made by Shaker apprentices were sold by mail order. Especially popular were chests, baskets, fabrics, and chairs. The chairs were noted for their lightness and durability. Spartan Shaker tastes did not, however, appeal to the English writer Charles Dickens, who complained that the "stiff, high-backed chairs . . . partook so strongly of the general grimness, that one would much rather have sat on the floor."

Shaker baskets *and a wooden storage chest reflect the society's insistence on the meticulous "care and management of temporal things." Domestic order was further enforced by the rule that all bedclothes and utensils in a Shaker dwelling be put out of sight when not in use.*

work of Joseph Richardson, Sr. In New York the fashion called for a heavy look, and William B. Heyer was a master of that style. Simple or ornate, every silver piece was designed individually, and silver objects were intended as much for display as for use. Pewter continued to be used for everyday pieces, and although the number of craftsmen using the alloy increased, the style of pewter work changed very little.

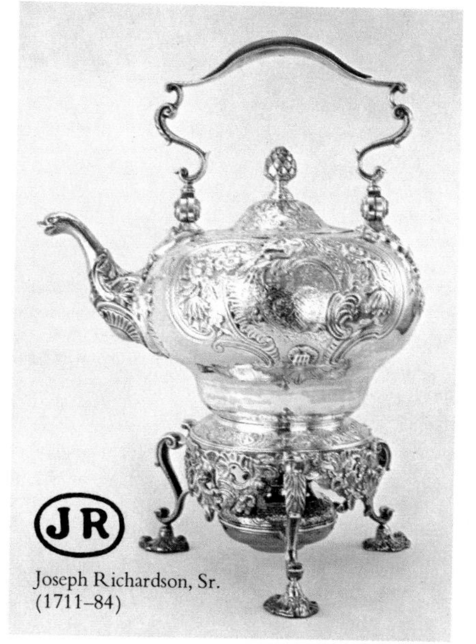

This richly ornamented *teakettle on a stand was made about 1760 by Joseph Richardson, Sr., for the widow of a Philadelphia mayor.*

Iron, Brass, and Other Metals

Early American craftsmen also worked in less elegant metals. The blacksmith was more than a shoer of horses. He produced many of the iron tools and housewares necessary for daily life: Tongs and andirons for the fireplace; kettles and cutlery for the kitchen; warming pans to take the chill from winter-cold bedsheets; hinges and latches for doors and cupboards; and gates and weather vanes for house exteriors. To the making of these mundane items he often brought an imaginative flair, adding graceful decorations to even the most prosaic objects. As life in the Colonies became less Spartan, the ironworker's craft became more refined. In the large homes of the wealthy, handsome wrought-iron railings added beauty to stairways; decorative cast-iron foot scrapers, which were placed just outside the front doors, often took the forms of animals or plants.

The first successful ironworks in the Colonies was established about 1645 at Saugus, Massachusetts, by Joseph Jenks. Copper was not mined until 1709, but thereafter it became popular and was used interchangeably with iron for many purposes. Shem Drowne, whose grasshopper weather vane first graced Boston's Faneuil Hall in 1749, was one of the best known early coppersmiths.

Since brass was not manufactured in the Colonies until the second half of the 18th century, many of the early brass articles were made from old pots and pans that had been melted down. Most of these did not even bear the name of the maker, but one whose name has survived was Caspar Wistar, who arrived in Philadelphia in 1717. (He founded his famous glassworks in Salem County, New Jersey, 22 years later.) Among the objects that he fashioned were brass buttons. In addition to their use in domestic articles, brass and copper were also used for firearms, tools, and parts of ships. The durability and sheen of brass commended it for wider use; and pewterers and silversmiths—among them Paul Revere—began to work in brass also, producing candlesticks, andirons, and other decorative as well as practical objects.

This gilded copper *weather vane in the form of a strutting rooster was made in the 19th century; such weathercock designs had been popular since colonial times. The kitchen fireplace at right is surrounded by typical 18th-century cooking utensils: Tin molds, heavy iron pots, and kettles of iron and copper. A crane with adjustable hooks holds cooking pots and swings them over the fire; a portable tinned reflector oven stands on the hearth.*

Pennsylvania German

Lively Motifs of a Traditional Folk Art

A sgraffito dish *made in 1786 for one Cadarina Raeder is decorated with a double-headed eagle, a traditional emblem introduced in Europe during the Crusades and adopted by the German Hapsburg emperors. Sgraffito, a specialty of Pennsylvania German potters, originated in China and received its name in Italy. It was made by scratching or cutting through the outer glaze to expose the red clay beneath.*

Attracted by the promise of religious freedom and the hope of rich farmland, German Protestant immigrants began streaming into William Penn's "Promised Land" of Pennsylvania in the late 17th and early 18th centuries. Most of them were from the German Palatinate—the Rhine Valley and adjacent lands—where they had long suffered from overcrowding, religious persecution, heavy taxation, and numerous foreign invasions. Conservative, pious, and industrious, these German settlers could bring along few possessions on the cramped ships that carried them to the New World, but they did bring their own cherished folk traditions and a determination to preserve them. Many who survived the long, chancy sea voyage—9,000 "Palatines" reached Philadelphia in 1738 alone—were skilled artisans, and they were soon busy duplicating the traditional crafts of their homeland. They painted dower chests and other furniture with unicorns, birds, flowers, fruit, and intricate geometric forms. They inscribed their gaily decorated pottery with such homely legends as, "Rather would I single live than my wife my breeches give." They even revived the hand illumination of manuscripts, an art that had been neglected after the invention of movable type.

But the Pennsylvania "Dutch" were not just pious, naive, tradition-bound folk artists. They were among the earliest and most accomplished makers of musical instruments in the American Colonies, and they were also responsible for two innovations of great significance. German artisans in Lancaster and Reading, Pennsylvania, developed the deadly accurate but inaccurately named Kentucky rifle, so beloved of frontier sharpshooters. And canny German farmers devised that most American form of transportation, the rugged, picturesque Conestoga wagon.

Fractur, a form *of illuminated calligraphy reminiscent of the Middle Ages, is shown in a detail of the 34th Psalm, made by George Geistweite in 1801. Birth, baptismal, and marriage certificates, as well as prayer books and hymnals, were often illuminated in this manner by Pennsylvania German folk artists, who executed their designs on paper in ink and watercolor. The term "fractur" is also used to designate these artists' highly stylized ornamental drawings of birds, animals, and flowers.*

Painted tinware *adorns the entrance hall of the Red Lion Inn, a Delaware tavern originally built in 1800 and reconstructed by the Winterthur Museum. The row of shelves and the painted Pennsylvania chest below them display gaily painted coffeepots and trays of the kind often sold by itinerant tinkers or peddlers in the early 1800's. Colonial tinware was usually imported from England, but in the post-Revolutionary period American whitesmiths, as workers in tin were called, began making a variety of utensils, toys, and boxes. Pennsylvania German whitesmiths used traditional birds, flowers, stars, and fruit clusters to decorate their pieces, which were made of thin sheets of iron dipped into molten tin.*

Ceramics in the Colonies

Along with carpentry, pottery making is probably the oldest American craft. Every colonial family needed dishes, mugs, pitchers, cooking vessels, and storage containers. And virtually every colonial community had its resident potter. Until well after the Revolution most American-made pottery was glazed redware, formed from clay containing high concentrations of iron oxide. This clay, found in abundance along the Atlantic seaboard, was also used in making bricks and tiles.

The earliest potters whose names we know—Philip Drinker, William Vincent, and John Pride—arrived in New England in 1635. Like their anonymous colleagues, these three men were less concerned with elegance than with sturdiness. They shaped their simple forms on the potter's wheel. Some pieces were decorated with zigzag, dotted, or wavy patterns made by trailing across them a thin line of slip (clay thinned to a creamlike consistency). Others had patterns incised by holding a stick against the vessel while it was being turned. The commonest glaze was a mixture of red lead and ground glass, but other color effects were achieved by adding ground metal particles. Although few of these early products of the potter's wheel have survived intact, many pieces have been found at pottery sites. Among the earliest sites are those at Jamestown, Virginia, and Danvers, Massachusetts—at the latter location James Kettle turned out redware from about 1687 to 1709. Delftware (white-glazed earthenware, often painted with colorful designs) was produced briefly in these early years at Burlington, New Jersey, by a pottery owned by an absentee proprietor, one Daniel Coxe, who lived in London.

Exuberant relics *of the woodcarver's art include ships' figureheads, carousel animals, cigar-store Indians and other storefront figures, some of which were carved from single tree trunks. This collection dates from the last half of the 19th century.*

These stoneware jars *date from the late 18th century. The teapot, possibly from Philadelphia, may have been made as early as 1750. Heavy, nonporous, and opaque, stoneware is made of a hard clay paste, which vitrifies when fired at high temperatures. At the peak of the firing process, the potter often throws salt into the kiln to give the surface of this highly durable pottery its characteristic roughness.*

The end of the 17th century saw the introduction of stoneware. Although it never replaced redware in popularity, it was often used for crocks, jugs, and other containers. The gray and tan pieces were usually decorated with blue slip formed into loops, flowers, animals, fish, or birds. Some of the best stoneware came from the kilns of John Rommey and William Crolius in New York City, beginning in 1735; their skills were carried on by their sons. James Morgan of Cheesequake, New Jersey, made blue-slip stoneware in the 1770's. George Huebener, a potter who emigrated from Germany and settled near Philadelphia, is known for his decorative earthenware. Shortly before the Revolution the Philadelphia potters Bonnin & Morris made refined pieces of porcelain (distinguished from pottery in that it is translucent). Their venture was short-lived, however.

Carvers in Wood

Encouraged by the abundance of wood, the wood-carver undoubtedly practiced his craft from early colonial times, whittling and painting dolls, rocking horses, tops, and

The Mountain Dulcimer

The dulcimer, a musical instrument that is basically a wooden box with a variable number of strings stretched over it, has been known in one form or another since ancient times. But the so-called mountain dulcimer made in the Appalachians is uniquely American. Probably evolved from the *scheitholt,* a stringed instrument made by the Pennsylvania Germans, and the French *épinette,* mountain dulcimers are usually carved from walnut, spruce, or cherry; they are still painstakingly fashioned by hand in the mountains of Virginia, West Virginia, and Kentucky. At right, dulcimer maker George Pickow, who learned his craft in Kentucky, is shown working in his shop in Port Washington, New York. Pickow's wife is folksinger Jean Ritchie, who often uses the dulcimer. Unlike the ancient dulcimer, which is played by striking the strings with small mallets, the mountain dulcimer is played by plucking the strings with a quill. The heart-shaped holes in the instruments are traditional.

other toys for children, and making simple decorative pieces for the home. But not until the latter half of the 18th century did the craft come to full flower. Simeon Skillin of Boston and his sons made wood carvings and figures to decorate the area's finest homes and public buildings. As shipbuilding increased in the 19th century, so did the demands for massive figureheads to grace the prows of the windjammers. Among the earliest to achieve fame in this field was William Rush of Philadelphia. Charles A. L. Sampson of Bath, Maine, dressed some of his female figureheads in the latest fashions. Another master ship carver was Isaac Fowle of Boston. Later in the century John Bellamy of Kittery, Maine, carved hundreds of American eagles with which to decorate ships. The eagle was also the favorite subject of Wilhelm Schimmel of Pennsylvania, an itinerant wood-carver. Other talented craftsmen carved signs and figures—including the familiar cigar-store Indian of the late 1800's—to signify a shopkeeper's wares. Some of the most delightful and whimsical work was done by the mostly anonymous craftsmen who carved and painted prancing horses for carousels.

The Homely Arts

Not all crafts were practiced by men. Fine needlework was a woman's art. But men did produce macrame work, and this knotting of threads and cords into designs was popular among 18th- and 19th-century sailors during their long sea voyages. Men also worked on home looms or as itinerant weavers until weaving became primarily a factory activity in the early 19th century.

This sheaf of wheat, *carved in wood by Clarke Noble about 1900, once decorated a bakery-shop front. Such recognizable symbols were especially helpful to illiterate customers.*

Embroidery was a required womanly skill. Bedspreads, chair covers, purses, and dresses were decorated with colorful stitching in crewel (worsted), silk, or linen. Every woman had a sampler—a long strip of cloth embroidered with various stitches. Originally a kind of sourcebook of stitches and motifs, the sampler later became a means of practice for young girls, who by the age of 8 were expected to be adept at needlework. At first the samplers might be restricted to the alphabet and a series of numbers, perhaps in two or three styles; then mottoes and verses were added; and finally intricate decorative patterns were executed, which might depict a house, an animal, or a landscape with figures, all stitched in beautiful and realistic detail. The mourning sampler commemorating friends, relatives, and heroes in pictures and verse appeared in the 19th century.

Hand hooking of rugs, using colorful strips of cloth or yarn pulled through a heavy meshed fabric, grew in popularity after 1820. Here again imagination and skill produced useful objects that were also lovely to look at. The making of bed quilts provided an opportunity to do intricate embroidery and appliqué, as well as to gather with neighbors at daylong quilting bees, during which the quilts were assembled and backed.

Early samplers *were almost as varied as the imaginations of their individual makers, usually young girls who were expected to demonstrate their proficiency in fancy needlework. A typical sampler combined the alphabet, lettered in several styles, with decorative designs, bits of homespun philosophy, and pious quotations.*

A patriotic hooked rug *celebrates America's Centennial. The art of hooking rugs, introduced to New England by early Scandinavian immigrants, was widespread in the United States by the 1850's. The designs were made by weaving brightly colored scraps of cloth or yarn through the homespun or burlap background fabric with a metal hook.*

Star of Bethlehem, *one of the most difficult of the patchwork patterns, was used for this magnificent show quilt, made about 1815 in Newburgh, New York. The complex design was formed by piecing together thousands of diamond-shaped bits of fine English chintz. Such bedcovers were commonly finished at festive quilting bees by a group of eight or more.*

Colonial crewelwork, *made by Mary Sarah Titcomb in 1760, depicts Eve's temptation in the Garden of Eden. Crewel patterns were stitched in woolen yarn, usually on a ground of bleached linen, and crewelwork was used to decorate everything from small cushions to elaborate bed curtains and rugs that were both handsome and extremely warm. Most colonial families could ill afford English textiles, and during the 1640's in Massachusetts and Connecticut they were required to grow their own flax or hemp. All women and girls were expected to become adept at spinning, weaving, dyeing, knitting, sewing, and several kinds of needlework.*

Indian Craftsmanship
A Natural Feeling for Beauty

Many Indian crafts served ritual functions; figurines portrayed the magical properties of a subject, its inner power or essence, rather than its outward form. Other works combined ritual and utilitarian purposes or were purely secular. Indian craftsmen tended to develop their skills around the natural materials at hand. The Plains tribes excelled in quillwork and the costume arts; the forest Indians, in woodcarving; and the Southwestern peoples, in metal and pottery work. White influences changed Indian crafts in ways both beneficial (by introducing new dyes, iron tools, and glass beads) and harmful. The growing white demand for Indian work led many artisans to mass-produce commercially acceptable imitations of primitive craftsmanship.

Inlaid shell ornament, Zuñi.

Making jewelry *in silver was a relatively late development among the Southwestern tribes; the Navahos learned metalwork from Mexican ironsmiths in the mid-19th century. Both Zuñi and Navaho craftsmen combined silver and turquoise. Navaho designs were usually massive; the Zuñis specialized in more delicate work.*

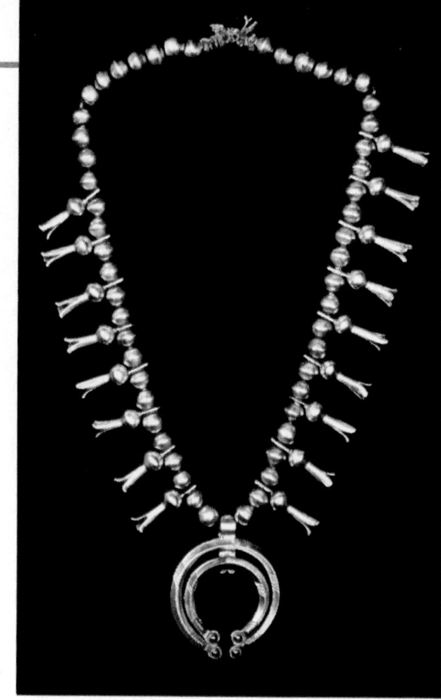

Silver "squash blossom" necklace, Navaho.

Carved cedar box front, Tlingit.

"Two Weavers" painting, Navaho.

Carving in wood, *metal, and stone was one Indian art that benefited greatly from the coming of the whites and the introduction of steel tools. The Tlingits of the Alaskan coast were masters of elaborately painted carvings in wood, such as the cedar box front above; they also worked in metal and horn. Carved stone pipe bowls with human or animal figures, like the steatite bowl below, have been found in many parts of the Southeast and were probably for ceremonial use. Similarly intended were the grotesque "False Face" masks of carved and painted wood made by the Iroquois tribes. Richly decorated* Kachina *figurines, like the Hopi "Cloud Being" at right, represented the mythical ancestors of the Southwestern Pueblo peoples and were used in fertility rituals.*

Kachina figurine, Hopi.

Pipe bowl with animal decoration, Cherokee.

Carved "crooked mouth" mask, Seneca.

The Navahos *learned weaving from the Pueblo textile artists, just as they later learned silversmithing from the Mexicans. Navaho sand paintings, used in healing rituals, were also adapted from Pueblo artwork. The Pueblo men did the weaving, but the Navahos, comparative latecomers to the Southwest, reversed the practice. Their women not only made blankets for home use but quickly built up a considerable trade with the whites. Many tribes had strict rules limiting the kind of work women could do, often prohibiting them from making or even touching any articles intended for religious use. The brightly colored geometric designs characteristic of Navaho weaving were apparently borrowed from Oriental patterns in carpets brought to the West by affluent white settlers. The painting of modern Navaho women spinning and weaving is by contemporary Navaho artist, Harrison Begay, who studied at the Santa Fe Indian School.*

Pottery olla, Acoma.

Pottery fetish jar, Zuñi.

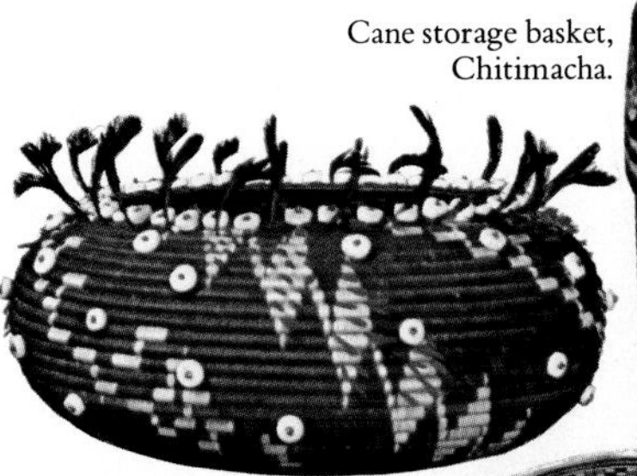

Gift basket, Pomo.

Cane storage basket, Chitimacha.

Grayware bowl with mountain lion, Mimbres.

Pottery and basketry *attained a rare quality among the tribes of California and the Southwest. Above left is an Acoma olla, or water jar; next to it is a Zuñi fetish jar, which was used to purify witches. The feather-and-shell gift baskets of the Pacific coast tribes, like the Pomo basket shown here, were famous for their fine weaving and for their use of bird plumage, which was woven into the baskets using a technique similar to that used by the ancient Peruvians and Polynesians. Unfortunately, since such baskets were often presented to the dead and burned on funeral pyres, few survive. The Mimbres bowl at right, with its painted mountain lion design, is from New Mexico; the polychrome cane basket above it was made by the Chitimachas, a Louisiana tribe.*

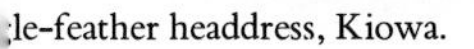

:le-feather headdress, Kiowa.

"Ghost Dance" dress, Pawnee.

Shoulder bag with beaded design, Chippewa.

Moccasins with quillwork decoration, Arikara.

Costume arts *reached their greatest heights among the Plains Indians, whose work with feathers, quills, beading, and painted hides embodies Indian craftsmanship in the minds of many people. A magnificent Kiowa eagle-feather war bonnet reflects the nomadic plainsmen's glorification of battle; their buffalo-hide shields and their horses' trappings were often equally lavish. The buckskin "Ghost Dance" dress was made for a Pawnee woman, a follower of the Paiute messiah who predicted the downfall of the whites during the 1890's; its designs show a decided familiarity with Christian symbolism. The elaborate Arikara moccasins, decorated with dyed porcupine quills, were worn only on important occasions. The shoulder bag above them is decorated with glass beading, which largely replaced quillwork after white traders brought in the beads.*

Cabinetmaker *and apprentices in a Williamsburg, Virginia, replica of an 18th-century woodworking shop use authentic methods of colonial days. Master furniture craftsmen often made and honed their own tools, whose cutting edges had to be kept razor sharp. The term "cabinetmaker" was first used in America around the end of the 17th century; earlier, such men were usually known as joiners—from their technique of fitting pieces together with mortise-and-tenon joints held by wooden pegs or pins. Those who used lathes to fashion chair and table legs were called turners. An elegant 18th-century highboy or secretary required months of painstaking labor, and the best American cabinetmakers might be booked up years in advance. Mahogany was one of the most popular woods for fine cabinetwork; it was strong, worm-resistant, easy to carve, and had a warm patina that improved with use.*

Craftsmen at Work for the World at Large

Despite regional differences, distinctive American designs developed early in the household crafts. (The Hadley chest, for example, dates from the 17th century.) The wealthier colonists, however, often preferred furniture styles virtually indistinguishable from those popular with their English counterparts. Until about 1725 the favorite style was the heavy, rectangular William and Mary; for the next 25 years it was the lighter, more graceful Queen Anne style. Thereafter, until the Revolution, the major force was the Georgian, most effectively expressed by the English cabinetmaker Thomas Chippendale, whose book of designs was widely circulated.

In the Georgian period American craftsmen began to add their own distinctive touches to styles that had a European origin. Chests and cabinets especially showed the mark of these innovations. William Savery of Philadelphia designed double chests that, despite their massiveness, conveyed a sense of grace and lightness not always found in European Chippendale. John Goddard and John T. Townsend of Newport originated the blockfront chest, with its carved shell motif. Perhaps the best known American modifications were in the design of the spindle-backed Windsor chair, which made it far more elegant and graceful than its English cousin. Originally known in this country as the Philadelphia chair, after the city in which it was first made, about 1725, it was one of the most popular pieces of furniture in America for almost a century and a half.

After the Revolutionary War American design and American designers came into their own. While the American Chippendale style continued to be popular, the lighter styles of the Classic Revival began to appear—exemplified abroad by the work of Adam, Sheraton, and Hepplewhite, and in the United States by the master cabinetmakers of New England, Philadelphia, and Baltimore. While these craftsmen were giving an American cast to European design, a New York cabinetmaker was producing a distinctive and widely imitated style of furniture. Duncan Phyfe, a Scot, came to this country with his family in 1783, when he was 15 years old; by 1792

Windsor chairs, *also known as Philadelphia or stick chairs, originated in England, but by the mid-1700's there was a flourishing trade in American-made Windsors, centering around Philadelphia. The American versions were generally much lighter and more delicately proportioned than their English counterparts. The Windsor's rails and tapering spindles were usually of hickory, the contour seats were of pine or whitewood, and the turned, splayed legs were of maple. Some chairs were painted in bright colors to disguise this assortment of woods. The comb-back Windsor armchair at left is of ash, hickory, and maple.*

Duncan Phyfe

Influential Cabinetmaker of the Classic Revival Period

The man who made New York the style capital of American furniture design in the early 1800's was a hard-working Scotsman whose elegant mahogany drawing-room pieces graced the homes of the city's most prominent families. Born in 1768, Duncan Phyfe immigrated first to Albany, New York. In 1795 he set up a shop in New York City on what later became Fulton Street. His popularity and industry are attested by the fact that, at his death in 1854, he left an estate of nearly half a million dollars—an impressive fortune for that time.

Phyfe's work was influenced by the English Regency and French Neoclassical styles, and by the Greco-Roman motifs used in both, but the restrained, curving lines of his furniture and the delicacy of its carvings were distinctly his own. Among his best known designs are lyre-back, or harp-back, side chairs, graceful settees and sofas with delicately carved classical motifs on their mahogany frames, and card tables with vase pedestals, inward-curving legs, and cloverleaf-shaped tops.

Phyfe's favorite carving motifs—stylized acanthus leaves and laurel branches, drapery swags, and reeds tied with ribbons—were often sketched out on paper and hung from the ceiling of his workroom, so that the busy cabinetmaker could quickly devise new design combinations for his apprentices to execute.

Phyfe was known as a strict taskmaster who begrudged his workers any time away from their jobs. He was equally strict with his family, who, according to one memoir, had to be in bed punctually at 9 o'clock.

A tool chest *of master cabinetmaker Duncan Phyfe holds saws, clamps, planes, chisels, and other implements of his trade, all arranged in meticulous order. At the height of Phyfe's success, his New York City workshop and salesroom employed more than a hundred people.*

The Phyfe room *at the Winterthur Museum in Delaware is furnished entirely in the restrained Neoclassical style of his best period. Most of the furniture in the room was made by Phyfe for a New York City client, William Bayard, in 1807. The caned settee and the two globe stands beside it feature the reed carvings and sweeping curves so characteristic of Phyfe's widely imitated designs. Complementing the furniture are the room's delicately modeled woodwork and the painted and gilded chimney glass, all taken from an elegant New York house of the period.*

This tall case clock *of walnut, chestnut, and yellow pine was made between 1770 and 1785 and is now part of the Williamsburg collection. During the 17th century most clocks were designed merely to strike the hour on a bell and had only a single hand, but by the early 18th century the accuracy of clocks had been greatly improved, and the minute hand was added. Tall case clocks were so named because they were housed within tall, standing cases, or cabinets, which protected the works and concealed the pendulum and weights. (They were not known as grandfather clocks until after the publication of the popular song "Grandfather's Clock" in 1875.) The engraved brass dials were usually imported from England, as were the delicate pierced-steel hands. But the inner works were made by American mechanics, who usually signed the clock faces, and the handsome cabinets were designed by American carpenters. The elaborate face of the clock at left, whose works were signed by Thomas Walker of Fredericksburg, Virginia, is framed by carved Doric columns supporting an elegant archway.*

he was well established at his trade in New York City, where he continued to work until the middle of the 19th century. Phyfe's work utilized classical motifs, particularly in the design of the klismos, or Greek, chair, the lyre-back chair, the Sheraton-style sofa, and the tripod table. Phyfe's early work was simpler and better than his later productions. From 1830 until his retirement in 1847, under pressure of increasing demand for the ornate, he produced what he called butcher furniture.

On the other hand, Phyfe's contemporary, Charles Honoré Lannuier, who also worked in New York, demonstrated that the ornate could be produced tastefully. Drawing largely on the Empire styles of his native France, Lannuier somehow managed to combine elaborate decoration in ormolu, brass, mirrors, and marble with elegant good taste.

Side by side with these trends to elaboration, two regional folk styles persisted. These were the Shaker and the Pennsylvania German, or "Dutch," both characterized by simplicity. This same simplicity was also found in the United States' first inexpensive factory-produced furniture: the wooden chair designed by Lambert Hitchcock, painted black and ornamented across its back with stenciled floral and geometric patterns; and the similarly stenciled, high-backed Boston chair and Boston rocker. All three pieces were extremely popular and were sold widely throughout the country.

With the Industrial Revolution, the products of American craftsmanship became increasingly standardized. But this loss in originality was offset by an increase in precision and transformation from a European to a distinctly American product. The development of finer tools and machinery gave the artisan greater control over his materials. In addition, the Industrial Revolution made the products of his craft more widely available and facilitated the development of a national style rather than a series of regional ones. It also had an influence on fashions in furniture and clothing—a good influence when it was tasteful, a bad one when it was not.

A change in public taste was particularly noticeable in the mid-19th century. The newly rich were attracted by the ostentatious and overelaborate. Mechanical lathes and jigsaws turned carving and decorating into machine skills, producing overornamental furniture. In what has been called the Grand Rapids era much American furniture was overstuffed and overdecorated, but, thanks to mass production, it was not overpriced.

Oases of Craftsmanship

During this period of pretentious design, which extended through the second half of the 19th century, designers and manufacturers of distinctive furniture could still be found. Among these was John Henry Belter, who immigrated to the United States from Germany and opened a workshop in New York City, where he made furniture for some of the most elegant homes of the 1850's and 1860's. Belter's furniture was ornate, for he followed the prevailing style of the Rococo Revival. But the refinement of his craftsmanship assured its good taste. Belter developed a technique for steaming laminated layers of rosewood veneer in molds to give them the graceful curved shapes that characterize all his work. In addition, every piece of his furniture was hand finished, with deep carving in floral and fruit motifs.

Contemporaneously with Belter, a new movement was beginning in England, and it was to have a significant effect in simplifying and improving American taste. The Arts and

This rocking chair *by Gustav Stickley (c. 1910) has the simple lines, straightforward design, and sturdy construction made popular by the English Arts and Crafts movement.*

John Henry Belter and the Rococo Revival

Talented Exponent of an Exuberant Style

The Rococo Revival style of the mid-19th century, with its extravagant curves and carvings, is so closely associated with the name of cabinetmaker John Henry Belter that all pieces of this genre are likely to be called Belter furniture. Belter was born in 1804. He was apprenticed as a cabinetmaker and carver in his native Germany during the period when French Rococo designs were becoming fashionable there. In 1844 he immigrated to New York City, and by 1858 he headed a prosperous furniture factory that employed 40 apprentices. The complex curves and ornamentation of Belter's furniture were achieved through a process in which an average of six to eight layers of wood were glued together, with the grains of alternate layers running at right angles. The wood was pressed and steamed into curving shapes, then pierced and carved. Further ornamental carvings were glued on to add depth and richness, often in the form of S- and C-shaped scrolls combined with fruit and flower motifs. Belter did not invent lamination, but he greatly improved the process. Although he patented his improvements, both his methods and his designs were frequently copied. In 1863 Belter died a poor man, and his company went bankrupt a few years after his death.

A fanciful love seat *by Belter exemplifies the taste of early Victorians. Such pieces, also known as "tête-à-têtes" or "conversationals," were popular novelties in an era with a passion for novelty. Although mid-19th-century craftsmen worked in many styles (among them various derivations and combinations of Greco-Roman, Elizabethan, and Gothic), the most popular was the Rococo revival of which Belter was the acknowledged master. The love seat above is of laminated rosewood, prized by Victorian cabinetmakers for its density, its durability, and the richness of its color and grain. It was during this period that upholstered furniture attained major importance. The coil spring, however, was not perfected until the 1880's, when wealthy customers were demanding more comfort.*

This parlor suite *designed by Belter is now on display at the Museum of the City of New York. The pieces shown here are among the few signed or documented Belter designs that survive today. The marble and rosewood table at center, with its ornate carvings of fruit and flowers, bears his label and the dates 1856–61. Belter's style is loosely derived from French Rococo designs of the 18th century, but the overall effect of his work is decidedly Victorian—a combination of romanticism and almost barbaric opulence. After visiting an 1854 exhibit of American furniture, Prof. Benjamin Silliman of Yale University noted regretfully that the ornamental carvings on Rococo Revival furniture were "very uninviting to human shoulders"; he was nonetheless a great admirer of the Belter style. During this period the field of cabinetmaking was dominated by German- and French-born craftsmen. One of them, Ernest Hagen of New York City, later observed that between 1840 and 1865 the city's "Colony of German mechanics" made quantities of furniture, "which is now sold for Antique to such as don't Know any better."*

Crafts movement, encouraged by John Ruskin and William Morris, reached the United States in 1872 with the publication in this country of Charles L. Eastlake's book, *Hints on Household Taste.* The book, which was an instantaneous success, decried the "silly knickknacks, crazy chairs, and tables, and all those shapeless extravagances which pass for elegance in the 19th century." To do away with them, Eastlake called for a return to the simple rectangular forms and restrained decoration of medieval times and to the careful construction and workmanship of the preindustrial period. The most influential of Eastlake's disciples in the United States was Gustav Stickley, who formed his own furniture manufacturing company in New York City in 1898 and 3 years later began *The Craftsman,* a magazine designed to promote the esthetics and philosophy of the new point of view.

In the 1920's and 1930's two European styles influenced American furniture design. One was that of the German Bauhaus school headed by Walter Gropius, who emigrated to the United States in 1937. Bauhaus furniture emphasized simplicity and severity and made use of metal as well as wood. The other influence was the Art Deco style. Originating in France, it was characterized by geometric shapes. Until the end of World War II these two styles dominated American furniture design.

Ceramics in the Young Republic

After the Revolution the United States continued to import fine china from Europe and found a new source of supply in China; American pottery remained everyday ware. In the Shenandoah Valley Peter Bell and his family made slip-decorated redware in the pre-Revolutionary tradition; in New Jersey Xerxes Price worked in stoneware. In New York the company founded by William Crolius in the colonial period continued until about 1870, with competition from another New York potter, Thomas Commeraw, whose stoneware was very similar to that made by Crolius.

It was in New England, however, that the potter's art reached its zenith. In Massachusetts Thomas Crafts made his fanciful jugs, in Connecticut Peter Cross was known for his stoneware, and in Bennington, Vermont, in 1793 John Norton began an enterprise that dominated American pottery for more than 50 years. Norton started with one kiln, expecting to do no more than supply pottery for himself and his neighbors. But the demand for his work grew, and when he retired in 1813, his sons, Luman and John, took over the business. About 15 years later Luman's son Julius joined the firm. Not content with making purely utilitarian wares, he began to turn out handsome decorative inkstands, flowerpots, and other

Christopher Webber Fenton
Bennington's Master Potter

America's best known ceramist in the mid-19th century was Christopher Webber Fenton, whose U.S. Pottery Co. in Bennington, Vermont, produced a remarkable array of designs in both earthenware and porcelain. Fenton started out in partnership with his brother-in-law, Julius Norton, but in 1847 he established his own works. There he made the mottled, brown-glazed Rockingham ware often described as typical Bennington pottery, and in 1849 patented flint enamel, in which a mixture of metallic oxides was sprinkled over the glaze to produce a multicolored effect. The Toby snuff jar, tulip vase, poodle, and standing stag shown here are all of flint enamel.

Fenton's most unusual pottery was "scroddled" ware, in which the marbled effects were achieved by mixing brown, blue, or gray clays with cream-colored clays. The pieces, such as the small pitcher in the grouping here, were then pressed into a mold and fired, usually with a coat of clear glaze. Fenton also made more elaborate, formal pieces—gilt-edged presentation pitchers, delicate ewers and

This Bennington pottery group *includes rare pieces in porcelain, flint enamel, graniteware, and "scroddled" ware. The flintware stag, made about 1850, is the only one of its kind.*

vases—in graniteware, glazed porcelain, and unglazed white parian ware. But by far the most prized, and most expensive, of the Fenton designs were the decorative animals—lounging cows, graceful deer, cocky poodles, and whimsical lions, whose "coleslaw" manes were made by pushing damp clay through a screen directly onto the figures. Also popular were Toby pitchers and snuff jars in the form of the fat, jolly little character called Toby Fillpot, hero of the popular song "Little Brown Jug."

Many of Fenton's ideas were not original—both the lions and the Toby pieces were inspired by English designs—but his firm produced an amazing variety of both functional and decorative pieces, executed with charm and exuberance.

Art pottery vases *designed around the turn of the century reflect the influence of the Arts and Crafts movement and its reaction against the drab uniformity of industrial products. Although art pottery was often made by commercially oriented firms, and many pieces were designed and executed cooperatively by a number of artists and craftsmen, the best work retains a creative, individual stamp. Shown above (clockwise from left) are an incised and reticulated vase, decorated with figures of knights, and designed and made by Frederick Hurten Rhead at Missouri's University City Pottery (1911); a vase with a columbine design by Artus Van Briggle of Colorado (1902); a daffodil-and-leaf-decorated vase from Boston's Grueby Pottery; two underglaze slip-painted vases with flower designs from the Rookwood Pottery of Cincinnati (late 1890's); the famous Lorelei vase by Van Briggle (1902); a covered cloisonné vase with a typically Craftsman moth design, also by the Grueby Pottery; and a porcelain vase with a crystalline glaze by Adelaide A. Robineau of Syracuse, New York (1904).*

display pieces. In 1845 Julius took his brother-in-law, Christopher Webber Fenton, into partnership. When Fenton left after 2 years to establish his own firm, later known as the U.S. Pottery Co., he took with him leadership in American ceramics. Other important potters of the early and mid-1800's were William Ellis Tucker of Philadelphia, the first American to work successfully in porcelain, and David Henderson, whose high standards and daring forms brought renown to the American Pottery Company.

As American potters became more skilled, their work became more elaborate. The United States began turning out menageries of ceramic animals—curly-maned lions, poodles carrying baskets in their mouths, horses, monkeys, bears, and even bird whistles. These extravagant forms served the Victorian taste for knickknacks, and they dominated the potter's art until the arrival of the Arts and Crafts movement, which influenced ceramics much as it influenced furniture.

This Losanti vase *with swirling Art Nouveau designs is by Mary Louise McLaughlin. Her vases were hand thrown and carved with a needle after drying.*

One of the most successful of the late-19th-century ventures in ceramics affected by the British movement was the Rookwood Pottery, founded in 1880 by Maria Longworth Nichols Storer, a prominent Cincinnati woman who became interested in ceramics through a class in china painting. Rookwood pottery is distinguished for its simple, elegant shapes, its beautiful glazes, and its finely painted decorations. Another Cincinnati woman, Mary Louise McLaughlin, experimented with many types of decorative porcelain. She is best known for her Losanti ware—a creamy-white, very translucent porcelain that she developed in 1898 and named after Losantiville, Cincinnati's original name. Also a successful exponent of the Arts and Crafts movement was William H. Grueby, who established a pottery in Boston. His work was all handcrafted—hand thrown, hand decorated, and hand glazed. Grueby introduced mat, or nonshiny, glazes to the United

States, and much of his work is glazed in a soft, watermelon-rind green.

The Art of Glassmaking

Although history records that the first settlers established a glassworks in Jamestown in 1609, nothing remains of its work. The first American glass of which examples exist was not made until more than a hundred years later, when Caspar Wistar, a German immigrant, founded a glassworks in New Jersey, and Henry "Baron" Stiegel, also from Germany, opened three successively in Pennsylvania. Wistar's plant originally made bottles and window glass, but it also produced blown table glass—bowls, jars, and pitchers of what has come to be called the South Jersey type, in which the decorative effects were achieved by imposing colored glass on the original blown base. Stiegel's glass was often pattern-molded. In this technique the pattern is imposed on the molten glass in a mold, and the glass is blown; it is then decorated with either engraving or enameling in deep blue. Stiegel's factories made a variety of fine glass tableware: Saltcellars, creamers, sugar bowls, tumblers, and decanters. Despite the high quality of their work, both Wistar's and Stiegel's ventures failed. The greatest of the early American glassmakers, John Frederick Amelung, established his New Bremen Glass Manufactory in Maryland in 1784, but a few years later he also went bankrupt.

This covered goblet *of engraved glass was made in 1788 as a presentation piece by John Frederick Amelung of New Bremen, Maryland.*

About a quarter of a century later, Deming Jarves of the Boston and Sandwich Glass Company designed a three-piece mold, with patterns engraved on it, into which hot glass could be blown. At first the patterns were forced onto the glass by the air pressure created when the mold was closed; later a machine was invented to press the glass into the mold. Because the patterns in the machine-pressed glass were so much sharper than those of the blown-mold glass, it was known as lacy glass. Many American companies made pressed glass—lacy and otherwise—throughout the 19th century, all of them seeking to produce a cheap facsimile of cut glass. The most famous was the one with which Jarves was associated and which has given the name "Sandwich glass" to all 19th-century pressed glassware.

A glass collection *from the mid-19th century includes a blown-glass pitcher of the South Jersey type, a pressed-glass decanter, salt holder, and lacy dish, and an Ohio compote and sugar bowl.*

Like every other craft, glassmaking was influenced by the Victorian mania for decorative detail. Again, it was the Arts and Crafts movement that reversed this trend to the ornate. A leading figure in the revival of simplicity was Louis Comfort Tiffany, who had originally planned to become a painter. Tiffany designed exquisite stained-glass windows, leaded and patterned with stylized landscapes, for the homes of the wealthy. For his Tiffany Glass and Decorating Company (later Tiffany Studios), he designed bowls and vases that were hand blown in what he called Favrile glass, distinguished by its graceful elongated shapes and its iridescent colors. The decoration on some pieces was made by carving through a layer of glass of one color, exposing a different-colored layer beneath. At the turn of the century Tiffany's Art Nouveau glassware was popular all over the world and today his pieces are treasured by many museums.

Among the early 20th-century glassmakers was English-trained Frederick Carder. His factory at Corning, New York, later became part of the Corning Glass Works; this organization, in turn, spawned Steuben Glass in 1933. From it has come handsome decorative glassware, both blown and molded, many of the pieces with engraved designs created by leading American artists. Steuben's glass, like Tiffany's, combines the best in design, craftsmanship, and industrial technique.

Louis Comfort Tiffany

Creator of a Sensuous New Art Form in Glass

As a young man, the romantic, flamboyant Louis Tiffany rejected a place in his father's business (New York's renowned Tiffany & Company) to devote himself to art. He later became America's leading exponent of Art Nouveau, a movement whose curvilinear, organic forms eminently suited his style.

Born in New York City in 1848, Tiffany began studying landscape painting seriously at 18. After traveling in Europe and North Africa, where he was captivated by Islamic art, he opened his own New York studio, but his interest and talents soon turned from conventional landscape painting to the decorative arts.

Tiffany began experimenting with stained glass in 1875 and opened a glass-making factory 3 years later. Dissatisfied with the creative limitations of traditional staining and leading, he conducted endless chemical experiments—during which his factory burned down three times—and finally devised techniques by which molten glass could be permeated with color from within. By treating the glass with fumes from vaporized metals and skillfully interweaving color and texture, Tiffany achieved effects of amazing subtlety and richness. With his new methods he created an enormous variety of designs, from delicate flower-shaped vases to intricate stained-glass windows. In 1893 he designed a modern Byzantine chapel, a glittering confection of black and white marble, stained glass, and luminous mosaics encrusted with pearls and semiprecious stones; it became the sensation of the World's Columbian Exposition in Chicago.

For a time Tiffany was remarkably successful in molding American taste to his concept of the beautiful. By 1900 his Tiffany Studios employed hundreds of skilled workers, who produced jewelry, desk sets, assorted bric-a-brac, stemware, and the famous cast-bronze Tiffany lamps with their intricate leaded-glass shades—a form later debased by mass-produced imitations. But by 1918, when he established a foundation in his name and converted his Long Island estate into an informal retreat for artists, his designs had gone out of fashion. Today, thanks to a renewed interest in Art Nouveau, Tiffany is again recognized as America's most original artist in glass.

These delicate vases *of opalescent Favrile glass were made by Tiffany about 1900. He used the word "Favrile," derived from the Latin* fabrica *("skillfully wrought object"), to describe a secret process of his own invention by which colors, designs, and textures were embedded into the glass before it was blown.*

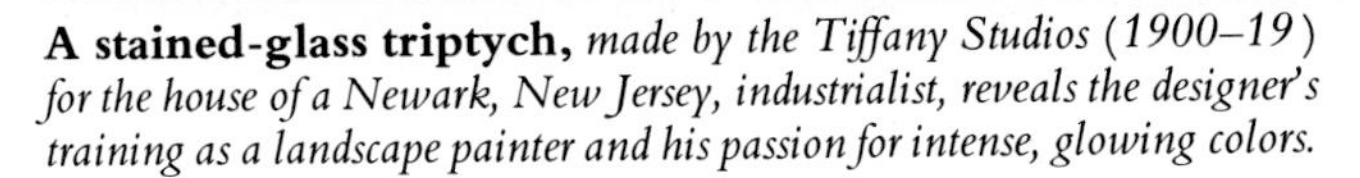

A stained-glass triptych, *made by the Tiffany Studios (1900–19) for the house of a Newark, New Jersey, industrialist, reveals the designer's training as a landscape painter and his passion for intense, glowing colors. Tiffany worked his pigments directly into the glass, rather than painting it and then burning or fusing the color into it, as was common; he produced variations in texture by forcing the molten glass into wrinkles or folds.*

The Dramatic Break With Tradition

Two major and diverse influences shape the work of craftsmen in the United States today. One derives from the same spirit that motivated the Bauhaus school: the attempt to use the methods and machines of modern industrial production to create objects that are both well designed and appropriate to contemporary life. Architect Frank Lloyd Wright was a major exponent of this point of view, and it has also found expression in such distinctive household objects as the dinnerware designed by Russel Wright for the Steubenville Pottery Company, and the molded chairs of laminated wood, plastic, and other materials designed by Charles Eames. These and other objects similarly designed by masters and executed by machines have made the best of modern design available to many Americans at reasonable prices.

The second major influence derives from the spirit that motivated the early leaders of the Arts and Crafts movement: the attempt to return craftsmanship to the hands of the individual craftsmen and to produce work designed and executed by the same person. The beautifully handcrafted and decorative objects so produced can transcend the usual definition of craft to become works of art, while retaining their basic function. The ceramics of Robert Arneson, the silver of John C. Marshall and Arline Fisch, the textiles of Alma W. Lesch, the glassware of Joel Philip Myers, and the furniture of Arthur Carpenter and Wendell Castle are examples of this approach.

Because these painstaking craftsmen produce one-of-a-kind pieces, their work can find its way into only a limited number of homes. But the artist-craftsmen of today can set examples for the mass-produced work within reach of everyone. They can remind us again that useful objects are worth all the care, taste, and skill that can be lavished upon them.

Ceramics. With textiles, metals, glass, and other handicrafts, ceramics have been influenced profoundly by the contemporary crafts movement, breaking free of traditional utilitarian forms to become a medium of individual creative expression. During the 1950's, California-based artist and ceramist Peter Voulkos, an Abstract Expressionist, encouraged other potters to use clay imaginatively and to discard the centuries-old concepts of utility and symmetry. One of the younger ceramists influenced by Voulkos' work—a craftsman whose earthy "Funk Art" forms are themselves highly influential—is Robert Arneson, whose "Alice House Wall" is shown at left. A polychromed earthenware design that serves no function but to please the eye, it demonstrates the increasingly blurred distinction between arts and crafts that characterizes the work of many studio craftsmen. Arneson's ceramics are often witty re-creations of the familiar objects of mass technology, transformed into vehicles of a deadpan social commentary—typewriters with red-painted ceramic fingernails for keyboards, ceramic six-packs and toasters, an earthenware bathroom sink with a clearly labeled hard-to-get-out stain next to the drain.

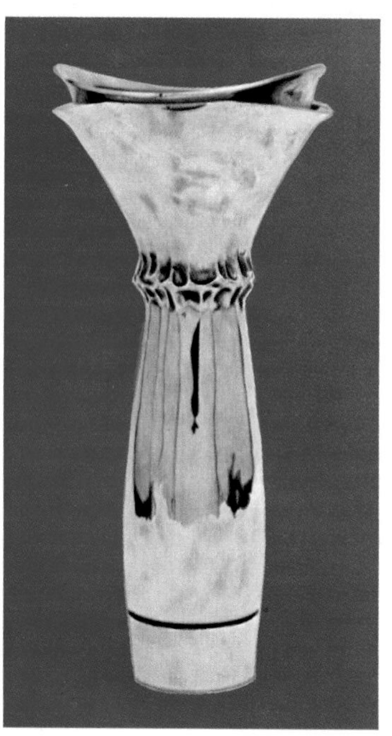

Silver. Popular with the modern artist-craftsman, silver expresses both elegance and strength in the hand-wrought objects shown at left. The tall chalice, with its flowing form and rich patina, is the work of silversmith John C. Marshall, who designed it not for a church but simply as a personal statement. The outside of the chalice was hammered to give it a slightly rough texture and avoid the excessive "coolness" Marshall finds in much contemporary silver; the inside was gold-plated and left smooth. The chased collar, or knob, is intended to symbolize Christ's crown of thorns. The spectacular, intricate body ornament was made by Arline Fisch, a California jeweler whose designs reflect the influence of Egyptian, pre-Columbian, and other ancient cultures. The interlocking parts of this piece move freely as the wearer moves, catching the changing light.

Textiles. Alma W. Lesch of Kentucky uses textiles in a startling way in this fabric collage, designed in 1967. Entitled "Like Father, Like Son," the work creates an effect both comic and nostalgic with its combination of stitching and familiar objects—a work shirt, overalls and overall jacket, wire-framed spectacles, a battered McGuffey *Reader,* and a blue bandanna handkerchief. Alma Lesch was one of the first American textile designers to incorporate random, commonplace items into decorative hangings.

Glass. With its clarity, brilliance, and volatility, glass has become a favorite medium of craftsmen like Joel Philip Myers, whose set of five free-blown goblets and decanter is shown above. Trained as a ceramist and industrial designer, Myers does not exhibit the broad disdain for the products of mass technology that characterizes some members of the contemporary crafts movement. He works both as a creative studio artist and as director of design for his own glass factory.

Wood. The flowing, organic forms inherent in wood take on a sculptural beauty in the hands of two self-taught woodworkers, Arthur Carpenter, known professionally as Espenet, and Wendell Castle. The walnut rolltop desk was designed by Espenet, who taught himself cabinetmaking in the 1950's and then established his own custom furniture concern. The laminated-wood music stand is by Wendell Castle, who also works in plastic. Castle builds up his pieces from 1-inch layers of glued and clamped wood, then carves, smooths, and finishes them as if they were single, solid blocks.

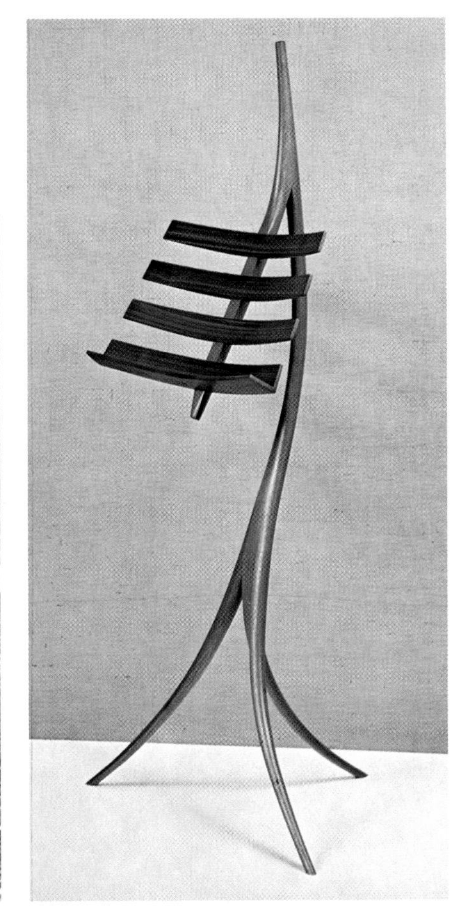

CHAPTER THIRTEEN

Achievement in Architecture and Planning

The story of architecture in America is one of variety ar change. When the earliest colonists arrived on our shore they first housed themselves in crude shelters that were lit more than roofed-over burrows in the earth and in bark covered huts patterned after the longhouses built by loc Indians. Today our architects can create such amazi structures as Chicago's sleek Sears Tower, which at 1,45 feet is one of the tallest buildings in the world.

The development of American architecture from tho primitive beginnings to the startling structures being bui today is a fascinating indication of our country's growth wealth and power. Some of the architects' creations are su

The Colonial Heritage

From the very beginning American architecture has been as varied as the settlers who came in search of a better life. Whether Spanish, German, French, English, or Dutch, each group of immigrants had its own traditions. Houses, barns, churches, and public buildings were built much as they were in the homeland.

The most enduring influence came from England. The earliest houses built by English colonists were simple, rural structures, but they grew more elaborate as the colonists prospered. To keep up with changing fashions, many in the early 1700's adopted the classically inspired style in vogue in London. Before long the new mode transformed townscape and countryside from rustic simplicity to formal elegance in favored places along the Eastern seaboard.

Although interest in the 18th-century colonial styles —often grouped together under the name Georgian— began to wane around 1800, neither they nor any of the earlier styles have faded entirely from the scene. The colonists might be startled by some of the changes that have taken place, but no doubt they would recognize the sources of inspiration if they could see the "Spanish colonial," "Dutch colonial," and "Georgian style" houses that contractors are building today.

Early Buildings That Set a Style

Spanish
Palace of the Governors
Santa Fe, N. Mex.
1612

English (Southern Colonial)
Adam Thoroughgood House
Princess Anne County, Va.
1640

Dutch
Domine Schaets House
Albany, N.Y.
1657

English (Northern Colonial)
Stanley Whitman House
Farmington, Conn.
c. 1660

French
Cahokia Courthouse
Cahokia, Ill.
1737

Spanish homebuilders in the Southwest borrowed freely from the Pueblo Indians to create a unique colonial style. Bricks molded from sandy clay and baked in the sun were fashioned into adobe houses, but with European-style wood-framed doors and windows. Elsewhere the settlers found no adaptable Indian architecture, so they tried to duplicate—with the available tools and within the bounds of simplicity and practicality—what they had left behind. As far as local conditions permitted, British colonial houses were built in the manner of houses in rural England. In the South houses tended to be of brick, in the North, of wood. The overhanging second story, common in the Northeast, is a feature of medieval English architecture. The Dutch in the Hudson Valley reproduced the narrow, step-gabled homes of Holland. The French in the Mississippi Valley favored hip-roofed, one-story buildings with a pillared *galerie*.

passingly beautiful, some are starkly functional, and others can only be considered bizarre. But all of them are products of their times. All inevitably reveal something of the values and aspirations of the people who built them. Wander the streets of any of the older cities in this country and you will find buildings dating from many periods in the city's history. Each building speaks of a changing way of life. Thus in broad outlines you will see the sweeping changes that have shaped the American architectural heritage and affected our history as a nation. On the following pages are traced some of the major developments that have occurred as that heritage has grown.

Thomas Cole's *"The Architect's Dream" was painted in 1840.*

Carter's Grove, *on the James River in Virginia, is one of the finest Georgian mansions in America. It was built between 1750 and 1753 for Carter Burwell. A builder from nearby Williamsburg supervised the construction, and the fine interior detail was done by an imported English carpenter. In 1928 the building was restored and the dependencies were connected to the main house, increasing the breadth of the facade to 200 feet. The focal point of the interior is the great hall, from which four rooms open—a conventional Georgian design.*

Buildings for a New Republic

The years following the Revolution were a time of exuberance and growth in America. The newly independent States and Nation needed buildings to house their governments, and the merchants, who were rising as a class, demanded distinguished homes that would proclaim their new status.

Most architects chose to break with the past, and built in the style called Federal architecture. Based on the mode popularized by the famous Scottish architect Robert Adam and his brother James, the Federal style was far lighter and more delicate than colonial designs of the 1700's. Columns and pilasters were slenderer, and windows were narrower in proportion. Curving staircases and delicate iron railings added to the feeling of restrained elegance. Characteristically, the focal point of the facade was a handsome doorway topped by an elliptical fanlight and flanked by narrow sidelights.

Interiors were different too. Most late colonial houses were rigidly symmetrical, with the central hall usually neatly balanced by two rectangular rooms on each side. In Federal-style houses, while facades remained symmetrical, floor plans became freer and far more varied. Wings and projecting bays were added, elegant oval and circular rooms were installed, and the main hall often featured a soaring spiral staircase. Even furniture became more delicate, with graceful Sheraton, Hepplewhite, and Duncan

The Massachusetts *State House in Boston was the most distinguished public building in the country when it was completed in 1798. It was also one of the most visible, with its great dome and its situation on Beacon Hill. The structure was designed by Charles Bulfinch, one of the first major exponents of the Federal style. Bulfinch submitted the plans in 1787, shortly after his return from a grand tour abroad. Preferring the lightness and elegance of Neoclassical buildings in England during the age of Robert Adam to the heavier classical structures he saw in Europe, Bulfinch modeled the State House on his impressions of Somerset House in London. Some years after the building's completion, the dome was gilded. A back wing was added to the State House late in the 19th century; the two side wings were built early in the 20th.*

The Rotunda *at the University of Virginia was designed by Thomas Jefferson to be the university library and the focal point of the campus. When Jefferson completed his plans for the university in 1821, the Greek Revival style was just beginning to sweep the North. Jefferson, however, preferred the buildings of ancient Rome. The Rotunda is a modified version of the Pantheon in Rome, at about half scale. Architect Stanford White changed the interior after it was destroyed by fire, along with the dome, in 1895. The Rotunda has been declared a National Historic Landmark, and in 1974 work was begun to restore it to Jefferson's original concept.*

Phyfe designs replacing the heavier and more richly carved Chippendale style. The result both inside and out was an air of refinement and quiet sophistication.

One of the early public buildings in the Federal style was the Massachusetts State House, designed by Charles Bulfinch. Good examples of Federal-style houses are most numerous in New England, but they can also be found as far south as Savannah, Georgia.

Thomas Jefferson, well known as the designer of his home, Monticello, was also the architect of some of the major new public buildings. Believing that the dignity, strength, and look of permanence of Roman architecture symbolized the virtues of the Roman Republic, he felt it was a suitable expression of the ideals of the new American Nation. When he designed a new capitol for his home State of Virginia, Jefferson used as his model the Maison Carrée, an ancient Roman temple he admired at Nîmes in southern France. His library for the University of Virginia, in turn, is virtually a half-size replica of the Pantheon in Rome. He also played a role in planning the classically inspired Capitol in Washington, D.C. Jefferson, the first American architect to reject English sources entirely and to turn to those of ancient Rome and France for his intensely personal, creative designs, led the Neoclassical movement and inspired the Greek and Gothic Revivals, both underway before his death.

The Nathaniel Russell House *in Charleston, South Carolina, built about 1809 by a wealthy merchant, is a superb example of the Southern Federal style. The delicately scaled flying (unsupported) staircase, one of the finest achievements of the Federal style, is a notable feature here, as in many homes of the period. This one spirals up for three stories, its curves echoing the ovoid shapes of the fanlight. A bay projecting into the garden provides space for a large oval room on each floor. The refined interior is Adamesque in its details.*

The Peirce-Nichols House *has a typical three-story McIntire facade and a central porch with a Doric pediment.*

Samuel McIntire *Architect of Salem*

Called the architect of Salem because he designed so many of the town's buildings, Samuel McIntire was an outstanding example of the many American craftsmen who became excellent architects despite a lack of formal training. McIntire learned his trade from his father, a carpenter-builder, and from English books on architectural detail and design. Jerathmeel Peirce gave him his first important commission when he was 22 years old. The Peirce House (later the Peirce-Nichols House), completed in 1782, was more imposing, and embellished with more classical detail than others in the town, and it assured McIntire wide patronage among the affluent merchants of the growing Massachusetts port.

McIntire's houses, like those of the pre-Revolutionary era, have symmetrical facades but are more attenuated in proportion and more delicate in scale. The exteriors show the influence of Charles Bulfinch's work, but McIntire developed his own style for the interiors, blending oval rooms, slender columns, and decorative carvings in high Adamesque style. McIntire's houses have more in common with the general character of the Federal style than the more individually designed houses of Bulfinch.

Inspirations From the Past

The 19th century was a time of revivals in American architecture. In their search for cultural identity, architects turned to the past and revived one historical style after another.

The first, the Greek Revival, swept the country from the 1820's to about 1850. Sympathizing with the Greek struggle for freedom from Turkish domination, Americans came to regard all things Greek as symbols of democracy, nobility, and virtue. Almost every town—some with such names as Athens, Syracuse, and Ithaca—had houses, banks, schools, and other buildings with columns, entablatures, and pediments that were carefully copied from Greek temples.

At the same time other, more romantic architects turned away from the formality of the Greek Revival. Favoring less regular, more energetic and original effects, they looked to the Gothic for models. Public response was enthusiastic: Gothic revivals in one form or another continued to the end of the century, and even in the 20th-century many college buildings and skyscrapers were adorned with elaborate Gothic ornament.

In the decades following the Civil War, architects continued to revive historical styles, sometimes with archaeological exactness, sometimes in a freer, more personal manner. Most individual of all was Henry Hobson Richardson, who in the latter part of the century took the Romanesque and made it tell of the energy and creativity of America, in a style now known as Richardsonian Romanesque. Richard Morris Hunt catered to the very rich, creating luxurious replicas of medieval and Renaissance châteaux and palaces. And a whole corps of disciples of the Parisian École des Beaux-Arts designed grandiose, classically inspired museums, libraries, rail terminals, and other monumental buildings in the style known now as Beaux-Arts Classic. Revivals in fact remained a major force in U.S. architecture into the 1930's, when architects no longer looked to the past and Modernism finally took root in American soil.

Greek Revival. *Despite an inauspicious start, Founders Hall, Girard College, Philadelphia, turned out to be one of the masterpieces of the style. Thomas U. Walter, the architect, won the competition for the commission with an entirely different design. However, the final plan had to conform to the specifications in the will of the college's founder and the requirements of Nicholas Biddle, president of the college's board of trustees. The result, completed in 1836, successfully overcame these limitations.*

Gothic Revival. *Tarrytown, New York, is the site of one of the earliest Gothic Revival mansions on the Hudson River. A leading proponent of the style, Alexander Jackson Davis, designed Lyndhurst in 1838 and planned its enlargement in 1864. A castle on a small scale, the gray marble mansion has a full complement of crenellations, turrets, and apparently vaulted ceilings. Lyndhurst was bought by Jay Gould in 1880. It is now owned by the National Trust for Historic Preservation.*

Italian Renaissance. *The Breakers, built for Cornelius Vanderbilt II in 1892–95, was designed by Richard Morris Hunt, architect of several other summer "cottages" in Newport, Rhode Island. Modeled after North Italian Renaissance palaces, which were copied by the French for their châteaux, the four-story edifice has 70 rooms arranged around a central grand hall. The interiors were profusely embellished in French and Italian styles of the 17th and 18th centuries by several architects and decorators working under Hunt's direction. The mansion is preserved as a monument to a bygone era of formal entertainment and showy wealth.*

Andrew Jackson Downing

Persuasive Advocate of Eclectic Architecture

One of the harshest critics of formalism in general and the Greek Revival in particular was Andrew Jackson Downing, America's first professional landscape architect. His first book on landscaping, *A Treatise on the Theory and Practice of Landscape Gardening, Adapted to North America,* published in 1841 when he was 26, became a classic. Like all his books, it continued to sell long after his untimely death at 37 in 1852. His theories strongly influenced landscape architects for the rest of the century.

Believing that a house should harmonize with its natural surroundings, Downing set out to improve the architectural taste of his countrymen. An ardent advocate of picturesque effects, he wrote two books on the subject of country houses. The books contained plans for homes of many types, often combining features of different styles. Not an innovator, Downing enlisted the help of his friend, the noted Gothic architect Alexander Jackson Davis, and incorporated the ideas of other architects and writers in his designs and in his books. He proposed many practical details in heating and construction and was an important force in bringing current ideas on good taste to a wider public. Downing disapproved of overdecoration, a stricture Americans all too often ignored. In the decades after 1850 architecture in America became increasingly varied. There were buildings modeled after Italian villas, Renaissance palaces, Chinese temples, Moorish castles, and Byzantine cottages—and sometimes bizarre combinations of several discordant motifs in the same structure.

A great admirer *of English cottages, Downing included this plan (left) for an Americanized version in a book published in 1842.*

ictorian Exuberance. *The enthusiasm in e late 19th century for complex shapes and ealth of ornamental detail can be seen in the 'arson Mansion in Eureka, California. Cometed in 1886, the house contains a variety of oods and is noted for the craftsmanship of its neling and moldings.*

Egyptian Revival. *Americans used this style mainly for cemeteries and prisons, but this fine example was built in 1845 for the Medical College of Virginia in Richmond.*

Italianate. *Richard Upjohn designed this villa in 1845 for a resident of Newport, Rhode Island. It influenced other builders after its plan appeared in Downing's last book.*

Romanesque. *The Ames Free Library in North Easton, Massachusetts (1877–79), is one of a series of libraries designed by Henry Hobson Richardson in his unique Romanesque style. The vitality and variety of his work show in the contrast between the massive stone entrance arch and the long windows to the left.*

Westward Ho! Housing on the Frontier

Generation after generation, Americans moved west, enticed by the lure of the frontier. With incredible optimism they packed their covered wagons with the bare essentials and headed into the wilderness.

Once there, their first priority was to throw up a roof of some sort over their heads. The form depended on their own backgrounds and on the indigenous building materials. In the eastern Appalachians, in the Northwest Territory, and in all the forested regions, they took their axes in hand, felled the trees, which were plentiful, and fashioned the trunks into logs to be fitted together into rude cabins—buildings that have become the very symbols of American resourcefulness. On the treeless plains they hacked the sod into blocks and stacked the blocks up to form snug shelters against the relentless wind. In the Southwest they mixed the soil with small amounts of the region's precious water to form bricks of adobe and laid the bricks layer upon layer to construct simple houses.

Most of the earliest buildings have crumbled to dust. But those that remain stand as inspiring reminders of the kind of grit that sustained the hardy pioneers who abandoned the comforts of civilization and traveled westward to conquer the unknown.

The Balloon-Frame House

The traditional house before the mid-1800's was built with hand-hewn beams let into heavy posts and held together by wooden pegs. This method was time-consuming and required skillful workmen with special tools. The balloon frame, said to have been invented in Chicago in 1833 by a carpenter newly arrived from Hartford, Connecticut, used lightweight "dimension" lumber, mostly 2 by 4 inches and 2 by 6 inches, which could be easily put together by any careful workman who could saw to a line and drive a nail.

This revolution in building was made possible by the advent of improved sawmill machinery that could cut lumber to standard sizes and of new machines that could produce inexpensive nails. Rafters for the roof were also made of lightweight lumber. The framework was covered with 1-inch siding, interior partitions were sheathed and plastered, and the exterior was shingled or sheathed. Skeptics prophesied that a good wind would send such houses flying through the air like balloons, and at first "balloon frame" was a term of derision. But the light frames proved practical, and houses have been built this way ever since.

The log cabin (*above*), *which has become a symbol of earliest America, belongs more to the late 18th century, although a few Swedish settlers in Delaware probably introduced it here as early as 1638. Some 80 years later Scotch-Irish immigrants began to make it a feature of the wooded frontier. It could be built with an ax, saw, and minimum skill.*

The sod house (*top right*) *of the prairie settlers was less durable. In a heavy rain the roof could cave in, and the soddy had to be weeded in spring before spreading roots broke it open. Still, it was cheap, easy to build, and cool in summer.*

False fronts (*right*) *were put on the wood buildings in the raw new Western towns to give the main street a more imposing character.*

The Beauty of Pure Function

Among the most refreshing features on our architectural landscape are the workaday buildings planned not for esthetic effect but to fulfill some specific, often prosaic function—and yet possessing grace, beauty, charm, and sometimes even monumental grandeur. Their builders, usually anonymous craftsmen rather than trained architects, looked at the job to be done and built the structure that would do it best. Their work was often drab and some was ugly. But sometimes through the builders' innate feeling for proportion and design, truly memorable results were achieved. Barns, silos, gristmills, covered bridges, and other structures of varied shapes and sizes emphatically proclaimed their functions; yet they enhanced rather than degraded their surroundings.

Then, too, there are the works of civil engineers and those hired to house industrial operations. While not architecture in the strictest sense, their creations sometimes are truly breathtaking. Gigantic grain elevators that thrust against Midwestern skies, sleek water towers, graceful suspension bridges curving over bays and rivers, oil refineries with mazes of tanks and pipes that look like sculpture on a grand scale—these constitute a kind of architecture that speaks a language all its own.

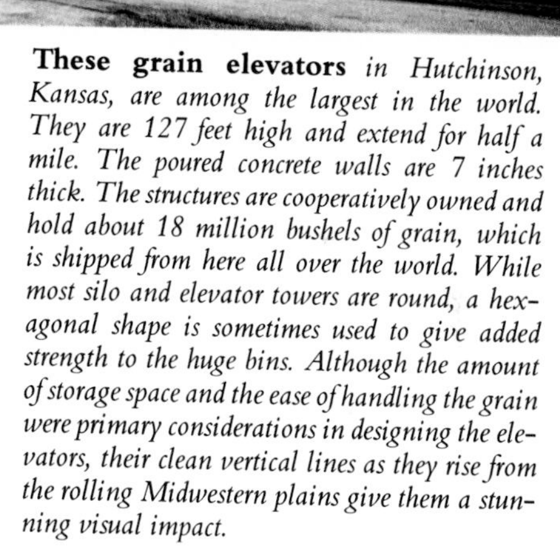

These grain elevators *in Hutchinson, Kansas, are among the largest in the world. They are 127 feet high and extend for half a mile. The poured concrete walls are 7 inches thick. The structures are cooperatively owned and hold about 18 million bushels of grain, which is shipped from here all over the world. While most silo and elevator towers are round, a hexagonal shape is sometimes used to give added strength to the huge bins. Although the amount of storage space and the ease of handling the grain were primary considerations in designing the elevators, their clean vertical lines as they rise from the rolling Midwestern plains give them a stunning visual impact.*

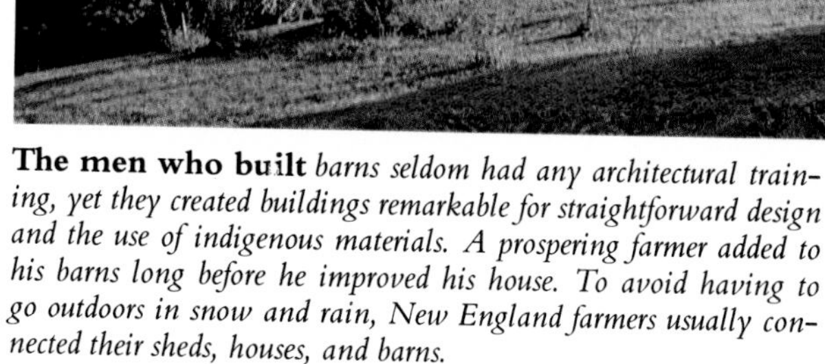

The men who built *barns seldom had any architectural training, yet they created buildings remarkable for straightforward design and the use of indigenous materials. A prospering farmer added to his barns long before he improved his house. To avoid having to go outdoors in snow and rain, New England farmers usually connected their sheds, houses, and barns.*

This Massachusetts mill *was built around 1640 and reconstructed in 1929. The water wheel and the long roofline of the shed behind it add a satisfying variation to the straight lines of the boxlike house. The mill has been used to process wool, to polish jewelry, and to make the cedar shingles that now cover it. Popular because they need little care, the shingles weather into a silvery gray on the seacoast and to darker colors in shady inland areas.*

The Race for the Sky

The most revolutionary development in 19th-century architecture—the skyscraper—has sometimes been called the American solution. It was not the invention of any single person. It simply evolved in response to changing circumstances. Cities were growing at an alarming rate. Businesses were becoming *big* businesses that needed ever larger buildings to house their burgeoning administrative staffs. New inventions—the telephone, the typewriter, the electric light, and, most important, the elevator—contributed to the efficiency of accommodating more people in larger structures.

But as more and more companies sought building sites in the large cities, real estate values skyrocketed, forcing builders to build up instead of out. So while New York City, for example, had few buildings of more than 5 floors in 1865, its skyline boasted several structures reaching 9 and 10 stories just a decade later.

These new buildings used traditional masonry construction methods with exterior load-bearing walls to support the upper stories. Thus, just as a dam must be thickest at its base, the taller a building, the thicker its lower walls had to be. Carried to the extreme, this could have meant a building the lower "floors" of which were solid masonry.

The breakthrough came in Chicago in the 1880's. In the building boom that followed the fire of 1871 a group of architects now known as the Chicago school began experimenting with new techniques. Their greatest discovery was that iron beams, which had long been used for interior support, could be joined to form a building's en-

Louis Sullivan
Skyscraper Pioneer

The most influential of the Chicago architects was Louis H. Sullivan. A restless genius who formulated a highly personal and purely American style, he was a pioneer of the modern movement in his profession and established a secure reputation as one of the most creative minds in the history of American architecture.

"Form follows function" was Sullivan's credo, but by this he meant something more than stark utilitarianism. The full import of his philosophy is revealed in nearly every building he ever designed. If a building had a steel skeleton, he believed it was pointless, even dishonest, to mask the truth with heavy masonry that only looked as if it were bearing the weight of the structure. Let the lines of the steel beams show, he declared, and become elements in the design. Shun historical styles and create buildings that reflect present-day conditions and current technology. If a structure must be tall, it should be made to *look* tall—a principle that was brilliantly realized in Sullivan's Wainwright Building in St. Louis, considered by some to be America's first successful skyscraper.

Sullivan never denied the validity of architectural ornament; he believed that beauty was a humanizing force that served an important function. Most of his creations are embellished with bas-relief friezes and other ornamentation in highly personal motifs that are a lovely mixture of Celtic and Art Nouveau designs.

Despite the innovations made in Chicago during the 1880's, a committee of architects planning the World's Columbian Exposition of 1893 in Chicago decided to revert to the historical eclecticism favored in the East. The resulting "White City" of Roman-style buildings so impressed the thousands of visitors to the fair that, according to Sullivan, American architecture was set back 50 years. Only Sullivan's vividly colored Transportation Building provided an example of the progressive architecture that had been originated by designers in the Midwest.

Sullivan was then 37 and at the height of his career. However, he was dependent on rich patrons, and he refused to compromise with their revived enthusiasm for historical themes. In 1895 Sullivan broke with his partner, Dankmar Adler, who possessed, along with technical knowledge, a tact and good business sense that Sullivan lacked. The two had designed more than 100 buildings in their 14-year partnership.

In his remaining 30 years Sullivan created only 20 more buildings, although many consider one of them, the Carson, Pirie, Scott & Company Building, completed in 1904, his masterpiece. Not until the modern movement came into full flower were Sullivan's pleas for rational architecture heeded and the scope of his accomplishments appreciated.

The Carson, Pirie, Scott & Company *Building in Chicago is reproduced from a 1906 photograph. The delicately detailed cast-iron foliage, depicted in a sketch by Sullivan (right), frames the show windows on the first two floors, in contrast to the clean horizontal lines above.*

tire framework. With this "metal cage" construction, the iron or, later, the steel skeleton held the building up. The exterior walls, relieved of their job of bearing the weight of the upper stories, became simply a skin enclosing the interior space. This principle has been carried to the ultimate in modern towers with curtain walls that are often great expanses of glass.

The progress from the first efforts of the Chicago architects to the sleek new skyscrapers of today was steady but slow. Better glass, improved concrete, and other technological advances all played a role in enabling architects to design taller and taller buildings. The result is universally acknowledged as a fitting symbol of American vigor and ingenuity—impressive urban skylines of elegant towers reaching ever higher.

Rise of the Skyscraper

Although it no longer seems like a skyscraper, Louis Sullivan's Wainwright Building towered over its neighbors in 1891. The buildings that followed grew taller but returned to the older style of historical eclecticism. For example, the Woolworth Building is lavishly Gothic. The depressed economy of the 1930's required a more austere style and also halted the race for the tallest building—a title held by the Chrysler Building very briefly until completion of the Empire State Building, which reigned supreme for the next 40 years. In the 1940's and 1950's tall buildings became common, but they were usually no more than about 60 stories high. Technology makes mile-high structures possible, but the advantages are questionable. Shown here are the steel-frame skyscrapers that were the world's tallest when built.

91 1892 1899 1908 1913 1930 1931 1972 1974

Higher and higher (*from left to right*): *1891, Wainwright Building, St. Louis, Missouri, 137 feet; 1892, Masonic Temple, Chicago, Illinois, 302 feet; 1899, Park Row Office Building, New York, New York, 390 feet; 1908, Singer Building, New York, New York, 612 feet; 1913, Woolworth Building, New York, New York, 792 feet; 1930, Chrysler Building, New York, New York, 1,046 feet; 1931, Empire State Building, New York, New York, 1,250 feet (1,472 feet with antenna); 1972, World Trade Center (twin towers), New York, New York, 1,350 feet (1,718 feet with antenna); 1974, Sears Tower, Chicago, Illinois, 1,454 feet (1,804 feet with antenna).*

The epitome of Wright's *prairie houses, and probably the best known example of the style, is the 1906 Robie House, in Chicago. Wright designed both the house and the furniture. In an era when most architects were still thinking in terms of historical revivals, the clean, sweeping horizontals and hovering rooflines of the house offended many contemporary observers, who compared the innovative dwelling to a steamship. While many of Wright's masterpieces have been razed or neglected, this one has been carefully preserved and is open to the public.*

Frank Lloyd Wright *An Amazingly Productive American Original*

Ask people to name an American architect, and most are likely to think first of Frank Lloyd Wright. In the long history of American architecture he alone achieved such fame that his name is almost universally recognized. Throughout a richly productive lifetime of 90 years Wright conceived scores of uniquely individual buildings—adventurous designs which profoundly affected the course of modern architecture.

Starting in the Chicago offices of Louis Sullivan, he adapted the master's principles and philosophy to his own visions. His first triumphs were his prairie houses, built in the early 1900's. Wright wanted them to echo the natural beauty of the rolling prairies of the Midwest. And they did; with their low horizontal lines and broad sheltering eaves, they seem to have grown from the earth.

To achieve his fundamental objective of harmonizing a building with its natural setting, Wright used indigenous materials and emphasized and contrasted their inherent textures and colors. The resulting warmth and humanity are his hallmarks, very different from the machine-honed precision of much modern architecture.

Humane, too, was his treatment of space. Deeply concerned with the physical and psychological needs of his clients, he abandoned the traditional rectangular floor plan for freer, more flexible layouts. Many of his prairie houses, for example, are cross-shaped, with wings radiating from a central core containing fireplace or stairwell. Spaces flow into one another and planes interpenetrate freely and often dramatically. Indoor and outdoor living areas merge without rigid boundaries.

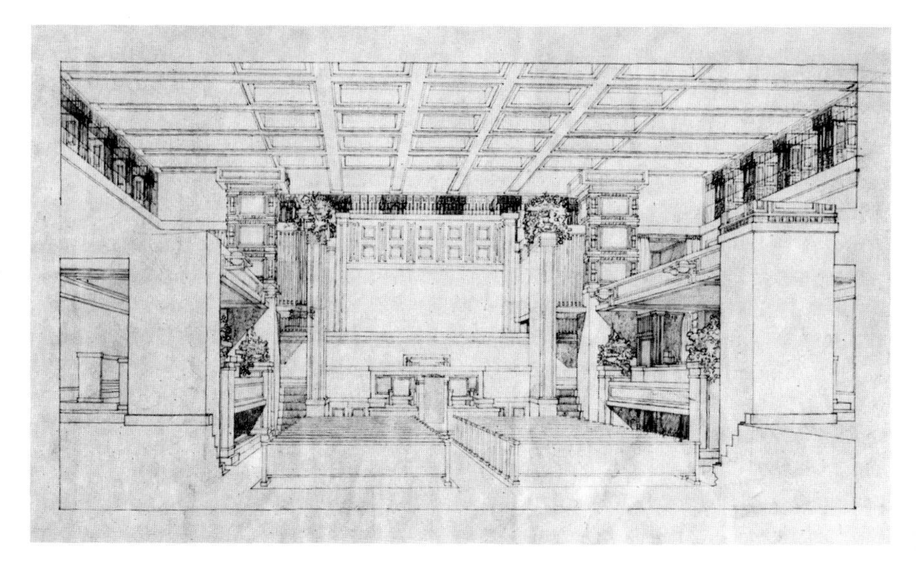

This rendering *of the interior of the Unity Temple in Oak Park, Illinois, done in brown ink with pencil shading on cream-colored paper, not only reveals Wright's masterful draftsmanship but also exemplifies the character of his work. Here you can see his powerful handling of the space itself: the ceiling as an uninterrupted sweep extending through the high windows to the outside, with the interior space divided only by freestanding screens and fixtures. Note, too, the unity of the large rectangular elements in contrast to the elegance of the decorative detailing. Wright inscribed on the drawing: "Sense of Space—to be lived in—the REALITY of the bldg. The big room coming through—the outside coming in." The drawing was made in 1904; the temple was completed in 1906.*

Fallingwater *(1936) at Bear Run, Pennsylvania, exemplifies Wright's genius for integrating a building with its setting. Spanning a waterfall in a wooded ravine, the dramatic horizontal planes and stone walls echo the stratified rock ledges at their base. Workmen predicted collapse when the supports were withdrawn, but the building proved sound.*

The 19-story Price Tower, *completed at Bartlesville, Oklahoma, in 1956, was the fruition of a 1929 project canceled by the Depression. Instead of using load-bearing walls, Wright cantilevered the floors from four interior columns. One of the quadrants is for apartments, the other three are for offices. Gold-tinted glass and 20-inch-wide copper louvers protect the inhabitants from the sun.*

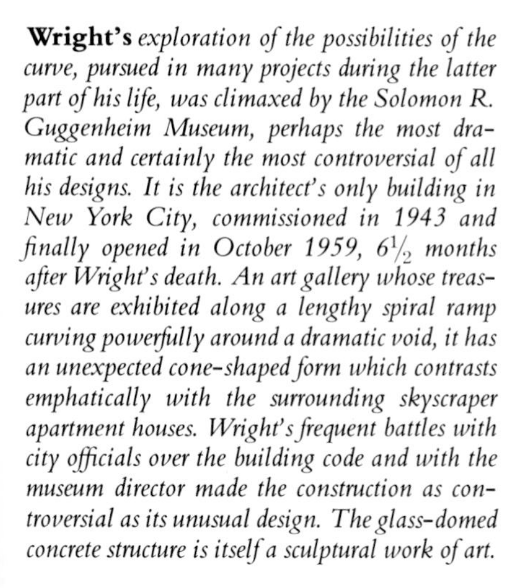

Wright's *exploration of the possibilities of the curve, pursued in many projects during the latter part of his life, was climaxed by the Solomon R. Guggenheim Museum, perhaps the most dramatic and certainly the most controversial of all his designs. It is the architect's only building in New York City, commissioned in 1943 and finally opened in October 1959, $6\frac{1}{2}$ months after Wright's death. An art gallery whose treasures are exhibited along a lengthy spiral ramp curving powerfully around a dramatic void, it has an unexpected cone-shaped form which contrasts emphatically with the surrounding skyscraper apartment houses. Wright's frequent battles with city officials over the building code and with the museum director made the construction as controversial as its unusual design. The glass-domed concrete structure is itself a sculptural work of art.*

Buildings for Today and Tomorrow

Although modern architecture is rooted in the works of Louis Sullivan, Frank Lloyd Wright, and other innovators of the Chicago school, the precedent-shattering messages they preached went unheeded for decades. Instead of seeking beauty through simplicity and functional design, most architects remained infatuated with the past. Instead of coping with contemporary reality, they continued to design skyscrapers that looked like Gothic spires, railroad terminals that imitated Roman temples, and suburban homes that vaguely resembled medieval English cottages.

It was not until the 1930's that modern architecture finally began to win acceptance in America. How did this exciting change come about? For one thing, the agonizing dislocations of the Great Depression shook the public's blind confidence in tradition. More and more people began to question the assumption that old ways are necessarily the best. Hitler played a role too. In 1933 the Nazis closed the Bauhaus, Europe's most progressive school of design, in Dessau, Germany. Seeking freedom of artistic expression, several of its ablest members—among them Walter Gropius, Ludwig Mies van der Rohe, and Marcel Breuer—emigrated to the United States. Besides winning commissions to design important buildings, several of them joined the faculties of American universities, where they inspired a younger generation with the principles of their International style. Gropius, the founder of the Bauhaus, became chairman of the Department of Architecture at Harvard's Graduate School of Design and later designed the university's Graduate Center. Mies van der Rohe became director of the school of architecture at the Illinois Institute of Technology and also designed a handsome complex of new buildings for the school. Cool, formal, almost cubistic in feeling, the austere glass and steel creations brought to the United States by the International architects were healthy antidotes to the lingering nostalgia in this country for Victorian eclecticism.

World War II caused a lull in construction, but the postwar building boom proved rich with opportunity for the new breed of architect. Some worked in pure International style. Others modified it, producing less severe, more decorative effects. Still others strove for dramatic expressionistic forms. But none save the most conservative could act as if the International style had never existed. Speculators might still build quaint Georgian-style shopping centers, and developers might cover acre upon acre with vaguely colonial split-level houses, but the main thrust of serious architecture today is truly contemporary. Architects now look to the present and future—not the distant past—for inspiration. And inspiration is needed. Our skyscrapers, for example, once the proud symbols of American architectural vigor, now tend to be sterile, look-alike towers of aluminum and glass. On the other hand, a few modern churches and schools are among the most imaginative structures in the country. Perhaps those who use these buildings for worship and study today will be advocates of good design in the future. Only through an enlightened public can creative architecture flourish.

The Ford Foundation Building *(right), designed by Kevin Roche, John Dinkeloo and Associates and completed in New York City in 1967, is a striking structure. Only 12 stories high in a city of much higher buildings, it is shaped in a C surrounding on three sides an enclosed garden of greenery (above). The thick glass walls and roof keep out the sounds of traffic but let in the light.*

The ultimate *in distilled architectural form—a glass box—was built by Philip Johnson for his home in 1949. The only enclosed area is the bathroom; other divisions in space are made by cupboards that do not reach the ceiling. The glass and steel house in New Canaan, Connecticut, brought its architect-owner wide renown.*

During his *career Eero Saarinen, one of the most prolific architects of the 1950's, showed remarkable diversity. At the outset starkly functional, rectilinear factories came off his drawing board. In the mid-1950's his forms became freer and more organic. The TWA Terminal at New York City's John F. Kennedy International Airport, opened in 1962, is an example of his later expressive period. In this case he wished to create a symbol of flight. From the exterior the two cantilevered curved shells of concrete suggest wings. Inside, the sculptured curves create an effect of free-flowing movement, an atmosphere far different from the rectangular monotony of most modern airport buildings.*

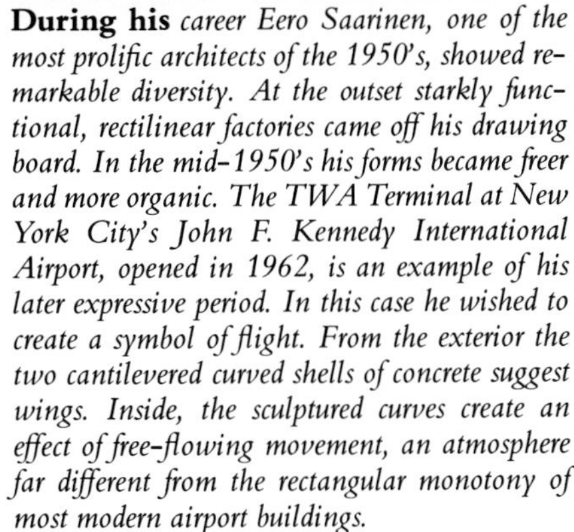

In 1894, when *The First Church of Christ, Scientist, headquarters was built in Boston's Back Bay section, it was a landmark. By 1964, when the Christian Science Church Center was begun, the original Romanesque church and the large-domed Byzantine-Renaissance extension added in 1906 were nearly hidden by other buildings. Moreover, the new Prudential Building nearby towered over the neighborhood. The goals of the project's architects were to focus attention on the mother church and the extension and to provide essential new facilities that would not be out of place. At the official opening in June 1973 the success of their planning was evident. The area, covering some 15 acres, had been opened up and landscaped. At the center of the plaza is a pool nearly 700 feet long and 110 feet wide. At one end is a large fountain, at the other the church and its extension. The 28-story administration building helps to maintain a sense of relative scale between nearby skyscrapers and the complex.*

The geodesic dome *(patented in June 1954) is Fuller's most famous creation. Elegant and light in appearance, it derives its strength not from weight but from tension. It consists of a series of tetrahedrons (pyramids of three triangular sides and a triangular base). These are assembled into a large skeletal frame that approximates a hemisphere. All stress is distributed equally throughout the frame, thus providing maximum strength with minimum weight. The framework can be covered with any lightweight material, and a heavy foundation is not necessary. Individual components are identical and easy to handle; thus an auditorium-sized dome can be erected in a few hours. Fuller's domes have appeared all over the world, including Antarctica. The United States has been using them in international fairs since 1956. Perhaps the most famous is this 200-foot-high dome built for Expo 67 in Montreal.*

Buckminster Fuller *And His Vision of the Spaceship Earth*

Mathematician, engineer, designer, inventor, and poet, Buckminster Fuller calls himself an explorer. He holds patents for many inventions, including the Dymaxion (from "dynamic" and "maximum") house (1927), an inexpensive transportable dwelling; the three-wheeled Dymaxion car (1932), which got 40 miles to a gallon of gasoline; and the Dymaxion world map (1940), which eliminates distortion and can be folded into a globe. These were concepts ahead of their time, and only the map was commercially successful. It was Fuller's development of the geodesic dome that established his reputation as a designer of genius.

From his birth in 1895, Richard Buckminster Fuller was extremely farsighted. He believes that spending his first 4 years without corrective glasses gave him the ability to see things in large-scale patterns. Certainly his ideas are on a large scale and have brought him a worldwide reputation for creative thinking. By the 1950's the one-time failure was in constant demand as lecturer, consultant, and teacher. Harvard University, which had expelled him for cutting classes, invited him to hold the Charles Eliot Norton Chair of Poetry for 1962–63, and, although not technically an architect, he was made a Fellow of the American Institute of Architects.

Fuller holds that energy cannot be increased, but knowledge can. He believes that as new knowledge engenders new research, more and more will be achieved with the energy available. He feels that as man learns to produce more from his limited resources, he will have more to share with others, and that sharing will bring an end to war.

Buckminster Fuller's concern with social issues, his stress on learning from the principles of nature, and his optimism about technology all combine to give him enormous public appeal. The world is beginning to appreciate the need for long-range plans for the Earth as a whole—a need that Fuller recognized long ago.

Fuller's lectures *are long (up to 6 hours), freewheeling, and often spellbinding. A consistent theme is the dome—to cover floating farms on the ocean or to shelter entire cities. The size of a dome is limited only by the money available for its construction. This 2-mile dome over midtown Manhattan, he suggests, would reduce the heating and cooling costs of the enclosed area by 90 percent and, simply in money saved on snow removal, would soon pay for itself.*

The Planners

The American landscape lay open before the first settlers. It was a place to build new settlements where and how they could. Sometimes villages just grew, and roads were made wherever they seemed most natural. The results can still be seen in the oldest parts of cities like Boston or in the financial district at the lower tip of Manhattan Island, where narrow streets crisscross at odd angles. More often, however, the early Americans chose to impose order on the land.

Among the most formal and specific of early town plans was that for Williamsburg, capital of Virginia. Echoes of this example are to be seen in almost any American town today. The plan, with the main thoroughfare and adjacent grid of streets, was probably conceived by Sir Francis Nicholson, who was governor when it was made in 1699. Minimum lot sizes were established. Along the Duke of Gloucester Street a standard setback of 6 feet, minimum house size (with "front alike"), specified roof pitch, and standard fencing were all required.

One of William Penn's first projects was to develop a plan for his model city of Philadelphia. Between the Schuylkill and Delaware Rivers he laid out a tidy grid of

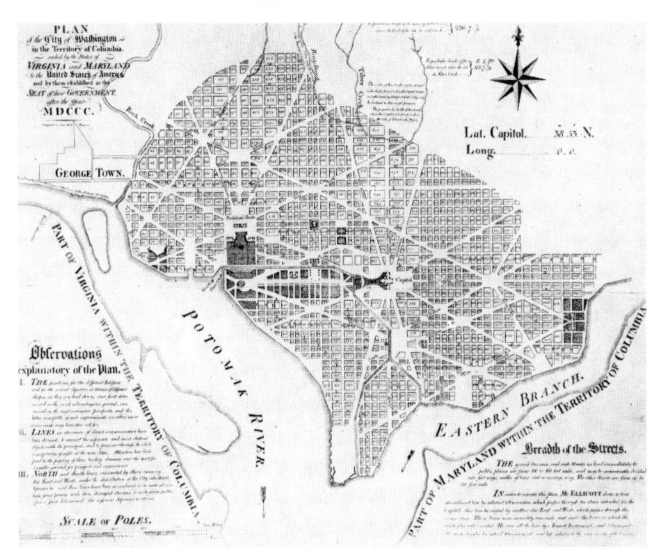

The plan for Washington, D.C. *(above), rendered by Andrew Ellicott, was conceived by Maj. Pierre Charles L'Enfant in 1791 and has proved remarkably resilient. The contemporary view (below) shows how the major avenues and axes have survived the impact of population expansion and the automobile. L'Enfant's "grand avenue," the Mall, has been jeopardized by such ill-advised incursions as a cross-city canal in the 1860's, a railroad station and train sheds in the 1870's, and "temporary" World War I office buildings that were not completely removed until 1970. But today the vista from the Capitol to the Washington Monument is clearly unobstructed.*

streets spotted with parks. Because of the generous open spaces he established, the order of the plan, and the beauty of the early buildings, this is still one of the most successful examples of town planning in America.

The 18th-century villages of New England are perhaps the most engaging of all American designs. They were built around the common land, or green, set aside as a protected place for sheep and cattle to graze. Spaced attractively around the common were the church or meetinghouse, school, town hall, a few shops, offices, and the homes of the leading citizens. Building sites were large enough for the house and a stable and other outbuildings, as well as the family orchard and vegetable garden. But the New England village offered few practical solutions to the problems of planning larger towns and cities.

Now and then more imaginative plans were adopted. In 1694 Sir Francis Nicholson, then Governor of Maryland, laid out the new capital of Annapolis with streets radiating from prominent focal points such as the capitol itself. Even more elaborate was the brilliant plan Pierre Charles L'Enfant developed for Washington, D.C., with a magnificent mall, parks, and grand diagonal avenues broken by circles, squares, and triangles superimposed on the basic grid of streets. As shown on the preceding page, the broad concepts of the plan survive.

One city, however, where the original plan has been maintained and even improved upon is Savannah. If James Oglethorpe could visit the first city of his Georgia Colony today, he would find the streets and squares much as he laid them out in 1733 but now lined with stately trees and handsome homes.

The automobile, which enables people to flee the cities in favor of the suburbs, has been greatly damaging to planning. Superhighways have slashed through established neighborhoods and eliminated precious parklands. Other roads have been lined with ugly strip developments of service stations, stores, and drive-in restaurants.

One good effort to cope with the automobile was made in 1928 by Clarence Stein and Henry Wright. In laying out Radburn (part of Fair Lawn), New Jersey, they clearly separated vehicular from pedestrian traffic. This example, however, has since been surrounded and overwhelmed by the usual grid of streets and sidewalks.

By the 1950's the situation of the cities had gotten out of hand. In attempting to cope with the growing problems of urban decay, new concepts of planning have been adopted. Vast urban renewal schemes have been undertaken. Public housing projects are replacing festering slums. Vest-pocket parks provide welcome oases for strollers in crowded commercial districts. Carefully planned new towns have been built in rural areas, while suburban housing has been designed in cluster developments to preserve green space.

The efforts are varied. The costs are high. And, so far, progress is limited and the effects are small. But the goal is admirable—to rebuild our towns and cities and make them worthy of our best new hopes and dreams.

Central Park *is so much a part of New York City today that few realize how long it took to acquire the land—about 5 years—and how much had to be done to reclaim what had been a marshy area littered with filth and shanties. The construction itself took some 16 years, but the park is so beautifully designed and the natural features so sensitively accentuated that it seems as if it has always been there. The supervisor and originator of this masterful plan was Frederick Law Olmsted, who with English-born landscape architect Calvert Vaux won the Central Park commission in 1857. The landscaping was so successful that many other growing cities commissioned them to create public parks; Olmsted designed more than 40 in all. He also landscaped many private estates and college campuses. Some of his innovations, such as the separation of pedestrian and vehicular traffic, have become standard practice. This 1863 engraving shows the park and some of its scenery.*

Reston, Virginia, *is a new town that is being built. Eventually it will be made up of seven villages and a manmade lake. A variety of styles is used for the town's houses and apartment buildings, and all are surrounded by trees and grass. Shopping centers and an industrial park are planned so that the inhabitants may walk to shops or to work, yet there is a feeling of spaciousness. The projected population is 75,000. Like other modern town plans, Reston's is designed to avoid both the hemmed-in, dehumanized feeling of a city and the sprawl of a suburb.*

A dream *that may hold a solution for urban life is slowly becoming a reality in the Arizona desert near Phoenix. Architect Paolo Soleri feels that the answer to preserving the land lies in expanding living space vertically—above and below the ground—rather than outward from the urban center. He has built models of cities designed for several million people in which cars and industry are underground and the living space is in tall towers surrounded by open country. Above, the plan for Acrosanti, a prototype being built by Soleri and his students, is superimposed on a photograph of the project's site. To the right is the work in progress. Acrosanti is designed to provide living space for 2,500 people on 8 acres, leaving the remaining 850 acres free for recreation.*

Great Fairs and Expositions *Extravaganzas Designed T*

By tradition, world's fairs have been joyous, colorful, colossal—and often wasteful—expressions of national pride and aspiration. Chicago's 1893 exposition, complete with a lavish amusement section, signaled the arrival of the superfair. This extravaganza was followed in 1904 by another in a similar vein at St. Louis. New York City's "World of Tomorrow," on the eve of World War II, marked the heyday of the superfair, but times were changing. More than 20 years passed before the United States staged another exposition—the small-scale 1962 Seattle fair, where, for the first time, some of the buildings were designed to become part of a permanent civic center. The second New York City fair, in 1964, was more ambitious than Seattle's, but the old flamboyance was missing—dimmed partly by economic necessity and partly, perhaps, by a change in the popular mood. The low-keyed Spokane Expo '74, with its theme of environmental protection, found a dignified way to reflect both national feeling and global human concern for the future. But in 1976 no single fair was planned to celebrate the Nation's bicentennial.

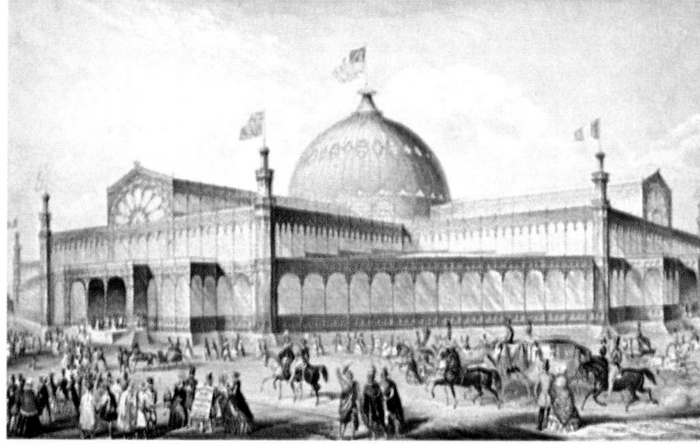

1853, Crystal Palace Exposition, New York, New York. The first American attempt to display "the industry of all nations," openly modeled after the Great Exhibition in London in 1851, was a fiasco. The roof of the exhibition hall, a domed structure that looked like a giant greenhouse, leaked badly, soaking spectators and ruining many of the nearly 5,000 exhibits. This, plus bad management and an excess of foreign exhibits, made the fair a financial disaster. Subsequent U.S. fairs took care to put more emphasis on American accomplishments.

1876, Centennial Exposition, Philadelphia, Pennsylvania. Intended to celebrate a century of American independence and to help heal Civil War wounds, this was the first major U.S. international exhibition to achieve popular success. It extolled American inventive genius and mass-production know-how, and featured the largest machinery hall in the world.

More than 10 million visitors were held spellbound by the typewriter, continuous-web printing press, self-binding reaper, Westinghouse airbrake, railway refrigerator car, giant Corliss steam engine (left), and, particularly, Alexander Graham Bell's "talking instrument." Here was promise of a Machine Age—a future of better farming, low-cost products from industry, safer and more comfortable transportation, even instant communication. One of the fair's 167 buildings stressed the contributions of women to American society.

Highlights of the exhibition were the painting "The Spirit of '76" by Archibald M. Willard and the hand and torch (above) of the as yet uncompleted Statue of Liberty.

1884–85, World's Industrial and Cotton Centennial Exposition, New Orleans, Louisiana. King Cotton reigned over Horticultural Hall, then the world's largest greenhouse (600 by 194 feet). The fair, despite its international overtones, was meant to revive the agricultural industries of the post bellum South. By disseminating new and more efficient methods of crop cultivation and production, this fair and others like it transcended local interests and helped rebuild cooperation between Northern and Southern business, thus bolstering the whole American economy.

1893, World's Columbian Exposition, Chicago, Illinois. This fair was a people's festival, epitomizing the Gilded Age and, at least nominally, commemorating the 400th anniversary of the discovery of America by Christopher Columbus.

Opened during a financial panic, it was nonetheless the first American fair of note to turn a profit. It featured architect Daniel Burnham's famous White City and attracted more than 27 million people. Its network of canals and artificial lagoons was fed by the waters of nearby Lake Michigan, and its exciting architecture embodied the new classicism of "the American Renaissance." The facades ranged from overly ornate splendor to the uncluttered lines of Louis H. Sullivan's Transportation Building (seen at left), although even that had a gilded entranceway.

Inventions such as the phonograph, Linotype, and Pullman car were on display. But the practical uses of electricity, demonstrated in an electrified house, made the deepest impression on fairgoers.

For the first time at a fair, machines became a source of fun. There was George Ferris' first wheel, terrifying but irresistible, as well as a balloon ride and artificial ice for summer skating.

The Midway amusement section was another fair first. Its features included Buffalo Bill's Wild West Show and perhaps the fair's most talked about attraction: Little Egypt, a hootchy-kootchy dancer who delighted some and horrified others.

Great Fairs and Expositions *(continued)*

1901, Pan-American Exposition, Buffalo, New York. Landscape City was a 350-acre complex of Spanish Renaissance architecture dominated by a 375-foot Electric Tower stressing the potential of electricity to everyday life. The fair was marred by tragedy when an anarchist fatally shot President William McKinley while he was attending a reception at the exhibition.

1904, Louisiana Purchase Exposition, St. Louis, Missouri. Featuring fountains and statuary in the grandiloquent French style, this fair, popularly known as the St. Louis Fair, outdid its predecessors in cost and size. It introduced the ice cream cone, iced tea, the hamburger, and the roller coaster, but its most popular exhibit was a display of more than 100 automobiles, one of which had been driven all the way from New York!

1915, Panama-Pacific International Exposition, San Francisco, California. This quietly cultural fair celebrating the opening of the Panama Canal featured graceful architecture—Italian and Spanish Renaissance and Spanish Baroque. Despite European immersion in World War I, it realized a profit.

1933–34, Century of Progress Exposition, Chicago. Efficient management and nearly 40 million Depression-defying visitors combined to make Chicago's centennial a resounding success. It emphasized technology, symbolized by the modernistic Hall of Science, which was prefabricated, air-conditioned, and evenly lighted throughout. Midway amusements abounded, and there was a new "rocket" sky ride to try out.

1939–40, Golden Gate International Exposition, San Francisco. Celebrating completion of the magnificent San Francisco-Oakland and Golden Gate Bridges, the "Pageant of the Pacific" took the form of a walled multicultural city on manmade Treasure Island in San Francisco Bay. Symbolized by the Tower of the Sun, which housed a 40-bell carillon, this impressive showcase for 11 Western States, British Columbia, and the Pacific Basin countries drew about 17 million visitors.

1939–40, New York World's Fair, New York. The spectacular "World of Tomorrow" introduced nearly 45 million people to nylon, home air-conditioning, and television. Taking part were 63 countries, 33 States, 2 U.S. Territories, and 600 businesses and other organizations, including the League of Nations. Its dedication by President Franklin D. Roosevelt on the 150th anniversary of George Washington's inauguration in New York City was broadcast over television.

The fair's two-part symbol was the Trylon, a soaring pyramid intended to reflect man's aspiration toward better living, and the Perisphere, a giant globe which housed a model of tomorrow's world. There was a rocketport from which a rocket ship was "shot into space," while General Motors' Futurama, which attracted 28,000 visitors daily, boldly visualized the super-highways of the future. The fair's most popular amusements were a parachute ride and the Aquacade.

1962, Century 21 Exposition, Seattle, Washington. Soaring above the courtyard of the five-building U.S. Science Pavilion, huge Gothic arches presented an image of technological poetry. The fair was devoted to man's search for truth through science. Its theme was "Man in the Space Age." Much of it was designed to remain standing as a permanent civic center, a new and creative idea in fair planning.

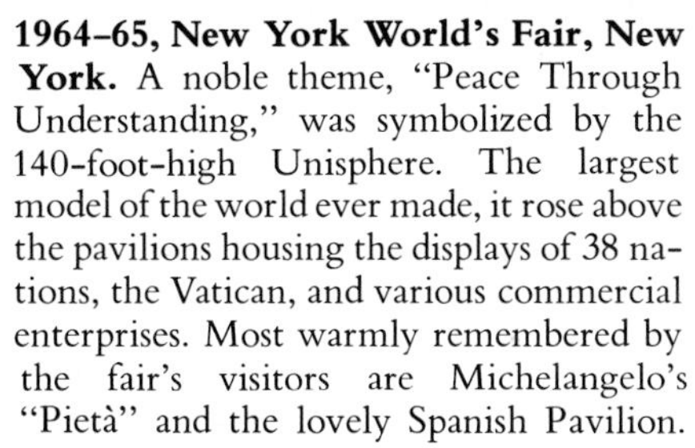

1964–65, New York World's Fair, New York. A noble theme, "Peace Through Understanding," was symbolized by the 140-foot-high Unisphere. The largest model of the world ever made, it rose above the pavilions housing the displays of 38 nations, the Vatican, and various commercial enterprises. Most warmly remembered by the fair's visitors are Michelangelo's "Pietà" and the lovely Spanish Pavilion.

1974, Expo '74, Spokane, Washington. A small international fair with an unusual theme—the protection of the environment—its 100-acre site was dominated by a tall tepee devoted in part to the history of the American Indian. While it presented traditional trade displays and fair diversions, this exposition's unique feature was a series of conferences on questions of environmental concern.

CHAPTER FOURTEEN

Great American Inventors

Today we travel in easy-chair comfort across the sky on ribbons of steel or concrete. With the flick of a fing we can have light wherever we want it and instant he to cook our meals. We set a thermostat to adjust the indc climate to our liking; turn a tap for hot water; dial a numb to talk with a friend 3,000 miles away. On a screen, color, in our own homes, we see events taking place all parts of the world and in outer space the moment th occur. Tools, clothing, food—all our material needs—a available on demand if we have the price.

Two hundred years ago a 40-mile trip meant 10 bon jarring hours through dust or mud behind a team of hors

Joseph Jenks and the Massachusetts Bay Patent

Joseph Jenks, born in England in 1602, was the prototype of those American inventor-capitalists who were to become so numerous and to play so important a role in developing and industrializing the country in the 18th and 19th centuries.

He was not the sort of man who could be content to work for others. Having got America's first ironworks going for settlers at Saugus, Massachusetts, he obtained permission to set up a forge and foundry of his own. In 1646 the Massachusetts General Court (the Colony's legislature) granted him a patent plus 14 years exclusive rights to operate water mills "for the speedy dispatch of much work with few men's labor in little time." While this was not the first patent granted in the New World—that distinction belonged to Samuel Winslow for a new method of processing salt—it was the first for a mechanical process. Its wording, furthermore, indicated that Jenks was a pioneer in the characteristically American endeavor to save time and labor.

Jenks' reputation as a skilled metalworker was growing. He cut the first coin dies in 1652. In 1654 the selectmen of the City of Boston asked him to make "an Ingine to carry water in case of fire." Jenks' fire engine is believed to have been the first made in America. He also designed an improved scythe whose shape and size have not been changed since then.

Jenks' son carried on the family tradition. Having completed an apprenticeship in his father's ironworks, he moved to Rhode Island, where he founded the city of Pawtucket and set up an ironworks of his own.

The elder Jenks was a trailblazer of American free enterprise. Looking at his inventiveness, his independence of spirit, his practical turn of mind, and his determination to succeed, one may fairly describe him as the precursor of Franklin, McCormick, Fulton, Edison, Henry Ford, and other such innovators.

If necessity is the mother of invention, the celebrated ingenuity of the early Yankees is not surprising, for their needs were many. Every colonist had to be a jack-of-all-trades. He was farmer, carpenter, blacksmith, cobbler, harnessmaker, hunter, and—if he lived by the sea—fisherman and boatbuilder. With whatever mechanical skills he could muster, he fashioned any tools and gadgets he could devise to lighten his daily labors. From that day to this, Americans have never lost the "do-it-yourself" spirit of the first colonists.

In colonial times any significant technological development was discouraged by the mother country. Britain considered her colonies sources of raw material, not competitors in manufacturing. Mercantile fortunes of the 18th century were built on monopoly, not on free trade. British law forbade the export of machinery, industrial drawings, or technical specifications, and made it difficult for skilled workmen to emigrate. As a result, American manufacturing was kept to a minimum, and practically all factory-made goods—from knives to silk fabrics—came from England.

Individual ingenuity, however, could not be outlawed. One of the first men to distinguish himself in this regard was Joseph Jenks, who arrived in America in 1643. Jenks developed an ironworks (now a National Historic Site) at Saugus, near Lynn, Massachusetts. He cut minting dies for the Pine Tree shilling, made what was probably the first fire engine in America, and developed a new type of scythe with a long, narrow blade and curving handle, or snath, that is still used today.

In 1735 Rowland Houghton, a Boston merchant, invented a surveying instrument, which he called the new theodolite. This was a small telescope, more precise than the surveyor's transit, with a scale for measuring horizontal and vertical angles. It was one of the first scientific instruments developed in America.

It took 4 to 6 days for a query of any kind to reach New York from Boston and as long again for the answer to come back; it took weeks for news to arrive from Paris or London, months from Asia. Clothing was handmade, mostly at home. Illumination was from an open flame. Tools were primitive and powered by hand. Providing food for a family required hard spadework, patience, and good aim.

The differences between daily life in 1776 and today are almost unimaginable. In no other equivalent span of history have there been so many or such far-reaching changes. Present-day Americans tend to take this veritable revolution for granted, along with the dislike of standing still and the predilection for problem solving that have brought it about. These qualities are amply documented in the files of the U.S. Patent Office, which has issued more than 4.5 million patents since it was established in 1790. Consider the impact on our lives of just a few: The cotton gin, the steel plow, the reaper, the telephone, the telegraph, the typewriter, the sewing machine, and—from the laboratory of one man—the electric light bulb, the phonograph, and motion pictures. Television was perfected in the United States, as were the computer and a most remarkable machine that could fly. It is no exaggeration to say that Americans have been the most inventive people in history.

Thomas Jefferson took time off from being a gentleman farmer, patriot, and statesman to invent a swivel chair, a dumbwaiter, a four-way music stand for string quartets, and other comforts and conveniences for Monticello, his home in Virginia. He also significantly improved the cutting edge of the plow and the shape of its moldboard—the part that actually turns over the soil. Plows were wooden then, but Jefferson's principles proved valid when iron and, finally, steel replaced wood.

Two other early inventors of note were David Bushnell and Jacob Perkins. Bushnell designed and built the *Turtle,* an ingenious prototype of the submarine that was tried out unsuccessfully in the Revolutionary War. Perkins devised a new way of silverplating shoe buckles, built a nailmaking machine, pioneered in the development of high-pressure steam boilers and engines, and made improvements on ship pumps and ventilators.

After the Revolution Americans were freed from the mother country's restrictions on technology, but they lost the privileges and price advantages formerly enjoyed in British ports. They soon realized that they had to draw on their own resources, and the new Government decided to promote an interest in invention. The Constitution empowered Congress "To promote the Progress of Science and useful Arts by securing for limited Times to Authors and Inventors the exclusive Right to their respective Writings and Discoveries." Accordingly, in 1790 the first Federal patent law was passed. Before independence, patents had been granted by the various colonial governments and legislatures. Under the new act the power of issuance was vested in a board that included the Secretary of State, the Secretary of War, and the Attorney General, with final approval required by the President of the United States. Fifty-five patents were granted under this act. The first went to Samuel Hopkins for an "Improved Method of Making Pot and Pearl Ashes"—a process that helped reduce the price of potash, a wood-ash extract used in making soap, glass, and other products.

In 1793 a new law gave the Secretary of State full authority over patents; but in 1802, when James Madison held that post, he made the Patent Office a separate bureau. In response to a charge by Senator John Ruggles of Maine that patents were issued "on every application" and many were "worthless and void," Congress passed the Patent Act of 1836. The Patent Office was reorganized and the foundations were laid for the modern U.S. patent system. The act obliged an applicant to prove the utility and originality of his invention and required him to "furnish a model . . . in all cases which admit of a representation by model of a convenient size to exhibit advantageously its several parts."

On December 15, 1836, fire destroyed the Patent Office and with it 168 volumes of records, almost 9,000 drawings, and some 7,000 models. Senator Ruggles immediately proposed that 3,000 of the most interesting models be replaced, and he appealed to the inventors for help in rebuilding them. The following year Congress appropriated $100,000 for this project.

At the end of the 18th century America was still at least 100 years behind Europe in the mechanical arts. The industrial revolution then going on in Europe had little immediate effect in the United States because Americans were not equipped to utilize its advances. Later, however, American inventors and mechanics would vastly improve the foreign-born factory system, with its efficient division of labor and specialization of skills.

The Versatile Mr. Franklin

Benjamin Franklin was a printer, publisher, writer, statesman, and scientist. He was also a gifted inventor. Some of his best known innovations are shown on the following page. Less well known but perhaps of greater

Benjamin Franklin

Scientist, Inventor, and Statesman Too

Franklin was easily the foremost American scientist of his day, and his ingenuity was immensely wide ranging.

Having established by observation and logic, and then by a practical kite test, that lightning is atmospheric electricity, he went on to invent the lightning rod, to this day a building's best protection against thunderbolts.

As a boy who loved to swim, he had devised primitive flippers shaped like artists' palettes for his hands and kick sandals for his feet. Many years later he invented watertight compartments for ships. He also devised improved designs for ships' hulls, helped define the Gulf Stream, and drafted plans for boats powered by jets of water.

His restless mind fixed on problems large and small. It is to Franklin that we are indebted for the grocer's claw, the mechanical hand attached to a pole used for reaching items stored on high shelves.

European audiences were delighted when he played for them on his "musical glass" machine, an assembly of glass bowls of graduated thicknesses that were revolved by means of a spindle and foot treadle and occasionally moistened.

Protean in *his interests, brilliant in his scientific methods, Franklin increased man's power over matter and made life more comfortable.*

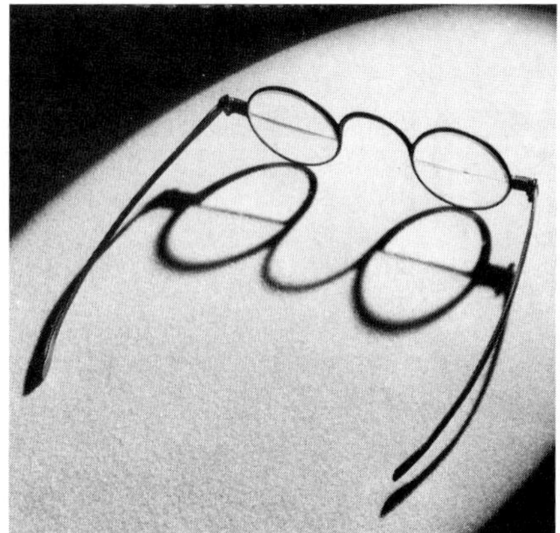

Bifocal Glasses. *At the age of 83, under the spur of his own nearsightedness, Franklin invented the bifocal. The top half of each lens was for distance viewing, the bottom half for reading.*
The Electric Generator. *Franklin invented this generator (left) for use in his experiments. A charge of electricity was built up in the globe.*
The Franklin Stove. *Americans had previously relied on the open fireplace, which sent most of the heat up the chimney, or the German stove, which made breathing uncomfortable by constantly reheating the air. Franklin pulled the stove away from the wall to increase its heating efficiency and gave it a flue that lost less heat and also served as a simple radiator.*

importance were Franklin's basic principles of investigation. A good example is his approach to the question of electricity. Before Franklin began his experiments, electricity seemed to be more in the realm of magic than science. It was known that when certain substances—such as amber, sulfur, or glass—were rubbed, they developed a force that could attract or repel paper, feathers, cork, and other lightweight materials. This force could also produce a spark, a crackling noise, and a physical shock. It was further known that an experimenter in Pomerania, E. G. von Kleist, and a physicist at the University of Leyden (now Leiden) in the Netherlands, Pieter van Musschenbroek, had accidentally discovered that this force could be accumulated in a glass jar filled with water and stoppered with a cork pierced by a nail or wire. What no one until Franklin had thought to ascertain was whether the charge in a Leyden jar was in the nail, the glass, or the water. By posing the right questions and answering them logically—the basis of the scientific method—Franklin determined that the static electricity was stored in the glass itself. This knowledge was basic to the later discovery of electromagnetism and the development of the electron theory. Franklin also originated much of the vocabulary of electricity, including such terms as "battery," "condenser," "charge" and "discharge," and "positive" and "negative."

Oliver Evans, Mechanical Genius

Franklin combined a talent for invention with an interest in the investigation of basic scientific principles. Others who have contributed to human comfort and convenience have been chiefly technicians. Such a man was Oliver Evans of Newport, Delaware. In 1769, at the age of 14, Evans was apprenticed to a wheelwright. After working all day he studied at night by the flame from burning wood shavings because he was not allowed to waste his master's money on candles.

While still in his early 20's, Evans created a machine to facilitate the automatic manufacture of the carders that combed wool and cotton before they were spun into yarn. Carders, imported from England until the Revolution, were being made by hand, mostly by women and children. The wire teeth had to be cut, bent, and attached to the leather backing. Evans' machine, which made the teeth and mounted them on leather, put an end to this tedious and painful manual work. He made little if any profit from his invention because there were no patent laws at the time. One of his most ingenious developments was a completely automatic mill for turning grain into flour, a drawing of which is shown below.

Another of Evans' significant contributions was his invention of the high-pressure steam engine. Until he put his mind to the problem, steam engines worked on principles developed in Britain by Thomas Newcomen and James Watt. In Newcomen's engine steam lifted a plunger contained in a cylinder; cold water sprayed into the cylinder, condensed the steam, and created a vacuum, thus enabling atmospheric pressure to drive the piston down. In 1763 Watt added a condensing chamber separate from the cylinder. These atmospheric engines were big and heavy, generated not more than 20 horsepower, and were used mostly to pump water out of mines.

Evans, however, had long dreamed of a "steam wagon," which he knew would require a smaller and more efficient power source than Watt's engine to propel it. With this in mind, he built a boiler to hold steam at high pressure, and he released the steam alternately at the ends of a closed cylinder to push a piston back and forth, instead of relying on the atmosphere to reverse the strokes. Here, at last, in the high-pressure reciprocating engine, was the breakthrough that would make steam practical for boats and railway trains.

Evans' most notable application of the engine was the *Oruktor Amphibolos,* or amphibious digger, commissioned by the Philadelphia Board of Health to dredge the harbor. Not only was the dredge steam powered, but Evans put wheels on the 15-ton scow and drove it to the Schuylkill under its own power. For the first time in America, in 1804, an engine had propelled a wheeled vehicle. When the scow had moved itself into the river, the drive belt was shifted to a paddle wheel and, still under its own power, the vessel steamed down the river to Philadelphia's harbor. At this point the little 5-horsepower en-

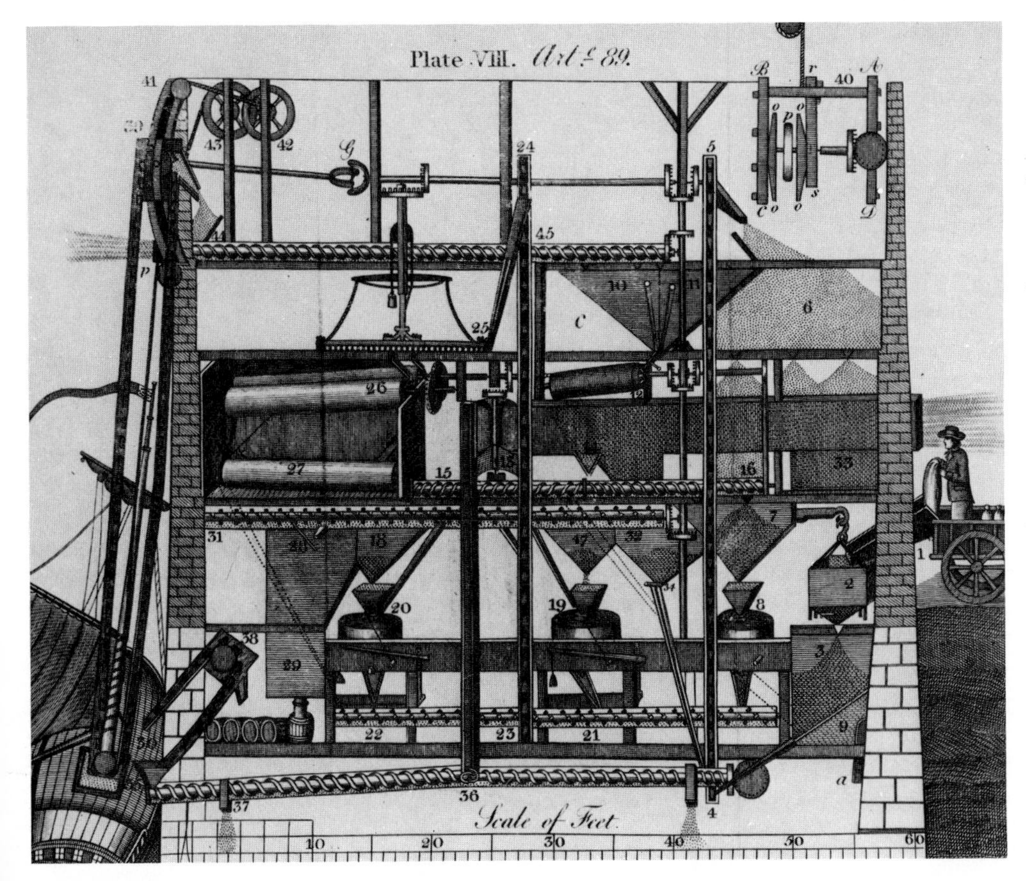

Oliver Evans' *automated flour mill, 1785, run by waterpower and controlled by one operator, combined five machines in one. To get an idea of how the process worked, follow the numbers on the drawing, starting at far right. The elevator, a revolving belt with wooden buckets attached, took the grain from a feeding hopper to the top of the mill. The conveyor, an endless screw, guided the grain to a chute leading to the grindstones. The drill, actually a belt, moved the meal horizontally or up an incline. A "hopper boy," or revolving rake, stirred the meal to cool it and included a device to separate bran from the flour. The descender, a belt mounted on rollers and moved by the weight of the flour, fed it to a loading point. The significance of the mill as a precursor of modern mass production lay in its mechanized, step-by-step combination of five processes. Millers were slow to adopt the Evans machine, but 1,200 of them were operating in the big grain-producing States of the Midwest by 1837.*

The U.S. Patent Office
Inventions Were a Form of Visual History

Many of the 7,000-odd models lost in the disastrous fire of 1
were replaced, although Senator John Ruggles' proposal to h
all the most interesting ones duplicated was never fully car
out. Meanwhile, fresh models continued to jam the tempor
quarters of the Patent Office.

The permanent new Patent Office, a handsome building
spired by the Parthenon, was begun in 1840. It acquired
wings shortly after it was completed, and still another section
added soon after that. Even so, by 1870 the chaos and congest
were such that Congress ruled out models as an automatic
quirement, though in some instances they might be reques
Then, in 1877, fire struck again, destroying about 87,000 m
els—a mere fraction of the whole collection, however. In 1
the laws were amended to discourage the sending of any mo
except those of aircraft and perpetual motion machines, un
they were specially requested. But not all inventors complied,
the collection continued to swell.

In 1907, after a congressional investigation had reveale
lack of public interest, it was decided to sell the lot, after lett
the Smithsonian Institution select the most valuable items. Sev
thousand models were auctioned; the rest found their way i
Government basements. Storage was costly, so in the 1920's
economy-minded Coolidge administration delivered the coup
grace. Many models went to the Smithsonian, the Ford Museu
the Edison Institute, and similar establishments; many were
claimed by their inventors; the rest were auctioned. Out of lo
unopened crates came models and drawings—one by Abrah
Lincoln.

Many of the models snapped up by collectors are things
beauty. But whether graceful, crude, or amusing, they illumin
a fascinating history. Inventions multiplied so rapidly in the f
half of the 19th century that Commissioner of Patents He
L. Ellsworth observed in 1844: "The advancement of the arts fr
year to year taxes our credulity and seems to presage the arri
of that period when human improvement must end." Ellswo
then resigned a job that he felt had no future. Within a few d
ades Elias Howe, Christopher L. Sholes, Thomas A. Edis
Alexander Graham Bell, and others were to belie his predicti
By the mid-1970's the scope of American inventiveness had b
officially documented by the 4.5 million-odd patents that w
then on record in the Patent Office.

gine was connected to the mechanical digger, and it proceeded with the job for which it had been built.

If the incredulous Philadelphians who saw it did not comprehend the importance of this lumbering monstrosity, Evans knew he had demonstrated the practicability of steam locomotion. In 1812 he wrote: "The time will come when people will travel in stages moved by steam engines from one city to another almost as fast as birds fly—fifteen to twenty miles an hour." Evans died 11 years before the first regular railway locomotive service in the United States was initiated in 1830.

The Slide Rest and the Stocking Lathe

Until the late 1700's metal could not be turned on a lathe to make it uniformly round and smooth. There was no way for the operator to guide the cutting tool evenly by hand against the turning piece. The problem was solved by David Wilkinson of Pawtucket, Rhode Island. In 1798 he obtained a patent for a machine in which the cutter was clamped into a movable slide that could be advanced precisely, by hand crank, parallel to the work. In precision metalwork the principle of the slide rest, as it is called, has many uses. It permits the manufacture of parts so uniform in size and shape that they can be interchanged. Without it, mass production could not have been achieved. As it turned out, the great English machinist Henry Maudslay had already developed a more refined version of the slide rest, but this was not known to Wilkinson and does not diminish his accomplishment.

Wilkinson also built an improved blast furnace for smelting iron and developed a method of boring cannon by rotating the barrel against a stationary bit. He foresaw correctly that greater precision could be achieved by turning the heavier, more stable barrel than by turning the lighter, more flexible bit.

One of New England's most precocious inventors was Thomas Blanchard, who was born in Sutton, Massachusetts, in 1788. At 13 he designed an apple parer and, at 18, a device to regulate the number of tacks in a packet. Later he developed a tackmaking machine. But his most significant contribution was the invention of the stocking lathe in 1818. This lathe not only could turn pieces of irregular shape but also could follow a pattern and make innumerable duplicates. It was developed for the manufacture of gunstocks but was later applied to making wooden lasts, which helped New England become the shoemaking center of the country. The invention that proved most profitable to Blanchard was a process for bending ships' timbers without splitting them.

A New Industry Is Started

While a few ingenious Yankees had successfully invented a variety of useful machines, no one yet knew how to put together an entire manufacturing system. As late as 1790 not one mill in America could profitably spin cotton into yarn or weave it into cloth. Because of Britain's ban on the export of spinning machines and the emigration of skilled mechanics, England held a virtual monopoly on the sale of cloth in America and intended to keep it. One man, the English-born Samuel Slater, broke this monopoly wide open.

In 1782, at the age of 14, Slater began work in Belper, Derbyshire, for Jedediah Strutt, inventor of a machine for making ribbed stockings, and a partner of Richard Arkwright, who in 1769 had perfected a spinning frame that could turn out strong cotton thread. Slater showed an uncommon aptitude for repairing and operating the machinery, and his advancement was rapid. When he heard that rewards were being offered in the United States to encourage the development of the textile business, Slater decided to emigrate. He memorized all the

Patent models. *Screw (1860) had a spiral edge to avoid splitting wood. The Selden Car (1895) figured in a George Selden–Henry Ford patent fight. A model of Otis' elevator (1880) featured an air cushion for safety. Abraham Lincoln's device (1849) was for buoying vessels over shoals.*

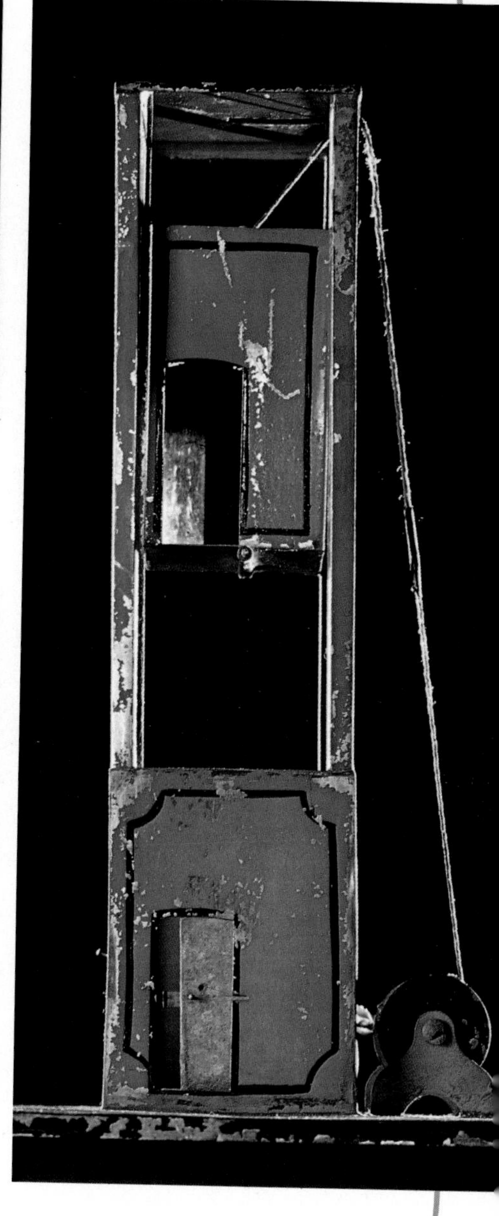

complicated details of Arkwright's spinning machinery, as well as the cotton machinery of James Hargreaves and Samuel Crompton, so that he would not have to risk carrying any incriminating plans. In 1789, disguised as a farmworker and under an assumed name, he sailed for New York. The next year, with the help of a skilled blacksmith, Oziel Wilkinson (father of David Wilkinson and Slater's future father-in-law), he built a replica of the Arkwright machinery in a mill owned by Almy & Brown in Pawtucket, Rhode Island. Slater can be called a founder of the textile industry in the United States, a title he shares with Francis Cabot Lowell. In 1814, at Waltham, Massachusetts, Lowell established the first American mill to combine carding, spinning, and weaving of cloth under one roof. After Lowell's death in 1817, his associates in Massachusetts developed the first American factory town and named it Lowell.

The Ubiquitous Byproduct of the Erie Canal

After years of wrangling and indecision the New York State Legislature authorized the digging of a canal from Lake Erie to the Hudson River to join the Great Lakes area with the port of New York. On July 4, 1817, the digging of the canal was begun. About a year later a promising young worker named Canvass White was sent to Europe to learn what he could about canal construction. He walked the towpaths for some 2,000 miles, sketching details of construction, and returned with the conviction that the only practical way to build the locks was with stone blocks sealed with hydraulic cement. This sealer was available only in Britain and was expensive.

While surveying for the canal in northern New York, however, White discovered an unusual deposit of lime rock, which he thought might have possibilities as a sealer. By burning, pulverizing, and mixing it with sand

American industry took a leap *forward when, in 1798, Eli Whitney began making rifles with interchangeable parts in this factory near New Haven, Connecticut. The attractive village of Whitneyville grew up around the plant to house the factory workers.*

The American System of Manufacture *A Brilliant Idea That Revolutionized Industry*

"A good Musket," said Eli Whitney, "is a complicated engine." As a gunmaker, he had reason to know. What made him one of the most important figures in the Industrial Revolution—a forefather, in fact, of mass production—was his role in developing the principle of interchangeable parts and then making it work.

The idea seems to have been brought to America from France by Thomas Jefferson in the 1780's. Whitney's contribution lay in making it practical. He was so far ahead of his time that some 50 years later a group of Britons, amazed by a demonstration of his techniques of gun manufacture, resolved to adopt this ingenious "American system" to production in their own plants.

Until Whitney's time a "manufactory" had been a workshop where each artisan, with or without assistants, made all the parts of a product by hand and then assembled the finished whole. But in 1798 Whitney, under pressure to fulfill his Government musket contract, saw to the core of the problem and concentrated not on the product itself but on the tools required to make it. It was his aim, he said, that "the tools themselves shall fashion the work and give to every part a just proportion." From this approach came interchangeable parts, each an exact duplicate of its thousands of mates. In application if not in concept this was revolutionary, for it meant that unskilled men could turn out precision products at speeds undreamed of under the individual craftsmanship system. Whitney became the first man to make and use power-driven precision tools. It took him 2 years to produce the drill presses, jigs, and templates for his Whitneyville plant, but, having done so, he was able to begin manufacture of the first effectively standardized musket.

Colt's 1835 patent *drawing shows his repeating pistol, which helped revolutionize war and tame the West. From 1856 to 1865 Colt's factory made more than 550,000 revolvers.*

Whitney never quite perfected a mass-produced musket; certain parts of the locks could not be interchanged. It was left to inheritors of his pioneering work to take up where he had left off. One of these was Samuel Colt, born in 1814, whose importance in the manufacture of firearms came finally to surpass that of all his rivals. Colt not only made the first revolving pistol, but he also improved the Whitney system of interchangeable parts and took it to its logical conclusion by developing an assembly line. With this crucial step he became a leader in employing the mass-production techniques used by modern industry.

Colt began manufacturing his revolver in Paterson, New Jersey, in 1836. It was both expertly made and easy to use: The six chambers of the revolving cylinder came in line with the barrel as the hammer was pulled back to full cock, and the barrel was carefully rifled to give the weapon greater accuracy. Colt's company failed in 1842, but the Mexican War brought a flood of orders. Colt got Whitney's son to make the revolvers for him and later built his own factory, which prospered immensely.

he made a material that would harden under water. He called it waterproof lime, and in 1820 patented his manufacturing process. It was used on the canal with great success. Natural cement, one of the three major types of cement now in use in making concrete, was developed from White's process. Few materials in history have had such a significant impact on construction.

A Genius With a Flair for Drama

Eli Whitney, perhaps more than any other individual, exemplified Yankee ingenuity and inventiveness. When still in his teens Whitney went into the nailmaking business with a machine of his own devising, in a shop on his father's Massachusetts farm. When cheaper imported nails came on the market, he turned to making walking sticks and women's hatpins. Yearning for an education and broader horizons, he entered Yale and headed south, after graduation in 1792, to take a tutoring job on a Georgia plantation. When the job failed to materialize, he was invited to stay with Mrs. Nathanael Greene, the widow of the Revolutionary War general. It was during his visit there that he became interested in finding a way to remove the seeds from cotton more rapidly than by slow and tedious handpicking. His brilliantly simple solution, the cotton gin, revolutionized agriculture in the South and revivified the waning institution of slavery. (For more about the cotton gin and its effects, see "Putting the Land to Work," pages 106–123.)

Whitney returned to New Haven and obtained a patent on his machine in 1794. But because of widespread pirating of his invention, he profited little from it. It did, however, establish his reputation for mechanical ingenuity and helped him get an order to make 10,000 muskets for the United States in 1798, when there was a threat of war with France. He rashly promised delivery in 2 years—a rate of production unheard of at the time; but his reputation and the support of influential fellow Yale alumni got him the contract.

Unable to deliver the muskets in the time promised, Whitney called on his flair for the dramatic. As the story goes, he took a pile of tooled metal castings to Washington and, before the unbelieving eyes of Government officials, picked up interchangeable parts at random and put together half a dozen complicated musket locks. After such a demonstration, he had little trouble in getting permission to extend the time of the contract.

In fact, it took Whitney more than 10 years to fill the order, and most of the actual production was in the last 2 years. (Even today when machine tools of every description are available, it can take longer to set up for a new product than to turn it out.) Whitney had to make—sometimes to invent—the machine tools he needed. By 1812, however, he could take an order for 15,000 muskets and deliver them all in 2 years.

Whitney, a compassionate man, did not live to see that slavery, which was given new life by his cotton gin, would precipitate a war, nor that the number and efficiency of the rifles manufactured by his system would serve to make that war the bloodiest in our history.

From Oars and Sail to the Power of Steam

The dream of boats driven by engines was not new in the 1790's, but in that era it began to come true. Various mechanics had worked on the idea; the most meaningful experiments were carried out by John Fitch, who had enough near-successes to keep him going, and enough failures to drive him to drugs, drunkenness, and—probably—suicide. Fitch was a mapmaker, surveyor, and clockmaker who became obsessed with steamboat design. His single-mindedness and rude manner alienated most potential backers. His basic principles were right, however, and as early as 1788 he built a workable paddle-wheel steamer. His *Thornton* ran some 20 miles on a test run and by 1790 had logged 3,000 miles. But even at 8 miles an hour it was not fast enough to compete with the stagecoaches of the day. Fitch eventually gave up his quest in despair. Bitter personal experience prompted him to write: "I know of nothing so perplexing and vexatious to a man of feelings as a turbulent wife and steamboat building."

Not the least of his troubles was a dispute with James Rumsey, who had developed a method of propulsion using a jet of steam. This was a concept that Benjamin Franklin had proposed. Samuel Morey, another pioneer, made an operable side-wheeler. The approaches of all these innovators have since been proved sound, but at that time there were no engines of practical size with the necessary power to run the boats profitably.

It remained for Robert Fulton and his *Clermont* to prove that the steamboat was here to stay. Fulton, the son of a Pennsylvania farmer, was born in 1765. He showed a talent for painting, and among his works was a portrait of Benjamin Franklin. In 1786 Fulton went to England to study with the American-born artist Benjamin West, and seemed headed for a promising career as a painter. Instead, he decided to develop his talent for engineering.

Fulton's interest in canals and aqueducts blossomed in England. While there he designed a power shovel to dig canals and an inclined railway to transport boats from one level of a canal to another. He also conceived the idea of casting iron sections for aqueducts right on the site—a remarkable advance at the time.

By 1793 Fulton was developing new ideas for the design of boats and by 1800 had actually launched a submarine, the *Nautilus*. He had built the craft for Napoleon, who hoped to nullify once and for all the British Navy's dominance of the seas. But when the *Nautilus* failed to overtake and sink a British warship, the French lost interest in the project. The British, who had been watching nervously, now asked Fulton for a demonstration. Defective torpedoes were the bugaboo this time, and the British refused to support further experiments.

Fulton had a gentleman's demeanor and access to financial backing that was unavailable to the truculent, impoverished John Fitch. He also had the advantage of his study of mechanics and engineering. While still in France, he tried out different hull shapes and paddles in a test tank and decided that side paddle wheels were best. He used them, with an English engine, on his first boat, the 133-foot *Clermont,* which left New York City on August 17, 1807, and steamed up to Albany in 32 hours. Dockside scoffers had dubbed the craft "Fulton's Folly" and compared it to a "floating sawmill caught on fire."

After a few modifications, the *Clermont* was soon in regular service on the Hudson and proved a profitable venture for Fulton and his wealthy sponsor, Robert R. Livingston. Before Fulton died in 1815 he designed at least 15 more successful steamboats for various clients, including the U.S. Navy. His *Demologos,* also called *Fulton the First,* was the first naval steamship ever launched.

The Livingston-Stevens Family Feud

In addition to providing financial backing, Livingston was able to ensure a monopoly of steamboat navigation on the Hudson, which he had received from the New York State Legislature. Before he met Fulton, he had formed a partnership with his brother-in-law, Col. John Stevens, to develop a steamboat for service on the river. When Livingston, as U.S. Minister Plenipotentiary, was in France negotiating the Louisiana Purchase, he became impressed with Fulton's mechanical experience and aptitude. Livingston made an agreement with Fulton that Stevens considered a breach of their previous partnership, and a bitter but gentlemanly feud developed.

While Livingston and Fulton were in France, Stevens had made significant advances in boilermaking and boat design. In 1808 he built his own boat, the *Phoenix,* and the following year he took it through the open ocean from New York to Philadelphia and into the Delaware River, where Livingston had no monopoly on navigation. This trip entailed the first sea voyage under the power of steam.

It became apparent in the ensuing years that monopolies on river routes were stifling trade. In 1824 a U.S. Supreme Court ruling handed down by Chief Justice John Marshall in a case argued by Daniel Webster declared that State-granted monopolies on waterways were illegal. Once the rivers were open to all, the profit would go to those with the most efficient vessels. The great Mississippi riverboats and the oceangoing steamers were soon to come. By the late 1800's the steamboat reigned supreme on the seas and the world's navigable rivers.

Applying Ingenuity to Agriculture

In 1793 Charles Newbold was awarded a patent for a cast-iron plow. It was more efficient than the wooden plow, but many farmers shunned it for fear it would poison the soil. As experience proved otherwise, iron was

Robert Fulton's North River Steamboat (*later the* Clermont) *chugs up the Hudson at about 4.5 miles per hour, smoke pouring from its pinewood-fueled engine, its sail little more than a salute to a passing age. With hull enlarged and engine improved, it became America's first commercially successful steamboat. Regular schedules for the 150-mile trip from New York City to Albany were established in the fall of 1807.*

Joseph Henry

The Reward Lay in the "Consciousness of Advancing Science"

American science owes an incalculable debt to Joseph Henry, who was born in Albany, New York, in 1797. The most distinguished native scientist since Franklin, Henry more than anyone showed how electricity—then generally regarded as a philosophic toy—could be put to work. As first secretary and director of the Smithsonian Institution, he set high standards for American research and stimulated and guided scientific talent throughout the land.

Henry was an austere man, reserved, unassuming, and endowed with strong Christian principles that enabled him to bear without complaint the disappointments that came when others got credit for his work, as they often did.

As a professor at Albany Academy and then at the College of New Jersey (now Princeton University), Henry discovered the principle of induction, on which generators and electric motors are based, and the relationship of electricity and magnetism. He built what was then the world's largest electromagnet (though weighing only 70 pounds, it could lift over a ton); devised the first telegraph system, based on his discovery of the relay principle; and did some of the research that led to the invention of the transformer and the development of wireless telegraphy. Michael Faraday, in England, had discovered induction independently and published his results. Henry not only confirmed Faraday's results, he went a step further by discovering self-induction—the fact that a current passing through a coil generates a charge in the coil itself. Henry also developed a system of transmitting weather reports by telegraph. This laid the groundwork for the U.S. Weather Bureau.

The young Henry *gazes out from an assemblage of personal effects that show his scientific interests: a surveyor's notebook, a battery, an induction coil, wire, pliers, and other tools.*

gradually accepted, and in 1819 Jethro Wood made an improved model of three sections; if one part broke or wore out it could be replaced. In 1837 John Deere, a young Vermont-born blacksmith working in Illinois, noticed the shine on a circular saw blade and wondered if polished steel might not be better than iron; perhaps soil would not cling to its smooth surface. Such proved to be the case. The thin steel of Deere's sharp new implement vibrated in use and became the "singing plow" that was soon turning the rolling land of the Indian and the buffalo into one of the greatest grain-producing regions in the world.

Three years before Deere designed the steel plow, Cyrus Hall McCormick patented a machine that would make it possible to harvest hundreds of thousands of acres in the short season when grain is prime for cutting. From the time of the Pharaohs, grain had been cut by hand with a curved blade. It is no wonder that every sweat-soaked farmer with a sickle or scythe in his blistered hands had dreamed of a machine that would do this backbreaking labor for him.

McCormick was born in 1809 on a Virginia farm, where his father over the course of some 20 years had developed a crude reaping machine that almost worked. The son had an interest in mechanics also, and in 1831 he began to improve his father's project. He devised the sickle bar, a series of V-shaped openings on a fixed bar under which triangular knives shuttle back and forth to shear off the standing grain at ground level. Other inventors were also making workable reapers, notably Obed Hussey, a Quaker from Maine. Hussey concentrated his work in the East, but McCormick moved to Chicago near the wide prairies, where his machines could really prove their worth. He established a partnership with the mayor of Chicago, who put up $50,000, and they soon began to harvest a profit. In the autumn of 1854 they sold 1,000 reapers. McCormick later bought out his partner and amassed a huge personal fortune. Much of his success was due to creative merchandising. He guaranteed his products and was one of the first to sell farm equipment on the installment plan.

During its early years of use the reaper was gradually improved. First, a canvas elevator was added to lift the cut grain into a wagon alongside. A few years later a platform was attached to the machine, and a man stood there to bind the grain into sheaves. A rake was added later to sweep the sheaves from the platform. Then, in 1874, came a big breakthrough. Charles B. Withington, of Janesville, Wisconsin, invented an ingenious device that bundled the grain into sheaves and tied them with wire. McCormick manufactured 50,000 of Withington's binders. But bits of wire sometimes got into the grain, with disastrous results to the livestock that ate it. When John F. Appleby came to McCormick with a twine-binding device, the reaper-harvester seemed perfect. It cut, bundled, and tied the grain by horsepower alone.

A threshing machine to separate the grain from straw and chaff was first built in Scotland in the 1790's. In America twin brothers Hiram and John Pitts of Winthrop, Maine, patented a thresher in 1837 and began manufacturing it. For the next 15 years they continued to improve it. By 1880 the reaper and thresher were coupled into a combine, which, operating with steam or mule power, cut, threshed, cleaned, and bagged the grain.

An Age of Innovation

No problem was too large or too small for 19th-century American inventors to tackle. In 1836 Alonzo D. Phillips developed a new method for making sulfur matches. Walter Hunt invented the safety pin in 1849. Joseph Henry was getting started on theories that would lead to amazing new applications for the power of electricity. This era also saw the emergence of Samuel Colt's improved pistol with a revolving chamber, the new barbed wire that could fence the prairies, and an ingenious system of wheels that enabled locomotives to negotiate the curving routes being built through mountain passes. The challenge of making the railways safe inspired a number of famous American inventors. Later in the century Thomas A. Edison turned out inventions by the hundreds, and his ideas won international renown.

Since ancient times iron ore had been heated and beaten into shape to make wrought iron or melted in a crucible at higher temperatures and poured into molds to make cast iron. Whether cast or wrought, iron is brittle because it has a carbon content of about 4 percent. This must be reduced to 2 percent or less to make steel, which is tough and resilient, can be worked into any shape, and will hold a sharp edge. Until the mid-1800's, however, there was no dependable or economical way to control iron carbon content.

Striving for Safety on the Rails

The Inventors Do Their Part

Even with all the safeguards that genius can devise, equipment can fail and human beings can err. But modern railroads are infinitely safer than the early-day trains, due, in large part, to the creation of the safety devices shown on these pages.

These inventions have mostly to do with keeping a train on the tracks, helping others know where it is at all times, and stopping it quickly when required. As can be seen by the dates, these developments did not come quickly. There is a span of more than 50 years between Robert L. Stevens' invention of the T-rail and the first workable installation of the automatic signal system developed by George Westinghouse.

In the late 1800's, when the railroads seemed particularly vulnerable to such occurrences, some of the spectacular wrecks were caused by inadequate understanding of the stresses and strains that heavy fast-moving equipment put on bridges and trestles. Construction techniques that would support structures for horse-drawn vehicles were too light for trains. The designers soon learned from their tragic mistakes, and such failures due to faulty design and construction were largely eliminated.

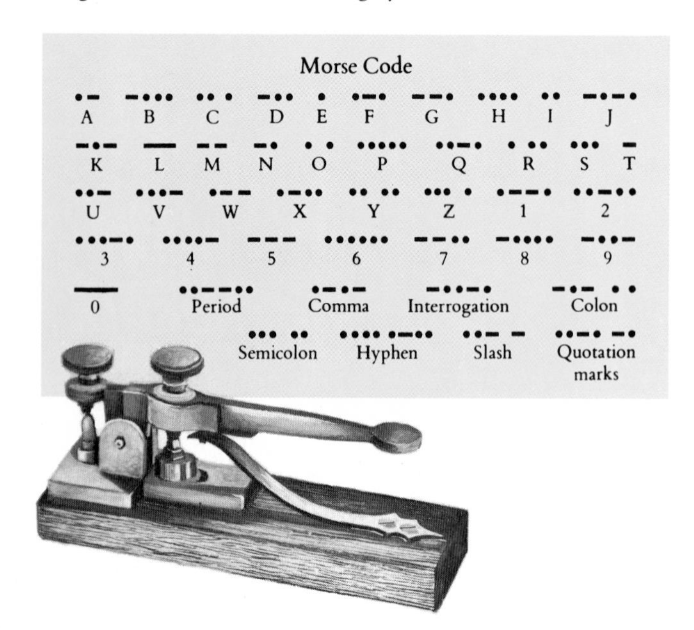

1830. The Iron T-rail. Robert L. Stevens, bound for England to order locomotives and track for the family railroad, developed an idea for a T-shaped track that would prove to be far superior to the equipment he was on his way to buy. His concept of a solid iron rail with a flat base and hook-headed spikes to hold it to wooden crossties has become the standard for railroads around the world. The ties were originally made of stone, but when the demand outstripped the stonecutters' rate of production, Stevens had to use wood. In the end the flexibility of wood ties proved to be a great advantage and wood is still the preferred material. Steel, which is tougher and more flexible than iron, was used for rails as soon as it became available after the Civil War. The drawing shows how the flanged wheel rides the track with minimum friction. The gravel base, or ballast, provides support and good drainage.

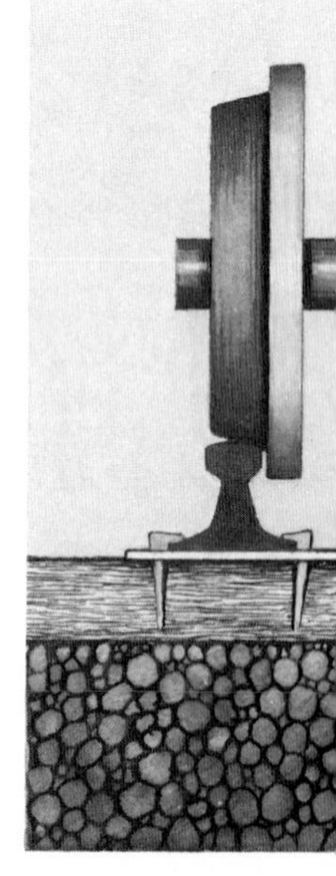

1844. The Telegraph. Samuel F. B. Morse gave up a successful career as a portrait painter to pursue his interest in telegraphy and gained more fame and wealth than he could have imagined as a painter. Before his invention of the unique dot-dash code that bears his name and the remarkable electromagnetic system that he assembled to transmit the message, as represented by the early-day telegrapher's key at left, the exact location of a fast-moving train was largely a matter of conjecture—and this lack of exactitude was frequently fatal.

Morse had completed a model of his system, including the all-important code, by 1835. The telegraph was not patented until 1844 and not put to practical use on the railroad until 1851. Although it immediately proved to be the best available method of communicating between way stations to determine whether or not a given train had arrived at that point or had already left, established practices die hard, and the telegraph system was not universally adopted for a full 20 years after its first use. The development of radio communication on the railroads spelled the end of the staccato tap-tap-tap of the telegrapher's key, but the principle established by Morse's invention remains the same. Instantaneous point-to-point communication is an essential element in making the railroads safe.

This changed when William Kelly, a Kentucky kettle manufacturer, discovered that when air is blown through molten iron, the carbon combines with the oxygen and burns off as carbon monoxide. The carbon content can thus be economically reduced to the small percentages required for steel. Kelly called this "air boiling." His neighbors could not believe that such an ancient and baffling problem could be solved so easily by a simple kettlemaker, and they gave him the sobriquet Crazy Kelly. But he had indeed made an important discovery, and he perfected his steel-making process in 1851.

About 6 years later Henry Bessemer, the English inventor, hit upon the same principle independently and was knighted for his achievement. That both men had made the same discovery did not come to light until an ambitious American engineer, Alexander Lyman Holley, applied for a license to bring Bessemer's process to this country. Although Kelly had a prior patent, he did not fight the matter in court; consequently, the process that revolutionized the steelmaking industry is called by the Englishman's name. And Bessemer did go on to make other important improvements in steelmaking.

Equipped with this new process the Nation—with its unprecedented potential for growth, its seemingly limitless mountains of ore, and at last a feasible means of production—began to roll out steel from blast furnaces

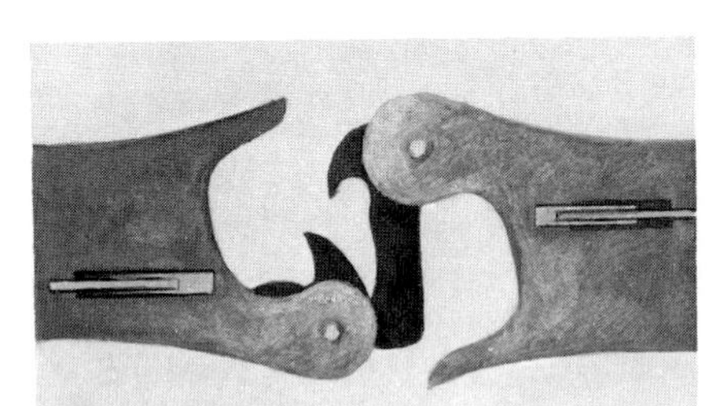

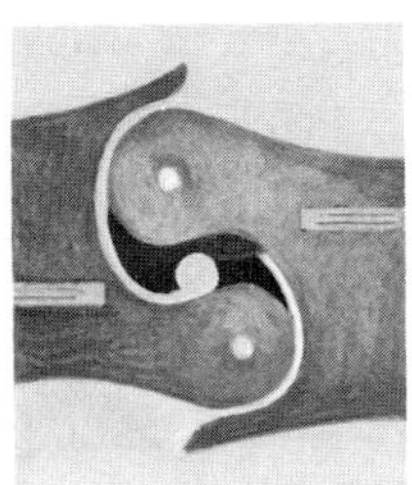

1868. The Safety Coupler. In the early days of railroading, the brakeman had the most dangerous job of all. Not only did he have to make his way along the catwalk on top of the swaying train to set the brakes by hand, he had to couple and uncouple the cars with a link and pin device, which, if not handled skillfully, could miss connecting and crush him to death between the cars. The man who put an end to this risky aspect of the brakeman's work was Confederate Army veteran Major Eli H. Janney. His knuckle couplers, so called for their fistlike shape when set in the open position, were designed to automatically engage and lock together upon impact. With the advent of the Janney coupler, the brakeman could stand safely to one side as the cars came crashing together. Some couplers today are remote controlled.

1869. The Air Brake. Not only was it dangerous to set brakes by hand, it was not an effective way to stop a train. This fact was widely recognized. But until George Westinghouse put his mind to it, no one had the foggiest notion of how to better the situation. Westinghouse realized that an effective system would permit the engineer to brake all the wheels of all the cars simultaneously. He considered various methods and decided that using compressed air, a relatively new concept, would be the best approach.

For the first demonstrations he attached a piston to a brake on each car. This was connected, by pipe and flexible hose, to an air compressor in the locomotive. With the turn of a valve, the engineer could set all the brakes at once. The system worked, but there were still problems: If one brake in the line failed, all those behind it would fail; and if part of the train became accidentally disconnected, the brakes would not work. By a stroke of genius Westinghouse solved both problems at the same time. He installed a reservoir of compressed air on each car sufficient to activate the brakes. He then used air pressure to hold the brake away from the wheels. When that pressure was released by the engineer, or by accident, pressure from the individual reservoirs would automatically apply the brakes and stop the train. This is basically the system still used today.

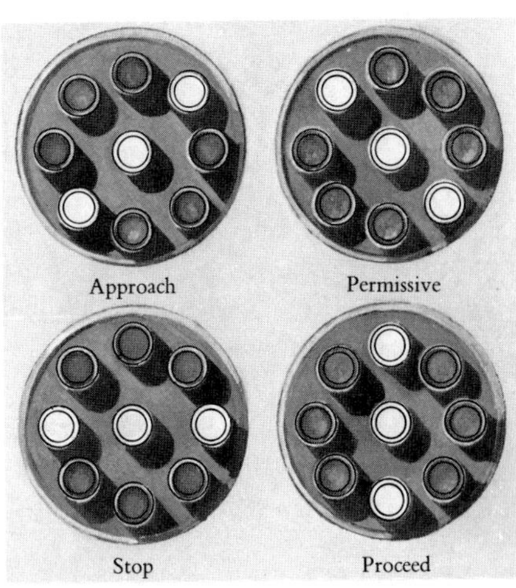

1882. Signals and Switches. George Westinghouse continued his interest in railroad safety and in 1880, at age 34, he founded the Union Switch and Signal Company in Pittsburgh, Pennsylvania. Within two years the company was selling complete systems for switching trains from track to track and indicating the position of every train with interlocked electrically controlled signals. There have been many improvements in the Westinghouse system, but his basic concepts still prevail.

On the tall semaphore shown at right the position of the arms, as well as the color of the lights, indicate to the engineer of an oncoming train whether or not the track in the block or zone ahead is clear and what action he should take. There are various signals that use yellow, green, red, and white lights in fixed or (see above) changing positions. Westinghouse's system not only helped prevent accidents, it helped speed up the movement of trains through marshaling yards where traffic was heaviest.

Modern centralized traffic control (CTC) systems have large lighted signal boards that use computers to further automate switching and signaling.

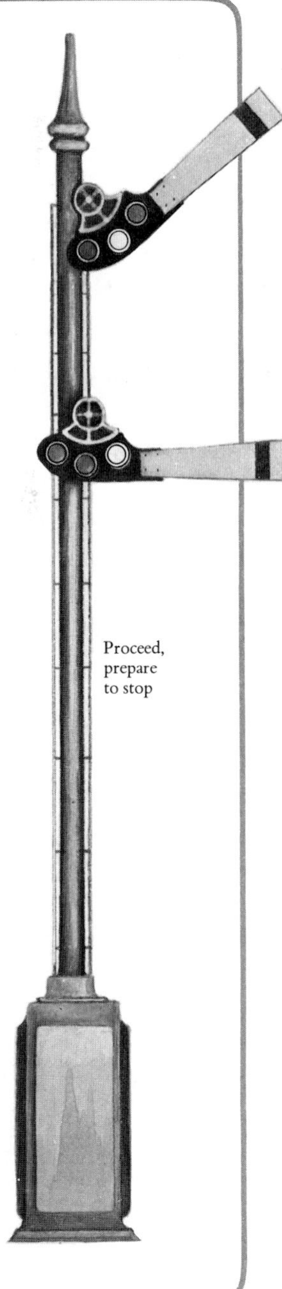

Proceed, prepare to stop

The Sewing Machine

Every Woman Her Own Seamstress

The sewing machine was the creation of many minds. In 1790 Thomas Saint, an Englishman, designed a leather-stitching machine, which was never built. In the 1820's Barthêlemy Thimonnier, a Frenchman, invented a machine with a crotchet-type needle that produced a chain stitch. Finally, the sewing machine as we now know it was developed in America during the innovative decade of the 1830's.

In 1832 or 1833 the inventor Walter Hunt built in his New York shop a machine that made a lock stitch. Instead of working to improve his invention, however, the kind-hearted Hunt abandoned it for fear it would throw seamstresses out of work. The less inventive but more single-minded Elias Howe first made the sewing machine a commercial proposition. In 1845 a hand-cranked machine Howe had made exceeded the combined output of five hard-working seamstresses. The following year Howe took out a patent on this machine and spent several unhappy years trying to market his product in England. Returning home, he was plunged into legal battles with those who in his absence had infringed the patent rights of his by then immensely popular innovation. Among his opponents was the machinist and promotional genius Isaac M. Singer, who had built a machine with several marked improvements on Howe's—in particular, a treadle, which left both hands free, and a vertically moving needle, which facilitated the sewing of a curved seam.

In prolonged litigation over patent rights, Howe emerged the victor in 1854. Two years later Howe, Singer, and two other competitors agreed to pool the best sewing machine patents and share the royalties. This reasonable approach to their problems proved to be a good idea: Singer and Howe both became millionaires.

The turn-of-the-century *housewife was enticed into buying a Singer sewing machine by this attractive advertisement.*

in mills in Pennsylvania, Ohio, Indiana, and Illinois. The steel was soon used to build transcontinental railroads and, later, steel-ribbed skyscrapers and suspension bridges that spanned distances previously impossible.

On the Homefront

Another great advance of the 1800's was a machine that could sew a straight seam as well as or better than a practiced seamstress—and even a man could run it. Today's sewing machine owes its success to many minds. Walter Hunt, probably the era's most prolific inventor, was one of the first to create a device that could sew. He built his machine about 1833, but thinking it would deprive seamstresses of their work, he withheld it from the market. Elias Howe had no such compunction; he patented his sewing machine in 1846 and spent years fighting to maintain the exclusive rights of his invention.

The typewriter also owes its origins to many contributors. The first machine in America was put together by William A. Burt in 1829. Dozens of other tinkerers worked on improvements, but it was not until the 1890's that the typewriter was mass-produced. Credit for developing the first model with the keyboard, lever action, and movable carriage that are standard today goes to Christopher L. Sholes, Carlos Glidden, and Samuel W. Soulé. Sholes and Glidden sold out in 1873 to Eliphalet Remington and Sons, who also made sewing machines and firearms. Mark Twain was one of the first users of the typewriter.

Christopher L. Sholes' *daughter demonstrates her father's typewriter in 1872. Sholes, Samuel W. Soulé, and Carlos Glidden had made the first practical typing machine in 1867.*

To the list of hardship-ridden individuals such as John Fitch and William Kelly, driven by their compulsive visions and considered by most of their contemporaries to be madmen, must be added the name of Charles Goodyear. His obsession was gum elastic, or "India rubber." In its natural state, the material was too soft for practical use in hot weather and too hard when it was cold. Goodyear was determined to stabilize it by some curing process, and he had a blind faith that he would hit on something if he kept trying every method he could think of. As it turned out, the process that made rubber a useful servant of man was discovered by accident. After patenting his process of vulcanization in 1844, Goodyear advocated rubber for almost every use including clothing, tobacco pouches, and bathtubs. He died in 1860, and was, therefore, not destined to see its universal use in automobile tires.

Some New Discoveries at Work

Once Samuel F. B. Morse turned to invention, he showed a doggedness fully equal to Charles Goodyear's. After enjoying considerable success as a portrait painter, Morse went to Europe for further study. On his voyage home in 1832 he heard talk of new developments in electromagnetism made in England by Michael Faraday. In a moment of insight Morse conceived the idea of using the newly discovered magnetic spark to send messages over a wire. He was not aware at that time that Joseph Henry had already built a telegraph system for his own use in Albany, New York.

Morse did some experimenting with his idea, but he had no scientific background, and to make a living he reverted to painting and then to teaching art. He continued working with the telegraph, however, and, hearing belatedly about Joseph Henry's work, turned to him for help. Henry generously gave Morse the idea of the relay, which Morse put to practical use. This was a device that could give new strength to a waning electrical impulse and send it along. In series, relays could extend a telegraph line for any distance.

By 1837 Morse had all the ingredients, but he failed to obtain British and French patents and lost financial backing in the United States. He was about ready to give up when in 1843 Congress voted $30,000 for an experimental line between Washington and Baltimore. The 40-mile test, on May 24, 1844, was successful; it covered the longest distance yet spanned by telegraph. The history-making words first sent over the line were: "What hath God wrought?"

Morse's Magnetic Telegraph Company was challenged by other systems, and by the end of the Civil War, Western Union dominated the business. Morse's name is remembered today mainly for the dot-dash code he devised with significant technical assistance and financial aid from the almost forgotten Alfred Vail.

Another name known in every household is Westinghouse, but many years and many products went into making it so. Prosperous, thanks to his development of air brakes for trains (1869) and a railroad signal system (1882), George Westinghouse bought a big house in a residential area in Pittsburgh and happened to hit natural gas on his property. This challenged his ingenuity; working to control gas safely and use it to best advantage for heating and lighting, he developed some 30 patents.

The "Men of Progress" *are shown here in an imaginary 1862 group portrait by Christian Schussele. From left to right they are: William T. G. Morton; James Bogardus; Samuel Colt; Cyrus Hall McCormick; Joseph Saxton; Charles Goodyear, elbow on table; Peter Cooper, behind Goodyear; Jordan L. Mott, seated; Joseph Henry, standing; Eliphalet Nott, seated; John Ericsson, standing; Frederick E. Sickels; Samuel F. B. Morse, hand on table; Henry Burden; Richard M. Hoe; Erastus B. Bigelow; Isaiah Jennings; Thomas Blanchard; and Elias Howe.*

Westinghouse thereupon addressed himself to the potential of electricity. Here he came into conflict with Thomas A. Edison. Edison and his supporters were committed to using direct current, which flows one way only. Westinghouse argued for the greater efficiency and adaptability of alternating current, which undergoes continuous reversals of direction in pulsing surges called cycles. Westinghouse had the better idea, mainly because the alternating system requires merely a simple transformer to increase or decrease the voltage. U.S. standard electrical current today alternates at 60 cycles a second.

The role of electricity and gas in the growth of America cannot be overstated, but the internal-combustion engine and its offspring, the automobile, affected our lives more than any other mechanical development.

Most of the early work on the engine was done in Europe. Prototypes of the standard four-cycle automobile engine were made in France as far back as 1862, and Gottlieb Daimler of Germany designed an effective engine in the 1880's. In 1893 in Springfield, Massachusetts, Charles E. and J. Frank Duryea operated the first gasoline-powered car in the United States.

In 1895 George B. Selden succeeded in patenting the first total concept for a "road locomotive." In 1901 Ransom E. Olds assembled more than 425 Oldsmobiles, and by 1914 Henry Ford was rolling the famous Model T from the most efficient assembly line yet devised.

With the automobile came the need for more gasoline and oil. One of the first men to drill for oil, in the face of ridicule and outright obstruction, was Edwin Drake, whose well near Titusville, Pennsylvania, produced as much as 1,000 gallons a day. The success of Drake's gamble, and of those who followed, created a demand for more efficient rigs to drill the rich Spindletop and east Texas oilfields. One man, Howard R. Hughes, Sr., produced 25 different types of rock-drilling bit. These were so superior that his Hughes Tool Company, started in 1908, established—and still holds—a virtual world monopoly on this vital piece of equipment.

Charles Goodyear

Vulcanization, the treating of crude rubber with sulfur under heat to give it strength and elasticity, proved crucially important to the world we live in. This process owed its discovery to phenomenal perseverance and a dash of good luck.

The magical year was 1839. For 4 years Charles Goodyear had been seeking a way of curing gum elastic so that articles made of it would not grow sticky with heat, brittle with cold, or yellow with age. Then one day he accidentally dropped a mixture of sulfur and rubber onto a hot stove. The next day he noted that the spilled mixture had hardened like leather, and he concluded that sulfur and heat were the vital elements that he and many others had been looking for.

Until then many uses had been found for natural rubber, and many more imagined. In 1823, in Scotland, Charles Macintosh had made a raincoat of rubberized cloth, which, in Britain's temperate climate, proved a commercial success. In the early 1830's many rubber products hit the American market, but none of them held up in the extremes of heat and cold characteristic of the U.S. climate. Goodyear's Yankee grit was reinforced by his belief that God intended him to devote his life to "trying to improve articles of necessity or convenience, for the use of man." He overcame his limited knowledge of chemistry and proceeded with his experiments despite great personal problems—including dire poverty and the deaths of some of his children—and despite the waning of his backers' patience and funds. He tried mixing rubber with salt, sugar, castor oil, pepper, nitric acid, and innumerable other substances until he stumbled onto the right answer. But after he had perfected his process, Goodyear failed to profit from it. Unhappily for him, he was a poor businessman. He set his royalty rates ridiculously low and had little skill in fending off patent pirates. Even though he managed to win a spectacular piracy case, in which his counsel was Senator Daniel Webster, Goodyear died a poor man. His discovery's benefit to mankind, however, can hardly be measured. It eventually led to the opening of giant factories all over the world adapted to the turning out of vulcanized rubber goods of bewildering variety.

On to Electronics and Chemistry

The era of essentially mechanical innovation and invention was symbolically ended in 1903 when the Wright brothers flew a contrivance, equipped with a small gasoline engine and two wooden propellers, off the ground under its own power. A new world of electronic and chemical marvels was about to unfold. Alexander Graham Bell's telephone, an incredibly sophisticated blending of established mechanical principles and newly discovered facts about electricity, had been a fitting precursor of things to come.

One creative pioneer in the art of applying electricity to new and useful purposes was Elmer A. Sperry. In 1879, when he was 19, he developed an electric arc lamp and an improved dynamo, and in 1880 he founded a company in Chicago to produce lamps, dynamos (for generating electricity), and electrically powered mining machinery and street railway cars. Among his more than 400 inventions, however, the most significant were related to the gyroscope, which was essentially a toy until Sperry saw its further possibilities. A gyroscope consists of a wheel, or rotor, suspended so that it can spin freely within a frame. When spinning, the rotor will hold true to the axis no matter how the frame is moved. When Sperry saw a gyroscope in France, where the principle was discovered, he realized what could be done if the power of electricity was applied to it. He developed a gyroscope

Thomas A. Edison
Wizard of the Age of Electricity

Edison once remarked that genius is "one percent inspiration and ninety-nine percent perspiration." Certainly neither inspiration nor industry were lacking in this prolific inventor, who was granted a total of 1,097 patents—an all-time record.

Thomas Alva Edison was born in Milan, Ohio, in 1847. He had but a few years of formal schooling, but his mother taught him at home, and he early developed an interest in science. He took his first job as a railroad newsboy and "candy butcher," and then became an itinerant telegrapher, an occupation that started him on the road to developing his amazing potentialities for electrical innovation. His first commercially successful invention was an improved stock ticker, used by speculators in gold and securities. He used the $40,000 he got for this—a small fortune for a 23-year-old—to open a factory in Newark, New Jersey. There he made telegraph instruments and stock tickers, and methodically set about turning out further inventions. These included paraffin paper; the "electric pen," a precursor of the mimeograph; and the multiplex telegraph, which could handle several incoming and outgoing messages simultaneously on one wire.

In 1876 Edison moved from Newark to Menlo Park, New Jersey, where he established his "invention factory," the first industrial research laboratory. A torrent of discoveries and inventions was soon pouring from his fertile brain. Within a year he invented the carbon telephone transmitter, which greatly improved Bell's original instrument. His one discovery in pure science came in 1883. While he was experimenting with his electric light, he observed what he called the Edison effect: the passage of electricity across space from a hot filament to a cold plate within a light bulb. Edison patented this discovery in 1884 but did not investigate it further. Other scientists used the Edison effect to develop the electronics industry, particularly radio and television. The facilities at Menlo Park proved inadequate for Edison's wide-ranging work, and he moved into a new laboratory at West Orange, New Jersey, in 1887.

Edison is shown *here at work in his West Orange laboratory about 1919. He originated the team approach to industrial research.*

Edison's character was not a simple one. As a young man he was handicapped by a progressive deafness, but the affliction may have served to isolate him from the usual social relationships and spurred his interest in science and invention. Although he assigned various aspects of a project to members of a team, he gave scant consideration to his workers, expecting them to match his own inexhaustible energy. He was not always successful. He lost a savage and wrong-headed campaign against the use of alternating current as opposed to direct current. But the urge to experiment and improve never lagged: At 80 he was busy experimenting with ways to produce rubber from goldenrod plants and had succeeded in the laboratory. When he died at 84, many people dimmed their lights in honor of the wizard who had extended their days with the incandescent light bulb.

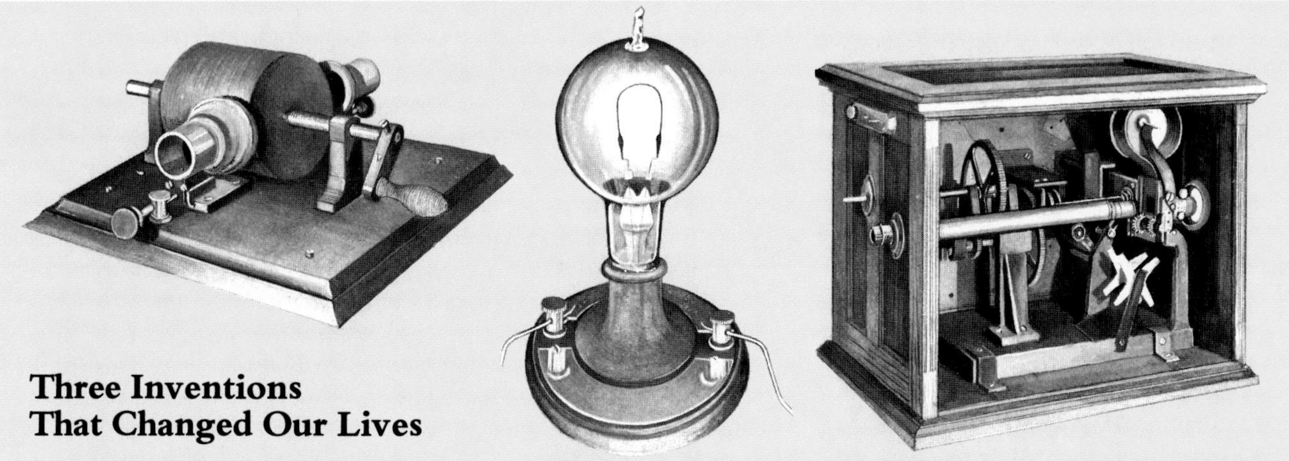

Three Inventions That Changed Our Lives

It would be hard to imagine life today without the phonograph, the light bulb, or motion pictures.

Edison's invention, in 1877, of a "talking machine" that could record, store, and reproduce human speech or music was revolutionary. Nothing had anticipated it. The inspiration came to Edison during experiments with the automatic telegraph. Noticing that an incoming signal made the needle of a telegraphic machine vibrate and hum, he had the idea that the vibrations of the human voice might be recorded, too, on the proper surface. His first models, such as the one above, left, used a cylinder covered with a sheet of tinfoil and were turned by a hand crank.

Men had worked for years to make a practical incandescent lamp, but it was Edison who found the answer in a filament of carbonized thread sealed in a vacuum. The lamp gave light for 40 hours. He patented this invention in 1880, then devised an electric generating system—which by 1882 was in use in his New York City power plant—to make it practical, thus beginning the great utility systems of today.

The movie camera resulted from Edison's attempt to do for the eye what the phonograph had done for the ear. Using a strip of George Eastman's new celluloid film, he took a series of photographs, which he projected on a screen in rapid succession to give the illusion of motion. He tested his first motion picture in his laboratory in 1889 and applied for a patent in 1891.

History in the making: *December 17, 1903, on the sands near Kitty Hawk, North Carolina.* The Wright Flyer *lifts off, and Wilbur Wright, who raced along holding on to a wingtip, watches anxiously as Orville makes man's first sustained, controlled powered flight in a heavier-than-air machine. The flight lasted 12 seconds and covered nearly 200 feet. The weather was unsuitable for flying, but the brothers were determined to make their attempt and be back home in Ohio for Christmas. They made three more flights that day, the longest covering 852 feet.*

with an electric motor to keep the rotor going, used electrical sensors to signal any departure from the fixed axis, and made electrical devices to correct the detected deviation. Here, for the first time in one ingenious package, was everything needed for an automatic guidance system. The gyroscope—to name but a few of its uses—is the basis for ship stabilizers, superaccurate compasses, and automatic piloting systems for aircraft, ships, missiles, and rockets. Although less well known than many other American inventors, Sperry made outstanding contributions to the modern era.

The first real indication of the role that chemistry might play in American progress was the result of work by Leo H. Baekeland, a Belgian chemistry professor who came to America in 1889 to further his future. His first success was with a superior photoprinting paper which he named Velox; he began to manufacture it in 1893. The paper so impressed George Eastman that in 1899 he paid Baekeland $1 million for the exclusive right to manufacture it. Velox was a bargain for Eastman and an astounding windfall for Baekeland. Financially secure, inventive, brilliant, and still young, Baekeland set himself a Herculean task. He decided to create a polymer. To accomplish this, small molecules had to be combined in such a way as to make larger molecules with the same structure. The result would be a solid amorphous mass, neither stratified nor crystalline in character. The only polymer produced up to that time had been glass, which was first made by man 3,000 years before, probably by accident.

Baekeland started by working with phenol and formaldehyde, two chemicals he knew could react in many unpredictable ways under various circumstances. He first repeated all previously recorded experiments to get the failures out of the way. After more than 2 years of constant experimentation, he created a resin that hardened to a stable material resistant to heat, cold, dampness, steam, or chemicals, and was also an excellent insulator. He called it Bakelite; its success triggered the development of plastic materials for every conceivable use.

Another genius in the new field of resins and plastics was Dr. Wallace H. Carothers. In 1934, working in the laboratories of E. I. du Pont de Nemours & Company, he developed a long-chain polymer, which he called polymer 66. It had qualities no natural material could duplicate. Five years later, when Du Pont marketed it, they called it nylon.

The chemical ramifications involved in the development of nylon called for the backing of a huge organization, and Carothers had a number of talented associates. Complexity was beginning to bring an end to the day of individual chemist-entrepreneurs like Baekeland, who worked alone in his basement and could solve by himself

The Wright Brothers
Man Takes to the Air

Orville *(left) and Wilbur Wright with their sister Katherine. The brothers never married. Wilbur died in 1912. Orville survived till 1948, the esteemed elder statesman of aviation.*

From earliest times men had dreamed of flying. In Greek mythology Daedalus, an artist and craftsman, flew by attaching feather-and-wax wings to his back. The Renaissance artist Leonardo da Vinci actually designed an aircraft. In the 18th century men finally got aloft in gas-filled balloons. In the 19th century others tried to ride kites and primitive gliders, strapped mechanical wings to their bodies, and even attached strings to geese. But the problem was not only to become freely airborne but to travel through the air with full control of direction, speed, and altitude. Around the beginning of the 20th century two Americans—Samuel P. Langley, secretary of the Smithsonian Institution, and Hiram Maxim—seemed close to success, but their heavily powered, kitelike contraptions came to grief for lack of stability. At about the same time several Europeans claimed to have gotten flying machines off the ground, however briefly.

To Wilbur and Orville Wright, however, must go the credit not only for the first controlled flight of a heavier-than-air machine but for the first construction of a practical airplane. The two brothers began their working partnership in a bicycle repair shop in Dayton, Ohio. Fascinated from boyhood with the idea of flying, they devoured all literature on flying and built many model gliders, which they tested in a homemade wind tunnel. Gliders large enough to support a man, first developed in Germany by Otto Lilienthal, came from their shop in due course. Convinced that powered flight was possible, the Wright brothers designed new gasoline engines that were surprisingly light for the power they delivered and devised reliable ways of controlling a plane in flight. Aware of the importance of tail control and wing-warping (changing the wing's curvature by twisting it), they resolved the essential aerodynamic and structural problems for gliders and determined that only a machine that would fly without an engine could also fly under power. In 1902 they built the motorless glider *No. 3,* a crucial step toward development of a motor-driven aircraft. *No. 3* had a wingspan of 32 feet, gently cambered wings, a movable tail made up of vertical planes for turning, an elevator in front for making the craft climb or dive, and a cradle for the pilot, who was able to maintain lateral stability by pulling on ropes that warped the wings.

The brothers were then ready for powered flight. *The Wright Flyer* had a 12-horsepower engine; a chain transmission, which drove two propellers in opposite directions; skids like sled runners; flattened wings; controllable wing tips; and a wingspan of just over 40 feet. On a December day in 1903, the Wright plane made the flight that changed the world—an event that went unheralded, however, by the press and the public. Nine days before, *The New York Times* had said man would not fly for 1,000 years.

For the next few years the Wrights worked hard to improve their plane. Not until 1908 did they begin giving public exhibitions. European aviation designers were inspired by the demonstrations, and the U.S. Army bought a Wright machine in 1909.

Bell demonstrates his telephone *at Salem, Massachusetts, on March 15, 1877. He has Boston on the line. By the turn of the century more than 1.5 million telephones were in use across the country. Its impact on business and industry was explosive.*

Alexander Graham Bell
The Telephone's First Voice

It is hard to imagine that until a century ago the world had to get along without the telephone. Its inventor, Alexander Graham Bell, was born in Scotland in 1847 and came to the United States at the age of 24. In 1873 he became professor of vocal physiology at Boston University. There he fell in love with Mabel Hubbard, a deaf student, whom he later married. Mabel's father, learning that Bell was trying to send several messages simultaneously over a single telegraph wire, offered financial backing.

Urged to concentrate on the telegraph, the inventor was nagged by the thought of transmitting the human voice. He had developed a "harmonic telegraph"—a wire linking two harplike assemblies of electrically activated reeds, with each reed tuned to a counterpart at the other end of the line. Bell had hooked the harps to magnetic diaphragms modeled on the human eardrum. One day his assistant, Thomas A. Watson, was tinkering with a stuck reed. Bell heard its twang over the connecting wire and drew conclusions that led to further tests. On March 10, 1876, he called over his transmitter: "Mr. Watson, come here. I want you." The assistant raced from the laboratory to Bell's bedroom, shouting that he had heard every word clearly. The invention was just in time to cause a sensation at the Philadelphia Centennial Exposition.

Bell became a wealthy man, but money had never been his goal. He plunged into other projects, building an early iron lung, devising hydrofoil speedboats, and inventing a number of airplane improvements, including the aileron.

Lee De Forest and the Amazing Audion Tube

As the son of a Congregationalist minister, young De Forest was expected to attend Yale, as did his father and grandfather, and become a clergyman. He was an imaginative youth fascinated by science and mechanics and as a teenager had already decided that he would become an inventor. After convincing his father that his true vocation was science, he did go to Yale and was awarded a doctorate in physics in 1899. The strong sense of individualism that set him on his professional course was a dominant characteristic all through his life. Many of the companies he started failed due, in some cases, to unscrupulous partners and, in others, to his lack of interest in the details of business. He was almost constantly embroiled in lawsuits, most of them related to the 300-odd patents in his name.

In 1904 De Forest was able to demonstrate the transmission of speech and music on the air. Six years later, from the stage of the Metropolitan Opera, his radio equipment sent forth the golden voice of Enrico Caruso to the few enraptured set owners in the New York area. In 1907 De Forest patented the audion, which established the principle of the vacuum tube. He is shown here with his invention, the flasklike object in the upper right-hand corner of the panel. While the tube was not perfected until efficient vacuum pumps were first made some years later, De Forest's breakthrough set the stage for development of radio, radar, television, computers, and all the other electronic marvels that are now so much a part of our daily lives. His later years were more peaceful, and he died in 1961 at the age of 88, well aware of his contributions to science.

such problems as he faced in those early days. The amazing improvements in photographic film and photographic processes, for example, are the fruits of millions of dollars spent on research and teams of researchers.

There seems to be no limit to the variety of ways in which inventions come to pass. Sometimes a neglected facet of one invention will become the focus of another, as was the case of the Edison effect and the vacuum tube. When Edison was working on improvements for his light bulb in 1883, carbon was one of the materials he tried for a filament. He observed that minute carbon particles, transmitted from the filament across the partial vacuum in the tube, adhered to a metal plate in the tube.

In 1904 Sir John Fleming, an English electrical engineer, determined that the Edison effect was caused by negatively charged electrons (discovered by physicist J. J. Thomson) "boiling off" the hot filament and flowing to the positively charged plate. He further discovered that if the charge on the plate was changed to negative, the electrons would not flow. He therefore developed a two-element valve to control the flow of electric current. Two years later the American inventor Lee De Forest inserted a third element, called a grid, into the Fleming valve, making it a triode (a tube with three electrodes), which could not only control an electric current but amplify it. In 1910 De Forest used his triode to strengthen radio signals, making commercial radio broadcasting possible. (Radio, of course, is also the result of the work of Italian inventor Guglielmo Marconi, who in 1895 found a way to send signals over the wireless telegraph, or radio, and of Reginald A. Fessenden, who made another great advance in 1900 when he discovered how to transmit the sound of a human voice by radio rather than just the dots and dashes of Morse code.) The triode was not only an indispensable element in the development of radio, but also in television, and the computer. The foundation of the electronics industry rests on the discoveries of a relatively few men of exceptional intelligence and perseverance. The phenomenon of electronics has proved to be remarkably adaptable. Such conveniences as pocket calculators, automatic cameras, electronic ovens, and push-button telephones are derived from thousands of other inventors and those with the faith to finance them.

Dr. Peter C. Goldmark *displays the final result of his research in this 1948 photograph. The long-playing records in front of him are equal to the two large stacks of 78s on either side.*

Photography for Everyone
George Eastman and Edwin H. Land Had the Answers

When George Eastman, a bank clerk in Rochester, New York, bought his first photographic equipment, it included a heavy camera and tripod, a dark tent for processing, and the necessary chemicals to sensitize, develop, and fix the glass plates before they dried. Such was wet-plate photography in 1877. Young Eastman was impatient with the inconvenience of the system. When he learned of a dry-plate process discovered in England, he began to experiment at night in his mother's kitchen, and he invented a machine for the manufacture of uniform gelatin-based dry plates in quantity. In 1879 he went to England and patented his machine. He got an American patent the following year and started the Eastman Dry Plate Company. Professional photographers were not as quick to switch to dry plates as Eastman had anticipated, and so he invented a camera (top, right) to create a market for his film. This breakthrough made picture taking a family institution. Improvements soon followed: roll film on a flexible transparent base; folding pocket cameras; and in 1900 the $1 box Brownie and a 6-exposure roll of film for 15 cents. With the invention of commercially successful color film in 1935 by two musicians, Leopold Mannes and Leopold Godowsky, Kodachrome came on the market, and in 1942 Kodacolor made inexpensive color prints possible.

The next significant advance in photography was a seeming miracle created by Edwin H. Land in 1947. Land's invention was a camera and film that would produce a finished print on the spot in a minute after exposure. Land started his career making polarizing filters for cameras and lenses for sunglasses. His Polaroid Corporation produced a self-developing color film in 1963 and, in 1973, the amazing automatic camera shown at right was put on the market. In terms of speed and convenience, one could hardly ask for more.

The first *Eastman camera was this Number One Kodak marketed in 1888. George Eastman coined the name Kodak for its easy spelling and pronunciation in any language and thought up the slogan "You press the button, we do the rest." The camera cost $25 and came loaded with film for 100 pictures. After exposure, both camera and film were sent to Rochester. The film was developed, the round prints were made, and the camera was reloaded and returned for $10. Eastman is shown here with his Kodak photographing the photographer who snapped his picture on shipboard.*

A new instant-picture system *was introduced by Polaroid in 1973. It features the self-printing techniques originally conceived by Edwin Land, but the SX-70 is more completely automatic than earlier systems. The photographer composes, focuses, and pushes the shutter button; less than 2 seconds later a properly exposed hard-dry "film unit" is ejected from the front of the camera. The picture continues to develop until it reaches full-color clarity.*

A New Era in Sound

Improved plastics, vacuum tubes, transistors, and new concepts of acoustics have come together in recent years to create a new era in sound. Few if any households in America are untouched by the phenomenon of high fidelity. Edison gets credit for starting it in 1877 with the phonograph, but the quantum jump in practicality was made in 1948 when Dr. Peter C. Goldmark, of the Columbia Broadcasting System, and others working with him developed the long-playing record. While phonographs and records had long been popular, the old 10-inch, 78-rpm shellac recordings left much to be desired. They played for about 3 minutes, the tonal range was limited, and surface scratch was audible. The improvements of Dr. Goldmark's group were based on the new technology in resins and plastics. Vinyl, in particular, made it possible to reduce greatly the width of the grooves, to eliminate almost all surface noise, and to slow the speed down to 33⅓ rpm. One side of a 12-inch record could then play for about 20 minutes, long enough to accommodate a full movement from a symphony. Recording on flexible tape was the next step taken in improving sound reproduction, and every year sees more improvements in the quality and convenience of tape recordings and recorders, most notably in the compact tape cassette and cartridge systems.

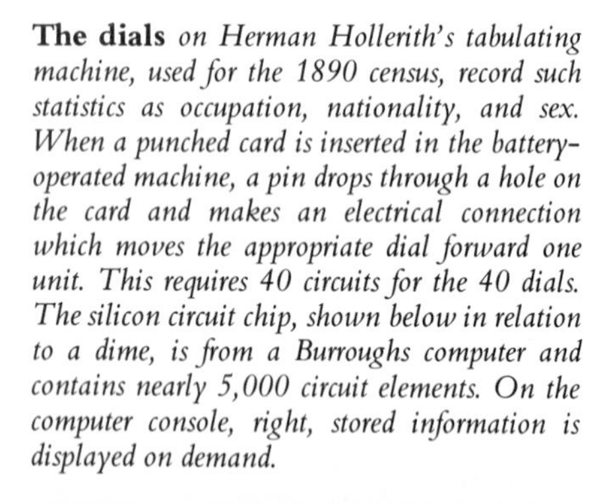

Electronic Computers

Machines That Are Changing the World

Despite the quaint appearance of the 1880's tabulating machine (left), it is a direct ancestor of today's sophisticated digital computers. Mechanical calculators go all the way back to 1642, when the French mathematician Blaise Pascal invented an adding machine that used wheels and other mechanical parts. But the almost incredible speed that has made the computer so indispensable to the modern world was achieved only after the development in the 20th century of such essential components as the transistor, magnetic tape, the logic circuit, and the memory core.

In essence, a computer stores information and retrieves or compares it when called on. It must be programed in meticulous detail as to the sequence of the steps it is to follow. The machine itself is remarkably efficient, but programers are human and prone to err—so much so that the acronym GIGO (Garbage In, Garbage Out) is a staple in computer jargon.

The first purely electronic computer, called ENIAC (Electronic Numerical Integrator and Computer), was built for the U.S. Army in 1946 by John W. Mauchly and J. Presper Eckert at the University of Pennsylvania. The transistor was still unknown, and the machine required 18,000 vacuum tubes. It filled a large room, and it could not store great amounts of information. Today computers no larger than a suitcase can do essentially the same job.

There are two basic kinds of computers. Digital computers deal with numerical relationships and perform such functions as predicting the cost of a spaceship. Analog computers work with comparisons of variable elements (analogies) and provide precise calculations, which could, for example, keep the ship on its projected course.

The dials *on Herman Hollerith's tabulating machine, used for the 1890 census, record such statistics as occupation, nationality, and sex. When a punched card is inserted in the battery-operated machine, a pin drops through a hole on the card and makes an electrical connection which moves the appropriate dial forward one unit. This requires 40 circuits for the 40 dials. The silicon circuit chip, shown below in relation to a dime, is from a Burroughs computer and contains nearly 5,000 circuit elements. On the computer console, right, stored information is displayed on demand.*

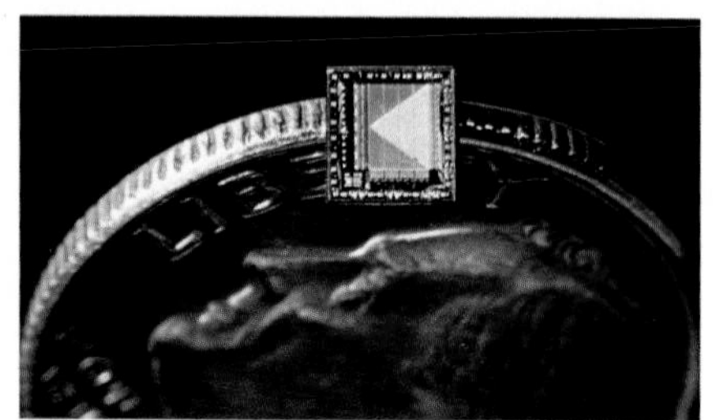

The Computer Comes of Age

The computer revolution of the past quarter-century has been so vast and all-pervading as to defy comprehension. This ubiquitous record-keeping calculator is strategically involved with the details of our lives—with the food we eat, the products we use, the entertainments we attend, and the money we have or do not have. There is no escaping its effect.

One of the most obvious precursors of today's computer was a punch-card tabulating machine invented by Herman Hollerith and used in the 1890 U.S. census. Hollerith's machine worked, was continually improved on, and was later applied to other problems of data storage and retrieval. With the development of electricity and electronics and, most particularly, the transistor, the present-day computer has evolved, based on principles established by Hollerith.

The transistor itself is a near-miraculous means of miniaturizing complicated electrical circuits. Its electronic complexities defy simple explanation. Suffice it to say that, without generating any heat, a minute piece of solid semiconducting material can switch, modulate, and amplify electronic impulses just as the vacuum tube does. Sponsored by Bell Telephone Laboratories, the transistor was called a corporate invention but it was created by the genius of individuals. The leaders of the team that developed it were John Bardeen, Walter H. Brattain, and William B. Shockley. The three inventors were awarded the Nobel Prize in physics in 1956 for their accomplishment. The tiny chip of germanium containing two wires, which was the first solid state transistor, fulfilled Bell's specifications beyond its developers' fondest dreams, and today the computer industry is based on this miniature component. It has since been further miniaturized and now nearly 5,000 computer circuit elements can be integrated on a single silicon chip $\frac{1}{10}$-inch square.

Television and the Future

The modern television set is the result of thousands of prior patents and theories, but the big breakthrough that made it possible can be credited to two men, Vladimir K. Zworykin and Philo T. Farnsworth.

Zworykin, born in Murom, Russia, in 1889, worked in the laboratory of Boris Rosing. Rosing was the first to design a television system using the cathode ray tube, which has since proved a key component of the electronic industry. When Zworykin immigrated to America in 1919, he was already deeply involved in the theory of television, and during the next 20 years became a leader in the field. His most important development was the iconoscope, basic to the TV camera.

Farnsworth, an Idaho farm boy, revealed an amazing grasp of science at an early age. In 1922, when he was 15, he conceived a television system more advanced than that of Rosing and Zworykin. By the early 1930's he had greatly increased the clarity of the television image and was ready for commercial production. Commercial telecasting began in 1941 but was interrupted by the war. Farnsworth went on to create other applications for his theories of electronics.

Although these two gifted scientists worked separately for competing companies, their theories were so interrelated that cross-licensing of patents was required before the best possible commercial television system could be developed.

These inventions had an unpredictable life of their own once their basic structure was established. When Herman Hollerith first started working with punched cards and Philo Farnsworth was developing his "image dissector," they could not possibly have foreseen the later improvements and the cultural and political impact that the computer and television would have on the world. As for today, who knows where the experiments with the laser and maser will lead? The genie is out of the bottle, still growing, and cannot be put back in.

We have made incredible progress in 200 years. We have proved that we can solve almost any mechanical or technical problem. Today the challenge is to discover better ways to live in harmony with the wonders we have wrought and those that are sure to come.

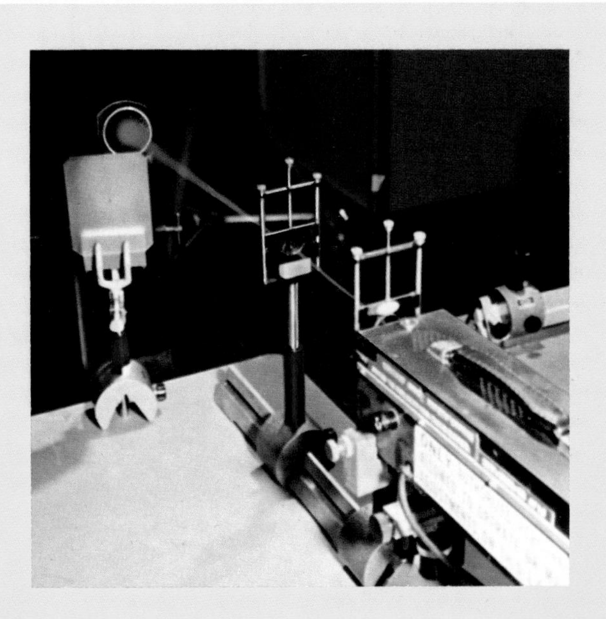

The Marvelous Masers and Lasers

Charles H. Townes had built up a wartime background with the Bell Telephone Laboratories in radar, which functions in the microwave portion of the electromagnetic spectrum. In 1948 Townes went to Columbia University to teach physics and to pursue his interest in microwaves. Experimenting with molecular vibrations, he found that ammonia molecules could create a stable wavelength. Normal ammonia molecules combined with others that had been "excited" by heat or electricity set up a chain reaction, producing a single intense form of radiation. The acronym for the process is maser (microwave amplification by stimulated emission of radiation). Other gases and crystals were used later, but all masers emit microwaves so stable that they could keep a clock accurate to a tenth of a second for 10,000 years. A maser-powered amplifier is so sensitive that it can pick up radar reflections from the planet Venus, 26 million miles from earth at its nearest.

An optical maser—one that operates in the visible spectrum—is called a laser (light amplification by stimulated emission of radiation). Shown above is a helium-neon laser testing a mylar membrane for optical distortion. When light is transmitted through a rod of ruby, or certain other materials, the waves are not diffused but maintain a narrow beam, and their intensity is vastly increased. Moreover, the tremendous energy compressed into a coherent beam projects the straightest line known to man and is used in surveying for bridges and tunnels and other situations where perfect alignment is critical. Laser beams can be used for surgery in hard-to-reach areas, such as the retina of the eye, and a minute beam can bore through a diamond so accurately as to make it into a die that can be used for drawing fine wire. The laser also is the basis for the holograph, which, with light alone, projects three-dimensional images of startling realism. The ultimate uses of this amazing force are yet to be discovered.

Setting New Standards *The American Penchant for Com*

In the past 100 years we Americans have made ourselves the most comfortably housed people on Earth. Much of what we take for granted here would be unimaginable luxury in other parts of the world. Our wealth of natural resources has had a great deal to do with the development of the comforts we enjoy, but the singular psychology of our people has had even more.

From the beginning settlers came to this land seeking a better way of life. For most the obstacles to this goal were relatively few. Land was available for the taking or for a small fee; tax assessments were few; trades and professions were open to all; free speech and free assembly prevailed. The Nation was founded on the principle that all men are created equal. Even in colonial New England, and, later, on the Western frontier, class lines were by no means as rigid as in Europe. Many a self-made man took pride in his humble origins. This was the land of opportunity, and, with a few glaring exceptions, most Americans had a good chance to succeed in their work and to make their fortunes.

In terms of industrial progress this new country was not tied to the concept that the old way was the best way. Our national character has always been one of enterprise. By the mid-1800's the power of steam had been harnessed, and we had the coal to use for fuel. After this it did not take long for us to demonstrate our ability as

The Kitchen. *The old-fashioned kitchen (right), with its hungry wood- or coal-burning stove, dingy sink, and varnished icebox, spelled drudgery for the housewife. In contrast is its modern successor (above), with an efficient gas or electric cooking unit, a dishwasher, electric refrigerator (often with icemaking machine), touch-latch cabinets, lighted work surfaces, and easy-to-clean floor.*

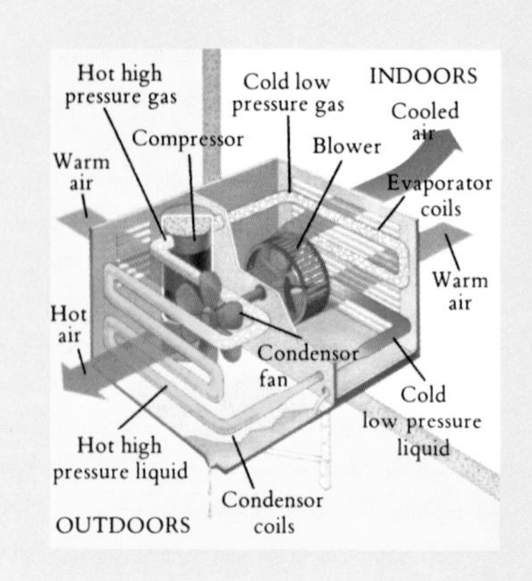

Conditioning the Air

In the summer of 1902 a publisher in Brooklyn was having trouble with his color printing because the paper on the press changed size with the weather. Willis Haviland Carrier, a young engineer assigned to solve the problem, found that air retained less moisture at lower temperatures. He designed a machine to blow air over chilled pipes, thus stabilizing the amount of moisture that was retained in the air. It was this concept that later made home air conditioning, as shown here, practical.

Heating. *Today's automatic gas, oil, or elect heating units are a far cry from this coal-eati giant. They supply heat or hot water, and summer may double as air conditioners.*

manufacturers and industrialists. The assembly line brought forth a wide range of commodities that, if available at all, had been reserved for the wealthy. Mass production, along with a newfound aptitude for advertising, created the vast market necessary to bring prices down.

In 1920 the Crane Co. spent more than $1 million—an unheard of sum for advertising in those days—to promote the idea of the modern bathroom. This was the beginning of the era of nationwide advertising campaigns that helped make household words of dozens of timesaving and worksaving conveniences.

The movies, which had an important influence on taste and style in the 1930's, were beginning to show elegant and luxurious domestic interiors. But the greatest impetus toward more comfort and convenience for the average householder was another unique American concept: the mail-order catalog. The two largest mail-order houses—Montgomery Ward & Co. (1872) and Sears, Roebuck and Co. (1893)—covered the country and brought to virtually every household the opportunity to order the latest fixtures and appliances for home delivery.

Products that often began as expensive luxuries and symbols of status soon seemed to be a necessity for every family. This has been an integral part of the American dream: What we want we invent or develop, and then we find new and better ways to bring it into our homes.

The Bathroom. *This has been rewarding territory for the imaginative designer. The sunken bath, its faucets streamlined, its contours molded to fit the reclining body, is an inviting sanctuary to the luxury minded. Soft carpeting for the unshod foot, frosted glass paneling, and potted plants can all help to transform the old, strictly functional washroom like the one at left into a glamorously appointed adjunct to comfortable living (above), more elaborate than most, but not unattainable.*

The Laundry Room. *Nowadays it is likely to be much smaller than its oldtime counterpart (left), and much easier on the muscles. The early washing machine, like the wringer, was hand-cranked; today, washer and dryer are electrified and automatic. The laundry is often placed near the back entrance, in an area that may also serve as a "mud room," a general utility space, sewing room, workshop, and playroom. Compact modern appliances leave ample space for the handy storage of linen or cleaning equipment; their clean-cut design harmonizes with carpeting and other decoration. Like the kitchen and the bathroom, the laundry has become an attractive feature of the well-planned house, its functional efficiency matched by its esthetic appeal.*

CHAPTER FIFTEEN

Growth of a National Economy

American economic history is a rough-and-tumble tal expansion and contraction, of boom and bust, of conser tism and innovation. Yet, from the beginning, despite sc backward steps, the United States has provided for m of its citizens a standard of living superior to that of th contemporaries of other nationalities, and well into 20th century wage earners in America continued to be highest-paid workers in the world.

The earliest settlers held the deep conviction that e nomic progress was both possible and desirable. As Ben min Franklin's Poor Richard put it, thrift and hard w assured the good and prosperous life.

North America's first permanent settlers ventured into a land with no cities, no roads, no communications systems, and no money. To tame a rich but formidable wilderness they had only their guns, a few domestic animals, and Old World agricultural techniques, which had to be modified or cast aside if the colonists were to survive on the new continent.

But the immigrants also brought with them a determination to enjoy fuller lives than those they had left behind. It was that ambition that fueled America's remarkable economic growth—a growth that began when the newcomers found they could trade their surpluses for the necessities and luxuries available in Britain.

Virtually all the early colonists sought a livelihood from the land. As late as the Revolution some 8 of every 10 workers were involved in agriculture. Gradually, as the settlers learned through trial and error and from the Indians how to raise such crops as maize, sweet potatoes, and tobacco, each region evolved its own occupational specialties. New England, with its rocky soil and harsh winters, turned to the sea—to fishing, shipbuilding, and overseas trade. The middle Colonies of New York, New Jersey, and Pennsylvania concentrated on grains and farm produce. In the warm and fertile South, where large-scale farming was both feasible and profitable, thriving plantations cultivated rice and tobacco, the "noxious weed" that for 150 years was the New World's most important agricultural export.

Throughout the Colonies labor was in short supply. The gap was filled by bondsmen—indentured whites and enslaved blacks. In the 18th century thousands purchased their passage across the Atlantic by contracting to work for 3 to 5 years as servants. Other thousands were given a choice between serving out their terms as convicts in British prisons or being shipped to America and indentured to masters for 7 years or more. Before the Revolution an estimated 75 percent of the immigrants were indentured servants of British stock. The tobacco and cotton planters looked to the African slave traders to man their fields, and by 1790 about 33 percent of the South's population and almost 18 percent of all persons in the newly independent Colonies were slaves.

Money and capital were as scarce as skilled labor in pre-Revolutionary America. Coins were rare, as the British forbade minting in the Colonies, and any foreign currency was quickly paid out for imports from overseas. Transportation was painfully slow in the dense, trackless forests of the East. A stagecoach journey from Boston to New York in the late 18th century took at least 3 days, and 2 weeks passed before news of the Battle of Lexington and Concord reached Charleston by swift messenger. Overland trade was limited, and so too was manufacturing, except for shipbuilding, some iron products, and clothing and utensils made at home. As late as the early 1800's a Southern backwoods farmer could live on $10 a year—the same amount, incidentally, that it took a plantation owner to maintain a slave for a like period.

Most purchases—whether of a bag of salt for a Massachusetts housewife, an ax for a frontier pioneer, or a Chippendale chair for a Maryland aristocrat—were obtained on credit. This was usually supplied by country storekeepers, by merchants established in Boston, New York City, or one of the other ports, or by commission agents, or factors, who extended credit to Southern planters until their crops were sold in England.

Some of the colonial gentry amassed sizable fortunes, however. An uncle of John Hancock, Thomas Hancock of Boston, who was involved in exporting and shipping (including a number of smuggling ventures), left an estate of more than £70,000 in 1764. The wealth of such men helped to build the Eastern cities and furnished the capital needed to start the Nation's first industries.

In the colonial era America was a collection of isolated extensions of Great Britain, supplying agricultural products and raw material to the mother country, and compelled to look to it for many finished goods. After independence was won, internal markets were widened by a network of transportation and communication facilities that gradually brought the country together. Factories and mills were established. The South, with its plantation system, grew tobacco and fed cotton into the looms of Britain and New England. The West became the Nation's breadbasket, while the North focused on commerce and industry and soon became a world leader in productive technology.

By the late 19th century a relatively few large firms had come to dominate American business. Thus far, free enterprise had been American gospel, but an increasingly urbanized, industrialized economy prompted Government attempts to regulate its hitherto unrestrained practices. Simultaneously, labor unions gained strength and successfully demanded a bigger share of the Nation's business profits for their workers. After the Great Depression most Americans took for granted—indeed, insisted on—active Government interest in the national economy, implemented by comprehensive policies designed to promote steady growth and to forestall massive unemployment.

The Old Tontine Coffee House *on the corner of Wall and Water Streets in New York was painted by Francis Guy, an English tailor and dyer who became an artist in his chosen land and painted city scenes with photographic fidelity. This building, put up in the early 1790's, was a central meeting place for brokers and merchants, and all ships were registered here upon arrival in the harbor. The name stems from the Tontine plan, a precursor of later life insurance plans, which was an agreement among members to pay premiums and to buy and hold real estate in common, the proceeds from which would be divided among surviving members after a certain time, usually 20 years. Such plans were often administered inefficiently and sometimes dishonestly. They were declared illegal in most States in the early 1900's.*

These same merchant capitalists, in alliance with the Southern landowners, provided much of the leadership of the Revolution. Britain had laws designed to restrict trade with the Colonies and to maintain North America as a source of cheap raw materials and as a ready market for the mother country's finished goods. The laws were not enforced until after 1762, but when they were and new taxes were levied, the revolutionary spark was struck. Indeed, some scholars argue that the economic clash between the colonists and the Crown not only precipitated the rebellion but permanently implanted in the American consciousness a distrust of all government intervention in matters that the public would prefer to regard as their private domain.

"In the growth of the American economy, the Revolution forms a watershed," historian Stuart Bruchey has written. Restrictions on trade and production were removed, and the last vestiges of feudalism—primogeniture (all inheritance to the eldest son) and the paying of feudal rents—were swept away in the confiscation of the great Tory estates. The severing of ties with Britain led in the 1780's to the establishment of the first banks to supply credit for the Nation's trade.

Most important, the new Constitution, by fashioning a larger sovereignty out of 13 separate jurisdictions and eliminating State barriers to the free flow of goods, established the basis for an American common market not unlike the one now operating in Europe. Congress assumed the sole power to regulate interstate commerce, ending the hodgepodge of State tariffs and fees on trade. In one of its first measures, Congress passed a tariff on imports to bring revenue into the Federal coffers. This act also protected infant American industries by levying duties on foreign products and encouraged American shipping by cutting duties on goods carried in U.S. ships. With its new right to tax and raise money, the Federal Treasury, under the brilliant Alexander Hamilton, soon established its credit abroad and began to attract the foreign capital required to finance the country's imports, internal improvements, and industry. By one estimate, $500 million from abroad, mainly from England, was invested in the United States between 1790 and 1861.

Hamilton's Vision

Alexander Hamilton was America's first Secretary of the Treasury—and, as such, the things in which he believed helped shape the evolving financial system of his country. Unlike Jefferson, he felt strongly that America should have a national bank to handle the Government's financing; similarly, he disagreed with Jefferson's emphasis on agrarian preeminence, stressing instead, as he did in his 1791 "Report on Manufactures," the benefits that would accrue from encouragement of a strong commercial sector in the economy. In this report Hamilton envisioned an industrial North, which would obtain raw materials from the agricultural South and sell it finished products. Hamilton believed in a vigorous government that would use its power to stimulate the privately owned enterprises of the economy.

But it was in purely financial matters that Hamilton's vision proved brilliant. In 1790 he explained to Congress his plan for funding the national debt, assuming the States' war debts, and creating a sound public credit. In recommending a national bank with money-creating powers, he appealed to commercial interests when he said, "it is a well-established fact that banks in good credit can circulate a far greater sum than the actual quantum of their capital in gold and silver."

By early 1791 America had Hamilton's dream: the chartering of the First Bank of the United States. Modeled on the Bank of England, it was authorized to issue currency as well as engage in commercial banking activities while serving as official depository of Federal funds. By threatening to demand that the paper money of State banks be redeemed in gold and silver, the Bank of the U.S. limited the amount of currency in circulation and stabilized the economy. Hamilton's vision—of a stable money supply—was on its way to realization.

Southern Farms and Northern Factories

In the South, after Eli Whitney's invention of the cotton gin in 1793 made the growing of short-staple cotton profitable, planters from Virginia to Georgia quickly made it the single most important export crop in the United States. Cotton was shipped to the textile mills of northern England, much of it by way of New York. This triangle earned more than half of all U.S. export returns between 1830 and 1860. Sixty cents of every cotton dollar went to the South, and 40 cents stayed with Northern bankers, shippers, and insurance brokers, many of whom began investing their profits in the Nation's industries.

The War of 1812, by closing the sealanes to American commerce, demonstrated the dangers of overdependence on foreign producers for essential items, and such Massachusetts families as the Lowells, the Lawrences, the Appletons, and the Jacksons turned to building a domestic textile industry. All along the Connecticut River Valley and elsewhere in New England new factories sprang up, run by cheap waterpower and the labor of women and girls from surrounding farms. By 1835 Lowell, Massachusetts, had become the textile capital of America, weaving 40 million yards of cotton cloth in a single year.

While most of the basic technology utilized in these factories came from England, American manufacturers, starved for skilled labor, were quick to introduce all the latest innovations and shortcuts. After a visit to the United States in the 1820's German political economist Georg Friedrich List wrote: "There is no clinging to old ways; the moment an American hears the word 'invention' he pricks up his ears." By the 1850's many Ameri-

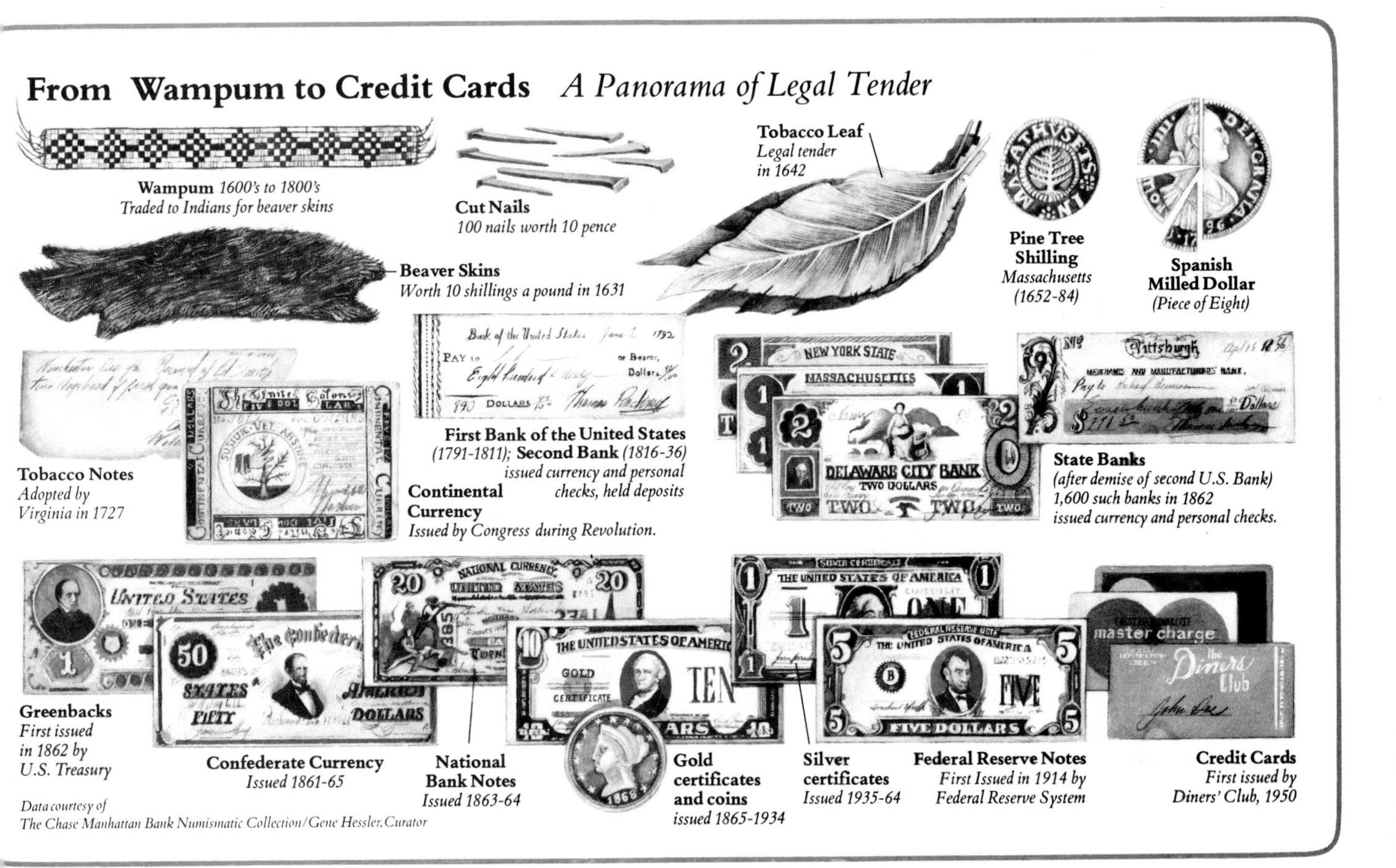

can factories, including those manufacturing furniture, small arms, and shoes, boasted the most mechanized and standardized production methods in the world. Mass production, marked by interchangeable parts and assembly-line operations, was pioneered by the Yankee ingenuity of such men as Whitney, Oliver Evans, and Samuel Colt, making for a phenomenal increase in output and lower unit costs. One New England company revolutionized the clock industry with the new techniques; by 1855 it was selling clocks for 75 cents. In Hartford, Connecticut, Colt six-shooters were streaming out of the world's largest arms plant to military men and gunslingers all over the globe.

In spite of its rapid growth, manufacturing remained a relatively small part of the U.S. economy before the Civil War. In 1860, when there were only 1.5 million workers in factories, there were nearly 6 million in agriculture. To the West the cheap, fertile land offered limitless opportunities for easier and quicker profits to farmers and speculators alike. But these promises could not be exploited until the vast food-producing regions of the Ohio Valley and beyond could be integrated with the cities and factories of the East, and the efforts to forge those ties produced a revolutionary series of innovations in transportation during the early 1800's.

Boats, Trains, and the Telegraph Link the Country
The essential task was to find a way across the Appalachian Mountains, which formed a solid barrier between the Eastern seaboard and the rest of the country. Roads and turnpikes were one solution, but land travel was so expensive that it cost about as much to send goods 100 miles overland in the United States as it did to ship them by sea to Europe. The first major breakthrough came with the steamboat, which in the 1820's linked the rich interior with the South and the East coast via the Mississippi River and the Gulf of Mexico. Even more important was the inland waterway that eventually connected the Midwest to New York through the Great Lakes, the Erie Canal, and the Hudson River.

After the Erie Canal was completed in 1825 a newspaper commentator wrote: "They have built the longest canal in the world, in the least time, with the least experience, for the least money, and to the greatest public benefit." Thanks to the canal, the cost of shipping a ton of goods from Buffalo to New York City fell from $100 to about $12, and the time was cut from 20 to 8 days. The canal not only opened up the Midwest for commercial farming but helped establish New York as the Nation's largest and most important business center.

Baltimore civic leaders, not to be outdone, sponsored the development of a new and unproved device: the steam locomotive. Beginning in 1830, the Baltimore and Ohio (B & O) Railroad began the first regular run: 13 miles between Baltimore and Ellicott's Mills. Iron horses with names like the B & O's *Tom Thumb* and the Philadelphia and Germantown Railway's *Old Ironsides* were soon routed all across the countryside. Within 10 years the Nation had more than 400 railroad companies and almost 3,000 miles of track—more than in all of Europe.

The West, supported by the South, sought Federal aid in improving transportation, but the Northeast balked. Henry Clay of Kentucky, in a House speech in 1824, proposed his American System, which linked the protective tariffs demanded by Northeast industries with the construction of roads and canals needed to facilitate the flow of commerce in the West and South. The Federal Government aided the West by building the National Road, which was started at Cumberland, Maryland, in 1811 and was completed to Columbus, Ohio, by 1833. It also dredged rivers and Great Lakes harbors and, beginning in the 1850's, indirectly supported the construction of railroads by giving them grants of public land.

Better communications provided another bond between the expanding frontier and the more settled parts of the country. By the late 1840's the telegraph was relaying Presidential speeches from Washington to St. Louis and market quotations from New York to Chicago.

Rapid advancements in technology had come to the farms, too, and was laying the groundwork for incredible growth in productivity. By 1860 well-run farms were already by one estimate using $500 worth of farm implements and machinery (harvesters and threshers), and the time required to produce a bushel of wheat had been cut in half since the beginning of the century.

The United States Becomes an Industrial Nation

The Civil War created feverish manufacturing activity to supply critical materials especially in the North. When the fighting ended, the stage was set for dramatic economic growth. Wartime taxes on production were gone, and the few taxes that remained leaned heavily on real property, not on business. The population flow from farm to city increased, and the labor force it provided was buttressed by millions of newly arrived immigrants willing to work for low wages in the mills of the North and on the railroad crews of the Midwest and West. Government was nothing if not accommodating: It established high protective tariffs, provided loans and land grants to build a transcontinental railroad, and, in addition, assumed a studied posture of nonintervention in private enterprise. The social Darwinism of British philosopher Herbert Spencer and American economist William Graham Sumner prevailed. The theory was that business, left to its own devices, would cull out the weak and nurture the strong. Competition and survival of the fittest became the watchwords of the day. But as business expanded and became nationwide, the competition grew rougher. In the 1880's five railroads operating between New York and Chicago were vying for traffic, and two more were under construction. As a result of the battle, the fare between the two cities plummeted to $1. The petroleum industry suffered from similarly savage competition, and in the 1870's many oil companies failed.

Trusts: Big Business Gets Bigger

To end this suicidal warfare and protect their profits, businessmen began forming pools—secret agreements to fix prices and share markets. John D. Rockefeller's Standard Oil Company took the lead. When exposure brought outraged howls from small businessmen and consumers, Rockefeller and his associates in 1879 devised the trust, a new and (from their vantage point) better way to control the oil industry. Under this plan the stockholders of 40 oil companies turned their shares over to nine trustees. The investors collected dividends while the trustees (Rockefeller and his associates) arranged to fix prices, crush competition, and limit production.

Soon trusts were being formed in a large number of industries, including meatpacking, rubber, lead, iron and steel, sugar, and whisky. Again there were widespread public protests, as well as civil lawsuits against the trusts, and Congress in 1890 passed the Sherman Anti-Trust Act to outlaw "every contract, combination in the form of trust or otherwise, or conspiracy in restraint of trade among the several states. . . ."

Before the Sherman Act was passed, however, big business had already found a way to get around it. New Jersey was persuaded in 1888 to pass a law permitting one corporation to own the stock of another; thus holding companies were born. A financier wishing to bring 20 sugar companies under his control would get the owners of those companies to exchange their shares of stock for shares of his newly formed holding company. Then he would induce the public to buy shares in the holding company and use that money to give him effective control of the 20 sugar companies. As this new dodge began to arouse public opposition, the popular humorist Finley Peter Dunne had his favorite character, Mr. Dooley, offer this definition of a holding company: "It's when you hand th' swag to someone else while th' police search yu."

Whether such a holding company would be ruled a conspiracy in restraint of trade under the Sherman Anti-Trust Act was uncertain, and the Government did not seem eager to settle the question by taking any of the companies to court. Furthermore, a series of U.S. Supreme Court decisions effectively blocking State and Federal efforts to regulate railroads convinced holding company barons that they had friends on the High Court.

Laws fixing railroad rates and banning unfair practices had been passed in the 1870's by several Midwestern States at the urging of the Grange, a powerful farm organization begun in 1867. At that time, freight charges often took the value of one bushel of wheat to pay the freight on another bushel. These rate laws were upheld by the Supreme Court in 1877, but 9 years later the Court gave itself the power to decide whether rates were being fixed so that the railroad could not make a reasonable profit. This action was followed within months by a de-

Giants of Finance and Industry

Farsighted Men With the Backing To Make Visions Come True

John Pierpont Morgan (1837–1913) was born in Hartford, Connecticut, the son of a prominent international banker. He began his career in his father's banking house and after the Civil War built a reputation as a reorganizer of railroads. By the end of the 19th century he controlled a vast transportation network. In 1895 Morgan had founded J. P. Morgan & Co. and that same year raked in a tidy profit by lending the hard-pressed U.S. Government $60 million in gold. In 1901 Morgan organized the first billion-dollar corporation—U.S. Steel—and when he died, he was the most powerful financial figure in America.

Andrew Carnegie (1835–1919), by contrast, was born in Scotland, son of a poor weaver. He came to America in 1848 and began work as a bobbin boy in a Pittsburgh cotton factory for $1.20 per week. But young Andrew soon was on the move, becoming a messenger, a telegrapher, and then secretary to Thomas Scott, then a division superintendent of the Pennsylvania Railroad. While rising to the post of superintendent of the line, he became wealthy investing in oil, ironmaking, and bridgebuilding. Then, in 1873, he concentrated his attentions on steel. The Carnegie Steel Company became America's biggest steel concern—and Andrew Carnegie, a ferocious competitor who could ruin a business rival or bust a union, wound up giving away most of his huge fortune for "the good of my fellow men."

John D. Rockefeller (1839–1937) also gave huge sums to charity before he died. His fortune was made in oil—the Standard Oil Co. that was first formed in 1870 to consolidate his investments. By the early 1880's his Standard Oil Trust controlled virtually all of the Nation's oil refineries. When the trust was ordered dissolved, Rockefeller formed Standard Oil of New Jersey, his huge holding company that survived 12 years until the Supreme Court broke it up in 1911. Rockefeller had retired earlier, his personal fortune of $1 billion making him the Nation's wealthiest man.

Edward H. Harriman (1848–1909), like Morgan, was born to wealth, but his career quickly eclipsed his father's. After a successful career on Wall Street, Harriman began to rebuild bankrupt railroads in 1881, including the troubled Illinois Central. The centerpiece of his railroading empire was to be the Union Pacific, where his word was law. But he also acquired controlling shares of other lines, including the huge Southern Pacific. When he died, Harriman was regarded as perhaps the most brilliant railroad strategist and administrator of his time.

James J. Hill (1838–1916) was also a railroader and matched Harriman in financial acumen and administrative ability. Born in Canada, Hill quickly headed for the United States and in the late 1870's became a partner in the St. Paul & Pacific Railroad. He later acquired this and other lines, and in 1890 consolidated his holdings in the Great Northern Railway. In the next decade he was involved in an epic battle for control of the Northern Pacific, a vital railroad running into Chicago: It was Hill and Morgan against Harriman and financier Jacob Schiff. Their clash led to the stock market panic of 1901. The rivals made peace by forming the Northern Securities Company, a holding company later dissolved under the Sherman Anti-Trust Act.

Who Were the Robber Barons?

As early as the mid-19th century, and even before, there developed in America a breed of businessmen who later became known as robber barons. Through financial doubledealing and stock manipulation these men bilked naive investors and plundered companies to enrich themselves. One such man was Jay Gould, who brought the cunning of a pickpocket and the audacity of a burglar to the world of high finance. In 1868 Gould and the high-living and equally corrupt James Fisk wrested control of the Erie Railroad from "Commodore" Cornelius Vanderbilt by tricking him into buying fake Erie stock. The next year the efforts of Gould and Fisk to corner the Nation's gold market resulted in the Black Friday financial panic that ruined other speculators but enriched Gould and his partner. Before he died in 1892, Gould, who admitted to being "the most hated man in America," was reputed to own 1 out of every 10 miles of railroad track in the country.

Modern scholars have concluded that the term "robber baron" should not be applied, as it has been, to all the biggest businessmen. While men like Rockefeller, Carnegie, and Morgan were fiercely competitive, their management of the Nation's resources lowered the cost of oil, steel, and other goods to America's consumers and created the modern corporation.

cision in a case involving the State of Illinois and the Wabash, St. Louis, and Pacific Railway Company, which forbade a State to regulate a railroad engaging in interstate commerce. Since most big railroads operated between States, they were thus placed beyond State reach.

Angry farmers called for legislative redress, and 4 months after the decision in the Wabash case Congress passed the Interstate Commerce Act of 1887. This act, a landmark in Federal regulation of private business, established the Interstate Commerce Commission (ICC) to control railroad rates and ban practices harmful to the public. But in the next few years the railroads appealed 16 cases involving the ICC and won 15 of them.

MAKING DEMOCRACY WORK

The Sherman Anti-Trust Act

Agitation by farm and labor groups for the curbing of industrial monopolies led to the passage by Congress of the Sherman Anti-Trust Act in 1890. On the face of it, the act flatly prohibited trusts or conspiracies in restraint of trade or commerce. But the language of the act was vague, and its force was blunted when the Supreme Court ruled against the Government in the Sugar Trust Case of 1895. In fact, it was labor, and not the trusts, that first felt the weight of the Sherman Act.

A year before the Sugar Trust decision, Eugene V. Debs' American Railway Union supported the striking workers of the Pullman Company by refusing to work on any train carrying a Pullman car. The Government obtained a court injunction against the union on the ground that its refusal to work was a conspiracy in restraint of trade and therefore a violation of the Sherman Act. When Debs and other union officials defied the injunction, they were convicted of contempt and jailed.

From 1894 on, employers regularly obtained court injunctions to stunt the growth of labor unions and break strikes. At the same time the Government's efforts to inhibit the growth of trusts were frequently stymied by Supreme Court decisions. Finally, in 1914, Congress passed the Clayton Act to specify more stringently the abuses that the Sherman Act had sought to outlaw. It prohibited exclusive sales contracts and local price discrimination among buyers to freeze out competition, and it banned intercorporate stock holdings and interlocking directorates, which could spawn monopolies. At the same time the Clayton Act was also expected to get the Sherman Act off labor's back by declaring that unions were not to be considered "illegal combinations in restraint of trade under the anti-trust laws," because "the labor of a human being is not a commodity or article of commerce."

Unfortunately, both the Government and labor found that, although Congress can pass a law, it is the Supreme Court that decides just what it means. And the Court soon weakened the Clayton Act's antitrust and labor-protection clauses by hostile decisions.

Turn-of-the-Century Depression

Businessmen appeared to be riding high in January 1893, but financial leaders were uneasy. Chronically low farm prices and crop failures plus strikes by steelworkers, miners, and railroadmen had caused a decline in production and sales. A severe depression in Europe and Australia had cut American exports. At the same time European bankers were selling the bonds of U.S. industries and refused to lend the companies more money. This action sent a shock wave through the country, and prices tumbled as people hoarded their cash and worried about the future. Railroads that had overextended their trackage on borrowed capital were the first to go under. The Philadelphia & Reading crashed in February 1893, and within 4 months 74 railroads operating more than 30,000 miles of track went broke. During 1893 more than 15,000 companies failed, and 574 banks closed.

Economic stability was further threatened by the initial successes of the farmer-supported People's Party, which advocated Government control of the railroads and the free coinage of silver. The "free silver" advocates believed that putting more money into circulation would force prices up—particularly for farm products.

With political and economic storms sweeping the country, in 1895 the Federal Government moved to use the Sherman Anti-Trust Act to break up the sugar trust, which controlled 98 percent of sugar refining in the Nation. The Supreme Court ruled against the Government, which is not surprising in view of the fact that Attorney General Richard Olney was representing a law that, in his own words, he ". . . believed to be no good." The decision was based on the contention that the act could control interstate commerce but not the refineries, which were regarded as local activities. This and other decisions against the act led to a proliferation of holding companies, mergers, and such. Between 1897 and 1904 there were 319 consolidations of companies, capitalized at $6.3 billion. Rockefeller's Standard Oil of New Jersey engulfed 20 separate oil companies and by 1904 controlled 85 percent of the domestic petroleum trade and 90 percent of oil exports. J. P. Morgan in 1901 put together 10 iron and steel companies to form the United States Steel Corporation, using the giant Carnegie Steel Company as the centerpiece. As an indication of the financial strength of U.S. Steel, it had enough ready cash aside from its marketable securities to have met all the obligations of the U.S. Government in 1800.

In 1902 big business had suffered a temporary setback when President Theodore Roosevelt dusted off the Sherman Act and used it to prosecute the Northern Securities Company, a railroad holding company monopoly engineered by Morgan, E. H. Harriman, and James J. Hill. The Supreme Court upheld the Government in 1904, but after this victory Roosevelt modified his attitude toward

Ups and Downs of the Economy *More Good Times Than Bad*

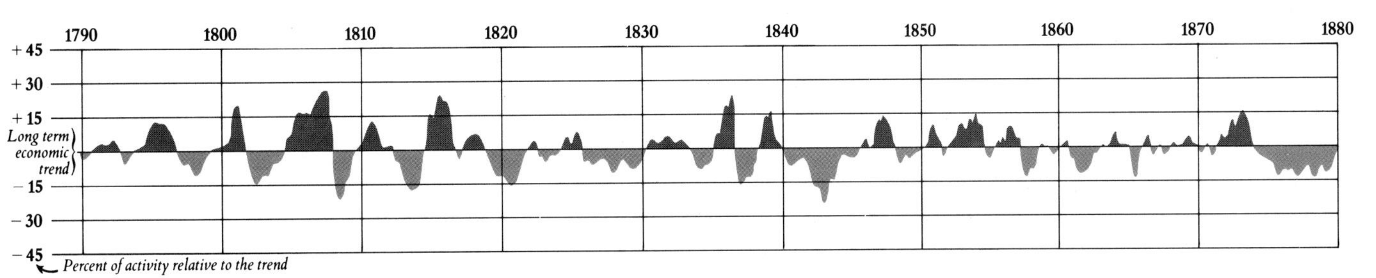

America's economic history has resembled a roller coaster—a movement from the peaks of prosperity to valleys of financial panic, recession, and depression. The reasons for the financial panics have varied, from the unwise financial ventures of one man (Jay Cooke in 1873), to excessive stock market speculation by banks (1907), to the complex web of social, political, and economic factors that led to the 1929 stock market crash and the Great Depression. Overextension of credit is usually also a factor.

The duration of a business cycle in America—from peak to valley and back again—has ranged from several months to several years. Before World War II, drops in production were sometimes enormous. But as this chart indicates, dips in the postwar years have been relatively small and short-lived. However, were the chart extended through the mid-1970's, it would show that 1974 and 1975 marked the sharpest decline since the 1930's. That there was little of the accompanying financial panic notable in earlier years is testimony to the efficacy of Government measures and to America's basic economic strength.

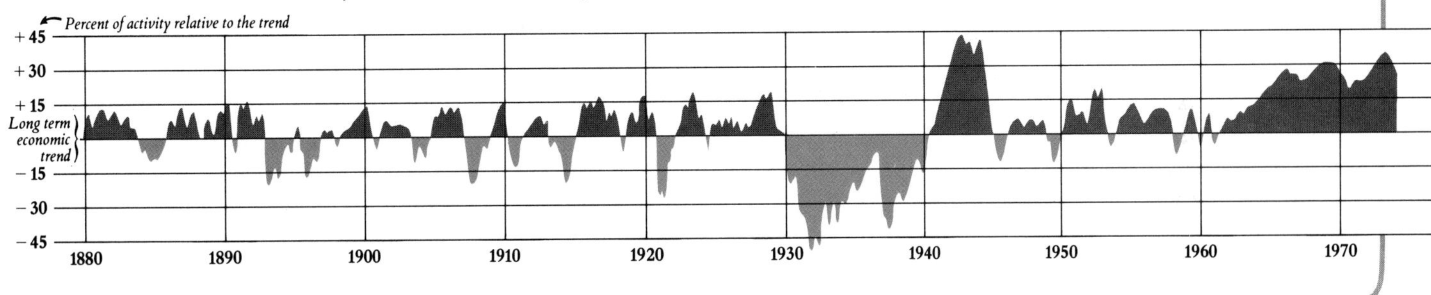

trusts, concluding that not all were bad or guilty of "unreasonable restraint of trade." A few years later the Federal Government moved against Standard Oil of New Jersey, and in 1911 the Supreme Court ordered its dissolution because it engaged in "unreasonable" restraint of trade. Thus the Court adopted the "rule of reason"—which had been vigorously promoted by big business lawyers—as a principle for applying the Sherman Act.

The Supreme Court continued using this guidepost to condone the growth of trusts until in 1914 President Woodrow Wilson asked Congress to clarify and strengthen the Sherman Act. That year Congress passed the Clayton Anti-Trust Act and established the Federal Trade Commission to ferret out business practices that restrained competition and spawned monopolies. But in a U.S. Steel Corporation case in 1920, the Supreme Court ruled that "mere size" was no offense against the antitrust laws, and in ensuing years it held that it alone had the last word on what business practices restrain trade. Between this dictum and the "rule of reason," the antitrust lawyers of the Department of Justice are constantly evaluating the effect and legality of the newest form of business combination, the conglomerate, which gathers companies from scores of unrelated industries under its corporate roof.

While the holding companies were busy building their industrial empires, business in the United States experienced sharp ups and downs. The Panic of 1907, which showed that New York banks were deeply involved in stock market speculation, caused Congress in 1908 to order a study of ways to reform the banking system. While this investigation was under way, the House of Representatives in 1912 set up a committee under Arsène Pujo of Louisiana to determine whether a "money trust"—a coalition of banks, insurance companies, and industrial firms—existed in America. The Pujo Committee dug deeply and reported that Morgan and his friends, along with bankers George Baker, James Stillman, and their associates, held 341 directorships in 112 concerns with resources or capitalization of more than $22 billion. The presence of one or two of these men on a board of directors did not necessarily mean that they could control the company's policies, but the facts assembled by Pujo did show that banking power in New York was becoming more concentrated and that the influence of a few central figures was powerful and far reaching.

The Pujo investigation and work by many other committees played important roles in the passage of an act in 1913 establishing the Federal Reserve System, consisting of 12 regional banks coordinated by the Federal Reserve Board. These "bankers' banks" enabled member institutions to borrow money in time of need and strengthened the currency by issuing Federal Reserve notes. The "Fed," which went into operation in 1914, quickly proved its value during World War I by mobilizing credit for war purchases and industrial expansion.

Henry Ford and the Automobile
New Mobility for All Mankind

In many ways the tale of Henry Ford and the product associated with his name is a microcosm of American economic history—a story of trial and error, of innovation and ultimate success. A farmer with a penchant for things mechanical, the young Ford quit school at 17, began building small steam engines, and drove his first bicycle-wheeled, engine-driven device in 1896.

It was a primitive affair, much simpler than cars already on the roads in Europe, and it wasn't until 1901 that the stubborn tinkerer, after several false starts, got enough financial support to start the Henry Ford Automobile Company. Financial disputes arose and Ford left. Two years later, with new backers, he established the Ford Motor Company. (Original investors reaped heady rewards when Ford bought all outstanding shares in 1919; a share that cost $100 was then worth $260,000.)

Henry Ford *sits in his first car, which he built in his backyard toolshed. It had a tiller instead of a steering wheel, and no reverse.*

Ford was convinced that he could produce a good car at a reasonable price, and on October 1, 1908, he realized his dream with the unveiling of the Ford Model T. This was a straightforward, sturdy machine made of the best metals young Henry could obtain and propelled by a single 4-cylinder, 22-horsepower, 167-cubic-inch engine.

The T was an instant success and within months was outselling all other American cars combined. What's more, Ford made good his pledge to reduce the Tin Lizzie's price. From $850 in 1909, the price dropped steadily to $260 for some models by 1924. By then, however, other manufacturers' inexpensive cars with better methods of changing gears and more speed were outperforming the T on America's improved roads.

Recognizing this, Ford and his engineers went to work, and in late 1927 they were ready with the company's second breakthrough—the Model A. The car people dubbed a "baby Lincoln" took America by storm. Some 4.5 million Model A's were built in 5 years, and even the most expensive version sold for under $600. But times were changing. The Detroit manufacturers realized that the mass market was not only growing but would buy a wide variety of cars. This trend was encouraged by General Motors, which began to make annual model changes, supported by intensive advertising campaigns. The Detroit design syndrome was soon established. Each year the new models had to be sufficiently different from the ones before to set them clearly apart (so that one's neighbors would be sure to know that a car was new); yet it could not be so drastically changed as to put it out of character with previous models.

Today the Big Three—General Motors, Ford, and Chrysler—manufacture many different products. But the automotive industry owes an enduring debt to a mechanical genius named Henry Ford, the man who first put Americans on wheels.

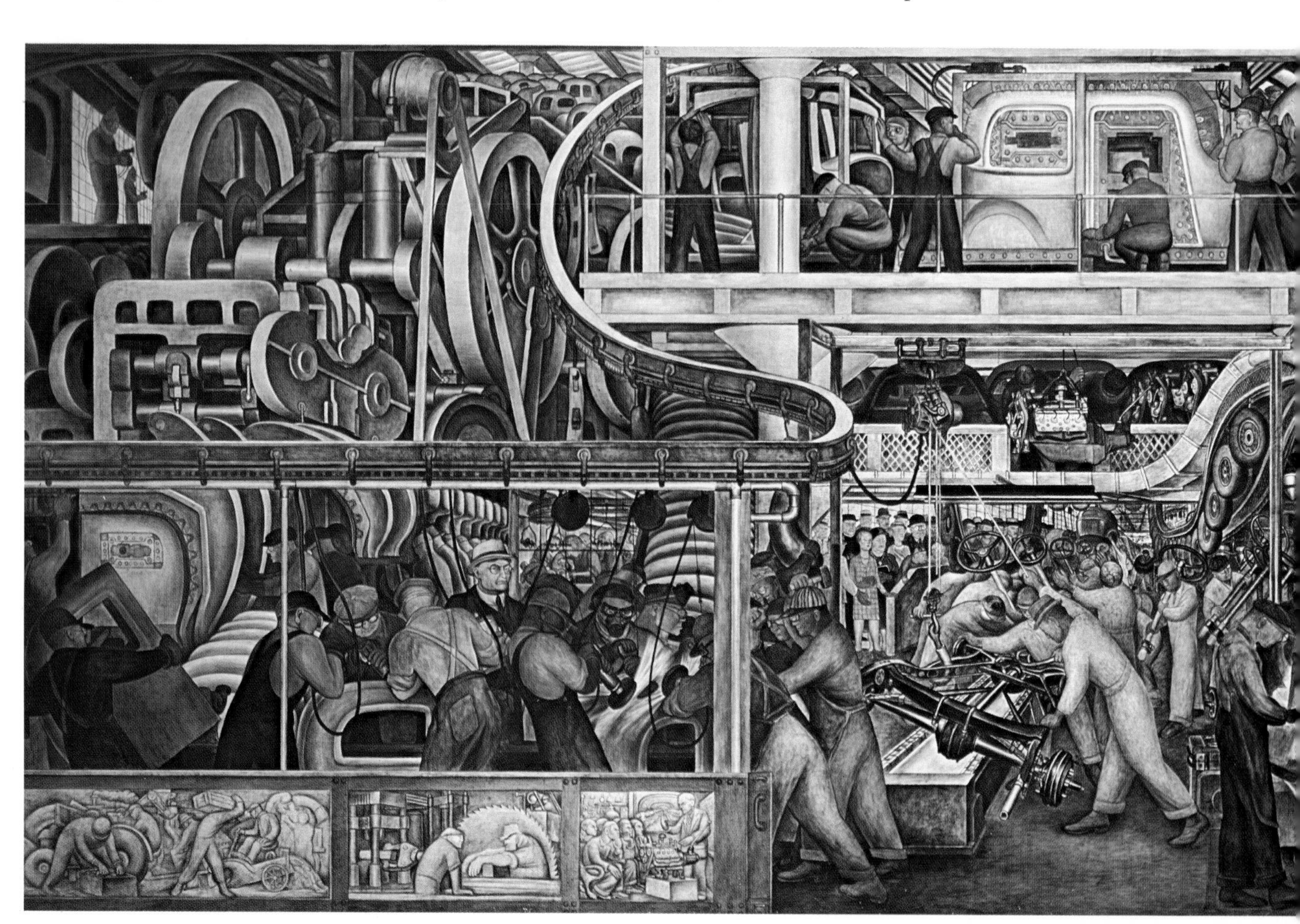

The Model T *(a 1909 model is pictured at the left) was the car that put Henry Ford and his fledgling auto company on the map. Contrary to popular belief, they weren't all black; the first Model T's, in fact, were Brewster green with red striping. But Ford had promised a car that would suit the pocketbook of America's burgeoning middle class. A certain uniformity of design, engine, and color clearly helped to produce the vehicle at the right price. To accomplish this feat, Ford moved quickly to standardize his production procedures. While he did not invent mass production and the assembly line (above), he used the concepts to maximum effect and set the pace for others. As early as 1913, his company was able to produce an astonishing 1,000 T's per day.*

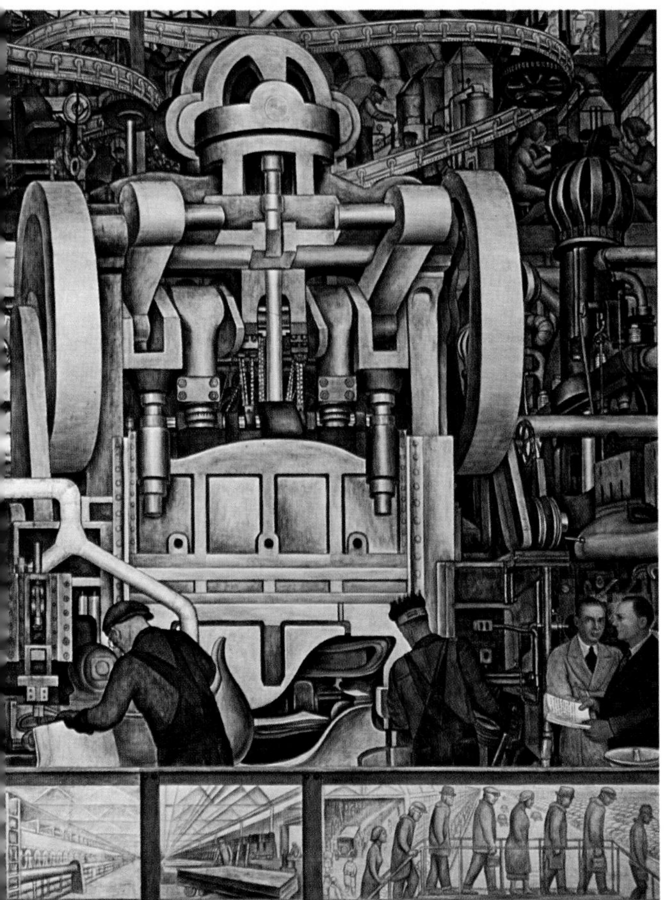

Ford's Model A *caught America's imagination, and like its predecessor, the Model T, was an instant success. There was nothing revolutionary about the engine, but the car's classic good looks and sturdiness endeared it to millions. Today the Model A Restorers Club has thousands of members, who proudly drive their prizes.*

Mass production, *even in its early days, was an awesome sight. It inspired the imagination of many artists, including the Mexican painter and muralist Diego Rivera, one of whose works appears here. Assembly lines still bombard human sensibilities. In cavernous plants, sometimes stretching a mile or more, the roar of machinery is deafening as cars jerk down the lines from one station to the next. Plants regularly produce 60 full-size cars an hour, although one plant turns out 100 cars, far more complex than the Model T.*

Department Stores and Mail-Order Houses
Ingenious Ways To Offer More Goods at Lower Prices

The American system of mass production met its test during the Civil War when huge amounts of war supplies and consumer goods were needed in a hurry. It was during the war years that the department store, a new concept in merchandising, was developed to bring the products of industry to the people at a fair price. What was probably the first such store, a collection of specialty shops under one roof, was opened by Alexander T. Stewart in New York City in 1862. Similar establishments were started about the same time by Marshall Field in Chicago and John Wanamaker in Philadelphia. Wanamaker's new Grand Depot store prospered during the Centennial Exposition of 1876, and by 1896 he had moved to New York and bought Stewart's store.

Meanwhile, mail-order houses were providing rural Americans with department store services. Aaron Montgomery Ward founded Montgomery Ward & Co. in 1872 and soon his catalog offering quality goods on a "money back guarantee" had an honored place in thousands of homes throughout the West. In 1893 a rival firm, Sears, Roebuck and Co., was started by Richard W. Sears who began in the mail-order business in 1886 selling watches. As the automobile offered greater mobility in the 1920's, farmers began patronizing city department stores. So Sears, and then Ward, countered by opening their own retail stores.

Rural families dreamed *of the wondrous goods illustrated in the Sears, Roebuck and Montgomery Ward catalogs, which were even used as textbooks in some rural schools.*

R. H. Macy & Co., *Inc., which now has six divisions and 70 stores across the country, got its start in 1858 when Rowland H. Macy opened his dry goods store at 14th Street and 6th Avenue in New York City. Macy's, as well as other department stores, featured fast service and low prices for cash purchases. But with the growth of chain stores, which spread from the grocery to the department store field in the late 1920's and brought intense competition, Macy's and others adopted charge accounts and time-payment plans to further accommodate their customers. In the early 1970's there were more than 6,000 department stores in the United States.*

An Economic World Power

World War I brought a tremendous increase in production, and by the time peace was restored, American industry was ready for even greater growth. In little more than half a century the United States had become the mightiest industrial force on Earth and the creditor of European nations that had once been the undisputed rulers of world economy.

In the postwar era the U.S. automobile industry came into its own—a fact that may have affected American society more profoundly than anything in its prior history. Henry Ford did not invent mass production based on relatively unskilled laborers working with interchangeable parts in central assembly units, but the former Detroit mechanic refined and perfected that process as never before. Ford's methods, soon adopted by other manufacturers and combined with installment buying on a previously unheard-of scale, brought the automobile within the budget of the ordinary wage earner.

The automobile industry, still in its infancy through World War I, matured quickly after 1918. By 1921 Americans were driving 10.5 million registered vehicles; 8 years later the number had jumped to more than 26 million—1 automobile for every 5 men, women, and children in the country. Autoworkers accounted for nearly 10 percent of all manufacturing wages, and directly or indirectly the industry affected the lives of some 5 million workers. Its impact was greater than that of any other element in the economy. Its growth soon brought major increases in petroleum production, tire manufacturing, road construction, and steelmaking. At the same time automobiles sharply cut the passenger business of the railroads and other common carriers.

Riding High

Automobiles in the 1920's led the way to America's first real consumer-buying spree. The number of metropolitan dry goods and department stores, which had come into being in the late 19th century, increased dramatically. R. H. Macy in New York, John Wanamaker in Philadelphia, and Marshall Field in Chicago carried a stunning array of goods. Montgomery Ward and Sears, Roebuck and Company—the great mail order houses whose catalogs and efficient service had earlier brought manufactured products into every rural community served by a post office—began to open retail stores as well.

Amid the rush to capture the consumer's attention, product identification grew in importance; advertising symbols and slogans sold everything from cigarettes to corsets. Ads blanketed billboards and filled newspapers as well as the airwaves of the newest wonder, radio. The fox terrier symbolizing the Radio Corporation of America became the best known dog in the world, and posters urged weight-watching smokers to "Reach for a Lucky instead of a sweet." By 1929 American businesses were spending $3.4 billion a year on advertising.

At the same time, corporate America, encouraged by the Supreme Court, was undergoing its second wave of mergers. During the 1920's some 7,000 manufacturing and mining companies and 5,000 utilities were amalgamated, and by 1929 some 200 giant corporations, controlled by an estimated 2,000 individuals, owned 38 percent of the Nation's business wealth. Of the 573 concerns whose securities were traded on the New York Stock Exchange, only 86 were not holding companies. The financial organisms assembled by such men as Samuel Insull (utilities), the Van Sweringen brothers (railroads), and A. P. Giannini (banking) were likened by Franklin D. Roosevelt to "a 96-inch dog wagged by a 4-inch tail."

Such men and some of their immediate predecessors had amassed their Croesus-like fortunes chiefly through shrewd financial manipulation rather than by building industries. No doubt they contributed to America's industrial growth by raising the money that helped finance expansion and technological development and made more jobs available at better pay. But their private manipulations sometimes meant rigged stock prices, which lured unsuspecting investors. As prosperity spread during the 1920's all sorts of "average citizens"—cabdrivers, grocery clerks, housewives, small businessmen—took fliers in the market, buying stock on margin (credit).

Danger signs were plentiful, however, even at the time of greatest prosperity. Commercial banks had cast prudent business practices aside and instead were financing stock market and real estate speculation. In rural America farm prices had fallen precipitously, and agricultural capital had dwindled, forcing hundreds of small banks into insolvency. The postwar housing boom was over. Auto and steel production had both declined.

Although industrial profits were rising by as much as 9 percent a year, and output per factory worker by 3.5 percent, the worker's earnings were increasing by only 2.4 percent annually in the 1920's; 78 percent of the U.S. population had family incomes below $3,000 a year or individual incomes of less than $1,500. More than half of that segment of the population had family incomes under $1,500, individual incomes under $750. More and more consumers were buying on the installment plan, going deeper into debt each year. Slowly but surely, the purchasing power of customers for the torrent of goods pouring from U.S. factories was declining.

1929: The Economy Falls Apart

In October 1929 Wall Street's house of paper profits began to fall apart. The sharpest downturn in stock prices in the Nation's history shattered American faith in a fadeproof economic rainbow. As the ensuing business contraction worsened in 1930, Congress voted a steep increase in tariffs on foreign imports. President Herbert Hoover signed the Smoot-Hawley bill, as this measure was known, despite a petition from 1,028 economists to veto it. Almost immediately America's European trading partners retaliated with higher tariffs of their own, accelerating what had already been a sharp decline in world trade. The tariff war deepened the Great Depression, a national—indeed, a worldwide—disaster.

For the United States it was unquestionably the worst of times. By many criteria, the Depression lasted until 1942, but the harshest years were the early ones. The Nation's gross national product fell from $104 billion in 1929 to $58 billion in 1932, and the following year, at the deepest point of distress, one-fourth of the labor force was jobless. In 1932 more than 1,400 banks failed, and the trend showed every sign of continuing.

In November 1932 Franklin D. Roosevelt was elected to the Presidency. His rapid-fire moves, labeled the "Hundred Days" because they occurred within a little more than 3 months of his inauguration, introduced the New Deal. A bank holiday was declared to shore up confidence. More credit was extended to farmers. The Glass-Steagall Act separated commercial and investment banking, broadened Federal Reserve Board control over stock market speculation, and created the Federal Deposit Insurance Corporation to protect depositors against losses due to bank failures. All gold and gold certificates were called in, and the currency was soon taken off a full gold standard. This action reduced the value of the dollar and caused prices to rise for the first time since 1929.

By the middle and late 1930's Roosevelt's "alphabet-soup" agencies were insinuating the Government into nearly every nook and cranny of private enterprise, from securities regulation (by the Securities and Exchange Commission) to control of agricultural production and prices. As the men whom Roosevelt branded the economic royalists grew more vehement in their protests, Roosevelt's popularity with America's working men and women increased. In addition to social security benefits, the National Industrial Recovery Act (NIRA) was pushed through Congress. Section 7(a) of this act guaranteed labor's right to form unions and bargain collectively with employers over wages, hours, and working conditions. When the Supreme Court invalidated the NIRA as an attempt to regulate local business, Congress passed the Wagner Act, which established the National Labor Relations Board (NLRB). When the Supreme Court approved this legislation in 1937, labor won a great victory. (The Depression and the New Deal are also discussed in "Turning Points," pages 353–355.)

The Growth of Labor Unions

The NLRB was the bill of rights the worker had been seeking almost from the first faint stirrings of American industry. Employer resistance had been stubborn. "Combinations of labourers" in early-19th-century America were held by the courts to be conspiracies against the public. By midcentury skilled craftsmen had formed a few local unions, but unskilled workers had no organization to improve their economic lot.

The number of industrial wage earners grew rapidly after the Civil War as the factory system spread west. And labor conflict intensified as employers, often with Government backing, moved to crush the unions. Secret agents, hired thugs, and even soldiers were used to deal with increasingly frequent strikes. There was, for instance, the Great Strike of 1877, a chain reaction that left dozens of railroad workers dead and caused property damage of close to $10 million; the Haymarket riot in Chicago in 1886, during which several policemen were killed; the bitter Homestead Strike of 1892, when steelworkers walked out of one of Carnegie's biggest plants; and the Pullman strike of 1894, which brought violent conflict between Federal troops and workers.

In this turbulent period two new organizations provided leadership for the struggling labor movement. The first was the Noble and Holy Order of the Knights of Labor, founded in 1869 as a "union of all trades and callings" and headed from 1883 to 1893 by Terence V. Powderly. The other was established in 1881 as the Federation of Organized Trades and Labor Unions and reorganized in 1886 as the American Federation of Labor (AFL). This affiliation of local and national craft unions of skilled workers was ruled by Samuel Gompers.

Between 1900 and 1920 the AFL quadrupled in size to 2 million members. But it was reluctant to tackle the huge, mass-production industries that had developed within the economy. In 1935 John L. Lewis, president of the United Mine Workers, formed the Committee for Industrial Organization to unionize these unskilled workers. After the AFL expelled the unions supporting Lewis, he formed the Congress of Industrial Organizations (CIO) in 1938. Under the leadership of Lewis, Philip Murray (who organized the steelworkers), and Walter Reuther (who helped to form the United Automobile Workers), the CIO (aided by the Wagner Act) proved a success, claiming around 4 million members by 1941, compared to 4.5 million in the AFL.

In 1955 the two groups buried past differences and merged, forming what then was an AFL-CIO of some 16 million members—more than 80 percent of all persons enrolled in U.S. unions. The merger seemed to symbolize just how far big labor had come and hinted where it was headed. Despite occasionally restrictive legislation, such as the Taft-Hartley Act (curbing some union activities and providing for Government intervention to halt strikes), union power grew steadily after the 1930's. The right to strike became sacrosanct, and persistent negotiation by labor leaders added significantly to the list of benefits enjoyed by union members. To the bread-and-butter issues of Gompers' day were added new concerns: The job inroads made by automation, the growing reluctance to perform unrelieved and tedious assembly-line work, and the need to integrate minority workers into all-white trade unions.

Many thoughtful commentators were asking whether the pendulum of advantage, once weighted so heavily in favor of the employers, was not swinging too far the other way. Labor disputes, which brought crippling strikes and wage increases, which contributed to ever-rising prices of consumer goods and services and further demands, were losing the sympathy of many Americans —at least among those who were not union members.

Government Steps In

While World War II finally ended the Depression and precipitated a fantastic industrial mobilization that meant jobs for everyone able to work, the grim memory of breadlines remained indelible in the American consciousness. The year after the war ended, the Nation underwrote its new goal of economic security for all when Congress passed the Employment Act of 1946, which committed the Federal Government "to promote maximum employment, production and purchasing power."

To achieve all three aims, the Government turned to the theories of British economist John Maynard Keynes, which held that governments, by using their fiscal and monetary tools, can guarantee prosperity and high employment. America entered a new economic era in which government made itself a partner of business and labor in assuring the economic well-being of the populace.

Business was changing, too, in the postwar era. The airlines, relatively unimportant during the first third of the 20th century, had come of age, altering the style of American transportation. The modern corporation, an extraordinarily efficient business structure, became the dominant force in American economic life, employing more than half of all workers and possessing assets valued at more than $1 trillion. And the managers of these corporations were coming to depend on new techniques and new devices to run their vast enterprises. The computer, a tool with seemingly limitless potential, began to perform scores of vital functions. Companies felt a need to diversify, many of them into areas wholly unrelated to their traditional businesses, with a central financial structure coupled with decentralized operations. For a while conglomerates, as these groupings are called, seemed to work, but the recession of the 1970's proved that they, too, were subject to the vagaries of business cycles.

The 1960's brought new and unparalleled prosperity to the Nation, but in the same period some glaring inequities and thinly veiled truths were exposed. Millions of Americans, victims of racial and sexual discrimination, had been forced to exist outside the economic mainstream. Concentration on civil rights legislation during the 1960's attempted to correct these injustices.

As its 200th anniversary approached, America was confronted with a new set of economic realities: Inflationary pressures that seemed resistant to the old curatives; pollution of air and water, suburban sprawl, traffic congestion, and the decay of the central cities; an uncoordinated transportation policy that overloaded multiplying highways while generally neglecting mass rapid transit and the railroads; depletion of resources and an energy crisis; and a foreign trade imbalance and wild gyrations in currency values, which emphasized the bewildering complexity of a world economy that locked nations together whether they liked it or not. In the past the Nation had surmounted depressions and wars, provided an ever-higher standard of living for more people, and made progress in healing social ills. In the next 200 years Americans will need even greater application of their famous know-how and their will to work if they are to meet the bewildering array of challenges ahead.

MAKING DEMOCRACY WORK

Legislating Economics

On December 23, 1913, President Wilson signed legislation that was to become a landmark in America's economic history: the Federal Reserve Act, which established the Federal Reserve System to provide a more effective supervision of banking. The "Fed"—as the Federal Reserve came to be known—today comprises a governing board in Washington and 12 regional banks, plus 24 smaller branches scattered throughout the country. The regional banks exercise a good deal of autonomy and perform many of the so-called "service" functions of the Federal Reserve System: making loans to member banks, holding their deposits, and issuing currency as commercial banks do for their customers.

The "control" functions of the system rest largely with the Board of Governors of the Federal Reserve in Washington. Since World War II, these functions have grown in importance, as economists have come to realize just how critical monetary management is in maintaining economic stability. The Fed sets an interest rate at which regional banks lend to member commercial banks; it establishes a level of reserves member banks must maintain; and it buys and sells Government securities in the open market. Using these tools of control, the bank can play an enormous role in determining just how much money there is in the economy at any one time—and thus is an equal partner with the Federal fiscal mechanism in influencing the direction of America's economy.

Less than one year after the passage of the Federal Reserve Act, Congress passed the Federal Trade Commission Act to buttress the Nation's antitrust laws. The act set up a five-man Federal Trade Commission to "prevent persons, partnerships or corporations, except banks and common carriers subject to the acts to regulate commerce, from using unfair methods of competition in commerce." The FTC would determine when such unfair practices existed in violation of the Sherman and Clayton acts and then issue cease-and-desist orders against their continuation.

Over the years the Supreme Court has weakened the FTC's drive against monopolistic practices by refusing to accept the Commission's "findings of fact" regarding antitrust violations and then setting aside its cease-and-desist orders. But the FTC has been credited with improving business ethics and limiting such practices as the mislabeling of products, false advertising, and price-fixing at a low rate to drive a competitor out of business.

One year after World War II ended, with the memory of the Great Depression still fresh in the collective mind of Congress, the Employment Act of 1946 was passed. This act broke new ground in economic planning by making the Government responsible for pursuing policies to assure full employment and the orderly growth of the national economy. The act created a Council of Economic Advisers in the Executive Office of the President and a Joint Economic Committee in the Congress. The idea was that these new governmental organs, especially the President's CEA, could help provide the best available advice to policymakers so that they might pursue fiscal and monetary goals necessary to implement the Employment Act. But after two decades of relative prosperity and price stability, the problems posed by the inflation-recession phenomenon of the 1970's underscored the difficulty of meeting the act's challenge.

CHAPTER SIXTEEN

The March of Medicine

In the mid-19th century France, Germany, and Brita were the centers of medical knowledge and progress; t United States was considered a backwater. Reputab American medical schools were few and far between; young man who was seriously interested in a career as doctor usually felt he had to attend a European universit In many cases this was the University of Edinburg Scotland since colonial times had been important for medi cal training. The rank and file of American physicia were all too often poorly trained. Even so, there were son significant early experiments in the science of healing i this country. Perhaps the most dramatic and controversi

Colonial Medicine's Modest Beginnings

In Britain's North American Colonies university-trained physicians were at a premium. At the time of the Revolution there were only about 400, plus some 3,000 practitioners who had had on-the-job training as barber-surgeons or physicians' apprentices. Whether university-trained or not, none had much knowledge of the causes of disease, and the "cures" that were often recommended—bleeding, blistering, and violent purgatives—were at best ineffective and at worst lethal.

Nonetheless, one medical advance can be credited to colonial medicine: the use of variolation, the direct inoculation of persons with live smallpox virus from a victim. The procedure was first employed with some success in Boston by Dr. Zabdiel Boylston in 1721. Variolation, however, ran the risk of spreading the disease it was supposed to prevent. Some years later, when it was administered to Continental soldiers already weakened by hunger and exposure, it probably killed more men than it protected. The Englishman Edward Jenner's far safer vaccination with cowpox virus replaced variolation in the early 1800's.

The colonials learned some medicine from the Indians, whose use of a variety of roots as well as herbs and other plants often proved beneficial in easing aches and pains, if not in effecting cures. Unfortunately, many physicians were unduly impressed with what they imagined to be the curative powers of tobacco, a plant introduced into the Colonies early in the 17th century. John Josselyn, an Englishman who twice visited the Colonies later in that century, described the medicinal properties of tobacco.

The vertues of tobacco are these. It helps digestion, the Gout, the Tooth-Ach, prevents infection . . . it heats the cold, and cools them that sweat, feedeth the hungry, spent spirits restoreth, purgeth the stomach, killeth nits and lice . . .

For the first settlers on America's shores, life held few certainties and one strong probability: an early death. As late as 1850 the life expectancy of the average American was less than 40 years. For the pioneers of the early 17th century, the outlook was far worse. Unprepared for the rigors of colonial life, many succumbed to Indian raids, starvation, and disease. Even in the comparatively mild climate at Jamestown, Virginia, more than half of the original settlers, who arrived in 1607, died before the end of a year. Of the 102 Pilgrims who landed at Plymouth Rock in December 1620, 44 were dead by the following spring. Set on an inhospitable foreign shore without even the limited cures that European medicine was then capable of providing, the colonists could only turn to the most educated of their group—usually the ministers—for medical advice. By and large, about all they could expect were folk remedies and prayer.

George Percy, one of the original Jamestown settlers, summed up in these words the insufferable conditions that confronted the colonists: "Our men are destroyed with cruel diseases, as swelling, flixes [dysentery], burning fevers . . . and some departed suddenly. . . . There were never Englishmen left in a foreign country in such misery. . . . Our food was but a small can of barley sod in water . . . our drink cold water taken out of the river, which was at flood very salty, at low tide full of slime and filth. . . . Our men night and day groaned in every corner of the fort most pitiful to hear. . . . Some departed out of the world, many times three or four a night, in the morning their bodies trailed out of their cabins like dogs to be buried."

For all their sufferings, the colonists gradually increased their numbers. By the mid-17th century a few university-trained physicians had joined them. These men enlisted apprentices from among the sons of settlers and taught them what little medical skills they had. As

as the use of inoculation for smallpox to control an epi-
'mic in colonial Boston in 1721.

By 1912, when an American won a Nobel Prize in edicine or physiology for the first time, the influence 'the United States in the world of medicine was beginning be felt. In the 62 years that followed, 46 of the 99 Nobel vards in that field went to Americans. This astounding cord is only one indication of the world leadership hieved by U.S. medicine in the 20th century. During e past several decades American medical schools, hospi-ls, research institutions, foundations, private individuals, nd companies have sponsored the scientific research that has resulted in discoveries helpful in eradicating numerous diseases and alleviating scores of chronic disabilities that once ranked with war and famine among man's scourges.

The preeminence of Americans in world medicine is relatively new, but even in the days when ignorance and ineffectiveness were the national condition, there were individual American physicians, scientists, and reformers who contributed to the improvement of care for the afflicted. These men and women laid the foundations of our present excellent—but improvable—position in the healing arts. It is this heartening story of small beginnings and steady growth that we celebrate here.

a result, the quality of health care slowly improved for the white men; but for the Indians contact with colonists brought on newfound miseries. For centuries these natives of America had lived in isolation, the vast oceans serving as a barrier against the infectious diseases to which Europeans were prey. Their bodies had built no immunities against these unfamiliar ills, and within a few years of white settlement this lack of resistance began to prove fatal as Indian tribes by the score fell victim to the bacteria and viruses the white man carried. Mysteriously, 2 years before the Pilgrims landed at Plymouth, an unidentified pestilence had decimated the Indians of New England, and some settlers saw in the red man's travail the hand of God himself, striking down the heathen to make way for the Christian.

The colonists as well as the Indians often fell victim to epidemics: Measles, yellow fever, malaria, diphtheria, dysentery, scarlet fever, and smallpox were among the commonest. It was in dealing with smallpox that American medicine made its first distinctive contribution. During a 1721 epidemic in Boston, the scholarly Congregational minister Cotton Mather prevailed on Dr. Zabdiel Boylston to inoculate the healthy with pus taken from the sores of smallpox patients—a practice little known in the Western World although common among the Turks. In spite of a public outcry, Boylston inoculated his own sons and 239 other people, of whom all but six escaped the dreaded disease.

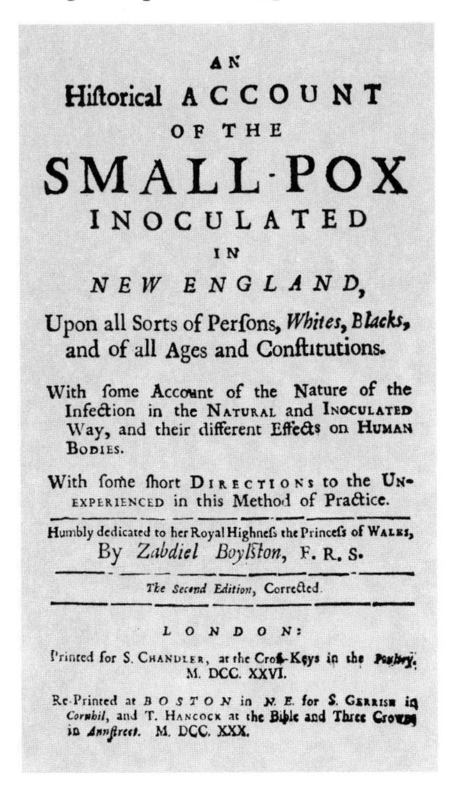
AN
Hiſtorical ACCOUNT
OF THE
SMALL-POX
INOCULATED
IN
NEW ENGLAND,
Upon all Sorts of Perſons, *Whites*, *Blacks*, and of all Ages and Conſtitutions.

With ſome Account of the Nature of the Infection in the NATURAL and INOCULATED Way, and their different Effects on HUMAN BODIES.

With ſome ſhort DIRECTIONS to the UNEXPERIENCED in this Method of Practice.

Humbly dedicated to her Royal Highneſs the Princeſs of WALES,
By *Zabdiel Boylſton*, F. R. S.

The Second Edition, Corrected.

LONDON:
Printed for S. CHANDLER, at the Croſs-Keys in the *Poultry*.
M. DCC. XXVI.

Re-Printed at *BOSTON* in *N. E.* for *S. GERRISH* in *Cornhil*, and T. HANCOCK at the Bible and Three Crowns in *Annſtreet*. M. DCC. XXX.

Dr. Zabdiel Boylston's *account of his smallpox inoculations was first published in 1726 in London, where he had gone to lecture. Four years later the book came out in Boston.*

Until 1751 not a single hospital existed in the Colonies, and it was not until 1765 that the first medical faculty for an American university was appointed at Philadelphia College (later the University of Pennsylvania). The great 19th-century essayist Oliver Wendell Holmes, himself a physician, described the practice of a typical medical man of a century before. "His pharmacopoeia," wrote Holmes, "consisted mainly of simples . . . St. John's wort and Clown's All-Heal with . . . Fennel, Saffron and Parsley . . . with opium in some form. . . . He would perhaps have a rheumatic patient wrapped in the skin of a wolf or a wild cat, and in cases of malignant fever . . . prescribed a certain black powder, which had been made by calcining toads in an earthen pot."

In the years just before the Revolution the Colonies first attempted to regulate and institutionalize medicine. In 1760 New York became the first colony to license physicians, and in that jurisdiction, at least, a man could no longer set up practice by merely giving himself the title of doctor. (In 1851, however, most States still had no licensing procedures for physicians.) In 1776 there were some 3,500 medical practitioners in America but only about 400 of these had attended medical schools. (Those who had studied formally had done so mostly in London or Edinburgh.) But doctors were al-

Cofounded by Benjamin Franklin *in 1751, the Pennsylvania Hospital, the first such facility in the Colonies, dominates the Philadelphia skyline in this late-18th-century print. In 1765 the Colonies' first medical school, at what is now the University of Pennsylvania, opened in Philadelphia. Before the century was out, two more medical schools and several hospitals were operating in east coast cities.*

ready gaining a degree of social standing and community leadership. Four signers of the Declaration of Independence were physicians; one of them, Dr. Benjamin Rush, founded the first public dispensary in Philadelphia and was one of the earliest doctors to characterize insanity as a medical problem rather than a scourge of the Devil.

Rush was nonetheless typical of his times in most other respects. Like many doctors, for example, he believed in the efficacy of bleeding, a treatment now regarded as generally having been worse than the ailments it was meant to relieve. This was the age of heroic medicine, when severe illness was thought curable only by administering severe shocks to the body. Rush's treatment for yellow fever, the disease that periodically ravaged Philadelphia, included such draconian measures as bloodletting, induced vomiting, and dousing the victim with icy water. During the 1793 yellow fever epidemic, some 5,000 of the nearly 24,000 Philadelphians who had been afflicted died, many succumbing to the far from tender ministrations of the city's medical attendants.

Some Progress Is Made

Still, there were occasional rays of light on the dark horizon. In 1809 a frontier surgeon, Ephraim McDowell, performed the world's first successful ovariotomy, removing a 22.5-pound ovarian tumor from a Kentucky woman—an operation all the more astounding as it was performed 33 years before another backwoods physician, Dr. Crawford Long, performed a minor operation using ether as an anesthetic for the first time. Yet another frontier doctor, Daniel Drake, brought institutional medicine to the Western wilderness, establishing a medical school in Cincinnati in 1819. Drake, however, is best remembered for his medical classic, . . . *the Principal Diseases of the Interior Valley of North America,* a study of the relation of disease to geography. A Boston dentist, William T. G. Morton, also experimented with the use of ether as an anesthetic. Under his direction it was used for a major surgical operation by Dr. John C. Warren, and a description of the new technique was published in a medical journal in 1846.

Clara Barton, *founder of the American Red Cross, is memorialized in this stained-glass window in Massachusetts for her pioneering work as a nurse to Civil War wounded.*

Oliver Wendell Holmes was a doctor who was well ahead of his day. In 1843—long before discoveries in bacteriology—he suggested that puerperal fever, a major cause of childbirth deaths among women, was spread by the unsanitary practices of doctors and midwives. A few years later a Hungarian obstetrician, Ignaz Semmelweis, was hounded from Vienna for attempting to impose antiseptic measures on his colleagues. But it was not until 1868 that the English surgeon Dr. Joseph Lister, influenced by the theories of French chemist Louis Pasteur, instituted a successful program of antisepsis during surgery at the University of Glasgow.

Women played an important role in promoting the care of the sick. About 1841 Dorothea Lynde Dix, a New Englander, began a decades-long campaign to reform institutions sheltering the insane. In Miss Dix's day the mentally ill were often held with criminals in local prisons. Although their only crime was their affliction, they were beaten and confined in chains. Ignoring popular ridicule, Miss Dix tirelessly exposed the horrible treatment the insane were forced to endure, and her dedication eventually led to reform in many States. During the Civil War she was appointed superintendent of Union Army nurses and, with Clara Barton, waged a campaign to improve treatment of the wounded and disabled and to give women a significant role in medical practice.

Another woman whose name belongs high on any list of pioneers was Elizabeth Blackwell, who in 1849 became America's first female physician. A few years later she opened a private dispensary staffed only by women in New York City. In 1857, after she had been joined by her sister, also a doctor, this institution became the New York Infirmary for Indigent Women and Children.

The Desperate Need for Reform

By the mid-19th century the urban centers of the United States, swollen with immigrants, had become little better than pestholes. The newcomers, pressed together in fetid slums, were prey to nearly every ill known to man. In many cities, New York among them, human wastes were routinely dumped from slop buckets onto the streets. Pedestrians ventured forth at their peril. Small wonder that malaria, yellow fever, and most of all tuberculosis swept these centers with plaguelike devastation. The cities of America had the dubious distinction of having the highest death rates of any in the Western World. Only slowly were the conditions that bred epidemics ameliorated.

Anesthesia
Surgery Without Pain

Most American contributions to the world's growing body of medical knowledge in the early 19th century were relatively minor. But in the 1840's, thanks to several American practitioners, one of mankind's age-old dreams—painless surgery—became a reality. For years physicians had known of the soporific qualities of ether (and of chloroform), but not until 1842 did anyone reach the conclusion that so powerful a sleep inducer might actually render a patient insensitive to pain.

The discoverer of the surgical uses to which ether might be put was a young Georgia physician, Crawford Long, who in January 1842 entertained several of his friends by having them breathe the gas in doses strong enough to numb them to pain but not so strong as to render them unconscious. The intoxicated revelers, unable to control their movements, bumped into furniture, fell over their own feet, and bruised themselves without making the slightest complaint.

After musing over this incident, the 27-year-old Long decided to experiment with ether in surgical cases and, in May 1842, administered the gas to a patient on whom he then operated to remove a small neck tumor. The results were as Long had hoped; the patient awoke without any memory of pain, and over the ensuing years Dr. Long used ether in many surgical procedures. Unfortunately, he neglected to publish his findings until December 1849. By then, a Boston dentist, William T. G. Morton, had publicly demonstrated the use of ether as the world's first truly effective surgical anesthetic. Soon after Morton's demonstration, Oliver Wendell Holmes suggested "anesthesia" as the name of the new medical procedure.

Distinguished physicians *at Massachusetts General Hospital watch William T. G. Morton anesthetize a patient by having him inhale ether. This public demonstration of ether's conquest of pain, on October 16, 1846, led one surgeon to declare: "Gentlemen, this is no humbug!"*

The use of ether was opposed by standpat surgeons who believed pain was a necessary evil, but in time it was recognized as a major advance in the practice of surgery. Later, however, surgeons noted that ether had unpleasant aftereffects and, in some cases, could be dangerous to a patient's health. For many operations, administering an anesthetic to deaden a specific portion of the body would be preferable to rendering the patient unconscious. In 1884 the great American surgeon William Stewart Halsted devised a method of injecting solutions of cocaine into nerve endings to anesthetize portions of the body, and a few years later Dr. James L. Corning used a similar substance to develop the first successful spinal anesthesia.

During the years that followed, dozens of substances—both natural and synthetic—were found useful as general and local anesthetics, and many of these were discovered by Americans. Often, however, the dangers inherent in these drugs were not recognized. Heroin, for example, was at first greeted as a safe, nonaddictive opiate, and for many years the delicate task of administering anesthetics was often left to interns or even medical students. Fortunately, such practices have stopped. Anesthesiology is now one of the most important specializations in American medical practice.

Most cities did not establish departments of health and sanitation until the early 20th century.

Farm and small-town dwellers were in most cases only marginally better off. Most of their physicians were products of the apprenticeship system of on-the-job training under established practitioners. By the last quarter of the 19th century America had plenty of institutions that conferred medical degrees, but few required more than 2 years of study, and many granted diplomas for nothing more than a fee. As late as the 1890's theological seminaries still received 15 times as much philanthropic aid as medical schools. Medical research was also sadly neglected. A physician who wished to pursue advanced studies had little choice but to go to Europe, particularly to Germany and France, where the basis of scientific medicine was then being laid.

Johns Hopkins Leads the Way

But in 1889 all this began to change. In that year the Johns Hopkins Hospital was founded in Baltimore, Maryland, and 4 years later the Johns Hopkins School of Medicine opened. Richly endowed by a Baltimore financier, Johns Hopkins attracted the best medical minds in America to its faculty, including pathologist William Henry Welch, surgeon William Stewart Halsted, Canadian-born internist William Osler, and Howard A. Kelly, professor of gynecology and obstetrics. Most of the Johns Hopkins faculty members had benefited from advanced training in Europe and had become committed to laboratory research. They imbued their students with the same commitment, as well as with a belief in the need for clinical training. Within a decade of its opening, Johns Hopkins had set standards of training for every other American medical school, had established the curriculum which, with minor changes, most medical schools followed, and had sent out hundreds of young doctors whose expertise became invaluable in the establishment of other first-rate medical schools.

The swift evolution of modern American medicine was given further impetus by a highly influential book, Abraham Flexner's 1910 study, *Medical Education in the United States and Canada.* Flexner's work threw light on the disgraceful conditions that existed in scores of American medical colleges, and amidst the public clamor that followed the book's publication, some 60 of these institutions closed their doors while others hurriedly reformed their academic practices.

It was during this age of medical reform that another institution began to play an ever-increasing role: the federally operated and financed U.S. Public Health Service. Chartered in 1798 as the Marine Hospital Service, its function limited to the care of sick and disabled merchant seamen, the service began to broaden its activities during the mid-19th century, when it was charged with examining prospective immigrants to determine if they were carriers of infectious diseases. Following a demonstration by Dr. Walter Reed of the U.S. Army that the mosquito *Aedes aegypti* was the carrier of yellow fever in Cuba, Public Health Service physicians and technicians played a primary part in tracking down the sources of epidemics

Physicians *gather on May 7, 1847, in the Academy of Natural Sciences of Philadelphia to form the American Medical Association. The AMA is one of America's most powerful professional associations—a watchdog over the quality of medical practice and a staunch defender of its members' social and financial interests. Its not too successful early campaigns to reform the Nation's medical schools and to insure uniformly high standards of professional competence and ethics began to pay off in the 1900's and now are largely responsible for establishing U.S. preeminence in medicine. Operating through county medical societies, the AMA still plays a primary role in maintaining and upgrading medical standards. Politically and economically, the AMA has been an active conservative force in opposing what it calls socialized medicine.*

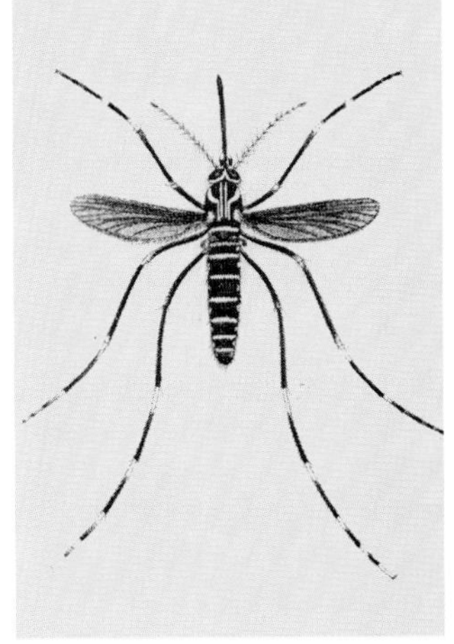

Victory Over Yellow Fever:
The End of a Scourge

Of all mankind's ailments, yellow fever was long among the most dreaded and the least understood. Epidemics in American cities killed thousands periodically from colonial times until 1905. During the middle and late 1800's, several investigators suggested that mosquitoes carried the disease, but these leads were not pursued. Finally, in 1900, a U.S. Army doctor, Walter Reed, adopted the theories of Cuban physician Carlos Juan Finlay and proved that the *Aedes aegypti* mosquito was the villain. Reed's colleague, Maj. William C. Gorgas, then undertook a massive campaign to wipe out the mosquito in Cuba by destroying its breeding grounds. So well did Gorgas succeed that in 1904 he was sent to Panama, where raging yellow fever epidemics had thwarted earlier efforts to build a canal. Overriding the protests of cost-conscious engineers, Gorgas went all out in a drive to rid Panama of *Aedes aegypti* by imposing strict sanitation measures and rooting out the mosquito's breeding places. Gorgas won his battle, and the Panama Canal was built. Even more important, his methods ended the yellow fever scourge in the United States and showed the way to fight the disease throughout the world.

Dr. Walter Reed *(below) examines Pvt. John Kissinger, the first volunteer patient in the program that proved that the* Aedes aegypti *mosquito (above) spread yellow fever. Thereafter, men were able to dig the Panama Canal (above left) without danger of contracting the disease.*

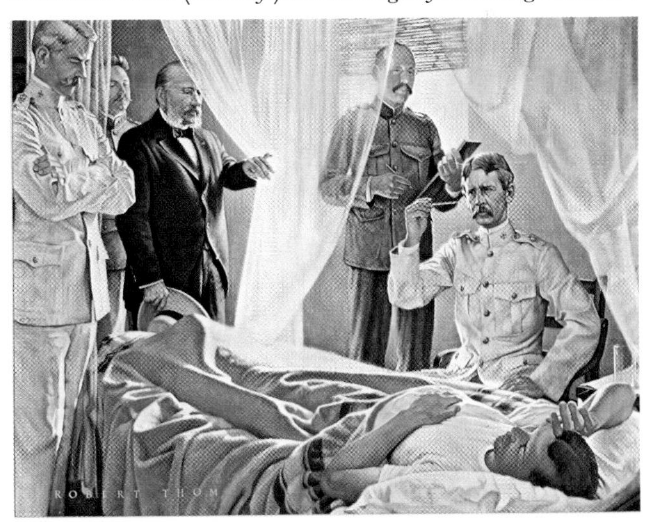

of yellow fever, typhoid, typhus, and infectious hepatitis in the United States. Today the 47,000 employees of the service, now a division of the Department of Health, Education, and Welfare, concentrate to a large extent on establishing doctors and medical facilities in parts of the country that do not have them. HEW and the National Institutes of Health have become increasingly active in the fields of preventive medicine and research.

Medicine's Quest for Causes and Cures

The Public Health Service, however, had a profound effect on the initiation and course of medical research in the past. In the 1890's the service began a search for the causes and cures of innumerable ailments, gradually increasing its staff over the decades. By the mid-1960's it was spending more than $1.2 billion annually for medical research, both in its own facilities and, through grants, in scientific foundations and medical schools. In fact some 40 percent of all medical research carried on in the United States was financed through the Public Health Service. Among the medical triumphs that the service can claim are vaccines against Rocky Mountain spotted fever and German measles—the latter a particularly dangerous disease when contracted by a pregnant woman, as it can cause deformity in her unborn child. Pellagra, once a widespread killer causing more than 10,000 deaths annually, is now practically unknown in the United States, thanks largely to the pioneering work of Dr. Joseph Goldberger of the Public Health Service and to later Public Health Service researchers who in 1938 discovered that it was caused by a niacin deficiency in the diet. Since then niacin has been routinely added to bread, cornmeal, and rice, eliminating the threat to those whose diets consist largely of such foods.

Major contributions to medical discovery have been made by privately endowed research centers such as the Rockefeller Institute for Medical Research (now the Rockefeller University), the Menninger Foundation for psychiatric research, and the Sloan-Kettering Institute for Cancer Research. In such institutions research physicians, biologists, biochemists, pharmacologists, physiologists, and other scientists and technicians work with all the complex tools of modern-day medical science to synthesize new drugs, discover new vaccines, devise new surgical procedures, and develop new diagnostic equipment. Research has been broadened by foundation grants to medical schools in a number of universities.

Medical Progress for the World

By the end of the 1960's American medicine was generally recognized as the most advanced in the world. The Nation's population of 208 million was being served by more than 322,000 physicians and approximately 7,000 hospitals with more than 1.5 million beds. Thanks to the ready availability of drugs and vaccines and a steady improvement in nutrition and sanitation, the life expectancy of the average American at birth had been increased from 47 years in 1900 to 71.3 years by 1973—one of the highest in the world. Diseases that were often fatal as recently as the 1930's are now routinely and successfully treated with such drugs as penicillin and streptomycin.

Some Highlights of Surgery's Progress

The Men Who Led the Way

From 1809, when Kentucky physician Ephraim McDowell made medical history by excising a patient's cancerous ovarian tumor, to the present day, when open heart surgery and kidney transplants are almost routine, American surgeons have been in the vanguard of medical progress. The list of their contributions is nearly endless, and though many of their names are unknown to the general public, millions of people the world over are in their debt.

Among America's earliest surgical pioneers was South Carolina-born James Marion Sims, the founder of modern gynecological practice in the United States. In the 1840's Sims devised surgical techniques for repairing uterine damages previously thought incurable. Through lectures and publications, he taught his procedures to scores of fellow physicians in the United States and abroad and gave new meaning to the role of the surgeon as a teacher. Another who combined teaching with surgery, and was unsurpassed in both fields, was Dr. William Stewart Halsted, a member of the original faculty of Johns Hopkins School of Medicine. In the late 19th century Halsted helped make Johns Hopkins one of the world's leading training grounds for physicians. He is famous for developing the technique of local anesthesia with cocaine and for his pioneering work in operations on breast cancers and hernias, but medicine owes as much to him for his emphasis on asepsis in surgery. He was the first surgeon to use rubber gloves, a seemingly small innovation that helped reduce post-operative infections to a minimum.

Among the hundreds whom Halsted helped to train was Harvey W. Cushing, the father of modern neurological surgery. Early in the 1900's Cushing, a revered teacher, devised revolutionary procedures for removing brain tumors and operating on the nervous and endocrine systems.

America's first Nobel Prize in physiology or medicine was won by the French-born surgeon and experimental biologist Alexis Carrel, who was honored in 1912. Dr. Carrel's pioneer work with transplants and implants provided the basis for today's advanced surgical techniques in this area. Electronic pacemakers and mechanical heart valves now keep thousands of victims of heart disease alive and active; healthy kidneys can replace those of sufferers from kidney failure with a high percentage of success, thanks to surgeons' skills.

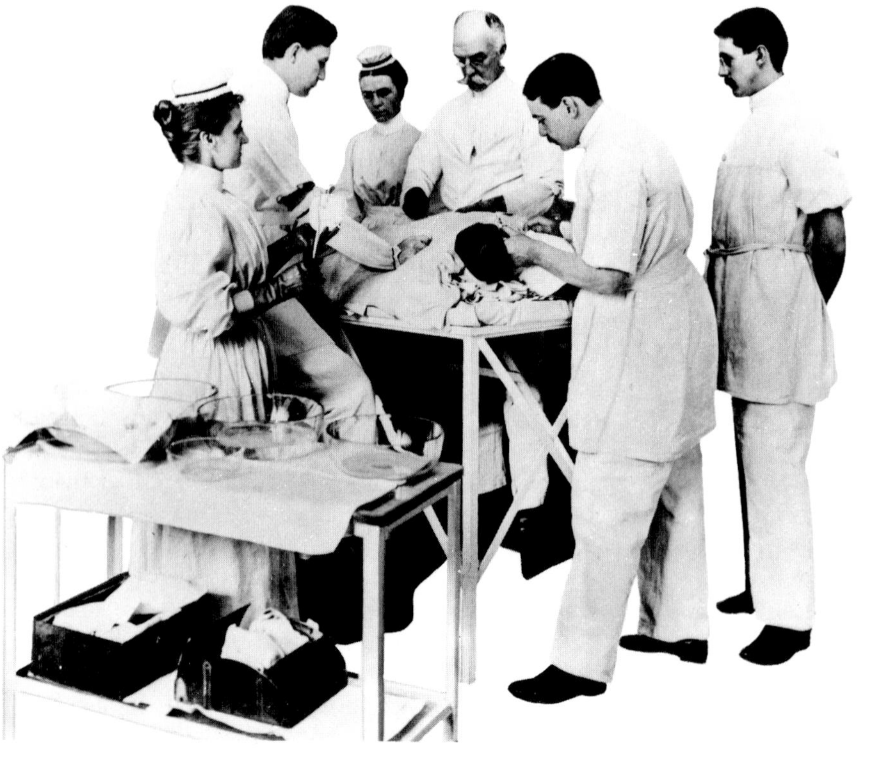

Surrounded by aides, *Dr. Charles McBurney operates at a New York hospital in 1901. His discovery of a pressure point on the abdomen (now called McBurney's point) greatly simplified the diagnosis of appendicitis, while the innovative "McBurney's incision" permitted surgeons to remove the appendix without destroying abdominal muscles.*

A puzzled *Dr. Joseph Goldberger of the U.S. Public Health Service watches youngsters eat at a Mississippi orphanage in 1914 as he seeks the answers to why pellagra singles out children between 3 and 12 years old as its victims. He later became convinced that the illness was caused not by infection or poisonous food, as was commonly thought, but by a nutritional deficiency in the diets of many poor children. After long experimentation Goldberger found that fresh milk, eggs, and meat added to their fare protected the children against pellagra. For almost a decade Goldberger had to battle public apathy and disbelief, but he lived to see the near extinction of the dreaded ailment. His work pointed the way to fruitful studies in nutrition and the importance of vitamins.*

The story of penicillin reflects the extent to which the world's medical establishment has become dependent on American resources. Although this antibiotic was discovered by an Englishman, Sir Alexander Fleming, Britain during World War II was unable to produce it in significant quantities. During the early 1940's three American pharmaceutical companies solved the problem of supplying penicillin in the vast amounts needed. The drug saved thousands of wartime wounded who might otherwise have died of bacterial infections, and it has been a major curative ever since.

During World War II another lifesaving drug, streptomycin, was discovered by Rutgers University's Dr. Selman A. Waksman. The first drug to prove effective in the treatment of tuberculosis, streptomycin was the father of a whole family of antibiotics used to combat a variety of infections. Other drugs for which Americans may claim credit are diphenylhydantoin, to ease epileptic seizures; ephedrine, to alleviate asthma; gramicidin D, to treat ear and throat infections; nitrogen mustards, effective against some cancerous tumors; quinacrine, to combat malaria; and steroids, to relieve the symptoms of such ailments as rheumatoid arthritis. Americans have also taken the leadership in the search for relatively safe methods of preventing conception. Drs. Gregory Pincus and Edward A. Doisy have made outstanding contributions in this field.

Like pharmacology, surgery has made unprecedented advances during the last several decades. In the early years of this century, the Rockefeller Institute's Alexis Carrel developed techniques for suturing the tiniest blood vessels and arteries, and neurosurgeon Harvey W. Cushing made numerous innovations in brain surgery. Their work, and that of today's giants of open-heart surgery—such men as Michael de Bakey, Denton Cooley, and Norman Shumway—have made American operating-room techniques the most sophisticated in the world. Such once radical procedures as the installation of electronic pacemakers and artificial heart valves and the transplantation of kidneys are now routine. Tens of thousands of people who a few decades ago would have died of brain tumors and other cancers, heart diseases, or kidney malfunctions are now alive and active thanks to methods and devices pioneered by American surgeons and technicians.

Dr. Albert Sabin, who developed the oral polio vaccine, has reported the discovery of two common viruses that seem to cause a variety of cancers in humans. This offers hope that a vaccine might be developed to control this scourge, which, after heart disease, is the leading cause of death in Americans.

Another important contribution has been the concept of specialists working as a team in the operating room. The cooperative approach, a particularly American inclination in many fields, is also practiced in other aspects of medicine. A most successful example is the Menninger Foundation in Topeka, Kansas. First established as a clinic in 1919 by Dr. Charles F. Menninger and his son Karl, it soon became a center for the sharing of information on mental illness and psychiatry. The practice of psychiatry has developed rapidly in recent decades and the onus once attached to this treatment has largely disappeared. In fact, in some circles, analysis has become fashionable.

Nobel Prize Winners in Physiology or Medicine

Some Prizes Were Shared. These Are the Recipients in America

When Swedish chemist and scientist Alfred Bernhard Nobel died in 1896, he left a fund of more than $8 million and specified that the interest be used for prizes in the fields of peace, science, and literature, the areas in which he was most interested. These were divided into five categories. A sixth was added for economics in 1968. Winners receive a gold medal, a citation, and a sum of money that has grown with the years, amounting to more than $100,000 each in 1974.

The first Nobel Prizes were given in 1901. Theodore Roosevelt, the first American to win, was awarded the Peace Prize in 1906. Since then the United States has won or shared in more prizes than any other country, mostly in the field of science. Many of the American winners were foreign-born, and in 12 of the years listed below the American winners shared the prize with distinguished colleagues from other countries. (For details on American winners in literature, see page 425.)

1912, Alexis Carrel. *"In recognition of his work on vascular suture and the transplantation of blood vessels and organs."* An accomplished surgeon, Dr. Carrel gained wide recognition in the 1930's as the coinventor, with Charles A. Lindbergh, of a mechanical heart. His award-winning work cleared the way for such presently commonplace procedures as blue baby operations.

1922, Otto F. Meyerhof. *"For his discovery of the fixed relationship between the consumption of oxygen and the metabolism of lactic acid in muscle."* A pioneer of modern biochemistry and the teacher of several Nobel laureates, Dr. Meyerhof demonstrated the nature of the chemical processes within working muscles.

1930, Karl Landsteiner. *"For his discovery of human blood groups."* Dr. Landsteiner, a distinguished physician, immunologist, bacteriologist, and chemist, discovered that human bloods differ and classified them into four basic groups. This knowledge removed most of the risk that had previously accompanied blood transfusion.

1933, Thomas Hunt Morgan. *"For his discoveries concerning the role played by the chromosome in heredity."* Dr. Morgan's study of the fruit fly (*Drosophila melanogaster*), a classic of modern experimental science, demonstrated that genes transmit hereditary elements from parents to offspring.

1934, George H. Whipple, George R. Minot, and William P. Murphy. *"For their discoveries concerning liver therapy in cases of anemia."* In the war on noninfectious diseases, the development of an effective treatment for pernicious anemia ranks second in its time only to the discovery of insulin in terms of human resources saved. Dr. Whipple's work on bile metabolism showed that adding liver to the diet significantly increased the regeneration of red blood corpuscles. Drs. Minot and Murphy demonstrated the rapid, lasting effect of liver in treating pernicious anemia.

1936, Otto Loewi. *"For discoveries relating to the chemical transmission of nerve impulses."* Dr. Loewi proved that the communication of commands to the muscles was triggered by a chemical substance released into the blood stream.

1937, Albert Szent-Györgyi. *"For his discoveries in connection with the biological combustion processes, with special reference to vitamin C and the catalysis of fumaric acid."* Dr. Szent-Györgyi's prize-winning research began as a study of the function of the adrenal glands but led to the identification of ascorbic acid (vitamin C).

1943, Edward A. Doisy. *"For his discovery of the chemical nature of vitamin K."* Vitamin K, isolated by a team working under Dr. Doisy at the St. Louis University School of Medicine, is vital to the proper clotting of the blood.

1944, Joseph Erlanger and Herbert S. Gasser. *"For their discoveries relating to the highly differentiated functions of single nerve fibers."* Dr. Erlanger and Dr. Gasser, one of his former students, adapted a cathode-ray oscillograph to record photographically the minute changes in potential that accompany the sending of messages from the brain to the muscles. Their findings—that different nerve fibers have their own conducting rates—have led to a clearer understanding of the peripheral and central nervous systems.

1946, Hermann J. Muller. *"For the discovery of the production of mutations by means of X-ray irradiation."* Dr. Muller's belief that "the great majority of mutations being undesirable . . . their further random production in ourselves should . . . be rigorously avoided" led to concern over exposure to X-rays and radioactive fallout from nuclear bomb tests.

1947, Carl F. Cori and Gerty T. Cori. *"For their discovery of the course of the catalytic conversion of glycogen."* The third husband-wife team to win a Nobel prize, the Coris worked chiefly on the catalytic and hormonal metabolism of carbohydrates, with special attention to breaking down into steps the detailed chemistry of the reactions involved in the function of muscle tissue.

Nobel medallions *show Alfred Nobel's likeness and birth and death dates on one side*

1950, Edward C. Kendall and Philip S. Hench. *"For their discoveries relating to the hormones of the adrenal cortex, their structure and biological effects."* Dr. Kendall's work with extracts of the adrenal cortex led in 1935 to the separation of compounds that he named A, B, E, and F, and which found limited clinical use in animals. Meanwhile, Kendall's colleague, Dr. Hench, who was head of the section for rheumatic disease at the Mayo Clinic, had begun inquiring into why pregnancy or the presence of jaundice tended to abate or even suspend the acute pain of rheumatoid arthritis. Their joint work demonstrated that the specific agent responsible was in fact Kendall's Compound E, since named "cortisone."

1951, Max Theiler. *"For his discoveries concerning yellow fever and how to combat it."* Dr. Theiler's development of the 17D attenuated vaccine finally relegated the ancient scourge of yellow fever to the level of a relatively minor disease.

1952, Selman A. Waksman. *"For his discovery of streptomycin, the first antibiotic effective against tuberculosis."* Although the award singled out one of his achievements, Dr. Waksman's lifelong work on microorganisms in the soil, carried on at Rutgers, created a new branch of microbiology and led to the identification of many other antibiotics, a word he coined.

1953, Fritz A. Lipmann. *"For his discovery of coenzyme A and its importance for intermediary metabolism."* Dr. Lipmann's work at Massachusetts General Hospital in Boston did much to explain the processes whereby carbohydrates, fats, and most of the protein

d a symbol of the field in which the award was *en (medicine or physiology) on the other.*

molecules are broken down by body chemistry to provide energy or change to fat.

1954, John F. Enders, Frederick C. Robbins, and Thomas H. Weller. *"For their discovery of the ability of poliomyelitis viruses to grow in cultures of various types of tissues."* By the late 1940's the strains of virus that cause polio had been identified, but the inability to grow them in the required quantities had frustrated attempts to prepare an immunizing agent. At the Children's Medical Center in Boston Dr. Enders and his colleagues devised a method that, as Dr. Jonas E. Salk noted, "was directly responsible for the development of a vaccine against infantile paralysis."

1956, André F. Cournand and Dickinson W. Richards, Jr. *"For their discoveries concerning heart catheterization and pathological changes in the circulatory system."* Drs. Cournand and Richards collaborated in adapting the technique of passing a tube into the heart by way of a vein to study the changes that take place in the circulatory system as a result of blood loss and burns, to examine heart defects, and to analyze pulmonary circulation.

1958, George W. Beadle and Edward L. Tatum. *"For their discovery that genes act by regulating definite chemical events."* **Joshua Lederberg.** *"For his discoveries concerning genetic recombination and the organization of the genetic material of bacteria."* It had long been suspected that the metabolic activity of living cells was related to genetic makeup. Drs. Beadle and Tatum, both of Stanford University, provided the needed proof by producing nutritionally deficient strains of organisms and showing that each deficiency was caused by the failure of a gene to form a necessary compound. Lederberg showed that the genetic basis of biochemical reactions extended to bacteria.

1959, Severo Ochoa and Arthur Kornberg. *"For their discovery of the mechanisms in the biological synthesis of ribonucleic acid [RNA] and deoxyribonucleic acid [DNA]."* The contribution of Drs. Ochoa and Kornberg was to identify the enzymes that are necessary for the synthesis of RNA and DNA, thereby permitting their laboratory production from easily obtainable smaller molecules.

1961, Georg von Békésy. *"For his discoveries of the physical mechanism of stimulation within the cochlea."* The first physicist to win a Nobel award in medicine. Dr. von Békésy, during his research on hearing, constructed a mechanical model that definitively established the physiology of the cochlea, the spiral tube in the inner ear.

1962, James D. Watson. *"For . . . discoveries concerning the molecular structure of nucleic acids and its significance for information transfer in living material."* The determination that deoxyribonucleic acid has the molecular form of an intertwined spiral (double helix) has been considered the greatest single discovery in molecular biology. Dr. Watson helped to develop a model in 1953.

1964, Konrad E. Bloch. *"For . . . discoveries concerning the mechanism and regulation of the cholesterol and fatty acid metabolism."* Cholesterol, suspect in circulatory ailments, is ubiquitous in animal tissues. Dr. Bloch showed how its molecules are built up.

1966, Charles B. Huggins. *"For his discoveries concerning hormonal treatment of prostatic cancer."* **Francis Peyton Rous.** *"For his discovery of tumor-inducing viruses."* Dr. Huggins' demonstration that injections of an artificial female sex hormone could be used to control cancer of the prostate gland was the first evidence that cancer could be controlled by chemical means. Dr. Rous showed that a tumor from one chicken could be used to cause malignant growth in another.

1967, Haldan K. Hartline and George Wald. *"For their discoveries concerning the primary physiological and chemical visual processes in the eye."* Dr. Wald showed that light created an image by activating specialized photoreceptive cells. Hartline was able, by recording the electric impulses generated from nerve cells and fibers, to demonstrate how the eye passes this image to the brain.

1968, Robert W. Holley, H. Gobind Khorona, and Marshall W. Nirenberg. *"For their interpretation of the genetic code and its function in protein synthesis."* The genetic code, which these laureates independently helped to decipher, is the name given to the biochemical process whereby information contained in body cells is translated into tangible physical traits. In simple terms, information stored within the cell's deoxyribonucleic acid determines the manufacture of certain enzymes required for reactions that in turn result in such individual characteristics as eye pigmentation or physical defects. Implicit in the discovery is the possibility of interfering with the code to the extent of curing or avoiding certain diseases or of modifying the effects of heredity.

1969, Max Delbrück, Alfred D. Hershey, and Salvador E. Luria. *"For their discoveries concerning the replication mechanism and the genetic structure of viruses."* In three decades of investigation, much of it at the Carnegie Institution's laboratory in Cold Spring Harbor, New York, Drs. Delbrück, Hershey, and Luria systematically laid the foundation of modern molecular biology. They developed the first effective method of purifying viruses and used it to demonstrate how a virus invades a living cell and reproduces itself in that environment.

1970, Julius Axelrod. *"For . . . discoveries concerning the humoral transmitters in the nerve terminals and the mechanism for their storage, release and inactivation."* The subject of the prize—the chemistry of nerve impulse transmission—has important implications for such phenomena as schizophrenia, mental depression, hypertension, sleep, and the instant summoning of energy under conditions of stress.

1971, Earl W. Sutherland, Jr. *"For his discoveries concerning the mechanisms of the action of hormones."* Working at the Vanderbilt University School of Medicine, Nashville, Tennessee, Sutherland discovered and identified cyclic adenosine 3′,5′-monophosphate (cyclic AMP), a substance apparently involved in the control and regulation of the metabolic activities of every cell.

1972, Gerald M. Edelman. *"For . . . discoveries concerning the chemical structure of antibodies."* Dr. Edelman deciphered the structure of the complex agents that defend the body against infection. The publication of his work led to renewed interest in immunology.

1974, Albert Claude and George Emil Palade. *"For their discoveries concerning the structural and functional organization of the cell."* Long associated with Rockefeller Institute (now Rockefeller University) in New York City, Claude was the first person to penetrate the subworld of the living cell by means of the electron microscope. His findings and those of Dr. Palade, who identified many of the cell's essential components, have provided a new approach to the control of arthritis and other degenerative diseases.

Impersonality, Rising Costs, and Other Problems
As in so many other fields of human endeavor, however, every advance in U.S. medicine has generated new problems and challenges. One such is the impersonality of modern practice. In earlier times the family physician was a supposed sage and a real friend: a tower of strength and kindly wisdom who appeared at one's bedside to deliver a baby, reduce a fever, or set a broken leg. With the help of the contents of his little black bag, he diagnosed one's ills, offered a comforting word, and prescribed a remedy. This familiar paragon, the general practitioner, has all but disappeared in America. In his place are a bewildering array of specialists: Internists, ophthalmologists, neurologists, psychiatrists, radiologists, allergists, dermatologists, cardiologists, surgeons of many kinds, and anesthesiologists. A person calling on a doctor, complaining of weakness or dizziness, will see four or five specialists on his way to a diagnosis. If the problem sounds serious or critical, rarely does the physician respond with a visit to the patient's home. Instead, he orders the patient taken immediately to a hospital where complete, up-to-date facilities and personnel are available.

This new way of conducting medicine has on the whole been beneficial, but the average American misses the personal touch that meant so much in the old days. Besides, the modern medical machine seems to have an insatiable appetite for money. A patient must pay for hospital rooms that may cost more than $100 a day and private nurses who may charge even more. In addition, surgical, medical, diagnostic, and therapeutic fees pile sky-high. To pay for all this, a family with one desperately ill member may have to mortgage its future for years to come. Malpractice suits against hospitals and physicians are another factor in rising costs. These have increased in the last few years, and so has the price of the insurance against them. Doctors have raised their fees commensurately and have organized protest work slowdowns to draw attention to them. In order to further protect themselves, doctors often insist on extra tests and opinions from two or three colleagues before going ahead with operations. These extra tests and the fees of the consultants add to the cost of being ill.

And so the problem of providing adequate medical care for every American has become a matter of national concern. Privately financed plans such as Blue Cross and Blue Shield have provided some defense against the high cost of moderate afflictions, and major-medical insurance programs have eased the financial burden of catastrophic illness for those who can afford the premiums or who work for companies or institutions enrolled in a group plan. Since 1965 the Government-financed programs of Medicare and Medicaid have relieved the elderly and the poor of many of the financial burdens imposed by ill health. But for many Americans, serious illness still brings worrisome financial problems, so much so that many doctors and most laymen now support some form of national health insurance.

A familiar scene *in early-19th-century rural America was the country physician making his rounds on horseback, his pockets filled with patent medicines, each of them a cure-all for a host of diseases and ailments. Here a practitioner prescribes for an anxious patient.*

Medicine faces new tests in other spheres as well. Emphysema, a slowly debilitating lung ailment believed to be caused by air pollution and cigarette smoking, was virtually unknown a quarter of a century ago; now it affects some 10 million Americans. Lung cancer, once rare, has become a major threat. Prosperity and soft living have weakened the health of many Americans. Sedentary occupations, fatty foods, cigarette smoking, and emotional stress have all been identified as causes of a soaring rate of heart disease; atherosclerosis (a fatty degeneration of the arteries) alone accounts for more than 40 percent of all deaths in the Nation. Coronary thrombosis, a leading cause of death today, was first described as recently as 1912 by Dr. James B. Herrick.

But as new problems arise, progress continues. At the beginning of this century one American baby in five died before its first birthday, but today that has been reduced to one in 40. As late as 1960 hundreds of children born with a biochemical disease called phenylketonuria (PKU) inevitably suffered severe brain damage, resulting in seizures, neurological disorders, and a short lifespan. In 1961 Dr. Robert Guthrie, an American researcher, devised a test to detect the ailment soon after birth, and a special diet now enables victims to develop normally and lead full lives. Only three decades ago infantile paralysis, or polio, was a national scourge, killing hundreds each year and crippling thousands. Today, thanks to vaccines developed in the 1950's by Jonas E. Salk and Albert Sabin, the disease has been all but eradicated. America has led the world in the rehabilitation of the disabled and the aged. With such achievements to build upon, there is hope that the guardians of the Nation's health will be able to meet successfully the challenges of the future.

Yankee Ingenuity
Keeping the Body Going

From the time of the first itinerant Yankee tinkers to the technicians who built a dune buggy to traverse the surface of the Moon, Americans have been exceptionally adept at solving mechanical problems. The human body has its mechanical aspects too, and knowledgeable American doctors and biomedical engineers have found ingenious ways in which to repair and replace worn and faulty parts.

The drawing shows some of the most dramatic innovations, but there are a number of other artificial (prosthetic) devices, artificial organs, and replacement parts that can extend useful and satisfying life. Even a complete artificial heart is a possibility.

Silicone is proving to be a boon. Researchers have found that it can be implanted or grafted in sacs in the body without ill effects. It is used for cosmetic purposes by plastic surgeons for breast implants, artificial ears, and the like. The artificial ears are done so artfully by Dr. Thomas Cronin of the Baylor College of Medicine in Houston, Texas, that they are hardly differentiated from the real thing.

Polyethelene and stainless steel are also proving to be at home in the human body. A technique developed in England and widely practiced here is the construction of hip joints with a stainless steel ball in a polyethelene socket. Other plastics too, including Dacron, Teflon, and epoxy, are used in various parts of the body. Successful artificial joints are also available for the shoulder, elbow, wrist, finger, ankle, and toe.

The artificial kidney pioneered by Dr. Willem Kolff, director of the Institute for Biomedical Engineering, University of Utah Medical Center, Salt Lake City, has saved thousands of lives. The dialysis machine literally duplicates the function of the kidney. It is connected to an artery in the arm, and the blood is circulated through a selective filter, cleansed of waste products, and returned through a vein in the arm.

The urinary sphincter uses a system of silicone-rubber tubing to compensate for bladder dysfunction. It can be implanted in the body and externally controlled. Developmental work was done by Dr. William E. Bradley and Dr. Gerald Timm of the Department of Neurology, University of Minnesota Hospitals in Minneapolis, with Dr. F. Brantley Scott, Department of Surgery, Baylor College of Medicine, Houston, Texas.

Experiments started in 1974 soon showed promising results for treatment of acute respiratory failure. A lung machine is used to circulate blood through a bedside oxygenator and sustain life for several days. This rest period for the respiratory system often proves sufficient for its recuperation.

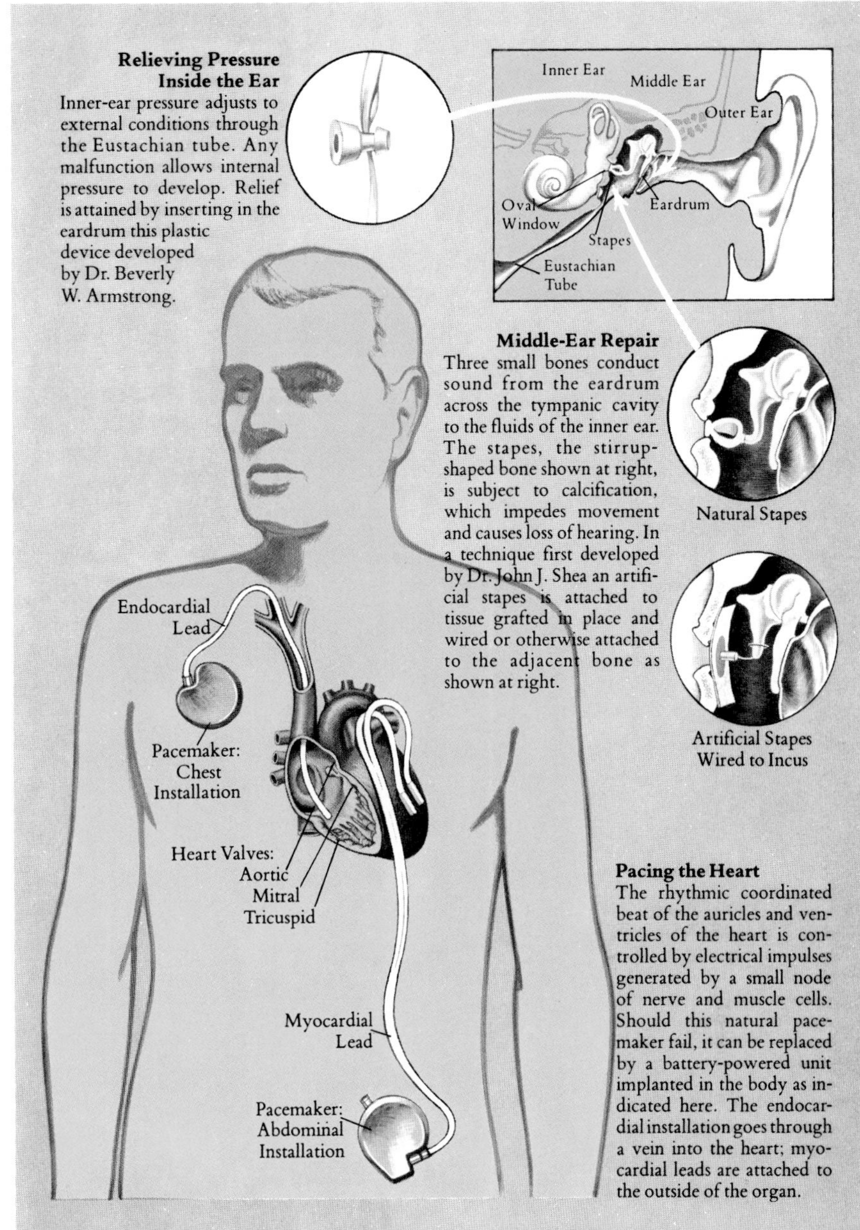

Relieving Pressure Inside the Ear
Inner-ear pressure adjusts to external conditions through the Eustachian tube. Any malfunction allows internal pressure to develop. Relief is attained by inserting in the eardrum this plastic device developed by Dr. Beverly W. Armstrong.

Middle-Ear Repair
Three small bones conduct sound from the eardrum across the tympanic cavity to the fluids of the inner ear. The stapes, the stirrup-shaped bone shown at right, is subject to calcification, which impedes movement and causes loss of hearing. In a technique first developed by Dr. John J. Shea an artificial stapes is attached to tissue grafted in place and wired or otherwise attached to the adjacent bone as shown at right.

Pacing the Heart
The rhythmic coordinated beat of the auricles and ventricles of the heart is controlled by electrical impulses generated by a small node of nerve and muscle cells. Should this natural pacemaker fail, it can be replaced by a battery-powered unit implanted in the body as indicated here. The endocardial installation goes through a vein into the heart; myocardial leads are attached to the outside of the organ.

Mechanical Assistance for the Most Vital Organ

The body lives for as long as the heart continues to beat, and some marvelous artifacts have been developed to keep it going. Among the first to make practical use of a mechanical pacemaker were Dr. C. Walton Lillehei and a team of doctors working at the University of Minnesota Medical Center in 1958; and Drs. William M. Chardack and Andrew A. Gage with engineer Wilson Greatbatch working in Buffalo, New York. In 1960 the Buffalo team developed a self-contained completely implantable unit as illustrated above. In this country alone there are more than 100,000 people with implanted pacemakers and some 15,000 operations are performed annually. A minor operation is required to replace the batteries every 2 or 3 years. Improved power sources are expected to extend battery life to 10 to 20 years or longer.

Heart valves are also subject to failure and until 1952, when the first artificial valves were successfully implanted, valvular disorders were

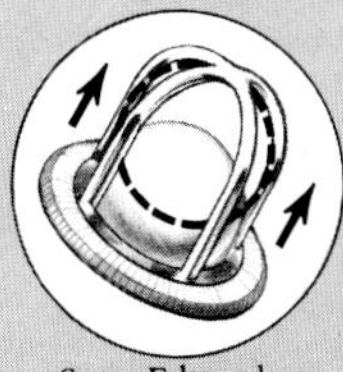
Starr-Edwards Ball Valve

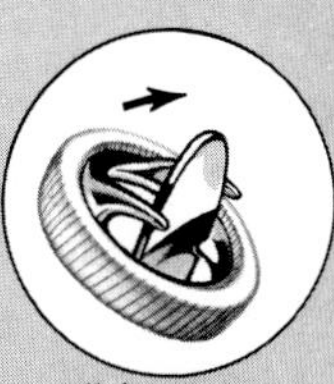
Lillehei-Kaster Pivoting Disc Valve

a major cause of death. The first operation was done by Dr. Charles Hufnagel of Georgetown University School of Medicine, who used a ball valve of his own design. The two most used modern valves are shown here, but valves from the hearts of pigs may prove to be most efficient of all. Many patients are doing well after 20 years with implanted valves. As a measure of the mechanical problem consider that a valve is subject to 100,000 openings and closings every 24 hours. Of the four heart valves the mitral, aortic, and tricuspid are most susceptible to disease. The pulmonary valve seldom needs replacement.

CHAPTER SEVENTEEN

A Scientific Revolution

Occupied as they were with the day-to-day concerns building a new life in a wild land, the earliest colon had limited time for scanning the heavens, recording varieties of birds, plants, and beasts, or pondering the sec of the universe. When they did concentrate on scient speculation and scholarly pursuits, their efforts, more of than not, were directed toward practical goals.

There were, however, a few "natural philosophers," the early-day scientists were called. In the late 160 Americans began making significant contributions to tronomy, a field in which they have excelled ever sin Benjamin Franklin, America's first great man of scient

Long before the first British colonists set foot in America, bands of Spaniards—many of them priests—were trudging across the wilderness collecting data on plants and animals to be used in a natural history of the New World they were preparing. They explored the empire of the King of Spain from Peru to what is now the Southwestern United States. As early as 1532 Gonzalo Fernández de Oviedo y Valdés began his *Historia General y Natural de los Indias Occidentalos,* in effect the first American encyclopedia. This rough survey was almost complete before the English arrived in America.

Only a few of the early English explorers and colonizers were interested in science. One of the foremost of these was Thomas Harriot, a skilled mathematician and astronomer. In 1585 Harriot, then 25 years old, was sent by Sir Walter Raleigh to make a statistical survey of Virginia. The following year he returned to England and published *A Briefe and True Report of the New-found Land of Virginia,* illustrated with drawings of 28 kinds of animals, 86 species of birds, and many plants.

A leading experimental scientist in colonial America was Dr. Lawrence Bohune, a physician, who came to Jamestown in 1610 with Lord De La Warr. Arriving in the midst of a strange epidemic, he started testing local plants and minerals to supplement his dwindling medical supplies. The aromatic sassafras plant proved so effective against colic—one aspect of the prevalent malady—that shiploads of the dried root were sent to England. This find spurred a search for other medicinal plants that continued well into the 19th century.

Science in the Age of Enlightenment

During the latter half of the 17th century and through most of the 18th century, philosophers in England, France, and other European countries were seriously questioning traditional doctrines and values and advocating individualism and the supremacy of reason. The thought of this period, which came to be known as the Age of Enlightenment, emphasized universal human progress and empirical methods of investigation. Scientific societies were formed throughout Europe, including the influential Royal Society of London for Improving Natural Knowledge, chartered by Charles II in 1662. Communication between members of these European societies and colonial correspondents encouraged scientifically inclined men on both sides of the Atlantic to venture farther afield in their quest for knowledge.

One of the first to be affected was John Winthrop the younger, a Governor of Connecticut, who initiated the serious study of astronomy in America. While on a trip to England, Winthrop met the renowned British chemist Robert Boyle and became the first colonial to be elected to the Royal Society. On Boyle's advice, Winthrop took back to Connecticut with him a telescope 3½ feet long. For the next 9 years he spent long nights peering at heavenly bodies until, in 1672, he gave the telescope to Harvard College. There the instrument was put to good use by Thomas Brattle, a Boston merchant. Brattle, who had studied mathematics and astronomy on his own, sent data on eclipses to Edmund Halley and Isaac Newton in England. Newton praised Brattle's work and included some of the New Englander's observations in his famous *Mathematical Principles of Natural Philosophy.*

Correspondence between the European scientific societies and the Colonies also spurred the international exchange of plants, seeds, minerals, and other specimens. This, in turn, resulted in an informal fellowship among naturalists. One member of this fellowship was botanist John Bartram, who in the mid-1700's walked through the Colonies with a pack on his back collecting plant specimens. The famous Swedish naturalist Carolus Linnaeus, one of Bartram's many European correspondents, *nt, advanced both the theoretical and practical aspects 'the study of the planets and stars. Franklin believed that l knowledge would sooner or later prove useful; it was ith this conviction that he founded the American Philo-ophical Society in 1743. After the Revolution U.S. in-ovators became more preoccupied than ever with practical ther than abstract concerns and turned to the develop-ent of an agricultural and industrial economy.*

A nation's wars, for all their waste and tragedy, invari-ly accelerate scientific research and development. The ivil War brought substantial progress in telegraphy and coping with the problems of medicine, surgery, and sanitation. World War I forced America to develop a chemical industry to provide drugs, dyes, and nitrates formerly imported from Europe. During World War II, with massive assistance from the Federal Government, tremendous advances were made in nuclear science, electronics, and medicine. Since then nuclear science, space exploration, and computer technology have made phenomenal gains. Science today, both pure and applied, is our chief weapon in the battle to conserve declining resources, to end pollution, and to find new sources of energy, the struggle that must be won if man is to live in harmony with his environment and indeed if he is to survive on this planet.

Dr. Lawrence Bohune, *the first practicing physician and scientist of record in the Colonies, is depicted in the early 1600's in the environs of Jamestown, Virginia, gathering native roots, soils, and herbs to determine their medicinal properties. In addition to discovering the curative values of sassafras, he reported that the gum of the white poplar was a useful balm to "heale any green wound." He was also interested in discovering which English fruits and plants would grow in Virginia. Bohune spent the winter of 1620–21 in England and was killed in the West Indies in March 1621 when a Spanish force attacked the ship on which he was returning to America.*

called him the greatest contemporary natural botanist. Bartram's work was carried on by his son William. John Ellis, a British naturalist, paid tribute to another 18th-century American naturalist (and physician), Alexander Garden, by naming the gardenia after him. Most of the natural data about the New World were funneled through England, and the grateful Royal Society honored 45 Americans with membership. The importance of New World naturalists is attested by the fact that about one-third of Linnaeus' published descriptions of plant and animal species were contributed by Americans.

Another product of the Age of Enlightenment was Benjamin Franklin, unquestionably colonial America's foremost man of science. His classic experiments on electricity were among the most important theoretical contributions of his time. European contemporaries hailed him as the Newton of electricity. What man knew about the nature of electricity in that day was fragmentary. Franklin unified the available data and presented a simplified theory that has stood the test of time. His roles as statesman and inventor are described elsewhere in this book, but he was also a physicist and meteorologist. He originated, among other things, the concept of atmospheric high and low pressures.

In 1743 Franklin founded the American Philosophical Society, the first significant scientific organization in the Colonies. The purpose of the society was to promote interest in and the spread of "useful knowledge" in the New World. The practitioners of what is now defined as pure science seek knowledge without regard to its immediate applicability; they seek to learn, for example, how the universe originated and how life arose. Applied science, or technology, deals with practical uses of theoretical knowledge. While technological applications

The American Philosophical Society
The Country's First of Its Kind, and Still One of the Best

America's oldest scientific body has what now seems an unlikely name: The American Philosophical Society held at Philadelphia for Promoting Useful Knowledge. After more than two centuries it is still an important force in our scientific life.

Benjamin Franklin founded it in 1743. Earlier, he had organized the Junto, also called the Leather Apron Club. This group of intelligent, curious-minded workingmen met to discuss scientific questions and incidentally lent support to some of Franklin's advanced ideas for city improvement, including the establishment of a fire department, a police force, and a circulating library. Franklin proposed formation of the Philosophical Society when he felt a need for a more scholarly organization. "The first drudgery of settling new colonies is now pretty well over," he wrote, "and there are many in every province in circumstances that set them at ease, and afford leisure to cultivate the finer arts, and improve the common stock of knowledge."

Despite Franklin's optimism, the society languished until 1769, when, through David Rittenhouse's new telescope, it achieved worldwide fame—and permanence—following its observations of the transit of Venus across the Sun. Most of the Republic's founders were early members: George Washington, John Adams, Thomas Jefferson, Alexander Hamilton, and Thomas Paine, as well as such distinguished foreign friends of America as the Marquis de Lafayette, Baron von Steuben, and Tadeusz Kosciuszko. Thomas Jefferson was among the society's early presidents.

Although the society was a private organization, during the first 50 years after independence it performed many of the functions of a national academy of science, a national library and museum, and even an embryonic patent office. Since the mid-1900's its approximately 600 members have concentrated on paleontology, geology, astronomy, and meteorology. As far back as 1789, when it took in Russian Princess Daskhov, president of the Imperial Academy of Sciences of St. Petersburg, the society has admitted women—among them, Maria Mitchell, the astronomer; Elizabeth Cary Agassiz, founder of Radcliffe College; and Marie Curie, codiscoverer of radium. The society pioneered serious study of the history, customs, and languages of American Indians. It also aids research in many fields with grants from its endowment. The society remains one of the Nation's most prestigious scholarly organizations.

Artist Charles Willson Peale, *director of the project to excavate a complete mastodon skeleton and portions of another near Newburgh, New York, recorded the event of 1801. The great wheel that turned the bucket chain to remove seepage water was powered by spectators walking inside like squirrels in a cage. The skeletons, the first mounted fossils exhibited in America, and this painting, "Exhumation of the Mastodon," were displayed in Peale's museum, located until 1802 in the hall of the American Philosophical Society in Philadelphia.*

usually flow from pure science, the reverse is sometimes true, too. The development of thermodynamics, for instance, followed the invention of the steam engine.

Like the other scientists and natural philosophers of the Age of Enlightenment, Franklin believed ardently in the ultimate utility of all knowledge. It was not surprising, then, that the American Philosophical Society could engage simultaneously and with equal enthusiasm in both astronomy and the improvement of agriculture.

Despite the encouragement of the scientific societies, there were not many outstanding scientists in colonial America. A few, however, were born near the end of the Age of Enlightenment and were active just before and after the American Revolution. David Rittenhouse, a Philadelphia instrument maker, mathematician, and astronomer, constructed the first telescope made in the Colonies and used it to track the transit of Venus across the Sun in 1769. From 1791 to 1793 mathematician Andrew Ellicott teamed with Negro scientist Benjamin Banneker to survey the 10 square miles now known as the District of Columbia. Banneker, who had become skillful in astronomy and mathematics largely through his own efforts, published a highly regarded almanac from 1791 until 1802, in which he gave astronomical data, weather forecasts, and other valuable information.

Another scientist born in the Colonies was Benjamin

Thompson, who, after siding with the British in the Revolution, was named Count Rumford by George III and pursued a successful political and scientific career in Europe. His primary discovery concerned the nature of heat, which he showed to be not a substance, as was then believed, but the product of particles in motion.

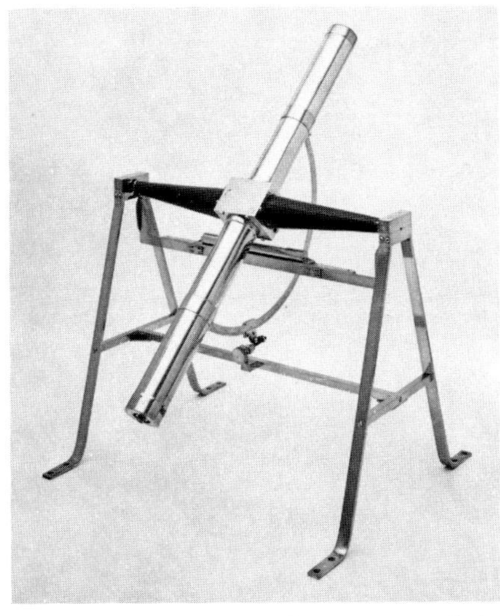

The first American *telescope was made by David Rittenhouse, who improved the focusing mechanism and used the instrument to track Venus across the face of the Sun in 1769.*

Independence Brings Problems

Independence gave American science a setback. Scientific communications with England were almost completely halted during the Revolution, and instruments were all but impossible to obtain. In the new spirit of nationalism, most Americans were reluctant to expand relations with England after the war. Contacts with other countries, such as France, were of limited help to the new Nation's scientists. Franklin, in his diplomatic post in Paris, did try to act as a relay point for communication between scientists of the two countries, but that was an inadequate substitute for direct ties.

Other reasons for the scarcity of scientists were the limited population of the new Nation compared with that of other countries and the even smaller number of students. Just before the Revolution there were fewer than 300 college students and scarcely 50 graduates a year, most of them trained primarily for the ministry. When the faculty at Yale College decided in 1802 to establish a professorship of chemistry and natural history, they picked for the post Benjamin Silliman, a 23-year-old lawyer with little training in science. Silliman protested that he was not qualified for the job, but the college president, Timothy Dwight, replied truthfully: "Neither is anyone else we can think of in this country." Before taking the Yale position, Silliman spent 2 years studying scientific subjects in Philadelphia and went on to a distinguished career in science.

Practicality became something of a fetish in post-Revolutionary America. The concept of elitism, the idea that the rich and the well-born were entitled to pursue such hobbies as pure science, fell into disrepute. The belief that everyone worth his salt must do useful work prevailed as never before. "Democratic nations," wrote the astute young Frenchman Alexis de Tocqueville after journeying across America in 1831–32, "will habitually prefer the useful to the beautiful, and they will require that the beautiful should be useful."

The high quality *of renderings by Louis Agassiz, Swiss geologist and zoologist who came here in 1846, is revealed in this study of variations in American turtle species.*

Soon after the Revolution a distinction began to be made between pure and applied science. "You are not to live in the Sun, nor Moon, nor to ride upon the tails of a comet," college graduates were admonished by the *Columbian Magazine* in 1790. "A *few* astronomers are enough for an age," was the author's opinion.

Nevertheless, the seeds of scientific investigation were planted in America during the early 19th century. John James Audubon, through his meticulously accurate paintings of birds, and Swiss-born Louis Agassiz, through his lectures and significant studies of the classification of animals, did much to further interest in the natural sciences. Asa Gray, an eminent botanist and professor of natural history at Harvard University, was so distinguished a figure that Charles Darwin confided his theory of evolution to the American botanist before it was published. Darwin's *On the Origin of Species* appeared in 1859. Gray became one of Darwin's defenders in the United States and encouraged other American scientists to consider the merits of Darwin's theories on evolution.

American diggings played no small part in furnishing the fossil proof of evolution. Othniel C. Marsh, who held Yale's first chair of paleontology, found fossils of birds with teeth, supporting the view that birds are descended from reptiles. Marsh also dug up fossilized remains of the ancestors of the horse and many of the first-discovered dinosaur skeletons.

American scientists recorded significant advances in other fields. John W. Draper, a chemist interested in applying photography to astronomy, took the first picture of the Moon in 1840; later he photographed solar and stellar spectra. But neither Draper nor his son Henry, who worked with him, could convince many Americans that their work was important.

There were good reasons for this emphasis on the practical. Imbued with a new sense of pride, the Nation was in a hurry to solve its practical problems. The natural philosophers who had thought they could success-

The Smithsonian
A Treasure-Filled Institution

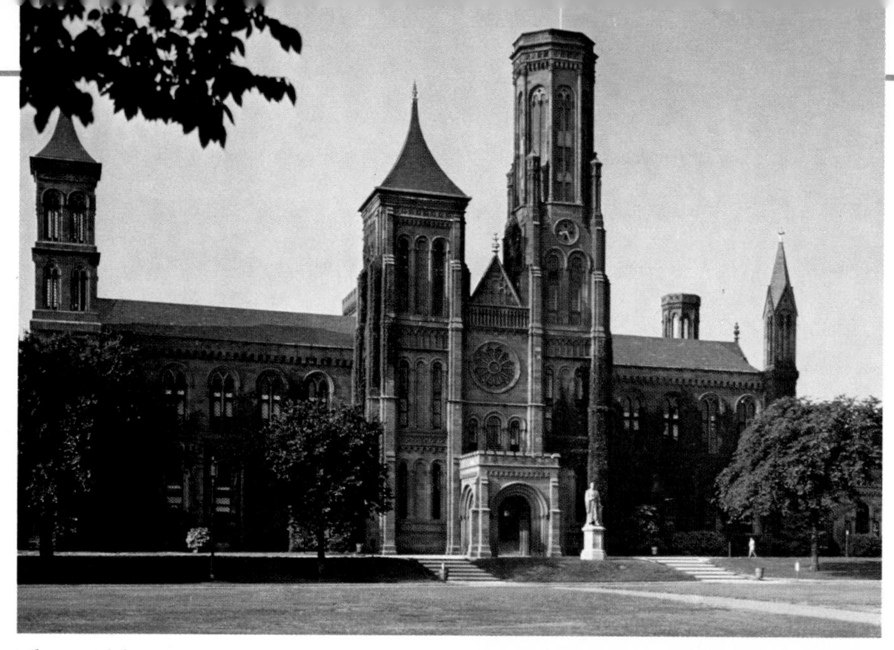

The Smithsonian's *ornate headquarters in Washington was also the home of its first secretary, Joseph Henry (right), who established the institution's dedication to original research, a dedication that continues to this day.*

Every year millions of Americans visit the Nation's Capital, and many of them pass fascinating hours there viewing such historic treasures as the Wright brothers' first airplane, Alexander Graham Bell's prototype telephone, and a wealth of American and foreign art at various museums scattered around the city. Few of these visitors realize that they are guests of the Smithsonian Institution, one of the world's most far-reaching societies of scholars and scientists, with interests in such diverse fields as astrophysics and music, painting and ethnology, drama and zoology. A vast complex of museums and galleries, laboratories and halls of learning, research centers and editorial offices, the Smithsonian Institution, though centered in Washington, also maintains a variety of facilities throughout the Nation and the world. From the Cambridge, Massachusetts, headquarters of its Astrophysical Observatory, for example, a vast network of research stations was established in both North and South America to study solar phenomena. Similarly, the institution's Bureau of American Ethnology has financed scores of anthropological field studies of the customs of American Indians, while its Canal Zone Biological Area has maintained an immense jungle reserve for research purposes.

But to the general public the Smithsonian is best known for its exhibition halls in the Nation's Capital. These include, among others, the National Gallery of Art, the Museum of Natural History, the Museum of History and Technology, the National Zoological Park, the John F. Kennedy Center for the Performing Arts, the Hirshhorn Museum and Sculpture Garden, and the National Air and Space Museum.

Supported in part by public funding and in part by private donations, the Smithsonian was established in 1846, thanks to a bequest of $508,000 from a British scientist, James Smithson, for "an establishment for the increase and diffusion of knowledge among men." In becoming one of the world's foremost institutes of research and enlightenment, and establishing its public displays, the Smithsonian has more than carried out its benefactor's charge.

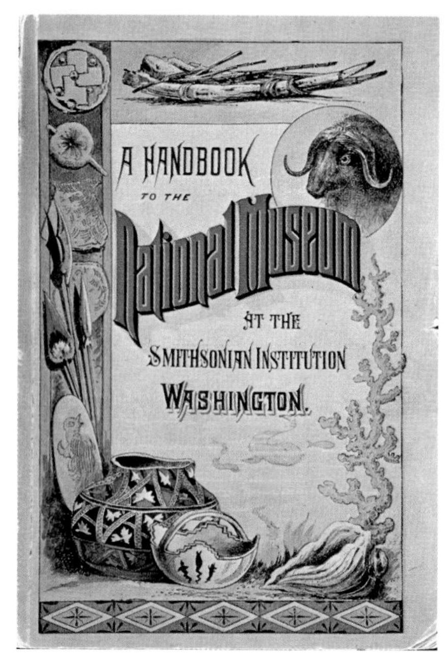

This 19th-century *guide is but one of the Smithsonian's thousands of publications.*

Early researchers *examine the fruits of a Smithsonian expedition. Today at the institution's Museums of Natural History and History and Technology there are 60 million cataloged items.*

fully divide their attention between astronomy and agriculture soon discovered they were mistaken. America's farmers badly needed help from full-time agronomists. Under such pressures, societies dedicated to practical ends began to emerge. In the early 1820's organizations devoted to specific technological objectives, such as improving farming and manufacturing methods, were operating in every State.

The general hunger for self-improvement and education was met through the lyceums, started by Josiah Holbrook in Millbury, Massachusetts, in 1826, when he began lecturing on scientific subjects. By 1834 nearly 3,000 lyceums had been organized throughout the country, and distinguished scientists (Benjamin Silliman and Asa Gray, for example), as well as poets, philosophers, and musicians, appeared on lyceum platforms.

Meanwhile America's experimental scientists were finding it difficult to gain recognition or to obtain support for serious research. Joseph Henry, the great American physicist, was discouraged when—through inability to publish his findings quickly enough—he lost the credit for discovery of the induction of electricity by magnetism to Michael Faraday, an English contemporary. In behalf of his fellow scientists, Henry urged stronger backing for abstract research, pointing out that the discovery of new truths is "a matter of great importance and eminently worthy of patronage and support." Nonetheless American enterprise put its weight mainly behind the development of technology. Proud achievements were registered, and during the 19th century the young Nation became known around the world for its technical inventiveness. "These very Americans who have not discovered one of the general laws of mechanics," marveled De Tocqueville, "have introduced into [marine] navigation the [steam] engine which changes the aspects of the world."

Beginnings of Federal Support

Congress was not easily convinced that Federal support for projects with no demonstrably practical value was justified. Funds for scientific inquiry had to be added in disguise to the Federal budget. In the face of congressional opposition to a Naval Observatory, the Secretary of the Navy obtained funds in 1830 to establish the Depot of Charts and Instruments to maintain navigational aids and equipment. In 1842 the depot was reorganized as the U.S. Naval Observatory, and 31 years later it obtained a 26-inch refracting telescope. Then, in 1955, when Washington had become so well lighted at night that astronomical observations were not practical, the Navy established an Astronomical Observing Station at Flagstaff, Arizona, with a 40-inch reflecting telescope.

Congress also voted funds for the Lewis and Clark expedition of 1804–06, and in 1807 it reluctantly authorized a "Survey of the Coast," giving it only temporary life. The project was revived in 1832, and Ferdinand Hassler, a Swiss-born immigrant, and later Alexander D. Bache, a great-grandson of Benjamin Franklin, vastly expanded the survey's scope beyond chartmaking. Terrestrial magnetism, the Gulf Stream, and studies of the ocean bottom all came within its purview. By 1854 the survey had a budget of $500,000, and there was nothing temporary about it. In 1878 it received its present name, U.S. Coast and Geodetic Survey.

A major indication of the Nation's interest in science, the Smithsonian Institution, was established in 1846 through the generosity of James Smithson, an English chemist. Ably led by Joseph Henry, it was of immediate value to science and scientists and has never faltered.

The Civil War dramatically upgraded the role of science in America. Scientists were involved in all sorts of well-publicized exploits, including manned balloons for aerial observation, measures to combat disease, and the development of new explosives. The scientific contributions of Joseph Henry and Alexander Bache proved vital to the war. Henry's basic research in electricity and magnetism greatly improved the telegraph, which was invaluable to the Union forces, and the complete mapping of the Atlantic coast, supervised by Bache, influenced Union naval strategy.

The Bureau of Agriculture, set up in 1862, and the new land-grant colleges, established under the Morrill Act of 1862, offered job opportunities to agronomists and other scientists, although the Government still made no provision for direct support of any aspect of basic science. In 1870 the National Weather Service was established as an adjunct of the U.S. Army Signal Corps. The Bureau of Standards, of vital importance to science, was not set up until 1901.

In the 1880's a group of wealthy, farsighted Americans—John D. Rockefeller, Andrew Carnegie, and James Lick—made a series of generous gifts to U.S. astronomic research. In a development probably unique in the history of science, a network of the greatest observatories the world had ever seen emerged from these endowments within a few decades. In the ensuing years many of the major discoveries about the universe were to come from American sources.

It was still difficult for an aspiring young scholar to get a first-class scientific education in the United States. Many went to Europe for their doctorates. In the 1890's graduate schools were still a new idea, and among all the U.S. universities there were no more than 26 graduate fellowships. The United States, after the Civil War, had miraculously boosted itself into a position of industrial leadership, but scientifically it remained backward.

Big changes were in the offing, however. For one thing, a revolution in physics was transforming the vision of the world around us. Intense investigations into the

Extending Our View of the Universe

Great American Contributions to Astronomy, Illustrated in Relative Scale

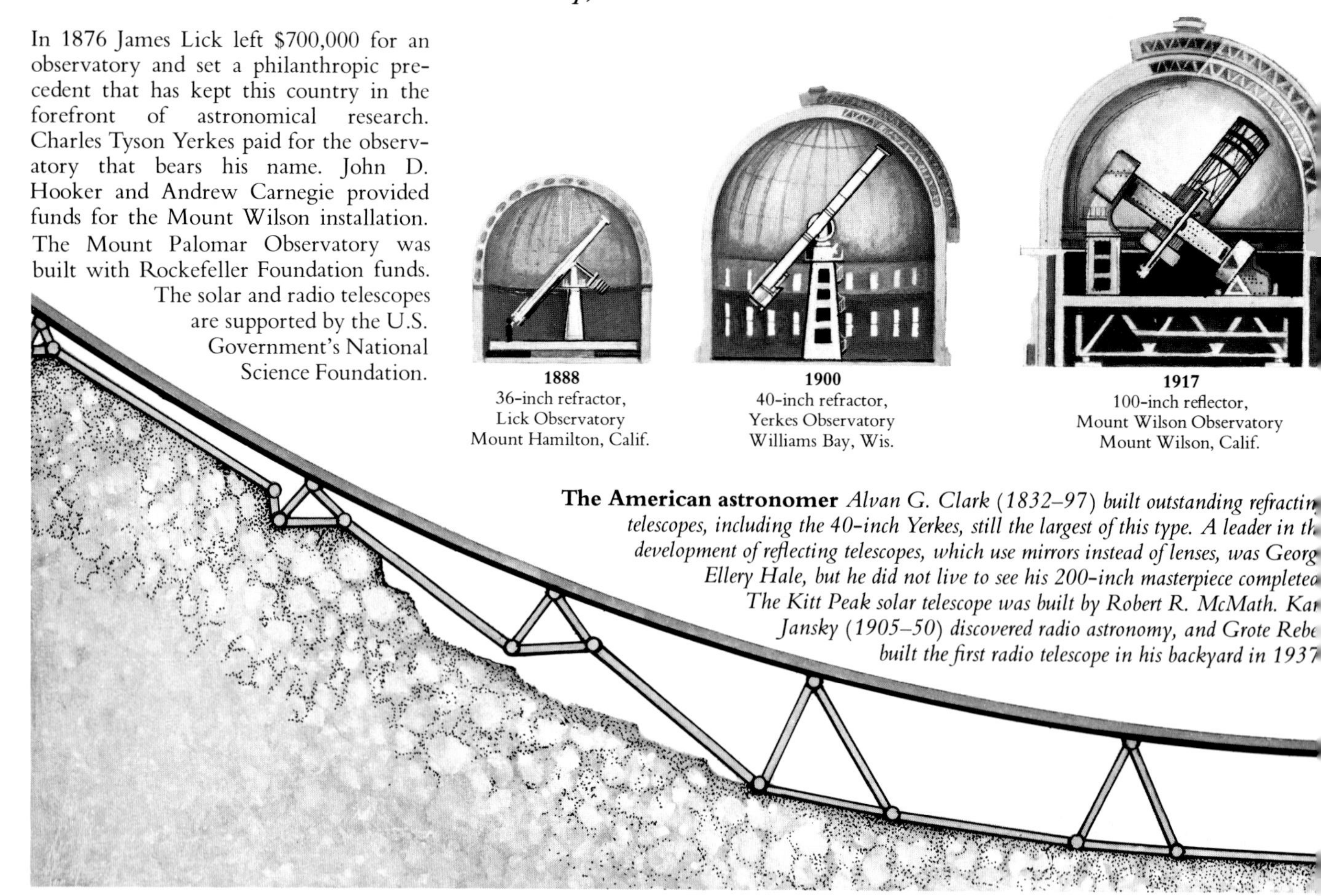

In 1876 James Lick left $700,000 for an observatory and set a philanthropic precedent that has kept this country in the forefront of astronomical research. Charles Tyson Yerkes paid for the observatory that bears his name. John D. Hooker and Andrew Carnegie provided funds for the Mount Wilson installation. The Mount Palomar Observatory was built with Rockefeller Foundation funds. The solar and radio telescopes are supported by the U.S. Government's National Science Foundation.

1888
36-inch refractor,
Lick Observatory
Mount Hamilton, Calif.

1900
40-inch refractor,
Yerkes Observatory
Williams Bay, Wis.

1917
100-inch reflector,
Mount Wilson Observatory
Mount Wilson, Calif.

The American astronomer *Alvan G. Clark (1832–97) built outstanding refractin telescopes, including the 40-inch Yerkes, still the largest of this type. A leader in th development of reflecting telescopes, which use mirrors instead of lenses, was Georg Ellery Hale, but he did not live to see his 200-inch masterpiece complete. The Kitt Peak solar telescope was built by Robert R. McMath. Kar Jansky (1905–50) discovered radio astronomy, and Grote Rebe built the first radio telescope in his backyard in 1937*

nature of matter, energy, and radiation were upsetting long-held theories. Americans began to emerge as important contributors to the new physics.

In the 1870's Albert A. Michelson, then a young instructor at the U.S. Naval Academy, devised a way to measure the speed of light. For his achievement Michelson was given the Nobel Prize in physics in 1907—the first American to receive the award in that field.

At the turn of the 20th century discoveries in physics continued at a remarkable pace. In Germany in 1895 Wilhelm C. Roentgen discovered X rays. In France Antoine Henri Becquerel investigated radioactivity, and the husband-wife team of Pierre and Marie Curie discovered radium. Meanwhile an almost reclusive professor of mathematical physics was siring a quiet revolution in scientific thinking. Josiah Willard Gibbs, who lectured and wrote at Yale from 1871 until his death in 1903, developed theories in the field of thermodynamics that, in time, evolved into a new branch of science known as physical chemistry. Although Gibbs performed few experiments, his formulas led to such practical results as the production of ammonia, dyes, drugs, and plastics.

Onto this receptive scene in 1905 burst the brilliant young Albert Einstein. With his special theory of relativity—expanded to the general theory in 1916—Einstein, at that time living in Switzerland, defined the relationship of space and time. He also theorized that matter is simply concentrated energy; that energy can be changed into matter, and matter into energy.

The War and Applied Science

World War I interfered with the full implementation of these momentous discoveries, but it speeded the growth of applied science in the United States. When the war started in Europe in 1914, only 528 workers were employed in U.S. plants making such coal-tar chemicals as dyes and drugs. America was importing more than 90 percent of its dyes, mainly from Germany. There was not one U.S. plant for extracting nitrogen from the air and transforming it into the chemicals so vital to our Armed Forces, to agriculture, and to industry in general. We depended on Chile for natural nitrates used in fertilizers and explosives. Starting almost from scratch to gain independence from foreign producers during the war, our chemical industry moved to a position of world leadership in the years thereafter.

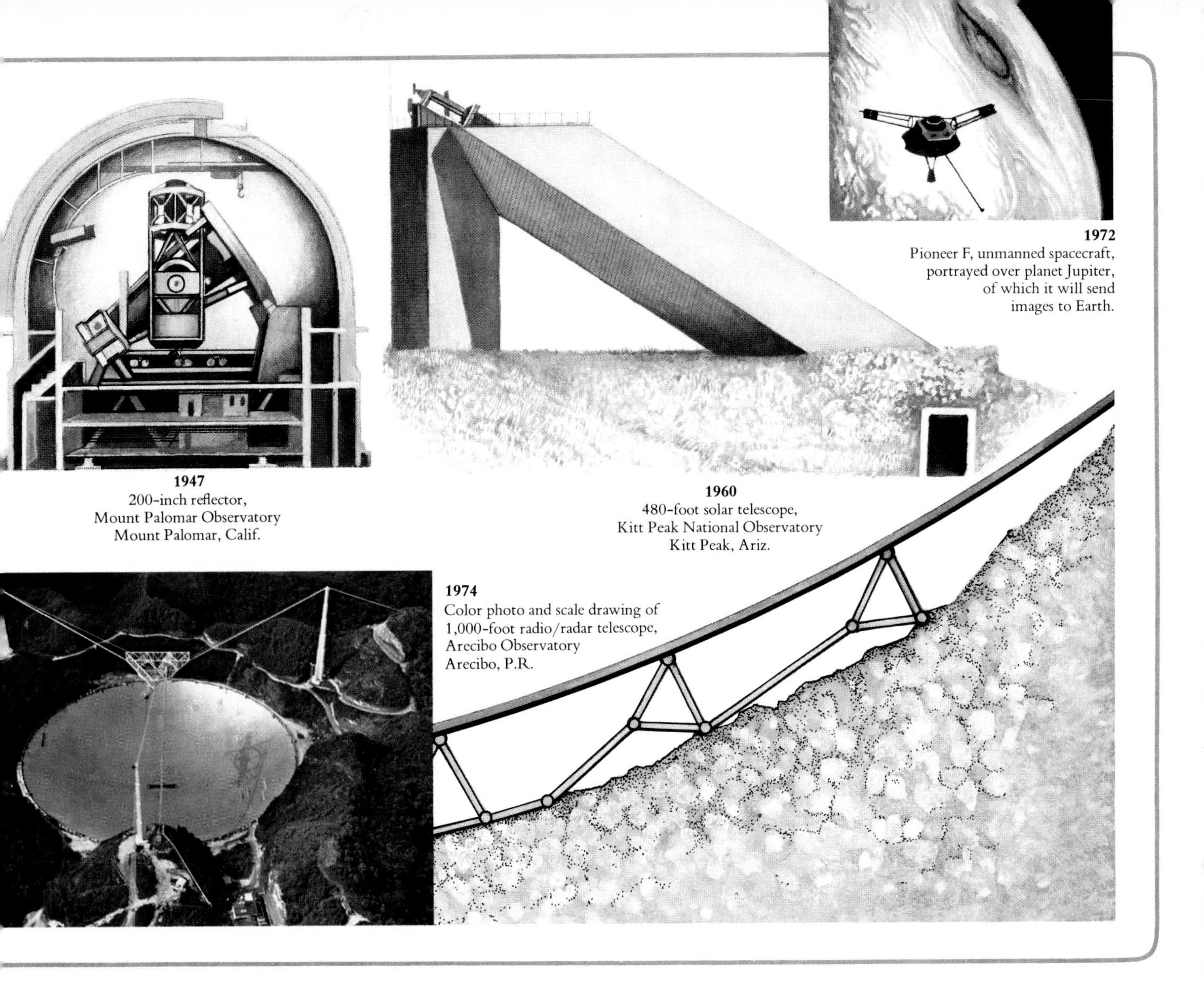

1947
200-inch reflector,
Mount Palomar Observatory
Mount Palomar, Calif.

1960
480-foot solar telescope,
Kitt Peak National Observatory
Kitt Peak, Ariz.

1972
Pioneer F, unmanned spacecraft, portrayed over planet Jupiter, of which it will send images to Earth.

1974
Color photo and scale drawing of 1,000-foot radio/radar telescope,
Arecibo Observatory
Arecibo, P.R.

After the war many large corporations established laboratories in which scientists were encouraged to seek knowledge for its own sake without worrying about whether their work would be of practical use. Most advances in the more abstract fields, such as physics, however, continued to be made in university environments.

The Development of Atomic Power

Since the time of ancient Greece, Democritus' theory that matter was made up of unsplittable atoms had been generally accepted, but all the developments of the new physics were inexorably headed toward disproving this idea. Scientists were beginning to learn that the most direct way of finding out about the composition of the atom was by chipping at it with subatomic particles—electrons, alpha particles, and deuterons. In 1930 Ernest O. Lawrence, a professor of physics at the University of California, built a cyclotron, or "atom smasher," which was used to whirl subatomic particles around under very high voltage and then fire them at atoms in the hope of breaking up the atoms. Atoms subjected to this bombardment were transformed into other atoms. Iron, for instance, had some of its atoms changed into cobalt or manganese. Other iron atoms remained the same, but they temporarily took on the quality of radioactivity.

The progress toward atom smashing was painfully slow, however, because the nucleus of the atom is surrounded by negatively charged electrons that capture or repel most high-speed particles shot at the nucleus. The few particles that reached the nucleus only chipped it. A particle might fly off the nucleus, releasing some energy, but far more was used in the bombardment than was turned loose. Then two important discoveries set the stage for the successful attempt to open the storehouse of energy in the atom.

In 1932 James Chadwick, of England, discovered the neutron, an electrically neutral particle that is stable in the nucleus of the atom. It can also become a free particle, in which state it has an average lifetime of about 17 minutes. The neutron came to public notice when it proved to be a useful tool in revealing the nature of the atom.

The first breakthrough was scored in 1939 when two German scientists, Otto Hahn and Fritz Strassmann, bombarded the metal uranium (which has radioactive potential) with neutrons and produced barium and krypton, a rare gas. Later that year Lise Meitner and Otto

Albert Einstein

Although Einstein was born in Germany, he spent some years studying, working, and teaching in Switzerland, and in 1902 became a Swiss citizen. He returned to Germany in 1913 to direct the Kaiser Wilhelm Institute of Physics in Berlin, where he spent most of his time in research, and resumed his German citizenship. When the Nazis came to power he immigrated to the United States, and in 1940 he became an American citizen.

Einstein's fame as one of the most creative of all scientists rests primarily on three theories he published in 1905 at the age of 26: his theory of Brownian motion relating to phenomena created by molecular collisions; his theory on photoelectricity concerning the emission of electrons from metal when it is illuminated; and his special theory of relativity (later expanded to the general). These three concepts are the foundation stones of the electronic, atomic, and subatomic wonders of today.

Best known are his theories of relativity, which boldly linked space with time through the factor of velocity. Einstein suggested that the geometry of space changed by a quantity related to the speed of the observer's motion. And—contrary to what had always been taken for granted about the constancy of intervals measured by clocks and calendars—Einstein proposed that time flowed at different rates, depending on the observer's motion; the faster the observer traveled, the slower his watch would run. As part of this theory, Einstein also broke down the distinction between mass and energy with his revolutionary concept that energy equals mass multiplied by the speed of light squared ($E = mc^2$). This principle suggested the enormous energy within the atom 34 years before it was first split.

Einstein spent his later years seeking a theory to unify the science of physics. His unified field theory was published in 1950 and 1953, the latter 2 years before his death. Experiments involving the theory continue.

Frisch, working in Sweden, performed the same experiment and announced that Hahn and Strassmann had, for the first time, split the atom's nucleus. Then they gave a world-shaking explanation of what had happened.

The two elements—barium and krypton—produced by the splitting of the atom (nuclear fission) had a combined weight much less than that of the original uranium atom. This loss in weight or mass during the split meant that enormous energy had been released, as predicted by Einstein when he wrote his famous equation $E = mc^2$. The energy of the neutron that split the atom was only $\frac{1}{30}$ volt, but it released 200 million volts. Clearly scientists had found a way to release incredible amounts of energy, which could lead to a bomb of horrifyingly destructive power. What if Nazi Germany, then on the threshold of war, should develop such a weapon? (As it turned out, Hitler did not give a high priority to development of an atom bomb.)

On August 2, 1939, two Hungarian-born scientists, Eugene P. Wigner and Leo Szilard, who were working with a group of atomic scientists in this country, sought the help of Albert Einstein. Deprived of his German citizenship by the Nazis, Einstein had accepted a post at Princeton's Institute for Advanced Study. Although a pacifist, he agreed to write to President Franklin D. Roosevelt and point out the potential of the new discoveries about the structure of the atom. Einstein wrote, in part: "Sir: Some recent work of E. Fermi and L. Szilard . . . leads me to expect that the element uranium may be turned into a new and important source of energy. . . ." Soon there began a "battle of laboratories" to determine the winner of World War II. British, Canadian, and U.S. talent was pooled in 1941, and in 1942 the Manhattan Project was organized. This $2 billion effort, the costliest single weapons project in history, led to the detonation of an atom bomb in 1945.

Scientists from many lands contributed to the Manhattan Project. Among them were Nobel Prize winners Niels Bohr from Denmark, who had escaped the Nazis, and Enrico Fermi, an Italian who had turned his back on fascism. Bohr and Fermi worked with J. B. Dunning and George B. Pegram of Columbia University. Fermi advanced the exciting and important theory that a "chain reaction" would be started when a uranium nucleus was hit by a neutron. The bombarded nucleus would, Fermi declared, release other neutrons, which would in turn bombard other nuclei, and so on and on.

The first chain reaction had been achieved under Fermi's direction on December 2, 1942, in a uranium and graphite pile set on the floor of a squash court under the stands of Stagg Field at the University of Chicago. The bomb was developed under the guidance of J. Robert Oppenheimer, a physics professor who had taken part in atomic research since the 1920's. When it was finally

Man's incessant search *for the fundamental structure of matter is being pursued here at Batavia, Illinois, in the Fermi National Accelerator Laboratory, the world's largest research instrument for high-energy physics. The idea of accelerating atomic particles and shooting them into various target materials to smash atomic nuclei was conceived in the 1920's by Ernest O. Lawrence. In 1930 he built the first atom smasher, which he called a cyclotron. It had a chamber the size of a frying pan. Since then cyclotrons have been enlarged, modified, and improved. The Fermi accelerator has a ring 4 miles in circumference in which proton particles (the atom's positive charge) can be accelerated to operate with a force of 500 billion electron volts. The proton beam travels in a vacuum tube around the ring at a rate of 200,000 miles per second. The beam is bent and focused by 1,014 magnets (encased in the blue housings at left) in this 8-by-10-foot tunnel 20 feet below the ground.*

tested on July 16, 1945, at a secret site near Alamogordo, New Mexico, "the whole country was lighted by a searing light with an intensity that of the midday sun," said a later War Department news release. "It was golden, purple, violet, gray, and blue. It lighted every peak, crevasse, and ridge of the near-by mountain range with a clarity and beauty that cannot be described. . . . The effects could well be called unprecedented, magnificent, beautiful, stupendous, and terrifying." The explosion was followed "by the strong, sustained, awesome roar which warned of doomsday and made us feel that we puny things were blasphemous to dare tamper with the forces reserved for the Almighty." In August two atom bombs were dropped on Japan in the belief that this devastating force would bring a quick end to the war. Japan signed surrender terms on September 2, 1945.

This event so shook men's hearts and minds that after the war some physicists turned to molecular biology—where, with their fresh views, they initiated further far-reaching studies. Others applied their skills to peaceful uses of the atom. Oppenheimer, who began to feel that scientists had "come to know sin," opposed the building of the even more destructive hydrogen bomb.

New Uses for the Atom and Other Advances

The Atomic Energy Commission (AEC) was created in 1946, and atomic energy development was placed under civilian control. From this research have come nuclear power reactors, applications of radioactive isotopes to medicine, and other advances. One of the most striking advances was the development in the late 1940's of radiocarbon dating by Willard F. Libby, then a chemist at the University of Chicago. By measuring the decay of atoms of radioactive carbon 14, the Libby method makes it possible to estimate the age of ancient relics more accurately than ever before. Radiocarbon dating has been hailed as a most significant American contribution to archeology, anthropology, and geology. One of the more surprising results of the use of this technique was the discovery that the most recent retreat of the ice, in the Pleistocene period, occurred only 11,000 years ago. New methods of dating have also challenged the assumption that civilization began in the Middle East.

Americans have made many other worthy contributions to geology and archeology. They discovered ruined cities built by the Mayan Indians in Central America and participated with British scientists in exploring the ancient Sumerian city of Ur in southern Iraq. They were also the first to probe deeply into man's transition from hunter to farmer. In addition, the worldwide emphasis on meticulous fieldwork can largely be attributed to the brilliant German-American anthropologist Franz Boas, who dominated the field of anthropology for the entire first half of the 20th century.

Out of World War II came not only atomic energy but computers, jet aircraft, radar, and many other advances. Because of wartime shortages, American chemists worked to produce various substitute materials, such as plastics and synthetic rubber. Many of these proved superior to the materials they replaced. In metallurgy, when imports of tungsten from China had been cut off during the war, molybdenum was successfully substituted for hardening steel. Because of its enormous contributions, American science seemed finally to have conquered the Government's established reluctance to support basic research. Vannevar Bush, who mobilized science for the war effort as head of the Office of Scientific Research and Development, argued forcefully for an agency to evolve national policy and to serve as a balance wheel in regulating financial support of science.

In 1950 Congress established the National Science Foundation, the first U.S. Government-supported body created to sponsor basic research. It was small compared to such giants as the AEC and the Defense Department, which together accounted for three-fourths of the research and development (R & D) budget at that time. The R & D budget covered such disparate elements as weapons development by the AEC and the Department of Defense and the appropriations for test tubes for a college chemistry laboratory.

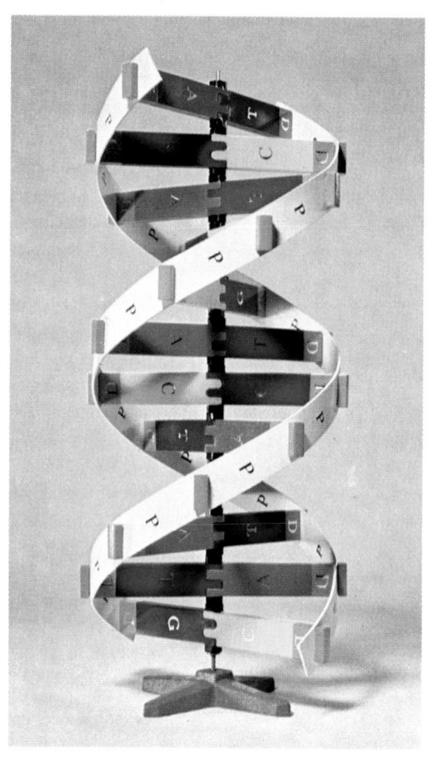

The master molecule *of the chromosomes, deoxyribonucleic acid (DNA), is a double helix, as this model shows. It contains a chemical code of life not yet fully understood.*

The Race for Space

Government expenditure on pure science skyrocketed however, as the Nation responded to the Soviet challenge in space by establishing the National Aeronautics and Space Administration. The commitment to land the first men on the Moon, successfully fulfilled in 1969, again boosted scientists onto the crest of a wave of popularity. Caught up in the excitement of the space race, no fewer than 20 Federal agencies, ranging from the Department of Agriculture to the Office of Naval Research, were supporting research and development in the 1960's.

The multiplicity of funding sources produced spectacular results as well as serious growing pains. Some critics have seen the thrust into space as more political than scientific in purpose, but it has unquestionably yielded exciting new knowledge about the nature of the planets and of our part of the universe. Electronics and computer technology have benefited. Indeed all Americans have been gainers from the great surge into space. Not only were we onlookers in a cosmic amphitheater as the race to the Moon was decisively won by the United States, but we have enjoyed the services of new and better electronic and medical devices that owe their existence, at least in part, to the needs of the space explorers.

The Biological Sciences Advance

In the second half of the 19th century Austrian monk Gregor Mendel established that physical traits are passed from generation to generation through units of heredity. Ever since his work gained recognition, American scientists have contributed mightily to the unraveling of the genetic puzzle. In 1902 Walter S. Sutton observed that Mendel's units were carried in the chromosomes. Then zoologist Thomas Hunt Morgan found that each chromosome consisted of a long string of genes, the units of heredity. Morgan received the Nobel Prize in physiology and medicine in 1933. In 1926 Herman J. Muller, a former student of Morgan's, used X rays to greatly increase the mutation rates in the genes of fruit flies, thus speeding up the study of such changes. Finally, in 1951, the very structure of the master substance of heredity, deoxyribonucleic acid (DNA), was deciphered by three men: James D. Watson, an American, and Francis H. C. Crick and Maurice H. F. Wilkins, both Englishmen. These three shared a Nobel Prize in 1962.

This discovery of the basic genetic material constituted a great advance in the understanding of living matter. The step was so great, in fact, that it touched off widespread anxieties over man's newfound ability to tinker with the code of life. More realistically, early advances in molecular genetics already made it possible to deal with hitherto intractable hereditary disease and promised improvement in the treatment of such killers as cancer and heart disease. In recent decades the largest proportion of Nobel Prizes in physiology and medicine have gone to molecular biologists, and most of them have been

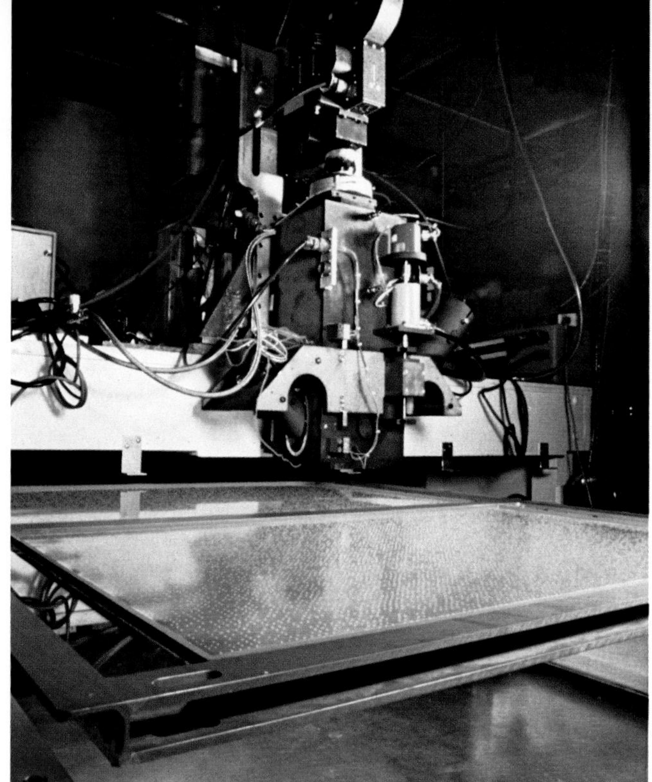

American technology *has led the way in creating sophisticated instruments of science. Dr. Donald A. Glaser, of the University of California at Berkeley, won a Nobel Prize in 1960 for his bubble chamber to record the tracks of elementary particles. Later, as a molecular biologist, he designed the revolutionary 40-foot-long, 2-story-high biological computer, details of which are shown here. Christened the Dumbwaiter, it handles 100 million microbial cultures at once, identifying, classifying, and manipulating them genetically and biologically.*

Americans. In health research this country led the world in the mid-1970's, although there was concern that government cutbacks in funding might slow its progress.

The High Cost of Atom Smashing

The demands of some branches of research for gargantuan tools to continue the exploration of both the atom and the universe have brought problems. High-energy physics, for instance, needs bigger and bigger atom smashers. In 1881 Albert Michelson, using a $200 grant from Alexander Graham Bell, had built an instrument called an interferometer, with which he disproved the existence of the mysterious ether that was supposed to fill all space. Today's atom smashers, in dramatic contrast, cost hundreds of millions of dollars to build and operate —and there is no guarantee that anything as momentous as Michelson's discovery will result. Consequently, in the late 1960's and early 1970's, there was increasing dissension and debate among scientists about the best ways to use research and development resources.

By the mid-1970's the honeymoon between science and Government had ended. Pressures on the Federal budget multiplied, and Congress was becoming tougher about spending, even as the scientists sought to convince the lawmakers that some portion of the annual gross national product should go to research to assure continuity of programs and progress. Once again science was bedeviled by its old bugaboo: practicality. Echoing De Tocqueville's insights of more than a century earlier, an influential Congressman who chaired a committee administering National Science Foundation funds said: ". . . the American people cannot afford to finance science as a hobby horse—science for the fun of it. They envision practical science as a workhorse for the people—research that produces a better quality of life. . . . Congress wants scientific research that gets results."

But science is not losing its forward motion. Nuclear fusion, for instance, incorporating the versatile laser, could eventually hold the key to the world's energy shortages. Fusion, as opposed to fission, involves the combining of atomic particles and is the process that powers the stars. Aside from powering the deadly hydrogen bomb, fusion could create an almost inexhaustible source of energy. And the new molecular biology looms as one of the most promising of all fields.

Clearly the United States, which once considered a few scientists as enough, has within a relatively short time built a scientific and technological establishment more productive, more diverse, and more brilliant than the world has ever seen. Manning the laboratories, observatories, atom smashers, and other research installations are 500,000 investigative scientists and 1 million engineers —probably three-fourths of the world's foremost specialists in science.

Wisely employed and generously supported, these men and women offer our best hope of uncovering new answers to the problems of finding all the energy we need, feeding ourselves more efficiently, enjoying longer and happier lives, coping with the world's exploding population, and living in harmony with our environment.

CHAPTER EIGHTEEN

The Saga of Immigration

The American continent was peopled by four great migrations. First to come were prehistoric hunters from the steppes of Asia who, most anthropologists believe, crossed a bridge of land that then extended across the Bering Sea and Strait. Their descendants, the American Indians, developed scores of complex and colorful cultures before the arrival of the white man in the early 17th century. The British and Western European settlers came to America seeking riches, land, and sanctuary. They conquered the wilderness, established the Thirteen Original Colonies, and eventually launched a new nation. With them came a massive and unwilling immigration of Negro slaves from West Africa.

Humorist Will Rogers was fiercely proud of his part-Indian heritage and enjoyed recounting that when the *Mayflower* landed at Plymouth in 1620, his ancestors met the boat. Yet even the first Americans—the more than 1 million Indians belonging to well over 200 tribes who lived north of Mexico at the time the Pilgrims landed—were probably all descended from "immigrants" who during the ice age left their frigid Siberian hunting grounds in search of game. At some time between 25,000 and 35,000 years ago, they are believed to have wandered across the land bridge that then linked Asia and Alaska. Over the centuries their descendants fanned out across the continent, adapting their ways of life to fit the forests, plains, deserts, and mountains in which they settled. By the time the white man arrived, Indian culture in North America, though in no instance as advanced as the complex Aztec, Mayan, and Inca civilizations destroyed in the Spanish conquest of Central and South America, was extremely diverse; it encompassed the powerful forest confederacy of the Eastern Iroquois; the roving, root-gathering simplicity of the Western Utes; the buffalo-hunting adeptness of the Plains Indians; the placid life of the pueblo-dwelling Zuñi; the agricultural skills of the Algonquians; and a host of other colorful peoples.

Jamestown, the first fragile *English foothold, as modern scholars believe it looked in 1607. The settlement was built on the bank of the James River in a malarial swamp. Its buildings were thatched and half-timbered, English style. The largest structure, in the center of the stockaded village, housed America's first Anglican church. Watchtowers with cannon were for protection from Indian or Spanish attack.*

he natural talents of these Negroes and their extraordi-ry powers of endurance enabled them to survive the hor-rs of slavery and the indignities of Jim Crow and to make calculable contributions to American civilization. Fi-lly, in increasing numbers throughout the 19th century d well into the 20th, came the outpouring of immigrants m almost everywhere that made a reality of poet Walt hitman's vision of America as "not merely a nation but teeming nation of nations."

Since the birth of the United States, some 44 million migrants have flocked to this country in search of oppor-nities denied them in their native lands. Among them have been men and women of every sort—seekers after land and freedom, religious and political dissidents searching for sanctuary, adventurers and misfits, merchants and artists. But most of them have been unlettered farmers from Europe's peasant heart, ordinary people with strong backs, hope, and a will to succeed. Through unshakable optimism, hard work, and grit, most have made a go of it. They have carved homes from America's wilderness, peopled her cities and towns, transformed her politics, and manned her farms and factories. The saga of the immigrant's struggle to fashion a new life in a foreign and often unfriendly land is among the most stirring chapters in America's story.

The earliest English settlers found the Indians "of a tractable, free, and loving nature, without guile or treachery," and willing to share their knowledge of the wilderness. Later, when the colonists' land hunger sparked violent conflict, tribal diversity worked against Indian survival; ancient intertribal enmities made a united defense impossible.

The Newcomers

Intrepid mariners from half a dozen European nations had explored America's coastal waters before England planted its first colonies on the Eastern shore. There were earlier visits by Portuguese, Danish, Italian, British, and Spanish seamen; armored Spanish conquistadores filed north from Mexico to explore the Southwest in the mid-1500's; and tonsured Franciscan friars from Spain established missions in Florida, Georgia, and the Carolinas late in the 16th century. But it was England that founded the first permanent Colonies, in the early 1600's, and the British, with their staying power, who outlasted all their colonial rivals and built the thriving American empire that eventually became the United States.

The motives that brought millions of Europeans to America were mixed, but most of the immigrants hoped to find wealth and a new start in life, or religious and political sanctuary. The three shiploads of English adventurers who anchored in the James River near the mouth of Chesapeake Bay in May 1607 came, in Sir Walter Raleigh's words, "to seek new worlds for gold, for praise, for glory." They found far more hardship than gold or glory, and many of them died of disease and malnutrition, but they did establish Jamestown, the first permanent English settlement in the New World. Tobacco, an Indian staple they began growing in 1612, became the vogue in Europe and the economic mainstay of Virginia and much of the colonial South.

MAKING DEMOCRACY WORK

The Mayflower Compact

Battered off course by Atlantic storms, the sturdy little *Mayflower* reached the Massachusetts coast in November 1620. This put her far outside the jurisdiction of the Virginia Company, which had granted a patent for a landing at the mouth of the Hudson River. The leaders (part of a religious group later called Pilgrims) resolved to land anyhow; but because of this deviation from course a majority of those aboard considered themselves freed of the contractual obligations made with the Virginia Company and threatened to go off on their own. To restore harmony, the leaders drew up the Mayflower Compact, which was signed by 41 male passengers. The Compact formed a "civil Body Politic . . . to enacte . . . just and equal laws" to which all promised "due Submission and Obedience. . . ." It remained in force as the keystone of the civil government of Plymouth Colony until 1691, when Plymouth became part of the Massachusetts Bay Colony. In the 19th-century painting by William Halsall reproduced below, the first colonizers are shown rowing ashore to their new land from the *Mayflower* anchored in Plymouth harbor.

Those who founded New England's first Colony at Plymouth in 1620 were hardly united in their aims. Their leaders were Protestant Separatists whose zeal for restoring the ruling Anglican Church to "its primative order, libertie & bewtie" had been met with royal persecution and banishment. After an unhappy decade in Holland these self-styled "saintes"—they were not known as Pilgrim Fathers until the 19th century—had resolved to sail for America where the "lordly & tyranous power" of the Anglican prelates could not reach them. But their backers, the wealthy merchants of the second Virginia Company, were less interested in saving souls than in reaping profits from fish and furs. And most of the 102 would-be colonists aboard the *Mayflower* were not Separatists but "strangers." They were a mixture of mostly Anglican farmers, servants, and soldiers, grudgingly willing to endure the pious leadership of the "saintes" in exchange for a chance at a new life in the wilderness. Once they were ashore, it was the Mayflower Compact that kept the Separatists in command and the Colony united.

As Jamestown, Plymouth, and the other British settlements that soon lined the Atlantic coast grew and prospered, and their restless inhabitants gradually worked their way inland to establish new outposts, England began almost two centuries of struggle with her colonial rivals. Only the final outcome of these conflicts need concern us here: After 1763 England, by treaty at least, was mistress of the wilderness from the east coast to the Mississippi. But the enclaves left behind by the Dutch, Swedish, and French were an important leaven in the American mix. Thus, well into the 19th century, whole villages along the Hudson spoke Dutch and no English; Swedes and Finns, the sturdy survivors of short-lived New Sweden, dwelt along the Delaware in America's first true log cabins; and French traders and trappers lent a strong Gallic flavor to Ohio Valley outposts.

Nor were the English settlements themselves ever exclusively English. There were Polish, German, and Italian artisans at Jamestown as early as 1609, and the first Negro slaves stepped off a Dutch trader at Jamestown's wharf just 10 years later. When English farmers proved reluctant to venture into what Plymouth Governor William Bradford called "a hidious & desolate wilderness, full of wild beasts & willd men," colonial promoters devised inventive schemes to lure new settlers from England and from other lands. They developed the indenture system, offering land and passage to men and women willing to work without pay for a specified term; brought in jailed debtors and convicts (some of whom reverted to form as soon as they came ashore); and circulated promotional books and pamphlets trumpeting the New World's advantages in strident, sometimes misleading, terms. There were plenty of takers in Western Europe, where ancient religious and political antagonisms, oppressive feudal landlords, and chronic overcrowding made life a nightmare for the poor. Quaker William Penn peopled much of Pennsylvania's wild interior with German religious dissidents grateful for a chance to escape the cruel

Apprenticeship and Indenture

A blacksmith and his apprentice hammer out implements in a shop at the Williamsburg, Virginia, restoration. In early America apprentices and indentured servants supplemented the scanty labor supply. A youth might be bound by indenture (contract) to a master craftsman for as long as 15 years in exchange for instruction in a trade, often wretched living conditions, and a severely restricted social life. In the South the heavy, back-breaking labor was done by Negro slaves; elsewhere, more often than not, by indentured servants. Some of these servants, known as redemptioners or free-willers, earned their passage to America by contracting to work from 2 to 7 years without pay. Thousands of others were debtors or felons who had been given a choice between the gallows and exile to America. On arrival at New York, Boston, or Philadelphia they were sold into service for terms ranging from 7 to 14 years.

The life of the indentured servant, whether a fieldworker or a craft apprentice, was often harsh and limited, but when the indenture expired, the worker was customarily given land, tools, and a gun with which to start out on his own. Consequently, such people came to America by the thousands from England, Germany, and elsewhere in Europe and helped to make the Colonies prosper.

New Americans from Ireland, *shown in this 1855 painting by Samuel Waugh, swarm ashore at Manhattan's southern tip. The ship that has brought them is far handsomer than were most immigrant vessels. The circular building at the left is Castle Garden; it served as the entry point to the New World for millions of newcomers from 1855 until 1892, when Ellis Island became immigration headquarters.*

persecutions of French occupation forces; these sturdy, pious farmers were the ancestors of today's misnamed "Pennsylvania Dutch." French Protestant Huguenots were also made welcome in almost every colony, while Jews from Spain and Portugal prospered in the coastal cities. Scotch-Irish Presbyterians, farmers and weavers mostly, also flocked to the American frontier to escape Anglican supremacy. (Among them were the ancestors of 11 U.S. Presidents.) No one knows the precise population of the Thirteen Original Colonies, but there are believed to have been 275,000 colonists by 1700, and well over 2 million at the outbreak of the Revolution. The first U.S. census, in 1790, recorded a population of almost 4 million. Of this number, about 700,000 were Negro slaves; almost one-quarter of the white population was of non-British ancestry.

While the Revolution was fought largely to reassert the "rights of Englishmen," non-English colonists played a major role on both sides. The war provided French and Scotch-Irish settlers with red-coated targets for their ancient, anti-English enmities. (Indeed, the lean Scotch-Irish frontiersmen of Pennsylvania were such enthusiastic rebels that one weary royal officer complained, "Call that war whatever name you may, only call it not an American rebellion; it is nothing more or less than a Scotch-Irish Presbyterian rebellion.") Among others who rallied to the revolutionary cause were a remarkable band of European officers, including the Germans Baron von Steuben and Johann Kalb (known as Baron de Kalb), the French Marquis de Lafayette, and Polish patriots Casimir Pulaski and Tadeusz Kosciuszko. While peaceable immigration virtually ceased as the fighting dragged on for 8 years, the British themselves unwittingly imported a new group of immigrants—German mercenaries, thousands of whom deserted or remained in America after the war ended. Incidentally, British defeat produced one phenomenon never seen before or since in America: massive immigration in reverse, as hundreds of ships laden with morose Loyalists, their families and possessions, set sail for England, Canada, and the West Indies.

Immigration Gathers Momentum

The turbulence spawned in Europe by the French Revolution and the Napoleonic wars almost stopped immigration to America between 1790 and 1820, affording the new Nation a welcome respite in advance of the problems of further assimilation soon to come.

The first great wave of 19th-century immigration, lasting roughly from 1830 to 1870, included thousands of English, Scottish, French, Dutch, Swiss, and Welsh settlers who melted with relative ease into American communities established by their predecessors. But it also encompassed large numbers of newcomers from three other places: Ireland, Germany, and Scandinavia.

Of the 2 million immigrants who had come by 1860, roughly half were Irish Catholics. Only a small number

Utopias on the Wabash

Scores of Utopias sprang up in 19th-century America, and two of them—one a success and the other a quick failure—occupied the same Indiana community. In 1814 George Rapp, a German pietist who preached celibacy, communalism, and the Second Coming, moved his followers from their thriving community at Harmony, Pennsylvania, to Indiana, where they founded a second Harmony. This tidy town prospered until 1824, when the inhabitants (known as Rappites or Harmonists) returned to Pennsylvania to establish the community of Economy, where Rapp died in 1847.

The British industrialist and philanthropist Robert Owen bought the Indiana town, renamed it New Harmony and, with his son Robert Dale Owen and an educator from Philadelphia, William Maclure, established a cooperative community in which labor and its fruits would be equally shared by all. Owen and Maclure attracted many leading scientists and educators to New Harmony with a promise of "universal happiness through universal education." Unfortunately, though thinkers were plentiful, there were too few skilled workers to provide enough food, shelter, and services for day-to-day living, and factionalism soon split the community into quarreling groups. His fortune depleted, Owen dissolved the experiment in 1827, but the Owenites, like the refugees from other failed Utopias, enriched the American mainstream with their idealism.

Pictured below is the altar of the Roofless Church, a modern edifice in New Harmony, designed by Philip Johnson as a nonsectarian memorial to both the Rappites and the Owenites. Inspired by the prophet Micah, who 700 years before Christ foretold the millennium with the words, ". . . the golden rose shall come," the structure is shaped like an inverted rosebud but casts a shadow of the full-blown flower. The sculpture in the center was created by Jacques Lipchitz.

of Irish settlers had arrived in colonial times, mostly as indentured servants. But conditions in Ireland after 1830 made mass emigration inevitable. Subjected to five centuries of English misrule and impoverished by their absentee landlords, most rural Irish were huddled in turf hovels on tiny tenant plots and subsisted mainly on potatoes. When a mysterious blight destroyed three successive potato crops in the late 1840's, a million persons starved to death in what came to be called the "great hunger." A million others sold their meager effects for the $20 or $30 needed for passage and trudged to the coastal ports to cross the Atlantic to "Ameriky" where, as a popular Irish song promised, "There's bread and work for all/ And the sun always shines."

In Germany, which had not yet attained nationhood, a revolution in 1848 attempted to overthrow feudalism and unite 38 quarrelsome states led by petty princes into a modern democracy. The movement failed, and thousands of its exiled leaders—students, intellectuals, and artisans—fled to America. They did not create a "new Germania" as many of them had hoped, but their efforts lent a tone of Old World culture and political idealism to the American communities in which they settled. By 1900 the "Forty-eighters" had been followed by some 5 million more Germans—peasants mostly, but also tradesmen and craftsmen. They had been lured by tireless real estate promoters, agents of land opened up in new Western States and Territories, and by widely circulated "America Letters" from earlier immigrants who had become successful and painted a rosy picture of the New World. Soon the roads to the wharves at Hamburg and Bremen were lined with hopeful emigrants, their belongings piled high on creaking ox carts.

Beginning in 1825, "America Fever" also swept Scandinavia and Finland, where political turmoil, overcrowding, feudalism, and a series of poor harvests spurred a peasant exodus that by 1920 would bring to the United States a million Swedes (one-sixth of Sweden's population) and another million Norwegians, Danes, and Finns.

Among the throngs of immigrants were tiny bands of earnest dreamers who saw in America's forests and prairies an ideal home for a variety of religious and secular Utopias. Those who tried and failed to create perfect societies in the wilderness included Rappites, Owenites, Millenarists, and Shakers. Few of these cults endured for long, but all left their mark.

The Rigors of the Journey

Hardship almost invariably attended the voyage to the promised land. Crooked passenger agents peddling fraudulent tickets fleeced many of these eager millions even before they embarked. Once aboard the aptly named "coffin ships," they found themselves packed into reeking, airless cargo holds without privacy or sanitary

In a race *to control traffic in the Salt Lake Valley, the rival Union Pacific (UP) and Central Pacific (CP) Railroads began digging parallel roadbeds only a few hundred feet apart. A majority of the UP work force was Irish, and the CP work force was predominately Chinese. There was much ill feeling between them. Neither side bothered to warn the other when firing dynamite blasts in rock cuts. Finally, after several UP and CP graders had been killed, a truce was called. Irish and Chinese laborers are shown together in this 1869 sketch by Alfred R. Waud. The artist's on-the-spot drawings of camp and battle scenes appeared in* Harper's Weekly *and* Frank Leslie's Illustrated Newspaper *during the Civil War.*

facilities for as long as 3 months. They had to carry and cook their own food, drink rationed water that was often green with slime, and live in terror of Atlantic storms and brutal crews. These rigors, plus the ravages of "ship fever" (typhus) and "rotten throat" (a streptococcal infection), killed an estimated 5 to 15 percent of those who set sail from Europe. The voyagers who endured to disembark at Boston, New York, Philadelphia, Baltimore, or Charleston were usually exhausted and filthy, not having been able to bathe for weeks. Upon landing they had to face the wiles of "emigrant runners" who haunted the wharves. These men were recent arrivals themselves who spoke the newcomer's language. They offered the bewildered immigrant a comforting link with the homeland, then cheated him of whatever money remained in his pockets. Conditions greatly improved with the coming of the steamship after 1860, and numerous hard-working immigrant aid organizations, such as New York's Shamrock Society, battled dockside corruption for decades. Nevertheless, the Atlantic crossing remained an ordeal for immigrants well into the 20th century. In anticipation of the freedom and the opportunity on this side of the Atlantic, however, most considered the risks well worth taking.

Once ashore, the immigrants pretty consistently followed ethnic patterns. The Germans and Scandinavians generally worked their way west. "Farmers without soil" in their homelands, as one historian wrote, "they had come to a land with soil but no farmers," and they prospered. While large numbers of Germans clustered in cities such as New York, Baltimore, Cincinnati, St. Louis, and particularly Milwaukee, most became Midwestern farmers, earning a well-deserved reputation for diligence and thrift. The Scandinavians shared the German love of the land, turning Wisconsin, Minnesota, and the Dakotas into the Nation's 19th-century breadbasket. German and Scandinavian immigrants endured the hardships encountered by all pioneers and the gibes sometimes provoked by their Old World ways, but they were generally accepted by the earlier settlers.

It was different for the Irish. Knowing nothing but tenancy and determined never again to be tied irrevocably to the unreliable land, eight out of ten went no farther inland than the fast-growing dockside slums. In 1840 Boston, which along with New York absorbed most of the Irish, was still little more than a large country town, with sheep and cattle grazing placidly on its grassy Common. The sudden rush of immigration transformed it into a crowded city where poverty and crime were constant problems. Between 1835 and 1845 only 5,500 immigrants settled in Boston, but in 1845 alone some 37,000 arrived in search of shelter. By 1850 New York City was one-third Irish, and the Irish-born made up more than 4 percent of the Nation's populace. Most Irish immigrants had no choice but to live in crude shacks—"a dozen rotten boards and a piece of stove pipe for a chimney," according to one appalled 19th-century New Yorker—in teeming, shanty towns. Jobs were scarce and poorly paid. Many businessmen refused to hire Irishmen. Women felt fortunate to work as domestics; men toiled in work gangs, building roads, canals, and railroads for as little as 50 cents for a 15-hour day. A few settled on farms and in towns along the route; others (in 1848 and after) headed for the Gold Rush in the California area. But most stayed in the stifling Eastern cities. It was against them (and to a lesser extent against their German fellow-immigrants, who were often considered radical revolutionaries) that the nativist agitation of the 1850's was directed.

The Involuntary Immigrants

Blacks Were Brought in Chains

"I tremble for my country when I reflect that God is just," Thomas Jefferson once wrote of slavery. "His justice cannot sleep forever." The author of the first draft of the Declaration of Independence, which boldly recognized that "all men are created equal," was himself a prosperous slaveowner who neatly personified the irony at the core of America. The nation that first proclaimed the essential dignity of man also officially sanctioned the ownership of one man by another. The enduring legacy of that initial contradiction remains—more than a century after the abolition of slavery itself—what Swedish sociologist Gunnar Myrdal has called "an American dilemma."

Slavery's searing question, *posed in a printer's device favored by abolitionists.*

Of all America's immigrant peoples, only the Africans came in chains. Although slavery had a long, bitter history in America, beginning with the arrival of "20 and odd negars" at Jamestown in 1619, it never really took root in the North, partly because the Quakers and other early abolitionists had moral qualms against it, but mostly because Northern farms and factories were initially too small to require large labor forces such as those provided by slaves. It must be said that Northern disapproval of slavery and slaveowning rarely came into play when a profit was at stake; many New England fortunes rested on the shipment and sale of slaves to buyers in Southern ports. Even in the South, however, white indentured servants outnumbered black slaves in every colony until 1700. But gradually the South developed great plantations of rice, sugar, tobacco, and indigo, which demanded large numbers of workers who were forced to endure arduous toil in searing heat. Consequently slavery became the very foundation of the Southern economy.

The sudden, soaring demand for Southern cotton after Eli Whitney invented the cotton gin in 1793 turned slave trading into an enormously profitable industry. Once ashore, the slaves were at the mercy of their masters' whims. Degradation was inherent in the definition of their lot. The best they could expect was unremitting toil; the worst was cruelty and even death. Although all Northern States had barred slavery by 1804, the "peculiar institution," as Senator John C. Calhoun called it, was maintained in the South until the end of the Civil War; by 1860 there were well over 4 million slaves in the United States.

These black Africans and their descendants proved an astonishingly resilient and resourceful people. Forced to work long hours, forbidden recourse to the courts, and kept even from learning to read the Bible for fear they would be inspired to rebel, they managed to establish their own clandestine churches, develop their own African-tinged music and folklore, and express in myriad ways their longing to be free. Slave revolts were rare. The few that did develop were brutally crushed, and white fears of bloody uprisings such as those that devastated Haiti between 1791 and 1803 spawned ever more severe repression on the plantations. Sabotage, malingering, and acts of defiance by individual slaves were quite common, and thousands ran away from their masters, seeking sanctuary in the swamps or fleeing northward.

Meanwhile, free Negroes—some 488,000 in 1860—clustered mostly in the Northern cities. These consisted mainly of former slaves and their descendants, and a few who had never been slaves at all. They, too, developed their own institutions, usually in the face of white hostility. Despite laws that barred black access to the ballot in all but six States, they fought bravely in every American war, published their own newspapers, formed their own churches and fraternal organizations, and contributed time and money to the antislavery movement. Among the best known black abolitionists were two former slaves: the imposing Frederick Douglass, who became the movement's finest orator and a powerful post-Civil War politician, and Harriet Tubman, an illiterate but indomitable woman who led more than 300 men, women, and children out of slavery via the Underground Railroad.

The conflict over slavery and States rights eventually came to dominate American politics and finally drove the Nation to a terrible and bloody Civil War. The Emancipation Proclamation and the Union Army—with the aid of some 186,000 black volunteers—finally freed the slaves (the 13th amendment made their freedom official), but the long-awaited liberation brought new problems. How were the former slaves to be brought into the American mainstream? Federal legislation in the Reconstruction period tried to provide answers. The 14th amendment granted blacks citizenship, and the 15th amendment gave them the right to vote; Congress also passed acts that forbade segregation in public facilities, provided for schooling, and guaranteed black recourse to the courts. White supremacy was brutally restored to the South in the late 1870's and 1880's through election fraud, widespread white terrorism, and the imposition of stringent Jim Crow laws.

Racial segregation by State law received official sanction in 1896, when the U.S. Supreme Court ruled in *Plessy* v. *Ferguson* that "separate but equal" public facilities were constitutional. (That fateful decision stood for 58 years, until the school desegregation ruling in 1954.) Southern legislatures emphasized the "separate" rather than the "equal" implications of the 1896 decision. They skimped on public expenditures for black education, health care, transportation, and welfare. Still tied to the soil, most freedmen in the South soon became pawns of the sharecropper and farm tenancy systems, or entered domestic or personal service. They were only marginally better off than they had been as slaves. A few sought to build new lives on the Western frontier; others headed north in search of work.

After 1900 about 70 percent of the Nation's Negro citizens moved to urban areas, almost half of them to cities outside the South. Factory jobs opened up to them when World War I stemmed the labor supply of European immigrants. Black ghettos in major cities became centers of a vibrant Afro-American culture in spite of the poverty, prejudice, crime, crowding, and disease that accompanied their growth. Despite the odds, increasing numbers of blacks worked their way into the professions, while others became prominent in sports and entertainment. Black Americans have had a lasting influence on the Nation's cultural and artistic life, while millions of Negroes in more prosaic callings—men and women, slave and free—have played an important role in building the economy.

Under the leadership of black and white civil rights champions and despite sporadic but shameful racial violence, the Negro march toward full citizenship and political equality gathered momentum with the passing years and continues today. The struggle is detailed in Chapter 19, "Developing a Social Conscience," pages 336–352; some major aspects in the history of black America are illustrated on the following pages.

In the big cities many people of Hispanic extraction, such as Puerto Ricans, as well as Jamaicans and other natives of the Caribbean islands, are also isolated in ghetto areas. While most of these minorities maintain their individual cultural identity, any gains that are made by one group serve to help them all.

Three 19th-century *English engravings depict the descent into bondage of members of an African tribe. Left to right: Arab invaders swoop down on an African village; lead their captives toward the coast; and herd them into boats to be rowed out to anchored transports.*

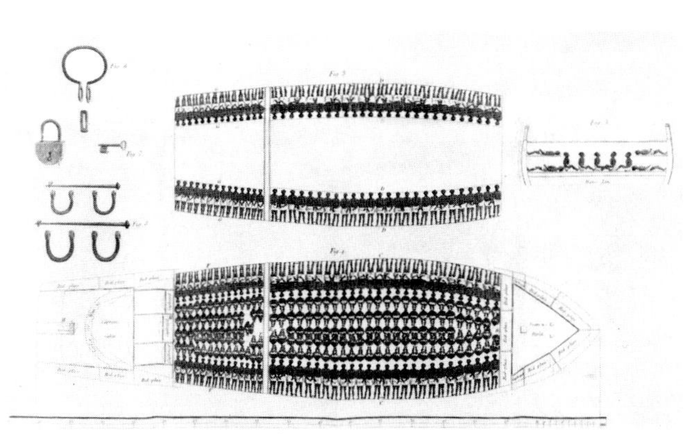

No one knows *how many African men, women, and children were shipped to the New World aboard slave vessels, but estimates range as high as 24 million. Most were taken to the West Indies and South America; by 1776 there were some 500,000 slaves in the Colonies. Perhaps one of every five died on the 10-week voyage. Shackled below deck in foul-smelling, tight-packed rows (as shown in the engraving at left and in the diagram above), they subsisted on stagnant water and stale provisions. Those who fell ill were thrown overboard. Many went mad or died struggling with their captors or by throwing themselves into the sea.*

The United States *barred the legal importation of slaves in 1808, although thousands were subsequently smuggled in before the Civil War. The ban caused a labor pinch at a time when the cultivation of cotton was booming and spreading into the Southwest. The price of prime field hands soared from between $300 and $350 in 1790 to an average of $1,500 in 1860, and traffic in bodies became a major Southern industry. Most sales followed a familiar pattern: Slaves were purchased by dealers from the worn-out plantations of the upper South, then "sold down the river" to markets in the burgeoning Southwest. Virginia became a leader in providing slaves for sales in that region. All Southern cities and most sizable towns in the South held regular public slave auctions like the one shown at right. At these, human beings were displayed, poked, and prodded like livestock, then sold to the highest bidder. Washington, D.C., was—as one writer put it—"seat and center" of the interstate slave trade until Congress banned sales of slaves in the District of Columbia in 1850.*

The Involuntary Immigrants
(continued)

Plantation life for the slaves *was as wretched or as comfortable as their owners saw fit to make it. The slave quarters shown at right were characteristic of those found on many plantations by Union troops during the Civil War. The often windowless, one-room cabins, usually made of chinked logs, had dirt floors and few furnishings. Most slaves, like those shown below, toiled in the fields from dawn to dark, planting, tending, and harvesting the cotton, sugar, rice, and tobacco that were at the heart of the Southern economy. Some became craftsmen and mechanics, keeping the equipment and installations of the nearly self-sufficient plantations in good repair. A privileged few worked, and sometimes lived, in the "big house" as family servants. Many were hired out by their masters as artisans, mechanics, and factory workers at rates that depressed the wages of white workers in the South. Food, clothing, housing, and health care were generally adequate to keep the work force productive—anything less would have been bad business practice. Brutality was not uncommon, and the hopelessness of life in captivity beclouded the slave's every moment.*

Some 75,000 slaves *fled northward before the Civil War, relying on an Underground Railroad of 3,000 or so active sympathizers for aid and shelter along the way. Runaways risked being flogged and returned to their masters if seized by the professionals who made a living hunting them down. Anyone who abetted a slave's escape risked arrest and imprisonment. The shivering refugees in the painting below are shown arriving at Quaker abolitionist Levi Coffin's Indiana farm, an important station on the railroad. Stations were located a night's march apart. The map at right shows the most frequent routes followed by the slaves.*

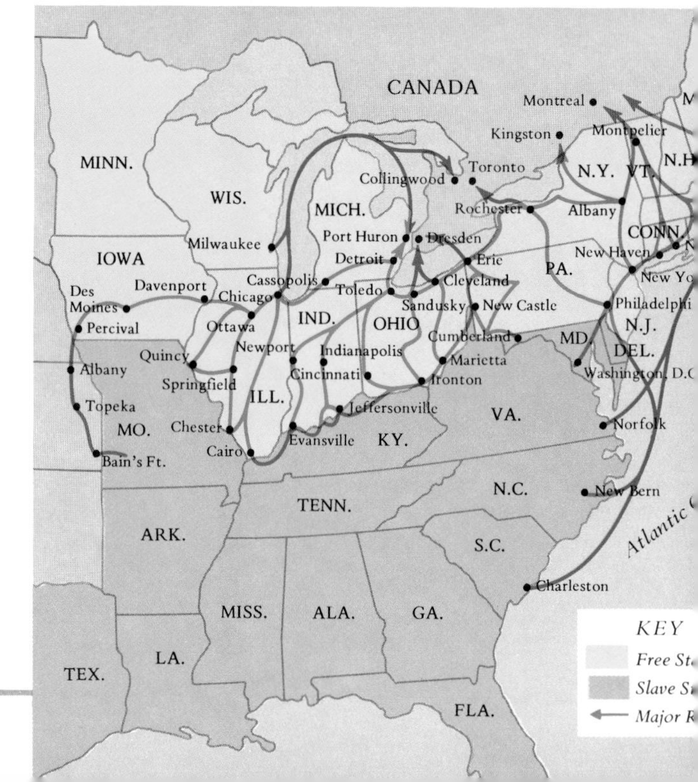

MAKING DEMOCRACY WORK

Black Americans Win the Right To Vote

"We have washed color out of the Constitution!" exulted abolitionist Wendell Phillips when the 15th amendment was ratified in 1870. In granting the ballot to all adult males regardless of "race, color or previous condition of servitude," the amendment made former slaves and their descendants full U.S. citizens—at least on paper. But the amendment was vitiated by Supreme Court decisions in the 1870's, by State statutes, and—on occasion—by violence and intimidation that in the South kept most blacks from the polls.

Among the most effective discriminatory statutes was the "grandfather clause," which enfranchised all persons whose fathers or grandfathers were qualified to vote on January 1, 1867. This measure permitted thousands of poor, illiterate whites to vote, but since no blacks could vote before 1867, they could qualify if at all only by meeting property-owning, tax-paying, and literacy requirements. The literacy test, monitored by prejudiced white registrars, disfranchised thousands of otherwise qualified blacks. But since the passage of the Voting Rights Act of 1965, blacks have been able to play a more active role in U.S. political life.

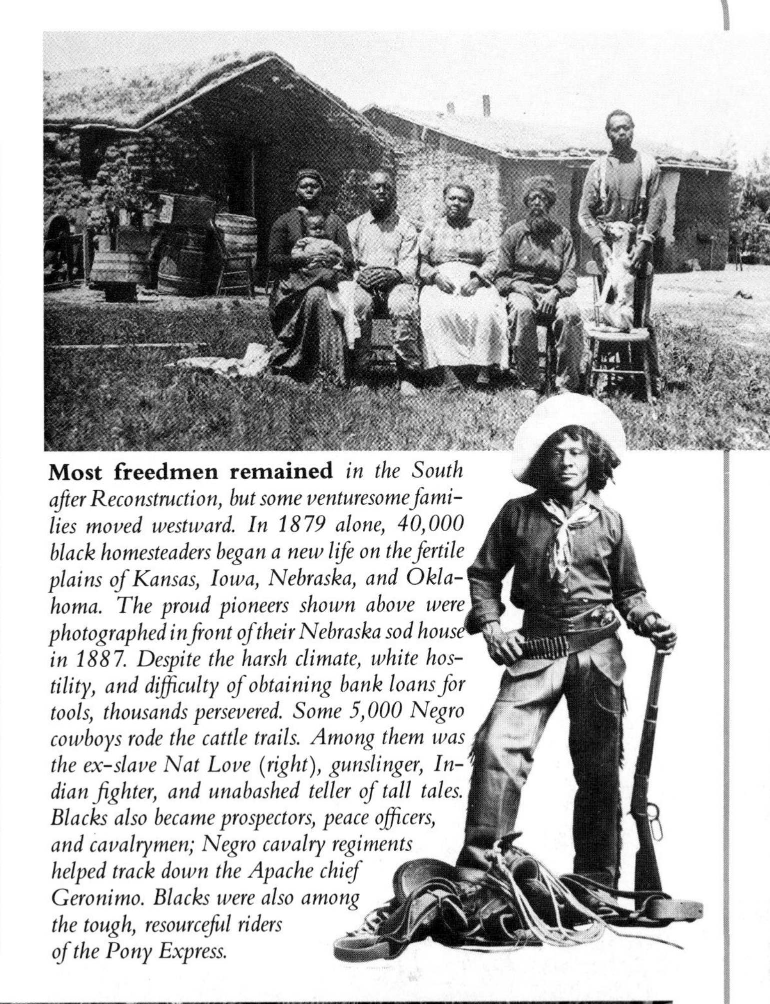

Most freedmen remained *in the South after Reconstruction, but some venturesome families moved westward. In 1879 alone, 40,000 black homesteaders began a new life on the fertile plains of Kansas, Iowa, Nebraska, and Oklahoma. The proud pioneers shown above were photographed in front of their Nebraska sod house in 1887. Despite the harsh climate, white hostility, and difficulty of obtaining bank loans for tools, thousands persevered. Some 5,000 Negro cowboys rode the cattle trails. Among them was the ex-slave Nat Love (right), gunslinger, Indian fighter, and unabashed teller of tall tales. Blacks also became prospectors, peace officers, and cavalrymen; Negro cavalry regiments helped track down the Apache chief Geronimo. Blacks were also among the tough, resourceful riders of the Pony Express.*

A massive population shift *brought millions of Southern blacks to Northern cities after 1900. In that year, 9 out of 10 Negroes still lived below the Mason-Dixon Line, most of them poor sharecroppers and tenant farmers. By 1970 almost half of the Nation's nearly 23 million blacks lived in the North and West. The overwhelming majority of these refugees from joblessness and Jim Crow settled in big-city neighborhoods like those shown in these photographs of Harlem, the heart of New York City's Negro community. Like earlier immigrants, they crowded into the decaying centers of the cities; unlike their predecessors, however, most blacks were blocked from improving their lot by discrimination in hiring, housing, and education. Although the Negro middle class has grown substantially in recent years, blacks and other nonwhites generally remain at the bottom of the economic ladder. How best to open up to all the full benefits of American life remains a central unfinished task of our democracy.*

The Era of the Know-Nothings

Fear and hostility toward newcomers were not new. Established Americans have always been ambivalent toward those who came later. Even George Washington tempered his enthusiasm for immigration. While declaring in 1783 that "the bosom of America is open to receive not only the Opulent and respectable Stranger, but the oppressed and persecuted of all Nations And Religions . . . ," he limited his welcome to those who "by decency and propriety of conduct . . . appear to merit the enjoyment." Although the Federal Government left immigration policy to the individual States, the Federalists sought to limit the influx through the Alien and Sedition Acts of 1798—ostensibly to thwart an alleged plot by French revolutionaries to overthrow the Republic, but actually to weaken immigrant support for Thomas Jefferson's emerging Democratic-Republican Party. These statutes, which expired in 1801, served only to cement the immigrant-Democratic alliance that has survived to modern times.

Traditional nativist anxieties might have remained manageable had most of the post-1830 immigrants been Protestants, for America remained an overwhelmingly Protestant Nation. As late as 1810, less than 1 percent of the population was Roman Catholic. But the Irish Catholic tide—216,000 in 1851 alone—frightened even mod-

The grim reality of steerage *is etched on the faces of these immigrants, photographed on the deck of the S.S.* Westernland *in 1890.*

Immigration Was Not Easy

Nor Was the Way of Life Upon Arrival

"All Europe is coming across the ocean," wrote a worried New Yorker as he surveyed the early immigrant tide in 1836. Goaded by grinding poverty at home, many set forth believing that in America the streets were paved with gold. They were swiftly disillusioned. Most of those who survived the grueling trip across the Atlantic in ships' steerage and the organized chaos of arrival soon found themselves in fierce competition for work and shelter in the appalling slums of the port cities. Others doggedly hacked out homes on the uncleared, sometimes savage frontier. Faced with America's rugged reality, many immigrants became embittered. Among those trapped in Manhattan sweatshops, "a curse on Columbus" became a common jibe. Edward Corsi recalled the lonely misery of his Italian-born mother, who spent her days and nights at her New York window, "staring up at the little patch of sky above the tenements." Nonetheless, most immigrants—or their children—adjusted and grew to think of their homelands with pride and nostalgia, but not with regret.

An apprehensive *Italian mother and children await processing at Ellis Island.*

Orchard Street *was the center of immigrant life on New York's Lower East Side.*

erate Protestants, as did tales of the newcomers' illiteracy, liking for alcohol, lack of marketable skills, and talent for political organization. Beginning in the 1830's secret anti-Catholic societies, with superpatriotic names such as "Order of the Star-Spangled Banner," joined with bigoted pamphleteers like inventor Samuel F. B. Morse to foment urban violence against the Irish. Soon nativist ruffians chanting "No Popery!" and Irishmen armed with brickbats clashed around big-city polling places; in the full-scale riots that often followed, churches and convents were razed and scores of lives were lost.

The rabble-rousing phrases and slogans were to become a familiar litany in American history. The immigrants were accused of threatening Protestantism; depressing wages and damaging unionism by their willingness to work cheaply; sending their meager savings home rather than plowing them back into the U.S. economy; filling jails and hospitals at public expense; and attempting to seize political power through corrupt party machines like New York's Tammany Hall. In 1854 several anti-immigrant groups merged to form the American Party, better known as the Know-Nothings because they were pledged to reply "I know nothing" to all queries about the party's secret doings. Know-Nothing candidates, vowing to bar Catholics and immigrants as office holders and to extend naturalization requirements from 5 to 21 years, had 48 congressional seats in 1855, and party leaders managed to persuade former President Millard Fillmore to run for the Presidency in 1856. He carried only one State (Maryland) and, like most single-issue parties, the Know-Nothings disintegrated thereafter, although some distrust of the foreign-born has endured to the present day.

Like the tormented Nation itself, the immigrant population was deeply divided by the Civil War. One Louisiana rebel regiment boasted of recruits from 37 foreign nations. The Union Army included Irish, German, Swedish, and multinational units, some commanded by officers barking orders in European languages. The Irish rallied to defend the Constitution in large numbers, but many resented risking their lives to free Negro slaves with whom they feared they would eventually compete for society's lowliest jobs. In July 1863, just 2 weeks after Irish troops had won almost universal Northern praise for gallantry at Gettysburg, Irish mobs roamed New York City, looting, burning, and lynching to protest the war and a draft that discriminated against the poor.

The Rising Tide

The dizzying rush of industrialization following the Civil War; the Homestead Act of 1862, which for a small filing fee offered 160 acres of public land to any man willing to become a citizen and live on the land for 5 years; and the growth of a railroad network that made

Ellis Island

Sturdy Italian immigrants step ashore (above) at New York's Ellis Island, the official entrance to America for half a century. After visiting the reception center in 1905 British author H. G. Wells wrote:

On they go, from this pen to that, pen by pen, towards a little metal wicket—the Gate of America. Through this wicket drips the immigration stream—all day long, every two or three seconds an immigrant, with a valise or bundle . . . into a new world.

Located in Upper New York Bay, Ellis Island was opened in 1892, after the immigrant flood had inundated a smaller facility called Castle Garden. Under its vast roof passed 25 million newcomers between 1892 and 1943. Long, shuffling lines of immigrants filed through a labyrinth of pipe-lined pens (below). Each one was given medical and intelligence tests and questioned about finances and job prospects. Those who seemed likely to become public charges were turned back, but most were admitted—as many as 5,000 a day.

"Where the Blame Lies," *an anti-immigration cartoon of the nativist 1890's. The diminutive mascot of the humor magazine* Judge *explains to Uncle Sam: "If immigration was properly restricted you would no longer be troubled with Anarchy, Socialism, the Mafia and such kindred evils!" The fear and hostility expressed here were shared by many Americans of older stock after the Civil War, when millions of peasants from Southern and Eastern Europe swelled the immigrant ranks to record numbers.*

virtually every region accessible to settlement—all these provided new allures for Europe's poor. Agents for U.S. railroads, shipping companies, and other industrial concerns fanned out across Europe. This contributed to history's most massive immigrant tide: An awesome 31 million people arrived in America between 1860 and 1930. At first most came from Northern and Western Europe and the British Isles, but the ratio began to change with startling swiftness in the mid-1880's as population pressure eased and prosperity increased in those areas. At the same time Southern and Eastern European markets were glutted with inexpensive grain and meat from America and Australia, threatening doom for local farmers and making emigration more attractive.

During the peak years (1900–20) more than 3 million immigrants came to the United States from Italy alone, mostly from the exhausted, sun-baked south. Another 3 million came from the heart of the crumbling Austro-Hungarian Empire (Austrians, Hungarians, Bohemians, Serbs, Slovaks, Czechs, and others). An additional 2.7 million arrived from Russia and Poland. Among them were entire villages of Jews, the weary targets of centuries of official and unofficial persecution, who hoped to find a better life in what they called the Golden Land. During these same two decades, well over 5 million more people came from Britain, Scandinavia, Germany, France, Portugal, Greece, Armenia, Syria, and other Old World nations—as well as from East Asia, Canada, and Mexico and other Latin American countries.

While these hopeful millions spoke scores of languages and came from all over the globe, they had some basic things in common: Most were uneducated, unskilled, poorly clothed, destitute or nearly so, and frightened. Without funds with which to purchase land, and bewildered by the fast-moving, fast-talking Americans they met, they tended to seek security and jobs among their fellow countrymen in the ethnic enclaves of the big cities. The vast majority settled in the industrial Northeast; most of the rest went to the industrial regions of the North Central States; a comparative few made their way west to farm colonies or homesteads. Soon virtually every Northern metropolis had its own "Little Italy" or "Little Warsaw," its foreign-language press, immigrant banks, and Old World holidays. The Lower East Side of New York—with more than 300,000 persons per square mile—was perhaps the most concentratedly cosmopolitan area on earth by 1890. By that year Chicago's stockyards and steel mills had made it a sprawling haven for newcomers from more than 40 lands, and the Nation's most international city, while Cleveland had 100,000 foreign-born residents, and Detroit had some 80,000. By 1910 two out of three New Yorkers had been born abroad. Most of those immigrants who did not settle in the cities swarmed into smaller industrial centers like the coal towns of Pennsylvania, the iron range of the northern Great Lakes, and the textile towns of New England. By 1912, for example, there were men and women from 25 nations, speaking 45 tongues, manning the looms of Lawrence, Massachusetts.

Despite the lofty hopes these immigrants carried with them, the conditions under which they lived and labored were often little better (and sometimes worse) than those they had left behind. As newcomers they started at the bottom of the American ladder. In New York's foulest slums, they were crowded into tiny, windowless tenement firetraps. The 12-hour workday and the 7-day week were standard for adults and children alike. Conditions in the coalfields and company towns were little better and were further complicated by bitter confrontations between union workers and unwitting immigrant strikebreakers, or by bloody rivalries between immigrant groups of differing origins.

A fed-up few actually returned to their homelands. But most endured; millions of unsung heroes and heroines stuck it out. "I am now in America," wrote one weary Jewish immigrant; "that means working." Through toil, patience, thrift, temperance, and self-denial, they overcame prejudice, poor pay, and despair to build better lives for themselves and their children. In this struggle they were sustained by the immigrant communities in which they lived and by ethnic newspapers, theaters, social clubs, and aid societies. Meanwhile, their children went to public schools—then still a rare privilege in much of Europe. "No application made, no questions asked," recalled one grateful immigrant, ". . . the doors stood open for every one of us." In the schools children of all nations mingled and were "Americanized." The language and skills they learned enabled many to break out of the ghetto into the American mainstream.

The New Nativism

Although the percentage of foreign-born Americans remained about the same (roughly 15 percent) throughout the period of the new immigration, its concentration in the cities and industrial centers of the North changed their character and shifted the balance of political power, to the dismay of many native Americans. The immigrant tide spawned a widespread resurgence of nativism. These newcomers *looked* different from their predecessors, and behaved differently. Many were dark haired, swarthy, and short. Most of them were Catholics. They spoke unfamiliar languages. They were unused to self-government and disposed to follow the ballot-box dictates of big-city bosses who, in return, provided jobs, handouts, and other favors unobtainable elsewhere. Alarmed by the crime, chaos, and crowding of the bloated cities, many rural Americans blamed the newcomers for the change. Anti-Catholics, notably the million-odd members of the Middlewestern American Protective Association, declaimed against the alleged menace of "the Catholic vote," and spread exaggerated tales of Italian criminal secret societies. Labor, too, opposed the newcomers, arguing that they lowered wages and took jobs from U.S. citizens. Management, which had eagerly backed unlimited immigration in order to ensure a ready supply of docile workers with whom to break strikes and offset the growing power of unions, began to question its wisdom as the newcomers themselves joined the unions, and foreign-born labor leaders—including a few anarchists and Socialists—rose to prominence.

The late 1800's and early 1900's, too, were the heyday of "Anglo-Saxonism," the widespread belief that what Massachusetts Senator Henry Cabot Lodge termed the unique "moral qualities of the English-speaking race" were threatened by an influx of "historically downtrodden, atavistic and stagnant races" from Eastern and Southern Europe. It was during this same period that the last Indian resistance was crushed in the West, Jim Crow laws

The Statue of Liberty

Ever since 1886, when her great torch was lifted into place 305 feet above Bedloe's (now Liberty) Island in New York harbor, the colossal statue of "Liberty Enlightening the World" has symbolized America for millions of eager newcomers. Many wept as they neared the American shore, recalling all they had left behind and apprehensive about what they might find in the new land. But with their first glimpse of the statue, one Italian immigrant recalled, they were "steadied . . . by the concreteness of the symbol of America's freedom, [and] they dried their tears."

The statue was the work of Alsatian sculptor Frédéric Auguste Bartholdi and was intended to commemorate both a century of amity between France and the United States and the concept of political freedom shared by the two nations. The book that Liberty holds in her left hand symbolizes the Declaration of Independence. The main figure is attached to an iron framework designed by Gustave Eiffel, builder of France's Eiffel Tower. The statue was paid for by French contributors; American schoolchildren participated in a nationwide drive to raise funds for the pedestal. On a tablet within are inscribed the last five lines of a sonnet, "The New Colossus," by Emma Lazarus, herself an immigrant:

Give me your tired, your poor,
Your huddled masses yearning to breathe free,
The wretched refuse of your teeming shore,
Send these, the homeless, tempest-tost to me,
I lift my lamp beside the golden door!

Shop signs along a single block *of Manhattan's multinational Ninth Avenue proclaim their owners' origins—Hispanic, Italian, French, Irish, and Jewish. Long the immigrant's entrance to the New World, New York remains the largest and most cosmopolitan city in the Nation; almost half of its 8 million citizens are foreign-born.*

were imposed to ensure white supremacy in the former Confederacy, and national enthusiasm for an overseas American empire reached its peak. The descendants of New England's Puritan founders, who for half a century had watched uneasily as newcomers assumed the power their ancestors had wielded, were the leading champions of the "old stock." In 1894 a group of Boston intellectuals established the influential Immigration Restriction League to try to turn the immigrant tide.

The Gates Begin To Close

"Wide open and unguarded stand our gates," wrote nativist poet Thomas Bailey Aldrich in 1892, "and through them presses a wild motley throng." It was to close those gates and keep out that throng that the new nativists worked so hard—and so successfully.

First to feel their wrath were the Pacific coast Chinese. The original Chinese immigrants had been attracted by the California Gold Rush. In the 1860's they were joined by some 75,000 fellow countrymen who worked as servants and gardeners, ran restaurants and laundries, and laid the tracks for the Central Pacific Railroad. Feared and scorned from the first because of his little-understood customs and willingness to work cheaply, the "heathen Chinee" became the target of widespread violence by competitive white workers during the 1870's. In 1882 Congress barred further Chinese immigration. This discriminatory law remained in effect until 1943, when the U.S. and China became wartime allies. Ironically, the exodus of Chinese that followed the 1882 action resulted in an influx of Japanese workers from Hawaii. They came initially to work in fields, factories, and canneries, and they stayed to prosper as truck farmers. The Japanese, too, aroused white resentment. They were unofficially barred by a so-called Gentlemen's Agreement in 1907 and new Japanese immigrants were excluded from citizenship by Congress in 1924. And in what Justice Frank Murphy denounced as "one of the most sweeping and complete deprivations of constitutional rights" in U.S. history, some 112,000 persons of Japanese descent were penned up in "detention centers" surrounded by barbed wire during most of World War II.

In 1882 Congress also imposed a head tax on each would-be immigrant and excluded paupers, idiots, and others likely to prove unable to fend for themselves. Three years later it curtailed contract labor. This was a much-abused practice, not unlike the colonial indenture system, by which U.S. contractors had been able to import work gangs willing to work at a specified job in exchange for their passage and wages far below the norm. Between 1897 and 1917 three congressional attempts to impose literacy tests aimed at barring most new immigrants were turned back by Presidential veto because, as Woodrow Wilson declared, the ability to read was "not a test of character, of quality or of personal fitness." Despite Wilson's veto, however, the last of these bills became law in 1917.

But the isolationist fervor that gripped the Nation after World War I finally proved irresistible. At the height of public alarm over subversion by "aliens and alien philosophies," in 1921 Congress passed a law that for the first time restricted the number of immigrants to this country. In 1924 a more comprehensive law limited immigration from any one nation to 2 percent of the estimated number of foreign-born persons from that nation living in the United States in 1890. Since up until that year the great majority of immigrants had come from Northern and Western Europe, the 1924 act favored them over immigrants from Eastern and Southern Europe.

The era of unchecked immigration was over—only 70,000 immigrants arrived during the Depression years of the 1930's. The quota system remained in effect for more than four decades, although its restrictions were temporarily eased several times to permit groups of refugees to find American sanctuary: These included displaced persons from war-torn Europe, Hungarians fleeing their country after the 1956 revolution, and Cubans escaping from Fidel Castro's government. The quota system was finally abandoned in 1965. Although the total number of immigrants allowed to enter the U.S. each year remains restricted, admittance is now based solely on a prospective immigrant's skills or profession or on his or her relationship to an American citizen.

But if immigration from abroad declined after 1924, the American populace remained restless and volatile. In the wake of Japanese exclusion, hundreds of thousands of Mexican families made their way north across the Rio Grande to toil in the fertile fields of the Pacific Coast States and the Southwest and to settle in the towns and cities along the way. Millions of Southern blacks—refugees from Jim Crow, the boll weevil, and the sharecropper system—sought jobs and shelter in the Northern cities. And almost a million Puerto Rican Americans who could not find jobs on their lovely but overcrowded island flocked to the continent in search of work.

Like the European immigrants who came before them, the Negroes, Puerto Ricans, and Mexicans brought with them distinctive cultures—as well as problems of assimilation and social and economic adjustment (further complicated by difference in color) that remain with us today.

MAKING DEMOCRACY WORK

The 1965 Immigration Act

For the signing of Public Law 89-326 on October 3, 1965, President Lyndon B. Johnson chose a fitting backdrop: the Statue of Liberty, symbol of America's welcome to the poor and oppressed of every land. Here was ended what Johnson termed "a cruel and enduring wrong"—the National Origins Quota System. Adopted in 1924 as a reaction to nativist fears of inundation by "undesirable aliens," quotas made race and ancestry rather than talents and skills the basis for the entry of a prospective American. Because of the quotas Africans, Asians, and Southern and Eastern Europeans were discriminated against in favor of immigrants from Northern and Western Europe.

Although the quota definitions were stretched repeatedly to provide sanctuary for political refugees in subsequent years, this discriminatory system prevailed for four decades. The 1965 act swept it away, making individual talents and skills or close relationship with U.S. citizens the criteria for admittance. "From now on," declared the President, "those who can contribute most to this country—to its growth, to its strength, to its spirit—will be the first that are admitted to this land."

The American People Today

"What then is the American, this new man?" Michel Guillaume Jean de Crèvecoeur, an enthusiastic French visitor, first posed that perplexing question in 1782. Even in his day his answer—that an American was "either an European or the descendant of an European"—was inadequate to describe a variegated people that already included Indians and Africans. But his prophecy that life in the New World would make sturdy, self-reliant, independent-minded citizens out of the persecuted peasants of the Old World and that their "labours and posterity will one day cause great changes in the world" has proved spectacularly accurate.

America's population remains richly diverse. Statistics tell part of the story. Of the Nation's more than 200 million citizens, 87.5 percent are classified as white by the U.S. Bureau of the Census; just over 11 percent are Negroes; the rest are Asians, Indians, and other nonwhite peoples. The majority, fully 65 percent, are other than "Anglo-Saxon." The celebrated WASP (White Anglo-Saxon Protestant) is in a distinct minority, although 2 out of 3 Americans belong to one of the more than 250 Protestant sects. About 1 out of 4 is Roman Catholic. Approximately 3 percent are Jewish.

It was once widely believed that the American "melting pot," fueled by the clash of immigrant cultures, would ultimately yield what Crèvecoeur called "a new race of man," free of all ancestral ties, concerned only with succeeding as Americans. Modern historians have shown, however, that the American crucible has proved healthily inefficient, producing an industrious, restless, patriotic American populace, which has nonetheless managed to hold on to much of its non-American heritage. In recent years the interest of America's myriad ethnic minorities in the customs and traditions of the lands from which their fathers came has grown, sparked in part by a new sense of self-esteem among black Americans. More accurate than "melting pot" might be the metaphor "salad bowl," implying that each ingredient contributes a distinctive texture and adds flavor to the whole.

As pollsters Richard Scammon and Benjamin Wattenberg have pointed out, "the only constant in the American recipe has been change in the mix." Once mostly English and Dutch, then one-fifth slave, then host to immigrants from a hundred lands, the American people have grown increasingly diverse as they have prospered. The national character has been immeasurably enriched by the special skills and outlooks each successive wave of newcomers has included in its ethnic luggage.

Despite sporadic setbacks and slowdowns, America continues to inch toward full realization of the ideal first expressed by Crèvecoeur almost two centuries ago. "Here," he wrote, "it is not asked what or who was your father, but . . . what are you?"

A Remembrance of Presidents Past

It has been the peculiar virtue of the highest post in the oldest republic on Earth that while some Presidents have done themselves little credit, none has dimmed the prestige of the office itself. Some, notably Washington, Lincoln, and the Roosevelts, enlarged the powers of the Presidency and were enlarged by their experiences in office. Others, who at first seemed too small for the Presidency, managed to fill it well. Only a few—notably, Grant, Harding, and Nixon—left tainted memories behind.

The Founding Fathers could not foresee the powers that would ultimately be given to the President, but they were wise enough both to allow for flexibility in the administration of the office and to establish limitations for it. Thus they left room for the occasional strong President, while ensuring that none could be other than an instrument of the people.

GEORGE WASHINGTON
1732–1799
FEDERALIST

President 1789–1797

Washington got the Nation off to a good start. Courageous, honest, decisive, and judicious, the hero of the Revolution addressed himself to the tasks of minimizing factionalism and setting worthy precedents in his every official act. Most modern historians agree he was neither a military nor a political genius. Yet he gave to the Presidency the aura of his own prestige.

JOHN ADAMS
1735–1826
FEDERALIST

Vice President 1789–1797
President 1797–1801

"Honest John" Adams was a philosopher and lawyer, a man of great intellectual gifts and solid accomplishments. Introspective and aloof, he never courted popularity. His legal defense of the British soldiers held responsible for the so-called Boston Massacre was a measure of his integrity. As President, he averted war with France.

THOMAS JEFFERSON
1743–1826
DEMOCRATIC-REPUBLICAN

Vice President 1797–1801
President 1801–1809

Scholar, writer, scientist, inventor, linguist, architect—Jefferson was amazingly versatile. Of his many achievements, two were preeminent: his authorship of the Declaration of Independence and his purchase of Louisiana from France. He was one of the most ardent champions of civil liberty of his day.

JAMES MADISON
1751–1836
DEMOCRATIC-REPUBLICAN

President 1809–1817

Madison, the "Father of the Constitution," worked out the system of checks and balances between the legislative, judicial, and executive branches that has proved the mainstay of American democracy. As President, Madison lost prestige during the War of 1812, but he regained it when the victorious end of the war brought a surge of national feeling and unity.

JAMES MONROE
1758–1831
DEMOCRATIC-REPUBLICAN

President 1817–1825

The last of Virginia's Revolutionary generation to lead the Nation, Monroe was honest and sensible. A successful diplomat, he proved a first-rate administrator as President. In 1823 he and John Quincy Adams enunciated, in the Monroe Doctrine, the principle of U.S. hegemony in the Western Hemisphere, warning European nations not to meddle in Latin America.

JOHN QUINCY ADAMS
1767–1848
DEMOCRATIC-REPUBLICAN

President 1825–1829

A brilliant Secretary of State, Adams refused to reward his friends when he became President. But his high-mindedness left his foes in control of Congress, and he could do little but wait for his ordeal of office to end. In 1831, however, he returned to the House, where "Old Man Eloquent" defended the right to petition, then denied to abolitionists by "gag rules."

ANDREW JACKSON
1767–1845
DEMOCRAT

President 1829–1837

"Old Hickory" brought a breath of fresh frontier air to the Presidency. Short-tempered and autocratic, the victor of New Orleans curbed congressional powers and expanded his own. Although he committed blunders in office, he had an instinctive feeling for the common people, many of whom had only recently gained the vote and who regarded Jackson as one of themselves.

MARTIN VAN BUREN
1782–1862
DEMOCRAT

Vice President 1833–1837
President 1837–1841

The diminutive, elegant Van Buren's unification of the Democratic Party helped Jackson win the Presidency in 1828 and 1832. When President himself, Van Buren proved courageous and farsighted. But his popularity declined when the Panic of 1837 brought on a severe depression, and Harrison easily defeated him in 1840.

WILLIAM HENRY HARRISON
1773–1841
WHIG

President March–April 1841
A genial, wealthy landowner and military hero, Harrison was the first Whig candidate to win the Presidency. His party chose him not for his political acumen but because of his reputation as the general who "saved the Northwest." Unfortunately for the Whigs, he died after a month in office, saddling them with a President, Tyler, who was more Democrat than Whig.

JOHN TYLER
1790–1862
WHIG

Vice President March–April 1841
President 1841–1845
Abruptly elevated to the highest office, Tyler determined to be President in fact as well as in name. The Virginia aristocrat was soon a President without a party. His impressive record in foreign affairs included settlement of parts of the Canadian border. He later became a Civil War secessionist.

JAMES KNOX POLK
1795–1849
DEMOCRAT

President 1845–1849
Small, neat, composed, cool, Polk seemed the antithesis of the frontiersman. Yet under the banner of Manifest Destiny he fulfilled the expansionist will of the people in acquiring California and New Mexico for the Union, establishing the Oregon boundary, and confirming possession of Texas. A tireless worker of rocklike integrity, he wore himself out in office.

ZACHARY TAYLOR
1784–1850
WHIG

President 1849–1850
A string of victories in the Mexican War hoisted "Old Rough and Ready" into the Presidency. Though a slaveholding southerner, he was above all a nationalist. Hampered by political inexperience, he was nevertheless determined to halt the spread of slavery and threatened to lead an army against any Southern rebellion. His sudden death smoothed the way for compromise.

MILLARD FILLMORE
1800–1874
WHIG

Vice President 1849–1850
President 1850–1853
Though against slavery, Fillmore enforced the unpopular, and unsuccessful, Compromise of 1850 as a means of saving the Union. He had more success in gaining foreign markets for American business, notably in Japan, through an expedition headed by Matthew C. Perry.

FRANKLIN PIERCE
1804–1869
DEMOCRAT

President 1853–1857
Although kindly, introspective, reasonable, and a skillful orator, Pierce was more follower than leader. Unable to see why northerners were so "fanatical" about slavery, he failed to grasp the burning moral issue of the day. He had some successes in foreign policy, but could not cope with civil strife in Kansas over the slave question, or the passionate sectionalism it aroused.

JAMES BUCHANAN
1791–1868
DEMOCRAT

President 1857–1861
Buchanan had shown skill in diplomacy, but as President he found himself in the eye of a domestic storm that he could not master. Bemused by legalisms (no State, he said, had the right to secede, but the Government had no right to coerce it), Buchanan marked time while the Union fell apart. History best knows him as "the President before Lincoln."

ABRAHAM LINCOLN
1809–1865
REPUBLICAN

President 1861–April 1865
Possibly the Nation's greatest President, Lincoln set standards of integrity and wisdom by which his successors are judged. A superb orator, he was essentially a loner; a believer in persuasion, he would fight for principle. Decisive in war, magnanimous in victory, putting the Union above even the Constitution, he answered America's need. His assassination caused worldwide grief.

ANDREW JOHNSON
1808–1875
NATIONAL UNION

Vice President March–April 1865
President 1865–1869
Both a southerner and a Unionist, this blunt, strong-minded former tailor seemed an ideal man to continue Lincoln's generous Reconstruction policy, but unfortunately he lacked political wisdom and tact. Republican radicals, enraged by his leniency toward the South, had him impeached. The Senate acquitted him—barely.

ULYSSES SIMPSON GRANT
1822–1885
REPUBLICAN

President 1869–1877
Victorious commander of the Union Army and one of America's ablest generals, Grant had neither a taste nor an aptitude for politics. He was an honest man with compassion for the oppressed, but he fell under the sway of the rich and powerful, and his administration was dogged by scandal. Dying of cancer, he completed his memoirs in 1883 to make his family financially secure.

Presidents Past *(continued)*

RUTHERFORD BIRCHARD HAYES
1822–1893
REPUBLICAN

President 1877–1881
Dignified and conservative, able if not brilliant, Hayes believed that the least government was the best—a view well suited to a people eager for a breathing spell and a chance to exploit vast new resources. He ended Reconstruction, chose his Cabinet for ability, defended Presidential authority against party encroachments, and defended the civil service from spoilsmen.

JAMES ABRAM GARFIELD
1831–1881
REPUBLICAN

President March–September 1881
A fiery orator, Garfield had been a teacher and preacher before entering politics. In the 4 active months of his Presidency he was preoccupied with trying to heal factionalism within his party and to halt the vicious jockeying for lucrative posts. His investigation of corruption in the postal system, and his assassination by a disappointed office seeker, spurred civil service reform.

CHESTER ALAN ARTHUR
1830–1886
REPUBLICAN

Vice President March–September 1881
President 1881–1885
Tall and stout, with a taste for good living, Arthur had the reputation of being a tool of the corrupt Republican Party machine. On acceding to the Presidency, however, he continued civil service reform and carried out his duties with dignity and honesty, to the chagrin of the party, which did not renominate him.

GROVER CLEVELAND
1837–1908
DEMOCRAT

President 1885–1889; 1893–1897
The only Democratic President elected between Buchanan and Wilson, Cleveland had won renown as a reform Governor of New York. Heavy-set and amiable, he was unshakably honest but obstinate and narrowminded. He did much to clean up the Government but failed to curb monopolies and had no solution for the Nation's pressing farm and labor problems.

BENJAMIN HARRISON
1833–1901
REPUBLICAN

President 1889–1893
Grandson of a former President, Harrison was an aloof, fastidious man who made a dignified but second-rate President. In foreign affairs he bettered pan-American relations, but domestically he took orders from party bosses and the industrialists and bankers who had poured money into his campaign. He also ignored the mounting unrest among farmers and workers.

WILLIAM McKINLEY
1843–1901
REPUBLICAN

President 1897–September 1901
McKinley's political rise was supported by millionaire industrialist Mark Hanna. A popular President who made a study of public opinion, McKinley promoted high tariffs and inaugurated a period of imperial expansion when, after the Spanish-American War, he annexed the Philippines and Hawaii. He was assassinated in his second term.

THEODORE ROOSEVELT
1858–1919
REPUBLICAN

Vice President March–September 1901
President 1901–1909
Born frail and asthmatic, popular Teddy developed into an outdoorsman of volcanic energy. Scholar and scientist as well as politician, he brought new dash to the Presidency. His domestic concerns were "trust busting," conservation, and a "square deal" for the worker. In foreign affairs he was an unashamed expansionist.

WILLIAM HOWARD TAFT
1857–1930
REPUBLICAN

President 1909–1913
Taft was a genial giant weighing over 300 pounds. His area of greatest expertise was the law. As President, he carried on the policies of his friend Roosevelt, prosecuting even more antitrust suits, but he did so in a spirit of legalistic conservatism that alienated his party's progressive wing. In 1921 he became Chief Justice of the United States, fulfilling a lifelong ambition.

WOODROW WILSON
1856–1924
DEMOCRAT

President 1913–1921
A man of academic background, austere manner, and self-righteous moral fervor, Wilson put his heart into a program of limited progressivism until world crises absorbed him. After ill-conceived intervention in Mexico, he applied U.S. force decisively in World War I. An advocate of a new world order, he could not persuade his own country to join the League of Nations.

WARREN GAMALIEL HARDING
1865–1923
REPUBLICAN

President 1921–1923
Affable, easygoing, and indecisive, Harding proved better at playing poker than at governing, and signally failed to fulfill his promise to set the Nation back on its "onward, normal way." A poor judge of character, he was betrayed by many of the cronies he put in office. After his sudden death on a tour of the West, widespread corruption was revealed in his administration.

CALVIN COOLIDGE
1872–1933
REPUBLICAN

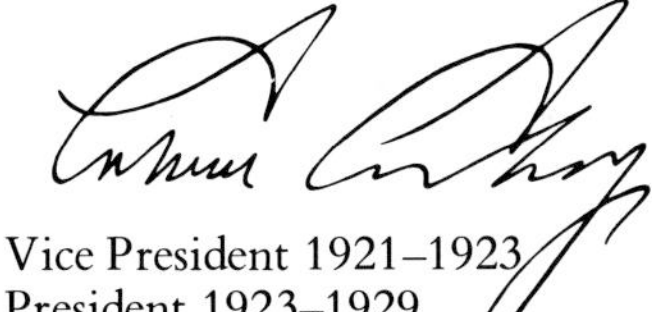

Vice President 1921–1923
President 1923–1929
This shy, upright, conservative Vermonter came to the White House like a whiff of fresh if rather chilling air. His belief that government should be unobtrusive and that "the business of America is business" paid off in the prosperous 1920's. He showed vigor in foreign affairs and appointed two capable Secretaries of State.

HERBERT CLARK HOOVER
1874–1964
REPUBLICAN

President 1929–1933
Hoover was a mining engineer and humanitarian of international repute before becoming President. In office he proved a skillful administrator, but his doctrinaire faith in self-reliance and free enterprise ill suited him to an understanding of the problems arising out of the Nation's worst depression. He reemerged as an honored public servant after World War II.

FRANKLIN DELANO ROOSEVELT
1882–1945
DEMOCRAT

President 1933–April 1945
Roosevelt's four-term Presidency was an American turning point. Forceful, imaginative, and charming—polio contracted at the age of 39 seemed to deepen and strengthen his spirit—he battled the Depression, expanded the powers of the Presidency, and committed America against Nazi-Fascist barbarism well before U.S. entry into World War II.

HARRY S. TRUMAN
1884–1972
DEMOCRAT

Vice President January–April 1945
President 1945–1953
Truman projected an image of the average man. He was far from that. Succeeding to the Presidency late in World War II, he guided his country into the atomic age. At home, though not always wise in his choice of advisers, he launched a wide liberal program. Abroad, he helped rehabilitate Europe and "contain" Russia.

DWIGHT DAVID EISENHOWER
1890–1969
REPUBLICAN

President 1953–1961
As Supreme Allied Commander in Western Europe in 1944, Eisenhower exhibited great tact and administrative ability. As a popular President, he tried both to contain communism and ease world tensions, delegating much authority to Secretary of State John Foster Dulles. His warnings against the power of the American "military-industrial complex" were farsighted.

JOHN FITZGERALD KENNEDY
1917–1963
DEMOCRAT

President 1961–1963
At 43 Kennedy was the youngest man and the first Roman Catholic elected President. His wit, grace, intelligence, and good looks; his dedication to national service; and his handpicked band of "New Frontiersmen" inspired enthusiasm and a sense of renewal. When he was assassinated, he was globally mourned, and something of his elan long outlived him.

LYNDON BAINES JOHNSON
1908–1973
DEMOCRAT

Vice President 1961–1963
President 1963–1969
Abruptly elevated to the world's most powerful office, Johnson swiftly took charge. Energetic and forceful, with a genius for political persuasion, he strove through enlightened civil rights legislation and other measures to realize his vision of a Great Society. But the war in Vietnam weakened his hold on the electorate.

RICHARD MILHOUS NIXON
1913–
REPUBLICAN

Vice President 1953–1961
President 1969–1974
Ambitious, managerial, vehemently anti-Communist during his early political career, Nixon worked long and hard to be President. He achieved striking successes in foreign affairs—most notably, détente with Russia and China—but the domestic Watergate scandal forced him to resign in the face of threatened impeachment.

Powers of the President

The Constitution states that "executive power shall be vested in a President" whose duty is to "take Care that the Laws be faithfully executed." From its brief outline of Presidential power, the Presidency has grown to be the unique institution it is today. The President is Commander in Chief of the Armed Forces. He can make treaties by and with the advice and consent of the Senate, provided two-thirds of the Senators present concur. He can name Ambassadors and receive Envoys from other countries. He can appoint Supreme Court Justices and other U.S. officers whose appointments are not otherwise provided for, and which shall be established by law. He may call for the written opinion of the principal officer of any executive department concerning any aspect of his work. He may summon Congress to special session and adjourn both Houses in case of disagreement between them with respect to the time of adjournment—a privilege never yet used. He can veto bills, although Congress may override him. He can grant pardons and reprieves. He may make recommendations to Congress.

CHAPTER NINETEEN

Developing a Social Conscience

America has long found her social problems perplexin and has faced them with mixed emotions and solutior In a country that has always cherished the ideal, if n the reality, of equal opportunity for all, we have unde standably respected and admired individual striving ar accomplishment. Most of us have been brought up to belie that industry, thrift, patience, and moderation are bour to bring rewards. The merits of such virtues were ea enough to document in the early years, even though fro the beginning substantial segments of our population we excluded from the American dream. As our numbers swell and the character and quality of our society became increa

John Woolman, Quaker— Apostle of Human Freedom

Son of a well-to-do New Jersey farmer and fruitgrower, John Woolman felt called to the Quaker ministry at a remarkably early age. Strong in his dislike of ostentation and in his advocation of moderation in all things, he conscientiously limited his earnings from his tailoring shop and from other profitable activities in which he engaged. At the age of 23 he began a series of journeys, extending over 30 years, which took him throughout the Colonies and as far as Yorkshire, England, preaching to Quakers and to whomever else would listen.

Although some of his efforts were spent converting Indians and opposing military conscription, Woolman's most urgent work was directed toward the abolition of slavery. Nearly 100 years before the Civil War, he was one of the first to raise his voice, warning:

> *The seeds of great calamity and desolation are sown and growing fast on this continent. Placing on men the ignominious title SLAVE . . . keeping them to servile labour in which they are often dirty, tends gradually to fix a notion in the mind that they are a sort of people below us in nature, and leads us to consider them as such.*

In his persuasive essay "Some Considerations on the Keeping of Negroes," Woolman counseled Quaker slaveholders to consider the moral and ethical implications of the control of one man's life by another.

Woolman mingled with his denunciations of slavery praises of voluntary simplicity in everyday life. In "A Plea for the Poor" he wrote movingly of the personal and social evils inherent in the ambitious pursuit of luxuries and fancy possessions. Woolman's teachings had little immediate effect, but they made a lasting impression. He is remembered both for his *Journal,* in which he tells of his self-doubts and religious concerns, and for his struggle to obtain social justice for all.

When illness or disaster struck the early settlers, the family and near neighbors pitched in to help, providing food, shelter, and financial aid. With the passage of time and the development of a more complicated society, communities began to recognize their responsibility for the victims of misfortune, and each town or parish took care of its own.

As early as the mid-1600's, both in New England and in the South, regulations governing relief to the needy —"poor laws," as they were called—and requirements for the education and care of the orphaned young had been passed. In Massachusetts it was common practice for the town selectmen to "put out" the aged or infirm to the care of willing local families, with money allotted from the town's taxes to ease the burden. In Virginia the vestrymen of the parish saw to the apprenticing of poor or orphaned youngsters to families where they would get a rudimentary education and learn a trade.

For the itinerant vagrant or those who would not work, however, there was no such compassion. In New England, heavily influenced by an unbending Protestant work ethic, rejection of the idle poor took the form of "warning out." Newcomers, even short-term visitors, had to establish their means of support before they were allowed to remain; otherwise they were warned out of town. As the tide of immigrants swelled and communities grew larger and more cumbersome to govern, the number of unemployed increased. The old remedies of whipping, imprisoning, or forcibly indenturing the unemployed as servants no longer sufficed. By the 18th century workhouses had been set up to put the jobless to honest labor. These, along with almshouses and jails, served at least to remove some of the unfortunates from the disapproving eyes of colonial society.

William Penn, arriving in his colony of Pennsylvania in 1682, encouraged the most humanitarian approach of *gly complicated, the inequities multiplied. Still, many mericans clung doggedly to the Jeffersonian concept that e best government is that which governs least, and insisted at social problems should be left in private hands.*

Despite mighty efforts on the part of individual reformers d philanthropists, no Promised Land hove into view for e poor and the homeless, the sick and the enslaved, the educated and the delinquent, or the "outsiders" doomed poverty and despair because of their racial or ethnic ori- ns. Growing numbers of Americans became convinced at only a concentrated, broad-based national attack on cial, economic, and political inequalities could reaffirm the lofty principles on which America was founded. This view broke into the open for the first time with President Franklin D. Roosevelt's dynamic social experimentation during the Depression. What many regarded at first as dangerous radicalism gradually came to be accepted in virtually all shades of political opinion. Government, at the State and the national level, found itself shouldering ever greater responsibility for the welfare of the people. America still fell far short of coping with her social problems, but an unprecedented national awareness of their existence gave hope that the groundwork was being laid for a better and more even-handed spreading of the good life.

any—significantly, he called his new capital Philadelphia, "City of Brotherly Love." Under the influence of the Society of Friends (Quakers), Pennsylvania continued to lead the way in social progress. Pennsylvania Hospital, the first public hospital in America, was founded in Philadelphia in 1751 by Benjamin Franklin and Dr. Thomas Bond. It had a section that endeavored to care for the mentally ill, instead of simply restraining them, as was common at the time. Quakers welcomed to the Colony all Christians regardless of nationality or social status. To the poor they gave aid and opportunity; to the religiously oppressed, freedom of worship; and to criminals, some hope for rehabilitation. All men within the Quaker sphere of influence were advised to avoid flaunting their wealth and to strive for a more equal distribution of wordly goods.

Noble in purpose, too, was the scheme, conceived by Englishman James Oglethorpe and several well-to-do associates, for the colonization of Georgia (1733–41). Here a selected group of adventurers, former inmates of English debtors' prisons, and German, Swiss, and Scottish artisans were given a fresh start in life. With free land, most got free passage; in return they pledged to defend the Crown in case of war with the neighboring Spanish colonies. Rules were strict: Slavery was forbidden, as was hard liquor, and the new settlers were expected to produce silk and wine. Frankly paternalistic and not a little despotic, Oglethorpe's daring exercise in benevolence sought radically to change the lot of the poor. As a practical undertaking, however, it was not a success. The silk and wine industries failed, and the settlers took up the growing of rice and indigo, using slaves for labor. In 1752 there were fewer than 2,000 white settlers. Oglethorpe, who had returned to England in 1743, and his associates gave up their charter, and Georgia became a royal province.

Often called the *universal reformer for his espousal of social causes,* New York Tribune *editor Horace Greeley was memorialized in this 1890 sculpture by John Quincy Adams Ward.*

The Spirit of Moral Reform

After the Revolution America entered a period of lively growth; her population swelled, the frontier continued to move westward, and new methods and machinery aided both industrial expansion and Southern agriculture. Such inevitable development caused immense changes in the quality of American life and occasioned, in the years between 1830 and 1860, the first ambitious moral and social stocktaking in our history.

The movement that developed emphasized the rights and aspirations of the individual. Its leaders were an enthusiastic and remarkably intelligent group of New Englanders, including Margaret Fuller, Horace Mann, Wendell Phillips, Catharine Beecher, Horace Greeley, Dr. Samuel G. Howe, and Theodore Weld. Taking their cue from the teachings of Unitarian ministers William Ellery Channing and Theodore Parker and from the philosophy of Transcendentalist writers Ralph Waldo Emerson and Henry David Thoreau, these social critics searched every corner of American life for evidence of

Champion of the Helpless

As a volunteer Sunday school teacher in a women's jail in East Cambridge, Massachusetts, in 1841, Dorothea Lynde Dix first stumbled on the terrible reality of America's treatment of the mentally ill. These unfortunates were, she charged in her *Memorial to the Legislature of Massachusetts* in 1843, "chained, naked, beaten with rods and lashed into obedience." Her report, based on months of visiting jails and almshouses, stunned everyone. She particularly condemned the practice of herding together criminals, the needy, and the mentally ill under one roof. A bill was finally passed providing separate and adequate space for the insane in Boston and Worcester, but for this indomitable New England spinster that was only the beginning. A chronic invalid whose ill health had forced her to give up schoolteaching, Miss Dix went from State to State, North and South, making her surveys and reporting the dreadful facts. Between 1845 and 1852 she was able to persuade the legislatures of Indiana, Illinois, Kentucky, Tennessee, Missouri, Mississippi, Louisiana, Alabama, South Carolina, North Carolina, and Maryland to build new State hospitals.

However, she was not always successful; a major disappointment was President Franklin Pierce's veto of a Federal bill allotting 5 million acres of Government-owned land to the States for the benefit of the indigent insane. Nevertheless, Miss Dix became, before her death in 1887, internationally famous for her effective labors in the cause of humane treatment for the insane everywhere in the world.

any impediment to the natural flowering and perfectibility of man's soul. Marriage, drinking habits, war, education, the treatment of mental and emotional ailments, industrial practices, women's rights, slavery, and prison conditions were all vigorously analyzed in spirited, argumentative meetings, pamphlets, and speeches. As Emerson wryly pointed out, "It was a day when almost every man you met might draw a plan for a new society or a new government from his pocket." The zeal displayed was sometimes obsessive, but the reform movement was more than mere hot air and heady words; real social progress developed, particularly on local and State levels.

In the field of education, Horace Mann and Henry Barnard worked to improve public schools; other educators devoted themselves to the handicapped. Thomas H. Gallaudet started America's first free school for the deaf in Hartford in 1817, while John Dix Fisher organized the Perkins Institution for the Blind in Boston in 1829. Dr. Samuel G. Howe, head of the school for 44 years, was able, for example, to demonstrate through 8-year-old Laura Dewey Bridgman, who was both deaf and blind, that a person thus handicapped was not necessarily mentally defective, but could be brought into meaningful communication with the rest of the world.

During this era workers too were showing signs of social discontent. In Philadelphia, New York, and Boston, journeymen shoemakers, printers, tailors, and carpenters formed societies (really trade unions) in the 1790's and early 1800's to demand a minimum wage and a 10-hour day. A Working Man's Party developed in Philadelphia in 1828 and in New York in 1829 to agitate for free public education and against imprisonment for debt. In the 1830's the National Trades' Union was organized by locals from six cities, but it collapsed during the Panic of 1837. The labor movement was hampered in its early stages by court decisions holding that unions were unlawful conspiracies to restrain trade. In 1842, however, Chief Justice Lemuel Shaw of the Supreme Judicial Court of Massachusetts overturned the conspiracy doctrine in a landmark case, *Commonwealth* v. *Hunt.* He ruled that unions were lawful institutions so long as the methods they used in attaining their ends were "honorable and peaceful."

Emigration to the West was one answer for the discontented, but land, though plentiful, was not cheap; 80 acres cost $100 in the 1820's—a price most farm tenants and laborers in the East could not afford. Under the sway of such partisans as land-reformer George Henry Evans ("Vote yourself a farm") and publisher Horace Greeley ("Go West, young man, go West"), a powerful political drive for free homesteads began. But it took years of intensive campaigning before Congress passed the Homestead Act of 1862.

Another alternative for those unhappy with American society was to join one of the many Utopian communities springing up. Here anarchists and religious fanatics as well as less radical reformers and idealists attempted to put their beliefs into practice by creating cooperative societies in which all members would share equally. Probably the best known and most intellectually fertile was Brook Farm in West Roxbury, Massachusetts. Begun by the Transcendentalist followers of Ralph Waldo Emerson, its members included Margaret Fuller, editor of *The Dial*; Charles A. Dana; John S. Dwight; and, for a brief stay, Nathaniel Hawthorne. These Utopias were often short lived. Bronson Alcott's austere, badly managed Fruitlands in the town of Harvard, Massachusetts, lasted barely 7 months. Occasionally the communities were downright radical. John Humphrey Noyes' Oneida Community in western New York advocated "complex marriage," in which no one had an exclusive right to a marriage partner. Nonetheless these experiments stirred many Americans to look critically at the character and promise of their own lives.

Women were often the most vocal and influential members of reform groups and were particularly active in the temperance movement. By the time the American Society for the Promotion of Temperance was founded in 1826, many advocates of the movement had hardened their positions and were calling for total abstinence on the grounds that liquor was one of the major causes of poverty and domestic strife among workers. In the 1840's the movement got a strong boost when a Washington, D.C., group headed by several reformed drunkards not only preached abstinence but offered to help keep the converted on the wagon, much as Alcoholics Anonymous does today. By 1851 there was a signal victory: Maine went dry. It was a portent of things to come.

Women's own plight—their sketchy education, their ambiguous legal status, their uncertain role in a growing America—was also much on the minds of both male and female reformers. At a 2-day convention in Seneca Falls, New York, in 1848, a bill of women's rights was adopted. Thereafter, the convention's leaders, Elizabeth Cady Stanton and Lucretia Coffin Mott, along with intellectuals such as Margaret Fuller, continued to argue and work forcefully for the full development of women as free, equal individuals.

Of all the issues that claimed the reformers' time and energies, none so bound them together in moral outrage and sorrow as the fight against slavery. In the years immediately following the Revolution there was little effective agitation for an end to slavery. A Federal law that banned the importation of slaves after 1808 was opposed by Southern planters and by prosperous New Englanders engaged in the slave trade, and Congress was reluctant to enforce the edict. It was not until 1831, when the fiery William Lloyd Garrison electrified the country with the first issue of his newspaper, *The Liberator,* that true battle lines were drawn. Garrison wrote: "I shall strenuously contend for the immediate enfranchisement of our slave population . . . I will be as harsh as truth and as uncompromising as justice . . . I will not retreat a single inch —AND I WILL BE HEARD." Organizing the first chapter of the New England Anti-Slavery Association the following year, he outlined his unyielding stand: Nothing short of immediate emancipation would satisfy him. He would have no truck with gradual emancipation or the return of blacks to Africa as advocated by others.

Abolition quickly found supporters in the North and West. By 1836 there were 500 local abolition societies and by 1840 memberships had risen to more than 150,000. Many abolitionists, however, held more moderate views than the militant, often abrasive Garrison. Among those who actively worked to bring real change were Wendell Phillips, Frances Wright, Horace Greeley, and Theodore Weld. Joining them from the South were some who had freed their slaves, including the famous Grimké sisters of South Carolina and James G. Birney of Alabama. Birney later moved to the North and ran for President twice (1840 and 1844) on the ticket of the Liberty Party, whose single issue was abolition. Also from the South came runaway slaves such as Frederick Douglass, perhaps the most articulate and effective of the blacks who fought for emancipation, and Sojourner Truth, a quick-witted and highly persuasive former slave who supported both abolition and women's rights. In the Midwest Presbyterian Charles G. Finney turned his talents and the considerable prestige of Oberlin College, of which he was president, not only to supporting abolition but also to creating equal opportunities and better living conditions for free blacks in the North. Two ardent abolitionists died for the cause: Elijah P. Lovejoy, who had edited a Presbyterian paper advocating gradual emancipation, was killed while defending his press from a mob in Alton, Illinois, and John Brown, leader of a raid on

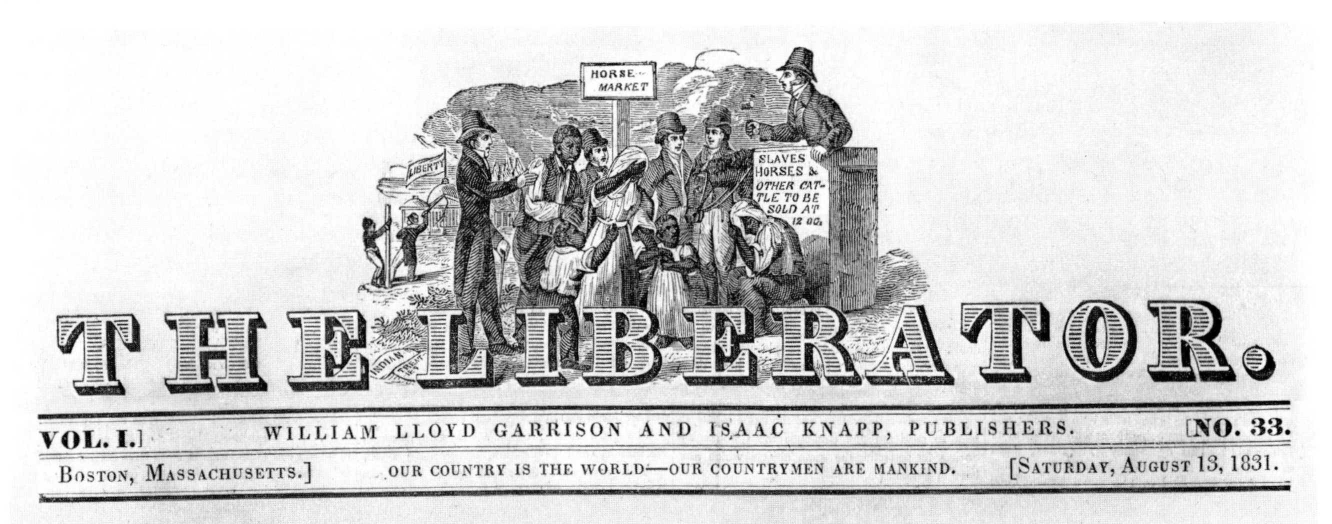

THE LIBERATOR.

VOL. I.] WILLIAM LLOYD GARRISON AND ISAAC KNAPP, PUBLISHERS. [NO. 33.

BOSTON, MASSACHUSETTS.] OUR COUNTRY IS THE WORLD—OUR COUNTRYMEN ARE MANKIND. [SATURDAY, AUGUST 13, 1831.

"The Liberator," *William Lloyd Garrison's influential abolitionist newspaper, appeared weekly from 1831 to 1865. Northern moderates were alarmed at its angry demands, southerners outraged. In its first year* The Liberator *had 450 subscribers, 400 of them black. The paper declared itself to belong not to the whites ("they do not sustain it") but "emphatically to the people of color—it is their organ."*

A Nobleman's View of Democracy

Among the many Europeans who came to record their impressions of the fledgling democracy in the New World, none made a more lasting impact than Alexis de Tocqueville, a young French nobleman. In 1831 and 1832 he and a friend traveled around the United States. The French Government had sent them to report on the U.S. penal system, but they were more interested in observing the evolution of the American democracy. Tocqueville's *Democracy in America,* the first parts of which were published in 1835 when he was 30, was immediately recognized as a major intellectual document analyzing the differences between aristocratic and democratic governments. Disillusioned with conditions in France and hopeful of finding a workable alternative, Tocqueville set out to study the political system and the day-by-day life of Americans. He found far more to praise than to criticize. Even today, though many of the practices and social customs he described have greatly changed, much of his astute commentary is as valid as when it was first written. Especially pertinent are his observations on the conflict over the right of the individual to be free and the duty of the government to promote the general welfare and to maintain order.

Perhaps his most telling insights are those dealing with the character and social relations of Americans. Describing as typically American the twin characteristics of individualism and a basic restlessness of spirit, Tocqueville was amazed at how well these qualities had been tempered by a love of equality and an insistence on political liberties and free institutions. As Americans participate in government, said the French commentator, they recognize that it is in their own interest, as well as their duty to be useful to other men. What begins as a necessity afterward becomes a choice, he found, and in the end Americans "acquire a habit and taste for serving their fellow citizens."

His chief concern for the social well-being of the United States centered on its treatment of the Indians and blacks. He foresaw that the Indians would ultimately be dispossessed as the whites continued to push westward. As for the blacks, he decried slavery as "one calamity which penetrated furtively into the world," and judging by what he saw in the North and the West, he predicted that discrimination would survive abolition. "Race prejudice seems stronger in those states that have abolished slavery than in those where it still exists," he wrote. "So the Negro is free, but he cannot share the rights, pleasures, labors, griefs, or even the tomb of him whose equal he has been declared."

On the whole, however, Tocqueville found Americans engagingly human, enormously vital, and not yet a tyranny of the majority. "The whole life of an American is passed like a game of chance, a revolutionary crisis, or a battle," he remarked. "The American taken as a chance specimen of his countrymen must then be a man of singular warmth in his desires, enterprising, fond of adventure and, above all, of novelty."

the arsenal at Harpers Ferry, Virginia, was hanged after his attempts to spark slave insurrections in the South.

Apart from such militancy there was considerable apathy toward the antislavery movement in the North. In the South abolitionist sentiment was attacked and finally suppressed. Holding firm to the conviction that slavery was a right as well as a necessity for its agricultural prosperity, the South turned its back on all proposals for change. Moderate proponents, of which there had been many in the South in the early days of the abolitionist movement, soon lost any prospect they might have had of working toward compromise.

As the break between North and South widened, political decisions, particularly those governing the new Western territories, began to overshadow the drama and excitement of militant rallies and the secret way stations along the Underground Railroad. With the publication of Harriet Beecher Stowe's *Uncle Tom's Cabin* in 1852 and the historic Dred Scott decision of 1857—which held that Negro slaves or former slaves could not become citizens—polarization became virtually complete. In 1860, on the eve of the Civil War, a new President who was a moderate on slavery, Abraham Lincoln, and a new political party, the Republican Party, won the leadership of the country. The abolitionists had sought a dramatic change in America's treatment of its black people, and largely through their perseverance a war that at first was waged to restore the Union evolved into a crusade to free a race from bondage.

Reconstruction and Its Aftermath

After the Civil War the most pressing social problem facing America was what to do to help the nearly 4 million ex-slaves. Well before his death Lincoln had noted the probable social consequences of the Emancipation Proclamation, and in March 1865 he had approved the congressional creation of the Freedmen's Bureau to aid the newly liberated Negroes, though privately hoping that many blacks would emigrate. Assuming the Presidency after Lincoln's assassination, Andrew Johnson, a southerner and a Democrat, attempted a continuation of Lincoln's moderate and compassionate view toward all Americans: "With malice toward none, with charity for all. . . ." Johnson proposed a mild reconstruction plan providing for modest political concessions by defeated Southern leaders, with little effective protection for the civil and political rights of the former slaves. Enraged northerners, particularly Radical Republicans such as Thaddeus Stevens and Charles Sumner, balked and, when they gained control of Congress in 1866, passed Radical Reconstruction measures over Johnson's veto.

The main thrust of Reconstruction, apart from imposing stringent military rule on the Southern States, was to guarantee the freedmen equality and opportunity. A newly strengthened Freedmen's Bureau proved a godsend to both bewildered and jobless blacks and poor whites. It furnished free food, clothing, and medical care, provided educational facilities, supervised employment, and exercised certain judicial powers in conflicts between freedmen and bosses. In reaction to this Northern interference, influential and disfranchised Southern whites formed vigilante groups such as the Ku Klux Klan, the Knights of the White Camelia, and other secret societies. They used whatever tactics they could to terrorize the freedmen, including night rides, ghostly costumes, and violence. An angry Congress replied with the 15th amendment to ensure every citizen the right to vote. This amendment, along with the 13th (abolishing slavery) and the 14th (granting citizenship and "the equal protection of the laws" to blacks), was vitiated by U.S. Supreme Court decisions in the 1870's and 1880's. Even though the Negroes' civil and political rights in the South were gradually eroded, at least some served in every Southern legislature, and from 1869 to 1901 a total of 22 Negroes was elected to both Houses of the U.S. Congress.

The economic situation of the great mass of blacks remained bleak. Uneducated and unskilled except in farming, they were seldom able to find anything but menial jobs. When they returned to their old masters, they were usually offered the dead-end arrangement of sharecropping. The owner whose land they farmed for a share of the crop and the storekeeper who sold them provisions against the next year's harvest effectively kept them in economic bondage. Hoping for a fairer deal, many freedmen went to the North, but there they generally found jobs only as unskilled laborers or as domestic servants and in most cases had to live in ghettolike slums.

HARPER'S WEEKLY
A JOURNAL OF CIVILIZATION
NEW YORK, SATURDAY, NOVEMBER 16, 1867.

Southern Negroes *cast their first votes in November 1867, under the Civil Rights Act. Since it could have been declared unconstitutional, Congress passed the 14th amendment.*

In the mid-1870's Radical Reconstruction was on the wane. By 1877, when Federal troops were withdrawn from the South, Northern attitudes toward the defeated white majority had become more conciliatory and southerners had begun to fashion their own new society. It was a dismal time for the freedmen. Discriminatory revision of State constitutions, making the right to vote contingent on payment of poll taxes and proof of literacy, effectively disfranchised them, particularly in the South. By 1902 barriers against black voters had been erected in all Southern States. Other steps were taken to guarantee white supremacy. Beginning with Tennessee in 1870, all Southern States enacted laws banning interracial marriage. In 1883 the Supreme Court invalidated the Civil Rights Act of 1875, which had sought to bar discrimination against blacks in theaters, hotels, restaurants, and trains. This decision touched off a determined effort to segregate the Negro in the South as well as in parts of the North and West. And in 1896, in *Plessy* v. *Ferguson,* the Supreme Court, with only one dissenting vote, further sanctified Jim Crowism by upholding a Louisiana law requiring all railroads to provide "equal but separate accommodations for the white and colored races."

The notorious practices ensuing from such decisions were to remain inviolate for nearly 60 years. Education —"separate but equal," as the euphemism for segregated schooling came to be written—was the one tangible benefit accorded to Southern blacks. Northern philanthropists contributed much to this system, flawed though it was. By 1870 nearly 250,000 black students were enrolled in more than 4,000 schools. Both day students and night students attended industrial schools and colleges. To Booker T. Washington, first president of Tuskegee Institute in Alabama, education, not violence nor agitation, was the surest path to full social and political equality. Urging his fellow blacks to learn skills by which they could gain economic independence, he chose to ignore publicly the evils of segregation and soon emerged, particularly among anxious whites, as the first acceptable black hero.

In the eyes of other blacks such as Massachusetts-born, Harvard-educated William E. B. Du Bois, however, Booker Washington's educated Negro was only half a man—a worker with no civil rights and no interest in trying to win them at the polls. In 1905 Du Bois organized the Niagara Movement, whose members pledged themselves to work for free speech, full suffrage, and the abolition of all racial discrimination. "We want full manhood suffrage," they declared, "and we want it now."

They were not alone in their fight. A distinguished group of white leaders, including Jane Addams, William Dean Howells, and John Dewey, joined Du Bois and others in 1909 to organize the National Association for the Advancement of Colored People (NAACP). Du Bois became editor of *The Crisis,* the NAACP's remarkably successful magazine. The publication espoused a broad program of job opportunities for all blacks, better police protection for Southern blacks, and, most important, a campaign of litigation to invalidate discriminatory laws. Another pivotal biracial organization, the National Urban League, founded in 1910, focused on the plight of urban blacks. It assisted new migrants from the South in finding homes, helped with employer and employee problems, and developed social training programs. These were hopeful beginnings, but it would take more, much more, to purge the poison of "separate but equal" Jim Crow thinking from American society.

The Age of Reform: 1880–1910

Immediately after the Civil War much of America enjoyed a burst of prosperity and progress. Industries expanded. Crossroads became boomtowns and villages blossomed into cities. In 1873, however, came the first serious depression since the Civil War, and ordinary Americans began to pay a price for the heady good times. The Nation was no longer a primarily agrarian society with easily traced lines of economic cause and effect between producer and buyer, between land yield and profit. It was caught in complex cyclical currents that brought severe, sometimes overwhelming, financial and personal hardship to vast numbers of Americans.

Social reformer Henry George sounded one of the most compelling alarms in his 1879 bestseller, *Progress and Poverty,* by showing how more and more wealth was going to fewer and fewer people. "It is as though an immense wedge were being forced, not underneath society, but through society. Those who are above are elevated, but those who are below are crushed down." When, George asked, would the promise to provide an equal opportunity and a good life for every American be kept?

Much of the blame could be laid on the newly rich industrialists and railroad tycoons. Operating under the guise of social Darwinism (Herbert Spencer's economic and social application of Charles Darwin's explosive 1859 theory of evolution), they touted "survival of the fittest" as a principle applicable in the marketplace as well as in biology. Some argued that they "deserved" to profit, unchecked by any regulation or moral responsibility, until the circumstances that produced their swollen gains ran a natural "evolutionary" course.

Opponents thought this philosophy little better than naked greed and they demanded practical social reforms in industry, in slum conditions, on farms, and in politics. An early leader in the post-Civil War fighting against privilege and chicanery in the Government was Carl Schurz, who, as Senator from Missouri (1869–75), attacked the corruption of the Grant Administration and helped organize the short-lived reformist Liberal Republican Party. Later, as Secretary of the Interior in the Cabinet of Rutherford B. Hayes, Schurz pushed for civil service reform, protection of national forest reserves, and justice for the Indians.

Organizing Labor

In the years just after the Civil War, the rudiments of modern American labor unions began to take shape. Many workers, skilled and unskilled, were convinced that their best interests lay in dealing collectively for higher pay, shorter working hours, and safer working conditions. They tried two approaches. Reform unionism, which theoretically shunned strikes and represented the worker as a producer who cooperated with management to get his just share of the wealth and benefits, spawned the highly successful Knights of Labor. Under the colorful leadership of Terence V. Powderly, Grand Master from 1879 to 1893, the organization welcomed men and women, blacks and whites, skilled and unskilled, even shopowners and farmers, and by 1886 boasted 700,000 members. That year seven policemen died during a labor riot in Haymarket Square in Chicago. The Knights were not responsible for the Haymarket riot, but it aroused a public outcry against union activity in general and caused the demise of the broad-based labor movement.

The other approach—trade unionism—found its greatest success in the American Federation of Labor (AFL). Under the spirited, iron-fisted control of New York cigarmaker Samuel Gompers, the AFL promoted organization along strict craft lines, gave considerable autonomy to member unions, and supported strikes and boycotts. Although he dominated the labor scene for 40 years, Gompers never sought to represent the working class as a whole. He chose to concentrate on organizing the craftsmen, whose skills gave them more bargaining power with management. The more radical Industrial Workers of the World (the IWW, also called the Wobblies) was founded by William Haywood to help unskilled workers. It organized and led strikes by such diverse groups as textile and silk workers in the East, lumbermen in the West, copper miners in Arizona, and dockhands on the west coast, but its antimilitarism during World War I brought charges of pro-Germanism, and many IWW leaders and members were jailed. The organization was further weakened when many Wobblies joined the Communist Party after 1917. Some minorities, such as blacks, Chinese, and Mexican Americans, were not represented by any labor organization.

The period was one of intense labor activity. Workdays were 10 to 12 hours long and sometimes the work week was 7 days. Industrial wages averaged a pitiful $650 a year. Strikes against such conditions often ended unsuccessfully and in violence. The Great Strike of 1877 against four Eastern railroads shocked the Nation with its miles of flaming railroad cars, its bloody battles between mobs and militia, and its scores of deaths. Detectives hired by Henry Frick of the Carnegie Steel Company were driven off by strikers at the Homestead Works near Pitts-

Although labor unrest *was common as early as 1805, it was not until some time after the Civil War that strikes on a nationwide scale began to grip the country. A famous one—the Great Strike of 1877 against certain railroads—supposedly inspired Robert Koehler to paint "The Strike" in 1886. The painting depicts angry workers, frustrated by low wages and mean working conditions, confronting their bosses. As violence spread, U.S. troops were called out by President Rutherford B. Hayes, the first time the Army was used to break a strike.*

burgh in 1892. The Pennsylvania National Guard took over the Homestead plant, strikebreakers were hired, and the union was finally beaten. Eugene V. Debs, one of the most humane and selfless of all the labor leaders, landed in jail for defying a Federal court injunction during a similar strike that he led against the Pullman Car Company 2 years later. Pondering the inability of workers to make even modest gains, Debs turned to socialism, which he believed would provide more benefits for the poor and uneducated.

Federal and State courts, influenced by the doctrine of social Darwinism, took a dim view of much labor legislation. The State courts of Pennsylvania, West Virginia, Illinois, Missouri, and Kansas outlawed legislation that forbade mineowners and other employers to pay their men in scrip instead of money. Generally the scrip could be spent only in company-owned stores, where the employer could charge what he pleased. A Pennsylvania court branded one antiscrip law "an insulting attempt" to put the worker under the protection of the State. This, it held, "was not only degrading to his manhood but invaded his rights as a citizen of the United States." It was not until 1902, when the United Mine Workers, led by youthful, magnetic John Mitchell, struck the coalfields of Pennsylvania, that the Government stepped in to aid labor. President Theodore Roosevelt's threat to seize and operate the mines forced the owners to accept arbitration, and the miners won a wage increase.

Though labor endured bitter days on the picket lines, some positive legislation was passed on its behalf. A Federal law establishing an 8-hour day for Government employees was enacted in 1892, a Bureau of Labor was created in 1884 and elevated to Cabinet rank in 1913, and the Erdman Act of 1898 provided for arbitration of railroad labor disputes. Massachusetts took the lead among the States in passing laws governing working hours for women and children as well as minimum wages. Still, a quarter century of agitation and strife, marked by defeats in the Supreme Court, lay ahead before lasting gains were to be realized by America's workers.

Aiding the Poor and Friendless

As cities swelled with immigrants from abroad, with refugees from America's failing farms, and with the chronically jobless and homeless, a whole new era in America's social problems began. New York, Boston, Chicago, and other large cities, plagued by political corruption and administrative incompetence, were ill equipped to handle the needs of their diverse populations, and the burden of reform fell increasingly on private groups and individuals. In the forefront were the settlement houses in the slums. The first of these, modeled after London's famous Toynbee Hall, was founded by Stanton Coit in New York City in 1886. Three years later Chicago's Hull House was established by Jane Addams; Lillian Wald's Henry Street Settlement opened in New York City in 1895. Originally created to ease class and cultural differences in the cities, settlement houses, of which there were nearly 100 by 1900, often evolved into active social service agencies. They provided essential help for bewildered widows, delinquent juveniles, and deserted women and children. Settlement house workers, angered by the hardship imposed on poor city dwellers by foul urban conditions, soon became leaders in such causes as the abolition of child labor, the education of immigrants, sanitary inspection, and the establishment of juvenile courts for cases involving young criminal offenders.

In 1890 Jacob Riis, a Danish-born journalist, contributed to the growing concern for urban ills by publishing *How the Other Half Lives,* a damning indictment of the teeming sidewalks and tenements of New York's Lower East Side. Theodore Roosevelt, Governor of New York

Jane Addams' Hull House
Hope for the Underprivileged

The original Hull House stood on Halsted Street, just off Polk, in teeming, immigrant-filled Chicago. When Jane Addams first saw the building in 1889, it housed a saloon, an office, a furniture factory's storage space, and—on its second floor—small, tenementlike rooms for lodgers. To her it was a perfect choice; within a small radius lived Bohemians, Italians, Germans, Polish and Russian Jews, and thousands upon thousands of Irish. Conditions were appalling: Dirty streets, unenforced sanitary laws, hundreds of houses unconnected to the street sewers, no fire escapes, an inadequate water supply. Chicago's city fathers, indifferent and often afraid of changing the political affiliations of the city's poor by improving their social conditions, spent their money elsewhere. Jane Addams was inevitably drawn to Chicago's meaner districts precisely because their inhabitants enjoyed neither privilege nor status.

She moved in with two old friends—Ellen Gates Starr, a teacher, and Mary Keyser, a housekeeper—and set about turning Hull House into a social center for the surrounding neighborhoods. Eager as they were to help the immigrants, the three women were searching, too, for ways of giving meaning to their own lives by furthering the social progress of American democracy. Soon Hull House was alive with clubs and educational programs for children and adults of all ages. Moving about in the community to explain and encourage participation, Jane Addams often found herself minding children, nursing the sick, washing newborn babies, even preparing the dead for burial. Her two-way street was working; she was gaining at least as much as she was giving her new-found friends.

Hull House grew steadily, both physically and in influence. Jane Addams and her enlarged staff began working for reform legislation to provide more and better social services and to improve the living and working conditions of the poor. Her own greatest devotion during those years was to the children of Chicago. She regarded nothing in the field of child welfare as out of her scope: Parent-child relations, strict child labor laws, and measures to protect children's health and, above all, to give them a better education.

Believing that reform legislation would be speeded if women could vote, Jane Addams also worked for woman suffrage. She found time to write books, to lecture, and to lead women's organizations working for world peace, both in her own country and abroad; in 1931 she shared the Nobel Peace Prize with Nicholas Murray Butler.

Settlement houses *attempted to relieve some of the sufferings of slum residents like those pictured in this crowded New York City scene, "The Cliff Dweller," by George Wesley Bellows.*

State at the turn of the century, had read it, and by 1901 the New York Tenement House Act had been passed to curb overcrowding in buildings and to establish plumbing and fire-prevention regulations. By 1916 most large American cities had taken similar steps. These laws served to slow the deterioration of many neighborhoods, but the failure to enforce them, especially in big-city ghettos, created countless social problems.

State and city boards of charity were organized to work in such areas as caring for dependent children, providing legal aid for the poor, fighting unscrupulous loan sharks, and seeking to ameliorate the worst slum conditions. The training of professional social workers was advanced by Mary Richmond's book, *Social Diagnosis* (1917). Earlier, as an outgrowth of the National Prison Congress at Cincinnati in 1870, new attitudes and laws concerning penal conditions had begun to emerge. Defense lawyer Clarence Darrow gave up a lucrative practice to champion "lost cause" cases after reading *Our Penal Machinery and Its Victims,* a devastating attack on prison conditions written in 1884 by John Peter Altgeld, later Governor of Illinois. Although America's concerned groups and individuals were far from solving the country's myriad urban social problems, they carried on the uphill fight with spirit and persistence. Today the problems are still running well ahead of workable solutions.

A Petition With Boots On

A flamboyant, if futile, attempt to force Federal Government measures against unemployment was a march on Washington organized by Jacob S. Coxey during the depression of the 1890's. A prosperous sandstone quarry operator of Massillon, Ohio, Coxey hoped to persuade Congress to enact a bill empowering the Government to print paper money with which to pay unemployed citizens to work on the construction of good roads throughout the United States. (The pay rate was to be $1.50 for an 8-hour day.) Coxey's "Army of the Commonwealth," 100 strong, began its march inauspiciously during a spring snowstorm in 1894. The participants were mostly hoboes looking for a hot meal, but as they advanced through Ohio and into Pennsylvania, they were joined by a more sober contingent of responsible unemployed. On May Day Coxey and 500 followers finally arrived in Washington, where nervous law enforcement officers confronted them. Since, except for the Populists, few Congressmen were eager to deal with the army, Coxey steered his band away from the Capitol. But he himself tried to speak on the Capitol steps and was promptly arrested, found guilty of walking on the grass and carrying a banner without a permit, and was jailed for 20 days.

Nothing immediate came from the long march. By the time Coxey was released from jail, his followers had scattered, and the lawmakers ignored his proposal. But long before his death at the age of 97 in 1951, Government-financed work programs for the jobless had become a well-established American principle.

The Farmers' Revolt

While all this ferment was going on in the cities, America's farmers were having their own difficulties. Life on the farm often meant isolation, unending toil, poverty and deprivation—hardships that were augmented by the vagaries of nature. The farmers, like the urban workers, were powerless to deal as individuals with the problems of soaring transportation rates, low prices for their produce, and mounting costs for everything they needed. In their search for relief they developed the Order of the Patrons of Husbandry, or the Grange, as it became familiarly known. Founded in 1867 by Oliver H. Kelley, a former clerk in the U.S. Bureau of Agriculture, the Grange was conceived as a network of social gathering places for farmers and their wives on lonely evenings. Mutual complaints were aired at these get-togethers, and soon the Grangers were electing representatives to State legislatures. Under Grange pressure, Illinois, Wisconsin, Iowa, and Minnesota all passed laws regulating railroad freight rates and banning practices that discriminated against the farmers. Grange cooperatives for both buying and selling were set up, and Grange factories produced excellent reapers, wagons, and sewing machines at prices far below those of the marketplace.

For about a decade all went well, but late in the 1870's the Grange ran into trouble. Most of its cooperative enterprises failed through overexpansion, mismanagement, and the bitter opposition of industrialists and bankers. Besides, the farmers were enjoying a period of prosperity, and membership dwindled as their sense of need diminished. The Grange revived somewhat in 1880, but thereafter stayed out of business and politics and became largely social.

The Grange's place on the political battlefield was taken over by two militant farm organizations: the National Farmers' Alliance and Industrial Union (known as the Southern Alliance) and the National Farmers' Alliance (called the Northwestern Alliance). These two alliances, along with delegates from Granges and labor groups, organized the national People's Party. The Populists, as they were known, angered and frightened the country's conservatives by advocating such radical notions as Government ownership of railroads, telephone, and telegraph; a graduated income tax; free and unlimited coinage of silver and gold; and direct election of U.S. Senators. The party was strong in the South even though it espoused the radical concept of cooperation of blacks and whites. In 1892 the newly formed Populists shook the two-party establishment when their candidate for the Presidency, James B. Weaver, polled more than 1 million

Prohibition
The "Noble Experiment" That Failed

During its 13-year span, the 18th amendment to the Constitution stood as a monument to the grim crusade for abstinence, which, from modest American beginnings in the mid-19th century, had slowly gathered force until in 1920 it became the law of the land. Touted by the Anti-Saloon League of America and other reform groups as a near-panacea for just about everything that ailed us—crime, marital discord, poverty, unemployment, child labor—the Prohibition amendment was passed by Congress in 1917. ("They put it over on us while the boys were away at war," its enemies said.) The required 36 States had ratified it by January 16, 1919, and it went into effect a year later. The moral fervor aroused by World War I, exploited for all it was worth by a dedicated band of "drys" skilled in the uses of publicity and propaganda, had carried the day.

Today the 1920's are often remembered with amused nostalgia as the heyday of peephole speakeasies, bathtub gin, and colorful bootleggers. On the darker side were the innumerable painful deaths and blindnesses inflicted by poisonous brews, the rise of organized crime and gangsterism as the underworld took charge of providing the citizenry with illegal booze, and the inadequacy of the undermanned and frequently corrupt enforcement agencies.

In 1929 President Herbert Hoover appointed a commission, headed by George W. Wickersham, to investigate how well the prohibition law was being enforced. Columnist Franklin P. Adams summed up the commission's report in this jingle:

Prohibition is an awful flop.
We like it.
It can't stop what it's meant to stop.
We like it.
It's left a trail of graft and slime,
It don't prohibit worth a dime,
It's filled our land with vice and crime.
Nevertheless, we're for it.

By the 1930's the people, badgered as they were by the Great Depression, had had enough of this unenforceable law. The 21st amendment, repealing the 18th, was speedily passed by Congress and ratified by the States in 1933. Alcoholic beverages returned legally to American life, subject only to the jurisdiction of individual States, all of which had abandoned statewide prohibition by 1966. The collapse of this attempt to impose abstinence on the American people demonstrated the difficulty of controlling moral conduct by law in the face of popular opposition.

Congress in October 1919 *passed the Volstead Act, which set up the machinery for enforcing national Prohibition. Under its terms, Federal agents, like the one shown at the right, were empowered to raid speakeasies, smash barrels of the then illegal liquor, and search for the bootleggers who trafficked in it.*

votes and won 22 electoral votes in the Western States.

In its brief span, the Populist movement was the most influential third party in U.S. history. Many of the reforms it proposed were later adopted by the two major parties. In 1896 it supported the losing Democratic Presidential candidate, William Jennings Bryan, who insisted that the free coinage of silver would solve all the Nation's ills; although it remained active through three more campaigns, it had lost its political power.

The Progressive Voice in Political Reform

With the demise of the Populists as an effective third party, the old order now faced a challenge from the Progressives, a more urban-oriented, middle-class movement. While espousing many of the farmers' and workers' demands for political and economic reform, the Progressives turned their energies to attacks on city and State political machines. They were influenced by Lincoln Steffens' series of articles in *McClure's Magazine* and his 1904 book, both published under the title *The Shame of the Cities,* which exposed the political corruption rampant in Philadelphia, Pittsburgh, St. Louis, Minneapolis, and other cities. The Progressives worked to modernize and expand the outdated administrative machinery that allowed boss-controlled political rings to flourish. Among the improvements they urged were the direct primary, extension and reform of the civil service, the secret ballot, and commission and city-manager plans for municipal governments. Winners in Progressive campaigns for clean politics included Robert M. La Follette, who became Governor of Wisconsin; Tom Johnson, Mayor of Cleveland; Hazen Pingree, Governor of Michigan; and Charles B. Aycock, Governor of North Carolina. Many of these men worked to break the influence of business in State and city governments and to set up public commissions to regulate industrial and railroad practices. Independent, democratic government on all levels was their goal, and although the Tammany Halls and the Boss Tweeds might never completely disappear from American politics, the Progressive reformers were fresh, welcome voices to most Americans. While Progressivism was not a successful movement, it did help to shift public opinion toward dramatic change soon to come.

The New Deal

From 1929 to 1941 America suffered the worst economic slump in her history—the Great Depression. Beginning with the stock market crash, the Depression rapidly engulfed the entire population—banker and servant, college graduate and tenant farmer, businessman and laborer—and stubbornly resisted Republican President Herbert Hoover's well-intentioned but conservative remedies. With the election in 1932 of Franklin D. Roosevelt, a Democrat and patrician who had never known a moment of economic anxiety, the stage was set for America's most daring adventure in social and economic experimentation: the New Deal.

A series of Federal work programs—the Civilian Conservation Corps, the Civil Works Administration, the Public Works Administration, and the Works Progress Administration, among others—all had one goal: putting employable men and women to work again. America had never seen such a massive Government attack on unemployment and, though not without bureaucratic tangles and mismanagement, the programs proved a bold and successful short-term solution to the hunger and poverty of millions of people. The farmers, for example, were paradoxically suffering amidst record crops. Roosevelt instituted price supports under the Agricultural Adjustment Act, aided tenant farmers, and gave all farmers some cushioning against the hazards of a marketing system they were unable to control.

At the urging of Secretary of Labor Frances Perkins, a noted social worker and the first woman Cabinet member, Roosevelt tried to compel industry, through the National Industrial Recovery Act, to raise wages, reduce hours, and accept unionization and collective bargaining. The U.S. Supreme Court invalidated this act, but the passage in 1935 of the Wagner Act, establishing the National Labor Relations Board, finally gave labor effective protection of its rights. As a direct outgrowth of this Government aid, tough, eloquent United Mine Workers president John L. Lewis set up the Congress of Industrial Organizations (CIO) to unionize unskilled factory workers, including for the first time large numbers of blacks. In 1938 the Fair Labor Standards Act was passed, outlawing "oppressive" child labor and setting the first national levels for minimum wages and maximum hours.

MAKING DEMOCRACY WORK

The Wagner Act

The 1935 National Labor Relations Act, more commonly known as the Wagner Act in recognition of its sponsorship by New York Senator Robert F. Wagner, supplanted the famous section 7(a) of FDR's short-lived National Industrial Recovery Act of 1933–35. The new law promised labor much the same wide-ranging guarantees as had been a part of the older act. These included the right to form unions free of company control and to bargain collectively over wages, hours, and working conditions. A three-man National Labor Relations Board was set up to enforce this code; it could summon employers to appear before it, hear reports from workers on alleged violations of their rights, affording them protection against punitive retaliatory measures by their employers, issue cease and desist orders, and sponsor elections enabling workers to select the collective bargaining agency of their choice. The board's decisions were enforceable through the courts. Unlike its predecessor, the Wagner Act was upheld in all aspects by a series of crucial Supreme Court decisions in 1937. The Court majority said that the right to organize for bargaining purposes was "a fundamental right" and "an essential condition of industrial peace."

MAKING DEMOCRACY WORK

Social Security

The Social Security Act of 1935 was America's first national welfare program. It authorized the allocation of funds to the States to assist people age 65 or older and required the States to produce aid plans that met Federal standards. An "Old-Age Reserve Account" funded by taxes from both employees and employers would accord benefits initially ranging from a fixed minimum of $10 to a maximum of $85 a month, depending on the individual's wage record during his working years. Unemployment compensation was provided under a system of Federal grants to the States, with benefits assured by a payroll tax collected from employers of eight or more persons. The States were also to receive funds for federally approved plans to help needy dependent children, to provide maternal and child welfare services, and to perform public health work. A three-member Social Security Board was established to carry out these provisions and to recommend other social legislation.

By 1960 Social Security had been greatly expanded. There were sizable increases in benefits, and more than 90 percent of working adults were covered. In the 1970's the originally small tax on payrolls was increased several times to boost the monthly payments in an effort to offset the steep rise in the cost of living.

For the old and the young, the poor and the helpless, Roosevelt showed particular concern. In 1935 America's landmark welfare bill—the Social Security Act—was passed to provide pensions for retired workers, insurance for the unemployed, help for mothers with young dependent children, and aid for the aged, crippled, and blind. Public insurance and support for millions of citizens who could neither handle the burden themselves nor look to private sources for relief was a radical departure for Americans. But the Depression itself was so traumatic, so economically and emotionally unsettling, that many of the country's old illusions about opportunity, self-reliance, and rugged individualism had been shattered. In their stead was the beginning of a permanent recognition that the Government had concrete, demonstrable responsibilities for the social and economic well-being of its people. The question was—and still is—whether or not the necessary perspective and funds could be established and maintained.

The Marshall Plan

At the end of World War II American leaders were quick to recognize that only rapid restoration of Europe's battered industries and economies could avert chaos and revolution. Accordingly, in June 1947, Secretary of State George C. Marshall proposed that the United States commit itself to supply Europe's most urgent needs for financial and economic assistance, as defined by the various European leaders themselves. In September 1947 representatives of 16 European nations, including Great Britain, met in Paris, where the United States agreed to underwrite a European Recovery Plan (ERP) amounting to the staggering sum of about $13 billion over a 4-year period. Although the door was open to them, the Soviet Union and its European satellites refused to participate and repeatedly applied diplomatic and economic pressure against the members of ERP. These actions failed to prove a deterrent, however, and the Marshall Plan restored economic and political stability to many Western European governments even faster than its sponsors had dared to predict—by 1952 European industrial production had risen to some 200 percent over its output of 1938. Moreover, joint international efforts in areas such as monetary planning, trade-barrier adjustments, and rebuilding industry and agriculture led to closer cooperation among the newly prospering nations and paved the way for what later became the Common Market.

Though the motive of the Marshall Plan was basically humanitarian, the stability and goodwill of a prosperous Europe brought inestimable benefit to the United States. In underwriting one of the most astonishing economic revivals ever recorded, Americans not only saved half a continent from poverty, economic depression, and pitiful physical hardship but proved democracy to be an effective political process even in times of deepest stress.

The Fair Deal

The problems facing a prosperous but inflation-ridden America after World War II were largely those of retooling a nation for peacetime progress. President Harry S. Truman, faced with a conservative, antagonistic Republican Congress, found little legislative support when he tried to extend the social advances of the New Deal. Labor, many people felt, had gained too much; to restore the balance between unions and industry, Congress passed the Taft-Hartley Act in 1947 over Truman's veto. Among its restrictive clauses were the outlawing of the closed shop, a mandatory 60-day "cooling off" period before a strike, and, symptomatic of the times, a requirement that all union leaders sign an oath that they were not members of the Communist Party.

On behalf of America's minorities Truman waged a strong fight for civil rights. Giving the cause a prominent place in his Fair Deal package, he appointed a biracial Committee on Civil Rights, which subsequently recommended, among other things, a permanent Fair Employment Practices Commission to eliminate discrimination in hiring. Unable to interest Congress in adopting the committee's suggestions, Truman acted on his own to speed desegregation in the Armed Forces and to outlaw discrimination in Federal hiring. Before his term was over he welcomed the passage of the Housing Act of 1949, which provided for the first massive slum clearance program and the building of low-income housing.

The Search for Equality

America in the 1950's, though otherwise enjoying the benign, hands-off policies of President Dwight D. Eisenhower, was beset by controversies over civil liberties and civil rights. Senator Joseph R. McCarthy dominated the headlines with his demagogic charges of alleged Communist infiltration in high places. Less publicized but infinitely more meaningful was the undercurrent of dissatisfaction and turmoil developing more strongly among America's growing black minority. Virtually unnoticed at the time by much of the country, this rose to a ground swell of agitation that was to become, before the next decade was over, a near revolution. Negroes, particularly those who had moved to the North, were at last beginning to demand some economic independence. Wartime jobs had provided many with new opportunities to learn skills and gain promotion, and when the AFL combined with the CIO in 1955, two noted black men—A. Philip Randolph and Willard Townsend—were elected vice presidents. Blacks were also gaining some political leverage; voting in blocs in such large cities as Detroit, Chicago, and Cleveland, they often held the balance of power in close elections. But while there was some progress, it was partial and erratic. Blacks, however, began to find unexpected allies and make strong gains among con-

The Warren Court
Justice for the People

"I would like the Court to be remembered as the people's court," said Earl Warren on his retirement as Chief Justice of the United States in 1969. And so it was, under his leadership. President Dwight D. Eisenhower appointed him Chief Justice in 1953. He and his eight colleagues, faced with the emotionally charged issues of civil liberties, interpreted the Constitution as the main protector of the rights of every American, no matter how obscure or powerless. The quality of Warren's leadership startled many people. As a law-and-order Attorney General of California, then as Governor of California for three terms, the genial politician had given little indication that he would so greatly change the social and political fabric of America.

The Court's decisions outraged conservatives everywhere. Many considered Warren virtually a traitor and talked of impeaching him. But to blacks, particularly in the South, and to the poor of every description, the Court's decisions opened new paths to long-denied social and political equality. Under Warren's leadership the Court ruled in 1963 that the States had to provide counsel for penniless defendants in all felony cases. In 1966 the Court upset convictions obtained in violation of the fifth and sixth amendments: the privilege of refusing to give self-incriminating testimony and the right to have legal counsel during police interrogation. Earlier, in what Warren considered the most significant decisions in his career, the Court used the "equal protection of the laws" clause of the 14th amendment to ban segregation in the public schools and to force the States to reapportion voting districts to conform to the principle of "one man, one vote." The Court's supporters saw in its record a rekindling of faith in the basic American tenet of "equal justice under law."

The U.S. Supreme Court *as it looked in June 1955. Seated, left to right: Felix Frankfurter, Hugo L. Black, Chief Justice Earl Warren, Stanley F. Reed, William O. Douglas. Standing, left to right: Sherman Minton, Harold H. Burton, Thomas C. Clark, and John Marshall Harlan.*

cerned religious groups, in the growing influence of biracial organizations, and, most importantly, in the courts.

Waging a quiet but persistent legal battle to destroy discriminatory legislation of all varieties, the NAACP, with experienced men such as Roy Wilkins and Walter White guiding its course, took more than a dozen major cases all the way to the Supreme Court and won most of them. Slowly but surely legal barriers to equality in everything from education and voting rights to sitting in bus terminals were declared unconstitutional. The most famous civil rights case, *Brown* v. *Board of Education of Topeka* (1954), argued so persuasively by the NAACP's Thurgood Marshall, was the most significant of the favorable decisions. Overruling the 58-year-old "separate but equal" doctrine of the *Plessy* v. *Ferguson* case, the Court unanimously held that "separate educational facilities are inherently unequal. . . ." The decision brought stiff resistance in the South, and the Court's ambiguously worded follow-up order of 1955 that schools must be desegregated "with all deliberate speed" was often given only token adherence.

Gradually school districts in the South began complying fully with Federal court desegregation orders. But although segregation was no longer sanctioned by law, many schools in both the North and South remained segregated in fact, because they were located in all-white or all-black neighborhoods. To achieve a more equitable racial balance, the Supreme Court during the late 1960's and early 1970's upheld lower Federal court orders in several States requiring the busing of students from one neighborhood school to another. But attempts to achieve still greater racial integration by busing students across district lines, thus mingling children from white suburban and black central-city neighborhoods, were all but banned by the highest court in a decision announced on July 25, 1974; and in any case such attempts were meeting with massive resistance in the political arena.

While the Federal courts were starting to deal with the problems of equality in education, Congress finally moved into the field of minority voting rights, passing the Civil Rights Act of 1957, the first legislation of its kind in 82 years, and the Civil Rights Act of 1960. Although these acts did little to assure minorities of their rights, they did establish the principle of the Government's responsibility in that area.

Negroes by this time had taken many of the issues into their own hands. A crucial step forward was the 1955–56 bus boycott in Montgomery, Alabama, led by a young Baptist minister, Martin Luther King, Jr. Although Dr. King and other ministers were thrown into jail for a brief time, segregated seating in Montgomery buses and, later, in all forms of transportation was ended, and a new era in nonviolent resistance to discrimination was begun. Such organizations as King's Southern Christian Leadership Conference and the Congress of Racial Equality organized scores of blacks and whites, many of them college students, to participate in demonstrations, sit-ins, and freedom rides. All were efforts to force businessmen—storekeepers, hotel managers, and bus line owners—to end discrimination. In some cases the reac-

MAKING DEMOCRACY WORK

Civil Rights Acts

The Civil Rights Act of 1957 established a bipartisan commission with authority to investigate the denial of voting rights and of equal protection under the law because of race, color, national origin, or religion. It also authorized injunctive proceedings in Federal courts when voting rights were in question.
The Civil Rights Act of 1960 empowered Federal courts to appoint referees to evaluate State voting qualification laws when citizens complained that their voting or registering rights had been denied. It authorized suits against States for such violations and imposed heavy penalties on private citizens who infringed on the civil rights of others.
The Civil Rights Act of 1964 guaranteed equal access to public accommodations, established commissions to assure equal rights to jobs and to help solve racial disputes, and empowered the Government to file suits and withhold Federal funds from schools practicing discrimination.
The Voting Rights Act of 1965 banned literacy tests and authorized Federal examiners to conduct the registration of voters and observe elections where there was evidence of a denial of voting rights. In 1970 Congress extended the act for another 5 years.
The Civil Rights Act of 1968 imposed heavier penalties for interference with rights of voting and education and strengthened regulations prohibiting discrimination in the sale or renting of housing.

tion of Southern whites was positive, and a number of chain stores, hotels, and eating places stopped segregation practices; in many instances, however, the demonstrators were booed, spat on, and even physically harmed.

Soon after his election in 1960 President John F. Kennedy showed his support of the civil rights movement by appointing three blacks to important posts: Thurgood Marshall to the U.S. Circuit Court (he later became the first black U.S. Supreme Court Justice), Robert C. Weaver to the sensitive Housing and Home Finance Agency, and Carl T. Rowan as Ambassador to Finland. Later he used Federal marshals to protect freedom riders who had been mobbed in Alabama, and he federalized the National Guard to ensure the admission of James Meredith, a black, to the University of Mississippi. Kennedy sensed the increasing anger of blacks over the slow rate of their progress, and in June 1963, a century after the Emancipation Proclamation, he urged Congress in an impassioned speech to pass further civil rights legislation. That same month Medgar Evers, the field secretary of the NAACP in Mississippi, was murdered. In late August 250,000 supporters of the bill before Congress marched on Washington, chanting the slogan "Free by '63" and singing their song of hope, "We Shall Overcome." But Congress did not act, and in the wake of its inaction a church in Birmingham, Alabama, was bombed, killing four small Negro girls. The forces at work—blacks desperately searching for true equality and whites retaliating with fear and violence—had begun to take on a new, more ominous character.

Strong leadership *has been called for to help minority groups attain the various degrees of equality they have today. Marcus Garvey proposed "uniting all the Negro peoples of the world into one great body to establish a country and government absolutely their own." Some concepts of separation have survived, although Garvey's specific plans failed. William Edward Burghardt Du Bois (1868–1963) helped organize the National Association for the Advancement of Colored People (NAACP) in 1909. Dismayed with the slow progress of blacks, he became an advocate of black separatism, left the United States for Ghana in 1962, and died there. The NAACP, primarily under the able leadership of Walter White and Roy Wilkins and with both blacks and whites as members, has won many notable victories for civil rights. One courageous woman was Mrs. Rosa Parks of Montgomery, Alabama, who in December 1955 refused to give up her seat and stand in the back of the bus. Her protest led to a bus boycott that lasted more than a year, brought Dr. Martin Luther King, Jr., to national prominence, and changed forever the pattern of segregation in public transportation and accommodations.*

Marcus Garvey as Provisional President of Africa

Dr. W. E. B. Du Bois addressing Congress of Partisans of Peace in Paris, 1949

A. Philip Randolph, labor le

Whitney M. Young as Director of th National Urban Le

Lyndon B. Johnson assumed the Presidency after Kennedy's assassination in November 1963 and urged Congress to pass the Civil Rights Act of 1964 as a memorial to his predecessor. It was by far the strongest bill yet. It prohibited discrimination in public places, strengthened voting rights, gave the Attorney General the right to sue for speedier school desegregation, and set up an Equal Employment Opportunity Commission to end job discrimination in hiring. It was soon followed by the Voting Rights Act of 1965. This bill was the direct outcome of an intensive voter registration campaign waged by Dr. King and of pressure by President Johnson. Disregarding the increasing white hostility that had caused the murder of three civil rights workers (Michael H. Schwerner, James E. Chaney, and Andrew Goodman) in 1964, Dr. King set up a protest march from Selma to Montgomery, Alabama, in March 1965 to publicize the continued inability of blacks to register to vote in the South. The murders of two more white sympathizers, the Rev. James Reeb of Boston and Mrs. Viola Liuzzo of Detroit, who had gone to Selma to help Dr. King, caused Johnson to exhort Congress to pass the Voting Rights Act.

A Great Society

Johnson was appalled by the degree of hardship and injustice in American life and vowed to build a Great Society by waging an unconditional war on poverty. Among his programs was the Office of Economic Opportunity (OEO). Its first director was Sargent Shriver, who had run Kennedy's Peace Corps, which sent Americans to foreign

MAKING DEMOCRACY WORK

Medicare and Medicaid

Under the Health Insurance Act for the Aged, passed in 1965 as an amendment to the Social Security Act, federally funded hospital insurance became available for the first time to most Americans who had reached or passed their 65th birthday. Popularly known as Medicare, this plan in 1974 paid all but $92 of a beneficiary's hospital costs for the first 60 days, and all but $23 for the next 30 days. In addition, it provided up to 100 days of care in a qualified nursing home, with the first 20 days completely covered and the patient paying $11.50 a day for the rest. The plan also covered in full up to 100 home visits by nurses or other health care workers (not doctors, however). Medicare is mainly concerned with inpatient care, but its members may also join, if they wish, a medical insurance program for outpatient services. Subscribers pay a small monthly premium, which is matched by the Federal Government. This covers most of the fees for the services of doctors and surgeons, a variety of diagnostic tests, the rental or purchase of medical equipment, and physical therapy.

Another amendment set up grants to States for medical assistance to the poor of any age. Under the provisions of Medicaid, as this program is known, the States must furnish help to residents whose income is below a set level: Such residents include families with dependent children, the blind, and the totally disabled. Medical rehabilitation programs designed to bolster the patients' independence and dignity are also available.

Dr. Martin Luther King, Jr., and wife, Coretta; Ralph Bunche; and (far left) the Rev. Ralph Abernathy

lm X as Muslim leader

Stokely Carmichael as leader of the Student Nonviolent Coordinating Committee

Roy Wilkins, Executive Director NAACP

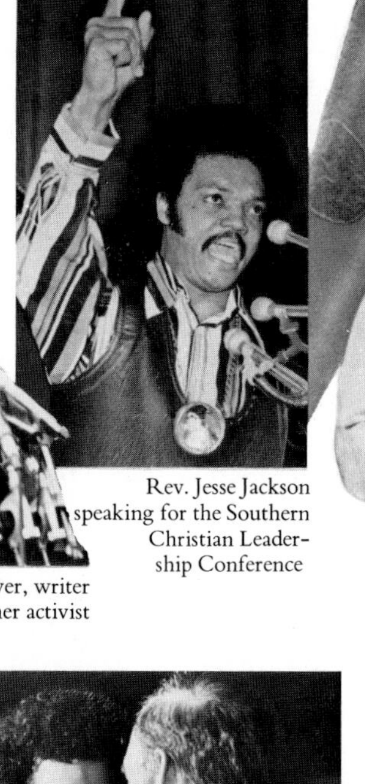

Eldridge Cleaver, writer and Black Panther activist

Rev. Jesse Jackson speaking for the Southern Christian Leadership Conference

Julian Bond, Georgia legislator

Cesar Chavez, United Farm Workers Union head

countries to aid in underdeveloped areas. Under Shriver the OEO set in motion such projects as VISTA, a domestic peace corps to fight poverty; Operation Head Start, a program to teach preschoolers; a Job Corps for school dropouts; a Neighborhood Youth Corps for unemployed teenagers; and a Community Action Program to encourage the poor to participate in the work of their own neighborhoods. For Appalachia, a long, narrow, and mountainous poverty belt extending from Pennsylvania to northern Alabama, Johnson obtained from Congress a far-reaching program that would provide highway construction, health centers, and resource development.

In the field of health, Johnson moved a step nearer to national insurance for all. Medicare, for older citizens, and Medicaid, for those too poor to pay, put Government-supported health care within reach of many more Americans than ever before. The Housing and Urban Development Act of 1965 was the first comprehensive attack on urban slums since the acts of 1949 and 1956. Other acts, providing Federal funds for a wide range of education programs at all levels, gave a strong boost to schools, particularly those with a large percentage of children from low-income families.

One long-neglected underprivileged group—the Mexican-American workers of California—gained a champion during the 1960's. Cesar Chavez, the son of migrant farmworkers, with the help of union leaders and national figures such as Robert F. Kennedy, organized many of California's Mexican-American grape pickers into a union. His United Farm Workers joined the AFL-CIO in 1966 and directed a nationwide boycott of table grapes that finally forced growers to sign contracts with them. In the early 1970's Chavez began to organize the lettuce pickers. In the meantime the Teamsters Union, which had separated from the AFL-CIO, began a campaign to win over the migrant workers, and Chavez found himself, temporarily at least, losing ground.

The Problems Grow

In the mid-1960's the problems of bettering the lot of the disadvantaged outran the progress achieved, and underlying frustrations began to surface. Some angry young black activists turned away from the nonviolent methods of the NAACP and the Urban League and joined various militant separatist groups. Black nationalism was encouraged by the Black Muslims, a religious group organized in Detroit in the 1930's, which had grown to impressive strength under the leadership of Elijah Muhammad. Marcus Garvey's Back to Africa campaign of the early 1920's had stressed the dignity and beauty of being black. The Muslims seized on this rallying cry and exhorted their supporters to strive for self-sufficiency and more influence in the businesses and institutions in the areas where they lived. Malcolm X, a Black Muslim who broke with Muhammad in 1963 and formed the Organization of Afro-American Unity, was eloquent in articulating the anger of his contemporaries. His following was on the increase when, in 1965, he was assassinated by black dissidents.

Stokely Carmichael, who became leader of the Student Nonviolent Coordinating Committee in 1966, was among the first publicly to advocate "black power" as a means of tipping the balance against the white establishment, which he believed was denying Negroes their constitutional and economic rights. This power was to be expressed by political and economic pressure.

Perhaps the most aggressive of the new militants were the Black Panthers. Starting in Alabama, they came to national prominence in Oakland, California, in 1966. The movement spread and attracted many restless young urban blacks. Objectives and methods varied with local leadership, and in some places there was violence.

In the long, hot summer of 1965, rioting broke out in the Watts section of Los Angeles. Buildings were burned, stores looted, and blacks and whites alike were killed in a tragic manifestation of the explosive forces bred by the oppressive conditions of life in the slums. Two years later, in similar conditions, violence erupted again, starting in the black ghettos of Newark, New Jersey, and Detroit, Michigan, and spreading to some 20 other communities.

In 1968 Dr. Martin Luther King, Jr., was assassinated (for motives never satisfactorily explained) as he stood on a motel balcony in Memphis, Tennessee. James Earl Ray, a white southerner, pleaded guilty to the murder and was sentenced to a 99-year prison term. The immediate effect of King's assassination was to diminish the influence of the black leaders who advocated nonviolence. However, it also moved Congress to pass the Civil Rights Act of 1968, which offered some protection to those working for racial equality and prohibited discrimination in the sale or rental of most private and public housing. As the tragedy-filled decade ended, the National Advisory Commission on Civil Disorders was moved to note in 1968: "Our nation is moving toward two societies, one black, one white—separate and unequal."

By the mid-1970's, although headway had been made in the battle for improvement, the social evils of discrimination against minority groups and the poor, lack of opportunity, unequal education and health care, unemployment, hunger, and slum living remained ugly realities in the eyes of all who cared to look. It was obvious that city, State, and National agencies were failing to cope with the growing problems. There was by no means general agreement on what to do, but most Americans had at least become aware that finding workable solutions was a matter of urgency and worthy of our utmost efforts.

Turning Points *The Depression and the Bomb*

In the life of every country certain developments so deeply penetrate the national consciousness that for long afterward no person is unaffected by them. For 20th-century America two such turning points were the Depression and the atomic bomb.

The Crash and the Depression

America began the year 1929 flushed with optimism. Business had never been better; the stock market continued to climb; and easy credit helped maintain a free flow of goods, jobs, and money. America, it appeared, had found the secret of prolonged prosperity. By autumn, however, clouds appeared. The stock market, that dependable fair-weather barometer, was the first to show storm signals. A sense of economic unease suddenly gripped the country, and prices on Wall Street plummeted. Speculators, frantically trying to get out before their narrow margins were erased, started a wild selloff. Black Thursday, October 24, saw the unloading of almost 13 million shares of stock. On October 29 the market took a further plunge. For the moment Americans could still chuckle at *Variety*'s black-humor verdict —WALL ST. LAYS AN EGG. But the laughter was short-lived. Soon the country was in the midst of the Great Depression, the worst in its history. Banks closed, businesses failed, mortgages were foreclosed, industrial production fell by half, and the number of unemployed persons approached an overwhelming 12 million. Hungry, often homeless, bitterly fearful of the future, Americans looked increasingly to Washington and President Herbert Hoover for help.

The effects of the American crash spread to Europe, and this in turn reinforced the downward trend here. Foreign investors withdrew funds from American banks and industry, and foreign trade dwindled. In an effort to help Europe's rapidly deteriorating economy, President Hoover in June 1931 proposed a 1-year moratorium on World War I debts and reparations.

Along with many leading businessmen, President Hoover had initially played down the gravity of the Wall Street crash; it was merely a stock-market panic, a temporary crisis of confidence, and it need not affect what he firmly believed was a sound economy. In a series of public statements Hoover urged people to forget their fears. Prosperity was "just around the corner." Bolstered by his conservative Republican philosophy of limited government intervention in economic matters, Hoover pinned his hopes for a quick economic recovery on voluntary relief efforts and promises by businessmen to maintain full staffs and steady wages. But as the Depression deepened, it became increasingly clear that words alone would not suffice. In 1932 Hoover signed the first measure providing for direct economic assistance to the country, (*continued*)

By the winter of 1932–33 *much of America was in the grip of despair. The hungry waited in long lines, such as the one in Kansas City (above top), for free bread and soup; the jobless searched in vain for employment and ended up, like the man with the empty tin cup in Dorothea Lange's bleak portrait (above), with nowhere to turn. In cities all over the country there were rickety shantytowns, called Hoovervilles by their unfortunate residents, and once-prosperous businessmen were peddling apples on street corners for a nickel apiece. Capturing the essence of the dramatic reversal of America's economic fortunes, a 1933* Vanity Fair *cover, using a newspaper's stock market quotations for its cutouts, depicts the meeting of the bloated 1929 market with its skeletal 1933 successor.*

Turning Points
(continued)

the Reconstruction Finance Corporation Act. RFC loans saved many banks, businesses, and railroads from failure, but to most beleaguered Americans Herbert Hoover was the villain of the Great Depression, who had proposed too little too late.

The Road to Recovery

In 1932 America's voters replaced Hoover with his Democratic opponent, Franklin D. Roosevelt, who was a strong, buoyant leader prepared to marshal the Government's powers in the public interest. In his inaugural address on March 4, 1933, Roosevelt demonstrated his flair for the dramatic—"the only thing we have to fear is fear itself"—and indicated his intention to use his executive power to the fullest. His first acts, declaring a national bank holiday and calling Congress into special session to pass emergency legislation, were followed 8 days later by a radio "fireside chat" in which he reassured the people that those banks ready to reopen the following day were sound and the money in them, safe. The impact of his calming words and decisive actions was immediate and profound.

Mar. 4, 1933
THE NEW YORKER
Price 15 cents

Peter Arno's *memorable* New Yorker *cover shows Roosevelt, the jaunty victor, and his glum predecessor riding together to the inaugural.*

Capitalizing on this initial lift, F.D.R. moved rapidly to implement his promise of "a new deal for the American people." In the 100 days it was in session, Congress passed a remarkable series of measures designed to strengthen the country's financial reserves and monetary practices, encourage agriculture and industry, protect home ownership, and provide jobs for the millions of people who were out of work.

The Emergency Banking Relief Act gave the President and the Secretary of the Treasury wide authority to regulate credit and the flow of gold, silver, and paper currency. The Agricultural Adjustment Act established parity prices for selected crops and gave subsidies to all the farmers who would voluntarily agree to limit their crop production. The Home Owners Loan Act put the credit of the Government behind mortgages that millions had been unable to meet, and saved their homes. The National Industrial Recovery Act enlisted the cooperation of industry in setting up codes of fair practice covering wages, working hours, and competition; the codes were widely violated, however, and in 1935 the Supreme Court declared them unconstitutional. Under the same act the Federal Emergency Administration of Public Works (later called the Public Works Administration) provided loans and grants for the construction of bridges, highways, and other works. The Civilian Conservation Corps recruited jobless youths for work camps, where they were kept busy with such endeavors as planting trees and cleaning up State parks. In the field of regional aid, the Tennessee Valley Authority was authorized to carry out flood control and land reclamation and to produce and distribute electric power; it was one of the most successful of all the programs.

Later congressional sessions continued to produce New Deal legislation. The Works Progress Administration (later known as the Work Projects Administration) used the unemployed for a variety of activities ranging from writing guidebooks and painting murals to building roads and schools. In 1935 President Roosevelt signed the historic Social Security Act, providing for old-age pensions, unemployment compensation, and aid to dependent children, the blind, and the totally disabled. Never in peacetime had Government played so decisive a role.

In the midst of the Depression, *the Works Progress Administration gave jobs to architects, artists, writers, and actors, as well as manual and white-collar workers. One of these artists, William Gropper, glorified the workingman in his WPA-funded mural "Construction of a Dam."*

The Bonus Army March

In May 1932, while an estimated 2 million homeless men were wandering the Depression-stricken land seeking jobs or handouts, about 15,000 bedraggled veterans of World War I, some with their wives and children, marched on Washington, D.C., to bring pressure on Congress. The veterans demanded full prepayment of their World War I bonus certificates, which were not scheduled to mature for another 13 years. The Bonus Army was permitted to camp along the Anacostia River while its leaders lobbied on Capitol Hill for the passage of a bill, sponsored by Texas Representative Wright Patman, that would give them the bonuses immediately.

When Congress rejected their appeal, most of the "Bonus Expeditionary Force" drifted out of town, but by late July there were still 2,000 people encamped in shacks near the Capitol. President Herbert Hoover, fearing that Communist agitators might incite the stragglers to violence, ordered the U.S. Army to disperse them. On July 28 Chief of Staff Douglas MacArthur led an attack by saber-wielding cavalrymen, tanks, and infantrymen with fixed bayonets. Tear-gas bombs scattered the veterans, and their shacks were burned. This harsh treatment of men who had served their country in wartime aroused bitter criticism against General MacArthur and President Hoover, but MacArthur insisted that a display of "obvious strength" had been necessary against what he termed "riotous elements."

On the morning of July 16, 1945, *in the barren desert south of Los Alamos, New Mexico, this, the first atomic bomb, was exploded. A second bomb, with a force equal to 20,000 tons of TNT, was dropped 3 weeks later over Hiroshima with devastating results—260,000 Japanese killed and 6,280 buildings destroyed. On August 9, Nagasaki was hit, ending World War II in a flash "brighter than a thousand suns."*

The Blast That Shook the World

It began conventionally enough as another avenue to be explored in man's continuing search for new, more efficient weapons of war. It culminated in a brilliant mushroom-shaped cloud of unimaginable consequences. For the first time in history man had a weapon that could destroy his entire kind. The use of these new bombs, with their radioactive fallout that could kill and maim far beyond the point of explosion, shook the world. Although beneficial uses for atomic energy were foreseen, a deep concern and regret began to develop over the dropping of atomic bombs on Hiroshima and Nagasaki near the end of World War II. Apart from any sense of guilt or remorse, the somber realization that there is no conceivable defense against atomic weapons inspired a fear deeper and more disturbing than men had ever known.

As scientists in other countries plumbed the secrets of the atom, nuclear warheads were stockpiled around the world. Incredibly sophisticated electronic brains could be harnessed to the most destructive weapons. Any target on Earth, no matter how small or how distant, could be pinpointed.

As technology advanced, men ought to have become happier and felt more fulfilled. Instead they became increasingly restless. Goods and gadgets, instruments and implements for personal comfort and gratification multiplied; but for many life seemed fragmented and curiously aimless. Crime, drugs (hard, soft, and hallucinatory), and crises of authority between the young and their elders shook people's confidence and faith. Although not all our difficulties could be traced to the ever-present threat of annihilation, the epidemic of woes besetting us from every direction appeared to many to be more than coincidental.

If man is to continue on this Earth, our most fearsome weapons must be controlled, and control is not without precedent. There has been no general use of poison gas since both sides used it with such deadly effect in World War I. Systems of biological warfare have been put aside as too terrible to use. Post-atomic bomb conflicts in Korea, Vietnam, and the Middle East have occurred without resort to the ultimate weapon. A series of Strategic Arms Limitation Talks (SALT) and efforts on other fronts have been initiated to avert the unthinkable.

Now that the nuclear genie has been let out of the bottle, the world can never again be the same. We know today that the challenge to the intelligence and compassion of mankind is basically different from anything ever encountered before. How we meet this grave challenge will determine our very survival.

CHAPTER TWENTY

The Power of the Press

On September 25, 1690, news-hungry Bostonians, wh had to wait months for papers from Britain, bought the fir copies of the American Colonies' first newspaper. It was $7\frac{1}{4}$-inch by $11\frac{1}{2}$-inch, four-page journal with one blan page on which readers could fill in their own news. Th paper was fairly sensational for its day, with reports o smallpox and fevers, a suicide, Indian raids, and a scan dalous story about the King of France. That first issue o printer Benjamin Harris' intended monthly, Publick Occurrences, Both Forreign and Domestick, *was also th last. Because Harris had not obtained the license require by law, Increase and Cotton Mather halted publication*

Benjamin Franklin, Printer

In 1718, at the age of 12, Ben Franklin was apprenticed to his half brother James, a Boston printer and publisher. Five years later he ran off, and, after working briefly as a printer in Philadelphia, spent 2 years in London at his trade. In October 1726 he settled in Philadelphia and set up shop as a printer. From his press came books, reprints of laws, religious tracts, and *The Pennsylvania Gazette,* a newspaper filled with his amusing essays. The paper "became extreamly profitable," Franklin observed, and soon, for a share of their profits, he was helping other printers start newspapers all along the east coast and even in the West Indies.

Franklin taught himself French, Italian, German, Spanish, and Latin. From his readings he gathered the world's aphorisms together with many of his own into various editions of his *Poor Richard's Almanack* (1733–58), which remains popular to this day. At 42 he left his printing concerns in a partner's charge and devoted the remaining half of his life to scholarly pursuits and statesmanship. Yet after many years as a diplomat, scientist, and author, this versatile citizen of a new Nation still described himself as "Benjamin Franklin, Printer."

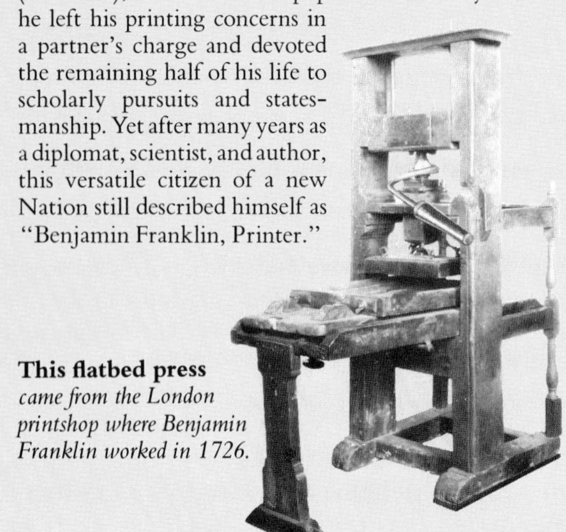

This flatbed press *came from the London printshop where Benjamin Franklin worked in 1726.*

The first true newspaper to appear after Benjamin Harris' short-lived venture was *The Boston News-Letter,* begun by John Campbell in 1704 and safely published "by authority" of the government. Campbell was a postmaster—as were many of his successors in American journalism—and filled the two sides of his sheet with news and with rumors he had heard from ship captains, sailors, and the postriders who carried the mail from town to town.

For 15 years the weekly *News-Letter* was the only paper in the Colonies, although its subscription list never contained more than 300 names. Then in 1719 another postmaster was appointed to Campbell's place. Campbell retained control of the *News-Letter,* and the new official began his own paper, *The Boston Gazette.* Two years later a third newspaper appeared in the city when James Franklin, with the aid of his 15-year-old half brother, Benjamin, established *The New-England Courant.*

The news that appeared in these early papers was usually from abroad. Aside from tiny boxed advertisements of articles lost, found, or for sale, domestic news was limited to notices of arriving and departing ships. But gradually the colonists became less reticent about their own "publick occurrences."

Perhaps the first truly important American story covered by the colonial press was the Stamp Act, passed in 1765 by the British Parliament, calling for the use of special stamped paper for written or printed materials in the Colonies. In most cases the tax would have doubled the cost of newspapers, which as often as not had to plead publicly with their readers to pay for their subscriptions. Several papers suspended or ceased publication; others continued to print on unstamped paper, claiming the stamped variety was impossible to find. No colonial newspaper ever appeared with a stamp, and the act was deemed unenforceable and soon repealed.

ys after the paper appeared. More than a decade passed ·fore Americans saw another native newspaper.

The press in the United States has followed a smoother ıth since 1690. Relations between press and government ave not always been the most cordial, for the press has aditionally tended to be its determined—but loyal— dversary. Since 1791 the first amendment to the Constiıtion has guaranteed freedom of the written word from ction by the Federal Government, a guarantee that has een tested and consistently upheld through the years.

The following pages tell of the personalities, ideas, and chnological changes that have shaped the American press—the freest and most vital in the world—from Publick Occurrences *to the "electronic village" created in the second half of the 20th century by radio and television. The power of the press has not always been used for noble purposes. From the very beginning there have been examples of sensationalism, gross inaccuracy, and, occasionally, slander. But for the most part the story is one of responsibility; for the press, whether in its staid journals, glossy ladies' magazines, or television documentaries, has on the whole dealt responsibly with the freedom guaranteed it by the Constitution and has fulfilled its primary duty: to inform the public of the truth.*

Most papers were in sympathy with the growing demand for more autonomy from England. Samuel Adams, James Otis, and other radical Patriots wrote for Isaiah Thomas' *Massachusetts Spy* and for *The Boston Gazette,* which was then edited by Benjamin Edes and John Gill—themselves among the leaders of the Boston Tea Party. The *Royal American Magazine* carried political cartoons by Paul Revere. Thomas Paine was editor of the *Pennsylvania Magazine* for a year and a half; the first of his *Crisis* essays, proclaiming that "These are the times that try men's souls," was originally printed in William Bradford's *Pennsylvania Journal.* In New York City, however, the Tory faction had the powerful *Royal Gazette.*

The Stamp Act *required that all printing be done on taxed paper bearing stamps like this.*

Communication among the Colonies was extremely limited. It took months for news to travel from Boston to Charleston, South Carolina. Because it was usually impossible to confirm or deny rumors with any speed, they were printed as fact or, oftener, under the heading "Important, If True." Solid facts were not ignored, however. Word of the completion of the Constitutional Convention's work traveled quickly, and the entire Constitution was soon printed and discussed in every newspaper. Final ratification of the Constitution hinged on the passage of the first 10 amendments to it—the Bill of Rights—one of which spelled out, for the first time in any country, the right of freedom of the press.

MAKING DEMOCRACY WORK

The Zenger Trial

By the time German immigrant John Peter Zenger began the *New-York Weekly Journal* in 1733, an American publisher no longer needed authorization from the Government to produce a newspaper. But the colonial Governors still kept close watch on the press and had a weapon to use against their critics: Publishers were subject to jail if they were found guilty of seditious libel (statements considered dangerous to the Government).

The *Journal* was financed by influential New Yorkers opposed to Gov. William Cosby, who was its chief target. After a year of scathing but accurate attacks on him and his administration, most of them written not by the poorly educated Zenger but by his backers, Cosby retaliated. Zenger, the legally responsible agent, was arrested on November 17, 1734, charged with seditious libel, and imprisoned.

When Zenger came to trial in the Supreme Court of New York after almost 9 months in prison, his backers engaged Andrew Hamilton, a brilliant and widely known Philadelphia lawyer, to defend him. Hamilton conceded Zenger's responsibility for printing the alleged libels, but he insisted that the issue before the court and jury was the truth or falsity of the printed material; if it could be proved true, Zenger was not guilty. Chief Justice James De Lancey sternly insisted that Hamilton could not "give the truth of a libel in evidence . . . for it is nevertheless a libel that it is true. . . ." But the jury accepted Hamilton's eloquent plea for Zenger and found him not guilty. Although the trial did not change the law at that time—truth as a defense in a libel suit was not formally recognized in New York State until 1805—it was the first public victory for freedom of the press in the Colonies.

Newspapers now began to adhere to one of the two party lines: Those of the strongly nationalist Federalist Party, which supported ratification, and the anti-Federalists (later the Democratic-Republicans), who opposed it because they were for States rights. During Washington's Administration the struggle between Federalist Alexander Hamilton and his chief opponent, Thomas Jefferson, was so intense that both had, in effect, their personal newspapers, two *Gazettes.* Their rivalry led, in 1798, to the passage of the Alien and Sedition Acts, which included penalties for false or malicious anti-Government writings and were invoked against several anti-Federalist publishers. This tradition of a highly partisan press continued into Andrew Jackson's Administration. One paper, the *National Intelligencer* of Washington, D.C., became the Government's spokesman and the source of news for the country's other papers.

The first U.S. census, taken in 1790, showed that fewer than 3 percent of the country's 3,929,214 inhabitants had ventured west of the Allegheny Mountains. By that date several papers had already been established in the small frontier settlements. Less than 40 years later the United States had 861 newspapers, more than any other nation.

The Penny Papers

Until the 1830's American papers were printed essentially for the elite. By that time many appeared daily and were sold only by subscription. Prices varied, but 6 cents was fairly standard—when 6 cents was more than 10 percent of a laborer's daily salary. Newspaper print runs were necessarily small; the papers were still being printed on slow, cumbersome presses. Then in 1833 Benjamin Day (father of Clarence Day, the subject of *Life With Father*) founded *The Sun* in New York. He installed the new Hoe cylinder press, which could print 1,500 papers of 4 to 8 pages an hour. Day, with the idea of gearing *The Sun* to the city's lower classes, decided to have newsboys hawk his paper on the street for a penny a copy. The news was colorful and local. For the first time New Yorkers were treated to crime reports—most of them of drunken brawls—and what became known as "human interest" stories: tales, often poignant, of typical, unknown city dwellers like themselves.

Day's penny paper was so successful that in 1835 Scottish-born James Gordon Bennett founded the New York *Morning Herald* (later simply the *Herald*) on the same principles. A sometime instructor of economics, Bennett introduced the country's most comprehensive financial reporting—his own "money articles," direct from Wall Street—and in addition printed exciting crime reports and theatrical and society news. The *Herald* was every bit as sensational as *The Sun,* and there was no news so important that it could knock a prostitute's murder off the front page. But Bennett stressed solid reporting and made every effort to get the news first, even dispatching speedboats and carrier pigeons out to sea to pick up reports from incoming European ships.

The fierce competition among the New York dailies led in 1849 to the creation of a combined news-gathering force, which in time became the Associated Press. Because the agency supplied stories to papers with widely varying viewpoints, its reports tended to be objective. Objectivity, then a new concept, went on to become the major thrust in American journalism. In the early 1900's Edward Wyllis Scripps formed the United Press Associations, which in 1958, after a merger with International News Service, became United Press International.

Both Day and Bennett were members of a new breed of newspaperman. Unlike the printer-publishers of earlier days, they were editors and reporters whose papers strongly reflected their personalities. Joining them in this era of personal journalism was one of the country's most discussed editors, Horace Greeley, who added a new dimension to the penny press—that of social reform.

Although Greeley wasn't actually the first person to urge young men to go West, his paper, the *New York Tribune,* founded in 1841, was the first to have national impact. Uncle Horace's often radical ideas for a better America were debated by every class of society, by Fifth Avenue dowagers as well as by the farmers and laborers whose champion he was. Political ambition drove Greeley throughout his life; he died in 1872, after having been badly defeated as the Liberal Republican and Democratic candidate for the Presidency.

While the penny press was popularizing spot news, periodicals began to appear with fiction by the leading American writers of the day. Serialized works by British authors continued in favor, but now such literary jour-

MAKING DEMOCRACY WORK

The First Amendment and the Press

Ratification of the Constitution by the States was contingent on a promise that the first Congress would approve amendments protecting the people's rights. By 1791, 10 amendments had been ratified by the States and added to the Constitution as the Bill of Rights. The first of these says in part: "Congress shall make no law . . . abridging the freedom of speech, or of the press. . . ." Court decisions have upheld this freedom through the years. In 1971 the Nixon administration sought to bar the publication of the "Pentagon Papers" by *The New York Times* and *The Washington Post,* claiming that this disclosure was harmful to "the nation's security." But the Supreme Court held that officials had not shown sufficient grounds for taking such action.

Thomas Jefferson

Alexander Hamilton

Jefferson, Hamilton, and the Two Gazettes
Doing Battle in the Public Press

Bitter dissension between political leaders marked the early days of our Republic. Secretary of the Treasury Alexander Hamilton and his supporters believed in a strong central government, perhaps even a monarchy, and thought the country would eventually be commercial and industrial rather than agrarian. Others, including Secretary of State Thomas Jefferson, favored the common man, States rights, and farming interests. Recognizing the growing power of the press, both Hamilton and Jefferson encouraged the establishment of newspapers that would give them sounding boards.

John Fenno began the *Gazette of the United States* in New York City in April 1789. Hamilton lent financial and editorial support, and the paper became the mouthpiece of the Federalist Party. When the Government moved to Philadelphia in 1790, the *Gazette* moved with it. The following year, with moral support from Jefferson and a supplementary job as a State Department translator, poet Philip Freneau started the *National Gazette* in the new capital. Soon Freneau was brazenly attacking President George Washington in his paper, and Hamilton was personally but anonymously answering Freneau's barbs in Fenno's *Gazette.*

Freneau suspended publication of the *National Gazette* in 1793 because of a lack of funds and because a yellow fever epidemic had practically closed down the city. Shortly afterward Jefferson retired from the Cabinet, and with the loss of his mentor Freneau decided not to start publishing the paper again. After Fenno's death in 1798 his son ran his paper for 2 years, then sold it.

nals as the *North American Review, United States Magazine and Democratic Review, Graham's Lady's and Gentleman's Magazine,* and the New York *Knickerbocker Magazine* published the works of such outstanding writers as Washington Irving, James Fenimore Cooper, Henry Wadsworth Longfellow, James Russell Lowell, John Greenleaf Whittier, and Nathaniel Hawthorne. In 1830 *Godey's Lady's Book,* which was to last for 68 years, 40 of them under the direction of feminist Sarah Josepha Hale, first went out to its women subscribers.

As more and more people moved west, the traveling printer moved with them. When the first miners rushed to California from the East in 1849, they had local papers to read. The national "news" printed in these papers was seldom new. California at first had to depend on ships, making the circuitous, three-month trip around Cape Horn, to bring papers from the East.

The rest of the country fared a bit better. By the 1850's the telegraph and the railroad reached as far west as Chicago. Papers no longer had to be weeks behind in news of national importance, and more and more of them began to take sides in the festering controversy between Northern and Southern States and pro- and anti-slavery factions. Abolitionist William Lloyd Garrison had begun *The Liberator* in Boston in 1831—and ceased its publication in December 1865, soon after the ratification of the 13th amendment abolished slavery in the United States. Two other famous abolitionist papers were founded in 1847: *The North Star,* published by Frederick Douglass, a former slave, and Gamaliel Bailey's *National Era* of Washington, D.C.

In the 1850's a colorful new form of periodical, the illustrated newspaper, appeared. *Frank Leslie's Illustrated Newspaper* and *Harper's Weekly,* both in New York, printed news, fiction, sports, and exposés, strikingly illustrated by such artists as Winslow Homer and Thomas Nast. (There was no way to reproduce photographs on newspaper presses, and the work of the great Civil War photographer Mathew Brady never appeared in the papers.) The illustrations, first done on paper, were copied onto wooden blocks. Wood engravers then painstakingly carved the drawings into the blocks.

During the Civil War Northern correspondents and illustrators flocked to the front lines—and provided some of the finest on-the-spot reporting ever seen. For the first time reporters became men of importance; individual papers no longer had to depend on news services and clippings from other, larger journals. The press itself became so powerful that it could make the reputation of some officers, destroy others, and create military strategy, even against the Army's better judgment.

The Southern papers simply didn't have the manpower to place their own reporters at the scene of action. Instead, they combined forces and began the Press Association of the Confederate States of America. Because 95 percent of the American paper mills were in the North, the Southern press also suffered a severe shortage of newsprint. Those Southern newspapers that were not forced to stop publication entirely had to do their printing on wrapping paper or on wallpaper.

Journalism in the Gilded Age

Tremendous advances were made in the publishing industry in the 1880's and 1890's. Ottmar Mergenthaler's Linotype machine set type three times faster than it could be done by hand. Instead of printing on a single flat sheet or one side of a roll of paper, the new web-perfecting press printed both sides of a continuous roll of paper at

Wood engravings assured *the success of the 19th-century weeklies after Frank Leslie revolutionized the production of illustrations in 1853. Instead of having one engraver incise a drawing on a block of wood—which could take several months—Leslie divided the sketch into separate blocks that a dozen or more engravers could work on, finishing the job in from 1 to 3 days. The blocks were then bolted together to form the picture. Civil War battle scenes re-created by this process helped boost the circulation of* Frank Leslie's Illustrated Newspaper.

once, using one-piece stereotyped plates that replaced the fragile columns of loose type. The need for column rules to hold in the type was thus eliminated, and bigger, bolder headlines began to stretch across the front pages. The invention of halftone engraving—a method of printing illustrations composed of shades and tones rather than simply of lines and solid areas of color—allowed newspapers to print photographs in place of line engravings. Cheaper and more accessible wood pulp paper gradually replaced the rag paper once common. Alexander Graham Bell's invention of the telephone in 1875 sped communication, and in the 1880's the typewriter came into widespread use to record the news that reporters phoned in.

The Gilded Age also saw the rise and expansion of humorous and literary magazines and children's and ladies' journals. *Puck, Judge,* and the original *Life* (with the famous Gibson Girl illustrations) made America laugh. Edwin Godkin's *The Nation,* begun in 1865, continued to make it think, as did the other journals of opinion, *Century* and *Scribner's* magazines among them. Two monthlies begun in the 1850's, *Harper's* (started by Harper and Brothers of the weekly magazine) and the *Atlantic,* still published the best of American writers. The *Literary Digest* became successful by reprinting articles from newspapers and other magazines. *The Ladies' Home Journal* appeared as a competitor with *Godey's Lady's Book* and is still published today.

The illustrated newspapers that began in the 1850's increased in popularity and took on political reform. *Harper's Weekly* joined *The New York Times* in a campaign against that city's notorious political organization, Tammany Hall, and helped to destroy it for a time. The cream that Boss Tweed's Ring skimmed off the top of the city's finances was so rich that the gang was able to offer George Jones, who had taken over the *Times* after the death of its founder, Henry Raymond, $5 million not to print damaging city records that had been given to the paper. The New York *Sun,* under the direction of Charles A. Dana, exposed the Crédit Mobilier scandal involving the building of the Union Pacific Railroad.

A new batch of periodicals became popular in the 1880's and 1890's. Popular fiction, general articles, profuse illustrations, and their low price—10 cents—made *Munsey's, McClure's,* and *Cosmopolitan* monthly magazines instant successes. *The Saturday Evening Post,* which could be bought every week for a nickel, was another bestseller.

Because of technological advances in printing, newspapers slowly became big businesses. One of the first men to set up a newspaper empire was Hungarian-born Joseph Pulitzer. After making a success of the *St. Louis Post-Dispatch,* Pulitzer proceeded to New York City, where he bought *The World* in 1883. By an entertaining and informative blend of sensationalism and solid reporting, he turned it into one of the greatest of all newspapers.

In 1895 a brash young Californian, fresh from his success with the *San Francisco Examiner,* went to New York, determined to beat Pulitzer at his own game. William Randolph Hearst had, in fact, based much of the *Examiner* on *The World,* and he intended to apply this experience to the *New York Journal,* which he bought from its foun-

THE NORTH STAR.

RIGHT IS OF NO SEX—TRUTH IS OF NO COLOR—GOD IS THE FATHER OF US ALL, AND ALL WE ARE BRETHREN.

VOL. I. NO. 33. | ROCHESTER, N. Y. FRIDAY, AUGUST 11, 1848. | WHOLE NO.—33.

Born in slavery on a Maryland plantation *in 1817, Frederick Douglass went on to become a brilliant speaker, writer, editor, and public servant. In 1847, after 9 years as a fugitive slave and one of the most successful lecturers of the Anti-Slavery Society, Douglass purchased his freedom. That same year he began* The North Star *(later* Frederick Douglass's Paper) *in Rochester, New York, and continued it until 1860. William Lloyd Garrison and his* Liberator *had greatly influenced Douglass, but establishment of* The North Star *led to a break between the two abolitionist editors. Garrison did not think a separate black press was necessary.*

der, Pulitzer's brother, Alfred. One of the first things Hearst did was to set up an office in *The World*'s building on Park Row—a *Journal* employment office for Pulitzer's experienced, carefully handpicked staff.

The feud that developed between the two editors gave rise to yellow journalism (named after a *World* comic-strip character, the Yellow Kid), which was to dominate the American press until about 1920. Sensational tales of murders, tragedies, disasters, and the famous—the more shocking, the better—were told in a new format that used bold "scare" headlines, lavish supplements, and numerous illustrations. Many of the stories were Hearst and Pulitzer creations, and the two papers have been accused of maneuvering the Nation into the Spanish-American War over Cuba in 1898.

While Hearst and Pulitzer were trying to outdo each other's comics, Sunday supplements, scandals, and stunts, Adolph Ochs was ignoring such frills and quietly redirecting his paper, *The New York Times,* on a course of serious news coverage—which the nationally read *Times* continues to follow today. Aided by his managing editor, Carr Van Anda, Ochs sought—and got—what the *Times'* slogan promised: "All the news that's fit to print" (a slap at the yellow journalists, who printed much that wasn't).

The Reformers

At the turn of the century papers and magazines again directed their attention to social and political reform. Jacob Riis, while a police reporter for the New York *Tribune* and the *Evening Sun,* had publicly exposed the horrors of New York City's slums. William Rockhill Nelson, founder and editor of the *Kansas City Evening Star* from 1880 to 1915, helped transform that city with his campaigns against corruption and for civic improvements such as parks and boulevards. *The Ladies' Home Journal* and *Collier's* took on the "cure-all" patent medicines; their efforts helped result in the passage of the first Pure Food and Drug Act in 1906. *Good Housekeeping* aided American consumers with its bureau and institute for testing products. With its January 1903 issue, *McClure's Magazine* started a trend that President Theodore Roosevelt later termed "muckraking." Although *McClure's* reporters wrote fair, balanced articles, allowing readers to draw their own conclusions from the facts presented, this type of reporting became simply abusive or sensational and died out almost entirely about 1912.

In 1919 the smaller, profusely illustrated, easy-to-read tabloid newspaper was first successful. Robert R. McCormick and Joseph M. Patterson, grandsons of Joseph Medill, who built *The Chicago Tribune,* founded the New York *Daily News.* William Randolph Hearst was quick to follow with his own tabloid, the *Daily Mirror,* and Bernarr Macfadden with the *Daily Graphic* (nicknamed the "Pornographic" because of its antics).

Thomas Nast: Cartoonist for All Seasons

While head of Tammany Hall, a political organization with headquarters in New York City, William M. "Boss" Tweed said: "I don't care so much what the papers write about me—my constituents can't read; but, damn it, they can see pictures!" Tweed's distrust of pictures proved well founded. In 1876, while hiding in Spain from New York justice, he was recognized and arrested by a policeman who had seen a drawing of him by Thomas Nast. Nast, whose scathing cartoons helped destroy the Tweed Ring, began his career at the age of 15. For $4 a week he depicted important events for *Frank Leslie's Illustrated Newspaper.* Several years later, commenting on his Civil War scenes in *Harper's Weekly,* President Lincoln called him "our best recruiting sergeant." Nast had a lighter side, too. In annual Christmas drawings, such as the one below, he created America's Santa Claus, basing the jolly, white-bearded figure on Pelze-Nicol (Fur-clad Nicholas) of his native Bavaria. The Democratic donkey, the Republican elephant, and Uncle Sam were also products of Nast's imagination.

About this period Frank Munsey, in the name of efficiency, began buying and merging papers; in the process he destroyed 4 of New York City's 15 dailies. At the same time other publishers were at work setting up chains of papers. Hearst, Edward Wyllis Scripps and Roy Howard, George C. Booth, and Herman Ridder were among those who established newspapers throughout the country.

Several popular new magazines appeared in the 1920's. In 1922 DeWitt and Lila Acheson Wallace brought out the first issue of *The Reader's Digest,* a small magazine with an unusual idea: lively, informative condensations of articles that had appeared in other magazines. The new format with its articles "of lasting interest" was an immediate success. Today the *Digest* is the most widely read magazine in the United States and, with its foreign editions, the largest-selling magazine in the world; every month almost 30 million are sold in 13 languages.

One year after the *Digest* began publication, Henry R. Luce and Briton Hadden started a breezy weekly news magazine which they called *Time.* It also found a huge audience immediately and was the inspiration for *Newsweek,* which appeared several years later. In 1925 Harold Ross founded *The New Yorker,* which continues to publish fine fiction, articles, and cartoons. In 1936 a new Luce magazine, *Life,* first showed the world that pictures are sometimes worth 10,000 words.

Along with the rest of the country the sensational, sometimes vulgar "jazz journalism" of the 1920's sobered up during the Depression. By the mid-1930's the "big" though unimportant story had given way to a careful analysis of the day's significant happenings. Readers had the opportunity to learn the background of an event, filled in by reporters who were specialists in their fields.

Besides learning the latest news, newspaper readers could also discover new recipes, test their skill at crossword puzzles, read reviews of new books, and ponder advice on health, love, and the care and feeding of pets. They could usually find something to laugh at in the syndicated columns of humorists George Ade, Don Marquis, and Franklin P. Adams, and something to approve of or disagree with in the columns of such political commentators as Walter Lippmann, Heywood Broun, Max Lerner, Westbrook Pegler, David Lawrence, and William L. White. Although his influence had waned, H. L. Mencken continued to excoriate the middle class—the "booboisie"—in the pages of the Baltimore *Sun.* Hedda Hopper, Louella Parsons, and Walter Winchell let ordinary mortals in on the doings of Hollywood and Broadway greats, and Grantland Rice, John Kieran, and Red Smith covered the sporting scene. Cartoonists such as John T. McCutcheon of *The Chicago Tribune* and C. D. Batchelor of the New York *Daily News* looked at America's political figures and affairs with trenchant eyes and depicted them with wicked pens.

Technology and the Press
Progress Has Been Slow in Coming

When Johann Gutenberg introduced his movable type a printing press in the 1440's, the scribes of Paris went on stri to protest an innovation which, as they accurately foresaw, v destined to put them out of work. In 1974 Typographical Uni No. 6 at the New York *Daily News,* America's most widely circ lated newspaper, struck for a similar reason. Their concern v a computer-based system that set type 50 times faster than t methods they were using and required far fewer operators. T printing trades have always tended to resist rapid progress. F almost 400 years printers followed Gutenberg's practice handsetting individual pieces of type, locking them into pla in a form, and printing on wooden flatbed handpresses like t one shown on page 356. A good rate of production was 300 500 sheets a day printed on one side.

It was not until the 1860's when the public demand for ne had swelled the circulations of the penny newspapers that stear powered rotary presses were developed which were capable printing both sides of the newsprint simultaneously. The ty however, was still set by hand, letter by letter, until Ottm Mergenthaler invented the Linotype, which considerably i creased the speed at which type could be set.

By the mid-1970's mammoth presses with newsprint rolli through at speeds up to a mile a minute could print, fold, c and assemble 70,000 copies of a 144-page newspaper in an hou The typesetting process has shifted from hot metal to cold type actually, to a computer-based system using photo images of ty that are transmitted from a keyboard to film and are nev touched by human hands. The speed is almost incredible. T complete Bible can be set into type in about 80 minutes. The sar job had taken Gutenberg almost 5 years on the press he develope but that press—crude as it was by today's standards—opened t door to the modern world of communication.

During World War I censorship had been too strong and communications too slow for reporters to provide the vivid coverage that had characterized the Civil War. World War II was another story. More than 1,500 reporters—colorfully exemplified by Scripps-Howard's Ernie Pyle, who was killed in the Pacific in the final months of the war—sent brilliant firsthand reports to their papers, while other correspondents spoke directly to anxious listeners over the radio.

Changing Times

In the 1950's and 1960's newspapers and magazines were attempting to recover the audiences and advertisers lost to radio and a postwar communications development, television. With this competition and the rising costs of paper, labor, services, and postage, many periodicals lost the battle. New York City, for example, had 10 general-interest dailies in 1960; a little more than 10 years later there were 3. (Lost in 1967 was the *World-Journal-Tribune,* a short-lived paper with memories of Pulitzer, Hearst, Dana, Day, and James Gordon Bennett and his son.) New periodicals keep appearing, however. There has been a great growth in suburban newspapers, which siphon readers from the big-city press. Most successful of these has been Long Island, New York's, *Newsday.*

The printing dynasty *founded in New York City by British-born Robert Hoe in 1805 supplied a world market with presses and other equipment for more than 100 years. The Hoe web-fed perfecting press (above) was featured at an 1870's exhibition of new machinery. It was capable of printing some 18,000 sheets an hour on both sides of the paper. The Linotype, invented in 1884 by Ottmar Mergenthaler, made such large, fast-moving presses practical. The early version of Mergenthaler's machine (top right) functioned much as do the Linotypes of today. The operator punched the typewriterlike keyboard, and the matrix, or mold, for each character dropped from its place in the sectioned magazine at the top of the machine and fell through the channels above the keyboard to the area where the matrices were assembled into a full, measured line. Molten lead then poured into the molds and cast a solid line of type. The woman in the photograph at right is operating the modern successor to the Linotype, similar to the equipment used to set the type for this book. Copy, which is stored on magnetic tape in the computer at her left, can be projected onto the video screen above the keyboard, which is used to make any corrections required.*

Founded in 1940, it is today one of the country's leading evening papers. At the same time, two newspapers have gained national circulation: *The Christian Science Monitor* has become known for its in-depth analyses of major news developments, while *The Wall Street Journal,* under Bernard Kilgore from 1940 to 1967, broadened from a strictly financial paper to one with general news interest. Although the foreign-language papers are dying out (in 1914 there were 140 such dailies; today there are about one-fourth that number), there has been a great surge in newspapers and magazines aimed at black Americans. *Ebony,* a pictorial modeled after *Life* and first published in 1945, was an early entrant in the black magazine field; the handsome fashion magazine *Essence,* begun in 1970, is one of the latest. Black newspapers founded at the turn of the century, such as the *Baltimore Afro-American,* the *Amsterdam News* of New York, and the *Pittsburgh Courier,* are still circulation leaders. Among numerous other publications aimed at special groups are *The National Geographic Magazine, Saturday Review, Women's Wear Daily, Ms., Field and Stream,* and *Gourmet.*

The Vietnam War was covered extensively by all media, and most of the reporting was adverse. In 1971 classified documents relating to the war came into the possession of *The New York Times* and *The Washington Post.* For the first time in U.S. history a national administration tried by legal means to prevent material from being published. The Supreme Court soon decided against the Government's attempt at prior restraint, ruling that newspapers could not be prevented from publishing the "Pentagon Papers" but were liable, after publication, for any breach of law.

In the 1970's the trend in newspaper reporting has been back to investigation, in the best tradition of the muckrakers. *The Washington Post* became involved in a second controversy in 1972 with its stories of the break-in at the Democratic headquarters in the Capital's Watergate complex, with its subsequent startling revelations. The role of the *Post* in this event, which may affect government and governmental policies for years to come, points up the need for continued vigilance on the part of the public and the press.

More and more the Nation seems to be getting its news from radio and television (see pages 368–370). But it is the newspapers and magazines that have the time and the space for the most careful interpretation of the news. The newspapers of the United States continue to deal most effectively with local news and to relate the national news to the locality. Despite persistent warnings of its imminent doom, the age of print is far from over.

The Drive for Circulation
News Wasn't Reported, It Was Manufactured

In this day of relatively responsible news reporting, it is hard to imagine the lengths to which the press lords of the 19th and early 20th centuries went to increase circulation. Some of the stunts were harmless enough. For example, in 1889 *World* reporter Nellie Bly circumnavigated the globe in 72 days, topping the record set by Jules Verne's fictional hero, Phineas Fogg. Other exploits of the unscrupulous sensationalists of the period contributed a disgraceful chapter to American journalism. Worst of all was the shameless warmongering that played so large a part in fomenting the conflict with Spain in 1898.

An early entry in the competition to manufacture news was the New York *Sun*. In 1835 *The Sun* offered a supposedly factual account of life on the Moon, complete with fantastic animals and winged humanoids. Only a few readers complained when *The Sun* was finally forced to admit that the story had been a hoax. If today's newspapers are less spectacular, they are more reliable. And at its best the American information industry has served as the Nation's conscience.

For 11 months *Henry M. Stanley, a Welsh-born reporter on the staff of the New York* Herald, *searched the African wilds for David Livingstone, a Scottish missionary and explorer who had not been heard from for 3 years. Their meeting at a village on Lake Tanganyika on November 10, 1871, made news throughout the world. Stanley's expedition was just one of many schemes that James Gordon Bennett, Jr., the erratic playboy son of the* Herald's *founder, had devised to promote the paper he now headed. Stanley stayed with Livingstone for 4 months; his enthusiastic but accurate reports won him support for later expeditions into the land he dubbed the Dark Continent. The engraving at the right was based on Stanley's description of the event. His greeting to the man he had sought so long survives as a classic example of understatement: "Dr. Livingstone, I presume?"*

"Remember the Maine!" *was the rallying cry when the United States plunged into war with Spain in April 1898. The U.S.S.* Maine *(above) had blown up in Havana Harbor 2 months earlier, and William Randolph Hearst and Joseph Pulitzer had made inflammatory use of the incident in their competing newspapers. For 2 years, in their battle for circulation, the sensationalist publishers had regaled their readers with lurid, often false tales of Spanish cruelties to Cuba's rebels. The story goes that when artist Frederic Remington, sent to the island to make sketches for Hearst's* New York Journal, *cabled, "There will be no war," Hearst replied: "You furnish the pictures and I'll furnish the war."*

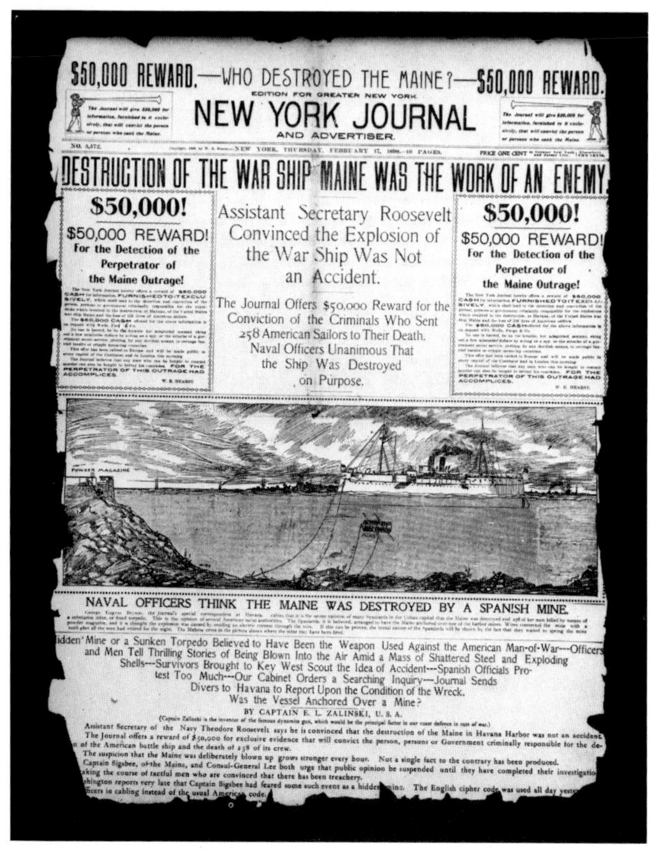

$50,000 REWARD.—WHO DESTROYED THE MAINE?—$50,000 REWARD.

EDITION FOR GREATER NEW YORK

NEW YORK JOURNAL

AND ADVERTISER.

NEW YORK, THURSDAY, FEBRUARY 17, 1898.—16 PAGES. PRICE ONE CENT

DESTRUCTION OF THE WAR SHIP MAINE WAS THE WORK OF AN ENEMY.

$50,000!

$50,000 REWARD! For the Detection of the Perpetrator of the Maine Outrage!

Assistant Secretary Roosevelt Convinced the Explosion of the War Ship Was Not an Accident.

The Journal Offers $50,000 Reward for the Conviction of the Criminals Who Sent 258 American Sailors to Their Death. Naval Officers Unanimous That the Ship Was Destroyed on Purpose.

$50,000!

$50,000 REWARD! For the Detection of the Perpetrator of the Maine Outrage!

NAVAL OFFICERS THINK THE MAINE WAS DESTROYED BY A SPANISH MINE.

[illegible]idden' Mine or a Sunken Torpedo Believed to Have Been the Weapon Used Against the American Man-of-War---Officers and Men Tell Thrilling Stories of Being Blown Into the Air Amid a Mass of Shattered Steel and Exploding Shells---Survivors Brought to Key West Scout the Idea of Accident---Spanish Officials Protest Too Much---Our Cabinet Orders a Searching Inquiry—Journal Sends Divers to Havana to Report Upon the Condition of the Wreck. Was the Vessel Anchored Over a Mine?

BY CAPTAIN E. L. ZALINSKI, U. S. A.

(Captain Zalinski is the inventor of the famous dynamite gun, which would be the principal factor in our coast defence in case of war.)

Assistant Secretary of the Navy Theodore Roosevelt says he is convinced that the destruction of the Maine in Havana Harbor was not an accident.

The Journal offers a reward of $50,000 for exclusive evidence that will convict the person, persons or Government criminally responsible for the de-[illegible]n of the American battle ship and the death of 258 of its crew.

The suspicion that the Maine was deliberately blown up grows stronger every hour. Not a single fact to the contrary has been produced.

Captain Sigsbee, of the Maine, and Consul-General Lee both urge that public opinion be suspended until they have completed their investigatio[illegible] [illegible]king the course of tactful men who are convinced that there has been treachery.

[illegible]shington reports very late that Captain Sigsbee had feared some such event as a hidden mine. The English cipher code was used all day yeste[illegible] [illegible]ficers in cabling instead of the usual American code.

The World.

A NEW HIGH MARK OF WORLD WANT SUPREMACY!

ALL TWO OTHER N. Y. NEWSPAPERS COMBINED.

"Circulation Books Open to All."

A WORLD WANT "CORNER" IN "SUMMER RESORT" ADVERTISING!

ALL THE OTHER N. Y. NEWSPAPERS COMBINED.

"Circulation Books Open to All."

VOL. XLVI. NO. 16,281. NEW YORK, WEDNESDAY, JUNE 27, 1906.

ARMOUR HOME; SAYS BIG PACKERS ARE SLANDERED.

HARRY THAW'S YOUNG BRIDE, AN ARTIST'S MODEL, SHOW GIRL, IN COSTUME, AND AS SHE HAS APPEARED IN SOCIETY SINCE HER MARRIAGE.

NOTE FROM WHITE TO HIS BRIDE DROVE HARRY THAW TO MURDEROUS REVENGE.

Evelyn Nesbit Thaw Begins a Loyal Fight for Her Husband's Life and, It Is Said, Has Furnished Letters from the Architect That Led to the Roof-Garden Tragedy.

$40,000,000 WILL BACK THE EFFORT TO ESCAPE DEATH CHAIR.

"I Am Not a Fugitive," Says Young Wife—Visits Lawyers and Leaves Over Roofs—Murderer Goes Through Police Routine and Lands in Tombs Cell—Pittsburg Folks and Friends Say He Has Long Been Known as "Crazy Harry."

OXEN END FLIGHT OF HOMEMADE BALLOON

HOW PATRICK HENRY AVENGED BOUNCE.

YALE MEN SHIP AS COMMON SAILORS.

HIT WALDO'S SMILE WITH BAD POTATO.

THAWS ROBBED OF $60,000 IN JEWELS.

A Day's Developments in the Tragedy of the Roof Garden.

NO MORE FRIDAY COUNTS.

INDEX TO ADVERTISEMENTS.

A field day *for yellow journalism followed the fatal shooting of Stanford White by millionaire Harry K. Thaw in 1906. White, an outstanding architect and a member of New York's high-living social set, had been Evelyn Nesbit's lover before her marriage to "Crazy Harry" Thaw. At the right is the New York* World's *front page as it appeared 2 days after the murder. White and Thaw are overshadowed by "artist's model, show girl" Evelyn Nesbit and the details of her private life. The story was kept alive for 2 years, through two trials, gaining new scandal-hungry readers for the sensational newspapers of the period. Hungarian-born Joseph Pulitzer, editor of* The World, *was a leading practitioner of this brand of journalism. Blind and with a nervous condition that made him overly sensitive to noise, he formally retired in 1890, but retained strict control of his paper's policies until his death in 1911. Under his direction the front page was a heady mixture of sensation, human interest, and an occasional serious story. On June 27, 1906, for example, the White murder shared the spotlight with a boy who threw a potato at the New York City Police Commissioner, a cat that tried to avenge the killing of its canine friend by another dog, and a meatpacker who denied muckrakers' charges against his industry. Inside were more human interest features, some solid news, and thoughtful, reform-minded editorials.* The World *did not hide its light under a bushel, as may be seen from boxes proclaiming the success of advertisements.*

The Comic Strips

Humorous drawings are an ancient way of portraying man's trials and triumphs, but the cartoon strip as a medium for a running account of the doings of an established cast of characters is an American innovation. In 1894 a young artist, Richard Felton Outcault, created "The Yellow Kid," a cartoon urchin in a sacklike garb—2 years later a yellow tint was added to his coat—whose weekly antics delighted the readers of Joseph Pulitzer's New York *World.* William Randolph Hearst hired Outcault away from Pulitzer in the battle for circulation and installed The Kid as a feature in his *New York Journal.* From "The Yellow Kid" came the term "yellow journalism," used ever since to describe sensationalism in the press. The popularity of the early comics led to new strips. The Kid was followed by "Buster Brown," "Happy Hooligan," and "The Katzenjammer Kids," the longest-lived characters of all cartoon features. Soon the funny papers became an American institution. In 1945, when a citywide strike shut down all the New York City papers, Mayor Fiorello LaGuardia kept his constituents informed of the adventures of Dick Tracy and Little Orphan Annie by reading the funnies over the radio. Despite the competition of television and radio, the comics have continued to enjoy wide appeal, with their never-ending sagas of slapstick, family life, adventure, pathos, suspense, satire, and popular psychology and philosophy.

A Magazine for Every Taste
The Trend Is Toward Specialization

In a single month some 9,000 different magazines appear in the United States. Americans all across the country buy millions of copies of these periodicals, which treat every imaginable subject in the range of human thought and endeavor. There are publications for farmers, apartment dwellers, cooks, dieters, weight lifters, and antique collectors, among many others. Men and women of every age group, adolescents, and children can all find magazines specifically aimed at them. Sports of every variety and special interests in every conceivable field are covered. Although individual magazines come and go, the magazine business continues to be the most zestful, competitive, and imaginative of all publishing endeavors, and there are no signs that the public appetite for its products is about to diminish.

While Americans want *a generous sprinkling of hometown fare . their newspapers, with the result that the United States has no gener newspaper with a large national circulation, many magazines ha achieved national readership. In recent years, however, many long-esta lished magazines of general interest have disappeared. A notable excepti is* The Reader's Digest, *which continues to enjoy the world's larg circulation.* The Saturday Evening Post *and* Collier's *were fixtu in several generations of American homes, but loss of advertising reven forced them to suspend, although the* Post *was later revived, first as quarterly and then as a bimonthly. Humorous magazines, such as* Judg College Humor, *and the old* Life *before Henry R. Luce pictorializ it, have also dropped from sight. Sex-oriented publications, however, ha sprouted like weeds, as permissiveness has gained ground.* TV Guic *a lusty offspring of the television age, increased its circulation by 6 milli readers between 1968 and 1972. A select few magazines are read by high percentage of America's pace setters and image makers. Among the are* The New Yorker, *with its outstanding cartoons and sophistica fiction and reportage;* The Atlantic Monthly *and* Harper's Magazin *both popular for more than a century;* Commentary, *the journal of t American Jewish Committee;* Commonweal, *a sounding board j advanced Catholic opinion; and* Saturday Review, *with its long trac tion of literary criticism and pioneering in the world of ideas.*

For more than 50 years one of America's most popular magazines.

Norman Rockwell was a favorite *Post* illustrator.

John Held's flappers graced *Judge*'s covers for many years.

Ladies, homes, and families are featured in the *Journal.*

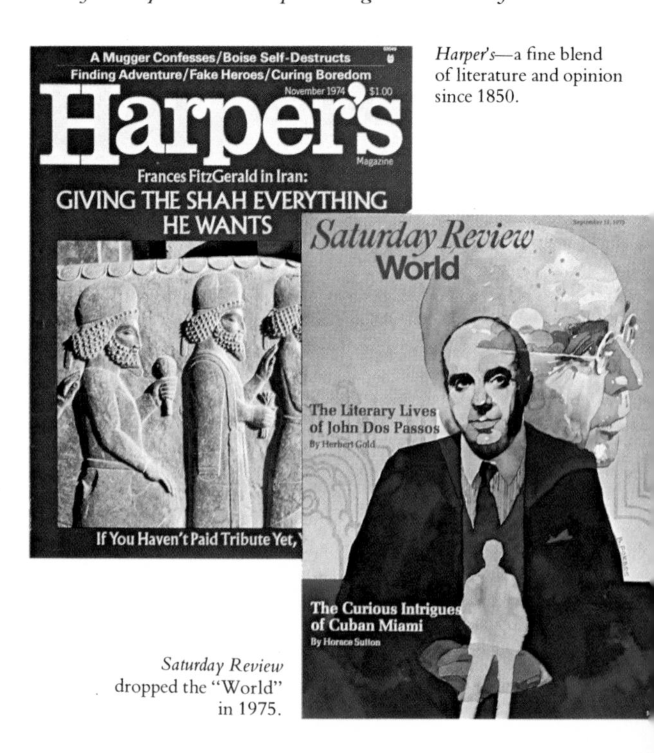

Harper's—a fine blend of literature and opinion since 1850.

Saturday Review dropped the "World" in 1975.

Hardest hit *by the competition of television were the picture magazines.* Life *and* Look *were both created in the 1930's to provide coverage of a kind that television would later overshadow and render obsolete. Loss of advertising revenue to TV combined with increasing postal rates proved fatal to the two magazines, even though they were still among the country's leaders in circulation when they folded—*Look *in 1971 and* Life *a year later.* Life, *created by* Time *publisher Henry Luce, provided America with an unequaled brand of photojournalism during its 36-year existence. Its photographers—Robert Capa, Margaret Bourke-White, Alfred Eisenstaedt, Carl Mydans, Gordon Parks, and David Douglas Duncan among others—covered the span of human experience so sensitively and excitingly for* Life's *readers that their pictures needed few words as accompaniment.*

The birth of *Life,* 1936.

An early *Look,* 1937.

There were a number *of news magazines and journals of opinion in America in the early 1920's—*Century, World's Work, Literary Digest, The Outlook, The Nation, *and* The New Republic *among them. Two brash young Yale graduates, Henry Luce and Briton Hadden, were convinced, however, that none had "adapted itself to the time which busy men are able to spend on simply keeping informed."* Time, *which they began in March 1923, set out to present the week's news concisely, interestingly, often wittily, and arranged in departments. The magazine never pretended to be objective or impartial in its reporting, but the editors hoped to achieve a degree of fairness in interpreting the facts.* Time's *success inspired a competitor.* Newsweek, *launched in 1933 with a similar format, differed in its intent to present the news free of editorial opinion. But* Time *retained the lead circulation. In the mid-1970's it had 4.3 million readers to* Newsweek's *2.7 million.*

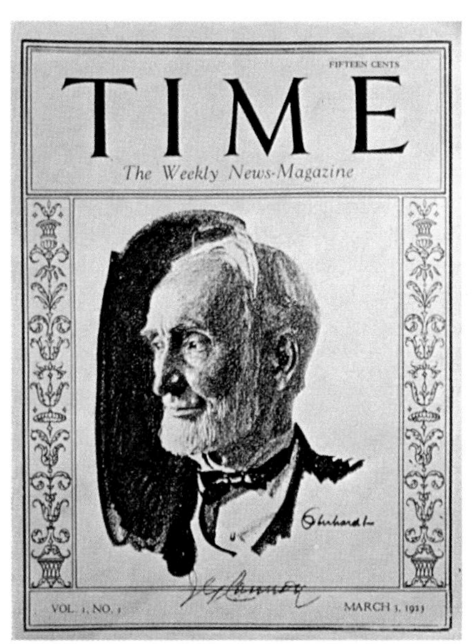

Time begins, 1923.

Newsweek first appears, 1933.

Journalism With a Conscience

The early 1900's in America saw gangsters controlling big-city politicians, monopolies destroying competitors and exploiting workers, groceries selling tainted food, and drugstores dispensing "medicines" that were mostly alcohol. These ills inspired some of the Nation's most exciting journalism in the popular magazines between 1903 and about 1912.

In a landmark issue in January 1903, *McClure's Magazine* published the third of 19 articles by Ida M. Tarbell on the Standard Oil Company, the first of a series by Lincoln Steffens on municipal corruption, and an article by Ray Stannard Baker on the plight of the workingman. *Arena, Everybody's, Collier's, The American Magazine, Cosmopolitan Magazine,* and other magazines joined the campaign to improve the quality of American life with hard-hitting articles by such writers as Samuel Hopkins Adams, Charles Edward Russell, David Graham Phillips, and Thomas W. Lawson. Novels and poetry by Upton Sinclair, Frank Norris, and Edwin Markham translated the ideals of reform into literature.

The writings turned out by the cream of this group were well researched, factual, and unbiased in approach. Unfortunately, sensationalism and abuse soon began to mar the landscape of crusade. President Theodore Roosevelt in a 1906 speech took disapproving notice. Taking his cue from a character in John Bunyan's *Pilgrim's Progress* who continually raked "the filth of the floor" rather than turn his eyes to the glories of heaven, T.R. used the term "muckrake" to lash out at the activities of the offenders. While the rebuke was justified in part, the first decade of the 20th century was an era that cried out for reform, and the best of the muckrakers helped America rediscover its conscience.

The Electronic Media

One day at the height of the Spanish-American War, in order to get the latest news to its readers and "scoop" the New York *World,* William Randolph Hearst's *Journal* printed 40 "extra" editions. For Hearst and his newspaper contemporaries, timeliness was next to godliness. Little did they know that soon the fastest press and the swiftest newsboy would be outmoded in the race for rapid communication. The last great series of newspaper "extras" were probably those concerning the kidnaping of Charles A. Lindbergh's baby in 1932. After that year most people listened to news flashes rather than read them.

The first commercial radio broadcast was made in 1920 when station KDKA, in Pittsburgh, Pennsylvania, broadcast the returns of the Presidential race between Warren G. Harding and James M. Cox. This new form of communication was at first welcomed by the press. The first regular daily programing also began in 1920, on a station sponsored by the Detroit *News.* By the end of 1922, 69 stations were owned by newspapers. Except for short news bulletins, which were intended to stimulate listeners to turn to their papers for more information, they usually featured recordings of musical favorites.

The first discontented rumbles from the press began in 1922, when the Associated Press warned its members against providing news for broadcasts. Opposition to the

The Early Days of Radio
Voices Known to All

David Sarnoff pioneered the promotion of the radio-telephone—at that time used only for communication between individuals—as a likely medium for broadcasting. Sarnoff first suggested in 1915 that his employer, the American Marconi Company, build "radio music boxes" to receive transmissions from central stations.

By the late 1920's Sarnoff's vision had materialized into the entertainment and information center of America's homes. Even during the Depression the radio industry prospered; some of its performers ranked in fame with movie stars.

Entertainment shows such as "Amos 'n' Andy" and Fred Allen's programs commanded massive audiences in the 1930's, but information programs—among them "The March of Time," which dramatized the week's news—gained wide favor, too. News commentators who attained tremendous influence included Graham MacNamee, Boake Carter, Gabriel Heatter, Lowell Thomas, Elmer Davis, and former Brooklyn *Eagle* editor H. V. Kaltenborn. In 1938 Prime Minister Neville Chamberlain of Britain went to Germany to discuss the fate of Czechoslovakia with Adolf Hitler and, after a series of meetings culminating at Munich, declared he had achieved "peace in our time." Kaltenborn was America's personal guide to the unfolding drama. Night and day, for 3 weeks, he remained in the Columbia Broadcasting System studios, bringing his vast audience a continuous flow of translations of Hitler's speeches, reports from other CBS correspondents in Europe, and his own analyses of the events.

World War II brought new radio correspondents prominence, among them Edward R. Murrow, William L. Shirer, Eric Sevareid, Bill Henry, and Arthur Mann. Commercial television broadcasts, suspended during the hostilities, were resumed in 1946. As receiving sets became more and more available, TV audiences soon dwarfed those of radio, but Murrow, Sevareid, and other personalities readily adjusted and built even bigger reputations now that they could be seen as well as heard.

Walter Winchell *(above) moved his newspaper gossip column onto the airwaves in 1932, electrifying audiences with his staccato greeting: "Good evening, Mr. and Mrs. America, and all the ships at sea!" H. V. Kaltenborn (right), the dean of radio newscasting, is shown in 1938 during a remarkable series on the Munich crisis, when he made 102 broadcasts in 21 days.*

competitor began to grow along with radio's fantastic development. By 1923, when the cost of a radio set was about one-fifth that of an automobile, there were 556 radio stations. (Fifty years later there were 7,331 AM and FM stations—more than 4 times the number of daily newspapers in the country.)

Between 1929 and 1933 radio advertising revenue doubled; that of newspapers fell by almost half. (Forty years later newspapers and magazines carried a little more than 37 percent of national advertising, television about 17 percent, and radio less than 7 percent.) Although papers had formerly featured listings of radio programs and extensive coverage of the new medium, they now refused to carry even the listings, and in 1933 the three major press services refused to sell their news to the stations. The Columbia Broadcasting System was the first network to retaliate by forming its own full-time news staff that same year.

In the 1930's radio began to realize its journalistic possibilities. Millions listened eagerly to King Edward VIII renouncing the British throne. Franklin D. Roosevelt spoke directly and effectively to the Nation in his "fireside chats," thereby offsetting much of the criticism he was receiving in the newspapers. The voices of radio commentators became familiar in millions of households across the country. Later, radio correspondents brought news of World War II to countless listeners. One of the most famous of this group of radio reporters was Edward R. Murrow. Murrow became famous for his compelling "This Is London" broadcasts from England during the war and for a later radio show, "Hear It Now" (in 1951, after television had found a niche in most homes, the show became "See It Now").

It was only after the war that television truly developed. Commercial operation was approved by the FCC in 1941, but production ceased entirely during the war, not to resume until 1946. In that year there were 6 television stations in the United States; in 1973 there were 927, and a TV set in almost every home.

Although both radio and television are geared more to entertaining than to informing, they have become increasingly concerned with the news. Certain radio stations are devoted entirely to news and opinion, with spot announcements, editorials, and in-depth reports. Howard K. Smith, Charles Collingwood, the late Chet Huntley, David Brinkley, Harry Reasoner, and Walter Cronkite were among the television news commentators whose names became household words during the 1950's and tumultuous 1960's. The Presidential press conference, a device introduced by Abraham Lincoln, who hoped to stop the disastrous criticism he was receiving from the press, was brought to its televised height a hundred years later by John F. Kennedy. One of our most media-conscious politicians, Kennedy probably owed his elec-

The Unforgettable Edward R. Murrow

In referring to television, E. B. White wrote: "It should be our Lyceum, our Chautauqua, our Minsky's and our Camelot. It should restate and clarify the social dilemma and the political pickle. Once in a while it does, and you get a quick glimpse of its potential." Edward R. Murrow did all he could to make television live up to the goals set forth by *The New Yorker's* distinguished essayist.

Once a week from 1951 to 1958 Murrow and his off-screen collaborator, Fred W. Friendly, put together a news documentary for CBS. Unlike other television news programs, "See It Now" made news by searching out stories that newspapers and magazines had not yet got around to or had not covered in depth. With his strong background of radio experience, Murrow emphasized the audio aspects of his reports. He placed stress on the facts, relationships, ideas, and implications behind a TV picture, and listeners always got his vivid, personal analysis of events.

"See It Now" reached its peak midway in its 7 years on the air with an exposé of Senator Joseph R. McCarthy. Video tape and film showed the Senator on the attack; live narration by Murrow refuted his unsubstantiated charges.

Murrow stayed at CBS until 1961. His 10 years as a television commentator were a bright period of effective informational programing. A dedication to speaking the truth—the traditional role of the conscientious journalist—was Murrow's most cherished wish for television, although he never overlooked the entertainment value of the medium. His program "Person to Person," on which he weekly interviewed celebrities in their homes, was a widespread favorite. Murrow objected to awards for news programing, asserting that "the only real award is public confidence." That much he certainly enjoyed, even from those who sometimes disagreed with his views.

Americans, stunned *by the assassination of President John F. Kennedy on November 22, 1963, were further shocked as television made them bystanders when nightclub owner Jack Ruby shot Kennedy's accused killer, Lee Harvey Oswald, 2 days later. Ruby was convicted of the crime, but died in 1967 while awaiting retrial.*

tion to his appearances on television. His famous debates with the then Vice President, Richard Nixon, helped to swing a small plurality to the Democrats.

No amount of print coverage can match the immediacy and thrill of certain television reporting. After President Kennedy's assassination in November 1963, the networks canceled their regular programing for 3 days to cover the aftermaths of the tragedy for horrified Americans. Television coverage of the Vietnam War brought the conflict home to the United States. Via satellite, television can bring the world live coverage of the Olympics from Japan, a Presidential visit to China, and unforgettably, the United States' historic men on the Moon.

Television's publicity value has become enormous. Street gangs hold press conferences for the television cameras. Televised congressional hearings have made national heroes of previously obscure Representatives and Senators. Politicians begin and dutifully end press conferences to fill allotted time slots in network programing. In order to eliminate the circus atmosphere that has prevailed at many trials, judges bar photographers and TV cameramen from their courtrooms. Television and newspapers have been forced to return to the practice of the 19th-century illustrated periodicals and to employ artists to depict the personalities in court trials.

Like print journalism, broadcast journalism has generated its share of controversy. Television stations have come under attack from local minority groups for ignoring their interests; congressional committees have investigated television programing such as CBS's documentary "The Selling of the Pentagon." Unlike newspapers and magazines, however, radio and television stations act under the implied restrictions of a Government license, granted by the Federal Communications Commission. The FCC, while it cannot censor program content, has the power to review a station's operations to determine if it is acting in the public interest and can suspend the license if it decides the station is not. There is always the possibility that threats of suspension may be used in attempts to intimidate stations. Fortunately the electronic media have in general followed in the tradition of public responsibility set by newspapers and magazines.

NASA's Apollo *program, completed in 1972 after 3½ years, provided some of television's most exciting coverage. Worldwide audiences watched as American astronauts became the first men to land on the Moon and as they went about the lunar surface exploring, gathering rocks and soil, taking photographs, and placing instruments that would transmit data back to Earth. Walter Cronkite of CBS provided some of the most compelling TV commentary. The first landing occurred on July 20, 1969, when Neil A. Armstrong and Edwin E. Aldrin, Jr., of* Apollo 11 *made the breathtaking ". . . giant leap for mankind." This view was taken during the landing of* Apollo 15. *Alfred M. Worden salutes the flag (of stiffened plastic, to keep it outstretched in the weightless environment). To his left is the lunar module* Falcon *and the dune buggy on which he and David R. Scott toured a small part of the Sea of Rains.*

The Business of Making Books

Constant Growth, From Hand-cut Type to Computers

A handprinted book published in Benjamin Franklin's Philadelphia shop usually ran to some 100 copies per volume. Today a hard-cover book may have a first print run of from 20,000 to 50,000 copies. The annual book output in America has become all but overwhelming, thanks to an insatiable public appetite, plus such mass production methods as stereotyping, high-speed presses, mechanical typesetting and typecasting, and new ways of reproducing illustrations. In 1973 alone there were some 20,000 titles with a total sale of more than 1.5 billion copies.

The books of Franklin's time were mostly on religious and legal subjects. Nowadays the spectrum is as broad as all human experience: encyclopedias, dictionaries, atlases, reference books of every imaginable description, along with what are called trade books—novels; travel books; treatments of religion, law, and history; biographies; elaborately illustrated art books; cookbooks representing every conceivable cuisine; and how-to-do-it books on everything from sex to Sanskrit. Trade books are sold in bookstores, department stores, and other establishments, as well as by book clubs, whose members purchase about 75 million volumes a year at prices substantially below retail. Despite technological advances, everything related to publishing has risen steeply in cost, especially paper—up from 7 percent of a book's cost in 1910 to as much as 40 percent in 1974. At the same time, in spite of competition from radio and television, Americans are more avid readers than ever before.

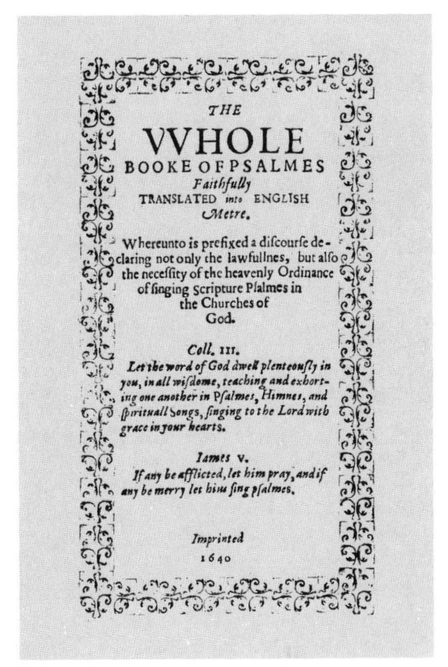

THE

VVHOLE

BOOKE OF PSALMES

Faithfully

TRANSLATED into ENGLISH

Metre.

Whereunto is prefixed a diſcourſe declaring not only the lawfullnes, but alſo the neceſſity of the heavenly Ordinance of ſinging Scripture Pſalmes in the Churches of God.

Coll. III.

Let the word of God dwell plenteouſly in you, in all wiſdome, teaching and exhorting one another in Pſalmes, Himnes, and ſpirituall Songs, ſinging to the Lord with grace in your hearts.

James V.

If any be afflicted, let him pray, and if any be merry let him ſing pſalmes.

Imprinted

1640

"The Whole Booke of Psalmes," *a hymnal known as the* Bay Psalm Book, *was the first book printed in the Colonies (1640).*

The Popularity of Paperbacks

A revolution in the book trade occurred in the late 1930's when, following an old European tradition and the example set by Britain's Penguin Books, American firms began publishing inexpensive, paperbound reprints of popular works. The first of these were issued by Pocket Books. They cost 25 cents and were such an immediate success that thousands were bought on their first day of sale.

Since then the paperback market has expanded enormously. The classics, modern novels, and nonfiction books on almost every subject imaginable are available in paperback. In the schools, textbooks with colorful paper covers have replaced their dull-looking predecessors. Paperbacks sell almost as readily as magazines; people can afford to buy them on impulse—at newsstands on the street, in railroad stations, and in airports; in drugstores; in variety stores; and in huge bookstores that specialize in them—and then discard them after they have been read. However, many of today's paperbacks are too large and too thick to be called pocketsize, and prices go as high as $7.50 or $10.00.

Writers often receive huge sums for paperback rights. In 1972, for example, a soft-cover edition of *The Joy of Cooking* brought its authors a record $1.5 million. Some publishers put out simultaneously soft- and hard-cover editions of a book for which they have high expectations. Surprisingly, in view of the current high cost of books, the hard-cover form of such a book often sells as well as the paperback.

CHAPTER TWENTY-ONE

Vigor in the Visual Arts

The year 1738 was an auspicious one for American art: it saw the births of Benjamin West near Springfield, Pennsylvania, and John Singleton Copley in Boston, Massachusetts. When he was 21, Benjamin West spent nearly a year studying art in New York City and then headed for Europe. There he enjoyed a meteoric rise to fame, became court painter to King George III, and inspired a long succession of American painters who came to his studio. Back at home, John Singleton Copley was painting dozens of superb portraits of his peers, an astonishing accomplishment for a virtually self-taught artist. But in 1774 he too left for Europe, never again to return to his native land.

The Creative Urge

America's artistic heritage has been greatly enriched by the works of men and women who painted not for profit but for pleasure. Usually self-taught, these folk artists, or Primitive painters, knew little of the intricacies of composition, perspective, and the other technical details that occupy professional artists. They simply painted what they saw in flat decorative patterns. But despite the naïveté of their visions, the best of the Primitives managed to capture the essence of people and of places with an innocence and a candor that continue to captivate the modern viewer.

The greatest output of Primitive painting came in the period between the Revolution and the Civil War, but Primitive painters have continued to express themselves to the present day. They have painted landscapes, portraits, still lifes, historical themes, and memorial pictures with equal directness and charm.

Having no artistic pretensions, many left their works unsigned. But others are known to us: Paul Seifert, who painted lively farm scenes; Joseph Pickett, who recorded views around New Hope, Pennsylvania; and Erastus S. Field, who is best known for his huge and fanciful "Historical Monument of the American Republic," which he painted for the Nation's first centennial.

Some received recognition late in life. At the age of 67, John Kane had a picture exhibited at Carnegie Institute's Pittsburgh International Exhibition of Contemporary Painting and Sculpture. His powerful self-portrait now hangs in the Museum of Modern Art in New York. Another who enjoyed a late success was Anna Mary Robertson Moses, better known as Grandma Moses. Her nostalgic views of New England farm life are among the most beloved paintings by any American artist.

On a pine panel *an unknown colonial artist created this captivating portrait (c. 1740) of a "Young Woman With a Bowl of Cherries." (Oil on wood.)*

Horace Pippin *(1888–1946), in "John Brown Going to His Hanging" (undated), showed his strong emotional reaction to the historic moment when the militant abolitionist was taken to the gallows. Pippin's ability to create rich surface patterns is in vivid evidence here. (Oil on canvas.)*

In these men colonial America produced its two great ative masters, and many others were to follow. In the vo centuries since the Revolution, painting and sculpture ave flourished in a fertile artistic climate that has nour-hed a remarkable variety of art. Portraits, landscapes, and ill lifes; realistic, romantic, and abstract art; murals, ionumental sculpture, and airy mobiles—all have been roduced by talented hands and inspired minds.

On the pages that follow is a survey of major trends that volved as our painting and sculptural heritage grew and atured. Not every American artist is mentioned, nor are orks by each and every one illustrated. The objective is to provide an overview of general developments and relate them to changes occurring in other areas of American life. Important works by many American artists can also be seen in other chapters in this book.

As the 20th-century painter Edward Hopper once remarked, "A nation's art is greatest when it most reflects the character of its own people." And American art has certainly reflected the character of the American people and their way of life. From the beginning America's painters and sculptors were preoccupied with the realities of the world around them. They created a superlative record of the changes taking place as the United States has matured.

Itinerant Quaker preacher *Edward Hicks (1780–1849) painted scores of versions of "The Peaceable Kingdom" (this one c. 1835). Illustrating the prophecy of Isaiah that the time would come when the lamb and the lion would lie down together, Hicks reinforced his message of brotherly love by including in the background William Penn signing a treaty with the Indians. (Oil on canvas.)*

Headhunters and Rebels

From earliest colonial times until the late 1700's portraits were virtually the only works of art produced in America. Colonists, in their struggles to tame the wilderness, had little time for such niceties as the fine arts; yet even they could not resist the urge to preserve their images for posterity. In early colonial times anonymous craftsmen traveled from town to town and painted likenesses for a fee. A tradition gradually matured and produced many capable artists who came to realize that portraits were what the public wanted. John Neagle, Samuel Lovett Waldo, Chester Harding, George Healy, and others willingly obliged and prospered accordingly. Painting portraits, in fact, remained many an artist's bread and butter until late in the 19th century, when the job was largely taken over by the camera.

But even in the early days of the new republic a few artists rebelled against portraiture, disdaining it as an inferior branch of art. Men like John Trumbull, who fancied himself *the* painter of the Revolution, and John Vanderlyn, an ardent disciple of the French Neoclassic movement, yearned to educate their contemporaries to the glories of noble themes from history, religion, and allegory. Unfortunately, the public was not interested in their efforts. Though their talents are appreciated today, these early rebels were sadly out of step with their times. It was their fate to have been born too soon.

In miniature *on pieces of ivory, Edward Greene Malbone (1777–1807) created scores of locket-size likenesses that became family heirlooms. This sensitive portrait (c. 1800) is of the artist Washington Allston, who is honored now as America's first romantic painter. (Watercolor on ivory.)*

His belief *that "no fault will be found with the artist—at least by the sitter—if he improve the appearance," helped make Thomas Sully (1783–1872) popular and prosperous. His romantic style was best suited to female subjects. Among his 2,000 portraits is a painting of Queen Victoria, done in 1838 while he was in England. His "Lady With a Harp: Eliza Ridgely" (1818) is shown here. (Oil on canvas.)*

Samuel F. B. Morse *(1791–1872) painted many portraits but longed for more inspiring subjects. His mission, he said, was to "revive the splendor of the 15th century"—and his treatment of the dramatic moment when the giant chandelier was being lighted during a night session in "The Old House of Representatives" (1822) carries out his purpose. He was well established as a painter in his time, but it was his development of the telegraph that eventually brought him fame and fortune. (Oil on canvas.)*

With dazzling brush strokes *Gilbert Stuart (1755–828) captured the delicate beauty of Mrs. Perez Morton (c. 802). The most sought-after portraitist of his day, Stuart was o intent on capturing his sitter's personality that once he inished the face he had only a perfunctory interest in the rest f the painting. (Oil on canvas.)*

This life-size *"Staircase Group" (c. 1795) by Charles Willson Peale (1741–1827) depicts his sons Raphaelle and Titian. Mounted in a door frame with a real step projecting at the bottom, the painting is so realistic that George Washington is said to have nodded to the boys as he passed by. A scientist and inventor as well as an artist, Peale opened America's first natural history museum in Philadelphia. There he exhibited—along with stuffed animals, fossils, and Indian relics—many portraits he and his sons had painted. (Oil on canvas.)*

Painters of a Virgin Land

The 19th century was the golden age of landscape painting in America. Inspired by the nature writings of Ralph Waldo Emerson and William Cullen Bryant, Americans began to look at their native scenery with a new sense of pride. In the mid-1800's a whole new generation of artists emerged and captured the public's imagination with reverent portrayals of the American landscape. The group came to be known as the Hudson River school, although its members ranged far beyond New York State's Hudson Valley in their search for subject matter. Their romantic renderings of the American scene are honored now as the first wholly indigenous movement in the history of American art.

The landscape tradition continued to the end of the century. Many artists—among whom were John W. Casilear, Jaspar F. Cropsey, and Worthington Whittredge—furthered the development of the Hudson River school. But others evolved quite different styles. At one extreme were Frederick Edwin Church and Albert Bierstadt, who painted huge theatrical canvases of awesome mountains and wilderness. George Inness, on the other hand, transmuted the Hudson River tradition into a highly individual style, imbuing intimate pastoral scenes with the lyrical beauty of his personal response. The results of his sensitive work include some of the finest landscapes ever painted by an American.

The versatile *Martin Johnson Heade (1819–1904) painted not only seascapes and landscapes, such as "Approaching Storm—Beach Near Newport" (c. 1860), but also sensuous still lifes of flowers and glowing, gemlike, natural compositions of hummingbirds and orchids. (Oil on canvas.)*

George Inness *(1825–94), a poetic interpreter of nature's changing moods, found his inspiration in the fields and meadows near his homes in New Jersey and Massachusetts. "June" (1882), shown here—and other paintings with such titles as "The Afterglow," "The Coming Storm," "The Sun Shower," and "Autumn Landscape, October"—reveal his preoccupation with atmospheric effects. In all these works he sought to achieve the objective of arousing in the viewer emotions similar to those he himself felt while contemplating the scene. (Oil on canvas.)*

At his best *with water scenes such as "Lake George" (1869), John Frederick Kensett (1816–72) also painted many serenely poetic landscapes aglow with luminous effects, mostly along the coast near Newport, Rhode Island. (Oil on canvas.)*

As a memorial *to his close friend and fellow painter Thomas Cole, Asher Brown Durand (1796–1886) in "Kindred Spirits" (1849) depicted Cole and the poet William Cullen Bryant admiring the beauty of a craggy Catskill mountain gorge. (Oil on canvas.)*

Thomas Cole *(1801–48) in "The Oxbow" (1836), a panorama encompassing miles of misty space, captured the idyllic beauty of the Connecticut River Valley. Cole, our first major landscape painter, was prominent in the Hudson River school of artists. The popularity of their paintings stemmed in part from the public's growing nostalgia for a wilderness that even then was beginning to disappear. (Oil on canvas.)*

Painters of the Common Man

With the rise of Jacksonian democracy in the 1830's, a new spirit surged through all areas of American life. Nationalism inspired the painters of the American landscape; democracy inspired the painters of the American people. Recognizing the common man as a suitable subject, more and more artists chose to portray ordinary people going about everyday activities in the storytelling pictures known as Genre art. The public responded enthusiastically to their straightforward uncondescending observations of human nature. People enjoyed pictures of men and women like themselves in familiar situations. Once the development of color lithography made inexpensive reproductions possible, prints of Genre paintings were favored for display in middle-class parlors throughout the country.

The Genre artists' subjects were as varied as the painters themselves. While William Sidney Mount portrayed Eastern farmers at work and play, George Caleb Bingham painted the fur trappers, riverboatmen, and electioneering politicians of the Missouri area. Richard Caton Woodville poked gentle fun at middle-class city folk, but David Gilmour Blythe, viewing society with a more jaundiced eye, chose pungent satire to mock the foibles of his fellowman. And John Quidor found the inspiration for his robust canvases in the tales of Washington Irving. While some of these works go beyond the usual definition of Genre painting, which does not allow for sentimental, romantic, religious, or historic content, they all reveal the artists' sensitivity to the intimate details of life in America. The paintings stand or fall on their qualities of design and color—and the familiarity of the scene. It is essentially a democratic art; its appreciation requires no special background or training.

Still lifes—in a sense, Genre paintings that told a story of things rather than of people—also found a ready market. From the lush tabletop arrangements of fruit and other decorative objects produced by Charles Willson Peale's remarkable family to the eye-fooling trickery of William M. Harnett and John F. Peto, still lifes remained very much in vogue throughout the 19th century.

William Sidney Mount *(1807–68), America's first full-time Genre artist, roamed rural Long Island, New York, in a trailerlike, horse-drawn studio, seeking subjects for his brush. He found many charming rustic scenes, such as the one shown in "Bargaining for a Horse" (1835). Like the works of other Genre artists, his paintings are timeless in appeal, not only for the stories they tell but also for their power to evoke a bygone era. (Oil on canvas.)*

With magical realism *and masterful design, William M. Harnett (1848–92) turned out many such narrative still lifes as "Old Models" (1892). Enchanted with textures, he re-created mellow wood, tattered book bindings, and timeworn brass so faithfully that the viewer is tempted to run a finger across the canvas. His wizardry appealed to the public, but some critics wrote it off as "mere imitation." Not until the mid-20th century did he receive wide expert acclaim. (Oil on canvas.)*

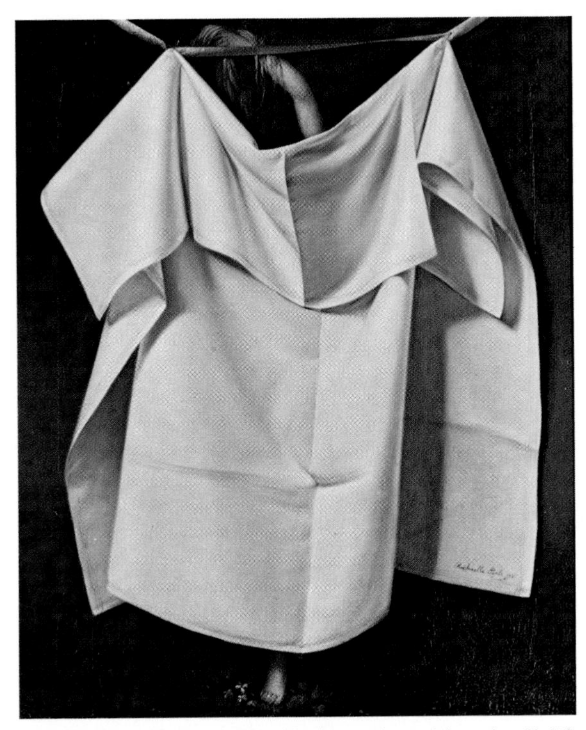

Raphaelle Peale *(1774–1825), in his celebrated still life "After the Bath" (1823), succeeded in his aim of deceiving the eye. When his wife saw the painting, she is said to have stalked out of the room in a rage, thinking he had draped a large white napkin across the canvas to hide the then-taboo subject of a female nude. (Oil on canvas.)*

John Quidor *(1801–81), a master of literary Genre, displayed ironic good humor in his earthy interpretations of such scenes as "The Return of Rip Van Winkle" (1829), based on the writings of Washington Irving. His exaggerated, almost grotesque figures, relaxed technique, and dramatic use of light and shadow all contribute to the emotional intensity of this vignette of the homecoming of the old man of the mountains. (Oil on canvas.)*

Sometimes sweetly sentimental, *sometimes coolly objective, Eastman Johnson (1824–1906) painted childhood memories, city life, and bucolic scenes of Maine with equal skill and enthusiasm. "The Old Stage Coach" (1871) is one of this popular artist's best known works. A versatile craftsman, Johnson painted portraits and landscapes as well as Genre subjects. (Oil on canvas.)*

New Frontiers

The lure of lands beyond the frontier was irresistible to many an artist, just as it was to generations of pioneers seeking new starts in new settings. One of the first artists to respond to the call of the wild was John James Audubon. He spent years in forests and swamplands stalking the birds of America, which he painted with an exuberance and beauty such as the world had never seen before. George Catlin, Seth Eastman, and Alfred Jacob Miller crossed the plains in search of a different but equally colorful kind of life—the Indians of the West. Their portraits and candid scenes of Indian activities have endured as invaluable records of a way of life that was already vanishing.

Albert Bierstadt and Thomas Moran, in contrast, found fame and fortune by painting the scenic wonders of a majestic new landscape that most easterners could only read about. And when the frontier disappeared once and for all, Frederic Remington, Charles Marion Russell, and a number of other artists mined the growing vein of interest in America's new heroes—the legendary cowboys of the Wild West. Strangest of the artists who drew their inspiration from the American frontier was Ralph Blakelock who, haunted by memories of a trip he had taken through the Far West, painted eerily romantic moonlit landscapes, mystifying to his contemporaries but appreciated by many today.

Although their subjects were as varied as their styles of painting, all the artists who followed the frontier as it stretched relentlessly across the continent filled a crucial need of their time and ours. They pictured the strange, the wonderful, and the unknown, and made them accessible to a curious public.

Thanks to the *realistic paintings of George Catlin (1796–1872), we have an unparalleled record of the customs of many Indian tribes, which are no longer practiced. Here, a bear claw necklace and other jewelry bedeck "The White Cloud, Head Chief of the Iowas" (undated). (Oil on canvas.)*

John James Audubon *(1785–1851) found immortality in his resolve to paint all the birds of wild America. With scientific objectivity combined with an artist's eye, he created bold designs, as in this undated painting of the bald eagle. (Watercolor on paper.)*

Albert Bierstadt *(1830–1902), a lover of nature on a grand scale, dazzled Eastern connoisseurs with gigantic wall-size canvases portraying the wonders of the West. Roaming through the awesome scenery of the Rocky Mountains and the High Sierra, he captured their overwhelming beauty for all time in vast, luminous panoramas such as "Yosemite Valley" (1868). Although in his heyday Bierstadt was among the country's best paid artists—with some of his paintings bringing fees as high as $35,000—he fell from critical favor late in life and his fortune gradually melted. Despite their romantic theatricality, the best of his works still have the power to stir the emotions of viewers today. (Oil on canvas.)*

Independent Visions

Every generation of artists produces a few mavericks, painters who belong to no school, reject all established traditions, and follow instead their own ideas of what art is all about. Oftener than not their ambitions outstrip their talents, and the rebels are doomed to obscurity. In the closing decades of the 19th century, however, America produced not one but three renegades who tossed the rule books aside and snared the greatest prize of all—immortality.

The first of them, Winslow Homer, is impossible to pigeonhole. He painted Genre scenes of rural and resort life. He portrayed hunters and fishermen in the Adirondack Mountains of New York. He dashed off sparkling watercolors in the Bahamas. In his later years he turned to the Maine coast, creating potent images of the sea. But whatever his subject, he executed his powerful compositions with absolute fidelity to the facts.

Thomas Eakins chose to paint everyday city life in Philadelphia—oarsmen sculling, boxers fighting, chess players pondering the next move—and portraits of his family and friends. Whereas Homer looked at his subjects with a cool, objective eye, Eakins peered into their very souls. Probing beneath surface appearances to explore the inner lives of his subjects, he produced profound psychological portraits with such uncompromising realism that his sitters sometimes refused to accept the paintings they had commissioned.

Unlike Eakins, Albert Pinkham Ryder plumbed his own soul for inspiration. His was a richly romantic imaginary world where lonely boats plied moonlit seas beneath dark clouds, and Biblical and literary themes sprang to life in ecstatic swirls of gemlike color.

Thomas Eakins *(1844–1916), a devotee of outdoor life, often found inspiration in sporting scenes such as "Max Schmitt in a Single Scull" (1871). With its meticulous attention to detail, the painting captures a specific moment with almost photographic candor. (Oil on canvas.)*

When he was *not painting mystical seascapes, Albert Pinkham Ryder (1847–1917) often found inspiration in the operas of Richard Wagner. This arresting vision of "The Flying Dutchman" (painted before 1890) combines these two themes. (Oil on canvas.)*

Winslow Homer *(1836–1910) in his later years concentrated on capturing the changing moods and relentless power of the sea. Although people appeared in most of his earlier paintings, such as "Breezing Up" (1876), human figures were rare in his late seascapes. (Oil on canvas.)*

The foremost *figurehead carver of his time, William Rush (1756–1833) is also considered America's first sculptor. This reclining, life-size "Charity" (c. 1811) is one of many vigorous naturalistic figures created by the talented Philadelphian. As in all his works, one senses the presence of a full, three-dimensional body beneath the intricately swirling robes. (Painted wood.)*

A Sequence of Sculptors

Sculpture was the orphan of the arts in early America. Except for ship figureheads and other folk art, there was little demand for it. A professional tradition developed in the early 1800's, when William Rush started carving portraits and allegorical figures in wood. With the 1820's came a great upsurge in sculpture. Important new public buildings demanded imposing monuments, and the owners of classic revival houses liked to embellish the decor with statues of marble goddesses and the like. The first commissions went to Italians, for no native sons had the necessary skills. But a few shrewd Americans soon endeavored to acquire them. Horatio Greenough, Thomas Crawford, and Hiram Powers traveled to Italy, learned their craft, and became rich and famous by catering to the public's taste.

The mania for idealized classical figures waned after the Civil War and more varied works appeared. John Quincy Adams Ward produced both Genre groups and fine highly realistic bronze portraits of Indians and public figures. William Rimmer, a devoted student of anatomy, combined absolute realism and intense emotion in his masterful interpretations of the human figure. Frederic Remington created energetic studies in bronze of cowboys and horses. At the turn of the century the two leading figures were Augustus Saint-Gaudens and Daniel Chester French, who treated traditional styles with a new sensitivity and skill.

To this day realism continues to be a major theme in American sculpture. But Malvina Hoffman, William Zorach, and the other realists broke completely with the conventions of the past. Working with new freedom and individuality, they interpreted their subjects in uniquely personal styles.

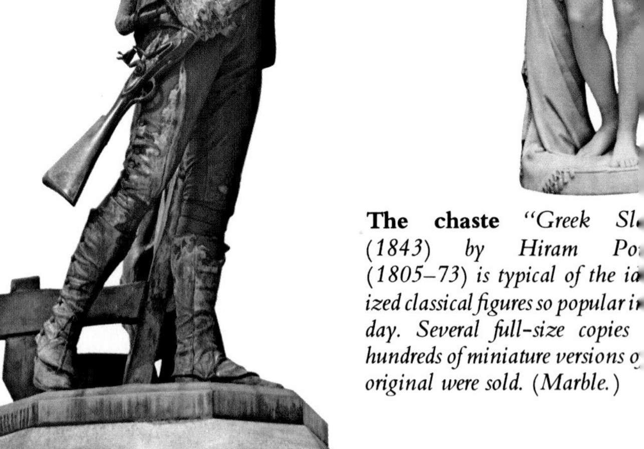

"The Minute Man *of Concord" (1874–75), by Daniel Chester French (1850–1931), has inspired generations of New England visitors. An instant success, this early work was the prelude to French's long career. (Bronze.)*

The chaste *"Greek Sl (1843) by Hiram Po (1805–73) is typical of the id ized classical figures so popular i day. Several full-size copies hundreds of miniature versions o original were sold. (Marble.)*

"Checkers up at the Farm" *(1877) by John Rogers (1829–1904) and similar Genre pieces found their way into thousands of Victorian parlors. Rogers mass-produced plaster copies from a bronze cast and sold them by mail order. (Plaster.)*

Horatio Greenough (1805–52)
"George Washington" (1833–41)
Marble

Thomas Crawford (c. 1813
"Seated Indian Chief" (185
Marble

Entranced *by the sensuous beauty of the female body, Gaston Lachaise (1882–1935) created this elegant, seemingly weightless "Floating Figure" (1927, cast 1935), one of a series of huge yet graceful images. (Bronze.)*

he most influential *sculptor at the close of the 19th ıtury was Augustus Saint-Gaudens (1848–1907). This Aemorial to Deacon Samuel Chapin" (1887) is one of : many public monuments. (Bronze.)*

The best known *works by Gutzon Borglum (1871–1941) are the carvings on South Dakota's Mount Rushmore. In this "Head of Abraham Lincoln" (1908) his sensitive realism can be more readily appreciated. (Marble.)*

Elie Nadelman *(1882–1946), reacting against the academic sculptors' attention to detail, stripped subjects of nonessentials to reveal basic structure. Above is "Man in the Open Air" (c. 1915). (Bronze.)*

olph Rogers (1825–
2) "Nydia" (1859)
Marble

Frederic Remington (1861–1909)
"The Bronco Buster" (1895)
Bronze

Jo Davidson (1883–1952)
"Gertrude Stein" (1920)
Bronze

Paul Manship (1885–1966)
"Prometheus," fountain figure (1933)
Bronze, gold leaf

The Expatriates

Even before the Revolution, aspiring American artists began trekking to Europe for training and inspiration and brought home word of new developments in art. In the late 19th century, however, three native masters chose to remain in Europe and there earned lasting fame.

John Singer Sargent, rightfully renowned for his dazzling brushwork, became the toast of two continents as the rich and fashionable flocked to his London studio to have their portraits painted.

James Abbott McNeill Whistler also worked in London, but the world did not exactly beat a path to his door. Though his talent was formidable, his abrasive wit alienated many potential patrons.

Meanwhile in Paris a Philadelphia socialite was making a mark of her own. In an age when women were supposed to raise children and do nothing more, Mary Cassatt decided to become an artist—and proved herself a very good one indeed. Befriended by Degas, she became a member of the French Impressionist group and helped introduce its work to wealthy Americans.

In "Symphony *in White N 1: The White Girl" (1862), in all his paintings, James M Neill Whistler (1834–1903) u mainly interested in arranging elements of the composition into artistically pleasing design. Beca of his meticulous attention to eve detail and his insistence that t artist must strive to create harmon ous arrangements of pattern a color, Whistler helped to bridge t gap between the literalism of t 19th century and 20th-centu abstraction. (Oil on canvas.)*

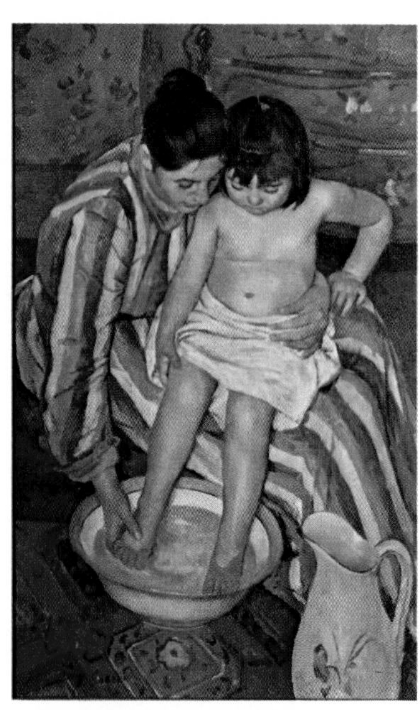

America's first *major woman artist, Mary Cassatt (1845–1926), returned time and again to the theme of motherhood, creating dozens of Impressionistic canvases. "The Bath" (c. 1891–92) is one of her best. (Oil on canvas.)*

John Singer Sargent *(1856–1925), who was to become famous for his polished portraits, first won esteem with "Daughters of Edward Boit" (1882), an inventively composed, mysteriously illuminated work. (Oil on canvas.)*

Down With the Academy

At the turn of the century art was stagnating in America. The National Academy of Design and other official tastemakers were rigidly conservative, giving uncritical approval to innocuous landscapes and other genteel subjects. One dynamic teacher, Robert Henri, however, was preaching a new credo. Paint reality, he demanded, no matter how seamy it might be. Four of his students took the message to heart and began painting city life with uncompromising realism. Because of their preoccupation with the mundane, they soon were dubbed the "Ashcan school." When the National Academy of Design rejected a number of their works as vulgar, the five joined forces with three other artists and opened an exhibit of their own in 1908. The critics were outraged, denouncing Henri and his disciples as "apostles of ugliness." But the public flocked to the show, and in time the group, who became known as The Eight, won acceptance. By rebelling against traditions that dictated "suitable" subject matter, the Ashcan painters struck an enduring blow for artistic freedom of expression.

John Sloan *(1871–1951), with obvious gusto, painted the life of the city—slums, tenements, and all—in strong compositions such as "Backyards, Greenwich Village" (1914). Like his colleagues in the Ashcan school—Robert Henri, George Luks, Everett Shinn, and William Glackens—he helped overcome academic strictures. (Oil on canvas.)*

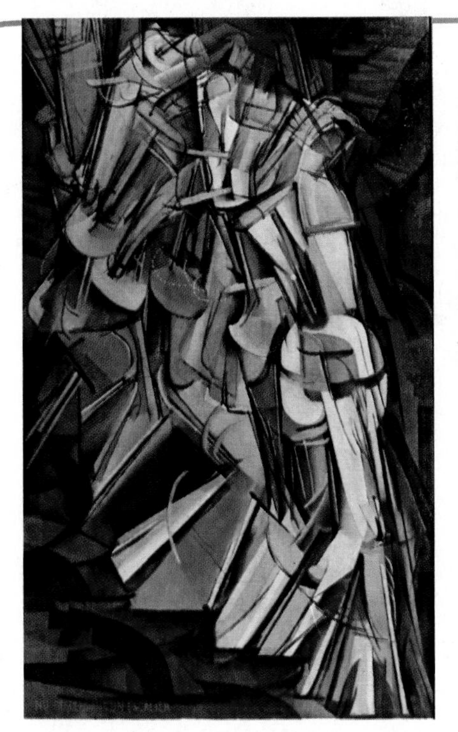

The gallery of foreign art *(above) at the Armory Show of 1913 held a wide range of styles, from the head of "Mlle. Pogany" (1913) by Constantin Brancuşi (1876–1957) and the "Kneeling Woman" (1911) and "Standing Woman" (1910) of Wilhelm Lehmbruck (1881–1919) to the classical "Girl With Pitcher" (1912) by Joseph Bernard (1866–1931). The oil-on-canvas painting (left), "Nude Descending a Staircase No. 2" (1912), by Marcel Duchamp (1887–1968) caused a furor; one critic called it "an explosion in a shingle factory."*

The Armory Show *America's Most Influential Exhibition*

In the first decades of the 20th century a full-scale artistic revolution was underway in Europe. Pablo Picasso, Georges Braque, and many others were rejecting the old forms and creating a new artistic language. Most Americans were not yet aware of the changing approaches to art. To introduce the new as well as more traditional contemporary works to the public, a group of American artists banded together and collected more than 1,300 paintings and sculptures in Europe and the United States. When their Exhibition of Modern Art opened in 1913 in New York's 69th Regiment Armory, it created unprecedented excitement and comment. The press poked fun at the Armory Show, as it became known, and some critics attacked the new art, but public interest was aroused. More than 300,000 saw the exhibit in New York and, later, in Chicago and Boston. For most it was their first glimpse of modern art, and many found they liked it. But the show's most important effects were on the subsequent course of American painting and sculpture, which were no longer isolated from international art trends.

The New Realists

While many American artists adopted modernism after the Armory Show in 1913, others rejected it in favor of the most enduring U.S. tradition of all, realism. But each interpreted the American scene in a different way. George Bellows combined the realism of the Ashcan school with the virtuoso brushwork of a John Singer Sargent. Walt Kuhn created haunting images of clowns and acrobats. Forlorn decaying towns in the Midwest provided Charles Burchfield with his major theme, while Reginald Marsh, Isabel Bishop, Raphael Soyer, and others found inspiration in New York City life.

The Depression, the Dust Bowl, and dire hints of war in the 1930's induced artists to look even more closely at American life. The regionalists—especially Thomas Hart Benton, Grant Wood, and John Steuart Curry—took an optimistic point of view, insisting that America's real strength lay in the homespun virtues of the Midwest. But the social commentators adopted an agonized view of our sadly dislocated society. Philip Evergood, William Gropper, and many others were painters with a message containing powerful, almost propagandistic thrusts at America's social ills.

Even today the realist tradition is flourishing. In recent decades two of the most popular artists, Edward Hopper and Andrew Wyeth, have been realists. And people enjoy their works in museums throughout the country.

Ben Shahn *(1898–1969) and other social-protest artists of the Depression era painted stark, bitter commentaries on the dilemma of the unemployed. In "Scott's Run, West Virginia" (1937) Shahn mourned tragically wasted lives. (Tempera on cardboard.)*

"Christina's World" *(1948), like many of the paintings by Andrew Wyeth (1917–), is pervaded with a sense of brooding melancholy. Combining photographic exactitude with dramatic design, his impressive works have a wide appeal. (Tempera on gesso panel.)*

The best known *and most durable of the regionalist painters, Thomas Hart Benton (1889–1975), usually painted bucolic scenes of life in the Midwest, but his "Arts of the West—Mural No. 2" (1932) celebrates the folklore of the cowboy and the almost mythical Wild West immortalized in present-day films and television. Like all his works, this intricate series of interlocking vignettes brims with restless exuberance and vibrant energy. (Tempera and oil on linen, mounted on panel.)*

An ardent athlete, *George Wesley Bellows (1882–1925) won new attention with this brutally realistic painting entitled "Stag at Sharkey's" (1907). As a young man he studied for 2 years with the Ashcan realist Robert Henri and was considered his most talented pupil. Filled with an immense zest for life, Bellows painted cityscapes, landscapes, and portraits with verve and affection. His lithographs, which he began to make in 1916, helped to repopularize that art form. (Oil on canvas.)*

Edward Hopper *(1882–1967) endowed commonplace scenes such as "Early Sunday Morning" (1930) with a poetic sense of silence and solitude. He observed his surroundings with a trenchant eye and often concentrated on the quality of light and pathos in a scene: The fading grandeur of Victorian mansions, dilapidated rowhouses, shabby hotel rooms, all-night diners, empty rooms in seaside cottages. Many of his paintings have no human figures in them. When people do appear, more often than not they are lost in reverie. (Oil on canvas.)*

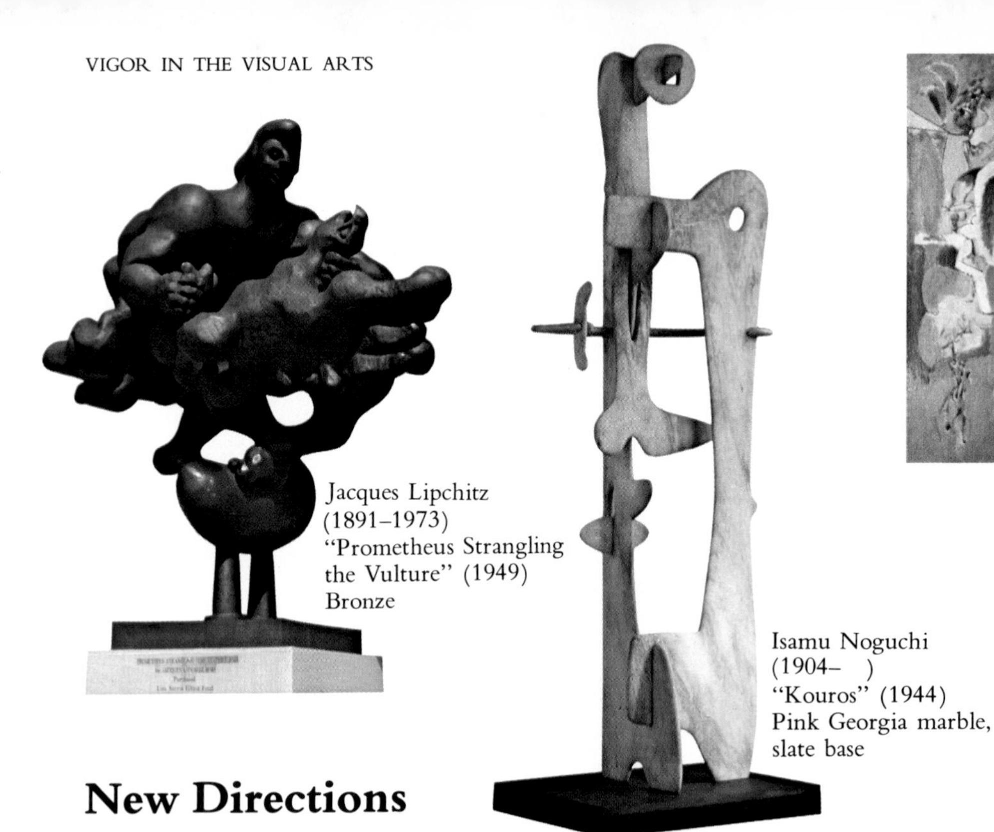

Jacques Lipchitz
(1891–1973)
"Prometheus Strangling the Vulture" (1949)
Bronze

Isamu Noguchi
(1904–)
"Kouros" (1944)
Pink Georgia marble, slate base

New Directions

The first wave of modernism in America faded in the 1920's. But with the rise of fascism in the 1930's many of Europe's most influential modern artists fled to the United States and, through their exhibits and teaching, exposed a rising generation of young Americans to free-form abstraction, geometric abstraction, precisionism, surrealism, and a variety of other new concepts. This time modern art really caught on here, with the public as well as with the museums which had formerly refused to exhibit abstract works.

By the late 1940's a group of New York painters had evolved a completely new interpretation of modernism —Abstract Expressionism, or action painting. With the appearance of their completely nonobjective, emotionally expressive works, America for the first time found itself in the vanguard of an international movement, one that remained dominant throughout the world until the 1960's. Reaction was bound to set in, of course. First came Pop Art and Op Art, then Minimal Art, post-painterly abstraction, conceptual art, and other new styles in dizzying succession. And the end is not in sight.

Changes in 20th-century sculpture have been just as dynamic. New materials and new forms have been adopted to produce Cubist sculpture, Expressionist sculpture, mobiles, stabiles, kinetic sculpture, assemblages, environmental art, earth sculpture, and many other innovative forms.

Which have been passing fads and which are genuine breakthroughs? Only time will tell. The important thing is that we have indeed achieved new vigor in the visual arts. True to the spirit of democracy, American artists enjoy full freedom of expression as they continue to experiment and seek new directions.

Arshile Gorky (1904–
"The Liver Is the Cock's Comb" (19
Oil on can

Alexander Calder (1898–
"Red Gongs" (19
Steel rod and wire, red pa

Jackson Pollock (1912–
"One" ("Number Thirty-one, 1950"; 19
Oil and enamel on can

Stuart Davis (1894–19
"Visa" (19
Oil on can

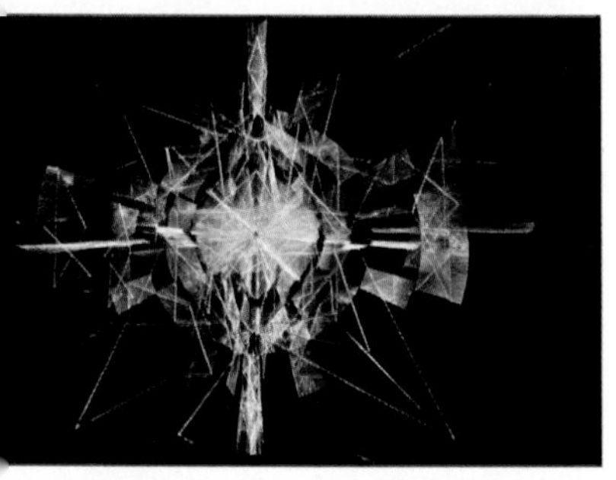

Richard Lippold (1915–)
ation Within a Sphere No. 10: the Sun"
(1953–56) Gold-filled wire

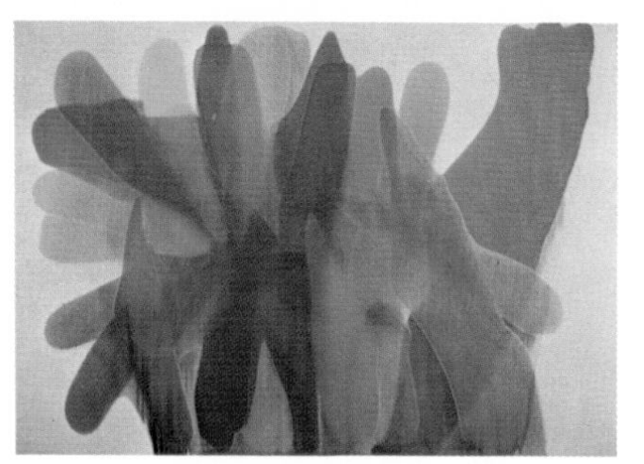

Morris Louis (1912–62)
"Floral" (1959)
Acrylic on canvas

Chryssa (1933–)
"Ampersand No. 3" (1965)
Neon and Plexiglas

Willem de Kooning (1904–)
"Gotham News" (1955)
Oil on canvas

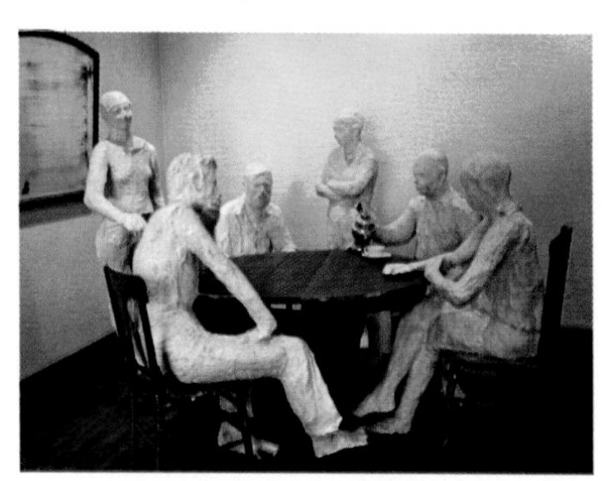

George Segal (1924–)
"The Dinner Table" (1962)
Plaster, wood, and metal

Frank Stella (1936–)
"Sinjerli Variation I" (1968)
Fluorescent acrylic on canvas

Richard Diebenkorn (1922–)
"Figure on a Porch" (1959)
Oil on canvas

Andy Warhol (c. 1930–)
"Campbell's Soup Can With Peeling Label"
(1962) Acrylic on canvas

Tony Smith (1912–)
"Moses" (1969)
Painted steel

Louise Nevelson (1900–)
"Sky Cathedral" (1958)
emblage: wood construction, black paint

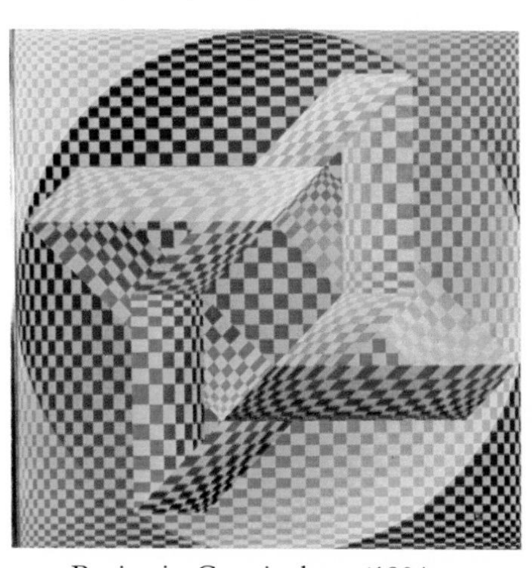

Benjamin Cunningham (1904–)
"Equivocation" (1964)
Synthetic polymer paint on composition board

Robert Cottingham (1935–)
"Art" (1971)
Oil on canvas

CHAPTER TWENTY-TWO

America's Music

Considering the forbidding aspect of their new land, it is not surprising that the music of the early settlers was essentially prayer set to song. The first music published in the Colonies appeared in the 1698 edition of the Bay Psalm Book. *In the early 1700's the well-to-do imported manuscripts of music from Europe to play for dancing and concerts. In the early 1800's more people had time and money for the pursuit of culture, and the music of European courts and concert halls was widely heard, especially in the cities. By the mid-1800's the piano was America's favorite instrument, and European romantic melodies the favorite music. Not until the "plantation songs" of Stephen Foster*

The hard and primitive life of the colonists was not conducive to the singing of madrigals or the delicate sounds of the lutes, virginals, and flageolets that graced the genteel English salons of the day. There was little room for instruments on the crowded ships, and only a sturdy and purposeful form of music was acceptable to the arbiters of colonial society.

For the Puritans who arrived in the early 1600's, solemn song was an integral part of their stern faith. Their psalms, intoned at home or at the meetinghouse, were intended to reinforce their dedication to the word of God. At first they sang from a psalter prepared by the Rev. Henry Ainsworth, who had "purified" a translation of the Book of Psalms that displeased the church elders and had set them to music. For the devout fundamentalists of the Massachusetts Bay Colony, however, even this was not close enough to the literal meaning of the Scriptures. In 1640 they published a new psalter, *The Whole Booke of Psalmes Faithfully Translated into English Metre,* better known as the *Bay Psalm Book.* Compiled by a committee of 30, it contained 150 psalms versified to correspond with the metrical patterns of familiar melodies. Only the words were printed because it was taken for granted that everyone knew the music. But by 1698 the oral transmission of tunes had produced so many different versions that the ninth edition of the *Bay Psalm Book* included the scores for 13 melodies.

Not many members of the growing Bay Colony could read music, however, so the practice of "lining out" became common. In this call-and-response style, the deacon reads or chants a line, and the congregation sings it back in unison. Some worshipers persisted with their own versions of the original melodies, and, out on the frontiers, away from clerical discipline, settlers were even enlivening the psalms with secular tunes of their own choosing.

Because "the tunes are now miserably tortured, twisted and quavered . . . into an horrid Medly of confused and disorderly Noises," as one minister complained, the Society for Promoting Regular Singing was formed in Boston in 1722. This and other "singing schools" went far beyond their original purpose of standardizing the psalms. Traveling teachers, mostly laymen, also taught the techniques of rounds, catches, and other forms of group singing, including some of their own compositions. In the collections they put together for their classes, these men created the first American music books.

Tunesmiths and Folksingers

William Billings, a Boston tanner, was the most notable of the Yankee tunesmiths, who were America's first composers. His book *The New England Psalm-Singer: or, American Chorister,* published in 1770, was a collection of settings for psalms, hymns, and anthems. He also wrote "fuguing tunes" with passages for voices that were brought into play one after another, as in a canon or round—a welcome departure from the unmodified unison singing that was still the general practice.

Even before the era of the Yankee tunesmiths, however, the colonists had begun to dilute their musical diet of straight psalmody. Literary historian Van Wyck Brooks reports a profusion of "sailors' chanties along the coast, ballads of village murders, rockaby songs, sugar-makers' songs, sung by weavers and carpenters, by farm wives and wandering fiddlers, by hunters, trappers, guides and lumbermen, snatches and refrains and longer pieces, brought over from the old world or natural outgrowths of the American soil."

Broadside ballads, so named because they were printed on newssheets or broadsides, were great favorites. These songs celebrated lurid, dramatic events. One, for example, told of a French and Indian attack on the Dutch town of Schenectady in the winter of 1690. Another, "Love-

d America begin to find a voice of its own. The Civil 'ar brought martial music, and the brass band, with Sun-y concerts in the park, became an American institution.

At the turn of the 20th century the music most widely presentative of this country was gaining a fast-growing idience. This appealing new freewheeling sound was lled jazz. Rooted in the field hollers and work songs of e plantations, levees, turpentine camps, and prisons, early zz and the blues had haunting echoes of an African past. 'his music, in all its cultural and ethnic permutations, has erhaps done as much to create understanding and respect mong all races as any other single force in our history.

The popular song, that tuneful product of Tin Pan Alley, and country Western music are two other American creations that have struck responsive chords around the world.

Until the early 1900's most classical music and most of the conductors and soloists came from Europe. Then a few American iconoclasts, such as Charles Ives and Henry Cowell, began to create new sounds in their own way inspiring interest in contemporary music. Encouraged by our outstanding schools of music, this interest has made the United States a leader in musical experimentation and innovation. Classical music composed here today is as American as our folk music and jazz.

Musical Inspiration From the Church
The First Influence Is Echoed to This Day

In colonial times, when the majority of the population was Protestant, most serious music was in the form of hymns. In the 19th century many styles of European religious music were brought over by immigrants of all faiths.

Meanwhile, black churches were developing their own spirituals and gospel songs, incorporating African rhythms and inflections with religious texts. The Queen of the Gospel Song, Mahalia Jackson, gained wide popularity and toured Europe to high acclaim. Other singers, such as Sister Rosetta Tharpe and Marion Williams, helped popularize the music of the black churches. The sound of gospel is an ingredient of jazz and a major element in the soul music of such popular contemporary singers as James Brown and Aretha Franklin.

Modern composers often turn to religious music. Virgil Thomson is one, as can be heard in his *Missa Pro Defunctis.* Alan Hovhaness delved into Armenian Catholic music for his *Saint Vartan* symphony. In his *New England Triptych,* William Schuman quoted from colonial composer William Billings' works, and Aaron Copland used a Shaker tune in *Appalachian Spring.*

The Puritans *always put religion first, even in their music. Although they did enjoy such entertainment as folksongs outside the church, most of the music in their lives was in the form of the psalms they sang at services, as shown above. Negro slaves were allowed some religious expression, and much of their music came out of their hymns and spirituals. After the Civil War black Americans began performing for paying audiences. The Fisk Jubilee Singers were organized to raise money for Fisk University in Nashville, Tennessee, a school started in 1866 to educate freed slaves. The Fisk singers were widely respected at home and abroad for their interpretations of Negro spirituals. The group gathered around the organ at right performed in the late 1800's.*

Stephen Foster
Authentic American Bard

For the brief span of a decade, the 1850's, Stephen Foster was blessed with a blaze of musical and poetic inspiration. During that time he wrote the songs that established him as the most popular composer of the 19th century. Foster's songs have memorable melodies that are easy to sing and lyrics that touch the wellsprings of the American life of his time. "Oh! Susanna," "Camptown Races," "Beautiful Dreamer," and many more of his works are irreplaceable in the American songbook.

Stephen Collins Foster was born in Pennsylvania, the descendant of Scotch-Irish immigrants. His grandfather had fought in the American Revolution, and his father, a Pittsburgh merchant, had been quartermaster and commissary of the U.S. Army during the War of 1812. Although the young Stephen Foster was drawn to music naturally, he received little formal musical education. Nevertheless he managed to learn music on his own and began composing at an early age. His song "Open Thy Lattice, Love" was published in 1844, but despite his demonstrations of talent, Foster was considered unfit for a musical career. In 1846 he was sent to Cincinnati, where he worked in his brother's commission house as a bookkeeper. Foster stayed in Cincinnati for 4 years, writing songs in his spare time. In 1848 he sold "Oh! Susanna" for $100, and it became a hit with the Forty-niners, who sang it on their way to the California goldfields. In 1850 Foster moved to Pittsburgh and married Jane Denny McDowell, who inspired the perennially popular "Jeanie With the Light Brown Hair."

Stephen Foster's *highly romanticized and idyllic vision of Negro life in the Old South is captured in "My Old Kentucky Home, Life in the South" (1859), a popular painting by Eastman Johnson.*

In 1851 Foster sold to Christy's Minstrels, the most popular minstrel troupe of all time, the right to introduce his songs before they were published. Many of his songs were "plantation songs," as he called them, which idealized life in the South, especially among the Negroes. Foster's only visit to Dixie probably was to New Orleans in 1852, although he had been impressed by Negro work songs heard on the Ohio River. The long list of songs for which he wrote both the music and the lyrics includes such favorites as "Old Folks at Home" ("Swanee River"), "Massa's in de Cold, Cold Ground," "Old Black Joe," and "My Old Kentucky Home."

Foster moved to New York City in 1860, and he wrote a large number of songs in the next few years. But they were failures, mostly ordinary, uninspired imitations of his past successes, and he sought refuge in alcohol. His wife left him, and he sank deeper into alcoholism and despair. Finally, in 1864, he died almost penniless in Bellevue Hospital after a fall in a Bowery flophouse. The Beautiful Dreamer thus ended the nightmare that had consumed the last years of his life.

well's Fight," described the ordeal of a Massachusetts Indian fighter and his party who were ambushed at Pigwacket, Maine, in 1725. The Revolution and the events leading up to it stimulated innumerable broadsides, some satirical and some inspirational. William Billings wrote an incendiary text for one of his best known fuguing tunes, "Chester," transforming it into what was widely accepted as the battle hymn of the Revolution.

Established Forms Are Heard

A sophisticated musical idiom in America was first developed by the Moravians who emigrated from German-speaking Bohemia and Moravia to Pennsylvania, Georgia, and the Carolinas during the middle of the 18th century. They presented the earliest concerts of public music for instrumental ensembles, choirs, and soloists, performing anthems, religious arias, and chorales. The Moravians encouraged their own composers, most of whom concentrated on sacred music.

In the 19th century as the frontier moved westward, the growing young cities of the East became increasingly conscious of their positions as centers of culture. Their tastemakers forsook the Yankee tunesmiths and the simple melodic heritage that had come from Britain and Ireland and turned to the more cultivated music of continental Europe's courts and concert halls. In the South and across the Appalachian Mountains, however, the old psalms, hymns, anthems, and ballads survived and became the backbone of rural music.

More and more religious verses were sung to popular melodies, patriotic airs, and dance tunes. These folk hymns were first collected by "Singin' Billy" Walker; his songbook *Southern Harmony,* published in 1835, sold 600,000 copies before the Civil War. Nine years later many of the hymns reappeared, along with such additions as "Wayfaring Stranger" and "The Old Ship of Zion," in *The Sacred Harp.* Both collections used shape, or character, notation, a simplified system in which the notes

The Story of the Banjo

The modern-day banjo is the one musical instrument that is undeniably American. Its ancestry is African, but the banjo as we know it is a far cry from the hollowed-out gourds with crude necks and strings first played here by slaves on the Southern plantations. Music was one of the few pleasures the slaves were allowed, and in the earliest days the homemade banjo was the only instrument they had. Played solo or as an accompaniment to their singing, which in itself became the wellspring of the Negroes' social and cultural life, the banjo soon came to the attention of the slaves' white masters. In his *Notes on Virginia,* written in 1784, Thomas Jefferson noted that the Negroes' musical instrument was "the Banjar, which they brought hither from Africa."

In the 19th century improved models of the banjo, with machined pegs for precise tuning and vellum heads with adjustable tension, were a staple instrument in the minstrel shows; virtuoso performers, both black and white, began to appear on the stage. The first banjos had a smooth neck, as does the violin. But early in the days of minstrelsy wire crosspieces, called frets, were added to the neck for more precise intonation. The banjo first had four strings. Later models had as many as nine, but by the minstrel days four strings were standard. Then, in the late 1800's, the five-string evolved. It has a short, unfretted drone string that is played with the thumb. This is the instrument that country singer Earl Scruggs took in hand and used to bring forth the propulsive sounds that have made the Scruggs-style banjo the backbone of the music known as bluegrass.

The four-string, or tenor, banjo had a remarkable resurgence in the 1920's. Inspired by the technical wizardry of Eddie Peabody and others, banjo bands, schools, and clubs flourished from coast to coast. In the late 1960's renewed interest in folk and country music brought the banjo into prominence again. While its musical stock may fluctuate, it will always be on the market.

of the staff are identified not only by their position but by four distinctive shapes—triangle, square, circle, and diamond. *The Sacred Harp,* complete with shape notes, is still widely used in rural Southern churches.

Such were the hymns sung at camp meetings in the late 1800's and early 1900's in isolated areas where there were no churches. These meetings, which went on for 4 or 5 days, featured rousing evangelical preaching, praying, and singing. The songs were revival hymns—simple, folklike, repetitious pieces that were often called spiritual songs and, later, spirituals. Negro religious songs, which blend African musical traditions with Christian themes, became known as spirituals, too, because of their similar use of repetition. Revival meetings also produced gospel hymns—songs with spirited melodies and sentimental, homespun lyrics. "Beautiful River" ("Shall we gather at the river?") was one of the most popular gospel hymns of the day.

In the 1840's American audiences were flocking to hear the offerings of the Hutchinsons, a singing family whose piece de resistance was a tearjerker called "The Lament of the Blind Orphan Girl." Into this sea of bathos sailed America's first great songwriter, Stephen Foster, who became famous in the 1850's for "My Old Kentucky Home" and other "plantation songs," as he called them. Although Foster's melodies were sung in the minstrel shows popular in his day, the lively banjo tunes created by Daniel Decatur Emmett were more typical of this medium. Of Emmett's more than 70 minstrel songs, the most popular was "Dixie," first performed in 1859 by Bryant's Minstrels. With the onset of the Civil War, "Dixie" became the anthem of the Confederate troops, although Emmett was a staunch supporter of the North. The favorite song of the Union soldiers was Julia Ward Howe's "Battle Hymn of the Republic."

The martial music of the war accelerated the development of the bright, compelling sound of the brass band, which became one of America's most popular musical institutions for the next half century. Interest in these bands was dramatically heightened by the grandiose initiatives of Patrick S. Gilmore, a cornet virtuoso and the probable composer of the Civil War song "When Johnny Comes Marching Home." Gilmore progressed from conducting military bands to the presentation of postwar "Peace Jubilees." These were massive spectacles involving thousands of singers and musicians. His most notable jubilee, held in Boston for 5 days in 1869, included 10,296 voices and more than 1,000 musicians and was climaxed by a performance of Verdi's "Anvil Chorus." Singers and instrumentalists were joined by 100 firemen striking 100 anvils, backed by all the church chimes in Boston and a fusillade of cannons fired in rhythm. What Gilmore did for an encore is not recorded.

Brass concert music was lifted to a new level in the 1880's when John Philip Sousa took over the U.S. Marine Band. Enthusiasm for martial ensembles spread so rapidly that by the turn of the century more than 20,000 amateur and professional brass bands were giving regular concerts in towns and villages throughout the country. Many played stirring marches composed by Sousa.

While the gleaming brass was resounding in the open air, the indoor musical scene was thriving as well. With the wave of German immigration in the mid-19th century came many trained musicians who—as performers, composers, and teachers—spread an enthusiasm for Romanticism and for that romantic instrument, the piano. The already growing piano business increased tremendously. The chief manufacturers were Jonas Chickering, of Boston, and two German immigrants, William Knabe and Henry Steinweg (who changed his name to Steinway). By 1860 there were 22,000 pianos in America. After the Civil War, as black musicians began to play European instruments previously unavailable to them,

John Philip Sousa, *leader of the U.S. Marine Corps Band (1880–92), composed many of our favorite marches, including "Semper Fidelis" and "Stars and Stripes Forever."*

Negroes created many minstrel songs and transposed the minstrel style to the piano. Negro talent, influenced by minstrel sounds applied to European-style melodies, ultimately produced a new form called ragtime. The term probably derived from the ragged, uneven sound of this syncopated piano music, which mixed Afro-Caribbean dance rhythms with the accents of the quadrille, the polka, the schottische, and the march. Scott Joplin's "Maple Leaf Rag," published in 1899, set off a craze that was sustained not only by the brass bands but by the popularity of Irving Berlin's "Alexander's Ragtime Band," a lively song (but not really a rag) written in 1911.

Ragtime faded during World War I but won a new audience in the 1960's when Max Morath, a pianist and singer, played ragtime classics on television shows and in personal appearances. Interest increased in the mid-1970's with the comeback of Eubie Blake, an early ragtime composer and pianist still remarkably agile at the age of 90. The revival reached a peak when Scott Joplin's "The Entertainer" was used as a theme in the Academy Award-winning score for the 1973 movie *The Sting.*

As ragtime was first finding favor at the turn of the century, the American popular song industry was also getting started. The melodic tunes and memorable lyrics to be written by Irving Berlin, Cole Porter, George and Ira Gershwin, and their peers were destined to be hummed, whistled, and sung the world around.

A New Kind of Music for All the World

Along with ragtime, another new kind of music, also played mostly by blacks, was gradually taking shape. It was not yet called jazz in the mid-1890's when Charles "Buddy the King" Bolden, a New Orleans barber and cornetist, was playing it at outdoor dances in Johnson Park and Lincoln Park. Indoors in such establishments as Come Clean Hall and Love and Charity Hall the new sound was heard on piano. Bolden's band—one or two cornetists, clarinet, trombone, bass, guitar, and drums—played music derived from African melodies and rhythms mixed with hymns, blues, quadrilles, funeral marches, ragtime, and even operatic arias. The rough-hewn, self-taught approach of onetime slaves or descendants of slaves blowing brass instruments and woodwinds was leavened by the technical precision and pure, warm tones of "Creoles of color," many of whom were trained musicians. After the passage of New Orleans' Legislative Code 111 in 1894, this population was forced to move from the city's French downtown section to a segregated quarter in the black uptown area.

The exciting effect of "singing horns," so called because the instrumentalists tried to reproduce the slurs and blue intonations of black singing, was not lost on white musicians. But when they tried to copy it, the emphasis shifted from the relaxed, blue tonality that came so naturally to the black musicians to a more staccato style of stricter tempo. This created the basis for the line of jazz still known as Dixieland, named after Tom Brown's Band from Dixieland, which, in 1915, was the first white band to take the music north to Chicago. "Jass," a sexual slang word, was applied to this new music by disgruntled musicians who could neither play nor understand it. But that connotation was soon lost.

Both blacks and whites used a basic instrumentation of trumpet (for melody), trombone (for foundation), and clarinet (for decoration), with a rhythm section of drums, string bass or tuba, banjo or guitar, and—when they played the dancehalls—the piano. The best piano players, particularly in New Orleans, tended to work as soloists in saloons or brothels.

After Bolden was committed in 1907 to a State mental hospital, where he remained until his death in 1931, cornetist Joe Oliver came to the fore among New Orleans' black musicians. King Oliver, as he quickly became known because of his virtuosity, was the idol of the young Louis Armstrong. In 1915 the 15-year-old Armstrong had been released from the Colored Waifs Home, where he had learned to play the cornet while serving time for a minor charge. Oliver was soon impressed by the boy and made him his protege. When the King left New Orleans for Chicago in 1918, he turned over his place as cornetist in Kid Ory's band to Armstrong. Four years later he called Louis to Chicago to join his Creole Jazz Band, the best of its kind.

By 1917 most of the good musicians in New Orleans played on the riverboats or had gone on to find work in such cities as Chicago, Kansas City, St. Louis, and New York. It was, however, a white group from New Orleans, the Original Dixieland Jass Band (ODJB), playing at Reisenweber's Restaurant in New York City in 1917, that established jazz in the national consciousness. This combination created such a sensation with what were then considered to be wild, cacophonic sounds and danceable rhythms that "jass" music became the rage of the moment. The word "jazz," in its variant spelling, was so firmly planted in the public mind that until the arrival of the swing era in the 1930's it was applied indiscrimi-

Echoes of Tin Pan Alley
Great Tunes Heard the World Around

The first songs to gain notable success in America were spawned in time of war. During the Revolution the favorite marching tune was "Yankee Doodle." In the Civil War "Battle Hymn of the Republic" and "Dixie" became the anthems of the warring sides. But it was not until the turn of the 20th century that the popular song industry began to flower.

In those days our grandparents and their friends would gather around the parlor piano on a typical social evening, squinting at the sheet music to follow the lyrics of the latest catchy tunes. New pieces were demonstrated daily in the music stores.

In the early 1900's most of the songs were published by firms in New York City's Broadway area, which came to be called Tin Pan Alley, a name possibly derived from the tinny sounds of the pianos heard on every side. Many of the hits came from the big musicals on Broadway and, later, in Hollywood. They were further popularized by the traveling dance bands that played all across the country and by phonograph records in the jukebox and on the radio. These songs, turned out by a succession of talented composers and lyricists, were whistled, hummed, and sung around the world.

One of the earliest of the great composers in the popular vein was George M. Cohan, who was also an actor, singer, dancer, producer, playwright, and director. Patriotism was his specialty. "Over There" was one of the most widely heard songs in the two World Wars. Other notable hits of his were "Yankee Doodle Boy" and "You're a Grand Old Flag."

In addition to those represented here with their sheet music, there are many bright stars in the songwriting firmament, such as Harold Arlen, Jule Styne, Frederick Loewe, Leonard Bernstein, Stephen Sondheim, and Meredith Willson, to name only a few who created popular songs that are classics of their kind.

nately to almost any form of music not exclusively an extension of traditional European concert forms. Beyond that, it was so interwoven with the upheaval in mores following World War I that the decade of the 1920's was known as the Jazz Age.

The young phonograph industry, which until then had never recorded a jazz band, decided to take a chance with the Original Dixieland Jass Band. ODJB recordings for the Victor Talking Machine Company in 1917 and 1918 took jazz for the first time beyond the environs of New Orleans and Chicago to middle-class communities throughout the country, exciting the interest of young musicians who might otherwise never have heard it. In Ogden, Utah, Loring "Red" Nichols, a music teacher's 13-year-old son who was studying to become a concert band cornetist, shifted to the popular new style and became one of the early white jazz celebrities.

In Davenport, Iowa, 15-year-old Leon Bix Beiderbecke, enthralled by the music he heard on the Mississippi riverboats that docked in his hometown, taught himself to play the cornet and polished his skills by playing the ODJB records over and over. Bix died in 1931 at 28, but his pure, singing tone and sensitive phrasing strongly influenced white musicians for several decades. His piano compositions, particularly the melody "In a Mist," were, harmonically, far ahead of their time.

In the mid-twenties records were made by King Oliver's Creole Jazz Band, by blues singer Bessie Smith, and by Louis Armstrong with his Hot Five and Hot Seven—a celebrated series of recordings. Almost equally significant were the disks of Ferdinand "Jelly Roll" Morton, a New Orleans pianist, composer, singer, and arranger whose structured orchestrations for his eight-piece group, the Red Hot Peppers, formed a bridge between the Oliver and Armstrong improvisations and the carefully organized jazz of the late twenties, played by the 10- and 12-piece bands of Fletcher Henderson and Duke Ellington. In New York, Henderson's 11-piece orchestra of relatively well-schooled musicians, specializing in dance arrangements, developed a strong jazz attack only after Louis Armstrong joined it late in 1924. During the year he spent with them, Louis communicated to the Henderson musicians his own soaring, freewheeling jazz spirit.

The Ellington Era Begins

Henderson's music in the Armstrong period impressed young Edward Kennedy "Duke" Ellington, who was leading his own six-piece group in New York. Ellington enlarged his band, creating arrangements around the unique guttural sounds produced by trumpeter Bubber Miley and trombonist Joe "Tricky Sam" Nanton. Three years later the Ellington band, grown to 10 pieces, was broadcasting nightly from the Cotton Club in New York, and the band's growling "jungle" style was providing the foundation for Ellington's long, innovative career as a bandleader, composer, and pianist. His popular songs ("Solitude," "Mood Indigo," "Sophisticated Lady"), his more extended works *Harlem, Night Creature*), and his series of Sacred Concerts were all colored by the distinctive style that grew directly from his early Cotton Club band.

Other jazz bands of 10 or more black musicians followed—bands led by Bennie Moten in Kansas City, by Earl "Fatha" Hines in Chicago, and by Don Redman (McKinney's Cotton Pickers) in Detroit. A few white, jazz-oriented big bands appeared in the twenties: The California Ramblers, a New York group; Jean Goldkette's Orchestra, whose stars (including Bix Beiderbecke) were absorbed by the semisymphonic dance band of Paul Whiteman, billed inaccurately as the King of Jazz; and, at the end of the decade, the Casa Loma Orchestra led by Glen Gray. In general, they perpetuated the earlier stylistic difference between small, white Dixieland groups and small, black blues-oriented groups. Then, in 1934, Benny Goodman, a clarinetist who had grown up in the Chicago jazz world of the twenties, formed a combination that used many arrangements originated by Fletcher Henderson for his own band. Goodman had an impact on the public's musical fancy comparable to that of the Original Dixieland Jass Band.

Goodman's success brought "swing" into popular parlance, although—as exemplified in Duke Ellington's "It Don't Mean a Thing If It Ain't Got That Swing"—the term had long been used by musicians to describe a rhythmic performance. The big white orchestras that played Goodman's exciting mixture of jazz and popular dance music—primarily Artie Shaw's and to a lesser extent Tommy Dorsey's and Glenn Miller's—were identified as swing bands.

But the swingingest band of the era was a black group out of Kansas City led by William "Count" Basie, a pianist trained by Thomas "Fats" Waller. Waller was also the musical inspiration for the blind genius Art Tatum, who became the acknowledged master of all jazz pianists. John Hammond, who helped put Benny Goodman's band together, also promoted Count Basie and provided him with a singer, Billie Holiday, whom Hammond first heard in Harlem in 1933. That year Billie Holiday made her first recording with a band led by Benny Goodman. Later she sang with Teddy Wilson, the pianist, saxophonist Lester Young, and a select group of other jazz stars. Their recordings have become classics.

New Sounds for Jazz

From the mid-thirties until America's involvement in World War II at the end of 1941, the white swing bands overshadowed the big black orchestras that had inspired them. But early in the forties black musicians in New York, "jamming" (improvising in impromptu groups) at afterhours clubs in Harlem and bored by stereotyped jazz routines, began to play complex new harmonies and rhythms that, unlike most earlier jazz, were based on a progression of chords instead of on the melody.

This new jazz, pioneered by alto saxophonist Charles Christopher "Bird" Parker and trumpeter John Birks "Dizzy" Gillespie, became known as bebop, an onomatopoetic simulation of a two-note phrase that appeared frequently in the music. By the mid-forties interest in the swing bands was dying out, and jazz had split into two opposing camps, the traditionalists and the beboppers. Although their disdain for each other has diminished over the years, the division in jazz styles has continued. The traditionalists, with roots in New Orleans jazz, Dixieland, and swing, still base their improvisations on a melody, while the post-World War II jazzmen, representing modern jazz—bebop and its successor styles—tend more to improvise on chord progressions.

No sooner had the nervous, frenetic sound of bebop, filled with rapidly executed flights of virtuosity, achieved its own identity than there was a reaction called cool jazz. This new music, as understated and unemotional as bebop was agitated, developed around Miles Davis, a trumpeter who had earned his credentials in Charlie Parker's quintet, and Gil Evans, an arranger who had helped to create

Pivotal Jazz Performers
A Few Who Set a Style

On almost every instrument there has been one musician, and sometimes more, of such surpassing originality that everything done before suddenly seems out of date. The standards they set will sometimes prevail for decades. Followers may add interesting nuances, but echoes of the seminal concepts of the pivotal performers are often so compelling that they become part of the idiom of the instrument.

In addition to the innovators shown at work here, there are a few others whose creativity has left an indelible mark on all who play the same instrument. The tenor saxophone did not come into its own as a jazz instrument until Coleman Hawkins evolved a rugged, deep-toned, driving attack in the mid-twenties, a style that was refined and reworked by other saxophonists over the years, leading eventually to the torrential lines and involved harmonics used by John Coltrane in the 1960's. Another saxophonist, Ornette Coleman, played the alto in a free form that often avoided set keys or chord structures and, starting in the 1960's, influenced performers on all instruments.

Louis Armstrong's stature as a trumpet player was reinforced by his followers: Roy "Little Jazz" Eldridge used Armstrong as the basis for fiery flurries of virtuosity, and John Birks "Dizzy" Gillespie used Eldridge as the starting point for his equally fiery and dazzling bebop style. Miles Davis condensed and simplified the virtuosic Armstrong-Eldridge-Gillespie style to create his own low-keyed approach.

Both the guitar and the bass were given new stature in 1940: Charlie Christian created a buoyant single-string solo idiom for electric guitar, and Jimmy Blanton's technical facility as a bassist also lifted that instrument from its monotonous timekeeper's role to a position of harmonic and melodic importance that is still expanding in the jazz ensemble.

Louis Armstrong *(1900–71) with the Creole Jazz Band in 1923. From left: Johnny Dodds, Baby Dodds, Honore Dutrey, Armstrong, Joe "King" Oliver, Lil Hardin (later Mrs. Armstrong), and Bill Johnson. Oliver led this band, but it was "Satchmo" who revolutionized trumpet playing.*

Charlie Parker *(1920–55). His virtuosity and advanced musical concepts brought new dimensions to the alto saxophone and to jazz.*

When Charlie Christian *(1919–42) started playing professionally in a band at age 15, the guitar was used mostly for rhythm. In the late 1930's he was one of the first to play an amplified guitar that had enough volume to be used as a solo instrument. He created a style of long melodic lines of eighth notes with subtle accents that almost every guitarist since has drawn upon.*

the unique sound for Claude Thornhill's popular dance band. The sounds of cool jazz were also heard in the early fifties among a west coast school led by saxophonist Gerry Mulligan and pianist Dave Brubeck.

During the 1950's there were several attempts to relate jazz to European concert music. Dave Brubeck's quartet, one of the most popular jazz groups of the decade, with a particularly loyal following on college campuses, employed elements that Brubeck had absorbed in his studies with the French composer Darius Milhaud. The Modern Jazz Quartet, guided by its pianist and musical director John Lewis, made good use of the Baroque tradition, particularly in the form of jazz fugues. And Gunther Schuller, a classically trained French horn player who had been part of Miles Davis' cool jazz clique, attempted to find a middle area of music between jazz and classical forms. Schuller's "third stream of music" was an interesting experiment that drew on the improvisational spontaneity and rhythmic vitality of jazz and the compositional procedures and techniques of classical music without being essentially one or the other.

But by the 1960's jazz innovators were moving not toward the established traditions of Western music but toward even greater freedom than had previously been enjoyed. Free jazz—music without a set key, a predetermined tempo, or even chord progressions—was pio-

The Changing Spectrum of Jazz
Created by Talent and Musical Taste

The essence of jazz is freedom, so it is not surprising that it covers a multitude of sounds. First played by black musicians in New Orleans at the turn of the century, jazz changes constantly as musicians master their instruments and are inspired by one another to push on to new plateaus. About every 10 years the cumulative change is sufficient to create a new spectrum. While the categories below are not meant to be definitive, they include the major permutations and reveal their relationship. Only the blues, that most basic of the roots of jazz, has steadily prevailed.

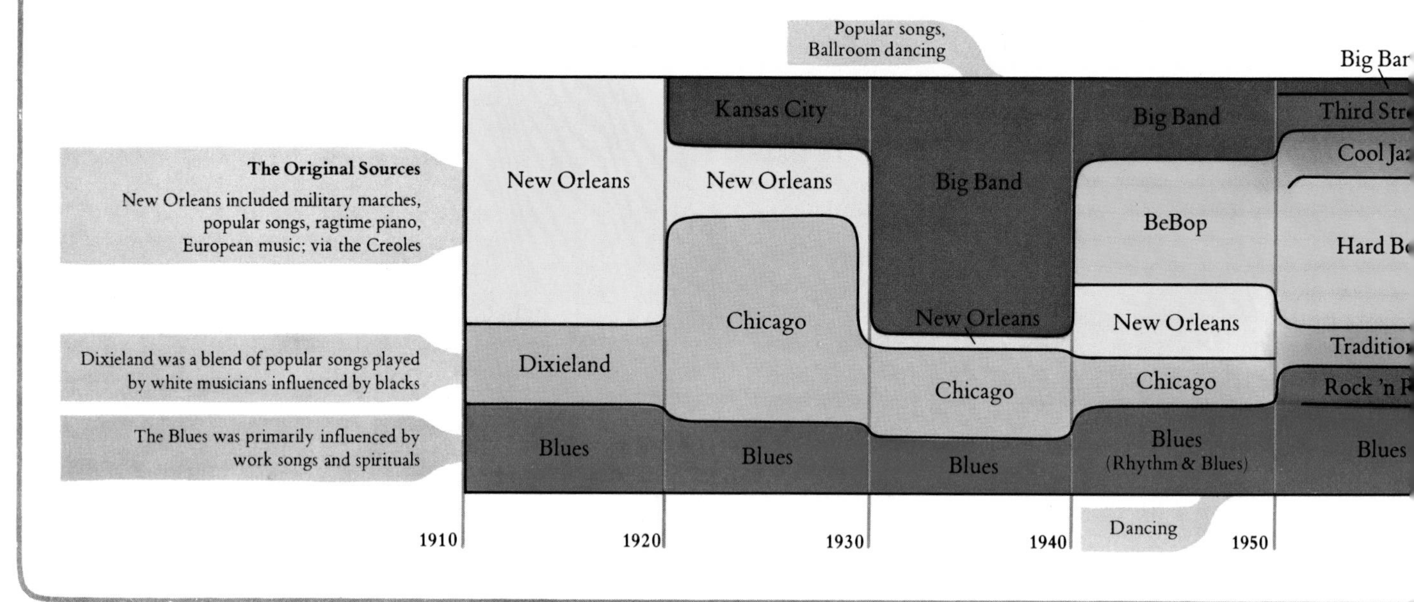

neered in the late 1950's by pianist Cecil Taylor but did not come into focus until the 1960's, when saxophonist Ornette Coleman spearheaded a bitterly argued change in the course of jazz. Another saxophonist, John Coltrane, became the standard bearer of avant garde jazz in the sixties. Strongly influenced by Eastern music, particularly Arabic and Indian, Coltrane's extended improvisations had an almost trancelike quality. To some of the black avant garde, this form of musical expression became a vehicle for aggressive ethnic assertions.

Country Music—Another First

While jazz, the first distinctively American music to emerge in this country, was winning adherents and acceptance, the ballads, broadsides, jigs, reels, and sacred songs that had come here with English, Scottish, and Irish settlers were evolving their own American forms. Abandoned by the culture-minded Eastern cities early in the 19th century, this music was nurtured in rural mountain areas of the Southeastern States. There it remained for a century, virtually unchanged except for slight coloration from contact with black music. Then, like jazz, it was spread beyond its narrow boundaries, first by the phonograph, and then by radio.

Between 1927 and 1933 recordings by Jimmie Rodgers, the Singing Brakeman, gave country music the same kind of forceful identity that Louis Armstrong's records were giving to jazz. Radio barn dance programs also whetted the public's appetite for the sound. The most notable of these programs was one started in 1925 on WSM, Nashville, Tennessee, which later became the Grand Ole Opry. Country music began to develop star performers such as the Singing Carter Family, Uncle Dave Macon, Roy Acuff, and the Monroe Brothers. Bill Monroe helped to establish a mixture of string band improvisation and vocal harmonizing, stressing a high, lonesome sound that became popular as bluegrass music.

Jimmie Rodgers, *a Mississippi railroadman, became famous as the Singing Brakeman in the late 1920's. He sang standard country tunes, Negro blues, and railroad songs.*

The performer who did most to take country music beyond the South and Midwest was Hank Williams, a singer and composer who, like Jimmie Rodgers, was steeped in Negro blues as well as in the country idiom. Such Williams favorites as "Cold, Cold Heart," "Jambalaya," and "Your Cheatin' Heart," recorded in the early 1950's by Tony Bennett, Jo Stafford, Joni James, and other established singers, helped to bridge the gap between country and pop. At about this time a new breed, conservatively dressed and with scarcely a touch of country twang in their voices, was exemplified by Eddy Arnold and Jim Reeves. In the mid-

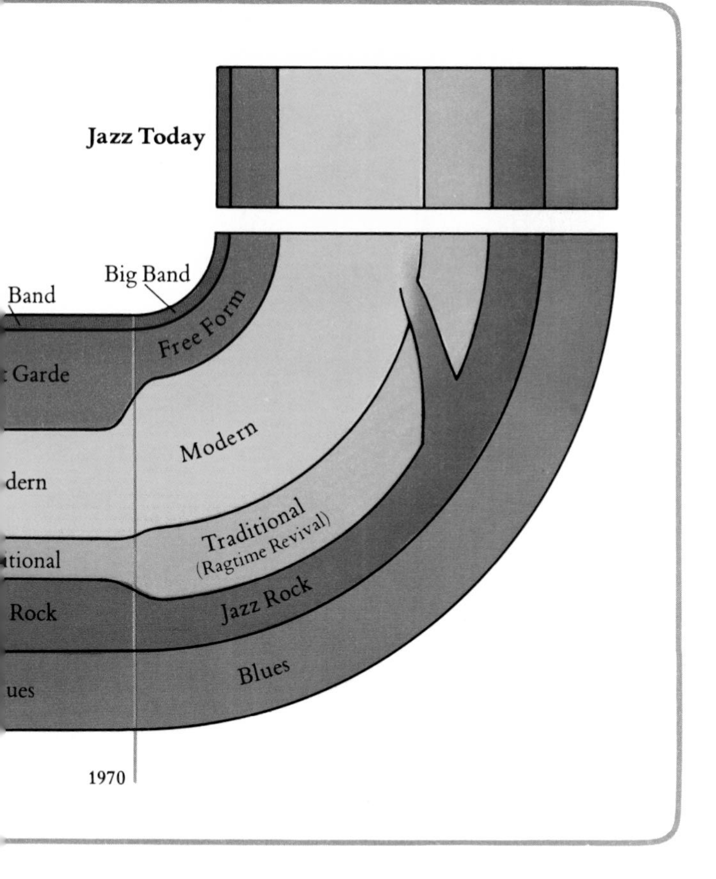

1960's Charley Pride became the first black to become popular exclusively as a country singer.

With the fusion of materials, styles, and audiences, as well as the growth of Nashville as a commercial music center, country music began to take on a gloss that sometimes threatened to obscure the regional individuality from which it had sprung.

By the 1970's John Denver, a pop-folk singer, was being hailed as a country artist, and Paul McCartney, one of the former Beatles, was accepted with enthusiasm by the local musicians in Nashville when he went there to record. Long before this happened, however, country music made an important contribution to a new phenomenon, to be formalized as rock 'n' roll.

From Rock 'n' Roll to Rhythm and Blues

While country music was being recorded in the twenties, thirties, and early forties specifically for its regional audiences, black performers were making so-called race records for Negro audiences in the big Northern cities as well as throughout the South. These records featured black singers of country blues, such as Robert Johnson and Big Bill Broonzy, and hard-driving little instrumental groups, often called jump bands. After World War II the blues singers began to move from the rural South to Northern cities, primarily Chicago, where they joined forces with the instrumental groups.

By the time they had come together, the race designation had fallen into disfavor, and this black music was broadly identified as rhythm and blues. Although there had always been some exchange between white and black country musicians in the South because of their proximity to each other, it had gone relatively unnoticed. In 1954 Bill Haley and the Comets, a white country group, made a rhythm and blues disk of "Rock Around the Clock," which had first been recorded 7 years earlier by Joe Turner, a black Kansas City blues singer.

From Haley's version, white listeners who had ignored Turner's recording became aware of the excitement and vitality this music could generate. The way was opened for another white performer, Elvis Presley, to project the essence of the black music, which became known as rock 'n' roll. As if to emphasize the music's sources, Presley's first records included "That's All Right, Mama," a blues number recorded 10 years earlier by Arthur "Big Boy" Crudup, and "Blue Moon of Kentucky," a country song composed by Bill Monroe.

Presley had an approach that helped to interest young audiences in this new concoction. His mixture of rhythm and blues, country ballads, and fundamentalist revival singing was accompanied by a show of open, aggressive sexuality—a far cry from the earlier, more genteel styles of Bing Crosby and Rudy Vallee or, for that matter, of Frank Sinatra who, in his time, could bring an audience to the verge of hysteria. Presley's performing style stirred so much anger in the adult world that teenagers made him a symbol of their beliefs, and rock 'n' roll became a musical expression of rebellion.

In England, Presley's success attracted attention to such rhythm and blues specialists as Chuck Berry and Little Richard. These performers were admired and copied by, among others, The Beatles and The Rolling Stones, the two most influential English rock groups of the 1960's. The Beatles, in particular, established popular standards for an entire era. They popularized the electronic amplification of instruments at piercingly high volumes and, through their example, revived long-hair styles for men. The trends they began outlasted the group itself.

As The Beatles and The Stones acknowledged their rhythm and blues sources, black American blues singers began to win wider audiences than ever before. Some, such as B. B. King and Muddy Waters, continued the old blues tradition. Janis Joplin, a white singer, reached back to classical blues artists of the 1920's, such as Bessie Smith and Ma Rainey, for her style. Jimi Hendrix flaunted an arrogance and sexuality similar to Elvis Presley's and won a wide following.

In the twenties and thirties black music was heard primarily by black audiences in segregated areas. Occasionally, a black performer became popular with white audiences. One of the most notable of all the performers in this category was actor, civil rights leader, and singer Paul Robeson, whose concerts of Negro spirituals drew enthusiastic white audiences. Robeson's powerful bass voice would have carried him even further had not his avowed Communist beliefs blighted his musical career.

Another, later aspect of black music called soul became a major force in the 1960's and 1970's. The spirit of soul was assimilated in blues, gospel, jazz, and even popular music. It was exemplified in the gyrating, hoarsely shouted, frenzied performances of James Brown, in the gospel-based singing of Aretha Franklin, and in the musical polemics of Nina Simone. It was heard in the blues-based singing of Ray Charles, and, as pop-soul, in the performances of Stevie Wonder, The Supremes, The Temptations, Smokey Robinson and the Miracles, and others who recorded for Detroit's Motown, the first major record company owned and directed by blacks.

The other basic brand of American music, kept alive by whites in the Southeastern mountains, produced contemporary versions of propaganda songs that had flourished during the Revolution. In the 1920's and 1930's they became songs of protest, stemming from the growth of the labor movement and from the social upheavals of the Depression. Woody Guthrie emerged as a leading chronicler of these troubled times. In New York before World War II, Guthrie inspired several like-minded singers, including Pete Seeger and his postwar group, The Weavers, who popularized many of Guthrie's songs, including "This Land Is Your Land." The Negro singer-guitarist Huddie "Leadbelly" Ledbetter was closer to these sociological sources than to the exponents of soul.

Aretha Franklin *toured as a gospel singer at age 14. This background combined with the blues and a voice of astounding range, has made her a soul music superstar.*

The Weavers developed a wide audience in the late fifties and stimulated other singers to such an extent that folksongs gained the status of popular music. Leading performers were The Kingston Trio, with "Tom Dooley"; and Peter, Paul, and Mary, who popularized "Blowin' in the Wind," a song written by Bob Dylan, a follower of Woody Guthrie.

Early in the 1960's Dylan's antiestablishment and antiwar songs won him almost as many avid young followers as Elvis Presley had attracted earlier. Dylan's audience, however, was more interested in the significance of the lyrics than in the music or the gyrations of the performer. Dylan shifted the emphasis in popular folk music from the traditional to original contemporary songs. He eventually turned from the folk style, but the poetic pop-folk manner that he had established was carried on by Tom Paxton, John Prine, Kris Kristofferson, and other singers and composers. Such artists as Joan Baez, Judy Collins, Arlo Guthrie, and James Taylor have so truly expressed the hopes, dreams and concerns of their peers that they have become celebrities.

Kristofferson was nominally part of the Nashville country music coterie. His songs—such as "Help Me Make It Through the Night"—had a sophistication and frankness that reflected a nationwide change in mores. In the seventies country music was carried a step further by Waylon Jennings, a country singer who merged rock with the realism of country music.

In the early seventies the influence of rock music—particularly the use of very loud, amplified electronic instruments—was also felt in jazz. Miles Davis, who had been in the forefront of new jazz developments since the mid-forties, turned to electronic jazz-rock. Electronic wizardry also changed the character of some music. Individual notes could be extended, distorted, or echoed to entirely new dimensions, and these effects were used to create new aural excitement.

During the period in which rock, folk, and country music were enjoying great popularity, large and faithful followings also continued to give their devoted patronage to long-established performers whom many young people and sophisticated listeners dismissed as vapid or overly sentimental. Liberace was a widely known pianist who used the trappings of show business—candelabra, a sequined jacket, and a winsome smile—to dramatize his repertory of classical, semiclassical, and tuneful popular music. Lawrence Welk conducted a dance band that offered a blend of flowing melodies and featured smiling, clean-cut choral singers and soloists. André Kostelanetz led a symphony-sized orchestra that played popular classics, operatic arias, marches, and semiclassical favorites with a bright, full sound.

The Evolution of Classical Music in America

The American colonists heard their first public concert of classical music in Boston in 1731. The following year there was a concert in Charleston, South Carolina, where the first music society was founded in 1761. Chamber music was popular in the Colonies. Thomas Jefferson played the violin, and Benjamin Franklin composed string quartets. Francis Hopkinson, a signer of the Declaration of Independence, composed an oratorio performed in 1781. But serious composers who wanted formal training usually went to France and Germany. They included Louis Moreau Gottschalk, who was this country's leading pianist-composer in the pre-Civil War years.

Gottschalk was born in New Orleans, where he lived for 13 years as a child and heard Negro and Latin American music in the Vieux Carré. When he went to Paris in 1842 to spend 11 years studying and performing, he drew on his background and wrote unique melanges of Afro-Caribbean rhythm and Creole melody, including "Bamboula" and "Le Bananier." With "Le Banjo" and other works based on American Negro songs, he became the first internationally known composer to make use of ideas stemming from the music of black Americans. Gottschalk toured Europe, South America, and the United States, performing his own compositions.

Only in the last 75 years or so have American composers generally begun to create classical music free of overwhelmingly European influence. They can be divided roughly into three groups: Those who established their individual melodic and tonal qualities on essentially European musical foundations, those who incorporated the indigenous sounds of folk music and jazz into their work, and the out-and-out iconoclasts who developed new sounds and systems—and even made new instruments.

Martha Graham *commissioned such ballets as Copland's* Appalachian Spring *and Barber's* Medea, *or* The Cave of the Heart, *and created her own powerful choreography.*

Echoes of Europe

The first full professor of music in America was John Knowles Paine, appointed to his post at Harvard University in 1875. He studied in Germany, and his music was based on major European forms. His finest compositions were conservative and coldly academic, but he later fell under the influence of the Romantic composers of the mid-19th century—particularly Robert Schumann and Richard Wagner—and his own works gained warmth and passion. Paine wrote a number of hymns and marches based on American themes and was working on a symphony, *Lincoln,* when he died in 1906.

Horatio Parker also studied in Germany and, starting in 1894, held the Chair of Music at Yale. An accomplished organist and composer of the traditional school, he is also remembered as the teacher of Charles Ives, the first influential composer of truly American music.

Walter Piston, who taught at Harvard, was another composer of distinctive talent. He was among the first of the traditionalists to break cleanly with the past and include dissonance and modern rhythmic patterns in his compositions. He won a Pulitzer Prize in 1948 for his Symphony No. 3 and another in 1961 for his Symphony No. 7. Leonard Bernstein, the composer and conductor who headed the New York Philharmonic from 1958 to 1969, was perhaps his most famous student.

Another traditionalist with an American slant is the Italian-American Gian Carlo Menotti, a consummate musical craftsman best known for his operas *The Medium* (1946), *The Consul* (1950), and *The Saint of Bleeker Street* (1954), and for his Christmas opera *Amahl and the Night Visitors,* written specifically for television.

Samuel Barber, essentially a romanticist of technical brilliance, won a Pulitzer Prize for his first opera, *Vanessa,* which has a libretto by Menotti. It was presented with great success at the Metropolitan Opera in 1958. Barber won a second Pulitzer Prize in 1963 for his Concerto for Piano and Orchestra, and his opera *Anthony and Cleopatra* opened the new Metropolitan Opera House in 1966. His ballet *The Cave of the Heart* was first danced by Martha Graham in 1946.

Another who composed for ballet, as well as the musical comedy stage, is Morton Gould. He also wrote more serious orchestral and solo works, particularly for his own instrument, the piano.

The works of Lukas Foss, a German-American conductor, composer, and pianist, show a gift for melody handled in brilliant personal style and include aspects of jazz as well as symphonic modernism.

New Sounds From America

One of the first to incorporate American Indian music into classical works was Edward MacDowell, who held the Chair of Music at Columbia College in 1896 and was considered the outstanding composer of his day.

John Alden Carpenter, a businessman-musician who studied with Paine at Harvard, used the sounds of jazz and ragtime in his compositions, particularly in his ballets. A folk legend about a famous American and a romantic version of the life of another American, together with some sounds of folk music, are the basis for two American operas, *The Devil and Daniel Webster* (1939) and *The Ballad of Baby Doe* (1958) by Douglas Moore. Some of the works of Roy Harris, such as *Cimarron* and *Folksong Symphony,* are specifically American, although his style is more personal than national.

Virgil Thomson, an influential critic and proponent of modern music, is often thought of as a folk-oriented composer; for example his two operas, *Four Saints in Three Acts* (1934) and *The Mother of Us All* (1947), include obvious echoes of American hymns and marches. Both of these operas have librettos by Gertrude Stein.

Persistent jazz rhythms are more evident in the early works of Aaron Copland than in those of any other classical composer. However, by the time the dean of American composers created his famous ballets, *Billy the Kid, Rodeo,* and *Appalachian Spring,* in the 1930's and 1940's, he was writing American music without such dependence on jazz. Louis Gruenberg composed *Jazzberries* and other jazz-related pieces; he is best known for his opera *Emperor Jones,* based on Eugene O'Neill's play. The opera was produced at the Metropolitan Opera in 1933 with the outstanding American singer and actor Lawrence Tibbett playing the title role.

Another composer steeped in Americana is Elie Siegmeister. Almost all his works, from the operetta *Hip-Hip-Hooray for NRA* (1933) to *American Sonata for Piano* (1944), reveal this interest.

Breaking New Musical Ground

Unlikely though it may seem, the first of the great American musical iconoclasts was a Connecticut insurance executive, Charles Ives. Ives' compositions were a tumultuous mixture of hymns, marches, ragtime, minstrel tunes, and European music scored for whatever instrumentation suited his fancy. He accepted wrong notes and off-key playing because he considered substance more important than technique. "If a man finds that the cadences of an Apache war dance come nearest his soul," said Ives, "he can use them fervently, transcendentally, inevitably, furiously in his symphonies, in his operas, in his whistlings on his way to work, [and] his music will be true to itself and, incidentally, American."

Ives' contribution to American music was not widely appreciated in his earlier years, but he was awarded a Pulitzer Prize in 1947, 7 years before his death, for his Symphony No. 3, which he had written in 1901–04 and revised in 1911. Ives was the first of several generations of Americans who have endeavored to push classical music beyond the limits of European tradition.

Carl Ruggles, born in 1876, was also a lifelong advocate of free musical expression and is best known for his symphony *Sun-Treader.* The next composer in the modern vein was Wallingford Riegger, who contributed some strong, pure, atonal pieces that are highly respected.

An admirer of Riegger and a vigorous advocate of all modern music was Henry Cowell. To get freedom of expression he used tone clusters, including sounds from the stroking and plucking of piano strings, oriental instruments and tonalities, and folksongs from everywhere.

Roger Sessions, a contemporary of Cowell's, wove a wide range of modern effects into more formal structures. One of his students, Vivian Fine, received a 1975 grant from the National Endowment for the Arts. Elliott Carter, a student of Walter Piston's, further broadened the scope of American classical music by successfully fusing modern dissonance and asymmetrical rhythms onto neoclassical frames. Carter had most of his training in America, although he also studied in France, as did his contemporary Louise Talma. Perhaps the most prolific woman composer in America, Talma has a long string of awards to her credit.

The most publicized of the avant garde Americans are Harry Partch and John Cage. Partch invented some 20 musical instruments and composed pieces for them using his own 43-tone scale. Cage, an accomplished composer in more conventional musical forms, is best known for his *Concerto for Prepared Piano.* Bobbypins, cellophane, and bits of wood and metal are put on the strings to create a random effect unique for each performance.

Inspirational Immigrants

America has long welcomed foreign artists in every field. Two of the world's most influential composers of modern music have strong American associations: Arnold Schoenberg, a Viennese, and Igor Stravinsky, a Russian. Schoenberg came to America in 1933 and became a U.S. citizen in 1940. He taught at the Malkin Conservatory in Boston and at the University of California. He died in Los Angeles in 1951. Schoenberg was an inspirational force all his life. His greatest influence, however, has been through his 12-tone (serial) music. Its dissonance and complexity found little popular acceptance, but his work has had a major influence on other modern composers. Schoenberg's development of serial composition forever changed the course of modern music.

Stravinsky lived in Russia, France, and Switzerland before he came to America in 1939. He became a U.S. citizen in 1945. Stravinsky created powerful works in every musical idiom. Among the major compositions he composed in America are two symphonies, a mass, two ballets, and the opera *The Rake's Progress* (1951). A writer as well, Stravinsky held the Charles Eliot Norton Chair of Poetry at Harvard in 1939–40.

Instrumentalists From Everywhere

America has been most receptive to the greatest of the European pianists and violinists, many of whom have become permanent residents. Such titans of the piano as Ignace Jan Paderewski, Artur Schnabel, Arthur Rubinstein, and Vladimir Horowitz, and violinists Fritz Kreisler, Jascha Heifetz, and, later, Isaac Stern—born in Russia, he received his musical training here—were perennial favorites of American audiences.

The Budapest String Quartet came here in the 1930's and made this country its base thereafter. In 1957 one of its members, Alexander Schneider, collaborated with the great Catalan cellist Pablo Casals in establishing

The Philadelphia Orchestra *gives a concert in its home, the Academy of Music, under Eugene Ormandy, its director since 1938. The pipes of the hall's great organ rise majestically in the background. Founded in 1900, the orchestra was the first to broadcast concerts and the first to make recordings. The hall itself has been the center for the performance of Philadelphia's concerts and operas since it opened in 1857.*

Puerto Rico's annual music festival, which is named in honor of Casals. Following the path of the Budapest Quartet, the Juilliard, La Salle, and Cleveland Quartets have earned devoted audiences.

Memories of Louis Moreau Gottschalk's foreign triumphs in the 1860's were revived by a young Texan pianist, Van Cliburn, who won the International Tchaikovsky Piano Competition in Moscow in 1958. Other young American pianists, such as Peter Serkin, Murray Perahia, Leon Fleisher, and André Watts, have established notable reputations both here and abroad. Among the younger violinists who have enjoyed wide acceptance are Erick Friedman, Eugene Fodor, and Pinchas Zukerman and Itzak Perlman (both of whom were born in Tel Aviv and came to this country to pursue their studies).

The Glory of the American Orchestras

Just as with instrumental soloists, the ensemble players in our symphony orchestras were at first drawn from Europe, but in recent years they have been largely replaced with American-trained musicians. The number of orchestras here has steadily grown, and today there are about 30 major orchestras. A major orchestra is classified as one that can play a full range of symphonic works, that has been active for at least 3 years, and that has had an annual budget of $1 million or more for at least 2 years. Other categories, also determined by budget, are metropolitan, urban, and community orchestras. There are more than 700 of these across the country.

The first American symphonic orchestra was the New York Philharmonic Society, organized in 1842. The orchestra, which is now the third oldest in the world, gained world renown in the late 1920's when Arturo Toscanini took the podium. His objective interpretations, his respect for the composer's intent, and his insistence on technical perfection set high standards for later conductors and musicians to live up to.

After Toscanini moved on to conduct radio's NBC Symphony, various eminent successors maintained the quality of the New York Philharmonic. The appointment of Leonard Bernstein as musical director in 1958 brought a new sense of power and excitement. The dynamic young Bernstein was the first American-born conductor to head a major symphony orchestra. His abundance of talent—as a composer of both classical and popular music and as a pianist, an educator, and a TV personality—made him one of the best known musical figures in the country. He retired from leadership of the Philharmonic in 1969 in order to have more time for composing. A noted successor was composer and conductor Pierre Boulez.

America's second oldest symphony orchestra is the Boston, founded in 1881. It had a succession of exceptional conductors. In its formative years the most influential of these were a Frenchman, Pierre Monteux, and a Russian, Serge Koussevitzky. Monteux, who led the orchestra from 1919 to 1924, was a man of elegance, charm, and impeccable musical taste. He encouraged the playing of new compositions and concentrated on broadening the orchestra's repertoire.

Koussevitzky, a powerful personality with an unceasing attention to detail and a sense of drama and color, raised the Boston Symphony Orchestra to new heights. It was during his tenure that the popular Berkshire Festival and Music Center were established at Tanglewood, in Lenox, Massachusetts. Orchestra members of the Boston Symphony also play summer concerts of popular and semi-classical music and short symphonic works. These appealing programs, the Boston Pops, began in 1930 and have been conducted from the outset by Arthur Fiedler, a fine musician of attractive modesty and good humor.

The third oldest of the great American orchestras is the Chicago Symphony. Established in 1891 as the Chicago Orchestra by Theodore Thomas, it developed one of the busiest and most ambitious schedules in its field. Its remarkable flexibility and responsiveness were created largely under the strict discipline and unerring technical facility of Fritz Reiner, its leader from 1953 until 1960. It reached a peak of excellence under Sir Georg Solti, who took over leadership in 1969.

Marian Anderson *sang at the Lincoln Memorial in 1939, after the Daughters of the American Revolution barred her from their Constitution Hall because she was black.*

The Philadelphia Orchestra, regarded by many critics as the world's most accomplished group of classical musicians, won much of its reputation during 24 years of forceful and colorful direction by Leopold Stokowski. Eugene Ormandy, who took over in 1938, maintained the Philadelphia's standing and added important modern works to its repertoire.

Also noted for its clean, clear sound and precise execution is the Cleveland Symphony Orchestra. Among its leaders have been Artur Rodzinski and Erich Leinsdorf, but the shaping force was George Szell, who was its musical director from 1946 until his death in 1970. Under Lorin Maazel the orchestra continued its distinctive heritage of musical excellence.

Opera in America

The first standard operas heard in this country were performed by a visiting French troupe in private homes in New Orleans in 1791. In the following years permanent theaters were built in New Orleans, including the French Opera (1859), which presented the American premieres of most of the important French works.

In New York the Park Theatre, which opened in 1825, was the first to be built for opera in that city. It was followed by the Italian Opera, the Astor Place Opera, and, in 1854, the influential Academy of Music. Philadelphia was introduced to opera in 1845 with a performance of William H. Fry's *Leonora,* the first grand opera written by an American. Chicago had its first full season of opera in 1865.

The Academy of Music in New York was sponsored by socialites who excluded the newly rich from the prestigious box seats. In retaliation a powerful group of millionaires built their own theater in 1883 and called it the Metropolitan Opera. The Met survived a series of buffeting changes in management and artistic points of view as well as a major fire and numerous financial crises to become America's principal opera house and to attract celebrated singers from all over the world.

Americans who helped make the Met one of the world's greatest houses were the colorful and charming Geraldine Farrar; Rosa Ponselle, a New Haven iceman's daughter who attained world renown; and Helen Traubel, who outraged her mentors by singing in nightclubs and appearing on television with comedian Jimmy Durante and others.

Tenor Roland Hayes was the first Negro classical singer to win international renown. He was soon followed by Marian Anderson, the matchless contralto for whose voice the critics could not find enough superlatives. Not far behind Miss Anderson in critical acclaim was soprano Dorothy Maynor. Both of these women were mainly recitalists, although Miss Anderson did make her debut at the Metropolitan in 1955. She also fostered the careers of other black artists by establishing the Marian Anderson Award in 1942. One of the winners was Grace Bumbry, a mezzo soprano of surpassing power. Another great Negro soprano is Leontyne Price, who sang at the Vienna State Opera and La Scala in Milan before making her Met debut in 1961. At the Met she was accorded one of the most resounding ovations ever heard in that demanding environment.

Among eminent white American singers were four whose origins lay in Hebrew liturgical music: tenors Jan Peerce and Richard Tucker and baritones Leonard Warren and Robert Merrill. Earlier baritones were Lawrence Tibbett and John Charles Thomas, both of whom went from opera to lucrative singing roles in the movies. American women who have won plaudits here and abroad for their singing of leading roles include Grace Moore, Gladys Swarthout, Risë Stevens, Regina Resnik,

Dorothy Kirsten, Eleanor Steber, Roberta Peters, Eileen Farrell, and Beverly Sills.

Interest in opera declined briefly in the United States in the mid-20th century but then rose to a new peak. In 1975 there were more than 50 U.S. opera companies with annual budgets of more than $500,000 and nearly 100 smaller companies. The largest American opera companies were the Metropolitan, the New York City Opera, the Lyric Opera of Chicago, and the San Francisco Opera Association. In addition to the regular companies, there were many annual festivals that included opera. Outstanding are programs of the Santa Fe Opera, the Saratoga (New York) Festival, and performances at the Wolf Trap Farm for the Performing Arts in Virginia.

Where Does the Music Start?

The emergence of American musicians and singers to positions of international prominence in both the popular and the classical fields can be traced to the unique character of U.S. musical education.

Training starts in kindergarten and is a continuing part of the ordinary school curriculum. Not the least of the incentives to take music courses in school is the lure of a place in a school orchestra, band, or singing group. Some 4.5 million students are active in school bands,

Electronic music, *a product of the mid-20th century, utilizes a variety of electronic equipment to create, shape, and control sounds and work them into ordered musical compositions. Above is composer Milton Babbitt working at the Columbia-Princeton Electronic Music Center in New York City with the RCA Mark II Synthesizer (installed in 1959). In the 1960's a portable commercial synthesizer was developed by Robert Moog. The Moog Synthesizer was used for the popular recording* Switched-On Bach, *created by Walter Carlos. In 1970 the first Pulitzer Prize ever given for a purely electronic composition was awarded to Charles Wuorinen for his* Time's Encomium.

choruses, and glee clubs. When Walter Camp established the rules for football in 1880, he could hardly have foreseen the effect the halftime break would have on the course of American music. The struggle for places in the marching bands that flourish during the football season can be as spirited as the competition for berths on the team itself. There are State and national contests for bands and soloists. For every Rose Bowl trombone player strutting before a national TV audience, there are thousands of aspirants practicing and hoping to be there some day.

Some 1,100 colleges offer degrees in music, and a number of schools are devoted entirely to the subject. A conservatory of music was established at Oberlin College in Ohio in 1867. Another pioneer in musical education was the Peabody Institute in Baltimore, founded in 1857 but delayed in opening until 1868 by the Civil War. The New England Conservatory of Music in Boston, founded in 1867, became one of the country's most prestigious music schools. Although the school was based on European standards, the appointment of Gunther Schuller as president in 1967 added a particularly American point of view. As a composer Schuller had been more successful than any other in blending jazz with classical as well as 12-tone and other serial music.

The Juilliard School of Music, established in 1920 in New York City, owes much to the influence of William Schuman, president from 1945 to 1962, and after Copland the most influential and frequently performed living composer. His successor, Peter Mennin, is also a distinguished composer. The Eastman School of Music of the University of Rochester (New York) flowered under the direction (1924–64) of the composer Howard Hanson, a staunch supporter of American music.

Another excellent school is the Curtis Institute of Music, founded in Philadelphia in 1924. The student orchestra has been conducted by such luminaries as Leopold Stokowski, Artur Rodzinski, and Fritz Reiner. The faculty has included pianist Josef Hofmann and violinists Leopold Auer and his pupil, Efrem Zimbalist, who became the institute's director. Zimbalist was succeeded as director by pianist Rudolph Serkin.

These and other schools are training the musicians who will create the sounds of tomorrow. While Beethoven, Brahms, and Bach are imperishable, their influence may well diminish as time passes. People who have grown up listening to the compositions of Babbitt, Cowell, Cage, or The Rolling Stones will generate music quite different from those whose idols were Handel, Mozart, or Duke Ellington. Music echoes the times. In America, a country of boundless variety, the music, too, has been diverse: From the tuneful melodies of Stephen Foster to the complex products of the 12-tone scale and the synthesizer. For the future it is likely that the classics, in every idiom, will survive and the search for new sounds will go on.

CHAPTER TWENTY-THREE

A Fresh Spirit in Literature

America's earliest literature flowed from the quill pens European explorers, and the wonder and promise told of proved a powerful lure to prospective settlers. Th Puritans, whose representatives colonized Massachuset and whose influence was felt in other Colonies, valued th written word primarily as a tool for religious instructio while they tolerated it as a medium for secular enlighten ment, they thoroughly condemned its use for frivolous en tertainment. Despite the limitations they set on writin the Puritans, as well as other colonists, placed a high val on education and laid an enduring foundation for literatur

By the time of the Revolution such native offerings

More than a century before the Pilgrims set foot on the forbidding New England coast, the most astonishing stories of America were circulated in the capitals of Europe. Spain's conquistadores wrote of the New World as a second Eden peopled by fascinating savages who dwelt in cities of solid gold and quaffed spring waters that conferred eternal youth. Later Jamestown's boastful Capt. John Smith, though more realistic than the Spanish dreamers, wrote romantically of a virginal continent. His intriguing writings on Virginia gave the new land a story that has passed into its folklore: the tale of the Indian princess Pocahontas who saved Smith's head from the chopping block—or so he said.

Wild and fanciful as this early literature may have been, it helped to entice the Pilgrims and other immigrants to America. And despite the unrelenting efforts of generations of realists who have brought the warts and blemishes of American life into sharp focus, the strain of optimism and hope first evidenced in the writings of the 16th and early 17th centuries has endured to this day. American literature has contributed mightily to the popular conviction that this is a land where men and women can start anew, a land where the only bounds to progress and self-improvement are the limitations of individuals themselves. This vision of America has been handed down from one generation of writers to the next. Sometimes it has been obscured by darker insights and observations, but it has never completely disappeared.

The Puritans Grow Eloquent

The Puritans may have been attracted by America's earliest chauvinists, but they did not permit their own authors to indulge in foolish optimism. The Puritan saw himself primarily as the instrument of his church and his God, and his view of mankind was not hopeful. He emphasized the fall of man through original sin and believed in the Calvinist doctrine of predestination: A man was either elected by God to go to heaven or was destined to go to hell; a virtuous life was the sign of the privileged elect. Although the Puritan considered the Bible a great source of worthwhile spiritual knowledge, he believed that salvation and a grasp of the eternal verities could not come from thumbing through books. "Jesus Christ is not got with a wet finger," Rev. Thomas Shepard cautioned in 1641 in *The Sincere Convert.*

But literature did have a role in Puritan Massachusetts. Its purpose, in sermons, religious tracts, and poetry, was twofold: to teach the flock and to keep the faithful on the straight and narrow path. Most often, the minister-authors of the time used the written word to instill the fear of everlasting damnation in their readers. Michael Wigglesworth's long poem *The Day of Doom* (1662), a New England bestseller that went through 10 editions in the century following its publication, prophesied a merciless Last Judgment. Wigglesworth painted a horrifyingly mechanistic God, who refused to heed the damned in their pleas for salvation. Even little children received no mercy—though they were consigned to "the easiest room in hell."

The Puritans shunned rich or elaborate imagery in their writing, as in their worship, but even the gloomy Wigglesworth could not always entirely smother his poetic impulses. Humanity, he wrote, was:

A restless Wave o' th' troubled Ocean,
A Dream, a lifeless Picture finely drest:
A Wind, a Flower, a Vapour, and a Bubble,
A Wheel that stands not still, a trembling Reed,
A Rolling Stone, dry Dust, light Chaff, and Stubble,
A Shadow of Something, but nought indeed.

Most of the poetry written by New England Puritans never found its way into print, however. Jotted in diaries or family albums, it was shown only to friends or rela-

enjamin Franklin's Poor Richard's Almanack *had elped to establish a sense of national identity among the olonists. In the Revolutionary epoch, fiery pamphleteers roved that literature could be highly effective in moving en to action. In the early and mid-1800's Washington ving, James Fenimore Cooper, and a remarkable group New Englanders gave voice to a fresh new culture that as no longer intellectually dependent on Europe.*

After the Civil War Bret Harte's colorful naturalism nd Mark Twain's native humor and delightful story-lling made indelible impressions on U.S. letters. Henry mes' novels were internationally recognized at the time the country was becoming a world power. Such post-World War I authors as Ernest Hemingway and T. S. Eliot gained worldwide recognition, as did William Faulkner and John Steinbeck in the 1930's. Eugene O'Neill's searching plays raised American drama to the level of literature and paved the way for the internationally known dramatists Arthur Miller and Tennessee Williams.

No more vivid record of the sum of a people's experience can be found than in their national literature. America's writers have given us living documents of all that has gone into the making of the greatest democracy in history, and the saga is still being written.

tives. The first book printed in the English Colonies was *The Whole Booke of Psalmes Faithfully Translated into English Metre* (1640), commonly known as the *Bay Psalm Book.* In their translations of the psalms, Richard Mather, John Eliot, and Thomas Weld, three of Massachusetts' leading Puritan divines, made no apology for the plainness of the language, declaring, "Gods Altar needs not our pollishings." But in the late 17th century iron Puritanism began to lose its grip. A flicker of rebellion was evident in the verses of Anne Bradstreet, who protested with gentle irony the Puritan fathers' low opinion of womankind. She came dangerously close to the heresy of questioning God's justice in one poem. Mourning the death of a grandchild, she wrote that it was the work of nature to cause trees to rot when they are grown,

But plants new set to be eradicate,
And buds new blown, to have so short a date,
Is by His hand alone that guides nature and fate.

More sharply at odds with Puritan taste was Rev. Edward Taylor, generally regarded today as the finest of the Puritan poets. Taylor published none of his poems while he lived and, according to tradition, even on his deathbed forbade their posthumous publication. Perhaps he feared the disapproval of his contemporaries. Fortunately, his writings survived in the collections of Yale University's library, where they came to light in 1937, more than 200 years after his death. To the modern reader Taylor's poetry seems hardly daring, but his evocation of the senses would have offended Puritan propriety.

Shall I not smell thy sweet, oh! Sharons Rose?
Shall not mine Eye salute thy Beauty? Why?
Shall thy sweet leaves their Beautious sweets upclose?
As halfe ashamde my sight should on them ly?

Even Cotton Mather, grandson of Richard and himself a renowned religious leader, did not restrict his prolific writings to the unvarnished prose style prescribed by the

The Poetic Riches of Puritan Edward Taylor

Although none of his poems were published during his lifetime, Edward Taylor is now considered the finest poet of the American Colonies. After his death his verse was handed down among his descendants. In 1883 it was finally given to Yale University's library, where it was put into an obscure corner and forgotten, a buried poetic treasure of high quality. Tradition has it that Taylor forbade publication. Perhaps he did so because most of his poems were deeply personal or because he feared that his sensual imagery might offend Puritan propriety. The poems were finally brought to light in 1937 and published for the first time 2 years later.

Edward Taylor was born in England, where he grew up under the rule of Oliver Cromwell's Commonwealth and became a staunch Puritan. After the Restoration Taylor refused to sign the Act of Conformity to accept the rites of the Anglican Church. In 1668 he came to America in search of religious freedom. He studied at Harvard and from 1671 to 1725 served as pastor and physician of the small farming community of Westfield, Massachusetts. He died there in 1729.

Taylor's major works are *God's Determinations Touching His Elect,* a long poem on the Calvinist doctrine of predestination, and *Preparatory Meditations,* a group of verses written to prepare himself for administering the Eucharist. The poems are full of extraordinary images and elaborate metaphors, in the tradition of England's Metaphysical poets. The *Meditations* begin with a prayer for guidance and a promise to praise God's works and make them "shine as flowers on stems/Or as in Jewellary Shops, do jems." In other poems Taylor depicts the soul as a bird in the cage of the body; describes himself as "God's gold" and begs God to "spend" him; and asks God to wash his soul in Zion's tub with holy soap. In *God's Determinations,* writing of the Creation, he asks: "Who in this Bowling Alley bowld the Sun?"

Puritans. His *Magnalia Christi Americana,* describing the ecclesiastical history of New England, was adorned with scholarly quotations and grandiloquent allusions. Although such Calvinist sermonizers as Jonathan Edwards, with their ever-present threats of hellfire and damnation, tried to stem the tide of romantic liberalism in the first half of the 18th century, it was to no avail.

A Southern Writer Mocks His Neighbors

In the South, meanwhile, a more gracious, more worldly literature was developing. Southern gentlemen, unhampered by dour religious training, were often educated in Britain and schooled in the classics. Southern poets, emulating such fashionable London writers as Alexander Pope and John Dryden, turned out sophisticated verse that could hardly be called American in flavor. The Southern colonial writer whose work has best stood the test of time is William Byrd the younger, the son of a wealthy Virginia planter. Byrd wrote perceptively and wittily of the planter's life and the frontier. He was a Virginia chauvinist who could be quite acid about other southerners. In *The History of the Dividing Line,* an account of a 1728 boundary survey, he mocked North Carolinians for their laziness:

When the Weather is mild, they stand leaning with both their arms upon the corn-field fence, and gravely consider whether they had best go and take a Small Heat at the Hough: but generally find reasons to put it off till another time. Thus they loiter away their Lives, like Solomon's Sluggard, with their Arms across, and at the Winding up of the Year Scarcely have Bread to Eat. To speak the Truth, tis a thorough Aversion to Labor that makes People file off to N[*orth*] *Carolina.*

Literature and the Struggle for Independence

In the Middle Colonies Benjamin Franklin was the dominant figure. After working as a printer under his half-brother James in Boston, Franklin ran away to Philadelphia and later went on to England. He returned to Philadelphia and in 1729 began publishing *The Pennsylvania Gazette.* Late in 1732 he brought out his first *Poor Richard's Almanack.* Richard's salty marginal comments made Franklin famous throughout the Colonies: "Three may keep a secret if two of them are dead." "Fish and visitors stink in three days." "A gloved cat can catch no mice." The pithy maxims, expressed in concise, no-nonsense language, did as much to create an image of an emerging American attitude as any writing in the decades before the Revolution. In *Poor Richard's Almanack* city shopkeeper and frontier farmer alike recognized elements of themselves. Here was a real American, not just a British subject 4,000 miles removed from "home." So, too, were those who heard their own voices in his words.

Franklin began his famous *Autobiography* in 1771, but years were to pass before he could return to it. Like other men of letters throughout the Colonies, he gave himself wholeheartedly to the struggle for independence. Never before had the written word been so important in moving men to action. The battle to win converts to the cause of national independence was waged with pamphlets and broadsides—a remarkable body of incendiary writings that was to inspire later revolutionists all around the world. Thomas Paine, whose *Common Sense* was the most powerful of the pamphlets, James Otis, John Dickinson, Thomas Jefferson, and others stirred the blood and fired the imagination. When the war had been won but the

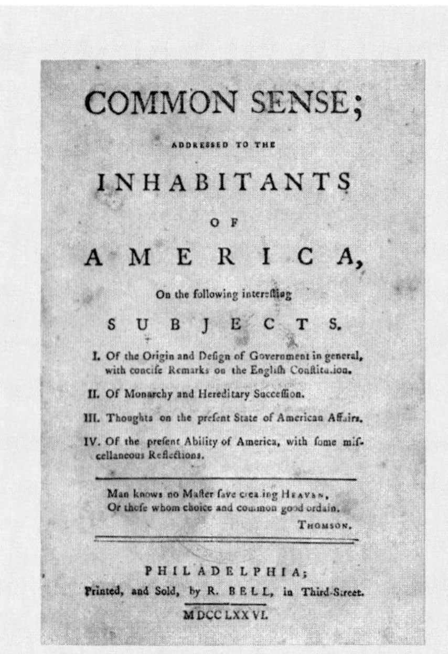

COMMON SENSE;

ADDRESSED TO THE

INHABITANTS

OF

AMERICA,

On the following interesting

SUBJECTS.

I. Of the Origin and Design of Government in general, with concise Remarks on the English Constitution.

II. Of Monarchy and Hereditary Succession.

III. Thoughts on the present State of American Affairs.

IV. Of the present Ability of America, with some miscellaneous Reflections.

Man knows no Master save creating HEAVEN,
Or those whom choice and common good ordain.
THOMSON.

PHILADELPHIA;
Printed, and Sold, by R. BELL, in Third-Street.
MDCCLXXVI.

Thomas Paine, Patriot Pamphleteer

A tempestuous, restless man, Thomas Paine became involved in the histories of three nations: his native England, France, and—especially—America. After losing a position as officer of the excise because he had written a fiery pamphlet about the corruption in the service resulting from poor salaries, he met Benjamin Franklin, who sent him to America. Paine arrived in late 1774 and became an editor of the *Pennsylvania Magazine* in Philadelphia. As soon as the Revolution broke out he began advocating separation from Britain.

In January 1776 he anonymously published *Common Sense.* The pamphlet charged that the Crown was hampering the economic growth of the Colonies, that a monarchy was a corrupt form of government, and that it was impossible to govern a land from 3,000 miles away. Paine's series of tracts, *The Crisis,* was so stirring that George Washington ordered the first one—which begins "These are the times that try men's souls"—to be read to all his troops in December 1776.

In 1787 Paine returned to England. After writing *The Rights of Man,* a defense of the French Revolution which urged the English to overthrow their monarchy, he was forced to flee to France. There he was elected to national office and ultimately got into trouble for voting against the execution of the deposed King Louis XVI. His *Age of Reason,* a deistic treatise opposing organized religion, alienated many of his friends. Paine returned to America in 1802 and died in 1809.

"The Legend *of Sleepy Hollow," by Washington Irving, tells of the humbling of Ichabod Crane, a humorless, self-centered schoolteacher whose lean, lanky frame conceals a greed for food and wealth. Ichabod visits the prosperous farmer Baltus Van Tassel, hoping to win his daughter Katrina's hand and eventually inherit the farm. After dinner, tales are told of the headless horseman who haunts the nearby Sleepy Hollow cemetery. Ichabod's chief rival for Katrina's affection, the mettlesome and mischievous Brom Van Brunt, known as Brom Bones because of his brawn, makes light of the dread specter, but Ichabod is frightened. While riding home through Sleepy Hollow, he senses that the ghostly rider is following him. Looking back, he sees the fiend wrench off his head and throw it at him. But, as George W. Jenkinson's painting "The Headless Horseman" suggests, the phantom Ichabod saw was only Brom Bones with a pumpkin. The schoolteacher flees town in disgrace.*

future of the Nation was still in grave doubt, another group of writers came to the fore in the cause of national unity and strength. In the brilliantly reasoned and strongly persuasive essays that formed *The Federalist* papers (1787–88), Alexander Hamilton, James Madison, and John Jay grappled with the problems of establishing a durable democracy. To this end, they urged the ratification of the new U.S. Constitution. As Hamilton put the issue in one essay:

The people of this country, by their conduct and example, will decide the important question, whether societies of men are really capable or not of establishing good government from reflection and choice, or whether they are forever destined to depend for their political constitutions on accident and force.

During the formative years of the Republic, the Nation produced some of the finest political writing in history, but fiction and poetry suffered. Poets such as John Trumbull, Timothy Dwight, and Joel Barlow, popularly known as the Hartford Wits, and Philip Freneau, often called the Poet of the American Revolution, were so absorbed in national issues that they scanted their writings. Most novels of the era were, in the European fashion, harrowing stories of mistreated damsels and conscience-stricken heroes, such as William Hill Brown's *The Power of Sympathy.* The novelist Charles Brockden Brown was widely praised for his Gothic tales of horror and violence, though his work suffered from the same ills that afflicted his lesser contemporaries: a marked imitativeness of such fashionable British authors as Horace Walpole, who wrote the first Gothic novel, *The Castle of Otranto* (1764), Mrs. Ann Radcliffe, and Matthew Lewis.

A Uniquely American Literature Emerges

Although America had ended its political dependency on Britain, it had not yet cut its literary ties. As British critic Sydney Smith pointed out in 1820:

Literature the Americans have none—no native literature, we mean. It is all imported. . . . But why should the Americans write books, when a six weeks' passage brings them in our own tongue, our sense, science and genius, in bales and hogsheads?

Smith was mistaken in his deduction; the eager reception given to Washington Irving and James Fenimore Cooper when they began publishing authentically native stories proved that Americans had been starved for a truly national literature.

Irving's *The Sketch Book,* containing "Rip Van Winkle" and "The Legend of Sleepy Hollow," began appearing in installments in the press in 1819. Its subsequent publication in London made Irving the first American writer to win international recognition. By the end of his career he had successfully staked his country's claim to literary significance. Even before *The Sketch Book,* Irving was known at home for *A History of New York,* written under the pen name of Diedrich Knickerbocker. Late in his life Irving reminisced that he had written this charming satire:

Natty Bumppo, *a hunter known as Leatherstocking because he wore deerskin leggings, disagrees with Judge Temple about who shot a stag. The illustration is from an 1862 edition of James Fenimore Cooper's* The Pioneers, *first of the Leatherstocking Tales, originally published in 1823.*

. . . to clothe home scenes and places and familiar names with those imaginative and whimsical associations so seldom met with in our new country, but which live like charms and spells about the cities of the old world, binding the heart of the native inhabitant to his home.

While weaving a unique fabric of American folklore, Irving accomplished still more. In *The Sketch Book* he created a new literary form: the short story. Virtually every 19th-century writer who came after him turned to Irving to learn the magic of this art. And in Rip Van Winkle, who slept for 20 years, Irving created a stock figure in American literature—the individual who rebels against the tyrannical mentality of the small town, with its pressures to succeed at any cost. (Rip was also rebelling against his shrewish wife.) This theme is still with us.

James Fenimore Cooper, Irving's contemporary, did even more to originate a uniquely American literature. In his Leatherstocking Tales, which appeared between 1823 and 1841 and included *The Last of the Mohicans, The Pathfinder,* and *The Deerslayer,* Cooper created the first great American hero, the frontiersman. Whether he went by the name of Natty Bumppo, Hawkeye, or Leatherstocking, Cooper's resourceful scout triumphed over the terrifying wilderness by wiles and skills he had learned from nature herself. Cooper's novels were bought as eagerly in Europe as at home.

In this same period the new Nation's first poet of stature emerged. William Cullen Bryant might have given up poetry had his father not discovered his manuscripts in an old desk and sent them to the *North American Review.* "Thanatopsis," which Bryant had written when he was only 16, appeared in the *Review* in 1817. Besides writing verse, Bryant also made his mark in journalism as editor of the *New York Evening Post.* He lectured widely, emphasizing the importance of poetry in the national culture and urging writers to break free of European influence. His pride in America is apparent in these lines from "The Prairies," written after a journey through the West:

These are the gardens of the Desert, these
The unshorn fields, boundless and beautiful,
For which the speech of England has no name.

Emerson and the Concord Group

In the first three decades of the 19th century luminaries such as Irving and Bryant made New York the literary capital of America, but in mid-century the center of gravity shifted back to New England. There a remarkable array of talents was to produce many of the works now recognized as classics. At the heart of this cultural flowering was the Concord Group, most of whose members were devoted followers of Ralph Waldo Emerson and his Transcendentalist philosophy. In 1837 Emerson, then 34 years old, delivered an address, "The American Scholar," before the Phi Beta Kappa Society at Harvard. It was later hailed as "Our Intellectual Declaration of Independence" by Oliver Wendell Holmes. "Our day of dependence, our long apprenticeship to the learning of other lands draws to a close," said Emerson. "We have listened too long to the courtly muses of Europe."

The Concord Group published a literary magazine, *The Dial,* and founded a pair of Utopian communities, Brook Farm and Fruitlands, which offered followers a chance to get away from the city, to work on the land, and to enjoy the intellectual stimulation of fellow Transcendentalists. First outlined in Emerson's 1836 essay "Nature" and further described in his later writings, Transcendentalism held that only human intuition could discern the truths of the universe. Man had to remove himself from the routines of ordinary experience and observation, and put himself in a quiet setting where his inner being could have free play. "The materialist takes his departure from the external world . . . the idealist . . . from his consciousness," Emerson wrote. Later he recognized that Transcendentalism was largely "the very oldest of thoughts cast into the mould of the new times." In this mood he could chide his followers for totally withdrawing from the labors of the world: ". . . they are not good citizens," he said, "not good members of society; unwillingly they bear their part of the public . . . burdens. They do not even like to vote."

Emerson and the other Transcendentalists steadfastly maintained their opposition to overemphasis on material progress, however. "Soon these . . . mechanical inventions will be superseded . . . these cities rotted," he wrote,

". . . but the thoughts which these few hermits strove to proclaim shall abide in beauty. . . ."

The most renowned of the "hermits" was Henry David Thoreau, who truly sought to practice Transcendentalist ideals in his daily life. His mistrust of most forms of social organization, particularly government, found expression in his essay "Civil Disobedience" (1849), which argued that citizens need not obey unjust laws. Thoreau inspired many of his contemporaries, and such later figures as Mahatma Gandhi of India and Rev. Martin Luther King, Jr., owed much to him. His most famous book, *Walden,* has the quality of Transcendentalist scripture. It describes the 2 years that Thoreau spent living as a virtual recluse in a simple cabin on the banks of Walden Pond, near Concord.

Titans of the Mid-19th Century

The era of Emerson was one of unparalleled literary ferment in the United States. Four men, especially, gave depth and power to American literature at that time: Nathaniel Hawthorne and Herman Melville, both novelists; Edgar Allan Poe, poet and short-story writer; and Walt Whitman, whose verse glorified his native land.

Nathaniel Hawthorne was a New Englander who spent some time at Brook Farm, a none too happy experience on which he drew for his fictional satire, *The Blithedale Romance.* Hawthorne shared little of the Transcendentalists' philosophy or approach to life. His masterpiece, *The Scarlet Letter* (1850), a psychological study of the New England mentality, is rich in symbolism and relentless in its exposure of the hypocrisy and repressiveness of Puritan society. The novel's heroine, Hester Prynne, is regarded by many critics as one of the most compelling figures in American fiction, and Hawthorne himself is acknowledged as the father of the American psychological novel.

While Hawthorne was at work on his own favorite novel, *The House of the Seven Gables,* he encouraged the younger writer Herman Melville, who had already published several books, including *Typee* and *Omoo,* based on his experiences aboard a whaling ship in the South Seas. These were adventure yarns, spiced with Polynesian trimmings. Under Hawthorne's influence, Melville set forth on his voyage into the seas of psychological obses-

Walden Pond, *so loved by Thoreau, is cloaked in legend. Long ago, it is said, Indians held a powwow on a high hill. They used so much profanity that the hill turned inside out and became Walden Pond.*

Thoreau and the Concord Group

Transcendentalism Comes Alive

From 1845 to 1847 Henry David Thoreau lived in the woods on Walden Pond, near Concord, Massachusetts, in a crude cabin he had built himself. He walked through the woods observing nature; worked to extract food, clothing, and a few primitive comforts from his natural environment; read a little; and on rare occasions received visitors. Later he wrote down his experiences, compressing them into a narrative spanning a single year beginning with spring. This book, *Walden,* published in 1854, reflected the inner and outer life of a man who had succeeded in putting into full practice the philosophy of Transcendentalism advocated by the Concord Group.

The group took its name from the hometown of its leader, Ralph Waldo Emerson. Besides Thoreau, it included author and educator Amos Bronson Alcott and his daughter Louisa May Alcott, who wrote the children's classic *Little Women;* the author, critic, and feminist Margaret Fuller; and novelist Nathaniel Hawthorne. All except Hawthorne adhered to the Transcendentalist views expounded by Emerson in his influential essays. According to Emerson, nature is another side of God, and every law of nature has a counterpart in the intellect. The soul of man is divine and identical in all men. In studying nature, therefore, man discovers truths about his own soul and about God. Emerson also emphasized the importance of self-reliance. Conformity, he claimed, deadened the soul and suffocated individuality; civilization's accoutrements have emasculated mankind, and man must return to nature and listen to the promptings of his soul.

Members of the Concord Group founded the communities of Brook Farm and Fruitlands, hoping to live their ideals there, working the land and discussing their philosophy. Both these utopias failed, but Thoreau, alone in the woods on Walden Pond, on land belonging to Emerson, proved that one determined man could turn Transcendentalism into a rewarding experiment.

Herman Melville, Literary Genius

From South Sea Romances to Works of Universal Significance

He might have spent his adult life among cannibals in the South Seas or—even worse—he might have perished there, but fortunately he managed to escape and ultimately wrote some of the finest novels in the English language. Herman Melville, one of eight children of a New York merchant, was only 12 years old when his bankrupt father died. Young Herman worked at various jobs to help support the family, even teaching elementary school, although he had had little formal education himself.

In 1837 he went to sea and found the life to his taste. In 1841 he signed aboard the whaling vessel *Acushnet,* but the life of a whaler was too grueling and after 18 months he jumped ship in the Marquesas Islands. After foraging through thick jungle for 5 days he was captured by local Typees, who were believed to be cannibals. Although Melville was treated well and lived a generally idyllic life among the natives, he escaped and eventually found his way home.

Back in America Melville wrote romantically of his adventures in the novels *Typee* (1846) and *Omoo* (1847). The books were so popular that he wrote a number of other novels of the sea and then created his masterpiece, *Moby-Dick.* Although acclaimed today, this probing, symbolic novel lost Melville many of his readers when it was published in 1851. But he persisted in writing works of great depth throughout the rest of his life. His later works include the stories "Benito Cereno" and "Bartleby the Scrivener," four volumes of poems, and the novels *Pierre; The Confidence Man, His Masquerade;* and *Billy Budd, Foretopman.*

Herman Melville (*1819–91*)

Captain Ahab *paces the deck of his ship, the* Pequod, *his soul possessed with the idea of destroying Moby-Dick, the white whale who took off his leg.* Moby-Dick *embodies realism, romance, adventure, symbolism, and psychological insight. It is a probing study of good and evil, of man against destructive nature, and of the problem of reconciling the existence of suffering and a good and just God. The work combines aspects of fiction, medieval drama, and Shakespearean tragedy and is a detailed account of daily life on a whaling vessel. Few works of literature approach it in its magnitude. These two illustrations are by Rockwell Kent for a 1930 edition of Melville's masterpiece.*

sion and the war between good and evil—his titanic masterwork, *Moby-Dick.* Although *Moby-Dick*'s brooding symbolism put off most readers at the time of its publication, as did his other later works, Melville's story of Captain Ahab's impassioned pursuit of the white whale is now considered a monument of American letters. Melville's story "Benito Cereno" and his short novel *Billy Budd, Foretopman,* which was discovered in manuscript form years after his death in 1891, rank with the world's finest psychological studies of virtuous innocence in conflict with entrenched wickedness.

No major American literary figure inspired such strong differences of judgment as did Edgar Allan Poe. The French saluted Poe as a great poet, and Britain's Alfred, Lord Tennyson, considered him the most original American writer of the time. But at home, partly because of his sometimes cutting literary criticism, Poe made more enemies than friends. Emerson disparaged him as "the jingle man," while Henry James later branded any enthusiasm for Poe as a mark of primitive taste. Although Poe was employed by various magazines and papers as editor and critic from time to time, he was hard pressed financially, and his alcoholic bouts and periods of extreme depression contributed to this condition. He wrote many of his best tales—including the detective stories "The Murders in the Rue Morgue" and "The Purloined Letter"—in a desperate effort to support himself. Publication of *The Raven and Other Poems* in 1845 brought him international fame as a poet. Poe hated most members of the New England establishment who then reigned supreme over American letters. Of the Transcendentalists he remarked: "The fact is, that in efforts to soar above our nature, we invariably fall below it. Your reformist demigods are merely devils turned inside out." To the end his pervasive theme was the inevitable ruin of mortal man. In "Annabel Lee," a poem that appeared just after his death in 1849, he wrote:

And so, all the night-tide, I lie down by the side
Of my darling, my darling, my life and my bride,
In her sepulchre there by the sea—
In her tomb by the side of the sea.

However much distaste the New England literary set may have felt for Poe, it soon had an appropriate candidate for its accolades. Emerson had expressed a wish for a poet who would sing of "our log-rolling, our stumps and their politics, our fisheries, our Negroes and Indians . . . the northern trade, the southern planting, the western clearing, Oregon and Texas. . ." When Walt Whitman published the first of nine editions of *Leaves of Grass* in 1855, Emerson proclaimed the advent of the man he had been looking for. Whitman set out to portray America through a single all-encompassing voice—a distillation of the American genius and personality. His narrator tells the reader in "Song of Myself":

I celebrate myself, and sing myself,
And what I assume you shall assume,
For every atom belonging to me as good belongs to you.

In an early draft of this important poem he had phrased the idea thus: "I am your voice—it was tied in you—in me it begins to talk." In unrhymed, meterless verse, Whitman chanted the praise of American democracy and the ordinary man. Unquestionably, he stands among the great innovators of American letters: For many he remains the greatest of the Nation's poets.

The most widely read author of the 1850's was Harriet Beecher Stowe, whose powerful novel *Uncle Tom's Cabin* was first serialized in *The National Era,* then published in book form in 1852. It sold more than 300,000 copies during its first year in print. Boston, where Mrs. Stowe published her diatribe against slavery, remained the national literary capital. America's cultural arbiters were the so-called Boston Brahmins, an elite group whose major voice was *The Atlantic Monthly.* The magazine was founded in 1857 by the cream of the Brahmin crop, including Henry Wadsworth Longfellow, Oliver Wendell Holmes, and James Russell Lowell. Longfellow won popularity at home and abroad with such poems as "The Village Blacksmith" and the epic *Evangeline* (1847). He is the only American honored in Westminster Abbey with a bust in the Poets' Corner. Holmes, a prominent physician, essayist, and poet who gave the magazine its name, was the leading intellectual tastemaker of his day.

The Atlantic Monthly was to have an incalculable effect on American letters. Under such editors as James Russell Lowell, briefly, and William Dean Howells for a longer period, the magazine discovered, published, and encouraged an extraordinarily varied list of native talents, including Bret Harte, Mark Twain (whose real name was Samuel Clemens), John Greenleaf Whittier, known as the Quaker Poet, Henry James, Stephen Crane, Frank Norris, Hamlin Garland, and Sarah Orne Jewett. Such writers brought into the mainstream of national literature the whole sweep of America: Jewett's decaying Maine seaports, Twain's Mississippi River towns, Garland's Midwestern farms and prairies, Harte's west coast mining camps. Both Lowell and Howells were distinguished writers themselves. Lowell was acclaimed by his contemporaries for his poetry and his social and political essays. Howells published 35 novels, among them *The Rise of Silas Lapham,* as well as poetry, dramas, and literary criticism.

By the middle of the 19th century a solid foundation had been laid for a broadly based, indigenous literature. Irving had given the infant Nation the confidence to take its first independent steps. Cooper and Whitman portrayed a national character combining frontier courage and resourcefulness, a sense of grand destiny, and boundless energy and optimism. The dark side of the

American dream was suggested in the hauntingly symbolic works of Hawthorne and Melville, who saw in the American character as much cause for worry as for hope. Bright promise and achievement existing side by side with doubt and self-criticism—this is a duality that constantly reappears in American literature.

The Civil War Spawns a New Realism

Reasons for the ascendancy of gloom soon became apparent. The Civil War has been called the Great Divide of American history. Brother took up arms against brother; the Southern dream of a prosperous and courtly gentility was brought to ruin; the ideal of equality for all men proved illusory; and, along with everything else, the war set in motion forces of industrialization that soon transformed American society. The virgin countryside was everywhere disappearing. In its place was a land crisscrossed by roads and steel rails. City slums were swollen with millions of immigrants. The once pure skies wore veils of soot and smoke. America's pastoral concerns were replaced by an awesome set of new problems: Big-city poverty, the violence of strikers confronting bosses, and the inroads of unbridled monopolies and trusts threatening the public interest. These phenomena were bound to encourage straightforward writing about social and economic conditions.

Curiously, the first expression of this new realism came not from the industrial cities of the North but from the still comparatively unspoiled West. In his short story "The Luck of Roaring Camp," published in *The Overland Monthly* in 1868, Bret Harte—an easterner who had gone west—painted a graphic picture of a mining camp, complete with profane roughnecks and degraded Indian prostitutes. On the strength of this and such other stories as "The Outcasts of Poker Flat," Harte's fame grew in Europe as well as in America and started the trend toward greater realism. Humor, too, was a flourishing literary genre. Artemus Ward (the pseudonym of Charles Farrar Browne) and Josh Billings (Henry Wheeler Shaw) had already made names for themselves when Mark Twain's humorous story "The Celebrated Jumping Frog of Calaveras County" appeared in 1865. Its quick popularity, together with the counsel and assistance of friends, caused Twain to turn from journalism to more fiction writing. His *The Adventures of Tom Sawyer, The Adventures of Huckleberry Finn,* and the autobiographical *Life on the Mississippi* stand today as landmarks of wit and wisdom and as reminders of the vitality and earthiness of the young American heartland.

Not all the writing in the era dominated by Bret Harte and Mark Twain was relentlessly realistic. Relief was provided in the romantic but honest Louisiana Creole novels of George Washington Cable and the charming Southern folklore of Joel Chandler Harris' Uncle Remus tales. But lusty and earthy works led in popularity, and this troubled many critics. The much respected editor Charles Dudley Warner wrote in the early 1880's:

The characteristics which are prominent, when we think of our recent fiction, are a wholly unidealized view of human society, which has got the name of realism; a delight in representing the worst phases of social life.

Bret Harte and Mark Twain were rebuked by numerous keepers of the public conscience for dwelling on unsavory heroes and thus teaching bad "moral lessons."

But the critics could not stop the best authors from exposing what was unhappy and—in the view of some of them—even rotten in American life. These writers were not merely exploiting seamy material; most of them were at heart reformers who hoped to prod the Nation into remedying its ills. Stephen Crane, considered by many to have set the laconic style later adopted by Ernest Hemingway and other leading 20th-century realists, lived only 28 years. But in *Maggie: A Girl of the Streets* he drew attention to the growing problem of prostitution among the big-city poor. And his spare, staccato prose in the Civil War novel *The Red Badge of Courage* (1895) brought home the horror of war more emphatically than had any previous American work on the subject. The torrent of unflinching realism culminated around the turn of the century in the sensational polemics of the muckraking era. Like the journalists of the period, such writers as Frank Norris, in *The Pit,* and Upton Sinclair, in *The Jungle* and *Oil!,* vented their anger against a wide spectrum of social and economic evils, ranging from urban poverty to the irresponsibility of big business.

The Romantic Introspectionists

All the while, however, a quieter brand of literary endeavor—a stream of more personal writing—had won its own adherents. The major figure of this group was Emily Dickinson, a New Englander virtually unknown in her lifetime but now regarded as one of our greatest poets. Much of her work was scrawled on scraps of paper, which she hid away. After her death in 1886 a devoted sister shepherded her poems into print, the first volume appearing in 1890. Intense honesty of feeling was Emily Dickinson's hallmark, as exemplified in this couplet:

I like a look of agony
Because I know it's true.

Unlike the frontier and urban realists, who fixed their attention on the consequences of human behavior, she dwelt on the hidden emotions that animate or destroy.

The masterful novelist of psychology and manners, Henry James, also saw his province as the inner life of the individual, or, as he put it, "an immense sensibility, a kind of huge spider web of the finest silken threads, suspended in the chamber of consciousness." James was a brother of the renowned pragmatist and psychologist

Mark Twain
A Man of the River

The Mississippi River cuts a strong, wide swath through the heartland of America. In the untrammeled flow of the Mississippi's waters, many see a symbol of the freedoms guaranteed by the Constitution; in the force of its currents, a reflection of the strength of the American character. Among the millions who have drawn inspiration from the mighty river, none is more dyed-in-the-wool American than Samuel Langhorne Clemens, better known to the world as Mark Twain.

Sam Clemens was raised in Hannibal, Missouri, a small town on the Mississippi. In 1847, when he was 12 years old, his father died; the boy quit school and started working for a printer. Stimulated by the material he was handling, he soon began writing stories of his own and later became a journalist. From 1857 to 1861 Clemens worked as a riverboat pilot. Judging from his later writings, his years on the Mississippi from boyhood through his career as a pilot were the happiest of Clemens' life. The observations he made on the river nourished much of his later work, and the people he knew there helped form his concepts of humanity and the world.

After serving a brief term with a company of confused Confederate volunteers—an experience hilariously recalled in "The Campaign That Failed"—Clemens in 1861 went to Nevada Territory. There—after unsuccessful attempts at prospecting—he returned to journalism and short-story writing. It was at that time that he adopted the pen name Mark Twain, a riverman's term for 2 fathoms deep. In 1867 Mark Twain left the West to tour Europe and the Holy Land, sending back humorous travel sketches later collected in *The Innocents Abroad.* On his return to America he settled in the Northeast, married, and spent the rest of his life writing, lecturing, and traveling. He died in 1910.

The Mississippi, *depicted in the Currier & Ives print at top, inspired the best writings of Mark Twain (above). At left is a Norman Rockwell illustration for* Tom Sawyer.

Mark Twain is generally recognized as America's greatest humorist. His many stories and sketches are colored with a caustic wit that penetrates to the core of his characters and shows up their foibles. He was a shrewd chronicler of his times and a fine novelist. His *Life on the Mississippi* is a magnificent study of what it was like on the river before and after the Civil War. *The Adventures of Tom Sawyer,* with its incident of the rascally Tom hoodwinking his friends into whitewashing his Aunt Polly's fence, is one of the most entertaining boys' books ever written. But *The Adventures of Huckleberry Finn* is Twain's masterpiece. On the surface it is also a book for juveniles, but ultimately it is a penetrating look at the human estate and the decaying civilization of the ante bellum South. It is a uniquely American work—the first major novel written in an idiom that is wholly American. Another great novelist, Ernest Hemingway, felt that all modern American literature stemmed from this one book by Mark Twain.

William James. For most of his adult life he lived in England and ultimately became a British subject, since he believed that only an "old civilization" offered fertile ground for the novelist's art. Among American writers he esteemed only the brooding Nathaniel Hawthorne; yet he considered even Hawthorne too provincial and preferred such European masters as Turgenev and Balzac for his own models. Nonetheless, James' most memorable characters were Americans. Like the heroine in *Daisy Miller* (1878), James' American characters are generally visiting or traveling in Europe. In this way James could use them to draw distinctions between American and European manners and attitudes. The author's slow, complex, analytical style, which subjected almost every thought and deed to many-sided questioning and explanation, won as many detractors as admirers.

Interestingly, while James was writing of Americans abroad, the Nation was flexing its muscles as a world power. If James' purpose was to Europeanize American letters, he fell short. But his finest novels, such as those written in the early 1900's—*The Wings of the Dove, The Ambassadors,* and *The Golden Bowl*—are recognized classics; they stand as milestones in America's intellectual journey toward international significance.

Henry James was not alone in his dissatisfactions with America. Historian Henry Adams, the direct descendant of two U.S. Presidents, deplored the quality of our national culture in his autobiography, *The Education of Henry Adams,* privately published in 1907. Hamlin Garland's brutal documentations of rural poverty, such as *Main-Travelled Roads,* flouted even the old dream of a land that yielded bountiful harvests in return for honest and intelligent labor. Edith Wharton, emulating James, moved abroad to aim her fire against her homeland's restrictive social conventions in such novels as *The House of Mirth* and *The Age of Innocence.* Her short novel *Ethan Frome* drew a stark picture of the bleak life and environment of a New England farmer. Even so confirmed a nativist and Marxian socialist as Jack London eventually turned his back on the domestic scene and wrote romances of the lost wilderness and the vanishing frontier. In his most popular novels, such as *The Call of the Wild,* he found virtue in animal heroes, not in men. Another writer to turn away from adverse circumstances in order to create romantic tales was O. Henry (William Sydney Porter), who had spent more than 3 years in an Ohio prison after being convicted of embezzlement. Settling in New York City—he nicknamed it Bagdad-on-the-Subway—in 1902, 8 years before his death, he achieved popular success with his short stories.

Why these evidences of disappointment in America, just when the United States was savoring its first taste of glory as a world power? Surely U.S. democracy, with all its imperfections, offered greater hope than anything before. Perhaps the answer lay in this very fact, which had engendered an excess of idealism and impatient optimism in literary circles. With the Nation entering adulthood, certain writers saw it to be prey to many of the same ills as those of the older countries, while remaining a raw, crude land, lacking the opulent trappings and rich cultural traditions of France or Britain.

If World War I did not clear away the pessimism pervading much of the Nation's literature, it did decisively establish the United States as a world power of the first magnitude. Respect for the country whose intervention had tipped the military balance in the war gained an almost automatic hearing for its artists, writers, and

MAKING DEMOCRACY WORK

"The Jungle" and the Pure Food and Drug Acts

Working conditions in the Chicago stockyards were incredibly bad. Hours were long, pay was low, and the work was backbreaking. In the fertilizer rooms the acids damaged the soles of the workers' feet. Men sometimes fell into the lard vats. Children were worked to the breaking point. One such child was Stanislovas.

Hour after hour, day after day, year after year, it was fated that he should stand upon a certain square foot of floor from seven in the morning until noon, and again from half-past twelve till half-past five, making never a motion and thinking never a thought, save for the setting of lard-cans. In summer the stench of the warm lard would be nauseating, and in winter the cans would all but freeze to his naked little fingers in the unheated cellar. . . . And for this, at the end of the week, he would carry home three dollars to his family, being his pay at the rate of five cents per hour.

These are only a few of the horrors described by Upton Sinclair in his brutally realistic novel of the Chicago stockyards, *The Jungle.* The book was written after the 27-year-old Sinclair, spurred by a strike that had been forcibly put down, went to the stockyards and lived and talked with the workers there.

The Jungle, first published serially in the Socialist paper *The Appeal to Reason,* was intended to arouse sympathy for the plight of the poor laborers. However, its publication in 1906, plus Dr. Harvey Wiley's earlier books reporting on the use of poisonous additives in manufactured foods, principally brought public demands for action to protect the consumer. President Theodore Roosevelt responded by getting Congress to pass two trailblazing laws: the Meat Inspection Act of 1906, providing strict Federal inspection of meats to eliminate unwholesome and unsanitary products, and the Pure Food and Drug Act of 1906, making illegal the interstate shipment of adulterated and mislabeled foods and drugs. *The Jungle* not only proved to be a powerful novel but also helped effect needed legislation.

The exquisitely refined *world of Henry James is reflected in Childe Hassam's "Washington Arch in Spring" (1890). James was born in this elegant New York City neighborhood, and it is the setting for his novel* Washington Square *(1881), later dramatized as* The Heiress.

intellectuals. But America, unlike most European nations, had gone to war in a mood of soaring idealism, epitomized in Woodrow Wilson's stated hope of "making the world safe for democracy." The war's destruction of lives and societies, followed by social upheaval and uncertainty, compounded the disillusionment of American thought, which was reflected in American letters.

The New Poets

Shortly before World War I the so-called New Poets had begun to emerge, aided by Harriet Monroe's magazine, *Poetry,* founded in 1912. Foremost among them were Robert Frost and Carl Sandburg, whose powerful conversational styles and unflinching views of life had a strong impact on their fellow writers. Both men lived long enough to survive many literary movements and to win widespread affection as beloved patriarchs. Frost settled in 1915 into an almost reclusive life on his farm. In such poems as "Stopping By Woods on a Snowy Evening," he wrote of nature's austere beauty and its harsh indifference to man. In another poem he wrote:

Well, there's—the storm. That says I must go on,
That wants me as a war might if it came.

For Frost, a poem was "never a put-up job" but began as "a lump in the throat, a sense of wrong, a homesickness, a loneliness. . . ."

Sandburg, whose verse reflects the vitality of the Midwest, spent some 30 years writing an epochal biography of Abraham Lincoln—a major contribution to U.S. history. In "Chicago," published in his book *Chicago Poems,* Sandburg celebrates even more vividly than Whitman the raw quality of a great city:

Hog Butcher for the World,
Tool Maker, Stacker of Wheat,
Player with Railroads and the Nation's Freight Handler;
Stormy, husky, brawling,
City of the Big Shoulders.

Sandburg and his fellow poets of the so-called Chicago school, Vachel Lindsay and Edgar Lee Masters, had a missionary zeal to win the hearts of their countrymen, which Lindsay from time to time carried out by wandering through the countryside exchanging his poems for bed and board. "What we want now is the *whole public,*" he wrote in 1922. But in the post-World War I years the poets were hard put to sustain their vision of America's resilient dignity in the face of changing public morals, snowballing prosperity, and their growing disenchantment with the materialism sweeping the country.

The Lost Generation Finds a Voice

A common refrain of despair—or, as Frost put it, "a sense of wrong"—ran through the testaments of the postwar writers, whom Gertrude Stein is said to have dubbed the Lost Generation. Many, notably Ernest Hemingway, John Dos Passos, T. S. Eliot, E. E. Cummings, and F. Scott Fitzgerald, seemed to doubt that the war had been worth winning. All deeply regretted what had happened to the American character in the process and in the ensuing economic boom. Many knowingly or unconsciously nurtured their own unhappiness, either by staying on in Europe after the war or by playing profligate roles in the Jazz Age society of the 1920's.

Even before the first of the Lost Generation writers gained prominence, similar sentiments had been apparent in other popular authors. In his controversial novel *Jurgen,* James Branch Cabell created a nihilistic pleasure seeker who withdrew from all civic responsibility. Sinclair Lewis, who in 1930 became the first American to win a Nobel Prize in literature, took the opposite approach. In *Main Street* and *Babbitt,* he drew disparaging caricatures of middle Americans who believed they were exemplary citizens—men and women who worshiped convention, money, and their own brand of community boosterism and bourgeois snobbery.

Most of the Lost Generation authors seemed to wish to turn back the clock to a simpler time. Ernest Hemingway, who won world fame beyond any previously enjoyed by an American writer, worked heroically to create a supple, direct prose style, which would in itself embody a plea for a return to basic values. He was rewarded with the enthusiastic approval of millions of readers. His novels of comparatively innocent Americans mired in war-ridden or decadent European surroundings—*The Sun Also Rises* and *A Farewell to Arms,* both appearing in the 1920's—are dark with despair. A sense of the lost cause, the hunt for some elusive Holy Grail, permeates his best writing, including *For Whom the Bell Tolls* and *The Old Man and the Sea.* Widely publicized exploits as big-game hunter, deep-sea fisherman, bullfight buff, and roving war correspondent gave "Papa" Hemingway a veneer of glamour, but he did not substitute these personal heroics for quality in his writing. More than any other novelist of his day he showed Americans that, as John Donne had written, "No man is an island"—that the United States could not isolate itself, no matter how much it might long to do so. In 1954 he was given the ultimate recognition: He was awarded the Nobel Prize in literature.

The young Hemingway had been a member of a glittering circle of expatriate writers and artists whom the American writer Gertrude Stein gathered around her in Paris after the war. They included the poet Ezra Pound, who had left America to settle in England in 1908. There he helped to found the Imagist movement, whose adherents turned against the romantic effusions of their British contemporaries to draw on classical, medieval, and oriental sources and to turn out verse that was characteristically brief, compact, and metrically balanced. Pound soon lost interest in the Imagists and in 1920 moved to Paris to follow his own private vision, perhaps best expressed in his *Cantos,* which appeared in several volumes between 1925 and 1970. While his poetry reached a relatively small audience, especially after his World War II broadcasts from Rome for the Fascist cause, his influence on other poets can hardly be exaggerated.

It was perhaps T. S. Eliot who, with Pound's coaching, best expressed the Lost Generation's mood. His *The Waste Land* and "The Hollow Men" described a postwar civilization that was a spiritual desert. The only possible hope for rebirth was to be found in the omnipresent decay. The old values must disintegrate before a new vitality could spring up from their humus. In one of the choruses from "The Rock" Eliot laments the decline of religion and the reliance on scientific knowledge:

Endless invention, endless experiment,
Brings knowledge of motion, but not of stillness;
Knowledge of speech, but not of silence;
Knowledge of words, and ignorance of the Word.
All our knowledge brings us nearer to our ignorance,
All our ignorance brings us nearer to death,
But nearness to death no nearer to God.
Where is the Life we have lost in living?
Where is the knowledge we have lost in information?

Like James before him, the Missouri-born Eliot chose to live in England and become a British subject rather than return to his homeland. He died in London in 1965.

One of the most ambitious innovators in this period was John Dos Passos. In his many novels, Dos Passos strove to break new ground. In *Manhattan Transfer* he employed numerous plots and a huge cast of characters. In a trilogy published under the title *U.S.A.* in 1937, he used devices such as the "camera eye" and "newsreels" to make his representation of the times more vivid. Along with Theodore Dreiser, best known for his novel *An*

John Dos Passos and the U.S.A.

The novels of John Dos Passos, more than those of any other writer, present the essence of life in the United States during the first half of the 20th century. The most important of these novels—especially the trilogy *U.S.A.*—give a broad view of manifold aspects of American life and politics.

Dos Passos, of Portuguese descent, was born in Chicago in 1896 and spent part of his childhood in Europe. He went to Harvard College and served as a volunteer in the ambulance corps in Europe during World War I. The rest of his life was devoted to writing, and he produced more than 40 books in all. His first important novel was *Manhattan Transfer* (1925), a sprawling work with a vast number of characters and plots, representing every facet of life in New York City. In 1930 Dos Passos published *The 42nd Parallel,* the first novel of his masterful trilogy. The sequels, *1919* and *The Big Money,* appeared in 1932 and 1936, and the novels were published together in 1937 as *U.S.A.*

U.S.A. combines several episodic narratives about fictitious characters from varying walks of life with a number of innovative devices that heighten the realism of the work and help give a true feeling of the change and restlessness in America from 1898 to 1929. Between episodes of the stories are brief biographies of prominent people; "newsreels," which give headlines and excerpts from newspapers, snatches of songs, and advertising slogans of the time; and sections called the "camera eye," in which the author gives his own views.

Dos Passos' second trilogy, *District of Columbia* (1939–49), is more conventional, centering on a single family: a Communist who is betrayed by the party; his brother, the spokesman for an ambitious and greedy Southern politician; and their father, a disillusioned liberal. *Midcentury* (1961), a novel in the style of *U.S.A.,* deals with the ills of society. Although his politics began at the extreme left and shifted in later life to the extreme right, Dos Passos always believed in the ordinary man's potential for decency and originality, and his villains were those who threatened it. He died in 1970, at a time when many of the patterns of social unrest described in *U.S.A.* seemed to be recurring in America.

Poets Are Women Too
From Versifying to Poetry

Despite the then-prevailing male chauvinist attitude that women were incapable of creating true poetry—that they could, at best, turn out only light love lyrics or sentimental novels—a number of outstanding women poets emerged in the first centuries of our history. The earliest was Anne Bradstreet, a Puritan who immigrated to Massachusetts from England in 1630. She won praise on both sides of the Atlantic for her poetry, which demonstrated an appreciation of beauty not generally found in Puritan verse.

Poets of the 19th century included Transcendentalist Margaret Fuller, a prominent member of the Concord Group, and Emily Dickinson, one of the three or four greatest American poets of all time. A virtual recluse, Dickinson wrote nearly 1,800 poems, only two of which were published in her lifetime. Many of the poems distill Biblical and Transcendental thought into deeply felt lines that come alive with imagery drawn from domestic objects, nature, and religious ritual. Her most common themes are destiny, death, and nature as teacher.

The woman suffrage movement seems to have had a positive effect on the self-confidence of women writers, and particularly of women poets. By the start of the 20th century more women were writing poetry, much of it of high quality, and more of it was being published. A strong advocate of women's rights and of women poets was the cigar-smoking New Englander Amy Lowell, who with Hilda Doolittle (known as H.D.) vigorously promoted the school of Imagist poetry, which they had helped to found. Another highly individualistic woman writer was Gertrude Stein, who, after she moved to Paris in 1903, produced a primitivistic style of poetry in which she attempted to probe the character of subconscious thought. Her most famous line reads: "A rose is a rose is a rose is a rose." Stein is more noted, however, for her prose and for the writers she gathered around her.

Marianne Moore *was one of the most acclaimed poets of the mid-20th century. She saw herself as a "literalist of the imagination." Her verse gently criticizes human foibles.*

Marianne Moore was recognized as a major American poet in the late 1920's. Her carefully crafted poems, full of gentle wit and warmth, often use the animal and plant worlds to point out characteristics of her fellow human beings. A more recent poet, Elizabeth Bishop, writes in a similar vein. Her poetry is simple, direct, and usually descriptive, but she often indulges in excursions into fantasy. Other important poets of the 1920's and 1930's include Louise Bogan, whose poems are exquisitely subtle and intellectual; Edna St. Vincent Millay, both a poet and a playwright; and Dorothy Parker, whose humorous verses have undercoatings of bitterness.

In the 1960's came Sylvia Plath, whose verse is haunted by the shadow of death. Her poem "Ariel" is one of the finest American poems of the post-World War II period. Anne Sexton's poetry is equally somber, dealing with her own personal struggle against emotional instability. In addition, a number of fine young poets began to emerge in the 1970's. One of the best of them is Karen Swenson, whose collection *An Attic of Ideals* is divided into three parts: poems about women alone, poems about men alone, and poems about the relationship between the sexes.

At least in the field of poetry, women have finally come to be accepted as equals to men. It is no longer valid to speak separately of men and women poets. A poet, today, is a poet.

American Tragedy, Dos Passos was an early practitioner of the politically aware social realism that later swept through American letters during the depressed 1930's.

Another star of the Lost Generation was F. Scott Fitzgerald. For a time both his work and his stormy marriage to Zelda Sayre mirrored the fast, loose living of the Jazz Age, as it is called. The Fitzgeralds were at the center of a group of wealthy sophisticates who frequented speakeasies and often traveled to Europe. Scott supported his extravagant way of life by publishing glossily polished stories and novels. But when he settled down to more serious writing, he created in *The Great Gatsby* a poignant scrutiny of the era's reckless values; and in the long novel *Tender Is the Night* (1934), he issued a crushing indictment of the destructiveness of the times.

Edna St. Vincent Millay, whose poetry reached its zenith in the 1920's, epitomized the way of life of the Fitzgeralds and their friends when she wrote the bittersweet "First Fig" for her collection *A Few Figs from Thistles:*

My candle burns at both ends;
It will not last the night;
But, ah, my foes, and, oh, my friends—
It gives a lovely light.

The most widely read poet of the period was probably Stephen Vincent Benét. His *John Brown's Body* challenged the complacent and materialistic to remember the Nation's greatest time of struggle and idealism, the Civil War. Benét's patriotic epic was out of tune with the output of the Lost Generation, however. Almost all his fellow writers were employing their scalpels to expose corruption in the United States.

Few writers exposed corruption as humorously as Ring Lardner did. Lardner wrote short stories about ordinary people (professional athletes, salesmen, barbers, songwriters, stenographers), and his ear for the vernacular was scathingly funny and unerring. Lardner's chief characters usually turned out to be mean, greedy, sadistic, dull, pretentious, or cruelly ambitious. With such acid portraits he showed his disgust for Jazz Age standards.

The Midwest was Sherwood Anderson's stamping ground. His collection of short stories *Winesburg, Ohio* sympathetically examined the often twisted, unhappy lives of smalltown inhabitants. Anderson wrote many volumes of short stories, including *The Triumph of the Egg,* as well as the fictionalized autobiography *Tar: A Midwest Childhood.* The Ohio-born author was hailed as a leader

Regionalism
America in Its Literature

Regionalism flourished as an active force in American fiction during the 1920's and 1930's—as it did, in fact, in all the arts. The two murals at the right—painted in 1930 by Thomas Hart Benton for New York City's New School for Social Research—offer glimpses into the lives of ordinary Americans of the period, at work and at play. All kinds of people in all parts of the Nation were subjects of fiction. John Steinbeck wrote in *The Grapes of Wrath* of Oklahoma farmers driven to California by the Dust Bowl drought. William Faulkner depicted rural and smalltown Mississippians in *Light in August* and other works. DuBose Heyward's *Porgy* described the sights and sounds of a black ghetto in South Carolina. Oliver La Farge's *Laughing Boy* centered on the Navaho Indians. The farms, mountains, and small towns of Virginia were the focus of Ellen Glasgow's *Barren Ground.* A Texas dairy farm was Katherine Anne Porter's choice of locale in *Noon Wine.* Sinclair Lewis' *Main Street* satirized life in a thinly disguised replica of his own hometown, Sauk Centre, Minnesota. In *Appointment in Samarra* John O'Hara vividly recounted the tragedy of a businessman in a Pennsylvania coal-country town. Countless other authors helped to bring home to millions of readers across the United States the rich tapestry and almost infinite variety of their multifaceted homeland.

of the so-called revolt from the village; but, as one critic put it, the former manager of a paint factory probably was rebelling "not against the village, but against the swallowing up of the village as it had once been by the monster of industrialism."

With the stock market crash of 1929, the curtain suddenly rang down on the extravagant Jazz Age. Concern over material decadence, sprawling industrialization, and the disillusioning aftermaths of war was overshadowed by even larger problems: poverty, unemployment, and civil strife, both in rural regions and in the cities.

Regionalism Flowers in the South and West

It was during the 1930's that the use of regional characters and backgrounds as proper grist for serious fiction blossomed and flowered. Twentieth-century American regionalism was, of course, older than the Great Depression. In 1913 Willa Cather had already published her first novel of the prairie, *O Pioneers!* Few writers surpassed Cather in narrative power, but her evocations of the prairie, the Southwest, and other locales were mainly historical works harking back to earlier times. So, too, was Margaret Mitchell's *Gone with the Wind,* a record-breaking bestseller about the South during the Civil War and Reconstruction. Other regional fiction of the 1930's told of the here and now, and much of it vividly described the poverty and degradation brought on, or aggravated, by the blight of economic depression. The leading writers of this type of fiction were William Faulkner, Erskine Caldwell, John Steinbeck, and, in a limited sense, Thomas Wolfe.

Wolfe was the first to win fame. He was teaching in New York City when he poured forth his first wordy, nearly formless, largely autobiographical novel, *Look Homeward, Angel,* in 1929. Wolfe's star rose suddenly, seeming to have come out of nowhere. As its title indicated, the novel was looking back into Wolfe's own roots: his North Carolina home and the experiences of his boyhood and youth. Often hauntingly poetic, his voice was in tune with the yearning, confused spirit of a rural and smalltown generation lured to the big cities by industrialism and beginning to sense that it had sacrificed its roots in a quest for prosperity. Wolfe followed with three more novels; the last, *You Can't Go Home Again,* was published in 1940, 2 years after his untimely death at the age of 37. While Wolfe's sprawling narratives were regional in emphasis, his psychological insights held significance for most uprooted Americans.

Erskine Caldwell's regionalism was narrower and his novels simpler and more naturalistic than Wolfe's. At first he shocked his readers with his down-to-earth, bawdy portraits of poor Southern whites. His characters in *Tobacco Road* and *God's Little Acre* were coarse, brawling, conniving, and greedy, and Caldwell portrayed them with the clear eye of a comic genius. But in Caldwell's hands they were more than entertaining clowns. They were filled with a lust for life, and their struggles to escape from grinding back-country poverty were curiously heroic.

William Faulkner was both a naturalist and a regional writer. His feet were firmly planted in the earthy soil of his imaginary Yoknapatawpha County in Mississippi, but his vision was trained on the problems and aspirations of all humanity. In his speech accepting the 1949 Nobel Prize in literature, Faulkner offered revealing testimony of an affirmative philosophy: "I decline to accept the end of man. . . . He is immortal, not because he alone among creatures has an inexhaustible voice, but because he has a soul, a spirit capable of compassion and sacrifice and endurance." The characters in the masterful short story "The Bear" and such novels as *Sanctuary* and *Intruder in the Dust* are hard pressed to salvage their sanity, if not their very lives, in a Southland haunted by violent obsessions and a legacy of racial hatred. In these and other Faulkner works, the air is dark with threats to human existence, and justice is a slippery thing. Starting with the novels *Sartoris* and *The Sound and the Fury,* both published in 1929, Faulkner wove an enormous tapestry of Southern lore. Central figures in the design are the aristocratic and once influential Sartoris family. The time frames shift back and forth from Civil War days to the contemporary South. Faulkner traced the decay of genteel bloodlines and the collapse of the Old South's dream of courtly grandeur; he depicted the rise of a new breed of acquisitive, sometimes unscrupulous whites, who were taking over the reins of political and economic power. Faulkner was so steeped in the tradition and history of his chosen settings that he was able to raise regional writing to the heights of legend and universal tragedy.

John Steinbeck, also a Nobel Prize winner (1962), grew up in California's Salinas Valley and labored as a boy in its fertile orchards and truck gardens. In his early novels, such as *Tortilla Flat,* he wrote sympathetically of farm workers near Monterey. As the Depression deepened, the plight of migrant workers fighting for a living wage inspired his novel *In Dubious Battle.* By 1939 he had produced *The Grapes of Wrath,* a searing portrayal of Dust Bowl poverty that firmly established him near the top of his craft. In the middle and late 1930's farmers by the thousands were streaming out of the drought-stricken Western plains, and Steinbeck traveled among them to gather the facts and the impressions for his masterwork. The novel recounts the trials of a poor Okie family, the Joads, during the trek to California. No other Depression novel more eloquently attests the courage of ordinary people caught in the era's shattering economic miseries.

Disillusionment Darkens the Literary Scene Again

The 1930's were an era in American literature that offered little cheerful reading. James T. Farrell's trilogy entitled *Studs Lonigan* describes the vicissitudes of big-city life. John O'Hara and J. P. Marquand, chroniclers of the east coast's upper crust, told tales of disillusionment, bitterness, and defeat in affluent surroundings. Richard Wright was writing powerful accounts of racial bitterness and the miseries of poor blacks at the other end of the social scale. Awarded the 1938 Nobel Prize for literature, Pearl Buck, in her novel *The Good Earth,* reported the Chinese struggle to survive in the face of famine and war. The American theater had only recently attained world recognition through the plays of the genius of psychological drama Eugene O'Neill. Clifford Odets, Lillian Hellman, Thornton Wilder, and Robert E. Sherwood, among others, were prominent and successful playwrights of the period.

All at once the concerns of the Depression were superseded by the demands of war. The Civil War, World War I, and the Great Depression had all proved to be turning points in American literature, and World War II was unmistakably another. For years after it ended American authors poured out a torrent of works about the effects of the war on its participants. James Jones, in *From Here to Eternity,* realistically detailed the sadistic, brutalizing quality of Army life in the years before Pearl Harbor. Perhaps the most popular of the war novels was Norman Mailer's *The Naked and the Dead,* an account of the degrading effects of combat on rank-and-file soldiers. There were no winners in Mailer's war, which dehumanized victors and vanquished alike. James Michener's *Tales of the South Pacific* reported on Americans at war in an exotic environment. Both Thomas Heggen, in *Mister Roberts,* and Herman Wouk, in *The Caine Mutiny,* told of the inanities of military life at sea. Aboard the *Caine* were reasonable men whose judgment was first beclouded by a vindictive and incompetent commander, Captain Queeg, then subjected to irrelevant scrutiny by inflexible military law. Joseph Heller, in his sometimes hilarious, sometimes tragic novel *Catch-22,* portrayed a half-world in which the soldier had as much to fear from the arbitrary nature and sheer magnitude of military operations on his own side as from the guns of the enemy, and cowardice and heroism were merely two sides of the same absurd coin. John Hersey's *Hiroshima* brought home to the reader the devastation and horror caused by the first atomic bomb dropped on Japan. It made most of the fiction of the decade look pale in comparison.

"The Grapes of Wrath" *is John Steinbeck's masterpiece and one of the best testimonies in all literature to man's strength in the face of suffering. It focuses on the Joads, a family of Oklahoma sharecroppers. When the land the Okies have been working in the Dust Bowl is laid to waste, the Joads hear that there is a demand for farmworkers in California, and they travel slowly westward, suffering endless miseries on the road. In California they find only migrant camps packed with thousands of others like themselves facing slow starvation. Episodes of the story are interspersed with evocative and poetic descriptions of the ravages in the Dust Bowl, the plight of the Okies, and the inhuman working conditions imposed by California landowners. At right is a scene from director John Ford's 1940 film version of the novel.*

"A Streetcar Named Desire," *Tennessee Williams' 1947 play, revealed the emotional disintegration of a genteel Mississippi schoolteacher in her encounter with a brutish brother-in-law in New Orleans' French Quarter. It starred Marlon Brando, Jessica Tandy, and Kim Hunter.*

Bestsellers dealing with World War II continued to win a broad audience into the 1970's, but by then most writers had turned to other preoccupations. Americans were streaming to the suburbs and enjoying comforts and technological advances which poured forth from booming factories in unprecedented volume. After suffering through two World Wars and the Great Depression in less than three decades, they wanted to concentrate on themselves and their families and friends. The onset of the Korean War in 1950 produced little good literature. Richard Condon's cold war spy novel, *The Manchurian Candidate,* the story of a brainwashed American captive sent home as an assassin, was a notable exception. The U.S.-Soviet rivalry and the terrifying prospect of a computerized world constantly in danger of global thermonuclear holocaust inspired a number of thrillers in much the same mold. But even when the country became embroiled in the divisive and protracted Vietnam disaster, fiction writers left the war reporting to journalists.

Even while World War II fiction was most popular, however, writers who mined other lodes were coming into prominence. In the theater of the 1940's Tennessee Williams picked up where Eugene O'Neill left off, exploring the psyches of a cast of characters in a part of the South he had staked out for himself. Williams' *The Glass Menagerie* and *A Streetcar Named Desire* continued a trend that led into the labyrinth of Freudian insights and 20th-century neuroses. Arthur Miller's *Death of a Salesman* harked back to the Depression through its central character, Willy Loman, whose realization of his failures as a businessman, husband, and father leads to his suicide.

A strange and brilliant stylist opened up a new world to fiction-lovers from the late 1940's through the 1960's. At first J. D. Salinger published shocking stories exposing the psychological wounds the war had left on his generation of returning veterans and their wives and girl friends. But with the *Catcher in the Rye* and *Franny and Zooey,* he became the pied piper to an entire generation that had reached maturity after the war. The personal experiences of these young people lay neither in the Depression nor on the battlefield but in schools and colleges rife with the tensions of academic competition. This audience, just coming to maturity and concerned primarily with its own survival, flocked to Salinger by the millions. John Knowles in *A Separate Peace,* his bittersweet novel of a boys' boarding school in the war years, appealed to the same generation. Calder Willingham, in his drama *End as a Man,* and Robert Anderson, with *Tea and Sympathy,* also spoke to readers whose primary testing ground had been in schools. John Updike—in such skillfully crafted novels as *Rabbit Run, Of the Farm,* and *Couples*—described their postgraduate tribulations.

A more exuberant, wider-ranging literary approach was also apparent in this period. Saul Bellow's *The Adventures of Augie March,* Nelson Algren's *The Man with the Golden Arm,* and Henry Miller's censor-plagued *Tropic of Cancer* (published in France in 1934 and in the United States in 1961) were all boisterous, free-swinging books that took their readers on wild rides. Bellow's hero Augie chased after fresh experience as though his life depended on it. The theme was as old as Cooper, Emerson, and Whitman; it reappeared in authors as far apart as Mark Twain and Dust Bowl balladeer Woody Guthrie. It was reflected, too, in the writings and Whitmanesque

"Death of a Salesman" *(1949) established Arthur Miller as a leading American playwright and was a Book-of-the-Month Club selection, unprecedented for a drama. The cast included Mildred Dunnock, Lee J. Cobb, Arthur Kennedy, and Cameron Mitchell.*

wanderings of the Beat Generation writers. Novelist Jack Kerouac's *On the Road,* which looked wide-eyed at America as if it were being seen for the first time, was the bible of an army of disciples. Kerouac and his friend poet Allen Ginsberg, author of "Howl," sang the praises of a startling pantheon of American heroes—parking lot attendants, waitresses in all-night diners, derelicts, drifters, freight-car vagrants, Times Square hustlers, bums, dope addicts, and homosexuals. By the 1960's such younger writers as Ken Kesey and Thomas Pynchon had broadened the "beat" definition to include all of society's underdogs. Among Kesey's protagonists were the helpless inmates of a mental hospital in *One Flew Over the Cuckoo's Nest.* Pynchon portrayed the outrageous anti-heroes who habitually thumbed their noses at respectability. To underscore his point, Pynchon, in his novel *V.,* named his main character Benny Profane.

Years of Turmoil

Young readers disillusioned with the Vietnam War and with middle-class values snapped up the books of these and other writers by the millions. College and high school dropouts began wandering across the country, fleeing from everything familiar and respectable to live in city slums, and joined the protest movement. When U.S. forces were finally withdrawn from Vietnam and conscription was discontinued in 1973, the protest subsided. But the Beat Generation and its fellow travelers had left its mark, and the literature that gave tongue to their complaints had been one of its moving forces.

The 1960's were a time of ferment and agitation for many causes: Peace in Vietnam, civil rights of ethnic minorities, and, ultimately, women's rights. Bellow moved on from *The Adventures of Augie March* to take his place in a long list of ethnic writers. He, Bernard Malamud, and Philip Roth were among the leading authors portraying both the dark and the light side of the Jewish experience in America. Indians joined the ranks of ethnic novelists in such books as *House Made of Dawn* by N. Scott Momaday.

But the most energetic outpouring came from the Negro community. Langston Hughes had set the pace with *The Weary Blues* in 1926. Richard Wright, in *Native Son,* created a Dostoievskian masterwork of racial anger. Ralph Ellison followed with his novel, *Invisible Man,* evincing the despair of a black intellectual embittered by white prejudices. James Baldwin, already well known for such naturalistic portraits of ghetto life as *Notes of a Native Son,* warned of a coming black rebellion in *The Fire Next Time.* Among the most artistically gifted American writers, Baldwin published his warning in 1963, when the civil rights movement was at a peak. The urban riots of 1967 and 1968 proved him sadly prophetic. Depictions of ghetto life by Claude Brown, Piri Thomas, and others were read by millions of Americans, black and white, as were the militant manifestos of such men as the poet-playwright LeRoi Jones, who now calls himself Imamu Amiri Baraka, and the revolutionary Eldridge Cleaver. In this same period white writers also turned to black themes, notably William Styron, whose *The Confessions of Nat Turner* was a fictionalized biography of the pre-Civil War Negro leader of a slave revolt.

Women writers had achieved recognition long before the 1960's, among them Lillian Hellman, author of such outstanding plays as *The Children's Hour* and *The Little Foxes;* Eudora Welty, who sensitively portrayed the agrarian aspects of Southern life; Carson McCullers, whose novel *The Member of the Wedding* became a successful play; and Flannery O'Connor, author of two novels and a volume of masterful short stories. In the 1970's there came such plainspeaking practitioners of the new freedoms with deep concern for accompanying problems as Erica Jong, whose blunt yet often poetic *Fear of Flying* became a runaway bestseller.

The golden thread of poetry continued to shine through the years of turmoil. Both Robert Lowell and John Berryman had been acclaimed for their distinctive writings since the 1940's, but in this period they achieved new power and stylistic originality. Lowell's *Notebook 1967–1968,* which he expanded into a volume called *History* in 1973, was especially memorable. Two women poets, Anne Sexton and Sylvia Plath, both students of Lowell's, explored the anguish and fear of mental breakdown, physical illness, and death.

In a limited space, no treatment of so broad a subject as the history of American literature could be complete or do justice to everyone who deserves mention. The names alone, if all were listed, would fill a book many times the size of this one. Various authors have played important roles in the development of American letters through their influence on others. Truman Capote's "nonfiction novel" *In Cold Blood,* which used fictional methods to flesh out actual happenings, and the works of Donald Barthelme, John Barth, and other daring experimentalists may influence future trends; so may the wordplay of the brilliant Russian émigré Vladimir Nabokov, whose novel *Lolita* (1955), one of several written during a 20-year sojourn in America, is a brilliant satire on our ways of life. It may be, too, that some trailblazer who in his own time was all but ignored will emerge one day as a giant of our era. The answers to such speculations will have to await the passage of time. What is clear from the record is that the living body of American literature offers powerful inspiration to the writers of today and tomorrow. Because we thrive on diversity of opinion and the freedom of expression, this country will continue to encourage the talent to carry on and enrich a proud literary tradition.

Nobel Prize Winners
American Masters of Literature

Alfred Bernhard Nobel, the Swedish scientist and inventor of dynamite, died in 1896. In his will he established a series of prizes to be awarded each year for the finest achievement in a number of stated fields. Since the first of the awards were made in 1901, the Nobel Prize winners have been esteemed the finest in their fields. In all the areas together, there have been more winners from the United States than from any other nation, and in the sphere of literature there have been six American winners. The American-born T. S. Eliot settled in England while a young man and became a British citizen in 1927, 21 years before he won the Nobel Prize. The six American winners are discussed below.

The Nobel Prize *in literature for 1936 was presented to Eugene O'Neill. The accompanying citation stated that O'Neill's dramatic works embody an original concept of tragedy.*

Sinclair Lewis (*1885–1951*), the son of a Minnesota country doctor, began writing while a student at Yale. His major novels are biting satires on life in the Midwest. *Main Street* (1920) depicted the restrictiveness of life in the fictional small Minnesota town of Gopher Prairie, which has become a symbol of self-willed provincialism. *Babbitt* (1922) focused on an unimaginative businessman, whose conformism, in Lewis' view, kept him from being free in a free country. *Arrowsmith* (1925) examined the medical profession, and *Elmer Gantry* (1927) chronicled the career of a corrupt traveling evangelist who preyed on the people who were taken in by him. Lewis was the first American writer to win the Nobel Prize, which he received in 1930.

Eugene O'Neill (*1888–1953*) was the son of actor James O'Neill. After brief careers as seaman, actor, and journalist, he began writing plays while recovering from a bout with tuberculosis. O'Neill became one of the pioneers of what has since become known as the off-Broadway theater movement, which promoted experimental American plays. His first Broadway play, *Beyond the Horizon* (1920), set a trend for literate American drama—almost nonexistent until then. The plays that followed were generally brooding psychological dramas of stark realism, including *Anna Christie* (1921) and *Strange Interlude* (1928). O'Neill often attempted to capture the essence of Greek tragedy in American settings, notably in *Mourning Becomes Electra* (1931). His only comedy was *Ah, Wilderness!* (1933). His most profound dramas were *The Iceman Cometh* (1946), about man's need for illusions, and the posthumously produced *Long Day's Journey Into Night* (1956), a soul-searching look at the tense relations in his own family caused in part by his mother's addiction to drugs. O'Neill won the Nobel Prize for 1936, the first American dramatist to be honored.

Pearl S. Buck (*1892–1973*) was taken to China by her missionary parents when she was only 5 months old. She spent most of her first 40 years in China, where she became a teacher and writer. Most of her novels and short stories are set in China, and she has been credited with giving Westerners their first look at life in the Chinese interior. Her masterpiece, *The Good Earth* (1931), is a sympathetic story full of vivid detail about a northern Chinese peasant family. The novel won her worldwide recognition and was largely responsible for her winning the Nobel Prize in literature for 1938, the first American woman to be so honored. Her other novels include *Dragon Seed* (1942) and *Pavilion of Women* (1946).

William Faulkner (*1897–1962*) was born in northern Mississippi and lived most of his life at Oxford, in his home State. After a limited formal education and service in the Royal Canadian Air Force in World War I, he published his first book, *The Marble Faun,* a collection of poems, in 1924. Faulkner then devoted himself to writing fiction, most of it rooted in the soil of the region in which he lived, often drawing on family history and local lore. His best novels—including *The Sound and the Fury* (1929), *As I Lay Dying* (1930), *Sanctuary* (1931), and *Absalom, Absalom!* (1936)—are written in a masterful style and probe deep beneath their sometimes sordid plots. Faulkner won the Nobel Prize for 1949.

Ernest Hemingway (*1899–1961*), affectionately known as Papa, was enormously popular for both his writings and his flamboyant personal life, which was highlighted by strenuous outdoor sports and dangerous stints as a war correspondent. The disillusioned generation of the 1920's considered him one of their spokesmen. In his fiction he emphasized virility and courage—which he defined as "grace under pressure"—and demonstrated that man could fight all the odds in life in such a way that even though he lost he maintained his dignity. Hemingway's terse, concise, and somewhat journalistic style greatly influenced later American writers. His best novels include *The Sun Also Rises* (1926), *A Farewell to Arms* (1929), *For Whom the Bell Tolls* (1940), and *The Old Man and the Sea* (1952), all of which contributed to his winning the Nobel Prize for 1954.

John Steinbeck (*1902–68*) was born and raised in California's Salinas Valley, and many of his novels are set there. Most of Steinbeck's works demonstrate his love for the common man who lives with integrity and dignity in a corrupt and often demeaning world. *Tortilla Flat* (1935), his first successful novel, and *Cannery Row* (1945) deal with Mexican-American agricultural and factory workers. *Of Mice and Men* (1937) is a pathetic portrait of two migrant farmhands, one a mentally deficient giant of a man. *The Grapes of Wrath* (1939) is a vivid account of the hardships endured by a family of Oklahoma farmers who migrate to California when their land is devastated by the Dust Bowl drought. The story of Cain and Abel is given a California setting in *East of Eden* (1952), and French politics are satirized in *The Short Reign of Pippin IV* (1957). Steinbeck was awarded the Nobel Prize for 1962. That same year he published *Travels with Charley,* an account of his trip across America in a pickup truck with his dog.

CHAPTER TWENTY-FOUR

Women's Role in the Making of America

In early colonial America women worked as hard as the husbands to hack homesteads out of the wilderness and rai sturdy families. Successful colonizing required a partnersh between the sexes. Life was hard and consequently ofte short, so it was not uncommon for a young widow to tak over her husband's duties or to find outside work to supple ment the family income.

As conditions became more settled and Old World tra ditions overtook America's women, they lost ground i their quest for equality. By the early 1800's, although few worked as millhands or schoolteachers, most wome stayed home and tended to the children and the hearth

In the earliest days of settlement America was, literally, a man's world. Explorers, fishermen, trappers, gold seekers, and other adventurers—all men—came to the New World to seek fortunes for themselves and their Old World backers. Only when the sponsoring merchant companies decided that American get-rich-quick schemes could profitably become long-range business endeavors did they encourage permanent colonization. Women were then needed to help establish homes and families. And they inevitably influenced the future.

In 1609, when 2-year-old Jamestown in Virginia was merely a cluster of small thatched shelters, 20 women joined the 2 who were already there—a planter's wife and her maid. In the ensuing 10 years there were many women among the boatloads of colonists who arrived. In 1619 one boat alone brought 90 women as wives-to-be for the hardy Jamestown settlers.

In 1620 the *Mayflower* headed for Virginia, crowded with religious refugees rather than fortune hunters. In December the ship landed off course on a bleak Massachusetts coast, which was inhabited only by native Indians. Of the 101 passengers aboard, 18 were married women and 11 were young girls. No friends were there to greet them or show them how to cope with a strange new life. With their ship-weary companions they went ashore and helped build homes as shelter against the winter. All the girls survived, but by spring 14 of the women had died. That first season foreshadowed the strenuous life that awaited many other colonial women.

As permanent settlements grew in size and multiplied up and down the Atlantic coast, colonists found marriage almost a necessity. It was a cooperative partnership in which husband and wife shared in the overwhelming amount of toil required to provide shelter, food, and clothing. A girl usually married in her teens, choosing —she hoped—an earnest and hard-working young man as a husband. She knew she was expected to be dutiful and enterprising and to bear strong babies. Although many children died in infancy, families grew, and all their members were taught to participate in useful tasks.

Because diseases were prevalent, medicines primitive, and childbearing frequent and hazardous, a wife or husband often died relatively young. In most cases the widow or widower remarried within weeks, or even days, so difficult was it to survive alone. Colonists commonly married four or five times rather than remain widowed. It was not unusual for a woman to bear 18 or 20 children in a lifetime. By the late 1600's the average New England family consisted of nine people, and for the next 200 years or so large families continued to be desirable.

The Pioneer Homemaker

As America's people began to move westward in the late 1700's, responding to new and challenging opportunities beyond the Appalachians, they made use of a variety of shelters: Dugouts, tepees, tents, sod houses, and (where trees were plentiful) log cabins.

Building a house was traditionally the man's job, but creating a home was the woman's. By this time some women on the Eastern seaboard had indentured servants or slaves to help them, but the pioneer woman undertook all her homemaking tasks by herself with the skill and dedication of her colonial forebears. Like the earliest settlers, she was wife, mother, housekeeper, family nurse, vegetable gardener, and animal tender, as well as household protector when her husband was away.

Keeping her family fed throughout the year was the homemaker's most demanding chore. Wild game, such as the buffalo roaming the Great Plains, deer, and rabbits, augmented whatever stocks of pigs, cattle, chickens, sheep, and goats were raised. She might gather wild huckleberries, blackberries, and grapes. Gardens, once *hat was their safest haven, so the menfolk thought, from e mind-straining demands of education and the sordid orlds of politics and business.*

The first women's rights convention, held in Seneca alls, New York, in 1848, denounced the platitudes em- oyed in keeping "the weaker sex" in a position of infe- rity and called on women to assert themselves. The press rided this initiative, but in time the cause espoused at neca Falls attracted eloquent new leaders and a growing mber of supporters. Having helped to build a strong na- n from its very beginning, women began in earnest to mand their rightful share in its life.

The first important breakthrough came in 1920 with ratification of the constitutional amendment giving women the right to vote. Meanwhile, as the battle for rights progressed, millions of women were responding to the ne- cessities of two World Wars and demonstrating capabilities matching those of their male counterparts in almost every field. Still, they remained the victims of discriminatory measures and practices, legal and otherwise, which inevi- tably spawned militant demands for full equality and liber- ation. As the liberation movement grew stronger its leaders vowed never to relax their efforts until they had eliminated the last vestiges of demeaning law and tradition.

The old-fashioned *kitchen, whatever its appeal to modern eyes, illustrates some harsh realities. Hours of toil went into the use of each picturesque object; and the in- viting hearth, while a haven from the cold of the other rooms in winter, could turn the kitchen into a sweat- box in summer. The 1820 example shown here differs little from kitchens of preceding centuries or those of the next several decades. The iron cooking pots, one of which might weigh as much as 40 pounds, hung on the swinging iron crane— an early Yankee invention to replace stationary iron bars. In early colo- nial days, the pots were slung on green-stick poles, which sometimes burned through, dumping the dinner onto the coals. Baking was begun by building a large fire in the brick oven to the right of the fireplace. The ashes were raked out in the evening, when bread, pies, and pots of beans were put into the chamber of hot bricks and left to bake slowly over- night. Hanging from the beams, along with dried apples and rings of dried pumpkin, are skeins of wool that represent the most time-consum- ing task of all, clothing the family. Both flax and wool required months of preparation before they could be dyed and spun into yarn. The dyes were homemade from flowers, bark, or berries. The bark of sassafras, red oak, or hickory made good yellow dye; dogwood could be used for red. Spinning was a highly regarded skill in the Colonies, and contests for quality and quantity were popu- lar social events.*

they were plowed and planted, yielded such staples as corn, squash, beans, and potatoes. But with no refrigeration except what nature provided in the winter, a woman had to dry, cook, smoke, pickle, salt, ferment, and otherwise preserve foods to assure an everyday supply.

None of the dozens of tasks a housewife constantly performed in preparing food was fast or easy. She had to boil the foods in heavy kettles, bake them in hot coals, or roast them on spits. She had to smoke large pieces of meat for several days over a slow-burning fire. Every housewife had to bake her own bread from sourdough, which she preserved in an earthen jar. From milk, which spoiled quickly, she made long-lasting cheeses—the process of warming and curdling the milk in pots over the fire, then turning and rubbing the finished cheeses was almost endless. She canned fresh fruits or made them into marmalades and jellies. Some fruits she boiled into a thin paste and dried the paste into leathery cakes, which she hung from the rafters until needed. She turned apples into delicacies like applesauce, apple butter, apple tarts, and apple pies—enough apple pies were baked to give them an American status all their own. Jerked venison, buffalo tongue, bear bacon, dried pumpkins, pickled cabbage, and candied nuts were among the myriad foods a resourceful woman prepared and kept in storage for her family's daily needs.

A homemaker also had to patch and darn the family's clothes and make new ones, sometimes fashioning them out of animal skins that had been tanned by the man in the family. Buffalo hides made handsome cloaks, beaver skins became warm mittens, raccoon and bearskins, fine caps. Especially popular was buckskin, which women's skillful hands made into durable shirts, breeches, petticoats, and moccasins. When buttons were needed, worn pewter spoons and plates were melted and recast in soapstone molds.

The pioneer woman usually made her own woolens, a complicated process that took weeks of part-time labor fitted between other tasks. After the fleece (wolf's fur was sometimes made to do when sheep's wool was not available) had been cleaned, it was dipped in a crude dye made from berries, roots, leaves, blossoms, or barks. Fibers were carded, and thread spun. Six skeins of yarn were considered a good day's output. After the yarn was ready, a full day at the loom produced only 3 yards of broadcloth.

Providing light for the home was another recurring chore. Splinters of pine, dried reeds soaked in fat, or rag wicks stuck in grease or lard served immediate needs, but candles—slow-burning and steady of flame—were the prized lights. For months the homemaker would collect the grease that was cooked out of beef, deer, or bear meat. This tallow was put into a kettle, mixed with water, and heated. Wicks, made from twisted hemp or milkweed silks, were carefully set in molds, and the hot tallow poured around them. When the oily concoction cooled and hardened, a new supply of candles was ready. Since candlemaking was a long, time-consuming process, this source of light was used sparingly by all but the well-to-do colonists.

To keep a pioneer household clean was also an onerous job. Since cabin walls were covered with rough bark or plaster, ceiling beams were left open for storing food, and floors were earth-packed or loosely planked, there was constant dust and dirt. If a housewife ran out of soap, more had to be made. Water for washing had to be carried from a well or a nearby stream. Brooms had to be made by binding twigs with wet strips of rawhide, which

Soapmaking

When we casually buy a bar of soap today, it is hard to imagine what an investment of planning and labor went into that commodity in an earlier time. The housewife collected the ingredients day after day: wood ashes from the fireplace, stored in a barrel, and grease and fat rendered from home-butchered animals and saved from daily cooking. Pounds of the grease and fat were set to boil in a large iron kettle. Water was poured over the ashes; it filtered down and trickled out of a hole near the bottom of the barrel, producing a brown alkaline substance called lye. The lye was added to the grease when it bubbled.

As indicated here, the hot, smelly job was done outdoors. Under Mother's watchful eye, the mixture slowly thickened to form a powerful, jellylike yellow soap. The fussy housewife might let this pasty substance cool, then reheat it, adding salt to drive out moisture and to promote hardening. Before the soap was cold again, she ladled it into rectangular molds, then pulled a wire through it to cut it into bars. Soap made by this process was cleansing but not notably kind to the skin—a fact that may help explain why bathing was infrequent in those days.

A paternalistic *system of factory operation flourished around Lowell, Massachusetts, from 1823 to about 1845. Millowners provided strictly run boardinghouses for the girls they employed. Most girls worked only a few years, saving up dowries for the day they married. At the factory they often had time to read or tend the flowers they planted in pots and window boxes; the hours of labor were no longer than a farm day. In the evenings there were lectures to attend. When Winslow Homer painted "The Morning Bell" in 1866, showing a girl crossing a footbridge over a canal to begin her life at a factory, new managers had cut wages, increased work, and overcrowded the boardinghouses. New England girls could go back home, but immigrant workers had no such option.*

shrank as they dried and made a tightly packed brush. Kettles were carried outside and scoured with sand, and clothes were washed either in water lugged from a well or in a stream.

The responsibilities of early housewives were endlessly demanding and required an extraordinary array of skills, such as tending and teaching the children, brewing an onion syrup (hopefully) to cure a cold, feeding the livestock, knitting a purse, stitching a quilt, and embroidering a petticoat. But the frontier women learned the art of homemaking at an early age. The diary of one young pioneer girl shows that in a single day her activities included dressmaking, carding wool, cheesemaking, ironing, milking, cooking, dyeing thread, knitting, scouring pewter, and weeding the vegetable garden.

From Home to Factory and Office Work

America's women earned their first pay from their homemaking skills. To increase the family income, they sold or bartered their surplus soap, candles, shoes, preserved foods, medicinal salves, and knitted garments. A celebrated example of such productivity occurred in 1775, on the eve of the Revolutionary War, when New England authorities asked the region's homemakers to turn out 13,000 winter coats for volunteer soldiers. The order was filled before the cold weather came—each woman sewing her name and the name of her town inside the homespun army coat.

In their homes women worked as barbers and hairdressers, made pies, bread, and other foods for sale, and set up shops to sell hardware and books, imported goods, and homemade clothing. Working alongside their husbands—or alone, if widowed—they learned dozens of profitable trades. Women became innkeepers, printers, gristmill operators, pewterers, glaziers, and land agents.

New England women developed one of the leading colonial industries—the production of linen and woolen cloth. As early as the end of the 17th century New England was producing a surplus of cloth for sale in the Southern Colonies and the West Indies. Mills were built to perform the more difficult processes of dyeing, carding, and fulling; but spinning and weaving remained home industries.

With the arrival of new inventions, around the beginning of the 19th century, women began to work away from home. In 1790, in Pawtucket, Rhode Island, waterpower had been used to spin cotton for the first time. By 1814 power-driven looms were operating in Massachusetts at Waltham and later at Fall River. These textile mills constituted America's first full-fledged industry. They were followed by a century-long procession of specialized factories that made such necessities as shoes, shirts, and trousers by machine. The output of these factories freed homemakers from some of their sewing chores and also became places of employment. Once they had tasted economic independence, girls and young women soon became eager wage earners.

Compared with performing the countless chores at home or hiring out as servants, working in a factory seemed a boon to single women who needed an income. The working hours were about the same as housework—12 to 15 hours a day—but spending all day at a spinning jenny or a power loom took relatively little exertion or skill. There were rest periods, Sundays off, and—best of all—regular pay. The building of factories in their neighborhoods created a source of income for married women, because piecework, such as stitching cuffs and collars or seaming trousers, could be done in

Technology and the Woman's Role

New Possibilities Open

Business expansion, accompanied by development of the typewriter and other clerical timesavers, spawned an increasing need for officeworkers during the last quarter of the 19th century. As a result, women began to be admitted into the male sanctum of the office. By 1890 twice as many girls as boys were finishing high school. With officework added to the short list of respectable occupations open to women, thousands of these graduates became typists, stenographers, secretaries, bookkeepers, and salesladies. Men willing to do clerical work demanded higher salaries, although they were usually not as well educated or as well qualified for such positions. Moreover, men were less docile.

The typewriter, when first put on the market, was considered too complicated for the "weaker sex," but by the 1890's female typists far outnumbered male, and, because of their manual dexterity, were thought to be better at the job. The first telephone switchboards were run by young men, but women soon took over because the pitch of their voices proved more suited to the early equipment. Women were accepted because the activities were new, and there were no preconceptions to be overcome concerning men's and women's roles. More recently, women and men have entered the field of computer programming in equal numbers.

Most young women *thought of their office jobs only as preludes to marriage. As wives they expected to stay happily at home.*

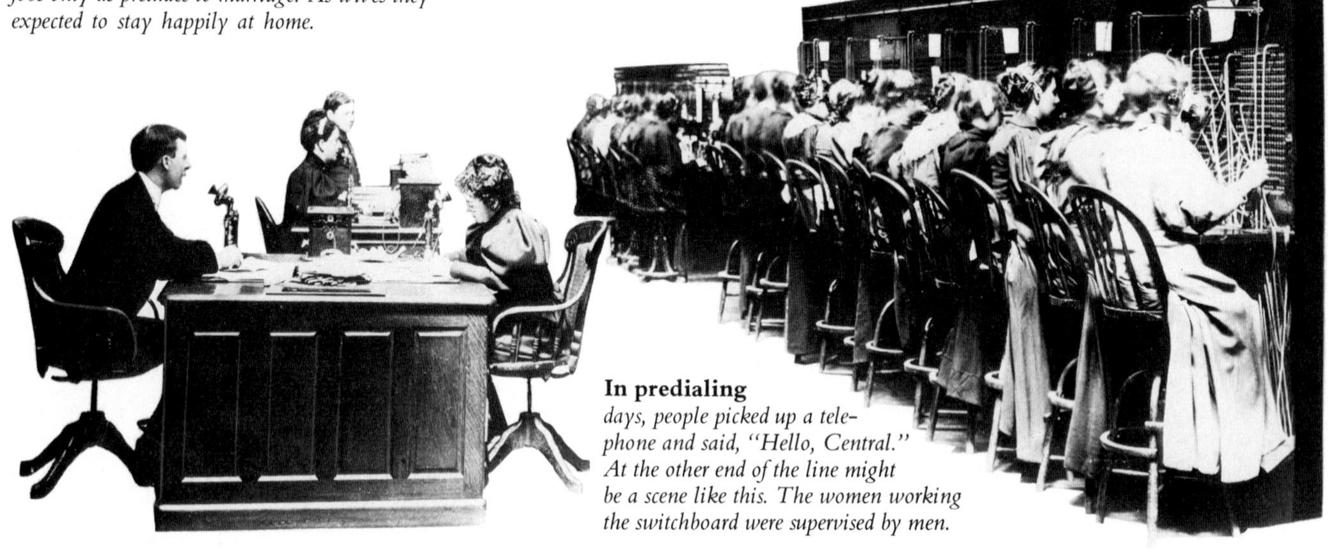

In predialing *days, people picked up a telephone and said, "Hello, Central." At the other end of the line might be a scene like this. The women working the switchboard were supervised by men.*

the home. By the late 1800's factory managers, in their efforts to increase production, even subsidized housewives' purchases of sewing machines. With the wages from their piecework the women made regular payments to the company. This was one of America's first installment-buying plans. Little did those early-day managers know that this merchandising technique would itself be as innovative as the machines they were financing.

Factory work, however, proved to be a mixed blessing. In the proliferating factories, especially the garment mills, women workers—who were minimally skilled and eminently exploitable—could be hired at one-third or at most one-half of the wages given men in similar jobs. Throughout the 19th century the supply of women who needed work was constantly being increased by the arrival of immigrants from Europe. The average young woman who worked in a mill earned $5 to $6 for a 60-hour week, and her room and board took more than half of that. Blessed with this vulnerable, cheap, and ever-growing pool of female labor, unscrupulous employers frequently imposed wage cuts and work speedups. They had little trouble finding replacements for those dissatisfied enough to leave. Nor was there any shortage of women to do piecework at home, in competition with factory employees. By 1870 in New York City alone there were some 20,000 women who relied on home piecework for their support, even though the rates for this work were scandalously low. A home-sewn shirt, for example, brought just 6 cents for labor. At such rates a woman could earn no more than about $3 a week.

During much of the 19th century there was little outside work for women apart from the factories, where they were caught up in a round of simple tasks, poor pay, and little chance of learning new skills or going on to better jobs. The chief alternative, except for women with some education, was domestic service. Household maids, cooks, and charwomen usually lived with the families they served and were on call from about 6 a.m. to 10 p.m. Their workday was even longer than that of the factory employees, and their pay, in addition to room and board, ranged from $2 to $5 for a 100-hour week in the cities of the Northeast.

One profession that welcomed women in the early 19th century was schoolteaching, and by the 1890's twice as many women taught as men. Since teaching demanded only 6 to 8 years of formal schooling and commanded some status in the community, it attracted a steady supply of young women. This, too, worked against equitable salary levels. Women teachers in city schools averaged $13 a week; men teachers, two or three times that. But most schools were in rural areas. Until the early 20th century 80 percent of America's schoolhouses were rough frame or log buildings consisting of one room, with one teacher supervising eight grades at a salary of about $10 a week. The teacher was usually a young, unmarried woman, often not much older than her eldest student. Although she officially worked shorter hours and under less tedious conditions than a factory worker or a domestic servant, she was expected to play the teacher's role at all times. In school she had to instruct a dozen or so students from 6 to 16 years old in all subjects. Outside school she was expected to be a model of decorous behavior: Pious, socially discreet, and impeccable in conduct.

The social and economic upheavals of America's wars gave women new work opportunities. With the men away from home during the Civil War, wives of farmers and plantation owners had to handle the duties of tending land and property in addition to keeping the family clothed and fed. In towns and cities many women took over their husbands' businesses. For the first time women in significant numbers were welcomed into government service, given office positions, and hired to work behind department store counters. New factories, short of manpower, drew women into jobs formerly reserved for men—jobs at which they could learn more intricate skills, perform more demanding tasks, and earn more rewarding salaries.

Women's greatest concern during the Civil War was the welfare of the soldiers. Women were active as fund raisers and fieldworkers for the Sanitary Commission, a Northern organization of volunteers with about 7,000 local branches. During the war the commission raised $15 million worth of supplies and almost $5 million in cash—used mostly for hospital services. Medicines, bandages, food, clothing, soap, letters to the families of the wounded, campaigns for better sanitation—there was little the workers did not tend to. The women volunteers in the war were mostly anonymous, but at least two became nationally famous. Dorothea Dix, already well known for her reform work in prisons and insane asylums, headed the Union Army's nurses and demanded tough new standards of professionalism among them. Clara Barton, a volunteer nurse in Union military hospitals and on battlefields, began the dedicated, demanding work that led to her pioneering contributions to the International Red Cross and, later, to the formation of the American Red Cross. In the South women were just as busy, collecting supplies and nursing the wounded. Outstanding among them were Sally Tompkins (the only woman to hold a regular commission from the Confederacy), Phoebe Pember, and Kate Cumming.

The Struggle for Equality

For much of the 19th century, as the frontier wilderness slowly but steadily disappeared, rugged pioneer ways yielded to ever more sophisticated manners and attitudes. While the arduous work of colonial and homesteading women had proved vital to family survival, many 19th-century women in settled, prospering communities found their tasks gradually lightened by the steadily growing output of household aids. As women adapted to their less essential roles in family life, prevailing social values tended to idealize them. The widely held image, shaped by shifting lifestyles and by imported Victorian manners, portrayed women as pious, cheerful, modest, tender, and tactful creatures given to attractive blushes and occasional emotional outbursts. That they were also pictured as fragile and subject to fainting spells reflected the Victorian customs of restrictive dress, delicate diet, and limited exercise and fresh air as much as it did the age's popular attitudes. In this era, too, one of the "weaker sex" was called a female rather than a woman. The word "woman" was considered common—to be applied only to a female of questionable character.

Given the stereotype of women as gentle custodians of society's most desirable traits, it is no wonder that 19th-century public sentiment regarded women who worked as somehow disreputable. The argument was many-sided. A woman should be the guardian of the home and all its moral values, not a competitor with men, whose aggressive natures were better suited to working conditions. Work was more demanding than a woman's delicate health and limited intelligence could endure, endangering her role as wife and mother. It was thought that most jobs, and certainly those in the rough company of men, threatened femininity and even encouraged immorality. In this age when legs were modestly called limbs, and even the legs of pianos were often hidden with prim ruffles, it was felt that a woman was physically, temperamentally, and intellectually better off at home. Only slowly, with the insatiable labor demands of factories and offices and the advent of wars, were women grudgingly given society's blessing to hold jobs away from home. And then their rights at work lagged far behind men's until the insistent rise of labor unions and the militant and effective emergence of feminists helped pave the way

A labor organizer *at 18 for the Industrial Workers of the World (IWW), Elizabeth Gurley Flynn appeared all over the country at rallies and strikes. Wearing a bright red tie, she harangued strikers, urging them to stick together and fight for better wages and improved working conditions. She is shown here at 23, encouraging silk-workers at a 1913 strike in Paterson, New Jersey.*

Elizabeth Cady Stanton *(above, left) and Susan B. Anthony (right) met in 1851. For the next half century they worked effectively together to lead the feminist movement, complementing each other in their abilities. Mrs. Stanton was excellent at public speaking and gaining friends for the movement. The austere Miss Anthony was a poor speaker but a superb organizer.*

Outstanding Reformers
Five Women Who Broke the Bonds of Convention

The cause of social justice was not limited by color, age, or social position. Harriet Tubman and Sojourner Truth were born into slavery. Elizabeth Gurley Flynn was a member of the working class. Elizabeth Cady Stanton and Susan B. Anthony belonged to the well-to-do. These women worked for many causes. Their refusal to accept the antifeminist conventions of their day often brought them scorn, yet they persevered in their efforts.

Harriet Tubman and Sojourner Truth spoke for woman suffrage in addition to leading the struggle for abolition and black education. Elizabeth Stanton and Susan Anthony also worked for abolition and were among the first to speak out against the inequities imposed on women. They espoused the revolutionary concept of equal pay for equal work and women's rights to keep their own earnings. Elizabeth Gurley Flynn, while supporting suffrage, saw this as part of a larger class struggle which included all workers and, in her impatience for change, joined the Communist Party in 1937. She died in Moscow in 1964.

Between 1850 and 1860, *Harriet Tubman, herself an escaped slave, made about 20 trips into the South to lead slaves north to freedom. She appears at the left (above) with one such group. Sojourner Truth (right) traveled around the country speaking for abolition and women's rights. With her deep, compelling voice and powerful personality, she was a famous lecturer.*

I Sell the Shadow to Support the Substance.

SOJOURNER TRUTH.

for more equitable pay and more challenging positions.

Nineteenth-century society was as reluctant to provide young women with educational opportunities as it was to see them work. Once beyond elementary school, girls might be instructed in such niceties as sewing, music, and manners, but not in such "manly" studies as higher mathematics, science, and history. With a few exceptions, it was not until after the Civil War that secondary schools for girls with more scholarly curricula began to appear in Boston, Philadelphia, and other cities.

One of the earliest and most influential advocates of education for women was Emma Willard, who taught herself algebra, geometry, geography, and history, and then, as a private tutor, instructed young ladies in those subjects. Encouraged by her students' enthusiasm for learning—and unimpressed by the general belief that intellectual pursuits would impair the girls' health—Mrs. Willard went on to fulfill an ambitious goal. After she had petitioned the Governor and the Legislature of the State of New York to vote her a charter, in 1819 at Waterford she opened a girls' school endowed with both private and public funds. Two years later she moved to Troy, where she founded the Troy Female Seminary. In addition to religion and domestic science, she taught subjects she herself had mastered, including a daring course in physiology. Mrs. Willard also supplied training for women teachers that enabled them to serve more competently and to seek salaries more comparable to those paid men. Always striving to make education for women as widely available as possible, she pioneered loans to needy prospective students, which were to be repaid after the students graduated and found positions.

Although Oberlin, in Ohio, was the first college in America to admit women as candidates for degrees (1837), the principal inheritors of Emma Willard's educational philosophy were the higher institutions established specifically for women. The first was Mount Holyoke Female Seminary in South Hadley, Massachusetts, founded in 1837 by Mary Lyon. Miss Lyon paved the way for the women's colleges of the 1860's and 1870's when she demanded that her school should be financially endowed; students should come from all income groups; and they should have the chance to pursue wide-ranging courses, not just those related to homemaking and teacher training. (For more on the important role that women have played in the field of education, see "Education for All," pages 126–139.)

Just as work and educational opportunities for women were limited in the 1800's, their legal rights were also severely circumscribed. Married women in particular were subject to what was traditionally, and accurately, called "civil death." A wife had no legal rights of her own. Her husband was lawfully sanctioned to exercise total authority over her person and property. Among the many inequities were these: A wife could not retain any wages she earned or hold and control her own property, even if her husband was a drunken spendthrift; she lost the guardianship of her children if she sought a divorce; and she could not sign a deed, a will, or any other legal document. During the late 19th century, as the result of agitation and petitions from feminists and reasoned arguments by writers and lecturers, many States adjusted their laws to recognize women's basic rights, but the slow, piecemeal job continues even today.

Women Begin To Fight for Civil Rights

Women's lack of political power was vividly dramatized in the 1830's, when they were working for the abolitionist cause. Many antislavery organizations would not accept women as members, and social convention would barely tolerate their speaking in public. Among the first to challenge and weaken this custom were two South Carolina sisters, Sarah and Angelina Grimké. Brought up in a slaveholding family, they despised what they saw of slavery, especially the demeaning role of the Negro women, who had to care for their masters' children but were denied the right to legal marriage and a stable family life of their own. The Grimkés ultimately left home for the North, where they gave eloquent speeches about the deplorable conditions they had witnessed firsthand. Public opinion, outraged at such audacious impropriety, relentlessly abused the Grimkés, awakening them to the need for freedom for women as well as for slaves. (For the contribution to the abolitionist cause made by another woman, Harriet Beecher Stowe, see "A New Literature From a New Land," pages 406–421.)

Two others whose support of abolition furthered their advocacy of women's rights were Lucretia Coffin Mott and Elizabeth Cady Stanton. Both were members of the American delegation to the World Anti-Slavery Convention held in London in 1840, but they, along with the other women on their team, were not only denied active participation in the 10-day meeting but actually forced to sit hidden behind a curtain. Mrs. Mott, already a well-known public figure in the United States, and Mrs. Stanton, the young, high-spirited wife of an abolition leader, vowed to hold a convention of their own to highlight the rights they so strongly felt were every woman's due.

On July 19 and 20, 1848, America's first women's rights convention was held in Mrs. Stanton's hometown, Seneca Falls, New York. Despite Mrs. Mott's concern that few would attend because it was harvesttime, the brisk little announcement in the local newspaper drew about 100 people, men as well as women. Mrs. Mott's husband, James, chaired the meetings, and in the course of 2 days the enthusiastic listeners heard a stunning Declaration of Sentiments, which was modeled after the

MAKING DEMOCRACY WORK

The 19th Amendment

In colonial times women of property could vote in a few Colonies, but after independence woman suffrage was denied in all States save New Jersey, which finally abolished it in 1807. The movement to regain the vote for women began at the Seneca Falls convention in 1848, on the insistence of Elizabeth Cady Stanton. Years of protest rallies, petitions, and lobbying in State and Federal legislatures bore fruit in 1869 when Wyoming Territory gave women the right to vote, and the right was retained when Wyoming became a State in 1890. By 1917 a total of 12 States had followed suit.

On January 9, 1918, President Woodrow Wilson gave his reluctant support to a constitutional amendment granting nationwide suffrage to women, and the House of Representatives passed it the next day, but the Senate failed to approve it. In May 1919 the House again approved the amendment and the Senate passed the measure on June 4, 1919.

The process of ratification by the States was begun, and the first to ratify was Wisconsin; Tennessee was 36th, providing the necessary three-fourths majority. On August 26, 1920, the Secretary of State certified the ratification of the 19th amendment to the Constitution. It proclaimed: "The right of citizens of the United States to vote shall not be denied or abridged by the United States or by any State on account of sex."

To have overcome the powerful forces opposed to woman suffrage was a particular triumph for Carrie Chapman Catt, who since 1887 had worked unceasingly for the cause, lecturing and organizing throughout the country and in Canada and Europe. Below, as president of the National American Woman Suffrage Association, she is shown at the victory celebration.

Declaration of Independence. The inferior status of women—legal, social, economic, religious, and political—was firmly decried, and a dozen resolutions were offered proposing recourses, in thought and action, against these injustices. After the impassioned speeches and agitated discussions were over, the audience unanimously passed every resolution but one: the advanced notion of woman suffrage was approved, but only by a slight margin.

The Seneca Falls convention crystallized the ideas and shaped the course of the women's movement for generations. It spawned similar meetings in other cities and other States, and publicized women's lack of basic human rights and opportunities. Even the satirical newspaper editorials and hostile church sermons that usually followed these gatherings served further to advertise women's restricted condition.

A small band of courageous, committed women—including Lucy Stone and Susan B. Anthony as well as Mrs. Mott and Mrs. Stanton—led and inspired the developing movement. At a time when traveling was a hardship, they journeyed widely to bring their message to men and women in farflung communities. They lectured, lobbied, campaigned, wrote articles, petitioned individuals and legislatures, and retained their dignity and purpose even under a barrage of public insults.

The women's rights movement, including the right to vote, was sidetracked by the Civil War and the ensuing crusades for Negroes' rights. It was diverted also by the cause of temperance, which attracted many women activists who felt that since existing laws did not protect women from the brutal abuses of drunken husbands, a restriction on alcohol might. The movement was often divided by disagreements over leadership, tactics, and ideology, and by the discordant demands of women in different sections of the country. Nevertheless, the feminists increased their organizational knowledge, sharpened their arguments, and hardened their determination.

By the turn of the 20th century, the fight for suffrage had taken precedence over the struggle for other rights. Among the most influential of the new generation of leaders was Carrie Chapman Catt. A superbly talented organizer, Mrs. Catt united the efforts of divergent individuals and groups in the single-minded pursuit of a constitutional amendment granting women the right to vote. She remained at odds with the aggressive militancy of feminists like Alice Paul and her followers, whose tactics included protest parades, hunger strikes, and jailings. But, like other suffragists, Mrs. Catt recognized their significant contribution to the women's cause. When the ratification of the 19th amendment was certified on August 26, 1920, 72 years after the Seneca Falls convention, it stood as a symbol of women's quest for true partnership in the American way of life.

Margaret Sanger (1883–1966)
Valiant Pioneer in the Appeal for Birth Control

Margaret Sanger coined the phrase "birth control" and spent a lifetime crusading for it. As a nurse in the slums of the Lower East Side of New York City, she had seen mothers, overburdened with children they were unable to care for, dying of self-induced abortions. In 1912 she set out to find and publicize the information about contraceptives, which she felt were so desperately needed. She believed that oversized families could cause poverty, and that in any case women should have rights over their own bodies that the law denied them.

In 1873 Anthony Comstock, secretary of the New York Society for the Suppression of Vice, had lobbied through Congress a law that labeled information about contraception obscene. Disregarding the law, Mrs. Sanger opened the country's first birth control clinic in Brooklyn, New York, in 1916. Hundreds of women lined up to see her until the vice squad closed the clinic. Jailed eight times, condemned by doctors, churches, and the press, Mrs. Sanger became a national symbol for protest against the anticontraception laws. Her trials forced the courts to interpret the laws leniently, permitting some use of contraceptive devices. As her concern for the problems of world overpopulation grew, she became an international figure.

Mrs. Sanger constantly sought a simple contraceptive, and in 1952 she persuaded a wealthy friend, Kate Dexter McCormick, to finance the research of Doctors Gregory Pincus, Min Chueh Chang, and John Rock. Their work resulted in the oral contraceptive known as the Pill, which was released for general use in 1960. Finally in 1965, the U.S. Supreme Court invalidated Connecticut's law banning the dissemination of birth control information and the prescribing of contraceptives. The concept of birth control is now accepted by most of the populace. But the question of abortion is still vigorously debated.

Supporters *encourage Mrs. Sanger after her arraignment in January 1917 following her arrest for running a birth control clinic. Her sister, who was arrested with her, made headlines by going on a hunger strike.*

A letdown followed the long struggle for the vote, and many suffrage groups disbanded, forfeiting the chance to gain and consolidate the legal, economic, and social advances that had concerned the original movement. Women tended to vote as did their menfolk—along educational, economic, and class lines. In the 1920's the emphasis seemed to shift from politics and economics to questions of freer moral and social conduct. Suddenly "nice" women were openly smoking, drinking, clothing themselves in more revealing apparel, and behaving generally with less cautious restraint than their predecessors.

During the Depression of the 1930's, women, like men, were primarily concerned with survival. A few individuals made significant advances: Frances Perkins, Secretary of Labor, became the first woman Cabinet member; Eleanor Roosevelt was in the forefront of work for New Deal recovery measures.

During World War I women served as fund raisers, nurses, and Red Cross workers, as they had in the Civil War. In addition, many substituted for men in industrial work, helping to make agricultural tools, military uniforms, explosives, armaments, airplanes, and automobiles. But it was World War II that opened almost unlimited work opportunities for women, who turned the manpower crisis into a work crusade. Six million women, twice as many as ever before, flooded the labor market. They joined the Armed Forces. They became pilots, engineers, chemists, economists, lawyers, and doctors. They cleaned blast furnaces, ran mammoth cranes, serviced cars, greased locomotives, cut precision tools, and operated lathes and drill presses. In shipyards women worked on everything from keels to radar antennae. In aircraft plants they assembled navigation equipment and welded fuselages. Rosie the Riveter became a heroine, symbolic of women's dedication to the war effort.

Posters like this *recognized and encouraged women's production efforts during World War II. Outstanding performance won acceptance in lines of work formerly unavailable to them.*

If wartime emergencies introduced women to new careers in the trades and professions, those years were also a catalyst that changed national values. Jobs outside the home had previously been considered appropriate chiefly for unmarried young women without households or children to manage, but the demands of World War II broke down barriers against wives and mothers in the labor force. The stage was set for a final push to establish equality.

Trailblazers in the Professional World

Women Prove Their Competence in a Variety of Fields

Maria Mitchell *in the Vassar observatory.*

Sarah Bagley (*active 1835–46*). A vital force in early labor reform, she was America's first professional woman labor leader. After working in the cotton mills of Lowell, Massachusetts, she protested against declining wages, long hours, and speedup of machine operations and fought those who said mere females must not question mill policies. Her conviction that the rights of female workers must be protected against the "driveling cotton lords" was shared by the 300-odd mill girls who joined the Lowell Female Labor Reform Association, which she founded in 1844. Two years later she gave up union activities to become probably the Nation's first female telegraph operator, opening another new field to women.

Louise Blanchard Bethune (*1856–1913*). In October 1881, when Louise Blanchard opened an architectural office in Buffalo, New York, with Robert A. Bethune, she became the first professional American woman architect. Marrying in December of that year, the Bethunes together designed a wide variety of public and private buildings, including a 225-room hotel and 18 schools. She worked to secure the passage of the architects' licensing law, designed to raise the standards of the profession, and as a women's advocate urged "equal pay for equal work." In 1888 she became the first woman to be elected to the American Institute of Architects.

Elizabeth Blackwell (*1821–1910*). "Trust a woman as a doctor? Never!" cried actress Fanny Kemble in 1857 when Dr. Blackwell asked her to help raise funds for a New York City hospital to be staffed by women. Such outspoken hostility was not new to Elizabeth Blackwell, who was by then America's first woman physician. She began studying medicine privately in 1845. Rejected repeatedly by leading colleges because of her sex, she kept applying until she was admitted to Geneva Medical College in Geneva, New York, in 1847. She graduated in 1849, then spent several years studying in Europe. She returned to America in 1853 with her sister Emily, by then also a physician, and in 1857 established the New York Infirmary for Indigent Women and Children. The two sisters trained Union Army nurses during the Civil War, and in 1868 Elizabeth helped found the Women's Medical College of the New York Infirmary. In 1869 she moved to England, where she spent the rest of her life teaching and working to advance medical opportunities for women.

Amelia Earhart *at the controls of her plane.*

Fanny Marion Jackson Coppin (*1837–1913*). Freed from slavery as a girl, she was one of the early pioneers in Negro education and the first black woman to become a school principal. At 14, propelled by a strong urge to "become a teacher to my people," she paid for private instruction out of the $7 a month she earned as a maid. One of the first Negro women to graduate from college, she received her degree from Oberlin in Ohio in 1865. Her most important contribution during her 33 years as teacher and later as principal at the Institute for Colored Youth in Philadelphia was to establish a department of industrial education where young black men and women could get training that would prepare them for an active role in an increasingly urbanized nation.

Amelia Earhart (*1898–1937*). On June 1, 1937, pilot Amelia Earhart and her navigator, Frederick Noonan, took off from Miami, Florida, intending to fly around the world. Miss Earhart had first won fame in 1928, when, as the first woman passenger on a transatlantic flight, she flew from Newfoundland to Wales with pilot Wilmer Stutz. In 1932 she flew the Atlantic alone; in 1935 she made the first solo flight over the hazardous route from Hawaii to California. But on the morning of July 2, 1937, after her plane had left New Guinea, as the world waited for news of her global flight, her last faint message that fuel was running low was received by the Coast Guard cutter *Itasca* in the mid-Pacific. Though extensive searches were made, no trace of the plane or its occupants was ever found.

Belva Ann Lockwood (*1830–1917*). On March 3, 1879, she became the first woman attorney to argue before the Supreme Court of the United States. After her petition for admission had been denied three years earlier, she worked effectively for congressional passage of a historic bill permitting women to plead before the High Court. Born in northern New York State, she taught school before moving in 1866 to Washington, D.C., where she began to study law. After several law schools rejected her because she was a woman, she was admitted to the National University Law School in Washington in 1871. She completed the course in 1873, but her diploma was withheld until she wrote a demanding letter to President Grant, the school's ex-officio president. A forceful lawyer who believed arbitration was the best way to solve world problems, she worked ardently for women's rights and international peace.

Mary E. Mahoney (*1845–1926*). The first black woman trained nurse was born in Roxbury, Massachusetts, and worked as a maid in the New England Hospital for Women and Children in Boston. She was accepted as one of 18 trial students in its school of nursing in 1878, a time when most such institutions were refusing Negro applicants. She was one of four students who graduated in 1879, and her record of competence and academic excellence encouraged the school to admit other black women. She was one of the first Negro members of the American Nurses Association. In 1909 in Boston she delivered an address and was elected chaplain at the first annual meeting of the Association of Colored Graduate Nurses, an organization raising standards and combating prejudice in that profession. Since 1951 the American Nurses Association has awarded the Mary Mahoney Medal to those making outstanding contributions to intergroup relations.

Maria Mitchell (*1818–89*). Her discovery of a new comet in 1847 brought her world fame and election as the first woman member of the American Academy of Arts and Sciences in 1848. Born on Nantucket Island, Massachusetts, she was taught astronomy by her father, a proficient amateur. She discovered the comet named for her while working as a librarian in Nantucket. In 1865 she became Vassar College's first professor of astronomy, a post she held until 1888. In honor of her scientific achievements and her interest in promoting the education of women, she was elected to the American Philosophical Society in 1869.

Frances Perkins (*1882–1965*). In 1965 W. Willard Wirtz, Secretary of Labor, said of the first woman Cabinet member: "Every man and woman in America who works at a living wage, under safe conditions and for reasonable hours . . . is Frances Perkins' debtor." Born in Massachusetts, Miss Perkins worked at Jane Addams' Hull House in Chicago and lobbied effectively in New York State in the early 1900's for consumer rights, improved working conditions, and factory safety. She served on the State Industrial Commission and from 1926 to 1929 was chairman of the State Industrial Board. She was then State Industrial Commissioner until appointed Secretary of Labor by President Franklin D. Roosevelt in 1933. After she resigned in 1945, she served 7 years on the U.S. Civil Service Commission. Later she lectured at many American universities on ways to improve labor relations.

Jeannette Rankin (*1880–1973*). She was a social worker in Seattle, Washington, and a campaigner for woman suffrage before she was elected to the U.S. House of Representatives from Montana in 1916, becoming the first woman to serve in Congress. A lifelong pacifist and isolationist, she voted against entering World War I—an act that cost her the Republican nomination to the Senate in 1918. In 1941 she was returned to Congress on an antiwar platform, but her lone vote in the House against the declaration of war on Japan after the attack on Pearl Harbor in 1941 ended her political career. Still active in the 1960's, she urged unilateral disarmament and lobbied for U.S. disengagement in Vietnam.

Secretary of Labor *Frances Perkins in 1934.*

Ellen Swallow Richards (*1842–1911*). A developer of the profession of home economics was the first woman in the United States to graduate from a scientific school. Her Bachelor of Science degree from the Massachusetts Institute of Technology in 1873 was a forward step in women's education, leading to regular admission of women students by MIT. Three years earlier she had received a degree from Vassar College, where she studied astronomy with Maria Mitchell. Appointed instructor of sanitary chemistry at MIT in 1884, she taught the practical application of chemistry to living conditions. In addition to teaching, she worked effectively to open scientific education and the scientific professions to women. Her work with her husband, a professor of metallurgy, resulted in her becoming the first woman to be elected to the American Institute of Mining and Metallurgical Engineers. A leading figure in the study of nutrition and hygiene, she became the first president of the American Home Economics Association in 1908 and helped establish its official *Journal.*

Lucy Hobbs Taylor (*1833–1910*). Known throughout Iowa in the 1860's as the woman who pulled teeth, she was the first woman in America to earn a dental degree. Born in western New York, she taught school and informally studied medicine before moving to Cincinnati in 1859. Dr. Jonathan Taft, dean of the Ohio College of Dental Surgery, taught her briefly until Dr. Samuel Wardle accepted her as an apprentice. In 1861, after rejection by the Ohio College of Dental Surgery, she opened her office without a diploma. (A degree was not yet required for private practice.) Moving to Iowa in 1862, she built a good clientele and was the first woman to be elected (1865) to a State dental society. Backed that year by the Iowa State Dental Society and secure in her undisputed reputation, she gained admission to the Ohio College of Dental Surgery, which granted her a degree in 1866. The next year she practiced in Chicago, where she married railroad-car painter James Taylor. After she taught him dentistry, the couple moved to Lawrence, Kansas, and, working together until his death in 1886, developed one of the most lucrative practices in the State.

Jeannette Rankin, *standing, with Carrie Chapman Catt at her right.*

What Does "Liberation" Mean?

"So widespread and pervasive are discriminatory practices against women, they have come to be regarded, more often than not, as normal," said a letter accompanying a 1970 report by a Presidential Task Force on Women's Rights and Responsibilities.

Although no one has yet formulated a manifesto that all women's liberationists would endorse in full, here are the changes most often asked for by those in the front lines of the battle against sexually based discrimination:

Equal pay for equal work.

Equal opportunity for on-the-job training and promotion.

Women's right to obtain credit and borrow money on their own merits, without the cosignatures of husbands or fathers.

A stronger legal voice in the management of a family's worldly goods. This would require revision of a formidable body of legislation based on the English common law doctrine that husband and wife are legally one—and that one is, for most purposes, the husband.

Ratification and implementation of the Equal Rights Amendment by States that have not yet done so.

Working wives and mothers, in particular, are concerned about the need for the following:

Maternity leave from jobs without loss of seniority.

Child care centers, publicly funded, so that mothers may be free to work outside the home whether or not they can afford babysitters.

Recognition of the economic importance of housework and child care and the right to Social Security benefits and disability insurance.

Far more controversial is the question of:

Unrestricted abortion and freedom from unwanted children.

Important, if less pressing, are such aspirations as these:

Revision of children's books to portray women and girls in more varied roles than those of wife and mother.

A new image in the media; abandonment of the time-honored habit of nearly always showing a woman in relation to a home or a man.

Better acknowledgment in history books of the contributions women have made in many fields.

Freedom in school for girls to take shop and for boys to take such courses as cooking if they wish.

Elimination of quotas that limit the number of women accepted into colleges and graduate schools.

An end to guidance counseling that advises high school girls to stick to such fields as teaching and nursing because other careers might interfere with marriage and raising a family.

A change in the attitude that housework should rest mainly on women's shoulders, whether or not they also work outside the home. In fact, many women insist that there should be no such thing as "men's work" and "women's work."

After the War: Back to the Home

Postwar attitudes, however, brought setbacks. Peacetime employment policies and practices often denied women responsible positions and wages comparable to men's. Persisting prejudices, rooted in 19th-century views of women's proper role in American society, were reinforced by the desire of both sexes to resume normal lives after the upheavals of the war. For most women this meant a retreat to domesticity. In women's magazines articles about career girls took second place to descriptions of the challenging life of the homemaker. A few women, such as Patsy Takemoto Mink, a young Hawaiian lawyer of Japanese descent, successfully entered local or national politics. Many women continued working, either because their families needed the additional income or because they enjoyed it. However, they found themselves carrying a double burden because they felt obliged to prove they were not depriving their families and could still be good housekeepers and mothers despite the demands of their jobs. Some were plagued by a sense of guilt for stepping out of what had long been regarded as women's role. Others, who stayed home, felt that their educations had been wasted—that, in acquiring such labels as "John's wife" or "Jennifer's mother," they had in effect lost their own identities.

In 1961 Esther Peterson, Assistant Secretary of Labor, persuaded President John F. Kennedy to establish a commission—the first of its kind—to research the status of women. Eleanor Roosevelt, a close friend of Mrs. Peterson's, became chairman. After 2 years of study the commission reported that necessity compelled many women to work for a living, that their recompense was uniformly low, and that many laws discriminated against them. The commission's greatest service was in stimulating interest in women's issues. By the time it was dissolved in 1963, most States had established commissions of their own.

That same year Betty Friedan's controversial best-seller, *The Feminine Mystique,* attacked the image of "the happy housewife." College-trained middle-class women throughout America read that thousands like themselves shared a dissatisfaction with a life made up of endless rounds of cooking, cleaning, chauffeuring, and serving husbands and children. Women's problems became a prime topic on television and in the press.

In 1964 the chairman of the House Rules Committee, Howard W. Smith, who opposed the civil rights bill then being debated in the House of Representatives, inadvertently helped the cause of women's rights. Assuming he could get the whole bill laughed off the floor by injecting a silly note, Mr. Smith suggested adding the word "sex" wherever the phrase "race, color, religion, or national origin" appeared in title VII, the section of the bill spelling out equal employment opportunities. So

Changing Hats
From Fashion to Function

The luxuriantly decorated straw bonnet of the mid-1800's and the close-fitting cloche of the 1920's evoke waves of nostalgia. The modern world of fashion has been stretched to include as well as decorative hats the many types of practical and protective headgear that are worn by growing numbers of women in the increasingly varied occupations opened up to them.

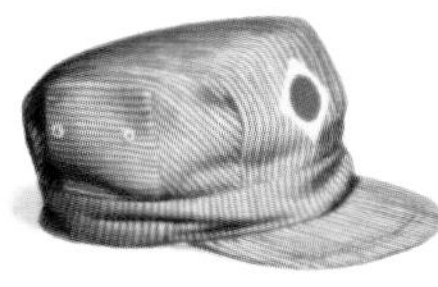

Train Engineer
In 1974 Christine Gonzales became the first woman railroad engineer, driving a 125-ton locomotive for the Santa Fe Railway.

Bricklayer
Maureen Harder was the first woman elected to office in the bricklayers' union. She was made financial secretary of a Nebraska local in 1975.

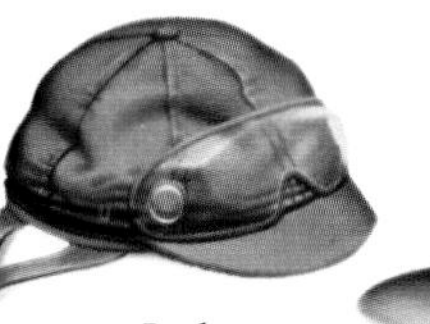

Jockey
The first woman to boot home a Thoroughbred winner on a parimutuel track was Diane Crump, at Miami's Hialeah Park in 1969. Kathy Kusner had become the first licensed woman jockey a year earlier, but a broken leg delayed her debut on a professional track.

Forester
The first women to work outdoors in the National Parks as foresters were hired by the Forest Service in the early 1960's. Many other women joined the service as scientists and landscape architects.

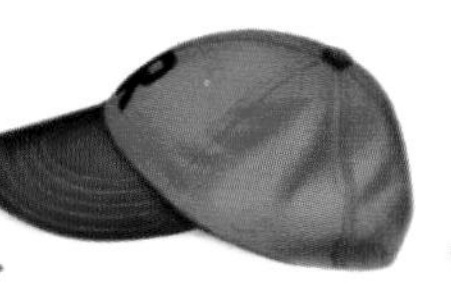

Baseball Player
In April 1974 Frances Pescatore won her lawsuit and Little League teams in New Jersey were ordered not to discriminate against girls. Faced by other suits, Little League, Inc., said girls would be allowed to play on their teams.

Airline Pilot
Bonnie Tiburzi graduated in 1973 from the Flight Academy of American Airlines, the first woman to become a certified pilot for a major airline. She flew a Boeing 727 and married an airline pilot.

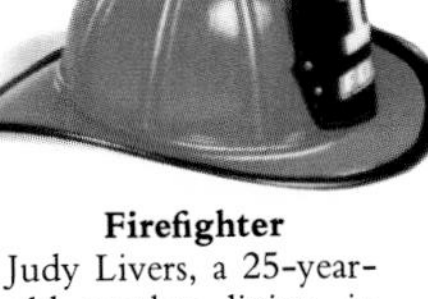

Firefighter
Judy Livers, a 25-year-old mother living in Arlington, Virginia, was the first woman to be hired as a firefighter in the United States. Starting her new career in July 1974, she was encouraged to enter the dangerous and strenuous work by her firefighting husband.

Merchant Marine
In 1974 the United States Merchant Marine Academy admitted its first women students. They will be the first licensed female deck and engineering officers in the service.

much laughter and joking followed his proposal that the occasion became known as Ladies Day. Nevertheless, the Civil Rights Act was passed with its "silly" addition, effective the next year. Although little publicized at first, title VII has since provided the legal basis for thousands of cases concerning employer discrimination against a worker because of sex.

The National Organization for Women (NOW), founded by Betty Friedan in 1966, attracted many active members but proved too conservative for some. Like the women who had battled for abolition more than a century earlier and had suddenly awakened to the fact that they too were in a sense legal "slaves," women civil rights activists of the 1960's concluded that they were being treated as second-class citizens by the very men at whose sides they had thought they were fighting as equals. The term "sex objects" began to be heard, and it became a fighting phrase among women demanding fuller recognition and a more respectful hearing in virtually every field. The groups that evolved from this experience were the first to use the label "women's liberation."

In an era in which values were being questioned, the women's liberation movement struck a responsive chord in Americans of all age groups (including many men) and at every level of society—from middle-aged mothers who found their lives empty after their children had left home to 10-year-old girls who wanted to play Little League baseball. Shirley Chisholm, the first black woman elected to Congress, remarked that her color had brought her less political discrimination than her sex. She and many others of like mind served notice that the day had passed when American women would accept lifelong subordination with passive acquiescence.

Every year from 1923 to 1948, a constitutional amendment to void hundreds of Federal, State, and municipal laws deemed discriminatory against women had been presented in Congress and rejected. For 12 years thereafter, the House Judiciary Committee had regularly tabled similar proposals. In the 1960's Representative Martha W. Griffiths of Michigan, a longtime advocate of women's rights, started getting signatures for a House petition that finally forced the equal rights measure out of committee in 1970. The House passed the measure by an overwhelming vote and sent it to the Senate, which failed to take action that year. In March 1972 the Senate approved the Equal Rights Amendment, but 3 years later it was still four States short of the number necessary for ratification.

Although the early-day stridency has subsided, women continue to press for equal treatment. Steadily growing numbers of women are seeking lifetime careers, as opposed to short-term jobs that serve as preludes to marriage. These women see no incompatibility between marriage and a career, nor between motherhood and a career. Today more women are entering business and enrolling in professional schools than ever before. There are record numbers of women candidates seeking public office. This new generation, of men as well as women, is not likely to bring up daughters conditioned from infancy to believe they are inferior to boys.

Fashions Through the Years *An Indication of Lifestyles*

1600's Early Colonial Period

1730–1770 Late Colonial Period

1795–1820 Empire Period

1820–1837 Era of Romanticism

1840–1869 Age of the Crinoline

In early colonial times fashions changed slowly. The difficulty of communication meant that even the wealthy were several decades behind their modishly dressed contemporaries in England and on the Continent. Favorite garments of costly materials were often mentioned in wills and handed on for two or three generations. Early in the 1800's the interest in ancient Greece and Rome, which had begun in the preceding century, had a strong influence on architecture, furniture, dress, and hairstyle. Women's gowns, straight and diaphanous, were more provocatively revealing than any garb of the previous 150 years. A topless outfit even made a brief appearance in Paris, although no one in America carried admiration of French styles so far as to try it.

In the 1830's, when the sensitive, drooping heroines of the romantic novels of Walter Scott and Victor Hugo were the rage, women began dressing in pastel colors. Faintness and fatigue brought on by tight lacing and heavy layers of petticoats encouraged a languid appearance. The hoop, which became the vogue in the 1850's, provided some relief from the weight of the skirts, but for several decades poor health remained stylish for women with the leisure and wealth to enjoy it.

At the end of the 19th century sports became fashionable, and higher education for women acceptable. The active young women of the new generation demanded less irksome clothing—although they did briefly don the hobble skirt, which forced the wearer to take tiny, mincing steps. During World War I, when women worked in factories and needed freedom of movement, skirts began rising—to the ankle, midcalf, and finally, in the flapper days of the 1920's, above the knee. After the war women deemphasized

1918–1929 Flapper Era

1930–1939 Return of Elegance

1939–1946 Austerity Years

1947–1957 New Look

1957–1964 Tailored Look

1965–1972 "Mod" Look

1869–1889
Victorian Period

1890–1910
Gibson Girl Look

1912–1918
Tubular Silhouette

their bosoms, cut their hair short, and wore short, straight dresses. Leg display fell out of favor during the Depresssion but returned with the cloth shortage of World War II. Slacks gained acceptance because they were convenient for wartime production work and continued to be worn at home even with the return to an emphasis on curves and femininity that came in with the New Look of 1947. The migration from city to suburbs required more casual clothes for both sexes. The women's movement of the 1960's and 1970's also affected clothing. Women wore pantsuits to work and in the evening, and men's fashions became more colorful. Comfort and function attained the upper hand. Informality was the keynote; people wore whatever they were in the mood to wear at any hour, and blue jeans and every variety of dress turned up on occasions that had previously demanded evening clothes.

1969
Relaxation of Dress Standards

1973
Fashions of Denim

A Few That Failed To Make It

Much like the automobile industry, which introduces a new model every year, the clothing business depends on change and planned obsolescence. It may come as no surprise that the fashion business has had its share of Edsels. In recent history a basic fashion, with variations, has usually lasted about 7 to 10 years. The degree of change from one model to the next must be carefully calculated. It must be different enough to make the last one seem out of date but not so different as to be outrageously unfamiliar. Extremes may catch on for a while, but they tend to disappear suddenly. Examples of short-lived fads appear below.

The zoot suit was reportedly first bought in Georgia in 1939 and soon became a favored symbol of defiance among young men. As fads go, it had an unnatural demise—killed not by lack of interest but by decree of the War Production Board in 1942 because the suit required an excessive amount of cloth. It was an exaggerated costume: the coat nearly knee length, the high trousers extra wide at the top and extra narrow at the bottom. Equally exaggerated accessories included a key chain long enough to trip over.

The bubble, along with the balloon, the barrel, and similar names, was a variation on the loose, straight sack or chemise, which appeared in 1958. By 1959 bubbles hung unworn in closets from coast to coast.

The Nehru jacket, which had been worn by Indian Prime Minister Jawaharlal Nehru and many other Indian men for years, suddenly became popular in 1966. During the less than 2 years the fad lasted, Nehru jackets and suits in many fabrics were worn at every sort of occasion.

As ephemeral as the bubble, hot pants arrived in midwinter and were gone by the end of the following summer. Most women found them too extreme.

1939–1942
Zoot Suit

1958
Bubble

1966–1968
Nehru Jacket

1971
Hot Pants

CHAPTER TWENTY-FIVE

Battles Fought in Foreign Lands

"Why quit our own to stand upon foreign ground? Wh by interweaving our destiny with that of any part of Eu rope, entangle our peace and prosperity in the toils of Eurc pean ambition, rivalship, interest, humor or caprice? George Washington asked these questions in his 179 Farewell Address. The vast majority of Americans in h time would have agreed wholeheartedly. Isolated from Eu rope and its wars by the breadth of the Atlantic, the wanted only to pursue their destiny without foreign inter ference or involvement. Blessed with more undeveloped ter ritory than they knew what to do with, they harbored n dreams of foreign conquest. Nonetheless, the realities

The Barbary Wars

Soon after independence, the United States reluctantly joined the European nations in a centuries-old practice of paying tribute to the rulers of Algeria, Morocco, Tripoli, and Tunis to protect Mediterranean shipping from the Barbary Coast pirates. The Pasha of Tripoli thought the American payments too low, however, and declared war on the United States in 1801. President Thomas Jefferson replied by sending warships but had to supplement this force in 1803. Among the reinforcements was the dashing Lt. Stephen Decatur, shown here in hand-to-hand combat with Algerian attackers. Tripoli signed a peace treaty in 1805, but the United States continued to pay tribute to the other Barbary States. The withdrawal of American warships encouraged new depredations; so in 1815 Decatur, then a commodore, led a squadron that forced all the pirate rulers to sign peace treaties. An American squadron remained in the area to enforce the agreements and see that U.S. ships in Mediterranean waters were not molested.

The Mexican War

The first full-fledged war fought on foreign soil by the United States began in the spring of 1846. On April 25 a strong Mexican cavalry force crossed the Rio Grande and surrounded a small squadron of American dragoons. The Mexicans killed 11 of the dragoons and captured most of the rest. The U.S. Army, commanded by Gen. Zachary Taylor, retaliated by beating the Mexicans at Palo Alto on May 8. Three days later, in a bristling message to Congress, President James K. Polk charged that Mexico had "shed American blood on American soil" and asked for a declaration of war. With anti-Mexican feeling sweeping the country, on May 13, 1846, both houses of Congress voted overwhelmingly for war.

The fight had been brewing for decades. As the aggressive, westward-moving Yankees bumped against the Mexicans, tempers flared. Lives and property were inevitably lost on both sides. Mexico, outraged at U.S. support for the Texans in their fight for independence, warned that there would be war if the United States annexed the Lone Star Republic. America not only annexed Texas but backed its claim to lands as far south and west as the Rio Grande. In this disputed territory the fighting began, provoking charges by Democratic President Polk's Whig Party foes and by some antislavery Democrats that the Nation had embarked on a war of conquest plotted by Southern planters to add slave States to the Union.

In the 2 years that followed, the Americans, though heavily outnumbered by the Mexicans, won a series of spectacular victories. Under the command of General Taylor they drove the Mexicans south of the Rio Grande and by the end of 1846 had seized most of northeast Mexico. Taylor's greatest victory came at Buena Vista, where his expert use of artillery enabled 4,700 Americans to *nternational power and politics have sometimes required J.S. soldiers to fight abroad, and on those occasions Americans picked up their guns, unfurled the Stars and Stripes, and marched off to alien battlefields.*

America's early ventures outside its borders were brief excursions, which brought glory at a relatively modest price. The United States easily punished the Barbary pirates, defeated Mexico, and humiliated imperial Spain. Later it used its growing might to police the newly independent nations of the Caribbean. But in the 20th century the price of foreign warfare rose dramatically. It was only at enormous cost in men and money that America tipped the scales in World War II—and at considerable cost in World War I—but both did end in unmistakable victory. Korea and Vietnam, however, took many thousands of American lives and billions of dollars without yielding conclusive military results. Vietnam exacted a heavy moral and psychological price besides, as our people found themselves bitterly divided on the merits of the war.

No nation's military history is completely untarnished, and the United States is not an exception. But Americans can take pride, on balance, in the way their countrymen have conducted six foreign wars and carried out many lesser military operations beyond U.S. borders.

It was the *first time the American flag had flown over a conquered enemy capital, and as Gen. Winfield Scott rode into Mexico City's Grand Plaza on September 14, 1847, the assembled American troops broke into loud cheering. Soon, however, the city was in turmoil. Snipers fired down on the Americans from the rooftops, while mobs rampaged through the streets hurling rocks and bottles. Scott ordered the disorders quelled, and his men zealously carried out the command. After 3 days of fighting, order was restored, and the Americans settled in for an occupation that was to last 9 months. The capture of Mexico City helped to build Scott's reputation as the ablest U.S. military commander of the period.*

rout a force of 20,000 under the command of Gen. Antonio López de Santa Anna. With the Mexicans thus occupied in trying to stop the invaders, other U.S. troops were able to wrest control of California and New Mexico from their country's southern neighbor.

It was Gen. Winfield Scott who struck the decisive blow of the war. On March 9, 1847, U.S. ships landed Scott's army near the gulf coast city of Vera Cruz. After taking Vera Cruz, the U.S. troops marched overland toward Mexico City. After a number of savagely fought battles, the Americans climbed through mountain passes 10,000 feet high on their trek to the Mexican capital. The battle around the city was the fiercest of the war, but Scott's men fought superbly, and on September 14 they marched into Mexico City and raised the Stars and Stripes. The war was over. The United States had won a brilliant victory, and in the Treaty of Guadalupe Hidalgo that followed, it formally annexed New Mexico and California (more than 520,000 square miles of land) and established the Texas border at the Rio Grande.

Early in the conflict, New England philosopher Ralph Waldo Emerson had said: "The United States will conquer Mexico, but it will be as the man swallows arsenic, which brings him down in turn. Mexico will poison us." Soon after the war ended, the North and South were at loggerheads over the fruits of victory. Southerners sought to keep Western lands open to slavery, and northerners adamantly opposed them. As debate sharpened in Congress, Representative Robert Toombs of Georgia warned: "If by your legislation you seek to drive us from the territories of California and New Mexico, I am for disunion!" It took a Civil War to resolve the dispute.

The Spanish-American War

On February 15, 1898, the American people were stunned by news from Cuba. The U.S. battleship *Maine,* anchored in Havana harbor on a peaceful visit, had been ripped apart by two explosions and sent to the bottom with the loss of some 260 lives. The cause of the blasts was never firmly established, but the U.S. public, goaded by jingoist newspapers, blamed the Spanish authorities in Havana and their superiors in Madrid.

Spanish rule in Cuba had long angered Americans. Since the 1870's Cuban patriots had been waging an almost continuous struggle for independence, and public opinion in the United States had been outraged by stories, often fictional, of Spanish ruthlessness in combating the rebels. The sinking of the *Maine* was a tragedy that brought renewed demands for action, and from New England to California Americans applauded when Assistant Secretary of the Navy Theodore Roosevelt declared: "We will have this war for the freedom of Cuba. . . ." Faced with the clamor for armed reprisal, President William McKinley abandoned his efforts toward a diplomatic settlement and on April 25 signed an act of Congress declaring a state of war with Spain.

To the surprise of most Americans, the first U.S. initiative came thousands of miles away in the Philippines. Before war had been officially declared, Roosevelt had secretly ordered Commodore George Dewey, commander of the U.S. Asiatic Squadron, to prepare for action. On May 1, 1898, Dewey's warships steamed boldly into Manila Bay and destroyed or crippled the Spanish fleet there. Only 7 Americans were wounded in the battle, but the Spanish had 381 casualties. A mere 6 days after the outbreak of the war America had a stunning victory to celebrate and a new hero to cheer.

In the Atlantic another American naval squadron,

The Roosevelt Corollary
Firepower and Good Works

In the early years of the 20th century a wave of political chaos in the republics of the Caribbean caused European powers with investments there to consider dispatching warships to collect their debts. That possibility disturbed President Theodore Roosevelt, who feared the Europeans might use such interventions to reestablish their power in this hemisphere and become a threat to the U.S.

In 1904 the President issued what became known as the Roosevelt corollary to the Monroe Doctrine. Having declared European intervention in the Americas intolerable, he reasoned the United States was obliged to see to it that the Latin republics put their houses in order. Reluctantly, said Roosevelt, this country would have to exercise "international police power" to keep peace and quiet in the Western Hemisphere.

Over the next few decades the United States did just that, sending troops to establish order in the Dominican Republic, Haiti, Cuba, and several republics of Central America. In some matters, such as collection of customs, roadbuilding, improved sanitation, and the establishment of schools, the American influence was constructive. But inevitably the Yankee initiatives created vast ill will in Latin America.

Beginning with Herbert Hoover, successive U.S. Presidents renounced the Roosevelt corollary—a hands-off trend that was interrupted in 1965 when Lyndon B. Johnson sent troops to put down alleged leftists in the Dominican Republic.

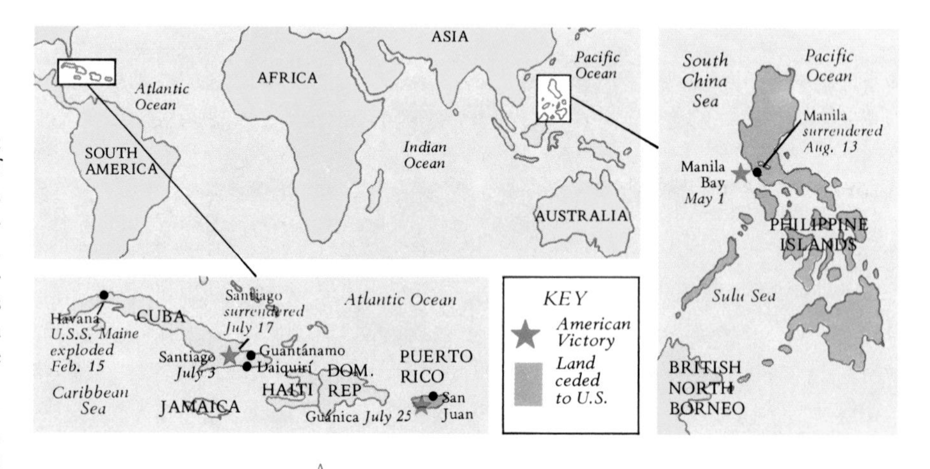

MAKING DEMOCRACY WORK

The Monroe Doctrine

In 1823 France and Spain were considering a combined expedition to South America to bring the recently independent republics there back under Spanish rule. Great Britain, which had a lucrative trade with the new nations, proposed to join with the United States in warning France and Spain to keep hands off Latin America. The United States, while needing British backing, preferred to issue its own statement. President James Monroe, in a message to Congress on December 2, 1823, outlined a position that was to become a vital and enduring element in U.S. foreign policy. "The American continents . . . are henceforth not to be considered as subjects for future colonization by any European powers . . . we should consider any attempt on their part to extend their system to any portion of this hemisphere as dangerous to our peace and safety."

The Battle of *San Juan Hill, on July 1, 1898, began in a most unpromising fashion. The Spaniards were deeply entrenched at the summit, and their rifles and artillery took a bloody toll of the Americans. Although Lt. Col. Theodore Roosevelt, his Rough Riders, and the black regiment the 9th Cavalry roared up neighboring Kettle Hill and routed those defenders, U.S. infantrymen made slow progress against the Spanish on San Juan Hill (shown in the painting by Charles Johnson Post). The "gallant but very foolish" thin blue line pushed through the hail of bullets and approached the top. Unable to halt the advance, the Spaniards threw down their arms and fled. The exhausted Americans had won the strategic heights above Santiago.*

under the command of Rear Adm. William T. Sampson, searched out a second Spanish fleet and bottled it up in the harbor of Santiago de Cuba. Marines landed at Guantánamo, about 40 miles east of Santiago, and established the first U.S. military base on Cuban soil, while the U.S. Army, far less prepared for action than the Navy, hastily organized an expeditionary force under the command of Maj. Gen. William R. Shafter. On June 14 General Shafter's force of some 17,000 men sailed out of Tampa Bay in Florida aboard 32 transports, which also carried 2,295 horses and mules and war-making equipment.

On June 22 the inadequate U.S. Army force disembarked about 15 miles east of Santiago, near the town of Daiquirí, to Cuban shouts of "¡Vivan los Americanos!" Meeting no immediate resistance from the Spanish, the invaders set out toward Santiago. They suffered their first casualties in pushing the Spaniards off the height of Las Guásimas. At El Caney on July 1 the entrenched Spanish defenders inflicted heavy losses, but Shafter's men fought gallantly and took the village. The same day, in what was overplayed at the time as the most heroic episode in U.S. military history, other troops, including Theodore Roosevelt's Rough Riders and a regiment of black cavalrymen, swarmed up Kettle Hill on foot and dislodged the Spaniards; infantrymen gained neighboring San Juan Hill after an arduous and bloody ascent.

On July 3, as the exhausted Americans paused to rest on the heights overlooking Santiago, the Spaniards tried a desperate gamble to avoid losing their fleet in case the city fell. They sailed their warships out of Santiago harbor toward the open sea. The U.S. naval force, which had more guns than the Spanish, attacked and after a few hours of fighting, blew the Spaniards out of the water; only one American was killed and one wounded. For Spain the situation was clearly hopeless, and after negotiations the Spanish surrendered not only the key seaport of Santiago but most of their military command in Cuba. On July 17 the Spanish flag, which had flown over Santiago for 384 years, was replaced by the Stars and Stripes.

With Cuba ready to fall to American forces, U.S. troops landed in Puerto Rico and seized the island after token Spanish opposition. On August 12, less than 4 months after the war had begun, Spain agreed to a cease-fire. In the Philippines U.S. troops took possession of Manila on August 13. The conflict, which had cost the United States fewer than 400 battle deaths (some 4,600 U.S. soldiers and sailors had, however, died of disease and exposure), was characterized by John Hay, U.S. Ambassador to Great Britain, as "a splendid little war."

Under the terms of the Treaty of Paris, signed in December 1898, Cuba became semi-independent under American protection, and the U.S. acquired Puerto Rico, Guam, and the Philippines. In expanding its dominion over people of alien races and languages, the United States became a world power and joined Great Britain and other imperialist nations as a self-appointed guardian of "the white man's burden." This proved a heavy load. On February 4, 1899, 2 days before the Senate had ratified the treaty with Spain, Emilio Aguinaldo and his Filipino patriots, who saw no advantage in exchanging one foreign master for another, launched an insurrection. Before the guerrilla warfare ended in July 1902, more than 4,200 Americans had been killed and hundreds had died of disease, while at home the American people were split into bitter imperialist and anti-imperialist camps. From this welter of blood, savagery, and recrimination finally emerged a workable U.S. colonial administration that brought independence to the Philippines on July 4, 1946.

Action Between Wars
Worldwide Involvement

A curious episode in American history came as a result of China's Boxer Rebellion. By the late 19th century U.S. trade with the ancient empire was sizable. More than 2,000 Americans and numerous Europeans lived in China, so the Western World was concerned when, in 1900, the Chinese secret society of Yi-Ho Ch'uan ("the righteous, harmonious fists") rose up against "the foreign devils" in an effort to expel them by force.

The Boxers, as the westerners called them, destroyed religious missions and killed a number of Chinese Christians and foreigners. Finally, encouraged by the Chinese imperial Government, they occupied Peking and laid siege to the British Legation and a Catholic church sheltering some 900 foreigners. Foreign powers with interests in China organized an international rescue expedition of 20,000 men, 2,500 of whom were Americans. They marched on Peking, entered the city in August 1900, and quickly put down the Boxers. Subsequently the Western nations forced enfeebled China to pay large indemnities. The United States used most of the $25 million it received to provide American scholarships for Chinese.

Another unexpected adventure for American soldiers came in the aftermath of the Russian Revolution of October 1917. Allied forces under British command, including a contingent of 5,100 Americans, occupied the ports of Archangel and Murmansk in northern Russia and for a time backed the counterrevolutionary White Russian armies in the war against the Bolsheviks. The American troops were all withdrawn by July 1919.

Troops of the U.S. infantry *parade on the Peking palace grounds, August 28, 1900. They had successfully helped to quell the Boxer uprising 2 weeks earlier and were now in control.*

The Allies intervened in Siberia on a bigger scale in the summer of 1918, ostensibly to rescue a large Czechoslovakian force that had deserted the Austro-Hungarian Army and was caught in the fighting between the Bolshevik and White Russian armies. At first President Wilson opposed U.S. involvement, but when the Allied command decided to send an expeditionary force and when it became apparent that the Japanese hoped to use the incident to further their own ambitions in the area, he reluctantly decided that this country should become involved. About 9,000 U.S. soldiers under Maj. Gen. William S. Graves were shipped to Siberia. Garrisoning Vladivostok and serving as railway guards, the Americans occasionally traded shots with Bolshevik troops, but for the most part concentrated on watching the Japanese and preventing them from permanently occupying strategic areas in Siberia. With their mission fulfilled, U.S. troops left Vladivostok in April 1920.

The rise of Japanese power *in the Pacific in 1905 alarmed many Americans, who saw a threat to U.S. interests. As a warning to Japanese expansionists, President Theodore Roosevelt dispatched the U.S. fleet on a round-the-world "practice cruise" in 1907. The Great White Fleet was greeted with enthusiasm in Latin America, Australia, and even Japan. The ships returned home through the Mediterranean and docked at Hampton Roads, Virginia, in early 1909 after a cruise of 46,000 miles—a spectacular stroke that enhanced U.S. prestige in the world.*

World War I

It was the Fourth of July, 1917. Parisians had not yet adopted the word "Yanks" into their vocabulary, so, when the first contingent of U.S. troops paraded in the streets of the French capital on American Independence Day, crowds lining the curbs shouted, "Vive les Teddies!"—using the nickname of the American best known to them, former President Theodore Roosevelt. Later, when Gen. John J. Pershing appeared at a ceremony before the tomb of the Marquis de Lafayette, the people of Paris responded with enthusiasm to his modest words: ". . . here on the soil of France and in the school of French heroes, our American soldiers may learn to battle and to vanquish for the liberty of the world." But it was another American officer, Col. Charles E. Stanton, who spoke the touching words that history best remembers: "Lafayette, we are here!"

The Americans had come to fight in a war that had convulsed Europe for nearly 3 years. On the one side stood France, Britain, Russia, Italy, and 8 other Allies.

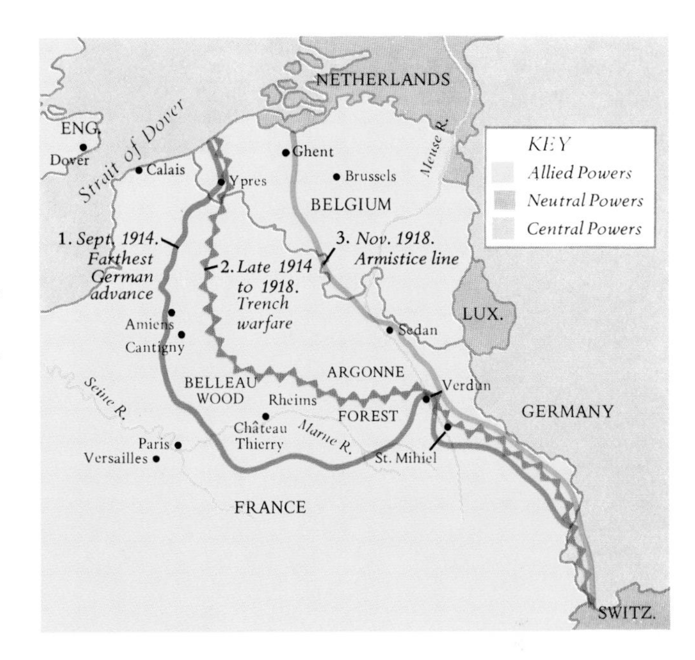

Opposing them were the Central Powers: Germany, Austria-Hungary, Turkey, and Bulgaria. Since 1914 the two sides had battered each other with the largest armies ever assembled in Europe. The great German offensives of 1914 had given way to the grinding attrition of trench warfare. Battlefields and new military cemeteries dotted the Continent, yet neither side had gained a decisive victory. The spring of 1917 had been a particularly dismal period for the Allies, but the arrival of the Americans gave French and British morale an enormous boost. Once again the Allies dared hope for victory.

It was a war America had done its best to avoid. At first there had been pro-German as well as pro-Allied sentiment in the country, and President Woodrow Wilson proclaimed a policy of neutrality. German atrocities in Belgium and the depredations of German U-boats did much to swing public opinion to the Allied side. Still, in 1916, Wilson won election to a second term with the slogan: "He kept us out of war."

In January 1917, however, the German Government made two moves that aggravated anti-German feeling in the United States: the dispatch of the so-called Zimmermann telegram and an order by the Kaiser for unrestricted submarine warfare. Although Wilson warned the Germans of dire consequences if U.S. merchant ships were attacked, the U-boats promptly sank a number of unarmed American ships. All across the country people burned with war fever. "Let's get the Hun!" and "Kill the Kaiser!" read the banners at "preparedness parades." On April 2 Wilson asked Congress to declare war, and 4 days later the legislators granted his request.

The United States was ill-prepared, but its raw draftees went off to World War I with fighting spirit high. During the summer and fall of 1917 more and more troop-

The Zimmermann Telegram

On March 1, 1917, with the opposition to U.S. involvement in World War I still showing considerable strength, a sensational story incriminating German Foreign Secretary Arthur Zimmermann in a fantastic scheme to enlist Mexico and perhaps Japan into hostilities against America was headlined in the newspapers.

The strange affair began on January 16, 1917, when Zimmermann sent a secret telegram by way of the German Embassy in Washington to the German Minister in Mexico. The envoy was instructed to propose an alliance with Germany to Mexican President Venustiano Carranza in the event the United States should join the Allies as a belligerent. The Mexicans' reward would be the recovery of their "lost territory in Texas, Arizona, and New Mexico" if they would attack their northern neighbor at a given moment. Carranza was also to be asked to invite "the immediate adherence of Japan" to the proposed alliance.

The telegram was intercepted and deciphered by British Naval Intelligence and turned over to Washington on February 24. President Woodrow Wilson, facing stiff Senate opposition to his measure to arm American merchant ships in response to unrestricted German submarine warfare, released the text to the press. Pacifists, neutralists, and pro-Germans denounced the telegram as a forgery and a British trick, but their efforts to discredit the story collapsed when Zimmermann himself said, "It is true."

The German gambit outraged American public opinion. Pro-Allied feeling in the Northeast reached new heights. Apathy toward the war in Europe gave way to anger in the Southwest and Midwest. On the Pacific coast, nervousness about expanding Japanese power was intensified. The Zimmermann telegram moved the United States one step closer to war.

May 7, 1915, *was a sunny day, and the passengers aboard the Cunard liner* Lusitania, *bound from New York to Liverpool, gathered on the decks to watch the approaching shores of Ireland. Then disaster struck. A torpedo fired at the unarmed British vessel by a German U-boat ripped through the hull, and within 18 minutes the* Lusitania *sank to the bottom with a loss of 1,198 lives. Among the dead were 128 Americans, many of them women and children. The sinking of the* Lusitania *outraged Americans and caused many to clamor for war. President Wilson refused to be pushed into the conflict by this emotional surge but denounced German policy as "subversive of the principles of warfare."*

ships arrived in French ports. The doughboys, as America's infantrymen had been called since the Civil War, were woefully ignorant of military ways, but once in France they experienced rigorous training in trench and open warfare. Later they were sent out on small raids, but although more than 175,000 of them were in France by the end of the year, few had yet taken part in combat.

The year 1918 began inauspiciously for the Allies. The Communists, who had seized power in Russia the preceding November, were suing for peace with Germany. On March 3, 1918, after the German Army had penetrated far into Russia, the Communists accepted the harsh terms of the Treaty of Brest-Litovsk and withdrew from combat. With Russia out of the way, Germany looked westward. On March 21 Gen. Erich Ludendorff, the guiding genius of the German Army, launched a series of major offensives. By late May the Germans had broken the Allied fronts in a number of sectors and were pushing deeply into France. They were only 56 miles from Paris, and the fall of the capital was thought likely by many Frenchmen. During this crisis Gen. Ferdinand Foch was appointed the Allied commander in chief to coordinate British, French, and American defensive efforts.

By now the Americans were ready for major action. On May 28 and 29 hard-fighting U.S. infantrymen slugged it out with the Germans and drove them from the village of Cantigny—the first clear-cut victory for the Americans. A few days later elements of the 3d Division checked the Germans at Château-Thierry on the banks of the Marne River, causing Gen. Henri Pétain of France to cite the Americans for their "valor and skill." Ludendorff, hoping to sustain his drive, wheeled his troops toward nearby Belleau Wood, where a U.S. infantry brigade and a do-or-die Marine brigade first stopped the Germans in their tracks and then launched a daring counterattack. On June 25 the doughboys drove the Germans out of Belleau Wood. It was the fiercest fighting the Americans had seen yet. Paris was saved, and

Air warfare *in World War I was primitive, romantic, and highly perilous. The major form of air combat was the dogfight, and its most celebrated practitioners—Germany's Manfred von Richthofen, France's René Fonck, and Britain's Edward Mannock—were men of spirit and daring. America's leading ace was Eddie Rickenbacker (right), a record-holding auto racer from Ohio. As leader of the Hat in the Ring squadron, Rickenbacker shot down 22 German planes and 4 observation balloons.*

they had earned some of the credit. French Premier Georges Clemenceau heaped praise on them, and the wood was renamed Bois de la Brigade de Marine, which infuriated the U.S. infantrymen who had played an important part in the battle. Even the German intelligence reports were laudatory; on June 17 they noted: "The personnel may be considered excellent. . . . The spirit of troops is fresh." The doughboys had proved themselves in battle and were a cocky lot, ready to take on the worst the enemy had to throw at them. It would not be long in coming, for Ludendorff was preparing another big drive. The Allies knew of the Germans' intentions, however, and Generalissimo Foch had his own plans for a counteroffensive. The American forces, now more than 1 million strong, were to play a major role.

After a massive artillery bombardment, the Germans began their offensive on July 15. They were able to cross the Marne near Rheims, but the Allies, stiffened by the Americans, generally held fast. The Germans took heavy losses, and on the second day Ludendorff was forced to abandon his offensive.

The Allied counterstroke began on July 18, when hundreds of thousands of French poilus and American doughboys went "over the top" and charged into the shell-pocked countryside around Soissons. The Germans were taken by surprise, and Americans and Frenchmen

Evidence of Patriotic Fervor
Posters, Slogans, and Songs To Inspire the Populace

James Montgomery Flagg, *World War I's leading poster artist, painted a number of appeals for volunteers. The one above is Flagg's classic.*

U.S. entry into the war against Germany touched off a frenzy of patriotism. Throughout the country young men responded eagerly to the powerful posters of James Montgomery Flagg and other famous illustrators of the day urging them to enlist in the Army, Navy, or Marines.

To keep the martial spirit at high pitch, the Government's Committee on Public Information commissioned such movies as *Pershing's Crusaders* and *America's Answer.* Tin Pan Alley turned out a succession of rousing tunes, and George M. Cohan's "Over There" stirred American hearts from Broadway to San Francisco's Telegraph Hill and was even recorded by opera immortal Enrico Caruso. Film stars Douglas Fairbanks, Charlie Chaplin, and Mary Pickford sold Liberty Bonds to cheering crowds at street-corner mass meetings. Never before had there been such a nationwide outpouring of patriotism.

In their enthusiasm to "crush the Kaiser," Americans learned to conserve gas and electricity and to teach their children not to waste food. So intense did the anti-German feeling become that sauerkraut was renamed "Liberty cabbage," the music of German composers was shunned, and many Americans of German descent were subjected to abuse and ridicule and sometimes they were physically assaulted.

Walter Whitehead *painted this poster to promote the sale of Liberty Bonds. More than half of the country's adults bought them.*

America's songwriters *poured forth a steady stream of wartime tunes. Some were martial; others told of the rigors of life in the Army.*

stormed into their trenches with bayonets fixed. Both sides took heavy losses, but all along the Soissons front thousands of demoralized German soldiers surrendered. By early August the Franco-American drive had carried from the Marne to the Vesle. On August 8—known as the Black Day for the German Army—Franco-British forces on the Amiens front launched an offensive that was to drive the Germans back along the Somme, capture nearly 30,000 prisoners, and convince Ludendorff and the Kaiser that defeat was just a matter of time.

Behind the scenes the Germans initiated peace negotiations. But there were battles still to be fought. Under Pershing's command American and French troops took St.-Mihiel on the Meuse River and snared 15,000 German prisoners in mid-September. The last great Franco-American offensive began on September 26, with Pershing's men striking between the Meuse and the Argonne Forest. The countryside was rugged and progress slow, but in early November the Americans advanced to the heights above Sedan. To the north the British and French advanced on a broad front, and it was now apparent that the enemy was crumbling. Bulgaria and Turkey had already concluded armistices with the Allies, and on November 3 Austria-Hungary followed suit. Four days later German and Allied representatives met in a railway car in the Forest of Compiègne for talks that terminated in virtually complete German capitulation.

On Armistice Day, November 11, 1918, at 11 a.m. the guns fell silent. The Great War was over. Germany had been defeated, and the Kaiser and his Crown Prince fled into exile in Holland. U.S. intervention had been a decisive factor. The United States was proud of the way the doughboys had fought and prayed that the war would be the last such massive bloodletting. In the more than 4 years of war, almost 10 million people had been killed; more than 115,000 Americans had died hoping to "make the world safe for democracy." As fate would have it, that fond hope could not be sustained.

On Armistice Day, *November 11, 1918, the crowds jammed Broad Street (right) in New York City's financial district. The war was over. One of the most celebrated of the returning Yanks was Sgt. Alvin C. York (below), who was awarded the Medal of Honor for singlehandedly killing 20 enemy soldiers and capturing 132 in 1 day.*

Smoke rises over Pearl Harbor *as Japanese planes carry out their attack on December 7, 1941. In the painting by U.S. Navy Comdr. Griffith Bailey Coale, bombs narrowly miss the* Nevada. *To the* Nevada's *stern is the* California. *In the foreground is the* Oglala.

World War II

Shortly before 8 a.m. on December 7, 1941, the Japanese struck Pearl Harbor in Hawaii without warning. Fighters and dive bombers emblazoned with the emblem of the Rising Sun attacked U.S. airfields, while Japanese high-level bombers and torpedo bombers mounted a furious attack on the assembled warships of the U.S. Pacific Fleet. The Americans, caught completely by surprise, could offer only feeble resistance. Of the eight heavy battleships at anchor at the naval base, seven were either sunk or severely damaged. Three cruisers and three destroyers were also crippled. Of the 394 U.S. aircraft in the area, almost all were badly damaged or demolished. In less than 2 hours the Japanese had greatly reduced the American striking power. Fortunately six U.S. aircraft carriers, which were later to play an all-important role in repulsing the Japanese in the Pacific, were not at Pearl Harbor on December 7.

The devastating sneak attack, which left 2,330 Americans dead and 1,145 wounded, sent a wave of shocked outrage across the United States. The next day President Franklin D. Roosevelt asked Congress to declare war on Japan—a request that was approved by an overwhelming vote of 470 to 1. Three days later Japan's Axis partners, Germany and Italy, declared war on the United States. Congress reciprocated, and the United States was at last drawn into World War II.

The largest war in history had been in the making since the early 1930's. As the rest of the world stood idle and the League of Nations churned in ineffectual debate at Geneva, a military clique in Japan, a Fascist dictatorship in Italy, and a brutal National Socialist (shortened to Nazi) regime in Germany created an international reign of terror. The Axis, as the three-power alignment called itself, swallowed up one country after another.

The Role of the Code Breakers

Cryptography, from the Greek words for *hidden* and *writing,* involves the putting of messages into a secret code or cipher. Those who do not have the key must unlock the secret by cryptanalysis. As early as 404 B.C. the Spartans used a transposition cipher in which the letters of the original message were scrambled. They wound a belt in a spiral around a stick and wrote the message on it. When the belt was unwound it appeared to be covered with meaningless letters. The recipient could read the message when he wound the belt around a rod of the same length and diameter. Julius Caesar was said to have invented the substitution cipher in which each letter in the original message was replaced by the letter three positions to the right in the alphabet. Thus a message ATTACK AT ONCE would encipher as DWWDFN DW RQFH. A code system, depending on its use, involves a specialized vocabulary of words and phrases. It employs a codebook, or dictionary of the code language, which is used to encode and decode messages. All known methods of enciphering and encoding messages are refinements or combinations of the code, the transposition cipher, or the substitution cipher. The combinations, however, can be very sophisticated.

The art of the cryptanalyst requires perspiration, luck, and extensive study of language characteristics. In solving, in 1940, the extremely complicated Japanese electronic machine cipher, known as the Code Purple, American cryptanalysts built a machine that duplicated the circuits of the enemy device. This code breaker consisted of an electric typewriter, the cryptographic assembly of plugboard and coding rings, and a printing unit. American cryptanalysts could not prevent the Pearl Harbor disaster because no message revealing Japan's intentions was intercepted. But later efforts by Army and Navy cryptanalysts broke the supersecret Japanese cryptographic system, and, in the words of a joint Congressional committee that investigated the attack on Pearl Harbor, "contributed enormously to the defeat of the enemy. . . ."

World War II *(continued)*

Finally Britain and France warned Nazi leader Adolf Hitler that an invasion of Poland would precipitate all-out war. Franco-British hopes of gaining Soviet aid against Germany were dashed when Hitler and Joseph Stalin signed a 10-year nonaggression pact in August 1939. On September 1 the Nazis launched a blitzkrieg against Poland, using dive bombers, tanks, and paratroopers in a concerted attack unparalleled in military history. World War II had begun.

Within days the U.S.S.R. joined the assault. Poland fell before the combined onslaught in 3 weeks and was dismembered by the two aggressors. In the spring of 1940 Denmark, Norway, Belgium, Luxembourg, the Netherlands, then France itself were overrun by the mighty Nazi war machine. Italy, which had stood by until then, allied itself in combat with its Axis partner shortly before France laid down arms. With nearly all Western Europe under their control, the Germans unleashed a massive air assault on Britain, but the tough island nation inflicted heavy losses on its attacker. Then, in rapid order, Hitler forced Rumania, Hungary, and Bulgaria to become satellites. In early 1941 the Nazis occupied Yugoslavia and Greece, while Germany's Afrika Korps, under Gen. Erwin Rommel, who was called the Desert Fox, was driving British desert troops back across North Africa toward Alexandria, Egypt. Flushed with success, Hitler then took a step of historic magnitude. Repudiating the nonaggression pact that he had signed with Stalin, he ordered an invasion of the Soviet Union. The invasion started on June 22, and by winter the German armies had penetrated deeply into Russia and were threatening Moscow.

As the Nazi juggernaut moved on, an alarmed America, step by hesitant step, abandoned its pretense of neutrality. The United States became "the arsenal of democracy" and embarked on a lend-lease program that eventually was to ship more than $50 billion worth of arms and other supplies to the Allies. The United States also began to prepare for direct action, gearing up its war industries and instituting the first peacetime draft. But the Nation was not yet fully ready, and the warlords in Tokyo, determined to put an end to American influence in the Pacific, decided that the time had come to strike.

The months that followed the disastrous attack on Pearl Harbor saw the Allied fortunes sink to their lowest point. In the Far East the Japanese overran Thailand; Burma; Hong Kong; British Malaya, including Singapore; the oil-rich Dutch East Indies; and dozens of Pacific islands. In the Philippines Gen. Douglas MacArthur and his badly outnumbered Filipino and U.S. troops fought gallantly, but early in May 1942 their resistance ended, and the Rising Sun flew over most of the western Pacific and Southeast Asia. In Europe the Nazis, who had been stalled for months by the weather and the Soviets, had also renewed their drive, reaching the Volga River near Stalingrad in the spring of 1942.

By midyear, however, the Allies had begun to stem the Axis tide. On May 7 and 8 American carrier-based warplanes outdueled a similar Japanese force in the Battle of the Coral Sea. A month later, in the Battle of Midway, U.S. planes battered a Japanese fleet, sinking 4 carriers and a cruiser and downing some 350 aircraft in 2 days of furious combat. Midway, Japan's first major setback, was an augury of things to come. Two months later U.S. Marines stormed ashore on Guadalcanal, and, reinforced by Army divisions, took the island after bloody fighting.

Despite the ravages of the German U-boats, huge amounts of American supplies were now reaching the British and Soviet armies. At the end of October the British in North Africa launched an armored offensive

In the Battle of Midway *the U.S. Navy gained a large measure of revenge. The painting by Commander Coale shows American dive bombers turning the Japanese carrier* Kaga *into an inferno in which 800 men died; the ship, along with four others, sank to the bottom.*

American Industry Meets the Challenge

Spanning the Oceans With Supplies

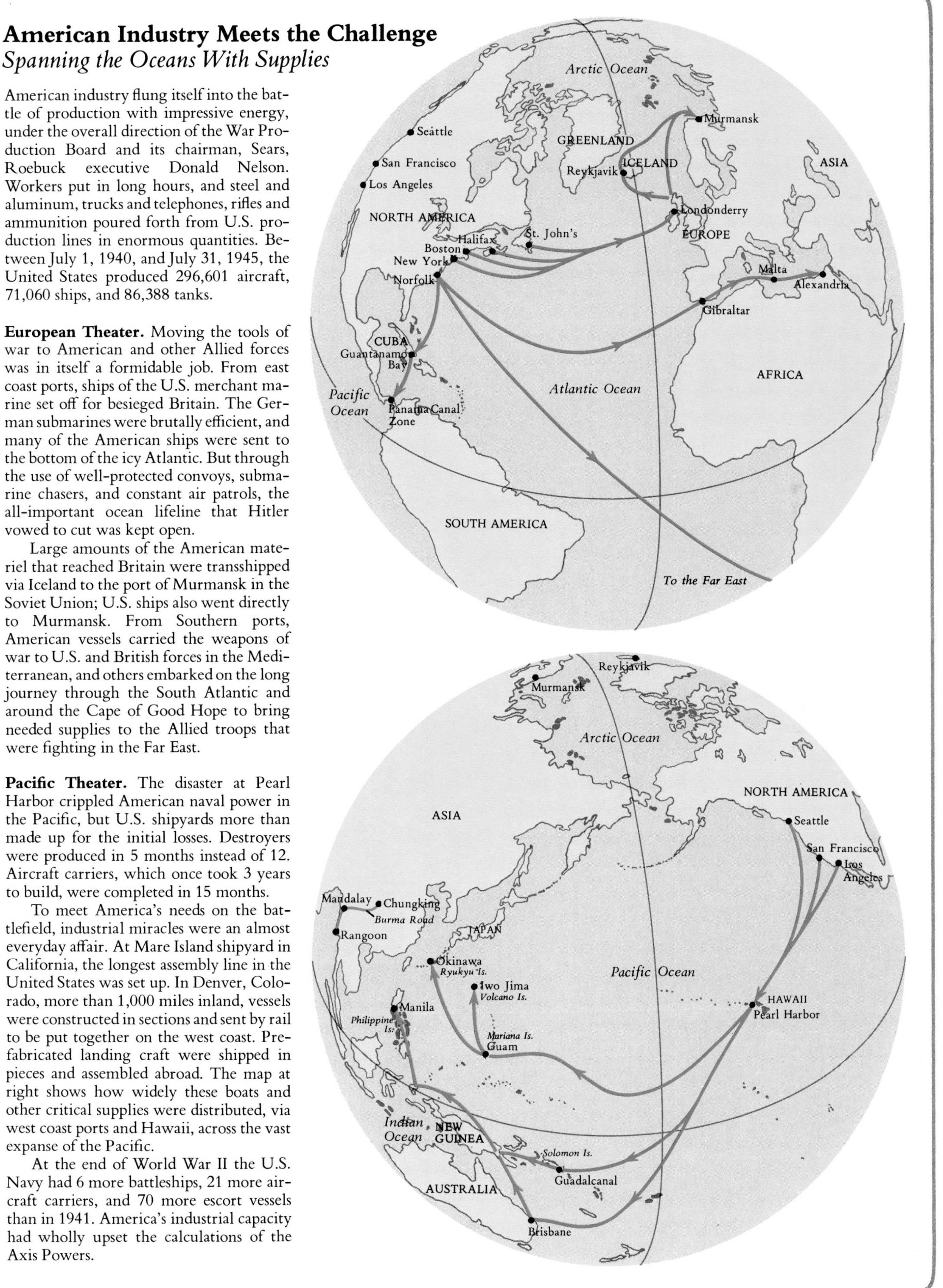

American industry flung itself into the battle of production with impressive energy, under the overall direction of the War Production Board and its chairman, Sears, Roebuck executive Donald Nelson. Workers put in long hours, and steel and aluminum, trucks and telephones, rifles and ammunition poured forth from U.S. production lines in enormous quantities. Between July 1, 1940, and July 31, 1945, the United States produced 296,601 aircraft, 71,060 ships, and 86,388 tanks.

European Theater. Moving the tools of war to American and other Allied forces was in itself a formidable job. From east coast ports, ships of the U.S. merchant marine set off for besieged Britain. The German submarines were brutally efficient, and many of the American ships were sent to the bottom of the icy Atlantic. But through the use of well-protected convoys, submarine chasers, and constant air patrols, the all-important ocean lifeline that Hitler vowed to cut was kept open.

Large amounts of the American materiel that reached Britain were transshipped via Iceland to the port of Murmansk in the Soviet Union; U.S. ships also went directly to Murmansk. From Southern ports, American vessels carried the weapons of war to U.S. and British forces in the Mediterranean, and others embarked on the long journey through the South Atlantic and around the Cape of Good Hope to bring needed supplies to the Allied troops that were fighting in the Far East.

Pacific Theater. The disaster at Pearl Harbor crippled American naval power in the Pacific, but U.S. shipyards more than made up for the initial losses. Destroyers were produced in 5 months instead of 12. Aircraft carriers, which once took 3 years to build, were completed in 15 months.

To meet America's needs on the battlefield, industrial miracles were an almost everyday affair. At Mare Island shipyard in California, the longest assembly line in the United States was set up. In Denver, Colorado, more than 1,000 miles inland, vessels were constructed in sections and sent by rail to be put together on the west coast. Prefabricated landing craft were shipped in pieces and assembled abroad. The map at right shows how widely these boats and other critical supplies were distributed, via west coast ports and Hawaii, across the vast expanse of the Pacific.

At the end of World War II the U.S. Navy had 6 more battleships, 21 more aircraft carriers, and 70 more escort vessels than in 1941. America's industrial capacity had wholly upset the calculations of the Axis Powers.

against the German lines at the Egyptian town of El Alamein. After a fierce tank duel the British broke through the enemy lines, sending Rommel's Afrika Korps fleeing across Libya in Germany's first big defeat of the war. On November 8 came the electrifying news that a powerful Anglo-American force under the command of Lt. Gen. Dwight D. Eisenhower had landed in Algeria and Morocco. On the Soviet front, too, the tide was turning. In November the Soviets mounted a major counteroffensive, trapping the entire German 6th Army at Stalingrad. It was forced to surrender on February 2, 1943.

In January 1943 President Roosevelt and British Prime Minister Winston Churchill met in Casablanca, on the Moroccan coast, to chart Allied strategy. The Western leaders ruled out a negotiated settlement with the Axis, declaring that nothing short of unconditional surrender would be accepted. They laid plans to step up the bombing of Germany and to reenter Europe through Sicily. In May, as a first step, British and American troops cornered and captured the remnants of the Axis armies in North Africa, bagging upward of a quarter of a million German and Italian prisoners.

In July the Allies landed on Sicily, which fell on August 8 after sharp encounters with the Germans and a spiritless defense by the Italians. As defeatism spread in Italy, an antiwar coup d'etat took place in Rome. Dictator Benito Mussolini was ousted and replaced by Marshal Pietro Badoglio, who opened secret negotiations with the Allies. In September the Allies made a triple landing at Reggio di Calabria, Taranto, and Salerno. Although deserted by their Axis partner, the Germans fought stubbornly and nearly threw the Allied force back into the sea at Salerno. After bloody fighting, however, the Allies took Naples on October 1 and advanced slowly toward Rome before coming to a standstill for the winter.

On the eastern front the Red Army, bolstered by fresh troops, new confidence, and a steady supply of food and supplies from the United States, also made dramatic gains in 1943. It drove the Germans out of the Caucasus, isolated them in the Crimea, and liberated such important cities as Kharkov, Smolensk, and Kiev.

In the Pacific theater the Americans had seized the initiative early in 1943. The American policy was to seize strategic islands, thus cutting off supplies to Japanese strong points and making them vulnerable to later attack. In the southwest Pacific, American and Australian troops under General MacArthur steadily pushed northward, punching their way up the coast of New Guinea against heavy Japanese resistance. American forces landed in the Bismarck Archipelago and leapfrogged across the Solomon Island chain, meeting fanatical enemy resistance at every point. In May, far to the north, the Americans retook the Aleutian Islands, which had been occupied by the Japanese the previous year. And in the Central Pacific, near the close of the year, U.S. troops seized the Gilbert Islands, though at heavy cost; more than 1,000 Marines, charging heroically into Japanese guns, lost their lives taking the atoll of Tarawa.

When Roosevelt, Churchill, and Stalin met at Teheran in November 1943, they agreed that the Italian campaign, though useful in diverting German troops, should not stand in the way of a major assault on Hitler's "Fortress Europe" across the English Channel. While this was being prepared for, the Allied forces in Italy inched northward in early 1944, and on June 4 the Americans entered Rome, Italy's capital, which had been declared an open city to preserve its historic treasures.

Two days later came D-day. An armada of Allied vessels, sheltered by an unprecedented air umbrella, landed

America's Wartime Leaders

Gen. Henry H. "Hap" Arnold, Commanding General of the U.S. Army Air Forces, had been taught to fly in 1911 by Orville Wright. Along with Gen. William Mitchell, Arnold was one of the Army's most fervent apostles of air power, and after the United States entered the war he became the guiding spirit behind the greatest air force ever to take to the skies.

Gen. Dwight D. Eisenhower, a magnetic Kansan, was Supreme Commander of the Allied Expeditionary Forces that stormed the fortress of Hitler's Europe. A natural arbitrator, Eisenhower was able to forge the often squabbling Allied commanders into a unified and victorious fighting team. The genial midwesterner also had the common touch, and to his troops—and to much of the world—he was known simply as Ike.

Adm. Ernest J. King was the starchy, exacting Commander in Chief, U.S. Fleet, and Chief of Naval Operations. A graduate of the U.S. Naval Academy at Annapolis, King—who possessed one of the sharpest strategic minds in the Allied camp—served as F.D.R.'s principal adviser on naval warfare.

Gen. Douglas MacArthur, Supreme Commander of Allied Forces in the Southwest Pacific, was—with the possible exception of Gen. George S. Patton, Jr.—the most flamboyant American military leader of the war. With his specially designed headgear, ever-present sunglasses, and corncob pipe, the outspoken general captured headlines around the world. But if MacArthur had a flair for self-publicity, he was also a great general who conducted the Allied comeback in the Pacific with admirable skill and audacity.

Gen. George C. Marshall, a quiet, patient man, was the principal organizer of the American military effort. As Chief of Staff of the Army, Marshall directed the recruitment and training of troops, the development of new weapons and equipment, and the selection of top commanders. A man of superb intellect, he was President Roosevelt's chief adviser on global military strategy and became the first man to hold the new rank of General of the Army.

On D-day *German resistance proved to be lighter than expected in most sectors. But on Omaha Beach two American divisions ran into a ferocious fight. As the Americans waded ashore they were open targets of crossfire from German troops on the bluffs above the beach, and the first U.S. units suffered fearful casualties. For a time it looked as if the Americans might be thrown back into the sea. But the GI's clung stubbornly to their foothold, regrouped their forces, and advanced up the heights in the face of murderous fire. After a bitter fight the Germans were dislodged—Omaha Beach was secured.*

thousands of troops on the Normandy coast of France. The greatest seaborne invasion in history, code-named Operation Overlord, had finally begun.

At the sector called Omaha Beach, withering German fire greeted the Americans, but, though hard pressed, they fought their way beyond the beach. The choice of a landing site seemed to have surprised the Germans, and the huge Anglo-American force under the overall command of General Eisenhower soon established a beachhead. With the British and U.S. Air Forces in command of the skies, the German Luftwaffe kept its distance as vast quantities of men and equipment were poured into the slowly expanding foothold on the Continent.

In late July U.S. tank forces under Gen. George S. Patton burst out of the Normandy beachhead and thrust with lightning speed into the heart of France. The Germans fell back rapidly, and on August 25 an Allied force, which included Free French units, liberated Paris. American troops pushed toward the German border while British and Canadian forces drove into Belgium and the Netherlands. Despite a terrific battering, however, the Germans were far from finished. In December Hitler launched a daring counterstroke, breaking through the American lines in the Ardennes Forest and winning important initial victories. The bitterly fought Battle of the Bulge was the Germans' last major offensive effort; ultimately the Americans repulsed them and sent them reeling toward their own border.

In the Pacific 1944 brought new Japanese reverses as U.S. forces hopped from island chain to island chain. The Americans took the Marshalls and the Marianas after heavy fighting. In the Battle of the Philippine Sea on June 19 and 20, U.S. submarines and carrier-based planes gave the Japanese a sound trouncing. In October General MacArthur's forces landed on Leyte, an island in the central Philippines. Three Japanese task forces converged in an attempt to trap the invasion transports and their escorts; but in the resulting Battle of Leyte Gulf, the largest sea action in history, the U.S. Navy battered the combined Japanese fleet so badly that thereafter the Japanese Navy could play no significant role in the war.

The year 1945 began auspiciously as the Red Army, which had driven the Nazis off Soviet soil the year before, penetrated the German border and drove to within 100 miles of Berlin. In early February Roosevelt, Churchill, and Stalin met near Yalta, in the Soviet Union, to prepare for Germany's surrender. Roosevelt died 2 months later, on April 12, and was thus spared the heavy criticism that later developed when the U.S.S.R. failed to honor certain terms that were agreed upon at the conference.

In early April, on the western front, U.S. troops swept to the Elbe, a scant 100 miles from Berlin, while the

In 1944, *with the tide of war turning dramatically in favor of the Allies, a caricaturist portrayed a jaunty F.D.R., a confident Churchill, and an amused Stalin winning their game of dominoes against the disconsolate Axis team of Hitler, Mussolini, and Emperor Hirohito.*

World War II *(continued)*

Russians were even closer to the city. From the skies U.S. and British bombers, which had hammered German industry over the past year, continued to rain destruction on most of Germany's major cities.

The end was now in sight. The Soviets were once again moving ahead and by April 25 had surrounded Berlin. On April 28 Benito Mussolini, Italy's deposed dictator, died at the hands of Italian partisans. Adolf Hitler, his mad dreams in a shambles, committed suicide, along with some of his supporters, in a Berlin bunker on April 30. German commanders began showing the white flag on all fronts. On May 2 the German forces in Italy gave up. On May 7 a formal surrender document was signed, ending the long war in Europe as of midnight on May 8.

In some of the *bloodiest fighting of the Pacific war, U.S. Marines took the Japanese island of Iwo Jima. In the above photo, Leathernecks plant the flag atop Mount Suribachi.*

In the Pacific the war had still to be won. In January, MacArthur, as he had promised, returned to the main Philippine island of Luzon with his liberating forces and after bitter fighting retook Manila on March 4, 1945. To the north other Americans captured Iwo Jima and Okinawa after months of battling for every rock and cave. In the Okinawa campaign (April 1–June 30) the U.S. suffered 12,500 dead and 36,500 wounded—the heaviest American loss of the Pacific war.

The situation was clearly hopeless for the Japanese. Their air force and navy were all but out of action. Their economy was shattered by devastating U.S. bombing raids and the loss of conquered territories that had supplied vital raw materials. Civilian morale was low to a point of despair. On July 26 the Allies broadcast an ultimatum threatening total destruction unless the Japanese surrendered unconditionally.

Tragically, Japan did not respond affirmatively to the ultimatum. President Harry S. Truman, still new in office, had a fateful decision to make: whether to mount a costly invasion of Japan's home islands or to unleash a secret weapon capable of hitherto-undreamed-of destructive power. Truman felt he had no real choice. On August 6 American aircraft dropped an atomic bomb on Hiroshima, and 3 days later another atomic bomb was dropped on Nagasaki. The resulting death and destruction shocked the world. On August 14 Emperor Hirohito announced that Japan had surrendered unconditionally; on September 2 the Japanese signed the surrender document aboard the U.S. battleship *Missouri* in Tokyo Bay.

After 6 years the most destructive war in history was over. Some 16 million military personnel and 18 million civilians had died. Though the United States had not entered the war until 1941, more than 400,000 Americans had given their lives. Americans of every race and ethnic group fought valiantly together to prevent the world from sinking back—as Winston Churchill expressed it—"into the abyss of a new Dark Age."

The war in the Pacific *ended on August 14, 1945, but Japan's formal surrender did not come until September 2—on the deck of the 45,000-ton battleship* Missouri *at anchor in Tokyo Bay. It was a moment of high drama. The* Missouri, *flagship of the U.S. Pacific Fleet, flew the same flag that waved over the Capitol in Washington the day Pearl Harbor was attacked. One by one, Japanese representatives and generals and admirals of the Allied military forces in the Pacific stepped forward to sign the surrender documents. In the photo at left, Japanese Gen. Yoshijiro Umezu affixes his signature under the watchful eye of Gen. Douglas MacArthur. After the signing MacArthur expressed the hope that "from this solemn occasion a better world shall emerge."*

The Korean War

On June 25, 1950, the North Korean Army—trained, equipped, and, many believed, inspired by the Soviet Union—plunged across the 38th parallel and invaded South Korea. The United Nations Security Council promptly branded the invasion a flagrant act of aggression and called on U.N. members to help South Korea. The Soviets, who could have prevented action by exercising their veto power, continued to boycott Security Council meetings. They had begun the boycott in January in protest over the U.N. refusal to seat Red China in place of Nationalist China on the Council. On June 27, after the South Korean capital of Seoul fell to the invaders, Truman ordered American air and naval forces in the area to join in resisting the Communists. Three days later, as the North Koreans menaced the southern port of Pusan, Truman sent U.S. ground troops stationed in Japan into the Korean battle.

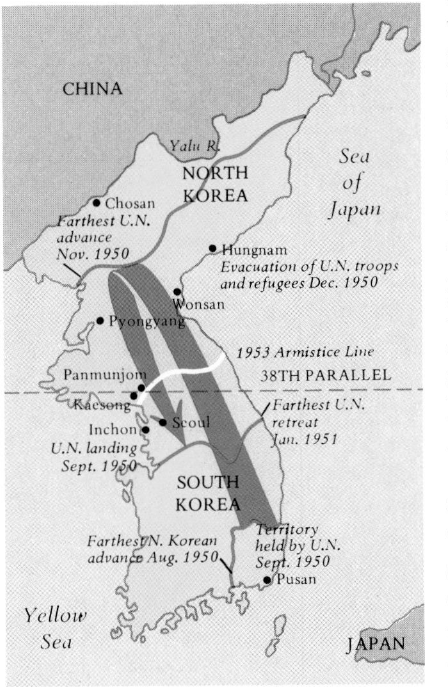

The decision to defend South Korea was popular at the time with both Congress and the American public. In the aftermath of World War II, Korea had been taken from Japan and occupied by the Soviet Union north of the 38th parallel and by the Americans south of that line. In their zone the Soviets set up a Communist dictatorship intent on reuniting the country by force; in the south the Americans tried with limited success to foster a democratic order. In the summer of 1949, after 4 years of occupation, the U.S. withdrew its troops, giving the North Koreans the chance they had been waiting for. In attacking South Korea, however, they seriously misjudged the mood in the United States. Most Americans, having seen Eastern Europe and China fall to the Communists in the postwar years, were convinced that it was time to draw the line.

The cold war had become a shooting war, and the early fighting went badly for the U.N. forces, at first composed chiefly of South Koreans and Americans. The North Koreans pushed southward and soon pinned the South Koreans and untried American troops into an enclave around Pusan. On September 15, in a masterful move, General MacArthur, who had been given the U.N. command on July 8, 1950, struck the Communists on their flank with a surprise amphibious landing near Inchon. The trapped North Koreans either surrendered en masse or fled northward across the 38th parallel.

At this point Communist China warned that it would not stand by "supinely" if North Korea were invaded. The warning was brushed aside as bluff, and MacArthur's forces pushed across the frontier and drove the enemy back toward the Chinese border. Some 300,000 Chinese "volunteers" had crossed the Yalu River and struck the Americans on the flank and in the rear on November 26, 1950. Stunned by the sudden assault, the Americans suffered heavy casualties and fell back in retreat through the bitter winter countryside.

South of the 38th parallel, the U.N. allies regrouped and dug in. The polyglot U.N. forces, although still composed mainly of Americans and South Koreans, by now included troops from 15 other nations and medical missions from several more. In early 1951 they beat off a number of enemy offensives, exacting a heavy toll and driving the Communists north of the 38th parallel once again. General MacArthur, convinced that there was "no substitute for victory," became more and more outspoken in calling for the bombing of China's supply depots in Manchuria. MacArthur's views, which raised the specter of full-scale war with China and perhaps with the Soviet Union, deeply disturbed America's allies and President Truman himself. Determined to assert civilian control over the military, Truman removed the popular war hero from his command and put Gen. Matthew B. Ridgway in charge.

Americans were dazed by this turn of events. By mid-1951 most of them were looking for an end to a war that appeared hopelessly stalemated. The Communists, who had endured fearful casualties, were also prepared to discuss a truce, so on July 10, 1951, negotiations began.

The talks dragged on for months while fighting men continued to die, and the conflict became an issue in the 1952 U.S. Presidential campaign. The Republican candidate, Gen. Dwight D. Eisenhower, promised if elected to go to Korea and bring the war to an end. He was elected in November, defeating Democratic candidate Adlai Stevenson, and in December, before his inauguration, he went to Korea. On July 27, 1953, an armistice was signed at Panmunjom, establishing a demilitarized zone at approximately the 38th parallel. Since then the armistice has remained in effect, marked frequently by skirmishes and charges of violations by both sides.

Although neither side claimed victory in Korea, American intervention under the U.N. banner was the first time that the Communists had been stopped by forces mobilized on an international scale.

The Vietnam War

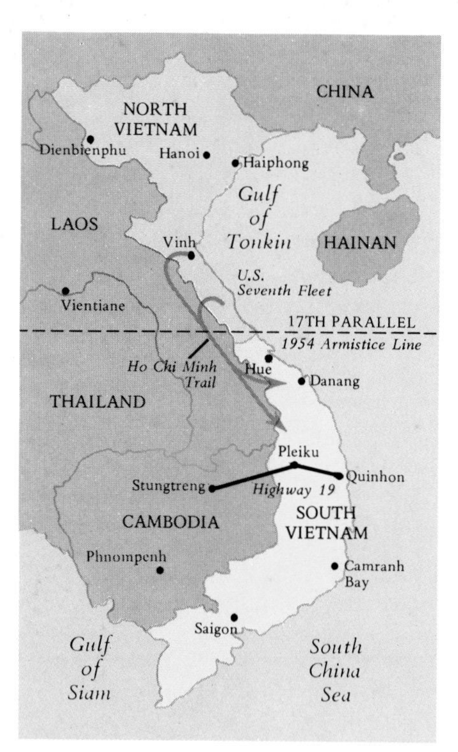

On March 6, 1965, 3,500 U.S. Marines splashed out of their landing craft and waded ashore near the South Vietnamese city of Danang to be greeted by smiling officials. The landing was to prove a fateful event for America. President Lyndon B. Johnson had come to the conclusion that large numbers of U.S. combat troops would have to be committed to the ground war in South Vietnam. The Marines were the advance guard of the 3 million American men who eventually would be deployed in the longest and most unpopular war in U.S. history.

President Johnson had inherited the problem of Vietnam from his predecessors. In the late 1950's President Eisenhower, fearful that the Communists would take over the former French colony, increased the number of U.S. military advisers to the Saigon government from 323 to 685. President Kennedy deepened the American commitment, raising the U.S. force to 23,000 and shipping much equipment to South Vietnam. Still, the Communists—chiefly local Vietcong, who were supported by disciplined cadres from North Vietnam—continued to gain strength.

Johnson, succeeding to the Presidency after Kennedy's assassination, was determined to prevent a Communist victory. In August 1964 the Navy reported an attack on two U.S. destroyers in the Gulf of Tonkin by North Vietnamese PT boats. Johnson used the incident as the basis for requesting blanket authority from Congress to take any military measures he deemed necessary in Southeast Asia. Early in 1965 he ordered U.S. aircraft into action against the Vietcong, and soon after he unveiled Operation Rolling Thunder—a massive bombing campaign against North Vietnam. By the end of the year 185,000 American troops were engaged in fighting.

The Americans fought well, but this was a new and unconventional kind of war. For the most part it was fought by small units in the jungles and rice paddies, and all too often it was impossible to tell who was a friendly villager and who was a Vietcong guerrilla. As the statistics of American dead and wounded rose, antiwar sentiment in the U.S. spread. Thanks to television, the horrors of war were brought home to the American public as never before. Peace groups demonstrated all across the country, and students fled into exile rather than serve in Vietnam. World opinion, seeing the struggle in terms of David and Goliath, turned against the U.S.

President Johnson made many attempts to initiate peace talks with Hanoi during 1966 and 1967, but the North Vietnamese refused to talk unless the United States first halted its bombing unconditionally. The U.S., in turn, would not agree to stop the bombing until North Vietnam curtailed military operations in the south. And so the fighting continued, with the North Vietnamese pouring in fresh forces and the United States bringing its troop strength to more than half a million. For a time it looked as if the Communists were beaten, but on January 30, 1968, during Tet, the Buddhist New Year, they struck at major cities across South Vietnam. The Communists held the city of Hué for 25 days and created havoc in Saigon, but were beaten back short of their objective of a popular uprising in Saigon.

The Tet offensive nevertheless had a profound impact on the United States, spurring the peace movement and dismaying administration supporters. Dejected and weary, President Johnson, on March 31, 1968, announced a partial unilateral halt to the bombing of North Vietnam and invited Hanoi to the peace table. At the same time he stated that he would not seek another term as President. Three days later Hanoi agreed to take part in preliminary talks, and in May those exchanges began in Paris. But the two sides haggled endlessly over procedural matters (including the size and shape of the conference table), and not until the early days of President Richard M. Nixon's administration did they start discussing substantive matters. The disclosure in 1970 of the massacre of civilians at Mylai by American troops and the publication in 1971 of the Pentagon Papers, detailing the dreary step-by-step involvement of America in Vietnam in the face of much contrary expert advice, further eroded support for the war in the United States.

In March 1972, after more than 3 years of talks in Paris, North Vietnam again tried for military victory, launching attacks in many sectors of the south. In retaliation President Nixon authorized punishing air raids on the north and had Navy planes mine Haiphong harbor. The Communists, after initial successes, were pushed back with terrible losses. Finally, on January 27, 1973, all parties to the war signed an accord calling for the withdrawal of U.S. troops (completed March 29, 1973) and the creation of a council to reconcile all factions. Soon a welter of charges of bad faith brought renewed fighting that ended early in 1975 with the surrender of South Vietnam. The U.S. legacy of a $150-billion war debt and 56,000 deaths left an indelible scar on the American consciousness.

Evolution of the U.S. Combat Soldier's Uniform

As War Became More Dehumanizing and Deadly, Its Panoply Disappeared

European-influenced field-service uniforms of traditional Army blue, with decorative touches appealing to regimental pride, were worn in the Mexican and Civil Wars, but after the conflict with Spain the Army recognized the need to make the soldier a less inviting target to a marksman armed with a modern rifle. By World War I armed combat had become a deadly science in which bright colors and gaudy decorations were an invitation to slaughter, as the French learned at heavy cost in the battles of 1914.

Modifications of uniforms were accompanied by changes in equipment. Steel helmets were introduced as a protection against shrapnel. Gas masks, essential in World War I, were carried in World War II but not used. As the use of automatic weapons increased, the soldier needed immediate access to his reserve ammunition, so compartmented belts were phased out and replaced by more pouches and bigger pockets.

Mexican War (*1846–48*). Yellow band on cap and yellow facing on jacket identify dragoon. Distinctive features include shoulder straps and white leather straps to which Hall carbine and saber are attached. Indian-style leggings were worn only in Southwest.

Spanish-American War (*1898*). Belt buckle, crossed rifles on campaign hat, and blue markings identify infantryman in New York regiment. Blanket roll and canvas-covered canteen are slung from shoulders. Ammunition for Springfield rifle is carried in cartridge belt at waist. Canvas leggings lace at sides.

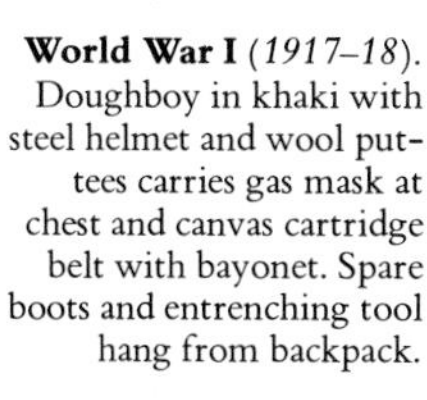

World War I (*1917–18*). Doughboy in khaki with steel helmet and wool puttees carries gas mask at chest and canvas cartridge belt with bayonet. Spare boots and entrenching tool hang from backpack.

World War II (*1941–45*). Helmeted GI in 1944-style olive-drab field jacket secures trousers in leather combat boots. Extra clips for M-1 Garrand rifle are carried in bandolier and canvas cartridge belt. Belt also supports bayonet scabbard and canvas-covered entrenching tool on left hip.

Korean War (*1950–53*). Infantryman wears winter-issue cap and field jacket lined with alpaca. Handgrenade hangs from shoulder strap, and extra clip for semiautomatic M-1 carbine is stuck into web belt, which also holds pistol holster, ammunition pouch, and bayonet. Boots are black leather.

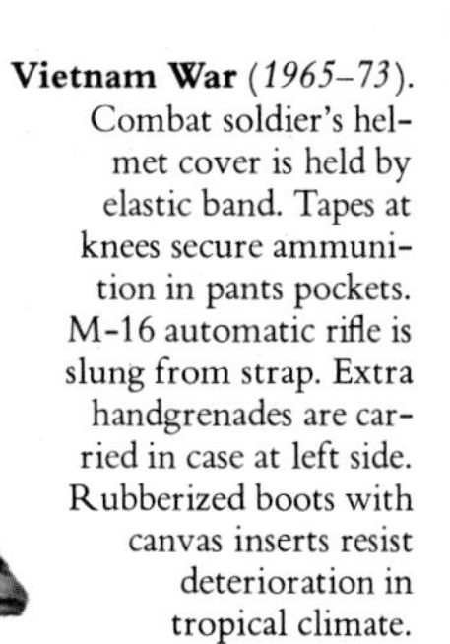

Vietnam War (*1965–73*). Combat soldier's helmet cover is held by elastic band. Tapes at knees secure ammunition in pants pockets. M-16 automatic rifle is slung from strap. Extra handgrenades are carried in case at left side. Rubberized boots with canvas inserts resist deterioration in tropical climate.

Reaching Out for New Horizons *Perry, Peary, and By*

The American urge to push on to the next frontier did not subside with the acquisition of Oregon (1846) and California (1848). Heretofore, the United States had expanded within North America; now the Nation began to think of exploring further horizons.

In 1854, after a carefully planned campaign, Navy Commodore Matthew C. Perry opened the long-barred gates of feudal Japan to American merchant ships. The prize Perry captured for his country was essentially a commercial one; more than half a century later, Arctic explorer Robert E. Peary scored a singular triumph on a different kind of mission—his heroic dash to the North Pole. And two decades after Peary, still another adventurous American, Richard E. Byrd, added new luster to the history of exploration when he made the first flights over both the North and South Poles.

Perry and the Opening of Japan. A gruff, spit-and-polish officer who was known to his men as Old Bruin, Commodore Matthew C. Perry proved an ideal choice for the delicate mission of opening the long-isolated Japanese Empire to U.S. trade. The commodore, the brother of Oliver Hazard Perry, was himself a veteran officer and a skilled diplomat who had seen 43 years of Navy service when President Millard Fillmore chose him in 1852 to negotiate a commercial treaty with Japan.

Carrying a letter from the President to the Japanese Emperor requesting the establishment of diplomatic relations, Perry anchored in Yedo (Tokyo) Bay on July 8, 1853, with an imposing squadron of four warships. His instructions from the U.S. State Department ruled out force unless absolutely necessary. Perry's plan was to outface all opposition to his demands with a display of power and to refuse to confer personally with any but the highest officials.

After 6 days of tense negotiations the Japanese finally gave in. On July 14, amid suitable pomp, Commodore Perry went ashore to deliver his message—and then tactfully sailed away to give his hosts time to reflect. The following February, his enlarged squadron again anchored off Japan, this time to a much more friendly reception. Aware that many influential Japanese now favored increased contact with the outside world, the Emperor had appointed five commissioners to discuss the U.S. proposals with Perry. On March 31, 1854, at the fishing village of Kanagawa (now Yokohama), the historic Treaty of Kanagawa was signed, granting the United States trading rights in two Japanese ports and the right to establish a consulate.

The painting above, done by the official artist for the expedition, shows Perry's 500-man force landing with splendid pageantry at Kanagawa to open negotiations with the Japanese commissioners. At far left is a Japanese portrait of the stern-faced "Old Bruin" in full dress uniform.

Peary Reaches the North Pole. For the iron-willed naval officer and Arctic explorer Robert E. Peary, a lifelong dream came true on April 6, 1909. He noted in his journal: "The Pole at last . . . I cannot bring myself to realize it. It all seems so simple and commonplace." With only his Negro assistant, Matthew A. Henson, and four Eskimos who drove the expedition's sled-dog teams, Peary had just made the final dash over the treacherous Arctic Ocean ice to latitude 90° N.—the North Pole.

Peary's triumph, the culmination of 20 years of Arctic exploration, was at first marred by a rival claim from physician-explorer Frederick A. Cook, who announced that he had reached the Pole in 1908. Cook had accompanied Peary on an earlier expedition. But his claim was eventually proved unfounded, and the indomitable Peary was recognized as the Pole's discoverer.

At left above, the 52-year-old Peary is shown aboard his Arctic exploration ship, the *Roosevelt,* in 1909; directly above are five other members of the expedition, photographed by Peary at the Pole. Henson holds Peary's much-patched U.S. flag.

Byrd Flies Over the South Pole. On November 28, 1929, Richard E. Byrd, pilot Bernt Balchen, and two other companions boarded a Ford trimotor, the *Floyd Bennett* (below), for their epoch-making flight over the South Pole. The sturdy plane (named after the pilot on Byrd's 1926 flight over the North Pole) had to fight fierce air currents and, laden with photographic and survival equipment, clear a 10,500-foot mountain pass. Byrd's team made it, returning to its Antarctic base in less than 19 hours.

The first man to fly over both Poles, Byrd was also renowned for a daring transatlantic flight made with Balchen in 1927. Late in 1928 he led a U.S. expedition to Antarctica and founded the famous base camp, Little America, from which he later explored and charted much of the continent. In 1955 Byrd was put in charge of all U.S. activities in the Antarctic, and that year he led his fifth and last expedition there. The photograph of Byrd at far left, in Antarctica with his dog Igloo, was taken in 1930, the year he was promoted to rear admiral.

CHAPTER TWENTY-SIX

Entertainment for All the People

The United States in its short history has contributed in remarkable variety to the entertainment of humankind. Blackface minstrels, glamorous motion picture stars, hard-riding cowboy heroes, glittering musical comedies, breathtaking three-ring circuses, and spectacular television shows—all are exuberant expressions of the innovative genius of American show business. (Jazz, that most American form of entertainment, is covered in "America's Music," pages 390–405.) The daytime radio serials, or soap operas, now adapted to television, were created here and, for better or worse, have captured an audience of millions. We have also become world renowned for imagina-

Show business got off to a slow start in America. Struggling to survive in a harsh wilderness, colonial pioneers had little time for entertainment. Cities and towns were too small and the distances between them too great to provide a steady theatergoing audience. In those Northern Colonies where grim Puritans and pious Quakers held sway, plays, games, lotteries, music, dancing, and all other secular "divertisements" were either discouraged or expressly forbidden as the Devil's work. The Puritans' disapproval of the bawdy, boisterous English theaters of Shakespeare's day and the Restoration had been passed down to later generations. Just the rumor of a stage performance in 1714 was enough to make Judge Samuel Sewall exhort his fellow citizens not to allow "Christian Boston [to] go beyond heathen Rome in the practice of shameful vanities."

In the South officialdom took a more worldly view. Three bold young men were arrested in Accomack County, Virginia, in 1665 for having put on a play called *Ye Beare and ye Cubb,* but after performing again before the court "in ye habilements which they had acted in," they were acquitted of having corrupted public morals.

Marathon sermons, parades by the local militia, cockfighting, and bullbaiting were acceptable forms of colonial entertainment. An occasional threadbare acrobat or juggler wandered from village to village to display his tricks before an entranced crowd, and oxen hauled caged wild animals (including camels, polar bears, lions, and at least one trained pig) from town to town on carts. Beginning in the early 1700's, bands of strolling English players appeared in the plays of Shakespeare, Addison, Steele, and others, performing in candlelit barns, taverns, coffeehouses, and in halls that were hastily built just outside the city limits to avoid prosecution.

Performances were very sporadic at America's first playhouse of record in Williamsburg (about 1716–45). Philadelphia's Southwark, which opened in 1766, was the hardiest of the early theaters, surviving for some 55 years. The most successful early showman was actor-manager Lewis Hallam, who landed at Yorktown, Virginia, in 1752 with a troupe of 10 actors and actresses, trunks filled with costumes and crudely painted scenery, and a repertoire of 24 plays. For two decades his "Company of Comedians from London" traveled the Eastern seaboard, introducing the pleasure of playgoing to thousands. Pledged to offer "nothing indecent or immoral," they and their imitators often circumvented local laws by advertising their performances as "moral dialogues" rather than as plays.

In Philadelphia during the Revolution bewigged British officers and elegant ladies of loyalist persuasion staged elaborate plays and pageants to while away their tedium during the British occupation of the city. These entertainments dazzled some Philadelphians, but others looked on the drama as a peculiarly British, even un-American, art form, and one to be avoided.

Amusements of an Infant Republic

Fervent patriotism marked the growth of the native theater, although until well into the 1800's all but a handful of the plays and star players were British. The stage character of the homespun but wise Yankee farmer who outwits the foppish European had his beginnings in 1787 as Jonathan in the first native American comedy, *The Contrast,* by Royall Tyler. The shrewd Yankee remained a stock theatrical character in this country for more than a century. A more important native-born playwright was William Dunlap, who used the Revolutionary War incident involving British spy Major John André as the basis for his 1798 blank verse tragedy, *André.*

America slowly developed its own performers, who worked hard to achieve a distinctively national style.

ve expression in modern dance and experimental theater.

Popular entertainment was a latecomer to America be-ause the piety and hardship of colonial days delayed its rowth. A few wandering players gave settlers their only age fare during the Colonies' first century, and throughout e 1700's many Americans regarded playgoing as an dulgence in sinful worldliness. By the 1800's, however, e high spirits of a fast-growing Nation were finding a atural outlet in the theater, while the hunger for self-nprovement encouraged flourishing lyceum and chautau-ua circuits, which combined education with entertainment.

America has originated many distinctive variations of show business and has breathed new life into older forms as well. Since the 19th-century heyday of P. T. Barnum, U.S. entertainment merchants have excelled at razzle-dazzle. They made turn-of-the-century theater big business, mapped transcontinental vaudeville circuits, transformed the movies from a peepshow novelty into a global industry, and, by creating national radio and television networks, brought much of the world into the American living room. Not only have these triumphs been accompanied by unprecedented commercial success, but since 1900 they have won international acclaim for American performers, playwrights, and filmmakers.

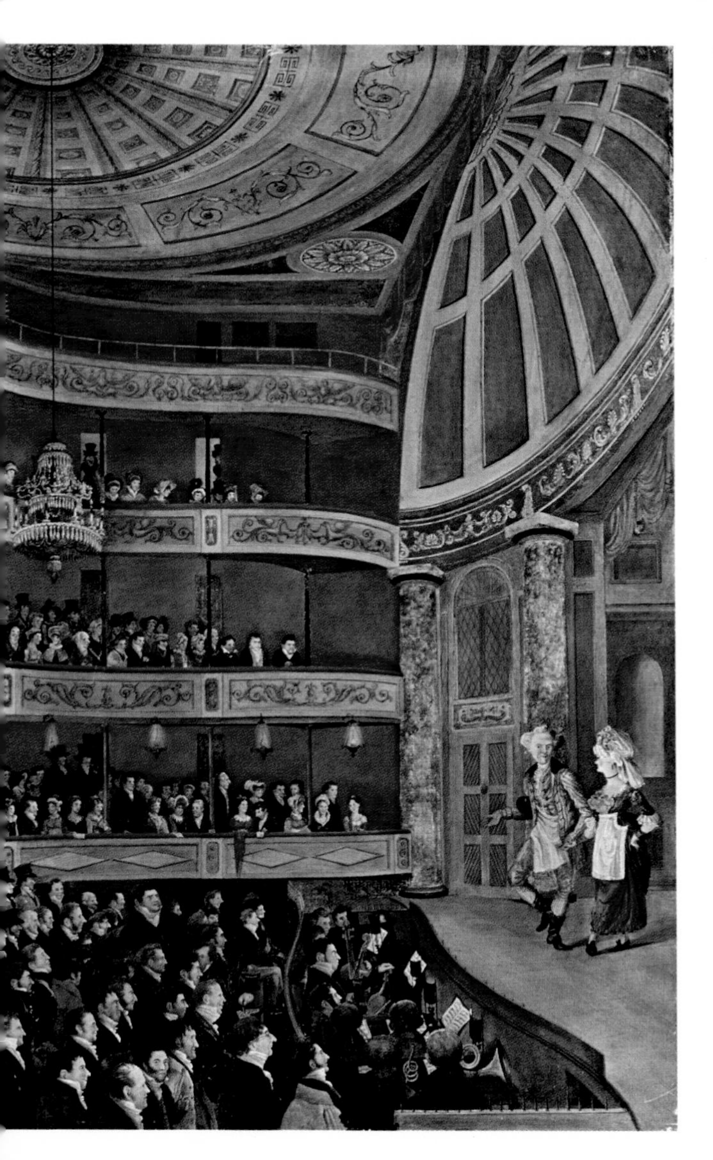

The Early Days of Show Business

Theatergoing Could Be an Adventure

Theatergoing in America before the Civil War was a lively, sometimes hazardous undertaking. Only a handful of fashionable, big-city theaters could boast well-dressed, well-behaved audiences. Most theaters were cold in winter, stifling in summer. Men in muddy boots sprawled across the seats, enjoying their chews and spitting tobacco juice. Heroes were cheered in midspeech. Villains were hissed and sometimes pelted with rotten fruit. Stage action often had to be stopped until fistfights in the audience subsided. Rats scuttled past the patrons' feet scratching for food. Cheap balcony seats were filled with thugs and prostitutes. Fire was always a danger although gaslights, introduced in 1825, were an improvement over candles.

An 1830 Cincinnati poster hints at what actors had to contend with. Patrons in the boxes and gallery are asked to "avoid the uncourteous habit of throwing nutshells, apples, etc. into the Pit," while "those in the Pit are cautioned against clambering over the balustrade into the Boxes, either during or at the end of the Performance." Gallery patrons are asked not to "disturb the harmony of the House by boisterous conduct, either in language or by striking with sticks on the seats or banisters. . . ."

British visitor Frances Trollope described her own visit to a Cincinnati theater at which her friends Mr. and Mrs. Alexander Drake were playing in 1828. In her book *Domestic Manners of the Americans,* published in 1832, she wrote:

> *The spitting was incessant, and the mixed smell of onions and whiskey was enough to make one feel even the Drakes' acting dearly bought. . . . Noises, too, were perpetual, and of the most unpleasant kind; the applause is expressed by cries and thumping with the feet instead of clapping; and when a patriotic fit seized them, and "Yankee Doodle" was called for, every man seemed to think his reputation as a citizen depended on the noise he made.*

Elegant playgoers *crowd New York's Park Theatre in this 1822 watercolor by amateur artist John Searle. The Park, which seated 2,500 patrons in cushioned comfort, was both larger and more luxurious than most American theaters of its time.*

Edwin Forrest, whose acting was characterized by broad gestures and a bellowing voice, was widely acclaimed for nearly 30 years. He was best known for playing the title role in *Metamora, or The Last of the Wampanoags,* a blood-and-thunder melodrama about a noble Indian chief. An unabashed flag-waver, who always billed himself as "the American tragedian" to distinguish himself from British rivals, Forrest sponsored contests to encourage U.S. playwrights to pen works on American themes. When William Macready, a leading English actor, dared to invade Forrest's territory and play New York City's Astor Place Opera House in 1849, the Yankee's jingoistic admirers stormed the theater. A riot ensued, and 22 persons were killed and at least 30 more were wounded before it was quelled.

Junius Brutus Booth *as he appeared in Massinger's* A New Way To Pay Old Debts. *His son Edwin was America's greatest Hamlet; another, John Wilkes, was Lincoln's assassin.*

Despite the international attention paid to U.S. artists, many Americans still regarded the stage with suspicion. One mid-19th-century minister denounced the theater as a "chandeliered and ornamented hell—a yawning maelstrom of perdition—whose dark foundations rest on the murderous souls of hundreds." This attitude persisted for decades. When the actor John Wilkes Booth assassinated President Abraham Lincoln at a performance of *Our American Cousin* in Ford's Theatre in 1865, one clergyman sermonized that "the theatre is one of the last places to which a good man should go." Yet the medium of live theater survived and prospered.

The infant Republic enjoyed other forms of entertainment in addition to that of the stage. The first European-style circus opened at Philadelphia in 1793, with British trick rider John W. Ricketts as its manager and star. It ran for years, gaining its largest audiences when George Washington's by then decrepit horse was a special attraction, and the show spawned countless imitators.

P. T. Barnum, Unrivaled Showman

"There's a sucker born every minute," exulted master showman Phineas T. Barnum, and his colorful career seemed to bear him out. After a short period as editor of an anticlerical newspaper, he began genially gulling the public in 1835, exhibiting an aged Negro woman named Joice Heth, who pretended to be George Washington's 161-year-old childhood nurse. (Somehow, enough people were taken in to turn a tidy profit for Barnum.)

Next he opened his American Museum, a Broadway tourist mecca for a quarter of a century. This internationally renowned repository of freaks and oddities, human and otherwise, real and contrived, included among its exhibits "Chang and Eng, the original Siamese Twins"; a troupe of "Shaking Quakers"; and the celebrated "Feejee Mermaid"—a leathery, 18-inch amalgam of fish scales and monkey skin that drew thousands, at 25 cents a head.

By claiming not to care what newspapers said about him, "provided they say *something,*" Barnum set the style followed by publicists ever since. In 1850 he ballyhooed a concert tour of America by soprano Jenny Lind, the Swedish Nightingale, whipping up a frenzy unmatched until the arrival of the Beatles more than a century later. Barnum became an international celebrity during two triumphal swings through Europe and the British Isles with General Tom Thumb, a multitalented midget whose real name was Charles Stratton. He appears here with Mr. and Mrs. Thumb (center) and two other midgets. In his last years Barnum managed a three-ring circus and its star, a 6½-ton African elephant named Jumbo. A promoter to the end, Barnum asked about the day's gate receipts on his deathbed in 1891.

The Minstrel Show

Burnt Cork, Tambourines, Broad Jokes, and Banjos

In today's era of increasing racial awareness it would be hard to imagine a 19th-century-style minstrel show as acceptable entertainment. But at the turn of the century the minstrels were the favorites of America's theatergoing public. During the heyday of minstrelsy, scores of troupes roamed the country, performing in big cities and small towns and aboard showboats that plied Southern rivers. Minstrel jokes, dances, songs, and comedy sketches presented Negroes as childlike objects of ridicule. As these posters show, white actors in blackface and wearing outlandish garb lampooned black men and women. Few modern audiences, black or white, could watch such spectacles without embarrassment. Crude satire centered around such stock themes as chicken stealing, malapropisms, the supposed shiftlessness of Southern blacks, and the airy pretensions ascribed to Northern Negroes.

Minstrelsy offered work to Negro entertainers willing to collaborate in projecting the white man's image of their people and enriched the popular culture with tuneful melodies, foot-tingling dances, and humorous catchphrases. But it also helped to keep alive a legacy of racism that still burdens the American conscience.

MECHANICS' HALL!
NO. 472 BROADWAY, BETWEEN GRAND AND BROOME STREETS.
OPEN EVERY NIGHT DURING THE WEEK!
CHRISTY'S
G. N. CHRISTY, W. PORTER, E. P. CHRISTY T. VAUGHN, J. RAYNOR, E. H. PIERCE
MINSTRELS
ORGANIZED, 1842.
THE OLDEST ESTABLISHED COMPANY IN THE WORLD
The First to Harmonize Negro Melodies, and originators of the present popular style of Ethiopian Entertainments, whose success in this City during the past THREE YEARS, is without Precedent in the annals of Public Amusements in this Great Metropolis; convincing evidence of their Superior Merit and Attractiveness.
The Company,
UNDER THE DIRECTION AND MANAGEMENT OF E. P. CHRISTY.
WENESDAY EV'ING, Sept. 19, 1849,
PROGRAMME—PART 1.
Medley Overture .... Full Band
Dinah's Wedding Day, from the Opera of Leonora .... Company
Come with me, my Dinah dear .... E. P. Christy
Stop that knocking, introduced with Happy and Light, from the Bohemian Girl .. Company
Julius's Bride .... George Christy
Rosa Lee, or don't be foolish Joe .... E. P. Christy
yrolean Solo, displaying a flexibility and volume of voice truly astonishing and hitherto unknown .... Christian
Phantom Chorus, or the Darkey's Apparition, from La Sonnambula .... Company
Masquerade Waltz, with Street Organ and Automaton Imitations .... Company
PART II.
The Original Burlesque, entitled
VOYAGE MUSICAL
Commencing "Somewhere" and ending "When 'tis done;" comprising a variety of AIRS PUT ON for the occasion. To give full effect to this most Stupendous Work,
The Celebrated and DISTIN-guished performers on the
SIX-HORNS
Will perform a grand POT POURRI &c.
For a Due appreciation of the above INCOMPREHENSIBLE MUSICAL COMBINATION, much and a little more is depending on the imagination of the audience.
After which, the Celebrated RONDO from the Finale of
"LINDA DI CHAMOUNI,"
Composed by MARETZEK, and sung by Mme. LABORDE, will be "Executed," by the
Prima Donna of the Troupe .... M. Zorer
Musical Director & Conductor ... Signor Johnsonio
ACCORDEON SOLO .... H. DONNELLY
MISS LUCY LONG .... GEORGE CHRISTY
ETHIOPIAN POLKA BURLESQUE .... T. VAUGHN & GEORGE CHRISTY
HUNGRY-ARIAN DUET, with Echo, "Burlesque," .... Christian & Zorer
G. N. CHRISTY, AS LUCY LONG
POLKA, BY T. VAUGHN & G. N. CHRISTY
PART III. Representing the peculiar Characteristics of the Southern or Plantation Negroes
Characteristic Banjo Song .... E. Peirce
Banjo Duet .... E. Peirce & T. Vaughn
That Good Old Coon, Quartette .... Vaughn, Raynor, Upson & George Christy
Sugar Cane Reel .... E. Peirce
Life by the Galley Fire .... E. P. Christy
The Skeeters do bite .... Company
Burlesque Lecture on Mesmerism .... W. Porter & George Christ
Down in Carolina, introducing Specimens of Ethiopian Statuary .... Geo. Christy and E. Pe
ADMISSION 25 CENTS.
Doors open at 7. To commence at 8 o'clock precisely.
AN AFTERNOON CONCERT EVERY SATURDAY, COMMENCING AT 3 O'CLOCK.
Herald Print.

Gaudy relics *of minstrelsy, these playbills indicate what two popular troupes were offering.*

Late in the 18th century museums also drew large urban throngs. In 1786, artist and naturalist Charles Willson Peale opened his pioneering natural history museum in Philadelphia. Its exhibits included Peale's own portraits of the Founding Fathers, the first complete skeleton of an American mastodon, and a stuffed cat that had once belonged to Benjamin Franklin.

Peale's phenomenal success inspired others to follow his lead. The greatest of these was Phineas T. Barnum, the self-styled "Prince of Humbugs." Owner and manager of the American Museum in New York from 1842 to 1866, he gathered together hundreds of curiosities.

The blackface minstrel show, a form of entertainment that would differ dramatically from the European arts of entertainment, evolved in the late 1820's and the 1830's. It began in 1828 when white song-and-dance man Thomas "Daddy" Rice scored a great success singing the satirical song "Jump, Jim Crow" and impersonating its subject, a black stablehand. Other white entertainers followed in Rice's shuffling footsteps. In 1843 the first permanent minstrel troupe, the Virginia Minstrels, was formed by Daniel Emmett, the composer of "Dixie." Dozens of imitators with such names as the "Ethiopian Serenaders" and the "Congo Melodists" soon fanned out across the continent. The best loved troupe was headed by Edwin P. Christy. The standard show included songs, dances, and racially slanted patter by 10 to 20 white performers caricaturing blacks. American minstrelsy reached its peak between 1850 and 1870 but remained a staple of amateur theatrical groups well into the 20th century. It spawned some of our most memorable songs —including the melodies of Stephen Foster—and indirectly helped popularize Negro music. It also established and perpetuated the worst kind of racial stereotype.

The Circus and the Wild West Show
Following the Sawdust Trail

The hunger for entertainment in out-of-the-way places spawned two unique show-business spectacles during the 19th century: the traveling three-ring circus and the Wild West Show.

The first U.S. circuses were modest affairs, staged in a single ring. But competition led to ever-gaudier extravaganzas. Master promoter P. T. Barnum concocted with W. C. Coup and Sam Costello in 1871 a lavish circus billed as "The Greatest Show on Earth." In 1881 it merged with that of James A. Bailey and began using two rings, then three, simultaneously. The crowds —especially the children—loved the clamor and confusion.

The Wild West Show helped keep alive the romantic legend of the frontier. William F. "Buffalo Bill" Cody set the style in 1883 with an action-packed show that eventually grew to include some 600 thundering "Rough Riders of the World." Cody and his rivals thrilled millions until soaring costs and competition from the movies ended the business after 1915.

This 9-ton steam calliope *wagon shrilly announced that the circus was in town during hundreds of smalltown parades. Brilliantly carved and painted wagons like this one, still surviving in museums around the country, are considered superb examples of folk art.*

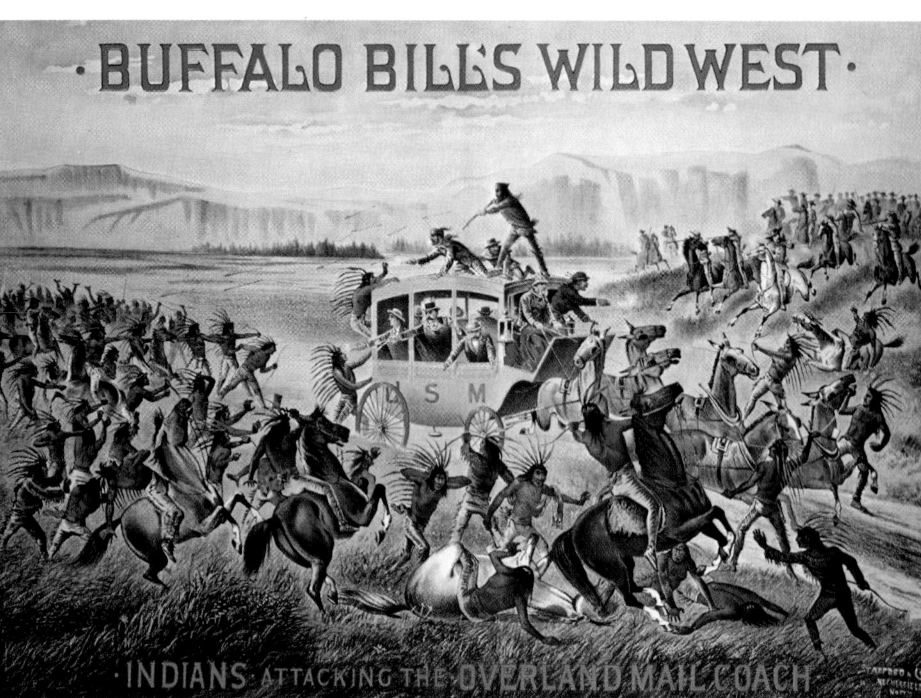

Former foes (*above left*) *Sitting Bull and Buffalo Bill were united by show business. During the 1880's the former leader of the Sioux performed in the Wild West Show's most popular feature—the reenactment of an Indian attack on a stagecoach, pictured in the poster above.*

Show Business Takes to the Road

America remained an overwhelmingly rural nation, and shrewd showmen soon saw that there was a fortune to be made in taking show business to the people. By 1820 there were some 30 small "mud show" circuses (so named because of the slimy goo through which their wagons often slogged) performing in backwoods barns or in the open air. Their numbers swelled after the first Big Top was hauled into place in 1826, enabling the show to go on rain or shine. Like the theater, early circuses had to struggle against churchly opposition. One famous pioneer animal trainer, Isaac van Amburgh, cleverly claimed Biblical sanction for his innovative act (which involved placing his head in a lion's mouth) by pointing out that Daniel had survived the lions' den.

The theater followed the frontier westward, reaching the Ohio and Mississippi Valleys by 1815, the wide-open California mining camps by 1850. By the 1830's cities and towns throughout the country were bursting with civic pride over their well-appointed theaters and concert halls, some seating up to 4,000 people. European luminaries, including the "Swedish Nightingale" Jenny Lind (first brought here by P. T. Barnum), and reigning stars of the London stage, such as Thomas Abthorpe Cooper, Fanny Kemble, Edmund Kean, and Henry Irving, swept on and off smalltown U.S. stages to tumultuous applause.

A schoolboy technique *for avoiding the circus ticket-taker is seen in William Hahn's 1868 painting "It's My Turn."*

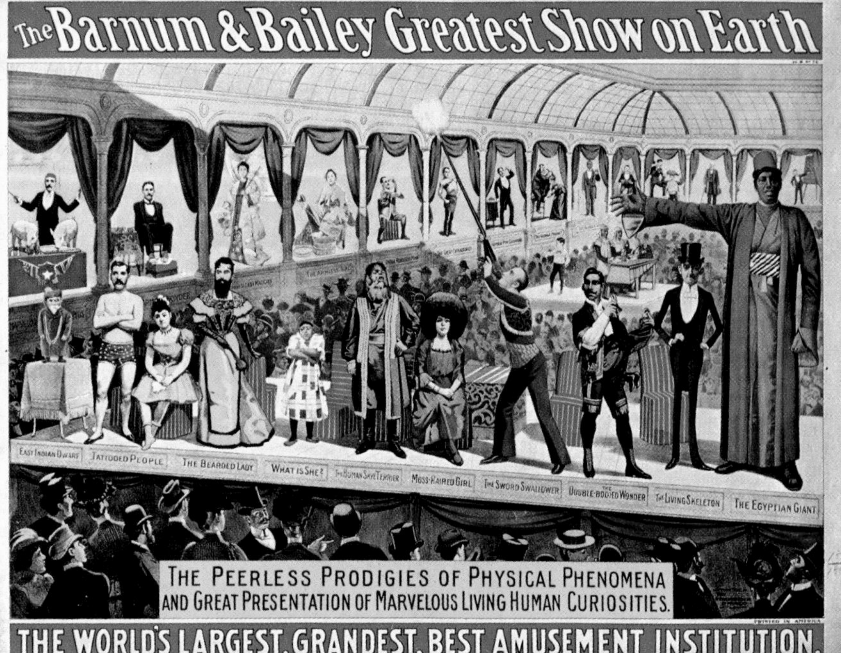

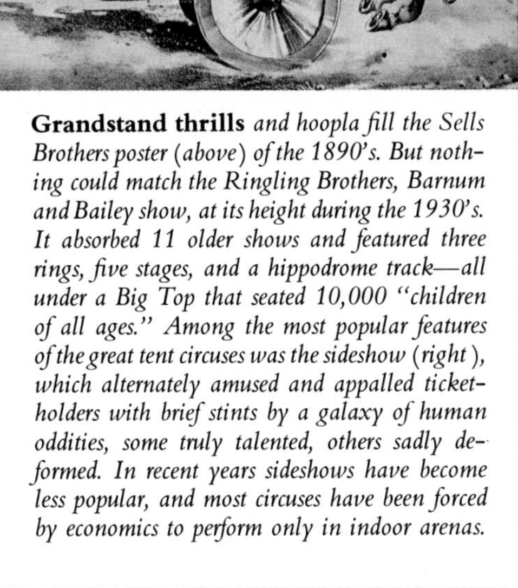

Grandstand thrills *and hoopla fill the Sells Brothers poster (above) of the 1890's. But nothing could match the Ringling Brothers, Barnum and Bailey show, at its height during the 1930's. It absorbed 11 older shows and featured three rings, five stages, and a hippodrome track—all under a Big Top that seated 10,000 "children of all ages." Among the most popular features of the great tent circuses was the sideshow (right), which alternately amused and appalled ticket-holders with brief stints by a galaxy of human oddities, some truly talented, others sadly deformed. In recent years sideshows have become less popular, and most circuses have been forced by economics to perform only in indoor arenas.*

The star system built around these popular performers produced some great one-man (and one-woman) shows, but very few good ensemble performances or great plays.

Audiences in cow towns and mining camps were a special challenge. Fueled by red-eye whisky and easily stirred to excess, they frequently showed their dislike of the villain by riddling the scenery with pistol bullets. Variety acts were inserted between scenes from Shakespeare to keep impatient frontiersmen from growing dangerously restless. The most popular productions in the woman-starved West featured scantily clad actresses. Buxom Adah Isaacs Menken was a perennial frontier favorite, starring season after season in *Mazeppa, or the Wild Horse,* a "grand equestrian melodramatic spectacle." She captivated her audiences by her daring appearance, clad in flesh-colored tights and a short tunic, strapped to the back of a plunging horse. A star-struck Mark Twain saw her in San Francisco and compared her to "a whole constellation" and "a vast spray of gas jets."

Patent medicine pitchmen brought their special brand of entertainment to every small town and crossroads community. They juggled, told jokes, performed Indian dances, or put on puppet shows—anything to attract a gullible crowd to their wagons. The profit lay in the alcoholic elixirs they sold; some were 80 proof, guaranteed to make even the sickest patient feel better long

Participants in the chautauqua experience *gather in the Hall of Philosophy on the shore of Lake Chautauqua, New York, in the summer of 1913 to watch the presentation of diplomas to members of the Literary and Scientific Circle. This first of all chautauquas has continued to attract thousands of visitors, some for a few days, others for the entire summer. Many own houses there, to which they return every year.*

enough for the peddler to hurry on to the next town. Other itinerant rural entertainers included primitive artists who displayed their vast, lurid dioramas depicting famous battles or scenic wonders, "guaranteed lifelike" and often accompanied by a vivid narration and stirring sound effects made with firecrackers and bird whistles.

Culture for the Millions

The lyceum and chautauqua circuits were typically American combinations of culture and inspiration. Educator Josiah Holbrook organized the first lyceum in Millbury, Massachusetts, in 1826, and urged other small towns to form associations that could arrange for lectures, concerts, debates, and demonstrations of the latest scientific wonders. By 1828 Holbrook's idea had taken hold in every State; 10 years later there were 3,000 active lyceums in the Nation, all eagerly vying for eminent speakers. Among those who appeared on lyceum platforms over the years were transcendentalist Ralph Waldo Emerson, reformer Frances Wright, abolitionist Wendell Phillips, clerical orator Henry Ward Beecher, and poet-physician Oliver Wendell Holmes, who privately compared a lecturer to "a literary strumpet," but made a comfortable supplementary income giving witty talks on health and medicine. Lecturers continued to be popular after the Civil War, their pervasive seriousness now leavened by comedy and music. Humorists such as Mark Twain and Artemus Ward and musical acts like the Fisk Jubilee Singers became the circuit's top draws. In a similar vein were the chautauquas that spread rapidly through the country after they were introduced in New York State in 1874. (For more information on the chautauqua assemblies, see "Education for All," pages 126–139.)

The Race Toward Realism

From the time when Edwin Booth and Joseph Jefferson began to dominate the American stage in the 1860's, actors and producers sought to make the theater more realistic. Three-dimensional box sets with sumptuous furnishings and elaborate props replaced flat, painted backdrops. Gas lighting and, after 1878, electricity allowed ever more dazzling atmospheric effects. The more natural style of performers such as Maude Adams, Ethel Barrymore, William Gillette, and Richard Mansfield gradually replaced the antiquated, scenery-chewing school of overwrought acting.

In a different vein *The Black Crook,* a frivolous musical fantasy that opened in 1866 and featured a bevy of beautiful, lightly draped dancers, ran for years and inspired dozens of similar shows. So did elaborately mounted operettas. Vaudeville and burlesque (considerably more decorous than it is today) also attracted large audiences.

After the Civil War touring theatrical companies crisscrossed the continent on the newly developed railroad lines, presenting knocked-down versions of Broadway hits and ever popular favorites such as *Uncle Tom's Cabin* and *East Lynne.* In 1895 there were 500 combinations (touring productions put together in New York by impresarios and theatrical combines) traveling through the country. For the most part this replaced the time-honored practice of bringing in Broadway stars to add luster to the performances of local groups. In that same year Charles Frohman and five other major agents joined forces to establish the Theatrical Syndicate, a mammoth trust that dominated the U.S. stage for more than a decade. It regulated the theater just as the oil and steel trusts controlled more down-to-earth industries.

Vaudeville and Burlesque

The "Two-a-Day" Had Something for Everyone

The wildfire growth of 19th-century cities gave birth to two new forms of entertainment aimed at urban audiences: vaudeville and its spicier sister, burlesque.

Vaudeville offered something for everyone. Acrobats, jugglers, dance teams, animal acts, magicians, monologists, singers, and comics all appeared on the weekly bills. Vaudeville had many roots: Between-the-acts specialties from the legitimate theater, minstrelsy, medicine shows, British music hall acts, and "concert saloons" that provided bawdy, backroom fare for all-male audiences.

Vaudeville's patron saint was Tony Pastor, a singer and saloonkeeper who opened his first theater on New York City's Broadway in 1861, promising a "straight, clean variety show" for the whole family. His recipe was an instant hit and soon had hundreds of imitators. Vaudeville became a national industry after 1900; B. F. Keith and Edward F. Albee alone controlled some 400 theaters in the East and Midwest, including New York City's legendary Palace, the goal of every vaudevillian.

Despite the vagabond life it imposed on performers, vaudeville was a spawning ground for show business stars. Among those who got their start on the "two-a-day" circuit were Jack Benny, Jimmy Durante, Al Jolson, the Marx Brothers, and George Burns and Gracie Allen.

After 1895, short films were often used at the end of the bill to "clear the house." Twenty years later the balance was reversed: Feature films were the main attraction, supplemented by a few live acts. Competition from movies, radio, and TV ultimately closed the vaudeville houses.

Burlesque was aimed mostly at adult males, not at the family. Originated as a spoof of the legitimate theater show, it soon developed a set of conventions that featured sparsely clad chorus girls and vulgar, baggy-trousered comedians. Burlesque reached its peak during World War I, when there were several flourishing circuits. Later, stripteasing was introduced. Considered daring in its day, burlesque would seem absurdly tame in the 1970's, when it had all but disappeared.

Will Rogers (*left*) *began as a trick lariat twirler, then added topical yarns to his routine. He went on to become the Nation's Cowboy Philosopher. Ed Wynn, the Perfect Fool of stage, radio, and, later, television, was famed for his fluttery manner and loony inventions.*

"Minsky's Chorus" *was painted by Reginald Marsh in 1935. New York's Minsky brothers were burlesque's most successful operators. Marsh, like many other artists and intellectuals of the 1930's, treasured the spectacle of the spangled burlesque line as an integral part of American life.*

Tapdancer *Bill "Bojangles" Robinson began in vaudeville in 1896, becoming nationally known in the all-Negro* Blackbirds *of 1928.*

Pistol-wielding bandits *invade the telegraph office in* The Great Train Robbery. *Written, directed, and photographed by Edwin S. Porter, an employee of inventor Thomas A. Edison, the movie appeared in 1903. Although it was not the first Western to be produced, it was the first U.S. film actually to tell a story. It introduced the all-important narrative technique that builds cinematic suspense by cutting swiftly from scene to scene. The movie was shot partly in a studio and partly in the New Jersey pine barrens, with amateur actors who had never ridden horses before. Its gunplay and exciting chase sequence thrilled filmgoers. The 8-minute movie proved so popular that it became the standard opening attraction for the nickelodeons that sprang up all over the Nation.*

Pictures That Move

The exalted place of the theater would not go unchallenged much longer. In 1889, 6 years before the Theatrical Syndicate was formed, William K. Dickson devised the first practical motion picture camera. Head of Thomas Edison's laboratory in West Orange, New Jersey, Dickson succeeded where hundreds before him had failed. He fulfilled the age-old dream of making pictures that move. Edison himself expressed little initial enthusiasm for the invention (called the kinetograph) because it could not easily be synchronized with his phonograph. But when Dickson developed the Kinetoscope, a peepshow device for viewing the flickering, quarter-minute films, Edison delightedly opened the first Kinetoscope Parlor in 1894. Soon the devices appeared in penny arcades all over the Nation. Patrons enthusiastically peered into the eyepieces of the coin-operated machines to see such shorts as an explosive sneeze by Edison's assistant Fred Ott, the gyrations of belly dancer Little Egypt, and Buffalo Bill waving from the back of an endlessly bucking horse.

Motion pictures had been achieved. How to get them out from behind a peephole and before a large audience was then the problem. The Lumière brothers of Paris in 1895 were among the first to utilize the Kinetoscope to project the picture onto a large screen. The following year Edison used the vitascope, developed by Thomas Armat, to project some movies on a screen in New York City's Music Hall. The triumphant presentation, in the midst of a series of vaudeville acts, delighted the audience with scenes of a burlesque boxing match, people dancing, and a very realistic angry sea. These 2-minute movies continued to be shown as bonus attractions in vaudeville houses and penny arcades until the early 1900's, when thousands of small theaters devoted solely to films, and called nickelodeons because they charged a nickel, opened across the country.

America's first *great movie director, David Wark Griffith, at work on the set. He created many silent-screen classics, among them* Birth of a Nation *(1915) and* Intolerance *(1916).*

But movies might have been only a temporary fad had European and American innovators not discovered the screen's enormous potential for storytelling. It was another Edison employee, Edwin S. Porter, who in 1903 made the first American film to spin a coherent story, *The Great Train Robbery.* Though this primitive horse opera lasted only about 8 minutes and seems embarrassingly crude to the modern eye, it would be hard to exaggerate its impact on contemporary audiences.

Despite clergymen who denounced "Nickel Madness" as "wholly vicious," the urban poor flocked to the movies in unprecedented numbers. Movies were cheap and lively, and even recent immigrants who were unable to read the English dialog found it easy to follow the stories because of the broad pantomime.

Within a few years the center of motion picture production had shifted to Hollywood, California, and shrewd entrepreneurs such as Adolph

Great Stars of the Silver Screen

There Were, and There Are, Others. But This Galaxy Includes Most of the Immortals

Left to right, *top row: Charlie Chaplin, Stan Laurel and Oliver Hardy, Rudolph Valentino, Lillian Gish, Clara Bow, Harpo, Chico, and Groucho Marx. Second row: Mary Pickford (in circle), Buster Keaton, Douglas Fairbanks, Sr. (in circle), Nelson Eddy and Jeanette MacDonald, Greta Garbo (in circle). Third row: William S. Hart (with revolver), Gloria Swanson, Jean Harlow (in circle), Ginger Rogers and Fred Astaire, W. C. Fields and Mae West. Fourth row: Joan Crawford, Rita Hayworth, Spencer Tracy (in circle), Marlene Dietrich, Bette Davis (in circle), Cary Grant, Clark Gable. Fifth row: Judy Garland, Edward G. Robinson, James Cagney, Marilyn Monroe, Shirley Temple, Gene Kelly, Humphrey Bogart. Sixth row: John Wayne, Gary Cooper, Elizabeth Taylor, Marlon Brando, Katharine Hepburn.*

The Oscar
Coveted Symbol of Excellence

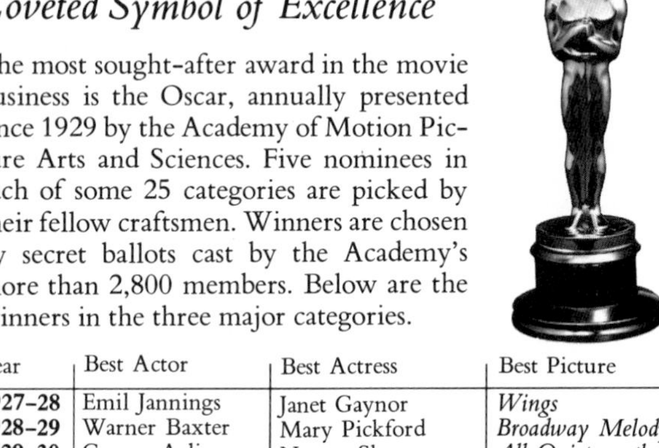

The most sought-after award in the movie business is the Oscar, annually presented since 1929 by the Academy of Motion Picture Arts and Sciences. Five nominees in each of some 25 categories are picked by their fellow craftsmen. Winners are chosen by secret ballots cast by the Academy's more than 2,800 members. Below are the winners in the three major categories.

Year	Best Actor	Best Actress	Best Picture
1927–28	Emil Jannings	Janet Gaynor	*Wings*
1928–29	Warner Baxter	Mary Pickford	*Broadway Melody*
1929–30	George Arliss	Norma Shearer	*All Quiet on the Western Front*
1930–31	Lionel Barrymore	Marie Dressler	*Cimarron*
1931–32	Wallace Beery, Fredric March	Helen Hayes	*Grand Hotel*
1932–33	Charles Laughton	Katharine Hepburn	*Cavalcade*
1934	Clark Gable	Claudette Colbert	*It Happened One Night*
1935	Victor McLaglen	Bette Davis	*Mutiny on the Bounty*
1936	Paul Muni	Luise Rainer	*The Great Ziegfeld*
1937	Spencer Tracy	Luise Rainer	*The Life of Emile Zola*
1938	Spencer Tracy	Bette Davis	*You Can't Take It With You*
1939	Robert Donat	Vivien Leigh	*Gone With the Wind*
1940	James Stewart	Ginger Rogers	*Rebecca*
1941	Gary Cooper	Joan Fontaine	*How Green Was My Valley*
1942	James Cagney	Greer Garson	*Mrs. Miniver*
1943	Paul Lukas	Jennifer Jones	*Casablanca*
1944	Bing Crosby	Ingrid Bergman	*Going My Way*
1945	Ray Milland	Joan Crawford	*The Lost Weekend*
1946	Fredric March	Olivia de Havilland	*The Best Years of Our Lives*
1947	Ronald Colman	Loretta Young	*Gentleman's Agreement*
1948	Laurence Olivier	Jane Wyman	*Hamlet*
1949	Broderick Crawford	Olivia de Havilland	*All the King's Men*
1950	Jose Ferrer	Judy Holliday	*All About Eve*
1951	Humphrey Bogart	Vivien Leigh	*An American in Paris*
1952	Gary Cooper	Shirley Booth	*The Greatest Show on Earth*
1953	William Holden	Audrey Hepburn	*From Here to Eternity*
1954	Marlon Brando	Grace Kelly	*On the Waterfront*
1955	Ernest Borgnine	Anna Magnani	*Marty*
1956	Yul Brynner	Ingrid Bergman	*Around the World in 80 Days*
1957	Alec Guinness	Joanne Woodward	*The Bridge on the River Kwai*
1958	David Niven	Susan Hayward	*Gigi*
1959	Charlton Heston	Simone Signoret	*Ben-Hur*
1960	Burt Lancaster	Elizabeth Taylor	*The Apartment*
1961	Maximilian Schell	Sophia Loren	*West Side Story*
1962	Gregory Peck	Anne Bancroft	*Lawrence of Arabia*
1963	Sidney Poitier	Patricia Neal	*Tom Jones*
1964	Rex Harrison	Julie Andrews	*My Fair Lady*
1965	Lee Marvin	Julie Christie	*The Sound of Music*
1966	Paul Scofield	Elizabeth Taylor	*A Man for All Seasons*
1967	Rod Steiger	Katharine Hepburn	*In the Heat of the Night*
1968	Cliff Robertson	Katharine Hepburn, Barbra Streisand	*Oliver!*
1969	John Wayne	Maggie Smith	*Midnight Cowboy*
1970	George C. Scott	Glenda Jackson	*Patton*
1971	Gene Hackman	Jane Fonda	*The French Connection*
1972	Marlon Brando	Liza Minnelli	*The Godfather*
1973	Jack Lemmon	Glenda Jackson	*The Sting*
1974	Art Carney	Ellen Burstyn	*The Godfather, Part II*

Zukor, Louis B. Mayer, Samuel Goldwyn, and Marcus Loew had built the movies into a national industry that grossed more than any other except agriculture, steel, and transportation. By 1925 motion pictures were more a necessity than a luxury for many Americans. More than 130 million people went to the movies each week. There were 20,000 motion picture theaters, many of unprecedented opulence, and some seating 7,000 persons.

The Movies Find a Voice

Only sound was lacking to make a reality of Edison's dream of true "talking pictures." From the first, audiences had come to expect musical accompaniment for the movies, either played on a house piano or an organ, or, in the more posh movie palaces, performed by a live orchestra. By 1923 it was possible to record sound on film, and soon movie shorts were enlivened by their own sound scores. Later, musical scores were added to feature films, and newsreels began to crackle with authentic sounds. The first full-length talkie, Warner Brothers' *The Jazz Singer,* appeared in 1927. It featured vaudeville veteran Al Jolson in the tearful saga of an Orthodox Jewish cantor's son who becomes a successful stage star. Jolson's first jaunty line, "You ain't heard nothing yet," was a prediction that was soon to come true.

Sound was an instant hit with moviegoers, who were glad to hear as well as see their screen favorites. The public would soon settle for nothing less than "all-talking, all-singing" movies. And when the voices of such film stars as John Gilbert failed to measure up to their looks, their careers collapsed.

In the 1930's Americans turned in unprecedented numbers to the movie screens for escape from their daily woes. Several new film genres delighted audiences and helped ensure Hollywood's preeminence in world mov-

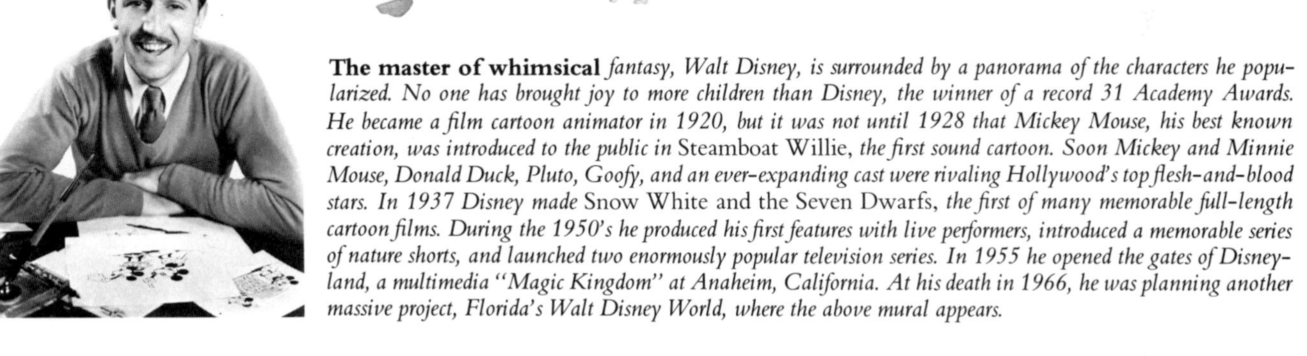

The master of whimsical *fantasy, Walt Disney, is surrounded by a panorama of the characters he popularized. No one has brought joy to more children than Disney, the winner of a record 31 Academy Awards. He became a film cartoon animator in 1920, but it was not until 1928 that Mickey Mouse, his best known creation, was introduced to the public in* Steamboat Willie, *the first sound cartoon. Soon Mickey and Minnie Mouse, Donald Duck, Pluto, Goofy, and an ever-expanding cast were rivaling Hollywood's top flesh-and-blood stars. In 1937 Disney made* Snow White and the Seven Dwarfs, *the first of many memorable full-length cartoon films. During the 1950's he produced his first features with live performers, introduced a memorable series of nature shorts, and launched two enormously popular television series. In 1955 he opened the gates of Disneyland, a multimedia "Magic Kingdom" at Anaheim, California. At his death in 1966, he was planning another massive project, Florida's Walt Disney World, where the above mural appears.*

iemaking. These included frothy, large-cast musicals (of which the best loved were the nine that paired dancers Fred Astaire and Ginger Rogers); gangster and detective films that made heroes of such professional tough guys as James Cagney and Humphrey Bogart; and a host of brilliant comedies, ranging from the frenetic carryings-on of the Marx Brothers and the boozy fraudulence of W. C. Fields to the witty sophistication of director Frank Capra's *It Happened One Night.* A scene in this film revealed Hollywood's powerful influence on the moviegoers of the day. When Clark Gable took off his shirt to reveal a bare chest, the sale of undershirts took a drastic drop. Producer David O. Selznick's 1939 Civil War epic, *Gone With the Wind,* became one of the most profitable films of all time. This classic film had pageantry, romance, tragedy, color, and four great stars—Gable, Vivien Leigh, Leslie Howard, and Olivia de Havilland.

Much of the prestige and profit accruing to both stars and studios depended on the genius of the directors. The first great one was David Wark Griffith, who started as an actor but by 1912 had made some 450 short films. He gave filming stature as an art and originated many now-standard moviemaking techniques, including the closeup, long shot, dissolve, soft focus, flashback, and the use of various camera angles in a single scene. In the idiom of comedy, Mack Sennett almost singlehandedly created a golden age in the silent era. He built the Keystone Studios where he orchestrated the hilarious pie-in-the-face and pratfall routines of the Keystone Kops and developed such stars as Mable Normand, Ben Turpin, Chester Conklin, and (for a time) Charlie Chaplin.

Cecil B. De Mille is remembered for his super spectaculars with casts of thousands, such as *The Ten Commandments,* first made in 1923. John Ford established the formula for the Western movie although his four Academy Awards were for non-Westerns—*The Informer, The Grapes of Wrath, How Green Was My Valley,* and *The Quiet Man.* Alfred Hitchcock became the master of spine-tingling thrillers. John Huston, who was to create many classic movies, began his career in 1941 with *The Maltese Falcon,* which set the style for the movie detective.

Production costs tripled between 1941 and 1961, and the postwar development of television signaled the end of the old Hollywood. Recently the surviving studios have concentrated on relatively inexpensive serials for television. Hollywood's days of glory are over, and American movie companies are now found on location almost anywhere in the world. But American moviemakers of a new generation, including Arthur Penn, Robert Altman, Peter Bogdanovich, and Mike Nichols, remain among the world's most innovative directors, and this country's interest in films is reviving.

The 20th Century on Stage

"Who reads an American book," scoffed London wit Sidney Smith in 1820, "or goes to an American play?" Early America was too raw, too rugged, too preoccupied with expanding its frontiers to develop much first-class theater. While in the 1800's many American performers rivaled Europe's best, U.S. playwrights and productions lagged far behind.

The lavish staging and shrewd commercial sense of such impresarios as David Belasco and Charles Frohman still dominated New York's many theaters during the early 1900's. The flossy, tuneful operettas of Victor Herbert, the brassy musicals of George M. Cohan, and the glorified girlie shows of Florenz Ziegfeld drew the most responsive crowds.

In tweeds and *deerstalker, actor-playwright William Gillette starred for decades in his own* Sherlock Holmes *(1899), an adaptation of the Arthur Conan Doyle stories.*

But growing numbers of young theater enthusiasts, scornful of Broadway's commercialism and inspired by the success of European and British "art" companies, such as Ireland's Abbey Theatre players, resolved to provide U.S. playgoers with more substantive fare. "Little theaters" sprang up around the country, devoted to producing and promoting the serious works of contemporary playwrights. Perhaps the best known were the Provincetown Players, who began their productions on a Cape Cod wharf and later moved to New York City. They were the first group to perform the brooding psychological works of America's most powerful playwright, Eugene O'Neill.

In 1919 some alumni of the little theater movement formed the New York City Theatre Guild, aimed at bringing serious contemporary drama to Broadway. The organization had a profound effect on the development of the American stage. In addition to introducing new techniques of staging, acting, and directing, the Guild encouraged a new generation of playwrights to examine American life. Among the best known were O'Neill, William Saroyan, Maxwell Anderson, and Robert E. Sherwood—all winners of Pulitzer Prizes.

The Theatre Guild was also instrumental in molding musical comedy, America's most distinctive contribution to world theater. More folksy than the operetta, and unlike the variety revue because it adheres to a plot, modern musical comedy draws upon a host of earlier sources. But it was the Guild productions of George Gershwin's folk

Ethel and John Barrymore, *outstanding members of the celebrated theatrical family, star together. The children and grandchildren of actors, the Barrymores began playing romantic leads and became preeminent American stage performers. Although they both appeared in Hollywood movies, the stage was their primary love.*

Actor-playwright Howard Lindsay *(left) plays the title role in* Life With Father, *the phenomenally popular play he coauthored with Russel Crouse in 1939. Based on Clarence Day's bestseller, it ran for 8 years.*

Claudia McNeil *and Sidney Poitier in Lorraine Hansberry's* A Raisin in the Sun *(1959). The success of this drama, dealing with a black family's move to an all-white suburb, broke new ground for Negro playwrights and performers.*

Jason Robards *(left) in Eugene O'Neill's* Hughie, *which opened in 1964. O'Neill demonstrated —in such plays as* The Emperor Jones, Anna Christie, Mourning Becomes Electra, The Iceman Cometh, *and* Long Day's Journey Into Night*—that drama can be as psychologically penetrating as the best fiction.*

Original cast *of* The Fantasticks, *the longest running show to appear on off-Broadway. Written by Harvey Schmidt and Tom Jones, it opened in 1960 and was still running 15 years later. Tomorrow's top performers and playwrights often get their start off-Broadway, where relatively low overhead allows for more experimentation.*

opera *Porgy and Bess* (1935) and Richard Rodgers and Oscar Hammerstein II's *Oklahoma!* (1943) that helped set the style for such great subsequent hits as *South Pacific, My Fair Lady, West Side Story,* and *Fiddler on the Roof.*

The 1929 stock market crash and the ensuing Great Depression were felt in almost every area of show business, but the live theater suffered most. In 1931 a number of talented Theatre Guild actors, directors, and writers formed the Group Theatre. They had two basic purposes: to present plays on distinctively American themes and to encourage a new style of introspective, intensely personal acting modeled upon the method taught by Russian actor and director Konstantin Stanislavski.

The Federal Theatre Project, established by the Works Progress Administration in 1935 as part of President Franklin D. Roosevelt's New Deal, provided jobs for some 10,000 unemployed theater people during its 4-year span. It brought every sort of theater—from the Greek classics to the left-wing topical satire of the "Living Newspaper" series—to some 25 million Americans all over the country, an estimated two-thirds of whom had never seen a professional dramatic production.

During the 1930's for the first time large numbers of American plays found audiences in European theaters. In the years since, the works of dramatists such as Tennessee Williams, Arthur Miller, and Edward Albee have become almost as familiar abroad as they are at home. American theater now ranks with the world's finest.

Despite soaring costs and shrinking Broadway audiences, the contemporary theater shows healthy signs of life. Adventurous playwrights, producers, and actors eke out a precarious living in small, enterprising "off-Broadway" playhouses. New repertory theaters are prospering in cities like Minneapolis. University theaters throughout the country have grown steadily in size and number. Summer stock companies and dinner theaters bring stage favorites to the suburbs and small towns.

New Directions in Dance

As befits a free country, freedom has been America's essential contribution to the world of dance. In 1905 Isadora Duncan outraged the balletomanes of the day by dancing to her own feelings rather than using classical forms. Her work and that of her contemporaries Ruth St. Denis and Ted Shawn, at their Denishawn School in Massachusetts, expanded the scope of modern dance.

Martha Graham, who studied with Ruth St. Denis, went even further in dramatic body movement. She also

Zero Mostel *(foreground) as Tevye, hero of* Fiddler on the Roof, *the longest running production in Broadway history. The musical was based on stories by Yiddish author Sholom Aleichem.* Fiddler *opened to critical acclaim on September 22, 1964, and closed on July 2, 1972, after 3,242 performances. Musicals have traditionally been favorites of American theatergoers. Each of the following ran more than 1,400 performances before Broadway audiences:* Hello, Dolly!; My Fair Lady; Man of La Mancha; Oklahoma!; South Pacific; Hair; The Sound of Music; *and* How To Succeed in Business Without Really Trying.

added story lines to this new kind of dance and made spatial relationships an important part of her productions. Her influential contributions to modern dance are echoed in the powerful, majestic expressions of José Limón and in the brilliance of such dance companies as those of Paul Taylor, Merce Cunningham, and Alvin Ailey.

The unique blend of theater and dance that established the American musical originated with Agnes De Mille in *Oklahoma!* (1943), which she choreographed for skilled dancers, not just hoofers. Both De Mille and the perfectionist Jerome Robbins, whose masterpiece *West Side Story* was produced in 1957, were strongly influenced by the dean of choreographers in America, George Balanchine, who brought new vigor and excitement to classical forms. Balanchine's New York City Ballet and the American Ballet Theater, under the direction of Lucia Chase and Oliver Smith, are among the most prestigious dance companies in the world today.

Opening the Airwaves

For all the importance of movies in shaping modern culture, the impact of radio has been just as great. The "wireless telephone" had become a reality in the late 1800's, and Lee De Forest's invention of the three-element vacuum tube in 1906 made long-distance transmission possible.

When Pittsburgh's KDKA, the first commercial station, took to the airwaves in 1920, it set off what can only be called a radio explosion. For the first time free entertainment and news reached into the average American parlor for nothing but the cost of the set. An early radio might have come to $100, and the minimum price of sets has since steadily fallen. At the beginning of 1922 there were 30 stations in operation; by the following year, more than 500. The creation of the first two multi-station networks, the National Broadcasting Company (NBC) in 1926 and the Columbia Broadcasting System (CBS) the following year, turned broadcasting into a coherent national medium. In 1930 more than 12 million U.S. families had radios; 20 years later 40 million families—nearly 92 percent of the American people—were avid listeners.

The earliest entertainers performed free, grateful for the publicity; the manufacturers of radio equipment paid for most programing. Then the idea of financing programs with advertising began to emerge. In 1922 Secretary of Commerce Herbert Hoover declared it "inconceivable that we should allow so great a possibility for service to be drowned in advertising chatter." Nonetheless this "chatter" soon proved profitable beyond its promoters' wildest dreams; by 1929 the Ford Motor Company was paying $1,000 a minute for prime time (the popular evening hours), and the price was climbing.

Mornings and early afternoons were devoted to the housewife. During the 1930's some 50 soap operas (so called because they were often sponsored by soap companies) chronicled the daily woes of a host of characters. The longest running daytime serial was *The Romance of Helen Trent,* broadcast five times a week from October 1933 through June 1960. Late afternoons were for children, who put aside their homework to follow the exploits of such heroes as the Lone Ranger, Captain Midnight, and Jack Armstrong, all-American boy.

Evenings offered more varied fare: News commentators; dance bands, crooners, and programs of classical and semiclassical music. Comedy stars included Fred Allen, Jack Benny, and two white dialect performers, Freeman Gosden and Charles Corell, better known as Amos 'n' Andy. Gosden and Corell's amusing but patronizing lampoons of what many whites conceived to be Negro life were so popular during the 1930's that some movie theaters turned off their projectors and played the 15-minute radio program for their audiences each evening rather than try to compete for patrons.

At Home With the Radio

More Than 19 Hours on the Air

From this cathedral-model set ($29.95—$1 down and $1 a week) poured some 200 programs in a single day's broadcasting when radio was at its peak. Four networks and innumerable local stations throughout the United States offered a remarkable variety of news and entertainment between 6:45 in the morning and 2 a.m., when the last dance band signed off. Here is a partial listing of shows that could have been tuned in on Wednesday, March 16, 1938, a day chosen at random.

MORNING

6:45	Bob Byron, Whistler
7:00	Morning Almanac
7:55	News; Salon Musicals
8:00	News Bulletins
8:15	Beauty Talk, Neil Vinick
8:30	Greenfield Village Chapel
8:45	Lucille and Lanny (Songs)
9:00	Breakfast Club (Variety)
9:55	Press-Radio News
10:00	Mrs. Wiggs of the Cabbage Patch (Sketch)
10:15	John's Other Wife (Drama)
10:30	Just Plain Bill (Drama)
10:45	Ma Perkins (Drama)
11:00	Larry Vincent and the Stewart Sisters (Songs)
11:15	Myrt and Marge (Sketch)
11:45	Aunt Jenny's Stories

AFTERNOON

12:00	Mary M. McBride (Talk)
12:15	Kidoodlers Quartet
12:25	News; Farm and Home Hour
12:30	Stella Dallas (Drama)
12:45	Student Science Clubs of America
1:00	Dramatized Health Talk; Music
1:15	Carson Robison Buckaroos
1:30	Ruth Lyon, Soprano; Charles Sears, Tenor
2:00	Swingtime Trio
2:15	The O'Neills (Sketch)
2:30	School of the Air (Education)
3:00	Pepper Young's Family
3:15	Ma Perkins (Drama)
3:30	Vic and Sade (Sketch)
3:45	Metropolitan Opera Guild: Milton J. Cross, Master of Ceremonies
4:00	Young Widder Brown (Drama)
4:15	From London: Sir Harry Lauder, Scotch Comedian
4:30	The Goldbergs (Comedy)
4:45	Dr. Allan Roy Dafoe (Talk)
5:00	Dick Tracy (Mystery)
5:15	Charlie Chan (Mystery)
5:30	Jack Armstrong (Adventure)
5:45	Tom Mix (Western)

EVENING

6:00	Uncle Don
6:30	Boake Carter, Commentator
6:45	Lowell Thomas, Commentator
7:00	Amos 'n' Andy (Comedy)
7:15	Mr. Keen, Tracer of Lost Persons (Drama)
7:30	Lone Ranger (Western)
7:45	Science on the March: Dr. Forest Ray Moulton
8:00	One Man's Family (Drama)
8:30	Eddie Cantor, Comedian; Deanna Durbin, Renard Orchestra, and others
9:00	Fred Allen, Comedian; Van Steeden Orchestra (Variety Revue)
10:00	Gang Busters (Mystery)
10:30	Minstrel Show
11:00	News; The Ink Spots
11:30	Dance Music
12:30	Lights Out (Drama)
1:00	Dance Music

The skilled radio dramatist's power to persuade was awesome. In 1938 Orson Welles and John Houseman broadcast a dramatized version of H. G. Wells' *War of the Worlds.* Thousands of listeners panicked and fled from their homes, fully convinced that Martians had actually landed and were laying New Jersey to waste.

For better or for worse, Americans in every corner of the continent were simultaneously laughing at the same jokes, listening to the same news, cheering the same teams, and dancing to the same music. Radio also affected the economy by introducing new products to millions of potential customers. President Roosevelt mastered the medium and used his "fireside chats" to help restore the Nation's confidence in its own future.

The World in Your Living Room

In many ways the story of television's phenomenal growth parallels that of radio. The technical knowledge existed long before commercial telecasting began. Development was interrupted by global war. And once full-scale telecasting was underway, its enormous popularity meant drastic change—in some cases, near disaster—for older forms of entertainment.

Independent researchers working on both sides of the Atlantic first transmitted tiny, blurred television images as early as 1925. Two years later WGY of Schenectady, New York, one of the earliest radio stations, began experimental telecasts for a few hours 3 days a week. The National Broadcasting Company started experimental broadcasts in New York City in 1930, and the Columbia Broadcasting System followed the next year. In 1932 WCBS-TV in New York City reported Presidential election returns to the fascinated owners of some 7,500 experimental sets. Seven years later NBC launched daily broadcasting with live coverage of Franklin D. Roosevelt's opening remarks at the New York World's Fair.

The first publicly available sets had round screens ranging in size from 5 to 9 inches, and viewers had to sit up close to see. The first commercial appeared in the summer of 1941. During a televised Dodgers-Pirates baseball game from Ebbetts Field in Brooklyn, the camera focused on a Bulova clockface while an announcer intoned the time. Total cost to Bulova: $9.

World War II postponed expansion of the medium. It was not until the winter of 1946–47 that broadcasters and set manufacturers renewed their efforts to get full-scale TV broadcasting underway. Tavern owners were the first to realize the potential of the new medium. Their business boomed during televised sporting events.

In 1947 there were just 14,000 sets in use. By 1949 there were nearly 1 million; by 1955, nearly 30 million; and by 1960, 60 million. Color and ever-larger screens added to TV's mass appeal, and by the early 1970's 96 percent of all American households had one or more sets.

Entertainment for the Millions

If the novelty of seeing moving images in their living rooms lured Americans to the TV screen, varied programing kept them there. The first TV "star" was a genial, red-haired marionette named Howdy Doody. His vast popularity among children led untold thousands of U.S. parents to buy their first sets out of sheer self-defense. The first human star was Milton Berle, a brash, burlesque comic whose slambang variety hour, the *Texaco Star Theatre,* earned him the honorary title "Mr. Television" during the early 1950's. The variety shows by Berle, Ed Sullivan, and others stemmed from vaudeville and were mainstays of the new medium.

Most early TV broadcasters were radio veterans, and many early shows (including *Amos 'n' Andy* with black actors) were carryovers. Some radio stars, such as Bob Hope and Jack Benny, made the transition to the small screen with little difficulty; others, including Fred Allen, radio's top draw, failed. While many movie stars tried the new medium, only the perennial favorite Lucille Ball achieved consistent success. Two enduring TV favorites, *Meet the Press* (begun in 1947) and *Today* (launched in 1952 with easygoing Dave Garroway at the helm), first demonstrated television's extraordinary ability to clarify national issues for a mass audience.

Television's sudden success caused widespread panic throughout the rest of the entertainment world. By 1951 movie theaters in cities with TV service had experienced a 20 to 40 percent drop in attendance. Theater owners tried desperately to hold on to their audiences by slashing ticket prices and giving away free sets of china, as they had done in the Depression years. Hundreds of theaters were forced to close their doors. Sports crowds dwindled. Other areas of the economy felt TV's impact during peak viewing hours: Cab drivers, librarians, restaurateurs, all reported steep declines in patronage. Radio networks, too, watched helplessly as longtime listeners abandoned their radios to watch television. They finally managed to survive by concentrating on programing for special audiences, such as teenagers, ethnic groups, and lovers of classical, jazz, or country music.

Virtually every area of American life was touched by the tension between the United States and the Soviet Union, and show business proved no exception. Television, which was coming into its own as the cold war became increasingly bitter in the early 1950's, was affected along with motion pictures and the theater. In an atmosphere of anxiety over internal spying and subversion—a fear that many Americans felt was exaggerated—legislative zealots and private citizens alike took it on themselves to rid show business of everyone who had been associated with Communist or Communist-front causes—directors, producers, writers, and performers. With few exceptions, network executives, studio bosses, and commercial sponsors went along, blacklisting scores of talented people on the basis of sometimes flimsy charges. During this period many powerful people in the entertainment industry did little or nothing to defend their colleagues under attack.

In its early days *television produced a very small image, as shown in this view of Edward R. Murrow on a Dumont Rumson table model, about 1949. This set included an FM radio and was obviously influenced by radio design. Regardless of the size, the cathode-ray tube was the all but unbelievable electronic wonder that it still is today. Color TV was introduced in 1951 but since a color set could not receive black-and-white broadcasts, it was discontinued until sets with such capabilities were produced in 1953.*

That television, along with the other media, should reflect the popular mood of the day is not surprising. Nor is it strange that with the number of hours to fill each year much of the programing is bland and mediocre. But at its finest, television has proved its ability to educate, uplift, and inform as well as to entertain. It has brought brilliant drama, superb music, sharp satire, and incisive documentaries to countless millions of viewers. From the televised investigation of organized crime chaired by Senator Estes Kefauver in 1950–51 to the probe of the Watergate scandal and the hearings on the impeachment of President Richard M. Nixon in 1973 and 1974, TV has brought more Americans closer to their Government than ever before in the history of the Republic. In times of crisis—perhaps most memorably in the aftermath of President John F. Kennedy's assassination—television has served to calm and unite a shocked people. It has also brought moments of human triumph into everyday lives: No dramatist could match the excitement experienced around the world when U.S. astronaut Neil Armstrong first stepped onto the surface of the Moon in 1969.

Meanwhile public television, funded by Government grants and private donations, provides a select blend of entertainment and information. Thanks to such programs as *Sesame Street* and *Electric Company,* it has also helped teach a whole generation to read.

Thanks to the performers and to the inventors and showmen who helped them display their talent, American entertainers have appeared in every major country. This would probably come as no surprise to the farsighted men of 1776; in the Declaration of Independence they deemed it self-evident that the pursuit of happiness ranked with life and liberty as worth fighting for.

Television Innovators *Big Entertainment on a Small Screen*

The Howdy Doody Show (1947–60), originally **The Puppet Playhouse.** The puppet Howdy Doody, Buffalo Bob, and Clarabell the Clown starred in the first popular children's TV show.

The Texaco Star Theatre, featuring Milton Berle (1948–53). So popular that he became known as Mr. Television, Berle had prominent guests on his variety show, but he was the main attraction.

The Toast of the Town (1948–55), changed to **The Ed Sullivan Show** (1955–71). Here Ed is with the Beatles. He also introduced Americans to the Moiseyev Dancers on television.

Your Show of Shows (1949–54). The team of Sid Caesar and Imogene Coca, with Howard Morris and Carl Reiner, brought memorable comedy and Broadway-quality revues into the home every week.

I Love Lucy (1951–57). Starring Lucille Ball and Desi Arnaz, seen here with Ethel Mertz and William Frawley (left), this comedy is among the leaders of the daytime reruns that have proliferated on every channel.

Dragnet (1952–59; 1969). Jack Webb produced, wrote, directed, and, with Ben Alexander, starred in this low-key, realistic crime detection show, which started a new trend in police dramas.

Gunsmoke (1955–75). Shown are James Arness and Dennis Weaver, two of the stars of what became the longest running Western on television. Gunsmoke was a forerunner among adult Westerns.

As the World Turns (1956–). Although not the oldest soap opera on television, this daytime serial attracted 10 million viewers. Some of its stars have been with the show since its inception.

Perry Mason (1957–66). Perry (Raymond Burr) and his secretary, Della Street (Barbara Hale), confer in a scene from this series, based on Erle Stanley Gardner's stories of a criminal lawyer who never lost a case.

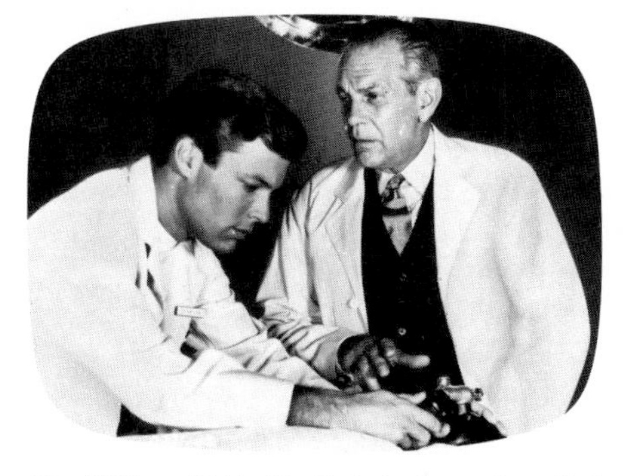

Dr. Kildare (1961–66). Typical of several medical series, this popular show starred Richard Chamberlain as Dr. Kildare and Raymond Massey as Dr. Gillespie. Some "Dr. Kildare" movies had preceded it.

The Tonight Show (1954–57), host Steve Allen; **The Jack Paar Show** (1957–62); **The Tonight Show Starring Johnny Carson** (photo) (1962–). This late-night show altered the habits of millions.

Super Bowl Joint Telecast (1967); **Super Bowl** (1968–). The climax of the professional football season attracted 56 million viewers in 1975, the largest audience up to then for a single sporting event.

CHAPTER TWENTY-SEVEN

Sports and Recreation

Considering America's infatuation with sports and recrea tion today, it is hard to imagine how little time our earl ancestors had for play. Baseball, generally recognized a the national pastime, did not begin to gain a sizable fol lowing until the 1840's and for many years was widel regarded as a game for the idle rich.

The Civil War helped democratize the game, as Unio Army recruits took to baseball and taught it to fellow sol diers and to their captors in prison camps in the South Soon after the war the first professional clubs were formed and thereafter baseball occupied an unchallenged positio as the Nation's No. 1 sport until the late 1940's. Footbal

The colonists who set out from the old country in the early 17th century had little time for fun and games. If they survived the 6-to-8-week voyage across the Atlantic, they found themselves 3,000 miles from home in a struggle for existence on the rim of an unfriendly continent, hemmed in by the ocean on one side and a hostile forest frontier on the other.

Of necessity, everybody—men, women, even children—worked hard from sunup to sundown to improve the crude dwellings, clear the land, plant crops, and hunt game. The colonists were in the main simple, God-fearing folk seeking livelihoods in an environment of political and religious freedom. Few had experienced the pleasures and diversions of upper-class Merrie England, which were generally regarded as sinful. On Christmas Day, 1621, William Bradford, Governor of the Plymouth Colony, came upon some young colonists pitching the bar, an Elizabethan sport similar to throwing the javelin, while others were playing a game of stoolball, a form of cricket. Bradford broke up the goings-on, stating that, "ther should be no gameing or revelling in ye streets." A few years later, in 1628, at Merry Mount, near Quincy, Massachusetts, a Maypole was chopped down and the dancers chastised for their "pagan idolatry."

The colonists' Indian neighbors had for centuries been playing their own native games, principally *baggataway* —more like a pitched battle than a sport, in which as many as 1,000 warriors took part. The French explorers named this game *la crosse* (French for "crosier") because they saw a resemblance between the playing stick and the bishop's staff. New England authorities dismissed these contests as fit only for heathens, but they did somewhat relax the blue laws against sports because of the militia system, which required that every able-bodied male bear arms against the threat of Indian attack. Periodic exercises were held to teach the men defensive tactics. Out of these drills evolved competitions in target shooting, wrestling, rough-and-tumble fighting, running, and jumping. Such activities were condoned as necessary for training purposes and were not considered pleasurable. But there was no slackening of laws against dancing and playing cards, quoits, and bowls. In 1677 a proclamation issued in Boston prohibited horseracing "within four miles of any town, or in any High way or common rode."

Sport of the Turf

In the worldlier Colonies down the Atlantic coast, horseracing was an established pastime, as were cockfighting, bull and bear baiting, skittles, and even a kind of golf. Informal horseraces had long been run over field and roads to settle local arguments or wagers, particularly in Maryland, Virginia, and the Carolinas. Col. Richard Nicolls, the first English Governor of New York, made horseracing America's first organized sport. In 1665, the year after the British captured New Amsterdam from the Dutch and renamed it, Colonel Nicolls had a 2-mile track laid out on Long Island's Hempstead Plains and instituted meets there. The innovation met with popular approval. By the early 1700's courses had been built in New York, in Rhode Island, which was untouched by the Puritan prejudice against racing, and in the South.

The racing horse in the early days was a hardy mixed breed called a short horse because of its speed over short distances. One distinctive Rhode Island type was the Narragansett pacer, believed to have been Paul Revere's mount on his famous ride. The year 1730 was a significant one for American racing because, according to some historians, it marked the shipment of the first Thoroughbred stallion, Bullee Rock, to Virginia. Around the end of the 17th century the Thoroughbred had been developed in England, the offspring of sturdy English mares and one of three imported Arab stallions. During the next century *in the early 1900's was essentially a college game and even then was criticized for its brutality. Boxing developed slowly, hampered by legal bans and public disapproval. Golf and tennis were dismissed as recreations for the wealthy. Eventually, all these sports attained great popularity. Bicycling became the rage in the 1890's, but interest diminished as the automobile took over. Basketball, a latecomer, was quickly accepted by players and the public.*

After World War II there were unprecedented opportunities for the enjoyment of leisure. Shorter workweeks, higher pay, and longer vacations encouraged travel and sightseeing. A growing interest in physical fitness sent people into the open. They learned to play golf, tennis, handball, softball, and volleyball. They bowled, skied, skated, and went camping, fishing, hunting, boating, hiking, jogging, bicycling, and swimming. When they were not out on the roads, waterways, beaches, or playing fields, they crowded into baseball parks, football stadiums, basketball and hockey arenas, and racetracks as spectators, and literally millions sat before their TV sets to watch highly paid athletic superstars perform.

The remarkable diversity of the American people is nowhere more dramatically illustrated than in the variety of sports they so enthusiastically pursue.

American Indians *ran, jumped, wrestled, and played a variety of games, the most popular of which was baggataway. The early French settlers, who thought the playing stick looked like a bishop's crosier, called the game* la crosse. *This drawing, made by George Catlin in 1834, shows a game of baggataway in progress between hundreds of braves of the Choctaw tribe. One team's players are covered with white body paint to distinguish them from their opponents. The object of the game was to propel a ball across the adversaries' goal line, marked by two upright posts. The ball was caught in a meshed loop at one end of the player's stick and carried forward. Sometimes each player wielded two sticks, at other times only one. As the Indians played it, baggataway was a vicious, warlike affair, and players were often maimed or killed.*

more than 300 Thoroughbred stallions and mares were brought over. Wealthy Southern landowners and Northern sportsmen opened breeding stables. In his younger years George Washington owned and bred Thoroughbreds and frequently officiated at races. The earliest turf organization was the Maryland Jockey Club, established in 1743, which operated a track at Annapolis.

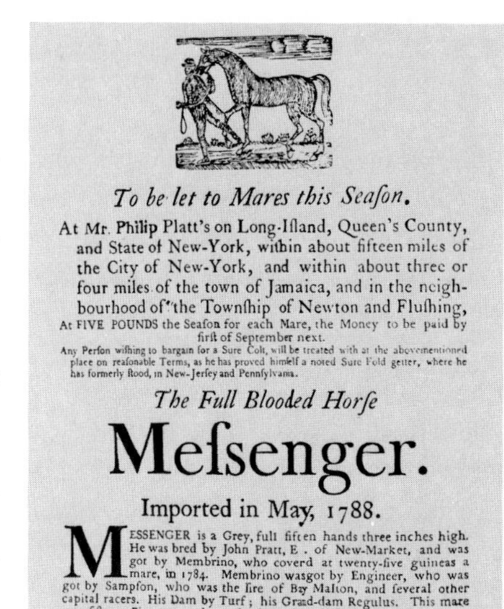

To be let to Mares this Seaſon.

At Mr. Philip Platt's on Long-Iſland, Queen's County, and State of New-York, within about fifteen miles of the City of New-York, and within about three or four miles of the town of Jamaica, and in the neighbourhood of the Townſhip of Newton and Fluſhing,

At FIVE POUNDS the Seaſon for each Mare, the Money to be paid by firſt of September next.

Any Perſon wiſhing to bargain for a Sure Colt, will be treated with at the abovementioned place on reaſonable Terms, as he has proved himſelf a noted Sure Fold getter, where he has formerly ſtood, in New-Jerſey and Pennſylvania.

The Full Blooded Horſe

Meſsenger.

Imported in May, 1788.

MESSENGER is a Grey, full fifteen hands three inches high. He was bred by John Pratt, E . of New-Market, and was got by Membrino, who coverd at twenty-five guineas a mare, in 1784. Membrino wasgot by Engineer, who was got by Sampſon, who was the ſire of Bay Malton, and ſeveral other capital racers. His Dam by Turf; his Grand-dam Regulus. This mare was ſiſter to Figerant, and was the dam of Leviathan, a capital racer

This early handbill *offers the breeding services of the English stallion Messenger, a founder of the American Standardbred horse.*

Although horseracing suffered setbacks during the Revolution and the War of 1812, it soon revived to become more popular than ever. Intersectional rivalry reached a peak in America's first sports spectacular: a match at the Union Race Course in Long Island, New York, on May 27, 1823, between American Eclipse, the North's unbeaten champion, and Henry, the South's fastest Thoroughbred. A crowd of 60,000 by some estimates packed the stands and the track's infield. American Eclipse won the $10,000 side bet. The famous track at Saratoga Springs, New York, was opened in 1863 in the midst of the Civil War. Churchill Downs, at Louisville, Kentucky, was established 12 years later with the first running of the Kentucky Derby.

About this time harness racing was becoming popular. Messenger, a Thoroughbred imported from England in 1788, proved of vital importance to the sport in America. Through some quirk of genetics, this fine Thoroughbred racer passed on to his progeny characteristics that made them superb trotters. Hambletonian, a third-generation descendant of Messenger, is regarded as the father of the modern American Standardbred (a horse bred for set speeds of trotting and pacing); he sired more than 1,300 foals, many of which became harness-racing champions. Another famous strain was founded in the 1790's by a stallion owned by a Vermonter named Justin Morgan.

What Thoroughbred racing was to the cities, harness racing was to American towns and villages. During the 19th century and into the 20th, practically every county and State fair featured Standardbred racing, which later became popular in the cities. By the 1970's horseracing in general, both Thoroughbred and harness, was by far the most heavily attended sport in the United States, well ahead of baseball, with close to 80 million persons passing through the turnstiles of the Nation's tracks each year and parimutuel betting hitting record totals of more than $6 billion a year.

Along with racing, horse shows have enjoyed popularity since the early 1700's. Annual shows (1,249 in 1974) are held in many communities, some in connection with State or county fairs, others as single events in spe-

Breeding lines *of practically all modern harness racehorses can be traced to the great stallion Hambletonian, shown in this painting with his owner, William M. Rysdyk. A great-grandson of Messenger, Hambletonian was foaled on Jonas Seeley's farm in Orange County, New York, in 1849 and was purchased with his dam for $125 by Rysdyk, a farmhand. Hambletonian became famous, not for his track performance—he was never officially raced—but as a sire. Before he died in 1876 at age 27, Hambletonian sired 1,331 foals, many of which became outstanding trotters. His stud fee, initially $10, went as high as $500, bringing wealth to his owner. The Hambletonian, considered the Kentucky Derby of harness horse racing, is named after the famed stallion.*

A typical scene *at almost any American State or county fair during the late 19th century is pictured in this Currier & Ives print. It was a close finish in the harness race run before a crowd of excited spectators. The type of sulky shown here, equipped with bicycle-size wheels and pneumatic tires, was introduced in 1892, replacing the heavier and slower high-wheeled vehicle that was popular until that time.*

cially built arenas or in showplaces such as Madison Square Garden in New York City. Thousands may watch as horses and riders go through their paces and receive awards for their skill in a variety of maneuvers.

Bat and Ball

Baseball had its early beginnings in America as a simple bat-and-ball game played first by children, then by adults. The game had a variety of names: Town ball, goal ball, round ball, one old cat, two old cat, baste ball, and base ball. It evolved from the old English sport of rounders, in which a batsman hit a thrown ball with a stick and then ran to bases marked by rocks or posts.

The rules of the American game were few. Any number could play, from 2 to 14 or 15 or more. The hitter ran the bases clockwise, with first base where third base is today. Counterclockwise base running was not adopted until 1839. A putout was made by catching the ball either on the fly or on first bounce, or by hitting, or "plugging," the batter with a thrown ball when he was running between bases. There were no sides and no teams. Each player had a turn and batted until he was put out.

Militiamen played during training days or while on standby duty. Team play may have begun at this time, when soldiers from one community or squad challenged another. The diary of one George Ewing, who served with General Washington during the Revolution, notes that on April 7, 1778, at Valley Forge, he "exercised in the afternoon in the intervals played at base."

College students took to the game enthusiastically as an alternative to soccer and cricket. Princeton records of 1787 mention ball playing, as does the 1827 diary of a Brown University student. The elder Oliver Wendell Holmes, who graduated from Harvard in 1829, wrote of participating in many ball games.

Interest in some form of baseball long preceded 1839, the year when, according to some now-discredited accounts, baseball was invented by Gen. Abner Doubleday at Cooperstown, New York. A better claim could be advanced in behalf of a New York surveyor and amateur ballplayer named Alexander Joy Cartwright.

The National Game

Cartwright was a charter member of the Knickerbocker Base Ball Club of New York City. Founded in 1845, the club was the first organization in the country composed entirely of ballplayers. In an endeavor to get some order into a sport that had such a conglomeration of rules and

The "Grand Match for the Championship" *at the Elysian Fields is shown in a Currier & Ives lithograph. In those early days the shortstop played inside the baseline, and the umpire stationed himself at one side of homeplate. The players did not wear gloves.*

Alexander Joy Cartwright and the Great American Game

The Rules Have Changed Little From the Original Concept—Now More Than 125 Years Old

Much of the credit for the present-day game of baseball belongs to Alexander Joy Cartwright. As a member of the New York Knickerbocker Base Ball Club, young Cartwright took it upon himself in 1845 to standardize a game that had evolved from the old English sport of rounders.

It was no easy task. One version of baseball was played in Boston, another in Philadelphia, still another in New York. There was no agreement as to the number of men on a team, how long a game should last, or the rules of play. Even the shape and dimensions of the playing fields varied.

Cartwright was by profession a draftsman and a surveyor, and he made good use of his talents when he designed a baseball field as he thought it should be. His "baseball square"—later called a diamond—turned out to be so right for the game that it is still used today, basically unaltered, in all ball parks and sandlots.

Even more astonishing is the fact that most of the rules that Cartwright set down more than 125 years ago remain unchanged: Nine players to a side, three strikes for an out, three outs per inning, no throwing the ball at the runner. Regulations on the foul ball and the pitcher's balk were also established.

The Cartwright-style diamond was laid out on the cricket grounds of the Elysian Fields in Hoboken, New Jersey, just across the Hudson River from New York City. There, on June 19, 1846, the first modern game of baseball was played. It pitted the Knickerbockers against a team called the New York Nine. The players and umpire wore their own clothes; the Knickerbockers first wore uniforms in 1849. The Knickerbockers went down to defeat, 23 to 1.

Alexander Cartwright did not participate as a player in the historic event. Instead he acted as the game's umpire, enforcing his own rules. In this role he may have been responsible for yet another baseball first when he fined one of the players for swearing. The fine amounted to 6 cents.

methods of play, Cartwright, who had experience as a draftsman, was assigned the task of laying out a baseball field and establishing a set of playing rules. Ultimately he came up with what is now the classic diamond. Among his rules was one limiting the number of players on a team to nine. (The first book of rules was formulated in 1859 by Henry Chadwick, a sportswriter.) The first game of baseball under Cartwright's rules was played on June 19, 1846, at Elysian Fields in Hoboken, New Jersey, between the Knickerbockers and the New York Nine; the latter triumphed 23 aces (runs) to 1.

As word of the newly designed game spread, groups of young men in the New York area formed amateur clubs and adopted the Knickerbocker version, which was soon referred to as the New York Game. A meeting of 22 clubs, held in New York in March 1858, resulted in creation of the National Association of Base Ball Players. Some modifications were made in the rules, such as limiting a game to nine innings and providing that a ball had to be caught on the fly to constitute an out. The codified game proved an unqualified success.

The Civil War did more than anything else to spread baseball. The volunteers who crowded Union Army training camps were eager converts. When some of them later became prisoners in Confederate stockades, they played when they could and taught the game to their captors. When peace came, baseball was soon flourishing in the South and the Midwest as well as in the East.

In 1869 the Cincinnati Red Stockings became the first ball club to turn professional. A year earlier they had made sartorial history when they adopted what was to become the accepted baseball uniform: knee-length pants and long stockings. The Cincinnatians made two exhibition tours of the country in 1869 and 1870, taking on all challengers. They won 130 of the 132 games played, tied 1 and lost 1.

The barnstorming tours drew overflow crowds everywhere and added immeasurably to the popularity of baseball. More and more clubs turned professional. The influence of the National Association of Base Ball Players, which represented only amateur teams, was so weakened that the organization was dissolved in 1871, to be replaced by the National Association of Professional Base Ball Players. In 1876 this was succeeded by what is now the National League (NL), which in turn was challenged by the American Association and later by the Western League, rechristened the American League (AL) in 1900. In 1903 the National and American Leagues recognized each other as the only major leagues in the sport and agreed to settle their competing claims to superiority on the baseball diamond.

The first World Series was held that autumn between the two pennant winners. The AL's Boston Red Sox defeated the NL's Pittsburgh Pirates, five games to three. New feuding prevented a 1904 meeting, but World Series play was resumed in 1905 and has been an autumn classic ever since.

Although plagued in its early days by professional gamblers, baseball had stayed relatively clean. Then in 1920 came the shocking revelation that in the 1919 World Series between the Chicago White Sox and the Cincinnati Reds some gamblers and some White Sox players had conspired to let Cincinnati win. Eight of the White Sox players were indicted for the conspiracy and were banned from baseball for life in what became known as the Black Sox scandal. In an effort to restore public faith, tough-minded Judge Kenesaw Mountain Landis was appointed commissioner of baseball and given almost unlimited powers. Much credit for the game's amazing comeback must go to Judge Landis for his rigorous handling of disciplinary matters, but a great share belongs to a slugger named George Herman "Babe" Ruth, who brought color, excitement, and crowds to the game with every home-run clout of his mighty bat.

Although there are many black players in the major leagues today, blacks had a difficult time breaking into the sport. In 1884, when the Toledo Mudhens were a major league club with the American Association, two black players were on their roster—Moses "Fleet" Walker and his brother, Welday Wilberforce Walker. After that, no major league club accepted a black player until 1947, when Jackie Robinson joined the Brooklyn Dodgers of the National League and became the first black player in modern major league history. Robinson's acceptance opened the way for a parade of great black stars—Larry Doby, Roy Campanella, Willie Mays, home-run king Henry Aaron, Roberto Clemente, from Puerto Rico, and many others. In 1974 Frank Robinson became manager of the Cleveland Indians, making him the first black manager of a major league baseball team.

From organized baseball's inception, fans have made folk heroes of the game's superstars. The names and records of these mighty men of the bat and glove—Honus Wagner, Ty Cobb, Christy Mathewson, Babe Ruth, and many immortals of more recent vintage are enshrined in the National Baseball Hall of Fame, established at Cooperstown, New York, in 1939.

The World Series of 1905 Was One of the Best Ever Played

The first modern World Series, played in 1903, pitted the pennant-winning Boston Red Sox of the American League against the National League champions, the Pittsburgh Pirates. Boston won, 5 games to 3, but it was in a sense a false start. The series failed to draw support from either the fans or baseball's national committee, so it was not played the following year. However, in 1905, the now celebrated fall classic was played again, this time with organized baseball's blessing, and it has continued uninterrupted ever since.

That first official series was one of the most dramatic ever held. It brought together tough John McGraw's National League New York Giants and mild-mannered Connie Mack's American League Philadelphia Athletics. At a time that has been called baseball's golden age of pitching, both clubs had superb mound aces. For the A's Charles A. "Chief" Bender and Eddie Plank were outstanding; for the Giants there was Christy "Matty" Mathewson, the darling of the crowd.

It was Matty who emerged the hero. He pitched the first, third, and fifth games and not only won them all but won them by shutouts. In so doing, Mathewson put a record in the books that has never been topped: the most consecutive shutouts in a World Series.

It is also of interest that Joseph J. "Iron Man" McGinnity won the fourth game for the Giants, 1–0, while Chief Bender pitched the Athletics to their only victory in the second game, blanking the Giants 3–0. The baseball championship of 1905 thus became a one of a kind—a shutout World Series. The Giants, of course, won it, 4 games to 1.

The five-game series drew a total of 91,723 spectators and grossed $68,436.81. Many grandstand seats went for a dollar, with bleacher admissions 50 cents. The world champion Giants each collected $1,142, while the Athletics ended up with $823 per share.

Other sports have had—and are having—their day in the sun. Yet, with an estimated 12 million people playing the sport from Little League to the major leagues and some 41 million attending a season's games, plus millions more watching on television, baseball remains, as it has been for more than a century, the national pastime.

The Gridiron

The first intercollegiate football game in the United States is generally said to have been played at New Brunswick, New Jersey, between Rutgers and Princeton on November 6, 1869 (Rutgers winning 6 goals to 4). It was Harvard more than any other college, however, that helped mold American football into the sport it is today. The Eastern colleges played a soccerlike game imported from England, but Harvard had a variation called the Boston Game. This was still essentially a kicking contest, but the rules also allowed the players to pick up the ball and run with it in certain situations.

When Harvard men learned that a different type of football was played at McGill University in Montreal, they arranged for two exhibition games with the Canadians at Cambridge, Massachusetts, in the spring of 1874. The first game, on May 14, under the Boston Game rules, was won by Harvard, 3 to 0; the second, on May 15, under the McGill rules, ended in a scoreless tie. What interested Harvard most was the kind of game the Canadians played. It was an English sport called rugby, which had little in common with soccer. The ball was elongated, not round, and a player could run with it, pass it to another player, and carry it across the goal line for a score. Furthermore, the ball carrier could be tackled.

Walter Camp of Yale

Father of Modern Football

The use of mass formations, *such as the flying wedge pictured here, turned college football from a kicking and running game into a brutal battering contest by the 1890's. Public outrage at the resulting toll in death and injuries brought about a revision of intercollegiate football rules.*

Walter Camp has been called the most influential figure in American football, and with good reason. No other person did so much to revolutionize the Rugby-type game of the middle 1800's and turn it into the truly American sport it is today.

Born in New Britain, Connecticut, April 7, 1859, Walter Chauncey Camp was a natural athlete. His ability was recognized when he entered Yale (class of 1880) and was quickly selected for a halfback position on the football team.

In those days a college football team consisted of 15 players—8 forwards, 4 halfbacks, and 3 fullbacks. What was called a scrimmage (scrum) occurred when the ball was put into play between the two opposing forward lines. In the ensuing free-for-all scramble the forwards of both sides endeavored to propel the ball to the rear and into possession of one of the backs. The back's task then was to advance the ball by running, passing, or kicking.

It was a wild sport with few rules and little or no strategy. After playing the game for a while, Camp began to envision ways of making football more scientific and the play controllable. He made suggestions to the rules committee, and they were for the most part accepted. Among them were recommendations that there be 11 players to a side; that a scrimmage take place with the center forward of one side putting the ball into play by snapping it back; and that "the man who receives the ball from the snapback . . . be called the quarterback." The creation of the position of quarterback was perhaps Camp's most significant innovation. The quarterback was soon calling out play signals—at first sentences, then letters, then numbers. Another dramatic change, at Camp's suggestion, was to allow tackling below the waist.

To counteract the prevailing tendency of teams to use up time by simply retaining possession of the ball without trying to advance it, Camp conceived the idea of a system of downs. His rule stated: "If on three consecutive downs a team shall not have advanced the ball five yards . . . they must give up the ball." This was later changed to four downs and 10 yards. With the adoption of downs, football fields began to be marked off with chalk lines, 5 yards apart, to assist game officials. From this striped appearance came the term "gridiron."

Camp excelled in other sports besides football. He was outstanding in baseball, track, swimming, and crew. After graduating he studied medicine for 2 years, then entered business. But he never allowed his career to interfere with his close ties to Yale. He remained active at his alma mater for many years as general director of athletics and advisory football coach. He also served on the Intercollegiate Football Rules Committee for 48 years.

Although the early All-American teams, beginning in 1889, were picked by Caspar Whitney, the selections were later made by Walter Camp (a custom he continued throughout his life) and published in *Collier's Weekly.* He died in New York on March 14, 1925.

In the days *of bareknuckle fighting in the 1800's, a bout was sometimes held between two teams of boxers, three to a side, as shown in this painting by George A. Hayes. Such a team fight usually continued until the members of one side were either knocked out or were otherwise put out of action. These bouts, often staged to settle local rivalries, attracted many spectators; few, if any, women were among them. Another type of multiple fight was known as the battle royal; in this a number of boxers fought each other until only one was left on his feet.*

The speed and freshness of the game so impressed the Harvard men that they tried it out among themselves and liked it. Word spread to other colleges. They, too, began to play rugby. When the U.S. Intercollegiate Football Association was formed in 1876, Rugby Union rules were adopted. Before long, changes were made and innovations were added—so many, in fact, that eventually a new game evolved. A young Yale undergraduate named Walter C. Camp was responsible for many of the imaginative suggestions.

In an astonishingly short time the revolutionized game had become wildly popular with players and spectators alike. Crowds thronged the fields to watch the college elevens do battle. The game turned violent with the introduction of massive power formations, such as Harvard's flying wedge of 1892. The bruising tactics became so savage that in 1905 alone 18 players were killed and 159 injured. After an investigation initiated by President Theodore Roosevelt, drastic reforms were made. The game was opened up, less emphasis was put on brute strength, and the forward pass was introduced.

Football became increasingly popular. Great stadiums were built, such as the Yale Bowl in 1914. Traditional rivalries developed between Army and Navy, Yale and Harvard, and dozens of other schools. By the 1970's more than 600 top college teams were competing for honors in a myriad of national collegiate conferences, climaxed by postseason games held in major cities, such as the Rose Bowl (first held in 1902), Sugar Bowl, Cotton Bowl, and Orange Bowl.

Professional football historically began in Latrobe, Pennsylvania, in 1895 but did not gain wide popularity until the late 1950's and early 1960's. National television has been responsible for its sweeping expansion. Today, with its efficiently run teams of highly paid athletes, it has become perhaps the top televised sport in the Nation.

The Fights

The English sport of bareknuckle prizefighting was introduced in America before the Revolution, when Southern plantation owners matched their strongest black slaves against one another for sizable stakes. But it was not until the early 1800's that boxing began to find favor among American sportsmen. During the next half century a number of self-proclaimed American champions fought top English boxers. The rules were few. The barefisted contestants wrestled, kicked, and gouged. A round lasted until there was a knockdown. The fallen fighter lost the match unless he could "come up to scratch" after 30 seconds' rest—that is, toe a line scratched on the ring floor and reengage his opponent.

Prizefighting was illegal in most of the United States, and bouts had to be held secretly. The fighter who brought a measure of respectability to the sport was the

Boston Strong Boy, John L. Sullivan. On February 7, 1882, Sullivan knocked out the champion, Paddy Ryan, at Mississippi City, Mississippi, to take the world heavyweight title. He won the last of the bareknuckle championship fights by overcoming Jake Kilrain in 1889.

Sullivan's popularity was enhanced by nationwide tours during which he offered $500 to anyone who could stay in the ring with him for 4 rounds. The Great John L. lost to Gentleman Jim Corbett, a former San Francisco bank clerk, in a 21-round title fight at New Orleans on September 7, 1892. This was the first world heavyweight championship fight held under the 12 rules drawn up in England by the Marquis of Queensberry in 1867. The rules established the use of padded gloves, 3-minute rounds with 1 minute's rest in between, and a referee's count over a floored fighter—a 10-second count meant a knockout and the end of the fight.

Early in the 20th century a number of talented black heavyweights came into prominence, but prejudice denied them a shot at the title and they had to fight each other for small purses. Jack Johnson of Galveston, Texas, widely considered one of the most accomplished boxers of all time, finally broke the color barrier by knocking out the reputed titleholder, Tommy Burns, at Sydney, Australia, in 1908. For Negroes everywhere, Johnson became a symbol of black power, but his flamboyant lifestyle and his marriages to two white women alienated white fans, who also resented his boxing skill. Jim Jeffries, who had retired undefeated in 1905, returned to the ring as "the great white hope," but Johnson easily defeated him in Reno, Nevada, in 1910, thus becoming the undisputed world heavyweight titleholder. Outrage at the black champion's ways mounted to such a pitch that in 1912 he was convicted on dubious evidence of having violated the Mann Act forbidding the transport of women across State lines for immoral purposes. Sentenced to a year in prison, he fled the country while out on bail. Johnson lost his title to Jess Willard in April 1915 in Havana, Cuba, in a 26th-round knockout that was regarded by many experts as questionable.

Jack Johnson, *the first black man to hold the world heavyweight title (1910–15), is regarded by many as the greatest fighter of them all. In a 28-year career, he lost only 7 of 114 bouts, and his losing title bout has been disputed.*

Boxing enjoyed great popularity during the heavyweight reigns of the colorful Jack Dempsey, Gene Tunney, and Joe Louis, the second black fighter to hold the world's title (from 1937 to 1949), who retired undefeated. But in the years after World War II interest in boxing sagged except for the highly publicized title matches. The smalltime neighborhood club fights drew few fans. Many local arenas and gyms went out of business, and some colleges even dropped the sport that earlier had been a popular collegiate event.

The one amateur boxing activity that continued unaffected was the Golden Gloves program, which had been initiated by the New York *Daily News* to promote the sport among the youth of America. The reputation of these tournaments for producing such great champions as Sugar Ray Robinson, Joe Louis, and Rocky Marciano still inspires youngsters to follow the rugged sport of self-defense. As always in the history of the sport, boxing appeals mostly to those who have few other opportunities to gain fame and fortune.

The Fabulous Twenties

Never again is one decade likely to see so many exceptional athletes in such a variety of sports as the 1920's produced. The 10-year span has rightly been called the Golden Age of Sports.

In baseball, Babe Ruth, with his booming home runs, revitalized a discredited game and packed the ball park stands with fans.

In boxing, Jack Dempsey, the Manassa Mauler, knocked out Georges Carpentier, France's Orchid Man (named for his favorite flower), on July 2, 1921, in the first sporting event to attract a million-dollar gate.

In football, Red Grange, the Galloping Ghost of Illinois, who worked as an iceman in his hometown of Wheaton during vacations, scampered for spectacular touchdowns (five against Michigan in one game), while Coach Knute Rockne and his Four Horsemen made gridiron history at Notre Dame.

In golf, amateur player Bobby Jones captured 13 national championships and swept golfdom's Grand Slam—the U.S. Open and Amateur and the British Open and Amateur titles—in 1930.

In basketball, Nat Holman and the Original Celtics earned national acclaim with their brilliant court play. The team was so good that it had difficulty finding opponents and eventually disbanded.

In swimming, Johnny Weissmuller, long before he became the movie Tarzan, streaked for records; and Gertrude "Trudy" Ederle conquered the riptides of the English Channel—the first woman to do so.

The greatest *American Thoroughbred, Man o' War, shown here with jockey Clarence Kummer, raced only 2 seasons (1919–20), winning 20 out of 21 races handily. Big Red's one loss resulted from bad riding.*

In track, an increasingly popular sport, Charley Paddock, whom sportswriters labeled the Fastest Human, was noted for his finishing leaps at the tape.

In horseracing, Man o' War thundered down the stretch to victory after victory, and the leading jockey was the competitive Earl Sande.

In tennis, Big Bill Tilden and Helen Wills—Little Miss Poker Face—dominated the courts.

There were outstanding performers not only in the major sports but in polo, in billiards and pool, in automobile and motorboat racing, in ice hockey and figure skating, in yachting, in rowing, and in 6-day bicycle racing. New sports were introduced. The mad, amazing, delightful decade kicked off the greatest expansion in sports and recreation America had ever known.

Made in U.S.A.

Of all the major sports played in the United States, the only purely indigenous game is basketball. It was invented in 1891 by Canadian-born James Naismith, who taught physical education in Springfield, Massachusetts, at the YMCA International Training School (now Springfield College, the site of basketball's Hall of Fame). Using a soccer ball and two peach baskets, he designed an indoor, no-contact sport to keep his students out of mischief during the winter. The game won swift acceptance, not only in American high schools and colleges but in many other countries, where it was introduced by YMCA workers trained at Springfield. Its growth was rapid. Soon the United States was laced with basketball leagues, and the players ranged from grammar school to college age. The game was made an official part of Olympic competition in 1936, when basketball teams from 22 countries participated.

Athletic director, *college professor, Presbyterian minister, Dr. James Naismith is shown here in his late 60's, holding a ball like the one used when he invented the game of basketball in December 1891. During his lifetime (1861–1939) Dr. Naismith witnessed the phenomenal growth of his game from a minor indoor recreation to a major American sport. Now internationally popular, basketball was made a part of Olympic competition at the 1936 games in Berlin, Germany. Dr. Naismith was present at the official ceremony honoring his game.*

Dr. James Naismith

A New Game With a Ball and Peach Basket

The origins of basketball, unlike those of many sports in America, have never been in doubt. It undoubtedly originated in this country and was undeniably the brainchild of one man, Dr. James Naismith.

Naismith was a Canadian, born in Almonte, Ontario, in 1861. After graduating from McGill University, he attended a Presbyterian theological college. Interested in athletics as well as in religion, Naismith declined a pastorate and instead became a member of the faculty of the International YMCA Training School (now Springfield College) in Springfield, Massachusetts, in 1890.

In his role as a physical-education instructor of young men preparing to serve in the association's overseas branches, Naismith saw a need for some sort of team game that would fill the winter gap between the football season in the autumn and baseball in the spring. Using a soccer ball and two peach baskets (from which came the game's name), Naismith invented the sport of basketball.

The game was an instant success with the Springfield students. Shortly thereafter it began to be played in YMCA gymnasiums across the country. Enthusiasm for basketball soon spread to schools and colleges in the United States and Canada. The game was also introduced in many countries throughout the world by graduates of the YMCA school in Springfield. By 1939 the rules of basketball had been printed in as many as 30 languages, and the game was played in more than 75 countries.

Professional basketball came into its own in 1949 with the merger of two competing leagues to form the National Basketball Association. The American Basketball Association began operations in 1967. Among the alltime great pro players are Wilt Chamberlain, Bob Cousy, Bill Russell, Jerry West, and Kareem Abdul-J'abbar, formerly known as Lew Alcindor.

Naismith remained at Springfield until 1895, then moved on to the YMCA at Denver, Colorado. Three years later Naismith was on the move again, this time to Lawrence, Kansas, where he became the ever-enthusiastic director of physical education at the University of Kansas. He died in Lawrence on November 28, 1939.

Bobby Jones, *shown here playing before an appreciative gallery, learned golf early. He won his first local tournament at age 8 and by his middle teens was regarded as a coming champion. Although Jones was a superb shotmaker, his game was flawed by outbursts of anger at himself when he made a misplay. Only after he conquered his tantrums did he win his first major championship, the 1923 U.S. Open. From then on the triumphs came fast. In 1930, he made his Grand Slam by taking the world's four major tournaments: the U.S. and British Open and Amateur. The feat had never been accomplished before and was still unmatched by the mid-1970's.*

Professional basketball, originally tried in the 1890's, failed to capture the public imagination until the advent of the Original Celtics of New York. In the 1920's the Celtics went on a barnstorming trip, displaying a fast-breaking style never seen before. The team toured the country for 7 years, sparked by the brilliant playing of Nat Holman, Joe Lapchick, and their stellar teammates.

Another famed professional team was the Harlem Globetrotters. This all-black quintet presented basketball as fun and entertainment, but with such players as Reese "Goose" Tatum, Marquis Haynes, and Wilt "the Stilt" Chamberlain in the lineup at various times, the Globetrotters could outscore many strong teams. Chamberlain went on to play superb ball in the National Basketball Association (NBA), scoring a record 4,029 points in the 1961–62 season for the Philadelphia Warriors.

With the founding of the NBA in 1949, basketball became one of America's big three professional team sports. The game's coverage was substantially increased in 1967 when a rival league, the American Basketball Association, came into existence. Nowadays millions of spectators pass through the turnstiles each year to attend high school, college, and professional basketball games, while millions more watch the action on their television screens—a far cry from the days of Dr. Naismith with his peach-basket goals and soccer ball.

On the Links

Records show that early Dutch settlers in New Amsterdam played a game called *het kolven* in which a club, or *kolf*, was used to hit a ball. Later, in the 1780's and 1790's, a game more like the modern version of golf (which originated in Scotland in the 15th century) was played on links in Georgia and South Carolina. But it was not until 1887 that the first permanent golf club with its own links was established in the United States, the Foxburg (Pennsylvania) Golf and Country Club. The next year the St. Andrews Club of Yonkers, New York, was founded. The course, laid out in a cow pasture, had a number of natural hazards. Other clubs soon followed, and in 1894 representatives of the five leading clubs met to form the United States Golf Association. The association standardized the game and in 1895 sponsored the first national amateur tournaments for men and women as well as the first official U.S. Open.

At first the American public regarded golf as a game for the well-to-do and ignored it. Then, in 1913, Francis Ouimet, an unknown 20-year-old ex-caddy from Boston, won the U.S. Open, defeating the top British professionals, Harry Vardon and Ted Ray. It was a victory straight out of Horatio Alger and received tremendous publicity. Young Ouimet's win has been credited with establishing American golf as a game for the people. New courses were laid out, club membership boomed, and public links were built for pay-as-you-play golfers. The game's popularity was further enhanced in the 1920's by the expertise and winning personality of the great amateur from Atlanta, Robert Tyre "Bobby" Jones.

Professional golf as a spectator sport was only modestly successful at first. When the Professional Golfers' Association was formed in 1916, tournaments for the playing professional were few, and cash prizes low. In 1934 the top money winner for the year collected $6,767, out of which he had to pay traveling and other expenses. By the mid-1970's Jack Nicklaus, the Golden Bear of golf, had picked up more than $300,000 in a single season and more than $2 million in his entire career to that time.

Professional golf, like other sports, has benefited enormously from television. While thousands of onlookers line the fairways to witness big tournaments, vastly larger numbers follow every tee shot and putt on their living room TV screens. Presidents Taft, Wilson, Harding, and Eisenhower were all golfers, but today it is a game for anyone who chooses to play or watch it.

The Net Game

Tennis, one of the fastest growing participant sports, was developed in England in 1873–74 by Maj. Walter C. Wingfield as a variation of the ancient indoor game of court tennis. Introduced to America via Bermuda shortly thereafter, it was first played during a garden party at the Staten Island (New York) Cricket and Baseball Club. Tennis-on-the-lawn, as it was called, soon became the rage in Newport, Rhode Island, and other fashionable Eastern resort centers as well as in California. In 1881 the United States Lawn Tennis Association was formed to prevent arguments by standardizing rules and equipment. The association held the first U.S. National Men's Singles championship the same year. The only interruption in this annual event came in 1917 when America entered World War I. A special "patriotic" tournament was substituted and was won in 1917 and 1918 by R. Lindley Murray. The U.S. National Women's championship, begun in 1887, has been held every year since.

Lawn tennis, like golf, was long considered a preserve of the privileged, and the best players came from the east coast. This changed just before World War I, when Maurice McLoughlin, a product of the asphalt public tennis courts of San Francisco, stunned opponents with his cannonball service and savage net game. The California Comet swept to the National Singles championship in 1912 and 1913 and prepared the way for the hard-hitting, crowd-pleasing brand of tennis played thereafter by Bill Tilden, Bill Johnson, Don Budge, and others.

Professional tennis came alive after World War II when television cameras began to zero in on the courts. The thin line between amateur and professional was swept aside when the prestigious amateur tournaments at Wimbledon, England, and Forest Hills, New York, capitulated to professionalism and held open championships beginning in 1968. As tournament prize money increased, promising young players who previously would have retained their amateur status turned pro, some of them while still in their teens. Women's tennis, under the leadership of champion Billie Jean King, won recognition and prize money equal to that of the men. Players' associations were formed, and world championship tours were organized.

The result was a tremendous increase in the popularity of tennis. Not only did more people watch tennis matches but more and more Americans began to play the game themselves—so many that they were expected to exceed 15 million by the end of the 1970's.

From a genteel game, *played in the 1890's by stylish ladies and dapper gentlemen and considered a sissy sport by nonplayers, lawn tennis soon spread from the East to become the most popular court game ever invented. Tennis reached new heights of popularity in the 1970's with such pro superstars as Billie Jean King, seen at right in a game with Bobby Riggs.*

Heroes of Professional Sports

A Colorful Array of Outstanding Athletes

Henry Aaron (*1934–*). Hit most home runs in baseball history. Aaron broke into organized baseball with Indianapolis Clowns, Negro American League. Sold to Braves, National League, 1952, for $10,000. Played with Braves in Milwaukee and Atlanta, 1954–74. Named league's Most Valuable Player, 1957. Traded to Milwaukee Brewers, American League, 1974. First player to earn $200,000 a season.

Muhammad Ali (*1942–*). Colorful, controversial heavyweight boxer. At first known as Cassius M. Clay, Jr., he took present name as member of Black Muslim sect. Won Olympic gold medal, light-heavyweight division, 1960. Defeated Sonny Liston, 1964, to gain world heavyweight title. Convicted of draft evasion, 1967, stripped of title; later won Supreme Court reversal. Regained world heavyweight crown, 1974, knocking out George Foreman at Kinshasa, Zaire.

Eddie Arcaro (*1916–*). The Master to other jockeys from 1930's to final ride at Pimlico in 1961 at age 45. Rode 24,092 mounts. Races won: 4,779; second place, 3,807; third, 3,302. Brought in five Kentucky Derby winners; two won Triple Crown (Derby, Belmont Stakes, and Preakness). Mounts earned $30,039,543 in purses.

Jim Brown (*1936–*). After starring at Syracuse University, became professional football's ranking running back in 9 seasons with Cleveland Browns, starting in mid-1950's. Upon retiring he left these records: Led National Football League in rushing 8 seasons, carried ball 2,359 times, gained 12,312 yards, scored 126 touchdowns, 106 by rushing.

Wilt Chamberlain (*1936–*). Seven-foot-one-inch height won him early nickname, Wilt the Stilt. Big man of basketball in 1960's with Philadelphia, San Francisco, Los Angeles. Scored 43 points, got 28 rebounds in professional debut. Tallied unprecedented 100 points against New York Knicks in 1962, averaging 50 points a game. Led sport to ever-greater status, packed galleries, earned fat paychecks.

Ty Cobb (*1886–1961*). Georgia Peach, coupled with Babe Ruth as baseball's all-time greatest. Joined Detroit Tigers as outfielder in 1905. Ended 24-year career with 4,191 hits, .367 average, 2,244 runs scored in 3,033 games. Led American League batters 9 years running, stole 892 bases, hit 118 homers.

Jack Dempsey (*1895–*). Manassa Mauler battered huge Jess Willard to win world heavyweight title in 1919. Knocked out Georges Carpentier in 1921 in first million-dollar gate. Outpointed by Gene Tunney in 1926. Almost regained title a year later, but Tunney survived historic "long count" to win again.

Joe DiMaggio (*1914–*). Jolting Joe. Postwar baseball's standout. Led New York Yankees from Babe Ruth era to be glorious 1940's center fielder. Batted .325 in 13 seasons, hit 361 home runs, averaged in 1,736 games 118 runs batted in per season, three times "Most Valuable." Set record by hitting safely in 56 straight games, 1941. Retired in 1951.

A. J. Foyt (*1935–*). Texas rancher, steered first racing car at age of 5, later won five national titles, three Indianapolis 500's, and $2,500,000. Drove all types of vehicles in a booming profession. On tracks from Le Mans to Indianapolis, he helped convert automobile racing into a big business in the 1950's and 1960's.

Lou Gehrig (*1903–41*). Iron Horse of baseball. Covered first base for New York Yankees in 2,130 consecutive games from 1925 till lateral sclerosis disabled him in 1939. He and Babe Ruth formed the game's most powerful hitting pair and led Yankees to dominance in the 1920's and beyond. Hit 493 home runs.

Harold "Red" Grange (*1903–*). The Galloping Ghost of the University of Illinois football team in 1920's and a running virtuoso. Scored 31 touchdowns, rolled up 3,637 rushing yards before turning professional. His most memorable game was Illinois versus the University of Michigan in 1924, when he scored five Illinois touchdowns in five consecutive ball carries. As a pro, he gave an instant lift to the struggling National Football League.

Sonja Henie (*1912–69*). Norwegian-born figure skater who captivated Europe during 1920's and 1930's and America in 1940's. Competed, but did not win, in 1924 Olympics at age of 12. She took gold medals in 1928, 1932, and 1936 and was world champion 10 times. As professional and as Hollywood star, she made skating a fad and surpassed all athletes of that era in earnings.

Ben Hogan (*1912–*). One of professional golf's great players of the 1940's and 1950's and one of its smallest (135 pounds). Won the PGA Open title in 1946 and 1948; the U.S. Open, 1948. Despite crippling auto accident in 1949, came back to take the U.S. Open in 1950 and 1951, the Masters in 1951, and in 1953 captured three major golf titles: the U.S. Open, the Masters, the British Open.

Bobby Hull (*1939–*). Golden Jet of modern game. Star of National Hockey League in 1960's with Chicago Black Hawks. A battering competitor, he scored 604 goals in 15 seasons with 119-mile-an-hour shots. Salary of $100,000 was put in shade by his more than $2½ million, 3-year contract in 1972 with Winnipeg of new World Hockey Association.

Joe Louis (*1914–*). Brown Bomber. Boxing king of 1930's, first black heavy-

weight champion since Jack Johnson. He turned pro in 1934, won title from Jim Braddock in 1937, defended it 25 times, held it 11 years, 8 months—longer than any modern champ. In 1938 he avenged pre-title loss to Max Schmeling of Germany with one-round knockout.

Willie Mays (*1931–*). Baseball's first black superstar after Jackie Robinson. Center fielder. Only Aaron and Ruth surpassed his career total of 660 home runs. Began with Birmingham Black Barons, joined New York Giants in 1951, sparked the Giants in New York and San Francisco, afield and at bat, for next 21 years. Ended playing days as New York Met in 1973.

George Mikan (*1924–*). First major gate attraction in postwar basketball. A 6-foot 10-inch All-American from DePaul University whose prowess brought prosperity to National Basketball Association. Led Minneapolis Lakers to five titles in 6 seasons and in 10 years scored 11,764 points with hook shots and muscular rebounds that changed the whole character of the game.

Helen Wills Moody (*1906–*). Queen of tennis in 1920's and 1930's. On-court imperturbability earned her nickname Little Miss Poker Face. Won at Forest Hills at 17, then took six more U.S. titles, plus eight at Wimbledon and four in France. Played memorable matches against Suzanne Lenglen, of France, and Helen Jacobs.

Bronko Nagurski (*1908–*). All-American fullback and tackle at Minnesota in 1929, became bruising star for Chicago Bears in Dark Ages of pro football in 1930's. After 6 years in retirement, returned to lead team to title. Highest salary was $5,000 under George Halas, pioneer of National Football League. Later Bronko won world wrestling title three times, refereed grunt-and-groaners 10 years.

Joe Namath (*1943–*). Broadway Joe, gimpy-kneed quarterback whose passing feats helped put American Football League on the map. Signed $427,000 contract with New York Jets, won first major victory for new league by leading Jets to victory over Baltimore Colts of National League in 1969 Super Bowl.

Jack Nicklaus (*1940–*). Premier pro golfer of the 1960's and 1970's. First played at age 10 in native Columbus, Ohio; won Ohio Open at 16, National Amateur at 19, turned pro at 21, won his first U.S. Open at 22, Masters and PGA at 23. Has since captured practically every major pro tournament, including his fifth Masters, in 1975, and been repeatedly on U.S. Ryder Cup team.

Bobby Orr (*1948–*). Boston Bruins of National Hockey League scouted him at 14, put him in its lineup at 18. Most versatile threat of the modern game: a defenseman who leads in scoring. Voted most valuable player 3 years running, best defenseman 5 years in a row. In 1969–70 led Boston to first Stanley Cup in 29 years; repeated in 1971–72.

Arnold Palmer (*1929–*). Instant hero of pro golf's surge in 1960's to mass-spectator status. Won 8 tournaments in 1960, finished among top five in 19 of 21 tournaments. Took U.S. Open that year with a fourth-round 65 that wiped out a seven-stroke deficit. First million-dollar winner of pro golf.

Sugar Ray Robinson (*1921–*). Born Walker Smith in Detroit, he fought for 24 years, starting in 1940, losing only 19 of his 202 professional fights. Won welterweight crown in 1946, middleweight title in 1951 (twice). Won it thrice more in next 7 years. A magnificent boxer whom many experts have acclaimed as, "pound for pound," the best fighter ever.

Babe Ruth (*1895–1948*). His bat revived baseball after 1919 Black Sox scandal. Lifetime total of 714 home runs stood 39 years as record. Broke into baseball with Baltimore Orioles of International League; entered the major leagues with Boston Red Sox as pitcher where he won 24 games; converted to outfielder. In 1920 moved to New York Yankees. With Ruth, the Yankees won seven pennants, four world championships in 15 years.

Willie Shoemaker (*1931–*). Four-foot-11-inch champion jockey. Rode 6,738 winners between 1949 and 1974 for more than $53 million in purses; brought in three Kentucky Derby champions: 1955, 1959, 1965. Eight times in his career rode six winners in a single day. Was elected to Jockey's Hall of Fame, 1959.

William T. Tilden II (*1893–1953*). Big Bill. Tennis titan in 1920's decade of sports giants. Won No. 1 ranking 10 straight years. First American to win men's singles at Wimbledon. Member of Davis Cup team 11 times and won 70 U.S. and international titles. Turned pro in 1931.

John Unitas (*1933–*). Baltimore Colts quarterback, 1956–72. Widely deemed football's foremost field general, deadliest passer. Set new records for completions (2,830), touchdown passes (290), and receiver's yardage (40,239). Hero of famous 1958 title game when Colts beat New York Giants in "sudden death" overtime, 23–17.

Mildred "Babe" Didrikson Zaharias (*1914–56*). Texas-born all-around phenomenon of 1930's and 1940's. Played basketball, excelled in track, later threw baseball 296 feet, and pitched exhibitions against Joe DiMaggio and Jimmy Foxx. Olympic star of 1932 and three-time Women's Open golfing champion. Married ex-wrestler George Zaharias. Cancer caused her untimely death.

The Automobile

The American fascination with automobile racing showed clearly when more than 30,000 persons gathered on Long Island to watch the first Vanderbilt Cup race in 1904. The event consisted of 10 laps around a 28.4-mile course. The race began with 18 cars, most of them foreign made and many of them stock cars—some stripped down for racing. Speeds remarkable for that time were registered, some cars traveling close to 100 miles an hour on the straightaways. The Vanderbilt Cup races were discontinued in 1910 as too many cars went out of control, killing or injuring drivers and spectators. In 1911 the annual event now known as the Indianapolis 500-mile Speedway Race, always held on Memorial Day, was held for the first time.

Automobile racing remained a popular sport through the first half of the 20th century and experienced an upswing in popularity during the late 1940's. The National Association for Stock Car Auto Racing, formed in 1947, has sanctioned many meets, chief among them the annual event at Daytona Beach, Florida.

The excitement *of America's famed Indianapolis Speedway Race is caught in this early poster. The first 500-mile classic was won by Ray Harroun, averaging 74.59 miles an hour.*

Today practically every type of car—from the powerful single-seater road racers to the sports cars and the midgets—has its own schedule of events and its own aficionados.

Motorcycling has also boomed as a competitive sport in recent times, with some 5,000 events held yearly. These include endurance runs, dirt-track and cross-country races, and hill climbing. The classic is the annual 200-mile national championship—the Indianapolis of motorcycling. It, too, is run on the hard-packed sands of Florida's Daytona Beach.

The American Scene

Sports and recreation in America are constantly changing. Activities and events popular in one period fade and give way to others. Back in the mid-1800's walking races and trap and rifle shooting were major sports. Archery, too, had its vogue. National and international contests in these sports were held before appreciative crowds. Rowing was another top sport, with oarsmen cheered by throngs along the waterways. Bicycle racing was enormously popular in the first third of the 20th century and drew large crowds as a spectator sport. Interest dropped sharply in the midcentury, but bicycling for exercise and transportation has recently enjoyed a comeback with the growing interest in health and ecology.

The League of American Wheelmen was formed in the 1880's and by 1898 had a membership exceeding 102,000. Charles Murphy, pedaling behind a railroad train in 1899, cycled a mile in 57.8 seconds, earning him the nickname of Mile-a-Minute Murphy. His amazing record was not beaten even by an automobile until 1909. Races and tournaments were held on carefully built tracks in velodromes in Newark, New Jersey; Hartford, Connecticut; and Springfield, Massachusetts. Bicycle racing reached its peak with the wild jamming sprints of the 6-day bicycle races in New York's Madison Square Garden in the 1920's and early 1930's.

On and in the water, canoeing, sailboating, motorboat racing, and yachting have attracted many Americans, as have swimming, diving, and water-skiing. In the winter, skiing, figure skating, speed skating, iceboating, and curling are enjoyed by many participants. Professional ice hockey, dominated by the Canadians, has become so popular that its attendance figures are close to those of the big three—baseball, football, and basketball. Lacrosse and soccer are played extensively in colleges, and professional soccer is growing in popularity.

The jet airplane has had a significant effect on major

Hero of the Stock Cars

Junior Johnson is given much of the credit for bringing stock-car racing to its present prominence. By the time he retired from National Association for Stock Car Auto Racing (NASCAR) competition in 1966 Johnson had chalked up 50 Grand National wins, among them victories at Daytona, Darlington, Atlanta, and Charlotte. Rated fifth on the roster of alltime GN champions, he was inducted into the Stock Car Hall of Fame at Darlington, South Carolina, in 1972.

Raised in the western North Carolina mountains, Johnson freely admitted that he had learned his hell-for-leather driving while delivering his father's moonshine whisky to Winston-Salem, Greensboro, and other cities. It took speed and daring to outwit and outrun the lawmen, and Johnson had both. "That was one race you couldn't afford to lose," he was quoted as saying.

His skill behind the wheel ultimately led him to enter stock-car races throughout the South, beginning in 1949 at the age of 17. His aggressive, charging style of hotfoot driving soon brought success and finally more than $500,000 in prize money.

Today Johnson operates a chicken farm and cattle ranch near Ronda, North Carolina, but as a builder and owner of successful race cars he is still part of the sport he did so much to develop.

The Olympic Games
For Worldwide Competition

When the ancient Olympic games were revived at Athens in 1896, through the efforts of the French sportsman Baron Pierre de Coubertin, the United States was represented along with a dozen other nations. Of the 285 athletes assembled, only 11 of them were from this country.

Members of the American team had come to Greece mainly on their own. There were no coaches, no U.S. Olympic Committee, no official sponsor, no training program. In spite of the lack of organization, the Americans went on to win 9 of the 12 track-and-field events. The world's first Olympic champion after a gap of some 1,500 years was a Harvard undergraduate, James B. Connolly, of Boston, Massachusetts, winner of the hop, step, and jump.

Held every 4 years after that 1896 Olympics (except during World Wars I and II), the games have taken place regularly, with the United States playing a leading role each time. The 4-year period between two sets of games is called an Olympiad. The first Olympic games on U.S. soil were staged at St. Louis, Missouri, in 1904. The United States again played host in 1932 at Los Angeles, California.

Winter Olympic games were inaugurated in 1924, with 293 athletes from 16 nations participating. The United States had a team on hand but was able to win only 1 of the 16 events: Charles Jewtraw captured the 500-meter ice-skating race. Competitors in the Winter Olympics have steadily increased in number; as many as 40 countries and more than 1,300 athletes have participated. The Winter Games were held in the United States at Lake Placid, New York, in 1932; at Squaw Valley, California, in 1960. The Americans were scheduled to play host to the winter athletes again in 1980, once more at Lake Placid.

When the first Olympic games were held by the Greeks in 776 B.C., women were not permitted even to witness the events, let alone take part. Women athletes had their first go in the second modern games, held in Paris in 1900, when six female contestants competed in lawn tennis. Since then the number of women entries, at the Summer and Winter Games, has risen to more than 1,000.

The great Olympic champion *Jesse Owens is shown here winning the broad jump at the 1936 games in Berlin. In the same games he also won gold medals (see insert) in the 100- and 200-meter sprints plus a fourth as a member of the victorious U.S. 400-meter relay team.*

Since the first modern Olympic games the United States has produced many great champions. Among them are Jesse Owens, pictured above, and the following:

In track and field: **Jim Thorpe,** all-round Indian athlete, winner of the decathlon (10 events) and the pentathlon (5 events), 1912, Stockholm. **Charley Paddock,** sprinter, 1920, Antwerp. **Babe Didrikson,** woman superstar, winner in hurdles and javelin throw, 1932, Los Angeles. **Bob Mathias,** winner of decathlon, 1948, London; 1952, Helsinki. **Al Oerter,** discus champion, 1956, Melbourne; 1960, Rome; 1964, Tokyo; 1968, Mexico City. **Wilma Rudolph,** sprinter, 1960, Rome.

In swimming and diving events: **Duke Kahanamoku,** Hawaiian swimming champion, 1912, Stockholm. **Johnny Weissmuller,** swimming, 1924, Paris; 1928, Amsterdam. **Pete Desjardins,** diving, 1924, Paris; 1928, Amsterdam. **Buster Crabbe,** swimming, 1932, Los Angeles. **Eleanor Holm,** swimming, 1932, Los Angeles. **Don Schollander,** swimming, 1964, Tokyo. **Debbie Meyers,**swimming, 1968, Mexico City. **Mark Spitz,** swimming (seven gold medals), 1972, Munich.

In winter sports: **Irving Jaffee,** speed skating, 1932, Lake Placid. **Dick Button,** figure skating, 1948, St. Moritz; 1952, Oslo. **Carol Heiss,** figure skating, 1960, Squaw Valley. **Peggy Fleming,** figure skating, 1968, Grenoble. **Andrea Mead Lawrence,** skiing, 1952, Oslo.

In boxing: **Floyd Patterson,** middleweight, 1952, Helsinki. **Cassius Clay** (Muhammad Ali), light heavyweight, 1960, Rome. **George Foreman,** heavyweight, 1968, Mexico City.

At the original Olympic games, an estimated 40,000 spectators packed the natural amphitheater. Today, thanks to television satellites, many millions all over the world are able to watch.

sports, making coast-to-coast competition in all sports commonplace. Air travel enabled baseball's major leagues to incorporate clubs representing every section of the country.

But television, more than any other factor, has brought the most profound change, especially to professional sports. Its ubiquitous influence ushered in the era of the superstar with the supersalary. Thanks largely to television, a new golden age of sports has emerged.

Better still, the flowering of high-powered spectator sports has inspired a golden age of recreation. Never before have the American people had so much leisure to enjoy indoor and outdoor activities devoted to health, exercise, and pleasurable relaxation. A listing of 20 popular forms of recreation with the estimated number of yearly participants is given below. (Activities such as hiking, swimming, and camping have been omitted because of their generalized character.)

1.	Bicycling	100,000,000
2.	Bowling	50,000,000
3.	Volleyball	50,000,000
4.	Tennis	33,900,000
5.	Table Tennis	33,000,000
6.	Billiards	32,000,000
7.	Boating	27,400,000
8.	Softball	26,300,000
9.	Fishing (*licensed*)	26,200,000
10.	Roller skating	19,000,000
11.	Hunting (*licensed*)	15,500,000
12.	Motorcycling	13,500,000
13.	Water skiing	12,000,000
14.	Golf	11,000,000
15.	Horseback riding	8,700,000
16.	Shuffleboard	8,500,000
17.	Bird watching	6,200,000
18.	Skiing	6,000,000
19.	Canoeing	4,500,000
20.	Handball	1,500,000

The Phenomenal Exhibitions

The American sporting scene has long been highlighted by special athletic events that are as much show business as sport. Since the early 1800's, people have thronged to see such exhibitions as challenge horse races, wrestling, championship boxing bouts, and, more recently, million-dollar tennis and golf matches.

The newspapers were the first to create an interest in the theatrics of sport. Radio further stimulated this trend. But it was television that brought about the final development of the great sports spectacular. The fans who could not get tickets or travel great distances to an event could watch the action in the comfort of their homes. And there, unlike the on-the-scene spectator, they had the services of skilled commentators who could explain the intricacies of the sport and repeat the action with instant replays. As a result large numbers of viewers who previously had had minimal interest in athletics became sports enthusiasts.

Furthermore, it was television that turned the traditional recreations of golf and tennis into highly popular spectator sports. (The Connors-Newcombe championship tennis match of April 26, 1975, drew an estimated 125 million TV viewers.) The appeal of such sports exhibitions lies in their ability to involve the emotions of the fans as they root for their favorites and are caught up in the sheer visual drama of the event.

One sport that capitalized on theatrics was professional wrestling. Originally an ancient and honored form of athletics, pro wrestling became sheer show business in the 1940's and 1950's, an era in which wrestling bouts enjoyed considerable popularity and television exposure. The wrestlers appeared under such fanciful names as Gorgeous George (shown here, peroxide locks flowing), the Masked Marvel, the Crusher, the Swedish Angel, and Chief Big Heart. Each affected appropriate costumes and mannerisms. The bouts, usually well rehearsed, saw one wrestler take the part of the good guy with his opponent cast in the role of the bad one. The villain resorted to head-butts, eye gouges and other illegal tactics, while the hero endeavored to win using legitimate holds. The action was often taken so seriously by the audiences that police riot squads had to be summoned to protect the participants.

In contrast to the slambang turmoil of wrestling and hockey, a billiard challenge match is played in almost churchlike quiet. Only the faint click of one ball against another is heard as the wizards of the cue make their precise moves. Billiards, a highly scientific game, is played by millions of Americans today. Some historians claim that the game evolved in England during the 15th century when the outdoor sport of lawn bowling was brought indoors and, eventually, played on a tabletop. Three types of billiards have developed in America: Pocket billiards, or pool; balkline; and 3-cushion. At left is Willie Mosconi, 15 times world champion of pocket billiards from 1941 to 1957. Most impressive of his many records is his high run of 526 balls. Mosconi acted as technical adviser on the 1961 motion picture *The Hustler.*

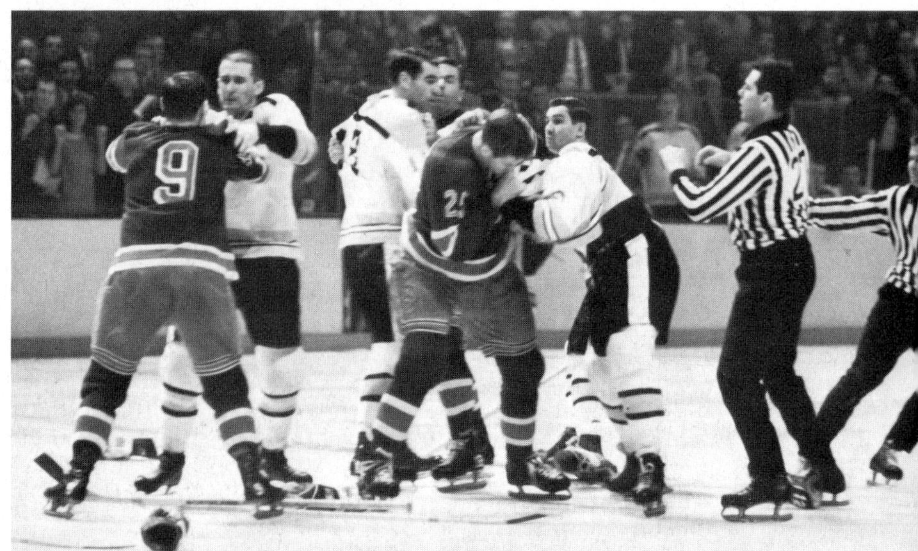

Hockey has been called, with reason, the most savage sport next to bullfighting. The very speed of play, with its 100-mile-per-hour shots and body-jarring checks, creates not only excitement among the spectators but also outbursts of fighting among the players. The melee shown here occurred in Madison Square Garden during a 1968 game between the New York Rangers and the Boston Bruins of the National Hockey League.

Crowds are drawn to basketball as performed by the famed Harlem Globetrotters because of the circuslike clowning of the players together with their razzle-dazzle ball handling and amazing trick shots. The organization, originally formed in the Middle West in 1927 by Abe Saperstein, was given the name Harlem Globetrotters not because the players came from the New York community but to indicate that it was an all-black team. The Globetrotters have barnstormed through America year after year, taking on all comers, both collegiate and professional. Their claim of being the "winningest team in sport history" is based on solid facts. Various units of the Trotters have made extended world tours, playing in as many as 94 countries. The picture at right shows the player-members of the 1974–75 Globetrotter teams.

To watch championship table tennis is to see wizardry in ball control. The game, ideally suited for small, lithe players, is popular in China and Japan. In 1971 so-called Ping-Pong diplomacy was inaugurated when a U.S. table tennis team played in China at the invitation of the People's Republic. Here Roberts Furando of the United States (left) plays China's Liang Ke-liang.

The roller derby is unique in that women as well as men take part in this high-speed, bruising, body-contact sport. Five men or five women compete against each other. The contestants race on roller skates around a banked wooden track, endeavoring to score points by gaining laps on opposing players. Spectator excitement is heightened by the fast action, the savagery of the body blocks, and the hair-raising spills. An outgrowth of 6-day bicycle races, the roller derby originated in Chicago in 1935 and gained in popularity, especially during the early 1950's. This spectacle was given widespread publicity when Raquel Welch played a roller derby heroine in the motion picture *Kansas City Bomber.*

Seven Wonders of the Modern World

The largest arch on Earth. *With both a span and a height of 630 feet, Eero Saarinen's majestic Gateway Arch of the Jefferson National Expansion Memorial in St. Louis, Missouri, commemorates the hardy westward-moving pioneers of the early 1800's. Made of stainless steel, it describes a curve remarkable for its delicacy and strength. A unique elevator system takes visitors to the top for a commanding view of the city and far beyond.*

Our tallest building. *Ever since 1885, with the completion in Chicago of the 10-story Home Life Insurance Building, designed by William Le Baron Jenney, American architecture has reached for the sky. The Chicago Sears Tower, opened in 1974, is 1,454 feet high—the tallest U.S. office building. Sheathed in black aluminum and bronze-tinted glass, its soaring stepped columns are complemented by the horizontal bands of windows.*

The longest span. *The world's longest single-span suspension bridge, the Verrazano-Narrows Bridge, stretches 4,260 feet across the entrance of New York Harbor from Staten Island to Brooklyn, exceeding the span of San Francisco's Golden Gate Bridge by 60 feet. End ramps lengthen the bridge another 2,430 feet. Its 700-foot towers and slender cables support a two-level roadway. Designed by Othmar H. Ammann and opened in 1964, it is considered one of the most beautiful bridges in the world. At night the lighted bridge glitters like a huge jeweled necklace.*

Made in America on a Scale That Dwarfs the Dreams of the Ancients

Most gigantic sculpture. *Chief Crazy Horse gallops into battle. When completed, this lifework of Korczak Ziolkowski near Custer, South Dakota, will be 561 feet high and 641 feet long; 5½ million tons of granite will have been moved in the process.*

Highest monumental column. *Built in 1936–39 near Houston, Texas, to commemorate the Battle of San Jacinto, this limestone-encased structure is 570 feet high, tapering gently from 47 feet square at its base to 30 feet square at its observation tower.*

Most massive concrete structure. *Grand Coulee Dam, on the Columbia River in Washington, contains 10½ million cubic yards of concrete. With its 151-mile-long reservoir, it provides hydroelectric power, flood control, and water for irrigation.*

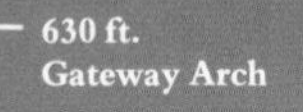

Our tallest tower. *The tallest manmade structure in the United States, this television transmitting tower, situated between Fargo and Blanchard, North Dakota, stands an amazing 2,063 feet high. The heights of three other structures are indicated for comparison.*

Inspiration for the Future

The preceding pages have been concerned with the past: with the people and events that have conspired to make this country what it is today. But what of the future? What can we expect? Where can we hope to find suggestions as to where we might go from here? It is tempting to think that a panel of experts in various fields could tell us what's in store. Tempting, that is, until one considers the predictions of experts in the past. It seems that the facts of the future unfold in defiance of the experts' fancy.

More valuable than hazarding guesses as to what the future may hold is to take still another look into the past. Only here will we find the concepts and practices that can serve us well on the path ahead. There is no "future" as such. There is only a succession of days. What we do today must, inevitably, be based on the experience of yesterday. Perhaps a consideration of these viewpoints and insights from various thoughtful leaders and commentators will help us, day by day, to make the most of the days to come.

Sustaining Freedom

BENJAMIN FRANKLIN
Historical Review of Pennsylvania, *1759*

They that can give up essential liberty to obtain a little temporary safety deserve neither liberty nor safety.

THOMAS JEFFERSON
Letter to James Monroe, June 17, 1785

. . . its soul, its climate, its equality, liberty, laws, people, and manners. My God! how little do my countrymen know what precious blessings they are in possession of, and which no other people on earth enjoy!

THOMAS JEFFERSON
First Inaugural Address, March 4, 1801

The will of the people is the only legitimate foundation of any government, and to protect its free expression should be our first object.

ALEXIS DE TOCQUEVILLE
Democracy in America, *1835*

American democracy frequently errs in the choice of the individuals to whom it entrusts the power of the administration; but the state prospers under their rule. If, in a democratic state, the governors have less honesty and less capacity than elsewhere, the governed are more enlightened and more attentive to their own interests. More vigilant in their affairs and more jealous of their rights, the people prevent their representatives from abandoning the general line of conduct which their interest prescribes. Furthermore, if the democratic magistrate is more apt to misuse his power, he possesses it for a shorter time.

MICHEL CHEVALIER
Society, Manners, and Politics in the United States, *1835*

The people of this country is eminently a working people; everyone is at liberty to work, to choose his profession, and to change it twenty times; everyone has the right to go and come on his business, at pleasure, and to transport his person and his industry from the centre to the circumference, and from the circumference to the centre. If the country does not enjoy the political advantages of administrative unity, neither is it hampered in the most petty details of industry by excessive centralisation.

SAMUEL GOMPERS
Address, 1898

Trades unions . . . were born of the necessity of workers to protect and defend themselves from encroachment, injustice and wrong. . . . To protect the workers in their inalienable rights to a higher and better life; to protect them, not only as equals before the law, but also in their rights to the product of their labor; to protect their lives, their limbs, their health, their homes, their firesides, their liberties as men, as workers, as citizens; to overcome and conquer prejudice and antagonism; to secure them the right to life, and the opportunity to maintain that life; the right to be full sharers in the abundance which is the result of their brain and brawn, and the civilization of which they are the founders and the mainstay; to this the workers are entitled.

FREDERICK JACKSON TURNER
The Frontier in American History, *1920*

Western democracy through the whole of its earlier period tended to the production of a society of which the most distinctive fact was the freedom of the individual to rise under conditions of social mobility, and whose ambition was the liberty and well-being of the masses. This conception has vitalized all American democracy, and has brought it into sharp contrasts with the democracies of history, and with those modern efforts of Europe to create an artificial democratic order by legislation. The problem of the United States is not to create democracy, but to conserve democratic institutions and ideals.

The arts cannot thrive except where men are free to be themselves and to be in charge of the discipline of their own energies and ardors. The conditions for democracy and for art are one and the same. What we call liberty in politics results in freedom of the arts. There can be no vitality in the works gathered in a museum unless there exists the right of spontaneous life in the society in which the arts are nourished. . . . Nourish the conditions of a free life and you nourish the arts, too.

FRANKLIN D. ROOSEVELT
Speech, New York City, May 10, 1939

The winning of freedom is not to be compared to the winning of a game—with the victory recorded forever in history. Freedom has its life in the hearts, the actions, the spirit of men and so it must be daily earned and refreshed—else like a flower cut from its life-giving roots, it will wither and die.

DWIGHT D. EISENHOWER
Speech, London, 1944

Our American heritage is threatened as much by our own indifference as it is by the most unscrupulous office or by the most powerful foreign threat. The future of this republic is in the hands of the American voter.

DWIGHT D. EISENHOWER
Speech, New York City, October 1949

Once a government is committed to the principle of silencing the voice of opposition, it has only one way to go, and that is down the path of increasingly repressive measures, until it becomes a source of terror to all its citizens and creates a country where everyone lives in fear.

HARRY S. TRUMAN
Message to Congress, August 8, 1950

We dare not forget today that we are the heirs of that first revolution. Let the word go forth from this time and place, to friend and foe alike, that the torch has been passed to a new generation of Americans—born in this century, tempered by war, disciplined by a hard and bitter peace, proud of our ancient heritage—and unwilling to witness or permit the slow undoing of those human rights to which this nation has always been committed, and to which we are committed today, at home and around the world. . . . The energy, the faith, the devotion which we bring to this endeavor will light our country and all who serve it—and the glow from that fire can truly light the world. . . . And so, my fellow Americans: Ask not what your country can do for you—ask what you can do for your country.

JOHN F. KENNEDY
Inaugural Address, January 20, 1961

With this faith we will be able to work together, to pray together, to struggle together, to go to jail together, to stand up for freedom together, knowing that we will be free one day. This will be the day when all of God's children will be able to sing with new meaning—"my country 'tis of thee; sweet land of liberty; of thee I sing; land where my fathers died, land of the pilgrim's pride; from every mountain side, let freedom ring"—and if America is to be a great nation, this must become true.

MARTIN LUTHER KING, JR.
Speech, Lincoln Memorial, August 28, 1963

Women are no longer imprisoned by manmade myths. We are coming down from our pedestal and up from the laundry room. We want an equal share in government and we mean to get it . . . although we seek not only equality for ourselves but also diversity. What is good for women will turn out to be good for our country.

BELLA S. ABZUG
Los Angeles Times, *November 20, 1972*

The ultimate by-product of women's liberation is the liberation of men from the incubus of having to seal themselves up in an office for 40 years to support a totally dependent wife.

MARYA MANNES
"W," *September 22, 1972*

Conserving Our Resources

ALEXIS DE TOCQUEVILLE
Democracy in America, *1835*

Everything about the Americans, from their social condition to their laws, is extraordinary; but the most extraordinary thing of all is the land that supports them. . . . There, there are still, as on the first days of creation, rivers whose founts never run dry, green and watery solitudes, and limitless fields never yet turned by the plowshare. . . . Now, at the time of writing, thirteen million civilized Europeans are quietly spreading over these fertile wildernesses whose exact resources and extent they themselves do not yet know. Three or four thousand soldiers drive the wandering native tribes before them; behind the armed men woodcutters advance, penetrating the forests, scaring off the wild beasts, exploring the course of rivers, and preparing the triumphal progress of civilization across the wilderness.

CAPT. FREDERICK MARRYAT
A Diary in America, *1839*

America is a wonderful country, endowed by the Omnipotent with natural advantages which no other can boast of; and the mind can hardly calculate upon the degree of perfection and power to which, whether the States are eventually separated or not, it may in the course of two centuries arrive. At present all is energy and enterprise; everything is in a state of transition, but of rapid improvement—so rapid, indeed, that those who would describe America now would have to correct all in the short space of ten years; for ten years in America is almost equal to a century in the old continent. Now, you may pass through a wild forest, where the elk browses and the panther howls. In ten years, that very forest, with its denizens, will, most likely, have disappeared, and in their place you will find towns with thousands of inhabitants; with arts, manufactures, and machinery, all in full activity. . . . Time to an American is everything and space he attempts to reduce to a mere nothing. By the steam-boats, rail-roads, and the wonderful facilities of water-carriage, a journey of five hundred miles is as little considered in America, as would be here a journey from London to Brighton. *"Go ahead"* is the real motto of the country; and every man does push on, to gain in advance of his neighbour. The American lives twice as long as others; for he does twice the work during the time that he lives. He begins life sooner: at fifteen he is considered a man, plunges into the stream of enterprize, floats and struggles with his fellows. In every trifle an American shews the value he puts upon time.

DANIEL WEBSTER
Remarks, Boston, January 13, 1840

Let us never forget that the cultivation of the earth is the most important labor of man. . . . When tillage begins, other arts follow. The farmers, therefore, are the founders of human civilization.

HENRY DAVID THOREAU
Walden, *1854*

I went to the woods because I wished to live deliberately, to front only the essential facts of life, and see if I could not learn what it had to teach, and not, when I came to die, discover that I had not lived.

JOHN MUIR
Our National Parks, *1901*

Any fool can destroy trees. They cannot run away; and if they could, they would still be destroyed—chased and hunted down as long as fun or a dollar could be got out of their bark hides, branching horns, or magnificent bole backbones. Few that fell trees plant them; nor would planting avail much toward getting anything like the noble primeval forests. During a man's life only saplings can be grown, in the place of the old trees—tens of centuries old—that have been destroyed. It took more than three thousand years to make some of the trees in these Western woods—trees that still stand in perfect strength and beauty, waving and singing in the mighty forests of the Sierra. Through all the wonderful, eventful centuries since Christ's time—and long before that—God has cared for these trees, saved them from drought, disease, avalanches, and a thousand straining, leveling tempests and floods; but He cannot save them from fools—only Uncle Sam can do that.

In this stage of the world's history, to be fearless, to be just, and to be efficient are the three great requirements of national life. National efficiency is the result of natural resources well handled, of freedom of opportunity for every man, and of the inherent capacity, trained ability, knowledge, and will—collectively and individually—to use that opportunity.

THEODORE ROOSEVELT
Message to Congress, January 22, 1909

Our objective must be so to manage the physical use of the land that we will not only maintain soil fertility but will hand on to the next generation a country with better productive power and a greater permanency of land use than the one we inherited from the previous generation. The opportunity is as vast as is the danger.

FRANKLIN D. ROOSEVELT
Message to Congress, January 30, 1936

Is a society a success if it creates conditions that impair its finest minds and make a wasteland of its finest landscapes? What does material abundance avail if we create an environment in which man's highest and most specifically human attributes cannot be fulfilled? . . . Each generation has its own rendezvous with the land . . . . we are all brief tenants on this planet. By choice, or by default, we will carve out a land legacy for our heirs. We can misuse the land and diminish the usefulness of resources, or we can create a world in which physical affluence and affluence of the spirit go hand in hand. . . . This, in brief, is the quiet conservation crisis. . . .

STEWART UDALL
The Quiet Crisis, *1963*

I look forward to a great future for America, a future in which our country will match its military strength with our moral restraint, its wealth with our wisdom, its power with our purpose. I look forward to an America which will not be afraid of grace and beauty, which will protect the beauty of our natural environment, which will preserve the great old American houses and squares and parks of our national past, and which will build handsome and balanced cities for our future. . . . And I look forward to an America which commands respect throughout the world not only for its strength but for its civilization as well.

JOHN F. KENNEDY
Speech, Amherst, Mass., October 26, 1963

The purpose of preservation is not to freeze history but to encourage a new humanism. What we need is an historical way of thinking. Our source material is all around us. It is our landmarks. They tell stories about society, politics, culture, economics and life. But up to now they were the most unexplored archives. If they are lost, they can tell us nothing. If there is no past, there is no future.

BEVERLY MOSS SPATT
Speech, New York City, May 9, 1974

Working Together

There is no wonder that this country has so many charms, and presents to Europeans so many temptations to remain in it. A traveler in Europe becomes a stranger as soon as he quits his own kingdom; but it is otherwise here. We know, properly speaking, no strangers. This is every person's country; the variety of our soils, situations, climates, governments, and produce, has something which must please everybody. No sooner does a European arrive, no matter of what condition, than his eyes are opened upon the fair prospect. When in England, he was a mere Englishman; here he stands on a larger portion of the globe. He does not find, as in Europe, a crowded society, where every place is overstocked; he does not feel that perpetual collision of parties, that difficulty of beginning, that contention which oversets so many. There is room for everybody in America. Has he any particular talent or industry, he exerts it in order to procure a livelihood, and it succeeds.

JEAN DE CRÈVECOEUR
Letters From an American Farmer, *1782*

HENRY CLAY
Speech, Senate, February 2, 1832

By competition the total amount of supply is increased, and by increase of the supply a competition in the sale ensues, and this enables the consumer to buy at lower rates. Of all human powers operating on the affairs of mankind, none is greater than that of competition.

MICHEL CHEVALIER
Society, Manners, and Politics in the United States, *1835*

If movement and the quick succession of sensations and ideas constitute life, here one lives a hundred fold more than elsewhere; all is here circulation, motion, and boiling agitation. Experiment follows experiment; enterprise succeeds to enterprise. . . . The existence of social order in the bosom of this whirlpool seems a miracle, an inexplicable anomaly. One is tempted to think that such a society, formed of heterogeneous elements, brought together by chance, and following each its own orbit according to the impulse of its own caprice or interest, one would think that after rising for one moment to the heavens, like a waterspout, such a society would inevitably fall flat in ruins the next; such is not, however, its destiny.

"Work," says American society to the poor; "work, and at eighteen you shall get, you a simple worker, more than a captain in Europe. You shall live in plenty, be well-clothed, well-housed, and able to save. Be attentive to your work, be sober and religious, and you will find a devoted and submissive wife; you will have a more comfortable home than many of the higher classes in Europe. From a journeyman, you shall become a master; you shall have apprentices and dependents under you in turn; you will have credit without stint, become a manufacturer or agriculturist on a great scale; you will speculate and become rich, found a town and give it your own name, you will be a member of the legislature of your State or alderman of your city, and finally member of Congress; your son shall have as good a chance to be made President as the son of the President himself. . . ."

ALEXIS DE TOCQUEVILLE
Democracy in America, *1835*

The free institutions of the United States and the political rights enjoyed there provide a thousand continual reminders to every citizen that he lives in society. At every moment they bring his mind back to this idea, that it is the duty as well as the interest of men to be useful to their fellows. Having no particular reason to hate others, since he is neither their slave nor their master, the American's heart easily inclines toward benevolence. At first it is of necessity that men attend to the public interest, afterward by choice. What had been calculation becomes instinct. By dint of working for the good of his fellow citizens, he in the end acquires a habit and taste for serving them.

In the United States the greatest industrial undertakings are executed without trouble because the whole population is engaged in industry and because the poorest man as well as the most opulent gladly joins forces therein. One is therefore in daily astonishment at the immense works carried through without difficulty by a nation which, one may say, has no rich men. The Americans arrived but yesterday in the land where they live, and they have already turned the whole order of nature upside down to their profit. They have joined the Hudson to the Mississippi and linked the Atlantic Ocean with the Gulf of Mexico across a continent of more than five hundred leagues.

JOHN RUSKIN
Pre-Raphaelitism, *1851*

In order that people may be happy in their work, these three things are needed: They must be fit for it; they must not do too much of it; and they must have a sense of success in it.

ABRAHAM LINCOLN
Remarks, Washington, D.C., March 2, 1864

Property is the fruit of labor; property is desirable; is a positive good in the world. That some should be rich shows that others may become rich, and hence is just encouragement to industry and enterprise. Let not him who is houseless pull down the house of another, but let him work diligently and build one for himself, thus by example assuring that his own shall be safe from violence when built.

Herein lies the tragedy of the age: not that men are poor—all men know something of poverty; not that men are wicked—who is good? Not that men are ignorant—what is truth? Nay, but that men know so little of men.

WILLIAM E. B. DUBOIS
The Souls of Black Folk, *1903*

Our employers can no more afford to be absolute masters of their employees than they can afford to submit to the mastery of their employees. Bluff and bluster have no place here. The spirit must be "Come, let us reason together."

LOUIS D. BRANDEIS
Business—A Profession, *1914*

The organized workers of America, free in their industrial life, conscious partners of production, secure in their homes and enjoying a decent standard of living, will prove the finest bulwark against the intrusion of alien doctrines of government.

JOHN L. LEWIS
Radio Address, September 3, 1937

I can conceive of nothing more alien to the American way of life than the denial of industrial freedom. And I say there is no more splendid vindication of democracy than the now-established practice of giving workers the chance to select their own representatives by secret ballot. Of course, we are always striving for greater industrial peace, but that can be done most successfully, experience shows, by recognition of the rights of workers as free men. If we wiped out labor unions and employers' associations, and settled all employer-employee disputes by government decree, there would perhaps be no more labor troubles, but there would also be no more democracy in America.

ROBERT F. WAGNER
I Am an American, *1941*

Our way of living together in America is a strong but delicate fabric. . . . It has been woven over many centuries by the patience and sacrifice of countless liberty-loving men and women. It serves as a cloak for the protection of poor and rich, of black and white, of Jew and Gentile, of foreign and native born. Let us not tear it asunder. For no man knows, once it is destroyed, where or when man will find its protective warmth again.

WENDELL L. WILLKIE
One World, *1943*

Of course I believe in free enterprise but in my system of free enterprise, the democratic principle is that there never was, never has been, never will be, room for the ruthless exploitation of the many for the benefit of the few.

HARRY S. TRUMAN
Congressional Record, *May 9, 1944*

Liberalism means an intelligent effort to keep the political and economic development of our nation abreast of the responsibilities that come from the atomic age. It means an extension of the use of our resources for the common good, the solving of the problem of maintaining democratic principles and free competitive enterprise in a day of big business, big unions and big government.

ESTES KEFAUVER
New Republic, *July 22, 1946*

The novelist in America today benefits, I think, from the versatility and power of his language, from the breadth of his landscapes, from the company of many brilliant, gifted and adventurous colleagues and from a group of readers who, beset with an unprecedented variety of diversions, continue to read with great taste and intelligence.

JOHN CHEEVER
Speech, quoted in The Writer, *September 1958*

. . . this free-enterprise system is made up of three parts—the man who has to invest the money, buy the machinery; the man who manages the men that work; and the men that work.

LYNDON B. JOHNSON
Press conference, Washington, D.C., April 19, 1964

"Here men from the planet Earth first set foot upon the Moon July 1969 A.D. We came in peace for all mankind." Inscription on the plaque taken to the Moon by the *Apollo 11* astronauts.

NEIL A. ARMSTRONG, MICHAEL COLLINS, *and* **EDWIN E. ALDRIN, JR.** *July 20, 1969*

Index

A

Main entries are in **bold** *type. Asterisks * indicate illustrations and subjects included in captions.*

Main entries are in **bold** *type. Asterisks * indicate illustrations and subjects included in captions.*

D

Main entries are in **bold** *type. Asterisks * indicate illustrations and subjects included in captions.*

E

F

G

Main entries are in **bold** *type. Asterisks * indicate illustrations and subjects included in captions.*

H

I

J

Main entries are in **bold** *type. Asterisks * indicate illustrations and subjects included in captions.*

M

Main entries are in **bold** *type. Asterisks * indicate illustrations and subjects included in captions.*

N

O

P

Main entries are in **bold** *type. Asterisks * indicate illustrations and subjects included in captions.*

Q

R

S

Main entries are in **bold** *type. Asterisks * indicate illustrations and subjects included in captions.*

Main entries are in **bold** *type. Asterisks * indicate illustrations and subjects included in captions.*

Credits

Art

James Alexander Cover embossing design.
Aspirin, Inc. **56–57, 398–399.**
Keith Batcheller **105** (*top*).
Howard Berelson **1, 27, 28–29, 106, 135, 165, 175, 178, 192, 198–199, 206–207, 232, 241, 264–265, 269, 276–277, 281, 310–311.**
Adolph Brotman **276, 303.**
Laura Karp **209.**
Gabor Kiss **5, 17, 21, 22, 34, 39, 48–49, 55, 64, 72, 75, 79, 82, 89, 93, 103, 109, 117, 147, 169, 194, 200–201, 285, 324, 444, 447, 453, 457, 458.**
Uldis Klavins **440–441.**
Rick McCallum **105** (*bottom*).
Nancy O'Hanian **54.**
Harriet Pertchik **283, 439, 471.**
Howard Rogers **10–11, 12–13, 14–15, 124–125, 172–173, 492–493.**
Edward Vebell **118, 146, 162, 459.**

Special appreciation for invaluable help in picture research is extended to the following organizations and their staffs: The Bettmann Archive; Brown Brothers; The New-York Historical Society; the New York Public Library's Picture Collection, Prints Division, and Rare Book Division; and Sandak, Inc.; and to the following individuals: Bob Jackson of Culver Pictures; William Glover of The Granger Collection; Gerald Kearns of the Library of Congress; Mark Sexton of the Peabody Museum of Salem; Gene Keesee of Photo Trends; and Jack Novak of Photri.

Photographs

2–3 Nebraska State Capitol. **8** John Veltri/Rapho Guillumette. **9** *top* The Bettmann Archive; *bottom left* The Granger Collection; *bottom right* New York Public Library. **18** *top* The Granger Collection; *lower* Culver Pictures. **19** *top* Photri; *bottom* Courtesy of the American Antiquarian Society. **20** Colonial Williamsburg Photograph. **22** *top and lower right* Courtesy of Kennedy Galleries, Inc. **23** Colonial Williamsburg Photograph. **24** Culver Pictures. **25** The John Carter Brown Library, Brown University. **26** Museum of Fine Arts, Boston. **27** *left* National Portrait Gallery, London; *right* National Army Museum. **28** *left* Fort Ticonderoga Museum Collection; *top* Delaware Art Museum; *bottom right* New York Public Library, Picture Collection, *Tinted by George Gray.* **29** Yale University Art Gallery. **30** Abbot Hall, Marblehead, Mass. **31** Yale University Art Gallery. **32** Library of Congress. **33** New York Public Library, Prints Division. **35** The Metropolitan Museum of Art, Gift of John Stewart Kennedy, 1897. **36** *top* Valley Forge Historical Society; *lower* Pennsylvania Historical and Museum Commission. **38** *top* U.S. Naval Academy Museum/Photri; *lower* The Pierpont Morgan Library. **40** Courtesy of the DAR Museum, Washington, D.C., Gift of Mrs. Charles Wesley Bassett. **41** The New-York Historical Society. **42** University Art Museum, Berkeley, Gift of Mrs. Mark Hopkins, San Francisco. **43** Archives of American Art, Smithsonian Institution. **44–45** Photo Musées Nationaux, Versailles Museum. **46** Courtesy of the Henry Francis duPont Winterthur Museum. **47** Culver Pictures. **48** *top* Fraunces Tavern Museum. **49** *top* Yale University Art Gallery. **52** Jack Zehrt. **53** The New-York Historical Society. **58** Virginia Museum of Fine Arts, Richmond. **60** National Gallery of Art, Washington, Gift of Edgar William and Bernice Chrysler Garbisch. **62** *top* The Granger Collection; *bottom* Private Collection. **65** Jack Zehrt. **66** U.S. Capitol Historical Society/Photri. **67** Jack Novak/Photri. **68** The Granger Collection. **69** Collection of Harry T. Peters, Jr. **70** *top* New York Public Library, Rare Book Division; *middle* Nebraska State Historical Society, Solomon D. Butcher Collection; *bottom* Steve Wilson/DPI. **71** The Granger Collection. **72** *top* Independence National Historical Park, National Park Service Photo; *middle* Missouri Historical Society. **72–73** *bottom* Montana Historical Society. **73** *top left* Thomas Gilcrease Institute of American History and Art, Tulsa, Okla.; *top right* Academy of Natural Sciences, Philadelphia. **76** © LDS. **77** *top* New York Public Library, Picture Collection; *center* Smithsonian Institution; *bottom* Peabody Museum of Salem/Mark Sexton. **78** *top and bottom* Thomas Gilcrease Institute of American History and Art, Tulsa, Okla.; *middle* Courtesy of the Bancroft Library. **79** *bottom and right* Photography Collection, University of Washington Library, Seattle. **80** U.S. Dept. of the Interior, National Park Service. **82** *top* Royal Ontario Museum, Toronto, Canada; *lower left* New York Public Library, Rare Book Division. **84** Oklahoma Historical Society. **85** *top* Smithsonian Institution; *bottom* National Archives. **86** *upper left* The Granger Collection; *upper right* New York Public Library, General Research and Humanities Division; *bottom* Library of Congress. **87** *top left* White House Historical Association; *top center* The New-York Historical Society; *top right* National Portrait Gallery, Smithsonian Institution; *middle* From the collection of the New Haven Colony Historical Society; *bottom* Chicago Historical Society. **88** *left* Anne S. K. Brown Military Collection, Brown University Library; *upper right* New York Public Library, Prints Division; *bottom* Courtesy of the National Park Service. **89** *middle* New Orleans Museum of Art, New Orleans, La.; *bottom* Philadelphia Chapter of the Masonic Lodge. **92** Culver Pictures. **93** *left* (*inset*) The Granger Collection; *right* David Muench. **95** Whaling Museum, New Bedford, Mass. **96** Thomas Gilcrease Institute of American History and Art, Tulsa, Okla. **97** The Granger Collection. **98** Joseph Delaney. **100** *center and* **101** *lower left* Brown Brothers. **100** *bottom and* **101** *top left* The Granger Collection. **101** *top right* Culver Pictures; *center* The Billy Graham Evangelistic Association. **103** Norman Rockwell, © Curtis Publishing Company. **107** The Granger Collection. **108** Courtesy of the Jamestown Foundation. **111** *left* National Archives; *right* The Granger Collection. **112** *top* Thomas Jefferson Memorial Foundation, Inc.; *bottom* Chicago Historical Society. **113** The Bettmann Archive. **114** *bottom left* United States Steel Corp.; *upper right* Nebraska State Historical Society, Solomon D. Butcher Collection; *bottom right* Deere & Company. **115** New York Public Library, Picture Collection. **116** *left and* **117** *top* Brown Brothers. **116** *bottom* U.S. Dept. of Agriculture. **117** *left and bottom* Montana Historical Society. **118** *top* Buffalo Bill Historical Center. **119** *top* Thomas Gilcrease Institute of American History and Art, Tulsa, Okla.; *middle* Western History Collections, University of Oklahoma Library; *bottom* Amon Carter Museum of Western Art, Fort Worth, Tex. **120** Tennessee Valley Authority. **121** *top* Library of Congress; *bottom* Dallas Museum of Fine Arts, Dallas Art Association Purchase. **123** *top* Grant Heilman; *bottom* UPI Photo. **127** Columbia University Library/Donna Harris. **128** *left* Butler Institute of American Art, Youngstown, Ohio; *upper right* St. Louis Art Museum; *bottom* Painted by Norman Rockwell for the Heritage Press edition of *The Adventures of Tom Sawyer;* the illustration is copyright © 1936, 1964 by The George Macy Companies, Inc., and reproduced by permission of *The Heritage Club,* Avon, Conn. **129** Columbia University Library/Donna Harris. **130** Philadelphia Museum of Art, Gift of Miss Willian J. Wyatt. **131** Courtesy of Mount Holyoke College/Michael Feinstein. **132** Culver Pictures. **134** *upper left* UPI Photo; *right and bottom* Whitby School, Greenwich, Conn. **136** Columbia University Library/Donna Harris. **137** Courtesy of Circle Gallery, Ltd. **138** SVE-Society for Visual Education. **139** Cummins Engine Co., Inc. **140** Philip B. Kunhardt, Jr. **141** Kansas State Capitol, Topeka/James L. Enyeart. **143** Library of Congress, *Tinted by George Gray.* **145** *top* West Point Museum Collections, U.S. Military Academy; *lower* Library of Congress. **148** Chicago Historical Society. **150** *top and middle* Library of Congress; *bottom* Peabody Museum of Salem/Mark Sexton. **153** National Park Service/The Lane Studio. **154** Library of Congress. **155** Clements Library of American History, University of Michigan. **156** *top and lower left* Library of Congress; *lower right* Anne S. K. Brown Military Collection, Brown University Library. **159** Museum of Fine Arts, Boston, M. and M. Karolik Collection. **160** Northern Natural Gas Company Collection, Joslyn Art Museum, Omaha, Nebr. **161** Washington University Gallery of Art, St. Louis. **163** Thomas Gilcrease Institute of American History and Art, Tulsa, Okla. **165** *top* Northern Natural Gas Company Collection, Joslyn Art Museum, Omaha, Nebr. **166–167** Thomas Gilcrease Institute of American History and Art, Tulsa, Okla. **170** *top* National Collection of Fine Arts, Smithsonian Institution/Photri; *bottom* Courtesy of Mercantile Library, New York. **175** *left and bottom* Peabody Museum of Salem/Mark Sexton. **177** *top* Maury: Pilot Charts, Vol. 2, 1846–49, Series A; *lower* The Granger Collection. **178** *top* From the Fine Arts Collection of the Seamen's Bank for Savings. **180, 181,** *and* **182** *bottom* Peabody Museum of Salem/Mark Sexton. **180** (*seal*) Courtesy of Essex Institute, Salem, Mass. **182** *top* Shelburne Museum, Shelburne, Vt. **183** Manuscript Collection, Mystic Seaport, Mystic, Conn. **184** *top* Peabody Museum of Salem/Mark Sexton; *bottom* New York Public Library, Picture Collection. **185** Private Collection. **186** United States Lines. **187** *and* **188** *lower left* General Dynamics. **188** *top left* Courtesy of the Henry Francis duPont Winterthur Museum; *top right* Peabody Museum of Salem/Mark Sexton; *bottom right* National Archives. **189** *top left* Parade Publications; *top right* The Granger Collection; *middle and bottom* Photri. **190** *bottom* The Granger Collection. **191** The Maryland Historical Society, Baltimore. **193** Bill Finney. **195** *top* The New-York Historical Society; *lower* Library of Congress. **196** *upper* Museum of the City of New York, the Harry T. Peters Collection; *bottom* The Metropolitan Museum of Art. **197** *left* From the Collections of the Louisiana State Museum; *right* From the Collection of Harnett T. Kane. **198** Museum of the City of New York, the Harry T. Peters Collection. **199** Brown Brothers. **200** *bottom* Index of American Design, National Gallery of Art, Washington. **201** *bottom* Bay Area Rapid Transit. **202** Automotive History Collection, Detroit Public Library. **203** *top and middle* Ralph Stein; *bottom* Magnum Photos. **204** *top* (*inset*) Mack Trucks, Inc.; *lower* Laurence Lowry/National Audubon Society. **207** *lower* Library of Congress. **208** Brown Brothers. **209** *top and bottom left* NASA. **210** *bottom* Colonial Williamsburg Photograph. **211** *and* **212** *top right* Courtesy of the Henry Francis duPont Winterthur Museum. **212** *top left* Beaker on loan from the First &

Second Church in Boston; Porringer from the Philip Leffingwell Spalding Collection; both courtesy of Museum of Fine Arts, Boston. **213** *left* Gift of Joseph W., William B., and Edward H. R. Revere, Courtesy of Museum of Fine Arts, Boston; *bottom* The Metropolitan Museum of Art, Bequest of A. T. Clearwater, 1933. **214** *top* Louis H. Frohman; *bottom* Jessie Walker. **215** *top* Philadelphia Museum of Art. **215** *bottom and* **216** *top* Index of American Design, National Gallery of Art, Washington. **215** *bottom right* © John T. Hopf. **216** *bottom left* Courtesy of the Henry Francis duPont Winterthur Museum; *bottom right* Philadelphia Museum of Art, the Titus C. Geesey Collection. **217** *left* From the collection of Mr. and Mrs. Charles F. Montgomery; *top* Photograph by Arnold Newman, © 1965 Smithsonian Institution. **218** *top* George Pickow; *bottom* Index of American Design, National Gallery of Art, Washington. **219** *top left* Philadelphia Museum of Art, Whitman Sampler Collection, Gift of Pet, Inc.; *top right* Shelburne Museum, Shelburne, Vt.; *bottom left* New York Graphic Society; *lower right* Wadsworth Atheneum, Hartford, Conn. **220** *middle right* Philbrook Art Center. **220** *remainder and* **221** Museum of the American Indian. **222** *top* Colonial Williamsburg Photograph. **222** *bottom and* **223** *bottom* Courtesy of the Henry Francis duPont Winterthur Museum. **223** *top* Private Collection/ Donna Harris. **224** *top* Colonial Williamsburg Photograph; *bottom* Collection of L. Thorne-Thomsen. **225** *top* The Metropolitan Museum of Art, Gift of Mrs. Charles Reginald Leonard, 1957; *bottom* Museum of the City of New York. **226** Photo by Frank Forward Color Productions from *A Color Guide to Bennington Pottery* by Richard Carter Barret. **227** Private Collection. **228** *top* The Metropolitan Museum of Art, Rogers Fund, 1928; *bottom* The Metropolitan Museum of Art, Photo by William F. Pons, 1972. **229** *top and middle left* Museum of Modern Art, Gift of Joseph H. Heil; *middle right* Museum of Modern Art, Phyllis B. Lambert Fund; *bottom* © Yale Joel, 1974. **230** *and* **231** *top* From *Objects: USA,* The Johnson Collection of Contemporary Crafts, assembled by the Johnson Wax Co. of Racine, Wisc. **231** *bottom left* Arthur (Espenet) Carpenter; *bottom right* American Crafts Council's Museum of Contemporary Crafts. **233** *top* The Toledo Museum of Art, Toledo, Ohio, gift of Florence Scott Libbey; *bottom* © Arnold Newman. **234** Sandak. **235** *left* Historic Charleston Foundation; *right* Essex Institute/Mark Sexton. **236** *left* Founders Hall, Girard College; *middle right* Louis H. Frohman. **236** *bottom right and* **237** *middle right* © John T. Hopf. **237** *top* Avery Library, Columbia University; *middle left and bottom* Sandak; *center* Medical College of Virginia. **238** *left* Illinois Dept. of Conservation; *middle right* Nebraska State Historical Society, Solomon D. Butcher Collection; *bottom right* Tom Myers. **239** *top* Alan Pitcairn/Grant Heilman; *middle* David Plowden; *bottom* Mark Sexton. **240** *center* Chicago Architectural Photographing Co.; *right* Avery Library, Columbia University. **242** *top* Frederick C. Robie House; *bottom* © 1962 The Frank Lloyd Wright Foundation by permission of The Frank Lloyd Wright Foundation. **243** *top left* W. E. Young; *top right* Western Pennsylvania Conservancy; *bottom* The Solomon R. Guggenheim Museum. **244** *left* The Ford Foundation; *right* Carroll C. Calkins. **245** *top left* Ezra Stoller © ESTO; *top right* Sandak; *bottom* Mark Sexton. **246** *top* Russ Kinne/Photo Researchers; *bottom* Courtesy of R. Buckminster Fuller. **247** *top* New York Public Library, Prints Division; *bottom* Jack Novak/Photri. **248** The New-York Historical Society. **249** *top* Courtesy of Gulf Reston, Inc.; *middle and bottom* Cosanti Foundation/Ivan Pintar. **250** *top* New York Public Library, Art and Architecture Division; *middle left* Sy Seidman/Photo Trends; *middle right* Library of Congress. **250** *bottom and* **251** *top* Culver Pictures. **251** *middle and bottom* New York Public Library, Picture Collection. **252** *top* Culver Pictures; *lower left* Private Collection; *bottom right* Paul Cret, Architect, Rendering by Joseph Urban. **253** *top* New York Public Library, Picture Collection; *middle* Anna L. Sobeck; *lower left* Seattle Center; *lower center* Brown Brothers; *lower right* Mike Roberts Color Productions. **256** *left, center, and lower right* The Franklin Institute; *top right* Philadelphia Museum of Art, Gift of Mr. and Mrs. Wharton Sinkler. **257** National Archives. **259** Bill Ray. **260** *top* Yale University Art Gallery, the Mabel Brady Garvan Collection; *bottom* Connecticut State Library Museum/Gus Johnson. **262** New York Public Library, Prints Division. **263** Photograph by Arnold Newman, © 1965 Smithsonian Institution. **266** *top* Courtesy of the Singer Co.; *bottom* The Bettmann Archive. **267** National Portrait Gallery, Smithsonian Institution. **269** *top* U.S. Dept. of the Interior, National Park Service, Edison National Historical Site. **270** Brown Brothers. **271** *top* UPI Photo; *bottom* The Granger Collection. **272** *top* Courtesy of Mrs. Mitchell Wilson; *bottom* Goldmark Communications Corp. **273** *top* International Museum of Photography at George Eastman House; *lower* Polaroid Corp. **274** *top* Smithsonian Institution; *lower* Burroughs Corp. **275** U.S. Army Ballistic Research Laboratories. **276** *upper left* Sub-Zero Freezer Co. **277** *upper right* Kohler Co.; *bottom right* Maytag Co. **279** The New-York Historical Society. **286** *top and* **287** *top right* Courtesy of the Ford Archives, Henry Ford Museum, Dearborn, Mich. **286–287** *bottom* Detroit Institute of Arts, Gift of Edsel B. Ford. **287** *top left and lower right* Ralph Stein. **288** *left* Sears, Roebuck and Co.; *center* Montgomery Ward; *right* R. H. Macy & Co. **293** New York Academy of Medicine Library. **294** *top* New York Public Library, Prints Division; *bottom* Unitarian Church, Winchester, Mass./Mark Sexton. **295** *and* **296** © 1961 Parke, Davis & Co. **297** *top left* Culver Pictures. **297** *top right and* **298** The Bettmann Archive. **297** *lower* © 1963 Parke, Davis & Co. **299** © 1964 Parke, Davis & Co. **300** *and* **301** Swedish Information Service. **302** Culver Pictures. **305** Sidney King. **306** The Peale Museum, Baltimore, Gift of Mrs. Harry White in memory of her husband. **307** *top* American Philosophical Society; *bottom* American Museum of Natural History. **308** *top* Lee Boltin; *middle* National Collection of Fine Arts, Smithsonian Institution; *bottom left and right* Smithsonian Institution. **311** *lower left* Cornell University. **312** Library of Congress. **313** Fermi National Accelerator Laboratory. **314** Fundamental Photographs/The Granger Collection. **315** Philip Spielman. **316** Sidney King. **317** Collection of Pilgrim Hall, Plymouth, Mass./Barney Burstein. **318** Colonial Williamsburg Photograph. **319** Museum of the City of New York. **320** Ezra Stoller Associates © ESTOL. **321** Library of Congress. **322** Culver Pictures. **323** *top and middle left* Courtesy of American Antiquarian Society; *middle right* Peabody Museum of Salem; *bottom* Chicago Historical Society. **324** *top* The New-York Historical Society; *middle* Culver Pictures; *bottom left* The Cincinnati Art Museum. **325** *top* Nebraska State Historical Society, Solomon D. Butcher Collection; *middle right* Denver Public Library, Western History Department; *bottom* Bill Smith. **326** *upper* Museum of the City of New York; *lower left* Culver Pictures; *bottom right* The Byron Collection, Museum of the City of New York. **327** *top* Culver Pictures; *bottom* New York Public Library. **328** Culver Pictures. **329** Tony Linck. **330** Donna Harris. **332–335** Bureau of Printing and Engraving. **337** Donna Harris. **339** Library of Congress. **341** The New-York Historical Society. **343** National Union of Hospital and Health Care Employees, from the Collection of Lee Baxandall, New York. **344** Los Angeles County Museum of Art. **346** Culver Pictures. **349** Harris-Ewing/Photo Trends. **350** *upper right* UPI Photo; *remainder* Wide World Photos. **351** *upper left, upper and lower center, and far right* UPI Photos; *remainder* Wide World Photos. **353** *upper left* Brown Brothers; *lower left* The Oakland Museum, Dorothea Lange Collection; *center* © 1933 Condé Nast Publications; *right* Wide World Photos; *bottom* Underwood & Underwood. **354** National Archives. **355** Los Alamos Scientific Laboratory. **356** *bottom and* **357** Smithsonian Institution. **359** Independence National Historical Park, National Park Service Photo. **360** *top* Smithsonian Institution; *bottom left* Collection of Robert A. Weinstein/J. R. Eyerman; *lower right* The New-York Historical Society. **361** The Granger Collection. **363** *left* Library of Congress; *top right* Brown Brothers; *lower* York Graphic Services. **364** *upper* The Bettmann Archive; *lower left* Old Print Center, Phyllis Lucas Gallery; *bottom right* The New-York Historical Society. **365** *top* New York Public Library; *lower* "The Yellow Kid," Private Collection; "The Katzenjammer Kids," "Bringing Up Father," "Krazy Kat," and "Blondie" reprinted by permission of King Features Syndicate, Inc.; "Mutt and Jeff" reprinted by permission of the McNaught Syndicate, Inc.; "Gasoline Alley," "Little Orphan Annie," "Dick Tracy," "Li'l Abner," and "Brenda Starr" reprinted by permission of The Chicago Tribune-New York News Syndicate, Inc. All rights reserved; "Pogo" © Walt Kelly, used by permission of Selby Kelly, executrix; The drawing of the character "Charlie Brown" from the "Peanuts" comic strip pictured on page 365 is the copyrighted property of United Feature Syndicate, Inc.; "Doonesbury" © G. B. Trudeau, distributed by Universal Press Syndicate. **366** *top* Donna Harris; *upper left, Reader's Digest; center* Norman Rockwell, © *The Saturday Evening Post; lower left* Culver Pictures; *bottom center* © 1948 Downe Publishing, Inc., Reprinted by permission of *Ladies' Home Journal; lower center, Harper's* magazine; *bottom right, Saturday Review.* **367** *top left, Life* magazine, © Time Inc.; *top right* Cowles Communications, Inc.; *lower left, Time* magazine, © Time Inc.; *lower right* Newsweek, Inc. **368** *and* **369** Culver Pictures. **370** *top* © 1963 Bob Jackson; *bottom* NASA. **371** *top* New York Public Library, Rare Book Division; *lower* Donna Harris. **372** *upper right* Courtesy of Kennedy Galleries, Inc.; *bottom* The Pennsylvania Academy of the Fine Arts. **373** Holger Cahill Collection. **374** *left* Museum of Fine Arts, Boston, Otis Norcross Fund; *right* National Gallery of Art, Gift of Maude Monell Vetlesen. **375** *top* Corcoran Gallery of Art; *lower left* Worcester Art Museum, Worcester, Mass.; *bottom right* Philadelphia Museum of Art, the George W. Elkins Collection. **376** *upper* Museum of Fine Arts, Boston, M. and M. Karolik Collection; *bottom* Brooklyn Museum, Bequest of Mrs. William A. Putnam. **377** *top left* The Metropolitan Museum of Art, Bequest of Maria De Witt Jesup, 1915; *top right* New York Public Library; *bottom* The Metropolitan Museum of Art, Gift of Mrs. Russell Sage, 1908. **378** *left* The New-York Historical Society; *right* Museum of Fine Arts, Boston, Hayden Fund. **379** *top left* William Rockwell Nelson Gallery of Art; *top right* National Gallery of Art, Washington, Andrew W. Mellon Collection; *bottom* Milwaukee Art Center, Layton Art Gallery Collection. **380** *upper left* National Gallery of Art, Washington, Collection of Mr. and Mrs. Paul Mellon; *upper right* The New-York Historical Soceity; *bottom* The Oakland Museum. **381** *top* The Metropolitan Museum of Art, Alfred N. Punnett Fund and Gift of George D. Pratt, 1934; *middle* National Collection of Fine Arts, Smithsonian Institution; *bottom* National Gallery of Art, Washington, Gift of the W. L. and May T. Mellon Foundation. **382** *top right* Masonic Temple,

Philadelphia, Pa.; top center Sandak; *top right* Corcoran Gallery of Art; *middle and bottom right* The New-York Historical Society; *bottom left* Smithsonian Institution. **383** *top right* City of Springfield; *top center* Museum of Modern Art, given anonymously in memory of the artist; *center* © Arnold Newman; *middle right* Museum of Modern Art, Gift of William S. Paley; *bottom left* The Metropolitan Museum of Art, Gift of James Douglas, 1899; *bottom center left* Joslyn Art Museum, N. P. Dodge Bequest Fund; *bottom center right* Collection of the Whitney Museum of American Art, New York; *bottom right* Sandak. **384** *top* National Gallery of Art, Washington, Harris Wittemore Collection; *left* Art Institute of Chicago; *bottom right* Museum of Fine Arts, Boston, Gift of the Boit daughters in memory of their father. **385** *left* Philadelphia Museum of Art, the Louise and Walter Arensberg Collection. **385** *top,* **386** *left, and* **387** *bottom* Collection of the Whitney Museum of American Art, New York. **385** *lower right and* **386** *upper right* Museum of Modern Art, New York. **386** *bottom* New Britain Museum. **387** *top* The Cleveland Museum of Art, Hinman B. Hurlbut Collection. **388** *left* Philadelphia Museum of Art, the Lisa Norris Elkins Fund; *top center and upper middle right* The Metropolitan Museum of Art, the Fletcher Fund; *top right* Albright-Knox Gallery, Gift of Seymour H. Knox; *lower middle* Museum of Modern Art, Gift of Sidney Janis; *bottom* Museum of Modern Art, Gift of Mrs. Gertrud A. Mellon. **389** *top left* The Metropolitan Museum of Art, The Fletcher Fund, 1956; *top center* Mr. and Mrs. Irwin Green Collection; *top right* Harry N. Abrams Family Collection, New York; *second row left* Albright-Knox Gallery, Gift of Seymour H. Knox; *second row center* Seymour Schweber Collection; *second row right* Harry N. Abrams Family Collection, New York; *third row left* The Oakland Museum; *third row center* Bruno Bischofberger Collection, Zurich and New York; *third row right* The Lt. John B. Putnam, Jr. Memorial Collection, Princeton University; *bottom left* Museum of Modern Art, Gift of Mr. and Mrs. Ben Mildwoff; *bottom center* Museum of Modern Art, Larry Aldrich Foundation Fund; *bottom right* O. K. Harris Works of Art. **391** *left* Religious News Service; *right* The Granger Collection. **392** The New-York Historical Society. **394** Library of Congress. **395** "Oh, What a Beautiful Mornin'" © Williamson Music, Inc.; "I've Got You Under My Skin" © Chappell & Co., Inc.; "Tea for Two" © Harms, Inc.; "White Christmas" © Irving Berlin, Inc.; "Bewitched" © Chappell & Co., Inc.; "They All Laughed" © Chappell & Co., Inc.; "Make Believe" © T. B. Harms Company; "What the World Needs Now Is Love" © Blue Seas Music, Inc., and Jac Music Co., Inc.; "The Way We Were" © Colgems Music Corp.; "Moon River" © Famous Music Corp. **397** *top* Culver Pictures; *lower left* Brown Brothers; *lower right* Courtesy of Robert Asen/Metronome Collection. **398** *High Fidelity.* **400** Queens Booking Corp. **401** Edward Steichen. **403** Adrian Siegel. **404** UPI Photo. **405** *Music Journal.* **408** Library of Congress. **409** Allston Jenkins Collection. **410** New York Public Library, Prints Division. **411** John A. Lynch. **412** *left and bottom right* The Rockwell Kent Legacies. **413** *top* Berkshire Athenaeum Public Library/Mark Sexton. **415** *top* Museum of the City of New York, the Harry T. Peters Collection; *lower left* Painted by Norman Rockwell for The Heritage Press edition of *The Adventures of Tom Sawyer;* the illustration is copyright © 1936, 1964 by The George Macy Companies, Inc., and reproduced by permission of *The Heritage Club,* Avon, Conn.; *lower right* UPI Photo. **417** The Phillips Collection, Washington. **419** Photo by George Platt-Lynes, Reprinted by permission of the Viking Press, Inc. **420** *and* **421** Courtesy of the New School for Social Research. **422** *and* **423** Culver Pictures. **425** The Eugene O'Neill Collection, Collection of American Literature, Beinecke Rare Book and Manuscript Library, Yale University. **427** © Arnold Newman. **428** Brown Brothers. **429** Yale University Art Gallery, Bequest of Stephen Carlton Clark. **430** *top* The Bettmann Archive; *lower* AT&T Photo Center. **432** *top left* Brown Brothers; *top center and bottom right* Sophia Smith Collection; *top right* Library of Congress; *bottom right* The Granger Collection. **434** *and* **435** *top* Sophia Smith Collection. **435** *bottom* Library of Congress. **436** *top* Vassar College Library; *bottom* Brown Brothers. **437** *top* Wide World Photos; *bottom* Sophia Smith Collection. **442** *bottom* Brown Brothers. **443** New York Public Library, Rare Book Division. **444** *bottom* Theodore Roosevelt Birthplace. **445** Time-Life Picture Agency/Herbert Orth. **446** *top* National Archives; *bottom* Brown Brothers. **448** *top* Culver Pictures; *bottom* Library of Congress. **449** *upper left* Culver Pictures; *bottom* "When the 'Yanks' Come Marching Home" © William Jerome Publishing Corp.; "Over There" © William Jerome Publishing Corp.; "Oh! How I Hate to Get up in the Morning" © Waterson, Berlin, & Snyder Co.; "How 'Ya Gonna Keep 'Em Down on the Farm" © Waterson, Berlin, & Snyder Co.: All courtesy of the Sy Seidman Collection/Photo Trends; *right* Edward Vebell Collection. **450** *left* Brown Brothers; *right* UPI Photo. **451** U.S. Navy Combat Art Museum/Mark Sexton. **452** Courtesy of U.S. Navy Combat Art Collection/Jack Novak. **455** *top* U.S. Navy Combat Art Museum/Mark Sexton; *bottom* Franklin D. Roosevelt Library. **456** *top* National Archives; *bottom* Larry Keighley. **460** *top* From the Collection of Mr. and Mrs. J. William Middendorf II, New York; *bottom* Chrysler Museum at Norfolk, Museum Purchase Fund. **461** *top left* Library of Congress; *top right and bottom left* © National Geographic Society; *bottom right* Culver Pictures. **463** The New-York Historical Society. **464** *top* Harvard Theatre Collection; *bottom* Circus World Museum. **465** *left* Library of Congress; *right* The Granger Collection. **466** *left* Edward Vebell Collection; *top* Circus World Museum; *lower right* Don Russell Collection. **467** *top left and lower right* Library of Congress; *top right* The Oakland Museum, the Kahn Collection. **468** Brown Brothers. **469** *top and bottom right* Culver Pictures; *bottom left* Collection of Mr. and Mrs. Albert Hackett. **470** Museum of Modern Art, Film Stills Archive. **471** *left* © Academy of Motion Picture Arts and Sciences. **471–472** Walt Disney World. **474** *top and bottom left* Culver Pictures; *bottom right* Museum of the City of New York, Theatre and Music Collection. **475** *and* **476** Friedman-Abeles. **477** *and* **478** Photri/Jack Novak. **479** *top left* Courtesy of the National Broadcasting Co., Inc.; *top center* The Bettmann Archive; *top right* Sullivan Productions, New York; *second row* Culver Pictures; *third row left* Culver Pictures; *third row center* CBS Television Network; *third row right* The Bettmann Archive; *bottom left* Culver Pictures; *bottom center* Courtesy of the National Broadcasting Co., Inc.; *bottom right* Jerry Cooke. **481** New York Public Library, Rare Book Division. **482** Hall of Fame of the Trotter. **483** Library of Congress. **484** Museum of the City of New York, the Harry T. Peters Collection. **486** The Bettmann Archive. **487** Collection of Edgar William and Bernice Chrysler Garbisch. **488** The Granger Collection. **489** *top* UPI Photo; *bottom* Wide World Photos. **490** Brown Brothers. **491** *left* Library of Congress; *right* UPI Photo. **494** The Bettmann Archive. **495** *top (inset)* UPI Photo; *lower* Brown Brothers. **496** *left* Culver Pictures; *upper right* UPI Photo; *bottom* Mickey Palmer/DPI. **497** *top* Harlem Globetrotters; *middle* UPI Photo; *bottom* George Skadding/Time-Life Books, © Time Inc. **498** *top left* Jack Zehrt; *top right* Hedrich-Blessing; *bottom* Tony Linck. **499** *left* Dennis Gad; *top center* Ed Stewart; *top right* Crazy Horse Memorial; *lower* U.S. Dept. of the Interior, Grand Coulee Project.

Acknowledgments for "Inspiration for the Future." 500 Alexis de Tocqueville, from *This Was America,* edited by Oscar Handlin. Harper & Row, Harper Torchbooks, the Cloister Library, 1964; Michel Chevalier, from *The Happy Republic: A Reader in de Tocqueville's America,* edited by George E. Probst. © 1962 by Harper & Brothers. **500–501** Frederick Jackson Turner, from *The Frontier in American History* by Frederick Jackson Turner. Copyright 1920 by Frederick Jackson Turner. Copyright 1948 by Caroline M.S. Turner. Reprinted by permission of Holt, Rinehart & Winston, Publishers. **501** Martin Luther King, Jr., from *I Have a Dream.* Copyright © 1963 by Dr. Martin Luther King, Jr. Reprinted by permission of Joan Daves; Bella S. Abzug, from an article by Jean Douglas Murphy. Copyright 1972 by the Los Angeles *Times.* Reprinted by permission. **502** Alexis de Tocqueville, in *Democracy in America,* taken from the translation by George Lawrence, edited by J. P. Mayer and Max Lerner. Harper & Row, Publishers, 1961; Capt. Frederick Marryat, from *The Happy Republic: A Reader in de Tocqueville's America,* edited by George E. Probst. © 1962 by Harper & Brothers. **503** Stewart L. Udall, from *The Quiet Crisis* by Stewart L. Udall. Copyright © 1963 by Stewart L. Udall. Reprinted by permission of Holt, Rinehart and Winston, Publishers. **504** Michel Chevalier, in *Society, Manners and Politics in the United States: Letters on North America.* Edited and with an introduction by John William Ward. Translated after the T. G. Bradford edition. Anchor Books, Doubleday & Co., Inc., 1961; Alexis de Tocqueville, in *Democracy in America,* taken from the translation by George Lawrence, edited by J. P. Mayer and Max Lerner. Harper & Row, Publishers, 1961. **505** Wendell L. Willkie, in *One World.* Copyright 1943 by Wendell L. Willkie. Simon & Schuster, Inc., 1943.

Marjorie Terrill Venable
1976